After a major restoration project that stabilized the structure, the Leaning Tower of Pisa has been shored up to a safe but still photogenic degree of tilt. Visitors are allowed to climb the tower once again. See chapter 7. © Harald Sund/The Image Bank.

Giotto's Campanile and Brunelleschi's red-tiled dome, which caps the Duomo, rise above the city of Florence. See chapter 6. © Kevin Galvin Photography.

Tuscany and Umbria are famed for their vineyards, which produce some of Italy's finest wines, including the renowned Chianti Classico. See chapters 1 and 7 for details on how to visit the top wineries. © Joe Englander/The Viesti Collection, Inc.

Siena is a city of the Middle Ages, with steep, twisting alleyways and stone buildings. Everything centers around the Piazza del Campo, arguably the most beautiful piazza in Italy and the setting for the Palio, a wild and exciting horse race full of pageantry and tradition. See chapter 7. © Kevin Galvin Photography.

Venice is one of the few places in Italy where you'll never hear an automobile. Yes, it's crowded and shockingly expensive, but it's also simply extraordinary and one of the world's most romantic cities. See chapter 9. © Gerard Pile/Tony Stone Images.

One of the loveliest spots in Verona is the 14th-century Giardino Giusti, with a "monster balcony" offering an incomparable view over the city of Romeo and Juliet. See chapter 10.
© Robert Essel/The Stock Market.

The peaks of the Dolomites, a mighty mountain range that dominates the north of Italy, offer terrific hiking in summer and great skiing in winter, when resort towns such as Cortina draw an international crowd. See chapter 10. © Ric Ergenbright Photography.

Milan's flamboyant Duomo is Italy's largest Gothic cathedral. On the roof, you can walk through a forest of pinnacles, turrets, and marble statuary. See chapter 11. © Jose Fuste Raga/ The Stock Market.

Lake Como, 20 miles north of Milan, is one of the most scenic spots in Italy, with colorful gardens, 17th- and 18th-century villas, lakeside promenades, and the peaks of the Alps towering above. See chapter 11. © Robert Everts/Tony Stone Images.

Italy's busiest port city, Genoa has a split personality. The narrow alleyways of the old town offer glimpses of the city's glory days, when it was one of the largest and wealthiest cities in Renaissance Europe. Modern Genoa stretches for miles along the coast, with parks and belvederes offering views over the sea. See chapter 13. © J. McDermott/Tony Stone Images.

With Mt. Etna looming in the background, the ancient Greek amphitheater is the major sightseeing attraction in Taormina, Sicily's prettiest beach resort. See chapter 16.
© James Marshall Photography.

A New Star-Rating System & Other Exciting News from Frommer's!

In our continuing effort to publish the savviest, most up-to-date, and most appealing travel guides available, we've added some great new features.

Frommer's guides now include a new **star-rating system.** Every hotel, restaurant, and attraction is rated from 0 to 3 stars to help you set priorities and organize your time.

We've also added **seven brand-new features** that point you to the great deals, in-the-know advice, and unique experiences that separate travelers from tourists. Throughout the guide, look for:

Finds	Special finds—those places only insiders know about
Fun Fact	Fun facts—details that make travelers more informed and their trips more fun
Kids	Best bets for kids—advice for the whole family
Moments	Special moments—those experiences that memories are made of
Overrated	Places or experiences not worth your time or money
Tips	Insider tips—some great ways to save time and money
Value	Great values—where to get the best deals

We've also added a **"What's New"** section in every guide—a timely crash course in what's hot and what's not in every destination we cover.

Here's what the critics say about Frommer's:

Other Great Guides for Your Trip:

Italy

2003

by Darwin Porter & Danforth Prince

Wiley Publishing, Inc.

About the Authors

A native of North Carolina, **Darwin Porter** was a bureau chief for the *Miami Herald* when he was 21 and later worked in television advertising. A veteran travel writer, he wrote Frommer's first-ever guide to Italy many years ago and has been a frequent visitor ever since. He is joined by **Danforth Prince,** formerly of the Paris bureau of the *New York Times,* who has lived in Italy and traveled there extensively. As a team, they've researched and written other best-selling Frommer guides, including *Frommer's Rome.*

Published by:

Wiley Publishing, Inc.

909 Third Ave.
New York, NY 10022

ISBN 0-7645-6655-5
ISSN 1044-2170

Editor: Kimberly Perdue
Production Editor: Tammy Ahrens
Cartographer: John Decamillis
Photo Editor: Richard Fox
Production by Wiley Indianapolis Composition Services
Chapter 2 illustrations by Rashell Smith

For information on our other products and services or to obtain technical support, please contact our Customer Care Department within the U.S. at 800-762-2974, outside the U.S. at 317-572-3993 or fax 317-572-4002.

Wiley also publishes its books in a variety of electronic formats. Some content that appears in print may not be available in electronic formats.

Manufactured in the United States of America

5 4 3 2 1

Italy

2003

by Darwin Porter & Danforth Prince

Wiley Publishing, Inc.

About the Authors

A native of North Carolina, **Darwin Porter** was a bureau chief for the *Miami Herald* when he was 21 and later worked in television advertising. A veteran travel writer, he wrote Frommer's first-ever guide to Italy many years ago and has been a frequent visitor ever since. He is joined by **Danforth Prince,** formerly of the Paris bureau of the *New York Times,* who has lived in Italy and traveled there extensively. As a team, they've researched and written other best-selling Frommer guides, including *Frommer's Rome.*

Published by:

Wiley Publishing, Inc.

909 Third Ave.
New York, NY 10022

ISBN 0-7645-6655-5
ISSN 1044-2170

Editor: Kimberly Perdue
Production Editor: Tammy Ahrens
Cartographer: John Decamillis
Photo Editor: Richard Fox
Production by Wiley Indianapolis Composition Services
Chapter 2 illustrations by Rashell Smith

For information on our other products and services or to obtain technical support, please contact our Customer Care Department within the U.S. at 800-762-2974, outside the U.S. at 317-572-3993 or fax 317-572-4002.

Wiley also publishes its books in a variety of electronic formats. Some content that appears in print may not be available in electronic formats.

Manufactured in the United States of America

5 4 3 2 1

Contents

List of Maps

An Invitation to the Reader

In researching this book, we discovered many wonderful places—hotels, restaurants, shops, and more. We're sure you'll find others. Please tell us about them, so we can share the information with your fellow travelers in upcoming editions. If you were disappointed with a recommendation, we'd love to know that, too. Please write to:

Frommer's Italy 2003
Wiley Publishing, Inc. • 909 Third Ave. • New York, NY 10022

An Additional Note

Please be advised that travel information is subject to change at any time—and this is especially true of prices. We therefore suggest that you write or call ahead for confirmation when making your travel plans. The authors, editors, and publisher cannot be held responsible for the experiences of readers while traveling. Your safety is important to us, however, so we encourage you to stay alert and be aware of your surroundings. Keep a close eye on cameras, purses, and wallets, all favorite targets of thieves and pickpockets.

New! Frommer's Star Ratings & Icons

Every hotel, restaurant, and attraction listing in this guide has been ranked for quality, value, service, amenities, and special features using a star-rating scale. In country, state, and regional guides, we also rate towns and regions to help you narrow down your choices and budget your time accordingly. Hotels and restaurants in the Very Expensive and Expensive categories are rated on a scale of one (highly recommended) to three stars (exceptional). Those in the Moderate and Inexpensive categories rate from zero (recommended) to two stars (very highly recommended). Attractions, towns, and regions are rated according to the following scale: zero stars (recommended), one star (highly recommended), two stars (very highly recommended), and three stars (must-see).

In addition to the rating system, we also use seven icons to highlight insider information, useful tips, special bargains, hidden gems, memorable experiences, kid-friendly venues, places to avoid, and other useful information:

(Finds   (Fun Fact   (Kids   (Moments   (Overrated   (Tips   (Value

The following abbreviations are used for credit cards:

AE	American Express	DISC Discover	V Visa
DC	Diners Club	MC MasterCard	

FROMMERS.COM

Now that you have the guidebook to a great trip, visit our website at **www.frommers.com** for travel information on nearly 2,500 destinations. With features updated regularly, we give you instant access to the most current trip-planning information available. At Frommers.com, you'll also find the best prices on airfares, accommodations, and car rentals—and you can even book travel online through our travel booking partners. At Frommers.com, you'll also find the following:

- Online updates to our most popular guidebooks
- Vacation sweepstakes and contest giveaways
- Newsletter highlighting the hottest travel trends
- Online travel message boards with featured travel discussions

What's New in Italy

In the vanguard of world tourism, Italy is always changing, but, like the city of Rome itself, Italy remains eternal. Here are some of the latest developments.

ROME Perhaps it was the attention it received during the Jubilee, but **Residenza Paolo VI,** via Paolo VI 29, 00193 Roma (© **06-68134108**), has recently become a coveted reservation. One reader claimed that from the terrace here he thought he was sitting at the Gates of Heaven, a reference to the panoramic view of St. Peter's Square. The rooms are comfortable too.

Deep in the heart of ancient Rome, **Boccondivino,** Piazza in Campio Marzio 6 (© **06-68308626**), is becoming increasingly fashionable. Against a backdrop of the ruins of imperial Rome, tasty Italian dishes from many regions of Italy are prepared to perfection and served with flair and zest, often with such luxurious culinary delights as black truffles. See chapter 4, "Settling into Rome," for more information about both establishments.

FLORENCE The dining picture of the City of the Renaissance has brightened considerably with the opening of **Taverna del Bronzino,** via della Ruote 27R (© **055-495220**), installed in the former studio of a 16th-century Renaissance artist. Offering a refined Tuscan cuisine, the kitchen manages to delight some of the most discerning palates of Florence.

At long last Florence has a top-rate vegetarian restaurant with the opening of the aptly named **Il Vegetariano,** via della Ruote 30R (© **055-475030**). At wooden tables freely shared, fellow vegetarian diners delight in some of the town's best antipasti. There's nothing finer than the kitchen's vegetable risottos.

For one of the best meals in Florence today, you can journey right outside the city to sample the wares at **Da Delfina,** via della Chiese 1 (© **055-871074**), in the medieval walled village of Artimino. On a table set on a terrace with a panoramic view of the Tuscan countryside, you can sample an array of homemade dishes from succulent pastas to fish grilled over a wood-burning fireplace. See chapter 6, "Florence," to find out more about all three restaurants.

TUSCANY In the medieval town of San Gimignano, fabled for its towers, **La Collegiata,** Località Strada 27, 53037 San Gimignano (© **0577-943201**), has burst on the scene surpassing the leading hostelries. The villa is from 1587 and has been beautifully restored, complete with an open-air swimming pool. A five-star hotel, **Grand Hotel Continental,** Banchi di Sopra, 53100 Siena (© **0577-56011**), has opened in the heart of this much-visited town. It's a faithful reconstruction of a baroque palace, maintaining many of its original features, including magnificent frescoes.

In ancient Gubbio, **Park Hotel Ai Cappuccini,** via Tifernate, 06024 Gubbio (© **075-9234**), has become the most important hotel in town. The hotel lies in the middle of a landscaped park and is surrounded by the ancient garden of a monastery.

The town of Spoleto has seen the opening of yet another historic hotel property to add to the cluster it already offers. **Palazzo Dragoni,** via del Duomo 13, 06049 Spoleto (℃ **0743-222220**), is a renovated 16th-century palace that's filled with antiques and tasteful fabrics in harmony with the well-preserved architecture.

Never known for the quality of its innkeeping, the art city of Assisi at last has a first-rate hotel, **Grand Hotel Assisi,** via Fratelli Canoni Canonichetti, 06081 Assisi (℃ **075-81501**). Its most dramatic feature is a roof garden terrace with panoramic views, and its bedrooms are the classiest in town.

To learn more about all of the offerings mentioned above, see chapter 7, "Tuscany & Umbria."

VENICE Visitors today can stay in the former house of the composer Antonio Vivaldi. **Locanda Vivaldi,** Riva degli Schiavoni, 4152–53, 30122 Venezia (℃ **041-2770477**), has been installed in this town house and decorated with baroque ornamentation and comfortably lush bedrooms.

There's a buzz centering on the Venetian cuisine offered at **Le Bistrot de Venise,** San Marco 4685, Calle dei Fabbri (℃ **041-5236651**). Based on time-tested recipes, dishes here are often inspired by the cookery of the 16th century. For more on both of these establishments, see chapter 9, "Venice."

MILAN This city of fashion isn't quite the same with the closing of La Scala for a much-needed restoration. However, opera in front of the world's most demanding audience is still presented in another location at the newly constructed **Teatro degli Arcimboldi,** Zona Bicocca, viale dell'Innovazione (℃ **02-72003744**), on the northern outskirts of Milan.

On the hotel front, the **Pierre,** via de Amicis 32, 20132 Milano (℃ **02-72000581**), is generating excitement. The hotel represents luxury on a small scale, and is filled with electronic objects to make your life easy.

Some of the most creative cookery in Milano today is offered at **Il Luogo di Aimo e Nadia,** via Montecuccoli 6 (℃ **02-416886**), in an avant-garde setting. Take the advice on wine from the best sommelier in Lombardy. Ingredients such as truffles in a series appear in beautifully showcased platters.

Acclaimed in both New York and London, **Nobu,** via Pisoni 1 (℃ **02-72318645**), has invaded Milan complete with one of its backers, Robert de Niro. A brilliant staff performs gastronomic pyrotechnics, turning out Northern Italy's finest Japanese cuisine.

See chapter 11, "Milan, Lombardy & the Lake District," for more information about the newcomers above.

POMPEII When some erotic frescoes were recently opened to the public for the first time here, it made headlines around the world. The ruins of the 2,000-year-old thermal bathhouse were discovered back in the 1980s, but it was just recently given world attention. The frescoes are amazingly well preserved, depicting various sex acts. Scholars and archaeologists disagree about their purpose, one group believing that they were intended to arouse viewers erotically, the other side asserting that the art was a satirical "camp" exercise intended for a laugh. See chapter 14, "Campania," for more about these recently unveiled discoveries.

SICILY The historic port of Siracua has restored the hotel grande dame that used to attract the royal of Europe. **Grande Hotel Villa Politi,** via Politi Laudien 2, 96100 Siracua (℃ **0931-412121**), has returned to its former glory and is the best address on the island, lying in the landmark gardens of Latomie dei Cappuccini.

In the island's capital, Palermo, the **Hotel Principe di Villafranca,** via G. Turrisi Colonna 4, 90141 Palermo (✆ **091-6118523**), has become the finest hotel in town, filled with Sicilian antiques, marble, silks, and vaulted ceilings—in all a museumlike aura but one that is nonetheless homey and inviting. See chapter 16, "Sicily."

1

The Best of Italy

Italy is so packed with attractions that it's hard to know where to start. But that's where we come in. In this chapter is our personal, opinionated list of what we consider to be Italy's top highlights. Our list will get you started and point you toward some of the possibilities for designing your own vacation. Whether this is your first trip or your tenth, you're bound to come away with your own favorites to add to the list.

1 The Best Travel Experiences

- **Visiting the Art Cities:** When Italy consisted of dozens of principalities, its art treasures were concentrated in many small capitals, each blessed with the patronage of a papal representative or ducal family. Consequently, these cities became treasure troves of exquisite paintings, statues, and frescoes displayed in churches, monasteries, and palaces, whose architects are now world-acclaimed. Although Rome, Florence, and Venice are the best known, you'll find stunning collections in Assisi, Cremona, Genoa, Mantua, Padua, Palermo, Parma, Pisa, Siena, Taormina, Tivoli, Turin, Verona, and Vicenza.

- **Dining Italian Style:** One of the most cherished pastimes of the Italians is eating out. Regardless of how much pizza and lasagna you've had in your life, you'll never taste any better than the real thing in Italy. Each region has its own specialties, some handed down for centuries. If the weather is fine and you're dining outdoors with a view of, perhaps, a medieval church or piazza, you'll find your experience the closest thing to heaven in Italy. *Buon appetito!*

- **Attending Mass in St. Peter's Basilica:** With the exception of some sites in Jerusalem, St. Peter's in the Vatican is Christendom's most visible and important building. The huge size of the church is daunting. For many visitors, attending Mass here is a spiritual highlight of their lives. In addition, many Catholic visitors to Rome eagerly await papal audiences every Wednesday morning, when the pope addresses the general public. If the day is fair, these audiences are sometimes held in St. Peter's Square. Your fellow faithful are likely to come from every corner of the world. See "St. Peter's & the Vatican," in chapter 5.

- **Riding Venice's Grand Canal:** The S-shaped Canal Grande, curving for 2 miles along historic buildings and under ornate bridges, is the most romantic waterway in the world. Most first-timers are stunned by the variety of Gothic and Renaissance buildings, the elaborate styles of which could fill a book on architecture. A ride on the canal will give you ever-changing glimpses of the city's poignant beauty. Your ride doesn't have to be on a gondola;

any public *vaporetto* (ferry) sailing between Venice's rail station and Piazza San Marco will provide a heart-stopping view. See chapter 9.

- **Getting Lost in Venice:** The most obvious means of transport in Venice is by boat; an even more appealing method is on foot, traversing hundreds of canals, large and small, and crossing over the arches of medieval bridges. Getting from one point to another can be like walking through a maze—but you won't be hassled by traffic, and the sense of the city's beauty, timelessness, and slow decay is almost mystical. See chapter 9.

- **Spending a Night at the Opera:** More than 2,000 new operas were staged in Italy during the 18th century, and since then, Italian opera fans have earned a reputation as the most demanding in the world. Venice was the site of Italy's first opera house, the Teatro di San Cassiano (1637), but it eventually gave way to the fabled La Fenice, which burned down in 1996 and is being restored; in the meantime, opera is presented under a tent at Palafenice. Milan's La Scala is historically the world's most prestigious opera house, especially for bel canto, and it will be again when it reopens after a much-needed restoration. There's also a wide assortment of outdoor settings, such as Verona's Arena, one of the largest surviving amphitheaters. Suitable for up to 20,000 spectators and known for its fine acoustics, the Arena presents operas in July and August, when moonlight and the perfumed air of the Veneto add to the charm.

- **Shopping Milan:** Milan is one of Europe's hottest fashion capitals. You'll find a range of shoes, clothing, and accessories unequaled anywhere else, except perhaps Paris or London. Even if you weren't born to shop, stroll along the streets bordering Via Montenapoleone and check out the elegant offerings from Europe's most famous designers. See "Milan," in chapter 11.

- **Experiencing the Glories of the Empire:** Even after centuries of looting, much remains of the legendary Roman Empire. Of course, Rome boasts the greatest share (the popes didn't tear down everything to recycle into churches)—you'll find everything from the Roman Forum and the Pantheon to the Colosseum and the Baths of Caracalla. And on the outskirts, the long-buried city of Ostia Antica, the port of ancient Rome, has been unearthed and is remarkable. Other treasures are scattered throughout Italy, especially in Sicily. Hordes of sightseers also descend on Pompeii, the city buried by volcanic ash from Mt. Vesuvius in A.D. 79, and Herculaneum, buried by lava on that same day. Our favorite spot is Paestum, along Campania's coast; its ruins, especially the Temple of Neptune, are alone worth the trip to Italy. See chapters 5, 14, and 16.

2 The Most Romantic Getaways

- **Todi:** For the ultimate escape, the hilltop of Todi, 126 miles south of Florence, will transport you back to the Middle Ages. You can lose yourself in its tangle of ancient streets and wine-dark alleys. Let the sun shine on you at its central square, where you might seriously contemplate moving there and living in a gentler time. See "Spoleto," in chapter 7.

- **Spoleto:** Spoleto is as ancient as the Roman Empire and as timeless as the music presented there every summer during its world-renowned arts festival. The architecture of this quintessential Umbrian hill town is centered on a core of religious buildings from the 13th century. It's even more romantic during the off-season, when the crowds are less dense. See "Spoleto," in chapter 7.

- **Bellagio:** Often called "the prettiest town in Europe," Bellagio is perhaps the loveliest town in Italy's stunningly beautiful Lake District. Its lakeside promenade, which follows the shores of Lake Como, is fragrant with flowers in bloom. Couples can spend their days exploring the arcaded streets and little shops, visiting lush gardens, and relaxing in the sun. See "Lake Como," in chapter 11.

- **Capri:** Floating amid azure seas south of Naples, Capri is called the "Island of Dreams." Everywhere, you'll find the aroma of lemon trees in bloom. Roman emperors Augustus and Tiberius both went there for R&R, and since the late 1800s celebrities have flocked to Capri for an escape. A boat ride around the island's rugged coastline is one of our favorite things to do. See "Capri," in chapter 14.

- **Ravello:** It's small, sunny, and loaded with notable buildings (such as its 1086 cathedral). Despite its choice position on the Amalfi coast, Ravello manages to retain the aura of an old-fashioned village. Famous residents have included writer Gore Vidal. See "Ravello," in chapter 14.

- **Taormina:** This resort, the loveliest place in Sicily, is brimming with regional charm, chiseled stonework, and a sense of the ages. Favored by wealthy Europeans and dedicated artists, especially in midwinter, when the climate is delightful, Taormina is a fertile oasis of olive groves, grapevines, and orchards. Visitors will relish the delights of the sun, the sea, and the medieval setting. See "Taormina," in chapter 16.

3 The Best Museums

- **The Vatican Museums** (Rome): Rambling, disorganized, and poorly labeled they might be, but these buildings are packed to the rafters with treasures accumulated over the centuries by the popes. Among them are the incomparable Sistine Chapel, such priceless ancient Greek and Roman sculptures as *Laocoön* and the *Belvedere Apollo,* buildings whose walls were almost completely executed by Raphael (including his majestic *School of Athens*), and endless collections of art ranging from (very pagan) Greco-Roman antiquities to Christian art by famous European masters. See p. 138.

- **Galleria Borghese** (Rome): This is one of the world's great small museums, reopened a few years ago after a full 14-year restoration that breathed new life into the frescoes and decor of this 1613 palace. And that's merely the backdrop for the collections, which include masterpieces of baroque sculpture by a young Bernini and paintings by Caravaggio and Raphael. See p. 160.

- **National Etruscan Museum** (Rome): Mysterious and, for the most part, undocumented, the Etruscans were the ancestors of the Romans. They left a legacy of bronze and marble sculpture, sarcophagi, jewelry, and representations of mythical heroes, some of which were excavated at Cerveteri, a stronghold north of Rome. Most startling about the artifacts is their sophisticated, almost mystical sense of design. The Etruscan collection is housed in a papal villa dating from the 1500s. See p. 161.

- **Uffizi Gallery** (Florence): This 16th-century Renaissance palace was the administrative headquarters, or *uffizi* (offices), for the Duchy of Tuscany when the Medicis controlled Florence. It's estimated that up to 90% of Italy's artistic patrimony is stored in this building, the crown jewel of Italy's museums. This is the world's greatest collection of Renaissance paintings. See p. 225.
- **Bargello Museum** (Florence): Originally built as a fortress palace in 1255, this imposing structure is now a vast repository of some of Italy's most important Renaissance sculpture. Donatello's bronze *David* is a remarkable contrast to the world-famous Michelangelo icon. See p. 232.
- **National Gallery of Umbria** (Perugia): Italian Renaissance art has its roots in Tuscan and Umbrian painting from the 1200s. This collection, on the top floor of the Palazzo dei Priori (parts of which date from the 1400s), contains a world-class collection of paintings, most executed in Tuscany or Umbria between the 13th and the 18th centuries. Included are works by Fra Angelico, Piero della Francesco, Perugino, Duccio, and Gozzoli, among others. See p. 314.
- **Academy Gallery** (Venice): One of Europe's great museums, this is an incomparable collection of Venetian painting, exhibited chronologically from the 13th through the 18th centuries. It's one of the most richly stocked art museums in Italy, boasting hundreds of works by Bellini, Carpaccio, Giorgione, Titian, and Tintoretto. See p. 423.
- **Peggy Guggenheim Collection** (Venice): A comprehensive and brilliant modern-art collection, assembled by legendary arts patron Peggy Guggenheim, is housed in an unfinished palazzo along the Grand Canal. The collection is a cavalcade of 20th-century art, including works by Max Ernst (one of Ms. Guggenheim's former husbands), Picasso, Braque, Magritte, Giacometti, and Moore. See p. 426.
- **Brera Picture Gallery** (Milan): Milan is usually associated with wealth and corporate power, and those two things can buy a city its fair share of art and culture. The foremost place to see Milan's artistic treasures is the Brera Picture Gallery, whose collection—shown in a 17th-century palace—is especially rich in paintings from the schools of Lombardy and Venice. Three of the most important prizes are Mantegna's *Dead Christ,* Giovanni Bellini's *La Pietà,* and Carpaccio's *St. Stephen Debating.* See p. 500.
- **National Archeological Museum** (Naples): Naples and the region around it have yielded a wealth of sculptural treasures from the Roman Empire. Many of these riches have been accumulated in a rambling building designed as a barracks for the Neapolitan cavalry in the 1500s. Much of the loot excavated from Pompeii and Herculaneum, as well as the Renaissance collections of the Farnese family, is in this museum, which boasts a trove of Greco-Roman antiquities. See p. 601.

4 The Best Cathedrals

- **St. Peter's Basilica** (Rome): Its roots began with the first Christian emperor, Constantine, in A.D. 324. By 1400, the Roman basilica was in danger of collapsing, prompting the Renaissance popes to commission plans for the largest, most impressive, most jaw-dropping cathedral the world had ever seen. Amid the rich decor of gilt, marble, and mosaics are countless artworks, including Michelangelo's *Pietà*. Other sights here are a small museum of Vatican treasures and the eerie underground grottoes containing the tombs of former popes. An elevator ride (or a rigorous climb) up the tower to Michelangelo's glorious dome provides panoramic views of Rome. See p. 136.

- **The Duomo of Florence:** Begun in the late 1200s and consecrated 140 years later, the pink, green, and white marble Duomo was a symbol of Florence's prestige and wealth. It's loaded with world-class art and is one of Italy's largest and most distinctive religious buildings. A view of its red-tiled dome, erected over a 14-year period in what was at the time a radical new design by Brunelleschi, is worth the trip to Florence. Other elements of the Duomo are Giotto's Campanile (bell tower) and the octagonal Baptistry (a Romanesque building with renowned bronze doors). See p. 233.

- **The Duomo of Siena:** Begun in 1196, this cathedral is one of the most beautiful and ambitious Gothic churches in Italy, with extravagant zebra-striped bands of marble. Masterpieces here include a priceless pavement of masterful mosaics, an octagonal pulpit carved by master sculptor Nicola Pisano, and the lavishly frescoed Piccolomini Library. See p. 294.

- **Basilica di San Francesco** (Assisi): St. Francis, protector of small animals and birds, was long dead when construction began on this double-tiered showcase of the Franciscan brotherhood. Giotto's celebrated frescoes reached a new kind of figurative realism in Italian art around 1300, long before the masters of the Renaissance carried the technique even further. Consecrated in 1253, the cathedral is one of the highlights of Umbria and the site of many religious pilgrimages. It took a direct hit from the 1997 earthquakes but has miraculously made a recovery. See p. 308.

- **The Duomo of Orvieto:** A well-designed transition between the Romanesque and Gothic styles, this cathedral was begun in 1290 and completed in 1600. It sheltered an Italian pope (Clement VII) when French soldiers sacked Rome in 1527. Part of the building's mystery derives from Orvieto's role as an Etruscan stronghold long before Italy's recorded history. The cathedral is known for its great fresco cycles by Fra Angelico and Luca Signorelli. See p. 334.

- **St. Mark's Basilica** (Venice): Surely the most exotic and Eastern of the Western world's churches, the onion-domed and mosaic-covered San Marco took much of its inspiration from Constantinople. Somewhere inside the mysterious candle-lit cavern of the 1,000-year-old church, which began as the private chapel of the doges, are the remains of St. Mark, revered patron saint of Venice's ancient maritime republic. See p. 416.

- **The Duomo of Milan:** It took 5 centuries to build this magnificent and ornate Gothic cathedral, the third-largest church in the world. It's marked by 135 marble spires, a stunning triangular facade, and thousands of statues flanking the massive but airy, almost fanciful exterior. See p. 496.

5 The Best Ruins

- **The Roman Forum** (Rome): Two thousand years ago, most of the known world was directly affected by decisions made in the Roman Forum. Today classicists and archaeologists wander among its ruins, conjuring up the glory that was Rome. What you'll see today is a pale, rubble-strewn version of the site's original majesty—it's now surrounded by modern boulevards packed with whizzing cars. See p. 146.

- **Palatine Hill** (Rome): According to legend, the Palatine Hill was the site where Romulus and Remus (the orphaned infant twins who survived in the wild by being suckled by a she-wolf) eventually founded the city. Although Il Palatino is one of the seven hills of ancient Rome, you'll find it hard to distinguish it as such because of the urban congestion rising all around. The site is enhanced by the Farnese Gardens (Orti Farnesiani), laid out in the 1500s on the site of Tiberius's palace. See p. 146.

- **The Colosseum** (Rome): Rome boasts only a handful of other ancient monuments that survive in such well-preserved condition. A massive amphitheater set incongruously amid a maze of modern traffic, the Colosseum was once the setting for gladiator combat, lion-feeding frenzies, and public entertainment whose cruelty was a noted characteristic of the Empire (just ask Russell Crowe). All three of the ancient world's classical styles (Doric, Ionic, and Corinthian) are represented, superimposed in tiers one above the other. See p. 143.

- **Villa Adriana** (near Tivoli): Hadrian's Villa slumbered in rural obscurity until the 1500s, when Renaissance popes ordered its excavation. Only then was the scale of this enormous and very beautiful villa from A.D. 134 appreciated. Its builder, Hadrian, who had visited almost every part of his empire, wanted to incorporate the widespread wonders of the world into one fantastic building site—and he succeeded. See p. 182.

- **Ostia Antica** (near Rome): During the height of the Roman Empire, Ostia ("mouth" in Latin) was the harbor town set at the point where the Tiber flowed into the sea. As Rome declined, so did Ostia; by the early Middle Ages, the town had almost disappeared, with its population decimated by malaria. In the early 1900s, archaeologists excavated the ruins of hundreds of ancient buildings, many of which you can view. See p. 183.

- **Herculaneum** (Campania): Legend says that Herculaneum was founded by Hercules. The historical facts tell us that it was buried under rivers of volcanic mud one fateful day in A.D. 79 after the eruption of Mt. Vesuvius. Seeping into the cracks of virtually every building in town, the scalding mud preserved the timbers of hundreds of structures that would otherwise have rotted during the normal course of time. Devote at least 2 hours to seeing some of the best-preserved houses from the ancient world. See "The Environs of Naples: The Phlaegrean Fields & Herculaneum," in chapter 14.

- **Pompeii** (Campania): Once it was an opulent resort filled with 25,000 wealthy Romans. In A.D. 79, the same eruption that devastated Herculaneum (above) buried Pompeii under at least 6m (20 ft.) of boiling volcanic ash and pumice stone. Beginning around 1750, Charles of Bourbon ordered the systematic excavation of the ruins—the treasures hauled out of Pompeii sparked a wave of interest in the classical era throughout northern Europe. See "Pompeii," in chapter 14.

- **Paestum** (Campania): Paestum was discovered by accident around 1750 when local bureaucrats tried to build a road across the heart of what had been a thriving ancient city. Paestum originated as a Greek colony around 600 B.C., fell to the Romans in 273 B.C., and declined into obscurity in the final days of the empire. Today amateur archaeologists can follow a well-marked walking tour through the excavations. See "Paestum & Its Glorious Greek Temples," in chapter 14.

- **The Valley of the Temples** (Sicily): Although most of the Valley of the Temples in Agrigento lies in ruins, it is one of Europe's most beautiful classical sites, especially in February and March when the almond trees surrounding it burst into pink blossoms. One of the site's five temples dates from as early as 520 B.C.; another (though never completed) ranks as one of the largest temples in the ancient world. See "Agrigento & the Valley of the Temples," in chapter 16.

- **Segesta** (Sicily): Even its site is impressive: a rocky outcropping surrounded on most sides by a jagged ravine. Built around 430 B.C. by the Greeks, Segesta's Doric colonnade is one of the most graceful in the ancient world. The site is stark and mysterious and is believed to have been destroyed by the Saracens (Muslim raiders) in the 11th century. See "Palermo," in chapter 16.

- **Selinunte** (Sicily): The massive columns of Selinunte lie scattered on the ground, as if an earthquake had punished its builders, yet this is one of our favorite ancient ruins in Italy. Around 600 B.C., immigrants from Syracuse built Selinunte into an important trading port. The city was a bitter rival of neighboring Segesta (above) and was destroyed around 400 B.C. and then again in 250 B.C. by the Carthaginians. See "Selinunte," in chapter 16.

6 The Best Wine-Growing Regions

- **Latium** (Lazio, outside Rome): The region around Rome is known for predominantly white wines that include Marino, Est! Est!! Est!!!, Colli Albani, and the famous Frascati ("the wine of the popes and the people"). All these are derived almost exclusively from Malvasia and Trebbiano grapes or, in some cases, from combinations of the two. The region's most famous producers of Frascati are **Fontana Candida,** Via di Fontana Candida 11, 00040 Monte Porzio Catone, Roma (© 06-9420066), whose winery, 14 miles southwest of Rome, was built around 1900; and **Gotto D'Oro–Cantina Sociale di Marino,** Via del Divino Amore 115, 00040 Frattocchie, Roma (© 06-93022211;

www.gottodoro.it). To arrange visits, contact the **Gruppo Italiano Vini,** Villa Belvedere, 37011 Calmasino, Verona (© **045-6269600**). See chapter 5.

- **Tuscany and Umbria:** Some of Italy's most scenic vineyards lie nestled among the verdant rolling hills of these two stately regions. In fact, the most famous kind of wine in Italy (Chianti) is indelibly associated with Tuscany, whereas the (usually white) Orivieto and the (usually red) Torgiano are closely associated with Umbria. One of Tuscany's largest vintners is **Banfi,** Castello Banfi, Sant'Angelo Scalo, Montalcino, 53020 Siena (© **0577-840111**). Near Siena are two other good choices: **Biondi-Santi,** Loc. Greppo, 53024 Montalcino (© **0577-848087**), and **Casa Vinicola L. Cecchi,** Loc. Casina dei Ponti 56, 53011 Castellina in Chianti (© **0577-743024**). See chapter 7.

- **Emilia-Romagna:** Composed of two distinct areas (Emilia, to the west of Bologna, around the upriver Po Valley; and Romagna, to the east, centered on the delta of the Po), the region is known to gastronomes as the producer of some of Italy's best food, with wines worthy of its legendary cuisine. Emilia's most famous wine is Lambrusco, 50 million bottles of which are produced every year near Modena and Reggio Emilia. Less well known but also highly rated are the Colli Piacentini wines, of which **Cantine Romagnoli,** Via Genova 20, Villo di Vigolzone 29020 (© **0523-870129**), is a rising star. Wines from Romagna are produced from Sangiovese, Trebbiano, and Albana grapes and are almost universally well respected, cropping up on wine lists throughout the country. See chapter 8.

- **The Veneto:** The humid flatlands of the eastern Po Valley produce memorable reds and whites in great abundance, including everything from soft white Soaves and Pinot Grigios to red Valpolicellas and Merlots. Important vineyards in the region are **Azienda Vinicola Fratelli Fabiano,** Via Verona 6, 37060 Sona, near Verona (© **045-6081111**), and **Fratelli Bolla,** Piazza Cittadella 3, 37122 Verona (© **045-8090911**). Smaller, but well respected because of recent improvements to its vintages, is **Nino Franco** (known for its sparkling prosecco), in the hamlet of Valdobbiadene, Via Garibaldi 147, 31049 Valdobbiadene, Treviso (© **0423-972051**). For information on these and the dozens of other producers in the Veneto, contact the **Azienda di Promozione Turistica,** Piazza Gabe, 37121 Verona (© **045-8000065**). See chapter 10.

- **Trentino–Alto Adige:** The two most important wine-producing regions of northwestern Italy are the Alto Adige (also known as the Bolzano or Sudtirol region) and Trento. The loftier of the two, the Alto Adige, was once part of the Austro-Hungarian province of the South Tirol. More Germanic than Italian, it clings to its Austrian traditions and folklore and grows an Italian version of the gewürztraminers (a fruity white) that would more often be found in Germany, Austria, and Alsace. Venerable wine growers include **Alois Lageder** (founded in 1855), Tenuta Loüwengang, Vicolo dei Conti 9, 39040 in the hamlet of Magré (© **0471-809500;** www.lageder.com), and **Schloss Turmhof,** Via Castello 4, Entiklar, Kurtatsch, 39040 (© **0471-880122**). The Trentino area, a short distance to the south, is one of the leading producers of Chardonnay and sparkling wines fermented using methods developed centuries ago. A winery worth a visit is **Cavit Cantina Viticoltori,** Via del Ponte 31, 38060 Ravina, Trento (✆ **0461-381711**). See chapter 10.

- **Friuli–Venezia Giulia:** This region in the cool alpine foothills of northeastern Italy produces a light, fruity vintage that's especially appealing when young. One of the largest and best-respected wineries here is **Livio Felluga,** Via Risorgimento 1, Brazzano di Cormons, 34071 Gorizia (✆ **0432-534040**). Another worthy producer known for its high-quality wines is **Eugenio Collavini Vini & Spumanti,** Via della Ribolla Gialla 2, 33040 Corno di Rosazzo, Udine (✆ **0432-753222**). See chapter 10.

- **Lombardy:** The Po Valley has always been known for its flat vistas, midsummer humidity, fertile soil, and excellent wines. The region produces everything from dry, still reds to sparkling whites with a champagnelike zest. **Guido Berlucchi,** Piazza Duranti 4, Borgonato di Cortefranca, 25040 Brescia (✆ **030-984381;** www.berlucchi.it), one of Italy's largest wineries, is especially willing to receive visitors. See chapter 11.

- **The Piedmont:** Reds with rich and complex flavors make up most of the wine output of this rugged high-altitude region near Italy's border with France. One of the most interesting vineyards is headquartered in a 15th-century abbey near the hamlet of Alba: **(Renato Ratti S.A.S.) Antiche Cantine dell'Annunziata,** Frazione dell'Annunziata 7, La Morra, 12064 Cuneo (✆ **0173-50185**). See chapter 12.

- **Campania:** The wines produced in the harsh, hot landscapes of Campania, around Naples in southern Italy, seem stronger, rougher, and, in many cases, more powerful than those grown in gentler climes. Among the most famous are the Lacryma Christi (Tears of Christ), a white that grows in the volcanic soil near Naples, Herculaneum, and Pompeii; Taurasi, a potent red; and Greco di Tufo, a pungent white laden with the odors of apricots and apples. One of the most frequently visited vineyards is **Mastroberardino,** 75–81 Via Manfredi, Atripalda, 83042 Avellino (✆ **0825-614111**). See chapter 14.

- **Sicily:** Because of its hot climate and volcanic soil, Sicily is home to countless vineyards, many of which just produce simple table wines. Of the better vintages, the best-known wine is Marsala, a sweet dessert wine produced in both amber and ruby tones. Its production was given a great boost by the British, whose fleet paid frequent calls in Sicily throughout England's Age of Empire. Lord Nelson himself was an avid connoisseur, encouraging its production and spurring local vintners to produce abundant quantities. One top producer is **Regaleali,** Contrada Regaleali, 93010 Vallelunga, Pratameno Caltanisetta (✆ **0921-542422**), a historic enterprise near Palermo run by the Tasca d'Almerita family; this winery is also known for its sauvignon-based Nozze d'Oro and such full-bodied reds as Rosso del Conte. Two other names that evoke years of wine-making traditions, thanks to their skill at producing Cerasuolo di Vittoria and Moscato di Pantelleria, are **Cantine Torrevecchia di Favuzza**

Giuseppe, Via Ariosto 10A, 90144 Ragusa (© **0932-865196**), and **Corvo Duca di Salaparuta,** a 19th-century winery in the hills above Palermo. For information, contact the **Casa Vinicola Duca di Salaparuta,** Via Nazionale, SS113, Casteldaccia, 90014 Palermo (© **091-953988**). See chapter 16.

7 The Best Luxury Hotels

- **Hotel Eden** (Rome; © **800/ 225-5843** in the U.S., or 06-478121; www.hotel-eden.it): The Eden offers great service and plush comfort, but without all the ostentation that comes with the package in many of Rome's grand hotels. Spacious, elegant guest rooms offer panoramic views over the Eternal City, and the Eden offers other perks such as a health club and one of the city's best restaurants. See p. 97.
- **Hotel de Russie** (Rome; © **800/ 323-7500** in North America, or 06-328881; www.roccofortehotels. com): Opulently furnished, this chic boutique hotel, which just opened in 2000, enjoys a spectacular location in a setting of terraced gardens near Rome's Piazza del Popolo. Almost three-quarters of the guest rooms are done in a stark and striking contemporary minimalist style. All are incredibly comfortable and offer all the high-tech gadgets and thoughtful touches you could want. See p. 101.
- **The Inn at the Spanish Steps** (Rome; © **06-69925657;** www. atspanishsteps.com): This intimate, upscale inn is a real find. The former Roman residence of Hans Christian Andersen has been transformed into a small inn of charm and grace, with each bedroom furnished with an authentic period decor and modern comforts. See p. 104.
- **Hotel Regency** (Florence; © **055-245247;** www.regency hotel.com): An intimate and luxurious hideaway in a tranquil part of Florence, this hotel is filled with stained glass, paneled walls, and reproduction antiques. The exquisite guest rooms boast thoughtful touches such as custom mattresses, double-glazed windows, thick carpeting, coffered or beamed ceilings, rich fabrics, and the most fabulous marble bathrooms in town. See p. 207.
- **Villa San Michele** (Fiesole, near Florence; © **800/237-1236** in the U.S., or 055-59451 or 055-567-200; www.orient-express hotels.com): This former 15th-century monastery is set behind a facade reputedly designed by Michelangelo. Brigitte Bardot once selected it for one of her honeymoons (no one remembers which husband she was with). With a decor that no set designer could ever duplicate, it evokes the charm of an aristocratic private villa. See p. 255.
- **Certosa di Maggiano** (Siena; © **0577-288180;** www.certosa dimaggiano.it): This early-13th-century Certosinian monastery has been impeccably restored and converted into an upscale Relais & Chateaux inn. The individually decorated guest rooms are spacious, with antiques, art objects, and sumptuous beds; one has a private walled garden. See p. 297.
- **Hotel Cipriani** (Venice; © **800/ 992-5055** in the U.S., or 041-5207744; www.orient-express hotels.com): This exclusive, elegant hotel is situated in a 3-acre garden on the isolated Isola della Giudecca, removed from the tourist bustle of Venice. It offers

chic, contemporary surroundings; sumptuous guest rooms; and a wealth of recreational facilities, including an Olympic-size pool, a first-rate health club, Venice's only tennis court, and much more. Service is the best in Venice, with two employees for every room. See p. 400.

• **Gritti Palace** (Venice; ✆ **800/ 325-3535** in the U.S., 416/ 947-4864 in Canada, or 041-794611; www.luxurycollection. com/grittipalace): The Gritti, in a stately, central Grand Canal setting, is the renovated palazzo of 15th-century doge Andrea Gritti. It's quite formal, but it simply oozes glamour and history. Expect superb service, and elegant rooms with nice touches such as hypoallergenic pillows, bottled water, two-line phones, and marble bathrooms with deep soaking tubs. See p. 385.

• **Four Seasons Hotel Milano** (Milan; ✆ **02-77088;** www. fourseasons.com): The building was first a 15th-century monastery, then the residence of the Hapsburg-appointed governor of northern Italy in the 1850s. The Four Seasons chain took over in the early 1990s and created one of Italy's finest hotels, incorporating the medieval facade, many of the frescoes and columns, and the original monastic details into a modern edifice accented with stone floors, pearwood cabinetry, Murano chandeliers, and acres of Fortuny fabrics. The guest rooms are cool, sleek, and spacious, with a sense of understated luxury and state-of-the-art bathrooms. Service is impeccable. See p. 507.

• **Grand Hotel Villa d'Este** (Cernobbio; ✆ **031-3481;** www. villadeste.it): Built in 1568, this splendid palace in the Lake District is one of Europe's finest resort

hotels. Step inside, and you're surrounded by frescoed ceilings, impeccable antiques, and many other exquisite details. Ten magnificently landscaped acres, parts of which have been nurtured since the 1500s, surround the hotel. Guests enjoy dining on outdoor terraces, swimming in the gorgeous pools, using the health club and reveling in spa treatments, and much more. Cool breezes are provided by nearby Lake Como. See p. 539.

• **Hotel Splendido and Splendido Mare** (Portofino; ✆ **800/223-6800** in the U.S., or 0185-267801;   www.orient-express hotels.com): Built as a monastery in the 14th century and abandoned because of attacks by North African pirates, this monument was rescued during the 19th century by an Italian baron, who converted it into a summer home for his family. The posh hillside retreat on the Italian Riviera now accommodates a sophisticated crowd, including many film stars. The views over the sea are stunning; you can enjoy the hotel's own lovely pool, or the staff will take you by boat to a private cove with changing cabins and lounge chairs. See p. 588.

• **Grand Hotel Quisisana Capri** (Capri; ✆ **081-8370788;** www. quisi.com): This is the grande dame of Capri's resort hotels, with glorious views, a posh style, and supremely comfortable rooms. See p. 638.

• **Hotel di San Pietro** (near Positano; ✆ **089-875455;** www.ilsan pietro.it): The only marker identifying this cliffside hotel is a 15th-century chapel set beside the winding road. The hotel doesn't advertise and offers a quiet place to escape from it all, but this Relais & Chateaux property, with its gorgeous views, is the most luxurious retreat in the south of Italy. Strands of bougainvillea twine around the dramatically terraced white exterior walls; the spacious rooms are superglamorous. An elevator takes you down to the cliff ledges to a private beach. See p. 646.

- **Grand Hotel Timeo** (Taormina; ✆ **0942-23801;** www.cormorano. net/framon/timeo): Hidden in a tranquil private park full of cypresses and magnolias, just below an ancient Greek amphitheater, the Timeo opened in 1873. Old-world elegance and Victorian antiques combine with contemporary conveniences. All rooms have balconies with a view of the snow-capped volcanic peak of Mount Etna or the sea. Guests relax on the hotel's private beach. See p. 692.

8 The Best Moderately Priced Hotels

- **La Residenza** (Rome; ✆ **06-4880789;** www.venere.it/roma/la_residenza): This town house hotel, close to Via Veneto, is elegantly old-fashioned and homey. With its ivy-covered courtyard, it is a successfully converted villa with spacious and tastefully furnished guest rooms. See p. 98.
- **Hotel Bellettini** (Florence; ✆ **055-213561**): If you're looking for a place with *A Room with a View* atmosphere, head for this Renaissance palazzo midway between the Duomo and the rail station. It's a family-run affair with an old-time atmosphere evoked by terra-cotta floors and stained-glass windows. The rooms are a bit plain but very comfortable. See p. 203.
- **Palazzo Ravizza** (Siena; ✆ **0577-280462;** www.palazzoravizza.it): Right in the heart of Siena, only a short walk from Piazza del Campo, you can stay in an elegant building that was successfully converted from a 19th-century palace. Every guest room has a few antiques along with ceiling frescoes. See p. 301.
- **La Residenza** (Venice; ✆ **041-5285315**): In a 14th-century building that looks a lot like a miniature Doge's Palace, this little hotel is on a residential square.

You'll enter through an enormous salon filled with antiques, 300-year-old paintings, and some of the most marvelously preserved walls in Venice. The guest rooms aren't as grand, but they're comfortable and offer remarkably good value for pricey Venice. See p. 394.

- **Hotel Menardi** (Cortina d'Ampezzo; ✆ **0436-2400;** www.hotel menardi.it): Built a century ago, this family-run alpine inn is adorable with its wooden balconies and shutters and blazing fireplaces. Its rear windows open onto a flowery meadow and a view of the Dolomite peaks. The Menardi is a great buy in a high-priced resort town. See p. 487.
- **Victoria Hotel** (Turin; ✆ **011-5611909;** www.hotelvictoria torino.com): One of Turin's best hotel buys, the Victoria has the distinct flavor of a British manor. You get touches of luxury and even a private garden. See p. 555.
- **Hotel La Villarosa** (Ischia; ✆ **081-991316**): In a semi-tropical garden setting, this is the island's finest pensione. It's like a Mediterranean-style country villa with antiques and tiles adorning bright, airy guest rooms. See p. 625.

9 The Best Restaurants

- **Relais Le Jardin** (Rome; ✆ 06-3613041): The restaurant of the dignified Lord Byron Hotel, in an upscale residential neighborhood a short drive from the center of Rome, the Relais is simply one of Italy's best. There are places in Rome with better views, but not with such an elegant setting. The service is impeccable, and the menu varies according to what's in season. See p. 131.
- **La Terrazza** (Rome; ✆ 06-478121): You get two winning elements here: some of the finest cuisine in Rome and a panoramic view toward Michelangelo's dome of St. Peter's. The constantly changing menu takes advantage of the best seasonal ingredients, and the chef is constantly dazzling discerning palates with new taste sensations. See p. 115.
- **Cibrèo** (Florence; ✆ 055-2341100): Fabio Picchi, the chef-owner, serves the most innovative cuisine in Florence. Cibrèo consists of a restaurant, a less formal trattoria, and a cafe/bar across the street. The impossibly old-fashioned small kitchen doesn't have a grill and doesn't turn out pastas; it specializes in sophisticated creations based on age-old Tuscan recipes with a twist. Don't miss the incredible flourless chocolate cake. See p. 222.
- **Antica Trattoria Botteganova** (outside Siena; ✆ 0577-284230): On the road leading north of Siena to Chianti, just outside the city walls, lies this outstanding restaurant. Chef Michele Sonentino gives standard Italian dishes a modern touch and uses the best seasonal ingredients from the Tuscan countryside. Try his tortelli stuffed with pecorino cheese and served with a hot parmigiano cheese sauce and truffled cream, and sample a regional vintage from the fine wine cellar. See p. 304.
- **San Domenico** (Imola, outside Bologna; ✆ 0542-29000): Foodies from all over Europe flock to the unlikely town of Imola to visit this, our pick as Italy's best restaurant. Convenient to both Bologna and Ravenna, San Domenico features a cuisine that seems to feature modern French influences. But owner Gian Luigi Morini claims that his heavenly offerings are nothing more than adaptations of festive regional dishes—they're just lighter, more subtle, and served in manageable portions. Enjoy a vintage from one of Italy's finest wine cellars to accompany your memorable meal here. Simply marvelous! See p. 353.
- **Harry's Bar** (Venice; ✆ 041-5285777): It's legendary, it's lighthearted, and it's fun. First made famous by writer Ernest Hemingway, Harry's Bar still serves sublime food in the formal dining room upstairs. The Bellini, peach juice with *prosecco* (Italian sparkling wine), was born here. See p. 403.
- **Antico Martini** (Venice; ✆ 041-5224121): Founded in 1720 as a spot to enjoy the newly developed rage of coffee drinking, this restaurant is one of the very best in Venice. Replete with paneled walls and glittering chandeliers, the Martini specializes in Venetian cuisine. See p. 403.
- **Ristorante il Desco** (Verona; ✆ 045-595358): Set in a former palazzo, this restaurant is the best in the Veneto region of northeastern Italy. Its culinary repertoire emphasizes a *nuova cucina* (nouvelle cuisine) that makes use of the

freshest ingredients. The wine selections are excellent. See p. 469.

- **Restaurant Joia** (Milan; ℂ 01-29522124): The vegetarian dishes here are among the best in Italy, but Swiss chef Pietro Leemann also excels in seafood. This is a hot dining ticket in Italy's city of fashion. See p. 513.
- **Vecchia Lugana** (Sirmione; ℂ 030-919012): Lake Garda's finest dining choice is found outside this resort. Visitors from all over northern Italy drive here for a first-rate culinary experience in which the chef is known for his deft use of market-fresh ingredients. See p. 535.
- **La Cantinella** (Naples; ℂ 081-7648684): The only Michelin-starred restaurant in Naples, La Cantinella serves some of the best and most refined seafood in Campania. Opening onto the bay of Santa Lucia, this will be the highlight of your culinary tour of the area. Time-tested Neapolitan classics are served here, along with an array of more imaginative dishes. Grilled fish can be prepared as you like it—and chances are, you'll like it a lot. See p. 612.

10 The Best Buys

- **Ceramics:** The town of Faenza, in Emilia-Romagna, has been the center of pottery making, especially majolica, since the Renaissance. Majolica, also known as faïence, is a type of hand-painted, glazed, and heavily ornamented earthenware. Of course, you don't have to go to Faenza to buy it because shops throughout the country carry it. Tuscany and Umbria are also known for their earthenware pottery, carried by many shops in Rome and Florence.
- **Fashion:** Italian fashion is world-renowned. Pucci and Valentino led the parade, to be followed by Armani, Missoni, Gucci, Versace, and Ferre. Following World War II, Italian design began to compete seriously against the French fashion monopoly. Today Italian designers such as Krizia are among the arbiters of the world fashion scene. Milan dominates with the largest selection of boutiques, followed by Rome and Florence. Ironically, a lot of "French" fashion is now designed and manufactured in Italy, in spite of what the label says.
- **Glass:** Venetian glass, ranging from the delicate to the grotesque, is famous the world over. In Venice you'll find literally hundreds of stores peddling Venetian glass in a wide range of prices. Here's the surprise: A great deal of Venetian glass today is manufactured not on Murano (an island in the Venetian lagoon) but in the Czech Republic. That doesn't mean that the glass is unworthy though. Many factories outside Italy turn out high-quality glass products that are then shipped to Murano, where many so-called glass factories aren't factories at all but storefronts selling this imported "Venetian" glass. See "Shopping," in chapter 9.
- **Gold:** The tradition of shaping jewelry out of gold dates from the time of the Etruscans, and this ancient tradition is going strong in Italy today, with artisans still toiling in tiny studios and workshops. Many of the designs they follow are based on ancient Roman originals. Of course, dozens of gold jewelers don't follow tradition at all but design original and often daring pieces. Many shops will even

melt down your old gold jewelry and refashion it into something more modern.

- **Lace:** For centuries, Italy has been known for its exquisite and delicate lace, fashioned into everything from women's undergarments to heirloom tablecloths. Florence long ago distinguished itself for the punto Firenze (Florentine stitch) made by cloistered nuns, although this tradition has waned over the years. Venetian lace is even more famous, including some of the finest products in the world, especially tombolo (pillow lace), macramé, and an expensive form of lace known as chiacchierino. Of course, the market today is also flooded with cheap machine-made stuff, which a trained eye can quickly spot. Although some pieces, such as a bridal veil, might cost hundreds of euros, you'll often find reasonably priced collars, handkerchiefs, and doilies in Venice and Florence boutiques. See "Shopping," in chapters 6 and 9.

- **Leather:** The Italians craft the finest leather in the world. From boots to luggage, from leather clothing to purses (or wallets), Italian cities—especially Rome, Florence, Venice, and Milan—abound in leather shops selling quality goods. This is one of Italy's best values, in spite of the substandard work that's now appearing. If you shop carefully, you can still find lots of handcrafted Italian leather products.

- **Prints and Engravings:** Wood engravings, woodcuts, mezzotints, copper engravings—you name it and you'll find it, especially in Rome and Florence. Of course, you have to be a careful shopper. Some prints are genuine antiques and works of rare art, but others are rushed off the assembly line and into the shops.

- **Religious Objects and Vestments:** The religious objects industry in Italy is big and bustling, centered mostly in the Greater Vatican area in Rome. The biggest concentration of shops in Rome is near the ancient Church of Santa Maria Sopra Minerva. These shops have it all, from cardinals' birettas and rosary beads to religious art and vestments.

A Traveler's Guide to Italy's Art & Architecture

by Reid Bramblett

Italy's art ranges from Roman mosaics and Renaissance masterpieces by Michelangelo and Leonardo to Bernini's baroque statues and Morandi's modern still lifes. Its architectural heritage encompasses Greek temples, Byzantine basilicas, Gothic cathedrals, baroque palaces, and postmodern stadiums that take their cue from the ancient Colosseum. This brief overview will help you make sense of it all.

1 Art 101

CLASSICAL: GREEKS, ETRUSCANS & ROMANS (5TH CENTURY B.C. TO A.D. 5TH CENTURY)

The **Greeks** settled Sicily and southern Italy centuries before the Romans expanded south, so their art, which celebrates the perfection of proportion, balance, harmony, and form, is an integral part of Italy's heritage.

Although those early tourists to the Italian peninsula, the **Etruscans,** arrived with their own styles from Asia Minor, by the 6th century B.C. they were borrowing heavily from the Greeks in their sculpture (and importing thousands of Attic painted vases, which displayed the most popular and widespread painting style of ancient Greece).

Although painting was used primarily for decorative purposes in ancient **Rome,** bucolic frescoes (the technique of painting on wet plaster) adorned the walls of the wealthy. Rome's sculptures tended to glorify emperors and the perfect human form, often copying famous Greek originals.

Examples of art from Classical eras include these:

- **Greek.** The world's best surviving ancient Greek murals are in Paestum's museum, including the famed Tomb of the Diver frescoes. There is also some fine sculpture in the archaeological museums of Syracuse, Palermo, and Taranto, as well as numerous Roman copies of Greek originals filling just about every Italian archaeology museum from Milan to Rome to Syracuse.
- **Etruscan.** Etruscan remains are mostly confined to museums (the best are in the Tuscan towns Volterra, Cortona, and Chiusi, and at Rome in the Villa Giulia and Vatican museums). Notable works include the bronze Chimera at Florence's archaeology museum, carved alabaster urns and the elongated bronze statuette *Shade of the Evening* in Volterra's Guarnacci museum, and terra-cotta sarcophagi covers of reclining figures in museums across Tuscany and in Rome's Villa Giulia. Some tomb paintings also survive at Tarquinia in Lazio and Chiusi in Tuscany.

- **Roman.** Along with an army of also-ran statues and busts gracing most archaeological collections in Italy, you'll find a few standouts. In Rome, look for the marble bas-reliefs (sculptures that project slightly from a flat surface) on the Arch of Constantine, the sculpture and mosaic collections at the Museo Nazionale Romano, and the gilded equestrian statue of Marcus Aurelius at the Capitoline Museums. The mosaics in the ancient villa of Sicily's Piazza Armerina are the most extensive in the world. Pompeii's Villa dei Misteri frescoes of religious rites are remarkably well preserved and expertly done. Also don't miss the Alexander mosaic from Pompeii, now at the archaeological museum in Naples.

BYZANTINE & ROMANESQUE (5TH TO 13TH CENTURIES)

Artistic expression in medieval Italy was largely church-related. Because Mass was recited in Latin, images were used to communicate the Bible's most important lessons to the illiterate masses. Bas-reliefs around the churches' main doors, and wall paintings and altarpieces inside, told key tales to inspire faith in God and fear of sin (*Last Judgments* were favorites). Otherwise, decoration was spare—what existed was often destroyed, replaced, or covered as tastes changed over the centuries and cathedrals were remodeled.

The **Byzantine** style of painting and mosaic was very stylized and static. This iconographic tradition was imported from the eastern half of the Roman Empire centered at Byzantium (its major political outposts in Italy were Ravenna and Venice). Faces (and eyes) were almond-shaped with pointy little chins; noses were long, with a spoonlike depression at the top; and folds in robes (always blue over red) were represented by stylized cross-hatching in gold leaf.

Romanesque sculpture was somewhat more fluid but still far from naturalistic. Often wonderfully childlike in its narrative simplicity, the work frequently mixes Biblical scenes with the myths and motifs from local pagan traditions that were being slowly incorporated into early medieval Christianity. Romanesque art was seen as crude in many later periods and usually was replaced or destroyed over the centuries; it survives mostly in scraps, as innumerable column capitals or carvings set above church doors, all across Italy.

The following are the best major examples of this era:

- **Ravenna.** The churches of Italy's Byzantine capital are covered in stylized Byzantine mosaics, especially at San Vitale and both Sant'Appollinare in Classe and Sant'Appollinare Nuovo.
- **Basilica di San Marco, Venice.** Venice's cathedral is a late Byzantine church of domes and an astounding number of mosaics (while the overall effect is indeed Byzantine, many of the mosaics are of various later dates).
- **Chiostro del Duomo di Monreale, Sicily.** This hillside hamlet above Palermo houses a cathedral swathed with Byzantine mosaics inside. Its cloister columns are topped with some of the most wonderful Romanesque carved capitals in Italy.
- **Il Duomo, Pisa.** Bonano Pisano's bronze Door of St. Ranieri (1180) on the cathedral's south side was the only door panel to survive a 16th-century fire.
- **Basilica San Zeno Maggiore, Verona.** The 48 relief panels of the bronze doors, one of the most important pieces of Romanesque sculpture in Italy, were cast between the 9th and the 11th centuries and are flanked by strips of 12th-century stone reliefs.

- **Baptistry, Parma.** The exterior sports a series of Romanesque allegorical friezes by Benedetto Antelami, who also carved the statues inside, while anonymous, 13th-century Romanesque artists painted frescoes on the walls.
- **Collegiata dei Santi Pietro e Orso, Aosta.** On the edge of town, this Romanesque church preserves part of an 11th-century fresco cycle and 40 remarkable 12th-century carved column capitals in the cloisters.

INTERNATIONAL GOTHIC (LATE 13TH TO EARLY 15TH CENTURIES)

Late medieval Italian art continued to be largely ecclesiastical. Church facades and pulpits were festooned with statues and carvings. In both Gothic painting and sculpture, figures tended to be more natural than in the Romanesque (and the colors used in painting were more rich and varied) but were highly stylized and rhythmic. The figures' features and gestures are exaggerated for symbolic or emotional emphasis. In painting, late Gothic artists such as Giotto started introducing greater realism, a sense of depth, and more realistic emotion into their art—characteristics that would later define the Renaissance.

The best examples of Gothic art include these:

- **Pisano Pulpits (1255–1311).** Father Nicola (1200–84) and son Giovanni (1245–1320) Pisano together crafted four relief-laden pulpits in Tuscany: in Pisa's Baptistry and Duomo, and in Siena's Duomo.
- **Andrea Orcagna (1344–68).** This painter/sculptor/architect left several examples of his work in Florence, including frescoes in Basilica di Santa Croce, the Strozzi altarpiece in Santa Maria Novella, the elaborate tabernacle in Orsanmichele, and the Loggia della Signoria, whose wide, rounded arches and simple proportions presage the Renaissance.
- **Ambrogio Lorenzetti (ca. 1290–ca. 1348).** The most important secular painting to survive from medieval Europe, his *Allegory of Good and Bad Government* (1338), is a complex Gothic allegory full of details from daily Sienese life. It hangs in Siena's National Picture Gallery. (Lorenzetti also left the gorgeous *Presentation at the Temple* [1342] in Florence's Uffizi Gallery.)
- **Giotto (1266–1337).** The greatest Gothic artist, Giotto lifted painting from its Byzantine funk and set it on the road to the realism and perspective of the Renaissance. His best works are fresco cycles in Assisi's Basilica di San Francesco, Padua's Chapel of the Scrovegni, and Florence's Basilica di Santa Croce. See also his *Ognissanti Maestà* (1310) in the Uffizi Gallery.

RENAISSANCE & MANNERISM (EARLY 15TH TO MID–17TH CENTURIES)

From the 14th to 16th centuries, the popularity of the Humanist movement in philosophy prompted princes and powerful prelates to patronize a generation of innovative young artists. These painters, sculptors, and architects experimented with new modes in art and broke with static medieval traditions in pursuit of a greater degree of expressiveness and naturalism. They began using such techniques as linear perspective, as pioneered by architect Brunelleschi and sculptors Donatello and Ghiberti. The term **Renaissance,** or "rebirth," was only later applied to this period in Florence (the epicenter from which the movement spread to the rest of Italy and Europe).

Eventually the High Renaissance began to stagnate, producing vapid works of technical perfection but little substance. Several artists sought ways out of the downward spiral. **Mannerism,** the most interesting attempt, was a movement that found its muse in the extreme torsion of Michelangelo's figures—in sculpture and painting—and his unusual use of oranges, greens, and other nontraditional colors, most especially in the Sistine Chapel ceiling. In sculpture, Mannerism produced twisting figures in exaggerated positions.

This list of Renaissance giants merely scratches the surface of the masters that Italy produced in the 15th and 16th centuries:

- **Ghiberti (1378–1455).** This sculptor labored for more than 50 years to complete two sets of doors, including those nicknamed "Gates of Paradise," full of relief panels for Florence's Baptistry. Because his competition piece to win this commission, crafted in 1401, won for its studied naturalism and dynamic action (two traits of Renaissance art), the event is taken to mark the beginning of the period. The competition piece is now in Florence's Bargello Museum.

- **Donatello (ca. 1386–1466).** The first full-fledged Renaissance sculptor, Donatello had a patented *schiacciato* technique of warping low-relief surfaces and etching backgrounds in perspective to create a sense of deep space. His bronze and marble figures are some of the most expressive and psychologically probing of the Renaissance. Among his many innovations, this unassuming artist cast the first freestanding nude (the Bargello Museum's *David*) since antiquity. A plethora of his masterpieces are in Florence's Bargello Museum, Duomo Museum, Basilica di San Lorenzo, and Palazzo Vecchio, with more in Siena's Duomo, Baptistry, and Duomo Museum.

- **Masaccio (1401–27).** Before he died at age 27, Masaccio produced the first example of painted perspective in the *Trinità* fresco (1427) in Florence's Basilica di Santa Maria Novella, as well as the famous fresco cycle in Florence's Brancacci Chapel (1424–27) of Santa Maria del Carmine. His work was studied assiduously by masters such as Michelangelo.

- **Botticelli (1444–1510).** His courtly, graceful paintings populated by languid figures have become among the most beloved of the Early Renaissance. His masterpieces are *The Birth of Venus* (ca. 1485) and *Allegory of Spring* (ca. 1481), both of which are in Florence's Uffizi.

- **Leonardo da Vinci (1452–1519).** A true Renaissance man, Leonardo dabbled his genius in a bit of everything from art to philosophy to science (on paper, he even designed machine guns and rudimentary helicopters). Little of his remarkable painting survives, however, because he often experimented with new pigment mixes that proved to lack the staying power of traditional materials. Leonardo invented such painterly effects as the fine haze of *sfumato*, which softens outlines and progressively blurs background details to create a sense of realism and vast distance within the painting. Unfortunately, the best example of this effect, his fresco of *The Last Supper* (1495–97) in Milan, is sadly deteriorated, and even the ongoing multidecade restoration is saving but a shadow of the fresco's glory. See his earlier *Annunciation* (1481) in Florence's Uffizi for a better-preserved example.

- **Raphael (1483–1520).** Rightfully considered one of Western art's greatest draftsmen, Raphael produced a body of work in his 37 short years that ignited European painters for generations to come. You'll find passels of his Madonnas and papal portraits in Florence's Uffizi and Palazzo Pitti and in Rome's National Gallery of Ancient Art. His ethereal *Transfiguration* (1520), which he had almost finished when he died, resides in the Vatican Museums. Also in the Vatican are perhaps his greatest works, a series of frescoed rooms (1508–20), including the *School of Athens,* which depicts the classical philosophers whose rediscovery spurred on the Renaissance—the various "philosophers" are actually portraits of Leonardo, Michelangelo, Raphael himself, and Bramante, a contemporaneous architect.

- **Michelangelo (1475–1564).** This heavyweight contender for world's greatest artist was a genius in sculpture, painting, architecture, and poetry. He marked the apogee of the Renaissance. A complex and difficult man, Michelangelo was intensely jealous, probably manic-depressive, and certainly homosexual. He enjoyed great fame in a life plagued by a series of never-ending projects. Many were commissioned by Pope Julius II, including the Sistine Chapel frescoes (ceiling 1508–12; *Last Judgment* 1535–41) and the tomb of Julius II, of which he finished only the powerful *Moses* (1513–15) in Rome's San Pietro in Vincoli and the *Slaves* (1513–16) in Florence's Galleria dell'Accademia. Others were commissioned by the Medicis, including the family tombs in Florence's Medici Chapels, which incorporate *Dawn, Dusk, Day,* and *Night* (1531–33). Michelangelo worshiped the male nude as the ultimate form and used *torsion* (twisting the body in one direction) or *contraposto* (twisting the body in contradictory directions) to bring out their musculature.

  When forced against his will to paint the Sistine Chapel, he broke almost all the rules and sent painting headlong in an entirely new direction, called Mannerism, marked by nonprimary colors, and twisting, elongated figures.

  Of Michelangelo's painting, Italy has only the *Sacra Famiglia* (1504) in Florence's Uffizi. Of his beloved sculpture, his hometown of Florence also preserves the famous *David* (1502–04) in the Galleria dell'Accademia and several early pieces in the Bargello Museum and Buonarroti's House. He sculpted three *Pietàs* (Mary mourning the dead Christ) over his long life—the first in Rome's St. Peter's Basilica, carved at age 25 (1500), and the second in Florence's Duomo Museum, created at age 75 (1550–53). He was still working on the oddly modern, elongated *Rondanini Pietà,* now in Milan's Museum of Ancient Art, when he died at age 89 (1564).

- **Titian (1485–1576).** The father of the Venetian High Renaissance, Titian imparted to the school his love of color and tonality and an exploration of the effects of light on darkened scenes. In Venice, you'll find his works everywhere, from canvases in the Academy Galleries to altarpieces decorating churches such as Santa Maria Gloriosa dei Frari to his early *Battle* (1513) scene in the Ducal Palace's Maggior Consiglio. He also has fine works in Florence, including the Uffizi's luminous *Flora* (1520) and famous *Venus of Urbino* (1538), which has had a great influence on European art (Manet's groundbreaking *Olympia* [1863] referenced this image), and the Palazzo Pitti's *Mary Magdalene* (1548) and *The Concert* (1510).

- **Mannerist artists.** Artists who took Michelangelo's ideas and ran them to their logical limits include painters **Andrea del Sarto** (1486–1530) and his students **Rosso Fiorentino** (1494–1540) and **Pontormo** (1494–1556). All three are well represented in Florence's Uffizi Gallery and Palazzo Pitti. **Il Parmigianino's** *Madonna of the Long Neck* (1534), in the Uffizi Gallery, is exemplary of the style, starring a waifish Virgin with a grotesquely long neck and pointy head.

  Sculptors fared better with the Mannerism idea, producing for the first time statues that needed to be looked at from multiple angles to be fully appreciated. A good example is **Giambologna**'s (1529–1608) *Rape of the Sabines* (1583) under Florence's Loggia della Signoria.

BAROQUE & ROCOCO (LATE 16TH TO 18TH CENTURIES)

The **baroque,** a more theatrical and decorative take on the Renaissance, mixes a kind of super-realism based on using peasants as models and an exaggerated use of light and dark, called *chiaroscuro,* with compositional complexity and explosions of dynamic fury, movement, color, and figures. The even more dramatic **rococo** is this later baroque art gone awry, frothy and chaotic.

The baroque period produced many fine artists, but only a few true geniuses, including the following:

- **Caravaggio (1571–1610).** Caravaggio started as a street urchin, rose to fame through the graces of a Borghese cardinal, became an honorary Knight of Malta, and ended his life on the run from murder charges in Rome. In between, he reinvented baroque painting, using peasants and commoners as models and including their earthy realism (dirty bare feet were a favorite) in his works. He added his chiaroscuro technique of playing areas of harsh light off deep, black shadows (this helped accent the deeply wrinkled faces that he loved to include). Among his masterpieces are the *St. Matthew* (1599) cycle in Rome's San Luigi dei Francesi, a series of paintings in Rome's Galleria Borghese, the *Deposition* (1604) in the Vatican Museums, and several more in Florence's Uffizi Gallery and Palazzo Pitti and in Naples's National Museum & Gallery of the Capodimonte.

- **Pietro da Cortona (1596–1669).** This Tuscan painter moved to Rome and became the progenitor of a fluffy, pastel baroque style, which he used to decorate the ceilings of Palazzo Barberini in Rome, including the allegorical *Glorification of the Reign of Urban VIII* (1635), and the Palatine Gallery (1641–47) of Florence's Palazzo Pitti for the Medici.

- **Bernini (1598–1680).** Bernini was the greatest baroque sculptor, a fantastic architect (see section 2, "Italian Architecture at a Glance"), and no mean painter. His finest sculptures are in Rome. In the Galleria Borghese are his *Aeneas and Anchises* (1613), *Apollo and Daphne* (1624), *The Rape of Persephone* (1621), and *David* (1623–24)—his version recalls a baroque man of action rather than a Renaissance man of contemplation like Michelangelo's *David.* His other masterpiece is the *Fountain of the Four Rivers* (1651) in Piazza Navona.

- **Tiepolo (1696–1770).** The best rococo artist, Tiepolo specialized in ceiling frescoes (and canvases meant to be placed in a ceiling) with frothy, cloud-filled heavens of light, angels, and pale early-morning colors. Although he painted many works for Veneto villas, including the sumptuous Villa Valmarana "Ai Nani" and Villa Pisani, he also spent much of his time traveling throughout Europe on long commissions (his work in Würzburg, Germany, enjoys distinction as the largest ceiling fresco in the world).

LATE 18TH CENTURY TO TODAY

After carrying the banner of artistic innovation for more than a millennium, Italy ran out of steam with the baroque, leaving countries such as France to develop the heights of **neoclassicism** (although Italy produced a few fine neoclassical sculptures) and the late-19th-century Impressionism (Italy had its own version, called the **Macchiaioli,** in Tuscany). Italy has not played an important role in late-19th- or 20th-century art, although it has produced a few great artists:

- **Antonio Canova (1757–1822).** Italy's top neoclassical sculptor, Canova was popular for his mythological figures and Bonaparte portraits (he even painted both Napoléon and his sister Pauline as nudes). You'll find his work in Venice's Correr Civic Museum, Rome's Galleria Borghese, Florence's Palazzo Pitti, and Milan's Brera Picture Gallery.
- **Giovanni Fattori (1825–1908).** Best of the *Macchiaioli,* Fattori painted battle scenes and landscapes populated by the Maremma's long-horned white cattle. His works grace Florence's Palazzo Pitti, Milan's Brera Picture Gallery, and Rome's National Gallery of Modern Art.
- **Amadeo Modigliani (1884–1920).** A sickly boy, only moderately successful in his short lifetime, Modigliani helped reinvent the portrait in painting and sculpture after he moved to Paris in 1906. He's known for his elongated, mysterious heads and rapidly painted nudes. Check them out at Milan's Brera Picture Gallery and Rome's National Gallery of Modern Art.
- **Futurist artists.** In 1909, Italian artists living in Paris made a spirited attempt to take the artistic initiative back into Italian hands, but what the futurist movement's **Umberto Boccioni** (1882–1916) came up with was similar to cubism (a painting style that depicted objects from all points of view at once) with an element of movement. Examples of his work can be seen in Milan's Brera Picture Gallery and Rome's National Gallery of Modern Art. **Gino Severini** (1883–1966) contributed a sophisticated take on color that rubbed off on the core cubists as well; you can view his works in Milan's Civic Gallery of Modern Art and Rome's National Gallery of Modern Art.
- **Giorgio de Chirico (1888–1978).** De Chirico founded freaky *Pittura Metafisica* ("Metaphysical Painting"), a forerunner of Surrealism wherein figures and objects are stripped of their usual meaning though odd juxtapositions, warped perspective, unnatural shadows, and other bizarre effects and a general spatial emptiness. Look for them at Milan's Brera Picture Gallery and Rome's National Gallery of Modern Art and Collection of Modern Religious Art in the Vatican Museums.
- **Giorgio Morandi (1890–1964).** In the painting of his eerily minimalist, highly modeled, quasi-monochrome still lifes, Morandi was influenced by *Pittura Metafisica.* His paintings decorate Bologna's Palazzo Comunale, where an entire section is devoted to him; Milan's Brera Picture Gallery; and Rome's National Gallery of Modern Art and Collection of Modern Religious Art in the Vatican Museums.

2 Italian Architecture at a Glance

While each architectural era has its own distinctive features, there are some elements, general floor plans, and terms common to many. Also, some features might appear near the end of one era and continue through several later ones.

From the Romanesque period on, most churches consist either of a single wide **aisle** or a wide central **nave,** flanked by two narrow aisles. The aisles are separated from the nave by a row of **columns** or by square stacks of masonry called **piers,** usually connected by **arches.**

This main nave/aisle assemblage is usually crossed by a perpendicular corridor called a **transept** near the far east end of the church so that the floor plan looks like a **Latin Cross** (shaped like a crucifix). The shorter, east arm of the nave is the holiest area, called the **chancel;** it often houses the stalls of the **choir** and the **altar.** If the far end of the chancel is rounded off, it's called an **apse.** An

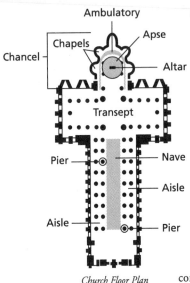

Church Floor Plan

ambulatory is a curving corridor outside the altar and choir area, separating it from the ring of smaller chapels radiating off the chancel and the apse.

Some churches, especially after the Renaissance when mathematical proportion became important, were built on a **Greek Cross plan,** with each axis the same length, like a giant "+" (plus sign). By the baroque period, funky shapes became popular, with churches built in the round or as ellipses.

It's worth pointing out that very few buildings (especially churches) were built in only one particular style. Massive, expensive structures often took centuries to complete, during which time tastes changed and plans were altered.

CLASSICAL: GREEKS & ROMANS (6TH CENTURY B.C. TO A.D. 4TH CENTURY)

The **Greeks** settled Sicily and Southern Italy, and left behind some of the best-preserved ancient temples in the world.

The **Romans** made use of certain Greek innovations, particularly architectural ideas. The first to be adopted was post-and-lintel construction (essentially, a weight-bearing frame, like a door). The Romans then added the load-bearing arch. Roman builders were inventive engineers, developing hoisting mechanisms and a specially trained workforce.

Identifiable Classical architectural features include these:

- **Classical orders.** These were usually simplified into types of column capitals, with the least ornate used on a building's ground level and the most ornate used on the top: Doric (a plain capital), Ionic (a capital with a scroll), and Corinthian (a capital with flowering acanthus leaves).

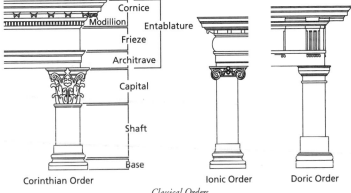

Corinthian Order   Ionic Order   Doric Order

Classical Orders

- **Brick and concrete.** Although marble is traditionally associated with Roman architecture, Roman engineers could also do wonders with bricks or even prosaic concrete—concrete seating made possible such enormous theaters as Rome's 6-acre, 45,000-seat Colosseum.

Most **Greek Temples** in the *Magna Graecia* of southern Italy were built in the 5th century B.C., Doric style, including those at **Paestum** south of Naples, and in Sicily at **Segesta** and **Agrigento,** including the remarkably preserved Temple of Concord. **Greek theaters** survive in Sicily at Taormina, Segesta, and Syracuse (which was the largest in the ancient world).

One of the best places to see **Roman** architecture, of course, is Rome itself, where examples of most major public buildings still exist. These include the sports stadium of the **Colosseum** (A.D. 1st c.), which perfectly displays the use of the Classical orders; Hadrian's marvel of engineering, the **Pantheon** (A.D. 1st c.); the brick public **Baths of Caracalla** (A.D. 3rd c.); and the **Basilica of Constantine and Maxentius** in the Roman Forum (A.D. 4th c.). By the way, Roman basilicas, which served as law courts, took the form of rectangles supported by arches atop columns along both sides of the interior, with an apse at one or both ends; the form was later adopted by early Christians for their first grand churches.

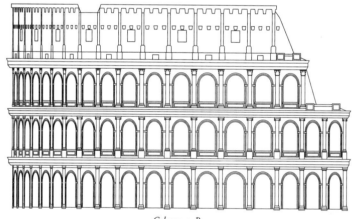

Colosseum, Rome

Three **Roman cities** have been preserved, with their street plans and, in some cases, even buildings remaining intact. These are famous, doomed **Pompeii** and its neighbor **Herculaneum** (both buried by Vesuvius's A.D. 79 eruption), as well as Rome's ancient seaport **Ostia Antica.**

ROMANESQUE (A.D. 800 TO 1300)

The Romanesque took its inspiration and rounded arches from ancient Rome (hence the name). Romanesque architects concentrated on building large churches with wide aisles to accommodate the masses, who came to hear the priests say Mass but mainly to worship at the altars of various saints. To support the weight of all that masonry, walls had to be thick and solid (meaning they could be pierced only by few and rather small windows), resting on huge piers, giving churches a dark, somber, mysterious, and often oppressive feeling.

Identifiable Romanesque features include:

- **Rounded arches.** These load-bearing architectural devices allowed architects to open up wide naves and spaces, channeling all the weight of the stone walls and ceiling across the curve of the arch and down into the ground via the columns or pilasters.
- **Thick walls.**
- **Infrequent and small windows.**
- **Huge piers.**
- **Blind arcades.** A range of arches was carried on piers or columns and attached to a wall. Set into each arch's curve was often a lozenge, a diamond-shaped decoration, sometimes inlaid with colored marbles.
- **Stripes.** Created by alternating layers of white and light-gray stones, this banding was typical of the Pisan-Romanesque style prominent in Pisa and Lucca. The gray got darker as time went on; by the late Romanesque/early Gothic period, the pattern often became a zebra of black and white stripes.
- **Stacked facade arcades.** Another typical Pisan-Romanesque feature was a tall facade created by stacking small, open-air loggias with columns of different styles on top of one another to a height of three to five levels.

Modena's Duomo (12th c.) marks one of the earliest appearances of rounded arches, and its facade is covered with great Romanesque reliefs. **Abbazia di Sant'Antimo** (1118), outside **Montalcino,** is a beautiful example of French Romanesque style. **Milan's Basilica di San Ambrogio** (11th–12th c.) is festooned with the tiered loggias and arcades that became hallmarks of the Lombard Romanesque.

Pisa's Cathedral group (1153–1360s) is typical of the Pisan-Romanesque style, with stacked arcades of mismatched columns in the cathedral's facade (and wrapping around the famous Leaning Tower of Pisa) and blind arcading set with lozenges. **Lucca's Cattedrale di San Martino and San Michele in Foro** (11th–14th centuries) are two more prime examples of the style.

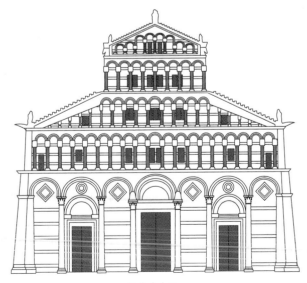

Cathedral, Pisa

GOTHIC (LATE 12TH TO EARLY 15TH CENTURIES)

By the late 12th century, engineering developments freed architecture from the heavy, thick walls of the Romanesque and allowed ceilings to soar, walls to thin, and windows to proliferate.

In place of the dark, somber, relatively unadorned Romanesque interiors that forced the eyes of the faithful toward the altar, where the priest stood droning on in unintelligible Latin, the Gothic interior enticed the churchgoers' gaze upward to high ceilings filled with light. The priests still conducted Mass in Latin, but now peasants could "read" the Gothic comic books of stained-glass windows.

The style began in France and was popular in Italy only in the northern region. From Florence south, most Gothic churches were built by the preaching orders of friars (Franciscans and Dominicans) as cavernous, barnlike structures. Identifiable features of the French Gothic include:

- **Pointed arches.** The most significant development of the Gothic era was the discovery that pointed arches could carry far more weight than rounded ones.
- **Cross vaults.** Instead of being flat, the square patch of ceiling between four columns arches up to a point in the center, creating four sail shapes, sort of like the underside of a pyramid. The X separating these four sails is often reinforced with ridges called ribbing. As the Gothic progressed, four-sided cross vaults became six-sided, eight-sided, or multisided as architects played with the angles.
- **Tracery.** These lacy spider webs of carved stone grace the pointy ends of windows and sometimes the spans of ceiling vaults.
- **Flying buttresses.** These freestanding exterior pillars connected by graceful, thin arms of stone help channel the weight of the building and its roof out and down into the ground. To help counter the cross forces involved in this engineering sleight of hand, the piers of buttresses were often topped by heavy pinnacles, which took the form of minispires or statues.
- **Stained glass.** Because pointy arches can carry more weight than rounded ones, windows could be larger and more numerous. They were often filled with Bible stories and symbolism written in the colorful patterns of stained glass.

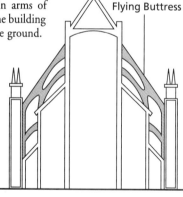

Cross Section of Gothic Church

The only truly French-style Gothic church in Italy is **Milan's massive Duomo & Baptistry** (begun ca. 1386), a lacy festival of pinnacles, buttresses, and pointy arches. **Siena's Duomo** (1136–1382), though started in the late Romanesque, has enough Giovanni Pisano sculptures and pointy arches to be considered Gothic. **Florence** has two of those barnlike Gothic churches: **Basilica di Santa Maria Novella** (1279–1357) and **Basilica di Santa Croce** (1294). The decorations inside **Santa Maria Sopra Minerva** (1280–1370), **Rome**'s only Gothic church, are all of a later date, but the architecture itself is all pointy arches and soaring ceilings (though, hemmed in by other buildings, its interior is much darker than most Gothic places).

Il Duomo, Milan

RENAISSANCE (15TH TO 17TH CENTURIES)

As in painting, Renaissance architectural rules stressed proportion, order, classical inspiration, and mathematical precision to create unified, balanced structures. It was probably an architect, **Filippo Brunelleschi,** in the early 1400s, who first truly grasped the concept of "perspective" and provided artists with ground rules for creating the illusion of three dimensions on a flat surface.

Some identifiable Renaissance features include:

- A sense of proportion
- A reliance on symmetry
- The use of classical orders

One of the first great Renaissance architects was Florence's Filippo Brunelleschi (1377–1476). He often worked in the simple scheme of soft white plaster walls with architectural details and lines in pale gray *pietra serena* stone. Among his masterpieces in **Florence** are the Basilica di Santa Croce's **Pazzi Chapel** (1442–46), decorated with Donatello roundels; the interior of the **Basilica di San Lorenzo** (1425–46); and, most famously, the ingenious **dome** capping **Il Duomo** (1420–46). This last truly exemplifies the Renaissance's debt to the ancients. Brunelleschi traveled to Rome and studied the Pantheon up close to unlock the engineering secrets of its vast dome to build his own.

Urbino architect **Bramante** (1444–1514) was perhaps the most mathematical and classically precise of the early High Renaissance architects, evident in his (much-altered) plans for **Rome's St. Peter's Basilica** (his spiral staircase in the Vatican Museums has survived untouched). Also see his jewel of perfect Renaissance architecture, the textbook **Tempietto** (1502) at San Pietro in Montorio on the slopes of Rome's Gianicolo Hill, where church officials once thought that St. Peter had been crucified (as a plus, the little crypt inside is a riotous rococo grotto).

Renaissance man **Michelangelo** (1475–1564) took up architecture late in life, designing **Florence's Medici Laurentian Library** (1524) and **New Sacristy** (1524–34), which houses the Medici Tombs at Basilica di San Lorenzo. In **Rome,** you can see his facade of the **Palazzo Farnese** (1566) and one of his crowning glories, the soaring **dome of St. Peter's Basilica,** among other structures.

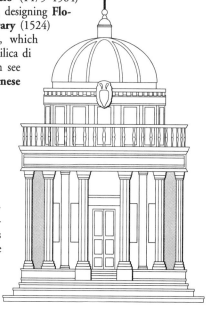

Tempietto, Rome

The fourth great High Renaissance architect was **Andrea Palladio** (1508–80), who worked in a much more strictly classical mode of columns, porticoes, pediments, and other ancient temple–inspired features. His masterpieces include **Villa Foscari** and the great **Villa Rotonda,** both in the **Veneto** countryside around Vicenza. His final work is **Vicenza's Olympic Theater** (1580), an attempt to reconstruct a Roman theater stage as described in ancient writings. Other designs include the Venetian church **San Giorgio Maggiore** (1565–1610). He had great influence on architecture abroad as well; his "Palladian" style informed everything from British architecture to Thomas Jefferson's Monticello.

BAROQUE & ROCOCO (17TH TO 18TH CENTURIES)

More than any other movement, the **baroque** aimed toward a seamless meshing of architecture and art. The stuccoes, sculptures, and paintings were all carefully designed to complement each other—and the space itself—to create a unified whole. This whole was both aesthetic and narrative, with the various art forms all working together to tell a single Biblical story (or often to subtly relate the deeds of the commissioning patron to great historic or Biblical events). Excessively complex and dripping with decorative tidbits, **rococo** is kind of a twisted version of the baroque.

Some identifiable baroque features include:

- **Classical architecture rewritten with curves.** The baroque is similar to Renaissance, but many of the right angles and ruler-straight lines are exchanged for curves of complex geometry and an interplay of concave and convex surfaces. The overall effect is to lighten the appearance of structures and add movement of line and vibrancy to the static look of the classical Renaissance.

- **Complex decoration.** Unlike the sometimes severe and austere designs of the Renaissance, the baroque was playful. Architects festooned exteriors and encrusted interiors with an excess of decorations intended to liven things up—lots of ornate stuccowork, pouty cherubs, airy frescoes, heavy gilding, twisting columns, multicolored marbles, and general frippery.

Trevi Fountain, Rome

- **Multiplying forms.** Why use one column when you can stack a half dozen partial columns on top of each other, slightly offset, until the effect is like looking at a single column though a fractured kaleidoscope? The baroque loved to pile up its forms and elements to create a rich, busy effect, breaking a pediment curve into segments so that each would protrude farther out than the last, or building up an architectural feature by stacking short sections of concave walls, each one curving to a different arc.

The baroque flourished across Italy. Though relatively sedate, Carlo Maderno's facade and Bernini's sweeping elliptical colonnade for **Rome's St. Peter's Square** make one of Italy's most famous baroque assemblages. One of the quirkiest and most felicitous baroque styles flourished in the churches of the Apulian city **Lecce.** When an earthquake decimated the Sicilian town of **Noto** near Syracuse, it was rebuilt from scratch on a complete baroque city plan; the streets and squares made viewing platforms for the theatrical backdrops of its churches and palaces.

For the rococo—more a decorative than architectural movement—look no further than **Rome's Spanish Steps** (1726), by architect de Sanctis, or the **Trevi Fountain** (1762), by Salvi.

NEOCLASSICAL TO MODERN (18TH TO 21ST CENTURIES)

As a backlash against the excesses of the baroque and rococo, architects began turning to the austere simplicity and grandeur of the classical age and inaugurated the **neoclassical** style by the middle of the 18th century. Their work was inspired by the rediscovery of Pompeii and other ancient sites.

In the late 19th and 20th centuries, Italy's architectural styles went in several directions. The **Industrial Age** of the 19th century brought with it the first genteel shopping malls of glass and steel. The country's take on the early-20th-century Art Nouveau movement was called **Liberty Style.** Mussolini made a spirited attempt to bring back ancient Rome in what can only be called **Fascist architecture.** Since then, Italy has built mostly concrete and glass skyscrapers, like the rest of the world, although a few architects in the medium have stood out.

Some identifiable features of each of these movements include:

- **Neoclassical.** The classical ideals of mathematical proportion and symmetry, first rediscovered during the Renaissance, are the hallmark of every classically styled era. Neoclassicists reinterpreted ancient temples as buildings and as decorative, massive colonnaded porticos.
- **Liberty Style.** Like Art Nouveau practitioners in other countries, Italian decorators rebelled against the era of mass production by stressing the uniqueness of craft. They created asymmetrical, curvaceous designs based on organic inspiration (plants and flowers), and they used such materials as wrought iron, stained glass, tile, and hand-painted wallpaper.
- **Fascist.** Deco meets Caesar. This period produced monumentally imposing and chillingly stark, white marble structures surrounded by statuary in the classical style.

Of the **neoclassical, Caserta's Royal Palace** (1752–74), outside Naples, was a conscious attempt to create a Versailles for the Bourbon monarchs, while the unbelievably huge (and almost universally derided) **Vittorio Emanuele Monument** (1884–1927) in Rome, which has been compared to a wedding cake or a Victorian typewriter, was Italy's main monument to reaching its *Risorgimento* goal of a unified Italy.

The **Industrial Age** created glass-domed shopping arcades in giant X shapes in both **Milan** and **Naples. Liberty** style never produced any surpassingly important buildings, although you can glimpse it occasionally in period storefronts.

Fascist architecture still infests corners of Italy (although most of the right-wing reliefs and the repeated engravings of DVCE—Mussolini's nickname for himself—have long since been chipped out). You can see it at its best in Rome's planned satellite community called **EUR,** which includes a multistory "square Colosseum" so funky that it has been featured in many a film and music video, and in **Rome's Stadio Olimpico** complex.

The **mid–20th century** was dominated by **Pier Luigi Nervi** (1891–1979) and his reinforced concrete buildings, **Florence's Giovanni Berta Stadium** (1932), **Rome's Palazzeto dello Sport stadium** (1960), and **Turin's Exposition Hall** (1949).

Vittorio Emanuele Monument, Rome

3

Planning Your Trip to Italy

This chapter is devoted to the where, when, and how of your trip—the advance planning required to get it together and take it on the road. Because you might not know exactly where in Italy you want to go or what surrounds the major city you want to see, we'll start off with a quick rundown of the various regions.

1 The Regions in Brief

Italy is about the size of the U.S. state of Arizona, but the peninsula's shape gives you the impression of a much larger area; the ever-changing seacoast contributes to this feeling, as do the large islands of Sicily and Sardinia. Bordered on the northwest by France, on the north by Switzerland and Austria, and on the east by Slovenia (formerly part of Yugoslavia), Italy is still a land largely surrounded by the sea.

Two areas within Italy's boundaries aren't under the control of the Italian government: the **State of Vatican City** and the **Republic of San Marino.** Vatican City's 109 acres were established in 1929 by a concordat between Pope Pius XI and Benito Mussolini, acting as head of the Italian government; the agreement also gave Roman Catholicism special status in Italy. The pope is the sovereign of the State of Vatican City, which has its own legal system and post office. (The Republic of San Marino, with a capital of the same name, strides atop the slopes of Mt. Titano, 23km/14 miles from Rimini. It's small and completely surrounded by Italy, so it still exists only by the grace of Italy.)

Here's a brief rundown of the cities and regions covered in this guide:

ROME & LATIUM
The region of **Latium** is dominated by **Rome,** capital of the ancient empire and the modern nation of Italy, and **Vatican City,** the independent papal state. Much of the civilized world was once ruled from here, going back to the days when Romulus and Remus are said to have founded Rome on April 21, 753 B.C. For generations, Rome was referred to as *caput mundi* (capital of the world). Its fortunes have fallen, of course, but it remains a timeless city, ranking with Paris and London as one of the top European destinations. There's no place with more artistic monuments—not even Venice or Florence. How much time should you budget for the capital? Italian writer Silvio Negro said, "A lifetime is not enough."

FLORENCE, TUSCANY & UMBRIA
Tuscany is one of the most culturally and politically influential provinces—the development of Italy without Tuscany is simply unthinkable. It was Tuscany, with its sun-warmed vineyards and towering cypresses, that inspired the artists of the Renaissance. Nowhere in the world is the impact of the Renaissance still felt more fully than in its birthplace, **Florence,** the repository of artistic works left by Leonardo and Michelangelo. Since the 19th century, travelers have been flocking to Florence to see the Donatello bronzes, the Botticelli

The Regions of Italy

0   100 Mi
0   100 Km

VALLE D'AOSTA
Courmayeur
Aosta
Alps
Lake Maggiore
Novara
Turin
Como
Milan
Vercelli
Bergamo
Asti
Brescia
PIEDMONT
Cremona
Cuneo
Savona
Genoa
LIGURIA
Rapallo
San Remo
Parma
Mantua
Modena
Gulf of Genoa
La Spezia
Ligurian Sea
Pisa
Livorno
Florence
Siena
TUSCANY
Elba
Viterbo
Civitavecchia
Perugia
Assisi
Orvieto
UMBRIA
Spoleto
Terni
VATICAN CITY
ROME
LATIUM

Merano
Bolzano
TRENTINO–ALTO ADIGE
Trent
Belluno
Cortina d'Ampezzo
Dolomites
Lake Garda
VENETO
Vicenza
Verona
Padua
Ferrara
Venice
Treviso
Udine
FRIULI–VENEZIA GIULIA
Trieste
Gulf of Venice
EMILIA-ROMAGNA
Bologna
Ravenna
Rimini
SAN MARINO
Pesaro
Ancona
Macerata
THE MARCHES
Terano
Adriatic Sea

Northern Appennines

L'Aquila
Pescara
Chieti
ABRUZZI
Campobasso
MOLIZE
Caserta
Gulf of Gaeta
Benevento
Foggia
Naples
Ischia
Pompeii
Mt. Vesuvius
Capri
Amalfi
Avellino
Sorrento
Salerno
Paestum
CAMPANIA
Potenza
APULIA
Bari
BASILICATA
Brindisi
Taranto
Gulf of Taranto
Lecce

Tyrrhenian Sea

SARDINIA
Sassari
Ólbia
Nuoro
Cagliari

Trapani
Marsala
Selinunte
Palermo
SICILY
Enna
Agrigento
Taormina
Mt. Etna
Messina
Reggio di Calabria
Catania
Ragusa
Syracuse
Aeolian Islands
CALABRIA
Cosenza
Catanzaro
Southern Appennines

Mediterranean Sea

Ionian Sea

smiles, and all the other preeminent treasures. Alas, it's now an invasion, so you run the risk of being trampled underfoot as you explore the historic heart of the city. To escape, head for the nearby Tuscan hill towns, former stomping ground of the Guelphs and Ghibellines. The main cities to visit are **Lucca, Pisa,** and especially **Siena,** Florence's great historical rival with an inner core that appears to be caught in a time warp. As a final treat, visit **San Gimignano,** northwest of Siena, celebrated for its medieval "skyscrapers."

Pastoral, hilly, and fertile, **Umbria** is similar to Tuscany, but with fewer tourists. Its once-fortified network of hill towns is among the most charming in Italy. Crafted from millions of tons of gray-brown rocks, each town is a testament to the masonry and architectural skills of many generations of craftsmen. Cities particularly worth a visit are **Perugia, Gubbio, Assisi, Spoleto** (site of the world-renowned annual arts festival), and **Orvieto,** a mysterious citadel once used as a stronghold by the Etruscans. Called the land of shadows, Umbria is often covered in a bluish haze that evokes an ethereal painted look. Many local artists have tried to capture the province's special glow, with its sun-dappled hills, terraced vineyards, and miles of olive trees. If you're short on time, visit Assisi to check out Giotto's frescoes at the Basilica di San Francesco (they've now been repaired after the 1997 earthquakes), and Perugia, the largest and richest of the province's cities.

BOLOGNA & EMILIA-ROMAGNA

Italians seem to agree on only one thing: The food in **Emilia-Romagna** is the best in Italy. The region's capital, **Bologna,** boasts a stunning Renaissance core with plenty of churches and arcades, a fine university with roots in the early Middle Ages, and a populace with a reputation for leftist leanings.

The region also has one of the highest standards of living. When not dining in Bologna, you can take time to explore its artistic heritage. Other art cities abound—none more noble than Byzantine **Ravenna,** still living off its past glory as the one-time capital of the declining Roman Empire.

If you can visit only one more city in the region, make it **Parma,** to see the city center with its Duomo and baptistry and to view its National Gallery. This is the home of Parmigiano-Reggiano cheese and prosciutto. Also noteworthy is the hometown of opera star Pavarotti, **Modena,** which is known for its cuisine, its cathedral, and its Este Gallery. The crowded Adriatic resort of **Rimini** and the medieval stronghold of **San Marino** are at the periphery of Emilia-Romagna.

VENICE, THE VENETO & THE DOLOMITES

Northeastern Italy is one of Europe's treasure troves, encompassing **Venice** (which is arguably the world's most beautiful city), the surrounding **Veneto** region, and the mighty **Dolomites** (including the **South Tirol,** which Italy annexed from Austria after World War I). The Veneto, dotted with rich museums and some of the best architecture in Italy, sprawls across the verdant hills and flat plains between the Adriatic, the Dolomites, Verona, and the edges of Lake Garda. For many generations, the fortunes of the Veneto revolved around Venice, with its sumptuous palaces, romantic waterways, Palazzo Ducale, and Basilica di San Marco. Aging, decaying, and sinking into the sea, Venice is so alluring that we almost want to say, visit it even if you have to skip Rome and Florence. Also recommended are three fabled art cities in the "Venetian Arc": **Verona,** of Romeo and Juliet fame; **Vicenza,** to see the villas of Andrea Palladio where 16th-century aristocrats lived; and **Padua,** with its Giotto frescoes.

The region of **Trentino–Alto Adige** is far richer in culture, artistic treasures, and activities than the Valle d'Aosta (see "Piedmont & Valle d'Aosta," below), and its ski resort, **Cortina d'Ampezzo,** is far more fashionable than Courmayeur in the northwestern corridor. Its most interesting base (especially if you want to see the Austrian version of Italy) is **Trent (Trento),** the capital of Trentino. In the extreme northeastern corner of Italy, the region of **Friuli–Venezia Giulia** is, in its own way, one of the most cosmopolitan and culturally sophisticated in Italy. Its capital is the seaport of **Trieste.** The area is filled with art from the Roman, Byzantine, and Romanesque-Gothic eras, and many of the public buildings (especially in Trieste) might remind you of Vienna.

MILAN, LOMBARDY & THE LAKE DISTRICT

Flat, fertile, prosperous, and politically conservative, **Lombardy** is dominated by **Milan** just as Latium is dominated by Rome. Lombardy is one of the world's leading commercial and cultural centers, and it has been ever since Milan developed into Italy's gateway to northern German-speaking Europe in the early Middle Ages. Although some people belittle Milan as an industrial city with a snobbish contempt for the poorer regions to the south, its fans compare it to New York. Milan's cathedral is Europe's third largest, its La Scala opera house is world-renowned, and its museums and churches are a treasure trove, with one containing Leonardo's *Last Supper.* However, Milan still doesn't have the sights and tourist interest of Rome, Florence, and Venice. Visit Milan if you have the time, though you'll find more charm in the neighboring art cities of **Bergamo, Brescia, Pavia, Cremona,** and **Mantua.** Also competing for your time will be the gorgeous lakes of **Como, Garda,** and **Maggiore,** which lie near Lombardy's eastern edge.

PIEDMONT & VALLE D'AOSTA

At Italy's extreme northwestern edge, sharing a set of alpine peaks with France (which, in some ways, it resembles), **Piedmont** was the district from which Italy's dreams of unification spread in 1861. Long under the domination of the Austro-Hungarian Empire, Piedmont enjoys a cuisine laced with alpine cheeses and dairy products. It's proud of its largest city, **Turin,** called the "Detroit of Italy" because it's the home of the Fiat empire, vermouth, and Asti Spumante, as well as the Borsalino hat. Although Turin is a great cosmopolitan center, it doesn't have the antique charm of Genoa or the sophistication, world-class dining, and chic shopping of Milan. Turin's most controversial sight is the *Sacra Sindone* (Holy Shroud), which many Catholics believe is the exact cloth in which Christ's body was wrapped when lowered from the cross.

Italy's window on Switzerland and France, the **Valle d'Aosta** (the smallest region) often serves as an introduction to the country, especially for those journeying from France through the Mont Blanc tunnel. The introduction is misleading, however, because Valle d'Aosta stands apart from the rest of Italy, a semi-autonomous region of towering peaks and valleys in the northwestern corridor. It's more closely linked to France (especially the region of Savoy) than to Italy, and its residents speak an ancient French-derived dialect. The most important city in this scenic region is the old Roman city of **Aosta,** which, except for some ruins, is rather dull. More intriguing are two of Italy's major ski resorts, **Courmayeur** and **Breuil-Cervinia,** which are topped only by

Cortina d'Ampezzo in the Dolomites (see "Venice, the Veneto & the Dolomites," above). Many of the region's villages are crafted from gray rocks culled from the mountains that rise on all sides. The best time to visit is in summer or the deep of winter. Late spring and fall get rather sleepy in this part of the world.

GENOA & THE ITALIAN RIVIERA

Comprising most of the **Italian Riviera,** the region of **Liguria** incorporates the steeply sloping capital city of **Genoa,** charming medieval ports (**Portofino, Ventimiglia,** and **San Remo**), a huge naval base (La Spezia), and five traditional coastal communities (**Cinque Terre**). There's also a series of beach resorts (**Rapallo** and **Santa Margherita Ligure**) that resemble the French Riviera. Although overbuilt and overrun, the Italian Riviera is still a land of great beauty. It's actually two Rivieras: the **Riviera di Ponente** to the west, running from the French border to Genoa, and the **Riviera di Levante** to the east. Faced with a choice, we always gravitate toward the more glamorous and cosmopolitan Riviera di Levante. Italy's largest port, Genoa, also merits a visit for its rich culture and history.

NAPLES, THE AMALFI COAST & CAPRI

More than any other region, **Campania** reverberates with the memories of the ancient Romans, who favored its strong sunlight, fertile soil, and bubbling sulfurous springs. It encompasses the anarchy of **Naples,** the elegant beauty of **Capri,** and the **Amalfi Coast.** The region also contains many sites specifically identified in ancient mythology (lakes defined as the entrance to the Kingdom of the Dead, for example) and some of the world's most renowned ancient ruins (including **Pompeii, Herculaneum,**

and **Paestum**). Campania is overrun, overcrowded, and over everything, but it still lures visitors. Allow at least a day for Naples, which has amazing museums and the world's worst traffic outside Cairo. Pompeii, Herculaneum, and Paestum are for the ruin collectors, while those seeking fun in the sun head for Capri or Portofino. The leading resorts along the Amalfi Drive (even though they're not exactly undiscovered) are **Ravello** (not on the sea) and **Positano** (on the sea). **Amalfi** and **Sorrento** also have beautiful seaside settings. However, their more affordable hotels tend to make them that much more crowded.

APULIA

Sun-drenched and poor, **Apulia** (depending on the dialect, Le Puglie or Puglia) forms the heel of the Italian boot. It's the most frequently visited province of Italy's Deep South; part of its allure lies in its string of coastal resorts. The *trulli* houses of **Alberobello** are known for their unique cylindrical shapes and conical flagstone-sheathed roofs. Among the region's largest cities are **Bari** (the capital), **Foggia,** and **Brindisi** (gateway to nearby Greece, with which the town shares many characteristics). Each of these is a modern disaster, filled with tawdry buildings, heavy traffic, and rising crime rates (tourists are often the victims). Most visitors pass right through Bari (though it's a favorite with backpackers), and the only real reason to spend a night in Brindisi is to catch the ferry to Greece the next morning.

SICILY

The largest Mediterranean island, **Sicily,** is a land of beauty, mystery, and world-class monuments. It's a bizarre mix of bloodlines and architecture from medieval Normandy, Aragonese Spain, Moorish North Africa, ancient Greece, Phoenicia, and Rome. Since the advent of modern times, part of the island's primitiveness has faded, as thousands of newly arrived cars clog the narrow lanes of its biggest city, **Palermo.** Poverty remains widespread, yet the age-old stranglehold of the Mafia seems less certain because of the increasingly vocal protests of an outraged Italian public. On the eastern edge of the island is Mt. Etna, the tallest active volcano in Europe. Many of Sicily's larger cities (**Trapani, Catania,** and **Messina**) are relatively unattractive, but areas of ravishing beauty and eerie historical interest include **Syracuse, Taormina, Agrigento,** and **Selinunte.** Sicily's ancient ruins are rivaled only by those of Rome itself. The Valley of the Temples, for example, is worth the trip here.

2 Visitor Information

For information before you go, contact the Italian State Tourism Board.

In the United States: 630 Fifth Ave., Suite 1565, New York, NY 10111 (📞 **212/245-4822;** fax 212/586-9249); 500 N. Michigan Ave., Suite 2240, Chicago, IL 60611 (📞 **312/644-0996;** fax 312/644-3019); and 12400 Wilshire Blvd., Suite 550, Los Angeles, CA 90025 (📞 **310/820-1898;** fax 310/820-6357).

In Canada: 175 Bloor St. E., South Tower, Suite 907, Toronto, ON, M4W 3R8 (📞 **416/925-4882;** fax 416/925-4799).

In the United Kingdom: 1 Princes St., London W1R 8AY (📞 **020/7408-1254;** fax 020/7493-6695).

You can also write directly (in English or Italian) to the provincial or local tourist boards of the areas you plan to visit. Provincial tourist boards (**Ente Provinciale per il Turismo**) operate in the principal towns of the provinces. Local tourist boards (**Azienda Autonoma di Soggiorno e Turismo**) operate in all places of tourist interest; you can get a list from the Italian State Tourism Board. If you are in Italy and need to get information, call the toll-free number (only within Italy, 📞 **800-117700**). If you are calling from another country, dial 📞 **06-87419007.** The service is available daily from 8am to 11pm in five languages, dispensing information concerning transportation, health assistance, events, museums, safety, hotels, information points, and tourist assistance.

On the Web, the Italian State Tourism Board sponsors the site **www.italiantourism.com** or **www.enit.it.** Other helpful sites include www.initaly.com and www.wandering.com.

3 Entry Requirements & Customs

ENTRY REQUIREMENTS

U.S., Canadian, U.K., Irish, Australian, and New Zealand citizens with a **valid passport** don't need a visa to enter Italy if they don't expect to stay more than 90 days and don't expect to work there. If after entering Italy you want to stay more than 90 days, you can apply for a permit for an extra 90 days, which as a rule is granted immediately. Go to the nearest *questura* (police headquarters) or to your home country's consulate. If your passport is lost or stolen, head to your consulate as soon as possible for a replacement.

CUSTOMS
WHAT YOU CAN BRING INTO ITALY

Foreign visitors can bring along most items for personal use duty-free, including fishing tackle, a pair of skis, two tennis rackets, a baby carriage, two hand cameras with 10 rolls of

Destination: Italy—Red Alert Checklist

- Did you remember your passport?
- If you are a woman intent on visiting Italy's churches, have you packed a long skirt and a garment to conceal bare shoulders? Men should also be sure to pack appropriate attire (no shorts allowed in St. Peter's Basilica, among others).
- If you plan to visit Rome's Galleria Borghese, have you made advance reservations through **Select Italy** (© **847/853-1661**; www.selectitaly.com)?
- If you purchased traveler's checks, have you recorded the check numbers and stored the documentation separately from the checks?
- Did you pack your camera and an extra set of camera batteries, and purchase enough film? If you packed film in your checked baggage, did you invest in protective pouches to shield film from airport X-rays?
- Do you have a safe, accessible place to store money?
- Did you bring your ID cards that could entitle you to discounts, such as AAA and AARP cards, or student IDs?
- Did you bring emergency drug prescriptions and extra glasses and/or contact lenses?
- Do you have your credit-card PIN numbers?
- If you have an E-ticket, do you have documentation?
- Did you leave a copy of your itinerary with someone at home?
- Did you check to see if any travel advisories have been issued by the **U.S. State Department** (http://travel.state.gov/travel_warnings.html) regarding your destination?
- Do you have the address and phone number of your country's embassy with you?

film, and 200 cigarettes or a quantity of cigars or pipe tobacco not exceeding 250 grams (0.05 oz.). There are strict limits on importing alcoholic beverages. However, for alcohol bought tax-paid, limits are much more liberal than in other countries of the European Union.

WHAT YOU CAN TAKE HOME

Returning **U.S. citizens** who have been away for at least 48 hours are allowed to bring back, once every 30 days, $400 worth of merchandise duty-free. You'll be charged a flat rate of 4% duty on the next $1,000 worth of purchases. Be sure to have your receipts handy. On mailed gifts, the duty-free limit is $100. You cannot bring fresh foodstuffs into the United States; tinned foods, however, are allowed. For more information, contact the **U.S. Customs Service,** 1300 Pennsylvania Ave., NW, Washington, DC 20229 (© **877/287-8867**), and request the free pamphlet *Know Before You Go.* It's also available on the Web at www.customs.gov. (Click on "Traveler Information," then "Know Before You Go.")

For a clear summary of **Canadian** rules, write for the booklet *I Declare,* issued by the **Canada Customs and Revenue Agency** (© **800/461-9999** in Canada, or 204/983-3500; www.ccra-adrc.gc.ca). Canada allows its citizens a Can$750 exemption, and you're allowed to bring back duty-free one carton of cigarettes, one can of tobacco, 40 imperial ounces of liquor, and 50 cigars. In addition, you're allowed to mail gifts to Canada valued at less than Can$60 a day, provided they are unsolicited and don't contain alcohol or tobacco (write on the package "Unsolicited gift, under $60 value"). All valuables should be declared on the Y-38 form before departure from Canada, including serial numbers of valuables you already own, such as expensive foreign cameras. *Note:* The $750 exemption can be used only once a year and only after an absence of 7 days.

Citizens of the U.K. who are returning from a European Community (EC) country will go through a separate Customs Exit (called the "Blue Exit") especially for EC travelers. In essence, there is no limit on what you can bring back from an EC country, as long as the items are for personal use (this includes gifts) and you have already paid the necessary duty and tax. However, customs law sets out guidance levels. If you bring in more than these levels, you may be asked to prove that the goods are for your own use. Guidance levels on goods bought in the EC for your own use are 800 cigarettes, 200 cigars, 1 kilogram smoking tobacco, 10 liters of spirits, 90 liters of wine (of this not more than 60 liters can be sparkling wine), and 110 liters of beer. For more information, contact **HM Customs & Excise,** Passenger Enquiry Point, 2nd Floor Wayfarer House, Great South West Road, Feltham, Middlesex, TW14 8NP (© **020/8910-3744;**

from outside the U.K. 44/181-910-3744), or consult their website at www.open.gov.uk.

The duty-free allowance in **Australia** is A$400 or, for those under 18, A$200. Personal property mailed back from Italy should be marked "Australian goods returned" to avoid payment of duty. Upon returning to Australia, citizens can bring in 250 cigarettes or 250 grams of loose tobacco, and 1,125 milliliters of alcohol. If you're returning with valuable goods you already own, such as foreign-made cameras, you should file form B263. A helpful brochure, available from Australian consulates or Customs offices, is *Know Before You Go.* For more information, contact **Australian Customs Services,** GPO Box 8, Sydney, NSW 2001 (© **02/ 9213-2000**).

The duty-free allowance for **New Zealand** is NZ$700. Citizens over 17 can bring in 200 cigarettes, or 50 cigars, or 250 grams of tobacco (or a mixture of all three if their combined weight doesn't exceed 250g); plus 4.5 liters of wine and beer, or 1.125 liters of liquor. New Zealand currency does not carry import or export restrictions. Fill out a certificate of export, listing the valuables you are taking out of the country; that way, you can bring them back without paying duty. Most questions are answered in a free pamphlet available at New Zealand consulates and Customs offices: *New Zealand Customs Guide for Travellers, Notice no. 4.* For more information, contact **New Zealand Customs,** 50 Anzac Ave., P.O. Box 29, Auckland (© **09/359-6655**).

4 Money

CURRENCY

The **euro,** the new single European currency, became the official currency of Italy and 11 other participating countries on January 1, 1999.

However, the euro didn't go into general circulation until early in 2002. The old currency, the Italian lire, disappeared into history on March 1, 2002, replaced by the euro, whose

The U.S. Dollar, the British Pound & the Euro

In January of 2002, the largest money-changing operation in history led to the deliberate obsolescence of many of Europe's individual national currencies, including the Italian lire. In its place was substituted the euro, a currency that, at this writing, was based on the fiscal participation of a dozen nations of Europe.

For American Readers   At this writing, 1 euro equals approximately 89 U.S. cents, and 1 U.S. dollar equals approximately 1.12€. This was the rate of exchange used to calculate the dollar values, each of which was rounded to the nearest nickel, throughout this book.

For British Readers   At this writing, Great Britain still uses the pound sterling, with 1 euro equaling approximately 70 pence, and £1 equaling approximately 1.43€. This was the rate of exchange used to calculate the pound sterling values laid out in the table below.

Note: The relative value of the euro fluctuates against the U.S. dollar, the pound sterling, and most of the world's other currencies, and its value might not be the same by the time you actually travel to Italy. Consequently, this table should be used only as an indication of approximate values.

Euro	US$	UK£	Euro	US$	UK£
1	0.89	0.70	75	66.98	52.50
2	1.79	1.40	100	89.30	70.00
3	2.68	2.10	125	111.63	87.50
4	3.57	2.80	150	133.95	105.00
5	4.47	3.50	175	156.28	122.50
6	5.36	4.20	200	178.60	140.00
7	6.25	4.90	225	200.93	157.50
8	7.14	5.60	250	223.25	175.00
9	8.04	6.30	275	245.58	192.50
10	8.93	7.00	300	267.90	210.00
15	13.40	10.50	350	312.55	245.00
20	17.86	14.00	400	357.20	280.00
25	22.33	17.50	500	446.50	350.00
50	44.65	35.00	1000	893.00	700.00

official abbreviation is "EUR." The symbol of the euro is a stylized *E:* €. Exchange rates of participating countries are locked into a common currency fluctuating against the dollar.

For more details on the euro, check out **www.europa.eu.int/euro**.

Exchange rates are more favorable at the point of arrival. Nevertheless, it's often helpful to exchange at least some money before going abroad (standing in line at the *cambio* [exchange bureau] in the Milan or Rome airport could make you miss the next bus leaving for downtown). Check with your local American Express or Thomas Cook offices or your bank. Or order euros in advance from the following: **American Express** (✆ **800/221-7282;** www.

americanexpress.com), **Thomas Cook** (📞 800/223-7373; www.thomas cook.com), or **Capital for Foreign Exchange** (📞 888/842-0880).

It's best to exchange currency or traveler's checks (for which you'll receive a better rate than cash) at a bank, not a cambio, hotel, or shop.

ATMS

ATMs are prevalent in all Italian cities and even the smaller towns. ATMs are linked to a national network that most likely includes your bank at home. Both the **Cirrus** (📞 800/424-7787; www.mastercard.com) and the **PLUS** (📞 800/843-7587; www.visa.com) networks have automated ATM locators listing the banks in Italy that'll accept your card. Or just search out any machine with your network's symbol emblazoned on it.

Important note: Make sure that the PIN access numbers for your bank cards and credit cards (see "Credit Cards," below) will work in Italy. You'll need a **four-digit code** (six digits won't work), so if you have a six-digit code you'll have to contact your card issuer to get a new PIN for your trip. If you're unsure about this, contact Cirrus or Plus (above) or your credit-card company. Be sure to check the daily withdrawal limit for each card at the same time.

TRAVELER'S CHECKS

These days, traveler's checks seem less necessary because most Italian cities and towns have 24-hour ATMs, allowing you to withdraw small amounts of cash as needed. But if you prefer the security of the tried and true, you might want to stick with traveler's checks—provided that you don't mind showing an ID every time you want to cash a check.

You can get traveler's checks at almost any bank. **American Express** offers denominations of $20, $50, $100, $500, and (for cardholders only) $1,000. You'll pay a service charge ranging from 1% to 4%. You can also get American Express traveler's checks over the phone by calling 📞 800/221-7782; Amex gold and platinum cardholders who use this number are exempt from the 1% fee. AAA members can obtain checks without a fee at most AAA offices.

Visa offers traveler's checks at Citibank locations nationwide, as well as at several other banks. The service charge ranges between 1.5% and 2%; checks come in denominations of $20, $50, $100, $500, and $1,000. Call 📞 800/732-1322 for information. **MasterCard** also offers traveler's checks. Call 📞 800/223-9920 for a location near you.

CREDIT CARDS

Credit cards are invaluable when traveling—they're a safe way to carry money and provide a convenient record of all your expenses. You can also withdraw cash advances from your cards at any bank (though you'll start paying hefty interest on the advance the moment you receive the cash). Keep in mind, though, that your credit-card company will likely charge a commission (1% or 2%) on every foreign purchase you make.

5 When to Go

April to June and **late September to October** are the best months for traveling in Italy—temperatures are usually mild and the crowds aren't quite so intense. Starting in mid-June, the summer rush really picks up, and from

July to mid-September the country teems with visitors. **August** is the worst month: Not only does it get uncomfortably hot, muggy, and crowded, but the entire country goes on vacation at least from August 15 to the end of the month—and many Italians take off the entire month. Many hotels, restaurants, and shops are closed (except at the spas, beaches, and islands, which are where 70% of the Italians head to). From **late October to Easter,** most attractions go on shorter winter hours or are closed for renovation. Many hotels and restaurants take a month or two off between **November and February,** spa and beach destinations become padlocked ghost towns, and it can get much colder than you'd expect (it might even snow).

High season on most airlines' routes to Rome usually stretches from June to the beginning of September. This is the most expensive and most crowded time to travel. **Shoulder season** is from April to May, early September to October, and December 15 to 24. **Low season** is November 1 to December 14 and December 25 to March 31.

WEATHER

It's warm all over Italy in summer; it can be very hot in the south, especially inland. The high temperatures (measured in Italy in degrees Celsius) begin in Rome in May, often lasting until sometime in October. Winters in the north of Italy are cold, with rain and snow, but in the south the weather is warm all year, averaging 50°F in winter.

For the most part, it's drier in Italy than in North America, so high temperatures don't seem as bad because the humidity is lower. In Rome, Naples, and the south, temperatures can stay in the 90s for days, but nights are most often comfortably cooler.

HOLIDAYS

Offices and shops in Italy are closed on the following **national holidays:** January 1 (New Year's Day), Easter Monday, April 25 (Liberation Day), May 1 (Labor Day), August 15 (Assumption of the Virgin), November 1 (All Saints' Day), December 8 (Feast of the Immaculate Conception), December 25 (Christmas Day), and December 26 (Santo Stefano).

Closings are also observed in the following cities on **feast days** honoring their patron saints: Venice, April 25 (St. Mark); Florence, Genoa, and Turin, June 24 (St. John the Baptist); Rome, June 29 (Sts. Peter and Paul); Palermo, July 15 (St. Rosalia); Naples, September 19 (St. Gennaro); Bologna, October 4 (St. Petronio); Cagliari, October 30 (St. Saturnino); Trieste, November 3 (St. Giusto); Bari, December 6 (St. Nicola); and Milan, December 7 (St. Ambrose).

Italy's Average Daily Temperature & Monthly Rainfall (Inches)

	Jan	Feb	Mar	Apr	May	June	July	Aug	Sept	Oct	Nov	Dec
Rome												
Temp. (°F)	49	52	57	62	72	82	87	86	73	65	56	47
Temp. (°C)	9	11	14	17	22	28	31	30	23	20	13	8
Rainfall	2.3	1.5	2.9	3.0	2.8	2.9	1.5	1.9	2.8	2.6	3.0	2.1
Florence												
Temp. (°F)	45	47	50	60	67	76	77	70	64	63	55	46
Temp. (°C)	7	8	9	16	19	24	25	21	18	17	13	8
Rainfall	3	3.3	3.7	2.7	2.2	1.4	1.4	2.7	3.2	4.9	3.8	2.9
Naples												
Temp. (°F)	50	54	58	63	70	78	83	85	75	66	60	52
Temp. (°C)	9	12	14	17	21	26	28	29	24	19	16	11
Rainfall	4.7	4	3	3.8	2.4	.8	.8	2.6	3.5	5.8	5.1	3.7

ITALY CALENDAR OF EVENTS

For major events in which tickets should be procured well before arriving, check with **Global Edwards & Edwards** in the United States at ✆ **800/223-6108.**

January

Epiphany celebrations, nationwide. All cities, towns, and villages in Italy stage Roman Catholic Epiphany observances. One of the most festive celebrations is the Epiphany Fair at Rome's Piazza Navona. January 6, 2003.

Festa di Sant'Agnese, Sant'Agnese Fuori le Mura, Rome. During this ancient ceremony, two lambs are blessed and shorn, and their wool is used later for palliums (Roman Catholic vestments). January 17, 2003.

Festival della Canzone Italiana (Festival of Italian Popular Song), San Remo, the Italian Riviera. At this 3-day festival, major artists perform the latest Italian song releases. Late January.

Foire de Saint Ours, Aosta, Valle d'Aosta. Observing a tradition that has existed for 10 centuries, artisans from the mountain valleys display their wares—often made of wood, lace, wool, or wrought iron—created during the long winter. Late January.

February

Carnevale, Piazza Navona, Rome. This festival marks the last day of the children's market and lasts until dawn of the following day. Usually February 4 to 5.

Almond Blossom Festival, Agrigento, Sicily. This folk festival includes song, dance, costumes, and fireworks. First half of February.

Carnevale, Venice. At this riotous time, theatrical presentations and masked balls take place throughout Venice and on the islands in the lagoon. The balls are by invitation only (except the Doge's Ball), but the street events and fireworks are open to everyone. Contact the **Venice Tourist Office,** San Marco, Giardinetti Reali, Palazzo Selva, 30124 Venezia (✆ **041/5298-711**). The week before Ash Wednesday, the beginning of Lent.

March

Festa di San Giuseppe, the Trionfale Quarter, north of the Vatican, Rome. The heavily decorated statue of the saint is brought out at a fair with food stalls, concerts, and sporting events. Usually March 19.

April

Holy Week observances, nationwide. Processions and age-old ceremonies—some from pagan days, some from the Middle Ages—are staged. The most notable procession is led by the pope, passing the Colosseum and the Roman Forum up to Palatine Hill; a torch-lit parade caps the observance. Sicily's observances are also noteworthy. Beginning 4 days before Easter Sunday; sometimes at the end of March but often in April.

Easter Sunday (Pasqua), Piazza di San Pietro, Rome. In an event broadcast around the world, the pope gives his blessing from the balcony of St. Peter's.

Scoppio del Carro (Explosion of the Cart), Florence. At this ancient observance, a cart laden with flowers and fireworks is drawn by three white oxen to the Duomo, where at the noon mass a mechanical dove detonates it from the altar. Easter Sunday.

Festa della Primavera, Rome. The Spanish Steps are decked out with banks of azaleas and other flowers; later, orchestral and choral concerts are presented in Trinità dei Monti. Dates vary.

May

Maggio Musicale Fiorentino (Musical May Florentine), Florence. Italy's oldest and most prestigious music festival emphasizes music from the 14th to the 20th centuries but also presents ballet and opera. Some concerts and ballets are presented free in Piazza della Signoria; ticketed events (concerts 15€–90€/$13.40–$80.35; operas 22.50€–100€/$20.10–$89.30; ballet 12.50€–27.50€/$11.15–$24.55) are held at the Teatro Comunale, Via Solferino 15, or the Teatro della Pergola, Via della Pergola 18. For schedules and tickets, contact the **Maggio Musicale Fiorentino/Teatro Comunale,** Corso Italia 12, 50123 Firenze (𝄞 **055-27791** or 055-211158). Late April to beginning of July.

Concorso Ippico Internazionale (International Horse Show), Piazza di Siena in the Villa Borghese, Rome. Usually May 1 to 10, but the dates can vary.

Corso dei Ceri (Race of the Candles), Gubbio, Umbria. In this centuries-old ceremony celebrating the feast day of St. Ubaldo, the town's patron saint, 1,000-pound, 30-foot wooden "candles" (*ceri*) are raced through the streets of this perfectly preserved medieval hill town. For more information, call 𝄞 **075-9220693.** May 15.

June

San Ranieri, Pisa, Tuscany. The town honors its patron saint with candlelit parades, followed the next day by eight rower teams competing in 16th-century costumes. For more information, call 𝄞 **050-42291.** June 16 to 17.

Festival di Ravenna, Ravenna, Emilia-Romagna. This summer festival of international renown draws world-class classical performers. A wide range of performances are staged, including operas, ballets, theater presentations, symphonic music concerts, solo and chamber pieces, oratorios, and sacred music. Tickets start at 12.50€ ($11.15), and reservations are needed for the most popular events. For details, call 𝄞 **0544-249244** (fax 055-36303; www.ravennafestival.org). Mid-June to July.

Calcio in Costume (Ancient Football Match in Costume), Florence. This is a revival of a raucous 16th-century football match, pitting four teams in medieval costumes against one another. There are four matches, usually culminating around June 24, the feast day of San Giovanni.

Festival di Spoleto, Spoleto, Umbria. Dating from 1958, this festival was the artistic creation of maestro and world-class composer Gian Carlo Menotti, who continues to be very visible and still presides over the event. International performers convene for 3 weeks of dance, drama, opera, concerts, and art exhibits in this Umbrian hill town north of Rome. The main focus is to highlight music composed from 1300 to 1799. For tickets and details, contact the **Spoleto Festival,** Piazza Duomo 8, 06049 Spoleto (𝄞 **0743-220320** or 0743-45028; fax 0743-220321). For further information, call 𝄞 **800-565600** (toll-free in Italy only) or 0743-44700, or visit www.spoletofestival.it. June 28 to July 15.

Gioco del Ponte, Pisa, Tuscany. Teams in Renaissance costume take part in a much-contested tug-of-war on the Ponte di Mezzo, which spans the Arno River. Last Sunday in June.

Festa di San Pietro, St. Peter's Basilica, Rome. This most significant Roman religious festival is observed with solemn rites. June 29, 2003.

Son et Lumière, Rome. The Roman Forum and Tivoli areas are dramatically lit at night. Early June to end of September.

Shakespearean Festival, Verona, the Veneto. Ballet, drama, and jazz performances are included in this festival of the Bard, with a few performances in English. June to September.

Biennale d'Arte (International Exposition of Modern Art), Venice. One of the most famous art events in Europe takes place during odd-numbered years. June to October.

July

Il Palio, Piazza del Campo, Siena, Tuscany. Palio fever grips this Tuscan hill town for a wild and exciting horse race from the Middle Ages. Pageantry, costumes, and the celebrations of the victorious *contrada* (sort of a neighborhood social club) mark the spectacle. It's a "no rules" event: Even a horse without a rider can win the race. For details, contact the **Azienda di Promozione Turistica,** Piazza del Campo 56, 53100 Siena (℡ **0577-280551**). July 2 to August 16, 2003.

Arena di Verona (Arena Outdoor Opera Season), Verona, the Veneto. Culture buffs flock to the 20,000-seat Roman amphitheater, one of the world's best preserved. Early July to mid-August.

Festa di Noantri, Rome. Trastevere, the most colorful quarter, becomes a gigantic outdoor restaurant, with tables lining the streets and merrymakers and musicians providing the entertainment. After reaching the quarter, find the first empty table and try to get a waiter—but keep a close eye on your valuables. For details, contact the **Ente Provinciale per il Turismo,** Via Parigi 11, 00185 Roma (℡ **06-48899253** or 06-48899255). Mid-July.

Umbria Jazz, Perugia, Umbria. The Umbrian region hosts the country's (and one of Europe's) top jazz festivals, featuring world-class artists. Mid- to late July.

Festa del Redentore (Feast of the Redeemer), Venice. This festival marks the lifting of the plague in July 1578, with fireworks, pilgrimages, and boating on the lagoon. Third Saturday and Sunday in July.

Festival Internazionale di Musica Antica, Urbino, the Marches. At this cultural extravaganza, international performers converge on Raphael's birthplace. It's the most important Renaissance and baroque music festival in Italy. For details, contact the **Azienda di Promozione Turistica,** Piazza del Rinascimento 1, 61029 Urbino (℡ **0722-2613**). July 18 to 28, 2003.

August

Torre del Lago Puccini, near Lucca, Tuscany. Puccini operas are performed in this Tuscan lakeside town's open-air theater, near the celebrated composer's former summertime villa. Throughout August.

Rossini Opera Festival, Pesaro, Italian Riviera. The world's top *bel canto* specialists perform Rossini's operas and choral works at this popular festival. Mid-August to late September.

Venice International Film Festival, Venice. Ranking after Cannes, this festival brings together stars, directors, producers, and filmmakers from all over the world. Films are shown more or less constantly between 9am and 3am in various areas of the Palazzo del Cinema on the Lido. Although many of the seats are reserved for international jury members, the public can attend virtually whenever they want, pending available seats. For information, contact the **Venice Film Festival,** c/o the La Biennale office, Ca' Giustinian, San Marco 1364A, 30124 Venezia. Call ©️ **041-5218838** for details on how to acquire tickets, or check out www.labiennale.org. August 29 to September 8, 2003.

September

Regata Storica, the Grand Canal, Venice. Here's a maritime spectacular. Many gondolas participate in the canal procession, although gondolas don't race in the regatta itself. First Sunday in September.

Giostra del Saracino (Joust of the Saracen), Arezzo, Tuscany. A colorful procession in full historical regalia precedes a reenactment of the tilting contest of the 13th century, with knights in armor in the town's main piazza. First Sunday in September.

Partita a Scacchi con Personnagi Viventi (Living Chess Game), Marostica, the Veneto. This chess game is played in the town square by living chess pieces in period costume. The second Saturday/Sunday of September during even-numbered years.

Sagra dell'Uva, Basilica of Maxentius, the Roman Forum, Rome. At this harvest festival, musicians in ancient costumes entertain and grapes are sold at reduced prices. Dates vary, usually early September.

October

Sagra del Tartufo, Alba, Piedmont. This festival honors the expensive truffle in Alba, Italy's truffle capital, with contests, truffle-hound competitions, and tastings of this ugly but very expensive and delectable fungus. For details, contact the **Azienda di Promozione Turistica,** Piazza Medford 3, 12051 Alba (©️ **0173-35833**). First Sunday of October.

December

La Scala Opera Season, Milan. The performances are held at the most famous opera house of them all, Teatro alla Scala. Even though opening-night tickets are close to impossible to get, it's worth a try; call ©️ **0272003744** for information or 02-860775 for reservations. The season opens on December 7, the feast day of Milan's patron St. Ambrogio, and runs into July.

Christmas Blessing of the Pope, Piazza di San Pietro, Rome. Delivered at noon from the balcony of St. Peter's Basilica, the pope's words are broadcast around the world. December 25.

6 Insurance, Health & Safety

TRAVEL INSURANCE AT A GLANCE

Since Italy is far from home for most of us, and a number of things could go wrong—lost luggage, trip cancellation, a medical emergency—consider the benefits of insurance.

Check your existing insurance policies before you buy travel insurance to cover trip cancellation, lost luggage, medical expenses, or car-rental insurance. You're likely to have partial or complete coverage. But if you need some, ask your travel agent about a comprehensive package. The cost of travel insurance varies widely, depending on the cost and length of your trip, your age and overall health, and the type of trip you're taking. Insurance for extreme sports or adventure travel, for example, will cost more than coverage for a European cruise. Some insurers provide packages for specialty vacations, such as skiing or backpacking. More dangerous activities may be excluded from basic policies.

For information, contact one of the following popular insurers:

- **Access America** (℡ 800/284-8300; www.accessamerica.com)
- **Travel Guard International** (℡ 800/826-1300; www.travelguard.com)
- **Travel Insured International** (℡ 800/243-3174; www.travelinsured.com)
- **Travelex Insurance Services** (℡ 800/228-9792; www.travelexinsurance.com)

TRIP-CANCELLATION INSURANCE (TCI)

There are three major types of trip-cancellation insurance—one, in the event that you prepay a cruise or tour that gets cancelled, and you can't get your money back; a second when you or someone in your family gets sick or dies, and you can't travel (but beware that you may not be covered for a pre-existing condition); and a third, when bad weather makes travel impossible. Some insurers provide coverage for events like jury duty; natural disasters close to home, such as floods or fire; or even the loss of a job. A few have added provisions for cancellations because of terror activities. Don't buy trip-cancellation insurance from the tour operator that may be responsible for the cancellation; buy it only from a reputable travel insurance agency. Don't overbuy. You won't be reimbursed for more than the cost of your trip. And keep in mind that in the aftermath of the September 11, 2001, terrorist attacks, a number of airlines, cruise lines, and tour operators are no longer covered by insurers. The bottom line: Always, always check the fine print before you sign on.

MEDICAL INSURANCE

Most health insurance policies cover you if you get sick away from home—but check, particularly if you're insured by an HMO. With the exception of certain HMOs and Medicare/Medicaid, your medical insurance should cover medical treatment—even hospital care—overseas. However, most out-of-country hospitals make you pay your bills up front, and send you a refund after you've returned home and filed the necessary paperwork. Members of **Blue Cross/Blue Shield** can now use their cards at select hospitals in most major cities worldwide (℡ 800/810-BLUE or www.bluecares.com for a list of hospitals).

Some credit cards (American Express and certain gold and platinum Visa and MasterCards, for example) offer automatic flight insurance against death or dismemberment in case of an airplane crash if you charged the cost of your ticket.

If you require additional insurance, try one of the following companies:

- **MEDEX International,** 9515 Deereco Rd., Timonium, MD 21093-5375 (℡ 888/MEDEX-00 or 410/453-6300; fax 410/453-6301; www.medexassist.com)
- **Travel Assistance International** (℡ 800/821-2828; www.travelassistance.com), 9200 Keystone Crossing, Suite 300, Indianapolis, IN 46240 (for general information on services, call the company's Worldwide Assistance Services, Inc., at ℡ 800/777-8710)

The cost of travel medical insurance varies widely. Check your existing policies before you buy additional coverage. Also, check to see if your medical insurance covers you for emergency medical evacuation. If you have to buy a one-way same-day ticket home and forfeit your nonrefundable round-trip ticket, you may be out big bucks.

LOST-LUGGAGE INSURANCE

On international flights (including U.S. portions of international trips), the airline's liability for baggage is limited to approximately $9.05 per pound, up to approximately $635 per checked bag. If you plan to check items more valuable than the standard liability, you may purchase "excess valuation" coverage from the airline, up to $5,000. Be sure to take any valuables or irreplaceable items with you in your carry-on luggage. If you file a lost-luggage claim, be prepared to answer detailed questions about the contents of your baggage, and be sure to file a claim immediately, because most airlines enforce a 21-day deadline. Before you leave home, compile an inventory of all packed items and a rough estimate of the total value to ensure you're properly compensated if your luggage is lost. You will be reimbursed only for what you lost, no more. Once you've filed a complaint, persist in securing your reimbursement; there are no laws governing the length of time it takes for a carrier to reimburse you. If you arrive at a destination without your bags, ask the airline to forward them to your hotel or to your next destination; they will usually comply. If your bag is delayed or lost, the airline may reimburse you for reasonable expenses, such as a toothbrush or a set of clothes, but the airline is under no legal obligation to do so.

Lost luggage may also be covered by your homeowner's or renter's policy. Many platinum and gold credit cards cover you as well. If you choose to purchase additional lost-luggage insurance, be sure not to buy more than you need. Buy in advance from the insurer or a trusted agent (prices will be much higher at the airport).

CAR-RENTAL INSURANCE (LOSS/DAMAGE WAIVER OR COLLISION DAMAGE WAIVER)

If you hold a private auto insurance policy, you probably are covered in the U.S., but not abroad, for loss or damage to the car, and liability in case a passenger is injured. The credit card you used to rent the car also may provide some coverage.

Car-rental insurance probably does not cover liability if you caused the accident. Check your own auto insurance policy, the rental company policy, and your credit-card coverage for the extent of coverage. Is your destination covered? Are other drivers covered? How much liability is covered if a passenger is injured? (If you rely on your credit card for coverage, you may want to bring a second credit card with you, because damages may be charged to your card and you may find yourself stranded with no money.)

Car-rental insurance costs about $20 a day.

THE HEALTHY TRAVELER

In general, Italy is viewed as a "safe" destination, although problems, of course, can and do occur anywhere. You don't need to get shots; most foodstuff is safe and the water in cities and towns potable. If you're concerned, order bottled water. It is easy to get a prescription filled in towns and cities, and nearly all places contain English-speaking doctors at hospitals with well-trained medical staffs, which are found through Italy.

WHAT TO DO IF YOU GET SICK AWAY FROM HOME

If you worry about getting sick away from home, consider purchasing **medical travel insurance** and carry your ID card in your purse or wallet. In most cases, your existing health plan will provide the coverage you need. See the section on insurance earlier in this chapter for more information.

If you suffer from a chronic illness, consult your doctor before your departure. For conditions like epilepsy, diabetes, or heart problems, wear a **Medic Alert Identification**

Tag (© 800/825-3785; www.medic alert.org), which will immediately alert doctors to your condition and give them access to your records through Medic Alert's 24-hour hotline.

Pack **prescription medications** in your carry-on luggage, and carry the medications in their original containers. Also bring along copies of your prescriptions in case you lose your pills or run out. Carry the generic name of prescription medicines, in case a local pharmacist is unfamiliar with the brand name.

Contact the **International Association for Medical Assistance to Travelers (IAMAT)** (© 716/754-4883 or 519/836-3412; www.sentex.net/ ~iamat) for tips on travel and health concerns in Italy and lists of local English-speaking doctors. The United States **Centers for Disease Control and Prevention** (© 800/311-3435; www.cdc.gov) provides up-to-date information on necessary vaccines and health hazards by region or country (their booklet, *Health Information for International Travel*, is $25 by mail; on the Internet, it's free). Any foreign consulate can provide a list of area doctors who speak English. If you get sick, consider asking your hotel concierge to recommend a local doctor—even his or her own. You can also try the emergency room at a local hospital; many have walk-in clinics for emergency cases that are not life-threatening. You may not get immediate attention, but you won't pay the high price of an emergency room visit (usually a minimum of $300 just for signing your name).

THE SAFE TRAVELER

The most common menace, especially in large cities, particularly Rome, is the plague of pickpockets and roving gangs of Gypsy children who virtually surround you, distract you in all the confusion, and steal your purse or wallet. Never leave valuables in a car, and never travel with your car unlocked. A U.S. State Department travel advisory warns that every car (whether parked, stopped at a traffic light, or even moving) can be a potential target for armed robbery. In these uncertain times, it is always prudent to check the U.S. State Department's travel advisories at http://travel.state.gov/ travel_warnings.html.

7 Tips for Travelers with Special Needs

TRAVELERS WITH DISABILITIES

Most disabilities shouldn't stop anyone from traveling. There are more options and resources out there than ever before. Laws in Italy have compelled rail stations, airports, hotels, and most restaurants to follow a stricter set of regulations about **wheelchair accessibility** to restrooms, ticket counters, and the like. Even museums and other attractions have conformed to the regulations, which mimic many of those presently in effect in the United States. Always call ahead to check on the accessibility in hotels, restaurants, and sights you want to visit.

With overcrowded streets, more than 400 bridges, and difficult-to-board *vaporetti*, Venice has never been accused of being too user-friendly for those with disabilities. Nevertheless, some improvements have been made. The Venice tourist office distributes a free map called *Veneziapertutti* (Venice for All), illustrating what parts of the city are accessible and listing accessible churches, monuments, gardens, public offices, hotels, and restrooms. According to various announcements, Venice will pay even more attention to this issue in the future, possibly adding retractable ramps operated by magnetic cards.

AGENCIES/OPERATORS

- **Flying Wheels Travel** (© 800/535-6790; www.flyingwheels travel.com) offers escorted tours and cruises that emphasize sports and private tours in minivans with lifts.
- **Access Adventures** (© 716/889-9096), a Rochester, New York–based agency, offers customized itineraries for a variety of travelers with disabilities.
- **Accessible Journeys** (© 800/TINGLES or 610/521-0339; www.disabilitytravel.com) caters specifically to slow walkers and wheelchair travelers and their families and friends.

ORGANIZATIONS

- **The Moss Rehab Hospital** (© 215/456-5995; www.moss resourcenet.org) provides helpful phone assistance through its **Travel Information Service.**
- **The Society for Accessible Travel and Hospitality** (© 212/447-7285; fax 212/725-8253; www.sath.org) offers a wealth of travel resources for all types of disabilities and informed recommendations on destinations, access guides, travel agents, tour operators, vehicle rentals, and companion services. Annual membership costs $45 for adults, $30 for seniors and students.
- **The American Foundation for the Blind** (© 800/232-5463; www.afb.org) provides information on traveling with Seeing Eye dogs.
- **Holiday Care** (© 01293/774-535; www.holidaycare.org.uk) is a national UK charity advising on accessible accommodations for the elderly and persons with disabilities. Annual membership is £30 ($38.30).

PUBLICATIONS

- **Mobility International USA** (© 541/343-1284; www.miusa.

org) publishes *A World of Options,* a 658-page book of resources, covering everything from biking trips to scuba outfitters, and a biannual newsletter, *Over the Rainbow.* Annual membership is $35.
- **Twin Peaks Press** (© 360/694-2462) publishes travel-related books for travelers with special needs.
- *Open World for Disability and Mature Travel* magazine, published by the Society for Accessible Travel and Hospitality (see above), is full of good resources and information. A year's subscription is $13 ($21 outside the U.S.).
- **Royal Association for Disability and Rehabilitation (RADAR)** (© 020/7250-3222; www.radar.org.uk) publishes three informative "fact packs" for travelers with disabilities. The cost is £2 ($2.55) each or £5 ($6.40) for all three.

GAY & LESBIAN TRAVELERS

Since 1861, Italy has had liberal legislation regarding homosexuality, but that doesn't mean it has always been looked on favorably in a Catholic country. Homosexuality is much more accepted in the north than in the south, especially in Sicily, although Taormina has long been a gay mecca. However, all major towns and cities have an active gay life, especially Florence, Rome, and Milan, which considers itself the "gay capital" of Italy and is the headquarters of **ARCI Gay,** the country's leading gay organization with branches throughout Italy. Capri is the gay resort of Italy, rivaled only by the gay beaches of Venice.

The **International Gay & Lesbian Travel Association (IGLTA)** (© 800/448-8550 or 954/776-2626; fax 954/776-3303; www.iglta.org) links travelers up with gay-friendly hoteliers, tour operators, and airline and cruise-line representatives. It offers monthly newsletters, marketing mailings, and a membership directory that's updated once a year. Membership is $150 yearly, plus a $100 administration fee for new members.

AGENCIES/OPERATORS
- **Above and Beyond Tours** (℃ 800/397-2681; www.above-beyondtours.com) offers gay and lesbian tours worldwide and is the exclusive gay and lesbian tour operator for United Airlines.
- **Now, Voyager** (℃ 800/255-6951; www.nowvoyager.com) is a San Francisco–based gay-owned and -operated travel service.
- **Olivia Cruises & Resorts** (℃ 800/631-6277 or 510/655-0364; http://oliviatravel.com) charters entire resorts and ships for exclusive lesbian vacations all over the world.

PUBLICATIONS
- *Frommer's Gay & Lesbian Europe* is an excellent travel resource.
- *Out and About* (℃ 800/929-2268 or 415/644-8044; www.outandabout.com) offers guidebooks and a newsletter 10 times a year packed with solid information on the global gay and lesbian scene.
- *Spartacus International Gay Guide* and *Odysseus* are good, annual English-language guidebooks focused on gay men, with some information for lesbians. You can get them from most gay and lesbian bookstores, or order them from **Giovanni's Room** bookstore, 1145 Pine St., Philadelphia, PA 19107 (℃ 215/923-2960;www.giovannisroom.com).

- *Gay Travel A to Z: The World of Gay & Lesbian Travel Options at Your Fingertips,* by Marianne Ferrari (Ferrari Publications), is a very good gay and lesbian guidebook series.

SENIOR TRAVEL
Mention the fact that you're a senior citizen when you first make your travel reservations. All major airlines and many Italian hotels offer discounts for seniors.

Members of **AARP** (formerly known as the American Association of Retired Persons), 601 E St. NW, Washington, DC 10049 (℃ 800/424-3410 or 202/434-2277; www.aarp.org), gets discounts on hotels, airfares, and car rentals. AARP offers members a wide range of benefits, including *Modern Maturity of My Generation* magazine and a monthly newsletter. Anyone over 50 can join.

The Alliance for Retired Americans, 8403 Colesville Rd., Suite 1200, Silver Spring, MD 20910 (℃ 301/578-8422; www.retiredamericans.org), offers a newsletter six times a year and discounts on hotel and auto rentals; annual dues are $13 per person or couple. *Note:* Members of the former National Council of Senior Citizens receive automatic membership in the Alliance.

AGENCIES/OPERATORS
- **Elderhostel** (℃ 877/426-8056; www.elderhostel.org) arranges study programs for those ages 55 and over (and a spouse or companion of any age) in the U.S. and in more than 80 countries around the world, including Italy. Most courses last 5 to 7 days in the U.S. (2 to 4 weeks abroad), and many include airfare, accommodations in university dormitories or modest inns, meals, and tuition.

- **Interhostel** (☎ 800/733-9753; www.learn.unh.edu/interhostel), organized by the University of New Hampshire, also offers educational travel for senior citizens. On these escorted tours, the days are packed with seminars, lectures, and field trips, with sightseeing led by academic experts. Interhostel takes travelers 50 and over (with companions over 40), and offers 1- and 2-week trips, mostly international.
- **European Walking Tours** (☎ 217/398-0058; www2.gorp. com/ewt/) sponsors tours for the mature traveler in Italy. The operator is a native of the Swiss Alps, and has charted specially discovered routes across alpine meadows, over mountain passes, or alongside serene lakes. The search is for wildflowers, birds, and mountain animals, with lessons in local architecture, traditions, and history thrown in as well.
- **Golden Escapes** (☎ 800/668-9125 or 416/447-7683 in Toronto) is a branch of Back-Roads Touring Company of Great Britain, sending out small tour groups of English-speaking people on customized tours to select European countries such as Italy. Tours, ranging from 10 to 17 days, usually are filled with mature travelers, though not restricted to them. Novel accommodations are provided in such places as working farmhouses, manors, castles, and historic inns.
- **Vantage Deluxe World Travel** (☎ 800/322-6677 or 617/878-6000; www.vantagetravel.com/trips/landTours.asp) offers out-of-the-ordinary vacation experiences to mature travelers in various European countries, including Italy. The deliberately small tour groups embark on luxurious river cruises and fully escorted land tours.

PUBLICATIONS

- *The Book of Deals* is a collection of more than 1,000 senior discounts on airlines, lodging, tours, and attractions around the country; it's available for $9.95 by calling ☎ 800/460-6676.
- *101 Tips for the Mature Traveler* is available from Grand Circle Travel (☎ 800/221-2610 or 617/350-7500; fax 617/346-6700).
- *The 50+ Traveler's Guidebook* (St. Martin's Press).
- *Unbelievably Good Deals and Great Adventures That You Absolutely Can't Get Unless You're Over 50* (Contemporary Publishing Co.).

STUDENT TRAVEL

When leaving the U.S., you'd be wise to arm yourself with an **international student I.D. card,** which offers substantial savings on rail passes, plane tickets, and entrance fees. It also provides you with basic health and life insurance and a 24-hour help line. The card is available for $22 from the **Council on International Educational Exchange,** or CIEE (www.ciee.org). The CIEE's travel branch, **Council Travel Service** (☎ 800/226-8624; www.council travel.com), is the biggest student travel agency in the world. If you're no longer a student but are still under 26, you can get a **GO 25 card** from the same people, which entitles you to insurance and some discounts (but not on museum admissions). **STA Travel** (☎ 800/781-4040; www. statravel.com) is another travel agency catering especially to young travelers, although their bargain-basement prices are available to people of all ages.

In Canada, **Travel Cuts** (☎ 800/667-2887 or 416/614-2887; www. travelcuts.com) offers similar services. In London, **Usit Campus** (☎ 0870/

240-1010; www.usitworld.com), opposite Victoria Station, is Britain's leading specialist in student and youth travel.

PUBLICATIONS
The Hanging Out Guides (www.frommers.com/hangingout/), published by Frommer's, is the top student travel series for today's students, covering everything from adrenaline sports to the hottest club and music scenes.

FAMILY TRAVEL
The family vacation is a rite of passage for many households, one that in a split second can devolve into a *National Lampoon* farce. But as any veteran family vacationer will assure you, a family trip can be among the most pleasurable and rewarding times of your life.

Most Italian hoteliers will let children 12 and under stay in a room with their parents for free; others do not. Sometimes this requires a little negotiation at the reception desk.

Italians love *bambini* but don't offer a lot of special amenities for them. For example, a kiddies' menu in a restaurant is a rarity. You can, however, order a half portion (*mezza porzione*), and most waiters will oblige.

At attractions inquire if a kids' discount is available, even if it isn't specifically posted. Italians call it *sconto bambino*. For European Community young people under 18, there's a big break offered. They are admitted free to all state-run museums.

The friendliest hotels in Italy are the 20 or so **Sheratons** (© **800/221-2340**). The downside to this kid-friendly hospitality? All of these Sheratons are expensive.

Throughout the guide, look for hotels, restaurants, and attractions marked with a Kids icon to discover good bets for your family.

AGENCIES/OPERATORS
Familyhostel (© **800/733-9753;** www.learn.unh.edu/familyhostel) takes the whole family on moderately priced domestic and international learning vacations. All trip details are handled by the program staff, and lectures, field trips, and sightseeing are guided by a team of academics. For kids ages 8 to 15 accompanied by their parents and/or grandparents.

PUBLICATIONS
- *How to Take Great Trips with Your Kids* (The Harvard Common Press) is full of good general advice that can apply to travel anywhere, including Italy.

WEBSITES
- **Family Travel Network** (www.familytravelnetwork.com) offers travel tips and reviews of family-friendly destinations, vacation deals, and thoughtful features such as "What to Do When Your Kids Are Afraid to Travel" and "Kid-Style Camping."
- **Travel with Your Children** (www.travelwithyourkids.com) is a comprehensive site offering sound advice for traveling with children.
- **The Busy Person's Guide to Travel with Children** (http://wz.com/travel/TravelingWithChildren.html) offers a "45-second newsletter" where experts weigh in on the bst websites and resources for tips for traveling with children.

8 Getting There

BY PLANE
High season on most airlines' routes to Rome is usually June to the beginning of September. This is the most expensive and most crowded time to travel. **Shoulder season** is April to May, early September to October, and December 15 to 24. **Low season** is November 1 to December 14 and December 25 to March 31.

FROM NORTH AMERICA   Fares to Italy are constantly changing, but you can expect to pay somewhere in the range of $400 to $800 for a direct round-trip ticket from New York to Rome in coach.

Flying time to Rome from New York, Newark, and Boston is 8 hours; from Chicago, 10 hours; and from Los Angeles, 12½ hours. Flying time to Milan from New York, Newark, and Boston is 8 hours; from Chicago, 9¼ hours; and from Los Angeles, 11½ hours.

American Airlines (© 800/433-7300; www.aa.com) offers daily non-stop flights to Rome from Chicago's O'Hare, with flights from all parts of American's vast network making connections into Chicago. **TWA** (© 800/221-2000; www.twa.com) offers daily nonstop flights from New York's JFK to Rome, Milan, and Venice. **Delta** (© 800/221-1212; www.delta.com) also flies from New York's JFK to both Milan and Rome; separate flights depart every evening for both destinations. **United** (© 800/241-6522; www.ual.com) has service to Milan only from Dulles in Washington, D.C. **US Airways** (© 800/428-4322; www.usairways.com) offers one flight daily to Rome out of Philadelphia (you can connect through Philly from most major U.S. cities). And **Continental** (© 800/525-0280; www.continental.com) flies twice daily to Rome from its hub in Newark.

Air Canada (© 888/247-2262; www.aircanada.ca) flies daily from Toronto to Rome. Two of the flights are nonstop; the others touch down en route in Montréal, depending on the schedule.

British Airways (© 800/AIR-WAYS; www.british-airways.com), **Virgin Atlantic Airways** (© 800/862-8621; www.fly.virgin.com), **Air France** (© 800/237-2747; www.airfrance.com), **Northwest/KLM** (© 800/374-7747; www.klm.com), and **Lufthansa** (© 800/645-3880; www.lufthansa-usa.com) offer some attractive deals for anyone interested in combining a trip to Italy with a stopover in, say, Britain, Paris, Amsterdam, or Germany.

Alitalia (© 800/223-5730; www.alitalia.com) is the Italian national airline, with nonstop flights to Rome from different North American cities, including New York (JFK),

---

⸢Tips⸣ **All About E-Ticketing**

Only yesterday **electronic tickets (E-tickets)** were the fast and easy ticket-free alternative to paper tickets. E-tickets allowed passengers to avoid long lines at airport check-in, all the while saving the airlines money on postage and labor. With the increased security measures in airports, however, an E-ticket no longer guarantees an accelerated check-in. You often can't go straight to the boarding gate, even if you have no bags to check. You'll probably need to show your printed E-ticket receipt or confirmation of purchase, as well as a photo I.D., and sometimes even the credit card with which you purchased your E-ticket. That said, buying an E-ticket is still a fast, convenient way to book a flight; instead of having to wait for a paper ticket to come through the mail, you can book your fare by phone or on the computer, and the airline will immediately confirm by fax or e-mail. In addition, airlines often offer frequent-flier miles as incentive for electronic bookings.

Newark, Boston, Chicago, and Miami. Nonstop flights into Milan are from New York (JFK), Newark, and Los Angeles. From Milan or Rome, Alitalia can easily book connecting domestic flights if your final destination is elsewhere in Italy. Alitalia participates in the frequent-flier programs of other airlines, including Continental and US Airways.

FROM THE UNITED KINGDOM

Operated by the European Travel Network, **www.discount-tickets.com** is a great online source for regular and discounted airfares to destinations around the world. You can also use this site to compare rates and book accommodations, car rentals, and tours. Click on "Special Offers" for the latest package deals. Students should also try **Usit Campus** (© **0870/240-1010;** www.usitcampus. co.uk).

British newspapers are always full of classified ads touting slashed fares to Italy. One good source is *Time Out.* London's *Evening Standard* has a daily travel section, and the Sunday editions of almost any newspaper will run many ads. Although competition is fierce, one well-recommended company that consolidates bulk ticket purchases and then passes the savings on to its consumers is **Trailfinders** (© **020/7937-5400;** www.trailfinders. com). It offers access to tickets on such carriers as SAS, British Airways, and KLM.

Both **British Airways** (© **0845/ 773-3377** in the U.K.; www.british airways.co.uk) and **Alitalia** (© **020/ 8745-8200;** www.alitalia.it/english/ index.html) have frequent flights from London's Heathrow to Rome, Milan, Venice, Pisa (the gateway to Florence), and Naples. Flying time from London to these cities is from 2 to 3 hours. British Airways also has one direct flight a day from Manchester to Rome.

NEW AIR TRAVEL SECURITY MEASURES

In the wake of the terrorist attacks of September 11, 2001, the airline industry began implementing sweeping security measures in airports. Expect a lengthy check-in process and extensive delays. Although regulations vary from airline to airline, you can expedite the process by taking the following steps:

- **Arrive early.** Arrive at the airport at least 2 hours before your scheduled flight.
- **Try not to drive your car to the airport.** Parking and curbside access to the terminal may be limited. Call ahead and check.
- **Don't count on curbside check-in.** Some airlines and airports have stopped curbside check-in altogether, whereas others offer it on a limited basis. For up-to-date information on specific regulations and implementations, check with the individual airline.
- **Be sure to carry plenty of documentation.** A government-issued photo ID (federal, state, or local) is now required. You may need to show this at various checkpoints. With an E-ticket, you may be required to have with you printed confirmation of purchase, and perhaps even the credit card with which you bought your ticket (see "All About E-Ticketing," above). This varies from airline to airline, so call ahead to make sure you have the proper documentation. And be sure that your ID is **up-to-date;** an expired driver's license, for example, may keep you from boarding the plane altogether.
- **Know what you can carry on— and what you can't.** Travelers in the United States are now limited to one carry-on bag, plus one personal bag (such as a purse or a briefcase). The Transportation Security Administration (TSA)

Tips   Travel Planning & Booking Sites

Keep in mind that because several airlines are no longer willing to pay commissions on tickets sold by online travel agencies, these agencies may add a $10 surcharge to your bill if you book on that carrier—or neglect to offer those carriers' schedules.

The list of sites below is selective, not comprehensive. Some sites will have evolved or disappeared by the time you read this.

- **Travelocity** (www.travelocity.com or www.frommers.travelocity.com) and **Expedia** (www.expedia.com) are among the most popular sites, each offering an excellent range of options. Travelers search by destination, dates, and cost.
- **Orbitz** (www.orbitz.com) is a popular site launched by United, Delta, Northwest, American, and Continental airlines. (Stay tuned: At press time, travel-agency associations were waging an antitrust battle against this site.)
- **Qixo** (www.qixo.com) is another powerful search engine that allows you to search for flights and accommodations from some 20 airline and travel-planning sites (such as Travelocity) at once. Qixo sorts results by price.
- **Priceline** (www.priceline.com) lets you "name your price" for airline tickets, hotel rooms, and rental cars. For airline tickets, you can't say what time you want to fly—you have to accept any flight between 6am and 10pm on the dates you've selected, and you may have to make one or more stopovers. Tickets are nonrefundable, and no frequent-flyer miles are awarded.

has also issued a list of newly restricted carry-on items; see the box "What You Can Carry On—and What You Can't" below.

- **Prepare to be searched.** Expect spot-checks. Electronic items, such as a laptop or cell phone, should be readied for additional screening. Limit the metal items you wear on your person.
- **It's no joke.** When a check-in agent asks if someone other than you packed your bag, don't decide that this is the time to be funny. The agents will not hesitate to call an alarm.
- **No ticket, no gate access.** Only ticketed passengers will be allowed beyond the screener checkpoints, except for those people with specific medical or parental needs.

FLYING FOR LESS: TIPS FOR GETTING THE BEST AIRFARE

Passengers within the same airplane cabin are rarely paying the same fare. Business travelers who need to purchase tickets at the last minute, change their itinerary at a moment's notice, or get home for the weekend pay the premium rate. Passengers who can book their ticket long in advance, who can stay over Saturday night, or who are willing to travel on a Tuesday, Wednesday, or Thursday after 7pm will pay a fraction of the full fare. Here are a few other easy ways to save:

- Airlines periodically lower prices on their most popular routes. Check the travel section of your Sunday newspaper for advertised discounts or call the airlines directly and ask if any **promotional rates** or special fares are available. You'll almost never see a sale during the peak summer vacation months of July and August, or during the Thanksgiving or Christmas seasons; but in periods of low-volume travel, you should pay no more than $400 for a domestic cross-country flight. If your schedule is flexible, say so, and ask if you can secure a cheaper fare by staying an extra day, by flying midweek, or by flying at less-trafficked hours. If you already hold a ticket when a sale breaks, it may even pay to exchange your ticket, which usually incurs a $100 to $150 charge.

Note: The lowest-priced fares are often nonrefundable, require advance purchase of 1 to 3 weeks and a certain length of stay, and carry penalties for changing dates of travel.

• **Consolidators,** also known as bucket shops, are a good place to find low fares, often below even the airlines' discounted rates. Basically, they're just big travel agents who get discounts for buying in bulk and pass some of the savings on to you. Before you pay, however, be aware that consolidator tickets are usually nonrefundable or come with stiff cancellation penalties.

We've gotten great deals on many occasions from **Cheap Tickets** ✦ (© 800/377-1000; www.cheaptickets.com). **Council Travel** (© 800/2COUNCIL; www.counciltravel.com) and **STA Travel** (© 800/781-4040; www. sta-travel.com) cater especially to young travelers, but their bargain-basement prices are available to people of all ages. Other reliable consolidators include **Lowestfare. com** (© 888/278-8830; www. lowestfare.com); **Cheap Seats** (© 800/451-7200; www.cheap-seatstravel.com); and **1-800/FLY-CHEAP** (www.flycheap.com).

⌐ Tips   What You Can Carry On—and What You Can't

The Transportation Security Administration (TSA), the government agency that now handles all aspects of airport security, has devised new restrictions for carry-on baggage, not only to expedite the screening process but to prevent potential weapons from passing through airport security. Passengers are now limited to bringing just one carry-on bag and one personal item onto the aircraft (previous regulations allowed two carry-on bags and one personal item, like a briefcase or a purse). For more information, go to the TSA's website, www.tsa.gov. The agency has released an updated list of items that passengers are not allowed to carry onto an aircraft.

Not permitted: Knives and box cutters, corkscrews, straight razors, metal scissors, golf clubs, baseball bats, pool cues, hockey sticks, ski poles, ice picks.

Permitted: Nail clippers, nail files, tweezers, eyelash curlers, safety razors (including disposable razors), syringes (with documented proof of medical need), walking canes and umbrellas (must be inspected first).

The airline you fly may have **additional restrictions** on items you can and cannot carry on board. Call ahead to avoid problems.

- Look into **courier flights.** These companies hire couriers to hand-deliver packages or mail, and use your luggage allowance for themselves; in return, you get a deeply discounted ticket—for example, $300 round-trip to Europe in winter. Flights often become available at the last minute, so check in often. **Halbart Express** has offices in New York (© **718/656-8189**), Los Angeles (© **310/417-9790**), and Miami (© **305/593-0260**). **Jupiter Air** (www.jupiterair.com) has offices in New York (© **718/ 656-6050**), Los Angeles (© **310/ 670-5123**), and San Francisco (© **650/697-1773**).

- Join a travel club such as **Moment's Notice** (© **718/234-6295;** www. moments-notice.com) or **Sears Discount Travel Club** (© **800/ 433-9383,** or 800/255-1487 to join; www.travelersadvantage.com), which supply unsold tickets at discounted prices. You pay an annual membership fee to get the club's hotline number. Of course, you're limited to what's available, so you have to be flexible.

BY CAR

If you're already on the Continent, particularly in a neighboring country such as France or Austria, you may want to drive to Italy. However, you should make arrangements in advance with your car-rental company.

It's also possible to drive from London to Rome, a distance of 1,810km (1,122 miles), via Calais/Boulogne/ Dunkirk, or 1,747km (1,083 miles) via Oostende/Zeebrugge, not counting channel crossings by Hovercraft, ferry, or the Chunnel. Milan is some 644km (399 miles) closer to Britain than is Rome. If you cross over from England and arrive at one of the continental ports, you still face a 24-hour drive. Most drivers play it safe and budget 3 days for the journey.

Most of the roads from western Europe leading into Italy are toll-free, with some notable exceptions. If you use the Swiss superhighway network, you'll have to buy a special tax sticker at the frontier. You'll also pay to go through the St. Gotthard Tunnel into Italy. Crossings from France can be through the Mont Blanc Tunnel, for which you'll pay, or you can leave the French Riviera at Menton and drive directly into Italy along the Italian Riviera toward San Remo.

If you don't want to drive such distances, ask a travel agent to book you on a Motorail arrangement where the train carries your car. This service, however, is good only to Milan, because there are no car and sleeper expresses running the 644km (399 miles) south to Rome.

BY TRAIN

If you plan to travel heavily on the European rails, you'll do well to secure the latest copy of the *Thomas Cook European Timetable of Railroads.* This 500-plus-page timetable accurately documents all of Europe's main-line passenger rail services. It's available from **Forsyth Travel Library,** 44 S. Broadway, White Plains, NY 10604 (© **800/FORSYTH;** www.forsyth. com), for $27.95 (plus $4.95 shipping in the U.S. and $6.95 in Canada), or at travel specialty stores such as **Rand McNally** (© **212/758-7488;** www. randmcnally.com).

New electric trains have made travel between France and Italy faster and more comfortable than ever. **France's TGVs** travel at speeds of up to 185 miles per hour and have cut travel time between Paris and Turin from 7 to 5½ hours and between Paris and Milan from 7½ to 6¾ hours. **Italy's ETRs** travel at speeds of up to 145 miles per hour and currently run between Milan and Lyon (5 hr.), with a stop in Turin. Visit **www.raileurope.com** for information (© **800/848-7245** in U.S.; 800/361-RAIL in Canada).

Frommers.com: The Complete Travel Resource

For an excellent travel-planning resource, we highly recommend **Frommers.com** (www.frommers.com). We're a little biased, of course, but we guarantee that you'll find the travel tips, reviews, monthly vacation giveaways, and online-booking capabilities thoroughly indispensable. Among the special features are our popular **Message Boards,** where Frommer's readers post queries and share advice (sometimes even our authors show up to answer questions); **Frommers.com Newsletter,** for the latest travel bargains and inside travel secrets; and Frommer's **Destinations Section,** where you'll get expert travel tips, hotel and dining recommendations, and advice on the sights to see for more than 2,500 destinations around the globe. When your research is done, the **Online Reservation System** (www.frommers.com/booktravelnow) takes you to Frommer's favorite sites for booking your vacation at affordable prices.

EUROPE-WIDE RAIL PASSES

EURAILPASS   Many travelers to Europe take advantage of one of the greatest travel bargains, the **Eurailpass,** which permits unlimited first-class rail travel in any country in western Europe (except the British Isles) and Hungary in eastern Europe. Oddly, it doesn't include travel on the rail lines of Sardinia, which are organized independently of the rail lines of the rest of Italy.

The advantages are tempting: There are no tickets; simply show the pass to the ticket collector and then settle back to enjoy the scenery. Seat reservations are required on some trains. Many of the trains have couchettes (sleeping cars), for which an extra fee is charged. Obviously, the 2- or 3-month traveler gets the greatest economic advantages. To obtain full advantage of a 15-day or 1-month pass, you'd have to spend a great deal of time on the train.

Eurailpass holders are entitled to considerable reductions on certain buses and ferries as well. You'll get a 20% reduction on second-class accommodations from certain companies operating ferries between Naples and Palermo or for crossings to Sardinia and Malta.

A **Eurailpass** is $572 for 15 days, $740 for 21 days, $918 for 1 month, $1,298 for 2 months, and $1,606 for 3 months. Children 3 and under travel free, provided that they don't occupy a seat (otherwise, they're charged half fare); children 4 to 11 are charged half fare. If you're under 26, you can buy a **Eurail Youthpass,** entitling you to unlimited second-class travel for $401 for 15 days, $518 for 21 days, $644 for 1 month, $910 for 2 months, and $1,126 for 3 months.

Eurail Saverpass, valid all over Europe for first class only, offers discounted 15-day travel for groups of three or more people traveling together April to September, or two people traveling together October to March. The price is $486 for 15 days, $630 for 21 days, $780 for 1 month, $1,106 for 2 months, and $1,366 for 3 months.

The **Eurail Flexipass** allows you to visit Europe with more flexibility. It's valid in first class and offers the same privileges as the Eurailpass. However, it provides a number of individual travel days you can use over a much longer period of consecutive days.

That makes it possible to stay in one city yet not lose a single day of travel. There are two passes: 10 days of travel in 2 months for $674, and 15 days of travel in 2 months for $888.

Having many of the same qualifications and restrictions as the previously described Flexipass is the **Eurail Youth Flexipass.** Sold only to travelers under 26, it allows 10 days of travel within 2 months for $473, and 15 days of travel within 2 months for $622.

Eurail Selectpass is a flexipass, meaning that travel days need not be consecutive. Passes are available for 5, 6, 8, or 10 days within a 2-month period. Prices vary, of course, depending on the days selected, beginning at $346 for a 5-day pass.

EUROPASS The **Europass** is more limited than the Eurailpass, but it could offer better value for visitors traveling over a smaller area. It's good for 2 months and allows 5 days of rail travel within three to five European countries (Italy, France, Germany, Switzerland, and Spain) with contiguous borders. For individual travelers, 5 days of travel costs $360; 6 days of travel, $400; 8 days of travel, $474; 10 days of travel, $544; and 15 days of travel, $710.

For travelers under 26, a **Europass Youth** is available. The fares are 35% to 55% off those quoted above, and the pass is good only for second-class travel. Unlike the adult Europass, there's no discount for a companion.

WHERE TO BUY A PASS In **North America,** you can buy these passes from travel agents or rail agents in major cities such as New York, Montréal, and Los Angeles. Eurailpasses are also available from the North American offices of **CIT Tours** (see section 10, "Getting Around Italy," below) or through **Rail Europe** (℡ **800/848-7245;** www.raileurope. com). No matter what everyone tells you, you can buy Eurailpasses in Europe as well as in America (at the major train stations), but they're more expensive. Rail Europe can also give you information on the rail/drive versions of the passes.

For details on the rail passes available in the **United Kingdom,** stop at or contact the **International Rail Centre,** Victoria Station, London SW1V 1JZ (℡ **08705/848-848**). The staff can help you find the best option for the trip you're planning. Some of the most popular are the **Inter-Rail** and **Under 26** passes, entitling you to unlimited second-class travel in 26 European countries.

Under 26 tickets are a worthwhile option for travelers under 26. They allow you to move leisurely from London to Rome, with as many stopovers en route as you want, using a different route southbound (through Belgium, Luxembourg, and Switzerland) from the return route northbound (exclusively through France). All travel must be completed within 1 month of the departure date. Under 26 tickets from London to Rome cost from £133 ($170) for the most direct route or from £209 ($267) for a roundabout route through the south of France.

9 Escorted Tours & Package Deals & Special-Interest Vacations

Before you start your search for the lowest airfare, you may want to consider booking your flight as part of a travel package such as an escorted tour or a package tour. What you lose in adventure, you'll gain in time and money saved when you book accommodations, and maybe even food and entertainment, along with your flight.

PACKAGE TOURS FOR INDEPENDENT TRAVELERS

Package tours are not the same thing as escorted tours. With a package tour, you travel independently but pay a group rate. Packages usually include airfare, a choice of hotels, and car rentals, and packagers often offer several options at different prices. In many cases, a package that includes airfare, hotel, and transportation to and from the airport will cost you less than just the hotel alone would have, had you booked it yourself. That's because packages are sold in bulk to tour operators—who resell them to the public at a cost that drastically undercuts standard rates.

RECOMMENDED PACKAGE TOUR OPERATORS

One good source of package deals is the airlines themselves. Most major airlines offer air/land packages, including **American Airlines Vacations** (© 800/321-2121; http://aav1.aavacations.com), **Delta Vacations** (© 800/221-6666; www.deltavacations.com), and **US Airways Vacations** (© 800/455-0123 or 800/422-3861; www.usairwaysvacations.com), **Continental Airlines Vacations** (© 800/301-3800; www.coolvacations.com), and **United Vacations** (© 888/854-3899; www.unitedvacations.com/). Another contender is **Italiatour,** a company of the Alitalia Group © 800/845-3365; fax 212/765-2183; www.italiatour.com), offering a wide variety of tours through all parts of Italy. It specializes in packages for independent travelers (not tour groups) who ride from one destination to another by train or rental car. In most cases, the company sells pre-reserved accommodations, which are usually less expensive than if you had reserved them yourself. Because of the company's close link with Alitalia, the prices quoted for air passage are sometimes among the most reasonable on the retail market.

Online Vacation Mall (© 800/839-9851; www.onlinevacationmall.com) allows you to search for and book packages offered by a number of tour operators and airlines. The **United States Tour Operators Association's** website (www.ustoa.com) has a search engine that allows you to look for operators that offer packages to a specific destination. Travel packages are also listed in the travel section of your local Sunday newspaper. **Liberty Travel** (© 888/271-1584; www.libertytravel.com), one of the biggest packagers in the Northeast, often runs full-page ads in Sunday papers. Or check ads in the national travel magazines such as *Arthur Frommer's Budget Travel Magazine, Travel & Leisure, National Geographic Traveler,* and *Condé Nast Traveler.*

ESCORTED TOURS (TRIPS WITH GUIDES)

Escorted Tours are structured group tours, with a group leader. The price usually includes everything from airfare to hotels, meals, tours, admission costs, and local transportation.

RECOMMENDED ESCORTED TOUR OPERATORS

The biggest operator of escorted tours is **Perillo Tours** (© 800/431-1515 or 201/307-1234; fax 201/307-1808 in the United States; www.perillotours.com), family operated for three generations—perhaps you've seen the TV commercials featuring the "King of Italy," Mario Perillo, and his son. Since it was founded in 1945, it has sent more than a million travelers to Italy on guided tours. Perillo's tours cost much less than you'd spend if you arranged a comparable trip yourself. Accommodations are in first-class hotels, and guides tend to be well qualified and well informed.

Trafalgar Tours (© 800/854-0103; www.trafalgartours.com) is one of Europe's largest tour operators, offering affordable guided tours with lodgings in unpretentious hotels. Check with your travel agent for more information on these tours (Trafalgar takes calls only from agents).

One of Trafalgar's leading competitors is **Globus+Cosmos Tours** (© 800/221-0090; www.globusandcosmos.com). Globus has first-class escorted coach tours of various regions lasting from 8 to 16 days. Cosmos, a budget branch of Globus, sells escorted tours of about the same length. Tours must be booked through a travel agent, but you can call the 800-number for brochures. Another competitor is **Insight Vacations** (© 800/582-8380; www.insightvacations.com), which books superior first-class, fully escorted motor-coach tours lasting from 1 week to a 36-day grand tour.

Abercrombie & Kent (© 800/323-7308 in the U.S., or 0845/0700-610 in the U.K.; www.abercrombiekent.com) offers a variety of luxurious premium packages. Your overnight stays will be in meticulously restored castles and exquisite Italian villas, most of which are government-rated four- and five-star accommodations. Several trips are offered, including tours of the Lake Garda region and the southern territory of Calabria. The oldest travel agency in Britain, **Cox & Kings** (© 020/7873-5000; www.coxandkings.co.uk), specializes in unusual, if pricey, holidays. Their Italy offerings include organized tours through the country's gardens and sites of historic or aesthetic interest, opera tours, pilgrimage-style visits to sites of religious interest, and food- and wine-tasting tours. The staff is noted for their focus on tours of ecological and environmental interest.

SPECIAL-INTEREST VACATIONS

If you have a special interest that you would like to experience in Italy, chances are there is a tour of it. Take tennis, for example.

Tennis fans set their calendars by the events that transpire every year within the Italian Open, which is conducted in mid-may at the Foro Italica, near Mussolini's Olympic site. A California-based company, **Advantage Tennis Tours** (© 800/341-8687 or 949/661-7331; fax 949/489-2837; www.advantagetennistours.com), conducts tours to the Open. The tours include 6 nights' accommodations in a deluxe Roman hotel, Center Court seats at three sessions of the tournament, city tours of ancient Rome, a farewell dinner, the organizational and communications skill of a tour hostess, and the opportunity to play tennis.

For travelers who want to experience and explore the homeland of Verdi, Toscanini, and Pavarotti, **Vermont Bicycle Tours** (© 800/BIKE-TOUR) offers 7-day vacations through the relatively flat terrain of the Parma and Po Valley region of Italy. Accommodations are included in the overall package deal.

The best mountain adventure tours are offered by **Mountain Travel-Sobek** (© 888/687-6235, 800/227-2384, or 510/527-8100; fax 510/525-7710; www.mtsobek.com). For both art and architecture and food and wine tours, **Amelia Tours International** (© 800/742-4591 or 516/433-0696; fax 616/822-6220; www.ameliainternational.com), is the leader of the pack. The best hiking tours of Italy are a feature of **Above the Clouds Trekking** (© 800/233-4499 or 802/482-4848; fax 802/482-5011; www.aboveclouds.com).

10 Getting Around Italy

BY PLANE

Italy's domestic air network on **Alitalia** (© **800/223-5730** in the United States or 020/8745-8200 in the U.K.; www.alitalia.it/english/index.html) is one of the largest and most complete in Europe. Some 40 airports are serviced regularly from Rome, and most flights take less than an hour. Fares vary, but some discounts are available. Tickets are discounted 50% for passengers 2 to 11 years old; for passengers 12 to 22, there's a youth fare. And anyone can get a 30% reduction by taking domestic flights departing at night.

BY TRAIN

Trains provide a medium-priced means of transport, even if you don't buy the Eurailpass or one of the special Italian Railway tickets (below). As a rule of thumb, second-class travel usually costs about two-thirds the price of an equivalent first-class trip. The relatively new InterCity trains (designated IC on train schedules) are modern, air-conditioned trains that make limited stops; compared to the far slower direct or regional trains, the supplement can be steep, but a second-class IC ticket will provide a first-class experience.

A couchette (a private fold-down bed in a communal cabin) requires a supplement above the price of first-class travel. Children 4 to 11 receive a discount of 50% off the adult fare, and children 3 and under travel free with their parents. Seniors and travelers under age 26 can also purchase discount cards. Seat reservations are highly recommended during peak season and on weekends or holidays; they must be booked in advance.

An **Italian Railpass** (known in Italy as a **BTLC Pass**) allows non-Italian citizens to ride as much as they like on Italy's entire rail network. Buy the pass in the United States or at main train stations in Italy, have it validated the first time you use it at any rail station, and ride as frequently as you like within the time validity. An 8-day pass is $299 first class and $199 second class, a 15-day pass costs $373 first class and $249 second class, a 21-day pass costs $433 first class and $289 second class, and a 30-day pass costs $522 first class and $348 second class. All passes have a $15 issuing fee per class.

With the Italian Railpass and each of the other special passes, a supplement must be paid to ride on certain rapid trains, designated **ETR-450** or **Pendolino trains.** The rail systems of Sardinia are administered by a separate entity and aren't included in the Railpass or any of the other passes.

Another option is the **Italian Flexirail Card,** which entitles you to a predetermined number of days of travel on any rail line in a certain time period. It's ideal for passengers who plan in advance to spend several days sightseeing before boarding a train for another city. A pass giving 4 possible travel days out of a block of 1 month is $239 first class and $159 second class, a pass for 8 travel days stretched over a 1-month period costs $334 first class and $223 second class, and a pass for 12 travel days within 1 month costs $429 first class and $286 second class.

You can buy these passes from any travel agent or by calling © **800/ 848-7245.** You can also call © **800/ 4EURAIL** or **800/EUROSTAR.**

BY BUS

Italy has an extensive and intricate bus network, covering all regions. However, because rail travel is inexpensive, the bus isn't the preferred method of travel. Besides, drivers seem to go on strike every 2 weeks.

Travel Times Between the Major Cities

Cities	Distance	Air Travel Time	Train Travel Time	Driving Time
Florence to Milan	298km/185 miles	55 min.	2½ hr.	3½ hr.
Florence to Venice	281km/174 miles	2 hr., 5 min.	4 hr.	3 hr., 15 min.
Milan to Venice	267km/166 miles	50 min.	3½ hr.	3 hr., 10 min.
Rome to Florence	277km/172 miles	1 hr., 10 min.	2½ hr.	3 hr., 20 min.
Rome to Milan	572km/355 miles	1 hr., 5 min.	5 hr.	6½ hr.
Rome to Naples	219km/136 miles	50 min.	2½ hr.	2½ hr.
Rome to Venice	528km/327 miles	1 hr., 5 min.	5 hr., 15 min.	6 hr.
Rome to Genoa	501km/311 miles	1 hr.	6 hr.	5 hr., 45 min.
Rome to Torino	669km/415 miles	1 hr., 5 min.	9–11 hr.	7 hr., 45 min.

One of the leading bus operators is **SITA** (℃ **055/47821**). SITA buses serve most parts of the country, especially the central belt, including Tuscany, but not the far frontiers. Among the largest of the other companies, with special emphasis in the north and central tiers, is **Autostradale** (℃ **02/801-161**). **Lazzi** (℃ **055/363-041**), goes through Tuscany, including Siena, and much of central Italy.

Where these nationwide services leave off, **local bus companies** operate in most regions, particularly in the hill sections and the alpine regions where rail travel isn't possible. For more information, see "Getting There" in the various city, town, and village sections.

BY CAR

U.S. and Canadian drivers don't need an **International Driver's License** to drive a rented car in Italy. However, if driving a private car, they need such a license.

You can apply for an International Driver's License at any **American Automobile Association (AAA)** branch. You must be at least 18 and have two 2-by-2-inch photos and a photocopy of your U.S. driver's license with your AAA application form. The actual fee for the license can vary, depending on where it's issued. To find the AAA office nearest you, check the local phone directory or contact **AAA's national headquarters** (℃ **800/222-4357** or 407/444-4300; www.aaa.com). Remember that an International Driver's License is valid only if physically accompanied by your original driver's license and only if signed on the back. In Canada, you can get the address of the **Canadian Automobile Association** closest to you by calling ℃ **613/247-0117** (www.caa.ca).

The **Automobile Club d'Italia (ACI),** Via Marsala 8, 00185 Roma (℃ **06/4998-2389**), is open Monday to Friday 8am to 2pm. The ACI's 24-hour **Information and Assistance Center (CAT)** is at Via Magenta 5, 00185 Roma (℃ **06-491716**). Both offices are near the main rail station (Stazione Termini).

RENTALS   Many of the loveliest parts of Italy lie away from the main cities, far away from the train stations. For that, and for sheer convenience and freedom, renting a car is usually the best way to explore the country. But you have to be a pretty aggressive and alert driver who won't be fazed by super-high speeds on the autostrade or by narrow streets in the cities and towns. Italian drivers have truly earned their reputation as bad but daring.

However, the legalities and contractual obligations of renting a car in

Italy (where accident and theft rates are very high) are a little complicated. To rent a car here, a driver must have nerves of steel, a sense of humor, a valid driver's license, and a valid passport and (in most cases) be over 25. Insurance on all vehicles is compulsory, though any reputable rental firm will arrange it in advance before you're even given the keys.

The three major rental companies in Italy are **Avis** (© **800/331-1212;** www.avis.com), **Budget** (© **800/ 527-0700;** https://rent.drivebudget. com), and **Hertz** (© **800/654-3131;** www.hertz.com). U.S.-based companies specializing in European car rentals are **Auto Europe** (© **800/ 223-5555;** www.autoeurope.com), **Europe by Car** (© **800/223-1516,** 800/252-9401 in California, or 212/ 581-3040 in New York; www.europeby car.com), and **Kemwel Holiday Auto** (© **800/678-0678;** www.kemwel. com).

In some cases, slight discounts are offered to members of the American Automobile Association (AAA) or the American Association of Retired Persons (AARP). Be sure to ask.

Each company offers a **collision-damage waiver (CDW)** at $15 to $25 per day (depending on the car's value). Some companies include CDWs in the prices they quote; others don't. This extra protection will cover all or part of the repair-related costs if you have an accident. (In some cases, even if you buy the CDW, you'll pay $200 to $300 per accident. Ask questions before you sign.) If you don't have CDW and have an accident, you'll usually pay for all damages, up to the car's replacement cost. Because most newcomers aren't familiar with local driving customs and conditions, we highly recommend you buy the CDW. (But first check your existing auto insurance and also see what's available through your credit cards. Note that credit cards might cover collision but will usually not cover liability.) In addition, because of Italy's rising theft rate, all three of the major U.S.-based companies offer theft and break-in protection policies (Avis and Budget require it). For pickups at most Italian airports, all three companies must impose a 10% government tax. To avoid that charge, consider picking up your car at an inner-city location. There's also an unavoidable 19% government tax, although more companies are including this in the rates they quote.

GASOLINE Gasoline (known as *benzina*) is expensive in Italy. Be prepared for sticker shock every time you fill up even a medium-size car with *super benzina,* which has the octane rating appropriate for most of the cars you'll be able to rent. It's priced throughout the country at around 1€ (90¢) per liter (about 3.75€/$3.35 per gallon). Gas stations on the autostrade are open 24 hours, but on regular roads gas stations are rarely open on Sunday; also, many close from noon to 3pm for lunch, and most shut down after 7pm. Make sure the pump registers zero before an attendant starts refilling your tank. A popular scam, particularly in the south, is to fill your tank before resetting the meter, so you pay not only your bill but also the charges run up by the previous motorist.

DRIVING RULES The Italian Highway Code follows the Geneva Convention, and Italy uses international road signs. Driving is on the right; passing is on the left. Violators of the highway code are fined; serious violations might also be punished by imprisonment. In cities and towns, the speed limit is 50 kilometers per hour (kmph), or 31 miles per hour (mph). For all cars and motor vehicles on main roads and local roads, the limit is 90kmph, or 56 mph. For the autostrade (national express highways), the limit is 130kmph, or 81 mph. Use the left lane only for passing. If a driver zooms up behind you on the autostrade with his or her lights on, that's your sign to get out of the way! Use of seat belts is compulsory.

BREAKDOWNS & ASSISTANCE
In case of car breakdown or for any tourist information, foreign motorists can call ✆ **116** (nationwide telephone service). For road information, itineraries, and all sorts of travel assistance, call ✆ **166-664477** (ACI's information center located near the Automobile Club d'Italia). Both services operate 24 hours.

11 Tips on Accommodations

Hotels are classified by stars in Italy, indicating their category of comfort: five stars for deluxe, four stars for first class, three stars for second class, two stars for third class, and one star for fourth class. Government ratings do not depend on the decoration or on frescoed ceilings, but rather on facilities, such as elevators and the like. Many of the finest hostelries in Italy are rated second class because they serve only breakfast (a blessing really, for those seeking to escape the board requirements of some hotels). Italy's government star-rating system is a separate rating device from the stars that we at Frommer's have awarded to the accommodations listed, though we note government ratings from time to time.

Note that all accommodations listed in this guide have private bathrooms unless specified otherwise. However, bathrooms can vary greatly from hotel to hotel, depending on the government class. Luxury hotels in Italy have some of the most deluxe bathrooms in the world, appealing to either Elizabeth Taylor or the Emperor Tiberius. However in one- or two-star choices, you'll often find bathrooms a bit quirky—that is, handheld faucets with no shower curtains, or else showerheads placed in the middle of the bathroom.

Most hotels in Italy do not have parking garages. For those that do, we have indicated any charges.

Reservations are advised, even in the so-called slow months from November to March. Tourist travel to Italy peaks from May to October, when moderate and budget hotels are full.

THE CHAINS   Italy has its share of chain hotels, the most noteworthy and luxurious of which are part of the **Sheraton/Luxury Collection** (✆ **800/ 221-2340** in the U.S) nearly two-dozen luxury properties from Rome to Venice. Information about more democratically priced hotels can be found through **Sheraton** (✆ **800/325-3333** in the U.S.; www.starwood.com).

The most popular chain throughout Italy is **Jolly** (✆ **800/221-2626** in the U.S.). There are 32 government-rated Jolly hotels in Italy. Even cheaper are some **Best Western**–affiliated hotels throughout Italy (✆ **800/528-1234** in the U.S; www.bestwestern. com). There are some 75 government-rated three- and four-star Best Westerns in the country.

For motorists seeking moderately priced hotels along the main highways of Italy, the most prominent chain is AGIP Motels. **Forte** (✆ **800/225-5843**; www.forte-hotels.com) represents some of the top-of-the-line AGIP properties.

Data about other international and American hotel chains in Italy can be found by contacting **Four Seasons** (✆ **800/332-3442;** www.four seasons.com); **Hilton** (✆ **800/445-8667;** www.Hilton.com); **Radisson** (✆ **800/333-3333;** www.Radisson. com); **Ramada** (✆ **800/228-2828;**

www.ramada.com); and **Holiday Inn** (*C* **800/465-4329;** www.basshotels. com).

RELIGIOUS INSTITUTIONS Convents, monasteries, and other religious institutions in Italy offer accommodations, generally of the fourth-class (one star) hotel or former pensione category. Some are just for men; others are for women only. Many, however, accept married couples. And admittedly these accommodations are not for everyone, certainly not "party animals" who've come to Italy seeking *la dolce vita*. They are mainly for those who want a clean, comfortable bed for the night and who plan to spend their days outside the convent, sampling the treasures of Italy. Italian tourist offices generally have abbreviated listings of these places, which are most commonplace in cities of religious pilgrimage such as Rome or Assisi. They range from comfortable convents to basic monastic cells. One of the main reasons for staying in a religious institution is economy, as the rooms are invariably cheaper than those in most hotels. Contact the local tourist offices for a listing.

FARMHOUSES   Another option is to stay in a farmhouse, an apartment, or a bedroom on a working Italian farm (wine-producing estates make up a large part of these) as part of a nationwide program known as *agriturismo*. Most of the farms lie in rural areas within easy reach of town centers or principal cities, such as those in Umbria, Tuscany, and Lazio. You can share the setup with the owner (staying in a guest bedroom in the main house) or have the place to yourself (free-standing converted stalls, mills, or workers' quarters on the grounds, all offering more privacy), the former being the less expensive, of course. Contact local tourist boards for a listing of local *agriturism* offerings for a do-it-yourself reservation. Daily double rates for a room on a farm usually start at 25€ ($22.35), with breakfast.

Tips   What's a Locanda, Albergo or Pensione?

Everyone knows what a hotel is, and, like people, they are good or bad, perhaps somewhere in between. An *albergo* is an old-fashioned Italian word for a hotel. More and more the word "hotel" is being used instead of "albergo," although some establishments still use the word albergo for its old-fashioned quaintness.

A *locanda* once suggested a rustic inn or even a carriage stop housing wayfarers for the night. The word is still used, especially in Venice, to mean an inexpensive inn, often a one-star hotel. But some establishments that are luxurious will use the word locanda, again because of the word's old-fashioned charm. So the word has taken on an increasingly broad definition in the Italy of today.

The word *pensione* is still in use but is dying out. In days of yore an Italian pensione was really a boardinghouse, in which you shared a bathroom and were required to eat three meals a day with the family. That institution is virtually gone with the Italian wind. Most of these boardinghouses are now one- or even two-star hotels, although some of these homes still prefer to call themselves a "pensione," even though no longer performing their original function.

A Home Away from Home: Renting Your Own Apartment or Villa

Increasingly popular is the option of renting an apartment, condo, or villa in Italy. Tuscany, especially the area south of Florence, is the most preferred region, but the Amalfi Coast from Salerno to Sorrento is another viable option, as is Umbria, the green heart of Italy. It's also possible to arrange apartment rentals in Florence, Venice, and Rome. For stays under a week, red tape and paperwork make renting an unrealistic option, but for longer stays, preferably of two or more weeks, renting can be an ideal way to experience Italian life.

One of the best rental agencies to call is **Rent Villas** (© 800/ 726-6702 or 805/641-1650; fax 805/641-1630; www.rentvillas.com). It's the representative for the Cuendet properties, some of the best in Italy, and its agents are very helpful in tracking down the perfect place to suit your needs. Cuendet's representatives in the United Kingdom, and one of the best all-around agents in London, is **International Chapters** (© 020/7722-0722). Marjorie Shaw's Insider's Italy (© 718/ 855-3878; www.insidersitaly.com) is a small, upscale outfit run by a very personable agent who's thoroughly familiar with all her properties and with Italy in general.

For some of the top properties, call the local representative of the **Cottages to Castles** group (© 1622/775-217). In the U.S., that's the **Parker Company, Ltd.** (© 800/280-2811 or 781/596-8282; fax 781/596-3125; www.theparkercompany.com). One of the most reasonably priced agencies is **Villas and Apartments Abroad, Ltd.** (© 800/ 433-3020 or 212/759-1025; www.vaanyc.com). **Vacanze in Italia** (© 800/533-5405 or 413/528-6610; fax 413/528-6222; www. homeabroad.com) handles hundreds of rather upscale rentals. A popular but very pricey agency is **Villas International** (© 800/221-2260 or 415/499-9490; www.villasintl.com).

If you want to stay in a historic palazzo, contact **Abitare la Storia,** Località L'Amorosa, 53048 Sinalunga, Siena (© 0577-632-256; fax 0577/632-160; www.abitarelastoria.it). This nonprofit organization represents owner-managed hotels, residences, restaurants, and convention centers around Italy, in the city and the country.

An average 1-bedroom villa or apartment costs $1,800 weekly, rising to $2,450 weekly for a 2-bedroom unit, each housing 2 to 4 guests. Most rentals include "the works," from toiletries to linens, though you'll need to go to local markets to fill your refrigerator.

The U.S.–based **Italy Farm Holidays (IFH),** 547 Martling Ave., Tarrytown, NY 10591 (© **914/631-7880;** fax 914/631-8831), represents about 50 working farms (a number owned by Americans or foreigners) scattered for the most part in the Piedmont, Tuscany, Umbria, Veneto, and Puglia, any of which would be suitable as a base for touring the region's art cities. Each farm or cooperative has passed inspection, and some of the most desirable ones lie just a few miles from the heart of Florence and Siena. Most properties require a minimum stay of 3 to 7 days and payment in full in advance. Many offer meals (usually breakfast) as part of the arrangement; others provide amenities like free use of bikes or optional horseback riding. Only a few of the places contain more than seven rentable accommodations, most have private bathrooms, and many contain kitchens of their own. Weekly rates for two begin at around $700 in low season in a modest apartment or B&B, and go way up for high-season villas or castles that accommodate up to eight or more occupants.

HOME EXCHANGES   One way to visit Italy is to exchange your home for someone else's. This is an especially attractive option in Umbria and Tuscany. Maintaining the greatest number of links is **Homelink International,** P.O. Box 47747, Tampa, FL 33647 (© **800/638-3841** or 813/975-9825; www.homelink.org). In business for 50 years, Homelink charges a membership of $50 a year ($106 if you want hard copies of three color directories), which grants access to a website that's loaded with photos. A competing organization, offering an equivalent kind of service, is **Intervac U.S,** P.O. Box 590504, San Francisco, CA 94159 (© **800/756-4663;** www.intervaucus.com). Prices with this service can range from $68 for access to their website to $157 for a rental offer and photo in the outfit's directory.

12 Tips on Dining

For a quick bite, go to a **bar.** Although bars in Italy do serve alcohol, they function mainly as cafes. Prices have a split personality: *al banco* is standing at the bar, while *à tavola* means sitting at a table where you'll be waited on and charged two to four times as much. In bars you can find *panini* sandwiches on various rolls and *tramezzini* (giant triangles of white-bread sandwiches with the crusts cut off). These both run 1€ to 3€ (90¢–$2.70) and are traditionally put in a kind of tiny press to flatten and toast them so the crust is crispy and the filling is hot and gooey; microwaves have unfortunately invaded and are everywhere, turning panini into something resembling a soggy hot tissue.

Pizza à taglio or *pizza rustica* indicates a place where you can order pizza by the slice—though Florence is infamous for serving some of Italy's worst pizza this way. Florentines fare somewhat better at *pizzerie,* casual sit-down restaurants that cook large, round pizzas with very thin crusts in wood-burning ovens. A *tavola calda* (literally "hot table") serves ready-made hot foods you can take away or eat at one of the few small tables often available. The food is usually very good. A *rosticceria* is the same type of place, and you'll see chickens roasting on a spit in the window.

A full-fledged restaurant will go by the name *osteria, trattoria,* or *ristorante.* Once upon a time, these terms meant something—*osterie* were basic places where you could get a plate of spaghetti and a glass of wine; *trattorie* were casual places serving full meals of filling peasant fare; and *ristoranti* were fancier places, with waiters in bow ties, printed menus, wine lists, and hefty prices. Nowadays, fancy restaurants often go by the name of *trattoria* to cash in on the associated charm factor; trendy spots use *osteria* to show they're hip; and simple, inexpensive places sometimes tack on *ristorante* to ennoble themselves.

The *pane e coperto* (bread and cover) is a .75€ to 5€ (65¢–$4.45) cover charge that you must pay at most restaurants for the mere privilege of sitting at the table. Most Italians eat a leisurely full meal—appetizer and first and second courses—at lunch and dinner and will expect you to do the same, or at least a first and second course. To request the bill, ask *"Il conto, per favore"* (eel *con*-toh, pore fah-*vohr*-ay). A tip of 15% is usually included in the bill these days, but if you're unsure, ask *"È incluso il servizio?"* (ay een-*cloo*-soh eel sair-*vee*-tsoh?).

You'll find at many restaurants, especially larger ones and in cities, a *menu turistico* (tourist's menu), sometimes called *menu del giorno* (menu of the day). This set-price menu usually covers all meal incidentals—including table wine, cover charge, and 15% service charge—along with a first course (*primo*) and second course (*secondo*), but it almost always offers an abbreviated selection of pretty bland dishes: spaghetti in tomato sauce and slices of pork.

Sometimes a better choice is a *menu à prezzo fisso* (fixed-price menu). It usually doesn't include wine but sometimes covers the service and *coperto,* and often offers a wider selection of better dishes, occasionally house specialties and local foods. Ordering a la carte, however, offers you the best chance for a memorable meal. Even better, forego the menu entirely and put yourself in the capable hands of your waiter.

The *enoteca* wine bar is a growing, popular marriage of a wine bar and an *osteria*, where you can sit and order from a host of local and regional wines by the glass (usually 1.50€–4€/ $1.35–$3.55) while snacking on finger foods (and usually a number of simple first-course possibilities) that reflect the region's fare. Relaxed and full of ambience and good wine, these are great spots for light and inexpensive lunches—perfect to educate your palate and recharge your batteries.

13 Recommended Reading

GENERAL & HISTORY   Luigi Barzini's *The Italians* (Macmillan) should almost be required reading for anyone contemplating a trip to Italy. The section on Sicily alone is worth the price of the book. Critics have hailed it as the liveliest analysis yet of the Italian character.

Edward Gibbon's 1776 *The History of the Decline and Fall of the Roman Empire* is published in six volumes, but Penguin issues a manageable abridgement. It has been hailed as one of the greatest histories ever written. No one has ever recaptured the saga of the glory that was Rome the way that Gibbon did.

One of the best books on the long history of the papacy—detailing its excesses, its triumphs and defeats, and its most vivid characters—is Michael Walsh's *An Illustrated History of the* *Popes: Saint Peter to John Paul II* (St. Martin's Press).

In the 20th century, the most fascinating period in Italian history was the rise and fall of Fascism, as detailed in countless works. One of the best biographies of Il Duce is Denis M. Smith's *Mussolini: A Biography* (Random House).

ART & ARCHITECTURE   The Renaissance period in Italy seems to capture the public's imagination more than any other art era, and one of the best accounts of this era is Peter Murray's *The Architecture of the Italian Renaissance* (Schocken). The same subject is covered by Frederick N. Hartt in his *History of Italian Renaissance Painting* (Agrams).

Giorgio Vasari's *The Lives of the Most Eminent Italian Architects, Painters, and Sculptors* was published in 1550 and, in spite of some fanciful inventions, it remains the definitive work on Renaissance artists—by one who knew many of them personally—from Cimabue to Michelangelo. Penguin Classics issues a paperback abridged version, called *Lives of the Artists.*

FICTION & BIOGRAPHY   Both foreign and domestic writers have tried to capture the peculiar nature of Italy—each seen from a completely different angle—in such notable works as Thomas Mann's *Death in Venice* (Random House) and E. M. Forster's *Room with a View* (Random House), the subject of a famous movie in the 1980s. Fred M. Stewart's books are so popular they're sold in supermarkets, and he spins a lively tale in his *Century* (NAL), tracing the saga of several generations of an Italian family.

Umberto Eco is popular worldwide, and his first blockbuster murder mystery *The Name of the Rose* (Harcourt Brace) can be an entertaining Italy primer—if a bit thick on theological philosophy—on the political and monastic world of medieval Italy.

Benvenuto Cellini's *Autobiography,* also available in Penguin Classics, was first printed in Italy in 1728, although Cellini lived from 1500 to 1571. It's a Renaissance romp, filled with gossip and interesting details, so much so that it has been compared to a novel. It launched the tide of the romantic movement.

The novels of Alberto Moravia (1907–90) are classified as neo-realism. Moravia is one of the best-known Italian writers read in English. Notable works include *Roman Tales* (Farrar, Straus, and Cudahy), *The Woman of Rome* (Penguin) and *The Conformist* (Greenwood Press).

Michelangelo's life was novelized (and later made into a movie) by Irving Stone in the *Agony and the Ecstasy* (Doubleday), which also offers an insight into Florentine politics at the time. The descriptions of the act of carving itself are powerful, even if his attempts to cast some aspects of the sculptor's life as strictly heterosexual are a bit tenuous.

Verdi: A Biography, by Mary Jane Phillips-Matz (Oxford University Press), is a towering work by an author who spent more than 30 years in research. Many new details about Verdi are revealed and some myths exploded—namely that Verdi had a poverty-stricken childhood (his father actually had substantial land holdings).

TRAVEL   H. V. Morton's *A Traveler in Italy* (Methuen) is by one of the world's most widely read travel writers who has a rare sense of history and is at his best in describing great centers of culture such as Florence and Venice.

Many great writers—when faced with the challenge of Italy—decided to become travel writers. These have included Charles Dickens, who wrote *Pictures from Italy* (Ecco Press), a classic 19th-century account of the Grand Tour, going from Tuscany to Naples via Rome. Wolfgang Goethe's *Italian Journey* (Penguin) devotes more attention to Roman antiquities, and Henry James's *Italian Hours* is young James at his best, capturing the special atmosphere of Italy.

D. H. Lawrence and Italy (Viking Press) is three classic Italian travelogues collected in a single volume that includes *Sea and Sardinia* and *Twilight in Italy.* It also includes *Etruscan Places,* which was published posthumously. Lawrence writes of a way of life that was disappearing even as he wrote.

Mary McCarthy gave Italian travel literature two distinguished works, *The Stones of Florence* (Harcourt Brace Jovanovich) and *Venice Observed* (Penguin). "The lady of the barbs" pulls no punches in observing these two famed tourist meccas with a sharp eye for detail. These two works were definitely researched on the streets and not in a library.

Within Tuscany: Reflections on a Time and Place, by Matthew Spender (Viking) is the work of a London-born sculptor who has lived in Tuscany for a quarter of a century. He spins a lively account of the cultural, artistic, and literary soul of the region.

About Florence The city of the Renaissance is one of the most written about in the world—from many points of view. Peter Burke's *Culture and Society in Renaissance Italy 1420-1540* (London: Batsford) received acclaim; it's often available in libraries. Florence is a backdrop for much of R. Coughlan's *The Life and Times of Michelangelo 1475-1564* (Time-Life International).

Florence and the Renaissance: The Quattrocento, by Alan J. Lemaître (Stewart, Tabori & Chang), combines high-quality illustrations and a critical background of the period that gave the world such towering art figures as Fra Angelico and Botticelli. Informed criticism is combined with intriguing details from the lives of the artists. *Florence: The Biography of a City,* by Christopher Hibbert (W. W. Norton), was hailed as a "lavish celebration" of an extraordinary city.

The City of Florence: Historical Vistas and Personal Sightings, by R. W. B. Lewis (Farrar, Straus & Giroux), the author of a Pulitzer Prize-winning biography of Edith Wharton, writes of the city where he lived for some half a century. One reviewer called the guide "treasurable."

About Venice John Ruskin wrote a definitive account of this city in his *The Stones of Venice,* first published in 1853 and in print by Little, Brown. Although Ruskin may have come to Venice to debunk (for example, he found San Giorgio Maggiore "contemptible"), his work has many notable sections, including "The Nature of Gothic."

Peter Lauritzen published *Venice, a Thousand Years of Culture and Civilization* (Atheneum), and John J. Norwich traces a *History of Venice* (Knopf).

About Naples *Naples: A Memoir of Love, Peace and War in Italy,* by Douglas Allanbrook (HoughtonMifflin), is one of the most memorable books published on Naples in recent years. Allanbrook does for Naples what Hemingway's *A Moveable Feast* did for Paris. Vividly evocative, he relates his experiences there in World War II and in the 1950s. It's particularly rich in detailing daily life among the Neapolitans.

 FAST FACTS: Italy

American Express Offices are found in Rome at Piazza di Spagna 38 (✆ 06/67-641), in Florence on Via Dante Alighieri 22 (✆ 055/50-981), in Venice at San Marco 1471 (✆ 041/520-0844), and in Milan at Via Brera 3 (✆ 02/7200-3693). See individual city listings.

ATM Networks See "Money," earlier in this chapter.

Business Hours Regular business hours are generally Monday to Friday 9am (sometimes 9:30am) to 1 and 3:30pm (sometimes 4) to 7 or 7:30pm. In July and August, **offices** might not open in the afternoon until 4:30 or 5pm. **Banks** are open Monday to Friday 8:30am to 1 or 1:30pm and 2 or 2:30 to 4pm, and are closed all day Saturday, Sunday, and national holidays. The *riposo* (mid-afternoon closing) is often observed in Rome, Naples, and most southern cities; however, in Milan and other northern and central cities, the custom has been abolished by some merchants.

Most shops are closed on Sunday, except for certain tourist-oriented stores that are now permitted to remain open on Sunday during the high season. If you're in Italy in summer and the heat is intense, we suggest that you, too, learn the custom of the *riposo*.

Car Rentals See "Getting Around," earlier in this chapter.

Climate See When to Go," earlier in this chapter.

Currency See "Money," earlier in this chapter.

Documents See "Visitor Information" and "Entry Requirements," earlier in this chapter.

Driving Rules See "Getting Around," earlier in this chapter.

Drugstores At every drugstore (*farmacia*) there's a list of those that are open at night and on Sunday.

Electricity The electricity in Italy varies considerably. It's usually an alternating current (AC), varying from 42 to 50 cycles. The voltage can be anywhere from 115 to 220. It's recommended that any visitor carrying electrical appliances obtain a transformer. Check the exact local current at the hotel where you're staying. Plugs have prongs that are round, not flat; therefore, an adapter plug is also needed.

Embassies & Consulates In case of an emergency, embassies have a 24-hour referral service.

The **U.S. Embassy** is in Rome at Via Vittorio Veneto 119A (© **06/46-741;** fax 06-467-422-17). **U.S. consulates** are in Florence, at Lungarno Amerigo Vespucci 38 (© **055/239-8276;** fax 055-284-088), and in Milan, at Via Principe Amedeo 2–10 (© **02/29-03-51-41**). There's also a consulate in Naples on Piazza della Repubblica 1 (© **081/583-8111**). The consulate in Genoa is at Via Dante 2 (© **010/58-44-92**). For consulate hours, see individual city listings later in the book.

The **Canadian Consulate** and passport service is in Rome at Via Zara 30 (© **06/445-981**). The **Canadian Embassy** in Rome is at Via G. B. de Rossi 27 (© **06/445-981;** fax 06/445-98754). The Canadian Consulate in Milan is at V.V. Pisani 19 (© 02/67581).

The **U.K. Embassy** is in Rome at Via XX Settembre 80A (© **06/482-5441;** fax 06/4890-3073). The **U.K. Consulate** in Florence is at Lungarno Corsini 2 (© **055/284-133;** fax 055/219-112). The **Consulate General** in Naples is at Via Dei Mille 40 (© **081/4238-911;** fax 081/422-434). In Milan, contact the office at Via San Paolo 7 (© **02/723-001**).

The **Australian Embassy** is in Rome at Via Alessandria 215 (© **06/852-721;** fax 06/852-723-00). The **Australian Consulate** is in Rome at Corso Trieste 25 (© **06/852-721**). The Australian Consulate in Milan is at Via Borgogna 2 (© 02/77-70-41).

The **New Zealand Embassy** is in Rome at Via Zara 28 (© **06/441-7171;** fax 06/440-2984). The **Irish Embassy** in Rome is at Piazza di Campitelli 3 (© **06/697-912;** fax 06/679-2354). For consular queries, dial © **06/697-91211.**

Emergencies Dial © **113** for ambulance, police, or fire. In case of a breakdown on an Italian road, dial © **116** at the nearest telephone box; the nearest Automobile Club of Italy (ACI) will be notified to come to your aid.

Holidays See "When to Go," earlier in this chapter.

Information See "Visitor Information," earlier in this chapter.

Language Italian, of course, is the language of the land, but English is generally understood at most attractions such as museums and at most hotels and restaurants that cater to visitors. Even if not all the staff at a restaurant, for example, speaks English, almost one person does and can be summoned. As you travel in remote towns and villages, especially in the south, a Berlitz Italian phrase book is a handy accompaniment.

Legal Aid The consulate of your country is the place to turn for legal aid, although offices can't interfere in the Italian legal process. They can, however, inform you of your rights and provide a list of attorneys. You'll have to pay for the attorney out of your pocket—there's no free legal assistance. If you're arrested for a drug offense, about all the consulate will do is notify a lawyer about your case and perhaps inform your family.

Liquor Laws Wine with meals has been a normal part of family life for hundreds of years in Italy. Children are exposed to wine at an early age, and consumption of alcohol isn't anything out of the ordinary. There's no legal drinking age for buying or ordering alcohol. Alcohol is sold day and night throughout the year because there's almost no restriction on the sale of wine or liquor in Italy.

Mail Mail delivery in Italy is notoriously bad. Your family and friends back home might receive your postcards in 1 week, or it might take 2 weeks (sometimes longer). Postcards, aerogrammes, and letters weighing up to 20 grams sent to the United States and Canada cost .75€ (65¢); to the United Kingdom and Ireland, .60€ (55¢); and to Australia and New Zealand, .75€ (65¢). You can buy stamps at all post offices and at *tabacchi* (tobacco) stores.

Newspapers/Magazines In major cities, it's possible to find the *International Herald Tribune* or *USA Today,* as well as other English-language newspapers and magazines, including *Time* and *Newsweek,* at hotels and news kiosks. The *Rome Daily American* is published in English.

Police Dial ⓒ **113,** the all-purpose number for police emergency assistance in Italy.

Safety See "Insurance, Health & Safety" earlier in this chapter.

Taxes As a member of the European Union, Italy imposes a **value-added tax** (called **IVA** in Italy) on most goods and services. The tax that most affects visitors is the one imposed on hotel rates, which ranges from 9% in first- and second-class hotels to 19% in deluxe hotels.

Non-EU (European Union) citizens are entitled to a **refund of the IVA** if they spend more than 150€ ($133.95) at any one store, before tax. To claim your refund, request an invoice from the cashier at the store and take it to the Customs office (*dogana*) at the airport to have it stamped before you leave. *Note:* If you're going to another EU country before flying home, have it stamped at the airport Customs office of the last EU country you'll be in (for example, if you're flying home via Britain, have your Italian invoices stamped in London). Once back home, mail the stamped invoice (keep a photocopy for your records) back to the original vendor within 90 days of the purchase. The vendor will, sooner or later, send you a refund of the tax that you paid at the time of your original purchase. Reputable stores view this as a matter of ordinary paperwork and are businesslike about it. Less-honorable stores might lose your dossier. It pays to deal with established vendors on large purchases. You can also request that the refund be credited to the credit card with which you made the purchase; this is usually a faster procedure.

Many shops are now part of the **"Tax Free for Tourists"** network (look for the sticker in the window). Stores participating in this network issue a check along with your invoice at the time of purchase. After you have the invoice stamped at Customs, you can redeem the check for cash directly at the Tax Free booth in the airport (in Rome, it's past Customs; in Milan's airports, the booth is inside the Duty Free shop) or mail it back in the envelope provided within 60 days.

Telephone To call Italy from the United States, dial the **international prefix, 011;** then Italy's **country code, 39;** and then the city code (for example, **06** for Rome and **055** for Florence), which is now built into every number. Then dial the actual **phone number.**

A **local phone call** in Italy costs around .10€ (10¢). **Public phones** accept precharged phone cards (*scheda* or *carta telefonica.* You can buy a *carta telefonica* at any *tabacchi* (tobacconists; most display a sign with a white *T* on a brown background) in increments of 2.50€ ($2.25), 5€ ($4.45), and 7.50€ ($6.70). To make a call, pick up the receiver and insert your card (break off the corner first). Most phones have a digital display that'll tell you how much money is left on the card. Dial the number, and don't forget to take the card with you after you hang up.

To **call from one city code to another,** dial the city code, complete with initial 0, and then dial the number. (Note that numbers in Italy range from four to eight digits in length. Even when you're calling within the same city, you must dial that city's area code—including the zero. A Roman calling another Rome number must dial 06 before the local number.)

To **dial direct internationally,** dial **00** and then the country code, the area code, and the number. **Country codes** are as follows: the United States and Canada, 1; the United Kingdom, 44; Ireland, 353; Australia, 61; New Zealand, 64. Make international calls from a public phone, if possible, because hotels almost invariably charge ridiculously inflated rates for direct dial—but bring plenty of *schede* to feed the phone. Calls dialed directly are billed on the basis of the call's duration only. A reduced rate is applied 11pm to 8am on Monday to Saturday and all day Sunday. Direct-dial calls from the United States to Italy are much cheaper, so arrange for whomever to call you at your hotel.

Italy has recently introduced a series of **international phone cards** (*scheda telefonica internazionale*) for calling overseas. They come in increments of 50, 100, 200 and 400 *unita* (units), and they're usually available at tabacchi and bars. Each *unita* is worth .15€ (10¢) of phone time; it costs 5 unita (.65€/55¢) per minute to call within Europe or to the United States or Canada, and 12 unita (1.55€/$1.50) per minute to call Australia or New Zealand. You don't insert this card into the phone; merely dial ℭ **1740** and then *2 (star 2) for instructions in English, when prompted.

To call the free **national telephone information** (in Italian) in Italy, dial ℭ **12. International information** is available at ℭ **176** but costs .60€ (55¢) a shot.

To make **collect or calling card calls,** drop in .10€ (10¢) or insert your card and dial one of the numbers here; an American operator will shortly come on to assist you (because Italy has yet to discover the joys of the touch-tone phone, you'll have to wait for the operator to come on). The following calling-card numbers work all over Italy: **AT&T** ☎ **172-1011, MCI** ☎ **172-1022,** and **Sprint** ☎ **172-1877.** To make collect calls to a country besides the United States, dial ☎ **170** (free), and practice your Italian counting in order to relay the number to the Italian operator. Tell him or her that you want it *a carico del destinatario.*

Don't count on all Italian phones having touch-tone service! You might not be able to access your voice mail or answering machine if you call home from Italy.

Time   In terms of standard time zones, Italy is 6 hours ahead of Eastern Standard Time in the United States. Daylight saving time goes into effect in Italy each year from the end of March to the end of September.

Tipping   This custom is practiced with flair in Italy—many people depend on tips for their livelihoods. In **hotels,** the service charge of 15% to 19% is already added to a bill. In addition, it's customary to tip the chamber-maid .50€ (45¢) per day, the doorman (for calling a cab) .50€ (45¢), and the bellhop or porter 1.50€ to 2.50€ ($1.35–$2.25) for carrying your bags to your room. A concierge expects about 15% of his or her bill, as well as tips for extra services performed, which could include help with long-distance calls. In expensive hotels, these amounts are often doubled.

In **restaurants and cafes,** 15% is usually added to your bill to cover most charges. If you're not sure whether this has been done, ask, *"È incluso il servizio?"* (ay een-*cloo*-soh eel sair-*vee*-tsoh?). An additional tip isn't expected, but it's nice to leave the equivalent of an extra couple of dollars if you've been pleased with the service. Checkroom attendants expect .75€ (65¢), and washroom attendants should get .35€ (30¢). Restaurants are required by law to give customers official receipts.

Taxi drivers expect at least 15% of the fare.

Toilets   All airport and rail stations, of course, have rest rooms, often with attendants, who expect to be tipped. Bars, night clubs, restaurants, cafes, gas stations, and all hotels have facilities as well. Public toilets are also found near many of the major sights. Usually they're designated as *WC* (water closet) or *donne* (women) or *uomini* (men). The most confusing designation is *signori* (gentlemen) and *signore* (ladies), so watch that final *i* and *e!* Many public toilets charge a small fee or employ an atten-dant who expects a tip, usually about .50€ (45¢). It's also a good idea to carry some tissues in your pocket or purse—they often come in handy.

Useful Phone Numbers   The number for the **U.S. Dept. of State Travel Advi-sory** is ☎ **202/647-5225** (manned 24 hr.). Call the **U.S. Passport Agency** at ☎ **202/647-0518.** Call the **Centers for Disease Control International Trav-eler's Hotline** at ☎ **404/332-4559.** Also see "Embassies & Consulates," above.

Water   Most Italians take mineral water with their meals; however, tap water is safe everywhere, as are public drinking fountains. Unsafe sources will be marked ACQUA NON POTABILE. If tap water comes out cloudy, it's only the calcium or other minerals inherent in a water supply that often comes untreated from fresh springs.

Settling into Rome

Rome is a city of images and sounds, all vivid and all unforgettable. You can see one of the most striking images at dawn—ideally from Janiculum Hill (Gianicolo)—when the Roman skyline, with its bell towers and cupolas, gradually comes into focus. As the sun rises, the full Roman symphony begins. First come the peals of church bells calling the faithful to Mass. Then the streets fill with cars, taxis, tour buses, and Vespas, with the drivers gunning their engines and blaring their horns. Next the sidewalks become overrun with office workers, chattering as they rush off to their desks, but not before ducking into a cafe for their first cappuccino. Added to the mix are shop owners loudly throwing up the metal grilles protecting their stores and the fruit-and-vegetable stands from being overrun with Romans out to buy the day's supply of fresh produce, haggling over prices and caviling over quality.

Around 10am, the visitors—you included, with your Frommer's guidebook in hand—take to the streets, battling the crowds and traffic as they wend from Renaissance palaces and baroque buildings to ancient ruins such as the Colosseum and the Forum. After you've spent a long day in the sun, marveling at the sights you've seen millions of times in photos and movies, you can pause to experience the charm of Rome at dusk. Find a cafe at summer twilight, and watch the shades of pink and rose turn to gold and copper as night falls. That's when a new Rome awakens. The cafes and restaurants grow more animated, especially if you've found one in an ancient piazza or along a narrow alley deep in Trastevere. After dinner, you can stroll by the lighted fountains and monuments (the Trevi Fountain and the Colosseum look magical at night) or through Piazza Navona and have a gelato—and the night is yours.

1 Essentials

ARRIVING

BY PLANE   Chances are, you'll arrive at Rome's **Leonardo da Vinci International Airport** (© **06-65951** or 06-65953640), popularly known as **Fiumicino,** 30km (19 miles) from the city center. (If you're flying by charter, you might land at Ciampino Airport, discussed shortly.)

After you leave Passport Control, you'll see two **information desks** (one for Rome, one for Italy; © 06-65956074). At the Rome desk, you can pick up a general map and some pamphlets Monday to Saturday 8:30am to 7pm; the staff can also help you find a hotel room if you haven't reserved ahead. A *cambio* (money exchange) operates daily 7:30am to 11pm, offering surprisingly good rates. **Luggage storage** is available 24 hours daily in the main arrivals building, costing 2.50€ ($2.25) per bag.

There's a **train station** in the airport. To get into the city, follow the signs marked TRENI for the 30-minute shuttle to Rome's main station, **Stazione**

Termini (arriving on Track 22). The shuttle runs 7:20am to 10pm for 8.50€ ($7.60) one way. On the way, you'll pass a machine dispensing tickets, or you can buy them in person near the tracks if you don't have small bills on you. When you arrive at Termini, get out of the train quickly and grab a baggage cart. (It's a long schlep from the track to the exit or to the other train connections, and baggage carts can be scarce.)

A **taxi** from Da Vinci airport to the city costs 45€ ($40.15) and up for the 1-hour trip, depending on traffic. The expense might be worth it if you have a lot of luggage or just don't want to be bothered with the train trip. Call ☎ **06-6645,** 06-3570, or 06-4994 for information.

If you arrive on a charter flight at **Ciampino Airport** (☎ **06-794941**), you can take a COTRAL bus, which departs every 30 minutes or so for the Anagnina stop of Metropolitana (subway) Line A. Take Line A to Stazione Termini, where you can make your final connections. Trip time is about 45 minutes and costs .75€ (65¢). A **taxi** from this airport to Rome costs the same as the one from the Da Vinci airport (above), but the trip is shorter (about 40 min.).

BY TRAIN OR BUS   Trains and buses (including trains from the airport) arrive in the center of old Rome at the silver **Stazione Termini,** Piazza dei Cinquecento (☎ **1848-88088**); this is the train, bus, and subway transportation hub for all Rome and is surrounded by many hotels (especially cheaper ones).

If you're taking the **Metropolitana** (subway), follow the illuminated red-and-white M signs. To catch a bus, go straight through the outer hall and enter the sprawling bus lot of **Piazza dei Cinquecento.** You'll also find **taxis** there.

The station is filled with services. At a branch of the **Banca San Paolo di Torino** (between Tracks 8 to 11 and Tracks 12 to 15), you can exchange money. **Informazioni Ferroviarie** (in the outer hall) dispenses information on rail travel to other parts of Italy. There's also a **tourist information booth** here, along with baggage services, newsstands, and snack bars.

BY CAR   From the north, the main access route is the **Autostrade del Sole (A1),** which cuts through Milan and Florence, or you can take the coastal route, **SSI Aurelia,** from Genoa. If you're driving north from Naples, you take the southern lap of the **Autostrade del Sole (A2).** All the autostrade join with the **Grande Raccordo Anulare,** a ring road encircling Rome, channeling traffic into the congested city. Long before you reach this road, you should study a map carefully to see what part of Rome you plan to enter, and mark your route accordingly. Route markings along the ring road tend to be confusing.

Warning: Return your rental car immediately, or at least get yourself to a hotel, park your car, and leave it there until you leave Rome. Don't even try to drive in Rome—the traffic is just too nightmarish.

VISITOR INFORMATION

Information is available at three locations maintained by the Azienda Provinciale di Turismo (APT): a kiosk at **Leonardo da Vinci International Airport** (☎ **06-65956074**), a kiosk in **Stazione Termini** (☎ **06-36004399**), and a kiosk and administrative headquarters at **Via Parigi 5** (☎ **06-48899253**). The headquarters are open Monday to Friday 8:15am to 7:15pm (Sat to 2pm). The office at the airport and the one at the Stazione Termini are open daily 8:15am to 7:15pm, but we've never found these locations to be great resources.

More helpful, and stocking maps and brochures, are the offices maintained by the **Comune di Roma** at various sites around the city. They're staffed daily 9am to 6pm, except the one at Termini (daily 8am to 9pm). Here are the addresses

Tips   A Few Train Station Warnings

In Stazione Termini, you'll almost certainly be approached by touts claiming to work for a tourist organization. They really work for individual hotels (not always the most recommendable) and will say almost anything to sell you a room. Unless you know something about Rome's layout and are savvy, it's best to ignore them.

Be aware of all your belongings at all times, and keep your wallet and purse away from professionally experienced fingers. Never ever leave your bags unattended for even a second, and while making phone calls or waiting in line, make sure that your attention doesn't wander from any bags you've set by your side or on the ground. Be aware if someone asks you for directions or information—it's likely meant to distract you and easily will.

Ignore the taxi drivers soliciting passengers right outside the terminal; they can charge as much as triple the normal amount. Instead, line up in the official taxi stand in Piazza dei Cinquecento.

and phone numbers: in Stazione Termini (© **06-48906300**); in Piazza dei Cinquecento, outside Termini (© **06-47825194**); in Piazza Pia, near the Castel Sant'Angelo (© **06-68809707**); in Piazza San Giovanni, in Laterano (© **06-77203598**); along Largo Carlo Goldoni, near the intersection of Via del Corso and Via Condotti (© **06-68136061**); on Via Nazionale, near the Palazzo delle Esposizioni (© **06-47824525**); on Largo Corrado Ricci, near the Colosseum (© **06-69924307**); on Piazza Sonnino in Trastevere (© **06-58333457**); on Piazza Cinque Lune, near Piazza Navona (© **06-68809240**); and on Piazza Santa Maria Maggiore (© **06-47880294**).

Enjoy Rome, Via Marghera 88 (© **06-4451843;** www.enjoyrome.com), was begun by an English-speaking couple, Fulvia and Pierluigi. They dispense information about almost everything in Rome and are far more pleasant and organized than the Board of Tourism. They'll also help you find a hotel room, with no service charge (in anything from a hostel to a three-star hotel). Summer hours are Monday to Friday 8:30am to 7pm, and Saturday 8:30am to 2pm; winter hours are Monday to Friday 8:30am to 1:30pm and 3:30 to 6pm.

CITY LAYOUT

Arm yourself with a detailed street map, not the general overview handed out free at tourist offices. Most hotels hand out a pretty good version at their front desks.

The bulk of ancient, Renaissance, and baroque Rome (as well as the train station) lies on the east side of the **Tiber River (Fiume Tevere),** which meanders through town. However, several important landmarks are on the other side: **St. Peter's Basilica** and the **Vatican,** the **Castel Sant'Angelo,** and the colorful **Trastevere** neighborhood.

The city's various quarters are linked by large boulevards (large, at least, in some places) that have mostly been laid out since the late 19th century. Starting from the **Vittorio Emanuele Monument,** a controversial pile of snow-white Brescian marble that's often compared to a wedding cake, there's a street running practically due north to **Piazza del Popolo** and the city wall. This is **Via del Corso,** one of the main streets of Rome—noisy, congested, always crowded with buses and shoppers, and called simply "Il Corso." To its left (west) lie the Pantheon, Piazza Navona, Campo de' Fiori, and the Tiber. To its right (east) you'll find the Spanish Steps, the Trevi Fountain, the Borghese Gardens, and Via Veneto.

Back at the Vittorio Emanuele Monument, the major artery going west (and ultimately across the Tiber to St. Peter's) is **Corso Vittorio Emanuele.** Behind you to your right, heading toward the Colosseum, is **Via del Fori Imperiali,** laid out in the 1930s by Mussolini to show off the ruins of the imperial forums he had excavated, which line it on either side. Yet another central conduit is **Via Nazionale,** running from **Piazza Venezia** (just in front of the Vittorio Emanuele Monument) east to **Piazza della Repubblica** (near Stazione Termini). The final lap of Via Nazionale is called **Via Quattro Novembre.**

THE NEIGHBORHOODS IN BRIEF

This section will give you some idea of where you might want to stay and where the major attractions are located. It might be hard to find a specific address, though, because of the narrow streets of old Rome and the little, sometimes hidden, *piazze* (squares). Numbers usually run consecutively, with odd numbers on one side of the street and evens on the other. However, in the old districts the numbers sometimes run up one side to the end and then run back in the opposite direction on the other side. Therefore, no. 50 could be opposite no. 308.

Near Stazione Termini The main train station, **Stazione Termini,** adjoins **Piazza della Repubblica,** and most likely this will be your introduction to Rome. Much of the area is seedy and filled with gas fumes from all the buses and cars, but it has been improving. If you stay here, you might not get a lot of atmosphere, but you'll have a lot of affordable options and a very convenient location, near the transportation hub of the city and not too far from ancient Rome. There's a lot to see here, including the **Basilica di Santa Maria Maggiore** and the **Baths of Diocletian.** Some high-class hotels are sprinkled in the area, including the **Grand,** but many are long past their heyday.

The neighborhoods on either side of Termini have been improving greatly, and some streets are now attractive. The best-looking area is ahead and to your right as you exit the station on the Via Marsala side. Most budget hotels here occupy a floor or more of a palazzo; many of their entryways are drab, although upstairs they're often charming or at least clean and livable. In the area to the left of the station as you exit, the streets are wider, the traffic is heavier, and the noise level is higher. This area off Via Giolitti is being redeveloped, and now most streets are in good condition. A few still need improvement; take caution at night.

Via Veneto & Piazza Barberini In the 1950s and early 1960s, **Via Veneto** was the swinging place to be, as the likes of King Farouk, Frank Sinatra, and Swedish actress Anita Ekberg paraded up and down the boulevard to the delight of the paparazzi. The street is still here and is still the site of luxury hotels and elegant cafes and restaurants, though it's no longer the happening place to be. It's lined with restaurants catering to those visitors who've heard of this famous boulevard from decades past, but the restaurants are mostly overpriced and overcrowded tourist traps. Rome city authorities would like to restore this legendary street to some of its former glory by banning vehicular traffic on the top half. It makes for a pleasant stroll, in any case.

To the south, Via Veneto comes to an end at **Piazza Barberini,** dominated by the 1642 **Triton Fountain (Fontana del Tritone),** a baroque celebration with four dolphins holding up an open scallop shell in which a triton sits blowing into a conch. Overlooking the square is the **Palazzo Barberini.** In 1623, when Cardinal Maffeo Barberini became Pope Urban VIII, he ordered Carlo Maderno to build a palace here; it was later completed by Bernini and Borromini.

Ancient Rome Most visitors explore this area first, taking in the **Colosseum, Palatine Hill, Roman Forum, Imperial Forums,** and **Circus Maximus.** The area forms part of the *centro storico* (historic district)—along with **Campo de' Fiori** and **Piazza Navona** and the **Pantheon,** which are described below (we've considered them separately for the purposes of helping you locate hotels and restaurants). Because of its ancient streets, airy piazzas, classical atmosphere, and heartland location, this is a good place to stay. If you base yourself here, you can walk to the monuments and avoid the hassle of Rome's inadequate public transportation.

This area offers only a few hotels—most of them inexpensive to moderate in price—and not a lot of great restaurants. Many restaurant owners have their eyes on the cash register and the tour-bus crowd, whose passengers are often hustled in and out of these restaurants so fast that they don't know whether the food is any good.

Campo De' Fiori & The Jewish Ghetto South of Corso Vittorio Emanuele and centered on **Piazza Farnese** and the market square of **Campo de' Fiori,** many buildings in this area were constructed in

Renaissance times as private homes. Stroll along **Via Giulia**—Rome's most fashionable street in the 16th century—with its antiques stores, interesting hotels, and modern art galleries.

West of Via Arenula lies one of the city's most intriguing districts, the old **Jewish Ghetto,** where the dining options far outnumber the hotel options. In 1556, Pope Paul IV ordered the Jews, about 8,000 at the time, to move into this area. The walls weren't torn down until 1849. Although ancient and medieval Rome has a lot more atmosphere, this working-class neighborhood is close to many attractions. You're more likely to want to dine here than to stay here.

Piazza Navona & The Pantheon One of the most desirable areas of Rome, this district is a maze of narrow streets and alleys dating from the Middle Ages and is filled with churches and palaces built during the Renaissance and baroque eras, often with rare marble and other materials stripped from ancient Rome. The only way to explore it is on foot. Its heart is **Piazza Navona,** built over Emperor Domitian's stadium and bustling with sidewalk cafes, palazzi, street artists, musicians, and pickpockets. There are several hotels in the area and plenty of trattorie.

Rivaling Piazza Navona—in general activity, the cafe scene, and nightlife—is the area around the **Pantheon,** which remains from ancient Roman times and is surrounded by a district built much later (this "pagan" temple was turned into a church and rescued, but the buildings that once surrounded it are long gone).

Piazza Del Popolo & The Spanish Steps Piazza del Popolo was laid out by Giuseppe Valadier and is one of Rome's largest squares. It's characterized by an obelisk brought from Heliopolis in lower Egypt during the reign of Augustus. At the end of the square is the **Porta del Popolo,** the gateway in the 3rd-century Aurelian wall. In the mid–16th century, this was one of the major gateways into the old city. If you enter the piazza along Via del Corso from the south, you'll see twin churches, **Santa Maria del Miracoli** and **Santa Maria di Montesanto,** flanking the street. But the square's major church is **Santa Maria del Popolo** (1442–47), one of the best examples of a Renaissance church in Rome.

Since the 17th century, the **Spanish Steps** (the former site of the Spanish ambassador's residence) have been a meeting place for visitors. Some of Rome's most upscale shopping streets fan out from it, including **Via Condotti.** The elegant **Hassler,** one of Rome's grandest hotels, lies at the top of the steps. This is the most upscale part of Rome, full of $500-a-night hotels, designer boutiques, and upscale restaurants.

Around Vatican City Across the Tiber, **Vatican City** is a small city-state, but its influence extends around the world. The **Vatican Museums, St. Peter's,** and the **Vatican Gardens** take up most of the land area, and the popes have lived here for 6 centuries. The neighborhood around the Vatican—called the "Borgo"—contains some good hotels (and several bad ones), but it's removed from the more happening scene of ancient and Renaissance Rome, and getting to and from it can be time-consuming. And the area is rather dull at night and contains few, if any, of Rome's finest restaurants. For the average visitor, Vatican City and its surrounding area are best for exploring during the day. Nonetheless, the area is very popular for those whose sightseeing or even business interests center around the Vatican.

Trastevere In Roman dialect, Trastevere means "Across the Tiber." For visitors arriving in Rome decades ago, it might as well have meant Siberia. All that has changed now, because this once medieval working-class district has been gentrified and overrun with visitors from all over the world. It started to change in the 1970s when expats and others discovered its rough charm. Since then Trastevere has been filling up with tour buses, dance clubs, offbeat shops, sidewalk vendors, pubs, and little trattorie with menus printed in English. There are even places to stay here, but as of yet it hasn't burgeoned into a major hotel district. There are some excellent restaurants here as well.

The original people of the district—and there are still some of them left—are of mixed ancestry, mainly Jewish, Roman, and Greek. For decades they were known for speaking their own dialect in a language rougher than that spoken in central Rome. Even their cuisine was spicier.

The area still centers on the ancient churches of **Santa Cecelia** and **Santa Maria** in Trastevere. Trastevere remains one of Rome's most colorful quarters, even if it is a bit overrun. Known as a "city within a city," it is at least a village within a city.

Testaccio & The Aventine In A.D. 55, Nero ordered that Rome's thousands of broken amphoras and terra-cotta roof tiles be stacked in a carefully designated pile to the east of the Tiber, just west of Pyramide and today's Ostia Railway Station. Over the centuries, the mound grew to a height of around 61m (200 ft.) and then was compacted to form the centerpiece for one of the city's most unusual working-class neighborhoods, **Testaccio.** Eventually, houses were built on the terra-cotta mound and caves were dug into its mass to store wine and foodstuffs. Once home to the slaughterhouses of Rome and its former port on the Tiber, Testaccio means "ugly head" in Roman dialect. Bordered by the Protestant cemetery, Testaccio is known for its authentic Roman restaurants. Chefs here still cook as they always did, satisfying local—not tourist—palates. Change is on the way, however, and this is a neighborhood on the rise. Nightclubs have sprung up in the old warehouses, although they come and go rather quickly.

Another offbeat section of Rome is **Avantine Hill,** south of the Palatine and close to the Tiber. According to records, in 186 B.C. thousands of residents of the area were executed for joining in "midnight rituals of Dionysos and Bacchus." These bloody orgies are a thing of the past today, and the Aventine area is now a leafy and rather posh residential quarter.

The Appian Way Via Appia Antica is a 2,300-year-old road that has witnessed much of the history of the ancient world. By 190 B.C., it extended from Rome to Brindisi on the southeast coast. Its most famous sights today are the **catacombs,** the graveyards of patrician families (despite what it says in *Quo Vadis?,* they weren't used as a place for Christians to hide out while fleeing persecution). This is one of the most historically rich areas of Rome to explore, but it's not a viable place to stay. It does contain some restaurants, however, where you can order lunch on your visit to the catacombs.

Prati The little-known **Prati** district is a middle-class suburb north of the Vatican. It has been discovered by budget travelers because of its affordable hotels, although it's not conveniently located for much of the sightseeing you'll want to do. The **Trionfale flower-and-food market** itself is worth the trip. The area also abounds in shopping streets less expensive than those found in central Rome, and street crime isn't much of a problem.

Parioli Rome's most elegant residential section, Parioli, is framed by the green spaces of the **Villa Borghese** to the south and the **Villa Glori** and **Villa Ada** to the north. It's a setting for some of the city's finest restaurants, hotels, and nightclubs. It's not exactly central, however, and it can be a hassle if you're dependent on public transportation. Parioli lies adjacent to Prati but across the Tiber to the east; like Prati, this is one of the safer districts. We'd call Parioli an area for connoisseurs, attracting those who shun the overrun Spanish Steps and the overly commercialized Via Veneto, and those who'd never admit to having been in the Termini area.

Monte Mario On the northwestern precincts of Rome, **Monte Mario** is the site of the deluxe **Cavalieri Hilton,** an excellent stop to take in a drink and the panorama of Rome. If you plan to spend a lot of time shopping and sightseeing in the heart of Rome, it's a difficult and often expensive commute. The area lies north of Prati, away from the hustle and bustle of central Rome. Bus no. 913 runs from Piazza Augusto Imperator near Piazza del Popolo to Monte Mario.

2 Getting Around

Rome is excellent for walking, with sites of interest often clustered together. Much of the inner core is traffic-free, so you'll need to walk whether you like it or not. However, in many parts of the city it's hazardous and uncomfortable because of the crowds, heavy traffic, and narrow sidewalks. Sometimes sidewalks don't exist at all, and it becomes a sort of free-for-all with pedestrians competing for space against vehicular traffic (the traffic always seems to win). Always be on your guard. The hectic crush of urban Rome is considerably less during August, when many Romans leave town for vacation.

BY SUBWAY

The **Metropolitana,** or **Metro,** for short, is the fastest means of transportation, operating daily 5:30am to 11:30pm. A big red M indicates the entrance to the subway.

Tickets are .75€ (65¢) and are available from *tabacchi* (tobacco shops), many newsstands, and vending machines at all stations. These machines currently accept 50L, 100L, and 200L coins, and some will take 1,000L notes. By the time you arrive, euros should also be accepted. Some stations have managers, but they won't make change. Booklets of tickets are available at tabacchi and in some terminals. You can also buy a **tourist pass** on either a daily or a weekly basis (see "By Bus & Tram," below).

Building a subway system for Rome hasn't been easy because every time workers start digging, they discover an old temple or other archaeological treasure, and heavy earth moving has to cease for a while.

BY BUS & TRAM

Roman buses and trams are operated by an organization known as **ATAC (Azienda Tranvie e Autobus del Comune di Roma),** Via Volturno 65 (© 06-46951 for information).

For .75€ (65¢) you can ride to most parts of Rome, although it can be slow going in all that traffic and the buses are often very crowded. Your ticket is valid for 75 minutes, and you can get on many buses and trams during that time by using the same ticket. Ask where to buy bus tickets, or buy them in tabacchi or bus terminals. You must have your ticket before boarding because there are no ticket-issuing machines on the vehicles.

At Stazione Termini, you can buy a special **tourist pass,** which costs 3€ ($2.70) for a day or 12€ ($10.70) for a week. This pass allows you to ride on the ATAC network without bothering to buy individual tickets. The tourist pass is also valid on the subway—but never ride the trains when the Romans are going to or from work, or you'll be smashed flatter than fettuccine. On the first bus you board, you place your ticket in a small machine, which prints the day and hour you boarded, and then you withdraw it. You do the same on the last bus you take during the valid period of the ticket.

Buses and trams stop at areas marked FERMATA. At most of these, a yellow sign will display the numbers of the buses that stop there and a list of all the stops along each bus's route in order, so you can easily search out your destination. In general, they're in service daily 6am to midnight. After that and until dawn, you can ride on special night buses (they have an "N" in front of their bus number), which run only on main routes. It's best to take a taxi in the wee hours—if you can find one.

Rome Metropolitana

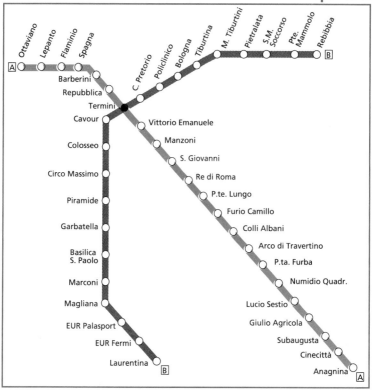

At the **bus information booth** at Piazza dei Cinquecento, in front of the Stazione Termini, you can purchase a directory complete with maps summarizing the routes.

Although routes change often, a few old reliable routes have remained valid for years, such as **no. 27** from Stazione Termini to the Colosseum, **nos. 75 and 170** from Stazione Termini to Trastevere, and **no. 492** from Stazione Termini to the Vatican. But if you're going somewhere and are dependent on the bus, be sure to carefully check where the bus stop is and exactly which bus goes there—don't assume that it'll be the same bus the next day.

BY TAXI

If you're accustomed to hopping a cab in New York or London, then do so in Rome. If not, take less-expensive means of transport or walk. Avoid paying your fare with large bills—invariably, taxi drivers claim that they don't have change, hoping for a bigger tip (stick to your guns and give only about 10%). Don't count on hailing a taxi on the street or even getting one at a stand. If you're going out, have your hotel call one. At a restaurant, ask the waiter or cashier to dial for you. If you want to phone for yourself, try one of these numbers: ✆ **06-6645,** 06-3570, or 06-4994.

The meter begins at 2.25€ ($2) for the first 3km (2 miles) and then rises .65€ (60¢) per kilometer. Every suitcase costs 1€ (90¢), and on Sunday a

---

> ## ⌐Tips Two Bus Warnings
>
> Any map of the Roman bus system will likely be outdated before it's printed. Many buses listed on the "latest" map no longer exist; others are enjoying a much-needed rest, and new buses suddenly appear without warning. There's also talk of completely renumbering the whole system soon, so be aware that the route numbers we've listed might have changed by the time you travel.
>
> Take extreme caution when riding Rome's overcrowded buses—pickpockets abound! This is particularly true on bus no. 64, a favorite of visitors because of its route through the historic districts and thus also a favorite of Rome's vast pickpocketing community. This bus has earned various nicknames, including the "Pickpocket Express" and "Wallet Eater."

1.05€ (95¢) supplement is assessed. There's another 2.50€ ($2.25) supplement 10pm to 7am.

BY CAR

All roads might lead to Rome, but you don't want to drive once you get here. Because the reception desks of most Roman hotels have at least one English-speaking person, call ahead to find out the best route into Rome from wherever you're starting out. You're usually allowed to park in front of the hotel long enough to unload your luggage. You'll want to get rid of your rental car as soon as possible or park in a garage.

You might want to rent a car to explore the countryside around Rome or drive on to another city. You'll save the most money if you reserve before leaving home. But if you want to book a car here, know that **Hertz** is at Via Vittorio del Gallopatoio 33, near the parking lot of the Villa Borghese (© **06-3216831;** Metro: Barberini); **Italy by Car** is at Via Ludovisi 60 (© **06-4870010;** Bus: 95 or 116); and **Avis** is at Stazione Termini (© **06-22935356;** Metro: Termini). **Maggiore,** an Italian company, has an office at Via di Tor Cervara 225 (© **06-229351;** Bus: 447). There are also branches of the major rental agencies at the airport.

 ___FAST FACTS:_ Rome__

American Express The Rome offices are at Piazza di Spagna 38 (© **06-67641;** Metro: Spagna). The travel service is open Monday to Friday 9am to 5pm, and Saturday 9am to 12:30pm. Hours for the financial and mail services are Monday to Friday 9am to 5pm. The tour desk is open during the same hours as those for travel services and also Saturday 2 to 2:30pm (May–Oct).

Banks In general, banks are open Monday to Friday 8:30am to 1:30pm and 3 to 4pm. Some banks keep afternoon hours from 2:45 to 3:45pm. There's a branch of **Citibank** at Via Abruzzi 2 (© **06-478171;** Metro: Barberini). The bank office is open Monday to Friday 8:30am to 1:30pm.

Currency Exchange There are exchange offices throughout the city, and they're also at all major rail and air terminals, including Stazione Termini, where the cambio beside the rail information booth is open daily 8am to 8pm. At some cambi, you'll have to pay commissions, often 1½%. Likewise, banks often charge commissions.

Dentists To find a dentist who speaks English, call the **U.S. Embassy** in Rome at © **06-46741.** You might have to call around to get an appointment. There's also the 24-hour **G. Eastman Dental Hospital,** Viale Regina Elena 287B (© **06-844831;** Metro: Policlinico).

Doctors Call the U.S. Embassy at © **06-46741** for a list of doctors who speak English. All big hospitals have a 24-hour first-aid service (go to the emergency room, *Pronto Soccorso*). You'll find English-speaking doctors at the privately run **Salvator Mundi International Hospital,** Viale delle Mura Gianicolensi 67 (© **06-588961;** Bus: 44). For medical assistance, the **International Medical Center** is on 24-hour duty at Via Firenze 47 (© **06-4882371;** Metro: Razza Republica). You could also contact the **Rome American Hospital,** Via Emilio Longoni 69 (© **06-22551**), with English-speaking doctors on duty 24 hours. A more personalized service is provided 24 hours by **MEDI-CALL,** Studio Medico, Via Salaria 300, Palazzina C, interno 5 (© **06-8840113;** Bus: 53). It can arrange for qualified doctors to make a house call at your hotel or anywhere in Rome. In most cases, the doctor will be a general practitioner who can refer you to a specialist, if needed. Fees begin at around $100 per visit and can go higher if a specialist or specialized treatments are necessary.

Drugstores A reliable pharmacy is **Farmacia Internazionale,** Piazza Barberini 49 (© **06-4871195;** Metro: Barberini), open day and night. Most pharmacies are open 8:30am to 1pm and 4 to 7:30pm. In general, pharmacies follow a rotation system, so several are always open on Sunday.

Embassies/Consulates See "Fast Facts: Italy," in chapter 3.

Emergencies Dial **113** for an ambulance or to call the police; to report a fire, call **115.**

Internet Access You can log onto the Web in central Rome at **Thenetgate,** Piazza Firenze 25 (© **06-6893445;** Bus: 116). Summer hours are Monday to Saturday 10:30am to noon and 3:30 to 10:30pm, and winter hours are daily 10:40am to 8:30pm. A 20-minute visit costs 2.50€ ($2.25), and 1 hour costs 5€ ($4.45). Access is free on Saturday 10:30 to 11am and 2 to 2:30pm. You can kill two birds with one stone just north of Stazione Termini at **Splash,** Via Varese 33 (© **06-49382073;** Metro: Termini), a do-it-yourself laundromat (6.50€/$5.80 per load, including soap) with a satellite TV and four computers hooked up to the Internet (2.50€/$2.25 per half hour).

Mail It's easiest just to buy stamps and mail letters and postcards at your hotel's front desk. Stamps (*francobolli*) can also be bought at tabacchi. You can buy special stamps at the **Vatican City Post Office,** adjacent to the information office in St. Peter's Square; it's open Monday to Friday 8:30am to 7pm and Saturday 8:30am to 6pm. Letters mailed at Vatican City reach North America far more quickly than mail sent from within Rome for the same cost.

Newspapers/Magazines You can get the *International Herald Tribune,* *USA Today, The New York Times,* and *Time* and *Newsweek* magazines at most newsstands. The expatriate magazine (in English) *Wanted in Rome* comes out monthly and lists current events and shows. If you want to try your hand at reading Italian, the Thursday edition of the newspaper *La Repubblica* contains "Trova Roma," a magazine supplement full of cultural and entertainment listings, and *Time Out* now has a Rome edition.

Police Dial ℭ 113.

Safety Pickpocketing is the most common problem. Men should keep their wallets in their front pocket or inside jacket pocket. Purse snatching is also commonplace, with young men on Vespas who ride past you and grab your purse. To avoid trouble, stay away from the curb and keep your purse on the wall side of your body and place the strap across your chest. Don't lay anything valuable on tables or chairs, where it can be grabbed up. Gypsy children have long been a particular menace, although the problem isn't as severe as in years past. If they completely surround you, you'll often literally have to fight them off. They might approach you with pieces of cardboard hiding their stealing hands. Just keep repeating a firm *no!*

Telephone The **country code** for Italy is **39.** The **city code** for Rome is **06;** use this code when calling from *anywhere* outside or inside Italy—you must add it even within Rome itself (and you must now include the 0 every time, even when calling from abroad). See "Fast Facts: Italy," at the end of chapter 3, or the front cover of this book for complete details on how to call Italy, how to place calls within Italy, and how to call home once you're in Italy.

Toilets Facilities are found near many of the major sights and often have attendants, as do those at bars, clubs, restaurants, cafes, and hotels, plus the airports and the rail station. (There are public restrooms near the Spanish Steps, or you can stop at the McDonald's there—it's one of the nicest branches of the Golden Arches you'll ever see!) You're expected to leave .10€ to .25€ (9¢ to 22¢) for the attendant. It's not a bad idea to carry some tissues in your pocket when you're out and about, either.

3 Where to Stay

You'll find Rome's hotels better than ever; many were recently renovated or spruced up to greet the hordes of visitors who arrived during Jubilee Year.

If you like to gamble and arrive without a reservation, head quickly to the **airport information desk** or, once you get into town, to the offices of **Enjoy Rome** (see "Visitor Information," in section 1 of this chapter), where the staff can help you reserve a room, if any are available.

See the section "The Neighborhoods in Brief," earlier in this chapter, to get an idea of where you might want to base yourself.

All the hotels listed serve breakfast (often a buffet with coffee, fruit, rolls, and cheese); but it's not always included in the room rate, so check the listing carefully.

Nearly all hotels are heated in the cooler months, but not all are air-conditioned in summer, which can be vitally important during a stifling July or

August. The deluxe and first-class ones are, but after that, it's a toss-up. Be sure to check the listing carefully before you book a stay in the dog days of summer!

NEAR STAZIONE TERMINI

Despite a handful of pricey choices, this area is most notable for its concentration of cheap hotels. It's not the most picturesque location and parts of the neighborhood are still transitional, but it's certainly convenient in terms of transportation and easy access to many of Rome's top sights.

VERY EXPENSIVE

Mecenate Palace Hotel *(Finds)*   A real gem, this little charmer lies 5 blocks south of the Termini. It's even more intimate and more professionally run than its closest competitor, the Artemide (see below), although it's also pricier. The hotel is composed of two adjacent buildings. One of them was designed by Rinaldi in 1887; the second one (on Via Carlo Alberto) was designed a few years later. The guest rooms, where traces of the original detailing mix with contemporary furnishings, overlook the city rooftops or Santa Maria Maggiore. The spacious marble bathrooms are sumptuous. Three suites offer superior comfort, authentic 19th-century antiques, and a fireplace. Except for these suites, the other rooms are fairly standardized in amenities and comfort.

Via Carlo Alberto 3, 00185 Roma. © **06-44702024.** Fax 06-4461354. www.mecenatepalace.com. 62 units. 340€ ($303.60) double; 600€ ($535.80) suite. Rates include buffet breakfast. AE, DC, MC, V. Parking 22.50€ ($20.10). Metro: Termini or Vittorio Emanuele. **Amenities:** Bar; cafe; room service; babysitting; laundry/dry cleaning. *In room:* A/C, TV, minibar, hair dryer, safe.

St. Regis Grand   This restored landmark is more plush and upscale than any hotel in the area—for comparable digs, you'll have to cross town to check into the Excelsior or Eden. And for sheer opulence, not even those hotels equal it. Its drawback is its location at the dreary Stazione Termini, but once you're inside its splendid shell, all thoughts of railway stations vanish.

When César Ritz founded this outrageously expensive hotel in 1894, it was the first to offer a private bathroom and two electric lights in every room. Today, a $35 million restoration has vastly improved it. Restored to its former glory, it is a magnificent Roman palazzo, combining Italian and French styles in decoration and furnishings. The lobby is decked out with Murano chandeliers, columns, and marble busts and cherubs. Guest rooms, most of which are exceedingly spacious, are luxuriously furnished. Hand-painted frescoes are installed above each headboard, and the large bathrooms are done in fabulous marble. For the best rooms and the finest service, ask to be booked on the St. Regis floor. Butler service is also available for an extra 90€ ($80.35) per night.

Via Vittorio Emanuele Orlando 3, 00185 Roma. © **06-47091.** Fax 06-4747307. www.stregis. com/grandrome. 161 units. 595€–755€ ($531.35–$674.20) double; from 1,890€ ($1,687.75) suite. AE, DC, MC, V. Parking 25€–30€ ($22.35–$26.80). Metro: Repubblica. **Amenities:** 2 restaurants; bar; fitness center; massage; babysitting; laundry/dry cleaning. *In room:* A/C, TV, minibar, coffeemaker, hair dryer, iron, safe.

EXPENSIVE

Hotel Artemide   While the Mediterraneo is a bustling business-oriented choice, the Artemide is a boutique hotel. Near the train station, it combines stylish simplicity with modern comforts against a backdrop of Art Nouveau motifs. The original stained-glass skylight dome was retained in the lobby. The guest rooms are furnished in natural colors and have tasteful furnishings, including elegantly comfortable beds, and spacious marble bathrooms. For those who

Where to Stay in Rome

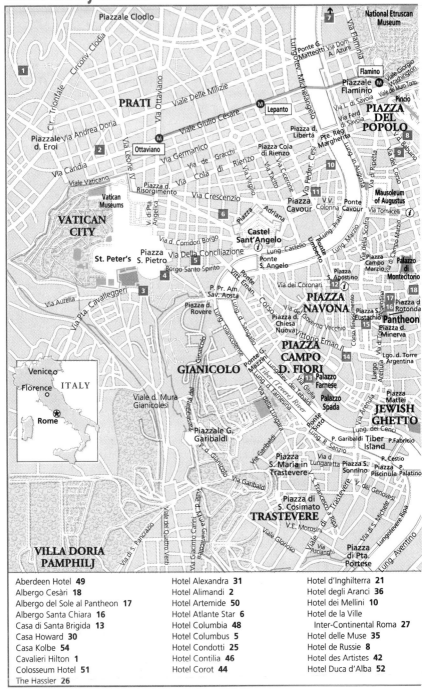

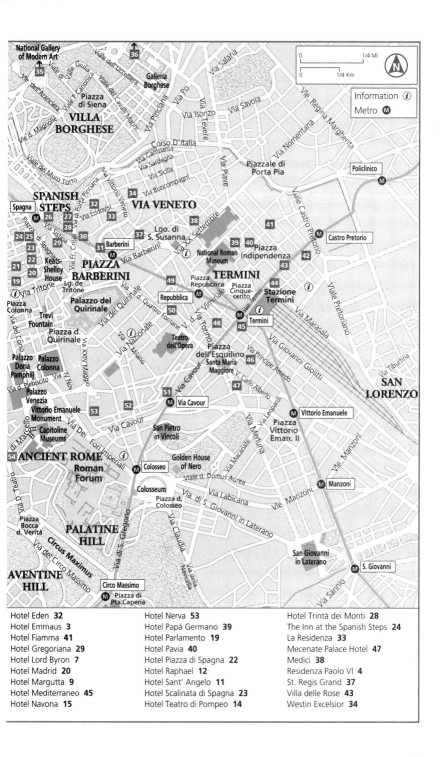

Hotel Eden 32
Hotel Emmaus 3
Hotel Fiamma 41
Hotel Gregoriana 29
Hotel Lord Byron 7
Hotel Madrid 20
Hotel Margutta 9
Hotel Mediterraneo 45
Hotel Navona 15

Hotel Nerva 53
Hotel Papà Germano 39
Hotel Parlamento 19
Hotel Pavia 40
Hotel Piazza di Spagna 22
Hotel Raphael 12
Hotel Sant' Angelo 11
Hotel Scalinata di Spagna 23
Hotel Teatro di Pompeo 14

Hotel Trintà dei Monti 28
The Inn at the Spanish Steps 24
La Residenza 33
Mecenate Palace Hotel 47
Medici 38
Residenza Paolo VI 4
St. Regis Grand 37
Villa delle Rose 43
Westin Excelsior 34

want to pay more, a series of deluxe rooms offer extra amenities such as VCRs and more deluxe bedding.

Via Nazionale 22, 00184 Roma. © **06-489911.** Fax 06-48991700. www.travel.it/roma/artemide. 85 units. 270€–280€ ($241.10–$250.05) double; 310€ ($276.85) suite. Rates include breakfast. AE, DC, MC, V. Parking 15€ ($13.40). Metro: Piazza Repubblica. **Amenities:** Unremarkable rooftop restaurant; bar; room service; laundry/dry cleaning. *In room:* A/C, TV, minibar, hair dryer, safe.

Hotel Mediterraneo (★ This golden oldie sports vivid Italian Art Deco styling. A recent influx of cash has returned the hotel to some of its former glory, although it doesn't compare to the lavish, plush St. Regis Grand (see above). Because it's located on the triumphant passageway through Rome along which Mussolini had planned to travel, local building codes were violated and approval was granted for the creation of this 10-floor hotel. Its height, coupled with its position on one of Rome's hills, provides panoramic views from the most expensive rooms on the highest floors (some with lovely terraces) and from its roof garden/bar (open May–Oct), which is especially charming at night. Views from here are far superior to those from the rooftop restaurant at the Artemide (see above).

Mario Loreti, one of Mussolini's favorite architects, designed the interior sheathing of gray marble, the richly allegorical murals of inlaid wood, and the Art Deco friezes ringing the ceilings of the enormous public rooms. The lobby is also decorated with antique busts of Roman emperors. Recent renovations have upgraded the guest rooms, most in Art Deco and all with bedside controls and large marble bathrooms. The most luxurious accommodations are the seven top-floor suites (even the phones are antique).

Via Cavour 15, 00184 Roma. © **800/223-9832** in the U.S., or 06-4884051. Fax 06-4744105. www.bettoja-hotels.it. 274 units. 279€ ($249.15) double; from 361€ ($322.35) suite. Rates include buffet breakfast. AE, DC, MC, V. Parking 17.50€ ($15.65). Metro: Termini. **Amenities:** 2 restaurants; bar; car-rental desk; room service; babysitting; laundry/dry cleaning. *In room:* A/C, TV, minibar, hair dryer, safe.

MODERATE

Aberdeen Hotel This completely renovated hotel near the opera and the train station stands in front of the Ministry of Defense. The guest rooms, ranging from small to medium, were renovated in 1998, with comfortable new queen or twin beds. The marble bathrooms are rather small but nicely appointed. Many inexpensive trattorie lie nearby.

Via Firenze 48, 00184 Roma. © **06-4823920.** Fax 06-4821092. www.travel.it/roma/aberdeen. 27 units (19 with shower only). 140€ ($125) double, 115€–150€ ($102.70–$133.95) suite. Rates include buffet breakfast. AE, DC, MC, V. Parking 19.75€ ($17.65). Metro: Repubblica. Bus: 64 or 170. **Amenities:** Laundry/dry cleaning. *In room:* A/C, TV, minibar, hair dryer, safe.

Hotel Columbia (★★ This is one of the newest hotels in the neighborhood, with a hard-working multilingual staff. A government-rated three-star choice, originally built around 1900, it underwent a successful, radical renovation in 1997. The interior contains Murano chandeliers and conservatively modern furniture. The compact and cozy guest rooms compare well to the accommodations in the best hotels nearby. Each contains a comfortable bed with fine linen, plus a medium-size tiled bathroom. The appealing roof garden has a view over the surrounding rooftops.

Via del Viminale 15, 00184 Roma. © **06-4744289** or 06-4883509. Fax 06-4740209. www.venere.it/roma/columbia. 45 units. 186.50€–251.50€ ($166.55–$224.60) double. Rates include buffet breakfast. AE, DC, MC, V. Parking nearby 20€ ($17.85). Metro: Repubblica. **Amenities:** Bar; room service; laundry service. *In room:* A/C, TV, minibar, hair dryer, safe.

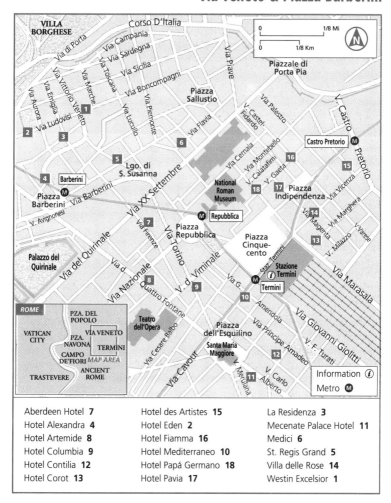

Aberdeen Hotel **7**	Hotel des Artistes **15**	La Residenza **3**
Hotel Alexandra **4**	Hotel Eden **2**	Mecenate Palace Hotel **11**
Hotel Artemide **8**	Hotel Fiamma **16**	Medici **6**
Hotel Columbia **9**	Hotel Mediterraneo **10**	St. Regis Grand **5**
Hotel Contilia **12**	Hotel Papá Germano **18**	Villa delle Rose **14**
Hotel Corot **13**	Hotel Pavia **17**	Westin Excelsior **1**

Medici Built in 1906, this hotel is near the rail station and the shops along Via XX Settembre. Many of its better guest rooms overlook an inner patio garden with Roman columns and benches. All rooms were renovated in 1997 in classic Roman style, with a generous use of antiques. The cheapest are a good buy because they're only slightly smaller than the others (but they have older furnishings and no air-conditioning). The bathrooms are small but well organized.

Via Flavia 96, 00187 Roma. *(C)* **06-4827319.** Fax 06-4740767. www.hotelmedici.com. 69 units (showers only). 150€–175€ ($133.95–$156.30) double. Rates include breakfast. AE, DC, MC, V. Parking 17.50€–20€ ($15.65–$17.85). Metro: Piazza della Repubblica. **Amenities:** Bar; room service; laundry/dry cleaning. *In room:* A/C, TV, minibar, hair dryer.

Villa delle Rose *(Kids)* Located less than 2 blocks north of the rail station, this hotel is an acceptable, if not exciting, choice. In the late 1800s, it was a villa with a dignified cut-stone facade inspired by the Renaissance. Despite many renovations, the ornate trappings of the original are still visible, including the lobby's Corinthian-capped marble columns and the flagstone-covered terrace that is part of the verdant back garden. The look is still one of faded grandeur. Much of the interior has been recently redecorated and upgraded with traditional wall coverings, new carpets, and tiled bathrooms. Breakfasts in the garden do a lot to add country flavor to an otherwise very urban setting. Families often book here asking for one of the three rooms with lofts that can sleep up to five.

Via Vicenza 5, 00185 Roma. ☏ **06-4451788.** Fax 06-4451639. www.villadellerose.it. 37 units (some with shower only). 90€–150€ ($80.35–$133.95) double. Rates include buffet breakfast. AE, DC, MC, V. Free parking (only 4 cars). Metro: Termini or Castro Pretorio. *In room:* A/C (23 rooms), TV, minibar (in some), hair dryer.

INEXPENSIVE

Hotel Contilia *Value* As the automatic doors part to reveal a stylish marble lobby with Persian rugs and antiques, you might step back to double-check the address. The popular old-fashioned Pensione Tony Contilia of yesteryear has taken over this building's other small hotels and upgraded itself to one of the best choices in the neighborhood. The guest rooms have been redone in modern midscale comfort, with perfectly firm beds and built-in units. Rooms overlooking the cobblestone courtyard are the most tranquil. The contemporary bathrooms are small but neat.

Via Principe Amadeo 79d–81, 00185 Roma. ☏ **06-4466942.** Fax 06-4466904. www.hotelcontilia.com. 40 units. 75€–175€ ($67–$156.30) double. Rates include buffet breakfast. AE, DC, MC, V. Parking 20€ ($17.85); free on street. Metro: Termini. **Amenities:** Bar; room service; laundry/dry cleaning. *In room:* A/C, TV, hair dryer, safe.

Hotel Corot This modernized hotel (last renovated in 1997) occupies the second and third floors of an early 1900s building that contains a handful of apartments and another inferior hotel. The Corot is a simple, safe haven north of the train station. You register in a small paneled street-level area and then take an elevator to your high-ceilinged guest room. Each room has simple but traditional furniture, including a good bed, and a modern bathroom.

Via Marghera 15–17, 00185 Roma. ☏ **06-44700900.** Fax 06-44700905. www.hotelcorot.it. 28 units (showers only). 95€–130€ ($84.85–$116.10) double; 120€–170€ ($107.15–$151.80) triple; 150€–200€ ($133.95–$178.60) quad. Rates include breakfast. AE, DC, MC, V. Parking 15€ ($13.40) for 1st night; 9.50€ ($8.50) for the 2nd. Metro: Termini. **Amenities:** Bar; lounge. *In room:* A/C, TV, minibar, hair dryer, safe.

Hotel des Artistes *Value* Completely renovated in 1997, this modest choice lies a few steps from Termini Station. It offers good-quality accommodations at a moderate price. One part of the hotel is a hostel with dormitory-style rooms, bathrooms in the corridors, and a TV in each room; rates for those accommodations range from 90€ ($80.35) for a triple to 110€ ($98.25) for a quad. Regular rooms range from small to medium in size, some of them decorated with Oriental rugs. The furniture is simple but classic, and the maid service is excellent. The hotel's rooms have private bathrooms, small but tidy and just renovated. The roof garden, open 24 hours, is an ideal place for socializing.

Via Villafranca 20, 00185 Roma. ☏ **06-4454365.** Fax 06-4462368. www.hoteldesartistes.com. 45 units (showers only). 95€–140€ ($84.85–$125) double; 110€–160€ ($98.25–$142.90) triple; 135€–180€ ($120.55–$160.75) quad. Rates include buffet breakfast. AE, DC, MC, V. Parking 12.50€–17.50€ ($11.15–$15.65) nearby. Metro: Castro Pretorio. Bus: 310. **Amenities:** Bar; babysitting. *In room:* A/C, TV, hair dryer, safe.

Hotel Fiamma Near the Baths of Diocletian, the Fiamma is in a renovated building, with five floors of bedrooms and a ground floor faced with marble and plate-glass windows. It's an old favorite, if a bit past its prime. The lobby is long and bright, filled with a varied collection of furnishings, including overstuffed chairs and blue enamel railings. On the same floor is an austere marble breakfast room. The comfortably furnished guest rooms range from small to medium in size, and the small bathrooms are tiled, with adequate shelf space.

Via Gaeta 61, 00185 Roma. *C* **06-4818436.** Fax 06-4883511. www.travel.it/roma/ianr. 79 units (showers only). 90€–175€ ($80.35–$156.30) double. Rates include breakfast. AE, DC, MC, V. Parking 17.50€ ($15.65) nearby. Metro: Termini. *In room:* A/C, TV, minibar, hair dryer.

Hotel Papà Germano   This choice is about as basic as anything in this book, but it's clean and decent. This 1892 building, on a block-long street immediately east of the Baths of Diocletian, has undergone some recent renovations yet retains its modest ambience. The pensione offers clean accommodations with plain furniture and well-maintained showers; it hosts a high-turnover crowd of European and North American students. The energetic English-speaking owner, Gino Germano, offers advice on sightseeing. No breakfast is served, but dozens of cafes nearby open early.

Via Calatafimi 14A, 00185 Roma. *C* **06-486919.** Fax 06-47825202. www.hotelpapagermano.com. 17 units, 7 with bathroom (showers only). 52€–62€ ($46.45–$55.35) double without bathroom; 67€–77€ ($59.85–$68.75) double with bathroom. 62€–70€ ($55.35–$62.50) triple without bathroom; 83€–93€ ($74.10–$83.05) triple with bathroom. AE, DC, MC, V. Metro: Termini. *In room:* TV, hair dryer.

Hotel Pavia ⭐ *Value*   In a renovated 100-year-old villa, this hotel is a popular choice on this quiet street near the gardens of the Baths of Diocletian. You take a wisteria-covered passage to reach the recently modernized reception area and tasteful public rooms. All the rooms are comfortable and fairly attractive, and the maids keep everything beautifully maintained, including the medium-size bathrooms with new showers. The quality of the rooms makes this a bargain.

Via Gaeta 83, 00185 Roma. *C* **06-483801.** Fax 06-4819090. www.hotelpavia.com. 20 units (showers only). 150€ ($133.95) double. Rates include breakfast. AE, DC, MC, V. Parking 12.50€ ($11.15). Metro: Termini. **Amenities:** Bar; room service. *In room:* A/C, TV, minibar, hair dryer, safe.

NEAR VIA VENETO & PIAZZA BARBERINI

If you stay in this area, you definitely won't be on the wrong side of the tracks. Unlike the dreary rail station, this is a beautiful and upscale commercial area, near some of Rome's best shopping.

VERY EXPENSIVE

Hotel Eden ⭐⭐⭐   It's not as grand architecturally as the Westin Excelsior, nor does it have the views of the Hassler, and it's certainly not a summer resort like the Hilton, but the Eden is Rome's top choice for the certain discerning traveler who likes grand comfort but without all the ostentation.

For several generations after its 1889 opening, this hotel, about a 10-minute walk east of the Spanish Steps, reigned over one of the world's most stylish shopping neighborhoods. Hemingway, Callas, Ingrid Bergman, Fellini—all checked in during its heyday. It was bought by Trusthouse Forte in 1989 and reopened in 1994 after 2 years (and $20 million) of renovations that enhanced its grandeur and added the amenities for which its government-rated five-star status calls. The Eden's hilltop position guarantees a panoramic city view from most guest rooms; all are spacious and elegantly appointed with a decor harking back to the late 19th century, plus marble-sheathed bathrooms with deluxe toiletries and makeup mirrors. Try to get one of the front rooms with a balcony boasting views over Rome.

Via Ludovisi 49, 00187 Roma. *C* **800/225-5843** in the U.S., or 06-478121. Fax 06-4821584. www.hotel-eden.it. 119 units. 385€–550€ ($343.80–$491.15) double; from 1,015€ ($906.40) suite. AE, DC, DISC, MC, V. Parking 50€ ($44.65). Metro: Piazza Barberini. **Amenities:** Restaurant (La Terrazza; see "Where to Dine in Rome," later in this chapter); bar; health club; room service; babysitting; laundry/dry cleaning. *In room:* A/C, TV, minibar, hair dryer, safe.

Westin Excelsior ⟨★⟩   If money is no object, here's a good place to spend it. It's architecturally more grandiose than either the Eden or the Hassler, but it is not as up-to-date or as beautifully renovated as either the Eden or the St. Regis Grand. The Excelsior has never moved into the 21st century the way some other grand hotels have. For our money today, we prefer the newer Hotel de Russie (see below), and we've always gotten better service at the Hassler (see below), but the Excelsior remains a favorite, especially among older visitors, who remember it from decades past. The baroque corner tower of this limestone palace, overlooking the U.S. Embassy, is a landmark in Rome. A string of cavernous reception rooms is adorned with thick rugs, marble floors, gilded garlands decorating the walls, and Empire furniture. Everything looks just a tad dowdy today, but the Excelsior endures, in no small part because of the hospitable staff.

The guest rooms come in two varieties: new (the result of a major renovation) and traditional. The older ones are a bit worn, while the newer ones have more imaginative color schemes and plush carpeting. All are spacious and elegantly furnished, always with antiques and silk curtains. Most rooms are unique; many have sumptuous Hollywood-style marble bathrooms with bidets. Ask for one of the larger doubles with spacious sitting areas; they're practically suites.

Via Vittorio Veneto 125, 00187 Roma. ⟨©⟩ **800/325-3589** in the U.S., or 06-47081. Fax 06-4826205. www.westin.com/excelsiorrome. 321 units. 605€–675€ ($540.25–$602.80) double; 1,045€–1,980€ ($933.20–$1,768.15) suite. AE, DC, DISC, MC, V. Parking 35€ ($31.25). Metro: Piazza Barberini. **Amenities:** 2 restaurants; bar; salon; room service; babysitting; laundry/dry cleaning. *In room:* A/C, TV, minibar, hair dryer, safe.

EXPENSIVE

Hotel Alexandra ⟨★⟩ *(Finds)*   This is one of your few chances to stay on Via Veneto without going broke (although it's not exactly cheap). Set behind the dignified stone facade of what was a 19th-century mansion, the Alexandra offers immaculate guest rooms. Those facing the front are exposed to roaring traffic and street noise; those in back are quieter but with less of a view. The rooms range from rather cramped to medium-size, but each has been recently redecorated, filled with antiques or tasteful contemporary pieces. They have extras such as swing-mirror vanities and brass or wooden bedsteads. The breakfast room is especially appealing: Inspired by an Italian garden, it was designed by noted architect Paolo Portoghesi.

Via Vittorio Veneto 18, 00187 Roma. ⟨©⟩ **06-4881943.** Fax 06-4871804. www.venere.it/roma/alexandra. 64 units (some with shower only). 210€ ($187.55) double; 325€ ($290.25) suite. Rates include buffet breakfast. AE, DC, MC, V. Parking 25€ ($22.35). Metro: Piazza Barberini. **Amenities:** Laundry/dry cleaning. *In room:* A/C, TV, minibar, hair dryer.

MODERATE

La Residenza ⟨★★⟩   In a superb but congested location, this little hotel successfully combines intimacy and elegance. A bit old-fashioned and homey, the converted villa has an ivy-covered courtyard and a series of upholstered public rooms with Empire divans, oil portraits, and rattan chairs. Terraces are scattered throughout. The guest rooms are generally spacious, containing bentwood chairs and built-in furniture, including beds. The dozen or so junior suites boast balconies. The bathrooms have robes and even come equipped with ice machines.

Via Emilia 22–24, 00187 Roma. ⟨©⟩ **06-4880789.** Fax 06-485721. www.venere.it/roma/la_residenza. 29 units. 175€–185€ ($156.30–$165.20) double; 200€–215€ ($178.60–$192) suite. Rates include buffet breakfast. AE, MC, V. Parking (limited) 5€ ($4.45). Metro: Piazza Barberini. **Amenities:** Lounge; room service; laundry. *In room:* A/C, TV, minibar, hair dryer, safe.

NEAR ANCIENT ROME
MODERATE

Hotel Duca d'Alba ⭐   A bargain near the Roman Forum and the Colosseum, this hotel lies in the Suburra neighborhood, which was once pretty seedy but is being gentrified. Completely renovated, the Duca d'Alba yet retains an old-fashioned air (it was built in the 19th c.). The guest rooms have elegant Roman styling, with soothing colors, light wood pieces, and luxurious beds and bedding. The most desirable rooms are the four with private balconies.

Via Leonina 14, 00184 Roma. © **06-484471.** Fax 06-4884840. www.hotelducadalba.com. 27 units (most with shower only). 100€–195€ ($89.30–$174.15) double; 175€–275€ ($156.30–$245.60) suite. Rates include breakfast. AE, DC, MC, V. Parking 20€–27.50€ ($17.85–$24.55). Metro: Cavour. **Amenities:** Dining area; bar; room service; babysitting; laundry/dry cleaning. *In room:* A/C, TV, minibar, hair dryer, safe.

Hotel Nerva   Some of the Nerva's walls and foundations date from the 1500s (others from a century later), but the modern amenities date only from 1997. The setting, above and a few steps from the Roman Forum, will appeal to any student of archaeology and literature, and the warm welcome from the Cirulli brothers will appeal to all. The decor is accented with wood panels and terracotta tiles; some guest rooms even retain the original ceiling beams. The furniture is contemporary and comfortable, with excellent beds. The tiled bathrooms have adequate shelf space.

Via Tor di Conti 3, 00184 Roma. © **06-6781835.** Fax 06-69922204. www.hotelnerva.com. 19 units. 115€–240€ ($102.70–$214.30) double. Rates include breakfast. AE, MC, V. Metro: Colosseo. **Amenities:** Bar; room service; babysitting; laundry. *In room:* A/C, TV, minibar, hair dryer, safe.

INEXPENSIVE

Casa Kolbe   Occupying an 1800 building, the Casa Kolbe (often full of bus tour groups from North America and Germany) holds a great position between the Palatine and the Campidoglio. The guest rooms are simple and well kept, even if some are worn and the bathrooms are small. Try to get a unit overlooking the small garden.

Via San Teodoro 44, 00186 Roma. © **06-6794974.** Fax 06-69941550. 65 units (showers only). 62€ ($55.35) double. AE, DC, MC, V. Metro: Circo Massimo. **Amenities:** Restaurant; lounge; babysitting; laundry/dry cleaning. *In room:* A/C, hair dryer, safe.

Colosseum Hotel   Two short blocks southwest of Santa Maria Maggiore, this hotel offers affordable and small but comfortable rooms. Someone with flair and lots of lire designed the public areas and upper halls, which hint at baronial grandeur. The drawing room, with its long refectory table, white walls, red tiles, and provincial armchairs, invites lingering. The guest rooms are furnished with well-chosen antique reproductions (beds of heavy carved wood, dark-paneled wardrobes, and leatherwood chairs); all have stark white walls, and some have old-fashioned plumbing in the bathrooms.

Via Sforza 10, 00184 Roma. © **06-4827228.** Fax 06-4827285. www.hotelcolosseum.com. 50 units (showers only). 115€–150€ ($102.70–$133.95) double. Rates include breakfast. AE, DC, MC, V. Parking 20€ ($17.85). Metro: Cavour. **Amenities:** Lounge; room service; babysitting; laundry/dry cleaning. *In room:* A/C, TV, hair dryer, safe.

NEAR CAMPO DE' FIORI
MODERATE

Hotel Teatro di Pompeo ⭐⭐ *(Finds)*   Built atop the ruins of the Theater of Pompey, this small charmer lies near the spot where Julius Caesar met his end on the Ides of March. Intimate and refined, it's on a quiet piazzetta near the

Palazzo Farnese and Campo de' Fiori. The rooms are decorated in an old-fashioned Italian style with hand-painted tiles, and the beamed ceilings date from the days of Michelangelo. The guest rooms range from small to medium in size, each with a tidy but cramped bathroom.

Largo del Pallaro 8, 00186 Roma. ℂ **06-68300170.** Fax 06-68805531. 13 units (showers only). 175€ ($156.30) double. Rates include breakfast. AE, DC, MC, V. Bus: 46, 62, or 64. **Amenities:** Bar; room service; babysitting; laundry/dry cleaning. *In room:* A/C, TV, minibar, hair dryer.

INEXPENSIVE

Casa di Santa Brigida (★ (Value) Rome's best and most comfortable convent hotel is run by the friendly sisters of St. Bridget in the house where that Swedish saint died in 1373. The hotel sits across from the Michelangelo-designed Palazzo Farnese on a quiet square a block from Campo de' Fiori. The place is similar to many traditional little pensiones, except that it's run by sisters (it's not a great place for carousing, obviously). Rooms where Santa Brigida lived and died are on the first floor. This convent hotel accepts people of every age and creed. The rates are justified by the comfy and roomy old-world guest rooms with antiques or reproductions on parquet (lower level) or carpeted (upstairs) floors. The bathrooms are a little old but at least have shower curtains, and the beds are heavenly firm. There are a roof terrace, library, and church.

Via Monserato 54 (off Piazza Farnese). (Postal address: Piazza Farnese 96, 00186 Roma.) ℂ **06-68892596.** Fax 06-68891573. www.brigidine.org. 20 units. 151€ ($134.85) double. Rates include breakfast. DC, MC, V. Bus: 46, 62, or 64. **Amenities:** Restaurant. *In room:* A/C, hair dryer.

NEAR PIAZZA NAVONA & THE PANTHEON

Travelers who want to immerse themselves in the atmosphere of ancient Rome, or those looking for romance, will prefer staying in this area over the more commercial Via Veneto area. Transportation isn't the greatest and you'll do a lot of walking, but that's the reason many visitors come here in the first place—to wander and discover the glory that was Rome. You're also within walking distance of the Vatican and the ruins of classical Rome. Many bars and cafes are within an easy walk of all the hotels located here.

VERY EXPENSIVE

Hotel Raphael (★★ With a glorious location adjacent to Piazza Navona, the Raphael is within easy walking distance of many sights. The ivy-covered facade invites you to enter the lobby, which is decorated with antiques that rival the cache in local museums (there's even a Picasso ceramics collection). The guest rooms (some quite small) were recently refurbished with a Florentine touch. Some of the suites have private terraces. The Raphael is often the top choice of Italian politicos in town for the opening of Parliament. We love its rooftop restaurant with views of all the major landmarks of Old Rome.

Largo Febo 2, 00186 Roma. ℂ **06-682831.** Fax 06-6878993. www.raphaelhotel.com. 65 units. 325€–425€ ($290.25–$379.55) double; 490€–600€ ($437.55–$535.80) suite. AE, DC, MC, V. Parking 22.50€ ($20.10). Bus: 70, 81, 87, or 115. **Amenities:** 2 restaurants; bar; fitness room; sauna; room service; babysitting; laundry. *In room:* A/C, TV, minibar, hair dryer, safe.

EXPENSIVE

Albergo Cesàri (★★ If you want to lose yourself on an ancient street in Old Rome, head here. Since 1787, this inn has stood in an offbeat location between the Pantheon and the Trevi Fountain, two of Rome's most enduring landmarks. Its well-preserved exterior harmonizes with the Temple of Neptune and many little antiques shops nearby. The guest rooms have mostly functional modern pieces, but there are a few traditional trappings to maintain character. In 1998, all the accommodations and the breakfast room were completely renovated.

Via di Pietra 89A, 00186 Roma. ℂ 06-6749701. Fax 06-67497030. 47 units (most with shower only). 220€ ($196.45) double; 260€ ($232.20) triple; 300€ ($267.90) quad. Rates include buffet breakfast. AE, DC, MC, V. Parking 25€ ($22.35). Bus: 175 or 492 from Stazione Termini. **Amenities:** Room service; babysitting. *In room:* A/C, TV, minibar, hair dryer, safe.

Albergo del Sole al Pantheon 🍷 You're obviously paying for the million-dollar view, but you might find that it's worth it to be across from the Pantheon. (Okay, so you're above a McDonald's, but one look at the Pantheon at sunrise, and you won't think about Big Macs.) This building was constructed in 1450 as a home, and the first records of it as a hostelry appeared in 1467, making it one of the world's oldest hotels. The layout is amazingly eccentric—prepare to walk up and down a lot of three- or four-step staircases. The guest rooms vary greatly in decor, much of it hit or miss, with compact, tiled bathrooms. The rooms opening onto the piazza tend to be noisy at all hours. The quieter rooms over-look the courtyard but are sans the view. We always opt to put up with the noise just to enjoy one of the world's greatest views from a hotel room. If you want the grandest view of the Pantheon, ask for room 106 or 108.

Piazza della Rotonda 63, 00186 Roma. ℂ 06-6780441. Fax 06-69940689. www.venere.com/it/roma. 25 units. 260€–325€ ($232.20–$290.25) double; 330€–454€ ($294.70–$405.40) suite. Rates include buffet breakfast. AE, DC, MC, V. Bus: 64. **Amenities:** Bar; room service; babysitting; laundry/dry cleaning. *In room:* A/C, TV, minibar, hair dryer, safe.

MODERATE

Albergo Santa Chiara This is a family-run hotel near the Pantheon in the very inner core of historic Rome. Since 1938, the Corteggiani family has been welcoming sightseers to classic Rome. The white walls and marble columns here speak of former elegance, although the rooms today are simply furnished, func-tional, yet comfortable. The size? They range from a broom closet to a suite large enough to be classified as a small Roman apartment. We go for those units fac-ing the piazza della Minerva, although you'll often have to listen to late-night revelers who don't know when to go home.

Via Santa Chiara 21, 00186 Roma. ℂ 06-6872979. Fax 06-6873144. www.albergosantachiara.com. 98 units (half with shower only). 150€–195€ ($133.95–$174.15) double; 230€ ($205.40) junior suite. Rates include breakfast. Metro: Piazza di Spagna. **Amenities:** Bar; room service; babysitting; laundry/dry cleaning. *In room:* A/C, TV, minibar, hair dryer, safe.

INEXPENSIVE

Hotel Navona This pensione is on a small street radiating from Piazza Navona's southeastern tip. The rooms aren't as grand as the exterior, but the Navona offers decent accommodations, many of which have been renovated and some of which open to views of the central courtyard. Run by an Australian-born family of Italian descent, it boasts ceilings high enough to help relieve the midsummer heat and an array of architectural oddities (the legacy of the con-tinual construction that this palace has undergone since 1360). The beds, most often twins or doubles, have fine linens. Each is equipped with a cramped bath-room. You can get an air-conditioned room by request for 20€ ($17.85) per night (only in the doubles with bathrooms).

Via dei Sediari 8, 00186 Roma. ℂ 06-6864203. Fax 06-68803802. www.hotelnavona.com. 35 units, 30 with bathroom (shower only). 90€ ($80.35) double without bathroom; 100€ ($89.30) double with bathroom; 142.50€ ($127.25) triple with bathroom. Rates include breakfast. No credit cards. Bus: 70, 81, 87, or 115. *In room:* A/C (some rooms), hair dryer.

NEAR PIAZZA DEL POPOLO & THE SPANISH STEPS

This is a great place to stay if you're a serious shopper, but expect to part with a lot of extra lire for the privilege. This is a more elegant area than the Via Veneto—think Fifth Avenue all the way.

VERY EXPENSIVE

The Hassler ★★   The Westin Excelsior is a grander palace, and the Eden and the de Russie are more up-to-date, but the Hassler has something that no other hotel can boast—a coveted location at the top of the Spanish Steps, which ensures glorious views and easy access to upscale designer shopping. The Hassler, rebuilt in 1944 to replace the 1885 original, is not quite what it used to be, but because it's such a classic, and because of that incredible location, it gets away with charging astronomical rates. The lounges and the guest rooms, with their "Italian Park Avenue" trappings, strike a faded, if still glamorous, 1930s note.

The guest rooms range from small singles to some of the most spacious suites in town. High ceilings make them appear larger than they are, and many of them open onto private balconies or terraces. The bathrooms are classy, complete with a range of deluxe body and hair products. The front rooms, dramatically overlooking the Spanish Steps, are often noisy at night, but the views are worth it. For panoramas of the Roman rooftops, ask for a room on the top floor. Although some of the accommodations remain a bit dowdy, those on the fourth floor have been recently and elegantly renovated and are the most desirable. Most requested is the famous corner room 403. For Rome's most spectacular hotel room with a view, we nominate this one.

Piazza Trinità dei Monti 6, 00187 Roma. ℂ 800/223-6800 in the U.S., or 06-699340. Fax 06-6789991. www.hotelhasslerroma.com. 100 units. 460€–656€ ($410.80–$585.80) double; from 1,478€ ($1,319.85) suite. AE, DC, MC, V. Parking 22.50€ ($20.10). Metro: Piazza di Spagna. **Amenities:** Restaurant; bar; free use of bicycles; room service; massage; babysitting; laundry/dry cleaning. *In room:* A/C, TV, minibar, hair dryer, safe.

Hotel de la Ville Inter-Continental Roma ★★   We prefer this place, designed in 1924 by Hungarian architect Jozef Vago, to the overpriced glory of the Hassler next door. The hotel looks deluxe (although it's officially rated first class) from the minute you walk through the revolving door, where a smartly uniformed doorman greets you. Once inside this palace, built in the 19th century on the site of the ancient Gardens of Lucullus, you'll find Oriental rugs, marble tables, brocade furniture, and an English-speaking staff. Endless corridors lead to a maze of ornamental lounges. Some of the public rooms have a sort of 1930s elegance, and others are strictly baroque; in the middle of it all is an open courtyard.

The guest rooms have been renovated in a beautifully classic style. The higher rooms with balconies have panoramic views of Rome, and you're free to use the roof terrace with the same view. Most units are small but boast chintz-covered fabrics and fine beds. The spacious bathrooms boast deluxe toiletries and generous shelf space.

Via Sistina 67–69, 00187 Roma. ℂ 800/327-0200 in the U.S. and Canada, or 06-67331. Fax 06-6784213. www.interconti.com. 192 units. 367.50€–484€ ($328.20–$432.20) double; from 650€ ($580.45) suite. Rates include continental breakfast. AE, DC, MC, V. Parking 25€ ($22.35). Metro: Piazza di Spagna or Barberini. **Amenities:** Restaurant; 2 bars; salon; room service; babysitting; laundry/dry cleaning. *In room:* A/C, TV, minibar, hair dryer, safe.

Where to Stay Near Piazza del Popolo & the Spanish Steps

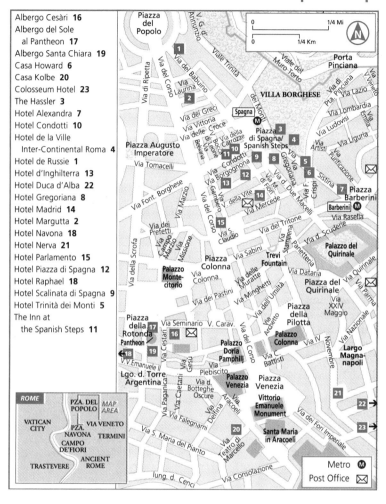

Albergo Cesàri **16**
Albergo del Sole
  al Pantheon **17**
Albergo Santa Chiara **19**
Casa Howard **6**
Casa Kolbe **20**
Colosseum Hotel **23**
The Hassler **3**
Hotel Alexandra **7**
Hotel Condotti **10**
Hotel de la Ville
  Inter-Continental Roma **4**
Hotel de Russie **1**
Hotel d'Inghilterra **13**
Hotel Duca d'Alba **22**
Hotel Gregoriana **8**
Hotel Madrid **14**
Hotel Margutta **2**
Hotel Navona **18**
Hotel Nerva **21**
Hotel Parlamento **15**
Hotel Piazza di Spagna **12**
Hotel Raphael **18**
Hotel Scalinata di Spagna **9**
Hotel Trinità dei Monti **5**
The Inn at
  the Spanish Steps **11**

Hotel de Russie ★★★ The new kid on the block is an old kid in new clothes, but this government-rated five-star hotel has raised the bar for every other hotel in the city. For service, style, and modern luxuries, it beats out the Eden, the Westin Excelsior, and the St. Regis Grand. Just off the Piazza del Popolo, it reopened in the spring of 2000 to media acclaim for its opulent furnishings and choice location. The hardworking, multilingual staff works to make your stay memorable and comfortable.

Public areas are glossy and contemporary. About 30% of the bedrooms are conservative, with traditional furniture, while the remaining 70% are more minimalist, with a stark and striking style. Each is equipped with every conceivable high-tech amenity and offers lots of deeply upholstered comforts and views over a verdant garden.

The signature feature is the extensive terraced gardens, which can be seen from many of the bedrooms. Nothing is finer on a summer evening than sipping a cocktail in the Stravinskij Bar, which opens to the fragrant blooming gardens, and then enjoying an alfresco meal in Le Jardin du Russie.

Via del Babuino 9, 00187 Roma. ℂ **800/323-7500** in North America, or 06-328881. Fax 06-3288888. www.roccofortehotels.com. 129 units. 425€–625€ ($379.55–$558.15) double; from 850€ ($759.05) suite. Rates include breakfast. AE, DC, MC, V. Metro: Flaminia. **Amenities:** Lovely restaurant and bar; gym; spa; room service; salon. *In room:* A/C, TV, minibar, hair dryer, safe.

Hotel d'Inghilterra ★★   The Inghilterra holds onto its traditions and heritage, even though it has been renovated. Situated between Via Condotti and Via Borgogna, this hotel in the 17th century was the guesthouse of the Torlonia princes. If you're willing to spend a king's ransom, Rome's most fashionable small hotel is comparable to the Hassler and Inter-Continental. The rooms have mostly old pieces (gilt and lots of marble, mahogany chests, and glittery mirrors), complemented by modern conveniences. The preferred rooms are higher up, opening onto a tile terrace, with a balustrade and a railing covered with flowering vines and plants. The bathrooms have been refurbished and offer deluxe toiletries.

Via Bocca di Leone 14, 00187 Roma. ℂ **06-69981**. Fax 06-69922243. www.charminghotels.it/inghilterra. 98 units. 245€–365€ ($218.80–$325.95) double; from 617.50€ ($551.45) suite. AE, DC, MC, V. Parking 22.50€ ($20.10). Metro: Piazza di Spagna. **Amenities:** 2 restaurants; bar; gym; room service; babysitting; laundry/dry cleaning. *In room:* A/C, TV, minibar, hair dryer, safe.

The Inn at the Spanish Steps ★★★ *Finds*   This intimate, upscale inn is the first new hotel to open in this location in years. The people who run Rome's most famous cafe, Caffé Greco, created it where Hans Christian Andersen once lived. Andersen praised the balcony roses and violets, and so can you. Every room is furnished in an authentic period decor, featuring antiques, elegant draperies, and parquet floors. The superior units come with fireplace, a frescoed or beamed ceiling, and a balcony. The hotel is completely modern, from its anti-allergic mattresses to its generous wardrobe space. Each marble-paneled bathroom comes with a full tub, and others also offer a Jacuzzi as well. Designer boutiques galore lie nearby.

Via dei Condotti 85, 00187 Roma. ℂ **06-69925657**. Fax 06-6786470. www.atspanishsteps.com. 24 units. 250€–600€ ($223.25–$535.80) double; 700€ ($625.10) suite. Rates include breakfast. Metro: Piazza di Spagna. **Amenities:** Bar; room service; babysitting; laundry/dry cleaning. *In room:* A/C, TV, minibar, hair dryer, safe.

EXPENSIVE

Hotel Scalinata di Spagna ★★★   This is Rome's most famous little boutique hotel. The deluxe Hassler is across the street but far removed in price and grandeur from this intimate, upscale B&B at the top of the Spanish Steps. Its delightful little building—only two floors are visible from the outside—is nestled between much larger structures, with four relief columns across the facade and window boxes with bright blossoms. The recently redecorated interior features small public rooms with bright print slipcovers, old clocks, and low ceilings.

The decor varies radically from one guest room to the next. Some have low beamed ceilings and ancient-looking wood furniture; others have loftier ceilings and more run-of-the-mill furniture. The tiled bathrooms range from small to medium but offer state-of-the-art plumbing. The best units are any overlooking the steps, but the best of the best are room nos. 10 and 12.

Piazza Trinità dei Monti 17, 00187 Roma. ℂ **06-6793006**. Fax 06-69940598. www.hotelscalinata.com. 16 units (tubs only). 200€–325€ ($178.60–$290.25) double; 325€–400€ ($290.25–$357.20) triple. Rates include breakfast. AE, MC, V. Parking 22.50€ ($20.10). Metro: Spagna. **Amenities:** Babysitting; laundry/dry cleaning. *In room:* A/C, TV, minibar, hair dryer, safe.

MODERATE

Casa Howard *★ Finds*   It's rare to make a new discovery in the tourist-trodden Piazza di Spagna area. That's why Casa Howard comes as a pleasant surprise. The little B&B occupies about two-thirds of the second floor of a historic structure. The welcoming family owners maintain beautifully furnished guest rooms, each with its own private bathroom (although some bathrooms lie outside the bedrooms in the hallway). The Pink Room is the most spacious, with its own en suite bathroom. Cristy at reception can "arrange anything" in Rome for you and will also invite you to use the house's private Turkish *hammam* (steam bath).

Via Capa le Case 18, 00187 Roma. ✆ **06-69924555.** Fax 06-6794644. www.casahoward.com. 5 units. 145€–180€ ($129.50–$160.75) double. MC, V. Metro: Piazza di Spagna. **Amenities:** Bar; babysitting; laundry/dry cleaning. *In room:* A/C, TV, hair dryer.

Hotel Condotti   The Condotti is small, choice, and terrific for shoppers intent on being near the tony boutiques. The born-to-shop crowd often thinks that the hotel is on Via Condotti because of its name—actually it lies 2 blocks to the north. The staff, nearly all of whom speak English, is cooperative and hardworking. The mostly modern rooms might not have much historic charm (they're furnished like nice motel units), but they're comfortable and soothing. Renovated in 1991, each is decorated with traditional furnishings, including excellent beds (usually twins). Room 414 is often requested because it has a geranium-filled terrace. Book here for the affordable price in a platinum-card neighborhood and a great location.

Via Mario de' Fiori 37, 00187 Roma. ✆ **06-6794661.** Fax 06-6790457. www.hotelcondotti.com. 16 units (showers only). 175€–265€ ($156.30–$236.65) double; 265€–309€ ($236.65–$275.95) minisuite. Rates include buffet breakfast. AE, DC, MC, V. Metro: Piazza di Spagna. **Amenities:** Car-rental desk; room service; laundry/dry cleaning. *In room:* A/C, TV, minibar, hair dryer.

Hotel Gregoriana *★ Finds*   The intimate Gregoriana has many fans, including many fashion-industry types. It's comparable to the Hotel Condotti. The matriarch of an aristocratic family left the building to an order of nuns in the 19th century, but they eventually retreated to other quarters. (There might be a heavenly vibe in Room C because it used to be a chapel.) The elevator cage is a black-and-gold Art Deco fantasy. The smallish guest rooms provide comfort and fine Italian design, and the door to each bears a reproduction of a fanciful Erté print. The bathrooms are a bit small but always spotless.

Via Gregoriana 18, 00187 Roma. ✆ **06-6794269.** Fax 06-6784258. 20 units. 200€ ($178.60) double. Rates include breakfast. AE, DC, V. Parking 25€ ($22.35). Metro: Spagna. **Amenities:** Babysitting; laundry/dry cleaning. *In room:* A/C, TV, hair dryer.

Hotel Madrid   Despite modern touches in the comfortable, if minimalist, guest rooms, the interior of the Madrid manages to evoke late-19th-century Rome. Guests often take their breakfast amid ivy and blossoming plants on the roof terrace with a panoramic view of rooftops and the distant dome of St. Peter's. Some of the doubles are large, with scatter rugs, veneer armoires, and shuttered windows. But other units are quite small, so make sure you know what you're getting before you check in. The small bathrooms were last renovated in 1998.

Via Mario de' Fiori 93–95, 00187 Roma. ✆ **06-6991511.** Fax 06-6791653. www.hotelmadridroma.com. 26 units (showers only). 181€ ($161.65) double; 274€ ($244.70) suite. Rates include breakfast. AE, DC, MC, V. Parking 17.50€–25€ ($15.65–$22.35) nearby. Metro: Piazza di Spagna. **Amenities:** Lounge; room service; babysitting; laundry. *In room:* A/C, TV, minibar, hair dryer.

Hotel Piazza di Spagna About a block from the downhill side of the Spanish Steps, this hotel is small but classic, with an inviting atmosphere made more gracious by the helpful manager, Elisabetta Giocondi. The guest rooms boast a functional streamlined decor; some even have Jacuzzis in the tiled bathrooms. Accommodations are spread across three floors, with very tidy bedrooms with high ceilings and cool terrazzo floors.

Via Mario de' Fiori 61, 00187 Roma. ✆ **06-6796412.** Fax 06-6790654. www.hotelpiazzadispagna.it. 17 units (some with shower only). 180€–260€ ($160.75–$232.20) double, 250€–300€ ($223.25–$267.90) triple. Rates include breakfast. AE, MC, V. Parking 17.50€ ($15.65) nearby. Metro: Piazza di Spagna. Bus: 590. **Amenities:** Bar; room service; laundry/dry cleaning. *In room:* A/C, TV, minibar, hair dryer.

Hotel Trinità dei Monti Between two of the most bustling piazzas in Rome (Barberini and Spagna), this is a friendly and well-maintained place. The hotel occupies the second and third floors of an antique building. Its guest rooms come with herringbone-pattern parquet floors and big windows, and are comfortable, if not flashy. Each has a tidy tiled bathroom. The hotel's social center is a simple coffee bar near the reception desk. Don't expect anything terribly fancy, but the welcome is warm and the location is ultraconvenient.

Via Sistina 91, 00187 Roma. ✆ **06-6797206.** Fax 06-6990111. www.trinitadeimonti.com. 25 units. 145€–185€ ($129.50–$165.20) double. Rates include breakfast. AE, DC, MC, V. Metro: Barberini or Piazza di Spagna. **Amenities:** Bar; room service; babysitting; laundry. *In room:* A/C, TV, minibar, hair dryer, safe.

INEXPENSIVE

Hotel Margutta The Margutta, on a cobblestone street near Piazza del Popolo, offers attractively decorated but tiny guest rooms, a helpful staff, and a simple breakfast room. You'll sacrifice space, but you'll get an affordable price and a chic location. The best rooms are the three on the top floor, offering a great view. Two of these three (nos. 50 and 51) share a terrace, and the larger room (no. 52) has a private terrace. (There's usually a 20% to 35% supplement for these.) Each room comes with a comfortable bed, plus a small but tidy bathroom.

Via Laurina 34, 00187 Roma. ✆ **06-3223674.** Fax 06-3200395. 24 units (showers only). 104€–145€ ($92.85–$129.50) double; 140€–160€ ($125–$142.90) triple. Rates include breakfast. AE, DC, MC, V. Metro: Flaminio. **Amenities:** Room service. *In room:* Hair dryer, no phone.

Hotel Parlamento The Parlamento has a four-star government rating at two-star prices. Expect a friendly pensione-style reception. The furnishings are antiques or reproduction, and the firm beds are backed by carved wood or wrought-iron headboards. Fifteen rooms are air-conditioned, and the bathrooms were recently redone with heated towel racks, phones, and (in a few) even marble sinks. Rooms are different in style; the best are no. 82, with its original 1800s furniture, and nos. 104, 106, and 107, which open onto the roof garden. You can enjoy the chandeliered and trompe l'oeil breakfast room, or carry your cappuccino up to the small roof terrace with its view of San Silvestro's bell tower.

Via delle Convertite 5 (at the intersection with Via del Corso), 00187 Roma. ✆ **06-6792082.** Fax 06-69921000. www.hotelparlamento.it. 23 units. 95€–115€ ($84.85–$102.70) double. Rates include breakfast. AE, DC, MC, V. Parking 15€–20€ ($13.40–$17.85). Metro: Spagna. **Amenities:** Restaurant; 2 bars; salon; room service; babysitting; laundry/dry cleaning. *In room:* A/C (some), TV, hair dryer, safe.

NEAR VATICAN CITY

For most visitors, this is a rather dull area in which to base yourself—it's well removed from the ancient sites, and it's not a great restaurant neighborhood. But if the main purpose of your visit centers on the Vatican, you'll be fine here, and you'll be joined by thousands of other pilgrims, nuns, and priests.

EXPENSIVE

Hotel Atlante Star ⭐⭐   This is the finest choice for those who'd like to lodge near the Vatican, with much more style and flair than its chief rival, the dei Mellini (see below). The Atlante Star is a first-class hotel with striking views of St. Peter's. The tastefully renovated lobby is covered with dark marble, chrome trim, and exposed wood; the upper floors will make you feel as if you're on a luxury ocean liner (no icebergs in sight). This stems partly from the lavish use of curved and lacquered surfaces, walls upholstered in printed fabrics, and wall-to-wall carpeting. Even the door handles are deco. The guest rooms are small but posh, with all the modern comforts, such as elegant beds with modern, full bathrooms. The royal suite has a Jacuzzi. If there's no room here, the owner will try to accommodate you in his less expensive and less desirable **Atlante Garden** nearby.

Via Vitelleschi 34, 00193 Roma. ✆ **06-6873233.** Fax 06-6872300. www.atlantehotels.com. 90 units. 290€ ($258.95) double; from 325€ ($290.25) suite. Rates include buffet breakfast. AE, DC, MC, V. Parking 35€ ($31.25). Metro: Ottaviano. Bus: 23, 64, or 492. **Amenities:** Superb restaurant; cafe; room service; babysitting; laundry/dry cleaning. *In room:* A/C, TV, minibar, hair dryer.

Hotel Columbus ⭐   This impressive 15th-century palace was once the home of the cardinal who became Pope Julius II and tormented Michelangelo into painting the Sistine Chapel. The building looks much as it must have centuries ago: a severe time-stained facade, small windows, and heavy wooden doors leading from the street to the colonnades and arches of the inner courtyard. The entranceway opens onto a reception hall and a series of baronial public rooms. Note the main salon with its walk-in fireplace, oil portraits, battle scenes, and Oriental rugs.

The guest rooms are considerably simpler than the salons, furnished with comfortable modern pieces. All are spacious, but a few are enormous and still have such original details as decorated wood ceilings and frescoed walls. The best and quietest rooms front the garden.

Via della Conciliazione 33, 00193 Roma. ✆ **06-6865435.** Fax 06-6864874. 92 units. 315€ ($281.30) double; 365€ ($325.95) suite. Rates include buffet breakfast. AE, DC, MC, V. Bus: 40, 62, or 64. **Amenities:** Restaurant; bar; room service; babysitting; laundry/dry cleaning. *In room:* A/C, TV, minibar, hair dryer, safe.

Hotel dei Mellini ⭐   Only slightly less desirable than Atlante Star, this neoclassical hotel is a choice place for Vatican pilgrims. It dates from the early 1900s, when it was a town house. In 1995, after years of neglect, it was turned into a first-class hotel with a certain charm and luxury. It consists of two interconnected buildings, one with four floors and one with six; the top is graced with a terrace overlooking the baroque cupolas of at least three churches. A small staff maintains the lovely guest rooms, whose decor includes Art Deco touches, Italian marble, mahogany furniture, and beds with fine linen. Accommodations with room numbers ending in "16" come with large sitting areas. The tiled full bathrooms have adequate shelf space.

Via Muzio Clementi 81, 00193 Roma. ✆ **06-324771.** Fax 06-32477801. www.hotelmellini.com. 80 units. 330€ ($294.70) double; from 480€ ($428.65) suite. Rates include breakfast. AE, DC, MC, V. Parking 22.50€ ($20.10). Metro: Lepanto or Flaminio. **Amenities:** Bar; room service; massage; babysitting; laundry/dry cleaning. *In room:* A/C, TV, minibar, hair dryer, safe.

Residenza Paolo VI ⭐⭐ *Finds*   Established on the premises of a former monastery, this hotel opened in 2000. With its marvelous panorama of St. Peter's Square, it offers one of the great views in Rome. One reader wrote, "I felt I was at the gates of heaven sitting on the most beautiful square in the Western world." In addition to its incomparable location, the hotel is filled with beautifully decorated and comfortable bedrooms, with modern bathrooms with tub and showers in the junior suites, showers in the regular doubles. In spite of its reasonable prices, the inn is like a small luxury hotel.

Via Paolo VI 29, 00193 Roma. ℂ 06-68134108. Fax 06-68677428. www.residenzapaolovi.com. 28 units. 186€–300€ ($166.10–$267.90) double; 413€–465€ ($368.80–$415.25) junior suite. AE, DC, MC, V. Metro: Ottaviano. Bus: 46, 64, 91, 916, or J5. **Amenities:** Restaurant; bar; room service; babysitting; laundry/dry cleaning. *In room:* A/C, TV, minibar, hair dryer, safe.

MODERATE/INEXPENSIVE

Hotel Alimandi   Named after the three brothers who run it (Luigi, Enrico, and Paolo), this friendly guesthouse was built as an apartment house in 1908 in a bland residential neighborhood. The guest rooms are comfortable, albeit a bit small, with unremarkable contemporary furniture and cramped but modern-looking bathrooms. All have been upgraded and fitted with new beds, which are mostly doubles. Each of the three upper floors is serviced by two elevators leading down to a simple lobby. The social center and most appealing spot is the roof garden, with potted plants and views of St. Peter's dome.

Via Tunisi 8, 00192 Roma. ℂ 06-39723948. Fax 06-39723943. www.alimandi.org. 35 units. 150€ ($133.95) double. AE, DC, MC, V. Parking 17.50€ ($15.65). Metro: Ottaviano. **Amenities:** Rooftop garden; bar; babysitting; laundry. *In room:* A/C, TV, hair dryer, safe.

Hotel Emmaus   Because of its relatively low prices and location near the Vatican, you might share this hotel with Catholic pilgrims from all over the world. Occupying an older building that was renovated in 1992, it offers unpretentious and basic but comfortable accommodations. The guest rooms have more recently been renovated but are still quite small, fitted with twin or double beds. Each comes with a small but efficiently organized bathroom.

Via delle Fornaci 25, 00165 Roma. ℂ and fax 06-635658. www.venere.it/roma/emmaus. 31 units (showers only). 150€ ($133.95) double. Rates include breakfast. AE, DC, MC, V. Parking 15€ ($13.40) nearby. Metro: Ottaviano. Bus: 65. **Amenities:** Breakfast room; lounge. *In room:* A/C, TV, minibar, hair dryer, safe.

Hotel Sant'Angelo   This hotel, right off Piazza Cavour (northeast of the Castel Sant'Angelo) and a 10-minute walk from St. Peter's, is in a relatively untouristy area. Maintained and operated by the Torre family, it occupies the second and third floors of an imposing 200-year-old building. The rooms are simple, modern, and clean, with wooden furniture and views of either the street or a rather bleak but quiet courtyard. Rooms are small but not cramped, each with a comfortable bed, plus a tiled bathroom.

Via Mariana Dionigi 16, 00193 Roma. ℂ 06-3242000. Fax 06-3204451. www.novaera.it/hsa. 31 units (showers only). 87.50€–170€ ($78.15–$151.80) double; 100€–190€ ($89.30–$169.65) triple. Rates include breakfast. MC, V. Parking 20€ ($17.85). Metro: Piazza di Spagna. **Amenities:** Breakfast room; bar; room service; babysitting. *In room:* A/C, TV, minibar, hair dryer.

IN PARIOLI

VERY EXPENSIVE

Hotel Lord Byron ★★★   Lots of sophisticated travelers with hefty wallets are forgetting about the old landmarks such as the St. Regis Grand and choosing this chic boutique hotel. The Lord Byron exemplifies modern Rome—an Art Deco villa set on a residential hilltop in Parioli, an area of embassies and exclusive town houses at the edge of the Villa Borghese. From the curving entrance steps off the staffed parking lot in front, you'll notice striking design touches. Flowers are everywhere, the lighting is discreet, and everything is on an intimate scale. Each guest room is unique, but most have lots of mirrors, upholstered walls, sumptuous beds, spacious full bathrooms with gray marble accessories, and big dressing room/closets. Ask for room nos. 503, 602, or 603 for great views.

Via G. de Notaris 5, 00197 Roma. ℰ 06-3220404. Fax 06-3220405. www.lordbyronhotel.com. 36 units. 284€–408€ ($253.60–$364.35) double; 651€–858€ ($581.35–$766.20) suite. Rates include breakfast. AE, DC, MC, V. Parking 22.50€ ($20.10). Metro: Flaminio. Bus: 52. **Amenities:** Restaurant (Relais Le Jardin; see "Where to Dine in Rome," later in this chapter); bar; room service; babysitting; laundry/dry cleaning. *In room:* A/C, TV, minibar, hair dryer, iron, safe.

MODERATE/INEXPENSIVE
Hotel degli Aranci   This former villa is on a tree-lined street, surrounded by similar villas that are homes of consulates and diplomats. Most of the accommodations have tall windows opening onto city views and are filled with provincial furnishings or English-style reproductions, including good beds (fitted with fine linen) and tiled bathrooms with adequate shelf space. Scattered about the public rooms are medallions of soldiers in profile, old engravings of ruins, and classical vases. From the glass-walled breakfast room, you can see the tops of orange trees.

Via Barnaba Oriani 11, 00197 Roma. ℰ 06-8085250. Fax 06-8070704. www.hoteldegliaranci.com. 55 units (showers only). 100€–187.50€ ($89.30–$167.45) double; from 225€ ($200.95) suite. Rates include breakfast. AE, DC, MC, V. Free parking. Metro: Piazza del Popolo. Bus: 3 or 53. **Amenities:** Restaurant; bar; laundry. *In room:* A/C, TV, minibar, hair dryer, safe.

Hotel delle Muse *Finds*   This little hotel, half a mile north of the Villa Borghese, is a winning but undiscovered choice run by the efficient English-speaking Giorgio Lazar. Most rooms have been renovated but remain rather minimalist. Nonetheless, there's reasonable comfort here, with tidy bathrooms.

Via Tommaso Salvini 18, 00197 Roma. ℰ 06-8088333. Fax 06-8085749. www.hoteldellemuse.com. 61 units (showers only). 80€–130€ ($71.45–$116.10) double; 110€–140€ ($98.25–$125) triple. Rates include buffet breakfast. AE, DC, MC, V. Parking 17.50€ ($15.65). Bus: 360. **Amenities:** Restaurant; bar; room service; babysitting; laundry/dry cleaning. *In room:* TV, hair dryer, safe.

IN MONTE MARIO
VERY EXPENSIVE
Cavalieri Hilton ★★ *Kids*   This is not the place for you if you want to be in the heart of Rome, near attractions, shopping, and nightlife. But if you want resort-style accommodations and don't mind staying a 15-minute drive from the center of Rome (the hotel offers frequent, free shuttle service), consider the Hilton. Because of its pools and array of facilities, it attracts a lot of well-heeled families from all over the globe. The Cavalieri Hilton overlooks Rome and the Alban Hills from atop Monte Mario. It's set among 15 acres of trees, flowering shrubs, and stonework, in the cooler hills above Rome.

The entrance leads into a lavish red-and-gold lobby, with sculptures, winding staircases, and massive windows. The guest rooms and suites, many with panoramic views, are contemporary and stylish. Soft furnishings in pastels are paired with Italian furniture in warm-toned woods, including beds with deluxe linen. Each unit has in-house movies, bedside controls for all the gadgets, and a spacious balcony. The bathrooms, sheathed in Italian marble, come with large mirrors, international electric sockets, vanity mirrors, piped-in music, and phones. There are facilities for travelers with disabilities.

Via Cadlolo 101, 00136 Roma. ℰ 800/445-8667 in the U.S. and Canada, or 06-35091. Fax 06-35092241. www.hilton.com. 371 units. 450€–625€ ($401.85–$558.15) double; from 900€ ($803.70) suite. AE, DC, DISC, MC, V. Parking 20€ ($17.85). **Amenities:** 2 restaurants; 2 bars; 2 pools; 6 tennis courts; fitness center; free shuttle to the center of Rome; room service; babysitting; laundry/dry cleaning. *In room:* A/C, TV, minibar, hair dryer, safe.

AT THE AIRPORT

EXPENSIVE

Hotel Hilton Rome Airport   At long last, Rome has a first-class airport hotel for late-night arrivals and early-morning departures. Only 200m from the air terminal, this hotel is approached via a skywalk. The Hilton doesn't pretend to be more than it is—a bedroom factory at the airport. Follow the broad hallways to one of the midsize to spacious "crash pads," each with deep carpeting, generous storage space, and large, full bathrooms. The best units are the executive suites with extra amenities such as separate check-in, trouser press, dataports, and voice mail.

Via Arturo Ferrarin 2, 00050 Fiumicino. ⒸⒸ **800/445-8667** in the U.S. and Canada, or 06-65258. Fax 06-65256525. www.hilton.com. 517 units. 270€–325€ ($241.10–$290.25) double; from 435€ ($388.45) suite. AE, DC, MC, V. Free parking. Metro: Fiumicino Aeroporto. **Amenities:** 2 restaurants; bar; coffee shop; pool; gym; sauna; room service; babysitting; laundry/dry cleaning. *In room:* A/C, TV, minibar, hair dryer, safe.

INEXPENSIVE

Hotel Cancelli Rossi   If you're nervous about making your flight, you could book into this very simple motel-style place, located 1½ miles from the airport. The hotel was built in 1994, and a full renovation was completed in 1999. Two floors are served with an elevator, and the decor is minimal. Rooms range in size from small to medium and are functionally furnished but reasonably comfortable, with good beds, along with perfectly clean, tiled bathrooms. The atmosphere is a bit antiseptic, but this place is geared more for business travelers than vacationers. A restaurant in an annex nearby serves Italian and international food.

Via R. La Valle 54, 00054 Fiumicino. ⒸⒸ **06-6507221.** Fax 06-65049168. www.cancellirossi.it. 50 units (showers only). 99€ ($88.40) double. Rates include breakfast. Free parking. **Amenities:** Restaurant; bar; free bus shuttle from/to the Leonardo Da Vinci airport (daily 7–9:45am and 5–8:45pm every 20 min.); room service; babysitting; laundry/dry cleaning. *In room:* A/C, TV, minibar, hair dryer, safe.

4 Where to Dine

Rome remains one of the world's great capitals for dining, with even more diversity today than ever. Most of its trattorie haven't changed their menus in a quarter of a century (except to raise the prices, of course), but there's an increasing number of chic, upscale spots with chefs willing to experiment, as well as a growing handful of Chinese, Indian, and other ethnic spots for those days when you just can't face another plate of pasta. The great thing about Rome is that you don't have to spend a fortune to eat really well.

Rome's cooking isn't subtle, but its kitchens rival anything that the chefs of Florence or Venice can turn out. The city's chefs borrow—and sometimes improve on—the cuisine of other regions. One of the city's oldest neighborhoods, Trastevere, is a gold mine of colorful streets and restaurants with time-tested recipes.

Refer to section 2 of appendix A to learn about Roman wines. Most of the wines on the Roman table are from the Castelli Romani, the little hill towns surrounding Rome.

Restaurants generally serve lunch between 1 and 3pm, and dinner between about 8 and 10:30pm; at all other times, restaurants are closed. Dinner is taken late in Rome, so although a restaurant might open at 7:30, even if you get there at 8pm, you'll often be the only one in the place. A heavier meal is typically eaten at midday, and a lighter one is eaten in the evening.

What if you're hungry outside those hours? Well, if you don't take continental breakfast at your hotel, you can have coffee and a pastry at any **bar** (really a cafe, although there will be liquor bottles behind the counter) or a *tavola calda* (hot table). These are stand-up snack bar–type arrangements, open all day long and found all over the city.

A *servizio* (tip) of 10% to 15% will often be added to your bill or included in the price, although patrons often leave an extra .50€ to 3€ (45¢–$2.70) as a token.

NEAR STAZIONE TERMINI
MODERATE

Taverna Flavia   ROMAN/INTERNATIONAL   This tavern is a robustly Roman restaurant, still serving the same food that once delighted the late Frank Sinatra and the "Hollywood on the Tiber" crowd in the 1950s. It's not chic anymore, but you can still enjoy the hearty classics here. Specialties are risotto with scampi, spaghetti with champagne, *osso buco* (veal shank) with peas, a delectable seafood salad, and a to-die-for fondue with truffles. There's a daily regional dish (it might be Roman-style tripe, much better than you might expect). A chef always prepares our favorite salad in Rome: Veruska, made with five kinds of lettuce and mushrooms, including fresh truffles.

Via Flavia 9 (a block from Via XX Settembre). ✆ 06-4745214. Reservations recommended. Main courses 11€–17.50€ ($9.80–$15.65). AE, DC, MC, V. Mon–Fri 12:30–3pm and 7:30–11pm; Sat–Sun 7:30–11:30pm. Metro: Repubblica.

INEXPENSIVE

Monte Arci   ROMAN/SARDINIAN   On a cobblestone street near Piazza Indipendenza, this restaurant is set behind a sienna-colored facade. It features cheap Roman and Sardinian specialties (you'll spend even less for pizza) such as *nialoreddus* (a regional form of gnocchetti); pasta with clams, lobster, or the musky-earthy notes of porcini mushrooms; green and white spaghetti with bacon, spinach, cream, and cheese; and delicious lamb sausage flavored with herbs and pecorino cheese. It's all home cooking, hearty but not that creative.

Via Castelfirdardo 33. ✆ 06-4941220. Reservations recommended. Main courses 8.50€–14€ ($7.60–$12.50); fixed-price menu 25€ ($22.35). AE, DC, MC, V. Mon–Fri 12:30–3pm and 7–11:30pm; Sat 7–11:30pm. Closed Aug. Metro: Stazione Termini.

Trimani Wine Bar   ✦ CONTINENTAL   Opened as a tasting center for French and Italian wines, spumantis, and liqueurs, this is an elegant wine bar with a lovely decor (stylish but informal) and comfortable seating. More than 30 wines are available by the glass. To accompany them, you can choose from a bistro-style menu, with dishes such as salad niçoise, vegetarian pastas, herb-laden bean soups (*fagiole*), quiche, and Hungarian goulash. Also available is a wider menu, including meat and fish courses. The specialty is the large choice of little "bruschette" with cheese and prosciutto—the chef orders every kind of prosciutti and cheese from all over Italy. The dishes are matched with the appropriate wines. The dessert specialty is chestnut mousse served with a sauce of white wine (*Verduzzo di Ronco di Viere*), covered by whipped cream and meringue.

Trimani maintains a well-stocked shop about 37m (40 yd.) from its wine bar, at V. Goito 20 (✆ **06-4469661**), where an astonishing array of Italian wines is for sale.

Via Cernaia 37B. ✆ 06-4469630. Reservations recommended. Main courses 6€–18€ ($5.35–$16.05); glass of wine (depending on vintage) 1.75€–10€ ($1.55–$8.95). AE, DC, MC, V. Mon–Sat 11:30am–3:30pm and 6pm–12:30am (in Dec open also on Sun). Closed 2 weeks in Aug. Metro: Repubblica or Castro Pretorio.

Where to Dine in Rome

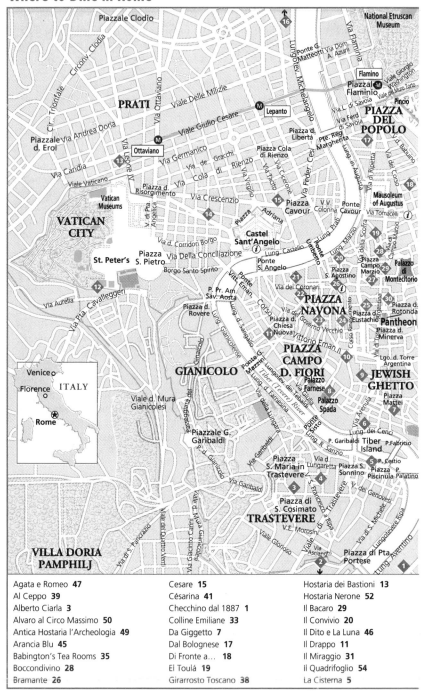

National Gallery of Modern Art

Viale dell'Uccelliera 39
40
Via Salaria

Galleria Borghese

Piazza di Siena

VILLA BORGHESE

Corso D'Italia

Piazzale di Porta Pia

Policlinico

SPANISH STEPS

Spagna 35 Piazza di Spagna

VIA VENETO

Lgo. di S. Susanna

Castro Pretorio

Barberini

National Roman Museum

Piazza Indipendenza

Keats-Shelley House

PIAZZA BARBERINI

Piazza Repubblica

TERMINI

Lg. del Tritone

Piazza Colonna

Palazzo del Quirinale

Trevi Fountain

Repubblica

Piazza Cinquecento

Stazione Termini

Piazza d. Quirinale

Teatro dell'Opera

Termini

Palazzo Doria Pamphilj

Palazzo Colonna

Piazza dell'Esquilino

Santa Maria Maggiore

Palazzo Venezia

SAN LORENZO 45

Vittorio Emanuele Monument

Via Cavour

Via Cavour

Vittorio Emanuele

46

Capitoline Museums

San Pietro in Vincoli

Piazza Vittorio Eman. II

ANCIENT ROME

Colosseo

Golden House of Nero

Roman Forum

Colosseum

Viale d. Domus Aurea

Via Labicana

Manzoni

Piazza d. Colosseo

Piazza d. S. Giovanni in Laterano

Piazza Bocca d. Verità

PALATINE HILL

Circus Maximus

San Giovanni in Laterano

S. Giovanni

AVENTINE HILL

Circo Massimo

Piazza di Pta.Capena

49

Information ⓘ
Metro Ⓜ

Take a Gelato Break

If you're craving luscious gelato, our top choice is **Giolitti,** Via Uffici del Vicario 40 (© **06-6991243**), the city's oldest ice-cream shop, open daily 7am to 2am. You'll find the usual vanilla (*vaniglia*), chocolate (*ciocco-lato*), strawberry (*fragola*), and coffee (*caffé*), but you'll also find fla-vors that you might not have heard of, such as *gianduia* (chocolate hazelnut), plus such treats as *cassata alla siciliana, zabaglione, mascar-pone,* and *marron glacé.* The preposterously oversize showpiece sun-daes have names such as Coppa Olimpico di Roma. Prices here and at each of the places below range from 1.50€ to 8€ ($1.35–$7.15).

A close second is **Tre Scalini,** Piazza Navona 30 (© **06-6879148**; see p. 125), which is celebrated for its *tartufo* (an intense chocolate cre-ation). Gelato connoisseurs say that you haven't really experienced Rome until you've enjoyed a tartufo here. It's open Thursday to Tues-day 9am to 1am. Another favorite is the **Palazzo del Freddo Giovanni Fassi,** Via Principe Eugenio 65–67 (© **06-4464740**). More than 100 years old, this ice-cream outlet (part of a gelato factory) turns out yummy concoctions and specializes in rice ice cream. It's open Tuesday to Sun-day, noon to 12:30am.

If you're fond of frothy *frullati* (fruit shakes) frappes, head to **Pas-cucci,** Via Torre Argentina 20 (© **06-6864816**), where blenders work all day grinding fresh fruit into delectable drinks. It's open Monday to Saturday, 6am to midnight.

IN SAN LORENZO
INEXPENSIVE

Arancia Blu ✦✦ (*Finds*) VEGETARIAN/ITALIAN   Fabio Bassan and Enrico Bartolucci offer Rome's best vegetarian cuisine. Under soft lighting and wood ceilings, surrounded by wine racks and university intellectuals, the friendly wait-ers will help you compile a menu to fit any dietary need. The dishes at this trendy spot are inspired by peasant cuisines from across Italy and beyond. The appetizers range from hummus and tabbouleh to zucchini-and-saffron quiche or salad with apples, gorgonzola, and balsamic vinegar. The main courses change seasonally and may be lasagna with red onions, mushrooms, zucchini, and gin-ger; couscous *con verdure* (vegetable couscous); or *ravioli ripieni di patate e menta* (ravioli stuffed with potatoes and mint served under fresh tomatoes and Sardin-ian sheep's cheese). They offer 250 wines and inventive desserts, such as dark-chocolate cake with warm orange sauce.

Via dei Latini 55–65 (at Via Arunci). © 06-4454105. Reservations highly recommended. Main courses 7€–10€ ($6.25–$8.95). No credit cards. Daily 8pm–midnight. Bus: 71.

Il Dito e La Luna ✦ SICILIAN/ITALIAN   This charming, unpretentious bistro has counters and service areas accented with lovely displays of fresh fruits and vegetables. The menu—divided between traditional Sicilian and creative contemporary dishes—includes orange-infused anchovies served on orange seg-ments, a creamy flan of mild onions and mountain cheese, and seafood couscous loaded with shellfish. The pastas are excellent, particularly the square-cut

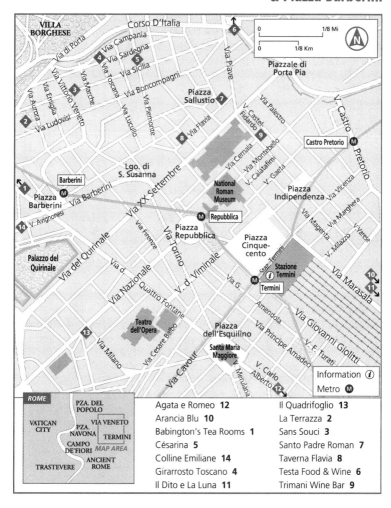

VILLA BORGHESE · Corso D'Italia · Via di Porta · Via Campania · Via Sardegna · Via Toscana · Via Sicilia · Via Boncompagni · Piazza Sallustio ⑦ · Via Marche · Via Piemonte · Via Luculio · Via Flavia · V. Castel Fidardo · V. Palestro · Piazzale di Porta Pia · Via Vittorio Veneto · Via Emiglia · Via Aurora · Via Ludovisi ② · ④ ⑤ · Via Piave · ⑧ ⑨ · Via Cernaia · Via Montebello · V. Calatafimi · V. Gaeta · Castro Pretorio Ⓜ · V. Castro Pretorio · Lgo. di S. Susanna · Barberini · Piazza Barberini Ⓜ ① · Via Barberini · Via XX Settembre · National Roman Museum · Piazza Indipendenza · Via Vicenza · Via Magenta · Via Margherita · V. Avignonesi ⑭ · Ⓜ Repubblica · Via Firenze · Piazza Repubblica · Piazza Cinquecento · V. Milazzo · V. Varese · Palazzo del Quirinale · Via del Quirinale · Via d. · Via Torino · Via d. Viminale · Staz. Termini · ⓘ Stazione Termini · Via Marasala · ⑩ ⑪ · Via Nazionale · Quattro Fontane · Via G. · Ⓜ Termini · Teatro dell'Opera · Via Cesare Balbo · Piazza dell'Esquilino · Santa Maria Maggiore · Amendola · Via Principe Amadeo · Via Giovanni Giolitti · V. F. Turati · ⑬ · Via Milano · Via Cavour · V. Merulana · V. Carlo Alberto · ⑫ · Information ⓘ · Metro Ⓜ · 0 ... 1/8 Mi · 0 ... 1/8 Km

ROME · VATICAN CITY · PZA. DEL POPOLO · PZA. NAVONA · VIA VENETO · CAMPO DE'FIORI · MAP AREA · TERMINI · TRASTEVERE · ANCIENT ROME

Agata e Romeo **12**
Arancia Blu **10**
Babington's Tea Rooms **1**
Césarina **5**
Colline Emiliane **14**
Girarrosto Toscano **4**
Il Dito e La Luna **11**

Il Quadrifoglio **13**
La Terrazza **2**
Sans Souci **3**
Santo Padre Roman **7**
Taverna Flavia **8**
Testa Food & Wine **6**
Trimani Wine Bar **9**

spaghetti (*tonnarelli*) with mussels, bacon, tomatoes, and exotic mushrooms. The specialty of the house is *caponata di melanzane,* chopped eggplant stewed in tomato sauce with onions and potatoes.

Via dei Sabelli 49–51, San Lorenzo. ✆ **06-4940726.** Reservations recommended. Main courses 12.50€–14€ ($11.15–$12.50). No credit cards. Mon–Sat 8pm–midnight. Metro: Vittorio Emanuele.

NEAR VIA VENETO & PIAZZA BARBERINI
VERY EXPENSIVE

La Terrazza ✿✿✿ ITALIAN/INTERNATIONAL   La Terrazza and Relais Le Jardin (see p. 131) serve the city's finest cuisine; here, you get the added bonus of a sweeping view over St. Peter's. The service is formal and flawless, yet not intimidating. Chef Enrico Derfligher, the wizard behind about a dozen top-notch Italian restaurants around Europe, prepares a seasonally changing menu that's among the most polished in Rome. You might start with zucchini blossoms stuffed with ricotta and black olives, or lobster medallions with apple purée and black truffles. Main courses may include red tortelli (whose coloring comes from tomato mousse) stuffed with mascarpone cheese and drizzled with lemon, or a sea bass baked in a crust of black olives and salt with oregano and potatoes.

In the Hotel Eden, Via Ludovisi 49. ☎ 06-478121. Reservations recommended. Main courses 35€–49€ ($31.25–$43.75); fixed-price menu 75€ ($67). AE, DC, MC, V. Daily 12:30–2:30pm and 7:30–10:30pm. Metro: Barberini.

Sans Souci ★★★ FRENCH/ITALIAN   Not long ago, Sans Souci was getting a little tired; but now it has bounced back, and Michelin has restored its coveted star. As you step into the dimly lit lounge, the maître d' will present you with the menu, which you can peruse while sipping a drink amid tapestries and glittering mirrors. The menu is ever changing, although the classics never disappear. A great beginning is the goose-liver terrine with truffles, one of the chef's signatures. The fish soup, according to one Roman restaurant critic, is "a legend to experience." The soufflés are popular (in varieties such as artichoke, asparagus, and spinach), as are the succulent truffle-filled ravioli, homemade foie gras, and tender Normandy lamb. Save room for a special dessert soufflé (prepared for two), in flavors such as chocolate and Grand Marnier.

Via Sicilia 20. ☎ 06-4821814. Reservations recommended. Main courses 29€–36€ ($25.90–$32.15). AE, DC, MC, V. Tues–Sun 8pm–1am. Closed Aug 10–30. Metro: Barberini.

EXPENSIVE
Colline Emiliane ★★ *Finds* EMILIANA-ROMAGNOLA   Serving the *classica cucina bolognese,* Colline Emiliane is a small, family-run place—the owner is the cook and his wife makes the pasta (about the best you'll find in Rome). The house specialty is an inspired *tortellini alla panna* (with cream sauce and truffles), but the less-expensive pastas, including *maccheroni al funghetto* and *tagliatelle alla bolognese,* are excellent, too. As an opener, we suggest *culatello di Zibello,* a delicacy from a small town near Parma that's known for having the world's finest prosciutto. Main courses include *braciola di maiale* (boneless rolled pork cutlets stuffed with ham and cheese, breaded, and sautéed) and an impressive *giambonnetto* (roast veal Emilian style with roast potatoes).

Via Avignonesi 22 (off Piazza Barberini). ☎ 06-4817538. Reservations highly recommended. Main courses 11€–15€ ($9.80–$13.40). MC, V. Sat–Thurs 12:45–2:45pm and 7:45–10:45pm. Closed Aug. Metro: Barberini.

MODERATE
Césarina *Kids* EMILIANA-ROMAGNOLA/ROMAN   Specializing in the cuisines of Rome and the region around Bologna, this place is named for Césarina Masi, who opened it in 1960 (many old-timers fondly remember her strict supervision of the kitchen and how she lectured regulars who didn't finish their tagliatelle). Although Césarina died in the mid-1980s, her traditions are kept going by her family. This has long been a favorite of Roman families. The polite staff rolls a trolley from table to table laden with an excellent *bollito misto* (an array of well-seasoned boiled meats) and often follows with misto Césarina—four kinds of creamy, handmade pasta, each with a different sauce. Equally appealing are the *saltimbocca* (veal with ham) and the *cotoletta alla bolognese* (tender veal cutlet baked with ham and cheese). A dessert specialty is *semifreddo* (ice cream with whipped cream) Césarina with hot chocolate, so meltingly good that it's worth the 5 pounds you'll gain.

Via Piemonte 109. ☎ 06-4880828. Reservations recommended. Main courses 10€–15€ ($8.95–$13.40). AE, DC, MC, V. Mon–Sat 12:30–3pm and 7:30–11pm. Metro: Barberini. Bus: 52, 53, 63, or 80.

Santo Padre *(Finds* ROMAN   Away from the tourist traps around the U.S. Embassy, this is a little gem managed by three brothers who have a great passion for good food and sports (one of them was a professional soccer player). Once you enter the modest dining room, you'll be surrounded by family pictures and you'll feel as if you're among friends. As soon as you're seated, the owners proudly present their fare of the day—perhaps grilled zucchini (one of our all-time favorites); slices from a whole, fresh mozzarella ball; or tender, sweet prosciutto. For a savory dish, ask for their small meatballs (*polpette*) served with an herb-flavored tomato sauce. Their pastas are worth a return visit, especially the linguine with shrimp, saffron, and *pachino* (a variety of cherry tomatoes from the Naples area). Count yourself lucky if you're there the day the cooks are preparing *maialino,* which translates as "little pig." The meat is crispy yet tender, and it's served with the freshest of seasonal vegetables.

Via Collina 18. C 06-4745405. Reservations required. Main courses 9€–15€ ($8.05–$13.40). No credit cards. Mon–Sat 7:30–10:30pm. Metro: Barberini or Termini.

Testa Food & Wine *(Finds* ITALIAN   Near Villa Borghese, this recently renovated restaurant draws discerning palates seeking food and wine at a reasonable price. It's a sophisticated setting for masterfully crafted dishes composed of fresh ingredients. The *orecchiette* (ear-shaped pasta) gratinée with broccoli and sautéed clams is one of the city's finest pasta dishes. If you're not on a diet, opt for strozza Preti with creamy cheese and bacon. Another excellent homemade pasta dish, *cacio e pepe,* is made with crunchy artichokes. The tuna steak with sun-dried tomatoes is a delight, as is the duck breast stuffed with foie gras and sprinkled with roasted almonds and served with plums marinated in port. The bar is one of the hottest places in Rome on Tuesday nights, when it features live jazz.

Via Tirso 30. C **06-85300692.** Main courses 12€–29€ ($10.70–$25.90). Mon–Sat noon–3pm and 8pm–midnight (bar open until 3am). Closed Aug. Bus: 3 or 19.

NEAR ANCIENT ROME
VERY EXPENSIVE
Agata e Romeo NEW ROMAN   One of the most charming places near the Vittorio Emanuele Monument is this striking duplex restaurant in turn-of-the-century Liberty style. You'll enjoy the creative cuisine of Romeo Caraccio (who manages the dining room) and his wife, Agata (who prepares her own version of sophisticated Roman food). Look for pasta garnished with broccoli and cauliflower and served in skate broth, as well as a crisp *sformato* (a type of soufflé) loaded with eggplant, parmigiano, mozzarella, and fresh Italian herbs. Sweet-tasting swordfish might be served thinly sliced as roulade and loaded with capers and olives; beans will probably be studded with savory mussels, clams, and pasta. For dessert, consider Agata's *millefoglie,* puff pastry stuffed with almonds and sweetened cream. There's a charming wine cellar with a wide choice of international and domestic wines.

Via Carlo Alberto 45. C **06-4466115.** Reservations recommended. All main courses 21€ ($18.75). AE, DC, MC, V. Mon–Sat 1–2:30pm and 8–10:30pm. Metro: Vittorio Emanuele.

EXPENSIVE
Trattoria San Teodoro *(Kids* ROMAN   At last there's a good place to eat in the former gastronomic wasteland near the Roman Forum and Palatine Hill. The helpful staff welcomes you to a shady terrace or a dimly lit dining room resting under a vaulted brick ceiling and arched alcoves. The chef handles seafood exceedingly well (try the mini baby squid sautéed with Roman

artichokes). His signature dish is seafood carpaccio made with tuna, turbot, or sea bass. Succulent meats such as medallions of veal in a nutmeg-enhanced cream sauce round out the menu at this family-friendly place. All the pastas are homemade.

Via dei Fienili 49–51. ℭ **06-6780933**. Reservations recommended. All main courses 21€ ($18.75). MC, V. Mon–Sat 12:30–3:30pm and 7:30pm–midnight. Closed Jan 15–Feb 15. Metro: Circo Massimo.

MODERATE

Alvaro al Circo Massimo ⭐ ITALIAN   Alvaro, at the edge of the Circus Maximus, is the closest thing you'll find in Rome to a genuine provincial inn, right down to the hanging corncobs and rolls of fat sausages. The antipasti and pastas are fine, the meat courses are even better, and the fresh fish is never over-cooked. Other specialties are tagliolini with mushrooms and truffles and briny roasted turbot with potatoes. Look for exotic seasonal mushrooms, including black truffles rivaling the ones you'd find in Spoleto. A basket of fresh fruit rounds out the meal. The atmosphere is comfortable and mellow.

Via dei Cerchi 53. ℭ **06-6786112**. Reservations required. Main courses 10€–17.50€ ($8.95–$15.65). AE, DC, MC, V. Tues–Sat 12:30–3:30pm and 7:30–11pm; Sun 12:30–3:30pm. Closed Aug. Metro: Circo Massimo.

Il Quadrifoglio NEAPOLITAN   In a grandiose palace, this well-managed restaurant lets you sample the flavors and herbs of Naples and southern Italy. You'll find a tempting selection of antipasti, such as anchovies, peppers, capers, onions, and breaded and fried eggplant, all garnished with fresh herbs and virgin olive oil. The pastas are made daily, usually with tomato- or oil-based sauces and always with herbs and aged cheeses. Try a zesty rice dish (one of the best is *sartù di riso*, studded with vegetables, herbs, and meats), followed by a hard-to-resist grilled octopus or a simple but savory *granatine* (meatballs, usually of veal, bound together with mozzarella). Dessert anyone? A longtime favorite is *torta caprese*, with hazelnuts and chocolate.

Via del Boschetto 19. ℭ **06-4826096**. Reservations recommended. Main courses 12.50€–16€ ($11.15–$14.30). AE, DC, MC, V. Mon–Sat 7pm–midnight. Closed Aug. Metro: Cavour.

Scoglio di Frisio NEAPOLITAN/PIZZA   This trattoria, a longtime favorite, offers a great introduction to the Neapolitan kitchen. Here you can taste a genuine plate-size Neapolitan pizza (crunchy, oozy, and excellent) with clams and mussels. Or perhaps you can start with a medley of savory stuffed vegetables and antipasti before moving on to chicken cacciatore or well-flavored tender veal scaloppine. Scoglio di Frisio also makes for an inexpensive night of hokey but still charming entertainment, as cornball "O Sole Mio" renditions and other Neapolitan songs spring forth from a guitar, mandolin, and strolling tenor. The nautical decor (in honor of the top-notch fish dishes) is complete with a high-ceiling grotto of fishing nets, crustaceans, and a miniature three-masted schooner.

Via Merulana 256. ℭ **06-4872765**. Reservations recommended. Main courses 9€–16€ ($8.05–$14.30). AE, DC, MC, V. Mon–Fri 12:30–3pm; daily 7:30–11pm. Metro: Manzoni. Bus: 16 or 714.

INEXPENSIVE

Hostaria Nerone ⭐ ROMAN/ITALIAN   Built atop the ruins of the Golden House of Nero, this trattoria is run by the energetic de Santis family, who cook, serve, and handle the large crowds of hungry locals and visitors. Opened in 1929 at the edge of the Colle Oppio Park, it contains two compact dining rooms, plus a terrace lined with flowering shrubs that offers a view over the Colosseum and the Bath of Trajan. The copious antipasti buffet represents the bounty of Italy's fields and seas. The pastas include savory spaghetti with clams and, our favorite, *pasta fagioli* (with beans). There are also grilled crayfish and swordfish and Italian sausages with polenta. Roman-style tripe is a local favorite, but maybe you'll skip it for the osso buco (braised veal shanks) with mashed potatoes and seasonal mushrooms. The wide list of some of the best Italian wines is reasonably priced.

Via Terme di Tito 96. ℂ **06-4817952.** Reservations recommended. Main courses 7.50€–12.50€ ($6.70–$11.15). AE, DC, MC, V. Mon–Sat noon–3pm and 7–11pm. Metro: Colosseo. Bus: 75, 85, 87, 117, or 175.

Ristorante al Cardello *(Value* ROMAN/ABRUZZI   Conveniently close to the Colosseum, this restaurant dates from the 1920s, when it opened in the semicellar of an 18th-century building. We always love the antipasti buffet, where the flavorful marinated vegetables reveal the bounty of the Italian harvest; at 6.25€ ($6) per person for a good serving, it's a great deal. You might follow with *bucatini* (thick spaghetti) *all'amatriciana* (with a pungent tomato sauce); tender roast lamb with potatoes, garlic, and mountain herbs; or a thick, hearty stew. A Roman food critic dining with us claimed that he always comes here when he wants to eat like a peasant (and that's a compliment).

Via del Cardello 1 (at the corner of Via Cavour). ℂ **06-4745259.** Reservations recommended. Main courses 6€–10€ ($5.35–$8.95); fixed-price menu 13.50€ ($12.05). AE, DC, MC, V. Mon–Sat noon–3pm and 7–11pm. Closed Aug. Metro: Cavour or Colosseo.

 Quick Bites

At **Dar Filettaro a Santa Barbara,** just off the southeast corner of Campo de' Fiori at Largo dei Librari 88 (ℂ **06-6864018**), you can join the line of people threading their way to the back of the bare room to order a filet of *baccalà* (salt cod), fried golden brown and served *da portar via* (wrapped in paper to eat as you take a *passeggiata,* or stroll). It costs 3€ to 9€ ($2.70–$8.05); it's closed Sunday.

Lunchtime offers you the perfect opportunity to savor Roman fast food: **pizza rustica,** by the slice (often called *pizza à taglio*), half-wrapped in waxed paper for easy carrying. Just point to the bubbling, steaming sheet with your preferred toppings behind the counter; 2€ ($1.80) buys a healthy portion of basil-and-cheese pizza *margherita. Pizza rossa* (just sauce) and *pizza con patate* (with cheese and potatoes) cost even less, as does the exquisitely simple *pizza bianca* (plain dough brushed with olive oil and sprinkled with salt and sometimes rosemary).

A *rosticceria* is a pizza à taglio with spits of chickens roasting in the window and a few pasta dishes kept warm in long trays. You can also sit down for a quick pasta or prepared meat dish steaming behind the glass counters at a **tavola calda** (literally "hot table") for about half the price of a trattoria. A Roman **bar,** though it does indeed serve liquor, is what we'd call a cafe, a place to grab a cheap *panino* (flat roll stuffed with meat, cheese, or vegetables) or *tramezzino* (large, triangular sandwiches on white bread with the crusts cut off, like giant tea sandwiches).

NEAR CAMPO DE' FIORI & THE JEWISH GHETTO

Vegetarians looking for monstrous salads (or anyone who just wants a break from all those heavy meats and starches) can find great food at the neighborhood branch of **Insalata Ricca,** Largo dei Chiavari 85 (© **06-68803656**). It's open daily 12:30 to 3:30pm and 6:45pm to 1:30am.

EXPENSIVE

Il Drappo ⚓ SARDINIAN   A favorite of the local artsy crowd, Il Drappo is on a narrow street near the Tiber and is run by a woman known to her regulars only as "Valentina." You have your choice of two tastefully decorated dining rooms festooned with patterned cotton draped from the ceiling. Flowers and candles are everywhere. Fixed-price dinners reflecting diverse choices might begin with wafer-thin *carte di musica* (sheet-music paper) topped with tomatoes, green peppers, parsley, and olive oil, and then followed with fresh spring lamb in season, fish stew made with tuna caviar, or one of the strong-flavored regional specialties. For dessert, try the *seadas* (cheese-stuffed fried cake in special dark honey). Valentina's cuisine is a marvelous change of pace from the typical Roman diet, showing an inventiveness that keeps us coming back.

Vicolo del Malpasso 9. © **06-6877365.** Reservations required. Main courses 9€–17.50€ ($8.05–$15.65); fixed-price menu 35€ ($31.25). AE, DC, MC, V. Mon–Sat 7pm–midnight. Closed Aug 15–31. Bus: 46, 62, or 64.

Piperno ⚓ ROMAN/JEWISH   This longtime favorite, opened in 1856 and now run by the Mazzarella and Boni families, celebrates the Jerusalem artichoke (which is not really an artichoke at all, by the way) and incorporates it into a number of recipes. You'll be served by a uniformed crew of hardworking waiters, whose advice and suggestions are worth considering. You might begin with aromatic *fritto misto vegetariano* (artichokes, cheese-and-rice croquettes, mozzarella, and stuffed squash blossoms) before moving on to a fish filet, veal, succulent beans, or a pasta creation. Many of the foods are fried or deep-fried, but they emerge flaky and dry, not at all greasy.

Via Monte de' Cenci 9. © **06-68806629.** Reservations recommended. Main courses 17.50€–20€ ($15.65–$17.85). AE, DC, MC, V. Tues–Sat noon–2:30pm and 8–10:30pm; Sun noon–2:30pm. Bus: 23.

MODERATE

Da Gigetto ROMAN/JEWISH   Da Gigetto is right next to the Theater of Marcellus, and old Roman columns extend practically to its doorway. Romans flock to this bustling trattoria for its special traditional dishes. None is more typical than *carciofi alla giudia,* baby-tender fried artichokes, a true delicacy. The cheese concoction called *mozzarella in carrozza* is another delight, as are the zucchini flowers stuffed with mozzarella and anchovies, our personal favorite. You could also sample shrimp sautéed in garlic and olive oil or one of Rome's best versions of saltimbocca (veal with ham).

Via del Portico d'Ottavia 21/A. © **06-6861105.** Reservations recommended. Main courses 11€–15€ ($9.80–$13.40). AE, DC, MC, V. Tues–Sun 12:30–3pm and 7:30–11pm. Closed last week of July, 1st week of Aug. Bus: 62, 64, 75, 90, or 170.

Ristorante da Pancrazio ROMAN   This place is popular as much for its archaeological interest as for its food. One of its two dining rooms is gracefully decorated in the style of an 18th-century tavern; the other occupies the premises of Pompey's ancient theater and is lined with carved capitals and bas-reliefs. In this historic setting, you can enjoy time-tested Roman food. Once a simple fishermen's dish, flavorful *risotto alla pescatora* (with seafood) enjoys a certain

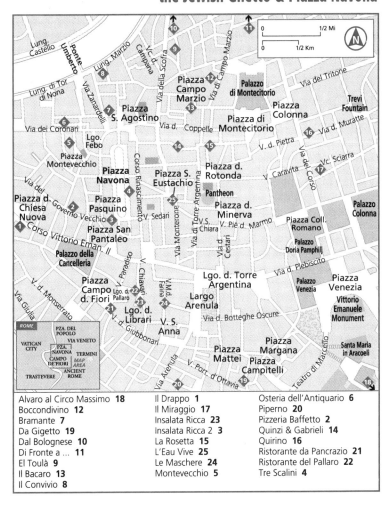

Alvaro al Circo Massimo **18**
Boccondivino **12**
Bramante **7**
Da Gigetto **19**
Dal Bolognese **10**
Di Fronte a ... **11**
El Toulà **9**
Il Bacaro **13**
Il Convivio **8**

Il Drappo **1**
Il Miraggio **17**
Insalata Ricca **23**
Insalata Ricca 2 **3**
La Rosetta **15**
L'Eau Vive **25**
Le Maschere **24**
Montevecchio **5**

Osteria dell'Antiquario **6**
Piperno **20**
Pizzeria Baffetto **2**
Quinzi & Gabrieli **14**
Quirino **16**
Ristorante da Pancrazio **21**
Ristorante del Pallaro **22**
Tre Scalini **4**

chic today, and the scampi is grilled to perfection. Two particular classics are prepared with great skill: saltimbocca and tender roast lamb with potatoes. For a superb pasta, opt for the ravioli stuffed with artichoke hearts.

Piazza del Biscione 92. ℂ **06-6861246.** Reservations recommended. Main courses 10€–20€ ($8.95–$17.85); fixed-price menu 25€ ($22.35). AE, DC, MC, V. Thurs–Tues noon–3pm and 7:30–11:15pm. Closed 2 weeks in Aug (dates vary). Bus: 46, 62, or 64.

Ristorante del Pallaro 🎇🎇 *Finds* ROMAN   The cheerful woman in white who emerges with clouds of steam from the bustling kitchen is owner Paola Fazi, who runs two simple dining rooms where value-conscious Romans go for good food at bargain prices. (She also claims—though others dispute it—that Julius Caesar was assassinated on this very site.) The fixed-price menu is the only choice and has made the place famous. Ms. Fazi prepares everything with love, as if she were feeding her extended family. As you sit down, your antipasto, the first of eight courses, appears. Then comes the pasta of the day, followed by roast veal, white meatballs, or (Fri only) dried cod, along with potatoes and eggplant. For your final courses, you're served mozzarella, cake with custard, and fruit in season. The meal also includes bread, mineral water, and half a liter of the house wine.

Largo del Pallaro 15. (C) **06-68801488.** Reservations recommended. Fixed-price menu 17.50€ ($15.65). No credit cards. Tues–Sun 1–3pm and 7:30pm–1am. Bus: 40, 46, 60, 62, or 64.

Vecchia Roma ROMAN/ITALIAN   Vecchia Roma is a charming, moderately priced trattoria in the heart of the Ghetto. Movie stars have frequented the place, sitting at the crowded tables in one of the four small dining rooms (the back room is the most popular). The owners are known for their *frutti de mare* (fruits of the sea), a selection of briny fresh seafood. The minestrone is made with fresh vegetables, and an interesting selection of antipasti, including salmon or vegetables, is always available. The pastas and risottos are savory, including linguine alla marinara with calamari—the "green" risotto with porcini mushrooms is reliably good. The chef's specialties are lamb and *spigola* (a type of white fish).

Via della Tribuna di Campitelli 18. (C) **06-6864604.** Reservations recommended. Main courses 12€–16€ ($10.70–$14.30). AE, DC. Thurs–Tues 1–3:30pm and 8–11pm. Closed 10 days in Aug. Bus: 64, 90, 90b, 97, or 774. Metro: Colosseo.

INEXPENSIVE

Le Maschere ★★ *(Finds* CALABRESE   This trattoria specializes in the fragrant, often-fiery cooking of Calabria's Costa Viola, with lots of fresh garlic and wake-up-your-mouth red peppers. In a cellar from the 1600s, decorated with artifacts of Calabria, it has enlarged its kitchen and added three dining rooms, all with fantastic medieval- and Renaissance-inspired murals. Begin with a selection of *antipasti calabresi*. For your first course, try one of the many preparations of eggplant or a pasta—perhaps with broccoli or with devilish red peppers, garlic, bread crumbs, and more than a touch of anchovy. The chef also grills meats and fresh swordfish caught off the Calabrian coast—and does so exceedingly well. If you don't want a full meal, you can visit just for pizza and beer and listen to the music at the piano bar, beginning at 8pm.

Via Monte della Farina 29 (near Largo Argentina). (C) **06-6879444.** Reservations recommended. Main courses 6€–15€ ($5.35–$13.40). AE, DC, MC, V. Tues–Sun 7:30–11pm. Closed Aug. Bus: 46, 62, or 64.

NEAR PIAZZA NAVONA & THE PANTHEON
VERY EXPENSIVE

La Rosetta ★★ SEAFOOD   You won't find any meat on the menu at this sophisticated choice near Piazza Navona, where the Riccioli family has been directing operations since the late 1960s. This is one of the leading seafood restaurants of Rome. Only Quinzi & Gabrieli (see below) does it better. An excellent start is *insalata di frutti di mare,* studded with squid, lobster, octopus, and shrimp. Menu items include just about every fish native to the Mediterranean, as well as a few from the Atlantic coast of France. There's even a sampling of lobster imported from Maine, which can be boiled with drawn butter or served Catalan style with tomatoes, red onions, and wine sauce. Hake, monkfish, and sole can be grilled or roasted in rock salt and served with potatoes. Everyone at our table agreed that the homemade spaghetti garnished with shrimp, squash blossoms, and pecorino cheese, with a drizzling of olive oil and herbs adding a savory zing, was tops.

Via della Rosetta 8. (C) **06-6861002.** Reservations recommended. Main courses 37.50€–60€ ($33.50–$53.60). AE, DC, MC, V. Mon–Fri 12:45–2:45pm and Mon–Sat 8–11:30pm. Bus: 70. Metro: Spagna.

Quinzi & Gabrieli ☆☆☆ SEAFOOD   We've never found better or fresher seafood than what's served in this 15th-century building. Don't be put off by the rough-and-ready service; come for the great taste instead. (And be prepared to pay for the privilege because fresh seafood is extremely expensive in Rome.) Alberto Quinzi and Enrico Gabrieli have earned their reputation on their simply cooked and presented fresh fish (heavy sauces aren't used to disguise old fish), such as sea urchin, octopus, sole, and red mullet. In fact, the restaurant is known for its raw seafood, including a delicate carpaccio of swordfish, sea bass, and deep-sea shrimp. The house specialty is spaghetti with lobster. Sometimes the headwaiters will prepare wriggling crab or scampi on the grill right before you. In summer, French doors lead to a small dining terrace.

Via delle Coppelle 5–6, 00185 Roma. © **06-6879389.** Reservation required as far in advance as possible. Main courses 25€–40€ ($22.35–$35.70). AE, DC, MC, V. Mon–Sat 7:30–11:30pm. Closed Aug. Bus: 44, 46, 55, 60, 61, 62, 64, or 65.

EXPENSIVE

Il Convivio ☆ ROMAN/INTERNATIONAL   This is one of the most acclaimed restaurants in Rome, and one of the very few to be granted a coveted Michelin star. Its 16th-century building is a classic setting in pristine white with accents of wood. The Troiano brothers turn out an inspired cuisine based on the best and freshest ingredients at the market. Their menu is seasonally adjusted to take advantage of what's good during any month. Start with their giant shrimp tossed with fresh greens. Among the pasta selections, their gnocchi stuffed with zucchini and dribbled with a well-seasoned seafood sauce is fabulous, as is one of the chef's specialties called *petto di faraona* (stuffed chicken spiced up with fresh olives).

Vicolo dei Soldati 31. © **06-6869432.** Reservations required. All main courses 24.50€ ($21.90). AE, DC, MC, V. Mon 8–11pm; Tues–Sat 1–2:30pm and 8–11pm. Bus: 40 and 64.

MODERATE

Bramante ROMAN   In an exquisite 18th-century structure on a cobblestone street behind Piazza Navona, this cafe-restaurant opens onto a delightful small square of vine-draped taverns. Behind the ivy-covered facade, the interior is completely hand-painted; white candles illuminate the marble bar, making for a cozy, inviting atmosphere. The owner, Mr. Giuseppe, tries to help visitors appreciate Italian food and traditions, and succeeds admirably. Almost all his dishes are handmade, and the cooks use only the freshest ingredients, such as parmigiano, fresh vegetables, and extra-virgin olive oil. Recipes are simple but rich in Mediterranean flavor. Try wonderful pastas made with fresh tomato sauce, garlic, and pasta, or opt for something heavier, such as braised beef or tender grilled steak flavored with herbs and served with potatoes.

Via della Pace 25. © **06-68803916.** Reservations recommended. Main courses 12.50€–16€ ($11.15–$14.30). AE, DC, MC, V. Mon–Sat 5pm–1am; Sun noon–1am. Closed Dec 24. Bus: 44, 46, 55, 60, 61, 62, 64, or 65.

L'Eau Vive ☆ *Finds* FRENCH/INTERNATIONAL   Here you'll find an elegant dining experience, with unique food and atmosphere. Fine French cuisine and a daily exotic dish are prepared and served by a lay sisterhood of missionary Christians from five continents who dress in traditional costumes. Nonsmokers can skip the plain stuccoed vaulting downstairs and head to the 17th-century Palazzo Lantante della Rovere, where the high ceilings are gorgeously frescoed. Pope John Paul II dined here when he was archbishop of Krakow, and today some jet-setters have adopted it as their favorite spot. You'll never know until you arrive what the dishes for the evening will be. On previous occasions we've enjoyed beef filet flambé with cognac, toasted goat cheese coated with mustard and almond slivers, and duck filet in Grand Marnier sauce with puff-fried potatoes. The homemade patés are always flavorful. At 10pm, when most customers are finished with dinner, the recorded classical music is interrupted so that the sisters can sing the "Ave Maria of Lourdes," and some evenings they interpret a short Bible story in ballet.

Via Monterone 85. ℂ **06-68801095**. Reservations recommended. Main courses 7.50€–19€ ($6.70–$16.95); fixed-price menus 7.50€ ($6.70), 11€ ($9.80), 15€ ($13.40), and 25€ ($22.35). AE, MC, V. Mon–Sat 12:30–2:30pm and 8–10:30pm. Closed Aug 1–20. Bus: 46, 62, 64, 70, or 115.

Montevecchio ROMAN/ITALIAN   To find this place, you have to negotiate the winding streets of one of Rome's most confusing neighborhoods, near Piazza Navona. The heavily curtained restaurant on this Renaissance piazza is where both Raphael and Bramante had studios and where Lucrezia Borgia spun many of her intrigues. The entrance opens onto a high-ceilinged room filled with country-style decorations and bottles of wine. Your meal might begin with a strudel of porcini mushrooms followed by the invariably good pasta of the day, perhaps a *bombolotti* succulently stuffed with prosciutto and spinach. Then you might choose roebuck with polenta, roast Sardinian goat, or veal with salmon mousse. Each of these dishes is prepared with flair and technique, and the food takes advantage of the region's bounty.

Piazza Montevecchio 22A. ℂ **06-6861319**. Reservations required. Main courses 18€–20€ ($16.05–$17.85). AE, MC, V. Tues–Sun 7:30pm–midnight. Closed Aug 10–25 and Jan 1–10. Bus: 60 or 64. Metro: Spagna.

Osteria dell'Antiquario 🍴 *(Finds* INTERNATIONAL/ROMAN   This virtually undiscovered osteria enjoys a good location a few blocks down the Via dei Coronari as you leave the Piazza Navona and head toward St. Peter's. In a stone-built stable from the 1500s, this restaurant has three dining rooms used in winter. In nice weather, try to get an outdoor table on the terrace; shaded by umbrellas, they face a view of the Palazzo Lancillotti. We like to begin with a delectable appetizer of sautéed shellfish (usually mussels and clams), but you might opt for the risotto with porcini mushrooms. For a main course, you can go experimental with the filet of ostrich covered by a slice of ham and grated Parmesan, or opt for shellfish flavored with saffron. The fish soup with fried bread is excellent, as is an array of freshly made soups and pastas. This is dining in the classic Roman style.

Piazzetta di S. Simeone 26/27, Via dei Coronari. ℂ **06-6879694**. Reservations recommended. Main courses 10€–22.50€ ($8.95–$20.10). AE, DC, MC, V. Tues–Sat 12:30–2:30pm; Mon–Sat 8–11pm. Closed 15 days in mid-Aug, Christmas, and Jan 1–15. Bus: 70, 87, or 90.

Quirino ROMAN/ITALIAN/SICILIAN   Quirino is a good place to dine after you've tossed your coin into the Trevi. The atmosphere is typical Italian, with hanging Chianti bottles, a beamed ceiling, and muraled walls. We're fond of the mixed fry of tiny shrimp and squid rings, and the vegetarian pastas are prepared only with the freshest ingredients. The regular pasta dishes are fabulous, especially our favorite: homemade pasta with baby clams and porcini mushrooms. A variety of fresh and tasty fish is always available and always grilled to perfection. For dessert, try the yummy chestnut ice cream with hot chocolate sauce or the homemade cannoli.

Via delle Muratte 84. ℂ **06-6794108**. Reservations recommended. Main courses 10€–17.50€ ($8.95–$15.65); fish dishes 12.50€–15€ ($11.15–$13.40). AE, MC, V. Mon–Sat 12:30–3:30pm and 7–11pm. Closed 3 weeks in Aug. Metro: Barberini, Spagna, or Colosseo.

Tre Scalini ROMAN/ITALIAN   Opened in 1882, this is the most famous restaurant on Piazza Navona—a landmark for ice cream as well as for more substantial meals. Yes, it's crawling with tourists; but its waiters are a lot friendlier and more helpful than those at the nearby Passetto, and the setting can't be beat. The cozy bar on the upper floor offers a view over the piazza, but most visitors opt for the ground-floor cafe or restaurant. During warm weather, try to snag a table on the piazza, where the people-watching is extraordinary.

The Lombard specialty of risotto with porcini mushrooms is excellent, the carpaccio of sea bass is worthy of a fine restaurant in Paris, and the roast duck with prosciutto wins many a devoted fan. One cook confided to us, "I cook dishes to make people love me." If that's the case, try his saltimbocca (veal with ham) and roast lamb Roman style—and you'll fall hard. No one will object if you order just a pasta and salad. The famous tartufo (ice cream coated with bittersweet chocolate, cherries, and whipped cream) makes a fantastic dessert.

Piazza Navona 30. ✆ **06-6879148.** Reservations recommended. Main courses 12€–17.50€ ($10.70–$15.65). AE, DC, MC, V. Thurs–Tues noon–3pm and 7–11pm. Closed Dec–Feb. Bus: 70, 87, or 90.

INEXPENSIVE

Il Miraggio ROMAN/SARDINIAN/SEAFOOD   You might want to escape the roar of traffic along Via del Corso by ducking into this informal spot on a crooked side street (about midway between Piazza Venezia and Piazza Colonna). It's a cozy neighborhood setting with rich and savory flavor in every dish. The risotto with scampi or the fettuccine with porcini mushrooms will have you begging for more. Some dishes are classic, such as roast lamb with potatoes, but others are more inventive, such as sliced stew beef with arugula. The grilled scampi always is done to perfection, or you might prefer a steaming kettle of mussels flavored with olive oil, lemon juice, and fresh parsley. We're especially fond of the house specialty, *spaghetti alla bottarga* with roe sauce, especially if it's followed by *spigola alla vernaccia* (sea bass sautéed in butter and vernaccia wine from Tuscany). For dessert, try the typical Sardinian seadas, thin-rolled pastry filled with fresh cheese, fried, and served with honey.

Vicolo Sciarra 59. ✆ **06-6780226.** Reservations recommended. Main courses 7.50€–14€ ($6.70–$12.50). AE, MC, V. Thurs–Tues 12:30–3:30pm and 7:30–11pm. Closed Nov 8–Dec 6. Metro: Barberini. Bus: 56, 60, 62, 81, 85, 95, 160, 175, 492, or 628.

Pizzeria Baffetto 🐕 *Kids* PIZZA   Our Roman friends always take out-of-towners here when they ask for the best pizza in Rome. Arguably, Pizzaria Baffetto fills the bill and has done so for the past 80 years. Pizzas are sold as *piccolo* (small), *media* (medium), or *grande* (large). Most pizza aficionados order the *margherita,* which is the simplest version with mozzarella and a delectable tomato sauce, but a wide range of toppings is served. The chef is proud of his pizza Baffetto, the house specialty. It comes with a topping of tomato sauce, mozzarella, mushrooms, onions, sausages, roasted peppers, and eggs. The pizza crusts are delightfully thin, and the pies are served piping hot from the intense heat of the ancient ovens.

Via del Governo Vecchio 114. ✆ **06-6861617.** Reservations not accepted. Pizza 3.50€–7.50€ ($3.15–$6.70). No credit cards. Daily 6:30pm–1am. Closed last 2 weeks in Aug. Bus: 46, 62, or 64.

NEAR PIAZZA DEL POPOLO & THE SPANISH STEPS
EXPENSIVE

Boccondivino 🐕 ITALIAN   Part of the fun of this restaurant involves wandering through historic Rome to reach it. Inside, you'll find delicious food and an engaging mix of the Italian Renaissance with imperial and ancient Rome, thanks to recycled columns salvaged from ancient monuments by 16th-century builders. Modern art and a hip staff dressed in black and white serve as a tip-off, though, that the menu is completely up-to-date. Dishes vary with the seasons, but you might find fettuccine with shellfish and parsley; carpaccio of beef; various risottos, including a version with black truffles; and grilled steaks and veal. Especially intriguing is whipped codfish resting on spikes of polenta; and taglioni with cinnamon, prosciutto, and lemon. If you're a seafood lover, look for either the marinated and grilled salmon or a particularly subtle blend of roasted turbot stuffed with foie gras. Desserts feature the fresh fruits of the season, perhaps marinated pineapple or fruit-studded house-made ice creams. The restaurant's name, incidentally, translates as "divine mouthful."

Piazza in Campo Marzio 6. ℂ 06-68308626. Reservations required. Main courses 14€–22.50€ ($12.50–$20.10). Fixed-price lunch 17.50€ ($15.65). AE, DC, MC, V. Mon–Sat 12:30–3:30pm and 7:30pm–midnight. Bus: 87.

El Toulà ★★ ROMAN/VENETIAN   El Toulà, offering sophisticated haute cuisine, is the glamorous flagship of an upscale chain that has now gone international. The setting is elegant, with vaulted ceilings, large archways, and a charming bar. The impressive, always-changing menu has one section devoted to Venetian specialties, in honor of the restaurant's origins. Items include tender *fegato* (liver) *alla veneziana* (vegetable-stuffed calamari), a robust baccala (codfish mousse with polenta), and *broetto,* a fish soup made with monkfish and clams. Save room for the seasonal selection of sorbets and sherbets (the cantaloupe and fresh strawberry are celestial); you can request a mixed plate if you'd like to sample several. El Toulà usually isn't crowded at lunchtime. The wine list is extensive and varied, but hardly a bargain.

Via della Lupa 29B. ℂ 06-6873498. Reservations required for dinner. Main courses 20€–25€ ($17.85–$22.35); 5-course menu degustazione 65€ ($58.05); 4-course menu veneto 55€ ($49.10). AE, DC, MC, V. Tues–Fri noon–3pm; Mon–Sat 7:30–11pm. Closed Aug. Bus: 81, 90, 90b, 628, or 913.

MODERATE

Babington's Tea Rooms ENGLISH/MEDITERRANEAN   This is a longtime landmark. When Victoria was on the throne in 1893, an Englishwoman named Anne Mary Babington arrived in Rome and couldn't find a place for "a good cuppa." With stubborn determination, she opened her own tearooms near the foot of the Spanish Steps, and the rooms are still going strong, although the prices are terribly inflated because of its fabulous location. You can order everything from Scottish scones and Ceylon tea to a club sandwich and American coffee. Brunch is served at all hours. Pastries cost 2.50€ to 7.50€ ($2.25–$6.70); a pot of tea (dozens of varieties available) goes for 6.50€ ($5.80).

Piazza di Spagna 23. ℂ **06-6786027.** Main courses 10.50€–19.50€ ($9.40–$17.40); brunch 27.50€ ($24.55). AE, DC, DISC, MC, V. Sept–June Wed–Mon 9am–8:30pm; July–Aug Mon–Sat 9am–8:30pm. Metro: Spagna.

Dal Bolognese ★ BOLOGNESE   This is one of those rare dining spots that's chic but actually lives up to the hype with truly noteworthy food. Young actors, shapely models, artists from nearby Via Margutta, and even corporate types on expense accounts show up, trying to land one of the few sidewalk tables. To begin, we suggest *misto di pasta:* four pastas, each with a different sauce, arranged on the same plate. Another good choice would be thin slices of savory Parma ham or the delectable prosciutto and vine-ripened melon. For your main course, specialties that win hearts year after year are *lasagne verde* and *tagliatelle* *alla bolognese.* The chefs also turn out the town's most recommendable veal cut-lets bolognese topped with cheese. They're not inventive, but they're simply superb.

You might want to cap your evening by dropping into the **Rosati** cafe next door (or its competitor, the **Canova,** across the street) to enjoy one of the tempt-ing pastries.

Piazza del Popolo 1–2. ⓒ **06-3611426.** Reservations required. Main courses 14€–19€ ($12.50–$16.95). AE, DC, MC, V. Tues–Sun 12:30–3pm and 8:15pm–midnight (last dinner order at 11:15pm). Closed 20 days in Aug. Metro: Flaminio.

Di Fronte a . . . ITALIAN   After a hard morning shopping in the Piazza di Spagna area, this is an ideal spot for a lunch break. Its name (which translates as "in front of . . .") comes from the fact that the restaurant lies right in front of a stationery shop (owned by the father of the restaurant's proprietor). We prefer the dining room in the rear, with its changing exhibitions of pictures. You'll be seated at a marble table on wrought-iron benches with leather cushions. The chef prepares a tasty cuisine that is simple but good—nothing creative, but a good boost of energy to hit the stores again. Salads are very large, as are the juicy half-pound burgers. You can also order more substantial food such as succulent pastas and tender steaks. The pizza isn't bad, either. For dessert, try the *pizza blanca,* which is a pizza crust topped with chocolate cream or seasonal fruits.

Via della Croce 38. ⓒ **06-6780355.** Reservations recommended for dinner. Main courses 10€–15€ ($8.95–$13.40). AE, DC, MC, V. Tues–Sun 12:30–4pm and 7:30–11:30pm. Metro: Spagna.

Il Bacaro ⭐ ITALIAN   Unpretentious and very accommodating to foreigners, this restaurant contains only about a half-dozen tables and operates from an ivy-edged hideaway alley near Piazza di Spagna. The restaurant is well known for its fresh and tasty cheese. This was a palazzo in the 1600s, and some vestiges of the building's former grandeur remain, despite an impossibly cramped kitchen where the efforts of the staff to keep the show moving are nothing short of heroic. The offerings are time-tested and flavorful: homemade ravioli stuffed with mushrooms and parmigiano (in season), grilled beef filet with roasted pota-toes, and an unusual version of warm carpaccio of beef. What dish do we prefer year after year? Admittedly, it's an acquired taste, but it's radicchio stuffed with Gorgonzola.

Via degli Spagnoli 27, near Piazza delle Coppelle. ⓒ **06-6864110.** Reservations recommended. Main courses 12€–19€ ($10.70–$16.95). DC, MC, V. Mon–Sat 8pm–midnight. Metro: Spagna.

INEXPENSIVE

Otello alla Concordia *Kids* ROMAN   On a side street amid the glamorous boutiques near the northern edge of the Spanish Steps, this is one of Rome's most consistently reliable restaurants. A stone corridor from the street leads into the dignified Palazzo Povero. Choose a table in the arbor-covered courtyard or the cramped but convivial dining rooms. Displays of Italian bounty decorate the interior, where you're likely to rub elbows with many of the shopkeepers from the fashion district. The *spaghetti alle vongole veraci* (with clams) is excellent, as are Roman-style saltimbocca (veal with ham), *abbacchio arrosto* (roast lamb), eggplant parmigiana, a selection of grilled or sautéed fish dishes (including swordfish), and several preparations of veal.

Via della Croce 81. ⓒ **06-6791178.** Reservations recommended. Main courses 7€–14€ ($6.25–$12.50); fixed-price menu 19€ ($16.95). AE, DC, MC, V. Mon–Sat 12:30–3pm and 7:30–11pm. Closed 2 weeks in Jan. Metro: Piazza di Spagna.

NEAR VATICAN CITY

The no. 6 branch of **Insalata Ricca,** a salad-and-light-meals chain, is across from the Vatican walls at Piazza del Risorgimento 5 (✆ **06-39730387**).

VERY EXPENSIVE

Les Etoiles ✿✿ MEDITERRANEAN Les Etoiles ("The Stars") is a garden in the sky where you'll have an open window over Rome's rooftops—a 360° view of landmarks, especially the floodlit dome of St. Peter's. A flower terrace contains a trio of little towers named Michelangelo, Campidoglio, and Ottavo Colle. In summer everyone wants a table outside, but in winter almost the same view is available near the picture windows. Savor the textures and aromas of sophisticated Mediterranean cuisine with perfectly balanced flavors, perhaps choosing quail in a casserole with mushrooms and herbs, delectable artichokes stuffed with ricotta and pecorino cheeses, Venetian-style risotto with squid ink, and roast suckling lamb perfumed with mint. The creative chef is justifiably proud of his many regional dishes, and the service is refined, with an exciting French and Italian wine list.

In the Hotel Atlante Star, Via dei Bastioni 1. ✆ **06-6873233**. Reservations required. Main courses 20€–35€ ($17.85–$31.25). AE, DC, MC, V. Daily 12:30–2:30pm and 7:30–11pm. Metro: Ottaviano.

MODERATE

Cesare ROMAN/TUSCAN The area around the Vatican is not the place to go in search of great restaurants. But Cesare is a fine old-world dining room known for its deft handling of fresh ingredients. You can select your fresh fish from the refrigerated glass case at the entrance. We come here for the fresh and tender seafood salad, brimming with cuttlefish, shrimp, squid, mussels, and octopus, and dressed with olive oil, fresh parsley, and lemon. Our table was blessed with an order of *spaghetti all'amatriciana* in a spicy tomato sauce flavored with hot peppers and tiny bits of salt pork. The *saltimbocca alla romana,* that classic Roman dish, is a masterpiece as served here—butter-tender veal slices topped with prosciutto and fresh sage and sautéed in white wine. Another specialty is smoked swordfish; you can order fresh sardines and fresh anchovies if you want to go truly Roman.

Via Crescenzio 13, near Piazza Cavour. ✆ **06-6861227**. Reservations recommended. Main courses 12.50€–25€ ($11.15–$22.35). AE, DC, MC, V. June 15–Aug 7 Mon–Sat 12:30–3pm and 7–11:30pm. Off-season Tues–Sat 12:30–3pm and 7–11:30pm; Sun 12:30–3pm. Closed 3 weeks Aug. Bus: 23, 46, 49, or 62. Metro: Lepanto.

Girarrosto Toscano ✿ *Value* TUSCAN Girarrosto Toscano, situated near the Vatican, draws large crowds, so you might have to wait for a table. Under a vaulted cellar ceiling, it serves some of Rome's finest Tuscan fare. Begin by trying the enormous selection of fresh antipasti, from little meatballs and melon with savory prosciutto to *frittate* (omelets) and delectable Tuscan salami. You're then given a choice of pasta, such as creamy fettuccine. Although expensive, the delicately flavored *bistecca alla fiorentina* (grilled steak seasoned with oil, salt, and pepper) is worth every euro if you're in the mood to splurge. Fresh fish from the Adriatic is served daily. Order with care if you're on a budget; both meat and fish are priced according to weight and can run considerably higher than the prices given below.

Via Germanico 58. ✆ **06-39725717**. Reservations required. Main courses 7.50€–15€ ($6.70–$13.40). AE, DC, MC, V. Tues–Sun 12:30–3:30pm and 7:30–11pm. Metro: Ottaviano.

Ristorante Giardinaccio ITALIAN/MOLISIAN/ROMAN This popular restaurant is only a stone's throw from St. Peter's. Unusual for Rome, it offers Molisian specialties from southeastern Italy. It's rustically decorated in the country-tavern style with dark wood and exposed stone. Flaming grills provide succulent versions of quail, goat, and other dishes, but perhaps the mutton goulash would be more adventurous. You can order many pastas, including homemade *taconelle* with lamb sauce. Vegetarians will like the large self-service selection of antipasti made from market-fresh ingredients. This is robust peasant fare, a perfect introduction to the cuisine of an area rarely visited by Americans.

Via Aurelia 53. ℂ **06-631367.** Reservations recommended, especially on weekends. Main courses 9€–20€ ($8.05–$17.85); fixed-price menus 8€–20€ ($7.15–$17.85). AE, DC, MC, V. Daily 12:15–3:15pm and 7:15–11:15pm. Bus: 46, 62, or 98.

INEXPENSIVE

Hostaria dei Bastioni ROMAN This simple but well-managed restaurant is about a minute's walk from the entrance to the Vatican Museums and has been open since the 1960s. Although a warm-weather terrace doubles the size during summer, many diners prefer the inside room as an escape from the roaring traffic. The menu features the staples of Rome's culinary repertoire, including fisherman's *risotto* (a broth-simmered rice dish studded with fresh fish, usually shellfish), a vegetarian fettuccine alla bastione with orange-flavored creamy tomato sauce, an array of grilled fresh fish, and saltimbocca. The food is first-rate—and a real bargain at these prices.

Via Leone IV 29. ℂ **06-39723034.** Reservations recommended Fri–Sat. Main courses 6€–10€ ($5.35–$8.95). AE, DC, MC, V. Mon–Sat noon–3pm and 7–11:30pm. Closed July 15–Aug 1. Metro: Ottaviano.

IN TRASTEVERE
EXPENSIVE

Alberto Ciarla 🕵🕵 SEAFOOD The Ciarla, in an 1890 building set in an obscure corner of an enormous square, is Trastevere's best restaurant and one of its most expensive. You'll be greeted with a cordial reception and a lavish display of seafood on ice. A dramatically modern decor plays light against shadow for a Renaissance chiaroscuro effect. The specialties include a handful of ancient recipes subtly improved by Signor Ciarla (such as the soup of pasta and beans with seafood). Original dishes include a delectable fish in orange sauce, savory spaghetti with clams, and a full array of delicious shellfish. The sea-bass filet is prepared in at least three ways, including an award-winning version with almonds.

Piazza San Cosimato 40. ℂ **06-5818668.** Reservations required. Main courses 15€–27.50€ ($13.40–$24.55); fixed-price menus 40€–70€ ($35.70–$62.50). AE, DC, MC, V. Mon–Sat 8:30pm–12:30am. Closed 1 week in Jan and 1 week in Aug. Bus: 44, 75, 170, 280, or 718.

Sabatini 🕵 ROMAN/SEAFOOD This is a real neighborhood spot in a lively location. (You might have to wait for a table even if you have a reservation.) In summer, tables are placed on the charming piazza, and you can look across at the church's flood-lit golden frescoes. The dining room sports beamed ceilings, stenciled walls, lots of paneling, and framed oil paintings. The spaghetti with seafood is excellent, and the fresh fish and shellfish, especially grilled scampi, might tempt you as well. For a savory treat, try *pollo con peperoni,* chicken with red and green peppers. The large antipasti table is excellent, and the delicious pastas, the superb chicken and veal dishes, and the white Frascati wine or the house Chianti continue to delight year after year. (Order carefully, though; your bill can skyrocket if you choose grilled fish or the Florentine steaks.) Diners overflow into the Sabatini annex nearby at Vicolo de Santa Maria in Trastevere 18 (same phone, hours, and prices).

Piazza Santa Maria in Trastevere 13. © 06-5812026. Reservations recommended. Main courses 12€–30€ ($10.70–$26.80). AE, DC, MC, V. Daily noon–3pm and 8pm–midnight. Closed 2 weeks in Aug (dates vary). Bus: 45, 65, 170, 181, or 280.

MODERATE

La Cisterna ROMAN   If you like traditional home cooking based on the best regional ingredients, head here. La Cisterna, named for an ancient well from imperial times discovered in the cellar, lies deep in the heart of Trastevere. For more than 75 years, it has been run by the wonderful Simmi family. In good weather, you can dine at sidewalk tables. From the ovens emerge Roman-style suckling lamb that's amazingly tender and seasoned with fresh herbs and virgin olive oil. The fiery hot *rigatoni all'amatriciana* is served with red-hot peppers, or you might decide on another delectable pasta dish, *papalini romana*, wide noodles flavored with prosciutto, cheese, and eggs. The shrimp is grilled to perfection, and there's also an array of fresh fish, including flaky sea bass baked with fresh herbs.

Via della Cisterna 13. © 06-5812543. Reservations recommended. Main courses 10€–17.50€ ($8.95–$15.65). AE, DC, MC, V. Mon–Sat 7pm–1:30am. Bus: 44, 75, 170, 280, or 710.

IN TESTACCIO
MODERATE

Checchino dal 1887 ⭐ ROMAN   During the 1800s, a wine shop flourished here, selling drinks to the butchers working in the nearby slaughterhouses. In 1887, the ancestors of the restaurant's present owners began serving food too. Slaughterhouse workers in those days were paid part of their meager salaries with the *quinto quarto* (fifth quarter) of each day's slaughter (the tail, feet, intestines, and other parts not for the squeamish). Following centuries of Roman traditions, Ferminia, the wine shop's cook, somehow transformed these products into the tripe and oxtail dishes that form an integral part of the menu. Many Italian diners come here to relish the *rigatoni con pajata* (pasta with small intestines), *coda alla vaccinara* (oxtail stew), *fagioli e cotiche* (beans with intestinal fat), and other examples of *la cucina povera* (food of the poor). In winter, a succulent wild boar with dried prunes and red wine is served. Safer and possibly more appetizing is the array of salads, soups, pastas, steaks, cutlets, grills, and ice creams. The English-speaking staff is helpful, tactfully proposing alternatives if you're not ready for Roman soul food.

Via di Monte Testaccio 30. © 06-5746318. Reservations recommended. Main courses 10€–20€ ($8.95–$17.85); fixed-price menu 30€–57.50€ ($26.80–$51.35). AE, DC, MC, V. Tues–Sat 12:30–3pm and 8–11pm; Sun 12:30–3pm. June–Sept closed Sun–Mon. Metro: Pyramide. Bus: 75 from Termini Station.

THE AVENTINE & THE SOUTH
MODERATE

La Dolce Vita ROMAN/ITALIAN   This trattoria draws pilgrims on a visit to St. Paul Outside the Walls. The trattoria is separated by a bridge that crosses the Tiber away from the basilica. Its owner, Giorgio Bodoni, has recently been named president of the association of Roman restaurateurs, and, if anything, his chefs are trying harder to impress with his sudden prominence. His fish is fresher and better prepared than ever; try the paper-thin slices of marinated salmon and octopus. No one makes a better skate broth with pasta, tomato, and Roman broccoli than La Dolce Vita.

Via Lungotevere di Pietra Papa 51. © 06-5579865. Reservations recommended. Main courses 10€–17.50€ ($8.95–$15.65). DC, MC, V. Tues–Sun 7:30pm–12:30am. Closed 2 weeks in Jan. Metro: Marconi.

ON THE APPIAN WAY
MODERATE
Antica Hostaria l'Archeologia ROMAN   A short walk from the catacombs of St. Sebastian, the family-run Hostaria l'Archeologia is like an 18th-century village tavern with lots of atmosphere, strings of garlic and corn, oddments of copper hanging from the ceiling, earth-brown beams, and sienna-washed walls. In summer, you can dine in the garden out back under the wisteria. From the kitchen emerges an array of first-rate dishes, such as gnocchi with wild boar sauce and a special favorite of ours—*veal alla massenzio* (with artichokes, olives, and mushrooms). A longtime favorite is braised beef, tender chunks cooked in a Barolo wine sauce. Of special interest is the wine cellar, excavated in an ancient Roman tomb, with bottles dating from 1800. (You go through an iron gate, down some stairs, and into the underground cavern. Along the way, you can still see the holes once occupied by funeral urns.)

Via Appia Antica 139. ℭ **06-7880494.** Reservations recommended Sat–Sun. Main courses 8€–22.50€ ($7.15–$20.10). AE, DC, MC, V. Wed–Mon 12:30–3:30pm and 7:30–11pm. Bus 218 from San Giovanni or 660 from colli Albani.

IN PARIOLI
VERY EXPENSIVE
Relais Le Jardin ✶✶✶ ITALIAN/TRADITIONAL   Relais Le Jardin is one of the best places to go for both traditional and creative cuisine, and a chichi crowd with demanding palates packs it nightly. The setting is elegant, inside one of the capital's most exclusive small hotels. The service is impeccable. The pastas and soups are among the finest in town. We were particularly taken with the tonnarelli pasta with asparagus and the smoked ham with concassé tomatoes. The chef can take a dish once served only to the plebes in ancient times, such as bean soup with clams, and make it something elegant. For your main course, you can choose a delectable roast loin of lamb with artichoke romana or the tender grilled beef sirloin with hot chicory and sautéed potatoes. The chef also creates a fabulous risotto with pheasant sauce, asparagus, black truffle flakes, and a hint of fresh thyme—it gets our vote as the best risotto around.

In the Hotel Lord Byron, Via G. de Notaris 5. ℭ **06-3613041.** Reservations required. Main courses 25€–30€ ($22.35–$26.80). AE, DC, MC, V. Mon–Sat 12:30–2:30pm and 8–10:30pm. Metro: Flaminio. Bus: 19 or 52.

MODERATE
Al Ceppo ✶✶ ROMAN   Because the place is somewhat hidden (although only 2 blocks from the Villa Borghese, near Piazza Ungheria), you're likely to rub elbows with more Romans than tourists. It's a longtime favorite, and the cuisine is as good as ever. "The Log" features an open wood-stoked fireplace on which the chef roasts lamb chops, liver, and bacon to perfection. The beefsteak, which hails from Tuscany, is succulent. Other dishes that we continue to delight in are *linguine monteconero* (with clams and fresh tomatoes); savory spaghetti with peppers, fresh basil, and pecorino cheese; swordfish filet filled with grapefruit, parmigiano, pine nuts, and dry grapes; and a fish carpaccio with a green salad, onions, and green pepper. Save room for dessert, especially the apple cobbler, pear-and-almond tart, or chocolate meringue hazelnut cake.

Via Panama 2. ℭ **06-8419696.** Reservations recommended. Main courses 15€–22.50€ ($13.40–$20.10). AE, DC, MC, V. Tues–Sun 12:30–3pm and 8–11pm. Closed last 2 weeks of Aug. Bus: 4, 52, or 53.

5

Exploring Rome

Whether Rome's ancient monuments are time-blackened or newly gleaming in the wake of the city's restoration efforts for the Jubilee Year in 2000, they are a constant reminder that Rome was one of the greatest centers of Western civilization. In the heyday of the Empire, all roads led to Rome, with good reason. It was one of the first cosmopolitan cities, importing slaves, gladiators, great art, and even citizens from the far corners of the world. Despite its carnage and corruption, Rome left a legacy of law; a heritage of great art, architecture, and engineering; and an uncanny lesson in how to conquer enemies by absorbing their cultures.

But ancient Rome is only part of the spectacle. The Vatican has had a tremendous influence on making the city a tourism center. Although Vatican architects stripped down much of the city's glory, looting ancient ruins for their precious marble, they created great Renaissance treasures and even occasionally incorporated the old into the new—as Michelangelo did when turning the Baths of Diocletian into a church. And in the years that followed, Bernini adorned the city with the wonders of the baroque, especially his glorious fountains.

SUGGESTED ITINERARIES

If You Have 1 Day

One day is far too brief—after all, Rome wasn't built in a day, and you can't see it in one—but you can make the most of your limited time. You'll basically have to choose between exploring the legacy of imperial Rome or taking in St. Peter's and the Vatican. We'll describe below how to see the best of ancient Rome, and we'll talk about the Vatican in Day 2; but if you have only 1 day, it's equally viable to spend it at St. Peter's and the Vatican Museums.

If you'll be in Rome for a few days, stop by the ticket office of the Galleria Borghese to make a reservation for later.

If you've come to see ancient Rome and the glory of the Caesars, start your stroll at Michelangelo's Campidoglio, or Capitoline Hill. From here you can look out over the Roman Forum area before venturing forth to discover on your own. After this overview, walk east along the Via dei Fori Imperiali, taking in a view of the remains of the Imperial Forums, which can be seen from the street. This route leads you right to the ruins of the Colosseum. After a visit to this amphitheater, cross over to spend the rest of the day exploring the ruins of the Roman Forum and Palatine Hill to the immediate west of the Colosseum. And you can detour north of the Colosseum to look at Domus Aurea, or the "Golden House" of the emperor, Nero.

For a change of pace, stop into the church of San Pietro in Vincoli, which is near ancient Rome. Pop in quickly just to see Michelangelo's *Moses*.

After your day of sightseeing, have dinner near the Pantheon, an area that's packed with restaurants, bars, and cafes. Toss a coin in the Trevi Fountain and promise a return visit to Rome.

If You Have 2 Days

If you elected to see the Roman Forum and the Colosseum on your first day, then spend Day 2 exploring St. Peter's and the Vatican Museums. The tiny walled "city-state of the Vatican," the capital of the Catholic world, contains such a wealth of splendor that you could spend more than a day seeing it all, but most people are content to hit the highlights in 1 busy day. After exploring the treasures of St. Peter's Basilica (including climbing Michelangelo's dome), take a lunch break and then stroll over to the Vatican Museums, which boast one of the most jaw-dropping collections of art and antiquities in the world, all of it culminating in the gloriously restored Sistine Chapel. By now, you'll probably be exhausted, but if you can keep

going, take in the Castel Sant'Angelo.

Have dinner that night in a restaurant in Trastevere.

If You Have 3 Days

On the morning of Day 3, go to the Pantheon in the heart of Old Rome; then, if you were able to make a reservation, take in the Galleria Borghese and spend an hour relaxing in this beautiful park afterward. If you don't have a ticket, head instead to another of Rome's top museums (perhaps the Capitoline Museum and Palazzo dei Conservatori, if you weren't able to squeeze in a visit during your Day 1 in ancient Rome). Have dinner at a restaurant on Piazza Navona.

If You Have 4 Days

Spend your first 3 days as previously indicated. On Day 4, you might want to take in one of the museums you didn't get to earlier (consider the National Etruscan Museum or the Galleria Doria Pamphilj). Another great option is to head out the Appian Way to take in the catacombs, an outing that will take up most of the day. Squeeze in a couple of hours of shopping and strolling around the Spanish Steps.

1 St. Peter's & the Vatican

If you want to know more about the Vatican, check out its website at **www.vatican.va**.

IN VATICAN CITY

In 1929, the Lateran Treaty between Pope Pius XI and the Italian government created the **Vatican,** the world's second-smallest sovereign independent state. It has only a few hundred citizens and is protected (theoretically) by its own militia, the curiously uniformed (some say by Michelangelo) Swiss guards (a tradition dating back to the days when the Swiss, known as brave soldiers, were often hired out as mercenaries for foreign armies).

The only entrance to the Vatican for the casual visitor is through one of the glories of the Western world: Bernini's **St. Peter's Square (Piazza San Pietro).** As you stand in the huge piazza, you'll be in the arms of an ellipse partly enclosed by a majestic **Doric-pillared colonnade.** Atop it stands a gesticulating

Rome Attractions

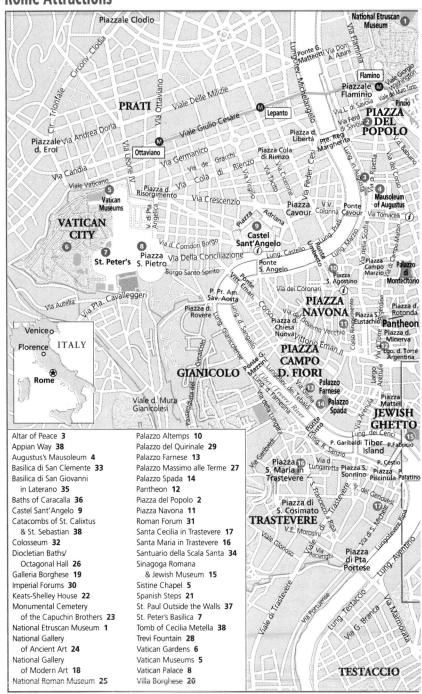

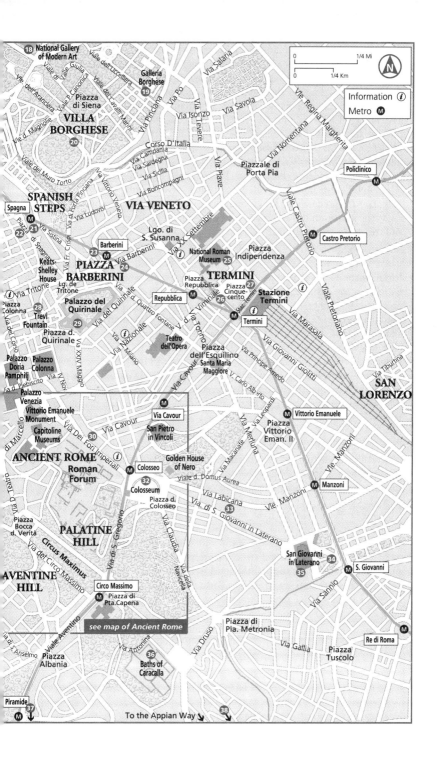

crowd of some 140 saints. Straight ahead is the facade of **St. Peter's Basilica** ✶✶✶ (Sts. Peter and Paul are represented by statues in front, with Peter carrying the keys to the kingdom), and, to the right, above the colonnade, are the dark brown buildings of the **papal apartments** and the **Vatican Museums** ✶✶✶. In the center of the square is an **Egyptian obelisk,** brought from the ancient city of Heliopolis on the Nile delta. Flanking the obelisk are two 17th-century **fountains.** The one on the right (facing the basilica), by Carlo Maderno, who designed the facade of St. Peter's, was placed here by Bernini himself; the other is by Carlo Fontana.

On the left side of Piazza San Pietro is the **Vatican Tourist Office** (✆ **06-69884466** or 06-69884866), open Monday to Saturday 8am to 6pm. It sells maps and guides that'll help you make more sense of the riches you'll be seeing in the museums. It also accepts reservations for tours of the Vatican Gardens and tries to answer questions.

Basilica di San Pietro (St. Peter's Basilica) ✶✶✶

In ancient times, the Circus of Nero, where St. Peter is said to have been crucified, was slightly to the left of where the basilica is now located. Peter was allegedly buried here in A.D. 64 near the site of his execution, and in 324 Constantine commissioned a basilica to be built over Peter's tomb. That structure stood for more than 1,000 years, until it verged on collapse. The present basilica, mostly completed in the 1500s and 1600s, is predominantly High Renaissance and baroque. Inside, the massive scale is almost too much to absorb, showcasing some of Italy's greatest artists: Bramante, Raphael, Michelangelo, and Maderno. In a church of such grandeur—overwhelming in its detail of gilt, marble, and mosaic—you can't expect much subtlety. It's meant to be overpowering.

In the nave on the right (the first chapel) stands one of the Vatican's greatest treasures: Michelangelo's exquisite *Pietà* ✶✶✶, created while the master was still in his early 20s but clearly showing his genius for capturing the human form. (The sculpture has been kept behind reinforced glass since a madman's act of vandalism in the 1970s.) Note the incredibly lifelike folds of Mary's robes and her youthful features (although she would've been middle-aged at the time of the Crucifixion, Michelangelo portrayed her as a young woman to convey her purity).

Much farther on, in the right wing of the transept near the Chapel of St. Michael, rests Canova's neoclassic **sculpture of Pope Clement XIII** ✶✶. The truly devout stop to kiss the feet of the 13th-century **bronze of St. Peter** ✶, attributed to Arnolfo di Cambio (at the far reaches of the nave, against a corner pillar on the right). Under Michelangelo's dome is the celebrated twisty-columned **baldacchino** ✶✶ (1524), by Bernini, resting over the papal altar. The 96-foot-high ultrafancy canopy was created in part, so it's said, from bronze stripped from the Pantheon, although that's up for debate.

⌐ *Tips* **A St. Peter's Warning**

St. Peter's has a strict dress code: no shorts, no skirts above the knee, and no bare shoulders. *You will not be let in if you don't come dressed appropriately.* In a pinch, men and women alike can buy a big, cheap scarf from a nearby souvenir stand and wrap it around their legs as a long skirt or throw it over their shoulders as a shawl. Taking photographs inside is also prohibited.

The Vatican

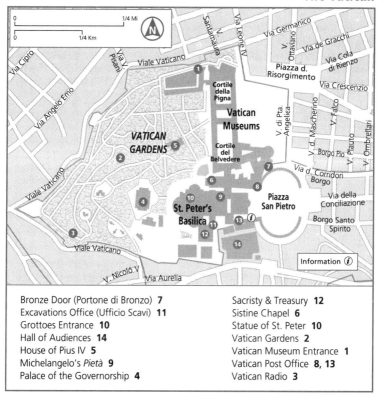

Bronze Door (Portone di Bronzo) 7	Sacristy & Treasury 12
Excavations Office (Ufficio Scavi) 11	Sistine Chapel 6
Grottoes Entrance 10	Statue of St. Peter 10
Hall of Audiences 14	Vatican Gardens 2
House of Pius IV 5	Vatican Museum Entrance 1
Michelangelo's *Pietà* 9	Vatican Post Office 8, 13
Palace of the Governorship 4	Vatican Radio 3

In addition, you can visit the **treasury** ⚘, which is filled with jewel-studded chalices, reliquaries, and copes. One robe worn by Pius XII strikes a simple note in these halls of elegance. The sacristy contains a **Historical Museum (Museo Storico)** ⚘ displaying Vatican treasures, including the large 1400s bronze tomb of Pope Sixtus V by Antonio Pollaiuolo and several antique chalices.

You can also head downstairs to the **Vatican grottoes** ⚘⚘, with their tombs of the popes, both ancient and modern (Pope John XXIII gets the most adulation). Behind a wall of glass is what's assumed to be the tomb of St. Peter himself.

To go even farther down, to the **necropolis vaticana** ⚘⚘, the area around St. Peter's tomb, you must apply in writing 3 weeks beforehand to the **excavations office.** Apply in advance at the Ufficio Scavi (✆ **06-69885318**), through the arch to the left of the stairs up the basilica. You specify your name, the number in your party, your language, and dates you'd like to visit. They'll notify you by phone of your admission date and time. For 8.50€ ($7.60), you'll take a guided tour of the tombs that were excavated in the 1940s, 7m (23 ft.) beneath the church floor. For details, check **www.vatican.va**.

After you leave the grottoes, you'll find yourself in a courtyard and ticket line for the grandest sight: the climb to **Michelangelo's dome** ⚘⚘⚘, about 114m (375 ft.) high. You can walk up all the steps or take the elevator as far as it goes. The elevator saves you 171 steps, and you'll *still* have 320 to go after getting off.

After you've made it to the top, you'll have an astounding view over the rooftops of Rome and even the Vatican Gardens and papal apartments—a photo op, if ever there was one.

Piazza San Pietro. ⓒ **06-69884466** or 06-69881662 (for information on celebrations). Basilica (including grottoes) free. Guided tour of excavations around St. Peter's tomb 8.75€ ($7.80); children younger than 15 are not admitted. Stairs to the dome 3.50€ ($3.15); elevator to the dome 4€ ($3.55); Sacristy (with Historical Museum) 4€ ($3.55). Basilica (including the sacristy and treasury) Oct–Mar daily 9am–5:15pm; Apr–Sept daily 9am–6:15pm. Grottoes daily 8am–5pm. Dome Oct–Mar daily 8am–5pm; Apr–Sept 8am–6pm. Bus: 46. Metro: Ottaviano/San Pietro, then a long stroll.

Vatican Museums (Musei Vaticani) & the Sistine Chapel (Cappella Sistina) ★★★

The Vatican Museums boast one of the world's greatest art collections. It's a gigantic repository of treasures from antiquity and the Renaissance, all housed in a labyrinthine series of lavishly adorned palaces, apartments, and galleries leading you to the real gem: the Sistine Chapel. The Vatican Museums occupy a part of the papal palaces built from the 1200s onward. From the former papal private apartments, the museums were created over a period of time to display the vast treasure trove of art acquired by the Vatican.

You'll climb a magnificent spiral ramp to get to the ticket windows. After you're admitted, you can choose your route through the museum from **four color-coded itineraries** (A, B, C, D) according to the time you have (1½–5 hr.) and your interests. You determine your choice by consulting large-size panels on the wall and then following the letter/color of your choice. All four itineraries culminate in the Sistine Chapel. Obviously, 1, 2, or even 20 trips will not be enough to see the wealth of the Vatican, much less to digest it. With that in mind, we've previewed only a representative sampling of the masterpieces on display (in alphabetical order).

Borgia Apartments ★: Frescoed with biblical scenes by Pinturicchio of Umbria and his assistants, these rooms were designed for Pope Alexander VI (the infamous Borgia pope). They may be badly lit, but they boast great splendor and style. At the end of the Raphael Rooms (see below) is the Chapel of Nicholas V, an intimate room frescoed by the Dominican monk Fra Angelico, the most saintly of all Italian painters.

Chiaramonti Museum: Founded by Pope Pius VII, also known as Chiaramonti, the museum includes the *Corridoio* (Corridor), the Galleria Lapidaria, and the *Braccio Nuovo* (New Side). The Corridor hosts an exposition of more than 800 Greek-Roman works, including statues, reliefs, and sarcophagi. In the Galleria Lapidaria are about 5,000 Christian and pagan inscriptions. You'll find a dazzling array of Roman sculpture and copies of Greek originals in these galleries. In the Braccio Nuovo, built as an extension of the Chiaramonti, you can admire *The Nile* ★, a magnificent reproduction of a long-lost Hellenistic original and one of the most remarkable pieces of sculpture from antiquity. The imposing statue of Augustus of Prima Porta presents him as a regal commander.

Collection of Modern Religious Art: This museum, opened in 1973, represents American artists' first invasion of the Vatican. Of the 55 rooms, at least 12 are devoted to American artists. All the works chosen were judged on their "spiritual and religious values." Among the American works is Leonard Baskin's 5-foot bronze sculpture of *Isaac*. Modern Italian artists such as De Chirico and Manzù are also displayed, and there's a special room for the paintings of the Frenchman Georges Rouault. You'll also see works by Picasso, Gauguin, Gottuso, Chagall, Henry Moore, Kandinsky, and others.

⌒ **Tips** **Buy the Book**

In the Vatican Museums you'll find many overpacked galleries and few labels on the works. At the Vatican Tourist Office (mentioned earlier), you can buy a detailed guide that'll help you make more sense of the incredible riches you'll be seeing here.

Egyptian-Gregorian Museum: Experience the grandeur of the pharaohs by studying sarcophagi, mummies, statues of goddesses, vases, jewelry, sculptured pink-granite statues, and hieroglyphics.

Etruscan-Gregorian Museum 🔆: This was founded by Gregory XIV in 1837 and then enriched year after year, becoming one of the most important and complete collections of Etruscan art. With sarcophagi, a chariot, bronzes, urns, jewelry, and terra-cotta vases, this gallery affords remarkable insights into an ancient civilization. One of the most acclaimed exhibits is the Regolini-Galassi tomb, unearthed in the 19th century at Cerveteri. It shares top honors with the *Mars of Todi,* a bronze sculpture probably dating from the 5th century B.C.

Ethnological Museum: This is an assemblage of works of art and objects of cultural significance from all over the world. The principal route is a half-mile walk through 25 geographical sections, displaying thousands of objects covering 3,000 years of world history. The section devoted to China is especially interesting.

Historical Museum: This museum tells the history of the Vatican. It exhibits arms, uniforms, and armor, some dating from the early Renaissance. The carriages displayed are those used by the popes and cardinals in religious processions.

Pinacoteca (Picture Gallery) 🔆🔆🔆: The Pinacoteca houses paintings and tapestries from the 11th to the 19th centuries. As you pass through room 1, note the oldest picture at the Vatican, a keyhole-shaped wood panel of the *Last Judgment* from the 11th century. In room 2 is one of the finest pieces—the *Stefaneschi Triptych* (six panels) by Giotto and his assistants. Bernardo Daddi's masterpiece of early Italian Renaissance art, *Madonna del Magnificat,* is also here. And you'll see works by Fra Angelico, the 15th-century Dominican monk who distinguished himself as a miniaturist (his *Virgin with Child* is justly praised—check out the Madonna's microscopic eyes).

In the **Raphael salon** 🔆🔆🔆 (room 8), you can view three paintings by the Renaissance giant himself: the *Coronation of the Virgin,* the *Virgin of Foligno,* and the massive *Transfiguration* (completed shortly before his death). There are also eight tapestries made by Flemish weavers from cartoons by Raphael. In room 9, seek out Leonardo da Vinci's masterful but uncompleted **St. Jerome with the Lion** 🔆🔆, as well as Giovanni Bellini's *Pietà* and one of Titian's greatest works, the *Virgin of Frari.* Finally, in room 10, feast your eyes on one of the masterpieces of the baroque, Caravaggio's **Deposition from the Cross** 🔆🔆.

Pio Clementino Museum 🔆🔆🔆: Here you'll find Greek and Roman sculptures, many of which are immediately recognizable. The rippling muscles of the **Belvedere Torso** 🔆🔆🔆, a partially preserved Greek statue (1st c. B.C.) much admired by the artists of the Renaissance, especially Michelangelo, reveal an intricate knowledge of the human body. In the rotunda is a large gilded bronze of *Hercules* from the late 2nd century B.C. Other major sculptures are under porticoes opening onto the Belvedere courtyard. From the 1st century B.C., one sculpture shows **Laocoön** 🔆🔆🔆 and his two sons locked in an eternal struggle with the serpents. The incomparable ***Apollo Belvedere*** ✶✶✶ (a late Roman reproduction of an authentic Greek work from the 4th c. B.C.) has become the symbol of classic male beauty, rivaling Michelangelo's *David.*

Raphael Rooms ✶✶: While still a young man, Raphael was given one of the greatest assignments of his short life: to decorate a series of rooms in the apartments of Pope Julius II. The decoration was carried out by Raphael and his workshop from 1508 to 1524. In these works, Raphael achieves the Renaissance aim of blending classic beauty with realism. In the first chamber, the Stanza dell'Incendio, you'll see much of the work of Raphael's pupils but little of the master—except in the fresco across from the window. The figure of the partially draped Aeneas rescuing his father (to the left of the fresco) is sometimes attributed to Raphael, as is the surprised woman with a jug balanced on her head to the right.

Raphael reigns supreme in the next and most important salon, the Stanza della Segnatura, the first room decorated by the artist, where you'll find the majestic ***School of Athens*** ✶✶✶, one of his best-known works, depicting such philosophers from the ages as Aristotle, Plato, and Socrates. Many of the figures are actually portraits of some of the greatest artists of the Renaissance, including Bramante (on the right as Euclid, bent over and balding as he draws on a chalkboard), Leonardo da Vinci (as Plato, the bearded man in the center pointing heavenward), and even Raphael himself (looking out at you from the lower-right corner). While he was painting this masterpiece, Raphael stopped work to walk down the hall for the unveiling of Michelangelo's newly finished Sistine Chapel ceiling. He was so impressed that he returned to his *School of Athens* and added to his design a sulking Michelangelo sitting on the steps. Another well-known masterpiece here is the *Disputa del Sacramento.*

The *Stanza d'Eliodoro,* also by the master, manages to flatter Raphael's papal patrons (Julius II and Leo X) without compromising his art (although one rather fanciful fresco depicts the pope driving Attila from Rome). Finally, there's the *Sala di Constantino,* which was completed by his students after Raphael's death. The loggia, frescoed with more than 50 scenes from the Bible, was designed by Raphael, but the actual work was done by his loyal students.

Sistine Chapel ✶✶✶: Michelangelo considered himself a sculptor, not a painter. While in his 30s, he was commanded by Julius II to stop work on the pope's own tomb and to devote his considerable talents to painting ceiling frescoes (an art form of which the Florentine master was contemptuous). Michelangelo labored for 4 years (1508–12) over this epic project, which was so physically taxing that it permanently damaged his eyesight. All during the task, he had to contend with the pope's incessant urgings to hurry up; at one point, Julius threatened to topple Michelangelo from the scaffolding—or so Vasari relates in his *Lives of the Artists.*

It's ironic that a project undertaken against the artist's wishes would form his most enduring legend. Glorifying the human body as only a sculptor could, Michelangelo painted nine panels, taken from the pages of Genesis, and surrounded them with prophets and sibyls. The most notable panels detail the expulsion of Adam and Eve from the Garden of Eden and the creation of man; you'll recognize the image of God's outstretched hand as it imbues Adam with spirit. (You might want to bring along binoculars so you can see the details better.)

The Florentine master was in his 60s when he began the masterly ***Last Judgment*** ✶✶✶ on the altar wall. Again working against his wishes, Michelangelo presented a more jaundiced view of people and their fate; God sits in judgment and sinners are plunged into the mouth of hell. A master of ceremonies under Paul III, Monsignor Biagio da Cesena, protested to the pope about the "shameless nudes" painted by Michelangelo. Michelangelo showed that he wasn't above petty revenge by painting the prude with the ears of a jackass in hell. When Biagio complained to the pope, Paul III maintained that he had no jurisdiction in hell. However, Daniele de Volterra was summoned to drape clothing over some of the bare figures, thus earning for himself a dubious distinction as a haberdasher.

On the side walls are frescoes by other Renaissance masters, such as Botticelli, Perugino, Signorelli, Pinturicchio, Roselli, and Ghirlandaio, but because they must compete unfairly with the artistry of Michelangelo, they're virtually ignored by most visitors.

The restoration of the Sistine Chapel in the 1990s touched off a worldwide debate among art historians. The chapel was on the verge of collapse, from both its age and the weather, and restoration took years, as restorers used advanced computer analyses in their painstaking and controversial work. They reattached the fresco and repaired the ceiling, ridding the frescoes of their dark and shadowy look. Critics claim that in addition to removing centuries of dirt and grime—and several of the added "modesty" drapes—the restorers removed a vital second layer of paint as well. Purists argue that many of the restored figures seem flat compared with the originals, which had more shadow and detail. Others have hailed the project for saving Michelangelo's masterpiece for future generations to appreciate and for revealing the vibrancy of his color palette.

Vatican Library ✦   The library is richly decorated, with frescos created by a team of Mannerist painters commissioned by Sixtus V.

Vatican City, Viale Vaticano (a long walk around the Vatican walls from St. Peter's Square). ℂ 06-69884341. Admission 10€ ($8.95); free for everyone the last Sun of each month (be ready for a crowd). Mid-Mar to late Oct Mon–Fri 8:45am–3:45pm; Sat and last Sun of the month 8:45am–1:45pm. Off-season Mon–Sat and last Sun of the month 8:45am–1:45pm. Closed all national and religious holidays (except Easter week) and Aug 15–16. Metro: Ottaviano/San Pietro, then a long walk.

Vatican Gardens ✦   Separating the Vatican from the secular world on the north and west are 58 acres of lush gardens filled with winding paths, brilliantly colored flowers, groves of massive oaks, and ancient fountains and pools. In the midst of this pastoral setting is a small summer house, Villa Pia, built for Pope Pius IV in 1560 by Pirro Ligorio. The gardens contain medieval fortifications from the 9th century to the present. Water spouts profusely from a variety of fountains.

To make a reservation to visit the Vatican Gardens, send a fax to **06-69885100.** Once the reservation is accepted, you must go to the Vatican information office (at Piazza San Pietro, on the left side looking at the facade of St. Peter's) and pick up the tickets 2 or 3 days before your visit. Tours of the gardens are Monday, Tuesday, Thursday, Friday, and Saturday at 10am; they last for 2 hours, and the first half hour is by bus. The cost of the tour is 9€ ($8.05). For further information, contact the **Vatican Tourism Office** (ℂ **06-69884466** or 06-69884866).

North and west of the Vatican. See previous paragraph for tour information.

NEAR VATICAN CITY

Castel Sant'Angelo ✦   This overpowering castle on the Tiber was built in the 2nd century as a tomb for Emperor Hadrian; it continued as an imperial mausoleum until the time of Caracalla. If it looks like a fortress, it should—that was its function in the Middle Ages. It was built over the Roman walls and

Papal Audiences

When the pope is in Rome, he gives a public audience every Wednesday beginning at 10:30am (sometimes at 10am in summer). It takes place in the Paul VI Hall of Audiences, although sometimes St. Peter's Basilica and St. Peter's Square are used to accommodate a large attendance. Anyone is welcome, but you must first obtain a **free ticket** from the office of the Prefecture of the Papal Household, accessible from St. Peter's Square by the Bronze Door, where the colonnade on the right (as you face the basilica) begins. The office is open Monday to Saturday 9am to 1pm. Tickets are readily available on Monday and Tuesday; sometimes you won't be able to get into the office on Wednesday morning. Occasionally, if there's enough room, you can attend without a ticket.

You can also write ahead to the **Prefecture of the Papal Household,** 00120 Città del Vaticano (*C* **06-69883114**), indicating your language, the dates of your visit, the number of people in your party, and (if possible) the hotel in Rome to which the cards should be sent the afternoon before the audience. American Catholics, armed with a letter of introduction from their parish priest, should apply to the **North American College,** Via dell'Umiltà 30, 00187 Roma (*C* **06-690011**).

At noon on Sunday, the pope speaks briefly from his study window and gives his blessing to the visitors and pilgrims gathered in St. Peter's Square. From about mid-July to mid-September, the Angelus and blessing take place at the summer residence at Castelgandolfo, some 26km (16 miles) out of Rome and accessible by metro and bus.

linked to the Vatican by an underground passage that was much used by the fleeing papacy, who escaped from unwanted visitors such as Charles V during his 1527 sack of the city. In the 14th century, it became a papal residence, enjoying various connections with Boniface IX, Nicholas V, and Julius II, patron of Michelangelo and Raphael.

But its legend rests largely on its link with Pope Alexander VI, whose mistress bore him two children (those darlings of debauchery, Cesare and Lucrezia Borgia). Even those on a rushed visit to Rome might want to budget time for a stopover here because it's a most intriguing sight, an imposing fortress that has seen more blood, treachery, and turmoil than any other left in Rome. It is Rome's chief citadel and dungeon. An audio guide is available to help you understand what you're seeing.

The highlight here is a trip through the Renaissance apartments with their coffered ceilings and lush decoration. Their walls have witnessed some of the most diabolical plots and intrigues of the High Renaissance. Later, you can go through the dank cells that once echoed with the screams of Cesare's victims of torture. The most famous figure imprisoned here was Benvenuto Cellini, the eminent sculptor/goldsmith, remembered chiefly for his candid *Autobiography.* Now an art museum, the castle halls display the history of the Roman mausoleum, along with a wide-ranging selection of ancient arms and armor. You can climb to the top terrace for another one of those dazzling views of the Eternal City.

The bumper-to-bumper cars and buses that once roared around Castel Sant'Angelo are now gone. The area around the castle has been turned into a new pedestrian zone. Visitors can now walk in peace through the landscaped section with a tree-lined avenue above the Tiber and a formal garden. In 2000, the moat under the ramparts was opened to the public for the first time. You can wander the footpaths and enjoy the new beeches providing shade in the sweltering summer.

Lungotevere Castello 50. ℂ **06-6819111.** Admission 5€ ($4.45). Tues–Sun 9am–7pm. Bus: 23, 46, 49, 62, 87, 98, 280, or 910. Metro: Ottaviano, then a long stroll.

2 The Colosseum, the Roman Forum & Highlights of Ancient Rome

THE TOP SIGHTS IN ANCIENT ROME

The Colosseum (Colosseo) ✪✪✪   Now a mere shell, the Colosseum still remains the greatest architectural legacy from ancient Rome. Vespasian ordered the construction of the elliptical bowl, called the Amphitheatrum Flavium, in A.D. 72; it was inaugurated by Titus in A.D. 80 with a bloody combat, lasting many long weeks, between gladiators and wild beasts. At its peak, under the cruel Domitian, the Colosseum could seat 50,000. The Vestal Virgins from the temple screamed for blood, as more exotic animals were shipped in from the far corners of the Empire to satisfy jaded tastes (lion versus bear, two humans vs. hippopotamus). Not-so-mock naval battles were staged (the canopied Colosseum could be flooded), and the defeated combatants might have their lives spared if they put up a good fight. Many historians now believe that one of the most enduring legends about the Colosseum (that Christians were fed to the lions) is unfounded.

Long after the Colosseum ceased to be an arena to amuse sadistic Romans, it was struck by an earthquake. Centuries later it was used as a quarry, its rich marble facing stripped away to build palaces and churches. On one side, part of the original four tiers remains; the first three levels were constructed in Doric, Ionic, and Corinthian styles, respectively, to lend variety. Inside, the seats are gone, as is the wooden floor.

The Colosseum has become the turnstile for Rome's largest traffic circle, around which thousands of cars whip daily, spewing exhaust over this venerable monument. Work completed in 2002 succeeded in reinforcing the structure, as well as cleaning off a layer of grime. Other renovations now allow visitors to explore the interior more fully than ever before (see "Hail to the Gladiator," below).

Arch of Constantine ✪✪, the highly photogenic memorial next to the Colosseum, was erected by the Senate in A.D. 315 to honor Constantine's defeat of the pagan Maxentius (A.D. 306). Many of the reliefs have nothing whatsoever

---

Hail to the Gladiator

Good news for fans of the Oscar-winning smash *Gladiator:* You can now get the same center-stage view of the Colosseum that the fighters had before they met a bloody death or glory in the ring. Recent renovations now allow visitors to wander spaces under the Colosseum where elephants, lions, and wild animals from North America once waited to be hoisted up in cages to take on the gladiators.

to do with Constantine or his works, but they tell of the victories of earlier Antonine rulers (they were apparently lifted from other, long-forgotten memorials).

Historically, the arch marks a period of great change in the history of Rome and thus the history of the world. Converted to Christianity by a vision on the battlefield, Constantine ended the centuries-long persecution of the Christians (during which many devout followers of the new religion had often been put to death in a most gruesome manner). While Constantine didn't ban paganism (which survived officially until the closing of the temples more than half a century later), he espoused Christianity himself and began the inevitable development that culminated in the conquest of Rome by the Christian religion.

After visiting the Colosseum, it's convenient to head over to the recently reopened **Domus Aurea (Golden House of Nero)** on the Esquiline Hill; it faces the Colosseum and is adjacent to the Forum (see below).

Piazzale del Colosseo, Via dei Fori Imperiali. ℂ **06-7004261**. Admission 6.50€ ($5.80) all levels. Oct–Jan 15 daily 9am–3pm; Jan 16–Feb 15 daily 9am–4pm; Feb 16–Mar 17 daily 9am–4:30pm; Mar 18–Apr 16 daily 9am–5pm; Apr 17–Sept daily 9am–7pm. Guided tours in English with an archaeologist 3 times per morning on Sun and holidays 3.50€ ($3.15). Tickets to Palatine Hill also sold at box office for 5€ ($4.45).

Golden House of Nero (Domus Aurea) ⚐   "Nero's Folly" finally reopened in 1999 after a 15-year restoration. After the disastrous fire of A.D. 64 swept over Rome (it has never been proven that Nero set the fire, much less fiddled while Rome burned), the emperor seized about three-quarters of the burned-out historic core (more than 200 acres) to create in just 4 years one of the most sumptuous palaces in history. Subsequent emperors destroyed much of the golden palace, but what remains is now on view.

The area that is the Colosseum today was a central ornamental lake reflecting the glitter of the Golden House. At the entrance Nero installed a 150-foot statue of himself in the nude. In the words of Suetonius, "all parts of it were overlaid with gold and adorned with jewels and mother-of-pearl." During the Renaissance, painters such as Raphael chopped holes in the long-buried ceilings to gain admittance and were inspired by the frescoes and small "grotesques" of cornucopia and cherubs. The word *grotto* comes from this palace because the palace is believed to have been built underground. Remnants of these almost-2,000-year-old frescoes and fragments of mosaics remain. Out of the original 250 rooms, 30 are now open to the public. Some of the sculptures that survived are also on view.

Practical matters: To visit the Domus Aurea, it's recommended that you make a reservation at Centro Servizi per l'Archeologia, Via Amendola 2 (Metro: Colosseo; open Mon–Sat 9am–1pm and 2–5pm). But it's easier to book your visit before you leave home through Select Italy (ℂ **847/853-1661** in the U.S.; www.selectitaly.com). Or, once you're in Rome, call ℂ **06-4815576**, to hear a recorded message in both Italian and English that will guide you through the reservation process. The guided tours, with a guide or with audio-guides, last about 1 hour from 9am to 7pm. Visitors enter in groups of no more than 25, with gaps of 15 minutes between groups.

Of particular interest are the Hall of Hector and Andromache (*Sala di Ettore e Andromaca*), once illustrated with scenes from Homer's *Iliad;* the Hall of Achilles (*Sala di Achille*), with a gigantic shell decoration; the Hall of Ninfeo (*Sala di Ninfeo*), which once had a waterfall; and the Hall of the Gilded Vault (*Sala della Volta Dorata*), depicting satyrs raping nymphs, plus Cupid driving a chariot pulled by panthers. You'll be amazed by the beauty of the floral frescoes along the *cryptoportici* (long corridors); the longest is about 61m (200 ft.). The

The Colosseum, the Forum & Ancient Rome Attractions

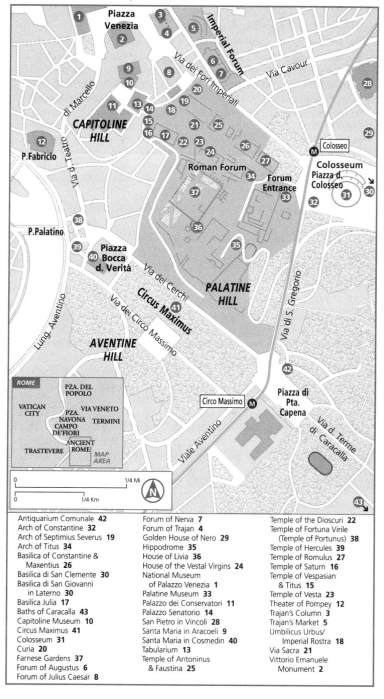

Antiquarium Comunale **42**
Arch of Constantine **32**
Arch of Septimius Severus **19**
Arch of Titus **34**
Basilica of Constantine &
  Maxentius **26**
Basilica di San Clemente **30**
Basilica di San Giovanni
  in Laterno **30**
Basilica Julia **17**
Baths of Caracalla **43**
Capitoline Museum **10**
Circus Maximus **41**
Colosseum **31**
Curia **20**
Farnese Gardens **37**
Forum of Augustus **6**
Forum of Julius Caesar **8**

Forum of Nerva **7**
Forum of Trajan **4**
Golden House of Nero **29**
Hippodrome **35**
House of Livia **36**
House of the Vestal Virgins **24**
National Museum
  of Palazzo Venezia **1**
Palatine Museum **33**
Palazzo dei Conservatori **11**
Palazzo Senatorio **14**
San Pietro in Vincoli **28**
Santa Maria in Aracoeli **9**
Santa Maria in Cosmedin **40**
Tabularium **13**
Temple of Antoninus
  & Faustina **25**

Temple of the Dioscuri **22**
Temple of Fortuna Virile
  (Temple of Portunus) **38**
Temple of Hercules **39**
Temple of Romulus **27**
Temple of Saturn **16**
Temple of Vespasian
  & Titus **15**
Temple of Vesta **23**
Theater of Pompey **12**
Trajan's Column **3**
Trajan's Market **5**
Umbilicus Urbus/
  Imperial Rostra **18**
Via Sacra **21**
Vittorio Emanuele
  Monument **2**

> ## *Tips* No More Lines
>
> The endless lines outside Italian museums and attractions are a fact of life. But new reservation services can help you avoid the wait, at least for some of the major museums.
>
> **Select Italy** offers the possibility to reserve your tickets for the Colosseum, the Palatine Forum & Museum, Palazzo Altemps, the Domus Aurea, the Galleria Borghese, and more, plus many other museums in Florence and Venice. The cost varies from 16.80€ to 26.90€ ($15–$24), depending on the museum, and several combination passes are available. Contact Select Italy at (© 847/853-1661 in the U.S.), or buy your tickets online at **www.selectitaly.com**.

most spectacular sight is the Octagonal Hall, Nero's banqueting hall, where the menu included casseroles of flamingo tongues and other rare dishes.

When Nero moved in, he shouted, "At last I can start living like a human being!"

Via della Domus Aurea. © 06-39749907. Admission 5€ ($4.45), plus 1€ (90¢) for a reservation. Wed–Mon 9am–7:45pm. Last admission 1 hr. before closing. Metro: Colosseo.

Roman Forum (Foro Romano), Palatine Hill (Palatino), and Palatine Museum (Museo Palatino) ✮✮✮   When it came to cremating Caesar, purchasing a harlot for the night, sacrificing a naked victim, or just discussing the day's events, the Roman Forum was the place to be. Traversed by the **Via Sacra (Sacred Way)** ✮, the Broadway of ancient Rome, the Forum was built in the marshy land between the Palatine and Capitoline hills, and flourished as the center of Roman life in the days of the Republic, before it gradually lost prestige to the Imperial Forums.

You'll see only ruins and fragments, an arch or two, and lots of overturned boulders, but with some imagination you can feel the rush of history here. That any semblance of the Forum remains today is miraculous because it was used for years (like the Colosseum) as a quarry. Eventually it reverted to what the Italians call a *campo vaccino* (cow pasture). But excavations in the 19th century began to bring to light one of the world's most historic spots.

By day, the columns of now-vanished temples and the stones from which long-forgotten orators spoke are mere shells. Bits of grass and weeds grow where a triumphant Caesar was once lionized. But at night, when the Forum is silent in the moonlight, it isn't difficult to imagine Vestal Virgins still guarding the sacred temple fire. (The maidens were assigned to keep the temple's sacred fire burning but to keep their own passions under control. Failure to do the latter sent them to an early grave—alive!) The best view of the Roman Forum at night is from Campidoglio or Capitoline Hill, Michelangelo's piazza from the Renaissance, which overlooks the Forum.

You can spend at least a morning wandering alone through the ruins of the Forum. If you're content with just looking at the ruins, you can do so at your leisure. But if you want the stones to have some meaning, buy a detailed plan at the gate (the temples are hard to locate otherwise).

Turn right at the bottom of the entrance slope to walk west along the old Via Sacra toward the arch. Just before it on your right is the large brick **Curia** ✮✮ built by Julius Caesar, the main seat of the Roman Senate (pop inside to see the 3rd-c. marble inlay floor).

The triumphal **Arch of Septimius Severus** 𝕽𝕽 (A.D. 203) displays time-bitten reliefs of the emperor's victories in what are today Iran and Iraq. During the Middle Ages, Rome became a provincial backwater, and frequent flooding of the nearby river helped to rapidly bury most of the Forum. This former center of the empire became a cow pasture. Some bits did still stick out above ground, including the top half of this arch, which was used to shelter a barbershop! It wasn't until the 19th century that people really became interested in excavating these ancient ruins to see what Rome in its glory must have been like.

Just to the left of the arch, you can make out the remains of a cylindrical lump of rock with some marble steps curving off it. That round stone was the **Umbilicus Urbus,** considered the center of Rome and of the entire Roman empire; and the curving steps are those of the **Imperial Rostra** 𝕽, where great orators and legislators stood to speak and the people gathered to listen. Nearby, the much-photographed trio of fluted columns with Corinthian capitals supporting a bit of architrave form the corner of the **Temple of Vespasian and Titus** 𝕽𝕽 (emperors were routinely turned into gods upon dying).

Start heading to your left toward the eight Ionic columns marking the front of the **Temple of Saturn** 𝕽𝕽 (rebuilt 42 B.C.), which housed the first treasury of Republican Rome. It was also the site of one of the Roman year's biggest annual blowout festivals, the December 17 feast of *Saturnalia,* which, after a bit of tweaking, we now celebrate as Christmas. Now turn left to start heading back east, past the worn steps and stumps of brick pillars outlining the enormous **Basilica Julia** 𝕽𝕽, built by Julius Caesar. Past it are the three Corinthian columns of the **Temple of the Dioscuri** 𝕽𝕽𝕽, dedicated to the Gemini twins, Castor and Pollux. Forming one of the most celebrated sights of the Roman Forum, a trio of columns supports an architrave fragment. The founding of this temple dates from the 5th century B.C.

Beyond the bit of curving wall that marks the site of the little round **Temple of Vesta** (rebuilt several times after fires started by the sacred flame housed within), you'll find the partially reconstructed **House of the Vestal Virgins** 𝕽𝕽 (A.D. 3rd–4th c.) against the south side of the grounds. This was the home of the consecrated young women who tended the sacred flame in the Temple of Vesta. Vestals were young girls chosen from patrician families to serve a 30-year-long priesthood. During their tenure, they were among Rome's most venerated citizens, with unique powers such as the ability to pardon condemned criminals. The cult was quite serious about the "virgin" part of the job description—if any of Vesta's earthly servants were found to have "misplaced" their virginity, the miscreant Vestal was summarily buried alive. (Her amorous accomplice was merely flogged to death.) The overgrown rectangle of their gardens has lilied goldfish ponds and is lined with broken, heavily worn statues of senior Vestals on pedestals (and, at any given time when the guards aren't looking, two to six tourists are posing as Vestal Virgins on the empty pedestals).

The path dovetails back to join Via Sacra at the entrance. Turn right and then left to enter the massive brick remains and coffered ceilings of the 4th-century **Basilica of Constantine and Maxentius** 𝕽𝕽. These were Rome's public law courts, and their architectural style was adopted by early Christians for their houses of worship (the reason so many ancient churches are called "basilicas").

Return to the path and continue toward the Colosseum, veering right to the second great surviving triumphal arch, the **Arch of Titus** 𝕽𝕽 (A.D. 81), on which one relief depicts the carrying off of treasures from Jerusalem's temple—look closely and you'll see a menorah among the booty. The war that this arch glorifies ended with the expulsion of Jews from the colonized Judea, signaling the beginning of the Jewish Diaspora throughout Europe. From here you can enter and climb the only part of the Forum's archaeological zone that still charges admission, the **Palatine Hill** (with the same hours as the Forum).

The Palatine, tradition tells us, was the spot on which the first settlers built their huts, under the direction of Romulus. In later years, the hill became a patrician residential district that attracted such citizens as Cicero. In time, however, the area was gobbled up by imperial palaces and drew a famous and infamous roster of tenants, such as Livia (some of the frescoes in the House of Livia are in miraculous condition), Tiberius, Caligula (he was murdered here by members of his Praetorian Guard), Nero, and Domitian.

Only the ruins of its former grandeur remain today, and you really need to be an archaeologist to make sense of them because they're more difficult to understand than those in the Forum. But even if you're not interested in the past, it's worth the climb for the panoramic view of both the Roman and the Imperial Forums, as well as the Capitoline Hill and the Colosseum.

The **Palatine Museum (Museo Palatino)** displays a good collection of Roman sculpture from the ongoing digs in the Palatine villas. In summer you can take guided tours in English Monday to Sunday at noon for 3€ ($2.70); call in winter to see if they're still available. If you ask the museum's custodian, he might take you to one of the nearby locked villas and let you in for a peek at surviving frescoes and stuccoes. The entire Palatine is slated for renewed excavations, so many areas might be roped off at first; but soon even more will be open to the public.

Via dei Fori Imperiali. © 06-6990110. Forum free admission; Palatine Hill 6€ ($5.35). Apr–Sept daily 9am–8pm; Oct–Mar daily 9am–3:30pm. Last admission 1 hr. before closing. Closed holidays. Metro: Colosseo. Bus: 27, 81, 85, 87, or 186.

Imperial Forums (Fori Imperiali) It was Mussolini who issued the controversial orders to cut through centuries of debris and junky buildings to carve out Via dei Fori Imperiali, thereby linking the Colosseum to the grand 19th-century monuments of Piazza Venezia. Excavations under his fascist regime began at once, and many archaeological treasures were revealed.

Begun by Julius Caesar as an answer to the overcrowding of Rome's older forums, the Imperial Forums were, at the time of their construction, flashier, bolder, and more impressive than the buildings in the Roman Forum. This site conveyed the unquestioned authority of the emperors at the height of their absolute power. On the street's north side, you'll come to a large outdoor restaurant, where Via Cavour joins the boulevard. Just beyond the small park across Via Cavour are the remains of the **Forum of Nerva,** built by the emperor whose 2-year reign (A.D. 96–98) followed that of the paranoid Domitian. You'll be struck by just how much the ground level has risen in 19 centuries. The only really recognizable remnant is a wall of the Temple of Minerva with two fine Corinthian columns. This forum was once flanked by that of Vespasian, which is now gone. It's possible to enter the Forum of Nerva from the other side, but you can see it just as well from the railing.

The next forum you approach is the **Forum of Augustus** , built before the birth of Christ to commemorate the emperor's victory over the assassins Cassius and Brutus in the Battle of Philippi (42 B.C.). Like the Forum of Nerva, you can enter this forum from the other side (cut across the wee footbridge).

Continuing along the railing, you'll see the vast semicircle of **Trajan's Market** , Via Quattro Novembre 94 (© **06-6790048**), whose teeming arcades stocked with merchandise from the far corners of the Roman world collapsed long ago, leaving only a few cats to watch after things. The shops once covered a multitude of levels, and you can still wander around many of them. In front of the perfectly proportioned facade (designed by Apollodorus of Damascus at the beginning of the 2nd c.) are the remains of a great library, and fragments of delicately colored marble floors still shine in the sun between stretches of rubble and tall grass. Trajan's Market is worth the descent below street level. To get there, follow the service road you're on until you reach the monumental Trajan's Column on your left; turn right and go up the steep flight of stairs leading to Via Nazionale. At the top, about half a block farther on the right, you'll see the entrance. It's open Tuesday to Sunday 9am to 4:30pm. Admission is 6€ ($5.35).

Before you head down through the labyrinthine passages, you might like to climb the **Tower of the Milizie** ✿, a 12th-century structure that was part of the medieval headquarters of the Knights of Rhodes. The view from the top (if it's open) is well worth the climb.

You can enter the **Forum of Trajan** ✿✿ on Via Quattro Novembre near the steps of Via Magnanapoli. Once through the tunnel, you'll emerge into the newest and most beautiful of the Imperial Forums, built between A.D. 107 and 113, and designed by Greek architect Apollodorus of Damascus (who laid out the adjoining market). There are many statue fragments and pedestals bearing still-legible inscriptions, but more interesting is the great Basilica Ulpia, whose gray marble columns rise roofless into the sky. This forum was once regarded as one of the architectural wonders of the world.

Beyond the Basilica Ulpia is **Trajan's Column** ✿✿✿, in magnificent condition, with intricate bas-relief sculpture depicting Trajan's victorious campaign (though, from your vantage point, you'll be able to see only the earliest stages). The next stop is the **Forum of Julius Caesar** ✿✿, the first of the Imperial Forums. It lies on the opposite side of Via dei Fori Imperiali. This was the site of the Roman stock exchange, as well as the Temple of Venus.

After you've seen the wonders of ancient Rome, you might continue up Via dei Fori Imperiali to **Piazza Venezia** ✿✿, where the white Brescian marble **Vittorio Emanuele Monument** dominates the scene. (You can't miss it.) Italy's most flamboyant landmark, it was built in the late 1800s to honor the first king of Italy. It has been compared to everything from a frosty wedding cake to a Victorian typewriter and has been ridiculed because of its harsh white color in a city of honey-gold tones. An eternal flame burns at the Tomb of the Unknown Soldier. The interior of the monument has been closed for many years, but you'll come to use it as a landmark as you figure your way around the city.

Via de Fori Imperiali. Free admission. Metro: Colosseo. Keep to the right side of the street.

Circus Maximus (Circo Massimo) The Circus Maximus, with its elongated oval proportions and ruined tiers of benches, still evokes the setting for *Ben-Hur* on the late show. Today a formless ruin, the once-grand circus was pilfered repeatedly by medieval and Renaissance builders in search of marble and stone. At one time, 250,000 Romans could assemble on the marble seats while the emperor observed the games from his box high on the Palatine Hill. What the Romans called a "circus" was a large arena enclosed by tiers of seats on three or four sides, used especially for sports or spectacles.

The circus lies in a valley formed by the Palatine on the left and the Aventine on the right. Next to the Colosseum, it was the most impressive structure in ancient Rome, located certainly in one of the most exclusive neighborhoods. For centuries, the pomp and ceremony of imperial chariot races filled this valley with the cheers of thousands.

When the dark days of the 5th and 6th centuries fell, the Circus Maximus seemed a symbol of the complete ruination of Rome. The last games were held in A.D. 549 on the orders of Totilla the Goth, who had seized Rome in 547 and established himself as emperor. He lived in the still-glittering ruins on the Palatine and apparently thought the chariot races in the Circus Maximus would lend credibility to his charade of an Empire. It must've been a pretty miserable show because the decimated population numbered something like 500 when Totilla recaptured the city. The Romans of these times were caught between Belisarius, the imperial general from Constantinople, and Totilla the Goth, both of whom fought bloodily for control of Rome. After the travesty of 549, the Circus Maximus was never used again, and the demand for building materials reduced it, like so much of Rome, to a great dusty field.

Between Via dei Cerchi and Via del Circo Massimo. Metro: Circo Massimo.

Capitoline Museum (Museo Capitolino) and Palazzo dei Conservatori ★★   Of Rome's seven hills, the Capitoline (Campidoglio) is the most sacred—its origins stretch way back into antiquity (an Etruscan temple to Jupiter once stood on this spot). The approach is dramatic as you climb the long, sloping steps by Michelangelo. At the top is a perfectly proportioned square, **Piazza del Campidoglio** ★★, also laid out by the Florentine artist. Michelangelo positioned the bronze equestrian statue of Marcus Aurelius in the center, but it has now been moved inside for protection from pollution (a copy was placed on the pedestal in 1997). The other steps adjoining Michelangelo's approach will take you to Santa Maria d'Aracoeli (see "Other Attractions Near Ancient Rome," below).

One side of the piazza is open; the others are bounded by the **Senatorium (Town Council),** the statuary-filled **Palace of the Conservatori (Curators),** and the **Capitoline Museum.** These museums house some of the greatest pieces of classical sculpture in the world.

The **Capitoline Museum,** built in the 17th century, was based on an architectural sketch by Michelangelo. In the first room is *The Dying Gaul* ★★, a work of majestic skill that's a copy of a Greek original dating from the 3rd century B.C. In a special gallery all her own is the *Capitoline Venus* ★★, who demurely covers herself. This statue was the symbol of feminine beauty and charm down through the centuries (also a Roman copy of a 3rd-c. B.C. Greek original). *Amore* (Cupid) and *Psyche* are up to their old tricks near the window.

The famous **equestrian statue of Marcus Aurelius** ★★, whose years in the piazza made it a victim of pollution, has recently been restored and is now kept in the museum for protection. This is the only bronze equestrian statue to have survived from ancient Rome, mainly because it was thought for centuries that the statue was that of Constantine the Great, and papal Rome respected the memory of the first Christian emperor. It's beautiful, although the perspective is rather odd. The statue is housed in a glassed-in room on the street level, the Cortile di Marforio; it's a kind of Renaissance greenhouse, surrounded by windows.

Palace of the Conservatori ★★, across the way, was also based on a Michelangelo architectural plan and is rich in classical sculpture and paintings. One of the most notable bronzes, a Greek work of incomparable beauty dating from the 1st century B.C., is *Lo Spinario* ★★★ (a little boy picking a thorn from his foot). In addition, you'll find *Lupa Capitolina* (*Capitoline*

Moments **A View to Remember a Lifetime**

Standing on Piazza del Campidoglio, walk around the right side of the
Palazzo Senatorio to a terrace overlooking the city's best panorama of
the Roman Forum, with the Palatine Hill and the Colosseum as a backdrop. At night, the Forum is dramatically floodlit and the ruins look even
more impressive and haunting.

Wolf) ★★★, a rare Etruscan bronze that could date from the 5th century B.C.
(Romulus and Remus, the legendary twins who were suckled by the wolf, were
added at a later date.) The palace also contains a *Pinacoteca* (Picture Gallery)—
mostly works from the 16th and 17th centuries. Notable canvases are Caravaggio's *Fortune-Teller* and his curious *John the Baptist; The Holy Family,* by Dosso
Dossi; *Romulus and Remus,* by Rubens; and Titian's *Baptism of Christ.* The
entrance courtyard is lined with the remains (head, hands, a foot, and a kneecap)
of an ancient colossal statue of Constantine the Great.

Piazza del Campidoglio. © **06-67102071.** Admission (to both) 6€ ($5.35). Free on last Sun of each month.
Tues–Sun 9am–7pm. Bus: 44, 81, 95, 160, 170, 715, or 780.

Baths of Caracalla (Terme di Caracalla) ★ Named for the emperor Caracalla, the baths were completed in the early 3rd century. The richness of decoration has faded, and the lushness can be judged only from the shell of brick
ruins that remain. In their heyday, they sprawled across 27 acres and could handle 1,600 bathers at one time. A circular room, the ruined caldarium for very
hot baths, had been the traditional setting for operatic performances in Rome,
until it was discovered that the ancient structure was being severely damaged.

Via delle Terme di Caracalla 52. © **06-5758626.** Admission 5€ ($4.45). Oct–Mar 1 daily 9am–4:30pm; Mar
2–Mar 30 daily 9am–5pm; Apr–Sept 31 daily 9am–6pm (every Mon 9am–1pm). Last admission 1 hr. before
closing. Closed holidays. Bus: 628.

OTHER ATTRACTIONS NEAR ANCIENT ROME

Basilica di San Clemente ★ From the Colosseum, head up Via San Giovanni in Laterano to this basilica. It isn't just another Roman church—far from
it. In this church-upon-a-church, centuries of history peel away. In the 4th century A.D., a church was built over a secular house from the 1st century, beside
which stood a pagan temple dedicated to Mithras (god of the sun). Down in the
eerie grottoes (which you can explore on your own), you'll discover well-preserved frescoes from the 9th to the 11th centuries. The Normans destroyed the
lower church, and a new one was built in the 12th century. Its chief attraction
is the bronze-orange mosaic (from that period) adorning the apse, as well as a
chapel honoring St. Catherine of Alexandria with frescoes by Masolino.

Via San Giovanni in Laterano at Piazza San Clemente, Via Labicana 95. © **06-70451018.** Basilica free; excavations 2.50€ ($2.25). Mon–Sat 9am–12:30pm and 3–6pm; Sun 10am–12:30pm and 3–6pm. Metro:
Colosseo. Bus: 85, 87, or 810.

Basilica di San Giovanni in Laterano ★ This church (not St. Peter's) is the
cathedral of the diocese of Rome, where the pope comes to celebrate Mass on
certain holidays. Built in A.D. 314 by Constantine, it has suffered the vicissitudes
of Rome, forcing it to be rebuilt many times. Only fragmented parts of the baptistry remain from the original.

The present building is characterized by its 18th-century facade by Alessandro Galilei (statues of Christ and the Apostles ring the top). A 1993 terrorist bomb caused severe damage, especially to the facade. Borromini gets the credit (some say blame) for the interior, built for Innocent X. It's said that, in the misguided attempt to redecorate, frescoes by Giotto were destroyed (remains believed to have been painted by Giotto were discovered in 1952 and are now on display against a column near the entrance on the right inner pier). In addition, look for the unusual ceiling and the sumptuous transept, and explore the 13th-century cloisters with twisted double columns. Next door, **Palazzo Laterano** (no admission) was the original home of the popes before they became voluntary "Babylonian captives" in Avignon, France, in 1309.

Across the street is the **Santuario della Scala Santa (Palace of the Holy Steps)**, Piazza San Giovanni in Laterano (© **06-7726641**). It's alleged that the 28 marble steps here (now covered with wood for preservation) were originally at Pontius Pilate's villa in Jerusalem and that Christ climbed them the day he was brought before Pilate. According to a medieval tradition, the steps were brought from Jerusalem to Rome by Constantine's mother, Helen, in 326, and they've been in this location since 1589. Today pilgrims from all over the world come here to climb the steps on their knees. This is one of the holiest sites in Christendom, although some historians say the stairs might date only to the 4th century.

Piazza San Giovanni in Laterano 4. © **06-69886433**. Basilica free; cloisters 2€ ($1.80). Summer daily 7am–6:45pm (off-season to 6pm). Metro: San Giovanni. Bus: 4, 16, 30, 85, 87, or 174.

National Museum of Palazzo Venezia (Museo Nazionale di Palazzo di Venezia)

The Palazzo Venezia, in the geographic heart of Rome near Piazza Venezia, served as the seat of the Austrian Embassy until the end of World War I. During the Fascist regime (1928–43), it was the seat of the Italian government. The balcony from which Mussolini used to speak to the people was built in the 15th century. You can now visit the rooms and halls containing oil paintings, porcelain, tapestries, ivories, and ceramics. No one particular exhibit stands out—it's the sum total that adds up to a major attraction. The State Rooms occasionally open to host temporary exhibits.

Via del Plebiscito 118. © **06-6798865**. Admission 4€ ($3.55). Tues–Sun 8:30am–7:30pm. Bus: 60, 64, or 70.

San Pietro in Vincoli (St. Peter in Chains)

This church, which has undergone recent renovations, was founded in the 5th century to house the chains that bound St. Peter in Palestine (they're preserved under glass). But the drawing card is the tomb of Pope Julius II, with one of the world's most famous sculptures: **Michelangelo's Moses**. Michelangelo was to have carved 44 magnificent figures for the tomb. That didn't happen, of course, but the pope was given a great consolation prize—a figure intended to be "minor" that's now numbered among Michelangelo's masterpieces. In the *Lives of the Artists*, Vasari wrote about the stern father symbol of Michelangelo's *Moses:* "No modern work will ever equal it in beauty, no, nor ancient either."

Piazza San Pietro in Vincoli 4A (off Via degli Annibaldi). © **06-4882865**. Free admission. Spring/summer daily 7am–12:30pm and 3:30–7pm (autumn/winter to 6pm). Metro: Colosseo or Cavour, then cross the boulevard and walk up the flight of stairs. Turn right, and you'll head into the piazza; the church will be on your left.

Santa Maria d'Aracoeli

On the Capitoline Hill, this landmark church was built for the Franciscans in the 13th century. According to legend, Augustus once ordered a temple erected on this spot, where a sibyl, with her gift of prophecy, forecast the coming of Christ. In the interior are a coffered Renaissance ceiling and a mosaic of the Virgin over the altar in the Byzantine style. If you're enough of a sleuth, you'll find a tombstone carved by the great Renaissance sculptor Donatello. The church is known for its **Bufalini Chapel,** a masterpiece by Pinturicchio, who frescoed it with scenes illustrating the life and death of St. Bernardino of Siena. He also depicted St. Francis receiving the stigmata. These frescoes are a high point in early Renaissance Roman painting. You have to climb a long flight of steep steps to reach the church, unless you're already on neighboring Piazza del Campidoglio, in which case you can cross the piazza and climb the steps on the far side of the Museo Capitolino (see above).

Piazza d'Aracoeli. ℂ **06-6798155**. Free admission. Daily 6:30am–noon and 3:30–5:30pm. Bus: 44, 46, or 75.

Santa Maria in Cosmedin   This little church was begun in the 6th century but was subsequently rebuilt, and a Romanesque campanile was added at the end of the 11th century, although its origins go back to the 3rd century. The church was destroyed several times by earthquakes or by foreign invasions, but it has always been rebuilt.

People come not for great art treasures, but to see the **"Mouth of Truth,"** a large disk under the portico. As Gregory Peck demonstrated to Audrey Hepburn in the film *Roman Holiday,* the mouth is supposed to chomp down on the hands of liars who insert their paws. (According to local legend, a former priest used to keep a scorpion in back to bite the fingers of anyone he felt was lying.) The purpose of this disk (which is not of particular artistic interest) is unclear. One hypothesis says that it was used to collect the faithful's donations to God, which were introduced through the open mouth.

Piazza della Bocca della Verità 18. ℂ **06-6781419**. Free admission. Summer daily 9am–8pm; winter daily 9am–5pm. Metro: Circo Massimo.

3 The Pantheon & Attractions Near Piazza Navona & Campo de' Fiori

THE PANTHEON & NEARBY ATTRACTIONS

The Pantheon stands on **Piazza della Rotonda,** a lively square with cafes, vendors, and great people-watching.

The Pantheon ✦✦✦   Of all ancient Rome's great buildings, only the Pantheon ("All the Gods") remains intact. It was built in 27 B.C. by Marcus Agrippa and was reconstructed by Hadrian in the early 2nd century A.D. This remarkable building, 43m (142 ft.) wide and 43m (142 ft.) high (a perfect sphere resting in a cylinder) and once ringed with white marble statues of Roman gods in its niches, is among the architectural wonders of the world because of its dome and its concept of space. Hadrian himself is credited with the basic plan, an architectural design that was unique for the time. The once-gilded dome is merely show. A real dome, a perfect, massive hemisphere of cast concrete, is supported by a solid ring wall. Before the 20th century, the dome was the biggest pile of concrete ever constructed. The ribbed dome outside is a series of almost weightless cantilevered brick. Animals were sacrificed and burned in the center, and the smoke escaped through the only means of light, the oculus, an opening at the top 5.5m (18 ft.) in diameter. Michelangelo came here to study the dome before designing the cupola of St. Peter's (whose dome is .5m [2 ft.] smaller than the Pantheon's). The walls are 7.5m (25 ft.) thick, and the bronze doors leading into the building weigh 20 tons each. About 125 years ago, Raphael's tomb was discovered here (fans still bring him flowers). Vittorio Emanuele II, king of Italy, and his successor, Umberto I, are interred here as well.

Piazza della Rotonda. © 06-68300230. Free admission. Mon–Sat 8:30am–7:30pm; Sun 9am–6pm. Bus: 46, 62, 64, 170, or 492 to Largo di Torre.

Galleria Doria Pamphilj 𝔸 This museum offers a look at what it was like to live in an 18th-century palace. It has been restored to its former splendor and expanded to include four rooms long closed to the public. It's partly leased to tenants (on the upper levels), and there are shops on the street level—but you'll overlook all this after entering the grand apartments of the Doria Pamphilj family, which traces its lineage to before the great 15th-century Genoese admiral Andrea Doria. The apartments surround the central court and gallery. The **ballroom, drawing rooms, dining rooms,** and **family chapel** are full of gilded furniture, crystal chandeliers, Renaissance tapestries, and family portraits. The **Green Room** is especially rich, with a 15th-century Tournay tapestry, paintings by Memling and Filippo Lippi, and a seminude portrait of Andrea Doria by Sebastiano del Piombo. The **Andrea Doria Room,** dedicated to the admiral and to the ship of the same name, contains a glass case with mementos of the great 1950s maritime disaster.

Skirting the central court is a **picture gallery** with a memorable collection of frescoes, paintings, and sculpture. Most important are the portrait of Innocent X, by Velázquez; *Salome,* by Titian; works by Rubens and Caravaggio; the *Bay of Naples,* by Pieter Brueghel the Elder; and a copy of Raphael's portrait of Principessa Giovanna d'Aragona de Colonna (who looks remarkably like Leonardo's *Mona Lisa*). Most of the sculpture came from the Doria country estates: marble busts of Roman emperors, bucolic nymphs, and satyrs.

Piazza del Collegio Romano 2 (off Via del Corso). © 06-6797323. Admission 7€ ($6.25) adults, 5.50€ ($4.90) students/seniors. Fri–Wed 10am–5pm. Private visits can be arranged. Metro: Barberini or Colosseo.

PIAZZA NAVONA & NEARBY ATTRACTIONS

Piazza Navona 𝔸𝔸𝔸, one of the most beautifully baroque sites in all Rome, is an ocher-colored gem, unspoiled by new buildings or traffic. Its shape results from the ruins of the Stadium of Domitian, lying underneath. Great chariot races were once held here (some rather unusual, such as the one in which the head of the winning horse was lopped off as it crossed the finish line and was then carried by runners to be offered as a sacrifice by the Vestal Virgins atop the Capitoline). In medieval times, the popes used to flood the piazza to stage mock naval encounters. Today the piazza is packed with vendors and street performers, and lined with pricey cafes where you can enjoy a cappuccino or gelato and indulge in unparalleled people-watching.

Besides the twin-towered facade of 17th-century Santa Agnes, the piazza boasts several baroque masterpieces. The best known, in the center, is Bernini's **Fountain of the Four Rivers (Fontana dei Quattro Fiumi)** 𝔸𝔸𝔸, whose four stone personifications symbolize the world's greatest rivers: the Ganges, Danube, della Plata, and Nile. It's fun to try to figure out which is which. (*Hint:* The figure with the shroud on its head is the Nile, so represented because the river's source was unknown at the time.) At the south end is the **Fountain of the Moor (Fontana del Moro),** also by Bernini. The **Fountain of Neptune (Fontana di Nettuno),** which balances that of the Moor, is a 19th-century addition; it was restored after a demented 1997 attack by two men who broke off the tail of one of its sea creatures.

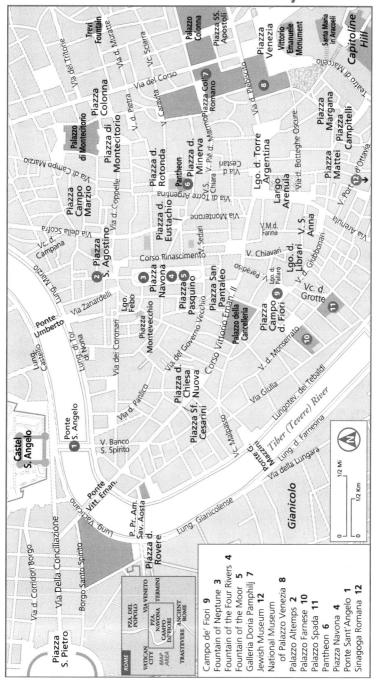

Trevi Fountain
Via del Tritone
Via d. Muratte
Via d. Sciarra
Vc. Sciarra
Palazzo Colonna
Piazza SS. Apostoli
Santa Maria in Aracoeli
Vittorio Emanuele Monument
Capitoline Hill

Via del Corso
Piazza Venezia

Palazzo di Montecitorio
Piazza di Montecitorio
Piazza Colonna
Via d. Pietra
V. Caravita
Piazza Col. Romano **7**
Via d. Plebiscito
8
Teatro di Marcello

Piazza Campo Marzio
Via di Campo Marzio
Via d. Coppelle
Piazza d. Rotonda
Pantheon **6**
Piazza d. Minerva
V. Piè di Marmo
V. d'Aracoeli
Piazza Margana
Piazza Campitelli

Vc. d. Campana
Via della Scrofa
Piazza S. Agostino **2**
Piazza d. Eustachio
V. S. Chiara
Via d. Cestari
Piazza Mattei
V. Port. d'Ottavia **12**

Lung. Marzio
V. Sediari
Via di Torre Argentina
Lgo. d. Torre Argentina
Via d. Botteghe Oscure
Via Arenula

Lgo. Febo
Corso Rinascimento
Piazza Navona **4**
Via Monterone
Largo Arenula
V.M.d. Farina
V.S. Anna

Ponte Umberto
Via Zanardelli
Piazza Pasquino **5**
Piazza San Pantaleo
V. Chiavari
Lgo. d. Librari
Vc. d. Grotte **11**

Lung. Castello
Via di Tor di Nona
Lgo. d. Pallaro
Lgo. d. Paradiso
Piazza Campo d. Fiori **9**
10

Via dei Coronari
Piazza Montevecchio
Via del Governo Vecchio
Corso Vittorio Eman. II
Palazzo della Cancelleria
V. d. Monserrato

Ponte S. Angelo **1**
Via d. Panico
Piazza Sf. Cesarini
Piazza Chiesa Nuova
Via Giulia
Via della Lungara

Castel S. Angelo
V. Banco S. Spirito
V. Malpasso
Lungotev. del Tebaldi
Lungotev. Tiber (Tevere) River

Ponte Vitt. Eman.
Lung. Vaticano
P. Pr. Am. Sav. Aosta
Piazza d. Rovere
Ponte G. Mazzini
Lung. d. Farnesina

Via d. Corridori Borgo
Via Della Conciliazione
Borgo Santo Spirito
Lung. Gianicolense
Via della Lungara
Gianicolo

Piazza S. Pietro

Campo de' Fiori **9**
Fountain of Neptune **3**
Fountain of the Four Rivers **4**
Fountain of the Moor **5**
Galleria Doria Pamphilj **7**
Jewish Museum **12**
National Museum of Palazzo Venezia **8**
Palazzo Altemps **2**
Palazzo Farnese **10**
Palazzo Spada **11**
Pantheon **6**
Piazza Navona **4**
Ponte Sant'Angelo **1**
Sinagoga Romana **12**

1/2 Mi
1/2 Km
0

Palazzo Altemps ☆   This branch of the National Roman Museum is housed in a 15th-century palace that was restored and opened to the public in 1997. It is home to the fabled Ludovisi Collection of Greek and Roman sculpture. Among the masterpieces of the Roman Renaissance, you'll find the *Ares Ludovisi*, a Roman copy of the original dated 330 B.C. and restored by Bernini during the 17th century. In the *Sala delle Storie di Mosè* is *Ludovisi's Throne*, representing the birth of Venus. The *Sala delle Feste* (the Celebrations' Hall) is dominated by a sarcophagus depicting the Romans fighting against the Ostrogoth Barbarians; this masterpiece, carved from a single block, dates back to the 2nd century A.D. and nowadays is called *Grande Ludovisi* (*Great Ludovisi*). Other outstanding art from the collection includes a copy of Phidias's celebrated *Athena*, which once stood in the Parthenon in Athens. (The Roman copy here is from the 1st c. B.C. because the original *Athena* is lost to history.) The huge *Dionysus with Satyr* is from the 2nd century A.D.

Piazza San Apollinare 44, near the Piazza Navona. (℃ 06-6833759. Admission 5€ ($4.45). Tues–Fri 9am–9pm, Sat 9am–midnight, Sun 9am–8pm. Closed Mon. Last admission 1 hr. before closing. Bus: 70, 81, 87, or 492.

CAMPO DE' FIORI & THE JEWISH GHETTO

During the 1500s, **Campo de' Fiori** ☆ was the geographic and cultural center of secular Rome, site of dozens of inns. From its center rises a statue of the severe-looking monk Giordano Bruno, whose presence is a reminder that religious heretics were occasionally burned at the stake here. Today, circled by venerable houses, the campo is the site of an **open-air food market** held Monday to Saturday from early in the morning until around noon (or whenever the food runs out).

Built from 1514 to 1589, the **Palazzo Farnese** ☆, on Piazza Farnese, was designed by Sangallo and Michelangelo, among others, and was an astronomically expensive project for the time. Its famous residents have included a 16th-century member of the Farnese family, plus Pope Paul III, Cardinal Richelieu, and the former Queen Christina of Sweden, who moved to Rome after abdicating. During the 1630s, when the heirs couldn't afford to maintain the palazzo, it became the site of the French Embassy, as it still is (it's closed to the public). For the best view of it, cut west from Via Giulia along any of the narrow streets (we recommend Via Mascherone or Via dei Farnesi).

Palazzo Spada ☆, Capo di Ferro 3 (℃ **06-6861158**), built around 1550 for Cardinal Gerolamo Capo di Ferro and later inhabited by the descendants of several other cardinals, was sold to the Italian government in the 1920s. Its richly ornate facade, covered in high-relief stucco decorations in the Mannerist style, is the finest of any building from 16th-century Rome. The State Rooms are closed, but the richly decorated courtyard and a handful of galleries of paintings are open. Admission is 5€ ($4.45) from Tuesday to Sunday 8:30am to 7:30pm. To get there, take bus no. 44, 56, 60, 65, 75, 170, or 710.

Also in this neighborhood stands the **Sinagoga Romana** (℃ **06-6840061**), open only for services. Trying to avoid all resemblance to a Christian church, the building (1874–1904) evokes Babylonian and Persian details. The synagogue was attacked by terrorists in 1982 and since then has been heavily guarded by *carabinieri* (a division of the Italian army) armed with machine guns. It houses the **Jewish Museum** (℃ **06-6840061**), open Monday to Thursday 9am to 4:30pm, Friday 9am to 1:30pm, and Sunday 9am to noon. Admission is 5€ ($4.45). Many rare and even priceless treasures are here, including a Moroccan prayer book from the early 14th century and ceremonial objects from the 17th-century Jewish Ghetto.

4 The Spanish Steps, the Trevi Fountain & Attractions Nearby

ON OR AROUND PIAZZA DI SPAGNA

The Spanish Steps ✦✦ (Scalinata di Spagna; Metro: Spagna) are filled in spring with azaleas and other flowers, flower vendors, jewelry dealers, and photographers snapping pictures of visitors. The steps and the square (Piazza di Spagna) take their names from the Spanish Embassy, which used to be headquartered here. Designed by Italian architect Francesco de Sanctis and built from 1723 to 1725, they were funded almost entirely by the French as a preface to Trinità dei Monti at the top.

The steps and the piazza below are always packed with a crowd: strolling, reading in the sun, browsing the vendors' carts, and people-watching. Near the steps, you'll also find an American Express office, public restrooms (near the Metro stop), and the most sumptuous McDonald's we've ever seen (cause for uproar among the Romans when it first opened).

Keats-Shelley House   At the foot of the Spanish Steps is this 18th-century house where John Keats died of consumption on February 23, 1821, at age 25. Since 1909, when it was bought by well-intentioned English and American literary types, it has been a working library established in honor of Keats and Percy Bysshe Shelley, who drowned off the coast of Viareggio with a copy of Keats in his pocket. Mementos range from the kitsch to the immortal. The apartment where Keats spent his last months, carefully tended by his close friend Joseph Severn, shelters a strange death mask of Keats as well as the "deadly sweat" drawing by Severn.

Piazza di Spagna 26. ✆ **06-6784235.** Admission 2.50€ ($2.25). Mon–Fri 9am–1pm and 3–6pm; Sat 11am–2pm and 3–6pm. Guided tours by appointment. Metro: Spagna.

Palazzo del Quirinale ✦✦   Until the end of World War II, this palace was the home of the king of Italy; before that, it was the residence of the pope. Despite its Renaissance origins (nearly every important architect in Italy worked on some aspect of its sprawling premises), it's rich in associations with ancient emperors and deities. The colossal statues of the Dioscuri Castor and Pollux, which now form part of the fountain in the piazza, were found in the nearby great Baths of Constantine; in 1793 Pius VI had the ancient Egyptian obelisk moved here from the Mausoleum of Augustus. The sweeping view of Rome

---

⎛ *Finds* Great Art in the Stables

Across from the Palazzo del Quirinale, the 18th-century Quirinale stables called the **Scuderie del Quirinale** or **Scuderie Papali,** via XXIV Maggio 16 (✆ **06-696270**), originally built for the pope's horses, have been transformed into an art gallery that hosts changing exhibitions. Recent exhibits have ranged from 100 masterpieces on loan from the Hermitage to Botticelli's drawings illustrating Dante's *Divine Comedy.* The stables were built on the site of the 3rd-century Temple of Serapis (some of the ruins can still be seen from the glass-enclosed stairs overlooking a private garden). The galleries are open Monday to Friday from 10am to 8pm; Saturday to Sunday 10am to 11pm. Admission is 8€ ($7.15).

from the piazza, which crowns the highest of the seven ancient hills of Rome, is itself worth the trip.

Piazza del Quirinale. No phone for visitor information; call Rome's tourist office. Free admission (but a passport or similar ID is required for entrance). Sun 9am–1pm. Metro: Barberini.

Trevi Fountain (Fontana dei Trevi) ✮✮ As you elbow your way through the summertime crowds around the Trevi Fountain, you'll find it hard to believe that this little piazza was nearly always deserted before the film *Three Coins in the Fountain* brought the stampede of tour buses. Today this newly restored gem is a must on everybody's itinerary.

Supplied by water from the Acqua Vergine aqueduct and a triumph of the baroque style, it was based on the design of Nicolo Salvi (who's said to have died of illness contracted during his supervision of the project) and was completed in 1762. The design centers on the triumphant figure of Neptunus Rex, standing on a shell chariot drawn by winged steeds and led by a pair of tritons. Two allegorical figures in the side niches represent good health and fertility.

On the southwestern corner of the piazza is a somber, not particularly spectacular-looking church, **SS. Vincenzo e Anastasio,** with a strange claim to fame. Within it survive the hearts and intestines of several centuries of popes. According to legend, the church was built on the site of a spring that burst from the earth after the beheading of St. Paul; the spring is one of the three sites where his head is said to have bounced off the ground.

Piazza di Trevi. Metro: Barberini.

AROUND VIA VENETO & PIAZZA BARBERINI

Piazza Barberini lies at the foot of several Roman streets, among them Via Barberini, Via Sistina, and Via Vittorio Veneto. It would be a far more pleasant spot were it not for the heavy traffic swarming around its principal feature, Bernini's **Fountain of the Triton (Fontana del Tritone)** ✮. For more than 3 centuries, the strange figure sitting in a vast open clam has been blowing water from his triton. Off to one side of the piazza is the aristocratic side facade of the **Palazzo Barberini,** named for one of Rome's powerful families; inside is the **Galleria Nazionale d'Arte Antica** (see below). The Renaissance Barberini reached their peak when a son was elected pope as Urban VIII; he encouraged Bernini and gave him great patronage.

As you go up Via Vittorio Veneto, look for the small fountain on the right corner of Piazza Barberini—it's another Bernini, the small **Fountain of the Bees (Fontana delle Api).** At first they look more like flies, but they're the bees of the Barberini, the crest of that powerful family complete with the crossed keys of St. Peter above them (the keys were always added to a family crest when a son was elected pope).

National Gallery of Ancient Art (Galleria Nazionale d'Arte Antica) ✮✮
Palazzo Barberini, right off Piazza Barberini, is one of the most magnificent baroque palaces in Rome. It was begun by Carlo Maderno in 1627 and completed in 1633 by Bernini, whose lavishly decorated rococo apartments, the **Gallery of Decorative Art (Galleria d'Arte Decorativa),** are on view. This gallery is part of the **National Gallery of Ancient Art.**

The bedroom of Princess Cornelia Costanza Barberini and Prince Giulio Cesare Colonna di Sciarra stands just as it was on their wedding night, and many household objects are displayed in the decorative art gallery. In the chambers, which boast frescoes and hand-painted silk linings, you can see porcelain from Japan and Bavaria, canopied beds, and a wooden baby carriage.

On the first floor is a splendid array of paintings from the 13th to the 16th centuries, most notably *Mother and Child,* by Simone Martini, and works by Filippo Lippi, Andrea Solario, and Francesco Francia. Il Sodoma has some brilliant pictures here, including *The Rape of the Sabines* and *The Marriage of St. Catherine.* One of the best-known paintings is Raphael's beloved *La Fornarina,* the baker's daughter who was his mistress and who posed for his Madonna portraits. Titian is represented by his *Venus and Adonis.* Also here are Tintorettos and El Grecos. Many visitors come just to see the magnificent Caravaggios, including *Narcissus.*

Via delle Quattro Fontane 13. ✆ 06-4814430. Admission 6€ ($5.35). Tues–Sun 9am–7pm. Metro: Barberini.

Monumental Cemetery of the Capuchin Brothers (Cimitero Monumentale dei Padri Cappuccini)   One of the most horrifying sights in all Christendom, this is a series of chapels with hundreds of skulls and crossbones woven into mosaic "works of art." To make this allegorical dance of death, the bones of more than 4,000 Capuchin brothers were used. Some of the skeletons are intact, draped with Franciscan habits. The creator of this chamber of horrors? The tradition of the friars is that it was the work of a French Capuchin. Their literature suggests that you should visit the cemetery while keeping in mind the historical moment of its origins, when Christians had a rich and creative cult for their dead and great spiritual masters meditated and preached with a skull in hand. Those who've lived through the days of crematoriums and other such massacres might view the graveyard differently, but to many who pause to think, this site has a message. It's not for the squeamish, however. The entrance is halfway up the first staircase on the right of the church.

Beside the Church of the Immaculate Conception, Via Vittorio Veneto 27. ✆ 06-4871185. Donation required. Daily 9am–noon and 3–6pm. Metro: Barberini.

NEAR PIAZZA DEL POPOLO

The newly restored **Piazza del Popolo** ★★ is haunted with memories. According to legend, the ashes of Nero were enshrined here, until 11th-century residents began complaining to the pope about his imperial ghost. The **Egyptian obelisk** dates from the 13th century B.C., removed from Heliopolis to Rome during Augustus's reign (it stood at the Circus Maximus). The piazza was designed in the early 19th century by Valadier, Napoleon's architect. The lovely **Santa Maria del Popolo** ★★, with two Caravaggios, is at its northern curve, and opposite are almost-twin baroque churches, overseeing the never-ending traffic.

Altar of Peace (Ara Pacis) ★   In an airy glass-and-concrete building beside the eastern banks of the Tiber rests a reconstructed treasure from the reign of Augustus. It was built by the Senate as a tribute to that emperor and the peace he had brought to the Roman world. On the marble wall, you can see portraits of the imperial family—Augustus, Livia (his second wife), Tiberius (Livia's son from her first marriage and Augustus's successor), and even Julia (Augustus's unfortunate daughter, who divorced her first husband to marry Tiberius and then was exiled by her father for her sexual excesses). The altar was reconstructed from literally hundreds of fragments scattered in museums for centuries. A major portion came from the foundations of a Renaissance palace on the Corso. The reconstruction (quite an archaeological adventure story in itself) took place during the 1930s.

Lungotevere Augusta. ✆ 06-36003471. Admission 2€ ($1.80). Tues–Sat 9am–7pm; Sun 9am–1pm. Bus: 70, 81, 186, or 628.

Augustus's Mausoleum (Mausoleo Di Augusto) This seemingly indestructible pile of bricks has been here for 2,000 years and will probably remain for another 2,000. Like the larger tomb of Hadrian across the river, this was once a circular marble-covered affair with tall cypresses, symmetrical groupings of Egyptian obelisks, and some of Europe's most spectacular ornamentation. Many of the 1st-century emperors had their ashes deposited in golden urns inside, and it was probably because of this crowding that Hadrian decided to construct an entirely new tomb (the Castel Sant'Angelo) for himself in another part of Rome. The imperial remains stayed intact here until the 5th century, when invading barbarians smashed the bronze gates and stole the golden urns, emptying the ashes on the ground outside. After periods when it functioned as a Renaissance fortress, a bullfighting ring, and a private garden, the tomb was restored in the 1930s by Mussolini, who might have envisioned it as a burial place for himself. You can't enter, but you can walk along the four streets encircling it.

Piazza Augusto Imperatore. ✆ **06-67103819.** Admission is 2.50€ ($2.25). Bus: 81, 115, or 590. Metro: Spagna.

5 In the Villa Borghese

Villa Borghese , in the heart of Rome, is 6km (3¾ miles) in circumference. One of Europe's most elegant parks, it was created by Cardinal Scipione Borghese in the 1600s. Umberto I, king of Italy, acquired it in 1902 and presented it to the city of Rome. With lovely landscaped vistas, the greenbelt is crisscrossed by roads, but you can escape from the traffic and seek a shaded area under a pine or oak tree to enjoy a picnic or simply relax. On a sunny weekend afternoon, it's a pleasure to stroll here and see Romans at play, relaxing or in-line skating. There are a few casual cafes and some food vendors throughout; you can also rent bikes here. In the northeast of the park is a small zoo; the park is also home to a few outstanding museums.

Galleria Borghese This legendary art gallery shut its doors in 1984 and appeared to have closed forever. However, in early 1997, after a complete restoration, it returned in all its fabulous glory.

This treasure trove includes such masterpieces as Bernini's *Apollo and Daphne,* Titian's *Sacred and Profane Love,* Raphael's *Deposition,* and Caravaggio's *Jerome.* The collection began with the gallery's founder, Scipione Borghese, who, by the time of his death in 1633, had accumulated some of the greatest art of all time, even managing to acquire Bernini's early sculptures. Some paintings were spirited out of Vatican museums and even confiscated when their rightful owners were hauled off to prison until they became "reasonable" about turning over their art. The great collection suffered at the hands of Napoleon's notorious sister, Pauline, who married Prince Camillo Borghese in 1807 and sold most of the ancient collection (many works are now in the Louvre in Paris). One of the most popular pieces of sculpture in today's gallery, ironically, is Canova's life-size sculpture of Pauline in the pose of *Venus Victorious.* (When Pauline was asked whether she felt uncomfortable posing in the nude, she replied, "Why should I? The studio was heated.")

Important information: No more than 300 visitors at a time are allowed on the ground floor, and no more than 90 are allowed on the upper floor. Reservations are essential, so call ✆ **06-328101** (Mon–Fri 9am–6pm). However, the number always seems to be busy. If you'll be in Rome for a few days, try stopping by in person on your first day to reserve tickets for a later day. Better yet, before you leave home, contact **Select Italy** (✆ **847/853-1661;** www.selectitaly.com).

Piazza Scipione Borghese 5 (off Via Pinciano). ✆ **06-8417645** for information. Admission 6€ ($5.35). Tues–Sun 9am–7pm. Bus: 56 or 910.

National Etruscan Museum (Museo Nazionale di Villa Giulia) ★★★

This 16th-century papal palace shelters a priceless collection of art and artifacts from the mysterious Etruscans, who predated the Romans. Known for their sophisticated art and design, they left a legacy of sarcophagi, bronze sculptures, terra-cotta vases, and jewelry, among other items. If you have time for only the masterpieces, head for room 7, with a remarkable 6th-century B.C. *Apollo from Veio* (clothed, for a change). The other two widely acclaimed statues here are *Dea con Bambino* (Goddess with a Baby) and a greatly mutilated but still powerful *Hercules* with a stag. In room 8, you'll see the lions' sarcophagus from the mid–6th century B.C., which was excavated at Cerveteri, north of Rome.

Finally, one of the world's most important Etruscan art treasures is the bride and bridegroom coffin from the 6th century B.C., also dug out of the tombs of Cerveteri (in room 9). Near the end of your tour, another masterpiece of Etruscan art awaits you in room 33: the *Cista Ficoroni,* a bronze urn with paw feet, mounted by three figures, dating from the 4th century B.C.

Piazzale di Villa Giulia 9. ✆ **06-3201951.** Admission 4€ ($3.55). Tues–Sat 8:30am–7pm; Sun 9am–2pm. Metro: Flaminio.

National Gallery of Modern Art (Galleria Nazionale d'Arte Moderna) ★

This gallery of modern art is a short walk from the Etruscan Museum (see above). With its neoclassic and Romantic paintings and sculpture, it makes a dramatic change from the glories of the Renaissance and ancient Rome. Its 75 rooms also house the largest collection in Italy of 19th- and 20th-century works by Balla, Boccioni, De Chirico, Morandi, Manzù, Burri, Capogrossi, and Fontana. Look for Modigliani's *La Signora dal Collaretto* and large *Nudo.* There are also many works of Italian optical and pop art and a good representation of foreign artists, including Degas, Cézanne, Monet, and van Gogh. Surrealism and expressionism are well represented by Klee, Ernst, Braque, Miró, Kandinsky, Mondrian, and Pollock. You'll also find sculpture by Rodin. Several other important sculptures, including one by Canova, are on display in the museum's gardens. You can see the collection of graphics, the storage rooms, and the Department of Restoration by appointment Tuesday to Friday.

Viale delle Belle Arti 131. ✆ **06-322981.** Admission 6€ ($5.35). Tues–Sun 8:30am–7:20pm. Bus: 19, 56, or 910.

6 The Appian Way & the Catacombs

Of all the roads that led to Rome, **Via Appia Antica** (built in 312 B.C.) was the most famous. It eventually stretched all the way from Rome to the seaport of Brindisi, through which trade with the colonies in Greece and the East was funneled. (According to Christian tradition, it was along the Appian Way that an escaping Peter encountered the vision of Christ, causing him to go back into the city to face subsequent martyrdom.) The road's initial stretch in Rome is lined with the great monuments and ancient tombs of patrician Roman families—burials were forbidden within the city walls as early as the 5th century B.C.—and, beneath the surface, miles of tunnels hewn out of the soft tufa stone.

Finds   Beneath It All: Touring Roma Sotteranea

Talk about the "underground," and a growing legion of Romans will excitedly take up the story, offering tidbits about where to go, who to talk to, what's been seen, and what's allegedly awaiting discovery around the next bend in the sewer. The sewer? That's right. **Roma Sotteranea (Subterranean Rome)** is neither a subway nor a trendy arts movement, but the vast historic ruins of a city that has been occupied for nearly 3,000 years, the first 2 millennia of which are now largely buried by natural sediment and artificial landfills. Archaeologists estimate that these processes have left the streets of ancient Rome as much as 18m (20 yd.) beneath the surface.

Consider this: Each year, an inch of dust in the form of pollen, leaves, pollution, sand, and silt from disintegrating ruins settles over Rome. That silt has really taken a toll in its own right. Archaeologists estimate that the ruins of a one-story Roman house will produce debris 2m (6 ft.) deep over its entire floor plan. When you multiply that by more than 40,000 apartment buildings, 1,800 palaces, and numerous giant public buildings, a real picture of the burial of the ancient city presents itself. You should also take note of the centuries-old Roman tradition of burying old buildings in landfills, which can raise the level of the earth up to several yards all at once. In fact, past builders have often filled up massive stone ruins with dirt or dug down through previous landfills to the columns and vaults of underlying structures, and then laid a foundation for a new layer of Roman architecture.

As a result, many buildings on the streets today actually provide direct access to Rome's inner world. Doorways lead down to hidden crypts and shrines—the existence of which are closely guarded secrets. Nondescript locked doors in churches and other public buildings often open on whole blocks of the ancient city, streets still intact. For example, take **San Clemente,** the 12th-century basilica east of the Colosseum, where a staircase in the sacristy leads down to the original 4th-century church. Not only that, but a staircase near the apse goes down to an earlier Roman apartment building and temple, which in turn leads down to a giant public building dating back to the Great Fire (A.D. 64). Another interesting doorway to the past is in the south exterior wall of **St. Peter's,** leading down to an intact necropolis. That crumbling brick entry in the gardens on the east side of Esquiline Hill carries you into the vast **Domus Aurea (Golden House),** Nero's residence, built on the ruins left by the Great Fire.

Don't expect a road map of this subterranean world; it's a meandering labyrinth beneath the streets. A guided tour can be useful, especially those focusing on Roman excavations and anything to do with church crypts. Several tour companies now offer selected subterranean views, lasting 90 to 120 minutes and costing 12.50€ to 25€ ($11.15–$22.35). The best are provided by **Itinera** (© 06-27800785) and **LUPA** (© 06-5741974), both run by trained archaeologists. **Città Nascosta** (© 06-3216059; www.cittanascosta.com) offers offbeat tours to less-visited churches and monuments, and advertises the week's schedule via a recorded phone announcement that changes every week.

These tunnels, or catacombs, were where early Christians buried their dead and, during the worst times of persecution, held church services discreetly out of the public eye. A few of them are open to the public, so you can wander through mile after mile of musty-smelling tunnels whose soft walls are gouged out with tens of thousands of burial niches (long shelves made for two to three bodies each). In some dank, dark grottoes (never stray too far from your party or one of the exposed light bulbs), you can still discover the remains of early Christian art. The requisite guided tours, hosted by priests and monks, feature a smidgen of extremely biased history and a large helping of sermonizing.

The Appia Antica has been a popular Sunday lunch picnic site for Roman families (following the half-forgotten pagan tradition of dining in the presence of one's ancestors on holy days). This practice was rapidly dying out in the face of the traffic fumes that for the past few decades have choked the venerable road, but a 1990s initiative has closed the Via Appia Antica to cars on Sundays, bringing back the picnickers and bicyclists—along with in-line skaters and a new Sunday-only bus route to get out here.

You can take bus 218 from the San Giovanni Metro stop, which follows the Appia Antica for a bit and then veers right on Via Ardeatina at Domine Quo Vadis? Church. After another long block, the 218 stops at the square Largo M.F. Ardeatine, near the gate to the San Callisto catacombs. From here, you can walk right on Via d. Sette Chiese to the San Domitilla catacombs; or, walk left down Via d. Sette Chiese to the San Sebastiano catacombs.

An alternative is to ride the Metro to the Colli Albani stop and catch bus 660, which wraps up the Appia Antica from the south, veering off it at the San Sebastiano catacombs (if you're visiting all three, you can take bus 218 to the first two, walk to San Sebastiano, and then catch bus 660 back to the Metro). On Sundays the road is closed to traffic, but bus 760 trundles from the Circo Massimo Metro stop down the Via Appia Antica, turning around after it passes the Tomb of Cecila Metella.

Of the monuments on the Appian Way, the most impressive is the **Tomb of Cecilia Metella** ⊛, within walking distance of the catacombs. The cylindrical tomb honors the wife of one of Julius Caesar's military commanders from the Republican era. Why such an elaborate tomb for such an unimportant person in history? Cecilia Metella happened to be singled out for enduring fame because her tomb has remained and the others have decayed.

Catacombs of St. Callixtus (Catacombe di San Callisto) ⊛⊛
"The most venerable and most renowned of Rome," said Pope John XXIII of these funerary tunnels. The founder of Christian archaeology, Giovanni Battista de Rossi (1822–94), called them "catacombs par excellence." These catacombs are often packed with tour-bus groups, and they have perhaps the cheesiest tour, but the tunnels are simply phenomenal. They're the first cemetery of the Christian community of Rome, burial place of 16 popes in the 3rd century. They bear the name of St. Callixtus, the deacon whom Pope St. Zephyrinus put in charge of them and who was later elected pope (A.D. 217–22) in his own right. The complex is a network of galleries stretching for nearly 19km (12 miles), structured in five levels and reaching a depth of about 20m (65 ft.). There are many sepulchral chambers and almost half a million tombs of early Christians. Paintings, sculptures, and epigraphs (with such symbols as the fish, anchor, and dove) provide invaluable material for the study of the life and customs of the ancient Christians and the story of their persecutions.

Entering the catacombs, you see at once the most important crypt, that of nine popes. Some of the original marble tablets of their tombs are still preserved. The next crypt is that of St. Cecilia, the patron of sacred music. This early Christian martyr received three ax strokes on her neck, the maximum allowed by Roman law, which failed to kill her outright. Farther on, you'll find the famous Cubicula of the Sacraments with its 3rd-century frescoes.

Via Appia Antica 170. ☏ 06-51301580. Admission 4€ ($3.55) adults, 2€ ($1.80) children 6–15; free for children 5 and under. Apr–Oct Thurs–Tues 8:30am–noon and 2:30–5:30pm (to 5pm Nov–Mar). Closed February. Bus: 118.

Catacombs of St. Sebastian (Catacombe di San Sebastiano) Today the tomb of St. Sebastian is in the basilica, but his original resting place was in the catacombs underneath it. From the reign of Valerian to the reign of Constantine, the bodies of Sts. Peter and Paul were hidden in the catacombs, which were dug from tufa, a soft volcanic rock. The big church was built in the 4th century. The tunnels here, if stretched out, would reach a length of 11km (6¾ miles). In the tunnels and mausoleums are mosaics and graffiti, along with many other pagan and Christian objects from centuries even before the time of Constantine. Unfortunately, though the catacombs are spectacular, the tour here is very restricted, one of the shortest and least satisfying of all the catacomb visits.

Via Appia Antica 136. ☏ 06-7850350. Admission 4€ ($3.55) adults, 2€ ($1.80) children 6–15; free for children 5 and under. Mon–Sat 9am–noon and 2:30–5:30pm. Closed Nov 13–Dec 11.

Catacombs of St. Domitilla (Catacombe di San Domitilla) ★★★ This oldest of the catacombs is also the hands-down winner for most enjoyable catacomb experience. Groups are small, most guides are genuinely entertaining and personable, and, depending on the mood of the group and your guide, the visit may last anywhere from 20 minutes to over an hour. You enter through a sunken 4th-century church. There are fewer "sights" than in the other catacombs—although the 2nd-century fresco of the Last Supper is impressive—but some of the guides actually hand you a few bones out of a tomb niche. (Incidentally, this is the only catacomb where you'll still see bones; the rest have emptied their tombs to rebury the remains in ossuaries on the inaccessible lower levels.)

Via d. Sette Chiese 280. ☏ 06-5110342. Admission 4€ ($3.55) adults, 2€ ($1.80) children 6–14. Tues–Sun 8:30am–noon and 2:30–5pm. Closed Jan.

7 More Attractions

AROUND STAZIONE TERMINI

Basilica di Santa Maria Maggiore ★ This great church, one of Rome's four major basilicas, was built by Pope Liberius in A.D. 358 and was rebuilt by Pope Sixtus III from 432 to 440. Its 14th-century **campanile** is the city's loftiest. Much doctored in the 18th century, the church's facade isn't an accurate reflection of the treasures inside. The basilica is especially noted for the 5th-century Roman mosaics in its nave, as well as for its coffered ceiling, said to have been gilded with gold brought from the New World. In the 16th century, Domenico Fontana built a now-restored "Sistine Chapel." In the following century, Flaminio Ponzo designed the **Pauline (Borghese) Chapel** in the baroque style. The church also contains the **tomb of Bernini,** Italy's most important baroque sculptor/architect. Ironically, the man who changed the face of Rome with his elaborate fountains is buried in a tomb so simple that it takes a sleuth to track it down (to the right near the altar).

Piazza di Santa Maria Maggiore. ☏ 06-483195. Free admission. Daily 7am–7pm. Metro: Termini.

MUSEO NAZIONALE ROMANO

Originally, this museum occupied only the Diocletian Baths. Today it is divided into four different sections: Palazzo Massimo alle Terme; the Terme di Diocleziano (Diocletian Baths), with the annex Octagonal Hall; and Palazzo Altemps (which is near Piazza Navona; see p. 156 for a complete listing).

Palazzo Massimo alle Terme ✸ If you'd like to go wandering in a virtual garden of classical statues, head for this palazzo, built from 1883 to 1887 and opened as a museum in 1998. Much of the art here, including the frescoes, stuccoes, and mosaics, was discovered in excavations in the 1800s but has never been put on display before.

If you ever wanted to know what all those emperors from your history books looked like, this museum will make them live again, togas and all. In the central hall are works representing the political and social life of Rome at the time of Augustus Caesar. Note the statue of the emperor with a toga covering his head, symbolizing his role as the head priest of state. Other works include an altar from Ostia Antica, the ancient port of Rome, plus a statue of a wounded Niobid from 440 B.C. that is a masterwork of expression and character. Upstairs, stand in awe at all the traditional art from the 1st century B.C. to the Imperial Age. The most celebrated mosaic is of the *Four Charioteers.* In the basement are a rare numismatic collection and an extensive collection of Roman jewelry.

Largo di Villa Peretti 67. ☎ **06-48903500.** Admission 6€ ($5.35); the same ticket will admit you to the Diocletian Baths. Tues–Sun 9am–7:45pm. Last admission 1 hr. before closing. Metro: Termini.

Terme di Diocleziano (Diocletian Bath) and the Aula Ottagona (Octagonal Hall) ✸ Near Piazza dei Cinquecento, which fronts the rail station, this museum occupies part of the 3rd-century A.D. Baths of Diocletian and part of a convent that may have been designed by Michelangelo. The Diocletian Baths were the biggest thermal baths in the world. Nowadays they host a marvelous collection of funereal art works, such as sarcophagi, and decorations dating back to the Aurelian period. The Baths also have a section reserved for temporary exhibitions.

The **Octagonal Hall** occupies the southwest corner of the central building of the Diocletian Baths. Here you can see the *Lyceum Apollo,* a copy of the 2nd-century A.D. work inspired by the Prassitele. Also worthy of a note is the *Aphrodite of Cyrene,* a copy dating back to the second half of the 2nd century A.D. and discovered in Cyrene, Libya.

Viale E. di Nicola 79. ☎ **06-4880530.** Admission to the Baths 4€ ($3.55); Octagonal Hall free. The same ticket will admit you to Palazzo Massimo alle Terme. Baths Tues–Sun 9am–7pm. Aula Ottagona Tues–Sat 9am–2pm; Sun 9am–1pm. Last admission 1 hr. before closing. Metro: Termini.

IN THE TESTACCIO AREA & SOUTH

St. Paul Outside the Walls (Basilica di San Paolo Fuori le Mura) ✸ The Basilica of St. Paul, whose origins go back to the time of Constantine, is Rome's fourth great patriarchal church; it's believed to have been erected over the tomb of St. Paul. The basilica fell victim to fire in 1823 and was subsequently rebuilt. It is the second-largest church in Rome after St. Peter's. From the inside, its windows may appear to be stained glass, but they're actually translucent alabaster. With its forest of single-file columns and mosaic medallions (portraits of the various popes), this is one of the most streamlined and elegantly decorated churches in Rome. Its most important treasure is a 12th-century candelabra by Vassalletto, who's also responsible for the remarkable cloisters, containing twisted pairs of columns enclosing a rose garden. Of particular interest is the *baldachino* (richly embroidered fabric of silk and gold, usually fixed or carried over an important person or sacred object) of Arnolf di Cambio, dated 1285, that miraculously wasn't damaged in the fire. The Benedictine monks and students sell a fine collection of souvenirs, rosaries, and bottles of Benedictine every day except Sunday and religious holidays.

Via Ostiense 184. ℂ 06-5410341. Free admission. Basilica daily 7am–6:30pm; cloisters daily 9am–1pm and 3–6pm. Metro: San Paolo Basilica.

IN TRASTEVERE

From many vantage points in the Eternal City, the views are panoramic, but one of the best spots for a memorable vista is the **Janiculum Hill (Gianicolo)** ★★, across the Tiber. It's not one of the "Seven Hills," but it's certainly one of the most visited (and a stop on many bus tours). The Janiculum was the site of a battle between Giuseppe Garibaldi and the forces of Pope Pius IX in 1870—an event commemorated with statuary. Take bus no. 41 from Ponte Sant'Angelo.

Santa Cecilia in Trastevere ★   A cloistered and still-functioning convent with a fine garden, Santa Cecilia contains *The Last Judgment,* by Pietro Cavallini (ca. 1293), a masterpiece of Roman medieval painting. Another treasure is a late-13th-century baldachino by Arnolfo di Cambio over the altar. The church is built on the reputed site of Cecilia's long-ago palace, and for a small fee you can descend under the church to inspect the ruins of some Roman houses, as well as peer through a gate at the stuccoed grotto beneath the altar.

Piazza Santa Cecilia 22. ℂ 06-5899289. Church free; Cavallini frescoes 1.50€ ($1.35); excavations 2€ ($1.80). Main church and excavations daily 9:30am–noon and 4–6:30pm; frescoes Tues and Thurs 10–noon, Sun 11:30am–noon. Bus: 44, 75, 170, or 181.

Santa Maria in Trastevere ★   This Romanesque church at the colorful center of Trastevere was built around A.D. 350 and is one of the oldest in Rome. The body was added around 1100, and the portico was added in the early 1700s. The restored mosaics on the apse date from around 1140, and below them are the 1293 mosaic scenes depicting the life of Mary done by Pietro Cavallini. The faded mosaics on the facade are from the 12th or 13th century, and the octagonal fountain in the piazza is an ancient Roman original that was restored and added to in the 17th century by Carlo Fontana.

Piazza Santa Maria in Trastevere. ℂ 06-5814802. Free admission. Daily 7:30am–8pm. Bus: 23, 280, or 780.

8 Organized Tours

Because of the sheer number of sights to see, some first-time visitors like to start out with an organized tour. While few things can really be covered in any depth on these overview tours, they're sometimes useful for getting your bearings.

One of the leading tour operators is **American Express,** Piazza di Spagna 38 (ℂ **06-67641;** Metro: Spagna). One popular tour is a 4-hour orientation of Rome and the Vatican, which departs most mornings at 9:30am and costs 40€ ($35.70) per person. Another 4-hour tour, which focuses on the Rome of antiquity (including visits to the Colosseum, the Roman Forum, the ruins of the Imperial Palace, and San Pietro in Vincoli), costs 37.50€ ($33.50). From April to October, a popular excursion outside Rome is a 5-hour bus tour to Tivoli, where tours are conducted of the Villa d'Este and its spectacular gardens and the ruins of the Villa Adriana, all for 45€ ($40.20) per person.

Enjoy Rome, Via Marghera 8A (ℂ **06-4451843;** www.enjoyrome.com), makes the 1-day sprint from Rome to Pompeii as inexpensive and painless as possible with a daily tour from 8:30am to 5:30pm round-trip by air-conditioned minivan (seating eight passengers); it costs 37.50€ ($33.50). The trip is 3 hours one way, with an English-speaking driver. You're on your own once you reach the archaeological site, and there's no imposed restaurant lunch—that's what keeps their prices the lowest around.

Another option is **Scala Reale,** Via Varese 52 (© **888/467-1986** in the U.S., or 06-4745673), a cultural association founded by American architect Tom Rankin. He offers small-group tours and excursions focusing on the architectural and artistic significance of Rome. Tours include visits to monuments, museums, and piazzas, as well as to neighborhood trattorie. Custom-designed tours are available. Prices begin at 25€ ($22.35). Children 12 and under are admitted free to walking tours. Tour discounts are available for a group of four.

Walks of Rome, Via Urbana 38 (© **06-484853**), features tours ranging from 1 to 5 hours. Some itineraries concentrate on major attractions, while other specialized tours take visitors to offbeat sights. Guides are young, native English speakers, usually art or history students, who know how to make the monuments come alive.

9 Shopping

Rome offers temptations of every kind. In our limited space below we've summarized certain streets known throughout Italy for their shops. The monthly rent on these famous streets is very high, and those costs are passed on to you. Nonetheless, a stroll down some of these streets presents a cross section of the most desirable wares in Italy.

Shopping hours are generally Monday 3:30 to 7:30pm, and Tuesday to Saturday 9:30 or 10am to 1pm and 3:30 to 7 or 7:30pm. Some shops are open on Monday morning, however, and some don't close for the afternoon break.

THE TOP SHOPPING STREETS

VIA BORGOGNONA   This street begins near Piazza di Spagna, and both the rents and the merchandise are chic and ultra-expensive. Like its neighbor, Via Condotti, Via Borgognona is a mecca for wealthy, well-dressed women and men from around the world. Its storefronts have retained their baroque or neoclassical facades.

VIA COLA DI RIENZO   Bordering the Vatican, this long, straight street runs from the Tiber to Piazza Risorgimento. Because the street is wide and clogged with traffic, it's best to walk down one side and then up the other. Via Cola di Rienzo is known for stores selling a wide variety of merchandise at reasonable prices—from jewelry to fashionable clothes and shoes.

VIA CONDOTTI   Easy to find because it begins at the base of the Spanish Steps, this is Rome's poshest shopping street. A few down-to-earth stores have opened recently, but it's largely a playground for the super-rich. For us mere mortals, it's a great place for window-shopping and people-watching.

Tips **A Pause Before Purchasing**

Although Rome has many wonderful boutiques, you'll find better shopping in Florence and Venice. If you're continuing on to either of these cities, hold off a bit.

VIA DEL CORSO   Not attempting the stratospheric image or prices of Via Condotti or Via Borgognona, Via del Corso boasts styles aimed at younger consumers. Some gems are scattered amid the shops selling jeans and sporting equipment. The most interesting stores are nearest the fashionable cafes of Piazza del Popolo.

VIA FRANCESCO CRISPI   Most shoppers reach this street by following Via Sistina (see below) 1 long block from the top of the Spanish Steps. Near the intersection of these streets are several shops well suited for unusual and less expensive gifts.

VIA FRATTINA   Running parallel to Via Condotti, it begins, like its more famous sibling, at Piazza di Spagna. Part of its length is closed to traffic. Here the concentration of shops is denser, although some aficionados claim that its image is slightly less chic and prices are slightly lower than at its counterparts on Via Condotti. It's usually thronged with shoppers who appreciate the lack of motor traffic.

VIA NAZIONALE   The layout recalls 19th-century grandeur, but the traffic is horrendous. It begins at Piazza della Repubblica and runs down almost to the 19th-century monuments of Piazza Venezia. You'll find an abundance of leather stores (more reasonable in price than those in many other parts of Rome) and a welcome handful of stylish boutiques.

VIA SISTINA   Beginning at the top of the Spanish Steps, Via Sistina runs to Piazza Barberini. The shops are small, stylish, and based on the tastes of their owners. The pedestrian traffic is less dense than on other major streets.

VIA VITTORIO VENETO   Via Veneto is filled these days with expensive hotels and cafes and an array of relatively expensive stores selling shoes, gloves, and leather goods.

SHOPPING A TO Z

ANTIQUES   Prices have risen to alarming levels as wealthy Europeans increasingly outbid one another in a frenzy. Any antiques dealer who risks the high rents of central Rome is acutely aware of valuations, so although you might find gorgeous pieces, you're not likely to find any bargains.

Beware of fakes, remember to insure anything that you have shipped home, and, for larger purchases—anything more than 156€ ($150) at any one store—keep your paperwork in order to obtain your tax refund (see "Fast Facts: Italy," in chapter 3).

Via dei Coronari, buried in a colorful section of the Campus Martius, is lined with stores offering magnificent vases, urns, chandeliers, chaises, refectory tables, and candelabra. To find the street's entrance, turn left out of the north end of Piazza Navona and pass the excavated ruins of Domitian's Stadium—it will be just ahead. There are more than 40 antiques stores in the next 4 blocks (most are closed 1–4pm).

Italian furniture from the days of Caesar through the 19th century is for sale at **Ad Antiqua Domus,** Via dei Coronari 41 (© **06-6861186;** bus: 70, 81, or 87). It's as much a museum of Italian furniture design through the ages as it is a shop.

A mecca for the antiques hound, **ArtImport,** Via del Babuino 150 at the corner with Via dei Greci (© **06-3221330;** Metro: Spagna), always has something for sale that's intriguing and tasteful, with an emphasis on silver.

A few minutes south of Piazza del Popolo, **via Laurina** lies midway between via del Corso and via del Babuino. It is filled with beautiful stores where you can find anything from an antique print to a 17th-century chandelier.

ART   Head for the **Studio d'Art Contemporanea di Pino Casagrande,** 7A via degli Ausoni (© **06-4463480;** Metro: Piazza Vittorio or Termini), to see what's hot and happening in the art world of Rome today. An industrial elevator carries you to the fifth floor of this battered, old former pasta factory. Pino Casagrande, the owner, displays some of the city's most avant-garde art on his all-white walls. Local artists hang out here, and it's fun to meet and talk to them, and perhaps purchase one of their works, which start at 1,000€ ($893).

BOOKSTORES   Staffed by Brits, Australians, and Americans, the **Economy Book and Video Center,** Via Torino 136 (© **06-4746877;** Metro: Repubblica; bus: 64, 70, or 170), sells only English-language books (new and used), greeting cards, and videos.

The **Lion Bookshop,** Via dei Greci 33 (© **06-32654007;** Metro: Spagna; bus: 116 or 117), is the oldest English-language bookshop in town, specializing in literature, both American and English. It also sells children's books and photographic volumes on both Rome and Italy. A vast choice of English-language videos is for sale or rent. It's closed in August.

COSMETICS & PERFUMES   Since the 18th century, **Antica Erboristeria Romana,** via di Torre Argentina 15 (© **06-6879493;** bus: 40, 46, 62, or 64), has dispensed "wonders" from its tiny wooden drawers, some of which are labeled with skulls and crossbones. You'll find scented paper, licorice, hellbane, and herbal remedies.

Since 1870, **Profumeria Materozzoli,** piazza San Lorenzo in Lucina 5 (© **06-68892686;** bus: 52, 53, or 58), has sold its elegant stock of scents, specializing in the Acqua di Parma line.

DEPARTMENT STORES   In Piazza Colonna, **La Rinascente,** Via del Corso 189 (© **06-6797691;** bus: 117), is an upscale store offering clothing, hosiery, perfume, cosmetics, housewares, and furniture. It also has its own line of clothing (Ellerre) for men, women, and children. This is the largest of the Italian department-store chains, with another branch at Piazza Fiume.

DISCOUNT STORES   **Discount System,** Via del Viminale 35 (© **06-4823917;** Metro: Repubblica), sells menswear and women's wear by many of the big names (Armani, Valentino, Cerruti, Fendi, and Krizia). Even if an item isn't from a famous designer, it often came from a factory that produces some of the best quality of Italian fashion. If you find something you like, it'll be priced at around 50% of its original price, and it just might be a cut-rate gem well worth your effort.

If you don't mind "last season's clothing," head for **Discount dell'Alta Moda,** via Gesù e Maria 16A (© **06-3613796;** Metro: Flaminio), where clothing is reduced by about 50% of its original tab. Top Italian designer labels are found here, including Krizia, Armani, and Donna Karan. The shop also sells irregulars and overstock at cut-rate prices.

FASHION   The exclusive **Angelo,** Via Bissolati 34 (© **06-4741796;** Metro: Barberini), is a custom tailor for discerning men and has been featured in *Esquire* and *GQ.* Angelo employs the best cutters and craftsmen, and his taste is impeccable. Custom shirts, dinner jackets, and even casual wear can be made on short notice. If you don't have time to wait, he'll ship anywhere. The outlet also sells ready-made items such as cardigans, cashmere pullovers, evening shirts, suits, and overcoats.

Battistoni, Via Condotti 61A (© **06-697611;** Metro: Spagna), is known for the world's finest men's shirts. It also hawks a cologne, *Marte* (Mars), for the "man who likes to conquer."

Emporio Armani, Via del Babuino 140 (© **06-36002197;** Metro: Spagna), stocks relatively affordable menswear crafted by the designer who has dressed perhaps more stage and screen stars than any other in Italy. If these prices aren't high enough for you, try the more expensive line a short walk away at **Giorgio Armani,** Via Condotti 77 (© **06-6991460;** Metro: Spagna). The merchandise here is sold at sometimes staggering prices that are still often 30% less than what you'd pay in the U.S.

Dating to 1870, **Schostal,** Via del Corso 158 (© **06-6791240;** bus: 117), is for men who like their garments (from underwear to cashmere overcoats) conservative and well crafted. The prices are more reasonable than you might think, and the staff is courteous and attentive.

Behind all the chrome mirrors is swank **Valentino,** Via Condotti 13 (© **06-6739420;** Metro: Spagna), where you can become the most fashionable woman in town—if you can afford to be. Valentino's men's haute couture is sold nearby at Via Bocca di Leone 15 (© **06-6795862;** Metro: Spagna).

The prices at **Sisley,** Via Condotti 59 (© **06-6749811;** Metro: Spagna), are a little more down to earth. It's famous for sweaters, tennis wear, blazers, and sportswear.

One of the hottest, hippest designer boutiques in Rome is **L'Anatra all'Arancia,** 105–109 Via Tiburtina (© **06-4456293;** Metro: Piazza Vittorio). In addition to some big and up-and-coming names, the owner, Donatella Baroni, stocks her own labels.

At **Gianfranco Ferré,** Via Borgognona 6 (© **06-6797445;** Metro: Spagna), you can find the adventurous women's line of this famous designer. There is also clothing for men.

Givenchy, Via Borgognona 21 (© **06-6784058;** Metro: Spagna), is the Roman headquarters of one of the great designer names of France. Here you'll find ready-to-wear garments for stylish women with warm Italian weather in mind. It also features tasteful shirts and pullovers for men.

Max Mara, Via Frattina 28 (© **06-6793638;** Metro: Spagna), is one of the best outlets in Rome for chic women's wear. The fabrics are appealing and the alterations are free.

Rapidly approaching the stratospheric upper levels of Italian fashion is **Renato Balestra,** Via Sistina 67 (© **06-6795424;** Metro: Spagna or Barberini), whose women's clothing attains standards of lighthearted elegance at its best. This branch carries a complete line of the latest ready-to-wear.

Baby House, Via Cola di Rienzo 117 (© **06-3214291;** Metro: Lepanto), offers stylish clothing for the under-15 set. This shop is for the budding young fashion plate, with threads by Valentino, Bussardi, and Biagiotti.

FLEA MARKETS   On Sundays 7am to 1pm, every peddler from Trastevere and the surrounding Castelli Romani sets up a temporary shop at the sprawling Porta Portese open-air flea market, near the end of Viale Trastevere (catch bus no. 75 to Porta Portese, and then take a short walk to Via Portuense). The vendors are likely to sell everything from secondhand paintings of Madonnas and bushels of rosaries to 1947 TVs, and books printed in 1835. Serious shoppers can often ferret out a good buy. If you've ever been impressed with the bargaining power of the Spaniard, you haven't seen anything until you've bartered with an Italian. By 10:30am, the market is full of people. As at any street market, beware of pickpockets.

"Underground" is a vast underground car park near the via Veneto. But for 2 days each month, it blossoms during the flea market, **Underground,** via Francesco Crispi 96 (© 06-36005345; Metro: Barberini), with stall after stall selling almost anything—from junk to genuine antiques. Collectors love this place. You can make some real finds here if you search diligently enough. It's open October to April the first Sunday of each month from 10am to 8pm.

FOOD & FOOD MARKETS   At old-fashioned **Castroni,** Via Cola di Rienzo 196 (© 06-6874383; bus: 32 or 81), you'll find an amazing array of unusual foodstuffs from around the Mediterranean. If you want herbs from Apulia, pepperoncino oil, cheese from the Valle d'Aosta, or an obscure brand of balsamic vinegar, Castroni will have it. It also carries foods that are exotic in Italy but commonplace in North America, such as taco shells, corn curls, and peanut butter.

Near Santa Maria Maggiore, Rome's largest market takes place Monday to Saturday 7am to noon at **Piazza Vittorio Emanuele** (Metro: Vittorio Emanuele). Most of the vendors at the gigantic market sell fresh fruit, vegetables, and other foodstuff, although some stalls are devoted to cutlery, clothing, and the like. There's probably little to tempt the serious shopper, but it's a fun glimpse into Roman life.

There's also a market Monday to Saturday 6am to noon at **Campo de' Fiori** (bus: 46, 62, or 64). It's Rome's most picturesque food market—but it's also the priciest. Things start bustling in the predawn as the florists arrange bouquets, and fruit and vegetable vendors set up their stalls.

GIFTS   Grispigni, Via Francesco Crispi 59 at Via Sistina (© 06-6790290; Metro: Spagna or Barberini), sells a large assortment of leather-covered boxes, women's purses, compacts, desk sets, and cigarette cases. There's also a constantly changing array of gifts if you're searching for some "small item" to take back.

Anatriello Argenteria Antica e Moderna Roma, Via Frattina 123 (© 06-6789601; Metro: Spagna), is known for new and antique silver. All the new items are made by Italian silversmiths, in designs ranging from the whimsical to the dignified. Also displayed are antique pieces from England, Germany, and Switzerland.

HOUSEWARES   Spazio Sette, hidden at Via d. Barberi off Largo di Torre Argentina (© 06-6869747), is far and away Rome's best housewares emporium, a design boutique of department-store proportions. It goes way beyond Alessi tea kettles to fill three huge floors with the greatest names, and latest word, in Italian and international design.

At **English Home,** via del Babuino 41A (© 06-36001721; Metro: Piazza di Spagna), it's amazing how so many intriguing items can be packed into such a small space. Here you'll find everything from painted pillows to handmade wooden frames, even mosaic incense holders or beaded jewelry.

Another good bet is **Bagagli,** Via Cam. Marzio 42 (© 06-6871406), offering a good selection of Alessi, Rose and Tulipani, and Villeroy & Boch china in a pleasantly kitschy old Rome setting that comes complete with cobblestone floors.

Bargain hunters should head to one of **Stock Market**'s two branches, at Via d. Banchi Vecchi 51–52 (📞 **06-6864238**), or near the Vatican at via Tacito 60 (📞 **06-36002343**). You'll find mouthwatering prices on last year's models, overstock, slight irregulars, and artistic misadventures in design that the pricier boutiques haven't been able to move. Most is moderately funky household stuff, but you never know when you'll find a gem of design hidden on the shelves.

If the big names don't do it for you, you may prefer **c.u.c.i.n.a.,** Via di Babuino 118A (no phone), a stainless-steel shrine to everything you need for a proper Italian kitchen, sporting designs that are as beautiful in their simplicity as they are utilitarian.

JEWELRY   Rome's most prestigious jeweler for more than a century, **Bulgari,** Via Condotti 10 (📞 **06-6793876**; Metro: Spagna), boasts a shop window that's a visual attraction in its own right. Bulgari designs combine classical Greek aesthetics with Italian taste, changing in style with the years yet clinging to tradition.

At **E. Fiore,** Via Ludovisi 31 (📞 **06-4819296;** bus: 95 or 115), you can choose a jewel and have it set to your specifications. Or you can make your selection from a rich assortment of charms, bracelets, necklaces, rings, brooches, corals, pearls, and cameos. Also featured are elegant watches, silverware, and gold ware.

One of the city's best gold- and silversmiths, **Federico Buccellati,** Via Condotti 31 (📞 **06-6790329;** Metro: Spagna), specializes in neo-Renaissance creations. The designs of the handmade jewelry and holloware recall those of Renaissance gold master Benvenuto Cellini.

Siragusa, Via delle Carrozze 64 (📞 **06-6797085;** Metro: Spagna), is more like a museum than a shop, specializing in unusual jewelry based on ancient carved stones or archaeological pieces. Handmade chains, for example, often hold coins and beads from the 3rd and 4th centuries B.C. discovered in Asia Minor.

LEATHER   Italian leather is among the very best in the world; it can attain butter-soft textures more pliable than cloth. You'll find hundreds of leather stores in Rome, many of them excellent.

At **Alfieri,** Via del Corso 1–2 (📞 **06-3611976;** bus: 117), you'll find virtually any garment you can think of fashioned in leather. Opened in the 1960s with a funky counterculture slant, it prides itself on leather jackets, boots, bags, belts, shirts, hats, pants for men and women, short shorts, and skirts that come in at least 10 (sometimes neon) colors. Although everything is made in Italy, the emphasis is on reasonable prices rather than ultrahigh quality, so check the stitching and workmanship before you invest.

Despite the postmodern sleekness of its shop, **Campanile,** Via Condotti 58 (📞 **06-6783041;** Metro: Spagna), bears a pedigree going back to the 1870s and an impressive inventory of well-crafted leather jackets, belts, shoes, bags, and suitcases. The quality is high.

If famous names in leather wear appeal to you, you'll find most of the biggies at **Casagrande,** Via Cola di Rienzo 206 (📞 **06-6874610;** bus: 32 or 81), such as Fendi and its youth-conscious offspring, Fendissime, plus Cerruti, Mosquino, and Valentino. This well-managed store has developed an impressive reputation for quality and authenticity since the 1930s. The prices are more reasonable than those for equivalent merchandise in some other parts of town.

Fendi, Via Borgognona 36–40 (📞 **06-696661;** Metro: Spagna), is mainly known for its avant-garde leather goods, but it also has furs, stylish purses, ready-to-wear clothing, and a new line of men's clothing and accessories. Fendi also carries gift items, home furnishings, and sports accessories.

Of course, **Gucci,** Via Condotti 8 (© **06-6790405;** Metro: Spagna), has been a legend since 1900. Its merchandise consists of high-class leather goods, such as suitcases, handbags, wallets, shoes, and desk accessories. It also has elegant menswear and women's wear, including beautiful shirts, blouses, and dresses, as well as ties and neck scarves. Prices have never been higher.

Saddlers Union, Via Condotti 26 (© **06-6798050;** Metro: Spagna), is a great place to look for well-crafted leather accessories. The wide selection of bags might lure you here, but there's plenty more—belts, wallets, shoes, briefcases, and other finely crafted items.

MOSAICS   Mosaics are an art form as old as the Roman Empire. And many of the objects displayed at **Savelli,** Via Paolo VI 27 (© **06-68307017;** Metro: Ottaviano), were inspired by ancient originals discovered in thousands of excavations, including those at Pompeii and Ostia. Others, especially the floral designs, depend on the whim and creativity of the artist. Objects include tabletops, boxes, and vases. The cheapest mosaic objects begin at around 140€ ($125) and are unsigned products crafted by students at an art school partially funded by the Vatican. Objects made in the Savelli workshops that are signed by the individual artists (they tend to be larger and more elaborate) range from 560€ to 28,000€ ($500–$25,000). The outlet also contains a collection of small souvenir items such as key chains and carved statues.

MUSIC   Head for **Disfunzioni Musicali,** 4–14 via degli Etruschi (© **06-4461984;** Metro: Piazza Vittorio), which is sought out by music lovers and used-vinyl collectors from Europe and America. Come here for the rarities. Was that Mick Jagger we spotted searching old labels?

PORCELAIN   One of the most prestigious retail outlets for porcelain in the city is **Richard Ginori,** Piazza Trinità dei Monti 18B (© **06-6793836;** Metro: Spagna). Anything you buy can be shipped.

PRINTS & ENGRAVINGS   At **Alberto di Castro,** Via del Babuino 71 (© **06-3613752;** Metro: Spagna), you'll find Rome's largest collection of antique prints and engravings. In rack after rack are depictions of everything from the Colosseum to the Pantheon, priced from 28€ to 22,400€ ($25–$20,000), depending on the age and rarity of the engraving.

Alinari, Via Alibert 16A (© **06-6792923;** Metro: Spagna), takes its name from the famed 19th-century Florentine photographer. Original prints and photos of Alinari are almost as prized as paintings in national galleries, and you can pick up your own here.

Giovanni B. Panatta Fine Art Shop, Via Francesco Crispi 117 (© **06-6795948;** Metro: Spagna or Barberini), sells excellent color and black-and-white prints covering a variety of subjects, from 18th-century Roman street scenes to astrological charts. There's also a selection of reproductions of medieval and Renaissance art that's attractive and reasonably priced.

Fava, Via del Babuino 180 (© **06-3610807;** Metro: Spagna), recaptures the era when Neapolitans sold 17th- and 18th-century pictures of the eruptions of Vesuvius, once highly sought after by collectors. This is really unusual art from the old attic.

SHOES   At **Dominici,** Via del Corso 14 (© **06-3610591;** bus: 117), a few steps from Piazza del Popolo, you'll find an amusing collection of men's and women's shoes in a pleasing variety of vivid colors. The style is aggressively young, and the quality is good.

Ferragamo, Via Condotti 66–73 (✆ **06-6798402;** Metro: Spagna), sells elegant footwear, plus women's clothing and accessories and ties, in an atmosphere full of Italian style. There are always many customers waiting to enter the shop; management allows them to enter in small groups. Figure on a 30-minute wait.

Fragiacomo, Via Delle Carrozze 28 (✆ **06-6798780;** Metro: Spagna), sells shoes for men and women in a champagne-colored showroom with gilt-painted chairs and big display cases.

Lily of Florence, Via Lombardia 38A off Via Vittorio Veneto (✆ **06-4740262;** bus: 80), has a shop in Rome, with the same merchandise that made the outlet so well known in the Tuscan capital. The colors come in a wide range, the designs are stylish, and the leather texture is of good quality. Lily sells shoes for both men and women and features American sizes with prices 30% to 40% less than in the U.S.

WINE & LIQUOR   At the historic **Buccone,** Via Ripetta 19 (✆ **06-3612154;** Metro: Piazza di Spagna), the selection of wines is among the finest in Rome.

Opened in 1821, **Trimani,** Via Goito 20 (✆ **06-4469661;** Metro: Castel Pretorio; bus: 3, 4, or 36), sells wines and spirits from Italy, among other offerings. Purchases can be shipped to your home.

Ai Monasteri, Piazza delle Cinque Lune 76 (✆ **06-68802783;** bus: 70, 81, 87, or 428), is a treasure trove of liquors (including liqueurs and wines), honey, and herbal teas made in Italian monasteries and convents. You can buy excellent chocolates and other candies as well. You make your selections in a quiet atmosphere reminiscent of a monastery, just 2 blocks from Bernini's Fountain of the Four Rivers in Piazza Navona. The shop will ship some items home for you.

10 Rome After Dark

When the sun goes down, Rome's palaces, ruins, fountains, and monuments are bathed in a theatrical white light. Few evening occupations are quite as pleasurable as a stroll past the solemn pillars of old temples or the cascading torrents of Renaissance fountains glowing under the blue-black sky.

The Fountain of the Naiads (*Fontana delle Naiadi*), on Piazza della Repubblica; the Fountain of the Tortoises (*Fontana della Tartarughe*), on Piazza Mattei; and the Trevi Fountain are particularly beautiful at night. The Capitoline Hill (or Campidoglio) is magnificently lit after dark, with its measured Renaissance facades glowing like jewel boxes. The view of the Roman Forum seen from the rear of the trapezoidal piazza del Campidoglio is the grandest in Rome, more so than even the Colosseum. Bus 48, 89, 92, 94, or 716 takes you here at night, or you can ask for a taxi. If you're across the Tiber, Piazza San Pietro (in front of St. Peter's) is impressive at night without the tour buses and crowds. And a combination of illuminated architecture, Renaissance fountains, and sidewalk shows and art expos enlivens Piazza Navona.

Even if you don't speak Italian, you can generally follow the listings of special events and evening entertainment featured in *La Repubblica,* a leading Italian newspaper. *Trova Roma,* a special weekly entertainment supplement (good for the coming week) is published in this paper on Thursday. The minimagazines *Metropolitan* and *Wanted in Rome* have listings of jazz, rock, and such and give an interesting look at expatriate Rome. The daily *Il Messaggero* lists current cultural news, especially in its Thursday magazine supplement, *Metro.* And *Un Ospite a Roma,* available free from the concierge desks of top hotels, is full of details on what's happening.

During the peak of summer, usually in August, all nightclub proprietors seem to lock their doors and head for the seashore, where they operate alternate clubs. Some close at different times each year, so it's hard to keep up-to-date. Always have your hotel check to see if a club is operating before you make a trek to it. (Dance clubs, in particular, open and close with freewheeling abandon.)

Be aware that there are no inexpensive nightclubs in Rome. Many of the legitimate nightclubs, besides being expensive, are highlighted by hookers plying their trade.

THE PERFORMING ARTS

CLASSICAL MUSIC   Concerts given by the orchestra of the **Academy of St. Cecilia,** Via della Conciliazione 4 (© **06-68801044;** bus: 23, 40, 62, 64, or 982), usually take place at Piazza Villa Giulia, site of the Etruscan Museum, from late June to late July; in winter, they're held in the academy's concert hall on Via della Conciliazione. Sometimes the orchestra performs elsewhere around the city, sometimes in historic churches.

Teatro Olimpico, Piazza Gentile da Fabriano 17 (© **06-3265991;** Metro: Flaminio), hosts a wide range of performances, from pop to chamber music to visiting foreign orchestras.

Check the daily papers for **free church concerts** given around town, especially near Easter and Christmas.

OPERA   If you're in the capital for the opera season, usually late December to June, you might want to attend the historic **Teatro dell'Opera,** Piazza Beniamino Gigli 1, off Via Nazionale (© **06-481601;** Metro: Repubblica). Nothing is presented in August; in summer, the venue usually switches elsewhere. Call ahead or ask your concierge before you go. Tickets are 15€ to 150€ ($13.40–$133.95).

DANCE   Performances of the Rome Opera Ballet are given at the **Teatro dell'Opera** (see previous entry). The regular repertoire of classical ballet is supplemented by performances of internationally acclaimed guest artists, and Rome is on the major agenda for troupes from around the world. Watch for announcements in the weekly entertainment guides about other venues, including the Teatro Olimpico, or even open-air ballet performances.

A MEAL & A SONG

Several restaurants offer tourist-oriented dinner shows full of folklore performances, sing-alongs, strolling musicians, and the like. Frankly, they're pretty cheesy, but thousands of visitors to Rome love this type of thing. Touristy or not, they're packed every night, so they seem to know what appeals to the masses. If you're interested in this kind of dinner and folklore show, try **Da Meo Patacca,** Piazza dei Mercanti 30, in Trastevere (© **06-58331086;** bus: 23). They serve bountiful "Roman country" meals along with the entertainment, starting at 35€ ($31.25). At **Fantasie di Trastevere,** Via di Santa Dorotea 6, in Trastevere (© **06-5881671;** bus: 23, 65, or 280), dinner and the show will run you about 40€ to 60€ ($35.70–$53.60).

BARS & CAFES

Unless you're dead set on making the Roman nightclub circuit, try what might be a far livelier and less expensive scene—sitting late at night on **Via Veneto, Piazza della Rotonda, Piazza del Popolo,** or one of Rome's other piazzas, all for the cost of an espresso, a cappuccino, or a Campari.

If you're looking for some scrumptious **ice cream,** see the entries for Café Rosati and Giolitti, below, as well as the box titled "Take a Gelato Break" on p. 114.

ON VIA VENETO Back in the 1950s (a decade that *Time* magazine gave to Rome, in the same way it conceded the 1960s and later the 1990s to London), **Via Vittorio Veneto** was the chic heart of Rome, crowded with aspiring and actual movie stars, their directors, and a group of card-carrying members of the jet set. Today the beautiful people wouldn't be caught dead on Via Veneto—it has become touristy. But visitors flock here by the thousands every night for cafe-sitting and people-watching.

Sophisticated **Harry's Bar,** Via Vittorio Veneto 150 (© 06-484643; Metro: Piazza di Spagna), is a perennial favorite for out-of-towners. Every major Italian city seems to have one, and Rome is no exception, although this one has no connection with the others. In summer, tables are placed outside. For those who want to dine outdoors but want to avoid the scorching sun, there's an air-conditioned sidewalk cafe open May to November. Meals inside cost about double what you'd pay outside. In back is a small dining room serving some of the finest (and priciest) food in central Rome. There's also a piano bar, with live music starting at 11pm.

Caffè de Paris, Via Vittorio Veneto 90 (© 06-4885284; Metro: Barberini), is popular in summer, when the tables spill right out onto the sidewalk and the passing crowd walks through the maze. This is perhaps the most famous cafe in all of Rome for people-watching along the via Veneto, although you'd be hard-pressed to ever meet a local here.

NEAR THE TERMINI A century-old bar, **Bar Marani,** 57 via dei Volsci (© 06-490016; Metro: Termini), has been compared to a Fellini movie set. By the marketplace, this is a coffee bar that attracts students, visitors, Japanese tourists, shopkeepers, artists, pickpockets, contessas, and rock stars, who come for espresso or delicious ice cream. Try to grab a table on the vine-covered terrace. Closed on Monday and in August.

Rive Gauche, 43 via dei Sabelli (© 06-4456722; Metro: Termini), is a sleek bar that attracts Roman yuppies, who are deserting their traditional glass of wine to sample the more than three dozen types of whisky or the rum-laced concoctions.

ON PIAZZA DEL POPOLO **Café Rosati,** Piazza del Popolo 5A (© 06-3225859; bus: 117), has been around since 1923 and attracts a crowd of all persuasions, both foreign and domestic, who drive up in Maseratis and Porsches. It's really a sidewalk cafe/ice-cream parlor/candy store/confectionery/ristorante that has been swept up in the fickle world of fashion. The later you go, the more interesting the action will be. It serves lunch and dinner daily noon to 11pm.

The management of **Canova Café,** Piazza del Popolo 16 (© 06-3612231; bus: 117), has filled this place with boutiques selling expensive gift items, such as luggage and cigarette lighters, yet many Romans still consider the Canova to be *the* place on the piazza. It has a sidewalk terrace for people-watching, plus a snack bar, a restaurant, and a wine shop. In summer, you can sit in a courtyard with ivy-covered walls and flowers growing in terra-cotta planters. A buffet meal is 21€ ($18.75) and up. Food is served daily noon to 3:30pm and 7 to 11pm, but the bar is open 8am to midnight or 1am, depending on the crowd.

Night & Day, Via Tuscolano 812 (© 06-768780; bus: 116), is a popular coffeehouse because it's open Monday to Saturday 24 hours a day. This laid-back cafe provides an after-hours hangout for club-goers left stranded by the 2am closing of most nearby night spots. Sandwiches go for anywhere up to 3.50€ ($3.15), and a cup of coffee for .60€ (55¢).

NEAR THE PANTHEON   The **Piazza della Rotonda,** across from the Pantheon, is the hopping place to be after dark, especially in summer. Although it's one of the most touristy places in Rome, locals come here, too, because it's a dramatic place to be at night when the Pantheon is lit up. Most cafes here are open until midnight or 2am.

Di Rienzo, Piazza della Rotonda 8–9 (© **06-6869097;** bus: 116), is the top cafe on this piazza. In fair weather, you can sit at one of the sidewalk tables (if you can find one free). There's a full menu, or you can just nurse a drink.

Tazza d'Oro, Piazza della Rotonda, Via degli Orfani 84 (© **06-6789792;** bus: 116), is known for serving its own brand of espresso. Another specialty, ideal on a hot summer night, is *granità di caffè* (coffee that has been frozen, crushed into a velvety, slushlike ice, and placed in a glass between layers of whipped cream).

Strongly brewed coffee is liquid fuel to Italians, and many Romans will walk blocks and blocks for what they consider a superior brew. **Caffè Sant'Eustachio,** Piazza Sant'Eustachio 82 (© **06-6861309;** bus: 116), is one of Rome's most celebrated espresso shops, where the water supply is funneled into the city by an aqueduct built in 19 B.C. Rome's most experienced espresso judges claim the water plays an important part in the coffee's flavor, although steam forced through ground Brazilian coffee roasted on the premises has a significant effect as well. Buy a ticket from the cashier for as many cups as you want; then leave a small tip for the counter-person when you present your receipt.

A longtime favorite, Hemingway's Pub, was recently transformed into the sleek **Riccioli Café,** Piazza delle Coppelle 10A (© **066-821-0313;** bus 64), a new and fast-rising oyster and champagne bar. In elegant yet informal surroundings, you can order drinks and oysters on the half shell (or more substantial meals). Many come here to see and be seen. The loftlike wine cellar has an excellent selection.

NEAR THE SPANISH STEPS   Since 1760, the **Antico Caffà Greco,** Via Condotti 86 (© **06-6791700;** Metro: Spagna), has been Rome's poshest coffee bar. Stendhal, Goethe, Keats, and D'Annunzio have sipped coffee here before you. Today you're more likely to see Japanese tourists and ladies who lunch, but there's plenty of atmosphere. In front is a wooden bar, and beyond is a series of small salons. You sit at marble-topped tables of Napoleonic design, against a backdrop of gold or red damask, romantic paintings, and antique mirrors. The house specialty is *paradisi,* made with lemon and orange. It's closed for 10 days in August.

One of the best places to taste Italian wines, brandies, and grappa is at **Enoteca Antica,** Via della Croce 76B (© **06-6790896;** Metro: Spagna). A stand-up drink in its darkly antique confines is the perfect ending to a visit to the nearby Spanish Steps. You can opt for a postage-stamp table in back or stay at the bar.

NEAR PIAZZA COLONNA   For gelato fans, **Giolitti,** Via Uffici del Vicario 40 (© **06-6991243;** bus: 81, 90, 175, or 492), is one of the city's most popular nighttime gathering spots and the oldest ice-cream shop. Some of the sundaes look like Vesuvius about to erupt. Many people take gelato out to eat on the streets; others enjoy it in the post-Empire splendor of the salon inside.

NEAR PIAZZA NAVONA   Head for the **Caffè della Pace,** 3–5 Via della Pace (✆ **06-6861216**), right off the heartbeat of Piazza Navona. It's a wild scene on Saturday night, when it's packed with a gorgeous young crowd who comes to see and be seen.

IN TRASTEVERE   Fans who saw *Fellini's Roma* know what **Piazza Santa Maria** in Trastevere looks like at night. The square, filled with milling throngs in summer, is graced with an octagonal fountain and a 12th-century church. Children run and play on the piazza, and occasional spontaneous guitar fests break out when the weather is good.

Café-Bar di Marzio, Piazza Santa Maria in Trastevere 15 (✆ **06-5816095**; bus: 8, 44, 75, or 170), is a narrow, wood-paneled coffee bar. It's strictly a cafe (not a restaurant), offering both indoor and outdoor tables at the edge of the square with the best view of its fountain. The crowd is a mix of blue collar and bohemia.

LIVE-MUSIC CLUBS

At **Alexanderplatz,** Via Ostia 9 (✆ **06-39742171**; bus: 23), you can hear jazz Monday to Saturday 9pm to 2am, with live music beginning at 10:30pm. The good restaurant here serves everything from *gnocchi alla romana* to Japanese fare. There's no cover; instead you pay a 3-month membership fee of 6€ ($5.35).

Big Mama, Vicolo San Francesco a Ripa 18 (✆ **06-5812551**; bus: 44, 75, or 170), is a hangout for jazz and blues musicians where you're likely to meet the up-and-coming stars of tomorrow and sometimes even the big names. For big acts, the cover is 10€ to 20€ ($8.95–$17.85), plus 10€ ($8.95) for a seasonal membership fee.

Fonclea, Via Crescenzio 82A (✆ **06-6896302**; bus: 32 or 39), offers live music every night: Dixieland, rock, and R&B. This is basically a cellar jazz place and crowded pub that attracts folks from all walks of Roman life. The music starts at 9:30pm and usually lasts until 12:30am. There's also a restaurant featuring grilled meats, salads, and crepes. A meal starts at 17.50€ ($15.65), but if you want dinner, it's best to reserve a table.

Berimbau, Via dei Fienaroli, 30B (✆ **06-5813249**; bus: 56 or 60), is a hot late-night spot that has tapped into the recent Roman craze for Brazilian music. The sounds of salsa and merengue fill the night. The live music eventually segues into blasting disco. Expect a cover of 5€ to 12.50€ ($4.45–$11.15).

Arciliuto, Piazza Monte Vecchio 5 (✆ **06-6879419**; bus: 42, 62, or 64), is a romantic candlelit spot that was reputedly once the studio of Raphael. From Monday to Saturday 10pm to 2am, you can enjoy a music-salon ambience, with a pianist, guitarist, and violinist. The presentation also includes live Neapolitan songs and new Italian madrigals, and even current hits from Broadway or London's West End. This place is hard to find, but it's within walking distance of Piazza Navona. The cover is 17.50€ ($15.65), including the first drink; it's closed July 15 to September 5.

NIGHTCLUBS & DANCE CLUBS

In a high-tech, futuristic setting, **Alien,** Via Velletri 13–19 (✆ **06-8412212**; bus 3, 4, or 57), provides a bizarre space-age dance floor, bathed in strobe lights and rocking to the sounds of house/techno music. The crowd is young. It's open Tuesday to Saturday 11pm to 5am, with a cover of 15€ to 17.50€ ($13.40–$15.65) that includes the first drink.

Gilda, Via Mario dei Fiori 97 (✆ **06-6784838**; Metro: Spagna), is an adventurous nightclub/disco/restaurant that attracts a post-35 set, most often couples.

In the past, it has hosted Diana Ross and splashy Paris-type revues. Expect first-class shows, and disco music played between the live acts. The disco (midnight–4am) presents music of the 1960s plus more current tunes. The attractive piano bar, Swing, features Italian and Latin music. The cover is 20€ ($17.85) and includes the first drink.

One of Rome's largest and most energetic nightclubs, **Alpheus,** Via del Commercio 36 (© **06-5747826;** bus: 713), contains three sprawling rooms, each with a different musical sound and an ample number of bars. You'll find areas devoted to Latin music, other areas playing rock, and an area devoted to jazz. Live bands come and go. Both locals and visitors frequent this club, and the clients represent a wide age range. It's open Tuesday to Sunday 10pm to 4am and charges a cover of 5€ to 15€ ($4.45–$13.40).

If you're looking for a little counterculture edge, where you might find the latest indie music from the U.K., head for **Black Out,** Via Saturnia 18 (© **06-70496791**), which occupies an industrial-looking site open only Thursday, Friday, and Saturday 10:30pm to 4am. The club lures a crowd, mainly Romans in their 20s and early 30s. The 5€ ($4.45) cover on Thursday and the 7.50€ ($6.70) cover on Saturday and Sunday include the first drink.

Everything about **Club Picasso,** Via Monte di Testaccio 63 (© **06-5742975;** bus: 95), seems straight out of L.A. R&B, rock, and funk blare out across a young Roman crowd that loves to dance. The door bouncer is extra-vigilant about screening out any troublemakers. Club Picasso is open Tuesday to Sunday 8pm to 4am. You can get affordable pizza and other fare to stave off the munchies. There is no cover.

Near the American Embassy and Via Veneto, **Jackie O,** Via Boncompagni 11 (© **06-42885457;** bus: 52, 53, 56, 58, 80, or 163), is a glittery club that draws an affluent, over-30 crowd, mostly foreign. It's less frenzied than the other spots mentioned here. It's open Tuesday to Sunday 8:30pm to 4am, and the 20€ ($17.85) cover includes the first drink.

Radio Londra, Via Monte Testaccio 67 (no phone; bus: 95), aims for London-style hip. Everyone tries to look and act as freaky as possible. Because Radio Londra is near the popular gay L'Alibi (see "Gay & Lesbian Clubs," below), the downstairs club attracts many brethren, although the young crowd is mixed, both Roman and foreign. Upstairs is a pub/pizzeria where bands often appear; you can even order a veggie burger with a Bud. The club is open Wednesday to Monday 11:30am to 4am, and the pub/pizzeria serves Sunday, Monday, and Wednesday to Friday 11:30am to 4am. Admission is free.

Don't be put off by the facade of **Locanda Atlantide,** 22B via dei Lucani (© **06-44704540;** bus: 71 or 492; Metro: Piazza Vittorio), thinking that you've arrived at a bunker for a Gestapo interrogation. This former warehouse in San Lorenzo is the setting of a nightclub, bar, concert hall, and theater. Every day there's something different—perhaps jazz on Tuesday, a play on Wednesday, or a concert on Thursday, giving way to dance-club action on Friday and Saturday

Tips A Nightlife Note

A neighborhood with an edge, **Testaccio** is radical chic—don't wander around alone at night. The area still has a way to go before regentrification. However, Testaccio is the place to ask about what's hot in Rome when you arrive because crowds are fickle.

with DJ music. The cover ranges from 2.50€ to 5€ ($2.25–$4.45), depending on the evening; hours are Tuesday to Sunday 10pm to 4am. It's closed June 15 to September 15.

GAY & LESBIAN CLUBS

Having survived since 1984, the **Hangar,** Via in Selci 69 (© **06-4881397;** Metro: Cavour), is a landmark on the gay nightlife scene. It's on one of Rome's oldest streets, adjacent to the Forum. Women are welcome any night except Monday, when the club features videos and entertainment for men. The busiest nights are Saturday, Sunday, and Monday, when as many as 500 people cram inside. It's open Wednesday to Monday 10:30pm to 2:30am (it's closed for 3 weeks in Aug). There's no cover, but a membership card of 2.50€ ($2.25) is needed.

L'Alibi, Via Monte Testaccio 44 (© **06-5743448;** bus: 95), in Testaccio, is a year-round stop on many gay men's agenda. The crowd, however, tends to be mixed, both Roman and international, straight and gay, male and female. One room is devoted to dancing. It's open Wednesday to Sunday 11pm to 4am, and the cover is 7.50€ to 12.50€ ($6.70–$11.15).

Angelo Azzuro, Via Cardinal Merry del Val 13 (© **06-5800472;** bus: 44, 75, or 170), is a gay hot spot deep in the heart of Trastevere, open Friday, Saturday, and Sunday 11pm to 4am. There's no food—men dance with men to recorded music. Women are also invited, and Friday is for women only. Cover, including one drink, is 5€ ($4.45) Friday and Sunday, 10€ ($8.95) Saturday.

A fixture on the lesbian nighttime scene, **Joli Coeur,** Via Sirte 5 (© **06-86216240;** bus: 52 or 56), attracts women from around Europe during its very limited hours (only Sat and Sun 11pm–5am). Saturday is reserved for women only, although on Sunday the crowd can be mixed. The cover is 10€ ($8.95) and includes the first drink.

11 Side Trips from Rome: Tivoli, Ostia Antica & More

TIVOLI & THE VILLAS

Tivoli, known as Tibur to the ancient Romans, is 32km (20 miles) east of Rome on Via Tiburtina, about an hour's drive with traffic. If you don't have a car, take Metro Line B to the end of the line, the Rebibbia station. After exiting the station, board an Acotral bus for the trip the rest of the way to Tivoli. Generally, buses depart about every 20 minutes during the day. For information about the town, check with **Azienda Autonoma di Turismo,** Largo Garibaldi (© **0774-334522**), Tivoli. Opening hours are Monday 9am to 1pm, Tuesday to Friday 9am to 1pm and 3 to 6pm, and Saturday 9am to 1pm.

EXPLORING THE VILLAS

Villa d'Este ✦✦   Like Hadrian centuries before, Cardinal Ippolito d'Este of Ferrara believed in heaven on earth, and in the mid–16th century he ordered this villa built on a hillside. The dank Renaissance structure, with its second-rate paintings, is not that noteworthy; the big draw for visitors are the **spectacular gardens** below (designed by Pirro Ligorio).

You descend the cypress-studded slope to the bottom and, on the way, are rewarded with everything from lilies to gargoyles spouting water, torrential streams, and waterfalls. The loveliest fountain is the Ovato Fountain (Fontana dell Ovato), by Ligorio. But nearby is the most spectacular achievement: the **Fountain of the Hydraulic Organ (Fontana dell'Organo Idraulico),** dazzling with its water jets in front of a baroque chapel, with four maidens who look

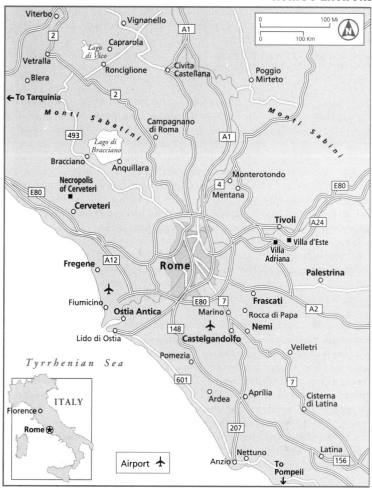

Viterbo
Vignanello
2
A1
Caprarola
Lago di Vico
Vetralla
Ronciglione
Civita Castellana
Poggio Mirteto
Blera
← To Tarquinia
2
M o n t i   S a b a t i n i
M o n t i   S a b i n i
Campagnano di Roma
493
A1
Lago di Bracciano
Bracciano
Anquillara
Monterotondo
E80
Necropolis of Cerveteri
4
E80
Mentana
Cerveteri
Tivoli
A24
Villa d'Este
Villa Adriana
Fregene
A12
Rome
Palestrina
Fiumicino
E80
7
Frascati
Ostia Antica
Marino
Rocca di Papa
A2
148
Nemi
Lido di Ostia
Castelgandolfo
Velletri
Pomezia
Tyrrhenian Sea
601
7
Ardea
Aprília
Cisterna di Latina
ITALY
207
Florence
Rome
Latina
156
Airport ✈
Nettuno
Anzio
To Pompeii
↓

0   100 Mi
0   100 Km

tipsy. The work represents the genius of Frenchman Claude Veanard. The moss-covered Fountain of the Dragons (Fontana dei Draghi), also by Ligorio, and the so-called Fountain of Glass (Fontana di Vetro), by Bernini, are the most intriguing. The best walk is along the promenade, with 100 spraying fountains. The garden is worth hours of exploration, but it's a lot of walking, with some steep climbs.

Piazza Trento, Viale delle Centro Fontane. ℂ **0774-312070**. Admission 6€ ($5.35). The bus from Rome stops near the entrance. Bus: Roma–Tivoli.

Villa Gregoriana ✮   The Villa d'Este dazzles with artificial glamour, but the Villa Gregoriana relies more on nature. The gardens were built by Pope Gregory XVI in the 19th century. At one point on the circuitous walk carved along a slope, you can stand and look out onto the most panoramic waterfall (Aniene) at Tivoli. The trek to the bottom on the banks of the Anio is studded with grottoes and balconies that open onto the chasm. The only problem is that if you do make the full descent, you might need a helicopter to pull you up again (the climb back up is fierce). From one of the belvederes, there's a panoramic view of the Temple of Vesta on the hill.

Largo Sant'Angelo. ✆ **0774-311249.** Admission 2.50€ ($2.25). May–Aug daily 10am–7:30pm; Sept daily 9:30am–6:30pm; Oct–Mar daily 9:30am–4:30pm; Apr daily 9:30am–6pm. The bus from Rome stops near the entrance.

Hadrian's Villa (Villa Adriana) 🐾🐾🐾   In the 2nd century A.D., the globe-trotting Hadrian spent the last 3 years of his life in the grandest style. Less than 6km (3¾ miles) from Tivoli, he built one of the greatest estates ever erected, and he filled acre after acre with some of the architectural wonders he'd seen on his many travels. Perhaps as a preview of what he envisioned in store for himself, the emperor even created a representation of hell. Hadrian was a patron of the arts, a lover of beauty, and even something of an architect. He directed the staggering feat of building much more than a villa: It was a self-contained world for a vast royal entourage and the hundreds of servants and guards they required to protect them, feed them, bathe them, and satisfy their libidos.

Hadrian erected theaters, baths, temples, fountains, gardens, and canals bordered with statuary throughout his estate. He filled the palaces and temples with sculpture, some of which now rest in the museums of Rome. In later centuries, barbarians, popes, and cardinals, as well as anyone who needed a slab of marble, carted off much that made the villa so spectacular. But enough of the fragmented ruins remains for us to piece together the story. For a glimpse of what the villa used to be, see the plastic reconstruction at the entrance.

After all the centuries of plundering, there's still a bit left. The most outstanding remnant is the **Canopo,** or Canopus, a re-creation of the town of Canope with its famous Temple of the Serapis. The ruins of a rectangular area, **Piazza d'Oro,** are still surrounded by a double portico. Likewise, the **Sala dei pilastri dorici,** or Doric Pillared Hall, remains to delight with its pilasters with Doric bases and capitals holding up a Doric architrave. The ruins of the **Baths** remain, revealing rectangular rooms with concave walls. The apse and the ruins of some magnificent vaulting are still found at the Great Baths. Only the north wall remains of the **Pecile,** or Poikile, which Hadrian discovered in Athens and had reproduced here. The best is saved for last—the **Teatro Marittimo,** a circular maritime theater in ruins with its central building enveloped by a canal spanned by small swing bridges. For a closer look at some of the items excavated, you can visit the museum on the premises and a museum and visitor center near the villa parking area.

Via di Villa Adriana. ✆ **0774-530203.** Admission 6€ ($5.35). Daily 9am–sunset (about 6:30pm in summer, 4pm Nov–Mar). Closed New Year's Day, May Day, and Christmas. Bus: 2 or 4 from Tivoli.

WHERE TO DINE

Albergo Ristorante Adriano ITALIAN   In a stucco-sided villa a few steps from the ticket office sits an idyllic stop for either before or after you visit Hadrian's Villa. It offers terrace dining under plane trees or indoor dining in a high-ceilinged room with terra-cotta walls, neoclassical moldings, and white Corinthian pilasters. The cooking is home-style, and the menu includes roast lamb, *saltimbocca* (veal cooked with ham), a variety of veal dishes, deviled chicken, salads and cheeses, and simple desserts. They're especially proud of their homemade pastas.

Via di Villa Adriana 194. ✆ **0774-535028.** Reservations recommended. Main courses 10€–16€ ($8.95–$14.30). AE, DC, MC, V. Mon–Sat 12:30–2:30pm and 8–10pm; Sun 12:30–2:30pm.

Le Cinque Statue ROMAN   This restaurant takes its name from the five old statues (Apollo Belvedere, gladiators, and so on) decorating the place. Today this comfortable establishment is maintained by a hardworking Italian family that prepares an honest, unpretentious cuisine. Everything is accompanied by the wines of the hill towns of Rome. Begin with a pastiche of mushrooms, or make a selection from the excellent antipasti. Try the rigatoni with fresh herbs, tripe fried Roman style, or mixed fry of cow's brains and vegetables. All the pasta is freshly made. The restaurant also has a wide array of ice creams and fruits.

Largo Santangelo 1. ☏ **0774-335366.** Reservations recommended. Main courses 10€–13€ ($8.95–$11.60). AE, DC, MC, V. Thurs–Sat 12:30–3pm and 7–11pm; Sun–Mon 12:30–3pm. Closed Aug 15–31. The Acotral bus from Rome stops nearby.

OSTIA ANTICA: ROME'S ANCIENT SEAPORT

Ostia Antica is one of the area's major attractions, particularly interesting to those who can't make it to Pompeii. If you want to see both ancient and modern Rome, grab your swimsuit, towel, and sunblock, and take the Metro Line B from Stazione Termini to the Magliana stop. Change here for the Lido train to Ostia Antica, about 26km (16 miles) from Rome. Departures are about every half hour, and the trip takes only 20 minutes. The Metro lets you off across the highway that connects Rome with the coast. It's just a short walk to the excavations.

Later, board the Metro again to visit the **Lido di Ostia,** the beach. Italy might be a Catholic country, but you won't detect any religious conservatism in the skimpy bikinis on the beach here. There's a carnival atmosphere, with dance halls, cinemas, and pizzerias. The Lido is set off best at Castelfusano, against a backdrop of pinewoods. This stretch of shoreline is referred to as the Roman Riviera.

Ostia Antica's Ruins ★★   Ostia, at the mouth of the Tiber, was the port of ancient Rome, serving as the gateway for all the riches from the far corners of the empire. It was founded in the 4th century B.C. and became a major port and naval base primarily under two later emperors, Claudius and Trajan.

A prosperous city developed, full of temples, baths, theaters, and patrician homes. Ostia flourished for about 8 centuries before it began to wither away. Gradually it became little more than a malaria bed, a buried ghost city that faded into history. A papal-sponsored commission launched a series of digs in the 19th century; however, the major work of unearthing was carried out under Mussolini's orders from 1938 to 1942 (the work had to stop because of the war). The city is only partially dug out today, but it's believed that all the chief monuments have been uncovered. There are quite a few visible ruins unearthed, so this is no dusty field like the Circus Maximus.

These principal monuments are clearly labeled. The most important spot is **Piazzale delle Corporazioni,** an early version of Wall Street. Near the theater, this square contained nearly 75 corporations, the nature of their businesses identified by the patterns of preserved mosaics. Greek dramas were performed at the **ancient theater,** built in the early days of the empire. The classics are still aired here in summer (check with the tourist office for specific listings), but the theater as it looks today is the result of much rebuilding. Every town the size of Ostia had a forum, and during the excavations a number of pillars of the ancient **Ostia Forum** were uncovered. At one end is a 2nd-century B.C. temple honoring a trio of gods, Minerva, Jupiter, and Juno (little more than the basic foundation remains). In addition, in the enclave is a well-lit **museum** displaying Roman statuary along with some Pompeii-like frescoes. Also of special interest are the ruins of **Thermopolium,** which was a bar; its name means "sale of hot drinks." The ruins of **Capitolium and Forum** remain; this was once the largest temple in Ostia, dating from the 2nd century A.D. A lot of the original brick remains, including a partial reconstruction of the altar. Of an insula, a block of apartments, **Casa Diana** remains, with its rooms arranged around an inner courtyard. There are perfect picnic spots beside fallen columns or near old temple walls.

Viale dei Romagnoli 717. ① 06-56358099. Admission 4€ ($3.55). Tues–Sun 9am–6pm. Metro: Ostia Antica Line Roma–Ostia–Lido.

THE CASTELLI ROMANI

For the Roman emperor and the wealthy cardinal in the heyday of the Renaissance, the Castelli Romani (Roman Castles) exerted a powerful lure, and they still do. The Castelli aren't castles, but hill towns—many of them with an ancient history. Several produce wines that are well-regarded.

The ideal way to explore the hill towns is by car. But you can get a limited review by taking one of the buses that leaves every 20 minutes from Rome's Subaugusta stop on Metro Line A.

NEMI

The Romans flock to Nemi in droves, particularly from April to June, for the succulent **strawberries** grown there, acclaimed by some gourmets as Europe's finest. In May, there's a strawberry festival. A COTRAL bus departs for Nemi and other hill towns from the Anagnina Metro stop in Rome. Service is about every 30 minutes during the day.

Nemi was also known to the ancients. A temple to the huntress Diana was erected on **Lake Nemi,** which was said to be her "looking glass." In A.D. 37, Caligula built luxurious barges to float on the lake. Mussolini drained Nemi to find the barges, but it was a dangerous time to excavate them from the bottom. They were senselessly destroyed by the Nazis during the infamous retreat.

At the **Roman Ship Museum (Museo delle Navi)** ⨯, Via di Diana 15 (① **06-9398040**), you can see two scale models of the ships destroyed by the Nazis. The major artifacts on display are mainly copies because the originals now rest in world-class museums. The museum is open daily 9am to 7pm. Admission is 2€ ($1.80). To reach the museum, head from the center of Nemi toward the lake.

The 15th-century **Palazzo Ruspoli,** a private baronial estate, is the focal point of Nemi, but the town itself invites exploration—particularly the alleyways that the locals call streets and the houses with balconies jutting out over the slopes.

Where to Dine

Ristorante Il Castagnone ROMAN/SEAFOOD   This well-managed dining room of the town's best hotel takes pride in its menu, with Roman-based cuisine that emphasizes seafood above meat. The attentive formal service is usually delivered with gentle humor. Amid neoclassical accessories and marble, you can order fine veal, chicken, beef, and fish dishes such as fried calamari; spaghetti with shellfish in garlicky tomato-based sauce; and roasted lamb with potatoes and Mediterranean herbs. There's a sweeping lake view from the restaurant's windows.

In the Diana Park Hotel, Via Nemorense 44. ① 06-9364041. Reservations recommended. Main courses 10€–20€ ($8.95–$17.85). AE, DC, MC, V. Tues–Sun noon–3pm and 8–10pm. Closed Nov.

Tips Reserving Winery Tours

While exploring the Castelli Romani, the hill towns around Rome, you might want to visit some of the better-known wineries. The region's most famous producers of Frascati are **Fontana Candida,** Via di Fontana Candida, 00040 Monte Porzio Catone, Roma (© **06-9420066**), whose winery, 14 miles southwest of Rome, was built around 1900. To arrange visits, contact the **Gruppo Italiano Vini,** Villa Belvedere, 37010 Calmasino, Verona (© **045-626-9600**).

FRASCATI ⚔

About 21km (13 miles) from Rome on Via Tuscolana and some 482m (1,281 ft.) above sea level, Frascati is one of the most beautiful hill towns. It's known for the wine to which it lends its name, as well as for its villas, which were restored after the severe destruction caused by World War II bombers. To get there, take one of the COTRAL buses leaving from the Anagina stop of Metro Line A. From there take the blue COTRAL bus to Frascati. Again, the transportation situation in Italy is constantly in a state of flux, so check your route at the station.

Although Frascati wine is exported, and served in many of Rome's restaurants and trattorie, tradition holds that it's best near the vineyards from which it came. Romans drive up on Sunday just to drink it.

Stand in the heart of Frascati, at Piazza Marconi, to see the most important of the estates: **Villa Aldobrandini** ⚔, Via Massala. The finishing touches to this 16th-century villa were added by Maderno, who designed the facade of St. Peter's in Rome. You can visit only the gardens, not the interior, but, still, with its grottoes, yew hedges, statuary, and splashing fountains, it's a nice outing. The gardens are open Monday to Friday 9am to 1pm and 3 to 5pm (to 6pm in summer), although you must go to the **Informazzione e Accoglienza Turistica,** Piazza Marconi 1 (© **06-9420331**), to ask for a free pass. The office is open Monday to Saturday 8am to 2pm, and also Tuesday to Friday 3 to 6pm in winter and 4 to 7pm in summer.

You also might want to visit the bombed-out **Villa Torlonia,** adjacent to Piazza Marconi. Its grounds have been converted into a public park whose chief treasure is the Theater of the Fountains, designed by Maderno.

Where to Dine

Cacciani Restaurant ROMAN Cacciani is the top restaurant in Frascati, where the competition has always been tough. It boasts a terrace commanding a view of the valley, and the kitchen is exposed to the public. To start, we recommend the pasta specialties, such as pasta *cacio e pepe* (pasta with caciocavallo cheese and black pepper), or the original spaghetti with seafood and lentils. For a main course, the lamb with a sauce of white wine and vinegar is always fine. Of course, there is a large choice of wine. If you call ahead, the Cacciani family will arrange a visit to several of Frascati's wine-producing villas, along with a memorable meal at their restaurant.

Via Armando Diaz 13. © **06-9420378**. Reservations required on weekends. Main courses 12.50€–32.50€ ($11.15–$29). AE, DC, MC, V. Tues–Sun 12:30–3pm and 7:30–10:30pm. Closed Jan 7–19 and Aug 15–26.

Moments   A Rare View

If you have a car, you can continue about 5km (3 miles) past the Villa Aldobrandini in Frascati to **Tuscolo,** an ancient spot with the ruins of an amphitheater dating from about the 1st century B.C. It offers what may be one of Italy's most panoramic views.

ETRUSCAN HISTORICAL SIGHTS
CERVETERI (CAERE)

As you walk through Rome's Etruscan Museum (Villa Giulia), you'll often see *Caere* written under a figure vase or sarcophagus. This is a reference to the nearby town known today as Cerveteri, one of Italy's great Etruscan cities, whose origins could date from as far back as the 9th century B.C.

Of course, the Etruscan town has long since faded, but not the **Necropolis of Cerveteri** (© 06-9940001). The effect is eerie; Cerveteri is often called a "city of the dead." When you go beneath some of the mounds, you'll discover the most striking feature: The tombs are like rooms in Etruscan homes. The main burial ground is the Necropolis of Banditacca. Of the graves thus far uncovered, none is finer than the **Tomba Bella** (or the Reliefs' Tomb), the burial ground of the Matuna family. Articles such as utensils and even house pets were painted in stucco relief. Presumably these paintings were representations of items that the dead family would need in the world beyond. The necropolis is open Tuesday to Sunday 9am to 4pm. Admission is 4€ ($3.55) for adults, 2€ ($1.80) for children.

Relics from the necropolis are displayed at the **Museo Nazionale Cerite,** Piazza Santa Maria Maggiore (© 06-9941354). The museum, housed within the ancient walls and crenellations of Ruspoldi Castle, is open Tuesday to Sunday 9am to 7pm. Admission is free.

You can reach Cerveteri by bus or car. If you're driving, head out Via Aurelia, northwest of Rome, for 45km (28 miles). By public transport, take Metro Line A in Rome to the Lepanto stop; from Via Lepanto, you can catch a COTRAL bus (© 06-3244724) to Cerveteri; the trip takes about an hour and costs 2.45€ ($2.20). Once you're at Cerveteri, it's a 2km (1¼-mile) walk to the necropolis; follow the signs pointing the way.

TARQUINIA

If you want to see tombs even more striking and more recently excavated than those at Cerveteri, go to Tarquinia. The medieval turrets and fortifications atop the rocky cliffs overlooking the sea seem to contradict the Etruscan name of Tarquinia. Actually, Tarquinia is the adopted name of the old medieval community of Corneto, in honor of the major Etruscan city that once stood nearby.

The main attraction in the town is the **Tarquinia National Museum**, Piazza Cavour (© 0776-856036), devoted to Etruscan exhibits and sarcophagi excavated from the necropolis a few miles away. The museum is housed in the Palazzo Vitelleschi, a Gothic palace from the mid–15th century. Among the exhibits are gold jewelry, black vases with carved and painted bucolic scenes, and sarcophagi decorated with carvings of animals and relief figures of priests and military leaders. But the biggest attraction is in itself worth the ride from Rome: the almost life-size pair of **winged horses** from the pediment of a Tarquinian temple. The finish is worn here and there, and the terra-cotta color shows through; but the relief stands as one of the greatest Etruscan masterpieces ever discovered. The museum is open Tuesday to Sunday 9am to 7pm, and charges 4€ ($3.55) admission.

An 4€ ($3.55) fee admits you to the **Etruscan Necropolis** ★★ (© **0766-856308**), covering more than 4.5km (2¾ miles) of rough terrain near where the ancient Etruscan city once stood. Thousands of tombs have been discovered, some of which haven't been explored even today. Others, of course, were discovered by looters, but many treasures remain even though countless pieces were removed to museums and private collections. The **paintings** on the walls of the tombs have helped historians reconstruct the life of the Etruscans—a heretofore impossible feat without a written history. The paintings depict feasting couples in vivid colors mixed from iron oxide, lapis lazuli dust, and charcoal. One of the oldest tombs (from the 6th c. B.C.) depicts young men fishing while dolphins play and colorful birds fly high above. Many of the paintings convey an earthy, vigorous, sex-oriented life among the wealthy Etruscans. The tombs are generally open Tuesday to Sunday 8:30am to 4:30pm. You can reach the grave sites by taking a bus from the Barriera San Giusto to the Cimitero stop. Or try the 20-minute walk from the museum. Inquire at the museum for directions.

To reach Tarquinia by car, take Via Aurelia outside Rome and continue on the autostrada toward Civitavecchia. Bypass Civitavecchia and continue another 21km (13 miles) north until you see the exit signs for Tarquinia. As for public transport, a diretto train from Roma Ostiense station takes 50 minutes. Eight buses a day leave from the Via Lepanto stop in Rome for the 2-hour trip to the town of Barriera San Giusto, 2km (1¼ miles) from Tarquinia. Bus schedules are available at the **tourist office** in Piazza Cavour 1 (© **0766-856384**), open Monday to Saturday 8am to 1pm.

6

Florence

Except for Venice, no other European city lives off its past like Florence (Firenze). After all, it was the birthplace of the Renaissance, an amazing outburst of activity from the 14th to the 16th centuries that completely changed the Tuscan town and the world. Under the benevolent eye (and purse) of the Medicis, Florence blossomed into an unrivaled repository of art and architectural treasures by geniuses such as Botticelli, Brunelleschi, Cellini, Donatello, Fra Angelico, Ghiberti, Giotto, Leonardo, Michelangelo, and Raphael. Since the 19th century, it has been visited by millions wanting to see Michelangelo's *David,* Botticelli's *Birth of Venus,* Brunelleschi's dome on the Duomo, and Giotto's *campanile* (bell tower).

At first glance, Florence might seem a bit foreboding. Architecturally, it's not a Gothic fantasy of lace like Venice. Many of its palazzi look like severe fortresses, a characteristic of the Medici style. (They were built, after all, to keep foreign enemies at bay.) But these facades, however uninviting, mask treasures within, drawing thousands of visitors who overrun the narrow streets. The locals bemoan the tourist crush and at the same time welcome it because it puts food on the table. "The visitors have crowded our city and strained our facilities," laments a local merchant, "but they make it possible for me to own a villa in Fiesole and take my children on vacation to San Remo every year."

The city officials have been wise to keep the inner Renaissance core relatively free of modern architecture and polluting industry. Florence has industry, but it has been relegated to the suburbs. The city proper is relatively clean and safe, as Italian cities go. You can generally walk the narrow cobblestone streets at night safely, although caution is always advised.

May and September are the ideal times to visit. The worst times are the week before and including Easter, and from June until the first week of September—Florence is literally overrun during these times, and the streets weren't designed for mass tourism. Temperatures in July and August hover in the 70s and 80s, dropping to a low of 45°F in December and January.

1 Essentials

ARRIVING

BY PLANE   From Rome, you can catch a short domestic flight to **Galileo Galilei Airport** at Pisa (© 050-5000707), 93km (58 miles) west of Florence. **Alitalia** (© 050-20221 for the airport office; www.alitalia.it) offers two flights a day from New York to Pisa with one stop in Rome. You can take an express train for the hour-long trip to Florence. There's also a small domestic airport, **Amerigo Vespucci,** on Via del Termine, near A-11 (© 055-373498), 5.5km (3½ miles) northwest of Florence, a 15-minute drive. From the airport, you can reach Florence by ATAF bus 62, which stops at the main Santa Maria Novella rail terminal. **Alitalia** also provides domestic air service and holds offices in Florence at Lungarno degli Acciaiuoli 10-12R (© **055-27881**).

BY TRAIN   If you're coming north from Rome, count on a 2- to 3-hour trip, depending on your connection. **Santa Maria Novella rail station,** in Piazza della Stazione, adjoins Piazza Santa Maria Novella. For railway information, call © **848-888088.** Some trains into Florence stop at the **Stazione Campo di Marte,** on the eastern side of Florence. A 24-hour bus service (no. 91) runs between the two rail terminals.

BY BUS   Long-distance buses service Florence, run by **SITA,** Viale Cadorna 105 (© **055-47821**), and **Lazzi Eurolines,** Piazza Stazione 3R (© **055-215155**). Both SITA and Lazzi Eurolines offer transfers to Florence from Arezzo, Pisa, and San Giminiano. A one-way ticket to Florence from Pisa, for example, costs 5.60€ ($5).

BY CAR   Florence enjoys good autostrada connections with the rest of Italy, especially Rome and Bologna. A1 connects Florence with both the north and the south. Florence lies 277km (172 miles) north of Rome, 105km (65 miles) west of Bologna, and 298km (185 miles) south of Milan. Bologna is about an hour's drive away, and Rome is 3 hours away. The Tyrrhenian coast is only an hour from Florence on A11 heading west.

Use a car only to get *to* Florence, not to get around once you're there. Most of central Florence is closed to all vehicles except those of locals. If your hotel doesn't have parking, head for one of the city-run garages. Although there's a garage under the train station, a better deal is the **Parterre** parking lot under Piazza Libertà, north of Fortezza del Basso. If you're staying at least 1 night in a hotel, you can park here and can use a free bike; after presenting your hotel receipt as you leave or the hotel's stamp on your parking receipt, you'll pay only 8€ ($7.15) per night.

VISITOR INFORMATION

Contact the **Azienda Promozione Turistica,** which has several branches: Via A. Manzoni 16 (© **055-23320**), open Monday to Saturday 8:30am to 1:30pm; Via Cavour 1R (© **055-290832**), open March to November Monday to Saturday 8:15am to 7:15pm, and Sunday 8:15am to 1:45pm, and December to February Monday to Saturday 8:15am to 1:45pm; and just south of Piazza Santa Croce, at Borgo Santa Croce 29R (© **055-2340444**), open the same hours as the one at Via Cavour. There's also a small **Uffizio Informazioni Turistiche** inside the main train terminal.

You might want to surf the Web before you leave home. Two useful sites are **www.mega.it/florence** and **http://english.firenze.net.**

CITY LAYOUT

Florence is a city designed for walking, with all the major sights in a compact area. The only problem is that the sidewalks are almost unbearably crowded in summer.

The *centro storico* (historic center) is split by the **Arno River,** which usually is serene but can at times turn ferocious with floodwaters. The major part of Florence, certainly its historic core with most of the monuments, lies on the north ("right") side of the river. But the "left" side isn't devoid of attractions, including some wonderful trattorie and some great shopping finds, not to mention the Pitti Palace and the Giardini di Boboli, a series of impressive formal gardens. In addition, you'll want to cross over to check out the panoramic views of the city from Piazzale Michelangiolo—especially breathtaking at sunset.

> ### *Tips* The Red & the Black
>
> Florence has two street-numbering systems—red (*rosso*) numbers and black (*nero*) numbers. Red numbers identify commercial enterprises, such as shops and restaurants. Black numbers identify office buildings, private homes, apartment houses, and hotels. Renumbering without the color system is on the horizon, although no one seems exactly certain when it will be implemented. In this chapter, red-numbered addresses are indicated by an "R" following the building number, as in "39R."
>
> Because street numbers are chaotic, it's better to get a cross street or some landmark if you're looking for an address along a long boulevard.

The Arno is spanned by eight bridges, of which the **Ponte Vecchio (Old Bridge),** lined with overhanging jewelry stores, is the most celebrated and most central. Many of these bridges were ancient structures until the Nazis, in a hopeless last-ditch effort, senselessly destroyed them in their "defense" of Florence in 1944. With tenacity, Florence rebuilt its bridges, using pieces from the destroyed structures whenever possible. The **Ponte Santa Trínita** is the second-most-important bridge. It leads to **Via dei Tornabuoni,** the right bank's most important shopping street (don't look for bargains, however). At the Ponte Vecchio you can walk, again on the right bank of the Arno, along **Via per Santa Maria,** which becomes **Via Calimala.** This leads you into **Piazza della Repubblica,** a commercial district known for its cafes.

From here, you can take **Via Roma,** which leads directly into **Piazza di San Giovanni,** where you'll find the baptistry and its neighboring sibling, the larger **Piazza del Duomo,** with the world-famous cathedral and Giotto bell tower. From the far western edge of Piazza del Duomo you can take **Via del Proconsolo** south to **Piazza della Signoria,** to see the landmark Palazzo Vecchio and its sculpture-filled Loggia della Signoria.

High in the olive-planted hills overlooking Florence is the ancient town of **Fiesole,** with Etruscan and Roman ruins and a splendid cathedral.

At the very least, arm yourself with a map from the tourist office (see "Visitor Information," earlier). Ask for the one *con un stradario* (with a street index), which shows all the roads and is better for navigation than their more generalized orientation version. But if you'd like to see Florence in any depth—particularly those little side streets—buy a **Falk map,** available at all bookstores and at most newsstands.

THE NEIGHBORHOODS IN BRIEF

Florence isn't divided into neighborhoods the way many cities are. Most locals refer to either the left bank or the right bank of the Arno, and that's about it, unless they head out of town for the immediate environs, such as Fiesole. The following "neighborhoods"—really just areas centering on a palace, church, or square—are therefore rather arbitrary.
This section will give you some idea of where you might want to stay and where the major attractions are.

Centro Centro could include all the historic heart of Florence, but mostly the term is used to describe the area southwest of the Duomo. This district isn't as important as it used to be because Piazza della Signoria (see below) now attracts more visitors. Centro's heyday was in the 1800s, when it was filled with narrow medieval streets that were torn down to make a grander city center. Lost forever were great homes of the Medicis and the Sacchettis, among others. **Piazza della Repubblica,** though faded, is still lively day and night with its celebrated cafes. Centro's **Via dei Tournabuoni** is the city's most elegant shopping street.

Piazza del Duomo In the heart of Florence, **Piazza del Duomo** and its surrounding area are dominated by the tricolored **Duomo,** site of the former local grain and hay markets. It's one of the largest buildings in the Christian world, and you come on it unexpectedly because the surrounding buildings weren't torn down to give it breathing room. Capped by Brunelleschi's dome, the structure now dominates the skyline. Every visitor flocks here to see not only the Duomo but also the neighboring **campanile** (bell tower), one of Italy's most beautiful, and the **baptistry** across the way (its doors are among the jewels of Renaissance sculpture). Also in this neighborhood is the **Museo dell'- Opera del Duomo,** which includes some of the most important works of Donatello.

The Duomo is a central location that's loaded with hotels in all price categories. The streets north of the Duomo are long and often full of traffic, but those to the south make up a wonderful medieval tangle of alleys and tiny squares heading toward Piazza della Signoria.

Piazza della Signoria The core of pre-Renaissance Florence, this heavily visited square is home to the **Loggia dei Lanzi,** with Cellini's *Perseus* holding up a beheaded Medusa, Florence's most photographed statue (the original was removed for restoration, and this is a copy), as well as Michelangelo's *David* (also a copy—the original was moved inside to protect it from the elements). To the south are the

Galleria degli Uffizi and the **Palazzo Vecchio.** This is the city's civic heart and perhaps the best bet for museum hounds. It's a well-polished part of the tourist zone yet still retains the narrow medieval streets where Dante grew up—back alleys where tour-bus crowds rarely set foot. The few blocks just north of the Ponte Vecchio have good shopping, but unappealing modern buildings were planted here to replace the district that was destroyed in World War II. The whole neighborhood can be stiflingly crowded in summer, but in those moments when you catch it empty of tour groups, it remains the most romantic part of Florence. Southwest of Piazza della Signoria is the **Ponte Vecchio (Old Bridge)** area. The oldest of Florence's bridges, it's flanked by jewelry stores and will carry you to the Oltrarno. This has always been a strategic crossing place, even when it was a stone bridge. In the Middle Ages, it was the center for leather craftsmen, fishmongers, and butchers, but over the years jewelers' shops have moved in. The **Vasari Corridor (Corridoio Vasariano)** runs the length of the bridge above the shops—built by Vasari in just 5 months. One of the most congested parts of Florence, this area is on every visitor's itinerary.

Piazza Santa Maria Novella & the Train Station On the northwestern edge of central Florence is the large Piazza Santa Maria Novella, with its church of the same name. This area isn't all art and culture, however. Northwest of Santa Maria Novella is the city's busiest section, centered at **Piazza della Stazione,** where the **Stazione di Santa Maria Novella** is located. Like all rail stations in Italy, it's surrounded by budget hotels. Leading off **Piazza dell'Unitá Italiana,** Via del

Melarancio goes a short distance east to **San Lorenzo,** the first cathedral of Florence. Beyond San Lorenzo is **Piazza Madonna degli Aldobrandini,** the entrance to the **Medici Chapels.** Thousands flock here to see Michelangelo's tombs, whose allegorical figures of *Day* and *Night* are among the most famous sculptures of all time. Southwest of Piazza Santa Maria Novella, toward the Arno, is **Piazza Ognissanti,** a fashionable (albeit congested) Renaissance square opening onto the river. On this square are two of the city's most legendary hotels: the **Grand** and the **Excelsior.**

Piazza San Marco Although Piazza San Marco has none of the grandeur of the square of the same name in Venice, the piazza and its surroundings on the northern fringe of Centro are nevertheless one of the most important in Florence—centered around its church, now the Museo di San Marco. Located in a former Dominican monastery, the museum houses a collection of the greatest works of Fra Angelico, who decorated the walls of the monks' cells with edifying scenes. This area is also overrun by visitors, most rushing to the Galleria dell'Accademia on Via Ricasoli to see the monumental figure of *David* (1501–04) by Michelangelo. Other area highlights include Piazza della Santissima Annunziata, Florence's most beautiful, graced by an equestrian statue of Ferdinand I de' Medici by Bologna.

Piazza Santa Croce This section and its Piazza Santa Croce are in the southeastern part of the old town, near the Arno, dominated by the Gothic church of Santa Croce (Holy Cross), completed in 1442. Once the scene of jousts and festivals, even *calcio* (a local game of football), the piazza in time became the headquarters of the Franciscans, who established a firm base there in 1218. The area is always full of visitors but isn't as congested as the areas previously mentioned. The church contains the tombs of Michelangelo and Machiavelli, among others. A little distance to the north of Santa Croce is the Casa Buonarroti, on Via Ghibellina, which Michelangelo acquired for his nephew. Today it's a museum with a collection of Michelangelo's works, mainly drawings, gathered by his nephew. From here you can follow Via Buonarroti to Piazza dei Ciompi, a lively square that's off the beaten track, filled with stalls peddling secondhand goods. Look for old coins, books, and even antique Italian uniforms.

Across the Arno The "left bank" of the Arno River, known as the Oltrarno, is home to the Palazzo Pitti, with its picture gallery and Giardini di Boboli; Massacio's frescoes in the church of Santa Maria del Carmine; artisans' workshops; some good restaurants; and the postcard panorama of Florence and its dome from Piazzale Michelangiolo. At the top of the gardens is an elegant fortress known as the Forte Belvedere (1590–95), with a panoramic view of Florence that's well worth the climb. The center of this district is Piazza Santo Spirito, a lovely, shady square.

2 Getting Around

Because Florence is so compact, walking is the ideal way to get around—and, at times, the only way because of numerous pedestrian zones. In theory, at least, pedestrians have the right of way at uncontrolled zebra crossings, but don't count on that if you encounter a speeding Vespa.

BY BUS

If you plan to use public buses, you must buy your ticket before boarding, but for 1€ (90¢) you can ride on any public bus for a total of 60 minutes. A 3-hour pass costs 2€ ($1.80) and a 24-hour ticket costs 4€ ($3.55). You can buy bus tickets at *tabacchi* (tobacconists) and newsstands. Once on board, you must validate your ticket in the box near the rear door, or you stand to be fined 40€ ($35.70)—no excuses accepted. The local **bus station** (which serves as the terminal for ATAF city buses) is at Piazza della Stazione (✆ **055-56501**), behind the train station.

Bus routes are posted at bus stops, but the numbers of routes can change overnight because of sudden repair work going on at one of the ancient streets—perhaps a water main broke overnight and caused flooding. We recently found that a bus route map printed only 1 week beforehand was already outdated. Therefore, if you're dependent on bus transport, you'll need to inquire that day for the exact number of the vehicle you want to board.

BY TAXI

You can find taxis at stands at nearly all the major squares. Rates are a bit expensive: The charge is .75€ (65¢) per kilometer, with a 3.25€ ($2.90) minimum. If you need a **radio taxi,** call ✆ **055-4390** or 055-4798.

BY BICYCLE & MOTOR SCOOTER

Bicycles and motor scooters, if you avoid the whizzing traffic, are two other practical ways of getting around. **Alinari,** near the rail station at Via Guelfa 85R (✆ **055-280500**), rents bikes for 2€ to 2.60€ ($1.80–$2.30) per hour, or 10€ to 15€ ($8.95–$13.40) per day, depending on the model. Also available are small-engined, rather loud motor scooters renting for 7.50€ ($6.70) per hour, 25€ ($22.35) per 5 hours, or 40€ ($35.70) per day. Renters must be 18 or over and must leave a passport, a driver's license, and the number of a valid credit card. Alinari is open Monday to Saturday 9:30am to 1pm and 3 to 7:30pm, and Sunday (Apr–Oct) 10am to 1pm and 3 to 7pm.

BY CAR

Just forget it. Driving in Florence is hopeless—not only because of the snarled traffic and the maze of one-way streets, but also because much of what you've come to see is in a pedestrian zone. If you arrive by car, look for prominently posted blue signs with the letter P that will lead you to the nearest garage. If your hotel doesn't have its own garage, someone on the staff will direct you to the nearest one or will arrange valet parking. Garage fees average 17.50€ to 22.50€ ($15.65–$20.10) depending on the size of your car, although vans or large luxury cars might cost as much as 35€ ($31.25).

The most centrally located garages are the **International Garage,** Via Palazzuolo 29 (✆ **055-282386**); **Garage La Stazione,** 3A Via Alamanni (✆ **055-284768**); **Autoparking SLL,** Via Fiesolana 19 (✆ **055-2477871**); and **Garage Anglo-Americano,** Via dei Barbadori 5 (✆ **055-214418**). If these are full, you can almost always find a space at the **Garage Porte Nuove,** Via delle Portenuove 21 (✆ **055-333355**).

You will, however, need a car to explore the surrounding countryside of Tuscany in any depth. Car-rental agencies include **Avis,** Borgo Ognissanti 128R (✆ **800/831-8000** in North America, or 055-213629 locally; www.avis.com); **Italy by Car,** Vorgo Ognissanti 134R (✆ **055-287161**); and **Hertz,** Via del Termine (✆ **800/654-3131** in North America, or 055-307370 locally; www.hertz.com).

FAST FACTS: Florence

American Express The office is at Via Dante Alighieri 22R (© **055-50981**); it's open Monday to Friday 9am to 5:30pm and Saturday 9am to 12:30pm.

Consulates The **U.S. Consulate** is at Lungarno Amerigo Vespucci 38 (© **055-2398276**), open Monday to Friday 9am to 12:30pm and 2 to 3:30pm. The **U.K. Consulate** is at Lungarno Corsini 2 (© **055-284133**), near Piazza Santa Trinità, open Monday to Friday 9:30am to 12:30pm and 2:30 to 4:30pm. Citizens of other English-speaking countries, including **Canada, Australia,** and **New Zealand,** should contact their diplomatic representatives in Rome (see chapter 3, "Planning Your Trip to Italy").

Currency Exchange Local banks have the best rates, and most are open Monday to Friday 8:30am to 1:30pm and 2:45 to 3:45pm. The tourist office (see section 1 of this chapter, "Essentials") exchanges money at official rates when banks are closed and on holidays, but a commission is often charged. You can also go to the Ufficio Informazione booth at the rail station, open daily 7:30am to 7:40pm. American Express (above) also exchanges money. One of the best places to exchange currency is the post office (below).

Dentists/Doctors For a list of English-speaking doctors or dentists, consult your consulate (above) or contact **Tourist Medical Service,** Via Lorenzo il Magnifico 59 (© **055-475411**). Visits without an appointment are possible only Monday to Friday 11am to noon and 5 to 6pm. After hours, an answering service gives names and phone numbers of dentists and doctors who are on duty.

Emergencies For fire, call © **115**; for an ambulance, call © **118**; for the police, call © **113**; and for road service, call © **116.**

Hospitals Call the **General Hospital** of Santa Maria Nuova, Piazza Santa Maria Nuova 1 (© **055-27581**).

Internet Access You can check your messages or send e-mail at **Internet Train,** Via dell'Orivolo 40R (© **055-2638968**; www.internettrain.it).

Pharmacies The **Farmacia Molteni,** Via Calzaiuoli 7R (© **055-215472**), is open 24 hours.

Police Dial © **113** in an emergency. English-speaking foreigners who want to see and talk to the police should go to the **Ufficio Stranieri station,** Via Zara 2 (© **055-49771**), where English-speaking personnel are available daily 9am to 2pm.

Post Office The **Central Post Office** is at Via Pellicceria 3, off Piazza della Repubblica (© **055-27361** for English-speaking operators), open Monday to Saturday 8:15am to 7pm. You can buy stamps and telephone cards at windows 21 and 22. A foreign exchange office is open Monday to Friday 8:15am to 6pm. If you want to send packages of up to 20kg (44 lb.), go to the rear of the building and enter at Piazza Davantati 4.

Safety Violent crimes are rare in Florence; most crime consists mainly of pickpockets who frequent crowded tourist centers, such as corridors of the Uffizi Galleries. Members of group tours who cluster together are often singled out as victims. Car thefts are relatively common: Don't leave your luggage in an unguarded car, even if it's locked in the trunk. Women should be especially careful in avoiding purse-snatchers, some of whom grab a purse while whizzing by on a Vespa, often knocking the woman down. Documents such as passports and extra money are better stored in safes at your hotel, if available.

Telephone The **country code** for Italy is **39.** The **city code** for Florence is **055;** use this code when calling from *anywhere* outside or inside Italy—even within Florence itself (and you must now include the 0 every time, even when calling from abroad). See the Fast Facts box at the end of chapter 3 (or the front cover of this book) for complete details on how to call Italy, how to place calls within Italy, and how to call home once you're in Italy.

You can place **long-distance and international calls** at the Telecom office north of the Duomo at Via Cavour 21R (open daily 8am–9:45pm).

Toilets Public toilets are found in most galleries, museums, bars and cafes, and restaurants, as well as bus, train, and air terminals. Usually they're designated as WC (water closet) or *donne* (women) or *uomini* (men). The most confusing designation is *signori* (gentlemen) and *signore* (ladies), so watch that final *i* and *e!*

3 Where to Stay

For sheer charm and luxury, Florence's accommodations are among the finest in Europe; many grand old villas and palaces have been converted into hotels. There aren't too many cities where you can find a 15th- or 16th-century palace—tastefully decorated and most comfortable—rated a second-class *pensione* (hotel). Florence is equipped with hotels in all price ranges and with widely varying standards, comfort, service, and efficiency.

During summer, there simply aren't enough rooms to meet the demand, so *reserve well in advance.* If you arrive without a reservation and don't want to wander around town on your own looking for a room, go in person (instead of calling) to the **Consorzio ITA office** (C 055-212245) in the rail terminal at Piazza della Stazione, open daily 8:45am to 8pm. The Consorzio ITA charges 2.25€ to 7.50€ ($2–$6.70) for the service and collects the first night's room charge.

The most desirable place to stay in terms of shopping, nightlife, sightseeing, and restaurants is the historic heart on the Arno's right bank, especially in Centro and around the Duomo and Piazza della Signoria. Yes, this area is touristy and often expensive, but staying here is a lot better than staying on the outskirts—inadequate public transport makes commuting difficult. Driving into the center is impossible because of the heavy traffic and because major districts are pedestrian-only zones.

The cheapest lodgings in Centro are around the rail station; these are also the least desirable, with a few notable exceptions. The area directly around the Termini and Santa Maria Novella, though generally safe during the day, is the center of major drug dealing late at night and should be avoided then. This area isn't all budget lodgings, however; also here is Piazza Ognissanti (south of Piazza Santa Maria Novella toward the Arno), one of Florence's most fashionable squares and the home of the city's two most famous hotels. Also in the historic center, but less tourist-trodden and a bit more tranquil, is the area around Piazza San Marco and the University quarter.

Where to Stay in Florence

Albergo Losanna **38**
Boscolo Hotel Astoria **7**
Gallery Hotel Art **20**
Grand Hotel **14**
Grand Hotel Cavour **27**
Grand Hotel Villa Medici **12**
Hermitage Hotel **19**
Hotel Abaco **8**
Hotel Albani Firenze **4**
Hotel Ariele **13**
Hotel Bellettini **6**
Hotel Berkleys **3**
Hotel Calzaiuoli **26**
Hotel Casci **29**
Hotel Cellai **32**
Hotel Cimabue **33**
Hotel Continental **21**
Hotel Elite **10**
Hotel Europa **28**
Hotel J and J **40**
Hotel La Due Fontane **36**
Hotel Le Vigne **9**
Hotel Malaspina **31**
Hotel Mario's **1**
Hotel Monna Lisa **41**
Hotel Morandi alla Crocetta **37**
Hotel Nuova Italia **5**
Hotel Porta Rossa **24**
Hotel Regency **39**
Hotel Tornabuoni Beacci **23**
Hotel Torre Guelfa **22**
Hotel Vasari **2**
Hotel Villa Carlotta **16**
Loggiato dei Servizi **35**
Orto de' Medici **30**
Pensione Annalena **17**
Piccolo Hotel **34**
Pitti Palace Hotel **18**
Plaza Hotel Lucchesi **42**
Ritz Hotel **43**
Savoy Hotel **25**
Villa Azalée **11**
Villa La Massa **45**
Villa Montartino **44**
Westin Excelsior **15**

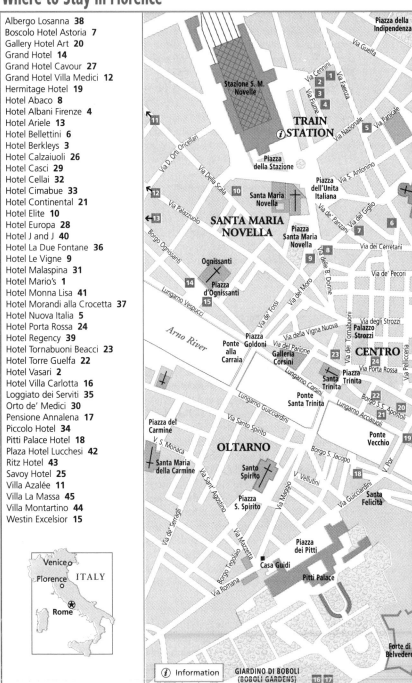

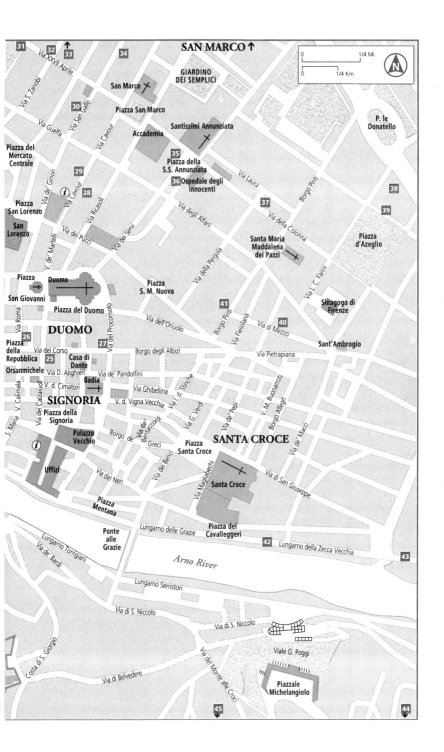

SAN MARCO ↑

GIARDINO
DEI SEMPLICI

San Marco ✠

Piazza San Marco

P. le
Donatello

Santissimi Annunziata ✠

Accademia

Piazza del
Mercato
Centrale

Piazza della
S.S. Annunziata

Ospedale degli
Innocenti

Via Laura

Piazza
d'Azeglio

Piazza
San Lorenzo

Via degli Alfani

San
Lorenzo

Santa Maria
Maddalena
dei Pazzi

Via dei Pucci

Piazza
S. M. Nuova

Via della Pergola

Sinagoga di
Firenze

Piazza
San Giovanni

Duomo

Piazza del Duomo

Via dell'Oriuolo

DUOMO

Borgo Pinti

Via di Mezzo

Sant'Ambrogio

Piazza
della
Repubblica

Via del Corso

Borgo degli Albizi

Via Pietrapiana

Orsanmichele

Casa di
Dante

Via D. Alighieri

Via de' Pandolfini

V. d. Cimatori

Badia

Via Ghibellina

SIGNORIA

V. d. Vigna Vecchia

Piazza della
Signoria

SANTA CROCE

Palazzo
Vecchio

Borgo de'
Greci

Piazza
Santa Croce

Uffizi

Via del Neri

Santa Croce

Via di San Giuseppe

Piazza
Mentana

Ponte
alle
Grazie

Lungarno delle Grazie

Piazza dei
Cavalleggeri

Lungarno della Zecca Vecchia

Arno River

Lungarno Serristori

Via di S. Niccolo

Via di S. Niccolo

Viale G. Poggi

Via di Belvedere

Piazzale
Michelangiolo

Once you cross the Arno, lodgings are much scarcer, although there are places to stay, including some pensioni. In general, prices are lower across the Arno, and you'll be near one of the major attractions, the Pitti Palace. Many luxury hotels exist on the outskirts of Florence, as do cheaper boardinghouses. Again, these are acceptable alternatives if you don't mind the commute. As a final option, consider lodging in Fiesole, where it's cooler and much more tranquil. Bus no. 7 runs back and forth between Fiesole and Centro.

IN CENTRO
MODERATE

Hotel Tornabuoni Beacci ⭐ Near Piazza Santa Trinita on the principal shopping street, this hotel occupies the three top floors of a 16th-century Strozzi family palazzo. Its public rooms have been furnished in an old Florentine style, with bowls of flowers, parquet floors, a formal fireplace, old paintings, murals, and rugs. Recently renovated, it still has an air of old-fashioned gentility. The roof terrace is for late-afternoon drinks or breakfast; in summer, dinner, typically Florentine and Italian dishes, is also served here (except in Aug, when it's closed). The view of the nearby Bellosguardo hills, churches, towers, and rooftops is panoramic. The guest rooms are moderately well furnished but worn, and top-floor rooms, though a bit cramped, open onto views of the rooftops. The loveliest part of the whole place is a cozy reading room with a 1600s tapestry and a large fireplace.

Via Tornabuoni 3, 50123 Firenze. ✆ **055-212645.** Fax 055-283594. www.bthotel.it. 30 units. 185€–220€ ($165.20–$196.45) double; 280€–360€ ($250.05–$321.50) suite. Rates include buffet breakfast. AE, DC, MC, V. Parking 22.50€–25€ ($20.10–$22.35). Bus: B, 6, 11, or 36. **Amenities:** Restaurant; bar; room service; babysitting; laundry/dry cleaning. *In room:* A/C, TV, minibar, hair dryer.

INEXPENSIVE

Hotel Porta Rossa ⭐ This hotel occupies the top three floors of a six-story building. Supposedly, this is the second-oldest hotel in Italy, dating from 1386. It's a bit dark, but on a hot Tuscan summer day, that's as good as air-conditioning. Despite the building's age, the hotel has installed modern conveniences, good beds, and ample bathrooms. Guest rooms are spacious, and the hotel has a little terrace offering a panoramic view.

Via Porta Rossa 19, 50123 Firenze. ✆ **055-287551.** Fax 055-282179. 79 units (some with shower only, some with tub only). 170€ ($151.80) double; 210€ ($187.55) suite for 3 or 4. Rates include breakfast. AE, DC, MC, V. Parking 20€–32.50€ ($17.85–$29). Bus: A. **Amenities:** Bar; babysitting; laundry/dry cleaning. *In room:* A/C, TV, minibar, hair dryer, safe.

NEAR PIAZZA DEL DUOMO
VERY EXPENSIVE

Savoy Hotel ⭐⭐ Everything is fresh and new again at Florence's most legendary hotel, which opened in 1896. It's just a notch below the Excelsior and the Grand in luxury, and it offers a great location for sightseers. Refined Italian elegance is the hallmark of this landmark, and its original architecture has been preserved through all its renovations. The Savoy has made a nod to the 21st century with such amenities as two-line phones, voice mail, interactive TVs, and fax machines in the sumptuously decorated guest rooms. Bathrooms are beautifully tiled. The corner accommodations (with room numbers ending in 06 and 07) are the most spacious and have the best views. Units on the second and fourth floors have small terraces.

Piazza della Repubblica 7, 50123 Firenze. © **055-27351**. Fax 055-2735888. www.roccofortehotels.com. 107 units (some with shower only). 412.50€–440€ ($368.35–$392.90) double; from 750€ ($669.75) suite. AE, DC, MC, V. Parking 27.50€ ($24.55). Bus: 22, 36, or 37. **Amenities:** Restaurant; bar; room service; babysitting; laundry/dry cleaning. In room: A/C, TV, minibar, hair dryer, safe.

EXPENSIVE

Hotel Calzaiuoli ⊛ Midway between the Duomo and the Uffizi, this hotel enjoys a fabulous location. Although the building is old (it was a home in the 1800s) and the location is historic, the interior has been modernized in a minimalist contemporary style. Its Pietra Serena staircase remains, however. This four-story hotel has an elevator to bring guests to their rooms, which are medium-size, with functional modern furnishings and good beds. Some rooms look out over the festive street scene (with its associated noise) or out back (either over the rooftops to the Bargello and Badia Towers or up to the Duomo's cupola). The recently renovated bathrooms are immaculately kept.

Via dei Calzaiuoli 6, 50122 Firenze. © **055-212456**. Fax 055-268310. www.calzaiuoli.it. 45 units (half with shower only). 180€–225€ ($160.75–$200.95) double. Rates include breakfast. AE, DC, MC, V. Parking 25€ ($22.35). Bus: 22, 36, or 37. **Amenities:** Lounge; laundry. In room: A/C, TV, minibar, hair dryer, safe.

MODERATE

Grand Hotel Cavour Opposite the Bargello, this 13th-century palace stands on one of Florence's noisiest streets (even double-glazed windows can't quite block out the sounds). Check out the coved main lounge, with its frescoed ceiling and crystal chandelier, and the chapel now used as a dining room (the altar and confessional are still there). The guest rooms are traditional and comfortable but a little too claustrophobic. The bathrooms have more than enough shelf space. On every floor is a bathroom specially fitted for travelers with disabilities.

At the front desk, the professional English-speaking staff can organize city tours upon request. The roof terrace, "Michelangelo," offers a panoramic sweep over the Duomo, Palazzo Vecchio, and more.

Via del Proconsolo 3, 50122 Firenze. © **055-282461**. Fax 055-218955. www.hotelcavour.com. 110 units (some with shower only). 166€–186€ ($148.25–$166.10) double. Rates include buffet breakfast. AE, DC, MC, V. Parking 25€ ($22.35). Bus: 14, 23, or 71. **Amenities:** Restaurant; wine cellar; lounge; car-rental desk; salon; room service; babysitting; laundry. In room: A/C, TV, minibar, hair dryer, safe.

NEAR THE PONTE VECCHIO
VERY EXPENSIVE

Gallery Hotel Art ⊛ The Ferragamo family has long been celebrated for setting styles in Florence. Founding father Salvatore was known as shoemaker to the stars, having shod such Hollywood royalty as Greta Garbo. One of the family's latest ventures is this unique boutique hotel near the Ponte Vecchio, which successfully combines the occasional antique with a sleek modern design sensibility. As befits its name, its art theme stretches from the public areas to the pin-striped guest rooms. Whimsical touches include the insect watercolors of Alberto Reggianini. The rectilinear armchairs are in suede and pigskin, and the books in the library were hand selected (often first editions of English classics). The good-size bedrooms sport clean, contemporary design, with leather headboards, fine linens, and Bulgari products in the well-maintained, tiled bathrooms.

Vicolo dell'Oro 5, 50123 Firenze. © **055-27263**. Fax 055-268557. www.lungarnohotels.com. 65 units. 225€–350€ ($200.95–$312.55) double; 380€–750€ ($339.35–$669.75) suite. Rates include buffet breakfast. AE, DC, MC, V. Bus: 1, 10, 11, 17. **Amenities:** Sleek bar; concierge; car-rental desk; room service; babysitting. In room: A/C, TV, minibar, hair dryer, safe.

Hotel Continental ⚗   At the Ponte Vecchio's entrance, the Continental, restored in 2002, occupies some select real estate. Through the lounge windows and from some of the rooms, you can see the little jewelry and leather shops flanking the bridge. The hotel was created in the 1960s, so its style is utilitarian, with functional furniture softened by decorative accessories. You reach your room by the elevator or a wrought-iron staircase (parts of the old stone structure have been retained). The guest rooms range from medium to large and offer all the standard comforts, including quality beds. Some have balconies opening onto panoramic views. The bathrooms are all well kept. The roof terrace is a perfect place for viewing Piazzale Michelangiolo, the Pitti Palace, the Duomo and campanile, and Fiesole. Artists fight to get the penthouse suite up in the Torre Guelfa dei Consorti (tower).

Lungarno Acciaiuoli 2, 50123 Firenze. ℂ 055-27262. Fax 055-283139. www.lungarnohotels.it. 48 units. 230€–255€ ($205.40–$227.70) double; from 475€ ($424.20) suite. Rates include buffet breakfast. AE, DC, MC, V. Valet parking 25€ ($22.35). **Amenities:** Bar; room service; massage; babysitting; laundry; dry cleaning. *In room:* A/C, TV, dataport, minibar, hair dryer, safe.

EXPENSIVE

Hermitage Hotel ⚗ *Finds*   On the Arno, at the foot of the Ponte Vecchio and near the Uffizi, the offbeat Hermitage is a charming place that has been recently renovated. It boasts a rooftop sun terrace offering a view of much of Florence, including the nearby Uffizi and the Duomo. You can take your breakfast under a leafy arbor surrounded by potted roses and geraniums. The success of this hotel has much to do with its English-speaking owner, Vincenzo Scarcelli, who has made it an extension of his home and furnished it in part with antiques and well-chosen reproductions. Best of all is his warmth toward guests, many of whom keep coming back. The small guest rooms are pleasantly furnished (if a little dark), many with 17th- to 19th-century Tuscan antiques, rich brocades, and good beds, plus double-glazed windows that cut down on noise. The tiled bathrooms are superb, with deluxe little shampoos and shower soaps; many have Jacuzzi tubs.

Vicolo Marzio 1, Piazza del Pesce I, 50122 Firenze. ℂ 055-287216. Fax 055-212208. www.hermitage hotel.com. 28 units. 187€–233€ ($167–$208.05) double; 208€–260€ ($185.75–$232.20) triple; 228€–285€ ($203.60–$254.50) family room. Rates include breakfast. MC, V. Parking 17.50€–22.50€ ($15.65–$20.10). Bus: B. **Amenities:** Bar; room service; laundry/dry cleaning. *In room:* A/C, TV, hair dryer, safe.

MODERATE

Hotel Torre Guelfa ⚗   One reason to stay in this atmospheric hotel is to drink in the panoramic 360° view from the hotel's 13th-century tower, the tallest privately owned tower in Florence's centro storico. Although you're just two steps from the Ponte Vecchio (and equidistant from the Duomo), you'll want to put sightseeing on hold and linger in your comfy canopied iron bed; your room is made even more inviting by pastel-washed walls and paisley carpeting (for a view similar to the medieval tower's, ask for room no. 15, with its huge private terrace). In 1998, all the bathrooms were renovated and given more shelf space.

Borgo SS. Apostoli 8 (between Via dei Tornabuoni and Via Per Santa Maria), 50123 Firenze. ℂ **055-2396338.** Fax 055-2398577. 21 units. 170€–200€ ($151.80–$178.60) double. Rates include breakfast. AE, MC, V. Bus: D, 11, 36, 37, 68. **Amenities:** Bar; room service; laundry/dry cleaning. *In room:* A/C, TV, minibar, hair dryer.

NEAR PIAZZA SANTA MARIA NOVELLA & THE TRAIN STATION
VERY EXPENSIVE

Boscolo Hotel Astoria ⚗   Despite its location in a sea of budget hotels, this choice is set in an impressive Renaissance palace, the nicely restored Palazzo Gaddi. In one of its rooms, John Milton wrote parts of *Paradise Lost*. The hotel has been renovated and turned into a serviceable choice, with a helpful staff and experienced management. From the guest rooms on the upper floors, you'll have a view over the terra-cotta rooftops. All rooms have stylish traditional furnishings, with quality linen and a monochromatic color scheme whose tones change on every floor. The front rooms, overlooking a busy street, are the noisiest, but double windows conceal much of the sound of traffic.

Via del Giglio 9, 50123 Firenze. © 055-2398095. Fax 055-214632. www.boscolohotels.com. 106 units. 205€–320€ ($183.05–$285.70) double; 300€–425€ ($267.90–$379.55) suite. Rates include buffet breakfast. AE, DC, MC, V. Parking 22.50€ ($20.10) nearby. Bus: 1, 9, 14, 17, 23, 36, and 37. **Amenities:** Restaurant; bar; car-rental desk; room service; babysitting; laundry. *In room:* A/C, TV, minibar, hair dryer, safe.

Grand Hotel ★★   The Grand is a bastion of luxury across from the even more luxurious Westin Excelsior (see below). The hotel was restored to some of its former glory when ITT Sheraton bought the CIGA chain, and its Belle Epoque lounges are truly grand. The guest rooms have a refined elegance meant to evoke 15th-century Florence, with silks, brocades, frescoes, and real or reproduction antiques; the most desirable units overlook the Arno. The large bathrooms, adorned in two types of Italian marble, are filled with amenities such as plush bathrobes, separate phone lines, and designer bidets.

Piazza Ognissanti 1, 50123 Firenze. © **800/325-3589** in the U.S. and Canada, or 055-288781. Fax 055-217400. www.luxurycollection.com/grandflorence. 107 units. 570€–770€ ($509–$687.60) double; from 1,099€ ($981.40) suite. AE, DC, MC, V. Parking from 30€ ($26.80). Bus: 6 or 17. **Amenities:** Restaurant; bar; valet; room service; babysitting; laundry/dry cleaning. *In room:* A/C, TV, minibar, hair dryer, safe.

Grand Hotel Villa Medici ★★   This old-time favorite occupies an 18th-century Medici palace 2 blocks southwest of the train station. Of all the government-rated five-star hotels of Florence, it is the only one with its own pool and health club. It generally appeals more to Europeans than to Americans, who might want more up-to-date facilities, although it was renovated in 2001 (when the guest rooms were spruced up and given such extras as electronic safes). Most rooms have twin beds. The most peaceful rooms front the garden, but during the day there's noise from the convent school next door. The Carrara-marble bathrooms are spacious and contain lots of extras. We prefer the sixth-floor accommodations because they open onto terraces. The staff is one of the best in Florence. Out back is a private garden, not Florence's finest, but with one of the only swimming pools in town.

Via il Prato 42, 50123 Firenze. © **055-2381331.** Fax 055-2381336. www.villamedicihotel.com. 103 units. 410€–440€ ($366.15–$392.90) double; 690€–900€ ($616.05–$803.55) suite. AE, DC, MC, V. Parking 17.50€–22.50€ ($15.65–$20.10). Bus: 1, 9, 14, 17, 23, 36, or 37. **Amenities:** 2 restaurants (including a romantic dining room and outdoor dining in summer); elegant piano bar; pool; fitness center with sauna; room service; babysitting; laundry/dry cleaning. *In room:* A/C, TV, dataport, minibar, hair dryer, safe.

Westin Excelsior ★★★ *Kids*   The sophisticated Westin Excelsior is Florence's prime luxury address, the first choice for those who like glamour and glitz. The sumptuousness will bowl you over (if the high prices don't get you first). This glamorous hotel, located near the Ponte Vecchio and the Uffizi, boasts the best service in town. Part of the hotel was once owned by Carolina Bonaparte, Napoléon's sister; the old palazzi were unified in 1927 and decorated with colored marbles, walnut furniture, Oriental rugs, and neoclassical frescoes.

The opulent, newly renovated guest rooms have 19th-century Florentine antiques, sumptuous fabrics, comfortable chairs, the Westin chain's signature "heavenly beds," and two-line phones; stereos and VCRs are available upon request. The bathrooms boast heated towel racks, deluxe toiletries, and high ceilings. In these old palaces, expect accommodations to come in a variety of configurations. The rooms on the top floor have balconies overlooking the Arno and the Ponte Vecchio. Parents will appreciate the special amenities for kids: safety kits that help childproof your room, spill-proof cups, bath toys, cribs, and kids' menus in the restaurants.

Piazza Ognissanti 3, 50123 Firenze. (✆) **800/325-3535** in the U.S. and Canada, or 055-264201. Fax 055-210278. www.westin.com/excelsiorflorence. 191 units. 570€–770€ ($509–$687.60) double; from 1,099€ ($981.40) junior suite. AE, DC, MC, V. Parking 30€ ($26.80). Bus: 6 or 17. **Amenities:** Restaurant; bar; valet; room service; babysitting; laundry/dry cleaning. *In room:* A/C, TV, minibar, hair dryer, safe.

EXPENSIVE

Hotel Albani Firenze ✮   In 1993, a respected nationwide chain transformed a run-down pensione, a 10-minute walk from the Duomo and close to the train station, into one of Florence's most appealing luxury hotels, set in a structure that was built around 1900 as a private villa. Today, you'll find up-to-date comforts, artwork, and architectural embellishments. The high-ceilinged interiors, outfitted in tones of soft terra-cottas and browns, sometimes verge on the theatrical but are never forbidding. The guest rooms, ranging from medium to spacious, possess style and grace, with mahogany beds.

Via Fiume 12, 50123 Firenze. (✆) **055-26030.** Fax 055-211045. www.hotelalbani.it. 100 units. 210€–300€ ($187.55–$267.90) double; from 500€ ($446.50) suite. Rates include breakfast. AE, DC, MC, V. Valet parking 20€ ($17.85). Bus: 10, 12, 25, 31, or 32. **Amenities:** Restaurant (Italian/international, with large wine list); bar; room service; laundry/dry cleaning. *In room:* A/C, TV, minibar, hair dryer, safe.

MODERATE

Hotel Ariele   A block from the Arno, the Ariele is a corner villa that has been converted into a roomy pensione. The late 1700s building is architecturally impressive, with large salons and lofty ceilings. The furnishings, however, combine the antique with the simply functional. The guest rooms are a grab bag of comfort; you can still get a good night's sleep even if the beds are a bit old (they're still firm). Although breakfast is the only meal served, the staff will provide you with the names of some restaurants nearby, where the hotel's guests receive discounts.

Via Magenta 11, 50123 Firenze. (✆) **055-211509.** Fax 055-268521. hotelariele@libero.it. 39 units (10 with shower only). 100€–140€ ($89.30–$125) double; 120€–176€ ($107.15–$157.15) triple. Rates include breakfast. AE, DC, DISC, MC, V. Parking 10€ ($8.95). Bus: A, B, or D. **Amenities:** Bar; room service; babysitting. *In room:* A/C, TV, hair dryer, safe.

Hotel Malaspina   A 10-minute walk north of the Duomo, this three-story hotel occupies a 19th-century structure (before that, it was a dorm for students at a nearby dentistry school). The interior has been carefully renovated and filled with traditional furniture that fits gracefully into the high-ceilinged public rooms and midsize to large guest rooms. The windows are big, and the floors tend to be covered in glazed or terra-cotta tiles.

Piazza dell'Indipendenza 24, 50129 Firenze. (✆) **055-489869.** Fax 055-474809. www.malaspinahotel.it. 31 units (some with shower only). 185€ ($165.20) double; 240€ ($214.30) triple. Rates include breakfast. AE, DC, MC, V. Parking: 21€ ($18.75). Bus: 1, 20, 23. **Amenities:** Lounge; babysitting; laundry. *In room:* A/C, TV, minibar, hair dryer, safe.

Hotel Mario's ✮ *Value*   Two blocks from the rail station, this is a winning choice. It's on the first floor of an old building that has been a hotel since 1872, when the *Room with a View* crowd started arriving in search of the glory of the Renaissance. This spotless, homey place has been completely restored and furnished in Florentine style. Mario Noce is a gracious host, and he and his staff speak English. Although you'll find cheaper inns in Florence, the service and hospitality make Mario's worth your euros. The guest rooms aren't very large but are furnished with taste; wrought-iron headboards frame firm beds. Several rooms open onto a small private garden. The bathrooms are neat, with shelf space. Breakfast is the only meal served; fresh flowers and fresh fruit are put out daily.

Via Faenza 89, 50123 Firenze. ⓒ 055-216801. Fax 055-212039. www.hotelmarios.com. 16 units (shower only). 93€–165€ ($83.05–$147.30) double; 114€–210€ ($101.80–$187.55) triple. Rates include breakfast. AE, DC, MC, V. Parking 17.50€ ($15.65). Bus: 10, 13, 17. **Amenities:** Bar; laundry. *In room:* A/C, TV, hair dryer, safe.

Hotel Vasari ⭐ *Value*   This inn enjoys a rather literary history; for several years, it was the home of 19th-century French poet Alphonse de La Martine. Built in the 1840s as a home, it was a run-down hotel until 1993, when its owners poured money into its renovation and upgraded it. Its three stories are connected by elevator, and the rooms are comfortable, albeit somewhat spartan. Nonetheless, the beds are firm and the linen is crisp. The tiled bathrooms are small but immaculate. Some of the public areas retain their elaborate vaulting.

Via B. Cennini 9–11, 50123 Firenze. ⓒ 055-212753. Fax 055-294246. 27 units (shower only). 145€ ($129.50) double. Rates include breakfast. AE, DC, MC, V. Parking 10€ ($8.95). Bus: 4, 7, 10, 13, 14, 23, or 71. **Amenities:** Bar; room service; babysitting; laundry/dry cleaning. *In room:* A/C, TV, minibar, hair dryer.

Villa Azalée   The handsome Villa Azalée, on the edge of the city near the train station with a big garden, is a remake of an 1870s home. The owners' personal touch is reflected in the atmosphere and the tasteful decor, featuring tall white-paneled doors with brass fittings, parquet floors, crystal chandeliers, and antiques mixed with good reproductions. We prefer the guest rooms in the villa to those in the more modern annex. They range from small to medium and boast an intimate, elegant style; the second-floor rooms are better furnished and command greater views. Our favorite is no. 24 because it's larger and has a huge ceiling fresco from the 19th century. In the 19th century, the annex was the *scuderia* (stables), and the rooms here have been given a sort of faux–Laura Ashley, cozy Cotswold cottage look; the finest rooms are on the ground floor because they're larger and more romantic, with heavy beamed ceilings. All the tiled bathrooms are small but well kept and come with robes.

Viale Fratelli Rosselli 44, 50123 Firenze. ⓒ 055-214242. Fax 055-268264. villaazalee@fi.flashnet.it. 25 units (shower only). 160€ ($142.90) double; 215€ ($192) triple. Rates include buffet breakfast. AE, DC, MC, V. Parking from 20€ ($17.85) nearby. Bus: 80. **Amenities:** Laundry/dry cleaning. *In room:* A/C, TV.

INEXPENSIVE

Hotel Abaco *Value*   This is a small, affordable choice in a Renaissance era townhouse near the train station. The rooms are immaculately kept, and the English-speaking owners are most helpful. One charming room, lacking a private bathroom, includes a fireplace. There is a communal refrigerator for your use, and breakfast is free for those who pay for their stay with cash.

Via dei Banchi 1, 50125 Firenze. ⓒ 055-2381919. Fax 055-282289. www.abaco-hotel.it. 7 units, 3 with bathroom (some with shower only, some with tub only). 63€ ($56.25) double without bathroom, 73€–83€ ($65.20–$74.10) double with bathroom. AE, DC, MC, V. **Amenities:** Bar; room service; laundry. *In room:* TV, hair dryer.

Hotel Bellettini ⭐ *Value*   The Bellettini's rates are very reasonable for the kind of historic ambience you'll find here (not to mention the convenient location, midway between the Duomo and the rail station). The palazzo was built in the 1300s, with a history of innkeeping at least 300 years old, and it is maintained by Tuscany-born sisters Marzia and Gina and their helpful staff. This place is so traditional—with terra-cotta floors, beamed ceilings, and touches of stained glass—that you expect Henry James or Elizabeth Barrett Browning to check in at any minute. The rooms are plain (some are almost stark) but comfortable, with queen or double beds. Many have sweeping views of Florence. The private bathrooms have adequate shelf space. Only two rooms per floor share the corridor bathrooms, so you'll rarely have to wait in line.

In 2001, the hotel acquired a small but charming annex, less than a 2-minute walk from the hotel's main core, and transformed its interior into five of what are today the best rooms in the hotel. If you stay here, you'll be given a key to the annex's front door, have telephone access to the main reception desk, and—in the public areas—have security coverage from a closed-monitor TV. Rooms in the annex are bigger than those in the hotel's main core, and they have large, Carrara marble-covered bathrooms, high ceilings, comfortable furnishings, and tea-making facilities.

Via di Conti 7, 50123 Firenze. ☏ **055-213561**. Fax 055-283551. www.firenze.net/hotelbelletini.com. 32 units, 28 with bathroom (shower only). 88€–97€ ($78.60–$86.60) double without bathroom, 112€–124€ ($100–$110.75) double with bathroom. Rates include buffet breakfast. AE, DC, MC, V. Parking 20€ ($17.85). Bus: 1, 9, 14, 17, 23, 36, and 37. **Amenities:** Lounge. *In room:* A/C, TV, safe.

Hotel Berkleys *(Kids)*   The pleasant but modest Berkleys, about a block east of the rail station, occupies the top floor of a 19th-century apartment building (there are two less-recommended hotels on the lower floors). The owners, the Andreoli family, are polite and friendly and are especially welcoming to frugal family travelers. The simple lobby leads into a breakfast nook and a bar area, where drinks are served on request. The guest rooms are a bit small but comfortable enough, and the bathrooms are tiny though neat. Some rooms open onto balconies with views of Florence.

Via Fiume 11, 50123 Firenze. ☏ **055-2382147**. Fax 055-212302. www.hotelberkleys.3000.it. 9 units. 85€–93€ ($75.90–$83.05) double; 107€–119€ ($95.55–$106.25) triple. Rates include breakfast. MC, V. Bus: 1, 10, 12, 14, 23, 25, 31, or 91. **Amenities:** Bar; room service; laundry/dry cleaning. *In room:* TV, hair dryer.

Hotel Elite   An attractive little pensione, the Elite is located two floors above street level in a 19th-century apartment building about 2 blocks from the rail station. It's convenient for exploring most of the major sights. Owner Maurizio Maccarini speaks English and is a welcoming host. The small hotel rents light and airy but small guest rooms, divided equally between singles and doubles. The shared corridor bathrooms are kept clean, and usually you don't have to wait to use them.

Via della Scala 12, 50123 Firenze. ☏ **055-215395**. 8 units, 5 with bathroom (3 with shower only). 50€ ($44.65) double without bathroom; 55€–68€ ($49.10–$60.70) double with shower; 70€–83€ ($62.50–$74.10) double with full bathroom. No credit cards. Parking 15€–17€ ($13.40–$15.20) nearby. Bus: 1, 2, 12, or 16. **Amenities:** Lounge. *In room:* TV, hair dryer.

Hotel Le Vigne   This inn offers comfortably furnished guest rooms and enjoys a prime location, with a sitting room that overlooks one of the city's most central piazzas. An Italian family took over this 15th-century building and restored it in the early 1990s, preserving the old features, including frescoes, whenever possible. The small hotel is on the first floor (the second floor, if you're American) of this old-fashioned building. The private bathrooms have adequate shelf space, and the hall bathrooms are fresh and neat.

Piazza Santa Maria Novella 24, 50123 Firenze. (C) **055-294449.** Fax 055-2302263. www.venere.it/ firenze/levigne. 26 units, 22 with bathroom (some with shower only). 60€–80€ ($53.60–$71.45) double without bathroom, 77.50€–105€ ($69.20–$93.75) double with bathroom; 105€–132.50€ ($93.75–$118.30) triple with bathroom; 122.50€–155€ ($109.40–$138.40) quad. Rates include buffet breakfast. AE, DC, MC, V. Parking 17.50€ ($15.65). Bus: 1, 2, 12, 16, 17, 22, or 29. **Amenities:** Lounge. *In room:* A/C, TV, safe.

Hotel Nuova Italia ✶ *Finds*   This little hotel lies in a renovated 17th-century building a block from the rail station. It has been welcoming Frommer's readers since 1958, when folks arrived with their dog-eared copies of *Europe on $5 a Day.* A Canadian guest, Eileen, met and fell in love with Luciano Viti, then a bellboy. Today they own the hotel and are grandparents with a new generation of Vitis waiting to take over one day. The guest rooms are pleasantly furnished and decorated with paintings and posters. Some large rooms are suitable for families, to whom the management grants special discounts. The furnishings, including the beds, were spruced up in early 1999. The bathrooms are small. The Vitis, who serve a fantastic cappuccino, will help you figure out how to get around Florence and offer tips on where to shop and what to do.

Via Faenza 26, 50123 Firenze. (C) **055-287508.** Fax 055-210941. www.hotelnuovaitalia.com. 20 units (shower only). 118€ ($105.35) double; 138€ ($123.25) triple. Rates include breakfast. AE, MC, V. Parking 15.60€ ($15) nearby. Bus: 10, 12, 25, 31, 32, or 91. **Amenities:** Lounge. *In room:* A/C, TV.

NEAR PIAZZA SAN MARCO
EXPENSIVE

Loggiato dei Serviti ✶   The amazing thing about this hotel is that it accepts paying guests at all—you'd think it could house a museum. But here you can wander through the premises of what was built in 1527 by Antonio da Samgallo as a monastery (a symmetrical foil for the Ospedale degli Innocenti across the square); it has been a hotel since the early 1900s. Once a run-down student hotel, it was transformed and upgraded in 1997. The guest rooms are artfully designed to emphasize the building's antique origins, usually with beamed or vaulted ceilings and terra-cotta floors. In 1999 and 2001, the canopies, tapestries, and curtains were replaced, and some antiques were added as well.

Piazza SS. Annunziata 3, 50122 Firenze. (C) **055-289592.** Fax 055-289595. www.loggiatodeiservitihotel.it. 29 units (some with shower only). 140€–201€ ($125–$179.50) double; 200€–284€ ($178.60–$253.60) suite. Rates include buffet breakfast. AE, DC, MC, V. Parking 17.50€–22.50€ ($15.65–$20.10). Bus: 1, 7, or 17. **Amenities:** Bar; laundry. *In room:* A/C, TV, minibar, hair dryer, safe.

MODERATE

Hotel Cellai   Since the 1930s, the Cellai family has been welcoming travelers to Florence. Eventually the enterprise grew into this large-scale place. Two blocks east of Piazza della Indipendenza, it boasts dignified public rooms, last renovated in 1999, with terra-cotta floors and nice architectural details. The guest rooms are individually decorated, some with appealing contemporary paintings. Try to get one with a varnished wooden ceiling supported by very old beams; these rooms seem more appealing and a bit warmer. The beds are comfortable, and the bathrooms are tiny but well organized.

Via 27 Aprile 14, 50129 Firenze. (C) **055-489291.** Fax 055-470387. www.hotelcellai.it. 47 units (some with shower only). 125€–190€ ($111.65–$169.65) double. Rates include breakfast. AE, DC, MC, V. Bus: 7, 20, 32, or 33. **Amenities:** Lounge; babysitting; laundry. *In room:* A/C, TV, minibar, hair dryer.

Hotel La Due Fontane   This hotel is a small 14th-century palace on a Renaissance square, right in the heart of all the sights. It has been completely renovated and modernized, and it offers simply but tastefully furnished guest rooms that are well kept, if a bit generic. The upper-floor rooms offer the most tranquil night's sleep. Each room is unique, and the bathrooms are a decent size.

Piazza SS. Annunziata 14, 50122 Firenze. ℂ **055-210185.** Fax 055-294461. 57 units (shower only). 135€–170€ ($120.55–$151.80) double; 190€–220€ ($169.65–$196.45) suite. Rates include breakfast. AE, DC, DISC, MC, V. Parking 17.50€–20€ ($15.65–$17.85). Bus: 1, 17, or 33. **Amenities:** Bar; car-rental desk; babysitting; laundry/dry cleaning. *In room:* A/C, TV, minibar, hair dryer.

Hotel Morandi alla Crocetta ⓐ This charming small hotel 2 blocks from the Accademia is run by one of Florence's most experienced hoteliers, the sprightly octogenarian Katherine Doyle, who came here from Ireland when she was 12. Although built in 1511 as a convent, it contains everything needed for a pensione and is on a back street near a university building. The rooms (small to medium in size) have been tastefully restored, filled with framed 19th-century needlework, beamed ceilings, and antiques. In the best Tuscan tradition, the tall windows are sheltered from the sun with heavy draperies. You register in an austere salon filled with Persian carpets.

Via Laura 50, 50121 Firenze. ℂ **055-2344747.** Fax 055-2480954. www.hotelmorandi.it. 10 units (shower only). 160€ ($142.90) double; 200€ ($178.60) triple. AE, DC, MC, V. Parking 16€ ($14.30). Bus: 6, 7, 10, 17, 31, or 32. **Amenities:** Lounge; babysitting; laundry. *In room:* A/C, TV, minibar, hair dryer, safe.

Orto de'Medici This hotel is within a 10-minute walk of the Duomo, yet this residential neighborhood seems a world away from the crush in the tourist district. The hotel occupies four high-ceilinged floors of a 19th-century apartment building, and its elegantly faded public rooms evoke the kind of family-run pensione you'd expect in a Merchant/Ivory film. A major renovation and refurbishment was completed in the summer of 2001. The homey rooms contain nice Florentine decorative touches and an eclectic array of semi-antique furniture. The tiny tiled bathrooms are neatly kept.

Via S. Gallo 30, 50129 Firenze. ℂ **055-483427.** Fax 055-461276. www.ortodeimedici.it. 31 units (some with shower only). 163€–180€ ($145.55–$160.75) double; 205€–227€ ($183.05–$202.70) triple. Rates include buffet breakfast. AE, MC, V. Parking 20€ ($17.85) in nearby garage. Bus: 1, 6, 7, 10, 11, 17, 25, 33, 67, or 68. **Amenities:** Lounge; room service. *In room:* A/C, TV, minibar, hair dryer, safe.

INEXPENSIVE

Hotel Casci This is a well-run little hotel 183m (200 yd.) from the rail station and 91m (100 yd.) from Piazza del Duomo. As one reader wrote, "For location, location, location, there's nothing better in Florence." It dates from the 15th century, and some of the public rooms (such as the breakfast room) feature the original frescoes. Giacchino Rossini, the famous composer of *The Barber of Seville* and *William Tell*, lived here from 1851 to 1855. The hotel is both traditional and modern, and the English-speaking reception staff looks after you very well. The guest rooms are comfortably furnished, and every year, four or five units are upgraded and renovated. The few units overlooking the street are soundproof.

Via Cavour 13, 50129 Firenze. ℂ **055-211686.** Fax 055-2396461. www.emmeti.it/casci.html. 25 units. 85€–135€ ($75.90–$120.55) double; 110€–175€ ($98.25–$156.30) triple; 135€–220€ ($120.55–$196.45) quad. Rates include buffet breakfast. AE, DC, MC, V. Parking 17.50€–25€ ($15.65–$22.35). Bus: 1, 7, 25, or 33. **Amenities:** Bar; babysitting; laundry/dry cleaning. *In room:* A/C, TV, minibar, hair dryer, safe.

Hotel Cimabue ⓐ This hotel was built in 1904 as a Tuscan-style palazzo, and the most charming guest rooms are the six with original frescoed ceilings. Four of these are one floor above street level, and the other two are on the ground floor. Rooms have comfortable beds and range from small to medium in size. The bathrooms are hardly spacious but have adequate shelf space. The hotel was recently renovated and has turn-of-the-century antiques that correspond to the building's age. Its Belgian-Italian management extends a warm multicultural welcome.

Via B. Lupi 7, 50129 Firenze. © 055-471989. Fax 055-475601. 16 units (shower only). 110€–135€ ($98.20–$120.55) double; 130€–160€ ($116.10–$142.90) triple. Rates include buffet breakfast. AE, DC, MC, V. Parking 15€ ($13.40). Bus: 17. **Amenities:** Lounge; room service; babysitting. *In room:* TV, hair dryer, safe.

Hotel Europa   Two long blocks north of the Duomo, this hotel occupies a 16th-century building. The Europa has been family-run since 1925. Despite the antique look of the simple exterior, much of the interior has been modernized, although it contains plenty of homey touches. All but four of the guest rooms overlook the back, usually opening onto a view of Giotto's campanile and Brunelleschi's dome; those facing the street are noisier but benefit from double-glazed windows. The rooms are small but decently furnished, with a tiny but well-organized bathroom.

Via Cavour 14, 50129 Firenze. © 055-2396715. Fax 055-210361. 20 units (shower only). 75€–125€ ($67–$111.65) double; 140€–167.50€ ($125–$149.60) triple. Rates include buffet breakfast. AE, MC, V. Parking 17.50€–20€ ($15.65–$17.85) in nearby garage. Bus: 1, 7, 25, or 33. **Amenities:** Babysitting; laundry/dry cleaning. *In room:* A/C, TV, hair dryer, safe.

Piccolo Hotel *(Value* Conveniently located near the railway station and all the top sights, this town house hotel offers an intimate atmosphere. You'll feel at home, thanks to Ms. Angeloni, the English-speaking manager, who's a font of advice about the city. Rooms are medium in size; some have balconies, while all have simple, tasteful furniture and flowered bed linens. Bathrooms are a little small but well organized and neat. The only meal served is the generous buffet breakfast, but the hotel is surrounded by good restaurants.

Via S. Gallo 51, 50129 Firenze. © 055-475519. Fax 055-474515. www.piccolohotelfirenze.com. 10 units (shower only). 90€–125€ ($80.35–$111.65) double; 130€–155€ ($116.10–$138.40) triple. Rates include buffet breakfast. AE, DC, MC, V. Parking 17.50€–20€ ($15.65–$17.85) nearby. **Amenities:** Lounge; room service; babysitting; laundry. *In room:* TV, safe.

ON OR NEAR PIAZZA MASSIMO D'AZEGLIO

Piazza Massimo d'Azeglio is a 10- to 15-minute walk northeast of the historic core.

VERY EXPENSIVE

Hotel Regency ✦✦✦   The Regency is a bastion of taste and exclusivity, a member of the Leading Hotels of the World group. It lies a bit apart from the shopping-and-sightseeing center (and thus offers peace and quiet), but it is only a 15-minute stroll from the cathedral and can be quickly reached by taxi or bus. This intimate hideaway, filled with stained glass, paneled walls, and reproduction antiques, offers exquisite accommodations, including some special rooms on the top floor with terraces. They boast numerous extras, such as double glazing, thick wool carpeting, coffered or beamed ceilings, rich fabrics, and private thermostats. The large bathrooms are the most luxurious in town, clad in marble and offering deluxe toiletries, heated towel racks, dual sinks, bidets, and phones.

Piazza Massimo d'Azeglio 3, 50121 Firenze. © 055-245247. Fax 055-2346735. www.regency-hotel.com. 34 units. 280€–420€ ($250.05–$375.05) double; 550€–680€ ($491.15–$607.25) suite. Rates include buffet breakfast. AE, DC, MC, V. Parking 25€ ($22.35). Bus: 6, 31, or 32. **Amenities:** Restaurant; bar; room service; babysitting; laundry/dry cleaning. *In room:* A/C, TV, minibar, hair dryer, safe.

EXPENSIVE

Hotel J and J ✦✦ A 5-minute walk from Santa Croce, this is a charming hotel. It was built in the 16th century as a monastery and underwent a massive restoration in 1990. You'll find many sitting areas throughout, including a flagstone-covered courtyard with stone columns and a salon with vaulted ceilings and preserved ceiling frescoes. The guest rooms combine an unusual mix of modern furniture with the original beamed ceilings. The suites usually contain sleeping lofts, and some have rooftop balconies overlooking Florence's historic core. Most of the rooms are surprisingly spacious, and the bathrooms contain a wealth of amenities; some even have whirlpool tubs.

Via di Mezzo 20, 50121 Firenze. © **055-263121.** Fax 055-240282. www.jandjhotel.com. 20 units. 268€–300€ ($239.30–$267.90) double; 352€ ($314.35) junior suite; 408€–435€ ($364.35–$388.45) suite. Rates include buffet breakfast. AE, DC, MC, V. Parking 25€ ($22.35). Bus: A. **Amenities:** Bar; room service; laundry/dry cleaning; babysitting. *In room:* A/C, TV, minibar, hair dryer.

Hotel Monna Lisa ✦ This hotel (yes, it's Monna with two *n*'s) once appeared in *Frommer's Europe on $5 a Day,* but its prices have skyrocketed over the years—you'll need a giant roll of $5 bills to afford a night here these days. However, for old-world elegance in the setting of a 14th-century Tuscan palazzo, it's virtually unbeatable. The palazzo once belonged to the Neri family, whose most famous member, St. Philip Neri, was born in room no. 19. The facade is forbiddingly severe, in keeping with the architectural style of its heyday, but when you enter the reception rooms, you'll find an inviting atmosphere. Most of the great old guest rooms overlook an inner patio or a rear garden. They vary greatly in style and decor—some are quite spacious, but others are a bit cramped. Each is handsomely furnished with fine antiques and oil paintings, including Giambologna's original competition piece for the *Rape of the Sabines.* There are other works by neoclassical sculptor Giovanni Dupré (1817–82)—the hotel is still owned by a member of his family. Painted wood and coffered ceilings are found in many rooms. The bathrooms have recently been renovated; some have Jacuzzis.

Borgo Pinti 27, 50121 Firenze. © **055-2479751.** Fax 055-2479755. www.monnalisa.it. 30 units. 175€–275€ ($156.30–$245.60) double; 225€–400€ ($200.90–$357.15) triple. Rates include breakfast. AE, DC, MC, V. Parking 10€ ($8.95). Bus: A, 6, 31, or 32. **Amenities:** Room service; babysitting; laundry/dry cleaning. *In room:* A/C, TV, minibar, hair dryer, safe.

INEXPENSIVE

Albergo Losanna The Losanna, a family-run place off Viale Antonio Gramsci, offers utter simplicity and cleanliness, as well as insight into a typical Florentine atmosphere—the hotel seemingly belongs in the 1800s. The rooms are homey and well kept, although the private bathrooms are cramped, without enough shelf space. The hall bathrooms are large and quite adequate—you rarely have to wait in line.

Via Vittorio Alfieri 9, 50121 Firenze. © and fax **055-245840.** www.albergolosanna.com. 8 units, 3 with bathroom (shower only). 52€ ($46.45) double without bathroom, 68€ ($60.70) double with bathroom. Rates include breakfast. AE, MC, V. Parking 15€–17.50€ ($13.40–$15.65). Bus: 6.

NEAR PIAZZA SANTA CROCE
EXPENSIVE

Plaza Hotel Lucchesi ✦ This hotel (often a favorite with tour groups) dates from 1860 but has been renovated many times since. It lies along the Arno, a 10-minute walk from the Duomo and a few paces from Santa Croce. Its interior decor includes lots of glossy mahogany, acres of marble, and masses of fresh flowers. The guest rooms, ranging from medium to spacious, have recently been renewed. Twenty of them open onto balconies with views. The bathrooms are of good size.

Lungarno della Zecca Vecchia 38, 50122 Firenze. Ⓒ 055-26236. Fax 055-2480921. www.plazalucchesi.it. 97 units (some with shower only). 199€–387€ ($177.70–$345.60) double; 450€ ($401.85) suite. Rates include buffet breakfast. AE, DC, DISC, MC, V. Parking 17.50€ ($15.65). Bus: B, 13, 14, or 23. **Amenities:** Restaurant; piano bar (where daily afternoon tea is served); car-rental desk; 24-hr. room service; babysitting; laundry/dry cleaning. *In room:* A/C, TV, minibar, hair dryer, safe.

MODERATE

Ritz Hotel ⭐ *(Finds)*   The Ritz of Florence has nothing to do with the pricey palaces of London or Paris. The local Ritz is a family-run hotel that has been given a new lease on life by its youthful owners, who have upgraded it and turned it into a reasonably priced alternative in a lethally priced city. They have restored and redecorated, offering well-furnished, medium-size bedrooms. It's a short walk to the Ponte Vecchio or the Uffizi, and the Ritz enjoys a lovely location right on the river, with nice views.

Lugarno Zeccia Vecchia 24, 50122 Firenze. Ⓒ 055-2340650. Fax 055-240863. www.florenceitaly.net. 32 units (some with shower only). 110€–180€ ($98.25–$160.75) double; 170€–280€ ($151.80–$250.05) suite. Rates include breakfast. AE, DC, MC, V. Bus: 23. **Amenities:** Bar; room service; babysitting; laundry/dry cleaning. *In room:* A/C, TV, minibar, hair dryer, safe.

ACROSS THE ARNO
EXPENSIVE

Hotel Villa Carlotta ⭐ *(Finds)*   This hotel from the Edwardian age was built as a villa and bought in the 1950s by Carlotta Schulmann. Her lavish renovations have transformed it into one of Florence's most charming smaller hotels. It's still very homey and stands in a residential neighborhood. Rooms have silk wallpaper and bedspreads, reproduction antiques, safes, and crystal chandeliers; each has a view of the garden. The bathrooms are exceedingly well maintained. The hotel is only a 10-minute walk from the Ponte Vecchio; by taxi, it's a 5-minute ride.

Via Michele di Lando 3, 50125 Firenze. Ⓒ 055-220530. Fax 055-2336147. www.panoramahotelsitaly.com. 32 units (some with shower only). 150€–270€ ($133.95–$241.10) double; 170€–305€ ($151.80–$272.35) triple. Rates include buffet breakfast. AE, DC, MC, V. Free parking. Bus: 11, 36, or 37. **Amenities:** Restaurant; bar; lounge; car-rental desk; room service; babysitting; laundry/dry cleaning. *In room:* A/C, TV, minibar, hair dryer, safe.

MODERATE

Pensione Annalena ⭐ *(Finds)*   This 15th-century building has known many owners, including the Medicis. In the past three-quarters of a century, it has been a haven for artists and writers (Mary McCarthy once wrote of its importance as a cultural center). During most of that time, it was the domain of the late sculptor Olinto Calastri, but now it's owned by Claudio Salvestrini. During World War II, the Annalena was the center of the underground, and many Jews and rebel Italians found safety hidden away in an underground room behind a secret door. Most of the simply furnished rooms overlook a secret garden; five face an open-air galleria on the loggia, evoking an idyllic landscape that might've been painted by Gozzoli. Don't be put off by the lack of air-conditioning; the high ceilings and thick masonry walls almost guarantee a relatively comfortable temperature in summer. The bathrooms are small but have adequate shelf space. The pensione is about a 5-minute walk from the Pitti and 10 minutes from the Ponte Vecchio.

Via Romana 34, 50125 Firenze. Ⓒ 055-222402. Fax 055-222403. www.hotelannalena.it. 20 units. 155€ ($138.40) double. Rates include breakfast. AE, DC, MC, V. Parking 17.50€–20€ ($15.65–$17.85). Bus: C, 11, 36, or 37. **Amenities:** Lounge; room service; babysitting. *In room:* TV, hair dryer.

Pitti Palace Hotel *Finds*   Right across the Ponte Vecchio on the left bank, this hotel occupies the Torre dei Rossi, a tower dating from the 13th century. Seven floors make the tower one of the taller buildings of Florence, and a suite crowns the hotel's top floor, offering a 360° view. From two spacious terraces, a panoramic vista of the city unfolds. All of medieval Florence is within walking distance. The decor is minimalist; each midsize room is well maintained and comfortably furnished.

Via Barbardori 2, 50125 Firenze. ☎ **055-2398711.** Fax 055-2398867. www.vivahotels.com. 72 units. 210€ ($187.55) double; 425€ ($379.55) suite. Rates include breakfast. AE, DC, MC, V. Parking 20€–25€ ($17.85–$22.35). Bus: D. **Amenities:** Room service; babysitting; laundry/dry cleaning. *In room:* A/C, TV, minibar, hair dryer, safe.

ON THE OUTSKIRTS
VERY EXPENSIVE

Villa La Massa *★★★*   The Villa d'Este on Lake Como, one of the most legendary hotels in Italy (see chapter 11, "Milan, Lombardy & the Lake District"), runs this palace of charm and grace 5 miles southeast of Florence. (Ask about packages combining stays at both hotels.) On the banks of the Arno, in a secluded spot near the edge of the Chianti region, this 16th-century Medicean villa was built by the powerful Giraldi family, who owned it until the 19th century. It became a luxury hotel in 1948 and has been extensively restored and refurbished by the Villa d'Este. The guest rooms are spacious and opulently furnished, often with antiques, and the marble bathrooms are state-of-the-art, with deluxe toiletries. Eleven units are in an annex; try to get a room in the main house, with a view of the Arno.

Via della Massa 24, 50012 Candeli, Firenze. ☎ **055-62611.** Fax 055-633102. www.villalamassa.com. 34 units. 330€–510€ ($294.70–$455.45) double; 700€–990€ ($625.10–$884.05) suite. Rates include breakfast. AE, DC, MC, V. Free parking. Free shuttle bus to and from the villa and Ponte Vecchio in Florence during the day. **Amenities:** Restaurant; bar; lounge; pool; tennis club; concierge; room service; laundry/dry cleaning. *In room:* A/C, TV, minibar, hair dryer, safe.

Villa Montartino *★★*   In the Florentine hills, always a source of inspiration for Tuscan poets, Villa Montartino is an oasis less than a mile from the Ponte Vecchio. A strategic tower during the 11th century and then a patrician villa from 1500, the villa still retains the charm of the past after recent renovations. Rooms range from medium to spacious, each with its own character, thanks to the wise choice of antiques matched with pieces of Florentine craftsmanship. Bathrooms are medium in size, with mosaic tiles and modern, efficient accessories. Travelers preferring more privacy can opt for an apartment.

Via Suor Maria Celeste 19/21 (corner with Via G. Silvani), 50125 Arcetri, Firenze. ☎ **055-223520.** Fax 055-223495. www.montartino.com. 7 units, 14 apts. (some with shower only). 181€–248€ ($161.65–$221.45) double; 232€–336€ ($207.20–$300.05) suite; 930€–1,653€ ($830.50–$1,476.15) apt per week. Rates include buffet breakfast. AE, DC, MC, V. Free parking. From Porta Romana, follow signs for Poggio Imperiale, and turn right on Via San Felice; you'll see the villa on your left. **Amenities:** Guests-only dining room; pool; babysitting; laundry. *In room:* A/C, TV, minibar, hair dryer, safe. Also kitchenette, coffeemaker, iron in apts.

4 Where to Dine

The Florentine table has always been set with the abundance of the Tuscan countryside. That means the region's best olive oil and wine (such as Chianti), wonderful fruits and vegetables, fresh fish from the coast, and game in season. Meat lovers all over Italy sing the praise of *bistecca alla fiorentina*, an inch-thick juicy steak on the bone, often served with white Tuscan beans. Tuscan cuisine (except for some of its hair-raising specialties) should please most North Americans because it's simply flavored, without rich spices, and based on the hearty produce from the hills. Florentine restaurants aren't generally as acclaimed by gourmets as those of Rome, although good, moderately priced places abound.

IN CENTRO
EXPENSIVE
Buca Lapi TUSCAN   This cellar restaurant (under the Palazzo Antinori) opened in 1880 and is big on glamour, good food, and fun. The vaulted ceilings are covered with travel posters from all over the world. The cooks know how to turn out the classic dishes of the Tuscan kitchen with finesse, and there's a long table of interesting fruits, desserts, and vegetables. (Skip the international fare.) Specialties include *scampi giganti alla griglia* (supersize shrimp) and bistecca alla fiorentina. In season, the *fagioli toscani all'olio* (Tuscan beans in native olive oil) are a delicacy. For dessert, try crêpes suzette or the local choice, *zuccotto,* a dome-shaped ice-cream cake studded with almonds and rich in chocolate. The wine list is full of reasonably priced Tuscan and Chianti wines.

Via del Trebbio 1R. ✆ **055-213768.** Reservations required for dinner. Main courses 12.50€–22.50€ ($11.15–$20.10). AE, DC, MC, V. Tues–Sat 12:30–2:30pm; Mon–Sat 7:30–10:30pm. Closed 2 weeks in Aug. Bus: 6, 11, 36, or 37.

MODERATE
Cantinetta Antinori ✸ *Finds* FLORENTINE/TUSCAN   Behind the severe stone facade of the 15th-century Palazzo Antinori is one of Florence's most popular restaurants and one of the city's few top-notch wine bars. It's no wonder that the cellars are so well stocked because Antinori is also the oldest (600 years) and most distinguished wine company in Tuscany, Umbria, and Piedmont. You can sample these wines by the glass at the stand-up bar or by the bottle as an accompaniment to the meals served at wooden tables in the dining room, decorated with floor-to-ceiling racks of aged and dusty wine bottles. You can eat a full meal or just snacks. The food is standard but satisfying, and many of the ingredients come directly from the Antinori farms. Especially good are the sausages with white haricot beans, fresh Tuscan ewe's cheese, tripe Florentine style (for the traditionalist), fettuccine in duck sauce, thick oven-roasted Chiana beef (a bit pricey but worth it), and *stracotto al vino Peppole* (beef braised in strong Italian red wine).

Piazza Antinori 3. ✆ **055-292234.** Reservations recommended. Main courses 12.50€–20€ ($11.15–$17.85). AE, DC, MC, V. Mon–Fri 12:30–2:30pm and 7–10:30pm. Closed Aug and Dec 24–Jan 6. Bus: 6, 11, 14, 36, 37, or 68.

Oliviero TUSCAN   This small but smart and luxurious dining room maintains the finest traditions of Tuscan cookery; highly select fresh ingredients are used in the seasonal menu. We've come across such appetizers as octopus salad with basil, string beans, and tomatoes; fried mussels and squash blossoms; and Tuscan ham with figs and bread coated with virgin olive oil. We recently enjoyed *pici* pasta with savory tomato sauce, fresh garlic, and spicy red peppers, followed by a grilled Tuscan sirloin steak, flavored with sage and rosemary and covered in a perfect Chianti sauce. For dessert, try the green-fig mousse with almonds and chocolate.

Via delle Terme 51R. ✆ **055-287643** or 055-212421. Reservations required. Main courses 16€ ($14.30). AE, DC, MC, V. Mon–Sat 7:30pm–midnight. Closed Aug. Bus: 14, 23, or 71.

Where to Dine in Florence

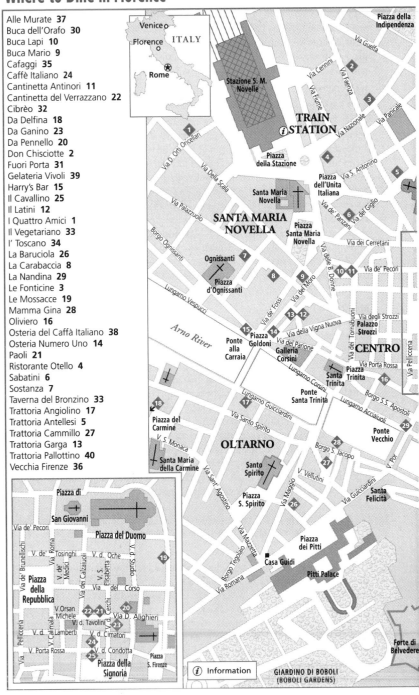

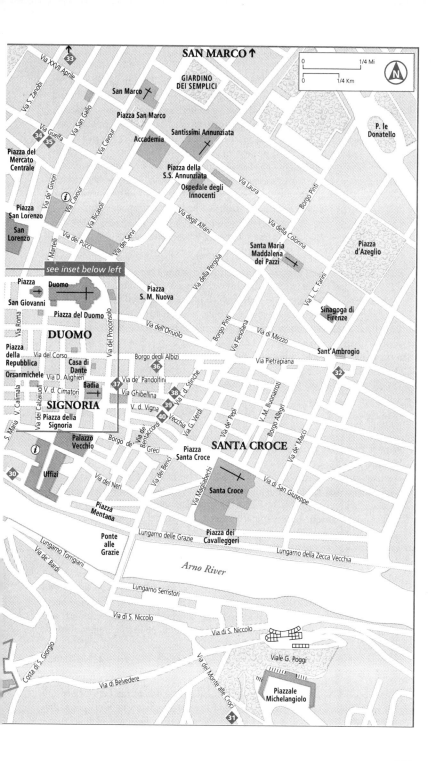

NEAR PIAZZA DEL DUOMO
INEXPENSIVE

Le Mossacce *Value* TUSCAN/FLORENTINE   The 35-seat Le Mossacce is midway between the Bargello and the Duomo. It opened in the early 1900s, and within its 300-year-old walls, hardworking waiters serve a wide range of excellent Florentine and Tuscan specialties, such as *ribollita* (thick vegetable soup), baked lasagna, and heavily seasoned baked pork. Bistecca alla fiorentina is a favorite—and you'll be hard-pressed to find it at a better price. Pasta buffs rightly claim that the cannelloni here is among Florence's finest—these baked pasta tubes are stuffed with spinach, a savory tomato sauce, and seasoned ground meat. For dessert, try the excellent *castagnaccio,* a cake baked with chestnut flour. Ask the waiters for advice and trust them; we had a great meal this way.

Via del Proconsolo 55R. ✆ 055-294361. Reservations unnecessary. Main courses 7.50€–12€ ($6.70–$10.70). AE, DC, MC, V. Mon–Fri noon–2:30pm and 7–9:30pm. Closed Aug. Bus: 14.

Vecchia Firenze FLORENTINE/TUSCAN   Housed in a 14th-century palace with an elegant entrance, this trattoria combines atmosphere and budget meals. Some tables are in the courtyard; others are in the vaulted dining rooms or the stone-lined cantina downstairs (which is usually reserved for groups). The place caters to students and working people, who eat here regularly and never tire of its simple but hearty offerings. You might begin with *tagliatelle Vecchia Firenze* (there's a different version every day), and then follow with a quarter of a roast chicken or sole in butter. Locals tend to go for the grilled rabbit, grilled sea bass, or else the expensive Florentine steak, on which the price can change weekly depending on the market. Almost any kind of meat you select can be grilled on a barbecue.

Borgo degli Albizi 18. ✆ 055-2340361. Main courses 7€–12.50€ ($6.25–$11.15); pizzas 5€–6€ ($4.45–$5.35). AE, DC, MC, V. Tues–Sun 11am–3pm and 7pm–midnight. Bus: 14, 23, or 71.

NEAR PIAZZA DELLA SIGNORIA
MODERATE

Da Ganino *Finds* FLORENTINE/TUSCAN   The intimate Da Ganino is staffed with waiters who take the quality of your meal as their personal responsibility. Someone will recite to you the frequently changing specials, which may include well-seasoned Tuscan beans, spinach risotto, grilled veal liver, and grilled veal chops. The *tagliatelle* (flat noodles) with truffles makes an excellent, if expensive, appetizer. We like the way the chef follows the seasons in his menu. In winter, that means lots of filling pastas and meat cooked with funghi, such as porcini mushrooms and white truffles; in spring, he dresses his pastas with fresh artichokes. You can order a classic T-bone Fiorentina steak that has won the praise of critics from *The New York Times* and the Paris *Herald Tribune.* "The food here is simple, flavorful, and reasonable, and who could ask for anything more?" an art historian from Lawrence, Kansas, told us. He dines here 3 nights a week when he's in town.

Piazza dei Cimatori 4R. ✆ 055-214125. Reservations recommended. Main courses 12.50€–17.50€ ($11.15–$15.65). AE, DC. Mon–Sat 1–3pm and 7:30–10:30pm. Bus: 14, 23, or 71.

Paoli *Finds* TUSCAN/ITALIAN   This restaurant is one of the best located in Florence. Paoli, between the Duomo and Piazza della Signoria, was opened in 1824 by the Paoli brothers in a building dating in part from the 13th century. It has a wonderful medieval-tavern atmosphere, with arches and ceramics stuck into the fresco-adorned walls. The pastas are homemade, and the chef does a superb *rognoncino trifolato* (kidney cooked with thinly sliced vegetables over pasta) and *sole meunière* (with a lemon, butter, and wine sauce). A recommended side dish is *piselli alla fiorentina* (garden peas). The ultrafresh vegetables are often served with olive oil, which your waiter will loudly proclaim as the world's finest.

Via dei Tavolini 12R. (C) **055-216215.** Reservations required. Main courses 11€–16€ ($9.80–$14.30). AE, DC, MC, V. Wed–Mon noon–2:30pm and 7–10:30pm. Closed 3 weeks in Aug. Bus: 14 or 23.

INEXPENSIVE

Da Pennello *(Value* FLORENTINE/ITALIAN   This informal trattoria offers many Florentine specialties on its a la carte menu and is known for its wide selection of antipasti; you can make a meal out of these delectable hors d'oeuvres. The ravioli is homemade, and one pasta specialty (loved by locals) is *spaghetti carrettiera,* with tomatoes and pepperoni. To follow that, you can have deviled roast chicken. The chef posts his daily specials, and sometimes it's best to order one of these because the food offered was bought fresh that day at the market. A Florentine cake, zuccotto, rounds out the meal. Da Penello is on a narrow street near Dante's house, about a 5-minute walk from the Duomo.

Via Dante Alighieri 4R. (C) **055-294848.** Reservations unnecessary. Main courses 7.50€–14€ ($6.70–$12.50); fixed-price menus from 17.50€ ($15.65). AE, DC, MC, V. Tues–Sat noon–2:30pm and 7–10pm. Closed 1st 3 weeks in Aug and Dec 24–Jan 2. Bus: 14, 22, or 23.

Il Cavallino TUSCAN/ITALIAN   A local favorite since the 1930s, Il Cavallino is on a tiny street (which probably won't even be on your map) leading off Piazza della Signoria at its northern end. There's usually a gracious reception at the door, especially if you called for a reservation. Two of the three dining rooms have vaulted ceilings and peach-colored marble floors; the main room looks out over the piazza. Menu items are typical hearty Tuscan fare, including an assortment of boiled meats in green herb sauce, grilled filet of steak, chicken breast Medici style, and the inevitable Florentine spinach. The portions are large. Most diners prefer the house wine, but a limited selection of bottled wines is also available. "Every drop is a pleasure," the waiter assured us as he placed our carafe on the well-set table.

Via della Farine 6R. (C) **055-215818.** Reservations recommended. Main courses 10€–16€ ($8.95–$14.30). AE, DC, MC, V. Mar–Oct daily noon–3pm and 7–10:30pm; off-season Thurs–Tues noon–3pm, Thurs–Mon 7–10:30pm. Bus: B.

⌐Finds Focaccia & Chianti on the Run

Owned by the Castello di Verrazzano, one of Chianti's best-known wine-producing estates, the **Cantinetta del Verrazzano,** Via dei Tavolini 18–20R (⌐(C) **055-268590**), helped spawn a revival of stylish wine bars as convenient spots for fast-food breaks. It promises a delicious self-service lunch or a snack of focaccia, plain or studded with peas, rosemary, onions, or olives; buy it hot by the slice or ask for *farcite* (sandwiches filled with prosciutto, arugula, cheese, or tuna). A glass of full-bodied Chianti priced at 3€ ($2.70) each makes this the perfect respite. Summer hours are from Monday to Saturday 8am to 3pm; winter hours are from Monday to Saturday 8am to 9pm.

NEAR THE PONTE VECCHIO
EXPENSIVE
La Nandina TUSCAN/INTERNATIONAL   Opened in 1924, this family-run restaurant is just off the Arno, about a 4-minute walk from the Uffizi, and is an old favorite with both Florentines and visitors. You can have a cocktail in the plush lounge and dine in the 14th-century cellar. The cuisine consists of dishes from the provinces as well as from Rome and Venice and might include ravioli with flap mushrooms, spinach crepes, curried breast of capon, veal piccatina, several kinds of beefsteak, and a changing array of daily specials. All the food is of high quality but not fussy.

Borgo SS. Apostoli 64R. ℂ 055-213024. Reservations recommended. Main courses 12.50€–20€ ($11.15–$17.85). AE, DC, MC, V. Mon 7–10:30pm; Tues–Sat noon–3pm and 7–10:30pm. Closed Aug. Bus: 23 or 71.

INEXPENSIVE
Buca dell'Orafo 🎖 *(Finds* FLORENTINE   This is an authentic neighborhood restaurant whose cuisine is firmly rooted in Tuscan traditions and inspired by whatever happens to be in season. Accessible via an alley beneath a vaulted arcade adjacent to Piazza del Pesce, it's named after the *orafo* (goldsmith shop) that occupied its premises during the Renaissance. The place is usually stuffed with regulars, who appreciate that the chef has made almost no concessions to international palates. Your pasta (usually *taglioni*) will probably be garnished with a seasonal vegetable, such as asparagus, broccoli rabe, mushrooms, peas, or asparagus. Florentine tripe and beefsteak are enduring favorites, as is *stracotto e fagioli* (beef braised in chopped vegetables and red wine), served with beans in tomato sauce.

Via Volta dei Girolami 28R. ℂ 055-213619. Main courses 10€–17.50€ ($8.95–$15.65). No credit cards. Tues–Sat 12:30–2:30pm and 7:30–10:30pm. Closed Aug and 2 weeks in Dec. Bus: B.

NEAR PIAZZA SANTA MARIA NOVELLA & THE TRAIN STATION
EXPENSIVE
Buca Mario 🎖 FLORENTINE   In business for a century, Buca Mario is one of Florence's most famous cellar restaurants, located in the 1886 Palazzo Niccolini. While diners sit at tables beneath the vaulted ceilings, the waiters (some of whom have worked in the United States) will suggest an array of fine-textured homemade pastas, grilled T-bone, Dover sole, or beef carpaccio, followed by a tempting selection of desserts, including "grandmother cake" (*Torta della Nonna*), a lemon-and-almond cake. We always like to begin with a medley of cured pork specialties called *affettati toscani*—the tastiest selection of "cold cuts" you'll likely encounter in Florence. There's a wonderful exuberance about the place, but in the enigmatic words of one longtime patron, "It's not for the faint-hearted."

Piazza Ottaviani 16R. ℂ 055-214179. Reservations recommended. Main courses 14€–20€ ($12.50–$17.85). AE, MC, V. Fri–Tues 12:15–2:30pm and Thurs–Tues 7:15–10:30pm. Closed Aug. Bus: 6, 9, 11, 36, 37, or 68.

Don Chisciotte 🎖🎖 ITALIAN/SEAFOOD   One floor above street level in a Florentine palazzo, this soft pink dining room is known for its creative cuisine and a changing array of fresh fish that emerges with a flourish from the kitchens. Flavors are often enhanced by an unusual assortment of fresh herbs, vegetables, and fish stocks. Choose from risotto of broccoli and baby squid; red taglioni with clams, pesto, and cheese; black ravioli colored with squid ink and stuffed with a purée of shrimp and crayfish; and filet of turbot with radicchio sauce.

Via Ridolfi 4R. ☎ 055-475430. Reservations recommended. Main courses 17.50€–25€ ($15.65–$22.35); *menu degustazione* 50€ ($44.65). AE, DC, MC, V. Mon 8–10:30pm; Tues–Sat 1–2:30pm and 8–10:30pm. Bus: 20.

Harry's Bar ✿ INTERNATIONAL/ITALIAN   Harry's Bar, in an 18th-century building in a prime position on the Arno, has hosted expats and well-heeled visiting Yankees since 1953. It's not as full of chic celebs as it was in the '50s and '60s, but it's still the only place in Florence to get a perfect martini. The international menu is select and beautifully prepared, including risotto or tagliatelle with ham, onions, and cheese and a tempting *gamberetti* (crayfish) cocktail. Harry has created his own tortellini, but his hamburger and his club sandwich are the most popular items. The chef also prepares about a dozen specialties daily: breast of chicken "our way," grilled giant scampi, and lean broiled sirloin. An apple tart with cream nicely finishes off a meal. From March to the end of October, outside tables are available.

Lungarno Vespucci 22R. ☎ 055-2396700. Reservations required. Main courses 17.50€–30€ ($15.65–$26.80). AE, MC, V. Mon–Sat noon–3pm and 7–11pm. Closed 1 week in Aug and Dec 18–Jan 8. Bus B.

I Quattro Amici ✿ SEAFOOD   Run by four Tuscan entrepreneurs who have known one another since childhood, this restaurant occupies the street level of a modern building near the rail station and has a vaguely neoclassical decor. Specialties include pasta with shrimp and grappa, fish soup, fried shrimp, squid Livorno style, and grilled, stewed, or baked versions of all the bounty of the Mediterranean. The roast sea bass and roast snapper, flavored with Mediterranean herbs, are among the finest dishes. The vegetables are fresh and flavorful. Every Thursday, Friday, and Saturday evening, diners are treated to live music.

Via degli Orti Oricellari 29. ☎ 055-215413. Reservations recommended. Main courses 15€–25€ ($13.40–$22.35). AE, DC, MC, V. Daily noon–2:30pm and 7–10:30pm. Bus: D, 26, 27, or 35.

Osteria Numero Uno ✿ INTERNATIONAL/FLORENTINE   This restaurant is in a 15th-century palazzo near the rail station. Many regulars (lawyers, civil servants, and reporters) prefer the main dining room, with its vaulted ceiling and oversize fireplace, to the two adjacent rooms. Well-prepared, well-presented menu choices include taglioni with mushrooms (with or without truffles); ravioli stuffed with ricotta and basil or fresh artichokes; risotto with asparagus or sweet peppers; carpaccio of beef or salmon; chicken with Marsala or Parmigiano-Reggiano; turbot baked with artichokes, herbs, and potatoes; and Florentine beefsteak, usually for two. The atmosphere is often rushed, with harried waiters darting about.

Via del Moro 22R. ☎ 055-284897. Reservations recommended. Main courses 12.50€–20€ ($11.15–$17.85). AE, DC, MC, V. Mon 7pm–12:30am; Tues–Sat 11am–3pm and 6pm–midnight. Closed 2 weeks in Aug. Bus: C, 6, 9, 11, 36, 37, or 68.

Sabatini ✿✿ FLORENTINE   Locals and visitors alike extol Sabatini as the finest of the city's typically Florentine restaurants. To celebrate our annual return here, we order the same main course we had on our first visit: boiled Valdarno chicken with a savory green sauce. Back then we complained to the waiter that the chicken was tough. He replied, "But, of course!" Florentines like chicken with muscle, not the hothouse variety so favored by Americans. Having eaten a lot of Valdarno chicken since then, we're more appreciative of Sabatini's dish.

But on subsequent visits, we've found some of the other main courses more delectable, such as the veal scaloppine with artichokes, sole meunière, classic beefsteak Florentine, and spaghetti Sabatini (a cousin of spaghetti carbonara but enhanced with fresh tomatoes). American-style coffee is served, following the Florentine cake called zuccotto.

Via de'Panzani 9A. ℂ **055-211559.** Reservations recommended. Main courses 12.50€–24€ ($11.15–$21.45). AE, DC, MC, V. Tues–Sun 12:30–2:30pm and 7:30–10:30pm. Bus: 1, 6, 14, 17, or 22.

Trattoria Garga ✦✦ TUSCAN/FLORENTINE   Some of the most creative cuisine in Florence is served here, about midway between the Ponte Vecchio and Santa Maria Novella. The thick Renaissance walls contain paintings by both Florentine and American artists, including those painted by owners Giuliano Gargani and his Canadian wife, Sharon, along with their son, Andrea. Both operatic arias and heavenly odors emerge from a postage stamp–size kitchen. Many of the Tuscan menu items are so unusual that Sharon's bilingual skills are put to good use: octopus with peppers and garlic, boar with juniper berries, grilled marinated quail, and "whatever strikes the mood" of Giuliano. One dish has earned a lot of publicity: *taglioni magnifico,* made with angel-hair pasta, orange and lemon rind, mint-flavored cream, and Parmigiano-Reggiano. One of the most delectable pastas is spaghetti with raw artichokes and red pepper served with extra-virgin olive oil. The chef prepares a cheesecake so well known in Florence that even New Yorkers give it a thumbs-up.

Via del Moro 48R. ℂ **055-2398898.** Reservations required. Main courses 15.60€–26€ ($15–$25). AE, DC, MC, V. Wed–Sun 7:30–11pm. Bus: 6, 9, 11, 36, 37, or 68.

MODERATE/INEXPENSIVE

Il Latini ✦ *Kids* TUSCAN/FLORENTINE   Il Latini is loud and claustrophobic, and the service borders on hysterical. Still, this is an enduringly popular place, with long lines. Diners pack the place for the enormous portions. A waiter will arrive to recite a list of items corresponding to antipasti, pasta, main course, and dessert. If you insist on seeing a printed menu, someone will probably find one, but it's more fun just to go with the flow. You can enjoy heaping portions of pastas such as penne with meat and cream sauce, deep-fried zucchini flowers or artichokes, and grilled meats that include veal, chicken, beef, rabbit, and pork. Don't expect decorative subtleties: The paintings are garish, and nobody is shy about displaying each and every framed award the place has ever earned.

Via del Palchetti 6R (off Via Vigna Nuova). ℂ **055-210916.** Reservations recommended. Main courses 10€–15€ ($8.95–$13.40). AE, DC, MC, V. Tues–Sun 12:30–2:30pm and 7:30–10:30pm. Closed Dec 24–Jan 7. Bus: C, 6, 11, 36, or 37.

La Carabaccia ✦ *Finds* FLORENTINE   Two hundred years ago, a *carabaccia* was a workaday boat, shaped like a hollowed-out half onion and used on the Arno to dredge silt and sand from the bottom. This restaurant still features the Medicis' favorite *zuppa carabaccia,* a creamy white onion soup with croutons (not in the French style, the chef rushes to tell you). You can, of course, eat more than onions here, and the menu changes daily. You might choose the soup of the day, followed by one of four or five pastas, such as a *crespelle* (crepe) of fresh vegetables, perhaps asparagus or artichokes. Our savory swordfish baked in parchment with essence of fresh tomato was perfect, especially when served with the house wine, a red Palazzuola (CQ) Chianti from Tuscany. You'll find the homemade breads irresistible (especially the onion variety).

Via Palazzuolo 190R. ℂ **055-214782.** Reservations recommended. Main courses 10€–17.50€ ($8.95–$15.65). AE, DC, MC, V. Tues–Sat noon–2:30pm; Mon–Sat 7–11pm. Bus: 6, 9, 11, 36, 37, or 68.

Take a Gelato Break

Opened in the 1930s and today run by the third generation of the Vivoli family, the **Gelateria Vivoli** ★★, Via Isola delle Stinche 7R (© 055-292334), on a back street near Santa Croce, produces some of Italy's finest ice cream and provides the gelati for many of Florence's restaurants.

Buy a ticket first and then select your flavor. Choose from blueberry (*mirtillo*), fig (*fico*), melon (*melone*), and other fruits in season, as well as chocolate mousse (*mousse al cioccolato*) or coffee ice cream flavored with espresso. A special ice cream is made from rice (*gelato di riso*). You can also choose from a number of flavors of *semifreddi*—an Italian ice cream with a base of cream instead of milk. The most popular flavors are *mandorla* (almond), *marengo* (a type of meringue), and *zabaglione* (eggnog). Others are *limoncini alla crema* (candied lemon peels with vanilla ice cream) and *aranciotti al cioccolate* (candied orange peels with chocolate ice cream). Prices range from 1.50€ to 5€ ($1.35–$4.45), and it's open Tuesday to Sunday 8am to 1am (it's closed in Jan and 3 weeks in Aug—dates vary).

Le Fonticine TUSCAN/BOLOGNESE   Today the richly decorated interior contains all the bounty of an Italian harvest, as well as the second passion of Signor Bruci's life: his collection of original modern paintings. The first passion, as a meal here reveals, is the cuisine that he and his wife produce from recipes she collected from her childhood in Bologna. Proceed to the larger of the two dining areas; along the way you can admire dozens of portions of fresh pasta decorating the table of an exposed grill. At the far end of the room, a wrought-iron gate shelters the extensive wine collection. The food, served in copious portions, is both traditional and delectable. Begin with a platter of fresh antipasti or with samplings of three of the most excellent pasta dishes of the day. Then follow with *fegatini di pollo* (chicken liver), veal scaloppine, or one of the other main dishes.

Via Nazionale 79R. © 055-282106. Reservations recommended for dinner. Main courses 8.50€–17.50€ ($7.60–$15.65). AE, DC, MC, V. Tues–Sat noon–3pm and 7–10pm. Closed Jan 1–15 and Aug. Bus: 7, 10, 11, 12, 25, 31, 33, or 70.

Ristorante Otello FLORENTINE/TUSCAN   This restaurant is carved out of part of a former convent and its garden. Located next to the train station, Otello serves an animated crowd in comfortably renovated surroundings. Its antipasti can hold their own with the best in town—this array of appetizing hors d'oeuvres is practically a meal in itself. The waiter urges you to *"Mangi, mangi, mangi!"* and that's what diners do. You might want to try one of the wonderful pasta dishes, such as spaghetti with baby clams or *pappardelle* with garlic sauce. The meat and poultry dishes are equally delectable, including sole meunière and veal pizzaiola with lots of garlic.

Via degli Orti Oricellari 36R. © 055-216517. Reservations recommended. Main courses 9€–17.50€ ($8.05–$15.65). AE, DC, MC, V. Daily noon–2:30pm and 7:30–10:30pm. Bus: D, 14, 17, 23, 26, 27, or 35.

Sostanza ★ *Value* FLORENTINE   Sostanza, the city's oldest (opened in 1869) and most revered trattoria, is where working people go for excellent moderately priced food. In recent years, however, it has also begun attracting a more sophisticated set, despite its somewhat funky atmosphere. (Florentines call the place *Troia,* a word that means "trough" but also suggests a woman of easy virtue.) The small dining room has crowded family tables, but when you taste what comes out of the kitchen, you'll know that fancy decor would be superfluous. Specialties include breaded chicken breast, a succulent T-bone, and tripe Florentine style (cut into strips and then baked in a casserole with tomatoes, onions, and *parmigiano*).

Via del Porcellana 25R. ✆ 055-212691. Reservations recommended. Main courses 8€–15€ ($7.15–$13.40). No credit cards. Mon–Fri noon–3pm and 7:30–10:30pm. Closed Aug and 2 weeks at Christmas. Bus: 12.

Trattoria Antellesi 🛪 *Finds* TUSCAN   Occupying a 15th-century historic monument just steps from the Medici Chapels and a 4-minute walk from the railway station, this place is devoted almost exclusively to well-prepared versions of time-tested Tuscan recipes. Managed by Joe Ranaudo, an Italian, French, and English-speaking Canadian from Montreal, and his Croatian wife, Renee, the restaurant changes its menu every 3 weeks, based on whatever is seasonal and fresh at the food market (Mercato San Lorenzo), which lies a short walk away. Dishes might include tagliatelle with porcinis or braised arugula, *crespelle alla fiorentina* (cheesy spinach crepe), *pappardelle* with wild boar, fresh fish (generally on Friday), Valdostana chicken, and superb *bistecca alla fiorentina* (local beefsteak). Expect a wide selection of high-quality Italian wines, mostly Tuscan, and most of them selected by Joe himself.

Via Faenza 9R. ✆ 055-216990. Reservations recommended. Main courses 10€–12.50€ ($8.95–$11.15). AE, DC, MC, V. Daily noon–3pm and 7–10:30pm. Closed Tues Dec–Apr. Bus: 1, 6, 7, 11, 17, 33, 67, or 68.

NEAR PIAZZA SAN MARCO
EXPENSIVE
Taverna del Bronzino 🛪 TUSCAN   It's a bit of an event to dine in the converted studio of a 16th-century Renaissance artist. You can do so in style where Santi di Tito, a student of Bronzino's, once painted. Against a backdrop of classic simplicity, you are served fine food from a menu that changes every week, based on the best produce in any given season. The waiters are among the most helpful in the city and will recommend the daily delights. In fair weather select a table on the patio, shaded by an arbor, or else dine inside under a vaulted ceiling. Start with one of the daily antipasti, guaranteed fresh. In season Tuscan asparagus appears in a creamy risotto. Among the main courses likely to be featured all year are veal scaloppine with fresh mushrooms from the fields or a beef filet Rossini (with truffles and duck liver). Desserts are prepared fresh every day, and are often rich and creamy, not good for dieting but exquisite.

Via delle Ruote 27R, near piazza Indipendenza. ✆ 055-495220. Reservations required. Main courses 22.50€–30€ ($20.10–$26.80). AE, DC, MC, V. Mon–Sat 12:30–2:30pm and 7:30–10:30pm. Closed Aug. Bus: 12 or 91.

MODERATE
Cafaggi TUSCAN/SEAFOOD   Atmospheric and charming, this 100-seat trattoria has flourished in a modestly proportioned palazzo since 1922. The tables are scattered between two old-fashioned dining rooms. The menu features Tuscan dishes, including Florentine beefsteak, steaming bowls of vegetarian soup, and very fresh salads and vegetables. Some of the newer menu items celebrate the robust quality of the Tuscan cuisine, notably a savory *risotto alla vedova* (widow's risotto) prepared with cuttlefish. *Caciucco* is a fish soup with shellfish served only in summer, and once you've tasted spaghetti with sardines, pine nuts, and raisins, it might become addictive. You can also order various fish,

such as scampi and swordfish, grilled to perfection. Forget the calories and try the *millefoglie alle creme* for dessert; it positively overflows with cream.

Via Guelfa 35R. ℂ 055-294989. Reservations recommended. Main courses 9€–14€ ($8.05–$12.50). AE, MC, V. Mon–Sat noon–3pm and 7–10pm. Bus: 1, 6, 7, 11, 17, 33, 67, or 68.

INEXPENSIVE

Il Vegetariano *Value* VEGETARIAN   At many Florentine restaurants, vegetarians can enjoy great antipasti made with fresh vegetables. But this is the city's only restaurant dedicated to glorifying the *legume*. The time-mellowed wooden tables are freely shared, and there is an informal, relaxed atmosphere. Daily specials—all from the fertile Tuscan fields—are changed daily. You make your selections, tell the staff what you want, pay in advance, and carry your tray to your table as in a cafeteria. The cooks emphasize the freshness of dishes and try to bring out the natural flavor in a vegetable, not concealing it too heavily with sauces. They make some of the best vegetable risottos in town, and their ovens turn out a country-style pizza with fresh olives, tomatoes, mushrooms, and ricotta. Their savory Chinese cabbage is another good choice, as is their tofu or their vegetable crepes. Their salads are always fresh, and their homemade cakes are a delight.

Via della Ruote 30R, near piazza Indipendenza. ℂ 055-475030. Reservations not taken. Main courses 7€–7.50€ ($6.25–$6.70). No credit cards. Tues–Fri 12:30–3pm, Tues–Sun 7:30pm–midnight. Closed 3 weeks in Aug. Bus: 12 or 91.

I' Toscano TUSCAN   Bouquets of flowers liven up this restaurant's plain interior, but despite the understated setting, the place is a magnet for foodies who appreciate its Tuscan specialties. Menu items change with the seasons but are often at their best in late autumn and winter, when mixed platters with slices of wild boar, venison, partridge, and (when available) pheasant are a worthy substitute for the antipasti that tempt visitors the rest of the year. Always popular are the spinach-stuffed ravioli and the several forms of gnocchi or tagliatelle. Fish (usually sea bass or monkfish, panfried or grilled) is most prominent on Friday, but veal, turkey, pork, and Florentine beefsteaks are also offered.

Via Guelfa 70R. ℂ 055-215475. Reservations recommended at dinner. Main courses 6.50€–13.50€ ($5.80–$12.05). AE, DC, MC, V. Wed–Mon 12:30–3pm and 7–11pm. Closed 1 week in Aug. Bus: 6, 11, or 14.

NEAR PIAZZA SANTA CROCE
EXPENSIVE

Alle Murate ★★ TUSCAN/SOUTHERN ITALIAN   Young Umberto Montano owns the sophisticated, softly lit Alle Murate and serves up some of the most creative Tuscan dishes in town. Yet the restaurant also offers classics of the south, such as *orecchiette* sauced with broccoli, fish poached *acqua pazza* (with tomatoes, garlic, and parsley), and five-bean purée with cooked chicory. The chefs make a truly memorable lasagna, with mozzarella and fresh tomatoes. Several soufflés are prepared with seasonal vegetables (leeks or artichokes), and handmade *tortelli* (a kind of ravioli) is stuffed with small eggplants and served with butter-and-thyme sauce. There's nothing finer here than the *brasato di chianina* (veal braised with Brunello di Montalcino red wine) or baked sea bream with crunchy potatoes. The wine selection is prodigious (ask and you might get to see the ancient wine cellar). In an adjacent smaller room, the Vineria, the menu is different and the service is not as good, but the food is slightly cheaper.

You might also want to check out Montano's **Osteria del Caffà Italiano** and **Caffè Italiano** (see below).

Via Ghibellina 52R. ℂ 055-240618. Reservations recommended. Main courses 17.50€–35€ ($15.65–$31.25). AE, DC, MC, V. Tues–Sun 7:30–11:30pm. Closed 15 days at Christmas. Bus: 14.

Cibrèo ✈✈✈ MEDITERRANEAN   Fabio Picchi, the chef-owner, serves the most innovative cuisine in Florence. Cibrèo consists of a restaurant, a less formal trattoria, and a cafe/bar across the street. The impossibly old-fashioned small kitchen doesn't have a grill and doesn't turn out pastas. Menu items include *sformato* (a soufflé made from potatoes and ricotta, served with parmigiano and tomato sauce), *inzimmino* (Tuscan-style squid stewed with spinach), and a flan of parmigiano, veal tongue, and artichokes. The cuisine is spicy, with plenty of garlic. Some of the staff members are expatriate New Yorkers who excel at explaining the menu. The restaurant takes its name from (and serves) an old Tuscan dish combining the organs, meat, and crest (or comb) of a chicken with lots of garlic, rosemary, sage, and wine. (Allegedly, it was so delectable it nearly killed Catherine de' Medici: She ate so much that she was overcome with near-fatal indigestion.) It's prepared only on request, usually for specially catered meals ordered in advance. Chocoholics can finish with the flourless chocolate cake, so sinfully good that it should be outlawed.

Via Verrocchio 8R. ✆ 055-2341100. Reservations recommended in the restaurant but not accepted in the trattoria. Aill main courses 30€ ($26.80) in the restaurant; 15€ ($13.40) in the trattoria. AE, DC, MC, V (restaurant only). Tues–Sat 12:30–2:30pm and 7:30–11pm. Closed late July to early Sept. Bus: B or 14.

MODERATE/INEXPENSIVE

Osteria del Caffè Italiano ✈ *Value* WINE BAR/TUSCAN   Housed in the 13th-century Palazzo Salviati, this wine bar/trattoria is the brainchild of Umberto Montano (see the listing for Alle Murate, above). The front room is warmed by burnished wood paneling and made even more welcoming when you see the prices. Beneath a wrought-iron chandelier hanging from the vaulted 6m (20-ft.) ceiling, you can sample delicious choices from the short menu. Look for the fresh *mozzarella di bufala,* specially couriered from a private supplier in Naples (not available June–Aug). Stop by any time the restaurant isn't serving meals for a by-the-glass introduction to Montano's renowned wine cellar and an assortment of Tuscan *salumi.* Or come back in the evening to dine in the elegant restaurant in the back room and splurge with excellently prepared entrees from the grill and a more serious sampling of wine.

Don't miss Montano's handsome **Caffè Italiano,** Via Condotta 56R, off Via dei Calzaiuoli (✆ **055-291082;** bus: 14, 23, or 71), which offers a delicious lunch and dinner to standing-room-only crowds (come early). It's open Monday to Saturday 12:30 to 3pm and 8 to 10pm.

Via Isola delle Stinche 11–13R (2 blocks west of Piazza Santa Croce). ✆ 055-289368. Reservations for restaurant (not wine bar) suggested. Wine bar: Small plates 7.50€–9€ ($6.70–$8.05). Restaurant: Main courses 14€–19€ ($12.50–$16.95). DC, MC, V. Tues–Sun noon–1am. Bus: A or 14.

Trattoria Pallottino TUSCAN/FLORENTINE   Less than a block from Piazza Santa Croce, on a narrow street, this distinctive restaurant contains two sometimes-cramped dining rooms. Flickering candles illuminate a timeless Italian scene where the staff works hard, usually with humor and style. Menu specialties are succulent antipasti, taglioni with cream and herbs, ravioli with spinach or pine nuts and cream sauce, *peposa* (a slab of beef marinated for at least 4 hours in a rich broth of ground black pepper, olive oil, and tomatoes), and *spaghetti fiacchiraia* (with spicy red chilies, olive oil, and tomatoes). Dessert might be vanilla custard drizzled with a compote of fresh fruit.

Isola delle Stinche 1R. ✆ 055-289573. Reservations recommended at dinner. Main courses 9€–15€ ($8.05–$13.40). AE, DC, MC, V. Tues–Sun 12:30–2:30pm and 7:30–10:30pm. Bus: 14, 23, or 71.

Finds Taking to the Hills: A Dining Secret

On Sunday nights, many of Florence's best restaurants are closed. For years we've driven 5km (3 miles) south to the little town of Arcetri to dine at **Omero,** via Plan de Giullarfi 11R (© **055-220053**). This is a small, rustic place, but every dish is perfumed with flavor. We can never resist the lip-smacking *pollo shiacciato* (grilled chicken). On a second visit, you're treated like a long-lost family friend. Closed Tuesday and in August.

ACROSS THE ARNO
MODERATE

Mamma Gina ⭐ TUSCAN   Mamma Gina is a rustic restaurant that prepares fine foods in the traditional manner. Although it's run by a corporation that operates other restaurants around Tuscany, this place is named after its founding matriarch, whose legend has continued despite her death in the 1980s. A few of the savory menu items are cannelloni Mamma Gina (stuffed with a purée of meats, spices, and vegetables), taglioni with artichoke hearts or mushrooms and whatever else is in season, and chicken breast Mamma Gina (baked northern Italian style with prosciutto and Emmenthaler cheese). This is an ideal spot for lunch after visiting the Pitti Palace.

Borgo San Jacopo 37R. © **055-2396009.** Reservations required for dinner. Main courses 10€–17.50€ ($8.95–$15.65). AE, DC, MC, V. Mon–Sat noon–2:30pm and 7–10:30pm. Closed 15 days in Aug. Bus: D.

Trattoria Cammillo TUSCAN   On the ground floor of a former Medici palace, the Cammillo is one of the most popular (and perhaps the finest) of the Oltrarno neighborhood's dining spots. Its most serious rival is Mamma Gina (listed earlier). Chic boutique owners cross the Arno regularly to feast here; they know they'll get specialties such as tagliatelle flavored with fresh peas and truffles (it sounds like such a simple dish, but when it's prepared right, it's a real treat). You'll also find excellent assortments of fried or grilled vegetables, fresh scampi and sole, fried deboned pigeon with artichokes, and chicken breast with truffles and parmigiano. Unfortunately, you're likely to be rushed through your meal.

Borgo San Jacopo 57R (between the Ponte Vecchio and Ponte Santa Trinita). © **055-212427.** Reservations required. Main courses 8€–25€ ($7.15–$22.35). AE, DC, MC, V. Thurs–Tues noon–2:30pm and 7:30–10:30pm. Closed mid-Dec to Jan and Aug 1–21. Bus: B, C, 6, 11, 36, or 37.

INEXPENSIVE

Fuori Porta ⭐ *Finds* TUSCAN   This is the city's best enoteca (wine tavern). As the name translates, it means "outside the gates," yet it's only a 15-minute taxi or bus ride from the landmark Piazza della Signoria, the historic core of Florence. The wine list ranks at the top in Florence, yet the prices are more than reasonable. Many of the finest selections are available by the glass. Discerning palates also appreciate the Tuscan fare served here, which is soul food to the Florentines. We recently started off an elegant repast with carpaccio of swordfish that was perfectly flavored, as was the sautéed calves' liver to follow. We especially like the loaves of bread that arrive freshly baked from the oven and are most often served with mozzarella and vine-ripened tomatoes.

Via del Monte alle Croce 10R. © **055-2342483.** Reservations recommended. Main courses 7.50€–9€ ($6.70–$8.05). AE, MC, V. Mon–Sat 12:30–3:30pm and 7pm–midnight. Closed 2 weeks Aug 10–20. Bus: 13 or 23.

La Baruciola TUSCAN   In a 16th-century building adjacent to the Pitti Palace, this restaurant celebrates the art of *cucina casalinga* (home cooking) and draws a busy crowd of Tuscans. In a pair of white dining rooms with understated decor, you can enjoy pastas such as homemade ravioli stuffed with dry mushrooms and penne with mushrooms and cream, or try ribollita, the heady vegetable soup of Tuscany, and a mixed platter of fish or smoked meat. The chef will even prepare a vegetarian lasagna. The place appeals to those who like simple, well-prepared dishes, brimming with flavor but low in price.

Via Maggio 61R. ✆ **055-218906.** Reservations recommended. Main courses 7.50€–17.50€ ($6.70–$15.65). AE, DC, MC, V. Daily 12:30–2:30pm and 7–10:30pm. Bus: B or C.

Trattoria Angiolino ITALIAN/TUSCAN   This restaurant thrives in a 14th-century building. Since the 1920s it has been going strong, feeding a friend or a relative of virtually everyone in Florence. The decor is old-fashioned and warm, with a potbellied stove and brick floors, and the menu includes dishes that many regulars remember from their childhood. Choose from an array of antipasti, steaming bowls of *pasta e fagioli* (pasta and bean soup), a roster of homemade pastas such as ravioli and taglioni, veal and chicken cutlets prepared either Milanese or parmigiana style, and rich homemade cakes and pastries.

Via San Spirito 36R. ✆ **055-2398976.** Reservations recommended. Main courses 10€–14€ ($8.95–$12.50). AE, DC, MC, V. Tues–Sun noon–2:30pm and 7–10:30pm. Bus: C, 6, 11, 36, 37, or 68.

AT ARTIMINO
MODERATE

Da Delfina ✦ *(Finds)* TUSCAN   Even on a short visit to Florence, give yourself a break and dip at least once into the countryside of Tuscany for a meal. Our candidate for an outing is this family-run restaurant in the medieval walled village of Artimino, just a 15-minute train ride from the center of Florence. Based on the freshest of local ingredients, the food has a wonderful, earthy taste, and some of it often comes from the nearby fields, including nettles, mushrooms, and wild herbs. Arriving in fair weather, request a table on the terrace with its classic view of a Tuscan landscape. The chefs, Carlo Cioni and his wife, Franca, turn out some of the region's best homemade pasta dishes, grilled fish over a wood-burning fireplace, and delectable sausages. We'd walk a mile or even more for a plate of their aged salami with its intense, meaty flavor. Raw fava beans appear with pecorino sheep-milk cheese, and homemade pasta with wild mushrooms should win an award. Baby goat or capretto is roasted to perfection in the oven.

Via della Chiesa 1, Artimino. ✆ **055-8718074.** Reservations recommended. Main courses 12€–15€ ($10.70–$13.40). No credit cards. Tues–Sun 12:30–2:30pm and Tues–Sat 8–9:30pm. From Santa Maria Novella station in Florence take the Signa train. At Signa take a taxi for the 5-min. ride to Da Delfina.

5 Seeing the Sights

Florence was the fountainhead of the Renaissance, the city of Dante and Boccaccio. For 3 centuries, the city was dominated by the Medici family, patrons of the arts, and masters of assassination. But it's chiefly through Florence's incomparable artists that we know of the apogee of the Renaissance: Ghiberti, Fra Angelico, Donatello, Brunelleschi, Botticelli, Leonardo da Vinci, and Michelangelo.

In Florence, you can trace the transition from medievalism to the age of "rebirth." For example, all modern painters owe a debt to an ugly, unkempt man named Masaccio (Vasari's "Slipshod Tom"), who died at 27. Modern painting began with his frescoes in the Brancacci Chapel in Santa Maria del Carmine, which you can see today. Years later, Michelangelo painted a more celebrated Adam and Eve in the Sistine Chapel, but even this great artist never realized the raw humanity of Masaccio's Adam and Eve fleeing from the Garden of Eden.

Group tourism has so overwhelmed this city that in 1996, officials demanded that organized tour groups book their visits in advance and pay an admission fee. No more than 150 tour buses are allowed into the center at one time (considering how small Florence is, even that's a stretch). Today there are more than seven tourists for each native Florentine. And that isn't counting the day-trippers, who rush off to Venice in the late afternoon. But despite all its traffic and inconveniences, Florence is still one of the world's greatest art cities.

If you have a limited amount of time or want to get an overall view before exploring on your own, many companies run guided bus tours of the main sights. The two virtually indistinguishable big names are **American Express** (© **055-50981**) and **SitaSightseeing** (© **055-219383**). They run morning tours of the major sights and separate afternoon tours of the top secondary sights; the cost is 30€ ($26.80) per person for each half-day tour, with museum admissions included. Both companies also run afternoon tours to Pisa (30€/$26.80) and the Chianti (30€/$26.80) and an all-day trip combining Siena and San Gimignano (50€/$44.65). To arrange any other kind of guided tour, visit the **CafTours** at Via Roma 4 (© **055-2302283**).

There's a daily walking tour, called **Enjoy Florence** (© **055-2341444** toll-free from anywhere in Italy), which departs daily at 10am (with a second tour on Mon, Wed, and Fri at 5pm) from the Thomas Cook exchange office just west of the Ponte Vecchio on the Duomo side of the river. It lasts 3 hours and costs 15€ ($13.40) for those over 26 and 12.50€ ($11.15) for those under 26.

THE TOP MUSEUMS

Uffizi Gallery (Galleria degli Uffizi) ★★★

When Anna Maria Ludovica, the last Medici grand duchess, died in 1737, she bequeathed to the people of Tuscany a wealth of Renaissance and even classical art. The paintings and sculptures had been accumulated by the powerful grand dukes during 3 centuries of rule that witnessed the height of the Renaissance. The collection is housed in an impressive palazzo commissioned by Duke Cosimo de' Medici in 1560 and initiated by Giorgio Vasari to house the Duchy of Tuscany's administrative offices (*uffizi* means offices).

Tips A Note About Museum & Church Hours

Most stores close for long lunch breaks, and many of the museums close for the day at 2pm or earlier (the last entrance is at least 30 min. before closing) and are closed on Monday. The Uffizi, the Accademia, the Palazzo Vecchio, the Duomo and the Duomo Museum, the Campanile di Giotto, Santa Croce, the Pitti Palace, and the Boboli Gardens are among the attractions that remain open during *il riposo*.

The first thing you should do is stop by the tourist office for an up-to-date listing of museum hours.

Churches and markets are good alternatives for spending your afternoons because they usually remain open until 7pm (however, churches, too, close for the long lunch break). The open-air Mercato San Lorenzo gets the lunch crowd; the stalls never close.

Florence Attractions

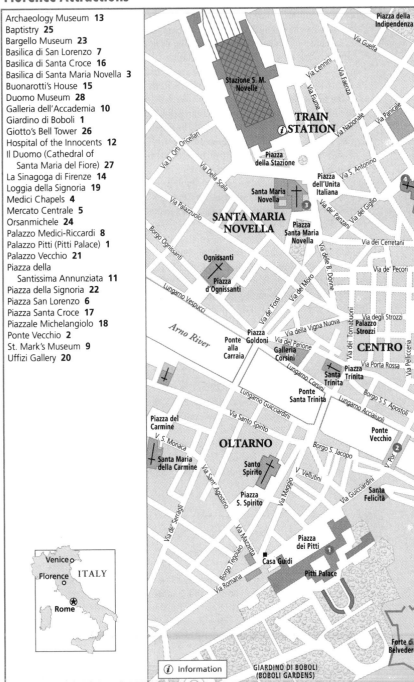

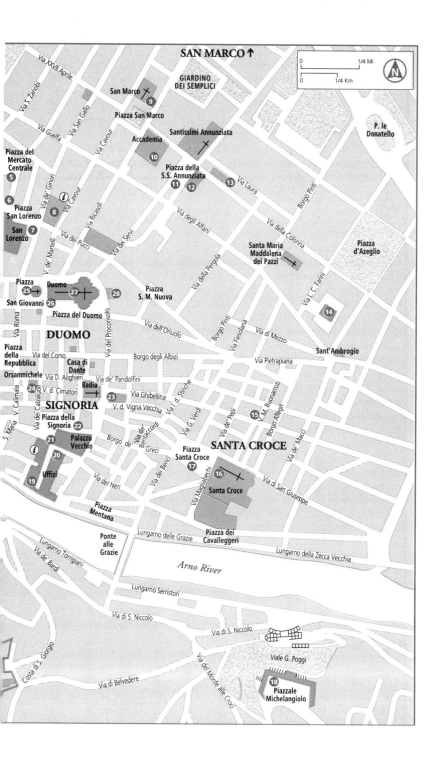

SAN MARCO ↑

GIARDINO
DEI SEMPLICI

San Marco ✝

Piazza San Marco

Via XXVII Aprile

Via S. Zanobi

Via San Gallo

Via Guelfa

Via Cavour

Accademia

Santissimi Annunziata ✝

10

Piazza della
S.S. Annunziata

11 12

13

Via Laura

P. le
Donatello

Piazza del
Mercato
Centrale

5

6

Piazza
San Lorenzo

San
Lorenzo

Via di Ginori

8 i

Via Cavour

Via Ricasoli

Via dei Servi

Via degli Affani

Via della Pergola

Via della Colonna

Borgo Pinti

Santa Maria
Maddalena
dei Pazzi

Piazza
d'Azeglio

7

Via dei Pucci

V. de' Martelli

Piazza
Duomo

25

San Giovanni 26

27 ✝

28

Piazza
S. M. Nuova

Piazza del Duomo

Via del Proconsolo

Via dell'Oriuolo

Borgo Pinti

Via Fiesolana

Via di Mezzo

14

DUOMO

Via Roma

Via del Corso

Casa di
Dante

Borgo degli Albizi

Via Pietrapiana

Sant'Ambrogio

Piazza
della
Repubblica

Orsanmichele

Via D. Alighieri

Badia ✝

Via de' Pandolfini

23

Via Ghibellina

V. d. Cimatori

SIGNORIA

V. d. Calzaiuoli

S. Maria

V. Calimala

Piazza della
Signoria 22

21

Palazzo
Vecchio

20

i

Uffizi

19

V. d. Vigna Vecchia

Borgo de'
Bentaccordi

Greci

Via de' Benci

Via G. Verdi

Via de' Pepi

Via Buonarroti

Borgo Allegri

Via de' Macci

15

SANTA CROCE

Piazza
Santa Croce

17

16

Santa Croce ✝

Via di San Giuseppe

Via del Neri

Via dei Macciabechi

Piazza
Mentana

Ponte
alle
Grazie

Lungarno delle Grazie

Piazza dei
Cavalleggeri

Lungarno della Zecca Vecchia

Lungarno Torrigiani

Via de' Bardi

Arno River

Lungarno Serristori

Via di S. Niccolo

Via di S. Niccolo

Viale G. Poggi

Costa di S. Giorgio

Via del Monte alle Croci

Via di Belvedere

18

Piazzale
Michelangiolo

0 ————————— 1/4 Mi
0 ————————— 1/4 Km
N

After several renovations following a terrorist bomb in 1993, the Uffizi now has a new look. A lobby has been added so that visitors don't have to wait in line outside; the galleries at the upper two floors are three times their previous size; the trompe l'oeil painting in the Loggiato sull'Arno has been restored to its original beauty; and walking down this hall, looking through the high windows, you'll have enchanting views of Florence. There's also a new bookstore on the premises.

You can buy tickets in advance online at **www.selectitaly.com**, or you can join a small tour that avoids the lines by logging onto **www.arca.net**, which has a full catalog of the museum's works on the Web. Any hotel in Florence that has a concierge can also make reservations for you, cutting down on the lines and hassle.

The Uffizi is nicely grouped into periods or schools to show the development and progress of Italian and European art.

Room 2: Here you'll meet up with those rebels from Byzantium, Cimabue and his pupil Giotto, with their Madonnas and bambini. Because the Virgin and Child seem to be the overriding theme of the earlier Uffizi artists, it's enlightening just to follow the different styles over the centuries, from the ugly, almost midget-faced babies of the post-Byzantine works to the red-cheeked chubby cherubs that glorified the baroque. One of the great works in the center of the salon is Giotto's masterful ***Ognissanti Maestà*** ✹✹ (1310).

Room 3: Look for Simone Martini's *Annunciation,* full of grace; the halo around the head of the Virgin doesn't conceal her pouty mouth. Fra Angelico of Fiesole, a 15th-century painter lost in a world peopled with saints and angels, makes his Uffizi debut with (naturally) *Madonna and Bambino.* A special treasure is the *Santa Trinita Madonna* by Masaccio, who died at an early age but is credited as the father of modern painting: In his Madonnas and bambini, we see the beginnings of the use of perspective in painting. Fra Angelico's *Coronation of the Virgin* is also in this salon.

Room 8: Here you'll find Friar Filippo Lippi's superior **Coronation of the Virgin** ✹, as well as a galaxy of charming Madonnas. Lippi was a rebel among the brethren.

Rooms 10 to 14: These are the **Botticelli rooms,** with his finest works. Botticelli ("little barrels") was the nickname of the great master of women in flowing gowns, Sandro Filipepi. Many come to contemplate his "Venus on the Half Shell": This supreme conception of life (the **Birth of Venus** ✹✹✹) really packs 'em in. Also check out *Minerva Subduing the Centaur,* which brought about renewed interest in mythological subjects. Botticelli's **Allegory of Spring, or Primavera** ✹✹, is a gem; it depicts Venus in a citrus grove with Cupid hovering over her head and Mercury looking out of the canvas to the left. Before leaving the room, look for Botticelli's *Adoration of the Magi,* in which you'll find portraits of the Medici (the vain man at the far right is Botticelli, with golden curls and a yellow robe), and his allegorical *Calumny.*

Room 15: Here you'll come across one of Leonardo da Vinci's unfinished paintings, the brilliant **Adoration of the Magi** ✹✹. Also here hangs Leonardo's *Annunciation,* reflecting the early years of his genius with its twilight atmosphere and each leaf painstakingly in place. The splendid Renaissance palace that he designed is part of the background.

Room 18: The most beautiful room in the gallery, with its dome of pearl shells, contains the **Venus of the Medici** ✹✹ at its center; it's one of the most reproduced of all Greek sculptural works, a 1st-century copy of a Greek original.

Room 19: This room is devoted to Perugino, especially his *Madonna* and his *Portrait of Francesco delle Opere,* and to Luca Signorelli's *Holy Family.* Signorelli was taught by his master, Piero della Francesca, to convey depth and perspective, as illustrated by this work.

Room 20: This room takes you into the world of German artists who worked in Florence, notably Lucas Cranach and Dürer, both intrigued with the Adam and Eve theme.

Room 21: You'll see the beginnings of important Venetian painting here, with works by Giambellino and Giorgione. The best example is Giovanni Bellini's *Sacred Allegory.*

Room 22: This room contains a cavalcade of works by northern Europeans, particularly Flemish and German works, especially Hans Holbein the Younger's ***Portrait of Sir Richard Southwell.***

Room 23: Correggio's ***Rest on the Flight to Egypt*** ✿ (1515) dominates this room, but the finest pieces are by Andrea Mantagna (1489): ***Epiphany, Circumcision,*** and ***Ascension*** ✿✿.

Room 25: The star here is Michelangelo's magnificent ***Holy Family*** ✿✿ (1506–08), but coming in second are Raphael's Leonardoesque *Madonna of the Goldfinch* (1505) and portraits of Pope Julius II and Pope Leo X. There are also works by Bartolomeo and Granacci.

Room 27: This room is devoted to works by Andrea del Sarto's star Mannerist pupils, Rosso Fiorentino and Pontormo, and by Pontormo's adopted son, Bronzino.

Room 28 and the rest: Masterpieces in the salons include two Venuses by Titian, Veronese's *Martyrdom of St. Justina,* Tintoretto's *Leda and the Swan,* Rubens's *Portrait of Philip IV of Spain* and *Judith and Holofernes,* and Caravaggio's *The Sacrifice of Isaac* and *The Head of Medusa.*

Vasari Corridor (Corridoio Vasariano): This corridor, commissioned from Vasari by Cosimo I after the Uffizi's completion, is an above-ground "tunnel" running along the rooftops of the Ponte Vecchio buildings and connecting the Uffizi with Cosimo's then-new residence in the Pitti Palace on the other side of the Arno (see below). The corridor is lined with portraits and self-portraits by a stellar list of international masters, including Bronzino, Rubens, Rembrandt, and Ingres.

Piazzale degli Uffizi 6. ✆ **055-23885.** www.uffizi.firenze.it. Admission 6€ ($5.35). Tues–Sun 8:15am–7pm (last entrance 45 min. before closing). Bus: 23 or 71.

Galleria dell'Accademia ✿

This museum boasts many paintings and sculptures, but they're completely overshadowed by one work: Michelangelo's colossal ***David*** ✿✿✿, unveiled in 1504 and now the world's most famed sculpture. It first stood in Piazza della Signoria but was moved to the Accademia in 1873 (a copy was substituted) and placed beneath the rotunda of a room built exclusively for its display. When he began work, Michelangelo was just 29. One of the most sensitive accounts we've ever read of how Michelangelo turned the 5m (17-ft.) "Duccio marble" into *Il Gigante* (the Giant) is related in Irving Stone's *The Agony and the Ecstasy.* Stone describes a Michelangelo "burning with marble fever" who set out to create a *David* who "would be Apollo, but considerably more; Hercules, but considerably more; Adam, but considerably more; the most fully realized man the world had yet seen, functioning in a rational and humane world."

Tips No More Lines

The endless lines outside the Italian museums are a fact of life. But new reservation services can help you avoid waiting, at least for some of the major museums.

Select Italy offers the possibility to reserve your tickets for the Uffizi, Boboli Gardens, Galleria dell'Accademia, and many other attractions in Florence, Rome, and Venice. The cost varies from 12.30€ to 26.90€ ($11–$24), depending on the museum, and several combination passes are available. Contact Select Italy at © 847/853-1661, or buy online at www.selectitaly.com.

If you're already in Florence and don't want to waste a half day waiting to enter the Galleria degli Uffizi, Galleria dell'Accademia, Boboli Gardens, Pitti Palace, and many others, call **Firenze Musei** (© 055-294883; www.firenzemusei.it). The service operates Monday to Friday from 8:30am to 6:30pm, and Saturday to 12:30pm. Requests must be made a minimum of 5 days in advance; you pick up the tickets at the museum booth on the day your visit has been approved. There's a service charge of 1.10€ ($1), plus, of course, the regular price of the museum admission. You can also join a small tour that avoids the Uffizi lines on the Web at **www.arca.net**. And if your hotel has a concierge, don't be shy about asking what he can do to get you tickets.

David is so overpowering in his majesty that many visitors head here just to see him and leave immediately afterward. (The wait to get in to see *David* can be up to an hour. Try getting there before the museum opens in the morning or an hour or two before closing time.) However, the hall leading up to him is lined with other Michelangelos, notably his quartet of celebrated *Prisoners* or *Slaves* ★★. The statues are presumably unfinished, although art historians have found them more dramatic in their current state as they depict the struggles of figures to free themselves from stone. Michelangelo worked on these statues, originally intended for the tomb of Pope Julius II, for 40 years because he was never pleased with them. The gallery also displays Michelangelo's statue of St. Matthew, which he began carving in 1504.

The Accademia also owns a gallery of paintings, usually considered to be of minor importance (works by Santi di Tito, Granacci, and Albertinelli, for example). Yet there are masterpieces as well, notably Lo Scheggia's 1440s *Cassone Adimari*, a panel from a wedding chest.

Via Ricasoli 60. © 055-2388609. Admission 7.50€ ($6.70). Tues–Sun 8:15am–6:20pm. Bus: 1, 6, 7, 11, 17, 20, 25, 31, 32, or 33.

Palazzo Pitti and the Giardini di Boboli (Boboli Gardens) ★★   The massive bulk of the **Palazzo Pitti** is one of Europe's greatest artistic treasure troves, with the city's most extensive coterie of museums embracing a painting gallery second only to the Uffizi. It's a virtual cavalcade of the works of Titian, Rubens, Raphael, and Andrea del Sarto. Built in the 16th century (Brunelleschi was probably the original architect), this was once the residence of the powerful Medici family. It's located across the Arno (a 5-min. walk from the Ponte Vecchio).

Of the several museums in this complex, the most important is the first-floor **Palatine Gallery (Galleria Palatina)** ★★, which houses one of Europe's great art collections and shows masterpieces hung one on top of the other as in the days of the Enlightenment. If for no other reason, you should come for its Raphaels. After passing through the main door, proceed to the Sala di Venere (Venus), where you'll find Titian's *La Bella,* of rich and illuminating color (entrance wall), and his portrait of Pietro Aretino, one of his most distinguished works. On the opposite wall are Titian's *Concert of Music,* often attributed to Giorgione, and his portrait of Julius II.

In the Sala di Apollo (on the opposite side of the entrance door) are Titian's **Man with Gray Eyes**★★, an aristocratic, handsome romanticist; and his luminously gold **Mary Magdalene**★, covered only with her long hair. On the opposite wall are Van Dyck portraits of Charles I of England and Henrietta of France. This salon also contains some of the grandest works of Andrea del Sarto, notably his *Holy Family* and his *Deposition.*

In the Sala di Marte (entrance wall) is an important *Madonna and Child* by Murillo of Spain and the Pitti's best-known work by Rubens, *The Four Philosophers.* Rubens obviously had so much fun with this rather lighthearted work that he painted himself in on the far left (that's his brother, Filippo, seated). On the left wall is one of Rubens's most tragic and moving works, **Consequences of War**★, an early *Guernica,* painted in his declining years.

In the Sala di Giove (entrance wall) are Andrea del Sarto's idealized *John the Baptist* in his youth and Fra Bartolomeo's *Descent from the Cross.* On the third wall (opposite the entrance wall) is the Pitti's second famous Raphael, **La Velata**★— the woman under the veil, known as La Fornarina, is his bakery-girl mistress.

In the following gallery, the Sala di Saturno, look to the left on the entrance wall to see Raphael's *Madonna of the Canopy.* On the third wall near the doorway is the greatest Pitti prize, Raphael's **Madonna of the Chair**★★, his best-known interpretation of the Virgin and what's probably one of the six most celebrated paintings in all Europe. In the Sala dell'Iliade (to your left on the entrance wall) is a work of delicate beauty, Raphael's rendition of a pregnant woman. On the left wall is Titian's *Portrait of a Gentleman,* which he was indeed. (Titian is the second big star in the gallery.) Other masterpieces are in the smaller rooms that follow, notably the Sala dell'Educazione di Giove, home to the 1608 *Sleeping Cupid* that "the divine" Caravaggio painted in Rome while escaping charges of murder in Malta.

The **Royal Apartments (Appartamenti Reali)** ★ boast lavish reminders of when the Pitti was a private residence. This was once the home of the Kings of Savoy, when they presided over a unified Italy. Reopened in 1993 after a restoration, these apartments in all their baroque sumptuousness, including a flamboyant decor and works of art by del Sarto and Caravaggio, can be viewed only on a guided tour, usually Tuesday and Saturday (also on an occasional Thurs) 9 to 11am and 3 to 5pm. Tours leave every hour. Reservations are needed, so call ✆ **051-2388614.**

The **Modern Art Gallery (Galleria d'Arte Moderna;** ✆ **055-2388601)** can easily be skipped if you're exhausted after all those Titians. Nevertheless, it contains an important collection of 19th-century proto-Impressionist works of the Macchiaioli school, embracing many romantic and neoclassic pieces. Even if you don't like the art, the panoramic view from the top floor is worth the visit.

Gallery of Costume (Galleria del Costume), housed in the Palazzina della Meridiana wing of the Modern Art gallery, traces the history of dress over 2 centuries, from the tight corsets and wide panniers of the 18th century to the beginning of the loose flapper dresses in the 1920s. Some of the costumes are even older.

The ground-floor **Museum of Silver (Museo degli Argenti)** ✿ displays the household wares of the Medicis, everything from precious ivory, silver, and rare gems to Lorenzo the Magnificent's celebrated collection of vases. These precious stone vases spawned a vogue for *pietra dura* (precious stonework) in the 19th century (the English called it Florentine mosaic). One writer called the entire collection here "a camp glorification of the Medici." Many of the exhibits are in dubious taste. The Museo degli Argenti has a separate number to call for information (© **055-294883**).

Behind the Pitti Palace are the **Boboli Gardens (Giardini di Boboli)** ✿, Piazza Pitti 1 (© **055-2651838**), through which the Medicis romped. These Renaissance gardens were laid out by Triboli, a great landscape artist, in the 16th century. Although plans were drawn up for them in 1549, they weren't completed until 1656 and weren't open to the public until 1766. The Boboli is everpopular for a stroll or an idyllic interlude in a pleasant setting. You can climb to the top of the Fortezza di Belvedere for a dazzling view of the city. The gardens are filled with fountains and statuary, such as *Venus* by Giambologna in the "Grotto" of Buontalenti. Our favorite? An absurd Mannerist piece depicting Cosimo I's court jester posing as a chubby Bacchus riding a turtle, next to the **Vasari Corridor** (see the previous entry for the Uffizi).

Piazza Pitti, across the Arno. © **055-2388611**. Palatina 7.50€ ($6.70); Modern Art Gallery 4€ ($3.55); Argenti 2€ ($1.80); Boboli Gardens 2.15€ ($1.90). Galleria Palatina and Appartamenti Reali Tues–Sun 8:15am–6:45pm. Museo degli Argenti and Modern Art Gallery daily 8:30am–1:30pm; closed the 1st, 3rd, and 5th Mon and the 2nd and 4th Sun of each month. Boboli Gardens June–Sept daily 8:30am–7:45pm; Apr–May and Oct daily 8:30am–6:45pm; Nov–Mar daily 9am–5:45pm; closed the 1st and last Mon of each month. Ticket office closes 1 hr. before the gardens. Bus: B or C.

Bargello Museum (Museo Nazionale del Bargello) ✿✿

A short walk from Piazza della Signoria, this is a 1255 fortress palace whose dark underground chambers resounded with the cries of the tortured when it served as the city's jail and town hall during the Renaissance. Today the Bargello is a vast repository of some of the most important Renaissance sculpture, including works by Michelangelo and Donatello.

Here you'll see **another Michelangelo *David*** (referred to in the past as *Apollo*), chiseled perhaps 25 to 30 years after the statuesque figure in the Accademia. The Bargello *David* is totally different, effete when compared to its stronger brother. The armory here displays Michelangelo's grape-capped and drunk *Bacchus* (one of his earlier works, carved when he was 22), who's tempted by a satyr. Among the more significant sculptures is Giambologna's *Winged Mercury* (ca. 1564), a Mannerist masterpiece looking as if it's ready to take flight.

The Bargello displays two versions of Donatello's ***John the Baptist*** ✿, one emaciated and the other a younger and much kinder man. Donatello was one of the outstanding and original talents of the early Renaissance, and in this gallery you'll learn why. His ***St. George*** ✿ is a work of heroic magnitude. According to an oft-repeated story, Michelangelo, upon seeing it for the first time, commanded it to "March!" **Donatello's bronze *David*** ✿✿ in this salon is truly remarkable; it was the first freestanding nude since the Romans stopped chiseling. As depicted, David is narcissistic (a stunning contrast to Michelangelo's later-day virile interpretation). For the last word, however, we'll have to call back our lady of the barbs, Mary McCarthy, who wrote: "His *David*, wearing nothing but a pair of fancy polished boots and a girlish bonnet, is a transvestite's and fetishist's dream of alluring ambiguity."

Look for at least one more work: another *David*, this one by Andrea del Verrocchio, one of the finest of the 15th-century sculptors. The Bargello also contains a large number of terra-cottas by the della Robbia clan.

Via del Proconsolo 4. *Ⓒ* 055-294883. Admission 5€ ($4.45). Daily 8:30am–1:30pm; 2nd and 4th Sun and 1st and 3rd Mon of the month 8:30am–1:50pm. Closed Jan 1, May 1, and Christmas. Bus: A, 14, or 23.

St. Mark's Museum (Museo di San Marco) ★★   This state museum is a handsome Renaissance palace whose cell walls are decorated with frescoes by the mystical **Fra Angelico,** one of Europe's greatest 15th-century painters. In the days of Cosimo de' Medici, San Marco was built by Michelozzo as a Dominican convent. It contained bleak, bare cells, which Angelico and his students brightened considerably with some of the most important works by this pious artist of Fiesole, who portrayed recognizable landscapes in vivid colors.

After buying a ticket, you enter the **Cloister of St. Anthony (Chiostro di Sant'Antonio),** designed by Michelozzo. Turn right in the cloister to enter the **Ospizio dei Pellegrini,** a virtual Fra Angelico gallery filled with painted panels and altarpieces. Here you'll see one of his better-known paintings, *The Last Judgment* ★★ (1431), depicting people with angels on the left dancing in a circle and lordly saints towering overhead. Hell, as it's depicted on the right, is infested with demons, reptiles, and sinners boiling in a stew. Much of hell was created by Angelico's students; his brush was inspired only by the Crucifixion, Madonnas, and bambini, or landscapes, of course. Henry James claimed that Angelico "never received an intelligible impression of evil; and his conception of human life was a perpetual sense of sacredly loving and being loved." Here also are his *Deposition* (ca. 1440), an altarpiece removed from Santa Trinita, and his *Madonna dei Linaiuoli,* commissioned by the flax workers' guild. Other works to look for are Angelico's panels from the life of Christ.

Now you can enter the courtyard, where a sign points the way to the **Chapter House (Capitolaire),** to the right of a large convent bell. Here you can see a large *Crucifixion and Saints* painted in 1442 by Fra Angelico. Returning to the courtyard, follow the sign into the **Refectory (Refettorio)** to see a *Last Supper* by Domenico Ghirlandaio, who taught Michelangelo how to fresco. This work is rather realistic, with the tragic faces of the saints evoking a feeling of impending doom.

From the courtyard, you can go up to the second floor to view the highlight of the museum: Fra Angelico's *The Annunciation* ★★★. The rest of the floor is taken up with dorm cells, 44 small cells once used by the Dominicans (nos. 12 to 14 were once occupied by Savonarola and contain portraits of the reformer by Bartolomeo, who was plunged into acute melancholy by the jailing and torturing of his beloved teacher). Most of the cells were frescoed by Angelico and his students from 1439 to 1445, and depict scenes from the Crucifixion.

Piazza San Marco 1. *Ⓒ* 055-294883. Admission 4€ ($3.55). Tues–Sun 8:15am–1:30pm. Ticket office closes 30 min. before the museum. Closed 1st, 3rd, and 5th Sun of the month; 2nd and 4th Mon of the month; Jan 1, May 1, and Christmas. Bus: 1, 6, 7, 10, 11, 17, or 20.

THE DUOMO, CAMPANILE & BAPTISTRY

In the heart of Florence, at **Piazza del Duomo** and **Piazza San Giovanni** (named after John the Baptist), is a complex of ecclesiastical buildings that form a triumvirate of top sights.

Il Duomo (Cattedrale di Santa Maria del Fiore) ★★★   The Duomo, graced by Filippo Brunelleschi's red-tiled dome, is the crowning glory of

Florence and the star of the skyline. Before entering, take time to view the exterior, with its geometrically patterned bands of white, pink, and green marble; this tricolor mosaic is an interesting contrast to the sienna-colored fortresslike palazzi around the city. The Duomo is one of the world's largest churches and represents the flowering of the "Florentine Gothic" style. Construction stretched over centuries: Begun in 1296, it was finally consecrated in 1436, although finishing touches on the facade were applied as late as the 19th century.

Volunteers offer **free tours** of the cathedral every day except Sunday 10am to 12:30pm and 3 to 5pm. Most of them speak English; if there are many of you and you want to confirm their availability, call © **055-2710757** (Tues–Fri, mornings only). Looking rather professorial and kindly, they can be found sitting at a table along the right (south) wall as you enter the Duomo. They expect no payment, but a nominal donation to the church is always appreciated. They also organize tours of Santa Croce and Santa Maria Novella.

Brunelleschi's efforts to build the **dome** ✸✸✸ (1420–36) could be the subject of a Hollywood script. At one time before his plans were accepted, the architect was tossed out on his derriere and denounced as an idiot. He eventually won the commission by a clever "egg trick," as related in Giorgio Vasari's *Lives of the Painters*, written in the 16th century: The architect challenged his competitors to make an egg stand on a flat piece of marble. Each artist tried to make the egg stand, but each failed. When it was Brunelleschi's turn, he took the egg and cracked its bottom slightly on the marble and thus made it stand upright. Each of the other artists said he could've done the same thing, if he'd known he could crack the egg. Brunelleschi retorted that they also would've known how to vault the cupola if they had seen his model or plans.

His dome, a "monument for posterity," was erected without supports. When Michelangelo began to construct a dome over St. Peter's, he paid tribute to Brunelleschi's earlier cupola in Florence: "I am going to make its sister larger, yes, but not lovelier." You can climb 463 spiraling steps to the ribbed dome for a view that's well worth the trek (however, you can climb only 414 steps and get the same view from Giotto's campanile, below).

Inside, the overall effect of the cathedral is bleak because much of the decoration has been moved to the Duomo Museum (see below). However, note the recently restored frescoes covering the inside of the cupola; begun by Giorgio Vasari and completed by Federico Zuccari, they depict the Last Judgment. The three stained-glass windows by Ghiberti on the entrance wall are next to Uccello's giant clock using the heads of the four prophets. Some of the stained-glass windows in the dome were based on designs by Donatello (Brunelleschi's friend) and Ghiberti (Brunelleschi's rival).

Also in the cathedral are some terra-cottas by Luca della Robbia. In 1432 Ghiberti took time out from his "Gates to Paradise" for the Baptistry (see below) and designed the tomb of St. Zenobius. Excavations in the depths of the cathedral have brought to light the remains of the ancient Cathedral of Santa Reparata (tombs, columns, and floors), which was probably founded in the 5th century and transformed in the following centuries until it was demolished to make way for the present cathedral. The entrance to the excavations is via a stairway near the front of this cathedral, to the right as you enter (look for the sign SCAVI DELLA CRIPTA DI SANTA REPARATA).

Incidentally, during some 1972 excavations, Brunelleschi's tomb was discovered, and new discoveries indicate the existence of a second tomb nearby.

Giotto's tomb, which has never been found, might be in the right nave, beneath the campanile bearing his name.

Piazza del Duomo. ℭ **055-2302885.** Cathedral free; excavations 2.50€ ($2.25); cupola 5€ ($4.45). Mon–Sat 10am–5pm; Sun 1:30–5pm. Bus: B, 6, 7, 11, 14, or 23.

Giotto's Bell Tower (Campanile di Giotto) ★★

If we can believe the accounts of his contemporaries, Giotto was the ugliest man ever to walk the streets of Florence. It's ironic, then, that he left to posterity Europe's most beautiful campanile, rhythmic in line and form. That Giotto was given the position of *capomastro* and grand architect (and pensioned for 100 gold florins for his service) is remarkable in itself because he's famous for freeing painting from the confinements of Byzantium. He designed the campanile in the last 2 or 3 years of his life and died before its completion.

The final work was admirably carried out by Andrea Pisano, one of Italy's greatest Gothic sculptors (see his bronze doors on the baptistry). The "Tuscanized" Gothic tower, with bands of the same colored marble as the Duomo, stands 84m (274 ft.); and you can climb 414 steps to the top for a panorama of the sienna-colored city. After Giotto's death, Pisano and Luca della Robbia did some fine bas-relief and sculptural work, now in the Duomo Museum (see below).

If you can make the tough climb up (and up and up) the cramped stairs, the **view** ★★★ from the top of Giotto's bell tower is unforgettable, sweeping over the city, the surrounding hills, and Medici villas.

Piazza del Duomo. ℭ **055-2302885.** Admission 5€ ($4.45). Daily 8:30am–6:50pm. Closed Jan 1, Easter, Sept 8, and Christmas. Bus: B, 6, 11, 14, 17, or 23.

Baptistry (Battistero San Giovanni) ★★★

Named after the city's patron saint, Giovanni (John the Baptist), the octagonal baptistry dates from the 11th and 12th centuries. It's the oldest structure in Florence and is a highly original interpretation of the Romanesque style, with bands of pink, white, and green marble to match the Duomo and campanile.

Visitors from all over the world come to gape at its three sets of **bronze doors** ★★★. In his work on two sets of the doors (the east and the north), Lorenzo Ghiberti reached the pinnacle of his artistry in *quattrocento* Florence. To win his first commission on the north doors, the 23-year-old sculptor had to compete against formidable opposition such as Donatello, Brunelleschi (architect of the Duomo's dome), and Siena-born Jacopo della Quercia. Upon seeing Ghiberti's work, Donatello and Brunelleschi conceded defeat. By the time he had completed the work on the north doors, Ghiberti was around 44. The gilt-covered panels (representing scenes from the New Testament, including the Annunciation, the Adoration, and Christ debating the elders in the temple) make up a flowing, rhythmic narration in bronze. To protect them from the elements, the originals were removed to the Duomo Museum (see below), but the copies are works of art unto themselves.

After his long labor, the Florentines gratefully gave Ghiberti the task of sculpting the east doors (directly opposite the Duomo entrance). Given carte blanche, he designed his masterpiece, choosing as his subject familiar scenes from the Old Testament, such as Adam and Eve at the creation. This time Ghiberti labored over the rectangular panels from 1425 to 1452 (he died in 1455). Upon seeing the finished work, Michelangelo is said to have exclaimed, "These doors are fit to stand at the gates of Paradise," and so they've been nicknamed the "Gates of

Paradise" ever since. Ghiberti apparently agreed: He claimed that he personally planned and designed the Renaissance—all on his own.

Shuttled off to adorn the south entrance and to make way for Ghiberti's "Gates of Paradise" were the baptistry's oldest doors, by Andrea Pisano, mentioned earlier for his work on Giotto's bell tower. For his subject, the Gothic sculptor represented the "Virtues" as well as scenes from the life of John the Baptist, whom the baptistry honors. The door was completed in 1336. On the interior (just walk through Pisano's door—no charge) the dome is adorned with 13th-century mosaics, dominated by a figure of Christ. Mornings are reserved for worship.

Piazza San Giovanni. ✆ 055-2302885. Admission 2.50€ ($2.25). Oct–June daily 8:30am–7pm; July–Sept daily 12:30–7pm. Bus: B, 6, 11, 14, 17, or 23.

Duomo Museum (Museo dell'Opera del Duomo) ✪✪ This museum, across from the Duomo but facing the apse of Santa Maria del Fiore, is beloved by connoisseurs of Renaissance sculpture. It houses the sculpture that was removed from the campanile and the Duomo, to protect the pieces from the weather and from visitors who want samples. A major attraction is an **unfinished** *Pietà* ✪✪, **by Michelangelo,** in the middle of the stairs. It was carved between 1548 and 1555, when the artist was in his 70s. In this vintage work, a figure representing Nicodemus (but said to have Michelangelo's face) is holding Christ. The great Florentine intended it for his own tomb, but he's believed to have grown disenchanted with it and to have attempted to destroy it. The museum has a Brunelleschi bust, as well as della Robbia terra-cottas. The premier attraction is the **restored panels of Ghiberti's "Gates of Paradise"** ✪✪✪, which were removed from the baptistry. In gilded bronze, each is a masterpiece of Renaissance sculpture, perhaps the finest low-relief perspective in all Italian art.

You'll see bits and pieces from what was the old Gothic-Romanesque fronting of the cathedral, with ornamental statues, as conceived by the original architect, Arnolfo di Cambio. One of Donatello's early works, *St. John the Evangelist,* is here—not his finest hour, but anything by Donatello is worth looking at. One of his most celebrated works, the *Magdalene* ✪✪, is in the room with the *cantorie* (see below). This wooden statue once stood in the baptistry and had to be restored after the 1966 flood. Dating from 1454 to 1455, it's stark and penitent.

A good reason for coming here is to see the **marble choirs (*cantorie*) of Donatello and Luca della Robbia** ✪✪ (the works face each other and are in the first room you enter after climbing the stairs). The della Robbia choir is more restrained, but it still "praises the Lord" in marble, with clashing cymbals and sounding brass that constitute a reaffirmation of life. In contrast, the dancing cherubs of Donatello's choir are a romp of chubby bambini. Of all Donatello's works, this one is the most lighthearted. But, in total contrast, lavish your attention on Donatello's *Zuccone,* one of his masterpieces, created for Giotto's bell tower.

Piazza del Duomo 9. ✆ 055-2302885. Admission 5€ ($4.45). Year-round Mon–Sat 9am–6:30pm; Sun 8:30am–1pm. Bus: B, 14, 23, 36, 37, or 71.

ON OR NEAR PIAZZA DELLA SIGNORIA

The L-shaped **Piazza della Signoria** ✪✪, though never completed, is one of Italy's most beautiful squares. It was the center of secular life in the days of the Medici and is today a virtual sculpture gallery. Through it pranced church robbers, connoisseurs of entrails, hired assassins seeking employment, chicken farmers from Valdarno, book burners, and many great men (including Machiavelli, on a secret mission to the Palazzo Vecchio, and Leonardo da Vinci, trailed by his entourage).

On the square is the controversial **Fountain of Neptune** (1560–75), with the sea god surrounded by creatures from the deep, as well as frisky satyrs and nymphs. It was designed by Ammannati, who later repented for chiseling Neptune in the nude. But Michelangelo, to whom Ammannati owed a great debt, judged the fountain inferior. Florentines used to mock it as *Il Biancone* ("big whitey"). Actually, the Mannerist bronzes around the basin aren't at all bad; many might have been designed by a young Giambologna.

Near the fountain is a **small disk in the ground,** marking the spot where Savonarola was executed. This zealous monk was a fire-and-brimstone reformer who rivaled Dante in conjuring up the punishment that hell would inflict on sinners. His chief targets were Lorenzo the Magnificent and the Borgia pope, Alexander VI, who excommunicated him. Savonarola whipped the Florentine faithful into an orgy of religious fanaticism but eventually fell from favor. Along with two other friars, he was hanged in the square in 1498. Afterward, as the crowds threw stones, a pyre underneath the men consumed their bodies. It's said that the reformer's heart was found whole and grabbed up by souvenir collectors. His ashes were tossed into the Arno.

For centuries, Michelangelo's *David* stood in this square, but it was moved to the Accademia in the 19th century. The work that you see on the square today is an inferior copy, commonly assumed by many first-timers to be Michelangelo's original. Near the towering statue stands Baccio Bandinelli's *Heracles* (1534). Bandinelli, however, was no Michelangelo, and his statue has been denounced through the centuries; Cellini dismissed it as a "sack of melons."

The 14th-century **Loggia della Signoria (or Loggia dei Lanzi)** ☆☆ houses a gallery of sculpture often depicting violent scenes. The most famous piece is a rare work by Benvenuto Cellini, the goldsmith and tell-all autobiographer. Critics have claimed that his exquisite but ungentlemanly *Perseus* ☆☆☆, holding up the severed head of Medusa, is the most significant Florentine sculpture since Michelangelo's *Night* and *Day.* However, what you see today is actually a copy; the original Perseus stood here from 1545 to 1996, when he was removed for restoration (the future of the original remains uncertain). Three other well-known pieces are Giambologna's bronze **statue of Duke Cosimo de' Medici on horseback,** celebrating the man who subjugated all Tuscany under his military rule; his *Rape of the Sabines,* an essay in three-dimensional Mannerism; and his *Hercules with Nessus the Centaur,* a chorus line of half a dozen Roman Vestal wallflowers.

Palazzo Vecchio ☆☆   The secular "Old Palace" is Florence's most famous and imposing palazzo. Gothic master builder Arnolfo di Cambio constructed it from 1299 to 1302, although it wasn't until 1540 that Cosimo I and the Medicis called it home. Its most remarkable architectural feature is the 94m (308-ft.) tower, an engineering feat that required supreme skill at the time. Today the palazzo is occupied by city employees, but much is open to the public.

The 16th-century **Hall of the 500 (Salone dei Cinquecento),** the most outstanding part of the palace, is filled with Vasari and company frescoes as well as sculpture. A tragic loss to Renaissance art, the frescoes originally done by Leonardo da Vinci in 1503 melted when braziers were brought in to speed up the drying process. The ever-inventive Leonardo had used wax in his pigments, and, of course, the frescoes melted under the heat. As you enter the hall, look for Michelangelo's *Victory* ☆, depicting an insipid-looking young man treading on a bearded older man (it has been suggested that Michelangelo put his own face on that of the trampled man). This statue (1533–34) was originally intended for the tomb of Pope Julius but was later acquired by the Medicis.

Later you can stroll through the rest of the palace, examining its apartments and main halls. You can also visit the private apartments of Eleanor of Toledo, the Spanish wife of Cosimo I, and a chapel that was begun in 1540 and frescoed by Bronzino. The palace displays the original of Verrocchio's bronze putto (1476) from the courtyard fountain, called both *Winged Cherub Clutching a Fish* and *Boy with a Dolphin*. You'll also find a 16th-century portrait of Machiavelli that's attributed to Santi di Tito. Donatello's famous bronze group, **Judith Slaying Holofernes** ⟨⚓⟩ (1455), once stood on Piazza della Signoria but was brought inside. The salons, such as a fleur-de-lis apartment, have their own richness and beauty.

Following his arrest, Savonarola was taken to the Palazzo Vecchio for more than a dozen torture sessions, including "twists" on the rack. The torturer pronounced Savonarola his "best" customer.

Piazza della Signoria. ⟨Ⓒ⟩ **055-2768325.** Admission 5.50€ ($4.90). Mon–Wed and Fri–Sat 9am–7pm; Thurs and Sun 9am–2pm. July 15–Sept 15 Mon and Fri 9am–11pm. Ticket office closes 1 hr. before palace. Bus: 23 or 71.

Orsanmichele ⟨⚓⟩   This 14th-century church is the last remnant of Florence's ornate Gothic architecture. It was first built as a covered market with an upstairs granary (hence its appearance as a converted warehouse). The downstairs was eventually converted to an oratory, the open archways were bricked up, and the outside's tabernacles were decorated with donations from the city's powerful *arti* (guilds): the tanners, bankers, silk weavers, furriers, and goldsmiths, whose patron saints fill the 14 niches surrounding the exterior. Masters such as Ghiberti, Donatello, and Giambologna were commissioned to cast the saints' images, which virtually compose a history of Florentine sculpture from the 14th to the 16th centuries (almost all have been relocated to the indoor museum and slowly replaced with copies).

In the candlelit interior, among the vaulted Gothic arches, stained-glass windows, and 500-year-old frescoes, is the encrusted 14th-century tabernacle by Andrea Orcagna, supporting and protecting the 1348 *Madonna and Child* painted by Giotto's student Bernardo Daddi. The entrance to the church's small museum (open daily 9am–1:30pm, with free admission, though this may change soon) is on the building's west side in what once housed the powerful Wool Guild. Upstairs, in the old granary rooms, are eight of the original statues from the church's niches.

Via de' Calzaiuoli at Via Arte della Lana (north of Piazza della Signoria). ⟨Ⓒ⟩ **055-284944.** Free admission. Mon–Fri 9am–noon and 4–6pm; Sat–Sun 9am–1pm and 4–6pm. Closed the 1st and last Mon of every month. Bus: 22, 36, or 37.

NEAR PIAZZA SAN LORENZO

Piazza San Lorenzo and its satellite, Piazza Madonna degli Aldobrandini, are lively and colorful. A huge market, the Mercato Centrale, forms around the church of San Lorenzo, continuing all the way to the area of San Marco. For details, see section 6, "Shopping," later in this chapter.

Medici Chapels (Cappelle Medicee) ⟨⚓⚓⟩   The Medici tombs are adjacent to the Basilica of San Lorenzo (see below). You enter the tombs, housing the "blue-blooded" Medici, in back of the church by going around to Piazza Madonna degli Aldobrandini. First you'll pass through the baroque **Chapel of the Princes (Cappella dei Principi)**, that octagon of death often denounced for its "trashy opulence." In back of the altar is a collection of Italian reliquaries.

The Ponte Vecchio

Spared by the Nazis in their bitter retreat from the Allied advance in 1944, the "Old Bridge" at Via Por Santa Maria and Via Guicciardini is the last remaining medieval *ponte* spanning the Arno (the Germans blew up the rest). It was again threatened in the 1966 flood, when the waters of the Arno swept over it and washed away a fortune in jewelry from the goldsmiths' shops flanking the bridge.

The Ponte Vecchio was built in 1220, probably on the Roman site of a bridge for the Via Cassia, the ancient road running through Florence on its way to Rome. Vasari claims that Taddeo Gaddi reconstructed it in 1354, and Vasari himself designed the corridor running over it (see the Uffizi entry, earlier). Once home to butchers, it was cleared of this stench by Ferdinand de' Medici, who allowed these "vile arts" to give way to goldsmiths and jewelers, who have remained ever since.

Today the restored Ponte Vecchio is closed to vehicular traffic. The little shops continue to sell everything from the most expensive of Florentine gold to something simple—say, a Lucrezia Borgia poison ring.

Hidden Gem: Discovered in a sepulchral chamber beneath the Medici Chapels with access via a trap door and a winding staircase was **Michelangelo's only group of mural sketches** ⭐. Apparently, he had used the walls as a giant doodling sheet. The drawings include a sketch of the legs of Duke Giuliano, Christ risen, and the *Laocoön,* the Hellenistic figure group. Fifty drawings, done in charcoal on plaster walls, were found. You can ask for a free ticket to view the sketches at the ticket office for the chapels.

The real reason you come here is to see the **New Sacristy (Nuova Sacrestia)** ⭐⭐⭐, designed by Michelangelo as a gloomy mausoleum. "Do not wake me; speak softly here," Michelangelo wrote in a bitter verse. Working from 1521 to 1534, he created the Medici tombs in a style that foreshadowed the baroque. Lorenzo the Magnificent—a ruler who seemed to embody the qualities of the Renaissance itself and was one of the greatest names in the history of the Medici family—was buried near Michelangelo's uncompleted *Madonna and Child* group, a simple monument evoking a promise unfulfilled.

Ironically, the finest groups of sculpture were reserved for two Medici "clan" members, who (in the words of Mary McCarthy) "would better have been forgotten." Both are represented by Michelangelo as armored, idealized princes of the Renaissance. In fact, Lorenzo II, duke of Urbino, depicted as "the thinker," was a deranged young man (just out of his teens before he died). Clearly, Michelangelo wasn't working to glorify these two Medici dukes. Rather, he was chiseling for posterity. The other two figures on Lorenzo's tomb are most often called *Dawn* and *Dusk,* with morning represented as a woman and evening as a man.

The two best-known figures, showing Michelangelo at his most powerful, are *Night* and *Day* ⭐⭐⭐ at the feet of Giuliano, the duke of Nemours. *Night* is chiseled as a woman in troubled sleep, and *Day* is depicted as a man of strength awakening to a foreboding world. These figures weren't the works of Michelangelo's innocence.

Piazza Madonna degli Aldobrandini 6. ℭ **055-294883**. Admission 5.50€ ($4.90). Mon–Sat 8:15am–5pm; Sun 8:30am–1:50pm. Closed 2nd and 4th Sun, and 1st, 3rd, and 5th Mon of each month. Bus: 1, 6, 7, 11, 17, 33, 67, or 68.

Basilica di San Lorenzo ★★   This is Brunelleschi's 1426 Renaissance church, where the Medicis attended services from their nearby palace on Via Larga, now Via Camillo Cavour. Critic Walter Pater found it "great rather by what it designed or aspired to do, than by what it actually achieved." Most visitors flock to see Michelangelo's New Sacristy with his *Night* and *Day* (see the Medici Chapels, above), but Brunelleschi's handiwork deserves some time, too.

Built in the style of a Latin cross, the church is distinguished by harmonious grays and rows of Corinthian columns. The **Old Sacristy (Vecchia Sacrestia;** walk up the nave and then turn left) was designed by Brunelleschi and decorated in part by Donatello (view his terra-cotta bust of St. Lawrence). The Old Sacristy is often cited as the first and finest work of the early Renaissance. Even more intriguing are the two bronze 1460 pulpits of Donatello, among his last works, a project carried out by students following his death in 1466. Scenes depict Christ's passion and resurrection.

After exploring the Old Sacristy, go through the first door (unmarked) on your right, and you'll emerge outside. A sign will point to the entrance of the **Medici Laurentian Library (Biblioteca Medicea Laurenziana)** ★★ (✆ **055-210760**), which you enter at Piazza San Lorenzo 9. Designed by Michelangelo to shelter the expanding collection of the Medicis, the library is a brilliant example of Mannerist architecture, its chief attraction a curving flight of stone steps. Michelangelo worked on it in 1524, but the finishing touches were completed in 1578 by Vasari and Ammannati. Michelangelo, however, designed the reading benches. The library is filled with some of Italy's greatest manuscripts, many of which are handsomely illustrated. In the rare book collection are autographs by Petrarch, Machiavelli, Poliziano, and Napoléon. You're kept at a distance by protective glass, but it's well worth the visit.

Piazza San Lorenzo. ✆ **055-214443.** Free admission; 2.50€–7.50€ ($2.25–$6.70) for special exhibitions. Fri–Mon 8:30am–1:30pm; Tues–Thurs 8am–5:30pm. Bus: 1, 6, 7, 11, 17, 33, 67, or 68.

Palazzo Medici-Riccardi ★   This palace, a short walk from the Duomo, was the home of Cosimo de' Medici before he took his household to the Palazzo Vecchio. At the apogee of the Medici power, it was adorned with some of the world's greatest masterpieces, such as Donatello's *David*. Built by Michelozzo in the mid–15th century, the brown stone building was also the scene, at times, of the court of Lorenzo the Magnificent. Art lovers visit today chiefly to see the **mid-15th-century frescoes by Benozzo Gozzoli** ★★ in the **Medici Chapel** (not to be confused with the Medici Chapels, above). Gozzoli's frescoes, depicting the journey of the Magi, form his masterpiece—they're a hallmark in Renaissance painting. Although he takes a religious theme as his subject, the artist turned it into a gay romp, a pageant of royals, knights, and pages with fun mascots such as greyhounds and even a giraffe. It's a fairy-tale world come alive, with faces of the Medici and local celebrities who were as famous as Madonna in their day but are known only to scholars today.

Another gallery, which you enter via a separate stairway, was frescoed by Luca Giordano in the 18th century, but his work seems merely decorative. The apartments, where the prefect lodges, aren't open to the public.

Via Camillo Cavour 1. ✆ **055-2760340.** Admission 4€ ($3.55). Thurs–Tues 9am–7pm. Bus: 1, 6, 7, 11, 17, 33, 67, or 68.

ON OR NEAR PIAZZA DELLA SANTISSIMA ANNUNZIATA

Lovely **Piazza della Santissima Annunziata** is surrounded on three sides by arcades. In the center is an equestrian statue of Grand Duke Ferdinand I, by

Giambologna. The Hospital of the Innocents stands on the eastern side. Once Brunelleschi wanted to create a perfectly symmetrical square here, but he died before his plans could be realized. The piazza is a popular student hangout.

Hospital of the Innocents (Ospedale degli Innocenti)   Opened in 1445, this was the world's first hospital for foundlings, although the Medici and Florentine bankers weren't known for welfare benefits. The building and the loggia with its Corinthian columns were conceived by Brunelleschi and marked the first architectural bloom of the Renaissance in Florence. On the facade are terracotta medallions done in blues and opaque whites by Andrea della Robbia, depicting babes in swaddling clothes.

Still used as an orphanage, the building no longer has its "lazy Susan," where Florentines used to deposit unwanted bambini, ring the bell, and then flee. It does contain an art gallery, and notable among its treasures is a terra-cotta *Madonna and Child,* by Luca della Robbia, plus works by Sandro Botticelli. One of its most important paintings is ***Adoration of the Magi,* by Domenico Ghirlandaio** (the chubby bambino looks a bit pompously at the Wise Man kissing his foot).

Piazza della Santissima Annunziata 12. ℂ **055-2491708.** Admission 2.50€ ($2.25). Thurs–Tues 8:30am–2pm; Sun 8:30am–2pm. Bus: 6, 31, or 32.

Archaeology Museum (Museo Archeologico) ⚜⚜   This museum, a short walk from Piazza della Santissima Annunziata, houses one of Europe's most outstanding Egyptian and Etruscan collections in a palace built for Grand Duchess Maria Maddalena of Austria. The Etruscan-loving Medicis began that collection, although the Egyptian loot was first acquired by Leopold II in the 1830s. Its Egyptian mummies and sarcophagi are on the first floor, along with some of the better-known Etruscan works. Pause to look at the lid to the coffin of a fat Etruscan (unlike the blank faces staring back from many of these tombs, this man's countenance is quite expressive).

One room is graced with three bronze Etruscan masterpieces, among the rarest objets d'art of these relatively unknown people. They include the *Chimera,* a lion with a goat sticking out of its back. This was an Etruscan work of the 5th century B.C., found near Arezzo in 1555. The lion's tail—in the form of a venomous reptile—lunges at the trapped beast. The others are *Minerva* and an *Orator,* ranging from the 5th to the 1st centuries B.C. Another rare find is a Roman bronze of a young man, the so-called *Idolino,* fished from the sea at Pesaro. The statue has always been shrouded in mystery; it might have been a Roman statue sculpted around the time of Christ. The François vase on the ground floor, from 570 B.C., is celebrated. A prize in the Egyptian department is a wood-and-bone chariot, beautifully preserved, that astonishingly dates back to a tomb in Thebes from the 14th century B.C.

Via della Colonna 38. ℂ **055-23575.** Admission 4€ ($3.55). Nov–Aug Mon 2–7pm; Tues–Fri 9am–7pm; Sat–Sun 9am–2pm. Sept also Sat 9pm–midnight; Oct also Sun 9am–8pm.

ON PIAZZA SANTA MARIA NOVELLA

Hardly the most beautiful or tranquil square, **Piazza Santa Maria Novella** overflows with traffic from the rail station. Vendors, backpackers, beggars, and buses and taxis vie for precious space. Visitors will want to tolerate this chaos for only one reason: to see the basilica.

Basilica di Santa Maria Novella ⚜⚜   Near the rail station is one of Florence's most distinguished churches, begun in 1278 for the Dominicans. Its geometric facade, with bands of white and green marble, was designed in the late 15th century by Leon Battista Alberti, an aristocrat and true Renaissance man (philosopher, painter, architect, poet). The church borrows from and harmonizes the Romanesque, Gothic, and Renaissance styles.

In the left nave as you enter, the third large painting is the great Masaccio's *Trinità* ⭐, a curious work that has the architectural form of a Renaissance stage setting but whose figures (in perfect perspective) are like actors in a Greek tragedy. If you view the church at dusk, you'll see the stained-glass windows in the fading light cast kaleidoscope fantasies on the opposite wall.

Head straight up the left nave to the **Gondi Chapel (Cappella Gondi)** for a look at Brunelleschi's wooden *Christ on the Cross* ⭐, said to have been carved to compete with Donatello's same subject in Santa Croce (see below). According to Vasari in *Lives of the Artists,* when Donatello saw Brunelleschi's completed Crucifix, he dropped his apron full of eggs intended for their lunch. "You have symbolized the Christ," Donatello is alleged to have said. "Mine is an ordinary man." (Some art historians reject this story.)

In 1485, Ghirlandaio contracted with a Tornabuoni banker to adorn the sanctuary behind the main altar with frescoes illustrating scenes from the lives of Mary and John the Baptist. Michelangelo, a teenager at the time, is known to have studied under Ghirlandaio (perhaps he even worked on this cycle).

In the north transept, a staircase leads to the remarkable **Strozzi Chapel (Cappella Strozzi)** ⭐, honoring St. Thomas Aquinas. Decorated between 1350 and 1357 by Nardo di Cione and Andrea Orcagna, it depicts Dante's *Purgatorio* and *Inferno.* On the left wall is *Paradiso.*

If time remains, you might want to visit the **cloisters,** going first to the Green Cloister and then to the splendid Spanish Chapel frescoed by Andrea di Bonaiuto in the 14th century (one panel depicts the Dominicans in triumph over heretical wolves).

Piazza Santa Maria Novella. ℭ 055-215918. Church free; Spanish Chapel and cloisters 2.50€ ($2.25). Church Mon–Fri 7am–noon and 3–6pm. Spanish Chapel and cloisters Sat–Thurs 8am–2pm. Bus: 6, 9, 11, 36, 37, or 68.

⌒*Moments* Catching the View from Piazzale Michelangelo

For a view of the wonders of Florence below and Fiesole above, climb aboard bus no. 12 or 13 at the Ponte alla Grazie (the first bridge east of the Ponte Vecchio) for a 15-minute ride to **Piazzale Michelangelo,** an 1865 belvedere overlooking a view seen in many a Renaissance painting and on many a modern-day postcard. It's reached along Viale Michelangelo. It's best at dusk, when the purple-fringed Tuscan hills form a frame for Giotto's bell tower, Brunelleschi's dome, and the towering hunk of stones that stick up from the Palazzo Vecchio. Another copy of Michelangelo's *David* dominates the square and gives the *piazzale* (wide piazza) its name. Crown your trip with a gelato at the **Gelateria Michelangelo** (ℭ 055-2342705), open daily 7am to 2am.

Warning: At certain times during the day, the square is overrun with tour buses and peddlers selling trinkets and cheap souvenirs. If you go at these times, often midday in summer, you'll find that the view of Florence is still intact—but you might be struck down by a Vespa or crushed in a crowd if you try to enjoy it.

ON OR NEAR PIAZZA SANTA CROCE

Every street leading to the famed **Piazza Santa Croce** seems to be lined with shops selling leather goods. The square has been an integral part of Florentine life for centuries, beginning when Franciscan friars used to preach here. The piazza used to be the playing field for calcio (a kind of football that's no longer played), and a marble disk in the center marks the center line of pitch. Today it's still devoted to popular gatherings such as games, events, and jousts.

Basilica di Santa Croce ✿✿ Think of this as Tuscany's Westminster Abbey. This church shelters the tombs of everyone from Michelangelo to Machiavelli, from Dante (he was actually buried at Ravenna) to Galileo, who at the hands of the Inquisition "recanted" his concept that the earth revolves around the sun. Just as Santa Maria Novella was the church of the Dominicans, Santa Croce, said to have been designed by Arnolfo di Cambio, was the church of the Franciscans.

In the right nave (the first tomb) is the Vasari-executed **monument to Michelangelo,** whose 89-year-old body was smuggled back to his native Florence from its original burial place in Rome, where the pope wanted the corpse to remain. Along with a bust of the artist are three allegorical figures representing the arts. In the next memorial, a prune-faced Dante, a poet honored belatedly in the city that exiled him, looks down. Farther on, still on the right, is the tomb of Niccoló Machiavelli, whose *The Prince* (about Cesare Borgia) became a virtual textbook in the art of wielding power. Nearby is Donatello's lyrical bas-relief *The Annunciation.*

The **Trecento frescoes** ✿✿ are reason enough for visiting Santa Croce—especially those by Giotto to the right of the main chapel. Once whitewashed, the Bardi and Peruzzi chapels were "uncovered" in the mid–19th century in such a clumsy fashion that they had to be drastically restored. Although badly preserved, the frescoes in the **Bardi Chapel (Cappella Bardi)** are most memorable, especially the deathbed scene of St. Francis. The cycles in the **Peruzzi Chapel (Cappella Peruzzi)** are of John the Baptist and St. John. In the left transept is Donatello's once-controversial wooden Crucifix—too gruesome for some Renaissance tastes, including that of Brunelleschi, who is claimed to have said: "You [Donatello] have put a rustic upon the cross." (Brunelleschi's "answer" to the Donatello version here can be seen in Santa Maria Novella, above.) Incidentally, the **Pazzi Chapel (Cappella Pazzi),** entered through the cloisters, was designed by Brunelleschi, with terra-cottas by Luca della Robbia.

Inside the monastery of this church, the Franciscan fathers established the **Leather School (Scuola del Cuoio)** ✿ at the end of World War II. The purpose of the school was to prepare young boys technically to specialize in Florentine leatherwork. The school has flourished and produced many fine artisans who continue their careers here. Stop in and see the work when you visit the church.

Piazza Santa Croce 16. ✆ **055-244619.** Church free; cloisters and church museum 4€ ($3.55). Church daily 9am–noon and 3–6pm. Museum and cloisters Thurs–Tues 10am–6pm. Bus: B, 13, 23, or 71.

Buonarroti's House (Casa Buonarroti) ✿ Only a short walk from Santa Croce is the house that Michelangelo managed to buy for his nephew, Lionardo. But it was Lionardo's son, named after Michelangelo, who turned the house into a virtual museum to his great uncle, hiring artists and painters to adorn it with frescoes. Turned into a museum by his descendants, the house was restored in 1964. It contains some fledgling work by the magnificent artist, as well as some models by him. Here you can see his *Madonna of the Stairs,* which he did when he was 16 (maybe younger), as well as a bas-relief that he did later, the *Battle of the Centaurs.* The casa is enriched by many of Michelangelo's drawings and models, shown to the public in periodic exhibits. A curiosity among them is the wooden model for the San Lorenzo facade that Michelangelo designed but never constructed.

Via Ghibellina 70. ✆ 055-241752. Admission 6€ ($5.35). Wed–Mon 9:30am–1:30pm. Bus: 14.

A SYNAGOGUE

La Sinagoga di Firenze   The synagogue is in the Moorish style, inspired by Constantine's Byzantine church of Hagia Sophia. Completed in 1882, it was badly damaged by the Nazis in 1944 but has been restored to its original splendor. A museum is upstairs, exhibiting, among other displays, a photographic record of the history of the ghetto that remained in Florence until 1859.

Via Farini 4. ✆ 055-245252. Admission 3€ ($2.70). Apr–Sept Sun–Thurs 10am–5pm; Fri 10am–3pm. Oct–Mar Mon–Thurs 10am–3pm; Fri and Sun 10am–3pm. Closed Sat and Jewish holidays. Bus: 6, 31, or 32.

6 Shopping

THE SHOPPING SCENE

Skilled craftsmanship and traditional design unchanged since the days of the Medicis have made this a serious shopping destination. Florence is noted for its hand-tooled **leather goods** and various **straw merchandise,** as well as superbly crafted **gold jewelry.**

The whole city strikes many visitors as a gigantic department store. Entire neighborhoods on both sides of the Arno offer good shops, though those along the medieval Ponte Vecchio (with some exceptions) are generally too touristy.

Florence isn't a city for bargain shopping, however. Most visitors interested in gold or silver jewelry head for the **Ponte Vecchio** and its tiny shops. It's difficult to tell one from another, but you really don't need to because the merchandise is similar. If you're looking for a charm or souvenir, these shops are fine. But the heyday of finding gold jewelry bargains on the Ponte Vecchio is long gone.

The street for antiques is **Via Maggio;** some of the furnishings and objets d'art here are from the 16th century. Another major area for antiques shopping is **Borgo Ognissanti.** Florence's Fifth Avenue is **Via dei Tornabuoni,** the place to head for the best-quality leather goods, for the best clothing boutiques, and for stylish but costly shoes. Here you'll find everyone from Armani to Ferragamo.

The better shops are largely along Tornabuoni, but there are many on **Via Vigna Nuova, Via Porta Rossa,** and **Via degli Strozzi** as well. You might also stroll on the *lungarno* along the Arno. For some of the best buys in leather, check out **Via del Parione,** a short, narrow street off Tornabuoni.

Shopping hours are generally Monday 4 to 7:30pm and Tuesday to Saturday 9 or 10am to 1pm and 3:30 or 4pm to 7:30pm. During summer, some shops are open Monday morning. However, don't be surprised if shops are closed for several weeks in August or for the entire month.

SHOPPING A TO Z

ANTIQUES   There are many outlets for antiques in Florence, many clustered along **Via Maggio** (ouch—those high prices!). If you're in the market for such expensive purchases or if you just like to browse, try these stores.

Chic **Adriana Chelini,** Via Maggio 28 (C 055-213471), specializes in 17th-and 18th-century furniture, from small to large pieces. It also carries some paintings and porcelain and glass items from later periods. The **Bottega San Felice,** Via Maggio 39R (C 055-215479), offers many intriguing items from the 19th century, sometimes in the style known as Charles X. The shop also sells more modern pieces, such as many Art Deco items and Biedermeier pieces.

Said to be the oldest antique dealer in Italy, **Galleria Luigi Bellini,** Lungarno Soderini 5 (C 055-214031), offers unusual, often one-of-a-kind selections of Florence antiques, paintings, and other objets d'art. The merchandise is tasteful and well chosen but not cheap. The founding father of the outlet, Mario Bellini, is one of the most respected names in Florentine antiques and the founder of the international antiques biennial.

The eclectic **Paolo Romano,** Borgo Ognissanti 20R (C 055-293294), carries furniture, accessories, and objets d'art from the 17th to the 19th centuries.

The amusingly named **Shabby Shop,** 12R Via del Parione (C 055-294826), definitely does not live up to its name. The store is packed with unusual or one-of-a-kind finds ranging from antique carafes to Renaissance-inspired statuary.

ART Opened in 1870 and thus Florence's oldest art gallery, **Galleria Masini,** Piazza Goldoni 6R (C 055-294000), is a few minutes' walk from the Excelsior and other leading hotels. The selection of modern and contemporary paintings by top artists is extensive, representing more than 500 Italian painters.

BOOKS If you'd like something to read while in Florence, head over to the **Paperback Exchange,** Via Fielsolana 31R (C 055-2478154), which isn't all Danielle Steele and John Grisham. If you don't want novels, you'll also find dozens of background books in English on Florence and Italy itself. The largest stock is in Penguin books. Many of the titles are used, as reflected in the low prices. Books are carried only in English, some 10,000 titles on all major subjects. The shop is also known as a "watering hole" for American and Italian students.

Other outlets for more artistic books are found at **FMR,** via delle Belle Donne 41R (C 055-283312), the domain of the locally known Franco Maria Ricci, who enjoys a worldwide reputation for his exquisite art books, particularly strong on the Renaissance. He also sells an exquisite selection of handmade papers. Another well-chosen selection of art books is found at **Libreria Salimbeni,** via Matteo Palmieri 16R (C 055-2340905).

CERAMICS & POTTERY **Richard Ginori,** via Rondinelli 17R (C 055-210041), has one of the most intriguing assortments of china and tableware, often in amusing designs and bright colors. In business in Florence since 1735, the shop features a changing array of merchandise from all parts of Italy. Sometimes you'll find especially good buys here in Murano (Venice) glassware. The wide inventory at **Menegatti,** Piazza del Pesce, Ponte Vecchio 2R (C 055-215202), includes pottery from Florence, Faenza, and Deruta. There are also della Robbia reproductions made in red clay like the originals. Items can be shipped home for you.

DEPARTMENT STORES The best outlet is **La Rinascente,** Piazza della Repubblica 2 (C 055-219113), right in the heart of Florence. This is where frugal but taste-conscious Florentines go to shop. Their clothing for men and women features some of the big names but also talented and lesser known Italian designers. You'll also find good buys in china, perfumes, and jewelry, along with a "made in Tuscany" department that sells everything from terra-cotta vases to the finest virgin olive oils. Another good store is **Coin,** Via Calzaiuoli 56R (© **055-280531**), which is particularly noted for offering good prices on fashionable ready-to-wear items.

FABRICS & EMBROIDERY   In business for more than half a century, **Casa di Tessuti,** Via de' Pecori 20–24R (© **055-215961**), has a huge, high-quality selection of linen, silk, wool, and cotton.

Although Florentine embroidery was once considered a dying art, **Cirri,** Via por Santa Maria 38–40R, near the Ponte Vecchio (© **055-2396593**), keeps it alive, with hundreds of beautiful designs in linen, cotton, and silk.

FASHION   Italian clothing from lesser-known designers such as Dream and Prima Ligna is available at **Glamour,** Borgo San Jacopo 49R (© **055-210334**). The style is first-rate, and the prices are more affordable than at most fashion houses in Florence. You'll find good-quality garments for both women and men in various fabrics and degrees of formality.

At **Loretta Caponi,** Piazza Antinori 4 (© **055-213668**), the arched ceiling and gilt trim create a perfect atmosphere in which to browse a wonderful selection of slip dresses, robes, linens, and children's wear in luxurious silks, velvets, and cottons.

Mariposa, Lungarno Corsini 18–20R (© **055-284259**), offers women's and men's fashions from such famous designers as Krizia, Ungaro, Rocco Barocco, Missoni, and Mimmina. Foreign customers are often granted a 20% discount on tax-free items.

Max Mara, Via del Pecori 23R (© **055-2396590**), features high-quality women's clothes, with classic elegance and even a touch of flamboyance. The selection covers everything from hats and coats to suits and slacks.

Like Milan, many of the biggest names in fashion are centered in Florence, including the flagship store for **Gucci,** via de Tournabuoni 73R (© **055-264011**). Saddlemaker Guccio Gucci (1881–1953) founded his first shop in Florence with almost no capital. On his dying day, he was objecting to his sons opening their first overseas boutique in New York, claiming that Americans would have no interest in Gucci leather products. How wrong he was. Not an Asian rip-off, Gucci leather products sold here, from classy shoes to clothing for both men and women, are the real thing.

Florence is the home not only of Gucci but also of Pucci. The descendent of a Florentine family famous since the Renaissance, Marchese Emilio Pucci di Barsento, a debonair Italian aristocrat, burst onto the fashion world in the 1950s with his rich colors, supple fabrics, and dramatic prints, as well as his couture collection that would cover some of the most celebrated women in the world, including Jacqueline Kennedy. Pucci led the post-war emergence of the casually chic jet-setter, adorning his fans with what came to be known as "the Italian look." It was a Pucci-designed flag that Apollo 15 carried to the moon. Pucci fashion today is directed by Julio Espada and is on display at their shop at via de Tournabuoni (look for the sign in lieu of a number; © **055-2658082**).

For that **Armani** look, patronize the outlets of that often rude, arrogant, but brilliantly talented workaholic, Giorgio Armani, at via de Tournabuoni 48 (© **055-219041**) and a branch at Piazza Strozzi 16R (© **055-284315**), the latter store offering less expensive items. The relaxed Armani designs for women are inspired by his menswear (for example, he uses menswear fabrics in his sophisticated, unstructured jackets and suits for women). And, of course, for men, an Armani suit is what you wear to the Academy Award presentations.

On a much more democratically priced level, **Enrico Coveri,** via de Tournabuoni 73R (℃ **055-211263**), is being celebrated as *il signore in rosso,* "the man in red," known as the urban cowboy of fashion. Women loved his "women in red look," and now Coveri fully expects thousands of fashionable young men to burst out in similarly flaming red wardrobes—long jackets, red pants, woolen sweaters, T-shirt, and even red mink coats. Get this: a red mink backpack.

GLASS   The small **Cose del '900,** Borgo Sant' Jacopo 45R (℃ **055-283491**), is full of glass items of every description from 1900 to 1950: shot glasses, drinking glasses, centerpieces, and many Art Deco pieces.

Dating back to the era of the grand dukes, the art of grinding and engraving glass is still carried out at **Paola Locchi,** Via Burchiello 10 (℃ **055-2298371**), with exquisite skill and craftsmanship. Seemingly every kind of engraved object is sold, some of it of stupendous size. You can even find engraved goblets that decorated the banqueting tables of the ancients.

HERBAL REMEDIES/BATH & BODY PRODUCTS   The **Antica Farmacia del Cinghiale,** Piazza del Mercato Nuovo 4R (℃ **055-282128**), in business for some 3 centuries, is an *erboristeria,* dispensing herbal teas and fragrances along with herbal potpourris. A pharmacy is also here.

The **Officina Profumo Farmaceutica di Santa Maria Novella,** Via della Scala 16N (℃ **055-216276**), is the most fascinating pharmacy in Italy. Northwest of Santa Maria Novella, it opened in 1612 and offered a selection of herbal remedies that were created by friars of the Dominican order. Those closely guarded secrets have been retained, and many of the same elixirs are still sold today. A wide selection of perfumes, scented soaps, shampoos, and potpourris, along with creams and lotions, is also sold. The store is closed for 2 weeks in August.

HOUSEWARES   **Viceversa,** Via Ricasoli 53R (℃ **055-2398281**), offers the latest kitchen gadgets: Robert Graves–designed teakettles, Alessi creations, Pavoni espresso machines, and much more, all produced with cutting-edge and whimsical design.

Mobili Bianchi, 117 Viale Europa (℃ **055-686118**), has revived the 17th-century art in which carved slate or marble is inlaid with colored paste from the powder of a regional stone, selenite. At his busy atelier, the artist, Bianco Bianchi, is turning out consoles, custom-made tabletops, and an amazing list of other decorative items.

Carmiche Ricceri, 14R Via dei Conti (℃ **055-291296**), has an unusual collection of terra-cotta tableware that it obtains from the town of Imruneta, 6 miles south of Florence. The region is known for its gray clay with a high content of aluminum and iron. This makes a very strong pottery for pitchers, platters, and the like.

JEWELRY   Proceed with caution. You'll find some stunning antique pieces and, if you know how to buy, some good values.

Befani e Tai, Via Vacchereccia 13R (℃ **055-287825**), is one of the most unusual jewelry stores in Florence; some of its pieces date from the 19th century. The store was opened after World War II by expert goldsmiths who were childhood friends. Some of their clients even design their own jewelry for special orders.

Tiffany, Via dei Tornabuoni 25R (℃ **055-215506**), draws a well-heeled patronage, looking for a branch of the fabled jewelry store in New York.

Located away from the Ponte Vecchio, **Mario Buccellati,** Via dei Tornabuoni 69-71R (✆ **055-2396579**), a branch of the Milan store that opened in 1919, specializes in exquisite handcrafted jewelry and silver. A large selection of intriguing pieces at high prices is offered, although you can find moderately priced items as well.

Modern 18K white gold jewelry—sometimes accented with diamonds—is the specialty at **Elisabetta Fallaci,** Ponte Vecchio 22 (✆ **055-213192**), all made in Florence. Another well-respected jewelry store, also named Elisabetta Fallaci (once but no longer associated with this original outlet, and now under separate ownership) lies a few steps away, at no. 10 Ponte Vecchio (✆ **055-294981**).

LEATHER Universally acclaimed, Florentine leather is still the fine product that it always was—smooth and well shaped, often in vivid colors.

Beltrami, Via della Vigna Nuova 7R (✆ **055-287779**), sells fine leather goods as well as expensive evening clothes, heavyweight silk scarves, and fashions of the best quality. This is one of several Beltrami shops in the area. High fashion, high prices, and high quality are what you'll find here, but prices are significantly lower than what you'll pay for Beltrami in the United States. The **Beltrami Spa,** Via del Panzani 11R (✆ **055-212661**), offers last season's fashions at discounts of 20% to 50%. There are further discounts for multiple purchases, and because the original prices are still on the items, you can tell how much you're saving.

Sergio Bojola, Via dei Rondinelli 25R (✆ **055-211155**), a leading name in leather, has distinguished himself in Florence by the variety of his selections, in both synthetic materials and beautiful leathers.

You'll find first-class quality and craftsmanship at **Cellerini,** Via del Sole 37R (✆ **055-282533**), one of the city's master leathersmiths. Silvano Cellerini has been called a genius in leather. Original purses, shoulder bags, suitcases, accessories, wallets, and even a limited number of shoes (for both women and men) are sold.

The branch of **Gucci** at Via Tornabuoni 73R (✆ **055-264011**) is the mother of all Gucci shops. In general, prices are a bit cheaper here than in Milan and a lot less expensive than in the United States. You'll find every Gucci item imaginable, from belts to shoes, to shawls, to the chic Gucci scarf.

Leonardo Leather Works, Borgo dei Greci 16A (✆ **055-292202**), concentrates on leather and jewelry. Leather goods include wallets, bags, shoes, boots, briefcases, clothing, travel bags, belts, and gift items, with products by famous designers. The jewelry department has a large assortment of gold chains, bracelets, rings, earrings, and charms.

Pollini, Via Calimala 12R, near the Ponte Vecchio (✆ **055-214738**), offers a wide array of stylized merchandise, including shoes for men and women, suitcases, clothing, and belts.

MARKETS Intrepid shoppers head for the **Mercato della Paglia** or **Mercato Nuovo** (**Straw Market** or **New Market**), 2 blocks south of Piazza della Repubblica. (It's called Il Porcellino by the Italians because of the bronze statue of a reclining wild boar, a copy of the one in the Uffizi.) Tourists pet its snout (which is well worn) for good luck. The market stands in the monumental heart of Florence, an easy stroll from the Palazzo Vecchio. It sells not only straw items but also leather goods (not the best quality), along with typical Florentine merchandise: frames, trays, hand-embroidery, table linens, and hand-sprayed and -painted boxes in traditional designs. The market is open Monday to Saturday 9am to 6:30pm.

Age-Old Leather Traditions

If you drop into The Church of Santa Croce, you're likely to get more than prayers and a communion wafer. It's also the site of one of Florence's most unusual leather-working facilities. The craft skills of Tuscany's Franciscan friars date back to the Middle Ages, when they were acknowledged as Italy's finest bookbinders, using fine leather touched with accents of gold. Shortly after World War II, the Franciscan friars of Santa Croce found themselves in a dilemma: The orphanages they sponsored were chock-full of high-energy adolescents without any marketable skills. The friars' response involved training them in their age-old leather-working traditions.

So copious was their productivity that by 1950, a sales outlet opened within the Church of Santa Croce, which remains there today, immediately adjacent to the church's sacristy and its Medici Chapel. You can reach it directly from the main entrance to the church itself, or—more conveniently, and open even during the lunch hour—you can reach it via the church's garden gate at Via San Giuseppe 5R.

Inside, there's a wide array of every conceivable kind of leather good, except shoes, as produced by the 20 apprentices. Each of these apprentices will presumably carry the leather-working craft off to faraway lands, thereby keeping the medieval Franciscan traditions alive. For information about becoming an apprentice for a prolonged study program, or for access to the organization's extensive inventories, contact Laura Gori, or her son Tommaso, at **Scuola del Cuoio Firenze (Leather School of Santa Croce),** Via San Giuseppe 5R, 1022 Firenze (© **055-244533;** www.leatherschool.it).

The school and its shop are open as follows: Mid-November to mid-March Monday to Saturday 9:30am to 6pm; mid-March to mid-November Monday to Friday 9:30am to 6:30pm, Saturday and Sunday 9:30am to 6pm.

Even better bargains await those who make their way through the pushcarts to the stalls of the open-air **Mercato Centrale (Mercato San Lorenzo),** in and around Borgo San Lorenzo, near the rail station. If you don't mind bargaining, which is imperative, you'll find an array of merchandise such as raffia bags, Florentine leather purses, sweaters, gloves, salt-and-pepper shakers, straw handbags, and art reproductions. It's open Monday to Saturday 9am to 6:30pm.

MOSAICS Florentine mosaics are universally recognized. Bruno Lastrucci, the director of **Arte Musiva,** Largo Bargellini 2–4 (© **055-241647**), is one of the most renowned exponents of this art form. In the workshop, you can see artisans—including some of Italy's major mosaicists—plying their craft, creating both traditional Florentine and modern designs. A selection of the most significant works is permanently displayed in the gallery.

There's also **Pitti Mosaici,** Piazza Pitti 23R (© **055-282127**), where the artistry reflects generations of family tradition.

PAPER & STATIONERY **Giulio Giannini & Figlio,** Piazza Pitti 37R (© **055-212621**), has been a family business for more than 150 years and is

Florence's leading stationery store. Foreigners often snap up the exquisite merchandise for gift-giving later in the year.

The specialty at **Il Papiro,** Via Cavour 55R (✆ **055-215262**), is parti-colored marbleized paper that's skillfully incorporated into everything from bookmarks to photo albums (which make valued wedding gifts). More unusual are the marbleized wood (like music boxes) and leather items (couture-style purses and bags), as well as the marbleized fabric. The staff is charming, and the prices are reasonable, considering the high quality. There are branches at Piazza del Duomo 24R (✆ **055-281628**) and Lugarno Acciaiuoli 42R (✆ **055-2645613**).

Opened in 1774 and maintained today by descendants of the original founders, **J Pineider,** Piazza della Signoria 13R (✆ **055-284655**), is the oldest store in Florence specializing in printing and engraving. The most aristocratic-looking greeting cards, business cards, stationery, and formal invitations come from this outfit. Because most orders take between 2 and 3 weeks to fill, you can arrange to have the final product shipped home. The store also stocks a wide range of gifts, such as beautifully crafted diaries, stationery, desk sets for your favorite CEO, portfolios, address books, photo albums, and etchings of vistas unique to Florence.

Scriptorium, Via dei Servi 5R (✆ **055-211804**), offers wonderful hand-sewn notebooks, journals, and photo albums made of thick paper and bound with soft leather covers.

PRINTS & ENGRAVINGS Ducci, Lungarno Corsini 24R (✆ **055-214550**), hawks the best selection of historical prints and engravings covering the history of Florence from the 13th century. Also available are marble fruit, wooden items, and Florentine boxes covered with gold leaf.

Giovanni Baccani, Via della Vigna Nuova 75R (✆ **055-214467**), has long been a specialist in this field. Everything that it sells is old. "The Blue Shop," as it's called, offers a huge array of prints and engravings, often of Florentine scenes. Tuscan paper goods are also sold.

SHOES Casadei, Via del Tornabuoni 33R (✆ **055-287240**), is an interesting shop that is painted white; its pillars make the room look like a small colonnade. This shop is one of four Casadei shops in Italy (others are in Milan, Ferrara, and Rimini). Locally produced women's shoes, boots, and handbags are sold.

Lily of Florence, Via Guicciardini 2R (✆ **055-294748**), offers both men's and women's shoes in American sizes. For women, Lily distributes both her own creations and those of other well-known designers.

Salvatore Ferragamo, Via dei Tornabuoni 14R (✆ **055-292123**), has long been one of the most famous names in shoes. The headquarters of this famed manufacturer were installed here in the Palazzo Ferroni, on the most fashionable shopping street of Florence, before World War II broke out. Ferragamo sells shoes for men and women, along with elegant boutique items such as men's and women's clothing, scarves, handbags, ties, and luggage.

SILVER Pampaloni, Borgo Santi Apostoli 47R (✆ **055-289094**), is headed by Gianfranco Pampaloni, a third-generation silversmith. The business was launched in 1902, and some of the classic designs turned out back then are still being made.

A fabled name among serious shoppers, **Brandimartre,** Via Bartolini 18R (✆ **055-239381**), is Florence's best-stocked workshop and silver showcase. This semiprecious metal is exquisitely handcrafted into a number of dazzling items, including signature goblets. The shop even does frivolous designs for the man or women who has everything (a silver cheese grater, for example).

WINES   Ristorante e Enoteca Il Cantinone, Via Santo Spirito 6R (© 055-218898), is a wine tavern that serves a typical Florentine menu, but the emphasis is on Tuscan wines, such as Black Label, Santo Cristo, and Villa Antinori. Purchase your choice by the glass or by the bottle to take with you. And don't forget to try the *vin santo,* a Tuscan dessert wine, with almond cookies. If you want a little more sustenance, fixed-price menus cost 15€ to 17.50€ ($13.40–$15.65).

Enoteca Gambi Romano, Borgo SS. Apostoli 21–23R (© 055-292646), is a centrally located outlet for olive oil, vino santo, grappa, chocolates, cheese, and (upstairs) lots of wine, including well-priced Tuscan labels.

7 Florence After Dark

Evening entertainment in Florence isn't an exciting prospect, unless you simply like to walk through the narrow streets or head toward Fiesole for a truly spectacular view of the city at night. The typical Florentine begins an evening early at one of the cafes listed below.

For theatrical and concert listings, pick up a free copy of *Welcome to Florence,* available at the tourist office. This handy publication contains information on recitals, concerts, theater productions, and other cultural offerings.

From May to July, the city welcomes classical musicians for its **Maggio Musicale** festival of cantatas, madrigals, concertos, operas, and ballets, many of which are presented in Renaissance buildings. Schedule and ticket information is available from **Maggio Musicale Fiorentino/Teatro Comunale,** Corso Italia 16, 50123 Firenze (© 055-27791). Tickets cost 20€ to 80€ ($17.85–$71.45). For further information, visit the theater's website, at www.maggiofiorentino.com.

THE PERFORMING ARTS

Teatro Comunale di Firenze/Maggio Musicale Fiorentino, Corso Italia 16 (© 055-211158), is Florence's main theater, with opera and ballet seasons presented September to December and a concert season January to April. This theater is also the venue for the Maggio Musicale (see above), Italy's oldest and most prestigious festival.

Teatro della Pergola, Via della Pergola 18 (© 055-2479651), is Florence's major legitimate theater, but you'll have to understand Italian to appreciate most of its plays. Plays are performed year-round except during the Maggio Musicale, when the theater becomes the setting for many of the festival events.

Teatro Verdi, Via Ghibellina 99 (© 055-212320), is a venue for prestigious dance and classical music events. Major operatic and ballet performances are often presented here as well, often by big-name performers.

Many cultural presentations are performed in churches. These might include open-air concerts in the cloisters of the **Badia Fiesolana** in Fiesole or at the **Ospedale degli Innocenti,** on summer evenings only. Orchestral offerings, performed by the Regional Tuscan Orchestra, are often presented at **Santo Stefano al Ponte Vecchio.**

LIVE-MUSIC CLUBS

May Day Club, Via Dante Alighieri 16R (© 055-2381290), is a relative newcomer to Florence's nightlife scene, defining itself as a pub with recorded music that's about as hip and cutting edge as anything else in Tuscany. Its mostly white walls are adorned with a collection of antique radios and television sets (its owners refer to it as "a museum" of antique radios) and party-colored lights that constantly change the predominant colors. Entrance is free, and clients range in age from around 23 to 45. It's open daily, year-round, from 8:30pm to 2am. Beer costs from 3€ to 4€ ($2.70–$3.55), depending on the brand.

In the cellar of an antique building in the historic heart of town, **Full-Up,** Via della Vigna Vecchia 2325R (✆ **055-293006**), attracts college students who appreciate the club's two-in-one format. One section contains a smallish dance floor with recorded dance music; the other is a somewhat more restrained piano bar. The place can be fun, and even an older crowd feels at ease. It's open Wednesday to Monday 9pm to 3am, charging no cover.

Red Garter, Via de' Benci 33R (✆ **055-2344904**), right off Piazza Santa Croce, has an American Prohibition–era theme and features everything from rock to bluegrass. The club is open Monday to Thursday 8:30pm to 1am, and Friday to Sunday 9pm to 2am. There's no cover.

Within a 10-minute cab ride from Piazza del Duomo, **Tenax,** Via Pratese 46A (✆ **055-308160**), is the premier venue for live rock and roll and grunge-rock bands in Tuscany, with individual musical styles varying widely, and each drawing a widely different crowd of loyal fans. Bands come from throughout Italy and the rest of Europe, but whenever they're not playing, a DJ will provide high-energy, highly danceable recorded music instead. Shows begin nightly except Monday at 10pm and continue to around 3am. The cover is 10€ to 17.50€ ($8.95–$15.65) and includes the first drink.

CAFES

Café Rivoire, Piazza della Signoria 4R (✆ **055-214412**), offers a classy and amusing old-world ambience with a direct view of the statues on one of our favorite squares in the world. You can sit at one of the metal tables on the flagstones outside or at one of the wooden tables in a choice of inner rooms filled with marble detailing and unusual oil renderings of the piazza outside. If you don't want to sit at all, try the bar, where many colorful characters talk, flirt, or gossip. There's a selection of small sandwiches, omelets, and ice creams, and the cafe is noted for its hot chocolate.

The oldest and most beautiful cafe in Florence, **Gilli's,** via Roma 1, adjacent to Piazza Repubblica 39R, Via Roma 1 (✆ **055-213896**), is a few minutes' walk from the Duomo. It was founded in 1789, when Piazza della Repubblica had a different name. You can sit at a brightly lit table near the bar or retreat to an intricately paneled pair of rooms to the side and enjoy the flattering light from the Venetian-glass chandeliers. Daily specials, sandwiches, toasts, and hard drinks are sold, along with an array of "tropical" libations.

The waiters at **Giubbe Rosse,** Piazza della Repubblica 13R (✆ **055-212280**), still wear the Garibaldi red coats, as they did when this place was founded in 1888. It has always been known as a literary cafe, where intellectuals and writers met to discuss Italian politics and literature. It survived the Mussolini era and continues to attract an artsy crowd. You can enjoy coffee, drinks, and also salads and sandwiches surrounded by turn-of-the-century chandeliers and polished granite floors. Light lunches and full American breakfasts are specialties.

Procacci, via de Tornabuoni 64R (✆ **055-211656**), is a little charmer of a cafe and bar on the chic shopping street of Florence. A city tradition since 1885, it has attracted the movers and shakers in Florentine couture. We once encountered Emilio Pucci here, who warned us, "Don't write anything about me. I'm too famous already!" This is a marvelously old-fashioned kind of food shop and bar known for its house special, a *panini tartufati,* a dainty glazed roll shaped like an egg and filled with the world's most delectable white truffle paste. You can also enjoy a creamy Brie with a nut sauce or else foie gras or smoked salmon. Ask for a glass of prosecco while surveying the food on the shelves, everything from Sicilian orange marmalade (which we consider Italy's finest) to the rarest of balsamic vinegars. Light fare is served only from noon to 3pm, although the bar itself is open from Monday to Saturday from 10:30am to 8pm.

BARS & PUBS

Donatello Bar, in the Westin Excelsior, Piazza Ognissanti 3 (© **055-264201**), is the city's most elegant watering hole. This bar and its adjoining restaurant, Il Cestello, attract well-heeled international visitors along with the Florentine cultural and business elite. The ambience is enlivened by a marble fountain and works of art, and piano music is featured daily 7pm to 1am.

The **Dublin Pub,** Via Faenza 27R (© **055-293049**), is very much of an Irish pub, with an Italian accent. Along with Fiddler's Elbow (see below), few other places in Tuscany mingle the Celtic and Mediterranean souls as seamlessly. Neither offers live music, but there's an ongoing medley of recorded music, often Irish. The pub serves Irish grub and Irish whiskey along with Guinness and Irish coffee—and lots and lots of beer. It's a rollicking, congenial spot near the Santa Maria Novella rail station.

After an initial success in Rome, **Fiddler's Elbow,** Piazza Santa Maria Novella 7R, near the rail station (© **055-215056**), an Irish pub, has invaded this city and has quickly become one of the most popular watering holes. Here you can get an authentic pint of Guinness.

La Dolce Vita, Piazza del Carmine (© **055-284595**), draws the beautiful people of Florence. It's a see-and-be-seen type of place, lying south of the Arno and west of the historic core. You come here to drink, gossip, and look ever so chic. To see how you're doing, the owners have wisely covered the walls in mirrors.

DANCE CLUBS

Rio Grande, Viale degli Olmi 1 (© **055-331371**), is Florence's best, biggest, and most international disco. A 15-minute cab ride from Piazza del Duomo, near the Parco della Cascine, it has an indoor/outdoor setting that includes century-old trees, a terrace, and three dance floors. The music includes everything from punk to rock to funk to garage. Gays mix with the mostly straight crowd with ease, and the typical age range is 18 to 32. The crowd in the restaurant here tends to be well dressed, but don't be surprised if someone decides to dance on your table after you've finished eating. Full meals are served here Tuesday to Sunday 8pm to midnight, with main courses costing from 15€ to 25€ ($13.40–$22.35). After midnight on those nights there is disco action until 4am. If you order dinner and then visit the disco, there is no cover. For the disco only, a 15€ ($13.40) cover is imposed.

At **Space Electronic,** Via Palazzuolo 37 (© **055-293082**), the decor consists of wall-to-wall mirrors and an imitation space capsule that goes back and forth across the dance floor. If karaoke doesn't thrill you, head to the new ground-floor pub, which stocks an ample supply of imported beers. On the upper level is a large dance floor with a wide choice of music and a high-energy row of laser beams. This place attracts a lot of foreign students who want to hook up with Florentine men and women on the prowl. The disco opens nightly at 11pm and usually goes until 4am. The 15€ ($13.40) cover includes the first drink.

Yab, Via Sassetti 5R (© **055-215160**), is right in the historic core of the city. Owned and operated by the same management as the larger and more raucous Rio Grande (see above), it offers much the same kind of music, albeit in a smaller and more cramped setting. Partly because it isn't well air-conditioned, it closes between May and October. Otherwise, hours are Wednesday to Saturday 9:30pm to 3am. The cover is 15€ ($13.40), which includes the first drink.

GAY & LESBIAN CLUBS

ArciGay/Lesbica (aka Azione Gay e Lesbica), Italy's largest and oldest gay organization, has a center in Florence at Via Manara 12 (© **055-671298;** www.agora.stm.it/gaylesbica.fi). It's open for visits from Monday to Thursday 6 to 8pm.

Tabasco, Piazza Santa Cecilia 3 (© **055-213000**), is Florence's (and Italy's) oldest gay dance club, open daily 10pm to 3am, with a 10€ to 12.50€ ($8.95–$11.15) cover. The crowd is mostly men in their 20s and 40s. Florence's leading gay bar, **Crisco,** Via San Egidio 43R (© **055-2480580**), is for men only, open Wednesday to Monday from 10:30pm to 3:30am and Friday and Saturday 10:30pm to 5 or 6am. Cover is 7.50€ to 12.50€ ($6.70–$11.15). The owners of Crisco (see above) have also opened a similar men's bar in Florence. Called **Tin Box Club,** it's at via dell'Orivolo 19–21R (no phone) and is open Tuesday to Sunday 2 to 11pm. Its "dark room" is the most active in Florence, and there are also hot videos. Admission is 7.50€ ($6.70).

8 A Side Trip to Fiesole ✦

For more extensive day trips, refer to chapter 7, "Tuscany & Umbria." But Fiesole, once an Etruscan settlement, is a virtual suburb of Florence and its most popular outing. Florentines often head for these hills when it's just too hot in the city. Bus no. 7, leaving from Piazza San Marco, will take you here in 25 minutes and give you a panoramic view along the way. You'll pass fountains, statuary, and gardens strung out over the hills like a scrambled jigsaw puzzle.

EXPLORING THE TOWN

In Fiesole you won't find anything as dazzling as the Renaissance treasures of Florence; the town's charms are more subtle. Fortunately, all major sights branch out within walking distance of the main square, **Piazza Mino da Fiesole,** beginning with the **Cattedrale di San Romolo (Duomo).** At first this cathedral might seem austere, with its concrete-gray Corinthian columns and Romanesque arches. But it has its own beauty. Dating from A.D. 1000, it was much altered during the Renaissance, and in the Salutati Chapel are important sculptural works by Mino da Fiesole. It's open daily 7:30am to noon and 4 to 7pm.

Bandini Museum (Museo Bandini) This ecclesiastical museum, around to the side of the Duomo, belongs to the Fiesole Cathedral Chapter, established in 1913. On the ground floor are della Robbia terra-cotta works, as well as art by Michelangelo and Pisano. On the top floors are paintings by the best Giotto students, reflecting ecclesiastical and worldly themes, most of them the work of Tuscan artists of the 14th century.

Via Dupré 1. © 055-59477. Admission (includes admission to Roman Theater and Civic Museum, below) 6.50€ ($5.80). Mar–Oct daily 10am–6pm; Nov–Feb daily 10am–5pm. Closed 1st Tues of each month.

Roman Theater and Civic Museum (Teatro Romano e Museo Civico) ✦ On this site is the major surviving evidence that Fiesole was an Etruscan city 6 centuries before Christ and later a Roman town. In the 1st century B.C., a theater was built, and you can see the restored remains today. Near the theater are the skeletonlike ruins of the bathrooms, which might have been built at the same time. Try to visit the Etruscan-Roman museum, with its many interesting finds that date from the days when Fiesole, not Florence, was supreme (a guide is on hand to show you through).

Via Portigiani 1. ✆ 055-59477. Admission (includes admission to Bandini Museum, above) 6.50€ ($5.80). For hours, see the Bandini Museum. Bus: 7.

Museum of the Franciscan Missionaries (Museo Missionario Francescano Fiesole) ⭐   The hardest task you'll have in Fiesole is to take the steep goat-climb up to the Convent of San Francesco. You can visit the Gothic-style Franciscan church, built in the first years of the 1400s and consecrated in 1516. Inside are many paintings by well-known Florentine artists. In the basement of the church is the ethnological museum. Begun in 1906, the collection has a large section of Chinese artifacts, including ancient bronzes. An Etruscan-Roman section contains some 330 archaeological pieces, and an Egyptian section also has numerous objects.

Via San Francesco 13. ✆ 055-59175. Free admission (but a donation is expected). Church daily 8am–noon and 3–6pm. Museum Mon–Fri 9:30am–noon and 3–5:30pm (to 7pm in summer); Sat–Sun 3–5pm. Bus: 7.

WHERE TO STAY

Hotel Villa Aurora ⭐   On Fiesole's main square, behind a facade of shutters and ocher-colored stucco, the Aurora was a private home in the 18th century. In 1890 it became a hotel that catered almost exclusively to Brits making their Grand Tour. The hotel continues to rent rooms, which have been modernized and simplified and now even include Jacuzzis. Views over faraway Florence are visible from the back rooms, which cost more than those overlooking the piazza. The rooms range from small to medium, each with comfortable beds fitted with fine linens. Connecting doors can be opened between some rooms to create suites. On the premises are a back terrace with hanging vines and a pergola.

Piazza Mino da Fiesole 39, Fiesole, 50014 Firenze. ✆ 055-59100. Fax 055-59587. www.aurorafiesole.com. 25 units. 98€–204€ ($87.50–$182.15) double. Rates include continental breakfast. AE, DC, MC, V. Free parking. Bus: 7. **Amenities:** Restaurant; room service; babysitting. *In room:* A/C, TV, minibar, hair dryer, safe.

Pensione Bencista   This has been the villa of the Simoni family for years. It was built around 1300, with additions made about every 100 years after that. In 1925, Paolo Simoni opened the villa to paying guests, and today it's run by his son, Simone Simoni. Its position, high up on the road to Fiesole, is commanding, with an unmarred view of the city and the hillside villas. The spread-out villa has many lofty old rooms furnished with family antiques. They vary in size and interest; many are without private bathrooms and have hot and cold running water only. In chilly weather, guests meet one another in the evening in front of a huge fireplace. It's a 10-minute bus ride from the heart of Florence.

Via Benedetto da Maiano 4, Fiesole, 50014 Firenze. ✆ and fax 055-59163. 45 units, 33 with bathroom. 90€ ($80.35) per person without bathroom; 95€ ($84.85) per person with bathroom. Rates include half-board. No credit cards. Free parking. Bus: 7. **Amenities:** Restaurant; bar; room service; babysitting.

Villa San Michele ⭐⭐⭐   This is an ancient monastery of unsurpassed beauty in a memorable setting on a hill below Fiesole, a 15-minute walk south of the center. It was built in the 15th century, damaged in World War II, and then restored. The facade and loggia were reportedly designed by Michelangelo. A curving driveway, lined with blossoming trees and flowers, leads to the entrance, and a 10-arch covered loggia continues around the view side of the building to the Italian gardens at the rear.

Most of the guest rooms open onto the view; the others face the inner court-yard. Each is unique, some with iron or wooden canopy beds, antique chests and chairs, formal draperies, old ecclesiastical paintings, candelabra, and statues. In the old friars' cells, the units are rather austerely decorated in the spirit of their former role. The most elaborate room is no. 10, with its gilded four-poster bearing a 1600s Virgin painted on the headboard. The Michelangelo Suite is the grand choice, a spacious room with a marble fireplace and a large whirlpool. All the rooms come with deluxe bathrooms.

Via Doccia 4, Fiesole, 50014 Firenze. ✆ **800/237-1236** in the U.S., or 055-59451 or 055-5678200. Fax 055-5678250. www.orient-expresshotels.com. 37 units. 994€–1,331€ ($887.50–$1,188.40) double; 1,663€–2,148€ ($1,484.80–$1,917.85) suite. Rates include half-board. AE, DC, MC, V. Closed mid-Nov to mid-Mar. Bus: 7. **Amenities:** Restaurant; lounge; pool; room service; babysitting. *In room:* A/C, TV, minibar; hair dryer; safe.

WHERE TO DINE

You might also want to dine at the fine restaurant of the **Villa San Michele** (listed above under "Where to Stay").

Trattoria le Cave di Maiano TUSCAN   This former farmhouse is at Maiano, a 15-minute ride east from the heart of Florence and just a short dis-tance south of Fiesole. The rustically decorated family-run trattoria is a garden restaurant, with stone tables and large sheltering trees. We highly recommend the antipasto and homemade green tortellini. For a main course, there's golden grilled chicken or savory herb-flavored roast lamb. For side dishes, we suggest fried polenta, Tuscan beans, and fried potatoes. As a final treat, the waiter will bring you homemade ice cream with fresh raspberries.

Via delle Cave 16. ✆ **055-59133**. Reservations required. Main courses 12.50€–19€ ($11.15–$16.95); fixed-price lunch 30€–37.50€ ($26.80–$33.50). AE, DC, MC, V. Tues–Sun 12:30–2:30pm; daily 7:30–10:30pm. Closed 2 weeks in Aug.

Tuscany & Umbria

Rome might rule Italy's body, but Tuscany (Toscana) presides over its heart. The Tuscan landscapes look just like Renaissance paintings, with rolling plains of grass, cypress trees, and olive groves; ancient walled hill towns; and those fabled Chianti vineyards.

Tuscany was where the Etruscans first appeared in Italy. The Romans followed, absorbing and conquering them. By the 11th century, the region had evolved into a collection of independent city-states, such as Florence and Siena, each trying to dominate the others. Many of the cities we'll visit reached the apogee of their economic and political power in the 13th century. The Renaissance reached its apex in Florence, but it was slow to come to Siena, which remains a gem of Gothic glory.

The Renaissance brought with it new titans of art: Giotto, Michelangelo, and Leonardo. Ever since these geniuses "invented" the Renaissance, the world has flocked to Tuscany to see not just the land, but also some of the world's greatest art. Critics claim, without much exaggeration, that Western civilization was "rediscovered" in Tuscany. Art flourished under the tutelage of the powerful Medicis, and the legacy remains of Masaccio, della Francesca, Signorelli, Raphael,

Donatello, Botticelli, and countless others, plus the engineering feats of architects such as Brunelleschi. Tuscany also became known for its men of letters, including Dante, Petrarch, and Boccaccio (who put the seal of approval on the Tuscan dialect by writing in the vernacular rather than in Latin).

Tuscany might be known for its Renaissance artists, but the small region of **Umbria,** at the heart of the Italian peninsula, is associated mainly with saints. Christendom's most beloved saints were born here, foremost among them St. Francis of Assisi, founder of the Franciscans. Also born here were St. Valentine, a 3rd-century bishop of Terni, and St. Clare, founder of the Order of Poor Clares.

However, Umbrian painters also contributed to the glory of the Renaissance. Il Perugino, whose lyrical works you can see in the National Gallery of Umbria in Perugia, is one such example.

Umbria's countryside, also the subject of countless paintings, remains as lovely as ever today: You'll pass through a hilly terrain dotted with chestnut trees, interspersed with fertile plains of olive groves and vineyards.

For more in-depth coverage of both regions, you might want to pick up a copy of *Frommer's Tuscany & Umbria.*

1 The Chianti Road

The Chianti Road (La Chiantigiana), as the SS222 is known, twists and turns narrowly through the hilly terrain of Tuscany's famous wine region. Chianti, once associated with cheap, sweet Italian wines, has finally captured the attention of connoisseurs with well-crafted *classicos* and *riservas*. This is the result of

Tuscany & Umbria

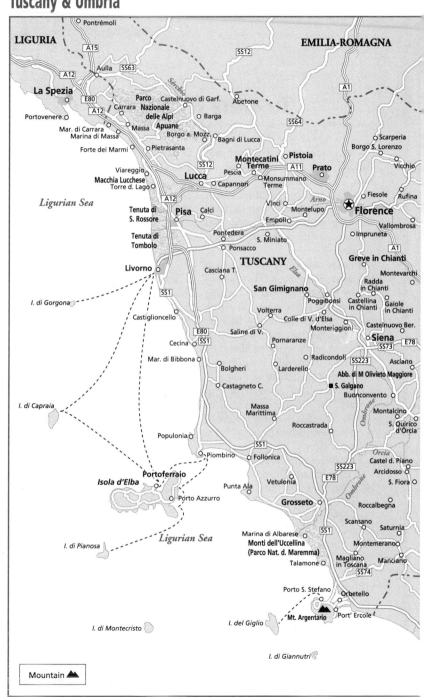

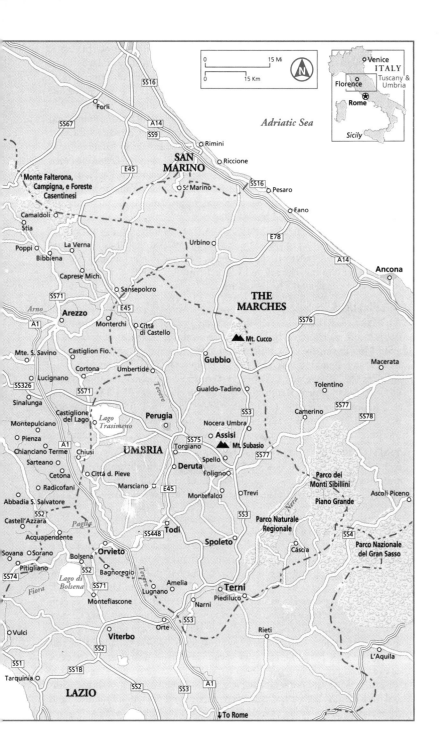

0 ⸺ **15 Mi**
0 ⸺ **15 Km**

Adriatic Sea

ITALY
o Venice
Florence o
Tuscany & Umbria
Rome ✪
Sicily

SS16
o Forli
SS67
A14
SS9
Rimini o
SAN MARINO
o Riccione
St Marino o
E45
SS16
Pesaro
Monte Falterona, Campigna, e Foreste Casentinesi
Fano o
Camaldoli o
Stia
E78
Poppi o
La Verna
Urbino o
A14
Bibbiena o
Ancona
Caprese Mich. o
Sansepolcro o
THE MARCHES
SS71
Arno
E45
Arezzo
SS76
A1
Monterchi
o Città di Castello
▲▲ Mt. Cucco
Mte. S. Savino o
Castiglion Fio.
Macerata
Cortona o
Umbertide o
Gubbio
Lucignano o
SS326
SS71
Tevere
Gualdo-Tadino o
Tolentino o
Sinalunga o
Camerino o
SS77
Castiglione del Lago o
Lago Trasimeno
Perugia
SS3
SS78
Montepulciano o
Nocera Umbra o
o Pienza
A1
SS75
Assisi
Chianciano Terme o
Chiusi o
Torgiano o
▲ Mt. Subasio
Sarteano o
UMBRIA
Spello o
SS77
Cetona o
Deruta
Foligno o
o Città d. Pieve
Radicofani o
Marsciano o
E45
Montefalco o
o Trevi
Parco dei Monti Sibillini
Abbadia S. Salvatore o
Nera
o Ascoli Piceno
SS2
Piano Grande
Castell'Azzara o
Paglia
SS3
Parco Naturale Regionale
Acquapendente o
SS448
Todi
SS4
Sovana o o Sorano
Bolsena o
Orvieto
Spoleto
Cascia o
Parco Nazionale del Gran Sasso
o Pitigliano
SS2
Bagnoregio o
Tevere
SS74
Lago di Bolsena
SS71
Amelia o
o Vulci
Montefiascone o
Lugnano o
Terni
Piediluco o
Fiora
Narni o
Rieti o
Orte o
SS3
Viterbo
o L'Aquila
SS2
Tarquinia o
SS1
SS1B
SS2
SS3
A1
LAZIO
↓**To Rome**

259

improved attention to growth and vinification techniques over the last 2 decades. The year 1990 proved to be a landmark, producing a vintage—some labels of which are highly prized by collectors—that quickly disappeared from world markets. The area is also home to *vin santo,* a dessert wine something like old sherry that's difficult to find elsewhere.

The entire area of Chianti is only 48km (30 miles) from north to south and 32km (20 miles) at its widest point. You could rent a bike or scooter for your tour, but you'd have to cope with hills, dust, and the driving habits of "road king" Italians. Renting an easily maneuverable small car is preferable, but even with an auto, you still must deal with road-hogging buses and flying Fiats. A car will let you stop at vineyards along the dirt lanes that stray from the main road, an option not provided by any bus tour. Still, be prepared for hairpin turns, ups and downs, and unidentified narrow lanes.

Signs touting DEGUSTAZIONE or VENDITA DIRETTA lead you to wineries that are open to the public and offer tastings. However, you should call ahead and make appointments at any of the wineries in this area. In other words, don't just show up. See also the Tuscany and Umbria entry in "The Best Wine-Growing Regions," in chapter 1, "The Best of Italy."

ESSENTIALS

GETTING AROUND　By far, the best way to explore the region is by rental car, but you can also do it by bike. You can reach the central town of Greve by a **SITA bus** leaving from the main station in Florence about every half hour. The trip takes an hour and costs 2.50€ ($2.25) one way. A SITA bus from Siena costs 3€ ($2.70) one way. Call ☎ **055-4782255** for information. Once you're in Greve, go to **Marco Ramuzzi,** Via Italo Stecchi 23 (☎ **055-853037**), and rent a mountain bike for 12.50€ to 17.50€ ($11.15–$15.65) per day or a scooter for 25€ to 40€ ($22.35–$35.70) per day. Armed with a map from the tourist office, you can set out, braving the winding roads of Chianti country.

VISITOR INFORMATION　The **tourist office** in the town of Greve, Viale 6 da Verrazzano 33 (☎ **055-8546287**), is a useful source of data for the entire area, offering maps and up-to-date listings about wineries that admit visitors. It's open Monday to Friday 9:30am to 1pm and 3:30 to 5pm, and Saturday 9:30am to 12:30pm.

TOURING THE WINERIES

Leaving Florence, get on SS222 off autostrada E35 and head south. At Petigli-olo, 4km (2½ miles) south of the city, turn left and follow the signs to the first attraction along the road—not a winery, but the vine-clad **Santo Stefano a Tiz-zano,** a Romanesque church. Nearby, 18km (11 miles) from Florence, stands the 11th-century **Castello di Tizzano** (☎ **055-6499234**), the prestigious cen-terpiece of sprawling vineyards and a consortium of farms producing Chianti Classico under the Gallo Nero label. To visit here, you should call ahead and ask for an appointment, as you should at all wineries. We cannot emphasize this strongly enough, because many readers who have arrived unannounced were not allowed visits here, or at other wineries in the region. Unless you come at a busy time, such as the autumn grape harvest, you may be allowed to visit the 15th- and 16th-century cellars and perhaps purchase some Chianti or vin santo and the estate's award-winning olive oil if supplies are available for retail.

About 2km (1¼ miles) farther along SS222 is **San Polo in Chianti,** at the heart of Italy's iris industry. So many flowers grow in this region that there's an

The Chianti Region

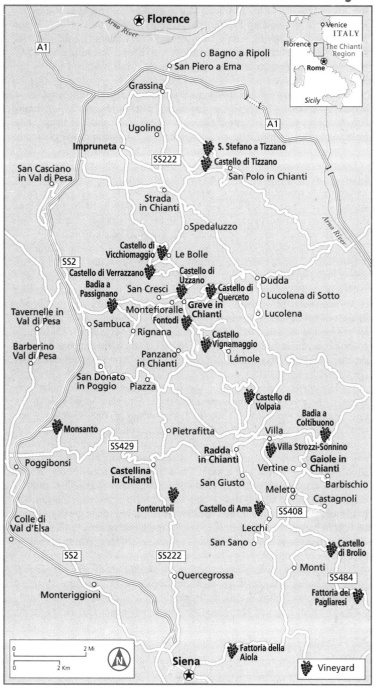

Florence

Arno River

A1

Bagno a Ripoli

San Piero a Ema

Grassina

Ugolino

A1

ITALY

Venice

Florence

The Chianti Region

Rome

Sicily

Impruneta

SS222

S. Stefano a Tizzano

Castello di Tizzano

San Polo in Chianti

San Casciano in Val di Pesa

Strada in Chianti

Spedaluzzo

Arno River

SS2

Castello di Vicchiomaggio

Le Bolle

Castello di Verrazzano

Castello di Uzzano

Dudda

Badia a Passignano

San Cresci

Castello di Querceto

Lucolena di Sotto

Montefioralle

Greve in Chianti

Tavernelle in Val di Pesa

Sambuca

Fontodi

Rignana

Lucolena

Castello Vignamaggio

Barberino Val di Pesa

Panzano in Chianti

Lámole

San Donato in Poggio

Piazza

Castello di Volpaia

Monsanto

Pietrafitta

Villa

Badia a Coltibuono

SS429

Villa Strozzi-Sonnino

Poggibonsi

Radda in Chianti

Vertine

Gaiole in Chianti

Castellina in Chianti

San Giusto

Meleto

Barbischio

Castagnoli

Colle di Val d'Elsa

Fonterutoli

Castello di Ama

SS408

SS2

SS222

Lecchi

San Sano

Castello di Brolio

Quercegrossa

Monti

SS484

Monteriggioni

Fattoria dei Pagliaresi

0   2 Mi

0   2 Km

N

Siena

Fattoria della Aiola

Vineyard

261

Iris Festival in May (dates vary according to weather patterns and the growing season). Far removed from the bustle and hordes of Florence, San Polo seems like a lonely time capsule, with a building that once belonged to the powerful Knights Templar. A church of ancient origins stands here, **San Miniato in Robbiana,** which, if you believe the inscription, was consecrated in 1077 by the bishop of Fiesole.

At San Polo, turn left and follow the signs back to SS222 and the village of **Strada in Chianti,** 14km (8½ miles) from Florence. *Strada,* which means "street," seems a strange name for a town—locals claim that the name came from an old Roman road that ran through here. The **Castello di Mugano,** one of the best preserved in Tuscany, stands guard over the region.

Continue along La Chiantigiana until reaching the isolated village of **Vicchiomaggio,** 19km (12 miles) from Florence, where an 11th-century castle once hosted the illustrious Leonardo da Vinci. You'll be following in his footsteps by visiting the **Fattoria Castello di Vicchiomaggio** (© **055-854078**), open Monday to Friday 9am to 1pm and 2:30 to 5:30pm. Here you can sample and buy wines, homegrown olive oil, vin santo, and grappa. The estate once sold Tuscany's greatest honey, although that was stopped several years ago because of stiff competition. Overall, the estate controls more than 300 acres, 70 of which are devoted to vineyards.

Nearby, 1.6km (about a mile) north of the hamlet of Greve, lies the hamlet of **Verrazzano,** a name that's more familiar to New Yorkers than to Tuscans because of the famous bridge bearing the name of Giovanni da Verrazzano. He left the land of the grape and set to sea in the service of François I of France. In 1524, he was the first European colonial to sail into the harbor of New York and the island of Manhattan before disappearing without a trace on his second voyage to Brazil.

His birthplace still stands on a hilltop overlooking Greve (4km/2½ miles from Greve, to be precise; take the route marked Via San Martino in Valle in the direction of Siena to reach it). **Castello di Verrazzano** (© **055-854243**) is centered in a 10th-century tower surrounded by other buildings from the 15th and 16th centuries. If you call ahead to make a reservation, the castle is open Monday to Friday 8am to 5pm. (Try to schedule your trip for 11am any day Mon–Fri, when you can join a tour.) Visits through the ancient caves usually include a sampling of the estate's great red and white wines, as well as complimentary platters of salami, cheese, and almond-scented biscuits. You can buy bottles of any of the wines. Unless the staff is rushed, you might get instructions on how to become a wine snob. If you didn't make reservations, you'll find that on SS222 heading south toward Greve is a *punto vendita* (sales outlet) open daily during daylight hours.

Lying just a mile to the west of Greve in Chianti is a little find off the beaten path. The small hilltop village of **Montefioralle** is the ancestral home of Amerigo Vespucci (1454–1512), the mapmaker and navigator for which America was named. It is said that Vespucci's niece, Simonette, was the model for *Venus* in Botticelli's celebrated *Primavera.* This village is sleepy except in mid-September when it hosts the Rassegna del Chianti Classico wine festival.

Consider spending at least an hour of your time here, exploring this partially restored hamlet with some of its octagonal walls still standing, along with its old tower houses and two Romanesque churches, Santo Stefano and Pieve di San Cresci a Montefioralle.

A signposted and potholed gravel road beyond Montefioralle continues for about 30 minutes to **Badia a Passignano** (© **055-8071278**), a 530-acre property set in the midst of some of the best vineyards for producing Chianti Classico. Antinori purchased the estate in 1987. In 1049, the Vallombrosian Order, a reformed branch of the Benedictines, moved in at this property. St. Giovanni Gualberto, who established the Vallombrosian order here, died in 1073, his relics still preserved in the abbey. The original Romanesque church where the saint was buried was given a baroque overlay in the 16th century. Ridolfo di Ghirlandio decorated the monks' refectory with one of his three representations of *The Last Supper* (1476). The order was suspended in 1866 when, following the unification of Italy, the government outlawed monastic orders and expropriated the property. The on-site castle tower is from the 19th century.

You can visit the bottega on the grounds and purchase wines from the Badia's vineyards and tour the historic cellars. La Bottega lies in an 18th-century building near the abbey gate. Next to the shop is a good restaurant, l'Osteria di Passignano. The bottega and osteria are open daily except Wednesday afternoon and Sunday from 10am to 11:30pm. Call for an appointment if you want to see the interior of the monastery, usually open Sunday from 2:30 to 5:30pm.

The road continues to **Greve in Chianti,** the region's unofficial capital, on the banks of the Greve River. Tuscany's grandest **wine fair** takes place here every September. Its central square is the funnel-shaped **Piazza del Mercatale,** with a statue honoring Giovanni da Verrazzano. Greve's castle long ago burned to the ground, but on Piazzetta Santa Croce you can visit the parish church, **Santa Croce,** containing a Bicci di Lorenzo triptych depicting the Annunciation. Greve is filled with wine shops (*enoteche*), yet we find it far more adventurous to buy from the wineries themselves.

Six kilometers (3¾ miles) from Greve, along the road signposted FIGLINE VAL D'ARNO, you'll find a tranquil estate, the **Castello di Querceto,** Via Dudda 61 (© **055-85921**). It boasts more than 125 acres of vineyards producing several grades of red Chianti and La Corte (made from the same Sangiovese grapes) and at least two whites (especially Le Giuncaie de Vernaccia). It's centered on a verdant park with an 11th-century castle that can be viewed only from the outside; the interior is not open to visitors. The staff is proud to show off the winery and cellars and will sell you wine, olive oil, and regional produce. Reservations are required.

About 9.5km (6 miles) south of Greve is **Fontodi,** Via San Leolino 89 (© **055-852005;** www.fontodi.com), accessible via SS222, near the village of Panzano, less than a meter (half mile) southeast of Sant'Eufrosino. Here you'll find 155 acres of vineyards radiating from a stone villa built between the 18th and 19th centuries, plus wine tastings and sales of several grades of Chianti and a reputable table wine known as Flaccianello della Pieve. Reservations are required; send a fax to © **055-852537.** Visits are possible Monday to Friday 8am to noon and 1:30 to 5:30pm.

South of Greve on SS222 is another highlight: **Vignamaggio** ⊛, Via Petriolo 5 (© **055-854661;** www.vignamaggio.com), boasting a beautiful Renaissance villa that was once the residence of La Gioconda (Lisa Gherardini). With her enigmatic smile, she sat for the most famous portrait of all time, Leonardo da Vinci's *Mona Lisa,* now in Paris's Louvre. You can tour the gardens (some of the most beautiful in Tuscany) Monday to Friday if you call in advance for a reservation. (The classical statues and towering hedges served as a backdrop for

Tuscan Tours: Biking, Horseback Riding & More

Florence-based **I Bike Italy** 🚲 (© 055-2342371; www.ibikeitaly.com) offers guided single-day rides in the Tuscan countryside, past olive groves, vineyards, castles, and vine-covered estates. Tours begin daily in Florence at 9am from the north end of Ponte alle Grazie. The company provides a shuttle service to carry you in and out of the city and also provides 21-speed bicycles, helmets, water bottles, and a bilingual guide to show you the way, fix flats, and so on. Tours cover scenic 24 to 48km (15–30 miles), at an average speed of 5kmph (3¼ mph), and return to Florence around 5pm. The cost is 60€ to 70€ ($53.60–$62.50) per person, with lunch included.

Ciclismo Classico (© 800/866-7314 in the U.S.; www.ciclismoclassico. com) has more than a decade of experience leading biking and walking tours in Italy. From April to November, the outfit runs several guided tours through Tuscany, always van-supported, or will help you arrange a do-it-yourself bike trip. Six- to 15-day trips usually include Italian and cooking lessons, along with wine tasting and cultural itineraries. Groups average 10 to 18 people, with all ages and ability levels welcome.

U.S.-based **Custom Tours in Tuscany** (© 847/432-1814), with up to 10 bilingual staff members familiar with Tuscany's art and culture, can customize a tour around your personal interests. You tell the company what you want to see and do, and it tailors a daylong guided tour. Its staff can help you visit Florence's monuments, guide you through its "secret" alleyways, and show you where to buy antiques, gold, leather, extra-virgin olive oil, or linens at unbeatable prices. Its Tuscan day tours include visits to Lucca, Siena, San Gimignano, and Pietrasanta. They begin and end in Florence, where you should plan to do a lot of walking; outside Florence, the guide accompanies you in your own rented car or arranges for a car and driver. Fees are $440 per day for Florence tours or $475 for tours in the countryside (6–7 hr.), for one or two people. Extra persons are $50 each. Transport, meals, highway tolls, museum admissions, and gratuities aren't included.

At the heart of Chianti in Barberino Val d'Elsa is one of Tuscany's top horse-riding clubs, **Il Paretaio** (© 055-8059218; ilparetaio@tin.it). Besides lessons, you can opt for half- and full-day outings (English-style) around the countryside on any of the 20 horses and can stay in one of the six guest rooms (private bathrooms) in an early-18th-century stone farmhouse with a view—even the pool is beautifully sited. Full-day trail riding with a picnic is 82.50€ ($73.65), room/board not included; and 1-week inclusive packages with 6 half days of trail riding and half-board are 650€ ($580.45) per person, based on double occupancy.

Only 20km (12 miles) from Florence in Pontassieve is the **Vallebona Ranch** (© 055-8397246; www.vallebona.org), where Western riding is the tradition. You can choose from lessons; full-day horseback rides returning daily to the six guest rooms (shared bathrooms) at the centuries-old farmhouse (1-week package with full board 475€, $424.20 per person, double occupancy); or weeklong inn-to-inn treks that begin and end at Vallebona (550€, $491.15 per person, double occupancy).

Kenneth Branagh's 1993 *Much Ado About Nothing*.) In 1404, the wine of this estate became the first red to be referred to as "Chianti." This is a private villa, and you can come here for a wine tasting, served along with snacks; it costs 30€ ($26.80), depending on your selection. Lovely, moderately priced apartments are available for rent here as well.

From Greve, continue 6km (3¾ miles) south along the winding Chiantigiana to one of the most enchanting spots in the Chianti, the little agricultural village of **Panzano.** It's worth a walk around the grounds and parts of its medieval castle, which once witnessed battles between Florence and Siena. The village women make the finest embroidery around, and you might want to acquire some from the locals. If you're so charmed by Panzano that you want to spend the night, contact the owners of the Torre Guelfa hotel in Florence (② **055-2396338;** fax 055-2398577) and ask about their **Villa Rosa di Boscorotondo,** Via San Leolino 59, Panzana (② **055-852577;** fax 055-8560835; villarosa@italyhotel.com).

Farther south is the delightful hill town of **Castellina in Chianti** ⚐, with a population of only 3,000. Once a fortified Florentine outpost against the Sienese, it fell to Sienese-Aragonese forces in 1478. But when Siena collapsed in 1555 to Florentine forces, sleepy little Castellina was left to slumber for centuries. That's how the town has preserved its *quattrocento* look, with its once-fortified walls virtually intact. Little houses were constructed into the walls and also nested on top of them. The covered walkway, Via della Volte, is the most historic in town. Although bottegas here sell Chianti and olive oils, you're better off delaying your purchases until later because you're on the doorstep of some of the finest wineries in Italy.

After Castellina, detour from SS222 and head east along a tortuous road to **Radda in Chianti,** with a population of 1,700. Radda is surrounded by the rugged region of Monti del Chianti and was the ancient capital of Lega del Chianti. The streets of the village still follow their original plan from the Middle Ages. The main square with its somber **Palazzo Comunale,** bearing a fresco from the 1400s, will make you feel as if you've traveled back in time.

Another winery is in the hamlet of Rentennano, near the village of Monti. Here the **Fattoria San Giusto a Rentennana** (② **0577-747121**) is the site of a 12th-century cellar that sits beneath a 15th-century villa. The centerpiece, 76 acres of vineyards, produces two grades of Chianti, as well as a simple table wine (Percarlo), which connoisseurs find surprisingly full of flavor. Tastings are possible, but only with a reservation and only for a minimum of three to four people. Hours are Monday to Friday 8:30am to noon and 3 to 7pm, and Saturday 8:30am to noon.

After a meal, continue 10km (6¼ miles) east to the market town of **Gaiole in Chianti,** with a population of 5,000. You'll come to a local cooperative, the **Agricoltori Chianti Geografico,** Via Mulinaccio 10 (② **0577-749489;** www.chiantigeografico.it), a branch of one of the region's largest associations of wine growers (more than 200). About 2km (1¼ miles) north of Gaiole in Chianti, it contains a modern wine-pressing facility with a prodigious output of (red) Chianti Classico and (white) Valdarbia. The local vin santo is made of trebbiano and malvasia grapes left to dry before pressing and then fermented in small oak barrels for about 4 years. The cooperative sells wine by the glass or the bottle, as well as olive oil, the Chianti Colli Senesi, and the (white) Gallestro wines produced on its lands near Siena.

Many other wineries in the area are easily reached by car from Gaiole. One of the best is the towering **Castello di Brolio** ✫ (© **0577-7301**), 10km (6¼ miles) south along SS484. This is the home of the Barone Ricasoli Wine House, famous since the 19th century for Ricasoli's experiments aimed at improving the quality of Chianti. Known as the Iron Baron, he inherited the property in 1829; in time he became one of the creators of a unified Italy and was elected its second prime minister. The property's history dates from 1141, when Florentine monks came here to live at a site whose vineyards go back to 1005. Caught up many times in the bombardments between the warring forces of Florence and Siena, the castle was later torn down, but then authorities in Florence ordered that it be reconstructed. Visiting hours are Monday to Friday 9am to noon and 3 to 6pm (Dec 1–Jan 15 it's open only on weekends); admission is 2.50€ ($2.25), and a tasting costs 10€ ($8.95; tastings are offered only to groups of five or more). A cantina sells the award-winning wines.

Another interesting stop is **Fattoria dei Pagliaresi,** in the village of Castelnuovo in Berardenga (© **0577-359070**), about 12km (7½ miles) southeast of Gaiole on SS484. In the mid-1990s, the charming English-speaking owner, Chiara Sanguineti, sold the cellars and vineyards to other growers, but the 300-year-old farmhouse that she maintains sits amid vineyards, near ancient olive groves. You can tour the farm; taste or buy wine, grappa, honey, and olive oil; visit lovely gardens; and (if you reserve in advance) enjoy a well-prepared Tuscan farmhouse lunch for 20€ to 25€ ($17.85–$22.35).

If you backtrack, taking SS408 to Siena, you can follow the signposts about 10km (6¼ miles) north to the **Fattoria della Aiola** (© **0577-322615;** fax 0577-322509), near the hamlet of Vagliagli, 20km (12 miles) southwest of Gaiole. Site of a ruined medieval castle (only a wall and a moat remain) and a 19th-century villa (not open to the public), it features 90 acres of vineyards that produce Chianti, Sangiovese, grappa, and Spumante "Aioli Brut" (a sparkling wine similar to champagne). The winery even produces olive oil and vinegar. This place receives a lot of visitors (including tour buses), so advance reservations or at least a phone call before arriving is a good idea.

WHERE TO STAY ALONG THE CHIANTI ROAD

The atmospheric Tuscan inns along the Chianti road are wonderful, and it's a good idea to break up a visit between Florence and Siena with a night at one of them. The best places to stay are Greve, Radda, Gaiole, and Castellina (our favorite). Many of these inns are also noted for their good food and wine. Even if you're not a guest, you might visit for a meal.

Albergo del Chianti ✫ (Value) At the edge of Greve's main square, with a facade and foundation as old as the square itself (more than 1,000 yr.), is this charming small inn with views over the countryside. Each cozy, simple guest room is painted a different color and is done in rustic Tuscan style, with a wrought-iron bedstead. Aside from breakfast, dinner is the only meal served (only to hotel guests). The Bussotti family takes good care of you in the restaurant; in warm weather, the food is served in a beautiful Mediterranean garden.

Piazza Matteotti 86, 50022 Greve in Chianti. © and fax 055-853763. www.albergodelchianti.it. 16 units. 95€ ($84.80) double. Rate includes buffet breakfast. Half-board 22.50€ ($20.10) per person. MC, V. **Amenities:** Restaurant; bar; outdoor pool; room service; babysitting. *In room:* A/C, TV, minibar, hair dryer.

Borgo Argenina ✫ From the flagstone terrace of Elena Nappa's hilltop B&B (she bought the whole medieval village), you can see the farmhouse where Bertolucci filmed his gorgeous *Stealing Beauty* in 1996. Against remarkable odds (she'll regale you with the anecdotes), she has created the rural retreat of her dreams—and yours too. Elena's design talents (she was a fashion stylist in Milan) are amazing, and the guest rooms boast antique wrought-iron beds, handmade quilts, hand-stitched lace curtains, and time-worn terra-cotta tiles. The bathrooms are made to look old-fashioned, although the plumbing is modern. The place isn't easy to find, so English-speaking Elena will fax you directions when you reserve.

Localiatà Argenina (near San Marcellino Monti), 53013 Gaiole in Chianti. ℂ and fax **0577-747117.** www.borgoargenina.it. 7 units. 130€ ($116.10) double; 160€–180€ ($142.90–$160.75) apt. Rates include country breakfast. Ask about off-season discounts. No credit cards. Ask for directions when reserving. **Amenities:** Lounge. In room: Minibar, hair dryer, safe.

Castello di Spaltenna ⚐ One of the region's unique hotels is on a hill above Gaiole. Opened during the Middle Ages as a monastery, it retains some medieval flair, despite several enlargements and modifications. In the compound are a small medieval chapel, two soaring towers, and several stone-sided annexes, one housing some of the junior suites. The guest rooms are cozy and traditionally furnished, with all the modern conveniences. Look for wrought-iron or wooden headboards and terra-cotta floors whose tiles might be as much as 1,000 years old. Some rooms have fireplaces, and all enjoy views over the peaceful countryside and classic cypress trees. Hiking, horseback riding, and tennis are available nearby. Dining is either indoors by candlelight in the old cloister or outdoors on a terrace.

Pieve di Spaltenna, 53013 Gaiole in Chianti. ℂ **0577-749483.** Fax 0577-749269. www.spaltenna.it. 37 units. 212€–274€ ($189.30–$244.70) double; 336€–491€ ($300.05–$438.45) suite. AE, DC, MC, V. Closed mid-Jan to mid-Mar. **Amenities:** Restaurant; bar; wine cellar; outdoor pool; exercise room; sauna; room service; babysitting; laundry. In room: A/C, TV, minibar, hair dryer, safe.

Hotel Salivolpi ⚐ *(Finds* In a classic farm setting that looks as if it's straight out of a Renaissance painting, the family-run Salivolpi stands only a 15-minute drive from Siena, or 30 minutes from Florence. The simple Tuscan-style guest rooms are spread across three buildings, each beautifully maintained and decorated with regional antiques. The bathrooms are spotless.

Via Fiorentina 89, 53011 Castellina in Chianti. ℂ **0577-740484.** Fax 0577-740998. www.hotelsalivolpi.com. 19 units (15 with shower only). 93€ ($83.05) double. Rates include buffet breakfast. AE, MC, V. **Amenities:** Bar; pool. In room: TV, hair dryer.

Hotel Tenuta di Ricavo ⚐⚐ Our favorite choice in the region, this place is a fantasy of what a Tuscan inn should look like. In fact, it's like a medieval village of stone houses. On nippy nights, guests gather in the atmospheric bar, with its fireplace. The innkeepers rent beautifully furnished and maintained guest rooms, each with a well-maintained bathroom. Surrounding the compound are 445 acres of woodlands, with paths that are ideal for taking long walks or riding a mountain bike.

Località Ricavo 4, 53011 Castellina in Chianti (3km/2 miles north of town). ℂ **0577-740221.** Fax 0577-741014. www.ricavo.com. 23 units (showers only). 170€–309€ ($151.80–$275.95) double; 221€–309€ ($197.35–$275.95) suite. Rates include breakfast. MC, V. Closed late Nov to early Apr. **Amenities:** Restaurant; lounge; 2 outdoor pools; small gym; room service; babysitting; laundry. In room: TV, minibar, hair dryer, safe.

Villa Casalecchi Almost as elegant as the Tenuta di Ricavo (listed previously), this government-rated four-star hotel is built against a hill. You arrive on the hilltop and enter into what's top floor. The hotel is composed of a trio of buildings; the main structure is an elegant villa whose 16 units are spread across two floors. The guest rooms range from small to medium, each furnished in part with 18th-century reproductions and often with canopied beds. The bathrooms are rather small. There's an elegant restaurant, offering outdoor dining in the evergreen garden in summer. The staff will help you arrange outings to nearby wineries on bike or horseback.

Località Casalecchi 18, 53011 Castellina in Chianti. ✆ **0577-740240.** Fax 0577-741111. www.villacasalec-chi.it. 25 units. 170€–210€ ($151.80–$187.55) double. Rates include buffet breakfast. AE, DC, MC, V. Closed Nov to 1 week before Easter. **Amenities:** Restaurant; bar; lovely outdoor pool; tennis court; room service; babysitting; laundry. *In room:* A/C, TV, minibar, hair dryer, safe.

Villa Miranda   The Miranda, which became a small inn in 1842, still retains its thick stone walls, brick arches, and old wooden beams. The reigning duenna is Donna Miranda herself, somewhat of a local legend. The rooms are intimate, antique-filled affairs, but make sure that you ask for a newer unit in one of the outbuildings nestled amid the vineyards, not one of the older guest rooms in the original 1842 post house. Some of the newer rooms have small terraces or whirlpool tubs.

The **restaurant** ✿ is one of the finest in the area, specializing in regional fare such as wild boar cooked in white wine. Mamma Miranda claims that her *ribol-lita* is the best vegetable soup in Tuscany, and no one disagrees! Her homemade ravioli and tender Florentine beefsteak are equally delectable. If you've always resisted ordering mutton, try Mamma Miranda's.

Località Villa, 53107 Radda in Chianti. ✆ **0577-738021.** Fax 0577-738668. 49 units (some with shower only). 75€–125€ ($67–$111.65) double; 125€–140€ ($111.65–$125) suite. MC, V. **Amenities:** Outstanding restaurant; 2 bars; 2 pools; tennis court; room service. *In room:* A/C, TV, minibar, hair dryer, safe.

WHERE TO DINE ALONG THE CHIANTI ROAD

Some of the best food in Italy is served in Chianti, and all dishes are accompanied by the wine of the region. See also the hotel listing for **Villa Miranda,** above; its restaurant is one of the best in the region.

Antica Trattoria La Torre ✿ TUSCAN   This old family-run dining room is on the town's main square in an 18th-century building, next to a medieval tower. The kitchen depends on the harvest from the field, stream, and air to keep its cooks busy. The Tuscan game, the fowl (such as pigeon and guinea), and the local beef are the finest in the area. The Florentine beefsteak alone is worth the trip. Other typical dishes are delicious ribolitta (thick vegetable soup), pasta with game sauce, and meat grilled over charcoal with mushrooms. The best dessert is the homemade pine-nut cake.

Piazza del Comune 13, Castellina in Chianti. ✆ **0577-740236.** Reservations required in summer and weekends. Main courses 7.50€–17.50€ ($6.70–$15.65). AE, DC, DISC, MC, V. Sat–Thurs noon–2:30pm and 7:30–9:30pm. Closed Sept 1–15.

Borgo Antico ✿ *(Finds* TUSCAN   Opened more than 30 years ago in a 200-year-old compound of farmhouses and barns, this country inn is more upscale than you might think, thanks to the hardworking Marunti family, who haul in fresh produce from nearby farms every morning. The pastas are made fresh on the premises, and the desserts, especially such relatively simple concoctions as crema cotta and tiramisu, are wonderful. The Florentine-style beefsteaks are among the best in the region, tender and loaded with Mediterranean herbs and olive oil. The turkey filet grilled with olive oil and the veal scallops with lemon juice or wine are worth the drive. As you dine, you'll enjoy views of the nearby slopes of Monte San Michele.

The Maruntis rent three simple guest rooms. The solid stone wall facade and old-time setting more than compensate for the lack of luxuries. Each has a private bathroom, although in one case it's outside the bedroom. Doubles are 40€ to 45€ ($35.70–$40.20). No breakfast is served.

Via Case Sparse 115, Lucolena (16km/10 miles northeast of Greve). ℂ 055-851024. Reservations recommended. Main courses 9€–17.50€ ($8.05–$15.65). AE, MC, V. Apr–Oct Wed–Mon noon–3pm and 7–9:30pm; Nov–Dec and Feb–Mar Fri–Sat 7–9:30pm, Sat–Sun noon–3pm.

Bottega del Moro ⚡ TUSCAN   Our favorite restaurant in Greve's center occupies an old stone blacksmith's shop. (Locals referred to the blacksmith as "The Moor" because of the charcoal that blackened his face, and ever since, the nickname "Lair of the Moor" has been associated with this restaurant.) Run by English-speaking Elizabeth Tassi and her husband, Sergio, who oversees the kitchen, this restaurant specializes in light Tuscan fare that goes easy on the olive oil. Menu items include homemade ravioli with butter and sage; Florentine-style tripe, beefsteaks, and roasted rabbit from nearby fields; and skewered meat grilled to perfection. The unusual modern paintings in the two dining rooms are by a well-known local artist, Alvaro Baralie, a friend of the owners. A flowering terrace provides limited extra seating on the square during clement weather.

Piazza Trieste 14R, Greve in Chianti. ℂ 055-853753. Reservations required. Main courses 10€–16€ ($8.95–$14.30). AE, DC, MC, V. Thurs–Tues 12:15–2:30pm and 7:15–9:30pm. Closed Nov and 1st week of June.

Il Vignale TUSCAN   This rustic yet elegant place is the area's best family-run dining room, turning out home-style Tuscan cuisine that's flavorful and prepared with fresh ingredients. Every day something new appears, and the cuisine is quite creative. You can start with a typical crostini as an appetizer (similar to a small bruschetta, with different kinds of prosciutto on top). Among the main courses are homemade soups and pastas, such as *tagliatelle* (flat noodles) with wild boar sauce. In autumn, some of the region's finest game dishes are offered, and you can order roast lamb stuffed with artichokes and aromatic herbs.

Via XX Settembre 23, Radda in Chianti. ℂ 0577-738094. Reservations recommended. Main courses 17.50€–22.50€ ($15.65–$20.10). AE, DC, MC, V. Fri–Wed 12:30–3pm and 7:30–9:30pm. Closed Dec–Mar.

La Cantinetta TUSCAN   To experience rural Tuscany, stop for a meal in the garden of this stone-sided restaurant built around 1800 as a farmhouse. It has been serving generous portions of pastas, risottos, and *peposo* (chunks of beef stewed in red wine with tomatoes and peppers) since the 1970s and is popular with locals. Tagliata with truffles or porcinis is a sure winner, as is chicken cooked with Tuscan vegetables. Adventurous palates sometimes enjoy the stuffed rabbit or stuffed pigeon. The setting, surrounded by the agrarian bounty of Tuscany, seems to enhance the food.

Via Mugnana 93, Spedaluzzo (1km/¹/₂ mile north of Greve). ℂ 055-8572000. Reservations recommended. Main courses 6.50€–15€ ($5.80–$13.40). AE, DC, MC, V. Tues–Sun 12:30–2:30pm and 7:30–10:30pm (open daily July–Aug).

Montagliari ⚡ *Finds* TUSCAN   Associated with a local vineyard, Montagliari is full of rustic charm and serves up authentic regional fare. Tables are set out in a garden, and the place is decorated like an old Tuscan farmhouse. The specialty here is wild boar cacciatore. You can also order roasted lamb or rabbit with potatoes, penne with raw chopped tomatoes and homegrown basil, tortellini stuffed with minced meat, or roasted lamb in the age-old style of the Tuscan hills.

Via di Montagliari 29, Panzano (between Montagliari and Greve, 1km/¹/₂ mile north of Panzano). ℂ 055-852184. Reservations recommended. Main courses 10€–15€ ($8.95–$13.40). AE, DC, MC, V. Tues–Sun 12:30–2:30pm and 7:30–9:30pm.

Tenuta Badia a Coltibuono ⋆ TUSCAN   This restaurant occupies a medieval building adjacent to the winery recommended earlier in this section. It's very much a family affair, with owner Paolo Stucchi Prinetti the host in the dining room. The chef prepares recipes given a touch of originality by the mistress of the domain, Lorenza de' Medici (a cookbook author who also runs a cooking school next to the restaurant). The dishes are based on simple seasonal ingredients whose flavors are accented by fresh herbs and greens. Fresh pasta is made daily, and regional meat specialties include rabbit, lamb, and the extraordinary Chianina beef of Tuscany. Local goat- and sheep-milk cheeses are served, and homemade desserts conclude the meals. The wine list highlights the vintages of Coltibuono.

From Radda, continue along the winding road, signposted GAIOLE IN CHIANTI. ☎ **0577-749031.** Reservations required. Main courses 13€–16€ ($11.60–$14.30); fixed-price menu 17€–40€ ($15.20–$35.70); platters from 12.50€ ($11.15). MC, V. May–Oct daily 12:15–2:30pm and 7:15–9:45pm; Nov–Apr Tues–Sun 12:15–2:30pm and 7:15–9:45pm.

2 Montecatini Terme: Italy's Top Spa ⋆

31km (19 miles) NE of Florence, 42km (26 miles) NE of Pisa

The best known of all Italian spas, Montecatini Terme has long drawn crowds seeking its curative waters and scenic location. It's a peaceful Tuscan town set among green hills in the valley called Valdinievole. By 1890, it was a regular stop for some of the titled aristocrats of Europe. In the 20th century, it drew such luminaries as Gary Cooper, Rose Kennedy, and Gabriel D'Annunzio and was further immortalized in Fellini's *8½.*

ESSENTIALS

GETTING THERE   From Florence, a **train** leaves for Montecatini every hour throughout the day. Trip time is 50 minutes, and a one-way ticket costs 4.40€ ($4.25). Montecatini is home to two rail stations, about a mile apart. The larger and closer to Florence is **Montecatini Terme Monsummano,** Piazza Italia. More central to most of the hotels of the town center is **Montecatini Centro,** which might save a bit of transit time for passengers headed to the resort's center. For more details, call ☎ **848-888088** in Italy only.

Lazzi buses (☎ **0583-584877** or 0583-584877 in Italy only) from Florence run frequently to Montecatini; the trip takes less than an hour.

If you have a **car,** take the A11 highway from Florence or Pistoia, exiting at the signposted turnoffs to the spa.

VISITOR INFORMATION   The **tourist office** is at Viale Verdi 66–68 (☎ **0572-772244**), open Monday to Saturday 9am to 12:30pm and 3 to 6pm (Apr–Oct, also Sun 9am–noon).

SEEING THE SPA & TAKING THE CURE

Many visitors are just regular tourists who enjoy a quick stop in a spa town; others come to lose weight, to take the mud baths, and to visit the sauna-cum-grotto. The mineral waters are said to be the finest in Europe, and the most serious visitors go to the 19th-century **Tettuccio spa,** with its beautiful gardens, to fill their cups from the curative waters.

Modern thermal centers, **Stabilimenti Termali,** await you at virtually every turn. The focus of the long grand promenade is the **Parco dei Termi,** with its neoclassical temples. The park lies above a series of underground hot springs, the most ancient of which appears in documents as far back as 1370. It's customary to come here every day to drink a healthful tonic from the fountains set up on marble counters. Spa treatments at the thermal centers cost 4€ to 10€ ($3.55–$8.95) for half a day (with tonics to drink), and 25€ to 37.50€ ($22.35–$33.50) for mud baths and other more elaborate treatments. Full information and tickets are available from the **Società delle Terme,** Viale Verdi 41 (**✆ 0572-7781;** www.termemontecatini.it). Most thermal houses are open May to October.

Montecatini is filled with dozens of hotels and pensiones, mostly Art Nouveau buildings from the beginning of the 20th century, and many would-be visitors to Florence, unable to find a room in that overcrowded city, base themselves here. The spa has a season lasting from April to October, and the town really shuts down in the off-season.

When you tire of all that rest, you can take a funicular from Viale Diaz up to **Montecatini Alto** to enjoy its panoramic view. This town was important in the Middle Ages, containing about two dozen towers that were demolished in 1554 on orders of Cosimo de' Medici. You can walk along narrow streets to the ruins of a fortress, paying a short visit to St. Peter's Church. From this hillside town, you can see all the way to Florence on a clear day.

Today Montecatini attracts some of the world's most fashionable people on the see-and-be-seen circuit, especially during the horse-racing season from April to October. It's filled with some of Europe's most expensive boutiques, so there's fun browsing but no bargains.

WHERE TO STAY

Grand Hotel Croce di Malta ⚔   Built in 1911 in a residential neighborhood near the spa, this hotel stands behind an imposing facade that rises from behind a screen of shrubbery. It's the best of the upper-middle-bracket hotels, with touches of polished marble around the guest rooms and public areas. A helpful staff and affordable prices make it a perennial favorite. In 1997, the hotel added a four-story wing (where rooms have Jacuzzis). Discounts on greens fees are available to guests at nearby golf courses.

Viale IV Novembre 18, 51016 Montecatini Terme. ✆ **0572-9201.** Fax 0572-767516 or 0572-772184. www.crocedimalta.com.   144   units.   160€–200€   ($142.90–$178.60)   double;   220€–240€ ($196.45–$214.30) suite. Rates include buffet breakfast. Half-board 20€ ($17.85) per person. AE, DC, MC, V. Parking 12.50€ ($11.15). **Amenities:** Restaurant; piano bar; outdoor pool; fitness center; room service. *In room:* A/C, TV, dataport, minibar, hair dryer, safe.

Grand Hotel & La Pace ⚔⚔   This is one of Italy's top spa hotels. A member of the Leading Hotels of the World group, the Grand has maintained its white-glove formality since 1869. It boasts frescoes, elaborate ceilings, flowered sun terraces, soaring columns, lots of gilt, and all the ornate detailing you'd expect. The guest rooms are less lavish than the public areas but are discreetly comfortable. Most are quite spacious, with high ceilings. The bathrooms are decked out in Italian tiles or marble, with deluxe toiletries.

Via della Toretta 1, 51016 Montecatini Terme. ✆ **0572-75801.** Fax 0572-78451. www. grandhotellapace.com. 144 units. 245€–285€ ($218.75–$254.45) double; 375€–425€ ($334.90–$379.55) suite. AE, DC, MC, V. Closed Nov–Apr 1. Free parking. **Amenities:** 2 restaurants; 2 bars; pool; 6 tennis courts; health club; spa offering massage and an array of treatments; concierge; room service; babysitting; laundry/dry cleaning. *In room:* A/C, TV, dataport, minibar, hair dryer, safe.

Grand Hotel Vittoria   This pleasantly old-fashioned hotel is a more affordable alternative to the choices above. Verdi stayed here shortly after the hotel opened, before it went through other transitions, including a brief stint as a monastery and as headquarters for the Nazis and then for the Americans during World War II. Away from the town center amid dignified homes, it's one of the best reasonably priced hotels in the area. Semiantique touches abound, including a double travertine stairway flanked by masses of flowers. The guest rooms are furnished in a refined but simple style, with all the standard comforts, such as fine linen. The bathrooms are a bit small. On the premises are a tranquil garden and a covered terrace.

Viale della Libertà 2A, 51056 Montecatini Terme. ℂ 0572-79271. Fax 0572-910520. www.hotelvittoria.it. 84 units. 125€–160€ ($111.65–$142.90) double; 250€ ($223.25) suite. Rates include breakfast. Half-board 25€ ($22.35). AE, MC, V. Parking 10€ ($8.95). **Amenities:** Bar; pool; spa; sauna; room service; babysitting; laundry. *In room:* A/C, TV, minibar, hair dryer, safe.

Hotel Manzoni   The Simoncini-Greco family is still here to welcome you, a tradition going back to 1921. They offer the best of both worlds, with 17th- to 19th-century furnishings and modern amenities, plus a landscaped garden, recreation room, and formal dining room. Most guest rooms are quite large and are furnished with elegant Tuscan styling. The tiled bathrooms are well maintained and frequently renovated. Free use of 18-speed touring bikes allows you to enjoy the surrounding parks and olive-covered hills.

Viale Manzoni 28, 51016 Montecatini Terme. ℂ 0572-70175. Fax 0572-911012. www. italway.it/alberghi/manzoni. 75 units. 100€ ($89.30) double. Rates include breakfast. AE, DC, MC, V. Free parking. Closed late Sept to late Mar. **Amenities:** Fine restaurant; bar; pool; free use of bicycles; room service. *In room:* A/C, TV, minibar.

Hotel Villa Ida *(Value)*   Bargain-hunting spagoers gravitate to this 19th-century building that was radically upgraded in the late 1980s. It offers simple comforts, but everything is cozy and refined. A modern decor now graces the place, and the guest rooms and bathrooms are small but immaculately maintained. The hotel offers two terraces ideal for an alfresco breakfast or dinner.

Viale G. Marconi 55, 51016 Montecatini Terme. ℂ 0572-78201. Fax 0572-772008. www.hotelvillaida.it. 21 units (showers only). 60€ ($53.60) double with breakfast; 90€ ($80.35) double with half-board. AE, DC, MC, V. Free parking (25 spaces). **Amenities:** Restaurant; bar; room service; babysitting. *In room:* A/C, TV, minibar, coffeemaker.

WHERE TO DINE

Gourmet *(★★)* ITALIAN   Located in a 19th-century building with a Liberty-style (the Italian term for Art Nouveau) interior, this is the best nonhotel restaurant in town. It prides itself on formal service and a cuisine that's more unusual than run-of-the-mill pastas. Menu items change seasonally and with the availability of ingredients, but you'll often find a spectacular array of antipasti ("antipasti fantasia") with seafood and fresh vegetables, ravioli stuffed with pulverized sea bass and herbs, risotto with scampi, and a medley of fruit garnishes (melon slices with lobster and honey-vinegar sauce, for example). Most items are delicious and beautifully presented. The desserts are made fresh daily and might include a Grand Marnier soufflé.

Via Amendola 6. ℂ 0572-771012. Reservations recommended. Main courses 17.50€–25€ ($15.65–$22.35). AE, DC, MC, V. Wed–Mon noon–2pm and 8–11pm. Closed Jan 7–20 and Aug 1–20.

Ristorante Pietre Cavate *(Finds)* TUSCAN   The Bertini and Menchi families are the creative forces behind this warmly hospitable farmhouse less than a mile north of the town center, where there are three rustic-looking dining rooms. The cuisine is a celebration of Tuscany, with special emphasis on macaroni with tomato and *parmigiano* sauce, pappardelle with chunks of rabbit, stuffed onions, savory stews, and chunky cuts of veal, pork, and beef. Come here with an appetite and enjoy the view over the rooftops of Montecatini.

Via Pietre Cavate 11. (C) **0572-954258.** Reservations recommended. Main courses 7.50€–20€ ($6.70–$17.85). AE, MC, V. Daily 7:30pm–midnight. Closed Wed Nov–Mar.

3 Lucca ✮✮✮

72km (45 miles) W of Florence, 21km (13 miles) E of Pisa, 336km (208 miles) N of Rome

In 56 B.C., Caesar, Crassus, and Pompey met in Lucca and agreed to rule Rome as a triumvirate. By the time of the Roman Empire's collapse, Lucca was virtually the capital of Tuscany. Periodically in its valiant, ever-bloody history, this town was an independent principality, similar to Genoa. This autonomy attests to the fame and prestige it enjoyed. Now, however, Lucca is largely bypassed by time and travelers, rewarding those who venture off the beaten track.

In the late 1600s, Lucca's third and final set of city walls was erected. This girdle of ramparts is largely intact and is one of the major reasons to visit the town, where the architecture ranges from Roman to Liberty.

Today, Lucca is best known for its *olio d'oliva lucchese,* the quality olive oil produced in the region outside the town's walls, and shoppers will be delighted to find a number of upscale boutiques here as well, testimony to an affluence not dependent on tourism. Thriving, cosmopolitan, and perfectly preserved, Lucca is a sort of Switzerland of the south: The banks have latticed Gothic windows, the shops look like well-stocked linen cupboards, children play in landscaped gardens, and geraniums bloom from the roofs of medieval tower houses.

ESSENTIALS

GETTING THERE   At least 20 **trains** travel daily between Florence and Lucca. The trip takes 1¼ hours and costs 3.15€ ($2.80) each way. The rail station is about .5 km (a quarter mile) south of Lucca's historic core, a short walk from the city's ramparts. For rail information, call (C) **848-888088.** If you don't have a lot of luggage, you can walk into the center; otherwise, most of the city's buses (notably, nos. 3 and 6) and lots of taxis stand ready to take you there.

The **Lazzi bus** company ((C) **0583-584877**) operates buses traveling between Florence and Lucca. They take less time than the train (50 min.–1 hr.), and, unlike the train, they carry passengers to a point within the city walls. Bus transit between Florence and Lucca, however, costs a bit more than the train: 4.30€ ($3.85). Buses pick up passengers in front of the rail station in Florence and drop them off in Lucca at both the rail station and the historic core at Piazzale Verdi, near the tourist office.

If you have a **car,** leave Florence and take the A11 highway through Prato, Pistoia, and Montecatini before reaching the outskirts of Lucca. If you're in Pisa, take SS12.

VISITOR INFORMATION   The Lucca **tourist office** is on Piazza Santa Maria 35 ((C) **0583-419689**), open daily 9am to 7pm April to October (off-season to 6pm).

GETTING AROUND   Lucca is a great place to rent a bike, especially because you can ride along the ancient city walls. Try **Antonio Poli,** Piazza Santa Maria 42 ((C) **0583-493787**), which is open daily from 8:30am to 7:30pm, except for Sunday in winter and Monday morning year-round. Expect to pay about 2€ ($1.80) per hour or 10€ ($8.95) for a whole day to rent a good mountain bike.

SPECIAL EVENTS Sleepy Lucca comes to life during July and August at the time of the classical music festival, the **Estate Musicale Lucchese.** Venues spring up everywhere, and the tourist office keeps a list. The town also comes alive on July 12, when residents don medieval costumes and parade through the city, with the revelry continuing late into the night.

In Puccini's hometown, you'll find a devotion to opera, and in October and November his work is showcased at the **Teatro Comunale del Giglio,** Piazza di Giglio (© **0583-467521;** fax 0583-490317). More classical music performances fill the town in September during the **Settembre Lucchese Festival,** highlighted by Volto Santo feast day on September 13. The crucifix bearing the "face" of Christ (normally housed in a chapel in the Duomo) is hauled through town in a candlelit procession to commemorate its miraculous journey to Lucca. The last two weeks of September also bring an **agricultural market** to Piazza San Michele, featuring Lucca's wines, honeys, and olive oils.

One of Italy's top **antiques markets** is held the third Saturday and Sunday of every month in Piazza Antelminello and the streets around the Duomo. (Hotel and restaurant reservations are always harder to get on these weekends.)

EXPLORING THE TOWN

The **city walls** 🏛🏛 enclose the old town; they're the best-preserved Renaissance defense ramparts in Europe. The present walls, measuring 35m (115 ft.) at the base and soaring 12m (40 ft.) high, replaced crumbling ramparts built during the Middle Ages. They comprise a city park more than 4km (2½ miles) long but only about 18m (60 ft.) wide, filled with leafy trees. The shady paved paths of Lucca's formidable bastions are always filled with couples strolling hand-in-hand, families on outings, old men playing cards, and hundreds of people on bikes. You can enter from 1 of 10 bastions; try the one behind the tourist office at **Piazzale Verdi.** For orientation, you might want to walk completely around the city on the ramparts, the **Passeggiata delle Mura,** a distance of 4km (2½ miles).

Besides the major sights below, worth seeking out is the **Roman Amphitheater (Anfiteatro Romano),** at Piazza Anfiteatro, reached along Via Fillungo. You can still see the outlines of its arches in its outer walls, and within the inner ring only the rough form remains to evoke what must've been. Once the theater was adorned with many-hued Tuscan marble, but greedy builders hauled off its materials to create some of the many churches of Lucca, including San Michele and the Duomo. The foundations of the former grandstands, which once rang with the sound of Tuscans screaming for gladiator blood, now support an ellipse of houses from the Middle Ages. The theater is from the 2nd century A.D.

If you want to catch a glimpse of Lucca life, find a chair at one of the sleepy cafes and pass the day away. In July and August, you can come to the **Piazza Guidiccioni** nearby and see a screening of the latest Italian and U.S. hits in the open air.

Cattedrale di San Martino (Duomo) 🏛🏛 The Duomo is the town's main monument, dating back to 1060, although the present structure was mainly rebuilt during the following centuries. The facade is exceptional, evoking the Pisan-Romanesque style but with enough originality and idiosyncrasies to distinguish it from the Duomo at Pisa. Designed mostly by Guidetto da Como in the early 13th century, the west front contains three wide ground-level arches, surmounted by three scalloped galleries with taffylike twisting columns tapering in size.

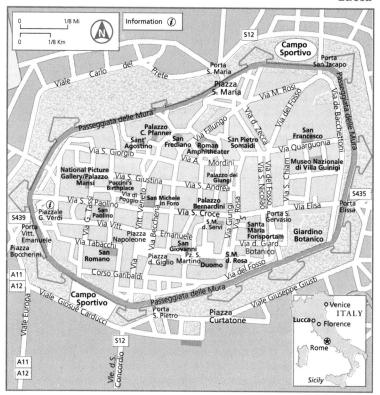

The main relic inside (in some ways the religious symbol of Lucca itself) is the **Volto Santo** ☆, a crucifix carved by Nicodemus (so tradition has it) from the Cedar of Lebanon. The face of Christ was supposedly chiseled onto the statuary.

The main art treasure lies in the sacristy: the **tomb of Ilaria del Carretto Guinigi** ☆☆, sculpted by Jacopo della Quercia. Ilaria was a local aristocrat and the wife of Paolo Guinigi; she died in 1405 while still young. Her marble effigy, in regal robes and guarded by chubby bambini, rests atop the sarcophagus; the diffused mauve afternoon light casts a ghostly glow on her face. (Long-term plans include moving the tomb to the Duomo Museum described below.) Also in the sacristy is the superb Domenico Ghirlandaio *Madonna and Saints* altarpiece (1494).

Adjacent to the Duomo is the **Duomo Museum (Museo della Cattedrale; ✆ 0583-490530)**. Admission is 3€ ($2.70); open daily. Here you'll find some rather dusty-looking memorabilia and mostly minor artworks, with the exception of Matteo Civitali's late-15th-century choir screen (removed from the cathedral in 1987) and Jacopo della Quercia's majestic early-15th-century sculpture *St. John the Evangelist*.

Piazza San Martino. ✆ **0583-957068**. Admission to cathedral free; sacristy and inner sanctum 2€ ($1.80). Apr–Oct daily 9:30am–6pm; Nov–Mar daily 9:30am–5pm.

San Frediano ⭐ Romanesque in style, this is one of Lucca's most important churches, built in the 12th and 13th centuries when the town enjoyed its greatest glory. The severe white facade is relieved by a 13th-century mosaic of Christ ascending, and the *campanile* (bell tower) rises majestically. The interior is dark, and visitors often speak in whispers. But the bas-reliefs on the Romanesque font add a note of comic relief: Supposedly depicting the story of Moses, among other themes, they show Egyptians in medieval armor chasing after the Israelites. Two tombs in the basilica (in the fourth chapel on the left) were the work of celebrated Sienese sculptor Jacopo della Quercia.

Piazza San Frediano. ℂ 0583-493627. Free admission. Mon–Sat 9am–noon and 3–6pm; Sun 9–11am and 3–5pm.

San Michele in Foro ⭐ This church often surprises first-timers, who mistake it for the Duomo. Begun in 1143, it's the most memorable example of the style and flair that the Lucchese brought to the Pisan-Romanesque school of architecture. The exquisite west front, employing the scalloped effect, is spanned by seven ground-level arches and then surmounted by four tiers of galleries, utilizing imaginatively designed columns. Dragon-slaying St. Michael, wings outstretched, rests on the friezelike peak of the final tier. Inside, seek out a Filippo Lippi painting, *Saints Sebastian, Jerome, Helen, and Roch,* on the far wall of the right transept. If you're here in September, the piazza outside, which was the old Roman forum, holds a daily colorful open market selling everything from olive oil to souvenirs of Tuscany.

Piazza San Michele. ℂ 0583-48459. Free admission. Daily 9am–noon and 3–5:30pm.

National Picture Gallery and Palazzo Mansi Museum (Pinacoteca Nazionale e Museo di Palazzo Mansi) This palace was built for the powerful Mansi family, whose descendants are still some of the movers and shakers in town. Although Tuscany has far greater art collections, there are some treasures, notably a portrait of Princess Elisa by Marie Benoist. Elisa Bonaparte (1777–1820), who married into a local wealthy family, the Bacceocchis, was "given" the town by her brother Napoleon in 1805 when he made her princess of Lucca and Piombino. Unlike her profligate sister, Pauline Borghese in Rome, Elisa was a strong woman with a remarkable aptitude for public affairs (she laid out Piazza Napoleone, among other accomplishments). The collection is enriched by works from Lanfranco, Luca Giordano, and Tintoretto, among others, although they're not their greatest works. There's a damaged Veronese, but Tintoretto's *Miracle of St. Mark Freeing the Slave* is amusing—the patron saint of Venice literally divebombs from heaven to save the day.

Via Galli Tassi 43. ℂ 0583-55570. Admission 4€ ($3.55). Tues–Sat 8am–7pm; Sun 8:30am–2pm.

⌐*Tips* **Travel Tip**

One mistake many people make when hopping from hill town to hill town is getting up early in the mornings to travel to their next destination. Because many of Tuscany and Umbria's sights are open only in the morning and almost all close for *riposo* from noonish to 3 or 4pm, this wastes valuable sightseeing time. Try to do your traveling just after noon, when everything is closing up. There's often a last train before *riposo* to wherever you're going; if you're driving, you can enjoy great countryside vistas under the noonday sun.

Puccini's Birthplace (Casa Natale di Puccini)   This unpretentious house was the birthplace of one of Italy's greatest operatic composers, Giacomo Puccini (1858–1924). More than any other Italian town (except Milan, where opera is viewed with passion), Lucca celebrates the memory and achievements of Puccini, whose operas are enthusiastically performed every September during the Festival of Santa Croce. Puccini's house, near Piazza San Michele, contains the piano at which he composed *Turandot* and has several of his librettos, letters, objets d'art, and mementos.

Corte San Lorenzo 9 ℂ 0583-584028. Admission 2.50€ ($2.25). Closed Jan–Feb; Mar–May Tues–Sun 10am–1pm and 3–6pm; June–Sept daily 10am–6pm; Oct–Dec Tues–Sun 10am–1pm and 3–6pm.

SHOPPING

The sunny, scenic hills around Lucca have been famous since the days of the Romans for producing fabulous amber-colored olive oil. You won't have to look far to find it—every supermarket, butcher shop, and delicatessen in Lucca sells a huge variety, in glass or metal containers. But if you want to travel into the surrounding hills to check out the production of this heart-healthy product, two of the best-known companies selling their products on rustic Tuscan farms are **Maionchi,** Via Tofori 81, in the hamlet of Tofori (ℂ 0583-978194), 18km (11 miles) northeast of Lucca; and **Camigliano,** V. per Sant'Andrea 49 (ℂ 0583-490420), 10km (6¼ miles) northeast of Lucca. Reservations are recommended.

Take a stroll along the town's top shopping streets, **Via Fillungo** and **Via del Battistero.** The best gift/souvenir shops are **Insieme,** Via Vittorio Emanuele 70 (ℂ 0583-419649), and **Incontro,** Via Buia 9 (ℂ 0583-491225), which places a special emphasis on Lucca's rustically appealing porcelain, pottery, tiles, and crystal.

The best wine shop in town is the **Enoteca Vanni,** Piazza Salvatore 7 (ℂ 0583-491902; www.enotecavanni.com), with hundreds of bottles of local and Tuscan vintages.

If you're in town on the right weekend, check out the wonderful **antiques market.** (See "Special Events," near the beginning of this section.)

WHERE TO STAY

Hotel Villa La Principessa ✦✦   Across from the Locanda l'Elisa (see below), this hotel from 1320 is also luxurious but less expensive. It's 3km (2 miles) south of the city walls, beside a meandering highway with sharp turns and limited visibility, but sheltered by hedges and flowering trees. Lodging here is like staying in an antique, aristocratic Luccan private villa. Its former owner and one of the dukes of Lucca, Castruccio Castracani (1281–1328), may have been the role model for Machiavelli's Ideal Prince. Later, when the hills around Lucca were dotted with the homes of members of the Napoleonic court, the house was rebuilt in dignified 18th-century style. The guest rooms were renovated in 2000, and you'll find quality linen on the luxurious beds.

Via Nuova Per Pisa 1616, 55050 Massa Pisana (Lucca). ℂ 0583-370037. Fax 0583-379136. www.hotel principessa.com. 40 units. 195€–245€ ($174.15–$218.80) double; from 400€ ($357.20) suite. AE, DC, MC, V. Closed Nov–Mar. Free parking. Bus: 2. **Amenities:** Restaurant; bar; outdoor pool; jogging track; room service; massage; babysitting; laundry. *In room:* A/C, TV, dataport, minibar, hair dryer, safe.

Locanda L'Elisa ✦✦✦   This Relais & Châteaux member is the region's most elegant hotel, 3km (2 miles) south of the city walls. In the mid–19th century, it was the home of an army officer who was the intimate companion of Napoleon's sister Elisa, who lived across the road. Today, both lovers' villas are upscale hotels

(Elisa's is now the Hotel Villa La Principessa, above). Behind a dignified neo-classical facade, Locanda l'Elisa offers verdant gardens, a worthy collection of antiques, discreet service, and large, plush guest rooms.

Via Nuova per Pisa 1952, 55050 Massa Pisana (Lucca). ℂ **0583-379737.** Fax 0583-379019. www.lunet.it/aziende/locandaelisa. 10 units. 230€–270€ ($205.40–$241.10) double; 260€–415€ ($232.20–$370.60) junior suite. AE, DC, MC, V. Free parking. Bus: 2. **Amenities:** Fine conservatory-style restaurant (see below); bar; outdoor pool; room service; babysitting; laundry/dry cleaning. *In room:* A/C, TV, minibar, hair dryer, safe.

Piccolo Hotel Puccini (Value Your best bet within the city walls is this palace built in the 1400s, across from the house where Puccini was born (Puccini music often plays in the lobby). Right off Piazza San Michele and one of the most enchanting spots in Lucca, this little hotel is better than ever now that an energetic couple, Raffaella and Paolo, has taken over. Intimate and comfortable, the rooms are beautifully maintained, with freshly starched curtains, good beds, crisp linens, and tasteful furnishings. Some windows open onto the small square in front with a bronze statue of the great Puccini.

Via di Poggio 9, 55100 Lucca. ℂ **0583-55421.** Fax 0583-53487. www.hotelpuccini.com. 14 units. 80€ ($71.45) double. AE, DC, MC, V. Free parking nearby. **Amenities:** Bar; room service; babysitting; laundry. *In room:* TV, hair dryer, safe.

WHERE TO DINE

Don't forget to drop in at the **Antico Caffè di Simo,** Via Fillungo 58 (no phone), where Puccini used to come to eat and drink and perhaps dream about his next opera. At this historic cafe you can order the best gelato in town while taking in the old-time aura of faded mirrors, brass, and marble. The cafe is open Tuesday to Sunday 8am to 8pm.

Buca di Sant'Antonio ★★ TUSCAN On a difficult-to-find alley near Piazza San Michele, this is Lucca's finest restaurant. The 1782 building was constructed on the site of a chapel (Buca di Sant'Antonio). The cuisine is refined and inspired, respecting the traditional but also daring to be innovative. Menu items include homemade ravioli stuffed with ricotta and pulverized zucchini, pork ragout, codfish, and roast Tuscan goat with roast potatoes and braised greens. Try the house-special dessert, *semifreddo Buccellato* (partially melted ice cream with local red berries).

Via della Cervia 15. ℂ **0583-55881.** Reservations recommended. Main courses 12.50€–17.50€ ($11.15–$15.65). AE, DC, MC, V. Tues–Sun noon–3pm; Tues–Sat 7:30–11pm. Closed 1st week of July and last 2 weeks of Jan.

Da Giulio in Pelleria LUCCHESE This cavernous restaurant holds fast to local traditions and time-honored recipes, with dishes such as great minestrones, pastas, veal, hearty soups, and chicken dishes served in robust portions. Some regional dishes might be a little too adventurous for most North American tastes, such as *cioncia* (veal snout and herbs). New food items include a Lucchese specialty, *farinata,* a soup with a base of minestrone and white flour; cuttlefish with beets; sausages with beans; and a fabulous almond torte for dessert.

Via della Conce 45. ℂ 0583-55948. Reservations recommended. Main courses 7.50€–11€ ($6.70–$9.80). AE, DC, MC, V. Tues–Sat and 3rd Sun of the month noon–2:30pm and 7:15–10:15pm. Closed Christmas and New Year's Eve.

Giglio ★ REGIONAL/TUSCAN In regional appeal and popularity, this place is rivaled only by the Buca di Sant'Antonio (see above). The secret to its appeal might be its rustic decor (including 16th-c. architectural detailing), its attentive staff, and its fine interpretations of time-honored recipes. Menu items usually include steaming bowls of *minestra di farro,* homemade tortellini with meat sauce, dried codfish with chickpeas, stewed rabbit with olives, and *tortes* made from carrots or other vegetables or with a base of cream and chocolate.

Piazza del Giglio 2. ℂ **0583-494058.** Reservations recommended. Main courses 10€–17.50€ ($8.95–$15.65). AE, DC, MC, V. Thurs–Tues noon–3pm; Thurs–Mon 7:30–10:30pm. Closed Feb 1–15 and July 15–30.

Il Gazebo ★ ITALIAN/TUSCAN   Set in one of Tuscany's most elegant hotels, 3km (2 miles) south of Lucca's center, the restaurant is a re-creation of an English conservatory. The wraparound windows in the almost-circular room offer garden views. The service, as you'd expect in a Relais & Châteaux, is impeccable. Menu items include upscale versions of Luccan recipes, such as *farro Lucchese,* a red-bean soup with locally grown greens. Other dishes include steamed scampi with tomato sauce, smoked swordfish with grilled eggplant, and ravioli stuffed with herbed eggplant and served with prawn sauce. Each is prepared with refinement and skill. The chefs also serve vegetarian and low-cholesterol dishes.

In the Locanda l'Elisa, Via Nuova per Pisa 1952. ℂ **0583-379737.** Reservations recommended. Main courses 14€–20€ ($12.50–$17.85); fixed-price menu 45€–65€ ($40.20–$58.05). AE, DC, MC, V. Mon–Sat 12:30–2:30pm and 7:30–10:30pm. Bus: 2.

Trattoria da Leo TUSCAN   In this unpretentious family-run spot, almost no one speaks English (although there's a menu in English). This is a pleasant trattoria in a 16th-century building close to Piazza San Michele. The decor of the dining rooms (one large, one very small) is vaguely 1930s. The savory menu items include an array of pastas, most made fresh; *minestra di Farro* (vegetable soup with pasta); fried chicken with fresh seasonal greens; steamed chicken with polenta; at least three versions of codfish; and liver with wild fennel.

Via Tegrimi 1. ℂ **0583-492236.** Reservations recommended. Main courses 9€–12.50€ ($8.05–$11.15). No credit cards. Mon–Sat noon–2:30pm and 7:30–10:30pm (daily Dec 8–31 and Aug 6–31). Closed last of Dec.

4 Pisa ★★

76km (47 miles) W of Florence, 333km (206 miles) NW of Rome

Few buildings in the world have captured imaginations as much as the Leaning Tower of Pisa, the single most instantly recognizable building in all the Western world (except, perhaps, for the Eiffel Tower). Perhaps visitors are drawn to it as a symbol of the fragility of people—or at least the fragility of their work. The Leaning Tower is a powerful landmark (and it draws hordes of day-trippers every midday).

There's more to Pisa than meets the usual visitor's eye, however. There are other historic sights. And there's also the present: Go into the busy streets surrounding the university and the market, and you'll find a town resounding with the exuberance of its student population and its residents as they make the purchases of everyday life.

ESSENTIALS

GETTING THERE   Both domestic and international flights arrive at Pisa's **Galileo Galilei Airport** (ℂ **050-500707;** www.pisa-airport.com). From the airport, trains depart every 15 to 30 minutes, depending on the time of the day, for the 5-minute trip into Pisa (about 1€, 90¢ each way). As an alternative, bus no. 3 leaves the airport every 40 minutes for the city (about .75€, 65¢).

Trains link Pisa and Florence every 1½ hours for the 1-hour trip, costing 4€ ($3.55) one way. Trains running along the seacoast link Pisa with Rome and require about 3 hours travel time. Depending on the time of day and the speed of the train, one-way fares are 18.50€ to 50€ ($16.50–$44.65). In Pisa, trains arrive at the **Stazione Pisa Centrale,** Piazza Stazione (© **1478-88088** for information in Italy), about a 10- to 15-minute walk from the Leaning Tower. Otherwise, you can take bus no. 1 from the station to the heart of the city.

If you're **driving,** leave Florence by taking the autostrada west (A11) to the intersection (A12) going south to Pisa. Travel time is about an hour each way.

VISITOR INFORMATION   The **tourist office** is at Via Cammeo 2 (© **050-560464**), open April to September Monday to Saturday 9:30am to 7pm, and Sunday 10:30am to 2:30pm (the rest of the year Mon–Sat 9am–5pm, and Sun 10am–2pm). A second branch is at Piazza della Stazione (© **050-42291**), open April to September Monday to Saturday 9:30am to 7pm, and Sunday 9:30am to 1:30pm (the rest of the year Mon–Sat 9am–5pm, and Sun 9am–1pm).

SPECIAL EVENTS   On summer evenings, **free classical music concerts** are presented on the steps of the Duomo. Music aficionados from all over the world can be seen sprawled out on the lawn. Concerts are also presented in the Duomo, which is known for its phenomenal acoustics. The tourist office has details.

The best time to be in Pisa is the last Sunday in June, when Pisans stage their annual tug-of-war, the **Gioco del Ponte,** which revives some of their pomp and ceremony from the Middle Ages. Each quadrant of the city presents richly costumed parades. Also in June is the **Festa di San Ranieri,** when Pisans honor their patron saint by lining the Arno with torches on the 16th and then staging a boat race on the 17th.

SEEING THE SIGHTS

In the Middle Ages, Pisa reached the apex of its power as a maritime republic before falling to its rivals, Florence and Genoa. As is true of most cities at their zenith, Pisa turned to the arts and made contributions in sculpture and architecture. Its greatest legacy remains at **Piazza del Duomo,** where you'll find the top three attractions: the Duomo, the baptistry, and the campanile (that famous Leaning Tower).

A 6€ ($5.35) **combination ticket** (you can buy it at any of the included attractions) allows you to visit two of these three sights: the baptistry, the cemetery, and the Duomo Museum. For 9.50€ ($8.50), you can visit the five major attractions: the baptistry, the Duomo, the cemetery, the Duomo Museum, and the Museum of Preliminary Frescoes.

Leaning Tower of Pisa (Campanile) ✸✸✸   In 1174, Bonnano began construction of this eight-story marble campanile, intended as a free-standing bell tower for the Duomo (see below). A persistent legend is that he deliberately intended the tower to lean. Another legend is that Galileo let objects of different weights fall from the tower, timing their descent to prove his theories of bodies in motion. The real story is that the tower began to tilt some time after the completion of the first three stories; only then did its builders discover that the foundation wasn't rock solid, but was water-soaked clay. Construction was suspended for a century and was eventually resumed, with completion in the late 14th century. The tower currently leans at least 4m (14 ft.) from perpendicular. If it stood straight, it would measure about 55m (180 ft.) tall.

Pisa

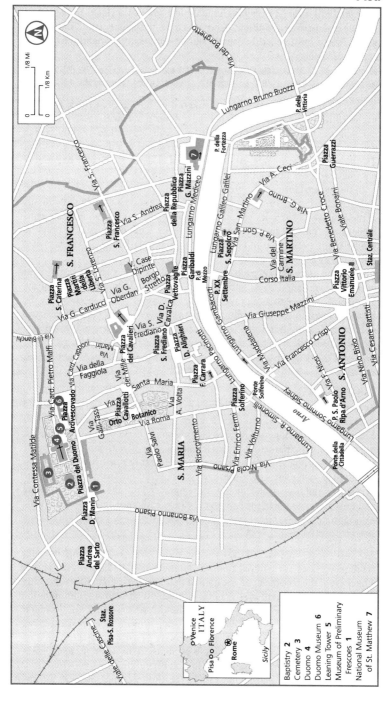

ITALY

Venice
Florence
Pisa
Rome
Sicily

Baptistry **2**
Cemetery **3**
Duomo **4**
Duomo Museum **6**
Leaning Tower **5**
Museum of Preliminary
Frescoes **1**
National Museum
of St. Matthew **7**

From 1990 until its reopening in 2001, the tower was closed to the public because of dangerous conditions. Since that time, to stabilize its tilt, tons of soil were removed from under the foundation, and lead counterweights were placed at the monument's base.

Piazza del Duomo 17. ℂ **050-560547.** Admission 15€ ($13.40). Phone for reservation, fax 050-560505, or use the Web at www.duomo.pisa.it. Only a group of 30 admitted at a time. Open daily 9am–4:20pm.

Il Duomo ✦✦ This cathedral was designed by Buschetto in 1063, although in the 13th century Rainaldo erected the unusual facade with its four layers of open-air arches diminishing in size as they ascend. It's marked by three bronze doors, rhythmic in line, that replaced those destroyed in a disastrous 1595 fire. The most artistic is the original south Door of St. Ranieri, the only one to survive the fire; it was cast by Bonnano Pisano in 1180.

In the restored interior, the chief treasure is the polygonal pulpit by Giovanni Pisano, finished in 1310. It was damaged in the fire and finally rebuilt (with bits of the original) in 1926. It's held up by porphyry pillars and column statues symbolizing the Virtues, and the relief panels depict biblical scenes. The pulpit is similar to an earlier one by Giovanni's father, Nicola Pisano, in the baptistry across the way.

There are other treasures too, including Galileo's lamp (which, according to unreliable tradition, the Pisa-born astronomer used to formulate his laws of the pendulum). At the entrance to the choir pier is a painting that appears to be the work of Leonardo but is actually *St. Agnes and Lamb,* in the High Renaissance style by the great Andrea del Sarto. In the apse you can view a 13th-century mosaic, *Christ Pancrator,* finished in 1302 by Cimabue (it survived the great fire).

Piazza del Duomo 17. ℂ **050-560547.** Admission 2€ ($1.80). Mar–Oct Mon–Sat 10am–8pm. Sightseeing visits are discouraged during masses and religious rites. Bus: 1.

Baptistry (Battistero) ✦✦✦ Begun in 1153, the baptistry is like a Romanesque crown. Its most beautiful feature is the exterior, with its arches and columns, but you should visit the interior to see the hexagonal pulpit (1255–60) by Nicola Pisano. Supported by pillars resting on the backs of three marble lions, the pulpit contains bas-reliefs of the Crucifixion, the Adoration of the Magi, the presentation of the Christ Child at the temple, and the Last Judgment (many angels have lost their heads over the years). Column statues represent the Virtues. At the baptismal font is a contemporary John the Baptist by a local sculptor. The echo inside the baptistry shell has enthralled visitors for years.

Piazza del Duomo. ℂ **050-560547.** Admission 5€ ($4.45). Apr–Sept daily 8am–8pm; Oct–Mar daily 9am–5pm. Closed Dec 25–Jan 1. Bus: 1.

Duomo Museum (Museo dell'Opera del Duomo) ✦✦ This museum exhibits works of art removed from the monumental buildings on the piazza. The heart of the collection, on the ground floor, consists of sculptures spanning the 11th to the 13th centuries. A notable treasure is an Islamic griffin from the 11th century, a bronze brought back from the Crusades as booty. For decades it adorned the cupola of the cathedral before being brought here for safekeeping. The most famous exhibit is the *Madonna and the Crucifix,* by Giovanni Pisano, carved from an ivory tusk in 1299. Also exhibited is the work of French goldsmiths, presented by Maria de' Medici to Archbishop Bonciani in 1616.

Upstairs are paintings from the 15th to the 18th centuries. Some of the textiles and embroideries date from the 15th century; another section of the museum is devoted to Egyptian, Etruscan, and Roman works. In the 19th century, Carlo Lasinio restored the Camposanto frescoes (see below) and made a series of etchings of each. These etchings were widely published, influencing the pre-Raphaelite artists of the time. When the Camposanto was bombed in 1944, the etchings were destroyed, but Lasinio's legacy provided an enduring record of what they were like.

Piazza Arcivescovado. ✆ **050-560547.** Admission 5€ ($4.45). Apr–Sept daily 8am–7:30pm; Oct–Mar daily 9am–5pm. Bus: 1.

Cemetery (Camposanto) ✸✸   This cemetery was designed by Giovanni di Simone in 1278, but a bomb hit it in 1944 and destroyed most of the famous frescoes that had covered the inside (the fresco sketches are displayed at the Museo delle Sinopie, below). Recently it has been partially restored. It's said that the crusaders shipped earth from Calvary here on Pisan ships (the city was a great port before the water receded). The cemetery is of interest because of its sarcophagi, statuary, and frescoes. One room contains three of the frescoes from the 14th century that were salvaged from the bombing: *The Triumph of Death,* *The Last Judgment,* and *The Inferno,* with the usual assortment of monsters, reptiles, and boiling caldrons. *The Triumph of Death* is the most interesting, with its flying angels and devils. In addition, you'll find lots of white-marble bas-reliefs, including Roman funerary sculpture.

Piazza del Duomo. ✆ **050-560547.** Admission 5€ ($4.45). Nov–Feb daily 9am–5pm; Mar and Oct daily 9am–6pm; Apr–Sept daily 8am–8pm. Bus: 1.

Museum of Preliminary Frescoes (Museo delle Sinopie) ✸   Next to the baptistry, this is a showcase for the *sinopie* (preliminary sketches or frescoes) that were discovered under the charred remnants of the badly damaged frescoes at the cemetery (see above). Before World War II, the finished frescoes were one of the major attractions of Tuscany, but they were mainly destroyed in a 1944 air raid. From the wreckage, Pisans discovered the preparatory sketches that the artists had created, which had been covered for centuries by the originals. The museum here also displays remnants of the finished frescoes, all rescued from the bomb site.

The museum is housed in medieval rooms of the New Hospital of Mercy (*Ospedale Nuovo della Misericordia*). The most interesting sketches are by Veneziano, Gaddi, and Traini, all from the 14th century. Displays also reveal how the fresco artists went about their work. In the 19th century, Carlo Lasinio made engravings of what the finished frescoes looked like, and these have been placed before the preliminary sketches to give you an idea of how the artists changed their conceptions along the way.

Piazza del Duomo. ✆ **050-560547.** Admission 5€ ($4.45). Apr–Sept daily 8am–8pm; Oct–Mar daily 9am–5pm. Closed Dec 25–Jan 1. Bus: 1.

Arsenale Medici ✸✸   One of Tuscany's most important new museums made its debut in 2000, in a 12th-century storehouse along the Arno that once housed weapons and other merchandise for the Medici. Today the high point of its collection is a series of 12 Roman wooden ships, one of which dates back to the 1st century B.C. (others are from the reigns of such emperors as the mighty Augustus).

The wooden ships, including an intact wooden warship, were discovered by construction workers digging to extend the San Rossore rail terminal in 1998. The find was heralded around the world, with some journalists calling it "a nautical Pompeii." In the 10th and 11th centuries, Pisa was a major port city until its waters were buried by silt in the 12th century. The shore now is some 5 miles to the west. Archaeologists believe that the ships were sunk in a flash flood. Much of the contents of the ships has been preserved, including clay vases—even wine some 20 centuries old. The contents of these rare finds, including personal paraphernalia and clothing of the sailors, are on display along with the ships.

Lungarno Simonelli. (C) 050-21441. Admission 2.50€ ($2.25). Tues–Sun 10am–1pm and 2–6pm.

National Museum of St. Matthew (Museo Nazionale di San Matteo) 🏛
This well-planned museum contains a good assortment of paintings and sculptures, many from the 13th to 16th centuries. You'll find statues by Giovanni Pisano; Simone Martini's *Madonna and Child with Saints,* a polyptych; Nino Pisano's *Madonna del Látte* (Madonna of the Milk), a marble sculpture; Masaccio's *St. Paul,* painted in 1426; Domenico Ghirlandaio's two *Madonna and Saints* depictions; and works by Strozzi and Alessandro Magnasco.

Piazzetta San Matteo 1 (near Piazza Mazzini). (C) 050-541865. Admission 4€ ($3.55). Tues–Sat 8:30am–7:30pm; Sun 8:30am–2pm. Bus: 1.

SHOPPING

On the second weekend of every month, an **antiques fair** fills the Ponte di Mezzo. Virtually everything from the Tuscan hills is for sale, from fresh virgin olive oil to what one dealer told us was the "original" *Mona Lisa* (not the one hanging in the Louvre).

If you're not in town for the antiques fair, head for **Piazza Vettovaglie,** just off Via Borgo Stretto, which has a market daily 7am to 1:30pm. You'll find everything from old clothing to fresh Tuscan food products. The market sprawls outside its boundaries, spilling onto Via Domenio Cavalca. You can skip the restaurants for lunch and eat here; an array of little trattorie will fill you up at an affordable price. You can also pick up the makings for a picnic to enjoy later in the Tuscan hillsides.

Intriguing stores line **Via Borgo Stretto,** an arcaded street where mimes and street performers often entertain the shoppers.

WHERE TO STAY

Hotel d'Azeglio   A safe nest for the night but not a lot more, this is an unremarkable first-class hotel near the rail station and the air terminal. It's viewed as the second best in town, at least by Michelin, but don't expect too much; competition in innkeeping isn't too keen in Pisa. There's a roof garden with a panoramic city view. The standard guest rooms are well maintained and comfortable, with small bathrooms.

Piazza Vittorio Emanuele II 18B, 56125 Pisa. (C) 050-500310. Fax 050-28017. www.pisaonline.it/hotel-dazeglio. 29 units. 121€–134€ ($108.05–$119.65) double. Rates include breakfast. AE, DC, MC, V. Parking 12€ ($10.70). **Amenities:** Bar; room service; babysitting; laundry. *In room:* A/C, TV, minibar, hair dryer, safe.

Jolly Hotel Cavalieri   A generic chain-run property that hosts lots of business travelers, this seven-story hotel opens onto a view of the train station and its piazza. The guest rooms are filled with time-worn furniture, fine mattresses, paneling, and lots of glass. The best ones are on the fifth floor because they have balconies with good views. Parking is often possible in the square in front of the station or in a nearby garage.

Piazza della Stazione 2, 56125 Pisa. (C) 800/221-2626 in the U.S., or 050-43290. Fax 050-502242. www.jollyhotels.it. 100 units. 152.50€–200€ ($136.20–$178.60) double. Rates include breakfast. AE, DC, MC, V. Parking 15€–20€ ($13.40–$17.85). **Amenities:** Restaurant; bar; room service; babysitting; laundry. *In room:* A/C, TV, dataport, minibar, hair dryer.

Royal Victoria ☆ *Finds*   This isn't Pisa's most luxurious hotel, but it's our favorite, thanks to its sense of history (it occupies several medieval towers and houses, and is Pisa's only inn of real character). Adjacent to the Arno and within walking distance of most of the jewels in Pisa's crown, it was opened in 1839 by ancestors (five generations ago) of the genteel manager, Nicola Piegaja, who runs the place with his brother and oversees the most helpful staff in town. The guest rooms are old-fashioned and well kept. The best accommodations are the three with balconies.

Lungarno Pacinotti 12, 56126 Pisa. © 050-940111. Fax 050-940180. www.royalvictoria.it. 48 units, 40 with private bathroom. 68€ ($60.70) double without bathroom; 102€ ($91.10) double with bathroom; 111€ ($99.10) triple with bathroom; 116€ ($103.60) quad with bathroom. Rates include breakfast. AE, DC, MC, V. Parking 15€ ($13.40). Bus: 3, 4, or 7. **Amenities:** Bar; room service; babysitting. *In room:* TV, hair dryer.

WHERE TO DINE

Al Ristoro dei Vecchi Macelli ☆ INTERNATIONAL/PISAN   This is Pisa's best and most formal restaurant, in a comfortably rustic 1930s building near Piazzetta di Vecchi Macelli. Locals claim that the cuisine is prepared with love, and they prove their devotion by returning frequently. After selecting from a choice of two dozen seafood antipasti, you can enjoy homemade pasta with scallops and zucchini, fish-stuffed ravioli in shrimp sauce, gnocchi with pesto and shrimp, or roast veal with velvety truffle-flavored cream sauce.

Via Volturno 49. © 050-20424. Reservations required. Main courses 10€–15€ ($8.95–$13.40); fixed-price menu 40€ ($35.70). AE, DC, MC, V. Mon–Tues and Thurs–Sun noon–3pm and 8–10:30pm. Bus: 1.

Antica Trattoria Da Bruno PISAN   For around half a century, Da Bruno has flourished in this spot near the Leaning Tower. It's one of Pisa's finest restaurants, although it charges moderate tabs. It serves old-fashioned but market-fresh dishes of the Pisan kitchen, including hare with pappardelle, *zuppa alla paesana* (thick vegetable soup), and *baccalà con porri* (codfish with leeks and tomatoes). Some new specialties have appeared on the menu, such as *zuppa pisana* (minestrone with black cabbage) and wild boar with olives and polenta.

Via Luigi Bianchi 12. © 050-560818. Reservations recommended for dinner. Main courses 11€–17.50€ ($9.80–$15.65). AE, DC, MC, V. Mon noon–2:30pm; Wed–Sun noon–3pm and 7–10:30pm. Bus: 2, 3, or 4.

Emilio PISAN/ITALIAN   Because of its well-prepared food and its proximity to Piazza del Duomo, this place is always packed. Inside, a large high window, similar to what you'd find in a church, filters light down upon the brick-walled interior. The menu features a fresh assortment of antipasti, spaghetti with clams, risotto with mushrooms, fish dishes such as *branzini à l'Isolana* (oven-baked with tomatoes and vegetables), and Florentine beefsteaks. In season, try one of the game dishes with polenta. Grilled fish is always perfectly prepared. The chef's dessert specialty is *crema limoncello,* a mousse prepared with limoncello liqueur.

Via Cammeo 44. © 050-562141. Reservations recommended. Main courses 10€–17.50€ ($8.95–$15.65); fixed-price menu 9€–20€ ($8.05–$17.85). AE, DC, MC, V. Sat–Thurs noon–3:30pm and 7–10:30pm. Bus: 1.

5 San Gimignano: The Manhattan of Tuscany ☆☆☆

42km (26 miles) NW of Siena, 52km (32 miles) SW of Florence

This gem of the Middle Ages is called the Manhattan of Tuscany because it preserves 13 of its noble towers, giving it a "skyscraper" skyline. The approach to the walled town is dramatic today, but once it must have been fantastic: In the heyday of the Guelph and Ghibelline conflict, **San Gimignano** (aka San Gimignano delle Belle Torri/San Gimignano of the Beautiful Towers) had as many as 72 towers. Its fortresslike severity is softened by the subtlety of its harmonious squares, and many of its palaces and churches are enhanced by Renaissance frescoes because San Gimignano could afford to patronize major painters.

But despite its beauty and authenticity, the town is just packed with tourists during the day in the high season. Stay overnight, if you can, so that you can enjoy the late afternoon or early evening and get a sense of the town without the crowds. Go to one of the tasting rooms for a sample of the famous Vernaccia, the light white wine bottled in the region.

ESSENTIALS

GETTING THERE   The **rail station** nearest to San Gimignano is at Poggibonsi, serviced by regular trains from Florence and Siena. At Poggibonsi, buses depart from the front of the rail station at frequent intervals, charging 1.30€ ($1.15) each way to the center of San Gimignano. For information, call ℂ **0577-933646.**

Buses operated by TRA-IN (ℂ **0577-204111**) service San Gimignano from Florence with a change at Poggibonsi (trip time: 75 min.); the one-way fare is 7€ ($6.25). TRA-IN also operates service from Siena, with a change at Poggibonsi (trip time: 50 min.); the one-way fare is 6.50€ ($5.80). In San Gimignano, buses stop at Piazzale Montemaggio, outside the Porta San Giovanni, the southern gate. You'll have to walk into the center because vehicles aren't allowed in most of the town's core.

If you have a **car,** leave Florence (1½ hr.) or Siena (1 hr., 10 min.) by the Firenze-Siena autostrada and drive to Poggibonsi, where you'll need to cut west along a secondary route (S324) to San Gimignano. There are parking lots outside the city walls.

VISITOR INFORMATION   The **Associazione Pro Loco,** Piazza del Duomo 1 (ℂ **0577-940008**), is open daily: November to February 9am to 1pm and 3 to 6pm, and March to October 9am to 1pm and 3 to 7pm.

EXPLORING THE TOWN

In the town center is the **Piazza della Cisterna,** so named because of the 13th-century cistern in its heart. Connected with the irregularly shaped square is its satellite, **Piazza del Duomo** 🟅🟅, whose medieval architecture of towers and palaces is almost unchanged. It's the most beautiful spot in town. On the square, the **Palazzo del Popolo** 🟅 was designed in the 13th century, and its **Torre Grossa,** built a few years later, is believed to have been the tallest "skyscraper" (about 178 ft. high) in town (see the entry for the Civic Museum below for information on how to climb this tower).

One **combination ticket,** available at any of the sites below, allows admission to all of them for 10€ ($8.95) for adults and 9€ ($8.05) for children and students under 18.

Duomo Collegiata o Basilica di Santa Maria Assunta 🟅   Residents of
San Gimignano still call this a Duomo (cathedral), even though it was demoted to a "Collegiata" after the town lost its bishop. Don't judge this book by its cover, though: It might be plain and austere on the outside, dating from the 12th century, but it is richly decorated inside. Actually, the facade was never finished, for some reason.

To escape the burning Tuscan sun, retreat inside to a world of tiger-striped arches and a galaxy of gold stars. Head for the north aisle, where in the 1360s Bartolo di Fredi depicted scenes from the Old Testament. Two memorable ones

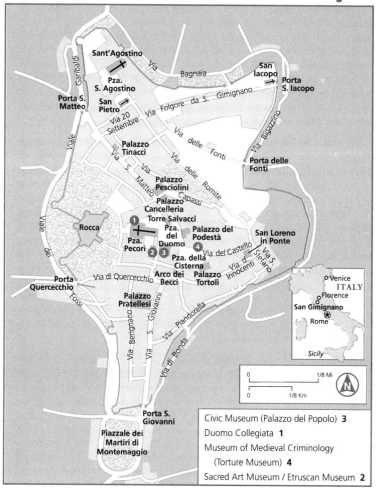

San Gimignano

Sant'Agostino
Pza. S. Agostino
Via Bagnaia
San Iacopo
Porta S. Iacopo
Porta S. Matteo
San Pietro
Via 20 Settembre
Via Folgore da S. Gimignano
Via delle Fonti
Via Bigazzino
Palazzo Tinacci
Via S. Matteo
Via delle Romite
Porta delle Fonti
Palazzo Pesciolini
Capassi
Palazzo Cancelleria
Torre Salvacci
Rocca
Pza. del Duomo
Palazzo del Podestà
San Loreno in Ponte
Pza. Pecori
Via del Castello
Pza. della Cisterna
Via d' Innocenti
Via S. Stefano
Arco dei Becci
Palazzo Tortoli
Porta Quercecchio
Via di Quercecchio
Fossi
Palazzo Pratellesi
Via S. Giovanni
Via Piandorella
Via di Bonda
Via Bergnano
Viale Garibaldi
Viale dei

Venice
ITALY
Florence
San Gimignano
Rome
Sicily

0   1/8 Mi
0   1/8 Km

N

Porta S. Giovanni
Piazzale dei Martiri di Montemaggio

Civic Museum (Palazzo del Popolo) **3**
Duomo Collegiata **1**
Museum of Medieval Criminology
(Torture Museum) **4**
Sacred Art Museum / Etruscan Museum **2**

are *The Trials of Job* and *Noah with the Animals.* Other outstanding works by this artist are in the lunettes off the north aisle, including a medieval view of the cosmography of the Creation. In the right aisle, panels trace scenes from the life of Christ: the kiss of Judas, the Last Supper, the Flagellation, and the Crucifixion. Seek out Bartolo's horrendous *Last Judgment,* one of the most perverse paintings in Italy. Abandoning briefly his rosy-cheeked Sienese Madonnas, he depicted distorted and suffering nudes, shocking at the time.

The chief attraction here is the **Chapel of Santa Fina (Cappella Santa Fina),** designed by Giuliano and Benedetto da Maiano. Michelangelo's fresco teacher, Domenico Ghirlandaio, frescoed it with scenes from the life of a local girl, Fina, who became the town's patron saint. Her deathbed scene is memorable. According to accounts of the day, the little girl went to the well for water and accepted an orange from a young swain. When her mother scolded her for her wicked ways, she was so mortified that she prayed for the next 5 years, until St. Anthony called her to heaven.

Spend a few minutes in the small **Sacred Art Museum/Etruscan Museum (Museo d'Arte Sacra/Museo Etrusco),** to the left of the Duomo (enter from Piazza Pecori and an arch to the left of the Duomo's entrance). Its medieval tombstones, wooden sculptures, and Etruscan artifacts prove that the city's roots run deeper than the Middle Ages. It's open April to October daily from 9:30am to 7:30pm; November to March, it's open Tuesday to Sunday from 9:30am to 5pm. Admission is 3.50€ ($3.15).

Piazza del Duomo. ℂ 0577-940316. Church free; chapel 3€ ($2.70) adults, free for children 5 and under. Mar–Oct daily 9:30am–7pm; Nov–Feb Mon–Sat 9:30am–5pm and Sun 1–5pm.

Civic Museum (Museo Civico) ✿   This museum is installed upstairs in the *Palazzo del Popolo* (town hall). Most notable is the **Dante Salon (Sala di Dante),** where the poet supporter of the White Guelph spoke out for his cause in 1300. Look for one of the masterpieces of San Gimignano: *La Maestà* (a Madonna enthroned), by Lippo Memmi (later touched up by Gozzoli). The first large room upstairs contains the other masterpiece: a *Madonna in Glory,* with Sts. Gregory and Benedict, painted by Pinturicchio. On the other side of it are two depictions of the *Annunciation,* by Filippino Lippi. On the opposite wall, note the magnificent Byzantine Crucifix by Coppo di Marcovaldo.

Passing through the Museo Civico, you can scale the **Torre Grossa** and be rewarded with a bird's-eye view of this most remarkable town. The tower, the only one you can climb, is open during the same hours as the museum. Admission is 4€ ($3.55) for adults and 3€ ($2.70) for students under 18 and children.

In the Palazzo del Popolo, Piazza del Duomo 1. ℂ 0577-990312. Admission 3.50€ ($3.15). Mar–Oct daily 9:30am–7:30pm; Nov–Feb Tues–Sun 10am–6pm.

Museum of Medieval Criminology (Museo di Criminologia Medioevale)   This bizarre place is also known as the Torture Museum. In this Tuscan chamber of horrors, some of the most horrendous instruments of torture are on display. In case you don't know just how the devices worked, descriptions are provided in English. The museum has a definite political agenda (including some pointed commentary on the continued use of capital punishment in the United States). The exhibits, such as cast-iron chastity belts, reveal some of the sexism inherently involved in torture devices, with the revelation that many have been updated for use around the world today, from Africa to South America. These include the garrote, that horror of the Inquisition trials of the 1400s. Fittingly enough, this chilling sight is housed in what locals call the *Torre del Diavolo* (Devil's Tower).

Via del Castello 1. ℂ 0577-942243. Admission 7.50€ ($6.70); free for children under 6. Apr–Oct daily 10am–8pm; off-season daily 10am–6pm.

WHERE TO STAY

You can learn about additional choices and see pictures of all the hotels by pointing your Web browser to www.sangimignano.com.

Hotel Bel Soggiorno *Value*   This hotel, though no longer the town's best, is still a good affordable alternative. The Gigli family has run it since 1886 (there's not as much old-fashioned charm as you'd think, though). The rear guest rooms and dining room open onto the lower pastureland and the bottom of the village. The medium-size rooms have cheap, functional furniture and beds verging on the oversoft, but the management is quite friendly. The best 10 rooms are those with private balconies. In summer, you'll be asked to take your meals at the hotel (no great hardship because the cuisine is excellent). The medieval-style dining room boasts murals depicting a wild boar hunt (see "Where to Dine," below).

Via San Giovanni 91, 53037 San Gimignano. ℂ **0577-940375.** Fax 0577-907521. www.hotelbel soggiorno.it. 22 units. 93€–120€ ($83.05–$107.15) double; 145€–155€ ($129.50–$138.40) suite. AE, DC, MC, V. Parking 10€ ($8.95). Closed Jan–Feb. **Amenities:** Recommended restaurant (see below); wine cellar; babysitting; laundry. *In room:* A/C, TV.

Hotel Leon Bianco ⭐

This restored 11th-century villa is San Gimignano at its best—the front rooms look out over medieval Piazza della Cisterna, and the rear rooms have a sweeping view of the Elsa Valley. The guest rooms are all different (one is rustically romantic, with vaulted ceilings and alcoves of rough brick) and range from small to medium, with tidy bathrooms. The sunny roof terrace is a good place to order breakfast or relax.

Piazza della Cisterna, 53037 San Gimignano. ℂ **0577-941294.** Fax 0577-942123. www.leonbianco.com. 21 units (some with shower only). 85€–112.50€ ($75.90–$100.45) double. Rates include breakfast. AE, DC, MC, V. Parking 10€ ($8.95). **Amenities:** Room service; laundry/dry cleaning. *In room:* A/C, TV, minibar, safe.

Hotel Pescille

This hotel conveys a sense of sleepy rural Tuscany, and although the blasé staff sometimes draws complaints, you might appreciate the tranquility. About 2 miles from town, it's surrounded by vineyards and olive trees. The guest rooms are outfitted in an old-time style, often with countryside views. All are comfortable and charming, but the most striking is the Tower Room, overlooking San Gimignano's towers. Only 16 rooms have balconies.

Località Pescille, 53037 San Gimignano. ℂ **0577-940186.** Fax 0577-943165. www.pescille.it. 50 units (showers only). 95€–100€ ($84.85–$89.30) double; 147.50€–155€ ($131.70–$138.40) suite. Rates include breakfast. AE, DC, MC, V. Closed Nov to mid-Mar. Head 2 miles north of San Giminiano, following the signs to Castel S. Giminiano and Volterra. **Amenities:** Bar; 2 pools; tennis court; room service; babysitting. *In room:* A/C, TV, minibar, hair dryer (in some).

La Collegiata ⭐⭐⭐

Outside of town and surrounded by a park of Tuscan cypresses, this elegant, refined choice is today the finest accommodation in the San Gimignano area, even surpassing Relais Santa Chiara (see below). The villa dates from 1587, when it housed Franciscan Cappuccini fathers. The red-brick Renaissance structure has been beautifully converted to receive guests, who live here far better than those monks. You can walk to the building through a beautifully planted Italian garden. After checking in, you can go for a dip in an open-air swimming pool and enjoy the Tuscan landscape so beloved by painters. The cloister opens into the reception area, a wine bar, a coffee shop, sitting rooms, and a reading room. Bedrooms are beautifully furnished, often with such decorative touches as mullioned windows or small balconies. Most of those on the first floor open onto the inner courtyard. The master bedroom in the tower offers a large Jacuzzi opening onto a scenic sweep of the valley. You dine under the Roman vaulting of an ancient chapel decorated in the red so evocative of the Renaissance in Sienna.

Località Strada 27, 53037 San Gimignano. ℂ **0577-943201.** Fax 0577-940566. www.lacollegiata.it/indexe.html. 20 units. 310€–415€ ($276.85–$370.60) double; 360€–465€ ($321.50–$415.25) junior suite. AE, MC, V. Free parking. **Amenities:** Restaurant; wine bar; coffee shop; pool; room service; babysitting; laundry/dry cleaning. *In room:* A/C, TV, minibar, hair dryer, safe.

L'Antico Pozzo ⭐⭐

This is the top inn within the historic walls, a 15th-century palazzo converted to a hotel in 1990. It has a medieval atmosphere and lovely antique touches, yet it provides all the modern comforts (you'll even have Internet access here). Accommodations vary in size and decor, but none is small.

Throughout, the furnishings are 19th-century wooden pieces, and the firm beds have cast-iron frames. "Superior" doubles have 17th-century ceiling frescoes, the smaller "standard" rooms on the third floor have wood floors and a view of the Rocca and a few towers, and the other rooms overlook the street or the rear terrace, where breakfast is served in summer.

Via San Matteo 87, 53037 San Gimignano (near Porta San Matteo). © **0577-942014.** Fax 0577-942117. www.anticopozzo.com. 18 units (some with shower only). 119€ ($106.25) double; 150€ ($133.95) junior suite. Rates include breakfast. AE, DC, MC, V. Parking 12.50€ ($11.15) in nearby garage or lot. Closed Feb. **Amenities:** Room service; babysitting; laundry/dry cleaning. *In room:* A/C, TV, minibar, hair dryer, safe.

Relais Santa Chiara 🌟🌟 This comfortable, upscale hotel lies in a residential neighborhood about a 10-minute walk south of the medieval ramparts. It's surrounded by elegant gardens, and its spacious public rooms contain Florentine terra-cotta floors and mosaics. The guest rooms are furnished in precious brierwood and walnut. Some enjoy views of the countryside; others overlook the hotel's garden. There's no restaurant, but the hotel serves a buffet breakfast and lunchtime snacks in summer.

Via Matteotti 15, 53037 San Gimignano. © **0577-940701.** Fax 0577-942096. www.rsc.it. 41 units (some with shower only). 108€–180€ ($96.45–$160.70) double; 160€–240€ ($142.90–$214.30) suite. Rates include buffet breakfast. AE, DC, MC, V. Free parking. **Amenities:** Bar; pool; room service; babysitting; laundry/dry cleaning. *In room:* A/C, TV, minibar, hair dryer, safe.

WHERE TO DINE

San Gimignano produces its own white wine, **Vernaccia.** You'll find one of the widest selections in town, as well as samplings of Chianti from throughout Tuscany, at **Da Gustavo,** Via San Matteo 29 (© **0577-940057**), which is run by the Beccuci family and has been thriving here since 1946. There's an informal stand-up bar where you can order by the glass. If you don't see what you're looking for on the shelves, ask—someone will probably haul it out from a storeroom the moment you mention its name.

Ristorante Bel Soggiorno TUSCAN   Its windows and terrace overlook the countryside, and its kitchen uses only fresh ingredients from nearby farms. Two of the most appealing specialties (available only late summer to late winter) are roasted wild boar with red wine and mixed vegetables, and pappardelle pasta, garnished with a savory ragout of pheasant. Other pastas are pappardelle with roasted hare, and risotto with herbs and seasonal vegetables. The main courses stress vegetable garnishes and thin-sliced meats that are simply but flavorfully grilled over charcoal, and breads are homemade and baked on-site. Many dishes hark back to medieval recipes.

In the Hotel Bel Soggiorno, Via San Giovanni 91. © **0577-940375.** Reservations recommended. Main courses 14€–16€ ($12.50–$14.30); fixed-price menu 36€ ($32.15). AE, DC, MC, V. Thurs–Tues 12:30–2:30pm and 7:30–10pm.

Ristorante Le Terrazze TUSCAN   One of this restaurant's two dining rooms boasts stones laid in the 1300s, and the other offers lots of rustic accessories and large windows overlooking the old town and the Val d'Elsa. The food features an assortment of produce from nearby farms. The soups and pastas make fine beginnings, and specialties of the house include delectable items such as sliced filet of wild boar with polenta and Chianti, goose breast with walnut sauce, *zuppa San Gimignanese* (a hearty minestrone), *vitello alla Cisterna* (veal) with buttered beans, Florentine-style steaks, and *risotto con funghi porcini.* A

superb dessert is a local sweet wine, vin santo, accompanied by an almond biscuit called a *cantucci.*

In La Cisterna, Piazza della Cisterna 24. ⓒ **0577-940328.** Reservations required. Main courses
12.50€–19€ ($11.15–$16.95). AE, DC, MC, V. Wed 7:30–10pm; Thurs–Mon 12:30–2:30pm and
7:30–9:30pm. Closed Jan 7–Mar 10.

EN ROUTE TO SIENA

Traveling from San Gimignano to Siena, you can take S324 east to Poggibonsi
and then turn south on S2, following the path of the ancient Roman highway
Via Cassia, now a little-traveled byway into Siena. Not only will you avoid the
heavily trafficked autostrada, but also you'll absorb more of the history, architecture, and geography of the region, taking in the sight of its hillside vineyards,
ancient walled villages, and historic tales of struggle. On SS323, 16km (10
miles) north of Siena, is the town of **Monteriggioni,** built as a Sienese lookout
fortress to guard against attack by the Florentines in 1213. The original walls are
still intact and contain the 14 towers that once gave it an imposing skyline,
looming up out of the wild, a symbol of Sienese might. A stop here will take you
back in time, wandering the streets of a village little changed after more than
700 years of civilization.

6 Siena ✶✶✶

34km (21 miles) S of Florence, 230km (143 miles) NW of Rome

After visiting Florence, it's altogether fitting, and certainly bipartisan, to call on
the city that in the past has been labeled its natural enemy. In Rome you see classicism and the baroque, and in Florence you see the Renaissance; but in the
walled city of Siena, you're transported back to the Middle Ages. Spread over
three sienna-colored hills in Tuscany's center, Sena Vetus lies in Chianti country.
Perhaps preserving its original character more markedly than any other city in
Italy, it's even today a showplace of the Italian Gothic.

Regrettably, Siena is too often visited on a quick day trip. But those who tarry
find that it is a city of contemplation and profound exploration, characterized
by Gothic palaces, almond-eyed Madonnas, aristocratic mansions, letter-writing
St. Catherine (patron saint of Italy), narrow streets, and medieval gates, walls,
and towers.

We're almost grateful that Siena lost its battle with Florence, although such a
point of view might be heretical. Had it continued to expand and change after
reaching the zenith of its power in the 14th century, it would be markedly different today, influenced by the rising tides of the Renaissance and the baroque
(which are represented here only in a small degree). But Siena retained its
uniqueness; in fact, certain Sienese painters were still showing the influence of
Byzantium in the late 15th century.

The university (founded in 1240) is still a major force in the town, and the
conversation you'll overhear between locals in the streets is the purest Italian
dialect in the country. However, you might have to wait until evening because
most residents retreat into the seclusion of their homes during the days full of
tour buses. They emerge to reclaim the cafes and squares at night, when most
visitors have gone. In a nod to its reputation as a commercial leader during the
Middle Ages, you can convert your dollars to euros at the **Monte dei Paschi,** the
oldest bank in the world.

The Palio: A Spectacle of the Middle Ages

Each year on July 2 and again on August 16, Siena comes alive in the intense, colorful **Palio delle Contrade,** part historical pageant and part horse race. Each bareback-riding jockey represents a *contrada* (one of the 17 wards into which the city is divided), and each is identified by its characteristic colors. The race, which requires tremendous skill, takes place on Piazza del Campo in the historic heart of the city. Before the race, much pageantry parades by, with colorfully costumed men and banners evoking the 15th century. The flag-throwing ceremony takes place at this time. Just as enticing is the victory celebration. All the pomp and ritual of the Middle Ages lives again.

Three days before the big race, trial races are held, with the final trial taking place on the morning of the event. There might be 17 contrade, but because Piazza del Campo holds only 10, the wards are chosen by lot. Young partisans, flaunting the colors of their contrada, race through the medieval streets in packs. Food and wine are bountiful on the streets of each contrada on the eve of the race.

The event could easily be considered all in good fun, but locals take it deadly seriously. There have been kidnappings of the most skilled jockeys, and bribery is commonplace. Jockeys have been known to unseat the competition, although a riderless horse is allowed to win. The event has been cited for its cruelty because horses are sometimes impaled by guardrails along the track, and jockeys have been caught on camera kicking the horses. In theory, riders are supposed to alternate whip strokes between their mounts and their competitors.

One Sienese who has attended 30 Palios has said, "Winning, not sportsmanship, is the only thing that's important. There are rules, but we Italians never bother to worry about rules. Instead of a horse race, you might call the event a rat race."

Don't buy expensive tickets for the day of the Palio. It's free—and a lot more fun—to stand in the middle of the square. Just get to Piazza del Campo *very early*—and bring a book and some refreshments because you'll be trapped there for hours. The square will soon become impossibly crowded, and the temperature can range from rainy and cold to blistering hot. If it's a sunny day, it's a good idea to bring some sort of head covering because most of the viewing area isn't shaded. For a memorable dinner and a lot of fun, join one of the 17 contrade holding a *cena* (supper) outdoors the night before the race. (You're likely to be invited by the first local you befriend. But while visitors are welcome, this is an event that's truly for the Sienese.)

ESSENTIALS

GETTING THERE   The **rail** link between Siena and Florence is sometimes inconvenient because you often have to change and wait at other stations, such as Empoli. But trains run every hour from Florence, costing 4.25€ ($3.80) one way. You arrive at the station at **Piazza Fratelli Rosselli** (© **0577-280115**).

This is an awkward half-hour climb uphill to the monumental heart; however, bus nos. 2, 4, 6, or 10 will take you to Piazza Gramsci near the center.

TRA-IN, Piazza San Domenico 1 (© **0577-204245**), offers bus service from all of Tuscany in air-conditioned coaches. The one-way fare between Florence and Siena is 6€ ($5.35). The trip takes 1¼ hours (actually faster than taking the train, and you'll be let off in the city center).

If you have a **car,** head south from Florence along the Firenze-Siena autostrada, a superhighway linking the two cities, going through Poggibonsi. (It has no route number; just follow the green autostrada signs for Siena.)

Trying to drive into the one-way and pedestrian-zoned labyrinth that is the city center just isn't worth the headache. Siena's parking (© **0577-22871**) is now coordinated, and all the lots charge 1.25€ ($1.10) per hour or 23.75€ ($21.20) per day (although almost every hotel has a discount deal with the nearest lot for anywhere from 40%–100% off). Lots are well-signposted, just inside several of the city gates.

VISITOR INFORMATION   The **tourist office** is at Piazza del Campo 56 (© **0577-280551**). It's open Monday to Saturday 8:30am to 7:30pm, Sunday 9am to 3pm. The office will give you a good free map.

EXPLORING THE MEDIEVAL CITY

There's much to see here. We'll start in the heart of Siena, the shell-shaped **Piazza del Campo** ✰✰✰, described by Montaigne as "the finest of any city in the world." Pause to enjoy the **Fonte Gaia,** which locals sometimes call the Fountain of Joy because it was inaugurated to great jubilation throughout the city, with embellishments by Jacopo della Quercia (the present sculptured works are reproductions—the badly beaten-up original ones are found in the town hall). The square is truly stunning, designed like a sloping scallop shell; you'll want to linger in one of the cafes along its edge.

Civic Museum (Museo Civico) & Torre del Mangia ✰✰✰   The Museo Civico, housed in the Palazzo Pubblico (1288–1309), is filled with important artworks by some of the leaders in the Sienese school of painting and sculpture.

In the **Globe Room (Sala del Mappomondo)** is Simone Martini's earliest-known work (ca. 1315) and his masterpiece, *La Maesta* ✰✰, the Madonna enthroned with her child, surrounded by angels and saints. The other remarkable Martini fresco (on the opposite wall) is the equestrian portrait of Guidoriccio da Fogliano, general of the Sienese Republic, in ceremonial dress.

The next room is the **Peace Room (Sala della Pace),** frescoed from 1337 to 1339 by Ambrogio Lorenzetti; the frescoes, perhaps the single most important piece of secular art to survive from medieval Europe, compose the **Allegory of Good and Bad Government and Their Effects on the Town and Countryside** ✰✰✰. In this depiction, the most notable figure of the Virtues surrounding the king is *La Pace* (Peace). To the right of the king and the Virtues is a representation of Siena in peaceful times. On the left, Lorenzetti showed his opinion of "ward heelers," but some of the sting has inadvertently been taken out of the frescoes because the evil-government scene is badly damaged. (Actually, these were propaganda frescoes in their day, commissioned by the party in power, but they're now viewed as among the most important of all secular frescoes to come down from the Middle Ages.)

Accessible from the courtyard of the Palazzo Pubblico is the **Torre del Mangia,** the most prominent architectural landmark on the skyline of Siena. Dating from the 14th century, it soars to a height of 102m (335 ft.). The tower takes its name from a former bell-ringer, a sleepy fellow called *mangiagaudagni* ("eat the profits"). Surprisingly, it has no subterranean foundations. If you climb this needlelike tower (more than 500 steps!), you'll be rewarded with a drop-dead gorgeous view of the red-tile roofs of the city and the surrounding Tuscan landscape. In the Middle Ages, this was Italy's second-tallest tower (Cremona has Siena beat). The tower is open the same hours as the Civic Museum and charges 3.50€ ($3.15) for you to climb it.

In the Palazzo Pubblico, Piazza del Campo. ℂ **0577-292263.** Admission 9€ ($8.05). Mid-Mar to Oct daily 10am–7pm; Nov to mid-Mar daily 10am–5pm. Bus: A, B, or N.

Il Duomo 🏵🏵🏵   At Piazza del Duomo, southwest of Piazza del Campo, stands an architectural fantasy. With its colored bands of marble, the Sienese Duomo is an original and exciting building, erected in the Romanesque and Italian Gothic styles in the 12th century. The dramatic facade, designed in part by Giovanni Pisano, dates from the 13th century, as does the Romanesque campanile.

The zebralike interior of black-and-white stripes is equally stunning. The floor consists of various inlaid works of art depicting both biblical and mythological subjects (many are roped off to preserve the richness in design). Numerous artists worked on the floor, notably Domenico Beccafumi. The octagonal 13th-century **pulpit** 🏵🏵🏵 is by Nicola Pisano (Giovanni's father), one of the most significant Italian sculptors before the dawn of the Renaissance. The Siena pulpit is his masterpiece; it reveals in relief such scenes as the slaughter of the innocents and the Crucifixion. The elder Pisano finished the pulpit in 1268, aided by his son and others. Its pillars are supported by four marble lions, reminiscent of the Pisano pulpit at Pisa.

In the chapel of the left transept (near the library) is a glass box containing an arm that tradition maintains is the one John the Baptist used to baptize Christ; the box also contains Donatello's bronze of John the Baptist. To see another Donatello work in bronze (a bishop's grave marker), look at the floor in the chapel to the left of the pulpit's stairway. Some of the designs for the inlaid wooden stalls in the apse are by Riccio. A representational blue starry sky twinkles overhead.

Inside the Duomo is the **Piccolomini Library** 🏵🏵, founded by Cardinal Francesco Piccolomini (later Pius III) to honor his uncle (Pius II); the library is renowned for its cycle of frescoes by the Umbrian master Pinturicchio. His frescoes are well preserved, although they date from the early 16th century. In Vasari's words, the panels illustrate "the history of Pope Pius II from birth to the minute of his death." Raphael's alleged connection with the frescoes, if any, is undocumented. In the center is an exquisite *Three Graces,* a Roman copy of a 3rd-century B.C. Greek work from the school of Praxiteles.

Piazza del Duomo. ℂ **0577-283048.** Duomo free; library 1.50€ ($1.35). Duomo Nov–Mar 15 daily 8am–1pm and 2:30–5pm (Mar 16–Oct to 7:30pm). Library Mar 15–Oct 31 daily 9am–7:30pm; Nov 1–Mar 14 daily 10am–1pm and 2:30–5pm. Closed Sun mornings, Jan 1, and Dec 25. Bus: A.

Baptistry (Battistero) 🏵   The Gothic facade was left unfinished by Domenico di Agostino in 1355. But you don't come here to admire that—you come for the frescoes inside, many of which are lavish and intricate and devoted mainly to depictions of the lives of Christ and St. Anthony.

The star of the place, however, is a **baptismal font** (1417–30), one of the greatest in all Italy. The foremost sculptors of the early Renaissance, from both

Central Siena

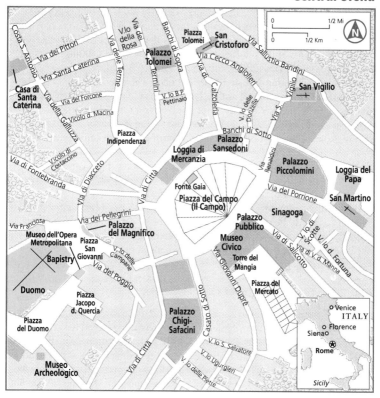

Florence and Siena, helped create this masterpiece. Jacopo della Quercia created *Annunciation to Zacharias,* Giovanni di Turino crafted *Preaching of the Baptist* and the *Baptism of Christ,* and Lorenzo Ghiberti worked with Giuliano di Ser Andrea on the masterful *Arrest of St. John.* Our favorite is Donatello's *Feast of Herod,* a work of profound beauty and perspective.

Piazza San Giovanni (behind the Duomo). ℂ **0577-283048.** Admission 2€ ($1.80). Apr–Sept daily 9am–7:30pm; Oct daily 9am–6pm; Nov–Mar daily 10:30am–1pm and 2–5pm. Closed Jan 1 and Dec 25. Bus: A.

Duomo Museum (Museo dell'Opera Metropolitana) ★★ This museum houses paintings and sculptures created for the Duomo. On the ground floor is much interesting sculpture, including works by Giovanni Pisano and his assistants. But the real draw hangs on the next floor: Duccio's fragmented *La Maestà* ★★ (1308–11), a Madonna enthroned, one of Europe's greatest late-medieval paintings. The majestic panel was an altarpiece by Duccio di Buonin-segna for the cathedral, filled with dramatic moments illustrating the story of Christ and the Madonna. A student of Cimabue, Duccio was the first great name in the school of Sienese painting. Upstairs are the collections of the treas-ury, and on the top floor is a display of paintings from the early Sienese school.

Piazza del Duomo 8. ℂ **0577-42309.** Admission 5€ ($4.45). Mar 16–Sept daily 9am–7:30pm; Oct daily 9am–6pm; Nov–Mar 15 daily 9am–1:30pm. Bus: A.

National Picture Gallery (Pinacoteca Nazionale) ★★ Housed in a 14th-century palazzo near Piazza del Campo is the National Gallery's collection of the Sienese school of painting, which once rivaled that of Florence. Displayed are some of the giants of the pre-Renaissance, with most of the paintings covering the period from the late 12th century to the mid–16th century.

The principal treasures are on the second floor, where you'll contemplate the artistry of Duccio in **rooms 3 and 4.** Duccio was the first great Sienese master. **Rooms 5 to 8** are rich in the art of the 14th-century Lorenzetti brothers, Ambrogio and Pietro. Ambrogio is represented by an *Annunciation* and a *Crucifix,* but one of his most celebrated works, carried out with consummate skill, is an almond-eyed *Madonna and Bambino* surrounded by saints and angels. Pietro's most important entry is an altarpiece, *Madonna of the Carmine,* made for a Siena church in 1329. Simone Martini's *Madonna and Child* (1321) is damaged but one of the best-known paintings here.

In the salons to follow are works by Giovanni di Paolo (*Presentation at the Temple*), Sano di Pietro, and Giovanni Antonio Bazzi (called Il Sodoma, allegedly because of his sexual interests). Of exceptional interest are the cartoons of Mannerist master Beccafumi, from which many of the panels in the cathedral floor were created.

In the Palazzo Buonsignori, Via San Pietro 29. ② **0577-281161.** Admission 4€ ($3.55). Mon 8:30am–1:30pm; Tues–Sat 8:30am–7pm; Sun 8:30am–1:30pm. Bus: A.

St. Catherine's Sanctuary (Santuario e Casa di Santa Caterina) Of all the personalities associated with Siena, the most enduring legend surrounds St. Catherine, acknowledged by Pius XII in 1939 as Italy's patron saint. Born in 1347 to a dyer, the mystic was instrumental in persuading the papacy to return to Rome from Avignon. The house where she lived, between Piazza del Campo and San Domenico, has now been turned into a sanctuary; it's really a church and an oratory, with many artworks. On the hill above is the 13th-century **Basilica di San Domenico,** where a chapel dedicated to St. Catherine was frescoed by Il Sodoma.

Costa di San Antonio. ② **0577-44177.** Free admission (a donation is expected). Daily and holidays 8am–12:30pm and 2:30–6pm. Bus: A.

Permanent Italian Library of Wine (Enoteca Italica Permanente) Owned and operated by the Italian government, this showcase for the finest wines of Italy would whet the palate of even the most demanding wine lover. An unusual architectural setting is designed to show bottles to their best advantage. The place lies just outside the entrance to an old fortress, at the bottom of an inclined ramp, behind a massive arched doorway. Marble bas-reliefs and wrought-iron sconces, along with regional ceramics, are set into the high brick walls of the labyrinthine corridors, the vaults of which were built for Cosimo de' Medici in 1560. There are several sunny terraces for outdoor wine tasting, an indoor stand-up bar, and voluminous lists of available vintages, for sale by the glass or the bottle. Special wine tastings for groups may be booked for 8€ ($7.15) for two wines or 9€ ($8.05) for three. Count yourself lucky if the bartender will agree to open an iron gate for access to the subterranean wine exposition; in the lowest part of the fortress, illuminated display racks contain bottles of recent vintages.

Fortezza Medicea. ② **0577-288497.** Free admission. Mon noon–8pm; Tues–Sat noon–1am. Bus: C.

SHOPPING

Although Siena's shopping scene can't compete with that in Florence, you'll still find a good selection of stores and boutiques. The best of the lot is **Arcaico,** Via di Citta 79–92 (© **0577-281144**), the centerpiece of three almost-adjacent shops stocking Siena's richest trove of ceramics and souvenirs (cachepots, religious figurines, decorative tiles, dinnerware painted in pleasing floral patterns, and wine and water jugs).

A worthy competitor is **Martini Marisa,** Via del Capitano 5 and 11 (© **0577-288177**), purveyor of gift items, local stoneware, and porcelain. Also try the nearby **Zina Proveddi,** Via di Città 96 (© **0577-286078**), smaller than either of the above but with a cozier feel and an emphasis on rustic and affordable handmade pottery and painted tiles set into wood.

Specializing in older jewelry, **Antichità Saena Vetus,** Via di Città 53 (© **0577-42395**), also handles furniture and paintings from the 1700s and 1800s, and always has smaller pieces reasonably priced for the bargain hunter. Utilizing the colors and designs of Renaissance Siena, **Siena Ricama,** Via di Città 61 (© **0577-288339**), is the place to order custom-made hand-embroidered table and bed linens. Call before going.

More contemporary is the intricately crafted knitwear at **Il Telaio,** Chiasso del Bargello 2 (© **0577-47065**). Most of the stock includes artfully tailored women's jackets, scarves, and jumpers, although there's a small collection of pullovers for men. Focusing on smaller leather goods, **Mercatissimo della Calzatura e Pelletteria,** Viale Curtatone 1 (© **0577-281305**), is the largest store of its type in Siena. You'll find discounted prices on upscale Italian-made leather goods (handbags, suitcases, briefcases, and men's and women's shoes), and there's an inventory of tennis and basketball sneakers imported from Asia.

Siena merchants also sell some of Tuscany's finest wines. Virtually every street corner has an outlet for local Chianti (sold in individual bottles and sometimes four-packs and six-packs). Many of the finer bottles are wrapped in the distinctive straw sheathing. For the largest selection, head to the **Enoteca Italica Permanente** (see above). A Tuscan gourmet's delight, the **Enoteca San Domenico,** Via del Paradiso 56 (© **0577-271181**), sells regional wines and grappa by the bottle, plus pasta, virgin olive oils, sauces, jams, and assorted sweets.

WHERE TO STAY

You'll definitely need hotel reservations if you're here for the Palio. Make them far in advance and secure your room with a deposit. If it looks as if Siena is full, you might want to check out some of the nearby accommodations in the Chianti region, north of Siena (see section 1, "The Chianti Road"). The **Siena Hotels Promotion** booth on Piazza San Domenico (© **0577-288084;** shp-net@novamedia.it) will help you find a room for a small fee.

VERY EXPENSIVE

Certosa di Maggiano ✦✦ This early-13th-century Certosinian monastery lay in dusty disrepair until 1969, when Anna Grossi Recordati fell in love with the property and set out on a long process of renovation and restoration. Now affiliated with Relais & Châteaux, it's an intimate, plush retreat. The stylish public rooms fill the spaces in what used to be the ambulatory of the central courtyard, and the complex's medieval church still holds Mass on Sunday. The individually decorated guest rooms are spacious, with antiques, art objects, and sumptuous beds; one has a private walled garden. The hotel isn't easy to find;

Siena

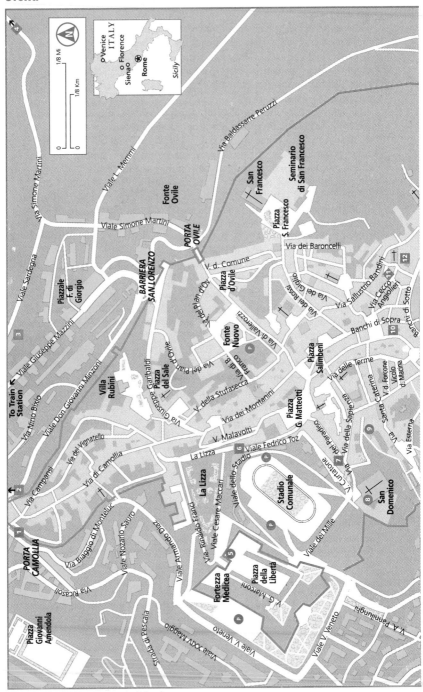

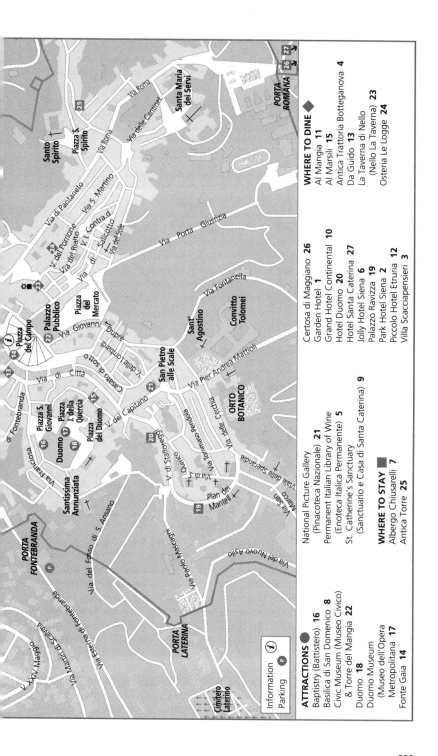

WHERE TO DINE ◆
Al Mangia **11**
Al Marsili **15**
Antica Trattoria Botteganova **4**
Da Guido **13**
La Taverna di Nello
  (Nello La Taverna) **23**
Osteria Le Logge **24**

Certosa di Maggiano **26**
Garden Hotel **1**
Grand Hotel Continental **10**
Hotel Duomo **20**
Hotel Santa Caterina **27**
Jolly Hotel Siena **6**
Palazzo Ravizza **19**
Park Hotel Siena **2**
Piccolo Hotel Etruria **12**
Villa Scacciapensieri **3**

National Picture Gallery
  (Pinacoteca Nazionale) **21**
Permanent Italian Library of Wine
  (Enoteca Italica Permanente) **5**
St. Catherine's Sanctuary
  (Sanctuario e Casa di Santa Caterina) **9**

WHERE TO STAY ■
Albergo Chiusarelli **7**
Antica Torre **25**

ATTRACTIONS ●
Baptistry (Battistero) **16**
Basilica di San Domenico **8**
Civic Museum (Museo Civico)
  & Torre del Mangia **22**
Duomo **18**
Duomo Museum
  (Museo dell'Opera
  Metropolitana) **17**
Fonte Gaia **14**

Information ⓘ
Parking Ⓟ

there are some signs, but you might want to phone ahead for directions. The staff can help you arrange for guided tours, wine tastings, and many other outings. Most guests take a taxi into the historic center of town, but there's also a shuttle.

Strada di Certosa 82, 53100 Siena. ☎ **0577-288180.** Fax 0577-288189. www.certosadimaggiano.it. 17 units. 517€–646€ ($461.60–$576.80) double; 775€–1,085€ ($692.10–$968.90) suite. Rates include half-board. Children under 12 are not accepted. AE, MC, V. Parking 30€ ($26.80). **Amenities:** Elegant and well-recommended restaurant; bar; outdoor pool; tennis court; jogging track; shuttle into the historic walls; room service; massage; babysitting; laundry/dry cleaning. *In room:* A/C, TV, minibar, hair dryer, safe.

Grand Hotel Continental 🏆🏆   A few steps from Piazza del Campo and the Duomo, this restored 1816 majestic building is the first government-rated five-star hotel to open in the very heart of Siena in 2002. After a faithful restoration of a palace designed by the baroque architect, Giovanni Fontana, this is now a deluxe and rather posh nest for big spenders. The restoration revealed many magnificent frescoes from the 1600s and decorative touches from the 19th century. Furnished with elegance and refinement, the midsize-to-spacious accommodations contain tiled bathrooms. Ideal are the panoramic junior suites on the top level with a terrace. Other junior suites contain a studio area on a loft level. Many rooms open onto views of the Duomo and are decorated with frescoes.

Banchi di Sopra 85, 53100 Siena. ☎ **0577-56011.** Fax 0577-56011555. www.grandhotelcontinentalsiena.it. 51 units. 325€–595€ ($290.25–$531.35) double; 522€–935€ ($466.15–$834.95) junior suite; 1,111€–1,230€ ($992.10–$1098.40) suite. AE, DC, MC, V. Parking: 25€ ($22.35). **Amenities:** Restaurant; bar; room service; babysitting; laundry/dry cleaning. *In room:* A/C, TV, minibar, hair dryer, safe.

EXPENSIVE

Jolly Hotel Siena 🏆   In the commercial center of Siena's newer section, this hotel is a member of a nationwide chain and caters to many business travelers. It was built as the Excelsior in the 1880s and was completely renovated about a century later. The high-ceilinged lobby is stylishly Italian, with terra-cotta accents and white columns. The guest rooms offer modern but generic furniture and many conveniences.

Piazza La Lizza, 53100 Siena. ☎ **800/221-2626** in the U.S., or 0577-288448. Fax 0577-41272. www.jolly hotels.it. 126 units (some with shower only). 155€–205€ ($138.40–$183.05) double; 180€–305€ ($160.75–$272.35) suite. Rates include breakfast. AE, DC, MC, V. Parking 22.50€–27.50€ ($20.10–$24.55). Bus: C. **Amenities:** Restaurant; lounge; room service; babysitting; laundry/dry cleaning. *In room:* A/C, TV, minibar, hair dryer, safe.

Park Hotel Siena 🏆🏆   This villa, about a 12-minute drive (2km/1¼ miles) north of the city center, was commissioned in 1530 by one of Siena's most famous Renaissance architects and was transformed into a luxury hotel around the turn of the century. A difficult access road leads around a series of hairpin turns to a villa with a view over green trees and suburban homes. Most public rooms have been redone in an opulent Belle Epoque style, while the guest rooms are more generic but plush and modern. The Park Hotel doesn't have the antique charm of the Certosa di Maggiano (see above), but it offers more services and facilities. The double-glazed windows, upholstered walls, and rich carpeting have set new standards around here. Several famous golf courses are nearby, in addition to the hotel's own links; golf packages are offered through the hotel. A local bus stops near the hotel entrance frequently during the day.

Villa Gori Golf Club, Via di Marciano 18, 53100 Siena. ☎ **0577-44803.** Fax 0577-49020. www.charming hotels.it. 70 units. 298€–441€ ($266.10–$393.80) double; from 523€ ($467.05) suite. AE, DC, MC, V. Free parking. Closed Dec 3–Feb. **Amenities:** Restaurant; bar; outdoor pool; 6-hole golf course; 2 tennis courts; business center; concierge; room service; babysitting; laundry. *In room:* A/C, TV, minibar, hair dryer, safe.

Villa Scacciapensieri ⚜ This is one of Tuscany's lovely old villas, where you can stay in a personal, if timeworn, atmosphere. Standing on the crest of a hill about 3km (2 miles) from Siena, the villa is approached by a private driveway under shade trees. Although it's not exactly state-of-the-art, it positively oozes tradition. The guest rooms vary widely in style and comfort, and your opinion of this hotel might depend on your room. If your accommodation opens onto the rear, you'll have a view of the sweet hills of Chianti. You won't be staying within the historic walls here, but a local bus passes by the hotel entrance every 15 minutes or so during the day (the ride into town takes 10 min.); you might want to simply take a taxi into the old town.

Via di Scacciapensieri 10, 53100 Siena. ℂ **0577-41441.** Fax 0577-270854. www.villascacciapensieri.it. 31 units (some with shower only). 170€–270€ ($151.80–$241.10) double; 200€–260€ ($178.60–$232.20) suite. Rates include breakfast. AE, DC, MC, V. Free parking. Closed Nov 15–Mar 15. Bus: 8 or 3. **Amenities:** Restaurant; bar; pool; tennis court; room service; babysitting; laundry. *In room:* A/C, TV, minibar, hair dryer, safe (in some).

MODERATE

Garden Hotel One of the really pleasant places to stay outside Siena, less than a mile north of the old city's fortifications, boasts an 18th-century core built as a villa by a Sienese aristocrat and expanded in the 1970s with an annex. Located on the ledge of a hill, with lovely gardens, the Garden Hotel commands a view of Siena and the countryside that has been the subject of many a painting. Its outstanding features are its garden and reasonable prices. The villa contains 25 guest rooms, high-ceilinged but less luxurious than the 100 in the conservatively modern annex. All rooms were completely renovated in 1998. Although the hotel doesn't lie within the historic walls, a local bus stops nearby every 10 minutes or so during the day; walking takes about 20 minutes.

Via Custoza 2, 53100 Siena. ℂ **0577-47056.** Fax 0577-46050. www.gardenhotel.it. 122 units. 145€–175€ ($129.50–$156.30) double. Rates include buffet breakfast. AE, DC, MC, V. Bus: 6 or 10. **Amenities:** Restaurant; bar; outdoor pool; tennis court; room service; babysitting; laundry. *In room:* A/C, TV, minibar, hair dryer, safe.

Hotel Santa Caterina This 18th-century villa is beautifully preserved, featuring original terra-cotta floors, sculpted marble fireplaces and stairs, arched entryways, beamed ceilings, and antique wooden furniture. Ms. Stefania Minuti runs this place, and she thinks of her guests as an extended family. The grounds include a terraced garden overlooking the valley south of Siena. When booking, ask for one of the 12 guest rooms with a garden view. Each room is filled with antique reproductions and chestnut furnishings.

Via Enea Silvio Piccolomini 7, 53100 Siena. ℂ **0577-221105.** Fax 0577-271087. www.hscsiena.it. 22 units. 125€ ($111.65) double. Rates include buffet breakfast. AE, DC, MC, V. Parking 12.50€ ($11.15) nearby (6 spaces). Bus: A, N, or 2. **Amenities:** Bar; room service; laundry. *In room:* A/C, TV, minibar, hair dryer.

Palazzo Ravizza ⚜⚜ This is an elegant small hotel, housed in a converted building from the 19th century. Every guest room has a few antiques along with ceiling frescoes. Some rooms also open onto a view of the garden. Each comes with a supremely comfortable bed and mattress, along with a small but tidily kept bathroom. The hotel lies within a short walk of Piazza del Campo, outside the very center of town but still within the walls. The free parking is a real plus.

Pian dei Mantellini 34, 53100 Siena. ℂ **0577-280462.** Fax 0577-221597. www.palazzoravizza.it. 38 units. 119€–227€ ($106.25–$202.70) double; 262€–307€ ($233.95–$274.15) suite. Rates include half-board. AE, DC, MC, V. Free parking. Bus: San Domenico. **Amenities:** Restaurant; bar; room service; babysitting; laundry/dry cleaning. *In room:* A/C, TV, minibar, hair dryer, safe.

INEXPENSIVE

Albergo Chiusarelli   Near Piazza San Domenico, the Chiusarelli is in an ocher-colored 1870 building with Ionic columns and Roman caryatids supporting a second-floor loggia. The interior has been almost completely renovated, and each functional, nondescript guest room contains a modern bathroom. Ask for a room in back to escape the street noise. The hotel is just at the edge of the old city, a 5-minute walk from the Campo and a half block from the bus station; it's not the prettiest area, but it's totally convenient.

Viale Curtatone 15, 53100 Siena. ℃ 0577-280562. Fax 0577-271177. 49 units. 105€ ($93.75) double; 135€ ($120.55) triple. Rates include breakfast. AE, MC, V. Free parking (10 spaces). Bus: C. **Amenities:** Restaurant; bar; room service; babysitting; laundry. *In room:* A/C, TV, hair dryer, safe.

Antica Torre ⭐   The Landolfo family extends a warm welcome to international visitors in its restored 17th-century tower within the city walls in the southeastern sector of town, a 10-minute walk from Piazza del Campo. Small and graceful, the tower sits on top of a centuries-old potters' workshop that's now the breakfast room. Take a stone staircase to the small but comfortable guest rooms, each with some Tuscan antiques, iron-filigree headboards, and marble floors. Try for one of the accommodations on the top floors for a panoramic view of the medieval city and the rolling Tuscan hills.

Via di Fieravecchia 7, 53100 Siena. ℃ and fax 0577-222255. 8 units (showers only). 100€ ($89.30) double. AE, DC, MC, V. Parking on street nearby. **Amenities:** Bar. *In room:* TV, hair dryer.

Hotel Duomo   With a fabulous location within the historic walls just south of its namesake, this hotel is in a 12th-century palazzo that once was the barracks for medieval troops (although the only reminders are the central staircase and the brickwork in the basement). The carpeted guest rooms are of a modest size but not cramped, and the modern furnishings are as tasteful as functional gets. If you want to secure one of the 13 rooms with Duomo views, ask when booking. The best choices are nos. 61 and 62, with terraces overlooking the Duomo. The friendly staff is polished and professional. The free parking is a huge plus in the crowded old city.

Via Stalloreggi 38, 53100 Siena. ℃ **0577-289088.** Fax 0577-43043. www.hotelduomo.it. 23 units (showers only). 93€–130€ ($83.05–$116.10) double. AE, DC, MC, V. Rates include buffet breakfast. Closed Jan–Feb. Free parking nearby. Bus: A. **Amenities:** Bar; room service; babysitting; laundry. *In room:* A/C, TV, hair dryer.

Piccolo Hotel Etruria ⭐ *Value*   This small family-run hotel could thumb its nose at the big corporate chains because it offers equally comfortable modern luxuries with twice the character and at a fourth of the price. In both the main building and the annex across the street, the guest rooms have tiled floors, wood-toned built-in furnishings with stone-topped desks and end tables, leather strap chairs, and quite decent beds. The rooms aren't very spacious, but they aren't small either. The only real drawback is the 12:30am curfew.

Via Donzelle 3, 53100 Siena. ℃ 0577-288088. Fax 0577-288461. 19 units (showers only). 73€ ($65.20) double. AE, DC, MC, V. Closed around Dec 10–27. Bus: A, B, N, 3, 9, or 10. **Amenities:** Lounge; room service (breakfast). *In room:* TV, hair dryer, safe

WHERE TO STAY NEARBY

Locanda dell'Amorosa ⭐⭐ *Finds*   This is a rural retreat about 45km (28 miles) from Siena. Until the 1960s, this compound of agrarian buildings was a working farm, with its own school, a priest (who conducted Masses in the chapel), and rich traditions of winemaking and olive-oil production. In the 1980s, the compound was transformed into a hotel resembling a small Tuscan village, with 14th-century stonework and a classic driveway lined with cypress trees. Today, thanks to substantial investments by local entrepreneur Carlo Citterio, it's a charming, atmospheric hotel. Still about 200 acres of farmland are associated with the hotel, about 20 of which are devoted to winemaking for the robust table wines (Sangioveto de Borgo) that continue to be produced here. What used to be the granary is now a convention center, favored for a weekend rendezvous by some of the region's corporations. The guest rooms are formal and lovely, with tasteful furnishings. Some open onto panoramic countryside views; others open onto the hotel's gardens.

Località Amorosa, 53048 Sinalunga. © 0577-677211. Fax 0577-632001. www.amorosa.it. 210€–300€ ($187.55–$267.90) double; from 325€ ($290.20) suite. Rates include breakfast. AE, DC, MC, V. Free parking. Closed Jan 6–Mar 5. From Siena, drive southeast 45km (28 miles) along SS326, following the signs first for Arezzo and then for Perugia. **Amenities:** 2 restaurants; bar; pool; room service; babysitting; laundry. *In room:* A/C, TV, minibar, hair dryer, safe.

Villa Belvedere ★ *Finds*   The Villa Belvedere, about 12km (7½ miles) from Siena and halfway to San Gimignano, occupies a 1795 building. In 1820, it was the residence of Ferdinand III, archduke of Austria and grand duke of Tuscany; in 1845, Grand Duke Leopold II lived there. Surrounded by a large park, the hotel offers a garden with a panoramic view. The warmly old-fashioned guest rooms, furnished partly with antiques, overlook the park.

Via Senese Belvedere, 53034 Colle di Val d'Elsa Siena. © 0577-920966. Fax 0577-924128. www.villa belvedere.com. 15 units (some with shower only). 137.50€ ($122.80) double. Rates include buffet breakfast. AE, DC, MC, V. Exit the autostrada from Florence at Colle di Val d'Elsa Sud, and follow the signs. **Amenities:** 2 restaurants; bar; pool; tennis court; room service. *In room:* TV, hair dryer.

WHERE TO DINE
EXPENSIVE/MODERATE

Al Mangia TUSCAN/INTERNATIONAL   Al Mangia, one of the historic center's most appealing restaurants, offers outside tables overlooking the town hall. It was constructed more or less continuously between 1100 and the late 1600s. The food is artfully cooked and presented by a relatively formal well-trained staff, with excellent menu items changing with the seasons. Look for *pici alla Sienese* (thick noodles made only with flour and water) with a sauce of fresh tomatoes, tarragon, and cheese; spicy spaghetti with baby spring onions and sausages; *filetto alla terra di Siena* (grilled steak with a Chianti-and-tarragon sauce); osso buco with artichokes; and roasted boar cacciatore (hunter's style, with mushrooms and onions, available only in season). The homemade desserts include *panforte*, a cake enriched with almonds and candied fruits.

Piazza del Campo 42. © 0577-281121. Reservations recommended. Main courses 15€–25€ ($13.40–$22.35). AE, DC, MC, V. Daily noon–3:30pm and 7–10pm. Bus: A.

Al Marsili SIENESE/ITALIAN   This beautiful restaurant stands between the Duomo and Via di Città. You dine beneath crisscrossed ceiling vaults whose russet-colored brickwork was designed centuries ago. The antipasti offer some unusual treats, such as polenta with chicken liver sauce; a medley of the best of Siena's cold cuts; and smoked venison, wild boar, and goose blended into a paté. The wide selection of first courses ranges from the typical vegetable soup of Siena (*ribollita alla senese*) to a risotto with four cheeses. For your main course, you might opt for wild boar with tomato sauce. The *panna cotta* is a cream pudding with fresh berries, and the *dolce Marsili* is a soft cake flavored with coffee and mascarpone cream.

Via del Castoro 3. © 0577-47154. Reservations recommended. Main courses 10€–16€ ($8.95–$14.30). AE, DC, MC, V. Tues–Sun 12:30–2:30pm and 7:30–10:30pm. Bus: A.

Antica Trattoria Botteganova ✿✿✿ TUSCAN   On the road leading north of Siena to Chianti, just outside the city walls, lies this outstanding restaurant. Chef Michele Sonentino's cuisine pleases discerning locals as well as visitors. In his presentation and his choice of first-class fresh ingredients, he tantalizes the palate based on the best of the season's offerings. Standard Italian dishes are given a modern touch; he serves old-time favorites along with more inventive platters. Try his tortelli, a kind of dumpling, stuffed with pecorino cheese and served with a hot parmigiano cheese sauce and truffled cream. Every day he offers perfectly baked or grilled fish along with the finest seasonal vegetables. Save room for *tortino di mele*, a little Sienese apple pie served warm. In the cellar is a choice of 400 wines, mainly Tuscan vintages.

Strada Chiantigiana 29 (reached via Porta Ovile, 1 mile north of the center of Siena). ✆ **0577-284230**. Reservations recommended. Main courses 20€–25€ ($17.85–$22.35); tasting menu 40€–50€ ($35.70–$44.65). AE, DC, MC, V. Tues–Sat 12:30–2:30pm and 8–10:30pm; Mon 8–10:30pm. Closed 10 days in Jan and 10 days in July. Bus: 8 or 12.

Osteria Le Logge ✿✿ SIENESE/TUSCAN   This trattoria deserves its long-time popularity. At the end of the 19th century, this place was a pharmacy, dispensing creams and medicines to cure the ill. Today it has been transformed into a bastion of superb cuisine in a refined and old-fashioned atmosphere. The menu, changed daily, overflows with freshness and flavor. Try the wild boar stew with spicy tomato sauce or the delectable baked duck stuffed with fennel or grapes. In autumn, try the pappardelle with game sauce. The tender veal steaks are among the best in town, and you can also order taglierini pasta with black truffle sauce. Save room for one of the desserts, which are made fresh each morning.

Via del Porrione 33. ✆ **0577-48013**. Reservations recommended. Main courses 14€–17.50€ ($12.50–$15.65). AE, DC, MC, V. Mon–Sat noon–2:45pm and 7–10:30pm. Closed Jan 7–31.

INEXPENSIVE

Da Guido SIENESE/INTERNATIONAL   Da Guido is a medieval Tuscan restaurant about 30m (100 ft.) off the promenade near Piazza del Campo. It's decked out with crusty old beams, aged brick walls, arched ceilings, and iron chandeliers. Our approval is backed up by the testimony of more than 300 prominent people who have left autographed photos to adorn the walls of the three dining rooms. Meals seem to taste best when begun with selections from the antipasti table. Pastas that appeal to anyone who loves the taste of spring vegetables include *rustici alla Guido* (spaghetti laced with mushrooms, truffles, and fresh asparagus). Some of the best meat dishes are grilled over the kitchen's charcoal grill and include spicy chicken breast with rosemary, sage, garlic, and Tabasco sauce; and *bistecca alla Guido,* grilled simply with a sauce of olive oil and rosemary.

Vicolo Pier Pettinaio 7. ✆ **0577-280042**. Reservations required. Main courses 12.50€–20€ ($11.15–$17.85). AE, DC, MC, V. Daily 12:30–3pm and 7:30–10pm. Bus: A.

La Taverna di Nello (Nello La Taverna) TUSCAN/VEGETARIAN   On a narrow stone-covered street half a block from Piazza del Campo, the 1930s restaurant offers a tavern decor with brick walls, lanterns, racks of wine bottles, and sheaves of corn hanging from the ceiling. Best of all, you can view the forge-like kitchen with its crew of uniformed cooks busily preparing your dinner from behind a row of hanging copper utensils. Specialties include a salad of fresh radicchio, green lasagna ragout style, and lamb cacciatore with beans. Freshly made pasta is served every day. Your waiter will gladly suggest a local vintage. The restaurant's wine bar offers more than 150 vintages from the south of Tuscany.

Via del Porrione 2830. ℂ **0577-289043**. Reservations required. Main courses 9€–15€ ($8.05–$13.40). AE, DC, MC, V. Mon–Sat noon–3pm and 7–11pm. Closed 15 days in Jan. Bus: A, B, or N.

SIDE TRIPS FROM SIENA
MONTALCINO ⚜

Forty-three kilometers (27 miles) south of Siena, Montalcino is the home of the robust DOCG Brunello wine and its lighterweight cousin, Rosso di Montalcino. Sleepy and small, Montalcino is still a well-to-do town that has remained unchanged since the 16th century, with lovely vistas.

From Siena, a dozen or so TRA-IN **buses** make the 60- to 90-minute trip, costing 3€ ($2.70) one way. The **tourist office** is on Via Costa del Municipio 8 (ℂ and fax **0577-849331**).

You'll find the best views from the 14th-century **Fortezza** ⚜ (ℂ **0577-288497**), which also moonlights as the town's *enoteca* (wine bar). Wines by the glass begin at 1.50€ ($1.35), but spend a little more to sample the region's famous Brunello at 5€ ($4.45); pair it with a savory plate of the local cheeses or salami at 7.50€ ($6.70) for a perfect lunch.

The other great place in town for wine tasting is in the Piazza del Popolo, at the **Caffè/Fiaschetteria Italiana,** no. 6 (ℂ **0577-849043**), open Friday to Wednesday 7:30am to midnight (open daily Apr–Nov). In the 19th-century ambience of the dining room, or at a few choice tables outside, you can revel in a self-styled Brunello tasting, with three or four varieties to choose from by the glass at 2.50€ to 10€ ($2.25–$8.95). Brunello's most revered producer, Biondi-Santi, had two stellar years in 1993 and 1990. You can buy a bottle at the Fiaschetteria to bring home with you, if you want to part with 50€ ($44.65).

In 1997, Montalcino's small **Civic Museum (Museo Civico)** moved its collection of Sienese paintings, which range from the 1400s to the Renaissance, to a new home, the handsomely restored former St. Augustine monastery on Via Ricasoli 31 (ℂ **0577-846014**). Admission is 4€ ($3.55). It's open Tuesday to Sunday from 10am to 1pm and 2 to 5:40pm.

Outside the town walls, the 12th-century Cistercian **Abbazia di Sant'Antimo** (ℂ **0577-835659**) rests in its own pocket-size vale amid olive trees and cypresses 10km (6¼ miles) south of Montalcino. One of Tuscany's most perfectly intact Romanesque churches, the abbey is especially worth visiting during the Gregorian chants performed daily by a handful of monks who still live there. Check the Montalcino tourist office for hours.

While at Sant'Antimo, follow the signs for the nearby **Fattoria dei Barbi** (ℂ **0577-848277**), which has been in the same family since the 16th century and is one of the area's most respected producers of the full-bodied Brunello. Wine tastings are available Monday to Friday (closed Wed), but so are excellent country meals, with most products direct from the estate's farm. Rustic accommodations at the inn will tempt you to stay on indefinitely.

PIENZA ⚜

This jewel of a Renaissance town 24km (15 miles) from Montalcino and 53km (33 miles) from Siena is easy to reach from Montalcino (to the west) by bus. (A rental car will make your life easier.)

When looking for a place to film *Romeo and Juliet* in 1968, director Franco Zeffirelli found the perfect backdrop awaiting him in Pienza, so he bypassed "fair Verona" as the obvious choice. Pienza was also used in the Oscar-winning epic *The English Patient*. Although it appeared as a medieval town on film, Pienza is more noteworthy as a testament to the ambitions and ego of a quintessential Renaissance man. Pope Pius II (of Siena's illustrious Piccolomini family) was born here in 1405 when the town was called Corsignano, and in 1459 (a year after he was elected pope), he commissioned Florentine architect Bernardo Rossellino to level the medieval core of the town and create the first stage of what would be the model High Renaissance city. He renamed it Pienza, in his own honor.

The grand scheme didn't get very far (the pope died in 1464), but what has remained is perfectly preserved and has become a UNESCO-protected site. The graceful **Piazza Pio II** is the star of the town. Visit its **Palazzo Piccolomini** (the pope's residence, lived in by descendents of the Piccolomini family until 1968) and the **Duomo;** then walk behind the Duomo for sweeping views of the dormant Mt. Amiata and the wide Val d'Orcia. The piazza is also the location for the **tourist office,** Corso Rossellino 59 (© and fax **0578-749071**). Ask about free guided tours of the town during summer.

You can see most of the town in half a day. It'll take only 5 minutes to cover Pienza's main drag, **Corso Rossellino,** whose food stores specialize in the gourmet products from this bountiful corner of Tuscany, namely wines, honey, and pecorino cheese (also known as *cacio*). Cheese tasting is more popular than wine tasting here, and stores offer their varieties of *fresco* (fresh), *semistagionato* (partially aged), *pepperocinato* (dusted with hot peppers), or *tartufi* (truffles). Taste as much cheese as you will, but by all means save room for lunch at the reasonably priced **Dal Falco,** Piazza Dante Alighieri 7 (© **0578-748551**), closed Friday. A meal of homemade *pici* pasta and a delicious grilled meat will cost around 16.50€ to 21€ ($14.75–$18.75). Upstairs are six simple doubles with a bathroom for 60€ ($53.60).

7 Arezzo

81km (50 miles) SE of Florence

The most landlocked of all the towns of Tuscany, Arezzo was originally an Etruscan settlement and later a Roman center. The city flourished in the Middle Ages before its capitulation to Florence.

The walled town grew up on a hill, but large parts of the ancient city, including native son Petrarch's house, were bombed during World War II before the area fell to the Allied advance in the summer of 1944. Apart from Petrarch, famous sons of Arezzo have included Vasari, the painter/architect remembered chiefly for his history of the Renaissance artists, and Guido of Arezzo (sometimes known as Guido Monaco), who gave the world the modern musical scale before his death in the mid–11th century.

Today, Arezzo looks a little rustic, as if the glory of the Renaissance has long passed it by. But this isn't surprising when you consider that it lost its prosperity when Florence annexed it in 1348. Arezzo might look a bit down at the heels, but it really isn't. The city today has one of the biggest jewelry industries in western Europe. Little firms on the outskirts turn out an array of rings and chains, and bank vaults are overflowing with gold ingots. However, the inner core, which most visitors want to explore, didn't share in this gold and looks as if it needs a rehab.

If Arezzo looks familiar to you, then you might've seen Roberto Benigni's wonderful *Life Is Beautiful*, which was partially filmed here.

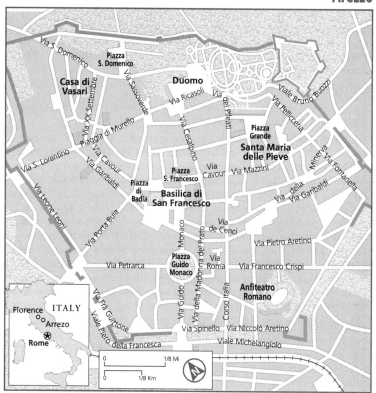

ESSENTIALS

GETTING THERE   A **train** comes from Florence at intervals of 20 to 60 minutes throughout the day. The trip takes between 40 and 60 minutes, costing 4.55€ to 6.50€ ($4.05–$5.80) one way, depending on its speed. In Arezzo, trains depart and arrive at the **Stazione Centrale,** Piazza della Repubblica (© **848-888088**). Because there are no direct trains from Siena to Arezzo, rail passengers from Siena are required to make hot, prolonged, and tiresome rail transfers at Chiusi. Therefore, unless it happens to be Sunday (see below), it's better to travel by bus if your point of origin is Siena.

Because of complicated transfers required en route and travel time of as much as 2½ hours each way, trips by **bus** from Florence to Arezzo aren't a good idea. Bus routes from Siena to Arezzo, however, are easier than the train transfers. From Monday to Saturday, five buses per day travel from Siena directly to Arezzo. On Sunday, however, you'll have to take the train. For information on bus routes and prices, call **ATAM Point** at © **0575-382651** in Arrezo.

If you have a **car** and are in Rome, head north on A1; from Florence, head south on A1. In both directions, the turnoff for Arezzo is clearly marked.

VISITOR INFORMATION   The **tourist office** is at Piazza della Repubblica 28 (© **0575-377678**). November to March, it's open Monday to Saturday 9:30am to 12:30pm and 3:30 to 6pm; April to October 30, hours are Monday to Saturday 9:30am to 1pm and 3:30 to 6:30pm.

SPECIAL EVENTS The biggest event on the Arezzo calendar is the **Giostra del Saraceno,** staged the third Sunday of June and the first Sunday of September on Piazza Grande. In a tradition unbroken since the 13th century, horsemen in medieval costumes reenact the lance-charging joust ritual, with balled whips cracking in the air.

EXPLORING THE TOWN

Stop by **Piazza Grande** to see the medieval and Renaissance palaces and towers that flank it, including the 16th-century loggia by Vasari.

Basilica di San Francesco ★★ This Gothic church was finished in the 14th century for the Franciscans. Inside is a Piero della Francesca masterpiece, a restored fresco cycle called *Legend of the True Cross* ★★★. His frescoes are remarkable for their grace, clearness, dramatic light effects, well-chosen colors, and ascetic severity. Vasari credited della Francesca as a master of the laws of geometry and perspective, and Sir Kenneth Clark called Piero's frescoes "the most perfect morning light in all Renaissance painting." The frescoes depict the burial of Adam, Solomon receiving the queen of Sheba at the court (the most memorable scene), the dream of Constantine with the descent of an angel, and the triumph of the Holy Cross with Heraclius, among other subjects.

Piazza San Francesco. ✆ 0575-20630. Free admission. Daily 8:30am–noon and 2–6pm. Guided 30-min. visits to the frescoes 5€ ($4.45). Mon–Sat 9:30–11:30am and 3–5pm; Sun 3–5pm; to make reservations call 0575-900404.

Santa Maria della Pieve ★ This Romanesque church boasts a front of three open-air loggias, with each pillar designed uniquely. The 14th-century bell tower is known as "the hundred holes" because it's riddled with windows. Inside, the church is bleak and austere, but there's a notable polyptych, *The Virgin with Saints,* by one of the Sienese Lorenzetti brothers (Pietro), painted in 1320.

Corso Italia 7. ✆ 0575-22629. Free admission. Mon–Sat 8am–1pm and 3–7pm; Sun 8am–1pm and 3–6:30pm.

Petrarch's House (Casa di Petrarca) A short walk away from Santa Maria della Pieve, this house was rebuilt after war damage. Born at Arezzo in 1304, Petrarch was a great Italian lyrical poet and humanist who immortalized his love, Laura, in his sonnets. Actual mementos are few, but the house displays books, engravings, sketches, and even some furnishings from Petrarch's time.

Via dell'Orto 28A. ✆ 0575-24700. Free admission (ring the bell to enter). Mon–Fri 10am–noon and 3–5pm; Sat 10am–noon. Closed Aug 1–25.

House of Vasari (Casa Vasari) This house was purchased by the artist (and the first art-history writer) in 1540. There are works by Vasari himself, but it's apparent that his fame rests on his *Lives of the Artists* more than it does on his actual artwork. His best works are *Virtue, Envy, and Fortune* and *Deposition.* Other works displayed are by Santi di Tito, Alessandro Allori, and Il Poppi.

Via XX Settembre 55. ✆ 0575-409040. Free admission. Wed–Mon 8:30am–7:30pm; Sun 8:30am–12:30pm.

Il Duomo The Duomo was built in the pure Gothic style, rare for Tuscany. It was begun in the 13th century, but the final touches (on the facade) weren't applied until the outbreak of World War I. Its art treasures include stained-glass windows (1519–23) by Guillaume de Marcillat and a main altar in the Gothic style. Its main treasure, though, is *Mary Magdalene* ★, a Piero della Francesca masterpiece.

Piazza del Duomo. ✆ 0575-23991. Free admission. Daily 7am–12:30pm and 3–6pm.

SHOPPING

Arezzo hosts one of Europe's biggest gold-jewelry industries. In the very center of town, around **Piazza Grande,** are dozens of antiques shops carrying these shiny wares.

If you happen to be in Arezzo the first Saturday and Sunday of the month, don't miss the **antiques street market.** It was started some 3 decades ago by the Italian antiques expert Ivan Bruschi. For 2 days, this little town becomes a center of interest for antiques connoisseurs, with more than 500 stalls scattered all over the Piazza San Francesco to Piazza Vasari (also known as Piazza Grande), going through Piazza della Libertá.

WHERE TO DINE

Buca di San Francesco ✦ ITALIAN   Located in the historic core, the city's finest restaurant is in the cellar of a building from the 1300s; it's decorated with medieval references and strong Tuscan colors of sienna and blue. Menu items include *pollo del Valdarno arrosto* (roast chicken from the Arno valley) flavored with anise, homemade tagliolini with tomatoes and ricotta, and calves' liver with onions. A popular first course is green noodles with a rich meat sauce, oozing with creamy cheese and topped with a hunk of fresh butter. All ingredients are fresh, many of the staples are produced in-house, and even the olive oil is from private sources not shared by other restaurants.

Via San Francesco 1. ✆ **0575-23271.** Reservations recommended. Main courses 8€–14€ ($7.15–$12.50). AE, DC, MC, V. Wed–Sun noon–2:30pm and 7–9:30pm; Mon noon–2:30pm.

8 Gubbio ✦✦

40km (25 miles) NE of Perugia, 217km (135 miles) N of Rome, 92km (57 miles) SE of Arezzo, 55km (34 miles) N of Assisi

Gubbio is one of the best-preserved medieval towns in Italy. It has modern apartments and stores on its outskirts, but once you press through that, you're firmly back in the Middle Ages. The best-known streets of its medieval core are **Via XX Settembre, Via dei Consoli, Via Galeotti,** and **Via Baldassini.** All these are in the old town (Città Vecchia), set against the steep slopes of Monte Ingino.

Because Gubbio is off the beaten track, it remains a fairly sleepy backwater today except for the intrepid shoppers who drive here to shop for ceramics (see "Exploring the Old Town," below). Gubbio is almost as well known for ceramics as is Deruta. The last time Gubbio entered the history books was in 1944, when 40 hostages were murdered by the Nazis. Today, the central **Piazza dei Quaranta Martiri** is named for and honors those victims.

ESSENTIALS

GETTING THERE   Gubbio doesn't have a rail station, so **train** passengers headed for Gubbio from other parts of Italy get off at Fossato di Vico, 12 miles away, and then transfer to one of the frequent buses that make the short trip on to Gubbio. One-way bus transfers to Gubbio from Fossato di Vico cost 2€ ($1.80).

Eight **buses** a day head to Gubbio from Perugia (see section 9, "Perugia"). Trip time takes about 65 minutes, and a one-way ticket costs 3.85€ ($3.45). Buses arrive and depart from Piazza 40 Martiri (✆ **075-9220066**), in the heart of town.

If you have a **car** and are coming from Rome, follow A1 to Orte and then take SS3 north 88 miles to its intersection with SS298 at Schéggia. Go southwest on SS298 for 8 miles to Gubbio. From Florence, take A1 south to Orte and then follow the directions above. From Perugia, this turnoff is 40km (25 miles) northeast on the SS298.

VISITOR INFORMATION   The **tourist office,** at Piazza Oderisi 6 (② **075-9220693**), is open October to February Monday to Friday 8am to 2pm and 3 to 6pm, and Saturday 9am to 1pm and 3 to 6pm; March to September Monday to Friday 8am to 2pm and 3:30 to 6:30pm, and Saturday 9am to 1pm and 3:30 to 6:30pm. Year-round, it's open Sunday 9:30am to 12:30pm.

SPECIAL EVENTS   The biggest annual bash is the **Corso dei Ceri** ⭐ on May 15, one of Italy's top traditional festivals. It starts out with solemn ceremonies in the Piazza Grande in the morning and then turns into a wild free-for-all as teams compete in races with giant candles, ringing bells, and vases hurled into the crowds to shatter, all culminating in a giant seafood banquet and a religious procession.

The last Sunday in May brings the **Palio della Balestra,** a traditional crossbow competition accompanied by an evening procession through the streets with lots of colorful medieval costumes.

The **Gubbio Festival** brings acclaimed international performers to town for 3 weeks of performances in late July; the town also stages free classical concerts in the ruins of the Roman theater.

EXPLORING THE OLD TOWN

If the weather is right, you can take a cable car up to **Monte Ingino,** at a height of 820m (2,690 ft.), for a panoramic view of the area. Service is available July to August Monday to Saturday 8:30am to 7pm, Sunday 8:30am to 8pm; September Monday to Saturday 9:30am to 7pm, Sunday 9am to 7:30pm; October to June Monday to Saturday 10am to 1:15pm and 2:30 to 5pm. A round-trip ticket costs 4.50€ ($4).

In Gubbio, you can set about exploring a town that knew its golden age in the 1300s. Begin at **Piazza Grande,** the most important square. Here you can visit the Gothic **Palazzo dei Consoli** ⭐ (② **075-9274298**), housing the famed bronze *tavole eugubine,* a series of tablets as old as Christianity that were discovered in the 15th century. The tablets contain writing in the mysterious Umbrian language. The museum has a display of antiques from the Middle Ages and a collection of not-very-worthwhile paintings. It's open daily: April to September, 10am to 1pm and 3 to 6pm; October to March, 10am to 1pm and 2 to 5pm. Admission is 3.50€ ($3.15).

The other major sight is the **Ducal Palace (Palazzo Ducale)** ⭐, Via Ducale (② **075-9275872**), built for Federico of Montefeltro. It's open Thursday to Tuesday 8:30am to 7:30pm; admission is 2€ ($1.80).

After visiting the palace, you can go inside **Il Duomo,** Via Ducale (② **075-9220904**), across the way. The cathedral is a relatively unadorned pink Gothic building with some stained-glass windows from the 12th century. It has a single nave. Inside, several arches support the ceiling. Of particular interest is the wood cross above the altar, an exquisite example of the Umbrian school of the 13th century. It's open daily 9am to 12:30pm and 3:30 to 8:30pm, and admission is free.

Shopping is the major reason many visitors flock here. Gubbio's fame as a ceramics center had its beginnings in the 14th century. In the 1500s, the industry rose to the height of its fame. Sometime during this period, Mastro Giorgio pioneered a particularly intense iridescent ruby red that awed his competitors. Today, pottery workshops are found all over town, with beautiful flowery plates lining the walls of shop doorways. You can't miss them.

Two of the best outlets are in the town center: **Ceramica Rampini,** at Via Leonardo da Vinci 94 (© **075-9272963**), where you can visit the workshop, and the Rampini store, at Via dei Consoli 52 (© **075-9274408**). Its largest competitor, **La Mastro Giorgio,** Piazza Grande 3 (© **075-9271574**), opens its factory at Via Tifernate 67 (© **075-9273616**), about 1km (half a mile) from the center, to visitors who phone in advance for a convenient hour.

Gubbio is known for more than pots and vases: Its replicas of medieval crossbows (*balestre*) are prized as children's toys and macho decorative ornaments by aficionados of such things. If you want to add a touch of medieval authenticity to your den or office, head for **Medioevo,** Ponte d'Assi (© **075-9272596**), or **Rafael & Giuliani Morelli,** Ponte d'Assi (© **075-9271065**). Your souvenir will cost from 12.50€ ($11.15) for a cheap version to as much as 75€ ($67) for something much more substantial.

WHERE TO STAY

Hotel Relais Ducale ✦✦   This new hotel occupies the guest quarters of the dukes of Urbino, between their Palazzo Ducale and Piazza Grande. Hanging gardens shaded by palms and scented by jasmine offer views over the city's main square, its palazzi, and a panorama. The elegant and spacious guest rooms boast parquet floors, damask bedspreads and curtains, and the occasional historical touch (stone vaulted ceilings) or modern luxury (such as heated towel racks and Jacuzzis in some rooms). Rooms on the upper floors have terrific views.

Via Ducale 2 (overlooking Piazza Grande), 06024 Gubbio. © **075-9220157.** Fax 075-9220159. www. mencarelligroup.com. 32 units (showers only). 103€–185€ ($92–$165.20) double; 196€–222€ ($175.05–$198.25) suite. Rates include breakfast. AE, DC, MC, V. **Amenities:** Restaurant (with outdoor dining on the main town square); bar; room service; babysitting; dry cleaning. *In room:* A/C, TV, minibar, hair dryer, safe.

Hotel San Marco ⓥalue   Its unpromising location on the busiest corner in town is the San Marco's only drawback. Otherwise, this is a worthwhile hotel near a municipal parking lot. Built of stone in stages between 1300 and the 1700s, it contains an arbor-covered terrace and traditionally furnished guest rooms that are comfortable and well maintained, with small bathrooms.

Via Perugino 5, 06024 Gubbio. © **075-9220234.** Fax 075-9273716. www.hotelsanmarcogubbio.com. 63 units (about half with shower only). 68€–88€ ($60.70–$78.60) double. Rates include breakfast. AE, DC, MC, V. Parking 13€ ($11.60) in nearby garage. **Amenities:** Restaurant; bar; room service; laundry. *In room:* A/C, TV, hair dryer.

Palace Hotel Bosone ✦   This hotel once housed Dante Alighieri when it was owned by a patrician Gubbian family, the Bosone clan. Set at the meeting point of a flight of stone steps and a narrow street in the upper regions of town, it was built in the 1300s, enlarged during the Renaissance, and converted from a private home into a hotel in 1974. Ever since, it has been welcoming guests into its generally spacious stone-trimmed rooms, especially the Renaissance suites with stucco ceilings and 17th-century frescoes.

Via XX Settembre 22, 06024 Gubbio. © **075-9220698.** Fax 075-9220552. www.mencarelligroup.com. 30 units (showers only). 85€–95€ ($75.90–$84.85) double; 140€–175€ ($125–$156.30) suite. Rates include breakfast. AE, DC, MC, V. Free self-parking nearby. Closed 3 weeks in Feb. **Amenities:** Bar; room service. *In room:* TV, minibar, hair dryer.

Park Hotel Ai Cappuccini ★★   This is the leading hotel of Gubbio, with the best facilities and the finest service in the area. The hotel grew from the ruins of a monastery—hence, its name. The entire structure has been reconstructed and renovated or often rebuilt in most cases. Set in the middle of a park, the hotel is still surrounded by the ancient garden of the friars. The bedrooms, ranging from midsize to spacious, have all the modern amenities and are the best accessorized in town. The on-site restaurant serves a superb international and regional cuisine.

Via Tifernate 06024. ② **075-9234.** Fax 075-9220323. 93 units. 145€–170€ ($129.50–$151.80) double; from 235€ ($209.85) suite. **Amenities:** Restaurant; bar; pool; gym; room service; babysitting; laundry/dry cleaning. *In room:* A/C, TV, minibar, hair dryer, safe.

Villa Montegranelli Hotel ★   The area's most tranquil retreat isn't in Gubbio—it's in this restored 18th-century manor house with a distant view of the town. The guest rooms are beautifully furnished, often with antiques, and the bathrooms are modern. The public rooms have been restored in keeping with their original architecture of wood ceilings and stone walls. The staff is among the most helpful and efficient in the area, providing such thoughtful extras as a basket of fresh fruit in your room every day. Even if you can't stay here, consider calling ahead and visiting for an excellent meal.

3km (2 miles) SW of Gubbio. ② **075-9220185.** Fax 075 9273372. www.villamontegranellihotel.it. 21 units. 110€–137.50€ ($98.25–$122.80) double; 155€ ($138.40) suite. AE, DC, MC, V. Free parking. **Amenities:** Recommended restaurant; bar; room service; babysitting; laundry/dry cleaning. *In room:* TV, minibar, hair dryer.

WHERE TO DINE

You can also dine at the Hotel Relais Ducale's refined **Caffè Ducale** or at the restaurant of the **Villa Montegranelli** (see "Where to Stay," above).

Ristorante Federico de Montefeltro ITALIAN/UMBRIAN   Named after the feudal lord who built the ducal palace, this restaurant stands beside steeply inclined flagstones in the oldest part of the city. Inside is a pair of tavern-style dining rooms ringed with exposed stone and pinewood planking. Many of the specialties are based on ancient regional recipes, although the selection of tasty antipasti covers the traditions of most of the Italian peninsula. Menu items include platters garnished with truffles, roast suckling pig, several types of polenta, and spaghetti with mushrooms and tomato. Fresh fish is available on Friday. You'll also be served a local version of unleavened bread fried in oil as part of the meal.

Via della Repubblica 35. ② **075-9273949.** Reservations recommended. Main courses 12.50€–17.50€ ($11.15–$15.65). AE, DC, MC, V. Fri–Wed noon–3pm and 7–11pm.

Taverna del Lupo ★ ITALIAN/UMBRIAN   This is the most authentically medieval of the many competing restaurants in Gubbio. Built in the 1200s, with unusual rows of tiles, it contains ceilings supported by barrel vaults and ribbing of solid stone, from which hang iron chandeliers. For such a relatively modest place, the menu is sophisticated and filled with the rich bounty from this part of Italy, each dish deftly prepared by a talented staff. Choose from a terrine of duck studded with truffles, supreme of pheasant, rich minestrones, or many of the pork, veal, and beef dishes that are distinctly Tuscan.

Via Giovanni Ansidei 21. ② **075-9274368.** Reservations recommended. Main courses 9€–17.50€ ($8.05–$15.65). AE, DC, MC, V. Tues–Sun noon–3pm and 7pm–midnight.

9 Perugia ⓐⓐ

81km (50 miles) SE of Arezzo, 188km (117 miles) N of Rome, 155km (96 miles) SE of Florence

Perugia was one of a dozen major cities in the mysterious Etruscan galaxy, and here you can peel away the epochs. For example, one of the town gates is called the **Arco di Augusto (Arch of Augustus).** The loggia spanning the arch dates from the Renaissance, but the central part is Roman. Builders from both periods used the reliable Etruscan foundation, which was the work of architects who laid stones to last.

Today the city, home to luscious Perugina chocolate, is the capital of Umbria; it has retained much of its Gothic and Renaissance charm, although it has been plagued with wars and swept up in disastrous events. The city is home to universities and art academies, and it attracts a young, vibrant crowd—some of whom can be seen in one of the zillions of local bars, pizzerias, music shops, or cafes enjoying the famous chocolate *baci* (kisses). To capture the essence of the Umbrian city, you must head for **Piazza IV Novembre** in the heart of Perugia. During the day, the square is overrun, so try to go late at night when the old town is sleeping. That's when the ghosts come out to play.

ESSENTIALS

GETTING THERE   Perugia has **rail** links with Rome and Florence, but connections can be awkward. Usually, two trains per day from Rome connect in Foligno, where, if you miss a train, you might face a wait of up to an hour or more. If possible, try to get one of the infrequent direct trains that take only 3 hours, or even an IC train that cuts the trip to 2½ hours. A one-way ticket from Rome costs 10€ to 17.50€ ($8.95–$15.65). Most trains from Florence connect in Terontola, although there are five daily direct trains as well. A one-way fare is 7.50€ ($6.70), but direct trains impose a supplement of about 4.50€ ($4). For information and schedules, call ⓒ **848-888088.** The train station is well away from the main historic center of town, at Piazza Vittorio Veneto. Bus nos. 6, 7, 9, 11, and 12 run to Piazza Italia, which is as close as you can get to the center.

A daily **bus** arrives in Perugia, pulling into Piazza Partigiani, a short walk from the city's historic core. One-way fares from Rome are 14€ ($12.50), and the trip takes 2½ hours. The several buses that pull into Perugia from Florence charge 9.50€ ($8.50) each way, for a trip that takes 2 hours. For information and schedules, call ⓒ **075-5009641.** Buses that operate exclusively in Perugia use Piazza Italia as their central base, departing and arriving there.

If you have a **car** and are coming from either Rome or Florence, Autostrada del Sole (A1) takes you to the cutoff east to Perugia. Just follow the signs. From Siena, SS73 winds its way to Perugia and connects with the autostrada. If you arrive by car, you can drive to your hotel to unload your baggage; after that, you'll be directed to a parking lot on the outskirts.

VISITOR INFORMATION   The **tourist office** is at Piazza IV Novembre 3 (ⓒ **075-5736458**), open Monday to Saturday 8:30am to 6:30pm, and Sunday 8:30am to 1:30pm.

SPECIAL EVENTS   The hottest time to visit Perugia is during Italy's foremost jazz festival, **Umbria Jazz** ⓐⓐ, held in mid-July. Jazz heavies such as Sonny Rollins and Keith Jarrett have shown up here to perform. For ticket sales and schedules, call ⓒ **075-5732432** (www.umbriajazz.com). Tickets cost 12.50€ to 100€ ($11.15–$89.30).

The weeklong **Eurochocolate Festival** ✫ is held annually from mid- to late October in Perugia. You can witness a chocolate-carving contest, when the scraps from the massive blocks are yours for the sampling, and entire multiple-course menus are created around the chocolate theme. Half-day lessons from visiting chefs are also available. For details, contact the **Eurochocolate Organization** (☎ 075-5732670; www.eurochocolate.perugia.it).

EXPLORING THE CITY

The central **Piazza IV Novembre** ✫✫ is one of the most beautiful squares in Italy. In the heart of the piazza is the **Grand Fountain (Fontana Maggiore)** ✫✫, built sometime in the late 1270s by a local architect, a monk named Bevignate. The fountain's artistic triumph stems from the sculptural work by Nicola Pisano and his son, Giovanni. Along the lower basin is statuary symbolizing the arts and sciences, Aesop's fables, the months of the year, the signs of the zodiac, and scenes from the Old Testament and Roman history. On the upper basin (mostly the work of Giovanni) is allegorical sculpture, including a figure who represents Perugia, as well as sculptures of saints, biblical characters, and even 13th-century local officials. The fountain emerged spectacularly from a major restoration in 1999, gleaming white as new.

Most of the other major attractions either open onto Piazza IV Novembre or lie only a short distance away.

An escalator will take you from the older part of Perugia at the top of the hill and the upper slopes to the lower city. During construction, the old **Rocca Paolina** ✫ fortress, Via Marzia, was rediscovered, along with buried streets. The fortress had been covered over to make the gardens and viewing area at the end of Corso Vannucci in the last century. The old streets and street names have been cleaned up, and the area is well lighted, with an old wall exposed and modern sculpture added. The fortress was built in the 1500s by Sangallo. The Etruscan gate, **Porta Marzia,** is buried in the old city walls and can be viewed from Via Baglioni Sotterranea. This street lies in the fortress and is lined with houses, some from the 1400s. The escalator to the Rocca operates daily 6am to 1am; the Rocca is open daily 8am to 7pm.

Il Duomo (Cathedral of San Lorenzo) ✫   The basilica was built in the Gothic style and dates from the 14th and 15th centuries. Its exterior is rather raw-looking, as if the builders had suddenly been called away and never returned. In the **Cappella di San Bernardino,** you'll find *Descent from the Cross,* by Frederico Barocchio. In the **Cappella del Sacremento** hangs Luca Signorelli's *Madonna,* an altarpiece created in 1484. Signorelli was a pupil of della Francesca.

Piazza IV Novembre. ☎ 075-5723832. Free admission. Church daily 7am–12:30pm and 4–6:45pm. Cappella Mon–Sat 9–9:30am, 10:30–11am, 11:45am–12:45pm, and 3:30–5:15pm; Sun 6–6:45pm.

National Gallery of Umbria (Galleria Nazionale dell'Umbria) ✫✫ Opposite Il Duomo is the Palace of the Priors (Palazzo dei Priori), one of the finest secular buildings in Italy, dating from the 13th century and containing both the National Gallery and the Collegio del Cambio (see below). The facade holds bronze copies of the 13th-century griffin (symbol of Perugia) and the Guelph (papal) lion, both holding the massive chains once used to close the city gates of Siena. These chains were looted from Siena when Perugia scored a military victory over the town in 1358. You can walk up the stairway (the Vaccara) to the pulpit. By all means, explore the interior, especially the vaulted *Sala*

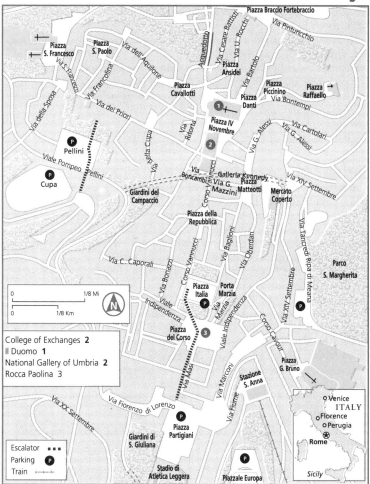

College of Exchanges **2**
Il Duomo **1**
National Gallery of Umbria **2**
Rocca Paolina **3**

Escalator ...
Parking P
Train ⊢━━━┥

ITALY
○ Venice
○ Florence
⊛ Perugia
⊛ Rome
Sicily

---

dei Notari, frescoed with stories of the Old Testament and from Aesop. From October to May, it's open Tuesday to Sunday 9am to 1pm and 3 to 7pm (June–Sept, it's open daily the same hours).

On the palazzo's third floor is the **National Gallery of Umbria,** containing the most comprehensive collection of Umbrian art from the 13th to 19th centuries. Among the earliest paintings of interest (room 4) is a *Virgin and Child* (1304), by Duccio di Buoninsegna, the first important master of the Sienese school. Also in this room is a small *Madonna and Child* (1405), by Gentile da Fabriano, one of the gems of the collection. In room 5, you'll see a masterpiece by Piero della Francesca, the *Polyptych of Sant'Antonio,* a massive altarpiece from the mid–15th century. Guarded by a medley of saints, the Virgin is enthroned in a classical setting.

No one is exactly sure who painted the eight panels in room 8. Dating from 1473, the *Miracles of St. Bernardino of Siena* was created in a workshop of the time. Both Perugino and Francesco di Giorgio Martini might have worked on these panels.

In room 9 are works of native son Perugino, among them his *Adoration of the Magi,* from 1475. Perugino was the master of Raphael. He was often accused of sentimentality, and today Perugino doesn't enjoy the popularity that he did at the peak of his career. However, he remains a key Renaissance painter, noted for his landscapes, as exemplified by the 1517 *Transfiguration.* You'll also find art by Pinturicchio, who studied under Perugino and whose most notable work was the library of Siena's Duomo.

3rd floor of the Palazzo dei Priori, Corso Vannucci 19. ⓒ 075-5741247. Admission 6€ ($5.35). Daily 8:30am–7pm. Closed 1st Mon of every month.

College of Exchanges (Collegio del Cambio) ⭐   During the Middle Ages, this section of the sprawling Palazzo dei Priori was conceived as a precursor of today's commodities exchanges, where grains, cloth, foodstuffs, gold, silver, and currencies were exchanged by the savvy merchants of Perugia. Today, its artistic and architectural appeal is largely centered on the **Hall of the Audience (Sala dell'Udienza)** ⭐⭐, a meeting room whose frescoes were painted by Perugino and his assistants, one of whom was a 17-year-old Raphael.

On the ceiling, Perugino represented the planets allegorically. The Renaissance master peopled his frescoes with the Virtues, sibyls, and such biblical figures as Solomon. But his masterpiece is his own countenance. It seems rather ironic that (at least for once) Perugino could be realistic, even depicting a chubby face and double chins resting under a red cap. Another room of interest is the **Chapel of S. J. Battista (Cappella di S. J. Bastista),** which contains many frescoes painted by a pupil of Perugino, G. Nicola di Paolo.

Corso Vannucci 25, street level of the Palazzo dei Priori (listed previously). ⓒ 075-5728599. Admission 2.50€ ($2.25). Mar–Oct Mon–Sat 9am–12:30pm and 2:30–5:30pm, Sun and holidays 9am–12:30pm; Nov–Feb Tues–Sat 8am–2pm, Sun and holidays 9am–12:30pm. Closed New Year's Day, May Day, and Christmas.

SHOPPING

The most famous foodstuff in town comes from one of Italy's best-loved manufacturers of chocolates and bonbons, **Perugina.** Displays of the foil-wrapped chocolates crop up at tobacco shops, supermarkets, newspaper kiosks, and sometimes gas stations around the city. The selection includes *cioccolato al latte* (milk chocolate) and its darker counterpart, *cioccolato fondente,* both sold in everything from mouth-size morsels (*baci*) to romance-size decorative boxes. One always-reliable place to buy is from the factory itself, which offers tours to those who phone in advance: The **Fabbrica Nestle Perugina** (ⓒ 075-52761), 5km (3 miles) west of Perugia's historic core, forms the centerpiece of the hamlet of San Sisto. It's open Monday to Friday 9am to 1pm and 2 to 5pm (Sat and Sun by arrangement). Admission is free. Call to book your visit.

Looking for ceramics and souvenirs that'll last longer than chocolate? Head for one of Perugia's most interesting shops, **La Bottega dei Bassai,** Via Baglioni 32 (ⓒ 075-5723108).

If you're searching for fashion, particularly the cashmere garments that are tailored and often designed in Perugia, consider a jaunt 6km (3¾ miles) south to the village of Ponta San Giovanni, where one of the largest inventories of cashmere garments (coats, suits, dresses, and sweaters) for men and women is stockpiled at **Big Bertha,** Via Industria 19, Ponte San Giovanni (ⓒ 075-5997572).

WHERE TO STAY

Brufani Palace ✦   This deluxe hotel is Perugia's finest choice. Situated at the top of the city, part of this deluxe hotel was built by Giocomo Brufani in 1884 on the ruins of the ancient Rocca Paolina, a site known to the ancient Romans that later served as a papal address. The Brufani combined with the much larger Palace Hotel Bellavista to form the hotel you see today. The Bellavista was built in the late 1800s as a home for a prominent English family, the Collinses, who eventually married into the aristocratic Brufanis. Now there's a wedding again with the marriage of the two structures. Many of the guest rooms open onto wonderful views of the countryside. Some of the grander rooms have antiques and frescoed ceilings, but all are elegant and filled with modern luxuries. The best accommodations are on the second and third floors. Avoid the cramped cells, nos. 129 and 229, however.

Piazza Italia 12, 06121 Perugia. ℂ **075-5732541**. Fax 075-5720210. www.brufanipalace.com. 94 units. 253€–300€ ($225.90–$267.85) double; 413€–775€ ($368.80–$692.10) suite. AE, MC, V. Parking 27.50€ ($24.55). **Amenities:** 3 restaurants; 2 bars; cafe; pool; exercise room; sauna; room service; babysitting; laundry/dry cleaning. *In room:* A/C, TV, minibar, hair dryer, safe.

Hotel Fortuna Perugia *Value*   Here's a chance to stay at a government-rated four-star hotel that in 1996 deliberately "downgraded" itself to three-star status and lowered its prices. In the heart of town, it dates from the 13th century but has been extensively reconstructed over the years. Today, arched leaded-glass doors lead to an interior of hardwood floors and tasteful art. The guest rooms boast sleek contemporary styling (often blond woods and flamboyant fabrics) and are filled with modern amenities. Even better than the rooms are the views, some of which might have inspired Perugino himself. The hotel has a rooftop terrace opening onto the tile roofs of the town and the Umbrian landscape. When the weather is right, guests take their cappuccinos and croissants here.

Via Bonazzi 19, 06123 Perugia. ℂ and fax **075-5722845**. www.umbriahotels.com. 34 units. 73€–114€ ($65.20–$101.80) double; 123€–145€ ($109.85–$129.50) suite. Rates include buffet breakfast. AE, DC, MC, V. Parking 20€ ($17.85) nearby. **Amenities:** Bar; room service; babysitting; laundry. *In room:* A/C, TV, minibar, hair dryer, safe.

Hotel La Rosetta   From humble beginnings, this is now one of Perugia's leading inns. Since this Perugian landmark opened in 1927, it has expanded from a seven-room pensione to a labyrinthine complex (it's the big hangout for the musicians in town for the jazz festival). Guest rooms vary from cramped to palatial, with curving Empire bed frames in some and modular units in others. With its frescoed ceiling, Suite 55 has been declared a national treasure. (The bullet holes that papal mercenaries shot into the ceiling in 1848 have been artfully preserved.) Each unit is peaceful, clean, and comfortable, though the bathrooms could be better outfitted for these prices.

Piazza Italia 19, 06121 Perugia. ℂ and fax **075-5720841**. 90 units. 115€ ($102.70) double; 160€ ($142.85) suite. Rates include breakfast. AE, DC, MC, V. Parking 15€ ($13.40). **Amenities:** Restaurant; bar; room service; babysitting; laundry/dry cleaning. *In room:* A/C, TV, minibar, hair dryer, safe.

Locanda della Posta   This time-honored inn enjoys the town's most central location, in the heart of corso Vannucci, the main drag. Goethe and Hans Christian Andersen slept here—in fact, this used to be the only hotel in Perugia. It sits behind an impressive ornate facade sculpted in the 1700s. The della Posta's views might not be grand, but it's nostalgic and inviting. The guest rooms are generally spacious, with fabric-covered walls, Art Nouveau floral prints, and sturdy wood furnishings.

Corso Vannucci 97, 06121 Perugia. ℂ **075-5728925.** Fax 075-5732562. www.umbriatravel.com/locanda dellaposta. 40 units. 134€–170€ ($119.65–$151.80) double; 201€ ($179.50) suite. Rates include buffet breakfast. AE, DC, MC, V. Parking 15€ ($13.40) in nearby garage. **Amenities:** Bar; room service; babysitting; laundry. *In room:* A/C, TV, minibar, hair dryer, safe.

Sangallo Palace Hotel 🔆   Rivaled only by the Brufani, this palace in the historic zone is a contemporary classic, up-to-date and favored by local business travelers. A roomy interior and a lobby of marble columns and fine furnishings are immediately welcoming. The halls are lined with reproductions of the works of Perugino, and over each bed is a framed reproduction of a Perugino or Pinturicchio. The guest rooms boast many luxuries, such as extra wide beds, and some open onto panoramic views of the countryside.

Via Masi 9, 06100 Perugia. ℂ **075-5730202.** Fax 075-5730068. www.sangallo.it. 93 units (some with shower only). 110€–158€ ($98.25–$141.10) double; from 200€ ($178.60) suite. Rates include breakfast. AE, DC, MC, V. **Amenities:** Well-recommended restaurant; bar; pool; gym; room service; babysitting; laundry/dry cleaning. *In room:* A/C, TV, dataport, minibar, hair dryer, safe.

WHERE TO DINE

Antica Trattoria San Lorenzo UMBRIAN   This family-run spot is known for its fresh ingredients, culinary flair, and elegant presentation. The restaurant is housed in an antique building, whose interior is decorated in part with marble that came from the Duomo. An interesting feature here is a canteen where you can sample some 700 different labels of wine. Our favorite appetizer is filet of chicken with black truffles and porcini mushrooms. After that you might follow with pasta *mezza luna* ("half-moon" pasta tossed with duck in a tomato-and-bacon sauce). Many desserts make use of the famed chocolate of Perugia, and none is finer than the chocolate and hazelnut soufflé.

Piazza Danti 19A. ℂ **075-5721956.** Reservations recommended. Main courses 9€–10€ ($8.05–$8.95); tasting menu 25€ ($22.35). AE, DC, MC, V. Mon–Sat 12:30–2:30pm and 7:30–11pm. Open Sun May–Oct.

Il Falchetto 🔆🔆 UMBRIAN/ITALIAN   This restaurant, a short walk from Piazza Piccinino (where you'll be able to park), has flourished in this 19th-century building since 1941. The dining room in the rear has the most medieval ambience, with its stone walls dating from the 1300s. In summer you might like a table outside (during Umbria Jazz, it's like having free seats to the concerts on Piazza IV Novembre). Many of the dishes adhere to traditional themes and have a certain zest. Menu items include tagliatelle with truffles, grilled trout from the Nera River, prosciutto several ways, pasta with chickpeas, grilled goat filet, and filet steak with truffles. One special dish is *falchetti* (gnocchi with ricotta and spinach). Some of the best Umbrian wines are served.

Via Bartolo 20. ℂ **075-5731775.** Reservations recommended. Main courses 13.50€–30€ ($12.05–$26.80). AE, DISC, MC, V. Tues–Sun noon–2:30pm and 7:30–10:30pm. Closed Jan 15–31.

La Taverna 🔆 UMBRIAN   One of Umbria's most innovative restaurants, La Taverna occupies a medieval house, and offers the best regional cuisine. Its entrance is at the bottom of one of the narrowest alleys in town, in the heart of the historic center. (Prominent signs indicate its position off Corso Vannucci.) Three dining rooms, filled with exposed masonry, oil paintings, and a polite staff, radiate from the high-ceilinged vestibule. The cuisine is inspired by Claudio Brugalossi, an Umbrian chef who spent part of his career in Tampa, Florida, working for the Hyatt chain. The best menu choices include truffle-stuffed ravioli, tagliata with arugula, veal slices with raisins and pine nuts, and grilled red snapper. For something really local and really good, order the Colfiorito lamb and grilled local pecorino cheese.

Via delle Streghe 8. © 075-5724128. Reservations recommended. Main courses 10€–15€ ($8.95–$13.40). AE, DC, MC, V. Tues–Sun 12:30–2:30pm and 7:30–11pm.

Osteria del Bartolo ☆☆ MEDITERRANEAN In the heart of the city, Perugia's finest restaurant lies only a short stroll from the landmark Maggiore Fountain. The owner/chef, Ezio Maria Ciani, and his staff extend a hearty welcome to visitors and invite them to partake of their refined cuisine. Early each morning the shopping for fresh ingredients is completed, while the pots in the kitchen are bubbling with soups and sauces. Whenever possible they try to use the produce of the region, turning out dishes rich in olive oil, fresh tomatoes, garden-fresh basil, fish, and an array of luscious vegetables. One of their daily soups might be studded with the rare and delicate Norcia black truffle of the region. Lamb appears baked in a pastry case with fresh herbs and served with potatoes seasoned with hazelnut oil. For dessert, take delight in a dark Perugia chocolate mousse with a basil-flavored cream.

Via Bartolo 30. © 075-5731561. Reservations required. Main courses 15€–19€ ($13.40–$16.95). AE, DC, MC, V. Apr–Oct Mon–Sat 8pm–midnight. Off-season 12:30–3pm and 8pm–midnight.

PERUGIA AFTER DARK

Begin your evening by joining Italy's liveliest *passeggiata* (a promenade at dusk) along **Corso Vannucci,** a pedestrian strip running north to south. Everyone, especially the students of Perugia, seems to stroll here. Many drop into one of the little cafes or enoteche for a drink. If you do a cafe hop or wine-bar crawl, you can sample as many as 150 wines from 60 Umbrian vineyards—providing that you can stay on your feet.

Two cafes outshine the rest: The better is chandelier-lit **Sandri Pasticceria,** Corso Vannucci 32 (© **075-5724112**), offering drinks, cakes, pastries, and sandwiches. You can also order full meals, including eggplant parmigiana and veal cutlet Milanese. It's another outlet for the city's famous chocolates. Sandri's main competitor is **Caffè del Cambio,** Corso Vannucci 29 (© **075-5724165**), a favorite of university students. The first room, with its vaulted ceiling, is most impressive; it contains racks of pastries, cones of ice cream, a long stand-up bar, and a handful of tiny tables. The low-ceilinged room in back is smoky, more crowded, and much livelier.

In **Hostaria del Lupo Mannaro,** Via Guardabassi 4, near Piazza Morlacchi (© **075-5736827**), you'll find an affordable Umbrian restaurant until about 10pm, when it transforms itself into a wine bar for a few hours. It's a funky, loud spot where, later in the evening, recorded music reverberates off the old stones of the very old vaulting. If you've got a hankering to go dancing, the best bet within Perugia's town center is **Velvet,** Viale Roma 20 (© **075-5721321**), which attracts a relatively young (in their 20s) crowd, who dance and interact with one another every night except Monday from 8pm to 3am. There's no cover charge, but someone will probably urge you to buy at least one drink before the night is over. Its most visible competitor, and more favored by night owls in their 30s and 40s, is **Disco Gradisco,** Ponte Valle Ceppi (© **075-5928611**). It lies almost immediately adjacent to the Ponte Valle Ceppi exit off the SuperStradale (superhighway) E45, about 5 miles east of Perugia. Charging 12.50€ ($11.15) for entrance, which includes one free drink, it's open only Thursday and Saturday from 11pm to at least 3am.

A SIDE TRIP TO DERUTA

One of the highlights of a trip to this part of Italy is shopping for a product that has been associated with Umbria since the days of the Renaissance painters. The manufacturing town of **Deruta,** 20km (12 miles) south of Perugia off Via Flaminia (beside E45 in the direction of Rome), has more than 300 ceramics manufacturers lining both sides of the town's main street. If you're not driving, you can catch one of six daily buses marked PERUGIA–DERUTA at Perugia's Piazza Partigiana.

By the way, don't even think of saying the word *porcelain* in town. (*Stoneware,* or, even better, *glazed terra cotta,* is preferred.) Terra-cotta clay is formed into sturdy bowls, umbrella stands, plates, cups, and art objects; they're fired and then glazed with distinctive arabesques and bright colors before being fired again. Especially popular is a design associated with the region since the Renaissance (when Raphael commissioned some of the ceramic ware here): a motif of dragons cavorting amid flowers and vines.

The largest manufacturer, with some of the most reliable shipping services and the biggest sampling of wares, is **Ubaldo Grazia,** Via Tiberina 181 (℡ **075-9710201**). It's a sophisticated place, selling fine copies of antique designs plus sleeker, more contemporary pieces. Many pieces of its colorfully painted stoneware are featured in Tiffany's, Bergdorf Goodman, and upscale mail-order catalogs such as Williams Sonoma. Specialties include cachepots, vases, and dinnerware. Anything that you buy on-site can be shipped via UPS to any destination in the world. The factory outlet is open Monday to Friday 9am to 1pm and 2:30 to 6:30pm, and Saturday 9am to 1pm. Free factory tours, lasting about half an hour, are sometimes offered to those who phone and reserve in advance.

A less comprehensive nearby competitor is **Antonio Margaritelli,** Via Tiberina 214 (℡ **075-9711572**). Founded in 1975, this factory outlet stocks material that's roughly equivalent to that at the Ubaldo Grazia factories but with a less diverse selection.

Before you buy, you can get a fast education in the town's ceramic traditions from the **Museo della Ceramica Umbra,** Palazzo del Comune, Piazza dei Consoli (℡ **075-9711100**). It's open Tuesday to Sunday 10am to 1pm and 3 to 6pm, charging 2.50€ ($2.25) for a view of ceramics produced in the region between the 1500s and today. The museum was enlarged and expanded in 1997, almost as a gesture of civic pride.

10 Assisi ✫✫✫

177km (110 miles) N of Rome, 24km (15 miles) SE of Perugia

Ideally placed on the rise to Mt. Subasio, watched over by the medieval Rocco Maggiore, the purple-fringed Umbrian hill town of Assisi retains a mystical air. The site of many a pilgrimage, Assisi is forever linked in legend with its native son, St. Francis. The gentle saint founded the Franciscan order and shares honors with St. Catherine of Siena as the patron saint of Italy. But he's remembered by many, even non-Christians, as a lover of nature (his preaching to an audience of birds is one of the legends of his life). Dante compared him to John the Baptist.

St. Francis put Assisi on the map, and making a pilgrimage here is one of the highlights of a visit to Umbria. Today, Italy's Catholic youth flock here for religious conferences, festivals, and reflection. But even without St. Francis, the hill town merits a visit for its interesting sights and architecture. Sightseers and

Assisi

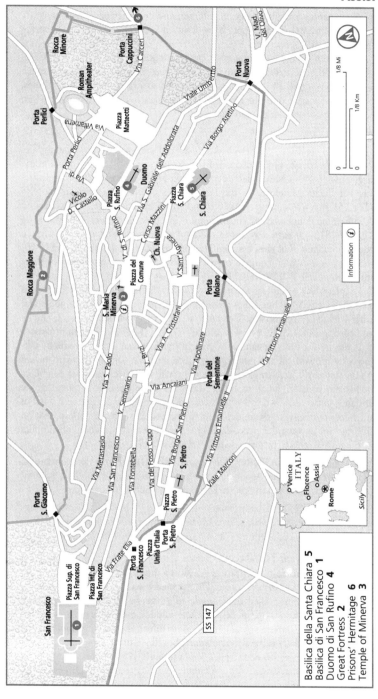

San Francesco

Piazza Sup. di
San Francesco

Piazza Inf. di
San Francesco

Porta
S. Giacomo

Via Frate Elia

Piazza
Unità d'Italia

Porta
S. Francesco

Piazza
S. Pietro

Porta
S. Pietro

S. Pietro

Via Borgo San Pietro

Via del Fosso Cupo

Via Fontebella

Via San Francesco

Via Metastasio

Via S. Paolo

V. Seminario

V. Brizi

Via A. Cristofani

Via Ancaiani

Via Apollinare

Viale Marconi

Via Vittorio Emanuele II

Porta del
Sementone

Porta
Moiano

S. Maria
Minerva

Piazza del
Comune

Ch. Nuova

V. di S. Rufino

V. Sant'Ana

V. S. Gabriele dell'Addolorata

Corso Mazzini

Via Nuova

Piazza
S. Rufino

Duomo

S. Rufino

Piazza
S. Chiara

S. Chiara

Via Borgo Aretino

Viale Umbertto

Porta
Nuova

V. Mad.
del Olivo

Rocca Maggiore

Vicolo
D. Castello

Via di
Porta Perlici

Via Villamena

Porta
Perlici

Piazza
Matteotti

Roman
Amphitheater

Rocca
Minore

Porta
Cappuccini

Via Carceri

SS 147

ITALY
Venice
Florence
Assisi
Rome
Sicily

Information

1/8 Mi
1/8 Km
0
0

Basilica della Santa Chiara **5**
Basilica di San Francesco **1**
Duomo di San Rufino **4**
Great Fortress **2**
Prisons' Hermitage **6**
Temple of Minerva **3**

pilgrims simply pack the town in summer, and at Easter or Christmas you're likely to be trampled underfoot. We've found it best and less crowded in spring or fall.

Assisi was hit by the devastating twin earthquakes that shook Umbria in 1997, but the recovery and restoration have been remarkable, although much remains to be done. Massive damage was caused to a great many historical sites, but the major attraction, the Basilica di San Francesco, reopened late in 1999 in time to greet visitors at the Jubilee.

ESSENTIALS

GETTING THERE Although there's no **rail station** in Assisi, the city lies within a 30-minute bus or taxi ride from the rail station in nearby Santa Maria degli Angeli. From Santa Maria degli Angeli, buses depart at 30-minute intervals for Piazza Matteotti, in the heart of Assisi. One-way fares are 12.50€ ($11.15). If you're coming to Assisi from Perugia by train, expect to pay around 1.75€ ($1.55) one way. If you're coming from Rome, expect to pay around 13.50€ ($12.05) each way. From either of those points, expect a transfer en route in Foligno. Rail fares between Florence and Assisi are about 13€ ($11.60) each way and usually require a transfer in the junction of Terontola. For more information call ☎ 075-8040272.

Frequent **buses** connect Perugia with Assisi; the trip takes 1 hour and costs 2.75€ ($2.45). One bus a day arrives from Rome; it takes about 3 hours and costs 16€ ($14.30) one way. Two buses pull in from Florence, taking 2½ hours and costing 11€ ($9.80) one way. Call ☎ **075-5731707** for more information.

If you have a **car,** you can make the trip from Perugia in 30 minutes by taking S3 southwest. At the junction of Route 147, just follow the signs toward Assisi. But you'll have to park outside the town's core because those neighborhoods are usually closed to traffic. (*Note:* The police officer guarding the entrance to the old town will usually let motorists drop off luggage at a hotel in the historic zone, with the understanding that you'll eventually park in a lot on the outskirts of town. Likewise, delivery vehicles are allowed to drop off supplies in the town's pedestrian zones daily 10am–noon and 4–6pm.)

VISITOR INFORMATION The **tourist office** is at Piazza del Comune 22 (☎ **075-812534**), open Monday to Friday 8am to 2pm and 3:30 to 6:30pm, Saturday 9am to 1pm and 3:30 to 6:30pm, and Sunday 9am to 1pm.

SPECIAL EVENTS The first weekend after May 1 brings the **Calendimaggio** spring festival, with processions, medieval contests of strength and skill, late-night partying in 14th-century costumes, and singing duels on the main piazza.

EXPLORING THE TOWN

Piazza del Comune, in the heart of Assisi, is a dream for lovers of architecture from the 12th to the 14th centuries. On the square is a pagan structure, with six Corinthian columns, called the **Temple of Minerva (Tempio di Minerva),** from the 1st century B.C. With Minerva-like wisdom, the people of Assisi turned the interior into a baroque church, so as not to offend the devout. Adjoining the temple is the 13th-century **Tower (Torre),** built by Ghibelline supporters. The site is open daily 7am to noon and 2:30pm to dusk.

Basilica di San Francesco ★★★ This important basilica, with both an upper church (1230–53) and a lower church (1228–30), houses some of the most important **cycles of frescoes** in Italy, including works by such pre-Renaissance giants as Cimabue and Giotto. The basilica and its paintings form the most significant monument to St. Francis, a focal point of both high art and intense spirituality. After a major restoration effort involving some of Europe's greatest craftsmen, the basilica reopened to the public late in 1999 after having been closed in the aftermath of the 1997 earthquake.

On the entrance wall, you can enjoy **Giotto's celebrated frescoes of St. Francis** ✶✶✶ preaching to the birds. In the nave is the cycle of 27 additional frescoes, some by Giotto, although the authorship of the entire cycle is uncertain. Many of these are almost surrealistic (in architectural frameworks), like a stage set that strips away the walls and allows you to see the actors inside. In the cycle, you can see pictorial evidence of the rise of humanism that led to Giotto's and Italy's split away from the rigidity of Byzantium.

The upper church also contains a damaged Cimabue masterpiece, his *Crucifixion* ✶. Time and quakes have robbed the fresco of its former radiance, but its power and ghostlike drama remain, at least on video. The cycle of badly damaged frescoes in the transept and apse are other works by Cimabue and his helpers.

The **lower church** was speedily reopened after the quakes, with only marginal damage. Reached by the entrance in Piazza Inferiore on the south side of the basilica, it's dark and mystical (if you're lucky enough to find a moment of calm between the arrival of fender-to-fender tour buses) and almost entirely covered with **frescoes** ✶✶✶ by the greatest pre-Renaissance painters of the 13th and 14th centuries. Look for Cimabue's faded but masterly *Virgin and Child* with four angels and St. Francis looking on from the far right; it's often reproduced in detail as one of Cimabue's greatest works. On the other side is the *Deposition from the Cross,* a masterpiece by Sienese artist Pietro Lorenzetti, plus a *Madonna and Child* with St. John and St. Francis (stigmata showing). In a chapel honoring St. Martin of Tours, Simone Martini of Siena painted a cycle of frescoes, with great skill and imagination, depicting the life and times of that saint. Finally, under the lower church is the **crypt of St. Francis,** with some relics of the saint. In the past, only scholars and clergymen were allowed access to the vaults containing these highly cherished articles, but now anyone can visit. Some of the items displayed are the saint's tunic, cowl, and shoes and the chalice and communion plate used by him and his followers.

Insider tip: The Franciscan community affiliated with the basilica offers free guided tours by English-speaking friars Monday to Saturday 9:30am to noon and 2 to 5:30pm (to 4:30pm in winter), and Sunday 2 to 6pm (to 4:30pm in winter). Stop by the office just left of the entrance to the lower church in Piazza Inferiore (✆ **075-8190084**). Tours don't go into the basilica itself to avoid disrupting worshippers (although the friar will tell you lots about the church), but do visit other sites and explore the life of St. Francis and today's religious community.

Tips A San Francesco Warning

The church has a strict dress code: Entrance to the basilica is absolutely forbidden to those wearing shorts or miniskirts or showing bare shoulders. You must remain silent and cannot take any photographs in the Upper Church.

From the lower church, you can also visit the **Treasury** ★★ and the **Perkins Collection.** The Treasury shelters precious church relics, often in gold and silver, and even the original gray sackcloth worn by St. Francis before the order adopted the brown tunic. The Perkins Collection is a limited but rich exhibit donated by a U.S. philanthropist who had assembled a collection of Tuscan/Renaissance works, including paintings by Luca Signorelli and Fra Angelico. The Treasury and the Perkins Collection are open daily 9:30am to noon and 2 to 6pm (closed Sun and Nov–March) and cost 1.50€ ($1.35).

Piazza San Francesco. © 075-819001. Free admission. Daily 8:30am–6pm.

Prisons' Hermitage (Eremo delle Carceri) ★★

This "prison," from the 14th and 15th centuries, is not a penal institution but a spiritual retreat. It's believed that St. Francis retired to this spot for meditation and prayer. Out back is a moss-covered, gnarled *ilex* (live oak) more than 1,000 years old, where St. Francis is believed to have blessed the birds; after the blessing, they flew in the four major compass directions to symbolize that Franciscans, in coming centuries, would spread from Assisi all over the world. The friary contains some faded frescoes. One of the handful of friars who still inhabit the retreat will show you through. (In keeping with the Franciscan tradition, they're completely dependent on alms for their support.)

About 4km (2½ miles) east of Assisi (out Via Eremo delle Carceri), on Via Eremo delle Carceri. © 075-812301. Free admission (donations accepted). Apr–Oct daily 7am–7pm; Nov–Mar daily 7am–5pm.

Great Fortress (Rocca Maggiore) ★★

The Great Fortress sits astride a hill overlooking Assisi. It's worth the visit, if only for the panoramic view of the Umbrian countryside from its ramparts. The present building (now in ruins but spared by the earthquakes' wrath) dates from the 14th century, and the origins of the structure go back beyond time. The dreaded Cardinal Albornoz built the medieval version to establish papal domination over the town. A circular rampart was built in the 1500s by Pope Paul III.

Reached by an unmarked stepped street opposite the basilica. © 075-815292. Admission 1.50€ ($1.35). Daily 10am–dusk.

Basilica della Santa Chiara (Clare) ★★

The basilica is dedicated to "the little plant of Blessed Francis," as St. Clare liked to describe herself. Born in 1193 into one of the noblest families of Assisi, Clare gave all her wealth to the poor and founded, together with St. Francis, the Order of the Poor Clares. She was canonized by Pope Alexander IV in 1255.

Although many of the frescoes that once adorned the basilica have been completely or partially destroyed (not as a result of the quakes), much remains that's worthy of note. Upon entering, your attention will be caught by the striking *Crucifix* behind the main altar, a painting on wood dating from the time of the church itself (ca. 1260). The work is by "the Master of St. Clare," who's also responsible for the beautiful icons on either side of the transept. In the left transept is an oft-reproduced fresco of the Nativity from the 14th century. The basilica houses the remains of St. Clare, as well as the crucifix under which St. Francis received his command from above.

The closest bus stop is near Porta Nuova, the eastern gate to the city at the beginning of Viale Umberto I. The bus doesn't have a number; it departs from the depot in Piazza Matteotti for its first run to the train station at 5:35am and concludes its final run at 11:59pm. Buses arrive at half-hour intervals.

Warning: The custodian turns away visitors in shorts, miniskirts, plunging necklines, and backless or sleeveless attire.

Piazza di Santa Chiara 1. ② **075-812282.** Free admission. Nov–Mar daily 6:30am–noon and 2–6pm; Apr–Oct daily 6:30am–12:05pm and 2–6:55pm.

Duomo di San Rufino ✦   Built in the mid–12th century, the Duomo is graced with a Romanesque facade, greatly enhanced by rose windows. This is one of the finest churches in the hill towns, as important as the one at Spoleto. Adjoining it is a bell tower (campanile). Inside, the church has been baroqued, an unfortunate decision that destroyed the purity that the front suggests. St. Francis and St. Clare were both baptized here. The church was spared any damage during the quakes.

Piazza San Rufino. ② **075-812285.** Church free; crypt and museum 1.50€ ($1.35). May–Oct daily 10am–noon and 2:30–6pm (weekends only Nov–Apr).

WHERE TO STAY

Space in Assisi tends to be tight, so book as far in advance as possible.

Albergo Ristorante del Viaggiatore *Value*   This budget choice offers a great deal. The ancient town house has been totally renovated, although the stone walls and arched entryways of the lobby hint at its age. The high-ceilinged guest rooms are spacious and contemporary, with cramped bathrooms.

Via San Antonio 14, 06081 Assisi. ② **075-816297** or 075-812424. Fax 075-813051. 16 units (showers only). 65€ ($58.05) double. Half-board 47.50€ ($42.40) per person. Rates include breakfast. DC, MC, V. **Amenities:** Restaurant; bar. *In room:* A/C, TV, hair dryer.

Grand Hotel Assisi ✦✦   At last Assisi—never known for its good hotels— has a front-ranking charmer, replacing the spot traditionally held by the Hotel Subasio. The latter continues to draw fire from readers but still basks in its glory of having sheltered Marlene Dietrich, Bette Davis, and Charlie Chaplin (that was a long time ago). The Grand's roof garden terrace is its most dramatic feature. It offers the most comfortable and best furnished rooms in town, the suites coming with a hydromassage tub and a balcony opening onto a panoramic view. The on-site restaurant is also one of the best in town, featuring homemade pastas, delicious truffles, and other succulent ingredients, plus the finest wines from the Umbrian hills.

Via Fratelli Canonichetti, 06081 Assisi. ② **075-81501.** Fax 075-8150777. www.grandhotelassisi.com. 156 units (some with tub only, some with shower only). 134€–170€ ($119.65–$151.80) double; 230€–439€ ($205.40–$392.05) suite. Rates include buffet breakfast. AE, DC, MC, V. Parking 20€ ($17.85). **Amenities:** 2 restaurants; 2 bars; indoor pool; fitness center; sauna; room service; babysitting; laundry/dry cleaning. *In room:* A/C, TV, minibar, hair dryer, safe.

Hotel dei Priori   Opened in 1923, this hotel occupies one of the town's most historic buildings, dating from the 16th century, when it was known as the Palazzo Nepis. A homey, somewhat old-fashioned atmosphere prevails. Marble staircases and floors, terra cotta, vaulted ceilings, and stone-arched doors remain from its heyday. Antiques and tasteful prints in both the guest rooms and the public areas add grace notes, along with a collection of Oriental rugs. Many of the rooms are a bit small, but each has a comfortable bed and a tidy bathroom.

Corso Mazzini 15, 06081 Assisi. ② **075-812237.** Fax 075-816804. www.assisihotel.net. 34 units. 75€–120€ ($67–$107.15) double; 125€–160€ ($111.60–$142.85) suite. Rates include breakfast. AE, DC, MC, V. Parking 10€ ($8.95) nearby. **Amenities:** Restaurant (only for hotel guests; closed Nov–Mar); bar; room service; babysitting; laundry/dry cleaning. *In room:* A/C, TV, minibar, hair dryer, safe.

Hotel Giotto ⭐ The Giotto is up-to-date and well run, built at the edge of town on several levels and opening onto panoramic views. Some of the foundations are 500 years old, but because of frequent modernizations, it's hard to tell. It offers spacious, modern public rooms and comfortable guest rooms; bright colors predominate, although many rooms look tatty. The small bathrooms still manage to offer adequate shelf space. There are small formal gardens and terraces for meals or sunbathing.

Via Fontebella 41, 06082 Assisi. ℂ 075-812209. Fax 075-816479. 68 units (showers only). 136€ ($121.45) double. Rates include breakfast. AE, DC, MC, V. Closed Nov–Mar. Free parking. **Amenities:** Restaurant; bar; room service; babysitting; laundry. *In room:* A/C, TV, minibar.

Hotel Sole *Value* For Umbrian hospitality and a general down-home feeling, the Sole is a winner. The severe beauty of rough stone walls and ceilings, terracotta floors, and marble staircases pays homage to the past, balanced by big-cushioned chairs in the TV lounge and contemporary wrought-iron beds and well-worn furnishings in the guest rooms. Some rooms are across the street in an annex. The hotel shows some wear and tear, but the price is right, the location is central, and the restaurant is a good choice even if you aren't a guest (you might want to take the meal plan, if you are).

Corso Mazzini 35, 06081 Assisi. ℂ 075-812373 or 075-812922. Fax 075-813706. www.italyhotels.it. 38 units (showers only). 60€ ($53.60) double; 72.50€ ($64.75) triple. Half-board (Apr–Nov) 47.50€ ($42.40) per person. AE, DC, MC, V. **Amenities:** Well-recommended restaurant (closed Dec–Mar); bar; room service. *In room:* TV, coffeemaker, safe.

Hotel Umbra ⭐ Only the odd pointed-stone Gothic arch and a few other architectural elements remain from the collection of 13th-century houses from which the Umbra was converted. The large whitewashed rooms contain agreeable old antique dressers, desks, and armoires. Many rooms have views over the valley and rooftops; some have balconies. The new bathrooms are sheathed in marble or feature brass fixtures.

Via dei Archi 6 (just off the west end of Piazza dei Commune), 06081 Assisi. ℂ 075-812240. Fax 075-813653. www.hotelumbra.it. 25 units (some with tub only, some with shower only). 98€–112€ ($87.50–$100) double. Rates include breakfast. AE, DC, MC, V. Closed Jan–Easter. Parking 10.50€ ($9.40). **Amenities:** Well-regarded restaurant; bar; babysitting; laundry/dry cleaning. *In room:* A/C, TV, minibar, hair dryer.

St. Anthony's Guest House This is not a traditional hotel, but a religious guesthouse. This special place provides economical, comfortable rooms in a medieval villa-turned-guesthouse operated by the Franciscan Sisters of the Atonement (an order that originated in Graymoor, New York) and located on the upper ledges of Assisi. The guest rooms are small and rather basic (so are the bathrooms), but everything was renovated after the earthquake.

Via Galeazzo Alessi 10, 06081 Assisi. ℂ 075-812542. Fax 075-813723. atoneassisi@tiscalinet.it. 21 units (showers only). 50€ ($44.65) double; 70€ ($62.50) triple. Rates include breakfast. No credit cards. Parking 2.60€ ($2.50). Closed Nov–Jan. **Amenities:** Restaurant; lounge; babysitting; laundry. *In room:* No phone.

WHERE TO STAY NEARBY

Castell di Petrata ⭐ *Finds* This ancient castle of the 16th century is now an elegantly furnished and completely renovated choice, lying on a peaceful hilltop in the resort area of Petrata, 4km (2½ miles) from the historic center of Assisi. From the castle you can enjoy a sweeping panorama of the Umbrian countryside. Each bedroom is comfortable and tastefully furnished; the suites come with a double-bedded loft. Some of the rooms contain fireplaces.

Pieve S. Nicolò 22, 06081 Loc. Petrata Assisi. *©* **075-815451**. Fax 075-815451. castellopetrata@libero.it. 21
units. 124€–166€ ($110.75–$148.25) double; from 206€ ($183.95) suite. AE, MC, V. **Amenities:** Recom-
mended restaurant; coffee bar; room service; babysitting; laundry. *In room:* TV, minibar, hair dryer, safe.

Hotel Palazzo Bocci *✦* Located in the historic center of nearby Spello, this
palace dates from the late 18th century. The owner bought it in 1989, renovated
it, and opened it as a hotel in 1992. Inside is a courtyard with a view of the valley, a beautiful fountain, and two age-old palms. Taste and restraint went into
designing the public rooms and guest rooms, some of which open onto
panoramic views. Each soundproof room has hydromassage, a well-kept bathroom, and a writing desk. There's a lush garden where drinks are served. The village has a pool and tennis courts within a 5-minute walk (there's a small fee to
use either).

Via Cavour 17, 06038 Spello. *©* **0742-301021**. Fax 0742-301464. www.emmeti.it/Pbocci.it.html. 23 units.
120€–140€ ($107.15–$125) double; 170€–240€ ($151.80–$214.30) suite. Rates include buffet breakfast.
AE, DC, DISC, MC, V. Head 10km (6¼ miles) southeast of Assisi along S147. **Amenities:** Restaurant; bar; room
service; babysitting; laundry. *In room:* A/C, TV, minibar, hair dryer, safe.

WHERE TO DINE

You might also want to try the wonderful restaurants at the **Hotel Sole** and the
Albergo Ristorante del Viaggiatore (see above).

Il Medioevo *✦* UMBRIAN/INTERNATIONAL Assisi's best restaurant is
one of the architectural oddities in the town's historic center, with foundations
at least 1,000 years old. It's an authentic medieval gem. Alberto Falsinotti and
his family prepare superb versions of Umbrian recipes, whose origins are as old
as Assisi itself. Specialties are tortellini stuffed with minced turkey, veal, and
beef, served with butter and parmigiano; roasted rabbit with red-wine sauce and
truffles; and roast lamb with rosemary, potatoes, and herbs.

Via Arco dei Priori 4B. *©* **075-813068**. Reservations recommended. Main courses 9€–14€ ($8.05–$12.50).
AE, DC, MC, V. Thurs–Tues noon–2:30pm and 7:30–10pm. Closed Jan 7–Feb 7 and July 1–20.

La Fortezza *✦✦* *Value* UMBRIAN Up a stepped alley from Piazza del
Comune, this lovely restaurant has been family-run for 40 years and is prized for
its high quality and reasonable prices. An exposed ancient Roman wall to the
right of the entrance immediately establishes the antiquity of this palazzo with
brick-vaulted ceilings; the rest dates from the 13th century. The delicious homemade pastas are prepared with sauces that follow the season's fresh offerings,
while the roster of meats skewered or roasted on the grill (*alla brace*) ranges from
veal and lamb to duck. La Fortezza also rents seven rooms upstairs.

Via della Fortezza 2B. *©* **075-812418**. Fax 075-8198035. Reservations recommended. Main courses
6€–12.50€ ($5.35–$11.15). AE, DC, MC, V. Mon–Wed and Fri–Sun 7–10:30pm. Closed Feb.

Ristorante Buca di San Francesco UMBRIAN/ITALIAN Evocative of the
Middle Ages, this restaurant occupies the premises of a cave near the foundation
of a 12th-century palace. Menu items change often, based on the availability of
ingredients, but you're likely to find spaghetti *alla buca,* with exotic mushrooms
and meat sauce; *umbricelli* (big noodles) with asparagus sauce; cannelloni with
ricotta, spinach, and tomatoes; *carlacca* (baked crepes) stuffed with cheese, prosciutto, and roasted veal; and *piccione alla sisana* (roasted pigeon with olive oil,
capers, and aromatic herbs). There are about a hundred seats in the dining room
and another 60 in the garden, overlooking Assisi's historic center.

Via Brizi 1. *©* **075-812204**. Reservations recommended. Main courses 7.50€–14€ ($6.70–$12.50). AE, DC,
MC, V. Tues–Sun noon–2:30pm and 7–10pm. Closed July 1–15.

11 Spoleto ⓐ★

129km (80 miles) N of Rome, 48km (30 miles) SE of Assisi, 209km (130 miles) S of Florence, 64km (40 miles) SE of Perugia

Hannibal couldn't conquer it, but Gian-Carlo Menotti did—and how! Before Maestro Menotti put Spoleto on the tourist map in 1958, it was known mostly to art lovers, teachers, and students. Today huge crowds flood this Umbrian hill town to attend performances of the world-famous **Spoleto Festival,** usually held in June and July. Menotti searched and traveled through many towns of Tuscany and Umbria before making a final choice. When he saw Spoleto, he fell in love with it—quite understandably.

ESSENTIALS

GETTING THERE **Trains** arrive several times a day from Rome, the fastest of which are IC (Inter-City) trains; they're a bit more expensive than ordinary trains, some of which might require a transfer. The one-way fare from Rome to Spoleto is 8€ to 11.50€ ($7.15–$10.25). The fastest train takes about 90 minutes; those requiring connections can take 2½ hours. Trains also run several times a day between Perugia and Spoleto; the ride lasts about an hour and costs 3.25€ to 6.25€ ($2.90–$5.60) each way. The **rail station** in Spoleto (✆ **0743-48516**) is at Piazza Polvani, just outside the historic heart. Notice the gigantic statue in front by Philadelphia-born artist Alexander Calder. Circolare bus A, B, C, or D will take you from the station into Piazza della Libertà in the town center, for a one-way fee of 6€ ($5.35). Buy your ticket for the Circolare at the bar, perhaps along with an espresso, in the rail station.

If you have a **car** and are coming from either Perugia or Assisi, continue along S3, heading south to the junction of Foligno, where you can pick up Highway 75 for the rest of the route into Spoleto. Driving time from Assisi is about 30 minutes.

VISITOR INFORMATION The **tourist office** is at Piazza della Libertà 7 (✆ **0743-220311**). From April to October, it's open daily 9am to 1pm and 4 to 7pm; November to March, hours are Monday to Saturday 9am to 1pm and 3:30 to 6:30pm, and Sunday 10am to 1pm.

SPECIAL EVENTS The **Spoleto Festival** ⓐ★★★ is an internationally acclaimed event. It's held annually, most often in June and July, and attracts the elite of the operatic, ballet, and theatrical worlds from Europe and America. Tickets for most events cost 12.50€ to 100€ ($11.15–$89.30), plus a 15% handling charge. For tickets in advance, contact the **Spoleto Festival,** Piazza Duomo 8, 06049 Spoleto (✆ **0743-220320** or 0743-45-028; fax 0743-220321). For further information, call ✆ **800-565600** or 0743-44700. Visit online at **www.spoletofestival.it.** Once in Spoleto, you can get tickets at the Piazza Liberte. Make your hotel reservations well in advance!

SEEING THE TOWN

Long before Tennessee Williams arrived to premiere a new play, Thomas Schippers to conduct the opera *Macbeth,* or Shelley Winters to do three one-act plays by Saul Bellow, Spoleto was known to St. Francis and Lucrezia Borgia (she occupied the 14th-. castle towering over the town, the Rocca dell'Albornoz). The town is filled with palaces, medieval streets, and towers built for protection at the time when visitors weren't as friendly as they are today. There are churches,

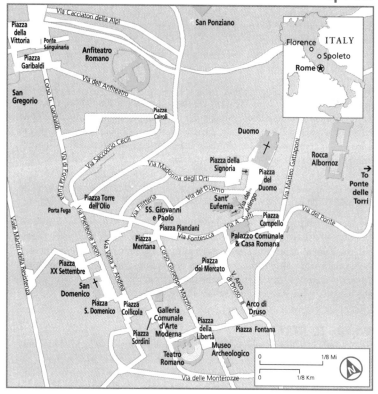

churches, and more churches—some of which, such as San Gregorio Maggiore, were built in the Romanesque style in the 11th century.

The tourist center of town is **Piazza del Duomo,** with its **Duomo.** A walk along Via del Ponte brings you to the **Ponte delle Torri** ★★, with nine towering pylons separating stately arches. The bridge is 80m (264 ft.) high and 232m (760 ft.) long, spanning a gorge. It's believed to date from the 13th century and is one of the most photographed sights in Spoleto. Even Goethe praised it when he passed this way in 1786.

If you have a car, continue up the hill from Spoleto around a winding road (about 8km/5 miles) to **Monteluco,** an ancient spot 762m (2,500 ft.) above sea level, where you'll enjoy a sweeping view. Monteluco is peppered with summer villas. The monastery here was once frequented by St. Francis of Assisi.

Il Duomo ★★   The cathedral is a hodgepodge of Romanesque and medieval architecture, with a 12th-century campanile. Its facade is of exceptional beauty, renowned for its 1207 mosaic by Salsterno. You should visit the interior, if for no other reason than to see the cycle of **frescoes** (1467–69) in the chancel by Filippo Lippi. His son, Filippino, designed the tomb for his father, but a mysterious grave robber hauled off the body one night about 2 centuries later. The keeper of the apse will be happy to unlock it for you. These frescoes, believed to have been carried out largely by students, were the elder Lippi's last work; he died in Spoleto in 1469. As friars went in those days, Lippi was a bit of a swinger; he ran off with a nun, Lucrezia Buti, who later posed as the Madonna in several of his paintings.

Piazza del Duomo (*C*) 0743-44307. Free admission. Daily 8am–12:30pm and 3–6:30pm (to 5:30pm off-season).

Sant'Eufemia & Diocese Museum (Museo Diocesano) The **Sant'Eufemia** church was built in the 11th century. Note the gallery above the nave, where women were required to sit, a holdover from the Eastern Church; it's one of the few such galleries in Italy. In the courtyard, double stairs lead to the **Museo Diocesano,** noted for its Madonna paintings, one from 1315. Room 5 contains Filippino Lippi's 1485 *Madonna and Child with Sts. Montano and Bartolomeo.*

Via Saffi 13, between Piazza del Duomo and Piazza del Mercanto. (*C*) 0743-23101 (museum). Admission to both 2.50€ ($2.25). By reservation only, Wed–Mon 10am–12:30pm and 3:30–7pm (to 6pm Nov–Feb).

Roman Amphitheater (Teatro Romano) & Archaeological Museum (Museo Archeologico) A setting for performances during the Spoleto Festival, the **Roman Amphitheater** dates from the 1st century A.D., and excavations began on it in 1891. For the same ticket, you can also visit the **Archaeological Museum** nearby, with a warrior's tomb dating from the 7th century B.C. Among the exhibits is Les Poletina, two tablets inscribed after 241 B.C.

Via Santágata. (*C*) 0743-223277. Admission to both 2€ ($1.80). Daily 8:30am–7:30pm.

WHERE TO STAY

Spoleto offers an attractive range of hotels, but when the crowds flood in at festival time, the going's rough (one year a group of students bedded down on Piazza del Duomo). In an emergency, the **tourist office** (see "Essentials," above) can arrange a list of where to stay in a private home at a moderate price, but it's imperative to lock up your reservation well in advance. Many of the private rooms are often rented well ahead to artists appearing at the festival. Innkeepers will raise their prices as high as the market will bear at festival time.

Albornoz Palace Hotel ⭐ In a residential neighborhood half a mile south of town, this five-story modern building is the largest and best equipped in Spoleto. However, the tiny Gattapone (below) is more luxurious and tranquil. The marble-trimmed lobby is decorated with large modern paintings by American-born artist Sol Lewitt. The guest rooms are well appointed, with fine linen, plus views over Spoleto, Monteluco, or the surrounding hills. There's a small garden in back.

Viale Matteotti, 06049 Spoleto. (*C*) 0743-221221. Fax 0743-221600. 96 units. 124€–217€ ($110.75–$193.80) double; 180€–345€ ($160.75–$308.10) suite. Rates include breakfast. AE, DC, MC, V. Free parking. **Amenities:** Restaurant; bar; pool; room service; babysitting; laundry/dry cleaning. *In room:* A/C, TV, minibar, hair dryer, safe.

Hotel Charleston This tile-roofed, sienna-fronted building is from the 17th century and today serves as a pleasant hotel in the historic center. It's a solid and reliable choice, with wood-beamed ceilings, terra-cotta floors, and open fireplaces. Each of the large guest rooms has a ceiling accented with beams of honey-colored planking. Many have been updated with new furnishings and bathrooms. The front desk usually has a movie or two in English that you can rent.

Piazza Collicola 10, 06049 Spoleto. (*C*) 0743-220052. Fax 0743-221244. www.hotelcharleston.it. 18 units (some with shower only). 70€–100€ ($62.50–$89.30) double. Rates include breakfast. AE, DC, MC, V. Parking 7.50€ ($6.70). **Amenities:** Bar; sauna; room service; laundry/dry cleaning. *In room:* A/C, TV/VCR, minibar, hair dryer.

Hotel Clarici   The Clarici is rated only third-class by the government, but it's airy and modern, the best of the budget bets. The hotel doesn't emphasize style, but focuses rather on the creature comforts: soft, low beds; built-in wardrobes; steam heat; and an elevator. Fourteen rooms open onto private balconies. There's a large terrace for sunbathing or sipping drinks.

Piazza della Vittoria 32, 06049 Spoleto. (C) **0743-223311**. Fax 0743-222010. 24 units (showers only). 82.50€ ($73.65) double; 95€ ($84.85) triple. Rates include breakfast. AE, DC, MC, V. Parking 5€ ($4.45). Bus: A, B, C, or D. **Amenities:** Bar; lounge; room service; laundry/dry cleaning. *In room:* A/C, TV, minibar, hair dryer, safe.

Hotel dei Duchi   This modern hotel is within walking distance of the major sights, yet it perches on a hillside with views and terraces. It lacks the style of the Gattapone and Albornoz Palace; its bland rooms seem geared to business travelers. Dei Duchi is graced with brick walls, open-to-the-view glass, and lounges with modern furnishings and original paintings. Some guest rooms have balconies, and all have bland bed coverings, wood-grained furniture, and built-in cupboards. The meal plan is required in high season.

Viale Giacomo Matteotti 4, 06049 Spoleto. (C) **0743-44541**. Fax 0743-44543. www.hoteldeiduchi.com. 49 units. 100€–150€ ($89.30–$133.95) double; 115€–275€ ($102.70–$245.60) suite. Rates include buffet breakfast. Half-board 60€ ($53.60) per person. AE, DC, MC, V. Free parking. **Amenities:** Restaurant; bar; room service; laundry. *In room:* A/C, TV, minibar, hair dryer.

Hotel Gattapone ★★ *Finds*   The stunning Gattapone is our first choice in town. It occupies two side-by-side stone 17th-century cottages among the clouds, clinging to the cliffs high on a twisting road leading to the ancient castle and the 13th-century Ponte delle Torri. It feels isolated and surrounded by nature, but it's only a couple of minutes' stroll to the Duomo. The interiors maximize views of the valley and the remarkable 14th-century arched bridge a few hundred feet away. The rooms are uniquely furnished, with comfortable beds, antiques, and plenty of space.

Via Del Ponte 6, 06049 Spoleto. (C) **0743-223447**. Fax 0743-223448. www.hotelgattapone.it. 14 units. 140€–230€ ($125–$205.35) double. AE, DC, MC, V. Free parking. **Amenities:** Lounge; room service; babysitting; laundry. *In room:* A/C, TV, minibar, hair dryer, safe.

Hotel San Luca ★   Occupying a restored building from the 19th century, this hotel is the most up-to-date in town, filled with ambience and style. Wherever you turn, there's a grace note of the past, such as a roof garden and a spacious courtyard with a 1602 fountain. All the elegant guest rooms are spacious and furnished in a sober yet comforting style, with all the amenities. The bathrooms are particularly welcoming, with extras such as phones and towel warmers. Many rooms are also fitted with a massage bath. The public rooms respect the style of the building, with period furniture. A garden solarium is a nice touch.

Via Interna della Mura 21, 06049 Spoleto. (C) **0743-223399**. Fax 0743-223800. www.hotelsanluca.com. 35 units. 104€–228€ ($92.85–$203.60) double; from 206€ ($183.95) suite. AE, DC, MC, V. Parking 12.50€ ($11.15). **Amenities:** Restaurant; bar; room service; babysitting; laundry. *In room:* A/C, TV, minibar, hair dryer, safe.

Il Vecchio Molino ★ *Finds*   Instead of staying in Spoleto, motorists may want to drive 9.5km (6 miles) to a site on the Clitunno River in the village of Fonti del Clitunno and stay at this undiscovered gem. In the heart of the Umbrian countryside, next to a paleochristian temple from the 4th century A.D., the landscape here has been phrased by poets ranging from Plinius the Young to Lord Byron. The inn incorporates the ruins of an ancient corn mill, including old grinding stones from the 15th century. You can walk through tree-shaded gardens along the river's bank. The interior is rustic, the rooms decorated with dark furnishings and handcrafted wool bedspreads. We prefer rooms 2, 4, and 10, opening onto the garden. Avoid 15, 16, and 19, opening onto the parking lot.

Via del Tempio 34, Loc. Pissignano, Campello sul Clitunno, 06042 Spoleto. ⓒ 0743-521122. Fax 0743-275097. www.perugiaonline.com. 13 units (showers only). 110€ ($98.25) double; 125€ ($111.65) suite. AE, DC, MC, V. Closed Nov–Mar. **Amenities:** Room service; babysitting. *In room:* A/C, minibar.

Palazzo Dragoni 👾👾 Near Piazza del Duomo, this is a lovingly renovated 16th-century palace once inhabited by the aristocracy of Spoleto. Skillfully converted into a hotel—more like a residence—it is one of the most atmospheric choices in the area, and it's filled with antiques and beautiful fabrics that are in harmony with the architecture. The rooms on the lower floors are the most evocative of palace living. We prefer rooms 3, 6, 8, and 10 because of their antiques, decorated ceilings, and views. Avoid no. 16 because it's cramped and without a view. Breakfast is taken on an open-air loggia with a panoramic view.

Via del Duomo 13, 06049 Spoleto. ⓒ 0743-222220. Fax 0743-222225. www.perugiaonline.com. 15 units (showers only). 119€ ($106.25) double; 145€ ($129.50) suite. AE, MC, V. **Amenities:** Room service; babysitting; laundry/dry cleaning. *In room:* A/C, TV, minibar, hair dryer, safe.

WHERE TO DINE

Enoteca Provinciale UMBRIAN   This is a local dive but a fun spot, often attracting celebrities visiting for the Spoleto Festival. You can dine modestly here while enjoying a selection of Umbrian wines by the glass. Many of the pastas are handmade, and we are especially fond of the spaghetti with a spicy hot tomato sauce. Many of the best dishes contain truffles. Start with a *zuppa di farro* with crushed grains, meat chunks, and vegetables. Sometimes a real special dish is a feature: wild boar simmered in red wine.

Via Aurelio Saffi 7. ⓒ 0743-220484. Reservations unnecessary. Main courses 5€–12.50€ ($4.45–$11.15). Wine from 1.50€ ($1.35) per glass. Tourist menu with wine 11€ ($9.80). AE, MC, V. Wed–Mon 11am–3pm and 7–11pm (to midnight in summer).

Il Tartufo 👾 UMBRIAN   At Il Tartufo, near the amphitheater, you might be introduced to the Umbrian *tartufo* (truffle)—if you can afford it. It's served in the most expensive appetizers and main courses at Spoleto's oldest restaurant. This excellent tavern serves at least nine regional specialties using the black tartufo. A popular pasta dish (and a good introduction for neophyte palates) is *strengozzi al tartufo*. Or you might want to start with an omelet, such as *frittata al tartufo*. Main dishes of veal and beef are also excellently prepared. For such a small restaurant, the menu is large.

Piazza Garibaldi 24. ⓒ 0743-40236. Reservations required. Main courses 9.50€–17€ ($8.50–$15.20); fixed-price menus 17.50€–40€ ($15.65–$35.70). AE, DC, MC, V. Tues–Sat noon–3pm and 7:30–10:30pm; Sun noon–3pm. Closed Jan 18–31 and July 15–31.

Ristorante Apollinare 👾👾 UMBRIAN   The most prestigious restaurant in Spoleto also serves the best cuisine and uses the finest ingredients. The dining room was created from an ancient church whose origins go back to the 12th century. Today the atmosphere is intimate and elegant with a summer gazebo. A dining tradition since 1991, the restaurant serves imaginative dishes that are carefully conceived. Roasted guinea fowl comes with artichokes flavored with balsamic vinegar, and a delectable pigeon appears in casserole. Eel from

Trasimeno Lake is smoked and makes an elegant appetizer. Stringozzi, the local pasta, appears with the black truffles of the region. Ravioli might appear stuffed with apples and nuts. Count on amusing variations of traditional dishes. For dessert, we prefer the chocolate flan in orange sauce.

In the Hotel Aurora, via Sant'Agata 14. © 0743-223256. Reservations required. Main courses 10€–17.50€ ($8.95–$15.65). AE, DC, MC, V. Apr–Oct daily 1–3pm and 7–10pm. Off-season Wed–Mon 1–3pm and 7–10pm.

A SIDE TRIP TO TODI ☆

For years, Todi lay slumbering in the Umbrian sun. Then the world moved in. Visa used it as a backdrop for a commercial, and the University of Kentucky keeps voting it "the most livable town in the world." This has brought a monied class from America rushing in to buy decaying castles and villas, hoping to convert them into holiday homes. And Todi has imitated Spoleto and now stages a **Festival di Todi,** attracting ballet, theatrical, and operatic stars during the first 10 days of each September.

Taking Route 418 out of Spoleto for 45km (28 miles) northwest will lead you to what the excitement is all about. At Acquasparta, get on Autostrada 3 northwest. Soon you'll come to this well-preserved medieval village, today a retreat for wealthy artists and diplomats. The setting is simply lovely.

Upon arrival, you'll enter the walled town through one of its three gates, named for the destinations of the roads leading away: **Rome** in the southwest wall, **Perugia** in the north, and **Orvieto** in the southeast. The remains of original Roman and Etruscan walls are also evident just inside the Rome gate. The central square, **Piazza del Popolo,** was built over a Roman forum. It contains the 12th-century Romanesque-Gothic **cathedral** and three beautiful palaces: the **Palazzo del Popolo,** built in 1213; the **Palazzo del Capitano,** dating from 1292; and the 14th-century **Palazzo dei Priori,** with its trapezoidal tower. Each summer, all three (and the piazza) are filled with the wares of the **National Exhibit of Crafts (Mostra Nazionale dell'Artigianato).**

Also on view are **Santa Maria della Consolazione,** standing guard over Todi with its domes and exquisite stained glass, and the 13th-century **San Fortunato,** in the **Piazza della Repubblica,** burial site of the town's most famous citizen, the monk/medieval poet Jacopone. To the right of the church, a path leads uphill to the ruins of a 14th-century castle known as **La Rocca.** From here, a walk up the Viale della Serpentina will reward you with a bird's-eye view of the surrounding valley. If the climb seems a bit much, check the view from **Piazza Garibaldi.**

Today the artisans of Todi are particularly renowned for their woodwork. Examples of historical as well as contemporary craft are available for perusal or purchase, especially during the **National Exhibit of Crafts** along Piazza del Popolo.

Our favorite place to stay in the area is **Tenuta di Canonica,** Località La Canonica 75–76 (© **075-8947545**), lying 5km (3 miles) northwest of Todi. Here Maria and Daniele Fano have converted a brick farmhouse and former medieval tower into a dining room with exposed stone walls, brick floors, and high ceilings. Their dining room is only for guests of one of their 11 attractively furnished bedrooms, with doubles going at 125€ ($111.65), including breakfast. There is also a pool.

12 Orvieto ★★

121km (75 miles) N of Rome, 76km (47 miles) SW of Perugia, 113km (70 miles) SW of Assisi

Built on a pedestal of volcanic rock above vineyards in a green valley, Orvieto is the Umbrian hill town closest to Rome and is often visited by those who don't have the time to explore other spots in Umbria. It lies on the Paglia, a tributary of the Tiber, and sits on an isolated rock some 315m (1,035 ft.) above sea level. Crowning the town is its world-famed cathedral.

The most spectacularly sited hill town in Umbria (but not the most spectacular town), Orvieto was founded by the Etruscans, who were apparently drawn to it because of its good defensive possibilities. Likewise, long after its days as a Roman colony, it became a papal stronghold. It was a natural fortress because its cliffs rise starkly from the valley below, even though Orvieto, when you finally reach it, is relatively flat. Although the tall, sheer cliffs on which the town stands saved it from the incursion of railroads and superhighways, time and traffic vibrations have caused the soft volcanic rock to disintegrate so that work is imminently necessary to shore up the town.

Orvieto is known for its white wine; the best place to enjoy it is at a wine cellar at Piazza del Duomo 2 as you contemplate the cathedral's facade.

ESSENTIALS

GETTING THERE   Three **trains** a day arrive in Orvieto from Perugia. Because of frequent stops, the trip takes 1½ hours. A one-way ticket costs 5.50€ ($4.90). From Florence, the handful of trains making the trip require 2 hours, with a one-way ticket costing 9€ ($8.05). From Rome, the train takes 1½ hours and costs 6.60€ ($5.90) each way. Orvieto's rail station (© 0763-300434) lies below the town in the valley; to get to the town center, take Bus A, which departs at intervals of 40 minutes or less throughout the day and most of the night, or via a small funicular that operates daily between 7:15am and 8:30pm. One-way transit from the rail station to the town by either bus or funicular costs .95€ (90¢). For information, call the tourist office (see below).

If you have a **car** and are coming from Rome, drive for about 90 minutes (a distance of around 121km/75 miles north along A1) to Orvieto. From Perugia, head 42km (26 miles) south on SS3bis to Todi, and then take SS448 for 25km (16 miles) southwest to the intersection of SS205; then drive 9km (5½ miles) to Orvieto.

VISITOR INFORMATION   The **tourist office,** at Piazza del Duomo 24 (© **0763-341772**), is open Monday to Friday 8:15am to 1:50pm and 4 to 7pm, Saturday 10am to 1pm and 4 to 7pm, and Sunday 10am to noon and 4 to 6pm.

EXPLORING THE TOWN

Il Duomo ★★★   Erected on the site of two older churches and dedicated to the Virgin, the Duomo was begun in 1288 (maybe even earlier) to commemorate the Miracle of Bolsena. This alleged miracle came out of the doubts of a priest who questioned the transubstantiation (the incarnation of Jesus Christ in the Host). However, as the story goes, at the moment of consecration, the Host started to drip blood. The priest doubted no more, and the Feast of Corpus Christi was launched.

The cathedral is known for its **elaborately adorned facade** ★★★, rich statuary, marble bas-reliefs, and mosaics. Pope John XXIII proclaimed that, on Judgment Day, God would send his angels down to earth to pick up this facade

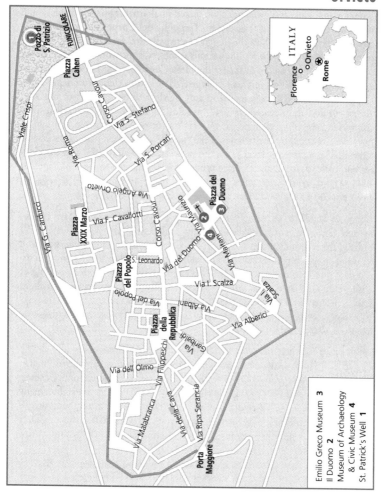

and transport it back to heaven. The modern bronze portals are controversial, and many art historians journey from around the world to see them. Installed in 1970, they were the work of eminent sculptor Emilio Greco, who took as his theme the Misericordia, the seven acts of corporal charity. One panel depicts Pope John XXIII's famous visit to the prisoners of Rome's Queen of Heaven jail in 1960. Some critics have called the doors "outrageous"; others have praised them as "one of the most original works of modern sculpture." You decide.

The west facade, divided into three gables, boasts richly sculptured marble based on designs of Lorenzo Maitani of Siena. Four wall surfaces around the three doors are adorned with bas-reliefs, also based on Maitani designs. Maitani worked on the facade until his death in 1330. The bas-reliefs depict scenes from the Bible, including the Last Judgment. After Maitani's death, Andrea Pisano took over, but the actual work carried on until the dawn of the 17th century.

Inside, the nave and aisles are constructed in alternating panels of black and white stone. You'll want to seek out the **Cappella del Corporale,** with its mammoth silver shrine based on the design of the cathedral facade. This 1338 masterpiece, richly embellished with precious stones, was the work of Ugolino Vieri of Siena and was designed to shelter the Holy Corporal from Bolsena (the cloth in which the bleeding Host was wrapped). The most celebrated chapel is the **Cappella di San Brizio,** which contains newly restored frescoes of the *Last Judgment* and the *Apocalypse* ★★, by Luca Signorelli, who was called in to complete them (they were begun by Fra Angelico). Michelangelo was said to have been inspired by the frescoes at the time he was contemplating the Sistine Chapel. The masterpiece was produced between 1499 and 1503, and cost $4.4 million to renovate. Only 25 persons at a time are allowed to see the chapel.

Piazza del Duomo. ✆ 0763-341167. Church free; chapel 1.50€ ($1.35). Apr–Sept daily 10am–1pm and 2:30–7:30pm; Oct and Mar daily 7:30am–1pm and 2:30–6:15pm.

Pozzo di San Patrizio (St. Patrick's Well) ★★ St. Patrick's Well is an architectural curiosity, and in its day it was an engineering feat. Pope Clement VII ordered the well built when he feared that Orvieto might come under siege and its water supply might be cut off. The well was entrusted to the design of Antonio da Sangallo the Younger in 1527. It's some 61m (200 ft.) deep and about 13m (42 ft.) in diameter, cut into volcanic rock. Two spiral staircases, with about 250 steps, lead into the wells. These spiral ramps never meet.

Viale Sangallo, off Piazza Cahen. ✆ 0763-343768. Admission 3€ ($2.70). Apr–Oct daily 10am–7pm; Nov–Mar daily 10am–6pm.

Museum of Archaeology & Civic Museum (Musei Archeologici Faina e Civico) This museum across from the cathedral contains many Etruscan artifacts found in and around Orvieto. In addition to the stone sarcophagi, terracotta portraits, and vials of colored glass left by the Etruscans, it exhibits many beautiful Greek vases. Three of the most important objects are amphorae attributed to one of the finest of the Attic vase painters, Exekias (550–540 B.C.). They were found in a necropolis near Orvieto and are a gauge of the wealth of this former city-state.

In the Palazzo Faina, Piazza del Duomo 29. ✆ 0763-341511. Admission 4.20€ ($3.75); 2.50€ ($2.25) for students and seniors. April 1–Sept 30 daily 9:30am–6pm; Oct 1–Mar 31 Tues–Sun 10am–5pm.

Emilio Greco Museum (Museo Emilio Greco) This museum opened in 1991 to house an important art collection donated to the city by eminent sculptor Emilio Greco. A devoted advocate of civic pride and an internationally recognized sculptor best remembered in Orvieto for his sculpting of the bronze doors in the front of the Duomo (see above), he died in 1996 in his mid-80s. You'll find 32 Greco sculptures and 60 graphic works (including lithographs, etchings, and drawings). The modern museum was designed by architect Giulio Savio on the ground floor of a 14th-century palazzo.

In the Palazzo Soliano, Piazza del Duomo. ✆ 0763-344605. Admission 2.50€ ($2.25). Apr–Sept daily 10:30am–1pm and 2:30–6:30pm; Oct–Mar Tues–Sat 10:30am–1pm and 2–5:30pm.

SHOPPING

Orvieto's local white wine, **Orvieto Classico,** is made from grapes that thrive in the local chalky soil and are sometimes fermented in caves around the countryside. You'll be able to buy glasses of the fruity wine ("liquid gold") at any tavern in town, but if you want to haul a bottle or two back to your own digs, try the town's best wine shop, **Foresi,** Piazza del Duomo 2 (✆ **0763-341611**).

You can also find lace and carved wooden objects here. For lace, go to **Duranti,** Via del Duomo 13–15 (© **0763-344606**), which carries tablecloths, handkerchiefs, and frilly curtains, along with an occasional baptismal robe. You'll also find imported European scents and locally distilled perfumes. You'll find a wide selection of hand-carved wooden items at **Michelangeli,** Via Gualverio Michelangeli 3 (© **0763-342660**), where you can find everything from full-scale furniture to an ornate cup and bowl.

Antonia Carraro, Corso Cavour 101 (© **0763-342870**), is a fabulous place to stock up for a picnic or just to buy locally made breads, olive oils, cheeses, salamis, wines, and biscotti.

Orvieto is also known for its pottery, which is best seen on Saturday mornings at the **pottery market** on Piazza del Popolo.

WHERE TO STAY

Albergo Filippeschi *(Value)*   If you're searching for a bargain, head here. Managed by its family owners, the Filippeschi is the most affordable property in the center. It occupies a historic mansion and has been restored with a certain style and grace by gutting a decaying structure and modernizing it. The guest rooms are generally spacious and, though lacking style, contain small refrigerators; the bathrooms are small but tidily kept.

Via Filippeschi 19, 05019 Orvieto. © and fax **0763-343275.** 15 units (showers only). 94€ ($83.95) double; 124€ ($110.75) triple. AE, DC, MC, V. Parking 5€ ($4.45) nearby. **Amenities:** Bar; room service. *In room:* A/C, TV, fridge, hair dryer.

Hotel Maitani   The stone-sided building that houses this family-run hotel is a palazzo dating from around 600 years ago. The guest rooms are mostly modern but do retain some reminders of their medieval origins. They're small but cozy and comfortable, with good beds. If you have a car, it's best to try to check in early because the hotel has parking space for only eight vehicles. The location is fabulous, although the service could be warmer.

Via Maitani 5, 05018 Orvieto. © and fax **0763-342011.** 40 units. 115€ ($102.70) double; 135€–155€ ($120.55–$138.40) suite. AE, DC, V. Parking 10€ ($8.95). Closed Jan 7–Feb 9. **Amenities:** Bar, lounge; laundry. *In room:* A/C, TV, minibar, hair dryer, safe.

Hotel Palazzo Piccolomini *(Value)*   A hotel since 1998, this inn was carved from a 16th-century Renaissance palazzo. Looking very pretty in pink, this was the Orvieto home of the illustrious Tuscan family that gave us two popes. The building has emerged from a complete refurbishment that has kept the historical shell and its grand dimensions of vaulted ceilings and wide halls, while creating a quasi-minimalist ambience with cool terra-cotta floors and white slip-covered furniture. The rooms are elegant but simple, with dark wood furnishings and canopied beds. Ground-floor rooms have high vaulted ceilings; those on the upper floors have nice views. The best rooms are the corner doubles 111, 211, and 311. The smallest and the less desirable rooms are nos. 6, 302, and 307.

Piazza Ranieri 36, 05018 Orvieto. © 0763-341743. Fax 0763-391046. www.hotelpiccolomini.it. 31 units. 114€–134€ ($101.80–$119.65) double; 219€ ($195.55) suite. AE, DC, MC, V. **Amenities:** Restaurant; bar; wine cellar; room service; babysitting; laundry/dry cleaning. *In room:* A/C, TV, dataport, minibar, hair dryer.

Villa Ciconia *(*   This beautiful 16th-century villa (the best hotel in the environs) sits in an 8-acre park at the confluence of the Chain and Paglia rivers, 4km (2½ miles) from Orvieto. It has the thick walls, terra-cotta floors, and beamed ceilings typical of its era. Huge chestnut beams run more than 12m (13 yd.)

along the ceiling of the lobby, and the main dining room features a great stone fireplace and a lacuna ceiling with ornate molding and frescoes around the walls. The spacious guest rooms have park views and period furnishings. You can use a nearby public sports center, which has an indoor Olympic-size pool, indoor and outdoor red-clay tennis courts, and horseback riding.

Via dei Tigli 69, 05019 Orvieto. © 0763-305582. Fax 0763-302077. 12 units. 124€–147€ ($110.75–$131.25) double. Rates include breakfast. AE, DC, MC, V. **Amenities:** Restaurant; bar; room service; babysitting; laundry/dry cleaning. *In room:* A/C (in some), TV, minibar, hair dryer.

WHERE TO DINE

Antica Trattoria dell'Orso ✦ UMBRIAN   The *umbricelli* (Umbria's homemade spaghettilike specialty) is best served here *alla campagnola* ("country style," with zucchini, eggplant, and onions). Any of the fresh pastas, in fact, is a must-try at this unassuming trattoria full of locals, partly free of tourists because of its location one step too far off the beaten path (it's a 10-min. stroll from the Duomo). The ingredients of fresh market offerings and homegrown herbs help confirm the impression of a day in the country. Even the simplest dish (a frittata of asparagus or potatoes) is full of flavor and bears the masterful touch of chef Gabriele di Giandomenico.

Via della Misericordia 18–20. © 0763-341642. Reservations recommended. Main courses 8.50€–13€ ($7.60–$11.60). AE, DC, MC, V. Wed–Sun noon–2:30pm and 7:30–10pm; Mon noon–2:30pm. Closed mid-Jan to mid-Feb and 3 weeks in July.

I Sette Consoli ✦✦ MEDITERRANEAN   In a dining room that was once the sacristy of the 18th-century church next door, Orvieto's finest cuisine is served at this Michelin-starred restaurant. We prefer the place in fair weather when we can sit in the garden, open only on summer nights, looking out onto the rear of Orvieto's monumental cathedral. Inventiveness and a solid culinary technique form a magic combination here. One of the most typical Umbrian regional dishes is young pigeon, or rabbit, cooked to perfection in the oven and served with vegetables recently gathered in the fields. Rabbit also appears cooked with bacon and served in a leek sauce with crunchy potato strings. Ravioli stuffed with duck and served in a nut sauce is another commendable dish. Our favorite is lamb chops stuffed with foie gras in a sesame crust.

Piazza Sant'Angelo 1A. © 0763-343911. Reservations required. Main courses 15€–17.50€ ($13.40–$15.65). AE, DC, MC, V. Thurs–Tues 12:45–2:15pm and 7:45–9:15pm. Closed Sun night in winter and last 2 weeks of Feb.

La Grotta del Funaro UMBRIAN/PIZZA   The cuisine is the type of fare Umbrian grandmothers have served for generations—fresh, flavorful, and nutritious, with no attempt to be creative. The setting, however, is a surprisingly dry cave below the city center that includes many eerie references to other times. No one seems to have any idea how long the cave has been in everyday use (the staff believes that it was part of the storerooms used by the ancient Etruscans). Menu items include an array of grilled meats (such as lamb or pork with potatoes and vegetables), pastas flavored with local mushrooms and truffles, and fresh vegetables. From a wood-burning oven emerge the most savory pizzas in town.

Via Ripa Serancia 41. © 0763-343276. Reservations recommended. Main courses 7€–15€ ($6.25–$13.40). AE, DC, MC, V. Tues–Sun noon–3pm and 7pm–1am.

Osteria San Patrizio *Value* TUSCAN/UMBRIAN   This is a little discovery that thrives in the midst of far more celebrated restaurants. The owner/chef and his wife are new to the local dining scene, and try harder than anybody in town to please their customers, hoping to gain a foothold. They have a limited but choice menu, and they gather the finest ingredients they can afford and shape them into an array of regional produce, including homemade pastas, polenta, rabbit, and beef dishes. Some of their dishes are of the type their grandmother made, especially the potatoes with cheese and pork. They do an excellent lamb on a bed of red pepper with potatoes or a risotto of pears and pecorino cheese in a red-wine sauce. Their faces light up when they serve you dessert. We'd walk a mile, even more, for their fig pastry with fresh figs and a caramelized sauce.

Corso Cavour 312. 🕐 **0763-341245.** Reservations unnecessary. Main courses 9€–11€ ($8.05–$9.80). Tues–Sun noon–2:30pm and Tues–Sat 7–11pm. AE, DC, MC, V.

Vissani ✩✩✩ MEDITERRANEAN   Gianfranco Vissani is the most celebrated chef of Umbria, and serious foodies make pilgrimages here from all over Italy. Not too prepossessing from the outside, the interior of the restaurant has a veranda with fireplace and a formal antique-filled dining room. This is a family affair, with Paola, Vissani's sister, turning out breads and pastry, including some of the most fragrantly flavored dinner rolls we've ever tasted. Vissani interprets Italian regional dishes with great imagination and uses only the freshest and finest of ingredients. Since the restaurant is on the banks of Lake Corbara, and close to a region of fine white wines, you can order the "local grape" with your meals. Try his blue lobster with white asparagus and a green coffee sauce served with pumpkin and Amaretto quenelles. Newburg baby-sweet-corn soup comes with a song-thrush and juniper mousse, and local regional quail is stuffed with turnips and served with a fried leek julienne.

SS448 Todi-Baschi, Civitella del Lago. 🕐 **0744-950206.** Reservations required. Main courses 15€–25€ ($13.40–$22.35). AE, DC, MC, V. Mon–Wed and Fri–Sat 1–2:30pm and 8–10:30pm; Thurs 8–10:30pm; Sun 1–2:30pm. Lies 10 miles from the center of Orvieto; take Strade Statale signposted to Todi.

8

Bologna & Emilia-Romagna

In the northern reaches of central Italy, the region of Emilia-Romagna is known for its gastronomy and for its art cities, Modena and Parma. Here, such families as the Renaissance dukes of Ferrara rose in power and influence, creating courts that attracted painters and poets.

Bologna, the capital, stands at the crossroads between Venice and Florence and is linked by express highways to Milan and Tuscany. By basing yourself in this ancient university city, you can branch out in all directions: north for 52km (32 miles) to Ferrara; southeast for 50km (31 miles) to the ceramics-making town of Faenza; northwest for 40km (25 miles) to Modena, with its Romanesque cathedral; or farther northwest for 55km (34 miles) to Parma, the legendary capital of the Farnese family duchy in the 16th century. Ravenna, famed for its mosaics, lies 74km (46 miles) east of Bologna on the Adriatic Sea.

Most of our stops in this region lie on the ancient Roman road, **Via Emilia,** which began in Rimini and stretched to Piacenza, a Roman colony that often attracted invading barbarians. This ancient land (known to the Romans as Æmilia, and to the Etruscans before them) is rich in architecture (Parma's cathedral and baptistry) and in scenic beauty (the green plains and the slopes of the Apennines). Emilia is one of Italy's most bountiful farming districts and sets a table highly praised in Europe, both for its wines and for its imaginatively prepared pasta dishes.

1 Bologna ★★

52km (32 miles) S of Ferrara, 151km (94 miles) SW of Venice, 378km (234 miles) N of Rome

The manager of a hotel in Bologna once lamented: "The Americans! They spend a week in Florence, a week in Venice. Why not 6 days in Florence, 6 days in Venice, and 2 days in Bologna?" That's a good question.

Bologna is one of the most overlooked gems in Italy; we've found empty room after empty room here in summer, when the hotels in Venice and Florence were packed tight. Now it's true that Bologna boasts no Uffizi or Doge's Palace, but it does offer a beautiful city that's one of the most architecturally unified in Europe—a panorama of sienna-colored buildings, marbled sidewalks, and porticos. After fighting those crowds in Rome, Florence, and Venice, you might enjoy a few days away from the tourist crush.

Bologna's rise as a commercial power was almost ensured by its strategic location between Florence and Venice. And its university, the oldest in Europe (founded 1088), has for years generated a lively interest in art and culture. It features the nation's best medical school, as well as one of its top business schools. The bars, cafes, and squares fill up with students, and an eclectic mix of concerts, art exhibits, and avant-garde ballet and theater performances always marks the calendar.

Perhaps because the student population is so large, Bologna is a center of great tolerance, with the national gay alliance and several student organizations making their headquarters here. Politically, communism and socialism figure prominently in the voter profile, which could be why the region has been largely unscathed by the scandal and corruption of neighboring precincts, where blatant capitalism has led to Mafia-corrupted activity.

Bologna is also Italy's gastronomic capital. Gourmets flock here just to sample the cuisine: the pastas (tortellini, tagliatelle, lasagna verde), the meat and poultry specialties (zampone, veal cutlet bolognese, tender turkey breasts in sauce supreme), and the *mortadella*, Bologna's incomparable sausage, as distant a cousin to baloney as porterhouse is to the hot dog.

The city seems to take a vacation in August, becoming virtually dead. You'll notice signs proclaiming CHIUSO (closed) almost everywhere you look.

ESSENTIALS

GETTING THERE   The international **Aeroporto Guglielmo Marconi** (© **051-6479615**) is 6km (3¾ miles) north of the town center and serviced by such domestic carriers as Aermediterranea and ATI; all the main European airlines have connections through this airport. An **Aerobus** (no. 54) runs daily every 15 minutes from the airport to the air terminal at Bologna's rail station. A one-way ticket costs 4€ ($3.55).

Bologna's **Stazione Centrale rail station** is at Piazza Medaglie d'Oro 2 (© **051-6302111,** or 1478-88088 toll-free in Italy only). Trains arrive hourly from Rome (trip time: 3½ hr.) and from Milan (2½ hr.). Bus nos. 25 and 30 run between the station and the historic core of Bologna, Piazza Maggiore.

If you have a **car** and are coming from Florence, continue north along A1 until reaching the outskirts of Bologna, where signs direct you to the city center. From Milan, take A1 southeast along the Apennines. From Venice or Ferrara, follow A13 southwest. From Rimini, Ravenna, and the towns along the Adriatic, cut west on A14.

VISITOR INFORMATION   The **tourist office** is at Piazza Maggiore 1 (© **051-239660**), open Monday to Saturday 9am to 8pm. There are two other offices, one at the railway station, Piazza Medaglie d'Oro 2 (© **051-246541**), and the other one at the airport. Both are open Monday to Saturday from 8am to 8pm.

GETTING AROUND   Bologna is easy to cover on foot; most of the major sights are in and around Piazza Maggiore. However, if you don't want to walk, **city buses** leave for most points from Piazza Nettuno or Piazza Maggiore. Free maps are available at the storefront office of the **ATC (Azienda Trasporti Comunali)** at Piazza XX Settembre (© **051-290290**). You can buy tickets at one of many booths and tobacconists in Bologna. The ATC Customer Service Office is at Via IV Novembre 16A, open daily from 8am to 8pm. Tickets cost .90€ (80¢) and last 60 minutes. A **citypass**—a booklet of eight tickets, each valid for 1 hour—costs 6€ ($5.35). Once on board, you must have your ticket validated.

Taxis are on radio call at © **051-372727** or 051-543141.

SEEING THE SIGHTS

On Piazza del Nettuno (adjacent to Piazza Maggiore) stands the **Neptune Fountain (Fontana di Nettuno)** ✦✦, which has gradually become a symbol of the city, although it was designed in 1566 by a Frenchman named Giambologna

Emilia-Romagna

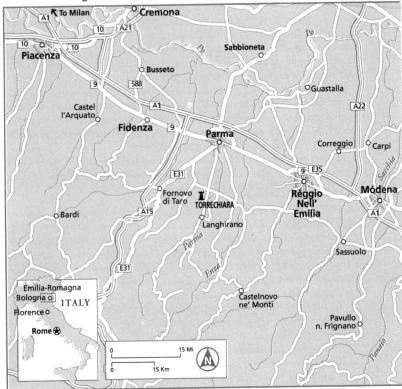

(the Italians altered his name). Viewed as irreverent by some, "indecent" by the Catholic Church, and magnificent by those with more liberal tastes, this 16th-century fountain depicts Neptune with rippling muscles, a trident in one arm, and a heavy foot on the head of a dolphin. The church forced Giambologna to manipulate Neptune's left arm to cover his monumental endowment. Giambologna's defenders denounced this as "artistic castration." Around his feet are four highly erotic cherubs, also with dolphins. At the base of the fountain, four very sensual sirens spout streams of water from their breasts.

Basilica di San Petronio ★★ Sadly, the facade of this enormous Gothic basilica honoring the patron saint of Bologna was never completed. Legend has it that the construction was greatly curtailed by papal decree when the Vatican learned that the Bologna city fathers had planned to erect a basilica larger than St. Peter's. Although the builders went to work in 1390, after 3 centuries the church was still not finished (nevertheless, Charles V was crowned emperor here in 1530). However, Jacopo della Quercia of Siena did grace the central door with a masterpiece Renaissance sculpture. Inside, the church could accommodate the traffic of New York's Grand Central Terminal. The central nave is separated from the aisles by pilasters shooting up to the ceiling's flying arches. Of the 22 art-filled chapels, the most interesting is the **Bolognini Chapel (Cappella Bolognini),** the fourth on the left as you enter; it's embellished with

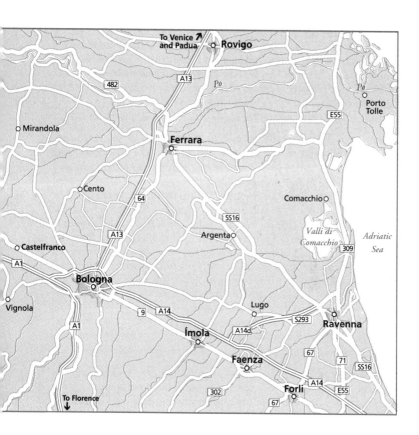

frescoes representing heaven and hell. The purity and simplicity of line represent some of the best of the Gothic in Italy.

Piazza Maggiore. ℂ 051-225442. Free admission. Daily 7:30am–1pm and 2–6:30pm (until 6pm Oct–Mar).

Palazzo Comunale ⊛   Built in the 14th century, this town hall has seen major restorations but happily retains its splendor. Enter through the courtyard; then proceed up the steps on the right to the **Communal Collection of Fine Arts (Collezioni Comunali d'Arte),** which includes many paintings from the 14th- to 19th-century Emilian school. Another section, the **Museum of Giorgio Morandi (Museo di Giorgio Morandi),** is devoted to the works of this famed painter of Bologna (1890–1964). His subject matter (a vase of flowers or a box) might have been mundane, but he transformed these objects into works of art of startling intensity and perception. Some of his finest works are landscapes of Grizzana, a village where he spent many lazy summers working and drawing. There's also a reconstruction of his studio.

Piazza Maggiore 6. ℂ 051-203111. Each museum separately, 4€ ($3.55) adults, free for children 14 and under. Tues–Sun 10am–6pm. Closed holidays. Bus: 11, 17, 25, 27, 30, or 37.

Basilica di San Domenico ⊛   The basilica dates from the 13th century but has undergone many restorations. It houses the beautifully crafted **tomb of St. Domenico,** in front of the Cappella della Madonna. The sculptured tomb, known as an *area,* is a Renaissance masterpiece, a joint enterprise of Niccolò Pisano, Guglielmo (a friar), Niccolò dell'Arca, Alfonso Lombardi, and the young Michelangelo. Observe the gaze and stance of Michelangelo's *San Procolo,* which appears to be the "rehearsal" for his later *David.* The **choir stalls,** the basilica's second major artistic work, were carved by Damiano da Bergamo, another friar, in the 16th century.

Piazza San Domenico 13. © 051-6400411. Free admission. Daily 8am–1pm and 2:30–7:30pm.

Tower of the Asinelli (Torre degli Asinelli) & Tower of the Garisenda (Torre degli Garisenda) 🏛🏛

Built by patricians in the 12th century, these leaning towers, the virtual symbol of Bologna, keep defying gravity year after year. In the Middle Ages, Bologna contained dozens of these skyscraper towers, predating Manhattan by several centuries. The towers were status symbols: The more powerful the family was, the taller its tower was. The smaller one, the Garisenda, is only 49m (162 ft.) tall, but because the Garisendas didn't prepare a solid foundation, it sways tipsily to the south, about 3m (10½ ft.) from perpendicular. In 1360, part of the tower was lopped off because it was viewed as a threat to public safety. Access to the Garisenda still isn't allowed. The taller one, the Asinelli (102m/334 ft. tall, a walk-up of nearly 500 steps), inclines almost 2.5m (7½ ft.). The reward for scaling the Asinelli is a panoramic view of the red-tile roofs of Bologna and the green hills beyond.

After visiting the towers, stroll down what must be the most architecturally elegant street in Bologna, **Via Strada Maggiore,** with its colonnades and mansions.

Piazza di Porta Ravegnana. Admission 2.50€ ($2.25). Summer daily 9am–6pm (to 5pm off-season).

Santo Stefano 🏛

From the leaning towers (above), head up Via Santo Stefano to see four churches linked together. A church has stood on this site since the 5th century, which even then was a converted Temple of Isis. Charlemagne stopped here to worship on his way to France in the 8th century.

The first church you enter is the 11th-century **Church of the Crucifix (Chiesa di Crocifisso),** relatively simple with only one nave and a crypt. To the left is the entrance to **Santo Sepolcro,** a polygonal temple dating principally from the 12th century. Under the altar is the tomb of San Petronio (St. Petronius), modeled after the Holy Sepulchre in Jerusalem and adorned with bas-reliefs. Continuing left, you enter the churches of **Santi Vitale e Agricola.** The present building, graced with three apses, also dates from the 11th century. To reenter Santo Sepolcro, take the back entrance, this time into the **Courtyard of Pilate (Piazza di Pilatus),** onto which several more chapels open. Legend has it that the basin in the courtyard was the one in which Pontius Pilate washed his hands after condemning Christ to death. (Actually, it's a Lombard bathtub from the 8th c.) Through the courtyard entrance to the right, proceed into the Romanesque **cloisters** from the 11th and 12th centuries. The names on the lapidary wall honor Bolognese war dead.

Piazza Stefano 24. © 051-223256. Free admission. Daily 9am–noon and 3:30–6:30pm.

San Giacomo Maggiore (St. James) 🏛

This church was a Gothic structure in the 13th century but, like so many others, was altered and restored at the expense of its original design. Still, it's one of Bologna's most interesting churches, filled with art treasures. The **Bentivoglio Chapel (Cappella Bentivoglio)** is the most sacred haunt, although time has dimmed the luster of its frescoes. Near the altar, seek out a *Madonna and Child* enthroned, one of the most outstanding works of Francesco Erancia. The holy pair is surrounded by

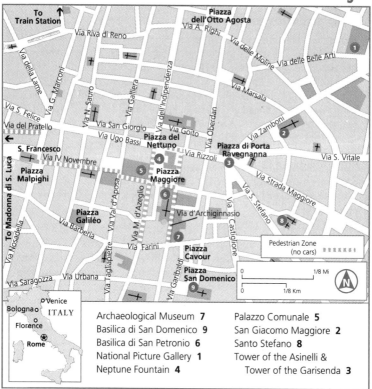

Archaeological Museum **7**
Basilica di San Domenico **9**
Basilica di San Petronio **6**
National Picture Gallery **1**
Neptune Fountain **4**

Palazzo Comunale **5**
San Giacomo Maggiore **2**
Santo Stefano **8**
Tower of the Asinelli &
   Tower of the Garisenda **3**

angels and saints, as well as by a half-naked Sebastian to the right. Nearby is a sepulchre of Antonio Bentivoglio, designed by Jacopo della Quercia, who labored so long over the doors to the Basilica of San Petronio. In the **Chapel of Santa Cecilia (Cappella di Santa Cecilia),** you'll discover important frescoes by Francia and Lorenzo Costa.

Piazza Rossini. ☎ 051-225970. Free admission. Daily 7am–noon and 2:30–6pm.

Archaeological Museum (Museo Civico Archeologico) ✦ This museum houses one of Italy's major Egyptian collections, as well as important discoveries dug up in Emilia. As you enter, look to the right in the atrium to see a decapitated marble torso, said to be Nero's. One floor below street level, a new Egyptian section presents a notable array of mummies and sarcophagi. The chief attraction in this collection is a cycle of bas-reliefs from Horemheb's tomb. On the ground floor, a new wing contains a gallery of casts, displaying copies of famous Greek and Roman sculptures. On the first floor are two exceptional burial items from Verucchio (Rimini). Note the wood furnishings, footrests, and throne of tomb 89, decorated with scenes from everyday life and ceremonial parades.

Upstairs are cases of prehistoric objects, tools, and artifacts. Etruscan relics constitute the best part of the museum, especially the highly stylized *Askos Benacci,* depicting a man on a horse that's perched on yet another animal. Also

---

Tips   Reserving Winery Tours

Emilia's most famous wine is Lambrusco, 50 million bottles of which are produced every year near Modena and Reggio Emilia. Less well known but also highly rated are the Colli Piacentini wines, one of the rising stars for which is **Cantine Romagnoli,** Via Genova 20, Villo di Vigolzone 29020 (© 0523-870129). If you'd like to venture out into the countryside, you might want to call ahead and make an appointment for a tour and tasting, and get directions.

---

displayed are terra-cotta urns, a vase depicting fighting Greeks and Amazons, and a bronze Certosa jar from the 6th century B.C. The museum's greatest single treasure is Phidias's head of Athena Lemnia, a copy of the 5th-century B.C. Greek work.

Via dell'Archiginnasio 2. © 051-233849. Admission 4€ ($3.55). Tues–Sat 9am–6:30pm; Sun 10am–6:30pm. Bus: 11, 17, 25, 30, or 37.

National Picture Gallery (Pinacoteca Nazionale di Bologna) ★★   The most significant works of the school of painting that flourished in Bologna from the 14th century to the heyday of the baroque have been assembled under one roof in this second-floor pinacoteca. The gallery also houses works by other major Italian artists, such as Raphael's *St. Cecilia in Estasi.* Guido Reni (1575–1642) of Bologna steals the scene with his *St. Sebastian* and *Pietà,* along with his penetrating *St. Andrea Corsini, The Slaying of the Innocents,* and idealized *Samson the Victorious.* Other Reni works are *The Flagellation of Christ, The Crucifixion,* and his masterpiece, *Ritratto della Madre* (a revealing portrait of his mother that must surely have inspired Whistler). Then seek out Vitale de Bologna's (1330–61) rendition of St. George slaying the dragon—a theme in European art that parallels Moby Dick in America. Also displayed are works by Francesco Francia, and especially noteworthy is a polyptych attributed to Giotto.

Via Belle Arti 56. © 051-243222. Admission 4€ ($3.55) adults, free for children 18 and under. Tues–Sun 9am–7pm. Closed holidays. Bus: 32, 33, 36, or 37.

SHOPPING

If you call puppeteer **Dimitrio Presini** ★ (© 051-6491837), you might be able to set up an appointment to see his creations, but your chances are better if you show up at his workshop at Via Rizzoli (no phone) between 1 and 6pm. Here you can tour the facilities and see how his puppets (including *burratini,* wooden puppets in handmade costumes) are made. You can't buy anything on the premises, but you can order a puppet that'll be made and shipped to you within 1 to 3 months. Presini specializes in local and regional characters but is capable of any custom work you want.

Galleria Marescalchi, Via Mascarela 116B (© 051-240368), features more traditional art, offering paintings and prints for view or sale by native son Morandi, Italian modern master De Chirico, and such foreigners as Chagall and Magritte.

An array of breads, pasta, and pastries makes **Atti,** Via Caprarie 7 (© 051-220425), tempting whether you're hungry or not. Among the pastries are the Bolognese specialty *certosino,* a heavy loaf resembling fruitcake, and an assortment of *gastronomie* (delectable heat-and-serve starters and main courses

Finds The World's Greatest China Shop

Faenza, 58km (36 miles) southeast of Bologna, has lent its name to a form of ceramics called faience, which originated on the island of Majorca, off Spain's coast. Faenza potters found inspiration in the work coming out of Majorca, and in the 12th century they began to produce their own designs, characterized by brilliant colors and floral decorations. The art reached its pinnacle in the 16th century, when the "hot-fire" process was perfected, during which ceramics were baked at a temperature of 1,742°F (950°C).

The legacy of this fabled industry is preserved today at the **International Museum of Ceramics (Museo Internazionale delle Ceramiche),** Via Corso Baccarin 1 (© **0546-21240;** www.racine.ra.it/micfaenza), called "the world's greatest china shop." Housed here are works not only from the artisans of Faenza but also from around the world, including pre-Columbian pottery from Peru. Of exceptional interest are Etruscan and Egyptian ceramics and a wide-ranging collection from the Orient, even from the days of the Roman Empire.

Deserving special attention is the section devoted to modern ceramic art, including works by Matisse and Picasso. On display are Picasso vases and a platter with his dove of peace, a platter in rich colors by Chagall, a "surprise" from Matisse, and a framed ceramic plaque of the Crucifixion by Georges Rouault. Another excellent work, the inspiration of a lesser-known artist, is a ceramic woman by Dante Morozzi. Even the great Léger tried his hand at ceramics.

From November to March, the museum is open Tuesday to Friday 9am to 1:30pm, Saturday 9am to 1:30pm and 3 to 6pm, and Sunday 9:30am to 1pm and 3 to 6pm. From April to October, hours are Tuesday to Saturday 9am to 7pm and Sunday 9am to 7pm. Admission is 5€ ($4.45). It's closed New Year's Day, May 1, August 15, and Christmas.

made fresh at the shop). If you want chocolate, head to **Majani,** Via Carbonesi 5 (© **051-234302**), which claims to be Italy's oldest sweets shop, having made and sold confections since 1796. A wide assortment of chocolates awaits you, accompanied by several types of biscuits; at Easter, the shop also makes chocolate eggs, rabbits, and lambs. At **Tamburini** ✮, Via Caprarie 1 (© **051-234726**), one of Italy's most lavish food shops, you can choose from an incredible array of gastronomie, including meats and fish, soups and salads, vegetables, and sweets, as well as fresh pasta to prepare at home. If you don't have anything to cook or serve your pasta in, **Schiavina,** Via Clavature 16 (© **051-223438**), sells every kitchen utensil you might need, such as cookware, silverware, glasses, dinnerware, and knives.

If you have hard-to-fit feet, walk to **Piero,** Via delle Lame 56 (© **051-558680**), for attractive footwear for men and women in large sizes, ranging up to European size 53 for men (American size 20) and size 46 for women. Bruno Magli quickly made a name for himself after opening his first shoe factory in 1934. Today, **Bruno Magli** shops selling leather bags, jackets, and coats for men and women—in addition to shoes—are at Galleria Cavour 9 (© **051-266915**) and Piazza della Mercanzia 2 (© **051-231126**).

A range of woman's clothing is available at **Paris, Texas,** Via Altabella 11 (© **051-225741**), including (but not limited to) designer eveningwear; the location at Via dell'Indipendenza 67B (© **051-241994**) focuses more on casuals such as jeans and T-shirts.

The Veronesi family has been closely tied to the jewelry trade for centuries. Now split up and competing among themselves, the various factions are represented by **F. Veronesi & Figli,** Piazza Maggiore 4 (© **051-224835**), which offers contemporary jewelry, watches, and silver using ancient designs; and **Giulio Veronesi,** with locations at Piazza di Re Enzo 1H (© **051-234237**) and Galleria Cavour 1 (© **051-234196**), which sells modern jewelry and Rolex watches.

WHERE TO STAY

Bologna hosts four to six trade fairs a year, during which hotel room rates rise dramatically. Some hotels announce their prices in advance; others wait to see what the market will bear. At trade fair times (dates vary yearly; check with the tourist office), business clients from throughout Europe book the best rooms, and you'll be paying a lot of money to visit Bologna.

An important note on parking: Much of central Bologna is closed to cars without special permits from 7am to 8pm daily (including Sun and holidays). When booking a room, be prepared to present your car registration number, which the hotel will then provide to the police to ensure that you are not fined for driving in a restricted area. Also ask about parking facilities as well as the most efficient route to take to reach your hotel because many streets in central Bologna are *permanently* closed to traffic. A permit is required to park in the center; hotel guests can purchase one through their hotel, if offered.

VERY EXPENSIVE

Grand Hotel Baglioni ★★★   The Baglioni boasts a location near Bologna's main square and is a superb atmospheric choice. Its four-story facade is crafted of the same reddish brick that distinguishes many of the city's older buildings, and the interior is noted for its wall and ceiling frescoes. Each soundproof guest room contains reproductions of antique furniture, good beds, and modern conveniences. They're generally spacious, with the fourth-floor units being the largest. The marble bathrooms come with deluxe toiletries.

Via dell'Indipendenza 8, 40121 Bologna. © 051-225445. Fax 051-234840. 125 units. 271€–416€ ($242–$371.50) double; 568€–930€ ($507.20–$830.50) suite. Rates include breakfast. AE, DC, MC, V. Parking 24€ ($21.45). **Amenities:** Excellent restaurant, I Carracci (see below); bar; concierge; salon; room service; babysitting; laundry. *In room:* A/C, TV, minibar, hair dryer, safe.

EXPENSIVE

Albergo Al Cappello Rosso   If you need a break from "rustic charm," this is the hotel for you. In the 14th century, the "Red Hat" in the hotel's name referred to the preferred headgear of the privileged tradesmen who stayed here. Now the hotel has been revamped into an ultramodern place with no hint of its past: The guest rooms tend to be rather modular, small to medium in size, each with a good bed. Bathrooms are smallish. Breakfast is the only meal served. The gracious staff is willing to help.

Via dei Fusari 9, 40123 Bologna. © 051-261891. Fax 051-227179. www.alcappellorosso.it. 34 units. 190€–330€ ($169.65–$294.65) double; 240€–390€ ($214.30–$348.25) suite. Rates include breakfast. AE, DC, MC, V. Parking 17.50€ ($15.65). **Amenities:** Room service; babysitting; laundry/dry cleaning. *In room:* A/C, TV, minibar, hair dryer, safe.

Hotel Corona d'Oro 1890 ✫ This fine palazzo, home of the noble Azzogu- idi family in the 15th century, preserves the architectural features of various peri- ods, from the Art Nouveau in the hall to the medieval coffered ceiling in the meeting room to the frescoes (coats of arms and landscapes) in the rooms. The guest rooms are decorated according to various periods, but all have fax and computer hookups. The bathrooms are small but well equipped. The hotel is a short distance from Piazza Maggiore.

Via Oberdan 12, 40126 Bologna. ℂ 051-236456. Fax 051-262679. www.bolognahotel.it. 35 units (shower only). 227€–284€ ($202.70–$253.60) double. Rates include buffet breakfast. AE, DC, DISC, MC, V. Parking 20€ ($17.85). **Amenities:** Bar; lounge; room service; babysitting; laundry/dry cleaning. *In room:* A/C, TV, mini- bar, safe.

Hotel dei Commercianti ✫ This hotel, located beside San Petronio in the pedestrian area of Piazza Maggiore, is near the site of the "Domus" (the first seat of the town hall) for the commune of Bologna in the 12th century. Recent restorations uncovered original wooden features, which you can see in the hall and the rooms in the old tower. Despite the centuries-old history, the atmos- phere is bright, and all modern luxuries are offered. The guest rooms, most small or medium in size, are decorated with antique furniture.

Via de' Pignattari 11, 40124 Bologna. ℂ 051-233052. Fax 051-224733. www.bolognahotel.it. 34 units (half with shower only). 196€–284€ ($175–$253.55) double; 284€–413€ ($253.60–$368.80) suite. Rates include buffet breakfast. AE, DC, DISC, MC, V. Parking 20€ ($17.85). **Amenities:** Bar; lounge; room service; babysitting; laundry/dry cleaning. *In room:* A/C, TV, minibar, hair dryer, safe.

Royal Hotel Carlton ✫✫ Some claim that the Carlton, only a few minutes' walk from many of the national monuments, is the best hotel in Bologna, but we feel that the honor goes to the Baglioni (see above). The Hilton-style Carl- ton is a rather austere place with a triangular garden, catering mainly to business travelers. It's modern all the way, with a balcony and a picture window for each room, although the views aren't particularly inspiring. The guest rooms range from medium to large, each with a comfortable bed. The midsize bathrooms are well equipped, with plenty of shelf space.

Via Montebello 8, 40121 Bologna. ℂ 051-249361. Fax 051-249724. www.monrifhotels.it. 251 units. 260€–360€ ($232.20–$321.50) double; from 415€ ($370.60) suite. Rates include buffet breakfast. AE, DC, MC, V. Parking 13.50€–17.50€ ($12.05–$15.65) in a garage; free outside. **Amenities:** Restaurant; bar; concierge; room service; babysitting; laundry/dry cleaning. *In room:* A/C, TV, minibar, hair dryer, safe.

MODERATE

Grand Hotel Elite Located on the city's northwestern edge, this hotel was built in the 1970s as a combination of private apartments and hotel rooms; in 1993, the entire structure was transformed into a hotel. The guest rooms are unremarkable but comfortable. The bathrooms are small but have adequate shelf space. Even if you're not staying here, you might want to dine in the **Cordon Bleu,** which features international cuisine of Emilia-Romagna (closed Sun).

Via Aurelio Saffi 36, 40131 Bologna. ℂ 051-6491432. Fax 051-6493539. www.hotelelite.it. 175 units (with shower only). 155€–248€ ($138.40–$221.45) double; 210€–351€ ($187.55–$313.45) suite. Rates include breakfast. AE, DC, MC, V. Parking 19€ ($16.95). **Amenities:** Well-regarded restaurant; bar; room service; babysitting; laundry/dry cleaning. *In room:* A/C, TV, minibar, hair dryer.

Hotel Orologio ✫ This charming small hotel faces the *orologio* (clock) on the civic center in the heart of medieval Bologna, with a view of Piazza Maggiore and the Podesà Palace. The guest rooms all have modern furnishings. Most are small but provide reasonable comfort, including tidy bathrooms. This is the ideal place for those who want a historic atmosphere without forfeiting modern comforts.

Via IV Novembre 10, 40123 Bologna. ℂ **051-231253**. Fax 051-260552. www.bolognahotel.it. 35 units (some with shower only). 165€–310€ ($147.30–$276.80) double, 258€–413€ ($230.40–$368.80) suite. Rates include buffet breakfast. AE, DC, DISC, MC, V. Parking 22€ ($19.65). **Amenities:** Bar; lounge; room service; babysitting; laundry/dry cleaning. *In room:* A/C, TV, minibar, hair dryer, safe.

Hotel Regina   A good, plain choice with moderate comfort, the Regina dates from the 1800s, but it was modernized in the 1970s. The guest rooms range from small to medium but come with comfortable furnishings. The bathrooms are a bit cramped. The staff is helpful, and the maids keep everything spotless.

Via dell'Indipendenza 51, 40121 Bologna. ℂ **051-248878**. Fax 051-247986. 61 units (shower only). 130€–160€ ($116.10–$142.90) double. Rates include breakfast. AE, DC, MC, V. Parking 10€ ($8.95). **Amenities:** Bar; lounge; room service; laundry. *In room:* A/C, TV, minibar, hair dryer.

Hotel Roma 𝒦 (Value)   This is one of the best buys in Bologna; it also enjoys one of the most scenic locations (despite the heavy traffic). Most of the guest rooms are roomy yet old-fashioned, with large closets, comfortable armchairs, and excellent beds with fine linen. The bathrooms are small but contain adequate shelf space and stall showers. The best units are on the top floor, where there's a terrace overlooking the city rooftops.

Via Massimo d'Azeglio 9, 40123 Bologna. ℂ **051-226322**. Fax 051-239909. hotelroma@mailbox.dsnet.it. 86 units. 144€ ($128.60) double. AE, MC, V. **Amenities:** Restaurant; lounge; room service; babysitting; laundry/dry cleaning. *In room:* A/C, TV, minibar, hair dryer, safe.

Hotel Tre Vecchi   This 1970s hotel lies in a century-old building, a 5-minute walk from the train station. The guest rooms are clean, bright, and soundproof. They're a bit cramped but still comfortable. The bathrooms are small. The best room is called Prestige—it's bigger than the others and boasts a Jacuzzi and a private terrace. The gentle humor in the name of the hotel ("Three Geriatrics") was the idea of the trio of aging entrepreneurs who founded the hotel.

Via dell'Indipendenza 47, 40121 Bologna. ℂ **051-231991**. Fax 051-224143. 96 units (most with shower only). 163€–241€ ($145.55–$215.20) double, 212€–282€ ($189.30–$251.85) triple. Rates include buffet breakfast. AE, DC, MC, V. **Amenities:** Cafe; room service; babysitting; laundry/dry cleaning. *In room:* A/C, TV, minibar, hair dryer, safe.

WHERE TO DINE
EXPENSIVE/MODERATE

Antica Osteria Romagnola ITALIAN   In a building dating from 1600, the Romagnola offers cuisines from throughout Italy. You might begin with one of the well-flavored risottos or choose from a savory selection of antipasti. The variety of pastas is impressive—for example, ravioli with truffle essence, garganelli with zucchini, and pasta whipped with asparagus tips. You might also select a terrine of ricotta and arugula (the latter was considered an aphrodisiac by the ancient Romans). For your main course you might try a springtime specialty, *capretto* (roast goat) with artichokes and potatoes, or filet mignon with aromatic basil.

Via Rialto 13. ℂ **051-263699**. Reservations recommended for dinner. Main courses 10€–17.50€ ($8.95–$15.65). AE, DC, MC, V. Tues 7:30–11pm; Wed–Sun 12:30–2:30pm and 7:30–11pm. Closed Dec 25–Jan 2 and Aug.

Diana 𝒦 REGIONAL/INTERNATIONAL   Occupying a late medieval building in the heart of town, the Diana has been popular since 1920. This restaurant offers three gracefully decorated dining rooms and a verdant terrace. It was named in honor of the goddess of the hunt because of the many game dishes it served when it first opened. In recent years, although game is still featured in season, the restaurant has opted for a staple of regional and international cuisine, all competently prepared. Begin with one of the city's most delicious appetizers: *spuma di mortadella,* a paté made of mortadella sausage served on dainty white toast. You'll never eat baloney again.

Via dell'Indipendenza 24. (C) 051-231302. Reservations recommended. Main courses 9€–20€ ($8.05–$17.85). AE, DC, MC, V. Tues–Sun noon–2:30pm and 7–10:30pm. Closed Jan 1–10 and Aug 1–28.

Grassilli BOLOGNESE/INTERNATIONAL   Grassilli is a good bet for conservative regional cooking prepared with time-tested recipes. It's in a 1750s building on a narrow cobblestone alley, a short block from the leaning towers. There's also a street-side canopy for outdoor dining. At night the place can be festive, and your good time will be enhanced if you order a specialty such as tortellini in mushroom cream sauce, the chef's special tournedos, tortellini *alla Bologna,* or grilled or roasted meat.

Via del Luzzo 3. (C) 051-237938 or 051-222961. Reservations required. Main courses 11.50€–15€ ($10.25–$13.40). AE, DC, MC, V. Thurs–Sat and Mon–Tues 12:30–2:30pm and 8–10:30pm; Sun 12:30–2:30pm. Closed July 15–Aug 10, Jan 9–21, and for dinner on holidays.

I Carracci ⊛ ITALIAN/INTERNATIONAL   The chic Carracci is named after the family of artists who decorated the premises with frescoes. Its cuisine equals that of Nuovi Notai (see below), and the service is impeccable. The elegant dining room dates from the 16th century, with ceiling frescoes of the seasons painted in the 1700s by the Carracci brothers. The seasonally adjusted menu features the freshest produce and highest-quality meat, poultry, and fish. Dishes we've enjoyed are tortellini in *brodo* (broth), tagliatelle in ragout, veal scallop *alla bolognese,* wild boar cacciatore, and grilled salmon filet. The wine list is among the region's finest.

In the Grand Hotel Baglioni, Via dell'Indipendenza 8. (C) 051-225445. Reservations required. Main courses 15€–25€ ($13.40–$22.35). AE, DC, MC, V. Daily 12:30–2:30pm and 7:30–10:30pm.

Montegrappa da Nello *(Finds* BOLOGNESE/INTERNATIONAL   This wonderful trattoria is one of the few restaurants still doing classic Bolognese cuisine. Hosts Franco and Ezio Bolini insist that all the produce be fresh. The menu's signature dish is *tortellina Montegrappa,* a pasta favorite served in cream-and-meat sauce. The restaurant is also known for its fresh white truffles and mushrooms. A good example is the *graminia,* a very fine white spaghetti presented with mushrooms, cream, and pepper. A heavenly salad is made with truffles, mushrooms, *parmigiano,* and artichokes.

Via Montegrappa 2. (C) 051-236331. Reservations recommended for dinner. Main courses 7.50€–22.50€ ($6.70–$20.10). AE, DC, MC, V. Tues–Sun noon–3pm and 7–11:30pm. Closed Sat–Mon in July and Aug.

Nuovi Notai ⊛ ITALIAN/TUSCAN/UMBRIAN   Behind a lattice- and ivy-covered facade next to the cathedral, within view of one of Italy's most beautiful squares, this sublime restaurant draws a loyal crowd. In summer, you can dine outside. Music lovers and relaxing businesspeople appreciate the piano bar. The decor combines the Belle Epoque with Italian flair and includes hanging Victorian lamps and clutches of flowers on each table. The fine cooking is based on the best local products, and menu items include a flan of cheese fondue, a gratin of gnocchi with truffles, beef filet cooked in a *cartoccio* (a paper bag) and garnished with porcini mushrooms, and breast of wild goose.

Via de' Pignattari 1. (C) 051-228694. Reservations required. Main courses 10€–17.50€ ($8.95–$15.65); fixed-price menus 27.50€–35€ ($24.55–$31.25). AE, DC, MC, V. Mon–Sat noon–2:30pm and 7–11pm.

Ristorante al Pappagallo ✩✩✩ BOLOGNESE   Foodies might disagree on which is the very best restaurant in Bologna, but this upscale choice always surfaces at or near the top of everyone's list. It has drawn a faithful following for decades; in past years, it has hosted Einstein, Hitchcock, and Toscanini (not at the same time). "The Parrot," still going strong, is on the ground floor of a Gothic mansion across from the 14th-century Merchants' Loggia (a short walk from the leaning towers). Start off with *lasagne verde al forno* (baked lasagna that gets its green color from minced spinach). For the main course, try the specialty: *filetti di tacchino,* superb turkey breasts baked with white wine, parmigiano, and truffles. The menu also features some low-calorie offerings. The restaurant boasts an impressive wine list and serves amber-colored Albana wine and sparkling red Lambrusco.

Piazza della Mercanzia 3C. ✆ 051-232807. Reservations recommended. Main courses 17.50€–20€ ($15.65–$17.85). AE, DC, MC, V. Mon–Sat 12:30–2:30pm and 7:30–10:30pm.

Ristorante Luciano ✩ 𝘝𝘢𝘭𝘶𝘦 BOLOGNESE   This restaurant, within walking distance of the city center, serves some of Bologna's best food at moderate prices. It has an Art Deco style and a real Bolognese atmosphere. We prefer the front room, opening onto the kitchen. As a novelty, on the street is a window looking directly into the kitchen. To begin your gargantuan repast, request the tortellini in rich cream sauce. Well-recommended main dishes are the *fritto misto all'Italiana* (mixed grill), *scaloppe con porcini* (veal with mushrooms), and *cotoletta alla bolognese* (veal layered with ham and parmigiano and then baked). A dramatic dessert is crepes flambé.

Via Nazario Sauro 19. ✆ 051-231249. Reservations recommended. Main courses 11€–27.50€ ($9.80–$24.55). AE, DC, MC, V. Thurs–Tues noon–2pm and 7:30–10:30pm. Closed Aug.

INEXPENSIVE

Enoteca Italiana, Via Marsala 2/B (✆ **051-235989**), is an inviting and aromatic shop-cum-wine bar on a side street just north of Piazza Maggiore. You can stand at the bar and sip a local wine while enjoying a sandwich. For a moveable feast, you can stock up on ham, salami, and cheese at the deli counter, and enjoy a picnic at the nearby Neptune fountain. Open Monday to Saturday 7:30am to 8pm.

On a stroll through the **Pescherie Vecchie,** the city's market area near the Due Torri, you can assemble a meal. Along the Via Drapperie and adjoining streets, salumerias, cheese shops, bakeries, and vegetable markets are heaped high with attractive displays. The stalls of Bologna's other food market, the **Mercato delle Erbe,** Via Ugo Bassi 2, are open Monday to Wednesday and Friday and Saturday from 7:15am to 1pm, and Monday to Wednesday again from 5 to 7pm.

Bar Roberto at Via Orefici 9/A, near Bologna's central market, is probably the only smoke-free cafe in Italy. It turns out delicious homemade pastries that attract a loyal breakfast clientele.

Osteria dell'Orsa ITALIAN   The restaurant, which offers some of the best *ragú alla bolognese* in town, occupies a 15th-century building near the university. Most diners opt for the high-ceilinged, medieval-looking main floor, though an informal cantinalike cellar room is open for additional seating. You won't go wrong if you preface a meal with any kind of pasta labeled *bolognese*. Other options are homemade tagliolini, veal cutlet fiorentina, and tortelloni with cheese, ham, and mushroom sauce. If you feel adventurous, you can always try grilled donkey meat (*somarino*).

Via Mentana 1F. ✆ 051-231576. Reservations recommended. Main courses 7€–10€ ($6.25–$8.95). AE, DC, MC, V. Daily noon–3pm and 7pm–1am (closes 1 hr. earlier Sat–Sun).

Osteria del Moretto BOLOGNESE   This is a simple trattoria and bar, operating since 1900 with few changes. Built as a convent in the 13th century, it lies
near the Porto San Mamolo, in the historic core. Most of the stand-up patrons
drink wine and often segue from drinks into a working-class meal. This might
include selections from a platter of local cheese as an antipasto, *pasta e fagiole* (a
tomato-based bean and pasta soup), spaghetti bolognese, *salata Trentino* (a cold
salad of meat and vegetables), eggplant parmigiana, and chicken—but no fish of
any kind.

Via di San Mamolo 5. ℂ 051-580284. Reservations recommended Fri–Sat. Main courses 7€–10€
($6.25–$8.95). No credit cards. Daily 7pm–3am.

A STANDOUT RESTAURANT IN NEARBY IMOLA

San Domenico ★★★ ITALIAN   Foodies from all over Europe and America
travel to the unlikely village of Imola to savor the offerings of what some food
critics (ourselves included) consider the best restaurant in Italy. San Domenico
can also be easily reached from Ravenna. The cuisine is sometimes compared to
France's modern creations. However, owner Gian Luigi Morini claims his delectable offerings are nothing more than adaptations of festive regional dishes,
except that they're lighter, more subtle, and served in manageable portions.

A tuxedo-clad member of his talented young staff will escort you to a table
near the tufted leather banquettes. Meals include heavenly concoctions made
with the freshest ingredients. You might select goose-liver paté studded with
white truffles, fresh shrimp in creamy sweet bell-pepper sauce, roast rack of lamb
with fresh rosemary, stuffed chicken supreme wrapped in lettuce leaves, or fresh
handmade spaghetti with shellfish. Signor Morini has collected some of the best
vintages in Europe for the past 30 years, with some bottles of cognac dating
from the time of Napoleon.

Via Gaspare Sacchi 1, Imola (34km/21 miles southeast of Bologna). ℂ 0542/29-000. Reservations recommended. Main courses 30€–45€ ($26.80–$40.15); fixed-price lunch 35€ ($31.25); fixed-price dinner 75€
($67). AE, DC, MC, V. Tues–Sun 12:30–2:30pm; Tues–Sat 8–10:30pm. Closed Jan 1–10 and 1 week in Aug.

BOLOGNA AFTER DARK

Because Bologna has a large population of students and graduate students, it has
a vibrant, diverse nightlife scene, including lots of cafes that are packed with a
young crowd. The Via del Pratello and, near the university, Via Zamboni and
Via delle Belle Arte and their surrounding areas are the usual haunts of night
owls. You can usually find a place for a drink, a shot of espresso, or a light meal
as late as 2am.

Facing the Duomo is **Bar Giuseppe,** Piazza Maggiore 1 (ℂ **051-264444**),
serving some of the best espresso and gelato in town. It stretches for at least a
block beneath the arcades facing the Piazza Maggiore.

At 10:30pm, make your way to the cellars of a 16th-century palazzo near the
university at **Cantina Bentivoglio** at Via Mascarella 4B (ℂ **051-265416**).
That's when you'll hear some of the best jazz in Bologna.

Cassero, Piazza Porta Saragozza 2 (ℂ **051-6446902**), is Bologna's most popular gay bar, with a noisy, discolike atmosphere and floor shows. The biggest
attraction here, though, is the setting—the club occupies one of Bologna's
medieval gates, the top of which serves as a roof garden and open-air dance floor
in good weather. Cassero is also the Bologna headquarters of Arcigay and
Arcilesbiche, a gay and lesbian center organizing cultural meetings and entertainment. Thursday is set aside for women, on Friday theatrical performances of

interest to the gay and lesbian community take place, and on Sunday disco fever takes over.

Osteria de Poeti, Via Poeti 1 (© **051-236166**), is Bologna's oldest osteria and has been in operation since the 16th century. The brick-vaulted ceilings, stone walls, and ancient wine barrels provide just the sort of ambience you would expect to find in such a historic establishment. Stop in to enjoy the live jazz and folk music that's on tap most nights. Closed Monday.

During July and August, the city authorities transform the **parks** along the town's northern tier into an Italian version of a German *biergarten* (beer garden), complete with disco music under colored lights. Vendors sell beer and wine from indoor/outdoor bars set up on the lawns, and others hawk food and souvenirs. Events range from live jazz to classical concerts. Ask any hotelier or the tourist office for the schedule of midsummer events, or try your luck by taking either a taxi or (much less convenient) bus nos. 25 or 91A from the main station to Arena Parco Nord.

The **Teatro Comunale,** Via Largo Respighi (© **051-529999**), is the venue for major cultural presentations, including opera, ballet, and orchestral presentations. The **Circolo della Musica di Bologna,** Via Galliera 11 (© **051-227032**), presents free classical music concerts in summer. For the rest of the year, there's always a cafe, bar, or pub nearby. Doors open daily at 8pm.

Another hot spot is the **Cantina Bentivoglio,** Via Mascarella 4B (© **051-265416**), off Via delle Belle Arti, a fairly up-market joint serving reasonably priced food and wine and staging great live jazz daily 8pm to 2am. The cover is 7.50€ ($6.70).

2 Ferrara ★

417km (259 miles) N of Rome, 52km (32 miles) N of Bologna, 100km (62 miles) SW of Venice

When Papa Borgia (Pope Alexander VI) was shopping for a third husband for the apple of his eye, darling Lucrezia, his gaze fell on the influential house of Este. From the 13th century, this great Italian family had dominated Ferrara, building up a powerful duchy and a reputation as patrons of the arts. Alfonse d'Este, son of the shrewd but villainous Ercole I, the ruling duke of Ferrara, was an attractively virile candidate for Lucrezia's much-used hand. (Her second husband was murdered, perhaps by her brother, Cesare, who was the apple of nobody's eye—with the possible exception of Machiavelli. Her first marriage, a political alliance, was to Giovanni Sforza, but it was annulled in 1497.)

Although the Este family might have had reservations (after all, it was common gossip that the pope "knew" his daughter in the biblical sense), they finally consented to the marriage. As the duchess of Ferrara, a position she held until her death, Lucrezia bore seven children. But one of her grandchildren, Alfonso II, wasn't as prolific and left the family without a male heir. The greedy eye of Pope Clement VIII took quick action, gobbling up the city as his personal fiefdom in the waning months of the 16th century. The great house of Este went down in history, and Ferrara sadly declined under the papacy.

Incidentally, Alfonso II was a dubious patron of Torquato Tasso (1544–95), author of the epic *Jerusalem Delivered,* a work that was to make him the most celebrated poet of the Late Renaissance. The legend of Tasso (who's thought to have been insane, paranoid, or at least tormented) has steadily grown over the centuries. It didn't need any more boosting, but Goethe fanned the legend through the Teutonic lands with his late-18th-century drama *Torquato Tasso.* It's said that Alfonso II at one time made Tasso his prisoner.

Ferrara is still relatively undiscovered, especially by North Americans, but it's richly blessed, with much of its legacy intact. Among the historic treasures are a great cathedral and the Este Castle, along with enough ducal palaces to make for a fast-paced day of sightseeing. Its palaces, for the most part, have long been robbed of their lavish furnishings, but the faded frescoes, the paintings that weren't carted off, and the palatial rooms are reminders of the vicissitudes of power.

Modern Ferrara is one of the most health-conscious places in all Italy. Bicycles outnumber the automobiles on the road, and more than half the citizens get exercise by jogging. In fact, it's almost surreal: Enclosed in medieval walls under a bright sky, everywhere you look, you'll find the people of Ferrara engaged in all sorts of self-powered locomotion. Beware of octogenarian cyclists whizzing by you with shopping bags flapping in the wind.

ESSENTIALS

GETTING THERE   Getting to Ferrara by **train** is fast and efficient because it's on the main line between Bologna and Venice. A total of 33 trains a day originating in Bologna pass through. Trip time is 40 minutes, and the fare is about 2.25€ ($2) one way. Some 24 trains arrive from Venice (1½ hr.); the one-way fare begins at 5.55€ ($4.95). Ravenna is just an hour's trip away, with hourly departures all day long. For information and schedules, call ℂ **1478-88088** (toll-free in Italy only).

If you're in Modena (see section 4 of this chapter), you'll find 11 **bus** departures a day for Ferrara. Trip time is between 1½ and 2 hours, and a one-way ticket is 4.50€ ($4). In Ferrara, bus information for the surrounding area is available at ℂ **0532-599492.**

If you have a **car** and are coming from Bologna, take A13 north. From Venice, take A4 southwest to Padua and continue on A13 south to Ferrara.

VISITOR INFORMATION   The helpful **tourist office** is at Castello Estense, Piazza del Castello (ℂ **0532-209370**), open daily 9am to 1pm and 2 to 6pm.

SPECIAL EVENTS   Not quite as dramatic as its counterpart in Siena, Ferrara's **Palio di San Giorgio** is a popular event held in the Piazza Ariostea the last Sunday of May. Two-legged creatures run first, in separate races for young men and young women. They are followed by donkeys and, finally, in the main event, horses ridden bareback by jockeys representing Ferrara's eight traditional districts.

During the summer, the streets of Ferrara seem like one great theater. Some excellent jazz and classical concerts are the main events of **Estate a Ferrara,** an outdoor festival that begins in early July and runs until late August, when the festivities are augmented by street musicians, mimes, and orators, who partake in the **Busker's Festival.**

EXPLORING THE TOWN

Ferrara's **medieval walls,** massive enough to be topped with trees and lawns, encircle the city with an aerie of greenery. The wide paths are ideal for biking, jogging, and strolling; they provide wonderful views of the city and surrounding farmland. Many hotels offer guests free use of bikes, or you can rent them from the lot outside the train station.

A cost-efficient way to tour Ferrara's many museums is to purchase a *biglietto cumulativo* for 12€ ($10.70), valid for 1 year and good for admission to most municipal museums. You can buy it at any of the participating museums.

Castello Estense ✪   A moated four-towered castle (lit at night), this proud fortress began as a bricklayer's dream near the end of the 14th century, although its face has been lifted and wrenched about for centuries. It was home to the powerful Estes, where the dukes went about their ho-hum daily chores: trysting with their own lovers, murdering their wives' lovers, beheading or imprisoning potential enemies, whatever. Today it's used for the provincial and prefectural administration offices, and you can view many of its once-lavish rooms—notably the **Salon of Games (Salone dei Giochi),** the **Salon of Dawn (Salone dell'Aurora),** and a **Ducal chapel** that once belonged to Renata di Francia, daughter of Louis XII. Parisina d'Este, wife of Duke Niccolò d'Este III, was murdered with her lover, Ugolino (the duke's illegitimate son), in the dank prison below the castle, creating the inspiration for Browning's "My Last Duchess."

Largo Castello. ✆ **0532-299233.** Admission 4€ ($3.55) adults. Tues–Sun 9:30am–5pm. Bus: 1, 2, 4, or 9.

Il Duomo ✪✪   A short stroll from the Este Castle, the 12th-century Duomo weds the delicate Gothic with a more virile Romanesque. Its outstanding feature is its **triple facade** ✪✪ with a magnificent porch. Over the tympanum the Last Judgment is depicted in stone in a style evocative of a French Gothic cathedral. The lunette over the main door is a sculpture by Nicholaus, depicting St. George. There are two splendid tiers of galleries on the upper section of the south side. Never finished, the bell tower (*campanile*) was built to the designs of Leon Battista Alberti. Inside, the massive structure is heavily baroqued. In decades to come, more artisans would be called in to festoon the cathedral with trompe l'oeil. Very little of the original decoration can be seen.

Piazza Cattedrale. ✆ **0532-207449.** Free admission but donation appreciated. Daily 7:30am–noon and 3–6:30pm. Bus: 1, 2, or 9.

Museo del Duomo ✪   In its new location, the Duomo Museum is worth a visit just to see works by Ferrara's most outstanding 15th-century painter, Cosmé Tura. Aesthetically controversial, the big attraction here is Tura's St. George slaying the dragon to save a red-stockinged damsel in distress. Opposite is an outstanding Jacopo della Quercia work of a sweet, regal Madonna with a pomegranate in one hand and the Christ child in the other. Also from the Renaissance heyday of Ferrara are some bas-reliefs, notably a Giano *bifronte* (a mythological figure looking at the past and the future), along with some 16th-century *arazzi* (tapestries) woven by hand.

Via San Romano 1–9. ✆ **0532-761299.** Admission 4€ ($3.55). Tues–Sun 9am–1pm and 3–8pm. Bus: 2, 3, or 11.

Civic Museum of Ancient Art (Museo Civico d'Arte Antica)   The Schifanoia Palace was built in 1385 for Albert V d'Este and then was enlarged by Borso d'Este (1450–71). The Ancient Art Museum was founded in 1758 and transferred to its present site in 1898. At first, only coins and medals were exhibited, but then the collection was enhanced by donations of archaeological finds, antique bronzes, small Renaissance plates and pottery, and other collections.

Art lovers are lured to the **Salon of the Months (Salone dei Mesi)** to see the astrological wall cycle, which represents the 12 months. Each month is subdivided into three horizontal bands: The lower band shows scenes from the daily life of courtiers and people, the middle shows the relative sign of the zodiac, and the upper depicts the triumph of the classical divinity for that myth. Humanist

Pellegrino Prisciani conceived the subjects of the cycle, although Cosmé Tura, the official court painter, was probably the organizer of the works. Tura was the founder of the Ferrarese School, to which belonged, among others, Ercole de' Roberti and Francesco del Cossa, who painted the March, April, and May scenes. The frescoes are complex, leading to varied interpretations of their meaning.

In the Palazzo Schifanoia, Via Scandiana 23. (✆ 0532-64178. Admission 4€ ($3.55) adults, free for those under 18. Tues–Sun 9:30am–6pm. Closed Mon and major holidays. Bus: 1, 2, or 9.

Palazzo dei Diamanti ⭐ The Palazzo dei Diamanti, another jewel of Este splendor, is so named because of the 9,000 diamond-shaped stones on its facade. Of the handful of museums sheltered here, the National Picture Gallery (Pinacoteca Nazionale) is the most important. It houses the works of the Ferrarese artists—notably the trio of old masters, Tura, del Cossa, and Roberti. The collection covers the chief period of artistic expression in Ferrara from the 14th to the 18th centuries. Next in importance is the Civic Gallery of Modern Art (Museo Civico d'Arte Moderne), which sponsors the most important contemporary art exhibits in town. The other three museums in the palazzo aren't really worth your time.

Corso Ercole d'Este 21. (✆ 0532-205844 or 0532-209988. Admission to Pinacoteca 4€ ($3.55); Civic Gallery of Modern Art 7€ ($6.25). Pinacoteca Tues–Sat 9am–2pm (open to 7pm Thurs); Sun 9am–1pm. Civic Gallery of Modern Art daily 9am–7pm, when exhibits are staged. Bus: 3.

Casa Romei ⭐ This 15th-century palace near the Este tomb was the property of Giovanni Romei, a friend and confidant of the fleshy Duke Borso d'Este, who made the Este realm a duchy. Giovanni was later set to marry one of the Este princesses, although we don't know if it was for love or power or both. In later years, Lucrezia and her gossipy coterie, riding in the ducal carriage drawn by handsome white horses, descended on the Romei house, perhaps to receive Borgia messengers from Rome. Its once-elegant furnishings have been carted off, but the chambers (many with terra-cotta fireplaces) remain, and the casa has been filled with frescoes and sculpture.

Via Savonarola 30. (✆ 0532-240341. Admission 2€ ($1.80) adults; free for ages 17 and under. Tues–Sun 8:30am–7pm. Bus: 3.

SHOPPING

Ferrara has a rich tradition of artisanship dating from the Renaissance. You can find some of the best, albeit expensive, products in the dozen or so antiques stores in the historic center.

You find beautifully designed, colorful ceramics at **Ceramica Artistica Ferrarese,** Via Baluardi 125 (✆ 0532-66093), and **La Marchesana,** Via Cortevecchia 38A (✆ 0532-240535).

More unusual is an outfit specializing in wrought iron: **Chierici,** Via Bartoli 17 (✆ 0532-67057), near the Ponte San Giorgio. Some of the smaller pieces, such as decorative brackets or fireplace tools, make good souvenirs.

The **Antica Salumeria Polesinati,** Via Mazzini 78 (✆ 0532-206833), and the **Enoteca Al Brindisi,** Via Adelardi 11 (✆ 0532-209142), stockpile the fruits of the Ferrarese harvest in historically evocative settings. Every month Tuesday to Sunday 9am to 1pm, the **open-air antiques and handcraft markets** feature lots of junk amid the increasingly rare treasures. The markets are conducted in Piazza Municipale (mostly antiques and bric-a-brac) and Piazza Savonarola (mainly handcrafts and bric-a-brac).

WHERE TO STAY

Hotel Duchessa Isabella ☆ Despite readers' complaints about staff attitude, this remains the town's leading inn. It opened in 1990 as a government-rated five-star hotel, named after the Este family's most famous ancestor, Isabella. The guest rooms are identified by the names of the flowers whose colors they most closely resemble. This might strike you as a bit gaudy if you end up in a room with pink pillows and enough satin to charm Mae West. Each boasts a sense of history and is outfitted with all the modern amenities, plus plush bathrooms. As a courtesy to guests, free horse-drawn tours are offered by the hotel—a romantic orientation to Ferrara and some of its most significant landmarks.

Via Palestro 68/70, 44100 Ferrara. ℂ **0532-202121.** Fax 0532-202638. www.duchessaisabella.com. 27 units. 285€ ($254.50) double; from 385€ ($343.80) suite. Rates include breakfast. AE, DC, MC, V. Free parking. Closed Aug. Bus: 1, 2, 3, or 9. **Amenities:** Excellent restaurant; lounge; free bicycles; horse-drawn tours; room service; babysitting; laundry/dry cleaning. *In room:* A/C, TV, minibar, hair dryer, safe.

Hotel Europa This is the leading moderately priced choice. In the 1600s, this palace was built near the Castello d'Estense. It was transformed into one of the most prestigious hotels in town in 1880, but during World War II, portions of the rear were bombed and then repaired in a less grandiose style. The government-rated three-star place continues today, with a well-trained staff, reasonable prices, and guest rooms that are clean and comfortable, with antique furnishings and modern comforts. A handful of rooms overlook the *corso* (they retain ceiling frescoes from the original construction). The bathrooms are small.

Corso della Giovecca 49, 44100 Ferrara. ℂ **0532-205456.** Fax 0532-212120. www.hoteleuropaferrara.com. 39 units (showers only). 86€–108€ ($76.80–$96.45) double; 110€ ($98.25) suite. Rates include breakfast. AE, DC, MC, V. Parking 8€ ($7.15). Bus: 1, 2, 3, or 9. **Amenities:** Bar; lounge; room service; laundry. *In room:* A/C, TV, minibar, hair dryer.

Locanda Borgonuovo ☆ *Finds* This is Ferrara's most elegant B&B, installed in a former 17th-century monastery near the Castello d'Estense. Your hostess is the charming Signora Adela Orlandini, who has restored the former quarters of her attorney father's offices and turned the space into an accommodating and stylish hostelry. Her most frequent guests are actors and musicians from the local theater who prefer this place to all others in town. Rooms are spacious and fashionably decorated, often with antiques and with comfortable beds and neatly tiled bathrooms. The best unit has a kitchenette, but that accommodation is usually rented to those seeking longer stays. In fair weather breakfast is served in the garden in back of this medieval palazzo. Reserve well in advance, because this is a very preferred address.

Via Cairoli 29, 44100 Ferrara. ℂ **0532-211100.** fax 0532-248000. www.borgonuovo.com. 4 units (showers only). 93€–103€ ($83.05–$92) double; 83€–166€ ($74.10–$148.25) apt. **Amenities:** Room service; babysitting; laundry/dry cleaning. *In room:* A/C, TV, hair dryer, safe.

Ripagrande Hotel ☆ The Ripagrande, one of the town's unusual hotels, occupies a Renaissance palace. Coffered ceilings, walls in Ferrarese brickwork, 16th-century columns, and a wide staircase with a floral cast-iron handrail characterize the entrance hall. Inside are two Renaissance courtyards decorated with columns and capitals. Half the guest rooms are junior suites with sleeping areas connected to an internal stairway. The rooms are spacious, with tasteful furnishings, which are often antique reproductions. Some are tri-level, with a garretlike bedroom above. The most desirable rooms are on the top floor, opening onto terraces overlooking the red-tile roofs. The bathrooms are a bit small but have adequate shelf space.

Via Ripagrande 21, 44100 Ferrara. ℂ **0532-765250.** Fax 0532-764377. www.ripagrandehotel.it. 40 units (showers only). 155€–175€ ($138.40–$156.30) double; 160€–205€ ($142.85–$183.05) junior suite. Rates include breakfast. AE, DC, MC, V. Parking free on street. Bus: 2, 3, 6, 9, or 11. **Amenities:** Restaurant; bar; room service; babysitting; laundry. In room: A/C, TV, minibar, hair dryer, safe (in some).

WHERE TO DINE

You might like to put together a picnic to enjoy atop Ferrara's medieval walls. Buy what you need on the **Via Cortevecchia,** a narrow brick street near the cathedral where locals shop for food. It's lined with salumerias, cheese shops, and bakeries. The nearby **Mercato Communale,** at the corner of Via Santo Stefano and Via del Mercato, is crowded with food stalls and open until 1pm Monday through Saturday, and 3:30 to 7:30pm Friday.

La Provvidenza FERRARESE/ITALIAN   The town's leading restaurant stands on the same street as the Palazzo dei Diamanti. It has a farm-style interior, with a little garden where you can dine in fair weather. The antipasti table is the finest we've sampled in Ferrara. Hearty eaters should order a pasta, such as fettuccine with smoked salmon, before tackling the main course, perhaps perfectly grilled and seasoned veal chops. Other specialties are *pasticcio alla Ferrarese* (macaroni mixed with a mushroom-and-meat sauce laced with creamy white sauce) and *fritto misto di carne* (mixed grill). Dessert choices are wide and luscious.

Corso Ercole d'Este 92. ℂ **0532-205187.** Reservations required. Main courses 10€–19€ ($8.95–$16.95). AE, DC, MC, V. Tues–Sun noon–2:30pm and 7–10:30pm. Bus: 3 or 9.

Trattoria La Romantica ★ *(Finds* FERRARESE   One of this city's most delightful dining experiences is found here in what used to be the stables of a 17th-century merchant's house. In a bright, fashionable decor, the well-trained chefs dazzle your palate with one taste sensation after another. Here is a chance to dine on several rare regional recipes not likely to be found anywhere else, including pasta in a tomato cream sauce (*cappellacci di zucca*) given added flavor by walnuts and Parmesan cheese. Another excellent pasta dish is garganelli with asparagus, or you can partake of a most intriguing salamilike local sausage, *salana da sugo,* which is sautéed to perfection and served with creamy mashed potatoes. Their spaghetti with shellfish is the town's best.

Via Ripagrande 36. ℂ **0532-765975.** Reservations recommended. Main courses 8€–15€ ($7.15–$13.40). AE, DC, MC, V. Thurs–Tues 12:30–2:30pm and 7–9:30pm.

FERRARA AFTER DARK

During July and August, concerts and temporary art exhibits are offered as part of the **Estate a Ferrara** program. The tourist office can provide a schedule of events and dates, which vary from year to year. During the rest of the year, you can rub elbows with fellow drinkers, and usually lots of students, at a refreshingly diverse collection of bars, pubs, and discos. The **Osteria Al Brindisi,** Via Adelardi 11 (ℂ **0532-209142**), claims, with some justification, to be the oldest wine bar in the world, with a tradition of uncorking bottles dating from the early 1400s. Wine begins at around 1.50€ ($1.35) per glass and seems to taste best when accompanied by a few of the dozen *panini* (sandwiches).

North of the historic center, **Pelledoca,** Via Arianuova 91 (ℂ **0532-248952**), is another hot club, luring young locals as well as foreign visitors. Hours depend on the crowd.

3 Ravenna & Its Dazzling Mosaics ★★★

74km (46 miles) E of Bologna, 145km (90 miles) S of Venice, 130km (81 miles) NE of Florence, 365km (226 miles) N of Rome

Ravenna is one of the most unusual towns in Emilia-Romagna. Today you'll find a sleepy town with memories of a great past, luring hordes of tourists to explore what remains. As the capital of the Western Roman Empire (from A.D. 402), the Visigoth Empire (from A.D. 473), and the Byzantine Empire under Emperor Justinian and Empress Theodora (A.D. 540–752), Ravenna became one of the greatest cities on the Mediterranean.

Ravenna achieved its cultural peak as part of the Byzantine Empire between the 6th and the 8th centuries, and it is known for the many well-preserved mosaics created during that time—the finest in all Western art and the most splendid outside Istanbul. Although it now looks much like any other Italian city, the low Byzantine domes of its churches still evoke its Eastern past.

ESSENTIALS

GETTING THERE   With frequent **train** service that takes only 1¼ hours from Bologna, Ravenna can easily be visited on a day trip; one-way fare is 4.30€ ($3.85). There's also frequent service from Ferrara, which connects to Venice; one-way fare from Ferrara is 3.90€ ($3.50). The train station is a 10-minute walk from the center at Piazza Fernini (© **848-88088**). The tourist office (below) has rail schedules and more details; or you can call © **0544-212755** or 0544-212816.

If you have a **car** and are coming from Bologna, head east along A14. From Ferrara, take the SS16.

VISITOR INFORMATION   The helpful **tourist office** is at Via Salara 8 (© **0544-35404**). From October to May, it's open Monday to Saturday 8:30am to 6pm, and Sunday 10am to 4pm; June to September, hours are daily 9am to 7:30pm. Stop in here first for a good map, free bicycle rental, and a discount combination ticket to the city's attractions.

SPECIAL EVENTS   If you're here in June and July, you can enjoy the **Ravenna Festival Internazionale.** Even Pavarotti and other greats might show up to perform. Tickets begin at 10€ ($8.95) but go much higher. For information, call © **0544-249211;** for tickets, call © **0544-32577.** A **Dante Festival** takes place the second week in September, sponsored by the church of San Francesco. Call © **0544-33677** for details.

EXPLORING THE TOWN

You can see all the sights in one busy day. The center of Ravenna is **Piazza del Popolo,** which has a Venetian aura. To the south, off the colonnaded Piazza San Francesco, you can visit the **Tomba di Dante** on Via Dante Alighieri. After crossing Piazza dei Caduti and heading north along Via Guerrini, you reach the **Battistero Neoniano** at Piazza del Duomo. Directly southeast and opening onto Piazza Arcivescovado is the **Museo Arcivescovile** and the **Chapel of San Andrea.**

Then you can head back to the tourist office, cutting west along Via San Vitale. This will take you to the **Basilica di San Vitale** and the **Mausoleum of Gallo Placidia** behind the basilica. Nearby is the **Museo Nazionale di Ravenna** along Via Fiandrini (adjacent to Via San Vitale). To cap off your day, you can

Ravenna

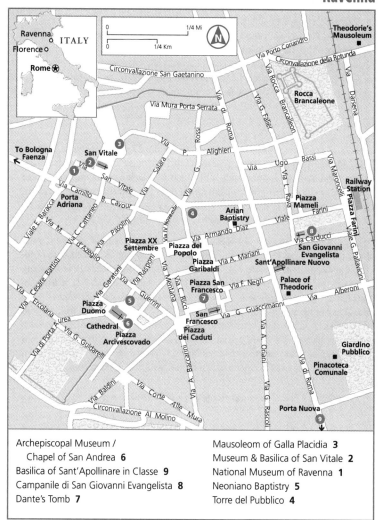

Archepiscopal Museum /
  Chapel of San Andrea **6**
Basilica of Sant'Appollinare in Classe **9**
Campanile di San Giovanni Evangelista **8**
Dante's Tomb **7**

Mausoleom of Galla Placidia **3**
Museum & Basilica of San Vitale **2**
National Museum of Ravenna **1**
Neoniano Baptistry **5**
Torre del Pubblico **4**

take bus no. 4 or 44 from the rail station or Piazza Caduti to visit the **Basilica of Sant'Appollinare in Classe,** reached along Via Romeo Sud.

If you're planning on seeing more than one sight, the most economical choice is to buy a **combination ticket** to visit these six monuments for 6€ ($5.35): the Battistero della Neoniano, Archepiscopal Museum/Chapel of San Andrea, Church of San Vitale, Mausoleum of Galla Placidia, and Basilica of Sant'Apollinare. The ticket is available at the tourist office. For more information on these sights, call © **0544-219938.**

Neoniano Baptistry (Battistero Neoniano)   This octagonal baptistry was built in the 5th century, and in the center of the cupola is a tablet showing John the Baptist baptizing Christ. The circle around the tablet depicts in dramatic

The Leaning Towers of Ravenna

North of Piazza del Popolo is a 12th-century leaning tower, the **Torre del Pubblico**. This tower (which you can't enter) leans even more than the Tower of Pisa. Nearby along Viale Farini is another leaning tower, the 12th-century **Campanile di San Giovanni Evangelista**, even tipsier than the Torre Pubblico. When Allied bombs struck the church in World War II, its apse was destroyed, but the mighty tower wasn't toppled.

mosaics of deep violet-blues and sparkling golds the 12 crown-carrying Apostles. The baptistry originally serviced a cathedral that no longer stands (the present-day Duomo was built around the mid–18th c. and is of little interest except for some unusual pews). Beside it is a campanile from the 11th century, perhaps earlier.

Piazza del Duomo. ✆ **0544-219938**. Admission (including admission to all sights) 6€ ($5.35). Mar–Oct daily 9:30am–5:30pm (to 4:30pm off-season). Closed Christmas and New Year's Day. Bus: MB.

Archepiscopal Museum & Chapel of San Andrea (Museo Arcivescovile e Cappella di San Andrea) ✿   This twofold attraction is housed in the 6th-century Archbishop's Palace. In the museum, the major exhibit is an ivory throne carved for Archbishop Maximian, from around the mid–6th century. In the chapel (oratory) dedicated to St. Andrea are brilliant mosaics. Pause in the antechamber to look at an intriguing mosaic above the entrance, an unusual representation of Christ as a warrior, stepping on the head of a lion and a snake; tough but haloed, he wears partial armor. The chapel, built in the shape of a cross, contains other mosaics that are "angelic," both figuratively and literally. Busts of saints and apostles stare down at you with the ox-eyed look of Byzantine art.

In the Archbishop's Palace, Piazza Arcivescovado. ✆ **0544-39196**. Admission 6€ ($5.35). Daily 9am–5:30pm (to 4:30pm in winter). Bus: 1 or 11.

Museum & Basilica of San Vitale (Museo e Basilica di San Vitale) ✿✿ This octagonal domed church dates from the mid–6th century. The **mosaics** ✿ inside—in brilliant greens and golds, lit by light from translucent panels—are among the most celebrated in the Western world. Covering the apse is a mosaic of a clean-shaven Christ astride the world, flanked by saints and angels. To the right is a mosaic of Empress Theodora and her court, and to the left is the figure of the man who married this courtesan/actress, Emperor Justinian, and his entourage.

Via San Vitale 17. ✆ **0544-219938**. Admission 6€ ($5.35). Daily 9am–4:30pm in winter and 9am–7:30pm in summer. Bus: 1 or 11.

Mausoleum of Galla Placidia ✿✿   This 5th-century chapel is so unpretentious that you'll think you're in the wrong place. But inside it contains some exceptional **mosaics** dating from antiquity, though they might not look it. Translucent panels bring the mosaics alive in all their grace and harmony, vivid with peacock blue, moss green, Roman gold, eggplant, and burnt orange. The mosaics in the cupola literally glitter with stars. Popular tradition claims that the cross-shaped structure houses the tomb of Galla Placidia, sister of Honorius, Rome's last emperor. Galla, who died in Rome in A.D. 450, is one of history's most powerful women. She became virtual ruler of the Western world after her husband, Ataulf, king of the Visigoths, died (only a virtual ruler because she became a regent for Valentinian III, who was only 6 at the time of his father's death).

Via San Vitale. (C) **0544-219938**. Admission 6€ ($5.35). Apr–Sept daily 9am–7pm (Oct–Mar to 5:30pm).

National Museum of Ravenna (Museo Nazionale di Ravenna)   This museum contains archaeological objects from the early Christian and Byzantine periods: icons, fragments of tapestries, medieval armaments and armory, sarcophagi, ivories, ceramics, and bits of broken pieces from the stained-glass windows of San Vitale.

Via Fiandrini (adjacent to Via San Vitale). (C) **0544-34424**. Admission 4€ ($3.55). Tues–Sun 8:30am–7:30pm. Bus: 1 or 11.

Basilica of Sant'Apollinare in Classe ★★   About 6km (3¾ miles) south of the city, this church dates from the 6th century and was consecrated by Archbishop Maximian. Dedicated to St. Apollinare, the bishop of Ravenna, the early basilica stands side by side with a campanile, symbols of faded glory now resting in a lonely low-lying area. Inside is a central nave flanked by two aisles, the latter containing tombs of ecclesiastical figures in the Ravenna hierarchy. The floor (once carpeted with mosaics) has been rebuilt. Along the central nave are frescoed tablets. Two dozen marble columns line the approach to the apse, where you'll find the major reason for visiting the basilica: The **mosaics** here are exceptional, rich in gold and turquoise, set against a background of top-heavy birds nesting in shrubbery. St. Apollinare stands in the center, with a row of lambs on either side lined up as in a processional; the 12 lambs symbolize the Apostles.

Via Romeo Sud. (C) **0544-473643**. Admission 6€ ($5.35). Daily 9am–5pm (to 5:30pm in summer). Bus: 4 or 44 from rail station (every 20 min.) or Piazza Caduti.

Dante's Tomb (Tomba di Dante)   Right off Piazza Garibaldi, the final monument to Dante Alighieri, "the divine poet," isn't much to look at, graced with a marble bas-relief. But it's a far better place than he assigned to some of his fellow Florentines. The author of the *Divine Comedy*, in exile from his hometown, died in Ravenna on September 14, 1321. To the right of the small temple is a mound of earth in which Dante's urn went "underground" from March 1944 to December 1945 because it was feared that his tomb might suffer from the bombings. Near the tomb is the 5th-century church of **San Francesco,** the site of the poet's funeral.

Via Dante Alighieri. (C) **0544-30252**. Free admission. Daily 9am–noon and 3–5pm.

SHOPPING

One of the best places to admire (and buy) mosaics is the **Studio Acomena,** Via Ponte della Vecchia ((C) **0544-554700**). Replicas of Christ, the Madonna, the saints, and penitent sinners appear in all their majesty amid more secular forms whose designs were inspired by Roman gladiators or floral and geometric motifs. Virtually anything can be shipped. **Scianna,** Via di Roma 34A ((C) **0544-37556**), and **Luciana Notturni,** Via Arno 13 ((C) **0544-63002**), are worthy competitors.

WHERE TO STAY

Hotel Bisanzio (Value)   The Bisanzio is cheaper and has more personality than the Jolly Hotel (see below). The small-to-midsize guest rooms at this pleasantly renovated modern hotel have attractive Italian styling, some with mottled batik

---

Tips A Day at the Beach

By taking bus no. 70 from Ravenna, in just 20 minutes you can enjoy white-sand beaches set against a backdrop of pine forests. Lined with beach clubs, snack shops, and ice-cream stands, these beaches are extremely overcrowded during the sultry summer. The most beautiful beaches are found along a stretch called the **Punta Marina di Ravenna.** The Marina di Ravenna is also lively at night, with pubs and discos open until the wee hours.

---

wall coverings. The uncluttered breakfast room has softly draped windows, and you have use of a garden.

Via Salara 30, 48100 Ravenna. ✆ **0544-217111.** Fax 0544-32539. www.bisanziohotel.com. 38 units. 124€–154€ ($110.75–$137.50) double. Rates include buffet breakfast. AE, DC, MC, V. Parking 12.50€ ($11.15). **Amenities:** 2 bars; room service; babysitting; laundry/dry cleaning. *In room:* A/C, TV, minibar, hair dryer, safe.

Hotel Centrale Byron   This Art Deco–inspired hotel is a few steps from Piazza del Popolo. The lobby is an elegant combination of white marble and brass detailing. The long, narrow public rooms include an alcove sitting room. The small guest rooms are simply but comfortably furnished, while the bathrooms are a bit cramped.

Via IV Novembre 14, 48100 Ravenna. ✆ **0544-212225.** Fax 0544-34114. 54 units (showers only). 75€–95€ ($67–$84.85) double. AE, DC, MC, V. Parking 12.50€ ($11.15). **Amenities:** Bar; lounge; room service; babysitting; laundry. *In room:* A/C, TV, minibar, hair dryer, safe.

Jolly Hotel   This hotel, built in 1950 in the postwar crackerbox style with a bunkerlike facade, contains a conservative decor of stone floors and lots of paneling. Ravenna doesn't have many first-class accommodations, so the Jolly has become a favorite of business travelers. Although the guest rooms are not style setters, they are of a decent size and are accompanied by well-kept bathrooms. They were last renovated in 1997, when the furnishings were upgraded. Five units are accessible for travelers with disabilities.

Piazza Mameli 1, 48100 Ravenna. ✆ **800/221-2626** in the U.S., or 0544-35762. Fax 0544-216055. www. jollyhotels.it. 84 units. 130€–152€ ($116.10–$135.75) double; from 182€ ($162.55) suite. Rates include buffet breakfast. AE, DC, MC, V. Parking 15€ ($13.40). **Amenities:** Restaurant; lounge; room service; babysitting; laundry. *In room:* A/C, TV, minibar, hair dryer, safe.

WHERE TO DINE

San Domenico (p. 353), in the nearby town Imola, is one of the finest restaurants in all of Italy and is well worth the 48km (30-mile) drive.

A walk through Ravenna's lively food market, the **Mercato Coperto,** will introduce you to the bounty of the land. It's near the center of town on Piazza Andrea Costa and is open Monday through Saturday from 7am to 2pm, and on Friday from 4:30 to 7:30pm.

Bella Venezia ROMAGNOLA/ITALIAN   Despite the name, the only Venetian dish prepared is delicious *fegato alla veneziana* (liver fried with onions). The repertoire is almost exclusively regional, with such dishes as risotto, *cappelletti alla romagnola* (cap-shaped pasta stuffed with ricotta, roasted pork loin, chicken breast, and nutmeg, served with meat sauce), and garganelli pasta served with whatever happens to be in season (baby asparagus, mushrooms, or peas). All pastas are made by hand, and the place is family-run and very old Italy. The Bella Venezia is a few steps from Piazza del Popolo and next to the Hotel Byron (see above).

Via IV Novembre 16. ② **0544-212746.** Reservations required. Main courses 9€–12.50€ ($8.05–$11.15). AE, DC, MC, V. Mon–Sat 12:15–2:30pm and 7:30–10pm. Closed Dec 23–Jan 23.

Ristorante La Gardèla ⭐ *Value* EMILIA-ROMAGNA/SEAFOOD   Considering the quality of the food and the first-rate ingredients, this is Ravenna's best restaurant buy. Located a few steps from one of Ravenna's startling leaning towers, La Gardèla is spread out over two levels, with paneled walls lined with racks of wine bottles. The waiters bring out an array of typical but savory dishes, including *tortelloni della casa* (made with ricotta, cream, spinach, tomatoes, and herbs) and *spezzatino alla contadina* (roast veal with potatoes, tomatoes, and herbs). Ravioli is stuffed with truffles, and one of the best pasta dishes, tagliatelle, is offered with porcini mushrooms. The chefs prepare more fresh fish than ever, most often from the Adriatic.

Via Ponte Marino 3. ② **0544-217147.** Reservations recommended. Main courses 6€–14€ ($5.35–$12.50). AE, DC, MC, V. Fri–Wed noon–2:30pm and 7–10pm. Closed Feb 10–20 and Aug 10–20.

Ristorante Villa Antica ⭐ INTERNATIONAL/EMILIAN/SEAFOOD This appealing spot keeps prices under control while magically combining solid technique and inventiveness. Specialties include tagliolini with fried shrimp, lamb with porcini mushrooms, and seafood dishes that are creative and tasteful. You might also enjoy the spaghetti in gorgonzola sauce with mushrooms and walnuts, or roast game when in season. There is also a very good collection of wines. The menu changes frequently.

Via Faentina 136. ② **0544-500522.** Reservations recommended. Main courses 7€–17.50€ ($6.25–$15.65). AE, DC, MC, V. Wed–Mon 7pm–1am (until 3am Sat–Sun). Closed Aug.

RAVENNA AFTER DARK

Beside the **Marina di Ravenna,** you'll find a handful of pubs and dance clubs. Our favorite of the bunch is the **Santa Fe,** Via delle Nazioni 180 (② **0544-438494**), an open-air dance club featuring recorded tunes: it attracts a crowd that's mainly in their 20s and early 30s.

Further entertainment is offered by the **Teatro Alighieri,** Via Mariani 2 (② **0544-249244**), which sponsors free summer concerts in the various squares and churches around town.

4 Modena ⭐

40km (25 miles) NW of Bologna, 403km (250 miles) NW of Rome, 130km (81 miles) N of Florence

After Ferrara fell to Pope Clement VIII, the Este family established a duchy at Modena in the closing years of the 16th century. This city in the Po Valley possesses many great art treasures evoking its more glorious past. On the food front, Modena's chefs enjoy an outstanding reputation in hard-to-please gastronomic circles. Traversed by the ancient Roman road, Via Emilia, Modena also is a hot spot for European art connoisseurs.

Modena is an industrial zone blessed with Italy's highest per-capita income, and it can seem as sleek as the sports cars it produces. This is partially because of its 20th-century face-lift, the result of the city being largely rebuilt following the destructive World War II bombings. These factors create a stark contrast to both the antiquity and the poverty so noticeable in other regions. Modena is home to automobile and racing giants Ferrari, Maserati, and De Tomaso, and is known for producing Lambrusco wine and balsamic vinegar. Locals also proudly claim opera star Luciano Pavarotti as one of their greatest exports.

Many visitors who care little about antiquities come here to do business with the Ferrari or Maserati car plant (both off-limits to the general public). However, you can visit a showroom, the **Galleria Ferrari,** Via Dino Ferrari 43 in Maranello (© **0536-949713**), a suburb of Modena. The showroom displays engines, trophies, and both antique and the latest Ferrari cars. It's open daily 9:30am to 12:30pm and 2:30 to 6pm, charging an admission of 9€ ($8.05) for adults and 5€ ($4.45) for youth ages 6 to 10. From the bus station on Via Bacchini in Modena, a bus marked MARANELLO departs hourly during the day. Ask at the tourist office (see below) for details and a map.

ESSENTIALS

GETTING THERE   There are good **train** connections to and from Bologna (one train every 30 min.); trip time is 20 minutes, and a one-way fare is 1.95€ ($1.75). Trains arrive from Parma once per hour (trip time: 40 min.); the one-way fare is 2.75€ ($2.45). For information and schedules, call © **848-88088,** toll-free in Italy only.

If you have a **car** and are coming from Bologna, take A1 northeast until you see the turn-off for Modena.

VISITOR INFORMATION   The **tourist office** is on Piazza Grande 17 (© **059-206660**). It's open Monday, Tuesday, and Thursday to Saturday from 9am to 1pm and 3 to 7pm, Wednesday from 9am to 1pm, and Sunday from 9:30am to 12:30pm.

SPECIAL EVENTS   In July and August, Modena presents a series of theater, ballet, opera, and musical performances called **Sipario in Piazza.** You might even get to see Pavarotti perform. For details, contact the tourist office (see above).

All of Modena seems to be a stage during 1 week each year at the end of June or beginning of July, when vendors, artists, mimes, and other performers take to the streets for the **Settimana Estense;** festivities culminate in a parade in which the town turns out in Renaissance attire.

SEEING THE SIGHTS

Il Duomo 🅐🅐   One of the glories of the Romanesque in northern Italy, Modena's cathedral was founded in 1099 and designed by an architect named Lanfranco. The cathedral, consecrated in 1184, was dedicated to St. Geminiano, the patron saint of Modena, a 4th-century Christian and defender of the faith. Towering from the rear is the **Ghirlandina,** a 12th- to 14th-century campanile, 87m (285 ft.) tall. Leaning slightly, the bell tower guards the replica of the Secchia Rapita (stolen bucket), garnered as booty from the defeated Bolognese.

The facade of the Duomo features a 13th-century rose window by Anselmo da Campione. It also boasts Wiligelmo's main entry, with pillars supported by lions, as well as Wiligelmo bas-reliefs depicting scenes from Genesis. The south door, the so-called Princes' Door, was designed by Wiligelmo in the 12th century and is framed by bas-reliefs illustrating scenes in the saga of the patron saint. You'll find an outside pulpit from the 15th century, with emblems of Matthew, Mark, Luke, and John.

Inside, there's a vaulted ceiling, and the overall effect is gravely impressive. The Modenese wisely restored the cathedral during the first part of the 20th century, so its present look resembles the original design. The gallery above the crypt is an outstanding piece of sculpture, supported by four lions. Two hunchbacks hold up the pulpit. And the crypt, where the body of the patron saint was finally taken, is a forest of columns; here you'll find Guido Mazzoni's *Holy Family* group in terra cotta, completed in 1480.

Piazza del Duomo. ℂ 059-216078. Free admission. Daily 7am–6pm. Bus: 7, 12, or 14.

Galleria Estense & Biblioteca Estense ★★   The **Galleria Estense** is noted for its paintings from the Emilian or Bolognese school from the 14th to 18th centuries. The nucleus of the collection was created by the Este family in the heyday of their duchies in Ferrara and then Modena. Some of the finest work is by Spanish artists, including a miniature triptych by El Greco of Toledo and a portrait of Francesco I d'Este by Velázquez. Other works are Bernini's bust of Francesco I and paintings by Correggio, Veronese, Tintoretto, Carracci, Reni, and Guercino.

One of the greatest libraries in southern Europe, the **Biblioteca Estense** (℃ **059-222248**) contains around 500,000 printed works and 13,000 manuscripts. An assortment of the most interesting volumes is kept under glass for visitors to inspect. Of these, the most celebrated is the 1,200-page *Bible of Borso d'Este*, bordered with stunning miniatures.

In the Palazzo del Musei, Piazza Sant'Agostino 48 (off Via Emilia). ℂ 059-4395711. Gallery admission 4€ ($3.55). Free admission to library. Gallery: Tues–Sun 8:30am–7pm. Library: Mon–Sat 9am–1pm. Bus: 7.

SHOPPING

Consider picking up a bottle or two of the item that changed the face of salad forever: balsamic vinegar. Right in the city center, **Fini,** Piazzale San Francesco (℃ **059-223314**), sells bottles of Modena's aromatic variety, plus other fabulous food products. **Justi,** Via Cucé (℃ **059-441203**), exports crates of the vinegar throughout Europe, and also sells bottles on the premises.

WHERE TO STAY

Canalgrande Hotel ★   Situated in the old town, the Canalgrande is housed in a 300-year-old stucco palace and has more atmosphere and charm than the more highly rated Real Fini. The Canalgrande boasts elaborate mosaic floors, Victorian-era furniture, elaborately carved and frescoed ceilings, and chandeliers. French doors open onto a beautiful garden with a central flowering tree that's always full of chirping birds (ask for a room facing it). The guest rooms are decorated in pastels and boast fine mattresses and marble bathrooms; ongoing renovations are bringing them all up-to-date. Some of the best rooms open onto balconies; the ones on the garden side are quieter.

Corso Canalgrande 6, 41100 Modena. ℂ 059-217160. Fax 059-221674. www.canalgrandehotel.it. 68 units (some with shower only). 160€ ($142.85) double; 248€ ($221.45) suite. Rates include breakfast. AE, DC, MC, V. Parking 10€ ($8.95). Bus: 7, 12, or 14. **Amenities:** Restaurant; bar; room service; laundry. *In room:* A/C, TV, minibar, hair dryer.

Hotel Daunia   Away from the city center, the recently built Daunia boasts an exterior in a modified 18th-century design. Inside, it's modern Italian all the way, with gleaming brass, polished woods, eclectic contemporary furniture, and marble and tiled floors. The bar is a pleasant place for a drink, but the breakfast room has a rather claustrophobic cafeteria feel. The guest rooms are comfortable but seem rather bare, with light-colored walls and neutral fabrics contrasting with the dark wood furnishings.

In an unusual arrangement, the hotel restaurant, Il Patriarca, is on the far side of the city center, and a free taxi shuttles you back and forth.

Via del Pozzo 158, 41100 Modena. © 059-371182. Fax 059-374807. 42 units (showers only). 85€ ($75.90) double. Rates include breakfast. AE, DC, MC, V. Free parking. Bus: 7, 12, or 14. **Amenities:** Restaurant; bar; room service; laundry/dry cleaning. *In room:* A/C, TV, minibar, hair dryer.

Hotel Libertà A modern hotel wrapped in an aged exterior, this lodge is mere steps from the cathedral and the Palazzo Ducale. Marble and terra-cotta floors run throughout. The guest rooms favor floral wallpapers and blond-wood furniture; some top-floor rooms are made cozy by sloping ceilings with skylights. Each room provides a good night's sleep. The tiled bathrooms are compact. Several restaurants are close, and the staff particularly recommends Da Enzo (see below), 23m (25 yd.) away.

Via Blasia 10, 41100 Modena. © **059-222365.** Fax 059-222502. www.hotelliberta.it. 51 units (with shower only). 105€ ($93.75) double; 175€ ($156.30) suite. AE, DC, DISC, MC, V. Parking 12.50€ ($11.15). Bus: 4 or 7. **Amenities:** Bar; room service; laundry. *In room:* A/C, TV, minibar, hair dryer.

Hotel Principe Located close to the heart of the city, the appealingly priced Principe attracts business travelers, but it also offers comforts for vacationers. Short on style, it's nonetheless a good choice. Rooms are well appointed and come with fine linen. The tiled bathrooms are small but have adequate shelf space. The impersonal look of the hotel is softened by the gracious reception of the staff.

Corso Vittorio Emanuele 94, 41100 Modena. © **059-218670.** Fax 059-237693. 51 units (showers only). 100€ ($89.30) double. Rates include breakfast. AE, DC, MC, V. Free parking. Bus: 4 or 6. **Amenities:** Cafe; room service; laundry; dry cleaning. *In room:* A/C, TV, minibar.

Real Fini We prefer the Canalgrande (see above) because it has more atmosphere and personal charm, but Real Fini is the top choice for most visiting businesspeople. The hotel offers the largest and best accessorized rooms in town, with medium-sized tiled bathrooms. The hotel is imbued with sleek modern Italian styling. The hotel also operates the finest restaurant in Modena, Fini (see below), in another location. The hotel's free limousine will take you there. The Fini name is famous in this part of Italy, having been launched in 1912 as a little Modena deli. The famous food company, Fini, was sold to Kraft in 1989, but the name lives on among the string of cafeterias labeled Fini along the Autostrada del Sole in Italy.

Via Emilia Est 441, 41100 Modena. © **059-238091.** Fax 059-364804. www.giuditta.it/hrf/hrf.htm. 181€–227€ ($161.65–$202.70) double; 284€–320€ ($253.60–$285.75) suite. AE, DC, MC, V. Parking 15€ ($13.40). **Amenities:** Bar; gym; sauna; room service; babysitting; laundry/dry cleaning. *In room:* A/C, TV, minibar, hair dryer, safe.

WHERE TO DINE

To put together a wonderful picnic, pick your way through the food stalls of the outdoor market on **Via Albinelli,** open weekdays from 6:30am to 2pm and Saturday afternoons in summer from 5 to 7pm.

Borso d'Este ITALIAN The movers and shakers of Modena often dine at this unheralded restaurant, which is known for its varied and unusual dishes and for its use of fresh ingredients. Although the place is filled with antiques, it is a contemporary setting, offering fine wines and impeccable service. To begin your repast, we'd recommend the tortelloni, pasta squares stuffed with fresh spinach and ricotta and served with a sauce made of mushrooms and regional truffles. Main dishes include *pesce alla sale,* or fish cooked encrusted in salt (to preserve its juices). You can order your fish steamed. Another good dish is the well-seasoned pork, which has a wonderful honey-nut taste.

Piazza Roma 5. ✆ 059-214114. Reservations recommended. Main courses 15€–40€ ($13.40–$35.70). AE, DC, MC, V. Mon–Fri noon–2pm and Mon–Sat 8–10:30pm. Closed Aug.

Fini ★★★ MODENESE/INTERNATIONAL   A visit to this restaurant is well worth the trip to Modena. Fini is one of the best restaurants in Emilia-Romagna and is Pavarotti's favorite. Its modernized Art Nouveau decor includes Picasso-esque murals and banquettes. For an appetizer, try the creamy green lasagna or the tortellini (prepared in six ways, including one with truffles). For a main dish, the *gran bollito misto* reigns supreme. A king's feast of boiled meats, accompanied by a selection of four sauces, is wheeled to your table. After all this rich fare, you might settle for the fruit salad for dessert. Lambrusco is the superb local wine choice.

Rua Frati Minori 54. ✆ 059-223314. Reservations recommended. Main courses 17.50€–30€ ($15.65–$26.80). AE, DC, MC, V. Wed–Sun 12:30–2:30pm and 8–10:30pm. Closed July 20–Aug 24 and Dec 22–Jan 3. Bus: 6 or 11.

Osteria Francescana ★★ INTERNATIONAL/VEGETARIAN   Osteria Francescana is worth a hundred-mile detour across Italy. In a city known for having some of the most demanding palates in Italy, chef Massimo Batturo satisfies. The iconoclastic chef doesn't seem to care whether he earns Michelin stars or rave reviews from guidebooks. He's more content to please his customers with his exciting food, which he serves on mismatched plates purchased in New York. Batturo's return to Italy follows a decade of work with Alain Ducasse, who, upon discovering Batturo's food in Modena, whisked him away to cook at his three-star Louis XV restaurant in Monte Carlo. Now released and "my own man" again, Batturo has taken all he learned from Ducasse and has used it to forge his own style and unique dishes. One reviewer called his cream sauce "edible gold." He still makes his heavenly Modenese tortellini based on his grandmother's recipe, but every other dish is his own invention. His langoustine risotto is a masterpiece.

Via Stella 222. ✆ 059-210118. Reservations required. Main courses 15€–20€ ($13.40–$17.85). AE, DC, MC, V. Mon–Fri 1–2:30pm and Mon–Sat 8–10:30pm.

Ristorante Da Enzo MODENESE   Well known in Modena, this restaurant is one floor above street level in an old building in the pedestrian zone. Specialties include all the classic dishes, such as *zampone* (stuffed pigs' trotters), lasagna verde, *pappardelle* (wide noodles) with rabbit meat, several kinds of tortellini, and an array of grilled meats liberally seasoned with herbs and balsamic vinegar.

Via Coltellini 17 (off Piazza Mazzini). ✆ 059-225177. Reservations recommended. Main courses 10€–17.50€ ($8.95–$15.65). AE, DC, MC, V. Tues–Sun noon–3pm and 7–10:30pm. Closed 3 weeks in Aug. Bus: 7, 12, or 14.

MODENA AFTER DARK

Opera arrives in winter at the **Teatro Comunale,** Corso Canal Grande 85 (✆ **059-206993** or 059-2136021 for reservations), and the summer brings a major opera festival.

Stroll through the neighborhood to the spot where everyone seems to gravitate on long, hot evenings, the **Parco Amendola,** south of Modena's historic core, filled with ice-cream stands, cafes, and bars.

5 Parma ★

457km (283 miles) NW of Rome, 97km (60 miles) NW of Bologna, 121km (75 miles) SE of Milan

Parma, straddling Via Emilia, was the home of Correggio, Il Parmigianino, Bodoni (of typeface fame), and Toscanini and has also given us *prosciutto* and *parmigiano* cheese. Parma rose in influence and power in the 16th century as the seat of the Farnese duchy, and even today it is one of the most prosperous cities in Italy.

Upon the extinction of the male Farnese line, Parma came under the control of the French Bourbons. Its most beloved ruler, Marie-Louise, widow of Napoleon and niece of Marie Antoinette, arrived in 1815 after the Congress of Vienna awarded her this duchy. Marie-Louise became a great patron of the arts, and much of the collection she acquired is on display at the Galleria Nazionale (see "Seeing the Sights," below). Rising unrest in 1859 forced her abdication, and, in 1860, following a plebiscite, Parma was incorporated into the kingdom of Italy.

The city has also been a mecca for opera lovers such as Verdi, the great Italian composer whose works include *Il Trovatore* and *Aïda.* He was born in the small village of Roncole, north of Parma, in 1813. In time, his operas echoed through the Teatro Regio, the opera house that was built under the orders of Marie-Louise. Because of Verdi, Parma became a center of music, and even today the opera house is jampacked in season.

ESSENTIALS

GETTING THERE   Parma is served by the Milan-Bologna **rail** line, with 20 trains a day arriving from Milan (trip time: 80 min.); the one-way fare starts at 5.85€ ($5.20). From Bologna, 34 trains per day arrive in Parma (1 hr.); the one-way fare is around 3.60€ ($3.20). There are seven connections a day from Florence (3 hr.); a one-way fare begins at 8€ ($7.15). For information and schedules, call ✆ **848-88088,** toll-free in Italy only.

If you have a **car** and are starting out in Bologna, head northwest along A1.

VISITOR INFORMATION   The **tourist office** is at Via Melloni 1A (✆ **0521-218889**), open Monday to Saturday 9am to 7pm and Sunday 9am to 1pm.

SPECIAL EVENTS   Parma celebrates its musical traditions in July and August with **Concerti Nei Chiostri,** when classical concerts are staged in churches, cloisters, and piazzas around the city. Admission is 12.50€ ($11.15) per event; the tourist office will provide a list of times and locations around the city.

SEEING THE SIGHTS

The gravel paths, wide lawns, and splashing fountains of the **Parco Ducale,** across the river from the Palazzo Pilotta, provide a nice retreat from Parma's more crowded areas.

Il Duomo ★★   Built in the Romanesque style in the 11th century, with 13th-century Lombard lions guarding its main porch, the dusty pink Duomo stands side by side with a campanile constructed in the Gothic-Romanesque style and completed in 1294. The facade of the cathedral is highlighted by three open-air loggias. Inside, two darkly elegant aisles flank the central nave. The octagonal cupola was frescoed by a master of light and color, Correggio (1494–1534), one of Italy's greatest painters of the High Renaissance. His fresco here, *Assumption* *of the Virgin,* foreshadows the baroque. The frescoes were painted from 1522 to 1534. In the transept to the right of the main altar is a somber Romanesque bas-relief, *The Deposition from the Cross,* by Benedetto Antelami, each face bathed in tragedy. Made in 1178, the bas-relief is the best-known work of the 12th-century artist, who was the most important sculptor of the Romanesque in northern Italy.

Piazza del Duomo. © 0521-235886. Free admission. Daily 9am–12:30pm and 3–7pm. Bus: 11.

Baptistry (Battistero) ✿✿✿   Among the greatest Romanesque buildings in northern Italy, the baptistry was the work of Benedetto Antelami. The project was begun in 1196, although the date it was actually completed is unclear. Made of salmon-colored marble, it's spanned by four open tiers (the fifth is closed off). Inside, the baptistry is richly frescoed with biblical scenes: a *Madonna Enthroned* and a *Crucifixion.* But it's the sculpture by Antelami that's the most worthy treasure and that provides the basis for that artist's claim to enduring fame.

Piazza del Duomo 7. © 0521-235886. Admission 2.50€ ($2.25). Daily 9am–12:30pm and 3–7pm. Bus: 11.

Abbey of St. John (San Giovanni Evangelista)   Behind the Duomo is this church of unusual interest. After admiring the baroque front, pass into the interior to see yet another cupola by Correggio. From 1520 to 1524, the High Renaissance master depicted the *Vision of San Giovanni.* Vasari, author of *Lives of the Artists* and a contemporary of Correggio, liked it so much that he became completely carried away in his praise, suggesting the "impossibility" of an artist conjuring up such a divine work and marveling that it could actually have been painted "with human hands." Correggio also painted a St. John with pen in hand, in the transept (over the door to the left of the main altar). Il Parmigianino, the second Parmesan master, did some frescoes in the chapel at the left of the entrance. You can visit the **abbey,** the **school,** the **cloister,** and a **pharmacist's shop,** where monks made potions for some 6 centuries, a practice that lasted until the closing years of the 19th century. Mortars and jars, some as old as the Middle Ages, line the shelves.

Piazzale San Giovanni 1. © 0521-235592. Free admission to church and cloisters; 2€ ($1.80) for the pharmacist's shop. Daily 9am–noon and 3–6pm; pharmacist's shop daily 8:30am–1:30pm. Bus: 11.

Arturo Toscanini Birthplace and Museum (Casa Natale e Museo di Arturo Toscanini)   This is the house where the great conductor was born in 1867. Toscanini was unquestionably the greatest orchestral conductor of the first half of the 20th century and one of the most astonishing musical interpreters of all time. He spent his childhood and youth in this house, which has been turned into a museum with interesting relics and a library containing all the recorded works he conducted. No more than 25 people at a time are permitted inside.

Via Rodolfo Tanzi 13. © 0521-285499. Admission 1.50€ ($1.35). Tues–Sat 9am–1pm and 2–6pm; Sun 9am–1pm. Bus: 3, 4, 5, 6, or 11.

National Gallery (Galleria Nazionale) & National Archaeological Museum (Museo Archeologico Nazionale) ✿✿   Palazzo della Pilotta once housed the Farnese family in Parma's heyday as a duchy in the 16th century. Badly damaged by bombs in World War II, it has been restored and turned into a palace of museums.

The **National Gallery** offers a limited but well-chosen selection of the works of Parma artists from the late 15th to 19th centuries, notably paintings by Correggio and Parmigianino. In one room is an unfinished head of a young woman attributed to Leonardo da Vinci. Correggio's *Madonna della Scala* (of the stairs), the remains of a fresco, is also displayed. But his masterpiece is *St. Jerome with the Madonna and Child.* Imbued with delicacy, it represents age, youth, and love—a gentle ode to tenderness. In the next room is Correggio's *Madonna della Scodella* (with a bowl), with its agonized faces. You'll also see Correggio's *Coronation,* a golden fresco that's a work of great beauty, and his less successful *Annunciation.* One of Parmigianino's best-known paintings is *St. Catherine's Marriage,* with its rippling movement and subdued colors.

You can also view **St. Paul's Chamber (Camera di San Paolo),** which Correggio frescoed with mythological scenes, including one of Diana. The chamber faces onto Via Macedonio Melloni. On the same floor as the National Gallery is the **Farnese Theater (Teatro Farnese),** a virtual jewel box, evocative of Palladio's theater at Vicenza. Built in 1618, the structure was bombed in 1944 and has been restored. Admission to the theater is included in the admission to the gallery; however, if you want to visit only the theater, there's a separate charge of 2€ ($1.80).

Also in the palazzo is the **National Archaeological Museum.** It houses Egyptian sarcophagi; Etruscan vases; Roman- and Greek-inspired torsos; Bronze-Age relics; and its best-known exhibit, the Tabula Alimentaria, a bronze-engraved tablet dating from the reign of Trajan and excavated at Velleia in Piacenza.

In the Palazzo della Pilotta, Piazzale della Pilotta 15. (© 0521-233309 (National Gallery) or 0521-233718 (Archaeological Museum). National Gallery admission 6.25€ ($5.60). Archaeological Museum admission 2€ ($1.80). National Gallery daily 8:30am–1:30pm. Archaeological Museum Tues–Fri 8:30am–2pm and Sat–Sun 8:30am–7:30pm. Bus: 9, 11.

SHOPPING

Parma's most famous food product—*parmigiano* (Parmesan) cheese, the best being *Parmigiano-Reggiano*—is savored all over the world. Virtually every corner market sells thick wedges of the stuff, but if you're looking to buy your cheese in a special setting, head for the **Salumería Garibaldi,** Via Garibaldi 42 (© 0521-235606). You might also take a walk through the city's **food market** at Piazza Ghiaia, near the Palazzo della Pilota; it's open Monday to Saturday from 8am to 1pm and 3 to 7pm.

Hoping to learn more about the region's famous hams and cheeses? There are well-funded bureaucracies in Parma whose sole functions are to encourage the world to use greater quantities of the city's tastiest products. They can arrange tours and visits to the region's most famous producers. For information about Parma cheeses, contact the **Consorzio del Parmigiano Reggiano,** Via Gramsci 26C (© 0521-292700). For insights into the dressing and curing of Parma hams, contact the **Consorzio del Prosciutto di Parma,** Via Marco dell'Arpa 8B (© 0521-243987).

Enoteca Fontana, Via Farina 24A (© 0521-286037), sells bottles from virtually every vineyard in the region, and the staff is extremely knowledgeable.

WHERE TO STAY

Hotel Button *Value*   The Button is a local favorite, one of the best bargains in the town center. This is a family-owned and -run hotel, and you're made to feel welcome. The guest rooms are simple but comfortably furnished and generally spacious, although the decor is dull. The bathrooms are a bit cramped but tidy. There's room service but no restaurant, and the bar never closes.

Strada San Vitale Borgo Salina 7 (off Piazza Garibaldi), 43100 Parma. ℂ **0521-208039.** Fax 0521-238783.
40 units (showers only). 103€ ($92) double. Rates include continental breakfast. AE, DC, MC, V. Free parking.
Closed July 5–31. Bus: 11. **Amenities:** Cafe; room service; babysitting; laundry/dry cleaning. *In room:* A/C, TV,
hair dryer.

Hotel Farnese International   This hotel is in a quiet area convenient to the
town center, the airport, and fairs. The guest rooms, ranging from small to
medium, are furnished in Italian marble. The tiled bathrooms are kept tidy.

Via Reggio 51A, 43100 Parma. ℂ **0521-994247.** Fax 0521-992317. www.farnesehotel.it. 76 units.
150€–180€ ($133.95–$160.75) double. Rates include breakfast. AE, DC, MC, V. Free parking outdoors;
7.50€ ($6.70) indoors. Bus: 11. **Amenities:** Restaurant; bar; cafe; room service; babysitting; laundry/dry
cleaning. *In room:* A/C, TV, minibar, hair dryer, safe.

Hotel Verdi ✱   Facing the Ducal Gardens, this Art Nouveau hotel preserves
the elegance of its era while meeting the needs of today's visitors. The guest rooms
feature parquet floors, brierwood furnishings, and fine linens. The marble-
lined bathrooms offer luxurious soaps, thick towels, and body oils. The adjacent
Santa Croce restaurant offers a refined yet cordial atmosphere resplendent with
period art, furnishings, and lighting in which to savor traditional cuisine and fine
Italian wines. In summer, a brick courtyard, alive with greenery, allows you to
dine outdoors. The parking garage at the rear of the hotel is guarded.

During the day, you can walk through the **Ducal Gardens (Parco Ducale),**
landscaped by the French architect Petitot and decorated with statues by another
Frenchman, Boudard. With its splashing fountains, wide expanses of greenery,
and gravel paths, the gardens make a great place to relax. Admission is free.

Via Pasini 18, 43100 Parma. ℂ **0521-293539.** Fax 0521-293559. 20 units (showers only). 175€–210€
($156.25–$187.50) double; 230€–256€ ($205.40–$228.60) suite. Breakfast 12€ ($10.70). AE, DC, DISC,
MC, V. Free parking. Bus: 11. **Amenities:** Bar; room service; babysitting; laundry/dry cleaning. *In room:* A/C,
TV, minibar, hair dryer, safe.

Palace Hotel Maria Luigia ✱   This hotel caters especially to business travel-
ers. Bold colors create an up-to-date mood, and the comfortable, modern rooms
are attractive, with amenities such as soundproof walls. The bar looks over a
pleasant patio-garden.

Viale Mentana 140, 43100 Parma. ℂ **0521-281032.** Fax 0521-2311126. www.sinahotels.com. 101 units.
225€ ($200.95) double; 325€ ($290.25) suite. Rates include buffet breakfast. AE, DC, MC, V. Parking 15€
($13.40). Bus: 11. **Amenities:** Restaurant (Italian/international); bar; fitness center; 24-hr. room service;
babysitting; laundry/dry cleaning. *In room:* A/C, TV, minibar, hair dryer, safe.

Park Hotel Stendhal   The Stendhal sits on a square near the opera house, a
few minutes' walk from many of the important sights and 6 blocks south of the
station. The guest rooms are well maintained and furnished with contemporary
pieces that are reproductions of various styles, ranging from rococo to provincial. Try for one of the traditional-looking rooms with classic furnishings. All
have well-maintained bathrooms.

Via Bodoni 3, 43100 Parma. ℂ **0521-208057.** Fax 0521-285655. www.bestwestern.com. 62 units (23 with
shower only). 196€ ($175) double. Rates include breakfast. AE, DC, MC, V. Parking 13€ ($11.60). **Amenities:**
Restaurant; bar; room service; babysitting; laundry/dry cleaning. *In room:* A/C, TV, minibar, hair dryer.

WHERE TO DINE
The chefs of Parma are acclaimed throughout Italy. Of course, Parmigiano-Reggiano has added just the right touch to millions of Italian meals, and the word
parmigiana is quite familiar to American diners.

At the atmospheric **Enoteca Fontana,** Via Farina 24A (© **0521-286037**), open daily 9am to noon and 3 to 9:45pm, you can stand at the ancient old bar or take a seat at one of the long communal tables and sample your choice of hundreds of wines from Emilia-Romagna, many of them from the immediate region. You might decide to order a light meal, too, from the short menu of panini, ham-and-cheese platters, and pastas.

The most popular pizzeria in Parma is open late (although it's closed Mon) and is almost always crowded. You might have to wait at **Pizzeria La Duchesa,** Piazza Garibaldi 1 (© **0521-235962**), especially if you want an outdoor table, but the pizzas are fabulous, especially when washed down with a carafe of Lambrusco.

Maxim's, in the Palace Hotel Maria Luigia (see "Where to Stay," above), is also worth seeking out, whether you're staying in the hotel or not.

Gallo d'Oro 🌟 *Value* PARMIGIANA   This is our favorite trattoria. It has an unpretentious decor with flea-market items such as antique cinema posters and old-fashioned toys. Downstairs is a bodega where locals pile in to taste the wine of the region, especially Lambrusco, which seems to go with anything served in Modena. Start with *salumi misti,* a variety of locally cured hams. All the pasta dishes are homemade, including *tortelli ripeini* (pasta stuffed with cottage cheese and fresh spinach). For a main course, we recommend the tender roasted lamb stuffed with bread, cheese, and eggs. A Parma classic is the chicken breast rolled with a delectable prosciutto and parmigiano and offered in a white-wine sauce.

Borgo della Salina 3. © **0521-208846.** Reservations recommended. Main courses 7€–9€ ($6.25–$8.05). AE, DC, MC, V. Mon–Sat noon–2:30pm and 7:30–11pm.

Parizzi 🌟🌟🌟 PARMIGIANA/ITALIAN   In the historic center of town, the building that houses Parizzi dates to 1551, when it first opened as an inn; the current restaurant was opened in 1958 by the father of the present owner. Seated under the skylit patio, you'll enjoy rich cuisine that's among the best in this region of Italy. After you're shown to a table in one of the good-size rooms, a trolley cart filled with antipasti is wheeled before you, containing shellfish, stuffed vegetables, and marinated salmon. Then you might be tempted by *culatelo,* cured ham made from sliced haunch of wild boar; a pasta served with a sauce of herbs and Parmigiano-Reggiano; a parmigiano soufflé with white truf-fles; roasted guinea fowl with Fonseca wine; or veal scaloppini layered with Fontina cheese and ham.

Strada della Repubblica 71. © **0521-285952.** Reservations required. Main courses 11€–18€ ($9.80–$16.05). AE, DC, MC, V. Tues–Sun noon–2:30pm and 7:30–10:30pm. Closed Jan 7–14.

Parma Rotta 🌟 *Finds* PARMIGIANA   This is a Parma classic if you don't mind driving 1 mile out of town along the road to Langhirano. This is the best neighborhood trattoria we know for tasting some of the hearty and flavor-filled dishes of the region. No one knows for sure how old the building housing the restaurant is, but everything has had a century or so to mellow out. The spit-roasted lamb or the roast pork is reason enough to come out here, although we're also fond of the grilled beef cooked in a wood-stoked oven. For a first course, many locals prefer *tortelli di erbetta,* pasta stuffed with fresh greens. We like it, too. There is also a wide selection of homemade desserts.

Via Langhirano 158. © **0521-966738.** Reservations recommended. Main courses 10€–17.50€ ($8.95–$15.65). AE, DC, MC, V. Sept–May Tues–Sun noon–2:30pm and 8–10:30pm; June–Aug Mon–Sat noon–2:30pm and 8–10:30pm. Bus: 7.

PARMA AFTER DARK

Life in Parma extends beyond munching on strips of salty ham and cheese. The **Teatro Regio,** Via Garibaldi, near Piazza della Pace (© **0521-218678**), is the site of concerts throughout the year, as well as the annual **Concerti Nei Chiostri** in June and July.

If you'd like to sample a glass or two of interesting wine, head for the bar section of a spot recommended in the "Where to Dine" section, above: the **Enoteca Fontana,** Strada Farina 24A (© **0521-286037**).

At **Bacco Verde,** Via Cavalloti (© **0521-230487**), sandwiches, glasses of beer, and a wide selection of Italian wines are dispensed in a cramped but convivial setting ringed with antique masonry.

In the mood for dancing? Head for **Dadaumpa,** Via Emilio Este 48 (© **0521-483802**), a stylish and light-hearted venue for European and New World dance tunes. More oriented toward students and the under-25 crowd is **Astrolabio,** Via Zarotta 86A (© **0521-460538**).

9

Venice

Venice is a preposterous monument to both the folly and the obstinacy of humankind. It shouldn't exist, but it does, much to the delight of thousands of visitors, gondoliers, lacemakers, hoteliers, restaurateurs, and glass blowers.

Centuries ago, in an effort to flee barbarians, Venetians left dry-dock and drifted out to a flotilla of "uninhabitable" islands in the lagoon. Survival was difficult enough, but no Venetian has ever settled for mere survival. The remote ancestors of the present inhabitants created the world's most beautiful city. To your children's children, however, Venice might be nothing more than a legend. The city is sinking at an alarming rate of about 2½ inches per decade, and at the same time, the damp climate, mold, and pollution here are contributing to the city's decay. Estimates are that, if no action is taken soon, one-third of the city's art will deteriorate hopelessly within the next decade or so. Clearly, Venice is in peril. One headline proclaimed, "The Enemy's at the Gates."

But for however long it lasts, Venice, decaying or not, will be one of the highlights of your trip through Italy. It lacks the speeding cars and roaring Vespas of Rome; instead, you make your way through the city either on foot or by boat. It would be ideal if it weren't for the hordes of tourists that descend every year, overwhelming the squares and making the streets almost impossible to navigate. In the sultry summer heat of the Adriatic, the canals become a smelly stew. Steamy and overcrowded July and August are the worst times to visit; May, June, September, and October are much better.

Although Venice is one of the world's most enchanting cities, you do pay a price, literally and figuratively, for all this beauty. Everyone leaves complaining about the outrageous prices, which can be double what they are elsewhere in the country. Since the 19th century, Venice has thrived on its visitors, but these high prices have forced out many locals. They've fled across the lagoon to dreary Mestre, an industrial complex launched to help boost the regional economy.

Today the city is trying belatedly to undo the damage that its watery environs and tourist-based economy have wrought. In 1993, after a 30-year hiatus, the canals were again dredged in an attempt to reduce water loss and reduce the stench brought in with the low tides. In an effort to curb the other 30-year-old problem of residential migration to Mestre, state subsidies are now being offered to the citizens of Venice as an incentive to not only stay, but also renovate their crumbling properties.

The greatest plan to save "Venice in peril" is to place mobile barriers at the three entrances to the port of Venice. The plan, drawn up decades ago and debated ever since, would cost anywhere from $2 to $4 billion. A huge mobile sluice gate regulating the movement of the tides was tested as late as 1992. The catch is the final project would need 79 of these sluice gates to save Venice from its own waters.

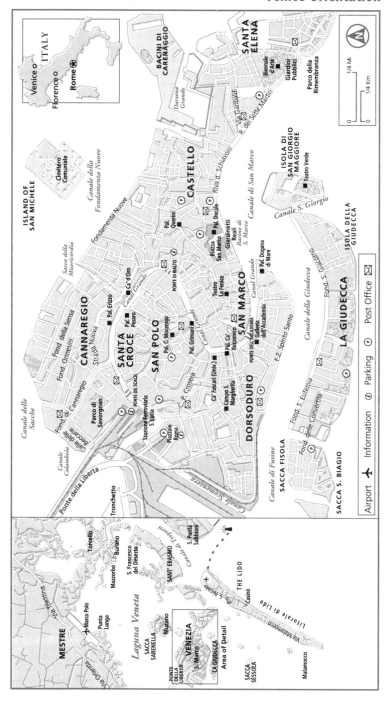

ITALY

Venice ○
Florence ○
Rome ✷

ISLAND OF SAN MICHELE

Cimitero Comunale

Canale della Fondamenta Nuove

BACINI DI CARENÀGGIO

Darsena Grande

SANTA ELENA

R. dei Sette Màrtiri

Via Garibaldi

Biennale d'Arte

Giardini Pùbblici

Parco della Rimembranza

¼ Mi
¼ Km

ISOLA DI SAN GIORGIO MAGGIORE

Teatro Verde

Canale S. Giorgio

CASTELLO

Fondamenta Nuove

Riva d. Schiavoni

Canale di San Marco

Pal. Querini

Pal. Ducale

Piazza San Marco

Giardinetti Reali

Bacino di S. Marco

Pal. Dogana di Mare

Sacca della Misericordia

Fond. della Sensa

CANNAREGIO

Fond. Ormesini

Strada Nuova

Ca' d'Oro

PONTE DI RIALTO

Pal. Pesaro

Pal. C. Mocenigo

SANTA CROCE

SAN POLO

Pal. Grimani

Canal Grande

Pal. Erizzo

Teatro La Fenice

SAN MARCO

PONTE DELL'ACCADEMIA

Galleria dell'Accademia

Pal. Ca' Rezzonico

DORSODURO

F.Z. Spirito Santo

Canale della Giudecca

ISOLA DELLA GIUDECCA

Fond. S. Giacomo

LA GIUDECCA

Canale delle Sacche

Fond. di Cannaregio

Parco di Savorgnan

Fond. delle Beccarie

PONTE DEI SCALZI

Ca' Foscari (Univ.)

S.P. Crosera

Campo S. Margherita

Canale Colombola

Stazione Ferroviaria S. Lucia

Piazzale Roma

Canale di Fusine

Fond. S. Eufemia

Fond. delle Convertite

SACCA FISOLA

SACCA S. BIAGIO

Ponte della Libertà

Tronchetto

Canale Scomenzera

✈ Airport   ⓘ Information   Ⓟ Parking   ⊙ Post Office ✉

MESTRE

Via Trentina

Via Orlanda

Laguna Veneta

Torcello

Mazzorbo

Buràno

S. Francesco del Deserto

SANT'ERASMO

S. Punta Sabbioni

THE LIDO

S. NICOLÒ

Casinò

Litorale di Lido

Marco Polo

Punta Lunga

SACCA SARENELLA

Muràno

PONTE DELLA LIBERTÀ

VENEZIA

S. Marco

LA GIUDECCA

Area of Detail

SACCA SESSOLA

Malamocco

Via Malamocco

1 Essentials

ARRIVING

The arrival scene at unattractive **Piazzale Roma** is filled with nervous expectation; even the most veteran traveler can become confused. Whether arriving by train, bus, car, or airport limo, everyone walks to the nearby docks (less than a 5-min. walk) to select a method of transport to his or her hotel. The cheapest way is by *vaporetto* (public motorboat); the more expensive is by gondola or motor launch (see section 2 of this chapter, "Getting Around").

BY PLANE   You can now fly nonstop from North America to Venice on Delta. You'll land at the **Aeroporto Marco Polo** (© 041-2606111) at Mestre, north of the city on the mainland. The **Cooperativa San Marco** (© 041-5222303) operates a *motoscafo* (shuttle boat) service that can deliver you from the airport directly to the center of Venice at Piazza San Marco in about 30 minutes. The boats wait just outside the main entrance, and the fare begins at 9.50€ ($8.50) for up to six passengers (if there are only two of you, find some fellow travelers to share the ride and split the fare with you). If you've got some extra euros to spend, you can arrange for a **private water taxi** by calling © 041-5415084. The cost of the ride to the heart of Venice is 70€ ($62.50).

Buses from the airport are less expensive, though they can only take you as far as Piazzale Roma; from there you will need to take a vaporetto to reach your hotel. The **Azienda Trasporti Veneto Orientale** (© 041-5205530) shuttle bus links the airport with Piazzale Roma for 2.50€ ($2.25). The trip takes about half an hour, and departures are about every 30 minutes daily 8:40am to 11:30pm. Even cheaper is a local bus company, **ACTV** (© 041-5287886), whose bus no. 5 makes the run for .70€ (65¢). The ACTV buses depart every half hour and take about a half hour to reach Piazzale Roma.

BY TRAIN   Trains pull into the **Stazione di Santa Lucia,** at Piazzale Roma (© 1478-88088 in Italy only). Travel time is about 5 hours from Rome, 3½ hours from Milan, 4 hours from Florence, and 2 hours from Bologna. The vaporetto departs near the station's main entrance. There's also a **tourist office** at the station (© 041-5298711).

Anyone between the ages of 14 and 29 is eligible for a **Rolling Venice pass,** entitling you to discounts for museums, restaurants, stores, language courses, hotels, and bars. Valid for 1 year, it costs 2.50€ ($2.25) and can be picked up at a special Rolling Venice office set up in the train station during summer.

BY CAR   The autostrada links Venice with the rest of Italy, with direct routes from such cities as Trieste (driving time: 1½ hr.), Milan (3 hr.), and Bologna (2 hr.). Bologna is 151km (94 miles) southwest of Venice, Milan is 266km (165 miles) west, and Trieste is 156km (97 miles) east. Rome is 526km (327 miles) southwest.

⸂Tips⸃ Travel Light

If your hotel is near one of the public *vaporetto* stops, you can probably manage to haul your own luggage to its reception area. If not, you'll have to pay a public porter a small fortune to carry your bags to and from the docks. Porters can't accompany you and your baggage on the vaporetto, however.

From the mainland, follow the signs leading to Venice, going to the Ponte della Libertà along S11, which links Venice to the mainland. The small island of Tronchetto appears on your right as the bridge comes to an end. Here you'll find the parking garages of Venice.

One of the most prominent is the **Garage San Marco,** Piazzale Roma (℘ **041-5235101**), near the vaporetto, gondola, and motor launch docks. You'll be charged 17.50€ to 24€ ($15.65–$21.45) per day or maybe more, depending on the car size. From spring to fall, this municipal parking lot is nearly always filled. You can fax a reservation for a space, however, at ℘ **041-5289969.** You're more likely to find parking on **Isola del Tronchetto** (℘ **041-5207555**), which costs 15€ ($13.40) per day. From Tronchetto, take vaporetto no. 82 to Piazza San Marco. If you have heavy luggage, you'll need a water taxi. Parking is also available at Mestre.

VISITOR INFORMATION

Visitor information is available at the **Azienda di Promozione Turistica,** San Marco 71/F (℘ **041-5298711**). Summer hours are daily 9am to 5pm; off-season hours are daily 9:30am to 3:30pm. Posters around town with exhibit and concert schedules are more helpful. Ask for a schedule of the month's special events and an updated list of museum and church hours because these can change erratically and often.

CITY LAYOUT

Venice lies 4km (2½ miles) from the Italian mainland (connected to Mestre by the Ponte della Libertà) and 2km (1¼ miles) from the open Adriatic. It's an archipelago of 118 islands. Most visitors, however, concern themselves only with **Piazza San Marco** and its vicinity. In fact, the entire city has only one piazza, which is San Marco (all the other squares are *campos*). Venice is divided into six quarters (*sestieri*): **San Marco, Santa Croce, San Polo, Castello, Cannaregio,** and **Dorsoduro.**

Many of Venice's so-called streets are actually canals (*rios*)—more than 150 in all, spanned by a total of 400 bridges. Venice's version of a main street is the **Grand Canal (Canal Grande),** which snakes through the city. Three bridges cross the Grand Canal: the white marble **Ponte Rialto,** the wooden **Ponte Accademia,** and the stone **Ponte degli Scalzi.** The Grand Canal splits Venice into two unequal parts.

South of Dorsoduro, which is south of the Grand Canal, is the **Canale della Guidecca,** a major channel separating Dorsoduro from the large island of La Guidecca. At the point where Canale della Guidecca meets the **Canale di San Marco,** you'll spot the little **Isola di San Giorgio Maggiore,** with a church by Palladio. The most visited islands in the lagoon, aside from the **Lido,** are **Murano, Burano,** and **Torcello.**

If you really want to tour Venice and experience that hidden, romantic trattoria on a nearly forgotten street, bring along a map that details every street and has an index on the back. The best of the lot is the **Falk map** of Venice, sold at many news kiosks and all bookstores.

A broad street running along a canal is a *fondamenta,* a narrower street running along a canal is a *calle,* and a paved road is a *salizzada, ruga,* or *calle larga.* A *rio terra* is a filled canal channel now used as a walkway, and a *sottoportego* is a passage beneath buildings. When you come to an open-air area, you'll often encounter the word *campo*—that's a reference to the fact that such a place was once grassy, and in days of yore cattle grazed there.

Tips **Finding an Address**

A maniac must've numbered Venice's buildings. Before you set out for a specific place, get detailed instructions and have someone mark the place on your map. Don't depend on street numbers; try to locate the nearest cross street. Because signs and numbers have decayed over 6 centuries, it's best to look for signs posted outside rather than for a number.

Every building has a street address and a mailing address. For example, a business at Calle delle Botteghe 3150 (3150 Botteghe St.) will have a mailing address of San Marco 3150 because it's in the San Marco *sestiere* (district), and all buildings in each district are numbered continuously from 1 to 6,000. (To confuse things, several districts have streets of the same name, so it's important to know the sestiere.) In this chapter, we give the street name first, followed by the mailing address.

THE NEIGHBORHOODS IN BRIEF

This section will give you some idea of where you might want to stay and where the major attractions are.

San Marco Welcome to the center of Venice. Napoleon called it "the drawing room of Europe," and it's one crowded drawing room today. It has been the heart of Venetian life for more than a thousand years. **Piazza San Marco (St. Mark's Square)** is dominated by **St. Mark's Basilica.** Just outside the basilica is the **campanile (bell tower),** a reconstruction of the one that collapsed in 1902. Around the corner is the **Palazzo Ducale (Doge's Palace),** with its **Bridge of Sighs.** Piazza San Marco itself is lined with some of the world's most overpriced cafes, including **Florian's** (opened 1720) and **Quadri** (opened 1775). The most celebrated watering hole, however, is away from the square: **Harry's Bar,** founded by Giuseppe Cipriani but made famous by Hemingway. In and around the square are some of the most convenient hotels in Venice (though not necessarily the best) and an array of expensive tourist shops and trattorie.

Castello The shape of Venice is often likened to that of a fish. If so, Castello is the tail. The largest and most varied of the six sestieri,

Castello is home to many sights, such as the **Arsenale,** and some of the city's plushest hotels, such as the **Danieli.** One of the neighborhood's most notable attractions is the Gothic **Santa Giovanni e Paolo (Zanipolo),** the Pantheon of the doges. Cutting through the sestiere is **Campo Santa Maria Formosa,** one of Venice's largest open squares.

The most elegant street is **Riva degli Schiavoni,** which runs along the Grand Canal; it's lined with some of the finest hotels and restaurants and is one of the city's favorite promenades.

Cannaregio This is Venice's gateway, the first of the six sestieri. At its heart is the **Santa Lucia Railway Station** (1955). It also shelters about a third of the population, some 20,000 residents. The area embraces the old **Jewish Ghetto,** the first one on the continent. Jews began to move here at the beginning of the 16th century, when they were segregated from the rest of the city. From here, the word *ghetto* later became a generic term used all

Impressions

Wonderful city, streets full of water, please advise.

—Robert Benchley

over the world. Attractions in this area include the **Ca' d'Oro,** the finest example of the Venetian Gothic style; the **Madonna dell'Orto,** a 15th-century church known for its Tintorettos; and **Santa Maria dei Miracoli,** with a Madonna portrait supposedly able to raise the dead. Unless you're coming for one of these attractions, this area doesn't offer much else because its hotels and restaurants aren't the best. Some of the cheapest lodging is found along **Lista di Spagna,** to the left as you exit the train station.

Santa Croce This area is on the opposite side of the Grand Canal from Cannaregio, between Piazzale Roma and a point just short of the Ponte di Rialto. It's split into two rather different neighborhoods. The eastern part is in the typically Venetian style and is one of the least crowded parts of Venice, although it has some of the Grand Canal's loveliest palazzi. The western side is more industrialized and isn't very interesting to explore.

San Polo This is the heart of commercial Venice and the smallest of the six sestieri. It's reached by crossing the Grand Canal at **Ponte di Rialto (Rialto Bridge).** The shopping here is much more reasonable than that around Piazza San Marco. One of the major sights is the **Erberia,** which Casanova wrote about in

his 18th-century biography. Both wholesale and retail markets still pepper this ancient site. At its center is **San Giacomo di Rialto,** the city's oldest church. The district also encloses the **Scuola Grande di San Rocco,** a repository of the works of Tintoretto. **Campo San Polo** is one of the oldest and widest squares and one of the principal venues for Carnevale. San Polo is also filled with moderately priced hotels and a large number of trattorie, many specializing in seafood. In general, the hotels and restaurants are cheaper here than along San Marco, but not as cheap as those around the train station in Cannaregio.

Dorsoduro The least populated of the sestieri, this funky neighborhood is filled with old homes and half-forgotten churches. Dorsoduro is the southernmost section of the historic district (from San Marco, take the Accademia Bridge across the Grand Canal). Its major sights are the **Accademia Gallery** and the **Peggy Guggenheim Foundation.** It's less trampled than the areas around the Rialto Bridge and Piazza San Marco. Its most famous church is **La Salute,** whose first stone was laid in 1631. The **Zattere,** a broad quay built after 1516, is one of Venice's favorite promenades. Cafes, trattorie, and pensiones abound in the area.

2 Getting Around

You can't hail a taxi—at least, not on land—so get ready to walk and walk and walk. Of course, you can break up your walks with vaporetto or boat rides, which are great respites from dealing with the packed (and we mean *packed*) streets in summer.

However, note that, in autumn, the high tide (*acqua alta*) is a real menace. The squares often flood, beginning with Piazza San Marco, one of the city's lowest points. Many visitors and locals wear knee-high boots to navigate their way. In fact, some hotels maintain a storage room full of boots in all sizes for their guests.

BY PUBLIC TRANSPORTATION

Much to the chagrin of the once-ubiquitous gondoliers, Venice's **motorboats** (*vaporetti*) provide inexpensive and frequent, if not always fast, transportation in this canal city. The vaporetti are called "water buses," and they are indeed the "buses" of Venice because traveling by water is usually faster than traveling by land. The service is operated by **ACTV (Azienda del Consorzio Trasporti Veneziano),** Calle Fisero, San Marco 1810 (© **041-5287886**). An *accelerato* is a vessel that makes every stop; a *diretto* makes only express stops. The average fare is 3€ ($2.70). Note that, in summer, the vaporetti are often fiercely crowded. Pick up a map of the system at the tourist office. They run daily up and down the Grand Canal, with frequent service 7am to midnight and then hourly midnight to 7am.

Visitors to Venice can buy a 10-ticket carnet costing 25€ ($22.35), which must be validated before use and shown together with the matrix (the last ticket of the booklet).

The Grand Canal is long and snakelike and can be crossed via only three bridges, including the one at Rialto. If there's no bridge in sight, the trick in getting across is to use one of the *traghetti* **gondolas** strategically placed at key points. Look for them at the end of any passage called Calle del Traghetto. Under government control, the fare is only .35€ (30¢).

BY MOTOR LAUNCH (WATER TAXI)

Motor launches (*taxi acquei*) cost more than public vaporetti, but you won't be hassled as much when you arrive with your luggage if you hire one of the many private ones. You might or might not have the cabin of one of these sleek vessels to yourself because the captains fill their boats with as many passengers as the law allows before taking off. Your porter's uncanny radar will guide you to one of the inconspicuous piers where a water taxi waits.

The price of a transit by water taxi from Piazzale Roma (the road/rail terminus) to Piazza San Marco begins at 40€ ($35.70) for up to four passengers and 50€ ($44.65) for more than four. The captains adroitly deliver you, with luggage, to the canal-side entrance of your hotel or on one of the smaller waterways within a short walking distance of your destination. You can also call for a water taxi; try the **Cooperativa San Marco** at © **041-5222303.**

BY GONDOLA

You and your gondolier have two major agreements to reach: the price and the length of the ride. If you aren't careful, you're likely to be taken on both counts. It's a common sight to see a gondolier huffing and puffing to take his passengers on a "quickie," often reducing an hour to 15 minutes.

The "official" rate is 50€ ($44.65) per hour, but we've never known anyone to honor it. The actual fare depends on how well you stand up to the gondolier, *beginning* at 75€ ($67) for up to 50 minutes. Most gondoliers will ask at least double the "official" rate and reduce your trip to 30 to 40 minutes or even less. Prices go up after 8pm. In fairness to them, we must say that their job is hard and has been overly romanticized: They row boatloads of tourists across hot, smelly canals with such endearments screamed at them as, "No sing, no pay!"

And these fellows have to make plenty of euros while the sun shines because their work ends when the first cold winds blow in from the Adriatic. Speaking of winds, hundreds of visitors get very seasick in a gondola on the open water on a windy day.

Two major stations where you can hire gondolas are **Piazza San Marco** (© 041-5200685) and **Ponte di Rialto** (© 041-5224904).

BY CAR

Obviously, you won't need a car in Venice, but you might want one when you leave, to head off to nearby cities such as Padua. Most of the car-rental agencies lie near the rail station in the traffic-clogged Piazzale Roma (you can return a rental car here as you arrive in Venice). You'll save the most money if you reserve from the U.S.

Hertz is at Piazzale Roma 496E (© **800/654-3131** in the U.S., or 041-5284091; www.hertz.com). From May to October, hours are Monday to Friday 8am to 6pm, and Saturday 8am to 1pm. From November to April, it's open Monday to Friday 8am to 12:30pm and 3 to 5:30pm, and Saturday 8am to 1pm. **Europcar** (associated with National in the U.S.) is at Piazzale Roma 496H (© **800/328-4567** in the U.S., or 041-5238616). From May to July and September, hours are Monday to Friday 8:30am to 1pm and 2 to 6:30pm, and Saturday and Sunday 8:30am to 1pm; in August, hours are Monday to Friday 8:30am to 12:30pm and 2:30 to 6pm, and Saturday 8:30am to noon; and October to April, hours are Monday to Friday 9:30am to 12:30pm and 2:30 to 6pm. **Avis** is at Piazzale Roma 496G (© **800/331-2112** in the U.S., or 041-5225825; www.avis.com). From April to October, it's open Monday to Friday 8am to 6:30pm, and Saturday and Sunday 8:30am to 12:30pm; November to March, hours are Monday to Friday 8:30am to 12:30pm and 2:30 to 6pm, and Saturday and Sunday 8:30am to 12:30pm.

 FAST FACTS: Venice

American Express The office is at Salizzada San Moisè, San Marco 1471 (© **041-5200844**; vaporetto: San Marco). The staff can arrange city tours and mail handling. From May to October, hours are Monday to Saturday 8am to 8pm for currency exchange, and 9am to 5:30pm for all other transactions; from November to April, hours are Monday to Friday 9am to 5:30pm, and Saturday 9am to 12:30pm.

Consulates The **U.K. Consulate** is at Dorsoduro 1051, at the foot of the Accademia Bridge (© **041-5227207**; vaporetto: Accademia), open Monday to Friday 10am to noon and 2 to 3pm. The **United States, Canada,** and **Australia** have consulates in Milan, about 3 hours away by train (see "Milan," in chapter 11).

Currency Exchange There are many banks in Venice where you can exchange money. You might try the **Deutsche Bank SPA,** San Marco 2216 (© **041-5207024**; vaporetto: San Marco). Hours are Monday to Friday 8:30am to 1:30pm and 2:45 to 4pm.

Dentist/Doctor Your best bet is to have your hotel set up an appointment with an English-speaking dentist or doctor. The American Express office and the British Consulate also have lists. Also see "Hospitals," below.

Drugstores If you need a drugstore in the middle of the night, call ℂ **192** for information about which one is open (pharmacies take turns staying open late). A well-recommended central one is **International Pharmacy,** Via XXII Marzo, San Marco 2067 (ℂ **041-5294111;** vaporetto: San Marco).

Emergencies Call ℂ **113** for the police, ℂ **118** for an ambulance, or ℂ **115** to report a fire.

Hospitals Get in touch with the **Ospedale Civile Santi Giovanni e Paolo,** Campo Santi Giovanni e Paolo in Castello (ℂ **041-52394517;** vaporetto: San Toma), staffed with English-speaking doctors 24 hours a day.

Laundry/Dry Cleaning One of the most convenient coin-operated laundromats and dry-cleaning enterprises is **Lavanderia Gabriella,** Calle Fiubera, San Marco 985 (ℂ **041-5221758;** vaporetto: San Marco), behind Piazza San Marco. Its washing machines are available daily 8am to 7pm, and its dry-cleaning facilities are open Monday to Saturday 8am to 12:30pm and 3 to 7pm.

Police See "Emergencies," above.

Safety The curse of Venice is the pickpocket. Violent crime is rare. But because of the overcrowding in vaporetti and even on the small narrow streets, it's easy to pick pockets. Purse-snatchers are commonplace as well. They can dart out of nowhere, grab a purse, and disappear in seconds down some narrow dark alley. Keep valuables locked in a safe in your hotel, if one is provided.

Telephone See "Fast Facts: Italy," in chapter 3, for full details on how to call Venice from home and how to place international calls once you're here. The **city code** for Venice is **041;** use this code for all calls—even within Venice itself (and you must now include the zero every time, even when calling from abroad).

Toilets These are available at Piazzale Roma and various other places, but they aren't as plentiful as they should be. A truly spotless one is at the foot of the Accademia Bridge. Often you'll have to rely on the restrooms in cafes, although you should buy something, perhaps a light coffee, because, in theory, the toilets are for customers only. Most museums and galleries have public toilets. You can also use the public toilets at the Albergo Diurno, Via Ascensione, just behind Piazza San Marco. Remember, *signori* means men and *signore* means women.

3 Where to Stay

Venice has some of the most expensive hotels in the world, but we've also found some wonderful lesser-known moderately priced places, often on hard-to-find narrow streets. However, Venice has never been known as an inexpensive destination.

Because of their age and lack of uniformity, Venice's hotels offer widely varying rooms. For example, it's entirely possible to stay in a hotel generally considered "expensive" while paying only a "moderate" rate—if you'll settle for a less desirable room. Many "inexpensive" hotels and boarding houses have two or three rooms in the "expensive" category. Usually these are more spacious and open onto a view. Also, if an elevator is essential for you, always inquire in advance; not every building has one.

The cheapest way to visit Venice is to book into a *locanda* (small inn), which is rated below the *pensioni* (boarding house) in official Italian hotel lingo. Standards are highly variable in these places, many of which are dank, dusty, and dark. The rooms even in many first-class hotels are often cramped because space has always been a problem in Venice. It's estimated that in this "City of Light," at least half of the rooms in any category are dark, so be duly warned. Those with lots of light and opening onto the Grand Canal carry a hefty price tag.

The most difficult times to find rooms are during the February Carnevale, around Easter, and from June to September. Because of the tight hotel situation, it's advisable to make reservations as far in advance as possible (months in advance for summer, and even a year in advance for Carnevale). After those peak times, you can virtually have your pick of rooms. If you ask at the reception desk, most hotels will grant you a 10% to 15% discount in winter (Nov–Mar 15). But getting this discount could require a little negotiation. A few hotels close in January if there's no prospect of business.

If you arrive without a reservation, go to one of the **AVA (Hotel Association) reservation booths** throughout the area at the train station, the municipal parking garage at Piazzale Roma, the airport, and the information point on the mainland where the highway comes to an end. The main office is at Piazzale Roma (© **041-5228640**). To get a room, you'll have to pay a deposit that's then rebated on your hotel bill. Depending on the hotel classification, deposits are 10€ to 45€ ($8.95–$40.20) per person. All hotel booths are open daily 9am to 10pm.

See "The Neighborhoods in Brief," in section 1 of this chapter, to get an idea of where you might want to base yourself, whether in less touristy San Polo or in Dorsoduro, or in the thick of things (and crowds too) in and around Piazza San Marco.

NEAR PIAZZA SAN MARCO
VERY EXPENSIVE

Gritti Palace ★★★   The Gritti, in a stately Grand Canal setting, is the renovated palazzo of 15th-century doge Andrea Gritti. Even after its takeover by ITT Sheraton, it's still a bit starchy and has a museum aura (some of the furnishings are roped off), but for sheer glamour and history, only the Cipriani (see the Cipriani listing, later in the chapter) tops it. (Stay at the Cipriani for quiet, isolation, and more recreational facilities, but stay here for a completely central location and service that's just as good.) Guests here are more pampered than those at the Danieli, the Gritti's closest rival in the heart of Venice, but expect to pay a great deal more at the Gritti for that extra notch in service. This was Hemingway's "home in Venice," and it has drawn some of the world's greatest theatrical, literary, political, and royal figures.

The variety of guest rooms seems almost limitless, from elaborate suites to small singles. But throughout, the elegance is evident. The most spacious rooms face the campo, but we prefer the big corner doubles (second and third floors) with balconies overlooking the canal. Elegant linen and hypoallergenic pillows grace the antique beds, and thoughtful extras include thermostats, bottled water, and two-line phones. Most of the bathrooms are sumptuous, sheathed in red

Where to Stay in Venice

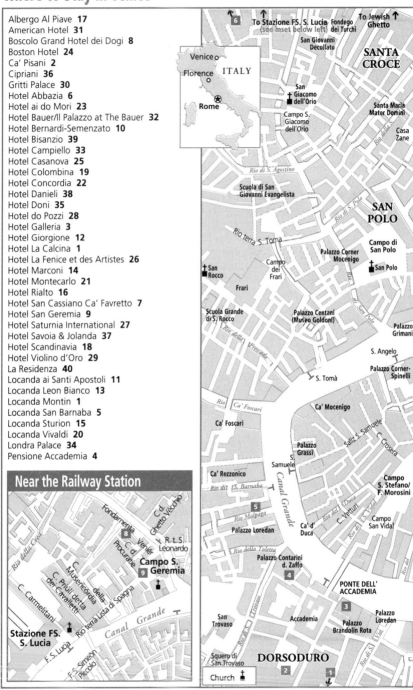

Near the Railway Station

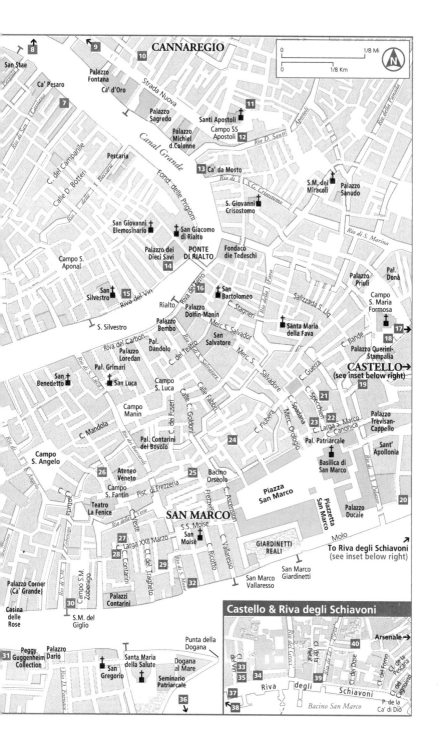

CANNAREGIO

San Stae

Ca' Pesaro

Palazzo
Fontana
Ca' d'Oro

Palazzo
Sagredo

Strada Nuova

Palazzo
Michiel
d.Colonne

Santi Apostoli
Campo SS
Apostoli

C. del Campanile

Pescaria

Canal Grande

Ca' da Mosto

Fond. delle prigioni

S. Giovanni
Crisostomo

S.G. Crisostomo

S.M. dei
Miracoli

Palazzo
Sanudo

Rio di S. Marina

San Giovanni
Elemosinario

San Giacomo
di Rialto

Campo S.
Aponal

Palazzo dei
Dieci Savi

PONTE
DI RIALTO

Fondaco
die Tedeschi

Palazzo
Priuli

Pal.
Donà

Campo
S. Maria
Formosa

San
Silvestro

Riva del Vin

Rialto

Rio della Fava

San
Bartolomeo

Salizzada S. Lio

Palazzo
Dolfin-Manin

C. Stagneri

Santa Maria
della Fava

C. Bande

Palazzo Querini-
Stampalia

S. Silvestro

Palazzo
Bembo

Merc. S. Salvador

San
Salvatore

CASTELLO →
(see inset below right)

Riva del Carbon

Palazzo
Loredan

Pal.
Dandolo

C. del Teatro

Merc. S. Salvatore

Merc. S. Salvadore

Salvadore

C. Guerra

San
Benedetto

Pal. Grimani

San Luca

Campo
S. Luca

Calle Fabbri

C. Fiubera

C. Specchieri

21

Palazzo
Trevisan-
Cappello

Campo
Manin

Calle dei Fuseri

Calle C. Goldoni

Merc. Orologio

C. Larga S. Marco
Canonica

22

23

Sant'
Apollonia

C. Mandola

Pal. Contarini
del Bovolo

24

Pal. Patriarcale

Basilica di
San Marco

Campo
S. Angelo

Ateneo
Veneto

Campo
S. Fantin

Pisc. di Frezzeria

25

Bacino
Orseolo

Frezzeria

Ascension

Piazza
San Marco

Piazzetta
San Marco

Palazzo
Ducale

20

Teatro
La Fenice

SAN MARCO

S.S. Moise

San
Moise

C. Vallaresso

GIARDINETTI
REALI

Molo

To Riva degli Schiavoni
(see inset below right)

Palazzo Corner
(Ca' Grande)

27

28

Larga XXII Marzo

Campo S.M.
Zobenigo

C. Contarini

C. del Traghetto

29

C. Ricotto

Rio d. S. Moise

San Marco
Vallaresso

San Marco
Giardinetti

Casina
delle
Rose

30

Palazzi
Contarini

S.M. del
Giglio

Castello & Riva degli Schiavoni

Peggy
Guggenheim
Collection

31

Palazzo
Dario

San
Gregorio

Santa Maria
della Salute

Punta della
Dogana

Dogana
al Mare

Seminario
Patriarcale

36

Rio d. Fornace

Arsenale →

40

Rio di Greci

Cl. Tetta
Pietà

C. del Dose

C. del Forno

33

34

35

39

Riva   degli   Schiavoni

37

38

Bacino San Marco

P. de la
Ca' di Dio

387

Carnevale

Venetians are once more taking to the open piazzas and streets for the pre-Lenten holiday of **Carnevale**. The festival traditionally marked the unbridled celebration that preceded Lent, the period of penitence and abstinence before Easter. It lasts about 5 to 10 days and culminates the Friday to Tuesday before Ash Wednesday (Mar 5 in 2003).

In the 18th-century heyday of Carnevale, well-heeled revelers came from all over Europe to take part in the festivities. Masks became ubiquitous, affording anonymity and pardoning 1,000 sins. They permitted the fishmonger to attend the ball and dance with the baroness. The doges condemned the festival and the popes denounced it, but nothing could dampen the Venetian Carnevale spirit until Napoleon arrived in 1797 and put an end to the festivities.

Resuscitated in 1980 by local tourism powers to fill the empty winter months, Carnevale is calmer now, though just barely. In the 1980s, it attracted an onslaught of what was seemingly the entire student population of Europe, backpackers who slept in the piazzas and train station. Politicians and city officials adopted a middle-of-the-road policy that helped establish Carnevale's image as neither a backpackers' free-for-all outdoor party nor a continuation of the exclusive private balls in the Grand Canal palazzi available to only a very few.

Carnevale was at its glorious best as it celebrated its 20th anniversary in 2000. Each year the festival opens with a series of lavish balls and private parties, most of which aren't open to the public. But the candlelit **Doge's Ball (Ballo del Doge)** is a dazzling exception, traditionally held the Saturday before Shrove Tuesday in the 15th-century Palazzo Pisani Moretta on the Grand Canal. Historic costumes are a must, and you can rent them. Of course, this ball isn't exactly cheap—the price for 2002 was 416€ ($371.50) per person including dinner—and you can expect it to rise for future years because organizers plan to make the ball ever more extravagant. If you're interested in finding out more and arranging for a costume rental, contact Antonia Sautter at the Ballo del Doge at ✆ **041-5233851** (fax 041-5287543).

Verona marble and amply stocked. For a splurge, ask for Hemingway's old suite or the Doge Suite, once occupied by W. Somerset Maugham.

Campo Santa Maria del Giglio, San Marco 2467, 30124 Venezia. ✆ **800/325-3535** in the U.S., 416/947-4864 in Canada, or 041-794611. Fax 041-5200942. www.luxurycollection.com/grittipalace. 93 units. 713€–909€ ($636.60–$811.60) double; from 1,653€ ($1,475.90) suite. Rates include breakfast. AE, DC, MC, V. Vaporetto: Santa Maria del Giglio. **Amenities:** Elegant restaurant and bar; 24-hr. concierge and butler service; private boat launches and sightseeing tours; salon; 24-hr. room service; babysitting; laundry/dry cleaning. *In room:* A/C, TV, minibar, hair dryer, safe.

Hotel Bauer/Il Palazzo at the Bauer ★   This deluxe hotel, known since 1880 as the Grand Hotel d'Italie Bauer Grunwald but now as simply the Hotel Bauer, is better than ever, although it can never obtain the pedigree of the Danieli and the Gritti. Long a favorite of prime ministers, royalty, and jet-setters, it's the combination of an ornate 13th-century palazzo facing the Grand

Even if you don't attend a ball, there's still plenty of fun in the streets. You'll find a patchwork of musical and cultural events, many of them free of charge, that appeal to all tastes, nationalities, ages, and budgets. At any given moment, musical events are staged in any of the city's dozens of piazzas—from reggae to zydeco to jazz to chamber music—and special art exhibits are mounted at numerous museums and galleries. The recent involvement of international corporate sponsors has met with a mixed reception, but it seems to be the wave of the future.

Carnevale is not for those who dislike crowds. The crowds are what it's all about. All of life becomes a stage, and everyone is on it. Whether you spend months creating an elaborate costume or grab one from the countless stands set up around town, Carnevale is about giving in to the spontaneity of the magic and surprise around every corner, the mystery behind every mask. Masks and costumes are everywhere, with the emphasis on the historical, because Venice's Carnevale is a chance to relive the glory days of the 1700s, when Venetian life was at its most extravagant. Groups travel in coordinated getups that range from a contemporary passel of Fellini-esque clowns to the court of the Sun King in all its wigged-out glory. You might see the Three Musketeers riding the vaporetto; your waiter might appear dressed as a nun. The places to be seen in costume are the cafes lining Piazza San Marco. Don't expect to be seated at a full-view window seat unless your costume is straight off the stage of the local opera house. The merrymakers carry on until Shrove Tuesday, when the bells of San Francesco della Vigna toll at midnight. But before they do, the grand finale involves fireworks over the lagoon.

The city is the quintessential set, the perfect venue; Hollywood could not create a more evocative location. This is a celebration about history, art, theater, and drama. Venice and Carnevale were made for each other.

Canal, a massive Stalinesque concrete wing that was "an architectural scandal" when it opened in the 1960s, and the new Bauer Palace, a VIP wing. The most evocative part of the complex is Il Palazzo, a separate boutique property within the workaday Bauer. Il Palazzo was coaxed out of an 18th-century residence with a stunning Gothic facade. Even the more modest accommodations are fitted with baroque furniture, walk-in closets, and marble floors in the bathrooms. The suites are totally sumptuous, almost "explosively" Venetian with their bacchanalian marble tubs, fireplaces, and Murano chandeliers, with balconies overlooking tourists in gondolas. The guest rooms are decorated in classic European style, with both French and Venetian pieces. No other luxury hotel has such a stunning location—just steps from Piazza San Marco.

Campo San Moisè, San Marco 1459, 30124 Venezia. © **041-5207022.** Fax 041-5207557. www.bauer venezia.com. 190 units. Hotel Bauer: 260€–500€ ($232.20–$446.50) double; 600€–950€

($535.80–$848.35) suite. Bauer Palace: 415€–685€ ($370.60–$611.70) double; from 930€ ($830.50) suite. AE, DC, MC, V. Vaporetto: San Marco. **Amenities:** 2 restaurants; bar; golf course; tennis courts; fitness center; watersports; concierge; business center; salon; room service; babysitting; laundry/dry cleaning. *In room:* A/C, TV, minibar, hair dryer, safe.

EXPENSIVE

Hotel Casanova ⋆   This former home is a few short blocks from Piazza San Marco. Although the name Casanova sounds romantic, the hotel doesn't have a lot of character; it does, however, contain a collection of church art and benches from old monasteries. For the most part, the modernized guest rooms are unremarkable, but they're well maintained. The accommodations vary considerably in size; some are quite small. The most intriguing units are on the top floor, with exposed brick walls and sloping beamed ceilings.

Frezzeria, San Marco 1284, 30124 Venezia. ✆ **041-5206855.** Fax 041-5206413. www.side7.it/casanova/. 49 units. 155€–256€ ($138.40–$228.60) double; 187€–292€ ($166.95–$260.70) triple. Rates include breakfast. AE, DC, MC, V. Vaporetto: Calle Vallareso. **Amenities:** Room service; babysitting; laundry/dry cleaning. *In room:* A/C, TV, hair dryer, safe.

Hotel Colombina ⋆*Finds*   A 5-minute walk from Piazza San Marco is a hard-to-find, recently renovated hotel that's a bit of a Venetian secret. After extensive 2-year-long renovation, this hotel is a little gem, offering rather luxurious and spacious bedrooms. The tasseled draperies and reproduction Venetian antiques give it some glamour. All is calm and tranquil inside, but the location is in a maze of narrowing alleys and massive international hordes going who knows where. A lovely buffet breakfast is set out every morning. The more expensive rooms are like suites—hence the very high price tag.

Calle del Remedio, Castello 4416, 30122 Venezia. ✆ **041-2770525.** Fax 041-2776044. www.hotelcolombina.com. 32 units. 170€–382€ ($151.80–$341.15) double; 216€–439€ ($192.90–$392.05) triple. AE, DC, MC, V. Vaporetto: San Marco. **Amenities:** Coffee bar; room service; babysitting; laundry/dry cleaning. *In room:* A/C, TV, minibar, hair dryer, safe.

Hotel Concordia ⋆   The Concordia, in a russet-colored building with stone-trimmed windows, is the only hotel with rooms overlooking St. Mark's Square (only a few do, and they command a high price). A series of gold-plated marble steps takes you to the lobby, where you'll find a comfortable bar area, good service, and elevators to whisk you to the labyrinthine halls. The (quite small) guest rooms are decorated in a Venetian antique style, with small Murano chandeliers, coordinated fabrics, hand-painted furnishings, and marble bathrooms.

Calle Larga, San Marco 367, 30124 Venezia. ✆ **041-5206866.** Fax 041-5206775. 57 units (some with shower only). 185€–380€ ($165.20–$339.35) double; 215€ ($192) suite. Rates include buffet breakfast. AE, DC, MC, V. Vaporetto: San Marco. **Amenities:** Restaurant; bar; room service; babysitting; laundry/dry cleaning. *In room:* A/C, TV, minibar, hair dryer, safe.

Hotel Saturnia International ⋆   Far superior to the Scandinavia (see below), this is one of Venice's most successful adaptations of a 14th-century palazzo. You're surrounded by richly embellished beauty: a grand hall with a wooden staircase, iron chandeliers, fine paintings, and beamed ceilings. The individually styled guest rooms are generally spacious and furnished with chandeliers, Venetian antiques, tapestry rugs, gilt mirrors, and carved ceilings. A few on the top floor have small balconies; others overlook the garden in back.

Calle Larga XXII Marzo, San Marco 2399, 30124 Venezia. ✆ **041-5208377.** Fax 041-5207131. www.hotelsaturnia.it. 95 units (a few with tub or shower only). 259.50€–450€ ($231.75–$401.85) double. Rates include breakfast. AE, DC, MC, V. Vaporetto: San Marco. **Amenities:** Restaurant; lounge; room service; babysitting; laundry/dry cleaning. *In room:* A/C, TV, minibar, hair dryer, safe.

Hotel Scandinavia ⭐ This hotel isn't actually in San Marco (it's in neighboring Castello, just off a colorful square), but it has a convenient location not far from Piazza San Marco. The public rooms are rococo, filled with copies of 18th-century Italian chairs and Venetian-glass chandeliers. The guest rooms are of a decent size and are decorated in the Venetian style, but modern comforts have been added. The bathrooms are a bit cramped; you can request a hair dryer at the front desk. The lobby lounge overlooks the campo. Breakfast is the only meal served, but the hotel staff will direct you to several good dining spots within a short walk of the entrance.

Campo Santa Maria Formosa, Castello 5240, 30122 Venezia. ℂ **041-5223507.** Fax 041-5235232. www.scandinaviahotel.com. 34 units (some with shower only). High season 300€ ($267.90) double; low season 150€ ($133.95) double. Rates include breakfast. AE, DC, MC, V. Vaporetto: San Zaccaria or Rialto. **Amenities:** Bar; room service; babysitting; laundry. *In room:* A/C, TV, minibar, safe.

Hotel Violino d'Oro ⭐ The 18th-century Palazzo Barozzi is now a restored three-story hotel. The midsize guest rooms are handsomely furnished with well-kept bathrooms. Two rooms and the junior suite open onto private terraces. Ms. Cristina and her family run the hotel with style and grace.

Campiello Barozzi, San Marco 2091, 30124 Venezia. ℂ **041-2770841.** Fax 041-2771001. www.violino doro.com. 26 units. 225€–275€ ($200.95–$245.60) double. Rates include breakfast. AE, DC, MC, V. Vaporetto: San Marco. **Amenities:** Bar; room service; babysitting; laundry. *In room:* A/C, TV, minibar, hair dryer.

MODERATE

Boston Hotel This is a battered but serviceable choice. Built in 1962, the hotel was named after an uncle who left to seek his fortune in Boston and never returned. For the skinny guest, there's a tiny self-operated elevator and a postage stamp–size street entrance. Most of the guest rooms, with parquet floors, have built-in features, plus chests and wardrobes. Some open onto tiny balconies overlooking the canal. The tiny bathrooms contain a basket of body-care products.

Ponte dei Dai, San Marco 848, 30124 Venezia. ℂ **041-5287665.** Fax 041-5226628. 42 units (most with shower only). 140€–210€ ($125–$187.55) double. Rates include breakfast. AE, DC, MC, V. Closed Nov–Feb. Vaporetto: San Marco. **Amenities:** Bar; room service; babysitting; laundry/dry cleaning. *In room:* A/C, TV, hair dryer, safe.

Hotel do Pozzi ⭐ A short stroll from Piazza San Marco, this small place feels more like a country tavern than a hotel. Its original structure is 200 years old, and it opens onto a paved courtyard with potted greenery. The sitting and dining rooms are furnished with antiques (and near-antiques) intermixed with utilitarian modern decor. Half the guest rooms open onto the street and half onto a view of an inner garden where breakfast is served in summer. Some have Venetian styling with antique reproductions; others are in a more contemporary and more sterile vein. A major refurbishment has given a fresh touch to the bathrooms.

Corte do Pozzi, San Marco 2373, 30124 Venezia. ℂ **041-5207855.** Fax 041-5229413. www.hoteldopozzi.it. 35 units (some with shower only). 120€–190€ ($107.15–$169.65) double. Rates include breakfast. AE, DC, MC, V. Vaporetto: Santa Maria del Giglio. **Amenities:** Dining room; bar; babysitting; laundry/dry cleaning. *In room:* TV, minibar, hair dryer.

Hotel La Fenice et des Artistes *Overrated* For decades one of the most famous hotels of Venice, this landmark is now in sad decline, although it still has its fans and one of the most desirable of all Venetian locations. Maintenance could be better, and the staff has grown complacent. This hotel offers widely varying accommodations in two connected buildings, each at least 100 years old. One is rather romantic, though timeworn, with an impressive staircase leading to the ornate rooms (one even has its own small garden and terraces). Your satin-lined room might have an inlaid desk and a wardrobe painted in the Venetian manner to match a baroque bed frame. The main building, site of the reception desk, is the more desirable, furnished in a more typically Venetian style, with nicely padded walls and art reproductions, gilt mirrors, Murano chandeliers, and spacious old bathrooms.

Campiello de la Fenice, San Marco 1936, 30124 Venezia. ℂ 041-5232333. Fax 041-5203721. fenice@fenicehotels.it. 69 units. 130€–210€ ($116.10–$187.55) double; 195€–275€ ($174.10–$245.55) suite. Rates include breakfast. AE, DC, MC, V. Vaporetto: San Marco. **Amenities:** Bar; room service; babysitting; laundry/dry cleaning. *In room:* A/C, TV, hair dryer, safe.

Hotel Montecarlo   Although still unremarkable, this hotel is in a vastly improved 17th-century building, just 2 minutes from Piazza San Marco. The upper halls are lined with paintings by Venetian artists. The guest rooms are decorated with Venetian-style furniture and Venetian-glass chandeliers. Some are quite dark, the curse of many Venetian hotels. All have well-kept bathrooms.

Calle dei Specchieri, San Marco 463, 30124 Venezia. ℂ 041-5207144. Fax 041-5207789. www.venice hotelmontecarlo.com. 48 units. 125€ ($111.65) standard double; 300€ ($267.90) deluxe double. Rates include buffet breakfast. AE, DC, MC, V. Vaporetto: San Marco. **Amenities:** Restaurant; bar; room service; babysitting; laundry. *In room:* A/C, TV, hair dryer, safe.

INEXPENSIVE
Hotel ai do Mori 🌟 *Value*   This 1450s town house lies about 10 paces from tourist central. You'll have to balance your need for space with your desire for a view (and your willingness to climb stairs because there's no elevator): The lower-level rooms are larger but don't have views; the third- and fourth-floor rooms are cramped but have sweeping views over the basilica's domes. The building is frequently upgraded by owner Antonella Bernardi. The furniture in the guest rooms is simple and modern, bathrooms are clean, and most of the street noise is muffled by double-paned windows. No meals are served, but there are dozens of cafes in the neighborhood.

Calle Larga San Marco, San Marco 658, 30124 Venezia. ℂ 041-5204817. Fax 041-5205328. www.hotel aidomori.com. 11 units, 9 with private bathroom (showers only). 80€ ($71.45) double without bathroom; 110€ ($98.25) double with bathroom. MC, V. Vaporetto: San Marco. **Amenities:** Lounge. *In room:* A/C, TV, hair dryer, safe.

CASTELLO/RIVA DEGLI SCHIAVONI
VERY EXPENSIVE
Hotel Danieli 🌟🌟🌟   The Cipriani is more exclusive and isolated, almost like a spa, and the Gritti coddles its guests a bit more, but the Danieli is clearly no. 3 among the fabulous palazzi hotels of Venice. Comparisons between the Danieli and the Gritti are inevitable. The Danieli broods, as the Gritti sparkles. The Danieli is more baronial, and the Gritti is more like home (that is, if your home is a palazzo). The Danieli sprawls, whereas the Gritti is intimate. The Danieli's rates are also a good deal lower than those of either of its two rivals, making it a better value (if $350-a-night rooms can be considered a good value).

The Danieli was built as a grand showcase by Doge Dandolo in the 14th century and in 1822 was transformed into a "hotel for kings." In a spectacular Grand Canal location, it has sheltered not only kings but also princes, cardinals, ambassadors, and such literary figures as George Sand and Charles Dickens. The atmosphere is luxurious; even the balconies opening off the main lounge are illuminated by stained-glass skylights. The guest rooms range widely in price, dimension, decor, and vistas (those opening onto the lagoon cost a lot more but are also susceptible to the noise of Riva degli Schiavoni). Alfred de Musset and Ms. Sand made love in room no. 10, the most requested accommodation. You're housed in one of three buildings: a modern structure (least desirable), a 19th-century building, and the 14th-century Venetian-Gothic Palazzo Dandolo (most desirable). On the downside, although the palazzo rooms are the most romantic, they also are the smallest.

Riva degli Schiavoni, Castello 4196, 30122 Venezia. © **800/325-3535** in the U.S. and Canada, or 041-5226480. Fax 041-5200208. www.hoteldanieli.it. 238 units. 565€–845€ ($504.45–$754.45) double; 2,200€ ($1,964.30) suite. AE, DC, MC, V. Vaporetto: San Zaccaria. **Amenities:** Elegant restaurant; lounge; bar; concierge; room service; babysitting; laundry/dry cleaning. *In room:* A/C, TV, minibar, hair dryer, safe.

Londra Palace ⭐⭐   It's no Danieli, but the Londra is a gabled manor on the lagoon, a few yards from Piazza San Marco. The hotel's most famous guest was arguably Tchaikovsky, who wrote his *Fourth Symphony* in room no. 108 in December 1877; he also composed several other works here. The cozy reading room is reminiscent of an English club, boasting leaded windows and paneled walls with framed blowups of some of Tchaikovsky's sheet music. The guest rooms are luxurious, often with lacquered Venetian furniture. Romantics ask for one of the two Regency-style attic rooms with beamed ceilings. The courtyard rooms are quieter and cheaper, opening onto rooftop views instead of the Grand Canal. The best units are those on the fifth floor, with beamed ceilings and private terraces. The bathrooms often have whirlpool tubs and come with deluxe toiletries and robes.

Riva degli Schiavoni, Castello 4171, 30122 Venezia. © **041-5200533.** Fax 041-5225032. www.hotel ondra.it. 53 units. 350€–700€ ($312.55–$625.10) double; 475€–1,000€ ($424.20–$893) junior suite. Rates include breakfast. AE, DC, MC, V. Vaporetto: San Zaccaria. **Amenities:** Restaurant; bar; concierge; room service; babysitting; laundry. *In room:* A/C, TV, minibar, hair dryer, safe.

EXPENSIVE

Hotel Bisanzio ⭐   A few steps from Piazza San Marco, this hotel in the former home of sculptor Alessandro Vittoria offers good service. It has an elevator and terraces, plus a little bar and a mooring for gondolas and motorboats. The lounge opens onto a traditional courtyard. The guest rooms are generally quiet, each in a Venetian antique style. The most requested rooms are the eight opening onto private balconies.

Calle della Pietà, Riva degli Schiavoni 3651, 30122 Venezia. © **041-5203100.** Fax 041-5204114. www.bisanzio.com. 50 units (half with shower only). 140€–290€ ($125–$258.95) double. Rates include breakfast. AE, DC, MC, V. Vaporetto: San Zaccaria. **Amenities:** Lounge; room service; babysitting; laundry/dry cleaning. *In room:* A/C, TV, minibar, hair dryer.

Finds **Your Own Apartment in Venice**

If you and your companions or friends are going to be in Venice for a minimum of 3 nights, consider renting your own apartment. **Venice Rentals,** P.O. Box 8711, Boston, MA 02114 (© **617/472-5392;** www.venicerentals. com), offers a wide selection of fine apartments to choose from within the city of Venice itself or at the beach, the Lido. Offered in a wide range of prices from moderate to very expensive, the agency lists one-, two-, and three-bedroom self-service apartments as well as luxury flats in all districts of Venice. Each unit is fully furnished and contains a kitchen.

Locanda Vivaldi ★ *Finds* Here is a rare chance to immerse yourself in a cliché of Venetian charm. The house of the composer Antonio Vivaldi (1678–1741) has been converted into a hotel. The most original and influential Italian composer of his day, Vivaldi was *maestro de' concerti* in Venice from 1716 to 1738, during which time he lived at this house. In keeping with the spirit of the maestro, the Locanda has been decorated with baroque ornamentation. Bedrooms are comfortably lush, evoking a time gone by but with modern conveniences such as tiled bathrooms. Standard doubles have a view of the Grand Canal, and superior double units offer a lagoon view and also contain a hydromassage tub. Anchor here and you'll be right in the heart of Venice.

Riva degli Schiavoni, 4152–4153, 30122 Venezia. © 041-2770477. Fax 041-2770489. www.locanda vivaldi.it/. 22 units (some with shower only). 170€–415€ ($151.80–$370.60) double; 232€–620€ ($207.20–$553.65) junior suite. Rates include buffet breakfast. AE, DC, MC, V. Vaporetto: San Zaccaria. *In room:* A/C, TV, minibar, safe.

MODERATE

Hotel Campiello This pink-fronted Venetian town house dates from the 1400s, but today you'll find cost-conscious Venetian-style accommodations. This government-rated two-star hotel is better than its rating implies because of a spectacular location and Renaissance touches such as marble mosaic floors and carefully polished hardwoods. The only room with a separate entrance is a ground-floor hideaway that, fortunately, has been flooded by high tides only once in the previous century. The guest rooms are cozy, with tidy bathrooms.

Campiello del Vin, Castello 4647, 30122 Venezia. © 041-5205764. Fax 041-5205798. www.hcampiello.it. 17 units (showers only). 93€–170€ ($83.05–$151.80) double; 142€–196€ ($126.80–$175.05) triple. Rates include breakfast. AE, DC, MC, V. Closed Jan. Vaporetto: San Zaccaria. **Amenities:** Lounge; babysitting. *In room:* A/C, TV, hair dryer, safe.

Hotel Savoia & Jolanda ★ The Savoia & Jolanda occupies a prize position on Venice's premier boulevard, with a lagoon as its front yard. Although its exterior reflects old Venice, the interior is somewhat spiritless; the staff, however, makes life comfortable. Most of the modern guest rooms have a view of the boats and the Lido; they contain desks and armchairs. All the rooms were last renovated in 1999. Some units are large enough to contain three or four beds.

Riva degli Schiavoni, Castello 4187, 30122 Venezia. © 041-5206644. Fax 041-5207494. www.elmoro.com. 75 units (some with shower only). 201€–346€ ($179.50–$309) double; 320€–599€ ($285.75–$534.90) suite. Rates include buffet breakfast. AE, DC, MC, V. Vaporetto: San Zaccaria. **Amenities:** Restaurant; lounge; room service; babysitting; laundry. *In room:* A/C, TV, minibar, hair dryer, safe.

La Residenza ★★ In a 14th-century building that looks a lot like a miniature Doge's Palace, this little hotel is on a residential square where children play soccer and older people feed the pigeons. You'll pass through a stone vestibule lined with ancient Roman columns before ringing another doorbell at the bottom of a flight of stairs. First an iron gate and then a door will open into an enormous salon filled with antiques, 300-year-old paintings, and some of the most marvelously preserved walls in Venice. The guest rooms are far less opulent, with contemporary pieces and good beds, plus small bathrooms. The choice rooms are usually booked far in advance, especially for Carnevale.

Campo Bandiera e Moro, Castello 3608, 30122 Venezia. © 041-5285315. Fax 041-5238859. 15 units (showers only). 100€–155€ ($89.30–$138.40) double. Rates include breakfast. MC, V. Vaporetto: Arsenale. **Amenities:** Lounge. *In room:* A/C, TV, minibar, safe.

INEXPENSIVE

Albergo Al Piave *(Value)* For Venice, this centrally located hotel is a real bargain, and the Puppin family welcomes you with style. Although the hotel is rated only one star by the government, its level of comfort is excellent, and its decor and ambience are inviting. Even some guests who could afford to pay more select the Piave for its cozy warmth. The small guest rooms come with clean bathrooms and good beds. A visit here is relaxed and enjoyable.

Ruga Giuffa, Castello 4838–4840, 30122 Venezia. ℂ 041-5285174. Fax 041-5238512. www.elmoro.com. 15 units (showers only). 135€–145€ ($120.55–$129.50) double; 195€–205€ ($174.15–$183.05) suite for 3. Rates include continental breakfast. AE, DC, MC, V. Vaporetto: San Zaccaria. **Amenities:** Lounge. *In room:* A/C, TV, fridge, hair dryer, safe.

Hotel Doni The Doni sits about a 3-minute walk from St. Mark's. Most of its very basic guest rooms overlook either a garden with a tall fig tree or a little canal where four or five gondolas are usually tied up. Simplicity and cleanliness prevail, especially in the down-to-earth rooms. The beds, often brass, are a little worn but still comfortable, and the plumbing is antiquated but still working fine.

Calle de Vin, Castello 4656, 30122 Venezia. ℂ and fax **041-5224267**. 13 units, 3 with private bathroom. 80€ ($71.45) double without bathroom; 105€ ($93.75) double with bathroom. Rates include breakfast. No credit cards. Vaporetto: San Zaccaria. **Amenities:** Lounge. *In room:* No phone.

NEAR THE PONTE DI RIALTO

The epicenter of this neighborhood is the bustling activity of the Rialto Market itself. This area is a mixed bag, with plenty of decaying apartment houses alongside tourist sights. There are some fine shops and restaurants, but also some of the worst tourist traps in Venice. Our recommendations will steer you clear of these.

MODERATE

Hotel Marconi This old relic is still going strong. The Marconi, less than 15m (50 ft.) from the Rialto Bridge, was built in 1500 when Venice was at the height of its supremacy. The drawing-room furnishings would be appropriate for visiting archbishops, and the Maschietto family operates everything efficiently. Only four of the lovely old guest rooms open onto the Grand Canal, and these are the most eagerly sought. The rooms vary from small to medium, each with a comfortable bed, and the small bathrooms are tiled. Meals are served in a room with Gothic chairs, but in fair weather the sidewalk tables facing the Grand Canal are preferred by many.

Riva del Vin, San Polo 729, 30125 Venezia. ℂ **041-5222068**. Fax 041-5229700. www.hotelmarconi.it. 26 units. 68€–310€ ($60.70–$276.85) double; 100€–403€ ($89.30–$359.90) triple. Rates include breakfast. AE, DC, MC, V. Vaporetto: Rialto. **Amenities:** Dining room; lounge; room service; babysitting; laundry/dry cleaning. *In room:* A/C, TV, minibar, hair dryer, safe.

Hotel Rialto The Rialto opens right onto the San Marco side of the Grand Canal at the foot of the Ponte di Rialto, the famous bridge flanked with shops. Its guest rooms combine modern or Venetian furniture with ornate Venetian ceilings and wall decorations. The hotel has been considerably upgraded to second class. All rooms have well-kept bathrooms. The most desirable and expensive doubles overlook the canal.

Riva del Ferro, San Marco 5149, 30124 Venezia. ℂ **041-5209166**. Fax 041-5238958. www.rialtohotel.com. 89 units (half with showers only). 155€–217€ ($138.40–$193.80) double; 207€–387€ ($184.85–$345.60) junior suite. Rates include buffet breakfast. AE, DC, MC, V. Vaporetto: Rialto. **Amenities:** Dining room; bar; room service; babysitting; laundry/dry cleaning. *In room:* A/C, TV, minibar, hair dryer, safe.

Locanda Sturion ★ The facade of this building seems familiar. Then you recognize it from a painting by Carpaccio hanging in the Galleria dell'Academia. In the early 1200s, the Venetian doges commissioned this site where foreign merchants could stay for the night. After long stints as a private residence, the Sturion continues to cater to visitors. A private entrance leads up four steep flights of marble steps, past apartments, to a labyrinth of cozy, clean, but not overly large guest rooms. Most have views over the terra-cotta rooftops of this congested neighborhood; two open onto Grand Canal views. The intimate breakfast room is homey—almost like a parlor, with red brocaded walls, a Venetian chandelier, and a trio of big windows overlooking the canal.

Calle del Sturion, San Polo 679, 30125 Venezia. ✆ 041-5236243. Fax 041-5228378. www.locanda sturion.com. 11 units. 125€–175€ ($111.65–$156.30) double; 175€–250€ ($156.30–$223.25) triple. Rates include continental breakfast. AE, MC, V. Vaporetto: Rialto. **Amenities:** Lounge; room service; babysitting; laundry. *In room:* A/C, TV, minibar, hair dryer, safe.

IN CANNAREGIO

This is one of our favorite sections of Venice because it affords you a chance to see some of the local life. Otherwise, you'd think that nobody lived in Venice except tourists. Nearly a third of the shrinking population of Venice calls Cannaregio home.

EXPENSIVE

Boscolo Grand Hotel dei Dogi ★★ *(Finds* Once an embassy and later a convent, this is one of the hotel secrets of Venice, definitely a hidden gem. On the northern tier of Venice, Dei Dogi looks across the lagoon to the mainland. As you sit in the beautiful little garden of rose bushes, you will think that you've arrived at a Venetian Shangri-La. Acquired by the Boscolo chain in 1998, the hotel lies just a short stroll down the canal from the Church of Madonna dell'Orto, where Tintoretto lies buried. Bedrooms are elegantly decorated in a palatial Venetian style, with gilt and polish. The bathrooms still retain their old-fashioned personality, pouring out either scalding hot or lethally cold water at their own unpredictable pace. Some 18th-century frescoes often decorate the walls of the bedrooms, as do antique mirrors, swag draperies, and doors intricately inlaid with veneer.

Fondamenta Madonna dell'Orto 3500, 30121 Venezia. ✆ **041-2208111.** Fax 041-722278. www.boscolo hotels.com/Dogi. 68 units. 284€–465€ ($253.60–$415.25) double; from 775€ ($692.10) suite. AE, DC, MC, V. Vaporetto: Madonna dell'Orto. **Amenities:** Restaurant; bar; room service; babysitting; laundry/dry cleaning. *In room:* A/C, TV, minibar, hair dryer, safe.

Locanda ai Santi Apostoli ★ *(Kids* If you can't afford the Gritti but you still fantasize about living in a palazzo overlooking the Grand Canal, near the Rialto, here's your chance. This inn isn't cheap, but it's a lot less expensive than the palaces nearby. The hotel is on the top floor of a 15th-century building, and the guest rooms, though simple, are roomy and decorated in pastels, and they often contain antiques. Naturally, the two rooms opening onto the canal are the most requested. The bathrooms are small but tidy. Extra beds can often be set up in the rooms to accommodate children. This is one of three 14th- or 15th-century Venetian palaces still owned by the family that built it.

Strada Nuova, Cannaregio 4391, 30131 Venezia. ✆ **041-5212612.** Fax 041-5212611. www.veneziaweb.com/santiapostoli. 11 units (showers only). 222€ ($198.25) double; 290€ ($258.95) double with Grand Canal view; 390€ ($348.25) suite. Rates include breakfast. AE, DC, MC, V. Vaporetto: Ca d'Oro. **Amenities:** Lounge; babysitting; laundry/dry cleaning. *In room:* A/C, TV, minibar, hair dryer.

MODERATE

Hotel Giorgione ⭐   Here's a modern hotel with traditional Venetian decor. The lounges and public rooms boast fine furnishings and decorative accessories, and the comfortable and stylish guest rooms are designed to coddle guests. Each accommodation comes with an excellent bed and a tiled bathroom. The hotel also has a typical Venetian garden. It's rated second class by the government, but the Giorgione maintains higher standards than many first-class places.

Campo SS. Apostoli, Cannaregio 4587, 30131 Venezia. ✆ **041-5225810.** Fax 041-5239092. www.hotel giorgione.com. 71 units (some with shower only). 130€–310€ ($116.10–$276.85) double; 200€–330€ ($178.60–$294.70) suite. Rates include buffet breakfast. AE, DC, MC, V. Vaporetto: Ca' d'Oro. **Amenities:** Bar; room service; babysitting; laundry. *In room:* A/C, TV, hair dryer, safe.

Hotel San Geremia   For years, the small Geremia was a government-rated one-star hotel that many guests considered worthy of two-star status. In 1997, the government raised it to two stars, justifying an increase in rates. Neither grand nor well-located, the Geremia still fills up every night because it offers value for the money. Located in a modernized early 1900s setting, this hotel is a 5-minute walk from the rail station. Inside, you'll find well-maintained pale-green guest rooms. They're often small, but each comes with a good bed. There's no elevator, but no one can deny that the price is appealing.

Campo San Geremia, Cannaregio 290A, 30121 Venezia. ✆ **041-716245.** Fax 041-5242342. 20 units, 14 with private bathroom (showers only). 90€ ($80.35) double without bathroom; 145€ ($129.50) double with bathroom. Rates include breakfast. Discounts of 20% in winter. AE, MC, V. Vaporetto: Ferrovia. **Amenities:** Lounge. *In room:* TV, hair dryer, safe.

INEXPENSIVE

Hotel Abbazia   The benefit of staying here is that there's no need to transfer onto any vaporetto—you can walk from the rail station, about 10 minutes away. This hotel was built in 1889 as a monastery for barefooted Carmelite monks, who established a verdant garden in what's now the courtyard; it's planted with subtropical plants that thrive, sheltered as they are from the cold Adriatic winds. You'll find a highly accommodating staff and comfortable but very plain guest rooms with well-kept bathrooms. Twenty-five rooms overlook the courtyard, ensuring quiet in an otherwise noisy neighborhood.

Calle Priuli ai Cavaletti, Cannaregio 68, 30121 Venezia. ✆ **041-717333.** Fax 041-717949. www.hotel abbazia.com. 39 units (some with shower only). 78€–212€ ($69.65–$189.30) double. Rates include buffet breakfast. AE, DC, MC, V. Vaporetto: Ferrovia. **Amenities:** Lounge; room service; laundry. *In room:* A/C, TV, minibar, hair dryer, safe.

Hotel Bernardi-Semenzato   This remains a budget favorite north of the Ponte Rialto. It doesn't please everyone, and it's hardly state-of-the-art in spite of mid-1990s renovations; but it's an affordable option in a ridiculously expensive city. The facade looks a little battered, but there is comfort to be found inside. Guests are housed in the main building, with lots of hand-hewn ceiling beams exposed, or else in an annex 3 blocks away. If you're given a room in the annex, you're not being sentenced to some Venetian Siberia; it evokes a Venetian nobleman's apartment. Bedrooms are tastefully furnished, with retiled bathrooms. Murano chandeliers and parquet floors add Venetian grace notes.

Calle de l'Oca, Cannaregio 4363, 30121 Venezia. ✆ **041-5227257.** Fax 041-5222424. 26 units (showers only). 70€–95€ ($62.50–$84.85) double; 85€ ($75.90) triple. AE, MC, V. Rates include breakfast. Vaporetto: Ca' D'Oro. **Amenities:** Room service; babysitting. *In room:* A/C, TV, hair dryer, safe.

Locanda Leon Bianco This converted 13th-century palazzo, north of the Rialto Bridge, offers spacious rooms, three of which provide stunning vistas of the Grand Canal. Each unit is furnished with antiques or reproductions and has a small- to medium-sized bathroom with a tiny stall shower. Some units are a little garish, but if you have a room with a view, you won't mind. The staff is quite helpful. Breakfast is served in your room.

Rio degli Apostoli, Cannaregio 5629. ℂ 041-5233572. www.leonbianco.it. 10 units (showers only). 130€ ($116.10) double with small canal view; 155€ ($138.40) double with view of Grande Canal or suite. Rates include breakfast. Credit cards accepted only to hold a reservation; payment must be in cash or by check. Vaporetto: Ca' D'Oro. **Amenities:** Lounge. *In room:* No phone.

SANTA CROCE

The eastern part of Santa Croce is rarely visited by most visitors, but it represents a slice of authentic Venetian life. Although Santa Croce sprawls all the way to Piazzale Roma, its heart is the Campo San Giacomo dell'Orio.

MODERATE

Hotel San Cassiano Ca' Favretto ⊛ The hotel's gondola pier affords views of the lacy Ca' d'Oro, perhaps Venice's most beautiful building. The hotel is a 14th-century palace (it contained the studio of 19th-c. painter Giacomo Favretto), and the owner has worked closely to preserve the original details, such as a 6m (20-ft.) beamed ceiling in the entrance. Fifteen of the conservatively decorated guest rooms overlook one of two canals, and many are filled with antiques or high-quality reproductions. Generally the housekeeping is excellent. The bathrooms are small but exceedingly well maintained.

Calle della Rosa, Santa Croce 2232, 30135 Venezia. ℂ **041-5241768.** Fax 041-721033. www.sancassiano.it. 35 units. 125€–275€ ($111.65–$245.60) double. Rates include breakfast. AE, DC, MC, V. Vaporetto: San Stae. **Amenities:** Dining room; bar; room service; babysitting. *In room:* A/C, TV, hair dryer, safe.

IN DORSODURO

On the opposite side of the Accademia Bridge from San Marco, Dorsoduro is one of our favorite neighborhoods of Venice, with a real flavor of the city and a dash of funky chic. Accommodations are limited but rather special and full of character.

EXPENSIVE

American Hotel ⊛ *Value* There's nothing American about this ocher building across the Grand Canal from the most heavily touristed areas. The modest lobby is filled with murals, warm colors, and antiques. The guest rooms are comfortably furnished in a Venetian style, but they vary in size; some of the smaller ones are a bit cramped. Each contains a small bathroom. Many rooms with their own private terrace face the canal. On the second floor is a beautiful terrace where guests can relax over drinks. The staff is attentive and helpful.

Campo San Vio, Accademia 628, 30123 Venezia. ℂ **041-5204733.** Fax 041-5204048. www.hotelamerican. com. 29 units. 100€–260€ ($89.30–$232.20) double; 150€–310€ ($133.95–$276.85) triple. Rates include buffet breakfast. AE, MC, V. Vaporetto: Accademia. **Amenities:** Lounge; room service; babysitting. *In room:* A/C, TV, hair dryer, safe.

Ca' Pisani ⊛⊛ *Finds* This is a new boutique hotel for Venice. Its style evokes the 1930s and 1940s, but the setting is a former Venetian nobleman's residence from the end of the 16th century. In the area of the Accademia gallery, accommodations come in a wide variety of styles and sizes, ranging from standard doubles to spacious suites. The style is unusual for Venice in that it concentrates on the avant-garde trends that blossomed "between the wars." The lobby, for example, recalls the forms of Futurism with a wealth of marble and walnut wood. The walls in the bedrooms evoke the graphics of Mondrian. We prefer the two studios with loft sleeping areas. The bedrooms are equipped with modern technology such as room darkening by electric curtains and remote-control door openings. The bathrooms are under "starlight," creating the effect of small shining stars. A roof terrace solarium opens onto the rooftops of Venice. On-site is a wine and cheese bar whose name, La Rivista, comes from an original flower design in 1925 by Fortunato Depero, the Futuristic painter.

Dorsoduro 979A, 30123 Benezia. ℂ 041-2401411. Fax 041-2771061. www.capisanihotel.it. 29 units. 198€–324€ ($176.80–$289.35) double; 271€–375€ ($242–$334.90) suite. Rates include breakfast. AE, DC, MC, V. Closed last 2 weeks of Jan and last 2 weeks of Aug. Vaporetto: Accademia. **Amenities:** Restaurant; bar; access to next-door gym; sauna; room service; babysitting; laundry/dry cleaning. *In room:* A/C, TV, minibar, hair dryer, safe.

MODERATE

Hotel La Calcina Recently renovated (and not a moment too soon), La Calcina lies in a secluded and less-trampled district that used to be the English enclave before the area developed a broader base of tourism. John Ruskin, who wrote *The Stones of Venice,* stayed here in 1877, and he charted the ground for his latter-day compatriots. This pensione is absolutely spotless, and the furnishings are well chosen but hardly elaborate. The guest rooms are cozy and comfortable, each with a comfortable bed and a compact tiled bathroom.

Zattere al Gesuati, Dorsoduro 780, 30123 Venezia. ℂ **041-5206466.** Fax 041-5227045. www.lacalcina.com. 29 units (showers only). 93€–176€ ($83.05–$157.15) double. Rates include buffet breakfast. AE, DC, MC, V. Vaporetto: Zattere. **Amenities:** Restaurant; bar; room service; babysitting; laundry/dry cleaning. *In room:* A/C, hair dryer, safe.

Locanda San Barnaba ⟨★⟩ ⟨*Value*⟩ Unpretentious yet exceedingly charming, this newly restored 16th-century palazzo is open for business again, after a 9-year restoration. Actually, it opened as a hotel in the unfortunate year of 1939 as Europe went to war. Its most winning architectural feature is its deluxe *piano nobile* on the second floor. This is a spacious salon, adorned with frescoes and surrounded by stained-glass windows. The large bedrooms are simply yet comfortably furnished. One of the staff told us, "We aimed for the pure essence of an old-fashioned Italian inn." Bedrooms are designed to evoke themes of long ago—the lover's nest, the philosopher's refuge, the artist's studio, or the playwright's chamber.

Calle del Traghetto 2785–2786 Dorsoduro, 30123 Venezia. ℂ **041-2411233.** Fax 041-2413812. www.locanda-sanbarnaba.com. 13 units (half with shower only). 120€–170€ ($107.15–$151.80) double; 160€–210€ ($142.85–$187.50) suite. Rates include breakfast. AE, DC, MC, V. Vaporetto: Carezzonico. **Amenities:** Bar; room service; laundry. *In room:* A/C, TV, hair dryer.

Pensione Accademia ⟨★★⟩ ⟨*Value*⟩ The Accademia is the most patrician of the pensioni, in a villa whose garden is bounded by the junction of two canals. The interior features Gothic-style paneling, Venetian chandeliers, and Victorian-era furniture, and the upstairs sitting room is flanked by two large windows. This place has long been a favorite of the *Room with a View* crowd of Brits and scholars; it's often booked months in advance. The guest rooms are airy and bright, decorated in part with 19th-century furniture.

Fondamenta Bollani, Dorsoduro 1058, 30123 Venezia. ℂ **041-5237846.** Fax 041-5239152. www.pensione accademia.it. 27 units (showers only). 120€–217€ ($107.15–$193.80) double. Rates include breakfast. AE, DC, MC, V. Vaporetto: Accademia. **Amenities:** Bar; room service; babysitting; laundry/dry cleaning. *In room:* A/C, TV, hair dryer, safe.

INEXPENSIVE

Hotel Galleria   If you've dreamed of opening your windows to find the Grand Canal before you, step through this 17th-century palazzo's leaded-glass doors. But reserve way in advance—these are the cheapest rooms on the canal and the most charming. Six guest rooms varying in size overlook the canal, and the others have partial views that include the Accademia Bridge. The bathrooms are small but were redone in 1998.

Dorsoduro 878A (at the foot of the Accademia Bridge), 30123 Venezia. ℂ **041-5232489.** Fax 041-5204172. www.hotelgaller`a.it. 10 units, 6 with private bathroom (showers only). 85€–90€ ($75.90–$80.35) double without bathroom; 100€–130€ ($89.30–$116.10) double with bathroom. Rates include continental breakfast. AE, DC, MC, V. Vaporetto: Accademia. **Amenities:** Babysitting. *In room:* Hair dryer.

Locanda Montin 🍷 *Finds*   The Montin is an old-fashioned Venetian inn whose adjoining restaurant is one of the area's most loved. The guest rooms are cozy and quaint. Only a few units have private bathrooms, and in-room extras are scarce aside from a phone. Most guests have to share the small corridor bathrooms, which are barely adequate in number, especially if the house is full. The inn is a bit difficult to locate (it's marked by only a small carriage lamp etched with the name) but is worth the search.

Fondamenta di Borgo, Dorsoduro 1147, 31000 Venezia. ℂ **041-5227151.** Fax 041-5200255. 11 units, 5 with bathroom. 100€ ($89.30) double without bathroom; 125€ ($111.65) double with bathroom. AE, DC, MC, V. Vaporetto: Accademia. **Amenities:** Restaurant; bar; laundry/dry cleaning.

ON ISOLA DELLA GIUDECCA

Even though this is traditionally a blue-collar neighborhood, it contains one of the grandest pockets of posh in northeast Italy, the Cipriani. You are isolated if you stay here (and can afford it), but you're just across the water from Piazza San Marco.

VERY EXPENSIVE

Cipriani ★★★   For old-world Venetian splendor, check into the Gritti or Danieli. But for chic, contemporary surroundings, flawless service, and refinement at every turn, the Cipriani is in a class by itself—as long as you can swing its jaw-dropping prices, some of the highest hotel rates in Europe.

Set in a 16th-century cloister on the isolated island of Giudecca (reached by private hotel launch from St. Mark's Square), this pleasure palace was opened in 1958 by Giuseppe Cipriani, the founder of Harry's Bar. The guest rooms range in design from tasteful contemporary to grand antique, but all have splendid views and are sumptuous. We prefer the corner rooms, the most spacious and most elaborately decorated. The bathrooms are large, with phones, deep tubs, robes, and deluxe toiletries.

The Cipriani is the only hotel on Giudecca. The location is either calm, quiet, and exclusive, or inconvenient for exploring the rest of the city, depending on how you look at it. Service is the best in Venice, with two employees for every room. The staff can arrange for tee times at golf courses about 40 minutes away by boat.

Isola della Giudecca 10, 30133 Venezia. ℂ **800/992-5055** in the U.S., or 041-5207744. Fax 041-5207745. www.orient-expresshotels.com. 110 units. 767€–1,177€ ($684.80–$1,050.90) double; from 1,588€ ($1417.85) suite. Rates include breakfast. AE, DC, MC, V. Closed Nov–Mar. Vaporetto: Zitelle. **Amenities:** 2 superb and very expensive restaurants; 3 bars (including a piano bar); Olympic-size swimming pool; Venice's only tennis court; fitness center; Turkish bath and sauna; private boat shuttle; room service; massage; babysitting; laundry/dry cleaning. *In room:* A/C, TV, minibar, hair dryer, safe.

ON THE LIDO

If you can balance it, you can have a beach holiday on the Lido with time out for sightseeing in the heart of Venice.

VERY EXPENSIVE

Hotel des Bains ⭑⭑   This is the best old-world spa hotel along this fabled strip of Adriatic sand. This hotel was built in the grand era of European resort hotels, but long ago lost its supremacy on the Lido to the Excelsior (see below). It has its own wooded park and beach with individual cabanas. Thomas Mann stayed here several times before making it the setting for *Death in Venice,* and later it was used as a set for the film. The renovated interior exudes the flavor of the leisurely life of the Belle Epoque. The guest rooms are large, each elegantly furnished with rich fabrics, Oriental rugs, antiques, and paneled walls.

Lungomare Marconi 17, 30126 Lido di Venezia. ℂ **800/325-3535** in the U.S. and Canada, or 041-5265921. Fax 041-5260113. www.sheraton.com. 191 units. 366€–616€ ($326.85–$550.10) double; from 843€ ($752.80) suite. Rates include breakfast. AE, DC, MC, V. Closed Nov–Mar. Vaporetto: Lido, then bus A, B, or C. **Amenities:** Restaurant; bar; pool; 2 tennis courts; private boat shuttle; room service; babysitting; laundry/dry cleaning. *In room:* A/C, TV, minibar, hair dryer, safe.

Westin Excelsior ⭑⭑⭑   This luxe palace caters to the most pampered beach crowd in Europe. When the Excelsior was built, it was the world's biggest resort hotel, and its presence helped make the Lido fashionable. Today it offers the most luxury on the Lido, although it doesn't have the antique character of the Hotel des Bains (see above). Its guest rooms range in style and amenities, but all have walk-in closets. The good-size bathrooms boast deluxe toiletries and deep tubs. Most of the social life takes place around the angular pool or on the flowered terraces leading up to the cabanas on the sandy beach.

Lungomare Marconi 41, 30126 Venezia Lido. ℂ **800/325-3535** in the U.S. and Canada, or 041-5260201. Fax 041-5267276. www.westin.com. 196 units. 422€–707€ ($376.85–$631.35) double; from 1,375€ ($1,227.90) suite. Rates include breakfast. AE, DC, MC, V. Parking 20€ ($17.85). Closed Nov–Mar 15. Vaporetto: Lido, then bus A, B, or C. **Amenities:** Restaurant; bar; pool; 6 tennis courts; boat rental; private boat shuttle; room service; babysitting; laundry/dry cleaning. *In room:* A/C, TV, minibar, hair dryer, safe.

EXPENSIVE

Hotel Quattro Fontane ⭑   The Quattro Fontane is one of the most charming hotels on the Lido. The trouble is, a lot of people know that, so it's likely to be booked. This former summer home of a 19th-century Venetian family is most popular with the British, who seem to appreciate the homey atmosphere, the garden, the helpful staff, and the rooms with superior luxuries, not to mention the good food served at tables set under shade trees. Many of the guest rooms are furnished with antiques, and all have tile or terrazzo floors and excellent beds.

Via Quattro Fontane 16, 30126 Lido di Venezia. ℂ **041-5260227.** Fax 041-5260726. www.quattro fontane.com. 60 units. 148€–320€ ($132.15–$285.75) double. Rates include buffet breakfast. AE, DC, MC, V. Closed Nov–Apr 4. Vaporetto: Lido, then bus A, B, or C. **Amenities:** Restaurant; bar; tennis court; room service; babysitting; laundry/dry cleaning. *In room:* A/C, TV, minibar, hair dryer, safe.

MODERATE

Hotel Belvedere *Kids*   The modernized Belvedere has been a family favorite since 1857. Right across from the vaporetto stop, the hotel is open year-round, which is unusual for the Lido, and offers simply furnished guest rooms, each with a good bed and tiled bathroom. As an added courtesy, the Belvedere offers guests free entrance to the Casino Municipale; in summer, guests can use the hotel's cabanas on the Lido.

You Oughta Be in Pictures

Venice International Film Festival is second only to Cannes for sheer glamour. It brings together stars, directors, producers, and filmmakers from all over the world during the first week or so of September. Films are shown more or less constantly between 9am and 3am in various areas of the Palazzo del Cinema on the Lido. Although a good number of the seats are reserved for international jury members, the public viewers can attend virtually whenever they want, pending availability. And there's always great people-watching all over the city. For information, contact the **Venice Film Festival,** c/o the La Biennale office, Ca' Giustinian, Calle del Ridotto 1364A, 30124 Venezia. Call ℭ **041-5218838** for details on getting tickets, or check out www.labiennale.org.

Piazzale Santa Maria Elisabetta 4, 30126 Lido di Venezia. ℭ **041-5260115.** Fax 041-5261486. hbelve@tin.it. 30 units (showers only). 125€–155€ ($111.60–$138.40) double. Rates include breakfast. AE, DC, MC, V. Vaporetto: Lido. **Amenities:** Restaurant; bar; room service; babysitting; laundry. *In room:* A/C, TV, hair dryer, safe.

Hotel Helvetia   This 19th-century building, on a side street near the lagoon side of the island, is an easy walk from the vaporetto stop. The quieter guest rooms face away from the street, and rooms in the older wing have Belle Epoque high ceilings and attractively comfortable furniture. The newer wing has a more conservative style. About half of the rooms have recently been renovated. Breakfast is served, weather permitting, in a flagstone-covered wall garden behind the hotel.

Gran Viale 4, 30126 Lido di Venezia. ℭ **041-5260105.** Fax 041-5268903. www.hotelhelvetia.com. 60 units. 100€–190€ ($89.30–$169.65) double. Rates include breakfast. AE, DC, MC, V. Closed Nov–Mar. Vaporetto: Lido. **Amenities:** Bar; room service; babysitting; laundry. *In room:* TV, hair dryer.

4 Where to Dine

Even though Venice doesn't grow much of its own produce, it's surrounded by a rich agricultural district and plentiful vineyards, and it specializes in fresh seafood. Venice's restaurants are among the most expensive in Italy, but we've found some wonderful moderately priced trattorie.

NEAR PIAZZA SAN MARCO
VERY EXPENSIVE

Da Ivo ☙   TUSCAN/VENETIAN   This trattoria draws a faithful crowd. The rustic atmosphere is cozy and relaxing, and tables are bathed in candlelight. Florentines head here for fine Tuscan cookery, but regional Venetian dishes are also served. In season, game, prepared according to ancient traditions, is cooked over an open charcoal grill. One cold December day, our hearts were warmed by homemade tagliatelle topped with slivers of *tartufi bianchi,* the unforgettable pungent white truffle from Piedmont. Dishes change according to the season and the availability of ingredients but are likely to include swordfish, beef carpaccio covered by arugula and parmigiana flakes, or cuttlefish in its own ink.

Calle dei Fuseri, San Marco 1809. ℭ **041-5285004.** Reservations required. Main courses 25€–35€ ($22.35–$31.25). AE, DC, MC, V. Mon–Sat noon–2:30pm and 7pm–midnight. Closed Jan 6–31. Vaporetto: San Marco.

Harry's Bar ★★★ VENETIAN   Harry's Bar serves the best food in Venice, although your tab will be painful. Harry, by the way, is an Italian named Arrigo, son of the late Commendatore Cipriani. Like his father, Arrigo is an entrepreneur extraordinaire known for his fine cuisine. His bar is a big draw for martini-thirsty Americans, but Hemingway and Hotchner always ordered Bloody Marys in their day. The most famous drink, which was originally concocted here, is the Bellini (prosecco and white-peach juice), wonderful when created properly, although we've had a watered-down horror here in the off-season (a real disappointment at 9.50€, $8.50). You can dine in the bar downstairs or the room with a view upstairs. We recommend the Venetian fish soup, followed by the scampi Thermidor with rice pilaf or the seafood ravioli. The food is relatively simple but absolutely fresh.

Calle Vallaresso, San Marco 1323. © 041-5285777. Reservations required. Main courses 40€–57.50€ ($35.70–$51.35). AE, DC, MC, V. Daily 10:30am–11pm. Vaporetto: San Marco.

Quadri ★★★ VENETIAN/INTERNATIONAL   One of Europe's most famous restaurants, Quadri is even better known as a cafe (see section 7 of this chapter, "Venice After Dark"); its elegant premises open onto Piazza San Marco, where a full orchestra often adds to the magic. Many diners come just for the view and are often surprised by the high-quality cuisine and impeccable service (and the whopping tab). Harry's Bar and the Antico Martini serve better food, although the skills of Quadri's chef are considerable. He's likely to tempt you with dishes such as octopus in fresh tomato sauce, salt codfish with polenta, marinated swordfish, and sea bass with crab sauce. Dessert specialties are "baked" ice cream and lemon mousse with fresh strawberry sauce.

Piazza San Marco, San Marco 120–124. © 041-5289299. Reservations required. Main courses 29.50€–38.50€ ($26.35–$34.40). AE, DC, MC, V. Tues–Sun noon–2:30pm (except for July–Aug) and 7–10:30pm. Vaporetto: San Marco.

EXPENSIVE

Antico Martini ★★★ VENETIAN/INTERNATIONAL   Antico Martini elevates Venetian cuisine to its highest level (although we still give Harry's a slight edge over it). Elaborate chandeliers glitter and gilt-framed oil paintings adorn the paneled walls. The courtyard is splendid in summer. An excellent beginning is the *risotto di frutti di mare* in a creamy Venetian style with plenty of fresh seafood. For a main dish, try the *fegato alla veneziana,* tender liver fried with onions and served with polenta. The chefs are better at regional dishes than at international ones. The restaurant has one of the city's best wine lists, featuring more than 350 choices. The yellow Tocai is an interesting local wine and is especially good with fish dishes.

Campo San Fantin, San Marco 1983. © 041-5224121. Reservations required. Main courses 20€–27.50€ ($17.85–$24.55); 4-course fixed-price menu 44.50€–49€ ($39.75–$43.75); 6-course menu degustazione 76€ ($67.85). AE, DC, MC, V. Wed 7–11:30pm; Thurs–Mon noon–2:30pm and 7–11:30pm. Vaporetto: San Marco or Santa Maria del Giglio.

La Caravella ★★ VENETIAN/INTERNATIONAL   This restaurant offers an overblown nautical atmosphere and a leather-bound menu that might make you think that you're in a tourist trap. But you're not. The restaurant contains four dining rooms and a courtyard that's open in summer. The decor is rustically elegant, with frescoed ceilings, flowers, and wrought-iron lighting fixtures. You might begin with an antipasti *misto de pesce* (fish) with olive oil and lemon juice, or prawns with avocado. Star specialties are *granceola* (Adriatic sea crab on

Where to Dine in Venice

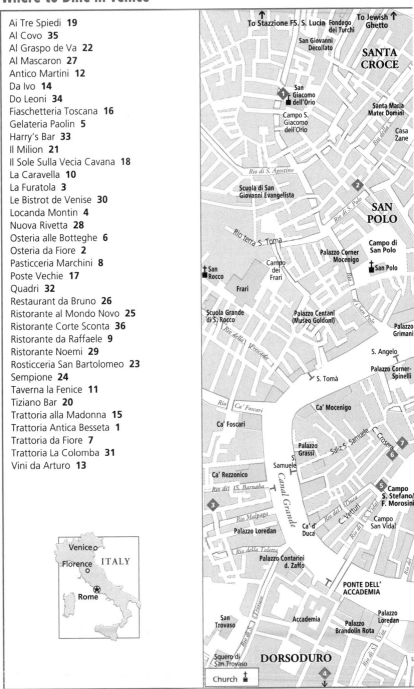

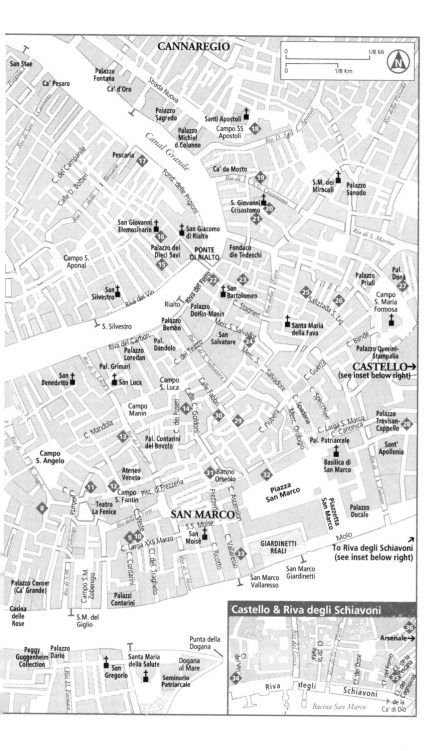

CANNAREGIO

San Stae

Ca' Pesaro

Palazzo Fontana
Ca' d'Oro

Strada Nuova

Palazzo Sagredo

Santi Apostoli
Campo SS Apostoli 18

Palazzo Michiel d.Colonne

Rio D. Sql

Canal Grande

Pescaria 17

C. del Campanile

Calle D. Botteri

Fond. delle Prigioni

Ca' da Mosto

Rio di

19

S.M. dei Miracoli

Palazzo Sanudo

S. Giovanni Crisostomo 20

21

Rio di S. Marina

San Giovanni Elemosinario 16

San Giacomo di Rialto

Palazzo dei Dieci Savi 15

PONTE DI RIALTO

Fondaco die Tedeschi

Campo S. Aponal

San Silvestro

Riva del Vin

Rialto

22

23

San Bartolomeo

C. Stagneri

25

Salizzada S. Liq

26

Palazzo Priuli

Pal. Donà 27

Campo S. Maria Formosa

S. Silvestro

Palazzo Dolfin-Manin

Merc S. Salvador

Santa Maria della Fava

Palazzo Querini-Stampalia

Riva del Carbon

Palazzo Bembo

San Salvatore 24

C. Bande

Palazzo Loredan

Pal. Dandolo

Rio di S. Luca

Pal. Grimari

San Benedetto

San Luca

Campo S. Luca

Calle Fabbri

Merc. S. Salvatore

C. Guerra

CASTELLO →
(see inset below right)

Campo Manin

C. dei Fuseri

Calle C. Goldoni

30

29

C. Fiubera

Merc. Orologo

Mercerie

Spaderia

C. Larga S. Marco

Palazzo Trevisan-Cappello 28

C. Mandola

Rio del Fenzetti

Pal. Contarini del Bovolo

13

C. Canonica

Sant' Apollonia

Campo S. Angelo

Ateneo Veneto

Bacino Orseolo 31

32

Pal. Patriarcale

Basilica di San Marco

Palazzo Ducale

11

12

Campo S. Fantin

Pisc. di Frezzeria

Frezzeria

C. Ascension

Piazza San Marco

Piazzetta San Marco

8

Teatro La Fenice

Rio della Verze

SAN MARCO

S.S. Moisè

San Moisè

C. Vallaresso

GIARDINETTI REALI

Molo

To Riva degli Schiavoni
(see inset below right)

C. Larga XXII Marzo

Cl. del Traghetto

C. Contarini

Rio di S. Moisè

C. Ricotto

33

Palazzo Corner (Ca' Grande)

Rio de S.M.

Campo S.M. Zobenigo

Palazzi Contarini

San Marco Vallaresso

San Marco Giardinetti

Casina delle Rose

S.M. del Giglio

Punta della Dogana

Castello & Riva degli Schiavoni

Arsenale →

Peggy Guggenheim Collection

Palazzo Dario

Rio D. Fornace

Santa Maria della Salute

San Gregorio

Dogana al Mare

Seminario Patriarcale

Cl. de la Pieta

Cl. del Dose

Cl. del Forno

36

34

Riva degli Schiavoni

35

Bacino San Marco

P. de la Ca' di Dio

carpaccio) and chateaubriand for two. The best item to order, however, is one of the poached fish, priced according to weight and served with a tempting sauce. The ice cream in champagne is a soothing finish.

In the Hotel Saturnia International, Calle Larga XXII Marzo, San Marco 2397. © **041-5208901.** Reservations required. Main courses 23.50€–46€ ($21–$41.10); fixed-price lunch 46€ ($41.10). AE, DC, MC, V. Daily noon–3pm and 7pm–midnight. Vaporetto: Santa Maria del Giglio.

Trattoria La Colomba ✿ VENETIAN/INTERNATIONAL   This is one of Venice's most distinctive trattorie, with its history going back at least a century. Modern paintings adorn the walls; they change periodically and are usually for sale. Menu items are likely to include at least five daily specials based on Venice's time-honored cuisine, as well as risotto with mushrooms from the local hills of Montello, and *baccalà alla vicentina* (milk-simmered dry cod seasoned with onions, anchovies, and cinnamon and served with polenta). The fruits and vegetables used are mostly grown on the lagoon islands.

Piscina Frezzeria, San Marco 1665. © **041-5221175.** Reservations recommended. Main courses 17.50€–32.50€ ($15.65–$29). AE, DC, MC, V. Daily noon–2:30pm and 7–11pm. Closed Wed Nov–Apr. Vaporetto: San Marco or Rialto.

MODERATE

Ristorante da Raffaele ✿ ITALIAN/VENETIAN   This is one of the best canal-side restaurants. It's often overrun with tourists, but the veteran kitchen staff handles the onslaught well. The restaurant offers the kind of charm and atmosphere unique to Venice, with its huge inner sanctum and high-beamed ceiling, 17th- to 19th-century pistols and sabers, wrought-iron chandeliers, a massive fireplace, and hundreds of copper pots. The food is excellent, beginning with a choice of tasty antipasti or well-prepared pastas. Seafood specialties include scampi, squid, and deep-fried fish. The grilled meats are wonderful, and the desserts will tempt you off your diet.

Calle Larga XXII Marzo (Fondamenta delle Ostreghe), San Marco 2347. © **041-5232317.** Reservations recommended Sat–Sun. Main courses 12.50€–22.50€ ($11.15–$20.10). AE, DC, MC, V. Fri–Wed noon–3pm and 7–10:30pm. Closed Dec 10 to mid-Feb. Vaporetto: San Marco or Santa Maria del Giglio.

Ristorante Noemi VENETIAN   The decor of this simple place includes a multicolored marble floor in abstract patterns and swag curtains covering big glass windows. The restaurant opened in 1927, named for the matriarch of the family that continues to own it. Specialties, many bordering on *nuova cucina,* include thin black spaghetti with cuttlefish in its own sauce, salmon crepes with cheese, and filet of sole Casanova, with a velouté of white wine, shrimp, and

---

⟮Tips⟯ Fishy Business

Venice's restaurants specialize in the choicest seafood from the Adriatic—but beware that the fish dishes are *very* expensive. On most menus, the price of fresh grilled fish (*pesce alla griglia*) commonly refers to the *etto* (per 100g) and thus is a fraction of the real cost. Have the waiter estimate it before you order, to avoid a shock when your bill comes.

The fish merchants at the Mercato Rialto (Venice's main open-air market) take Monday off, which explains why so many restaurants are closed on Monday. Those that are open on Monday are selling Saturday's goods—beware!

mushrooms. For dessert, try the special lemon sorbet, made with sparkling wine and fresh mint.

Calle dei Fabbri, San Marco 912. © **041-5225238.** Reservations recommended. Main courses 15€–22.50€ ($13.40–$20.10). AE, DC, MC, V. Daily 11:30am–midnight. Vaporetto: San Marco.

Taverna la Fenice ✪✪ ITALIAN/VENETIAN   Opened in 1907, when Venetians were flocking in record numbers to hear the bel canto performances in nearby La Fenice opera house (which burned down a few years ago), this taverna is one of Venice's most romantic dining spots. The interior is suitably elegant, but the preferred spot in fine weather is outdoors beneath a canopy. The service is smooth and efficient. The most appetizing beginning is the selection of seafood antipasti. You might enjoy the *risotto con scampi e arugula,* tagliatelle with cream sauce and exotic mushrooms, tagliatelle with a combination of shrimp and artichokes, turbot roasted with potatoes and tomato sauce, scampi with tomatoes and rice, or *carpaccio alla Fenice.*

Campiello de la Fenice, San Marco 1938. © **041-5223856.** Reservations required. Main courses 12.50€–20€ ($11.15–$17.85). AE, DC, MC, V. Mon–Sat noon–3pm and 7–11pm. Vaporetto: San Marco.

Trattoria da Fiore *(Value* VENETIAN   Don't confuse this trattoria with the well-known and much more expensive Osteria da Fiore. Start with the house specialty, *penne alla Fiore* (prepared with olive oil, garlic, and seven in-season vegetables), and you might be happy to call it a night. Or skip right to another popular specialty, *fritto misto,* comprising more than a dozen varieties of fresh fish and seafood. The *zuppa di pesce* is a soup stocked with mussels, crab, clams, shrimp, and chunks of fresh tuna. This is a great place for an afternoon snack or a light lunch at the Bar Fiore next door (10:30am–10:30pm).

Calle delle Botteghe, San Marco 3461. © **041-5235310.** Reservations suggested. Pasta dishes 6€–14€ ($5.35–$12.50); main courses 10€–20€ ($8.95–$17.85). MC, V. Wed–Mon noon–3pm and 7–10pm. Vaporetto: Accademia.

Vini da Arturo ✪ *(Finds* VENETIAN   Vini da Arturo attracts many devoted regulars to its seven tables, including an artsy crowd. You get delectable local cooking, not just the standard clichés (and not seafood, which could be unique for a Venetian restaurant). Instead of ordering plain pasta, try the tantalizing spaghetti alla Gorgonzola. The beef is also good, especially when prepared with a cream sauce flavored with mustard and pepper. The salads are made with fresh ingredients, often in unusual combinations; particularly interesting is the pappardelle radicchio.

Calle degli Assassini, San Marco 3656. © **041-5286974.** Reservations recommended. Main courses 20€–30€ ($17.85–$26.80). No credit cards. Mon–Sat noon–2:30pm and 7:30–10:30pm. Closed Aug. Vaporetto: San Marco or Rialto.

INEXPENSIVE

Le Bistrot de Venise ✪ VENETIAN   A classic Venetian cuisine, based on time-tested recipes handed down from generations, is served at this well-attended cafe-brasserie, which is also the site of occasional live music and poetry readings. It is countercultural hip, and attracts a lively crowd, often young and often local, until late at night. Many of the recipes are from the 16th century, and until the revival of this bistro were relatively forgotten by Venetian chefs. A soup, for example, is made with rice flour, pomegranates, chicken, and slivered almonds. Ever had baked eel in bay leaf with a rose pepper sauce, or a prawn and Treviso red chicory tartlet in a pumpkin sauce? One of the best dishes is a sausage made of fish and "fruits of the sea" served with a garlic-laced green herb sauce. We're especially fond of their pheasant and wild duck soup, beautifully spiced, and their baked sturgeon with grapes and prunes in a sour sauce. Most dishes except for fresh fish are priced at the lower end of the scale.

Calle dei Fabbri, San Marco 4685. ✆ **041-5236651.** Main courses 13€–25€ ($11.60–$22.35). MC, V. Daily noon–3pm and 7pm–1am. Vaporetto: Rialto.

Osteria alle Botteghe VENETIAN/ITALIAN   Once you've located the bigger-than-life Campo Santo Stefano, you'll find this osteria a great choice for a light snack or an elaborate meal. Hors d'oeuvres (*cichetti*) and fresh sandwiches can be enjoyed at the bar or the window-side counter; more serious diners can choose from pasta dishes or *tavola calda* (a buffet of prepared dishes such as eggplant parmigiana, lasagna, and fresh cooked vegetables in season, reheated when you order) and repair to tables in the back. Vegetarians will be happy with the vegetable lasagna. Classic dishes include a tender Venetian-style liver with polenta.

Calle delle Botteghe, San Marco 3454. ✆ **041-5228181.** Main courses 6€–10€ ($5.35–$8.95). AE, DC, MC, V. Sun–Fri 11am–5:30pm. Vaporetto: Accademia or Sant'Angelo.

CASTELLO/RIVA DEGLI SCHIAVONI
VERY EXPENSIVE

Do Leoni ★★ VENETIAN/INTERNATIONAL   This restaurant offers a panoramic view of a 19th-century equestrian statue ringed with heroic women taming (you guessed it) lions. The restaurant is filled with scarlet and gold, a motif of lions patterned into the carpeting, and reproductions of English furniture. The menu is something to savor. The chef isn't afraid to dip into Venice's culinary attic at times for inspiration—take the boneless sardines fried and left to marinate in onions before being served with fresh pine seeds and Cyprus sultanas. The risottos and pastas are delectable, especially the tagliatelle with scampi and fresh asparagus. We recently enjoyed the fresh filet of turbot with a Prosecco wine sauce. The tenderloin steak Do Leoni was prepared to perfection, but the winning dish at our table was the filet of duck served in a sauce of sweet raisin wine and blood oranges. If weather permits, you can dine out on the piazza.

In the Londra Palace, Riva degli Schiavoni, Castello 4171. ✆ **041-5200533.** Reservations required. Main courses 17.50€–20€ ($15.65–$17.85). AE, DC, MC, V. Restaurant daily noon–3pm and 7:30–10:30pm; bar daily 11am–1am. Vaporetto: San Zaccaria.

Something Sweet

If you're in the mood for some tasty gelato, head to the **Gelateria Paolin,** Campo Stefano Morosini (✆ **041-5225576**), which offers 20 flavors. It has stood on the corner of this busy square since the 1930s, making it Venice's oldest ice-cream parlor. April to October, it's open 8am to midnight; November to March, hours are daily 8am to 8:30pm.

One of the city's finest pastry shops is the **Pasticceria Marchini,** Ponte San Maurizio, San Marco 2769 (✆ **041-5229109**), whose cakes, muffins, and pastries are the stuff of childhood memories for many locals. The pastries include traditional versions of *torte del Doge,* made from almonds and pine nuts; *zaleti,* made from a mix of cornmeal and eggs; and *bigna,* akin to zabaglione, concocted from chocolate and cream. It's open Wednesday to Monday 8:30am to 8:30pm.

MODERATE

Al Covo VENETIAN/SEAFOOD   Al Covo has a special charm because of its atmospheric setting, sophisticated service, and the fine cooking of Cesare Benelli and his Texas-born wife, Diane. Look for a reinvention of a medieval version of fish soup, potato gnocchi flavored with local whitefish, seafood ravioli, linguine blended with zucchini and fresh peas, and delicious fritto misto with scampi, squid, a bewildering array of fish, and deep-fried vegetables such as zucchini flowers. Al Covo prides itself on not having any freezers, guaranteeing that all food is fresh every day.

Campiello della Pescaria, Castello 3968. ℂ 041-5223812. Reservations recommended for dinner. All main courses 21€ ($18.75); fixed-price lunch 29.50€ ($26.35). No credit cards. Fri–Tues 12:45–2pm and 7:30–10pm. Vaporetto: Arsenale.

Al Mascaron VENETIAN   Crowd into one of the three loud, boisterous din-ing rooms, where you'll probably be directed to sit next to a stranger at a long trestle table. The waiters will come by and slam down copious portions of fresh-cooked local specialties: deep-fried calamari, spaghetti with lobster, monkfish in a salt crust, pastas, savory risottos, and Venetian-style calves' liver (which locals prefer rather pink), plus the best seafood of the day made into salads. There's also a convivial bar, where locals drop in to spread the gossip of the day, play cards, and order vino and snacks.

Calle Lunga Santa Maria Formosa, Castello 5225. ℂ 041-5225995. Reservations recommended. Main courses 8€–25€ ($7.15–$22.35). No credit cards. Mon–Sat noon–3pm and 7:30–11pm. Vaporetto: Rialto or San Marco.

Nuova Rivetta *Value* SEAFOOD   Nuova Rivetta is an old-fashioned trattoria where you get good food at a good price. The most popular dish is *frittura di pesce*, a mixed fish fry that includes squid or various other "sea creatures" from the day's market. Other specialties are gnocchi stuffed with spider crab, pastic-cio of fish (a main course), and spaghetti flavored with squid ink. The most typ-ical wine is sparkling prosecco, whose bouquet is refreshing and fruity with a slightly sharp flavor; for centuries, it has been one of the most celebrated wines of the Veneto.

Campo San Filippo, Castello 4625. ℂ 041-5287302. Reservations required. Main courses 7€–15€ ($6.25–$13.40). AE, MC, V. Tues–Sun noon–10pm. Closed July 23–Aug 20. Vaporetto: San Zaccaria.

Ristorante Corte Sconta SEAFOOD   The Corte Sconta is behind a narrow storefront that you'd ignore if you didn't know about this place. This modest restaurant boasts a multicolored marble floor, plain wooden tables, and not much of an attempt at decoration. It has become well known, however, as a gathering place for artists, writers, and filmmakers. It's a fish restaurant, serving a variety of grilled creatures (much of the "catch" is largely unknown in North America). The fresh fish is flawlessly fresh; the gamberi, for example, is placed live on the grill. A great start is marinated salmon with arugula and pomegran-ate seeds in olive oil. If you don't like fish, a tender beef filet is available. The big bar is popular with locals.

Calle del Pestrin, Castello 3886. ℂ 041-5227024. Reservations required. Main courses 12.50€–20€ ($11.15–$17.85). AE, DC, V. Tues–Sat 12:30–2:30pm and 7:30–9:30pm. Closed Jan 7–Feb 7 and July 15–Aug 15. Vaporetto: Arsenale.

INEXPENSIVE

Restaurant da Bruno VENETIAN   On a narrow street about halfway between the Rialto Bridge and Piazza San Marco, this "country taverna" grills its meats on an open-hearth fire. You get your antipasti at the counter and watch your prosciutto being prepared—paper-thin slices of spicy ham wrapped around breadsticks (*grissini*). In season, Bruno does some of Venice's finest game dishes. If it's featured, try the *capriolo* (roebuck) or *fagiano* (pheasant). A typical Venetian dish prepared well here is zuppa di pesce. Other specialties are beef filet with pepper sauce, scampi and calamari, veal scaloppini with wild mushrooms, and squid with polenta.

Calle del Paradiso San Lio, Castello 5731. (C) **041-5221480.** Main courses 8€–13.50€ ($7.15–$12.05); fixed-price menu 12.50€ ($11.15). AE, DC, MC, V. Daily noon–3pm and 6:30–10pm. Vaporetto: San Marco or Rialto.

NEAR THE PONTE DI RIALTO
EXPENSIVE
Il Sole Sulla Vecia Cavana ★ *Finds* SEAFOOD   This restaurant is off the tourist circuit and well worth the trek through the winding streets. A *cavana* is a place where gondolas are parked, a sort of liquid garage, and the site of this restaurant was such a place in the Middle Ages. When you enter, you'll be greeted by brick arches, stone columns, terra-cotta floors, framed modern paintings, and a photo of 19th-century fishermen relaxing after a day's work. The menu specializes in seafood, such as a mixed grill from the Adriatic, fried scampi, fresh sole, squid, three types of risotto (each with seafood), and a spicy zuppa di pesce. *Antipasti di pesce Cavana* is an assortment of just about every kind of seafood. The food is authentic and seems prepared for the Venetian palate—not necessarily for the visitor's.

Rio Terà SS. Apostoli, Cannaregio 4624. (C) **041-5287106.** Reservations recommended. Main courses 20€–30€ ($17.85–$26.80); fixed-price menu 50€ ($44.65). AE, DC, MC, V. Tues–Sun noon–3pm and 6:30–10:30pm. Vaporetto: Ca' d'Oro.

MODERATE
Al Graspo de Va ★ SEAFOOD/VENETIAN   "The Bunch of Grapes" is a great place for a special meal. Decorated in old taverna style, it offers several air-conditioned dining rooms. One has a beamed ceiling, hung with garlic and copper bric-a-brac. Among Venice's best fish restaurants, it has hosted biggies such as Liz Taylor and Jeanne Moreau. You can help yourself to all the hors d'oeuvres you want (the menu tells you it's "self-service mammoth"). Next try the *gran fritto dell'Adriatico*, a mixed treat of deep-fried fish. The desserts are also good, especially the peach Melba.

Calle Bombaseri, San Marco 5094. (C) **041-5200150.** Reservations required. Main courses 25€–32€ ($22.35–$28.60). AE, DC, MC, V. Tues–Sun noon–3pm and 7–11pm. Closed Aug 5–20. Vaporetto: Rialto.

Fiaschetteria Toscana ★ *Value* VENETIAN   The service at this hip restaurant might be uneven and the staff might be frantic, but lots of local foodies come here to celebrate special occasions or to soak in the see-and-be-seen ambience. The dining rooms are on two levels, the upstairs of which is somewhat more claustrophobic. In the evening, the downstairs is especially appealing with its romantic candlelit ambience. Menu items include *frittura della Serenissima* (a mixed platter of fried seafood with vegetables), veal scallops with lemon-Marsala sauce and mushrooms, ravioli stuffed with whitefish and herbs, and several kinds of Tuscan-style beefsteak.

Campo San Giovanni Crisostomo, Cannaregio 5719. (C) **041-5285281.** Reservation required. Main courses 12€–33€ ($10.70–$29.45). AE, DC, MC, V. Wed–Sun 12:30–2:30pm and 7:30–10:30pm; Mon 12:30–2:30pm. Vaporetto: Rialto.

Il Milion VENETIAN   With a tradition extending back more than 300 years and a location near the rear of San Giovanni Crisostomo, this restaurant is named after the book written by Marco Polo, *Il Milion,* describing his travels. In fact, it occupies a town house once owned by members of the explorer's family. The bar, incidentally, is a favorite with some of the gondoliers. The menu items read like a Who's Who of Venetian platters, each fresh and well prepared. Examples are veal kidneys, calves' liver with fried onions, grilled sardines, spaghetti with clams, risotto with squid ink, and fritto misto of fried fish. The staff is charming and friendly.

Corte Prima al Milion, Cannaregio 5841. © 041-5229302. Reservations recommended. Main courses 11€–17.50€ ($9.80–$15.65). MC, V. Thurs–Tues noon–3pm and 6:30–11pm. Closed Aug. Vaporetto: Rialto.

Poste Vechie 🗲 SEAFOOD   This charming restaurant is near the Rialto fish market and is connected to the rest of the city by a small privately owned bridge. It opened in the early 1500s as a post office, and the kitchen used to serve food to fortify the mail carriers. Today it's the oldest restaurant in Venice, with a pair of intimate rooms (both graced with paneling, murals, and 16th-c. mantelpieces) and a courtyard. Menu items include superfresh fish from the nearby markets; a salad of shellfish and exotic mushrooms; tagliolini flavored with squid ink, crabmeat, and fish sauce; and the pièce de résistance, *seppie* (cuttlefish) *à la veneziana* with polenta. If you don't like fish, calves' liver or veal shank with ham and cheese are also well prepared. The desserts come rolling to your table on a trolley and are usually delicious.

Pescheria Rialto, San Polo 1608. © 041-721822. Reservations recommended. Main courses 12.50€–22.50€ ($11.15–$20.10). AE, DC, MC, V. Wed–Mon noon–3:30pm and 7–10:30pm. Vaporetto: Rialto.

Ristorante al Mondo Novo VENETIAN/SEAFOOD   This restaurant offers professional service and a kindly staff. Plus, it stays open later than many of its nearby competitors. Menu items include a selection of seafood, prepared as *frittura misto dell'Adriatico,* or charcoal grilled. Other items are *maccheroni alla verdura* (with fresh vegetables and greens), an antipasti of fresh fish, and beef filets with pepper sauce and rissole potatoes. Locals who frequent the place always order the fresh fish because the owner is a wholesaler in the Rialto fish market.

Salizzada di San Lio, Castello 5409. © 041-5200698. Reservation recommended. Main courses 12.50€–21€ ($11.15–$18.75). AE, DC, MC, V. Daily 11:30am–11pm. Vaporetto: Rialto or San Marco.

Rosticceria San Bartolomeo VENETIAN/ITALIAN   This *rosticceria* is Venice's most popular fast-food place and has long been a blessing for cost-conscious travelers. Downstairs is a tavola calda where you can eat standing up, but upstairs is a restaurant with waiter service. Typical dishes are *baccalà alla vicentina* (codfish simmered in herbs and milk), deep-fried mozzarella (which the Italians call *in carrozza*), and *seppie con polenta* (squid in its own ink sauce, served with polenta). Everything is accompanied with typical Veneto wine.

Calle della Bissa, San Marco 5424A. © 041-5223569. Main courses 10€–22.50€ ($8.95–$20.10). AE, DC, MC, V. Mon 9:30am–3:30pm; Tues–Sun 9:30am–9:30pm (for Carnevale open daily). Vaporetto: Rialto.

Sempione VENETIAN   Sempione does an admirable job of feeding locals and visitors and has done so for almost 90 years. Set adjacent to a canal in a 15th-century building near Piazza San Marco, it contains three dining rooms done in a soothingly traditional style, a well-trained staff, and a kitchen focusing on traditional cuisine. Examples are grilled fish, spaghetti with crabmeat, risotto with fish, fish soup, and delectable Venetian calves' liver that hasn't been significantly changed since the restaurant was founded. Try for a table by the window so you can watch the gondolas glide by.

Ponte Beretteri, San Marco 578. *©* 041-5226022. Reservations recommended. Main courses 12.50€–22.50€ ($11.15–$20.10). AE, DC, MC, V. Daily 11:30am–3pm and 6:30–10pm. Closed Thurs Nov–Dec. Vaporetto: Rialto.

INEXPENSIVE

Ai Tre Spiedi *(Finds)* VENETIAN   Venetians bring their visiting friends here to make a good impression without breaking the bank and then swear them to secrecy. Rarely will you find such a pleasant setting and such an appetizing meal as you will in this casually elegant trattoria. There's reasonably priced fresh fish plus selections to keep meat-eaters happy as well. If you order a la carte, ask the English-speaking waiters to estimate the cost of your fish entree because it'll typically appear priced by the *etto* (100g).

Salizzada San Cazian, Cannaregio 5906. *©* 041-5208035. Main courses 9€–15€ ($8.05–$13.40). AE, MC, V. Tues–Sat noon–2:30pm and 7–9:30pm; Sun 12:30–3:30pm. Vaporetto: Rialto.

Tiziano Bar SANDWICHES/PASTA/PIZZA   The Tiziano Bar is a tavola calda (hot table). There's no waiter service; you eat standing at a counter or sitting on one of the high stools. The place is known in Venice for selling pizza by the yard. From noon to 3pm, it serves hot pastas such as rigatoni and cannelloni. But throughout the day you can order sandwiches or perhaps a plate of mozzarella.

Salizzada San Crisostomo, Cannaregio 5747, in front of the Sanctuary. *©* 041-5235544. Main courses 7.50€–9€ ($6.70–$8.05). MC, V. Daily 7:30am–10:30pm. Vaporetto: Rialto.

Trattoria alla Madonna VENETIAN   No, this place has nothing to do with *that* Madonna. It opened in 1954 in a 300-year-old building and is one of Venice's most characteristic trattorie, specializing in traditional Venetian recipes and grilled fresh fish. A good beginning might be the antipasto frutti di mare. Pastas, polentas, risottos, meats (including *fegato alla veneziana,* liver with onions), and many kinds of irreproachably fresh fish are widely available.

Calle della Madonna, San Polo 594. *©* 041-5223824. Reservations recommended but not always accepted. Main courses 11€–20€ ($9.80–$17.85). AE, MC, V. Thurs–Tues noon–3pm and 7:15–10pm. Closed Dec 24–Jan and Aug 4–17. Vaporetto: Rialto.

IN SANTA CROCE
MODERATE

Trattoria Antica Besseta VENETIAN   If you manage to find this place (go with a good map), you'll be rewarded with true Venetian cuisine at its most unpretentious. Head for Campo San Giacomo dell'Orio; then negotiate your way across infrequently visited piazzas and winding alleys. Push through saloon doors into a bar area filled with modern art. The dining room is hung with paintings and illuminated with wagon-wheel chandeliers. Nereo Volpe and his wife, Mariuccia, and one of their sons are the guiding force, the chefs, the buyers, and even the "talking menus." The food depends on what looked good in the market that morning, so the menu could include roast chicken, fried scampi, fritto misto, spaghetti in sardine sauce, various roasts, and a selection from the day's catch. The Volpe family produces two kinds of their own wine, a Pinot Blanc and a Cabernet.

Campo SS. de Ca' Zusto, Santa Croce 1395. *©* 041-721687. Reservations required. Main courses 13€–17.50€ ($11.60–$15.65). AE, MC, V. Thurs–Mon noon–2:30pm and 7–10:30pm; Wed 7–10:30pm. Vaporetto: Rive di Biasio.

IN SAN POLO
EXPENSIVE
Osteria da Fiore ⭐ *(Finds)* SEAFOOD   The breath of the Adriatic seems to blow through this place, although how the wind finds this little restaurant tucked away in a labyrinth is a mystery. The imaginative fare depends on the availability of fresh fish and produce. If you love seafood, you'll find everything from scampi to *granceola* (a type of spider crab). In days gone by, we've sampled fried calamari, risotto with scampi, tagliata with rosemary, *masenette* (tiny green crabs that you eat shell and all), and *canoce* (mantis shrimp). For your wine, we suggest Prosecco, with a distinctive golden color and a bouquet that's refreshing and fruity.

Calle del Scaleter, San Polo 2202. © 041-721308. Reservations required. Main courses 32.50€–41€ ($29–$36.60). AE, DC, MC, V. Tues–Sat 12:30–2:30pm and 8–10:30pm. Closed 3 weeks in Aug and Dec 25–Jan 14. Vaporetto: San Tomà.

IN DORSODURO
MODERATE
La Furatola SEAFOOD   La Furatola is very much a neighborhood hangout that has captured the imagination of local foodies. It occupies a 300-year-old building, along a narrow flagstone-paved street that you'll need a good map and a lot of patience to find. Perhaps you'll have lunch here after a visit to San Rocco, a short distance away. In the simple dining room, the specialty is fish brought to your table in a wicker basket so that you can judge its size and freshness by its bright eyes and red gills. A display of seafood antipasti is set out near the entrance. A standout is the baby octopus boiled and served with a drop of red-wine vinegar. Eel comes with a medley of mixed fried fish, including baby cuttlefish, prawns, and squid rings.

Calle Lunga San Barnaba, Dorsoduro 2870A. © 041-5208594. Reservations required. Main courses 25€–42.50€ ($22.35–$37.95). AE, DC, MC, V. Fri–Sun and Tues–Wed 12:30–2:30pm and 7:30–10:30pm; Mon 7:30–10:30pm. Closed Aug and Jan. Vaporetto: Ca' Rezzonico.

Locanda Montin ⭐ INTERNATIONAL/ITALIAN   This mellow old inn offers the most authentic Venetian dining in the city. The Montin opened after World War II and has hosted Ezra Pound, Jackson Pollock, Mark Rothko, and the artist friends of the late Peggy Guggenheim. It's owned and run by the Carretins, who have covered the walls with paintings donated by or bought from their many friends and guests. The arbor-covered garden courtyard is filled with regulars, many of whom allow their favorite waiter to select most of the items for their meal. The frequently changing menu includes a variety of salads, grilled meats, and fish caught in the Adriatic. Desserts might include *semifreddo di fragoline,* a tempting chilled liqueur-soaked cake, capped with whipped cream and wild strawberries.

Fondamenta di Borgo, Dorsoduro 1147. © 041-5227151. Reservations recommended. Main courses 11€–20€ ($9.80–$17.85). AE, DC, MC, V. Thurs–Tues 12:30–2:30pm; Wed–Mon 7:30–10pm. Closed 10 days in mid-Aug and 20 days in Jan. Vaporetto: Accademia.

ON ISOLA DELLA GUIDECCA
VERY EXPENSIVE
Ristorante Cipriani ⭐⭐⭐ ITALIAN   The grandest of the hotel restaurants, the Cipriani offers a sublime but relatively simple cuisine, with the freshest of ingredients used by one of the best-trained staffs along the Adriatic. This isn't the place to bring the kids—in fact, children under 6 aren't allowed (a babysitter can be arranged). You can dine in the formal room with Murano

chandeliers and Fortuny curtains when the weather is nippy or on the extensive terrace overlooking the lagoon. Freshly made pasta is a specialty, and it's among the finest we've ever sampled. Try the *taglierini verdi* with noodles and ham au gratin. Chef's specialties include mixed fried scampi and squid with tender vegetables, and sautéed veal filets with spring artichokes. Come here in October for the last Bellinis of the white peach season and the first white truffles of the season served in champagne risotto.

In the Hotel Cipriani, Isola della Giudecca 10. ℂ 041-5207744. Reservations required. Main courses 33€–37€ ($29.45–$33.05). AE, DC, MC, V. Daily 12:30–3pm and 8–10:30pm. Closed Jan 7–Mar 15. Vaporetto: Zitelle.

EXPENSIVE
Harry's Dolci ☆ INTERNATIONAL/ITALIAN The folks behind famed Harry's Bar (see earlier in this section) have established their latest enclave far from the crowds of Piazza San Marco on this little-visited island. From the quayside windows of this chic place, you can watch seagoing vessels, from yachts to lagoon barges. White napery and uniformed waiters grace a modern room, where no one minds if you order only coffee and ice cream or perhaps a selection from the large pastry menu (the zabaglione cake is divine). Popular items are carpaccio Cipriani, chicken salad, club sandwiches, gnocchi, and house-style cannelloni. The dishes are deliberately kept simple, but each is well prepared.

Fondamenta San Biagio 773, Isola della Giudecca. ℂ 041-5208337. Reservations recommended, especially Sat–Sun. Main courses 16€–28.50€ ($14.30–$25.45); fixed-price menu 42.50€–47.50€ ($37.95–$42.40). AE, MC, V. Wed–Mon noon–3pm and 7–10:30pm. Closed Nov–Mar 22. Vaporetto: Santa Eufemia.

MODERATE
Cip's Club ☆ VENETIAN/ITALIAN On the island of Giudecca, site of the plush Hotel Cipriani, this is a hot new spot for dining. It's reached by private launch from the Piazza San Marco and makes for a delightful afternoon lunch. Cip's is informal and much more reasonable in price than Ristorante Cipriani. Tables are set out with a panoramic sweep toward San Marco. The menu makes the most of local ingredients and delights with freshly made antipasti, including barely cooked mantis shrimp over soft mesclun or tagliatelle with gorgonzola and that bitter but tasty radicchio from nearby Treviso. The Venetian-style liver served here, the city's specialty, is among Venice's finest—thin and tender. The fresh fish of the day is grilled to perfection. You can also order a wide variety of pizzas.

In the Hotel Cipriani, Isola della Giudecca 10. ℂ 041-5207744. Reservations required. Main courses 35€–38€ ($31.25–$33.95). AE, DC, MC, V. Daily noon–3pm and 7:30–10pm. Vaporetto: Zitelle.

ON THE LIDO
MODERATE
Favorita SEAFOOD Occupying two rustic dining rooms and a garden, Favorita is a Lido favorite. It has thrived since the 1920s, operated by the Pradel family, now in its third generation of ownership. Their years of experience contribute to flavorful, impeccably prepared seafood and shellfish, many of them grilled. Try the *trenette* (spaghettilike pasta) with baby squid and eggplant, potato-based gnocchi with crabs from the Venetian lagoon, and grilled versions of virtually every fish in the Adriatic, including eel, sea bass, turbot, and sole.

Via Francesco Duodo 33, Lido di Venezia. ℂ 041-5261626. Main courses 11.50€–30€ ($10.25–$26.80). AE, DC, MC, V. Tues 7:30–10:30pm; Wed–Sun 12:30–2:30pm and 7:30–10:30pm. Vaporetto: Lido.

Ristorante Belvedere VENETIAN   Outside the big hotels, the best food on the Lido is served at the Belvedere, across from the vaporetto stop. It attracts a lot of locals, who come here knowing that they can get some of the best fish along the Adriatic. The main dining room is attractive, with cane-backed bentwood chairs and big windows. In back is a busy cafe with its own entrance. Main dishes include the chef's special sea bass, grilled *dorade* (or sole), and fried scampi. You might begin with the special fish antipasti or *spaghetti en papillote* (cooked in parchment).

Piazzale Santa Maria Elisabetta 4, Lido di Venezia. ℂ 041-5260115. Reservations recommended. Main courses 8€–17.50€ ($7.15–$15.65); fixed-price menu 17.50€ ($15.65). AE, DC, MC, V. Tues–Sun noon–2:30pm and 7–9:30pm. Closed Nov 4–Easter. Vaporetto: Lido.

5 Seeing the Sights

Venice appears to have been created specifically to entertain its legions of callers. Ever since the body of St. Mark was smuggled out of Alexandria and entombed in the basilica, the city has been host to a never-ending stream of visitors, famous, infamous, and otherwise. Venice has perpetually captured the imagination of poets and artists. Wordsworth, Byron, and Shelley addressed poems to the city, and it has been written about or used as a setting by many contemporary writers.

In the pages ahead, we'll explore the city's great art and architecture. But, unlike Florence, Venice would reward its guests with treasures even if they never ducked inside a museum or church. Take some time just to stroll and let yourself get lost in this gorgeous city.

ST. MARK'S SQUARE (PIAZZA SAN MARCO) ✦✦✦

Piazza San Marco was the heart of Venice in the heyday of its glory as a seafaring republic. If you have only 1 day for Venice, you need not leave the square: Some of the city's major attractions, such as St. Mark's Basilica and the Doge's Palace, are centered here or nearby.

The traffic-free square, frequented by visitors and pigeons and sometimes even by Venetians, is a source of bewilderment and interest. If you rise at dawn, you can almost have the piazza to yourself; as you watch the sun come up, the sheen of gold mosaics glistens with a mystical beauty. At around 9am, the overstuffed pigeons are fed by the city (if you're caught under the whir, you'll think that you're witnessing a remake of Hitchcock's *The Birds*). At midafternoon the tourists reign supreme, and it's not surprising in July to witness a scuffle over a camera angle. At sunset, when the two Moors in the Clock Tower strike the end of another day, lonely sailors begin a usually frustrated search for those hot spots that characterized the Venice of yore. Deeper into the evening, the strollers parade by or stop for an espresso at the Caffè Florian and sip while listening to the orchestra play.

Thanks to Napoleon, the square was unified architecturally. The emperor added the Fabbrica Nuova facing the basilica, thus bridging the Old and New Procuratie on either side. Flanked with medieval-looking palaces, Sansovino's Library, elegant shops, and colonnades, the square is now finished—unlike Piazza della Signoria in Florence.

If Piazza San Marco is Europe's drawing room, then the piazza's satellite, **Piazzetta San Marco** ✦, is Europe's antechamber. Hedged in by the Doge's Palace, Sansovino's Library, and a side of St. Mark's, the tiny square faces the

Grand Canal. Two tall granite columns grace the square. One is surmounted by a winged lion, representing St. Mark. The other is topped by a statue of a man taming a dragon, supposedly the dethroned patron saint Theodore. Both columns came from the East in the 12th century.

During Venice's heyday, dozens of victims either lost their heads or were strung up here, many of them first subjected to torture that would've made the Marquis de Sade flinch. One, for example, had his teeth hammered in, his eyes gouged out, and his hands cut off before being strung up. Venetian justice became notorious throughout Europe. If you stand with your back to the canal, looking toward the south facade of St. Mark's, you'll see the so-called *Virgin and Child of the Poor Baker,* a mosaic honoring Pietro Fasiol (also Faziol), a young man unjustly sentenced to death on a charge of murder.

To the left of the entrance to the Doge's Palace are four porphyry figures, whom, for want of a better description, the Venetians called "Moors." These puce-colored fellows are huddled close together, as if afraid. Considering the decapitations and tortures that have occurred on the piazzetta, it's no wonder.

St. Mark's Basilica (Basilica di San Marco) ★★★   Dominating Piazza San Marco is the Church of Gold (*Chiesa d'Oro*), one of the world's greatest and most richly embellished churches, its cavernous candlelit interior gilded with mosaics added over some 7 centuries. In fact, it looks as if it had been moved intact from Istanbul. The basilica is a conglomeration of styles, although it's particularly indebted to Byzantium. Like Venice, St. Mark's is adorned with booty from every corner of the city's once far-flung mercantile empire: capitals from Sicily, columns from Alexandria, porphyry from Syria, and sculpture from old Constantinople.

The basilica is capped by a dome that, like a spider plant, sends off shoots—in this case, a quartet of smaller-scale bulbed cupolas. Spanning the facade is a loggia, surmounted by replicas of the four famous St. Mark's horses, the *Triumphal Quadriga.* The facade's rich marble slabs and mosaics depict scenes from the lives of Christ and St. Mark. One of the mosaics re-creates the entry of the evangelist's body into Venice—according to legend, St. Mark's body, hidden in a pork barrel, was smuggled out of Alexandria in A.D. 828 and was shipped to Venice. The evangelist dethroned Theodore, the Greek saint who up until then had been the patron of the city that had outgrown him.

In the **atrium** are six cupolas with mosaics illustrating scenes from the Old Testament, including the story of the Tower of Babel. The interior of the basilica, once the private chapel and pantheon of the doges, is a stunning wonderland of marbles, alabaster, porphyry, and pillars. You'll walk in awe across the undulating multicolored ocean floor, patterned with mosaics.

To the right is the **baptistry,** dominated by the Sansovino-inspired baptismal font, upon which John the Baptist is ready to pour water. If you look back at the aperture over the entry, you can see a mosaic of the dance of Salome in front of Herod and his court. Salome, wearing a star-studded russet-red dress and three

Tips **A St. Mark's Warning**

A dress code for men and women prohibiting shorts, bare arms and shoulders, and skirts above the knee is strictly enforced at all times in the basilica. You *will* be turned away. In addition, you must remain silent and cannot take photographs.

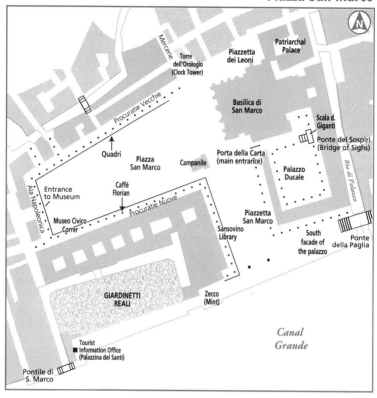

white fox tails, is dancing under a platter holding John the Baptist's head. Her glassy face is that of a Madonna, not an enchantress.

After touring the baptistry, proceed up the right nave to the doorway to the oft-looted **treasury (*tesoro*)** . Here you'll find the inevitable skulls and bones of some ecclesiastical authorities under glass, plus goblets, chalices, and Gothic candelabra. The entrance to the **presbytery** is nearby. In it, on the high altar, the alleged sarcophagus of St. Mark rests under a green marble blanket and is held by four Corinthian alabaster columns. Behind the altar is the rarest treasure at St. Mark's: the Byzantine-style **Pala d'Oro** , a golden altar screen measuring 3m by 1m (10 ft. by 4 ft.). It's set with 300 emeralds, 300 sapphires, 400 garnets, 100 amethysts, and 1,300 pearls, plus rubies and topazes accompanying 157 enameled rondels and panels. Second in importance is the 10th-century *Madonna di Nicopeia,* a bejeweled icon taken from Constantinople and exhibited in its own chapel to the left of the high altar.

After leaving the basilica, head up the stairs in the atrium to the **Marciano Museum** and the **Loggia dei Cavalli.** The star of the museum is the world-famous *Triumphal Quadriga* , four horses looted from Constantinople by Venetian crusaders during the sack of that city in 1204. These horses once sur-mounted the basilica but were removed because of pollution damage and were subsequently restored. This is the only *quadriga* (a quartet of horses yoked together) to have survived from the Classical era, believed to have been cast in

---

Impressions

Venice is like eating an entire box of chocolate liqueurs at one go.

—Truman Capote

---

the 4th century. Napoleon once carted these much-traveled horses off to Paris for the Arc de Triomphe du Carrousel, but they were returned to Venice in 1815. The museum, with its mosaics and tapestries, is especially interesting, but also be sure to walk out onto the loggia for a view of Piazza San Marco.

Piazza San Marco. ✆ 041-5225205. Basilica free; treasury 2€ ($1.80); presbytery 1.50€ ($1.35); Marciano Museum 1.50€ ($1.35). Basilica and presbytery Apr–Sept Mon–Sat 9:30am–5:30pm, Sun 2–5:30pm; Oct–Mar Mon–Sat 10am–4:30pm, Sun 2–4:30pm. Treasury Mon–Sat 9:30am–5pm; Sun 2–5pm. Marciano Museum Apr–Sept Mon–Sat 10am–5:30pm, Sun 2–4:30pm; Oct–Mar Mon–Sat 10am–4:30pm, Sun 2–4:30pm. Vaporetto: San Marco.

Campanile di San Marco ★★   One summer night in 1902, the bell tower of St. Mark's, suffering from years of rheumatism in the damp Venetian climate, gave out a warning sound that sent the fashionable coffee drinkers in the piazza below scurrying for their lives. But the campanile gracefully waited until the next morning, July 14, before tumbling into the piazza. The Venetians rebuilt their belfry, and it's now safe to climb to the top. Unlike Italy's other bell towers, where you have to brave narrow, steep spiral staircases to reach the top, this one has an elevator so that you can get a pigeon's view. It's a particularly good vantage point for viewing the cupolas of the basilica.

Piazza San Marco. ✆ 041-5224064. Admission 5€ ($4.45). Oct–Feb daily 9:30am–4pm; Mar–June daily 9am–7pm; July–Sept daily 9am–9pm. Closed Jan 7–31. Vaporetto: San Marco.

Clock Tower (Torre dell'Orologio)   The two Moors striking the bell atop this Renaissance clock tower, soaring over the Old Procuratie, are one of the most characteristic Venetian scenes. The clock under the winged lion not only tells the time but also is a boon to the astrologer: It matches the signs of the zodiac with the position of the sun. If the movement of the Moors striking the hour seems slow in today's fast-paced world, remember how many centuries the poor wretches have been at their task without time off. The "Moors" originally represented two European shepherds, but after having been reproduced in bronze, they've grown darker with the passing of time. As a consequence, they came to be called Moors by the Venetians.

The base of the tower has always been a favorite *punto di incontro* ("meet me at the tower") for Venetians and is the entrance to the ancient **Mercerie** (from the word for merchandise), the principal souklike retail street of both high-end boutiques and trinket shops that zigzags its way to the Rialto Bridge.

Piazza San Marco. ✆ 041-5224951. Admission 9€ ($8.05). Daily 9am–3:30pm. Vaporetto: San Marco.

Ducal Palace & Bridge of Sighs (Palazzo Ducale & Ponte dei Sospiri) ★★★   You enter the Palace of the Doges through the magnificent 15th-century **Porta della Carta** ★★ at the piazzetta. This Venetian Gothic palazzo gleams in the tremulous light somewhat like a frosty birthday cake in pinkish-red marble and white Istrian stone. Italy's grandest civic structure, it dates to 1309, although a 1577 fire destroyed much of the original building. That fire made ashes of many of the palace's masterpieces and almost spelled doom for the building itself because the new architectural fervor of the post-Renaissance was in the air. However, sanity prevailed. Many of the greatest Venetian painters of

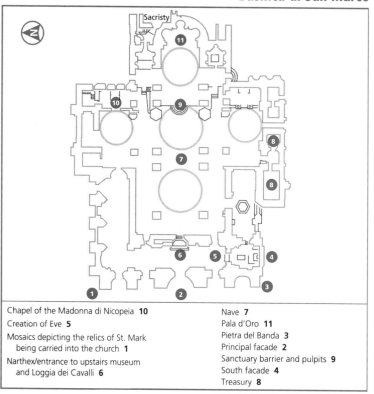

Chapel of the Madonna di Nicopeia **10**
Creation of Eve **5**
Mosaics depicting the relics of St. Mark
  being carried into the church **1**
Narthex/entrance to upstairs museum
  and Loggia dei Cavalli **6**

Nave **7**
Pala d'Oro **11**
Pietra del Banda **3**
Principal facade **2**
Sanctuary barrier and pulpits **9**
South facade **4**
Treasury **8**

the 16th century contributed to the restored palace, replacing the canvases or frescoes of the old masters.

If you enter from the piazzetta, past the four porphyry Moors, you'll be in the splendid Renaissance courtyard, one of the most recent additions to a palace that has benefited from the work of many architects with widely varying tastes. To get to the upper loggia, you can take the **Giants' Stairway (Scala dei Giganti),** so called because of the two Sansovino statues of mythological figures.

If you want to understand something of this magnificent palace, the fascinating history of the 1,000-year-old Maritime Republic, and the intrigue of the government that ruled it, search out the infrared **audioguide** at the entrance, which costs 3.50€ ($3.15). Unless you can tag along with an English-language tour group, you may otherwise miss out on the importance of much of what you're seeing.

After climbing the Sansovino stairway, you'll enter some get-acquainted rooms. Proceed to the **Sala di Anti-Collegio,** housing the palace's greatest works, notably Veronese's *Rape of Europa,* to the far left on the right wall. Tintoretto is well represented with his *Three Graces* and his *Bacchus and Ariadne.* Some critics consider the latter his supreme achievement. The ceiling in the adjoining **Sala del Collegio** bears allegorical paintings by Veronese. As you proceed to the right, you'll enter the **Sala del Senato o Pregadi,** with its allegorical painting by Tintoretto in the ceiling's center.

Venice Attractions

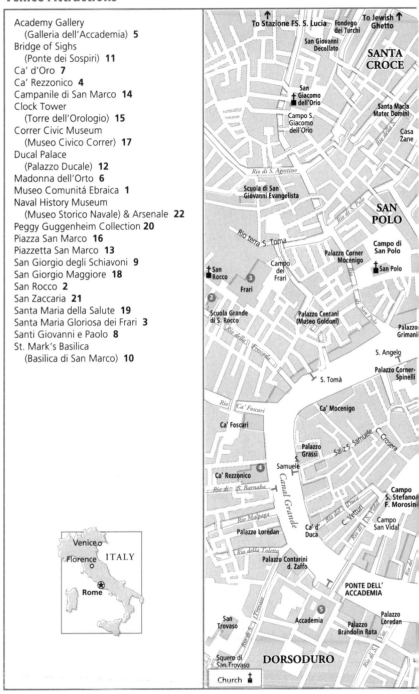

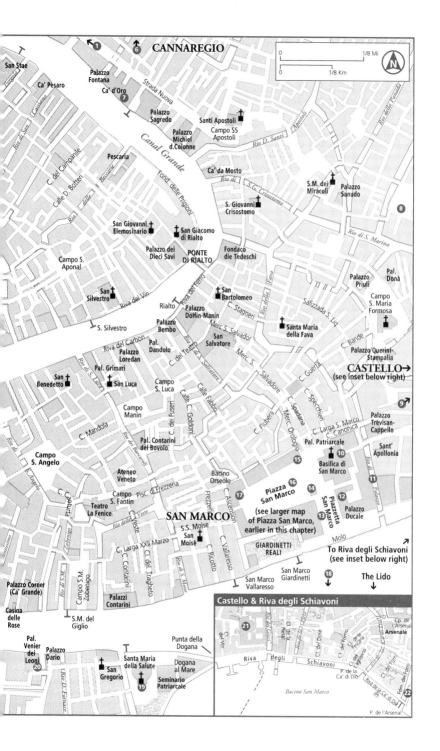

CANNAREGIO

San Stae

Ca' Pesaro

Palazzo
Fontana

Ca' d'Oro

Palazzo
Sagredo

Palazzo
Michiel
d.Colonne

Strada Nuova

Santi Apostoli

Campo SS
Apostoli

Pescaria

Canal Grande

Ca' da Mosto

S. Giovanni
Crisostomo

S.M. dei
Miracoli

Palazzo
Sanudo

C. del Campanile

Calle D. Botteri

Rio di San Cassiano

Fond. delle Prigioni

Rio di S. G. Crisostomo

Rio D. Santi

Rio dei Apostoli

Rio di S. Marina

San Giovanni
Elemosinario

San Giacomo
di Rialto

Palazzo dei
Dieci Savi

PONTE
DI RIALTO

Fondaco
die Tedeschi

Palazzo
Priuli

Pal.
Donà

Campo S.
Aponal

Campo
S. Maria
Formosa

San
Silvestro

Riva del Vin

S. Silvestro

Rialto

Riva del Ferro

San
Bartolomeo

Palazzo
Dolfin-Manin

C. Stagner

Merc S. Salvador

Santa Maria
della Fava

Salizzada S. Lio

C. Bande

Palazzo
Bembo

San
Salvatore

Palazzo Querini-
Stampalia

Riva del Carbon

Palazzo
Loredan

Pal.
Dandolo

Merc. S.

C. del Teatro

C. dei Fabbri

Rio de S. Luca

Pal. Grimari

San
Benedetto

San Luca

Campo
S. Luca

Salvadore

C. Guerra

CASTELLO →
(see inset below right)

Campo
Manin

Calle C. Goldoni

C. Flubera

Mercerie Orologio

Spadaria

C. Larga S. Marco

Palazzo
Trevisan-
Cappello

C. Mandola

Pal. Contarini
del Bovolo

C. dei Fuseri

Pal. Patriarcale

C. Canonica

Sant'
Apollonia

Campo
S. Angelo

Ateneo
Veneto

Campo
S. Fantin

Bacino
Orseolo

Piazza
San Marco

Basilica di
San Marco

Teatro
La Fenice

Pisc. d. Frezzeria

SAN MARCO

Frezzeria

C. Vallaresso

Piazzetta
San Marco

Palazzo
Ducale

Rio delle Veste

S.S. Moisè

San
Moisè

C. Ascension

C. Ricotto

GIARDINETTI
REALI

Molo

To Riva degli Schiavoni
(see inset below right)

C. Larga XXII Marzo

C. Contarini

Cl. del Traghetto

Rio di S. Moisè

San Marco
Vallaresso

San Marco
Giardinetti

The Lido

Palazzo Corner
(Ca' Grande)

Campo S.M.
Zobenigo

Palazzi
Contarini

Castello & Riva degli Schiavoni

Casina
delle
Rose

S.M. del
Giglio

Cp. de
l'Arsenale

Arsenale

Pal.
Venier
dei
Leoni

Palazzo
Dario

Punta della
Dogana

Cl. de la
Piazza

Cl. dei Dose

Cl. del Forno

Cl. de la
Pescaria

Cl. del Forno

San
Gregorio

Santa Maria
della Salute

Dogana
al Mare

Seminario
Patriarcale

Rio D. Fornace

Riva

degli

Schiavoni

P. de la
Ca' di Dio

Riva de Ca' di Dio

Bacino San Marco

P. de l'Arsenal

421

It was in the **Sala del Consiglio dei Dieci,** with its gloomy paintings, that the dreaded Council of Ten (often called the Terrible Ten, for good reason) assembled to decide who was in need of decapitation. In the antechamber, bills of accusation were dropped in the lion's mouth.

The excitement continues downstairs. You can wander through the once-private apartments of the doges to the grand **Maggior Consiglio,** with Veronese's allegorical *Triumph of Venice* on the ceiling. The most outstanding feature, however, is over the Grand Council chamber: Tintoretto's *Paradise,* said to be the world's largest oil painting. Paradise seems to have an overpopulation problem, perhaps reflecting Tintoretto's too-optimistic point of view (he was in his 70s when he began this monumental work and died 6 years later). The second grandiose hall, which you enter from the grand chamber, is the **Sala dello Scrutinio,** with paintings telling of Venice's past glories.

Reentering the Maggior Consiglio, follow the arrows on their trail across the **Bridge of Sighs (Ponte dei Sospiri)** ★★, linking the Doge's Palace with the Palazzo delle Prigioni. Here you'll see the cell blocks that once lodged the prisoners who felt the quick justice of the Terrible Ten. The changing roster of the Terrible Ten was a series of state inquisitors appointed by the city of Venice to dispense justice to the citizens. This often meant torture on the rack even for what could be viewed as a minor infraction. The reputation of the Terrible Ten for the ferocity of their sentences became infamous in Europe. The "sighs" in the bridge's name stem from the sad laments of the numerous victims forced across it to face certain torture and possible death. The cells are somber remnants of the horror of medieval justice.

If you're really intrigued by the palace, you might want to check out the **Secret Trails of the Palazzo Ducale (Itinerari Segreti del Palazzo Ducale).** These 12.50€ ($11.15) guided tours are so popular that they've recently been introduced in English (you must reserve in advance at the ticket-buyers' entrance or by calling). You'll peek into otherwise restricted quarters and hidden passageways of this enormous palace, such as the doge's private chambers and the torture chambers where prisoners were interrogated. The tour is also offered in Italian daily at 10am and noon.

Piazzetta San Marco. ✆ 041-5224951. Admission 9€ ($8.05) adults, 5€ ($4.45) students. Apr–Oct daily 9am–7pm; Nov–Feb daily 9am–5pm. Vaporetto: San Marco.

THE GRAND CANAL (CANAL GRANDE) ★★★

Paris has its Champs-Elysèes, and New York City has its Broadway—but Venice, for sheer uniqueness, tops them all with its Canal Grande. Lined with palazzi (many in the Venetian Gothic style), this great road of water is filled with vaporetti, motorboats, and gondolas. The boat moorings are like peppermint sticks. The canal begins at Piazzetta San Marco on one side and Longhena's La Salute church opposite. At midpoint, it's spanned by the Rialto Bridge. Eventually, the canal winds its serpentine course to the rail station.

Some of the most impressive buildings along the Grand Canal have been converted into galleries and museums. Others have been turned into cooperative apartments, but often the lower floors are now deserted. (Venetian housewives aren't as incurably romantic as foreign visitors. A practical lot, these women can be seen stringing up their laundry to dry in front of thousands of tourists.)

The best way to see the Grand Canal is to board vaporetto no. 1 (push and shove until you secure a seat at the front of the vessel). Settle yourself in, make sure that you have your long-distance viewing glasses, and prepare yourself for a view that can thrill even the most experienced world traveler.

(*Tips* **The Five Major Landmarks**

Time and again, you'll think you know where you're going, only to wind up on a dead-end street or at the side of a canal with no bridge to get to the other side. Just remind yourself that Venice's complexity is an integral part of its charm, and getting lost is part of the fun.

Fortunately, around the city are yellow signs whose arrows direct you toward one of five major landmarks: **Ferrovia** (the train station), **Piazzale Roma,** the **Rialto** (Bridge), (Piazza) **San Marco,** and the **Accademia** (Bridge). You'll often find these signs grouped together, with their arrows pointing off in different directions.

MUSEUMS & GALLERIES

Venice is a city of art. Decorating its palazzi and adorning its canvases were artists such as Giovanni Bellini, Carpaccio, Titian, Giorgione, Lotto, Tintoretto, Veronese, Tiepolo, Guardi, Canaletto, and Longhi, to name just the important ones. You'll even come across some modern surprises, such as those in the Guggenheim Collection.

Academy Gallery (Gallerie dell'Accademia) ★★★ The pomp and circumstance, the glory that was Venice, lives on in this remarkable collection of paintings spanning the 13th to 18th centuries. The hallmark of the Venetian school is color and more color. From Giorgione to Veronese, from Titian to Tintoretto, with a Carpaccio cycle thrown in, the Accademia has samples of its most famous sons—often their best works. Here we've highlighted only some of the most-renowned masterpieces for the first-timer in a rush.

You'll first see works by such 14th-century artists as Paolo and Lorenzo Veneziano, who bridged the gap from Byzantine art to Gothic (see the latter's *Annunciation*). Next, you'll view Giovanni Bellini's *Madonna and Saint* (poor Sebastian, not another arrow) and Carpaccio's fascinating yet gruesome work of mass crucifixion. As you move on, head for the painting on the easel by the window, attributed to the great Venetian artist Giorgione. On this canvas he depicted the Madonna and Child, along with the mystic St. Catherine of Siena and John the Baptist (a neat trick for Catherine, who seems to have perfected transmigration to join the cast of characters).

Two of the most important works with secular themes are Mantegna's armored *St. George,* with the slain dragon at his feet, and Hans Memling's 15th-century portrait of a young man. A most unusual *Madonna and Child* is by Cosmè Tura, the master of Ferrara, who could always be counted on to give a new twist to an old subject.

The Madonnas and bambini of Giovanni Bellini, an expert in harmonious color blending, are the focus of another room. None but the major artists could stand the test of a salon filled with the same subject, but under Bellini's brush each Virgin achieves her individual spirituality. Giorgione's *Tempest,* displayed here, is the single most famous painting at the Accademia. It depicts a baby suckling from the breast of its mother, while a man with a staff looks on. What might've emerged as a simple pastoral scene by a lesser artist comes forth as rare and exceptional beauty. Summer lightning pierces the sky, but the tempest seems to be in the background, far away from the foreground figures, who are menaced without knowing it.

You can see the masterpiece of Lorenzo Lotto, a melancholy portrait of a young man, before coming to a room dominated by Paolo Veronese's *The Banquet in the House of Levi.* This is really a "Last Supper" but was considered a sacrilege in its day, so Veronese was forced to change its name and pretend that it was a secular work. (Impish Veronese caught the hot fire of the Inquisition by including dogs, a cat, midgets, Huns, and drunken revelers in the mammoth canvas.) Four large paintings by Tintoretto, noted for their swirling action and powerful drama, depict scenes from the life of St. Mark. Finally, painted in his declining years (some have suggested in his 88th year, before he died from the plague) is Titian's majestic *Pietà.*

After an unimpressive long walk, search out Canaletto's *Porticato.* Yet another room is heightened by Gentile Bellini's stunning portrait of St. Mark's Square, back in the days (1496) when the houses glistened with gold in the sun. All the works in this salon are intriguing, especially the re-creation of the Ponte de Rialto and a covered wood bridge by Carpaccio.

Also displayed is the cycle of narrative paintings that Vittore Carpaccio did of St. Ursula for the Scuola of Santa Orsola. The most famous is no. 578, showing Ursula asleep on her elongated bed, with a dog nestled on the floor nearby, as the angels come for a visitation. Finally, on the way out, look for Titian's *Presentation of the Virgin,* a fitting farewell to this galaxy of great Venetian art.

Campo della Carità, Dorsoduro. ② 041-5222247. Admission 6€ ($5.35). Mon 8:15am–2pm; Tues–Sun 8:15am–7:15pm. Vaporetto: Accademia.

Correr Civic Museum (Museo Civico Correr) ★★

This museum traces the development of Venetian painting from the 14th to 16th centuries. On the second floor are the red-and-maroon robes once worn by the doges, plus some fabulous street lanterns and an illustrated copy of *Marco Polo in Tartaria.* You can see Cosmà Tura's *Pietà,* a miniature of renown from the genius in the Ferrara School. This is one of his more gruesome works, depicting a bony, gnarled Christ sprawled on the lap of the Madonna. Farther on, search out Schiavone's *Madonna and Child* (no. 545), our candidate for ugliest bambino ever depicted on canvas (no wonder his mother looks askance).

One of the most important rooms boasts three masterpieces: a *Pietà* by Antonello da Messina, a *Crucifixion* by Flemish Hugo van der Goes, and a *Madonna and Child* by Dieric Bouts, who depicted the baby suckling at his mother's breast in a sensual manner. The star attraction of the Correr is the **Bellini salon,** which includes works by founding padre Jacopo and his son, Gentile. But the real master of the household was the other son, Giovanni, the major painter of the 15th-century Venetian school (look for his *Crucifixion* and compare it with his father's treatment of the same subject). A small but celebrated portrait of St. Anthony of Padua by Alvise Vivarini is here, along with works by Bartolomeo Montagna. The most important work is Vittore Carpaccio's *Two Venetian Ladies,* although their true gender is a subject of much debate. In Venice, they're popularly known as "The Courtesans." A lesser work, *St. Peter,* depicting the saint with the daggers piercing him, hangs in the same room.

The entrance is under the arcades of Ala Napoleonica at the western end of the square.

In the Procuratie Nuove, Piazza San Marco. ② 041-5225625. Admission (including admission to the Ducal Palace above) 9€ ($8.05); 3€ ($2.70) children 6–14. Mar–Oct daily 9am–7pm; Nov–Feb daily 9am–5pm. Vaporetto: San Marco.

Tips **A Note on Museum Hours**

As throughout Italy, visiting hours in Venice's museums are often subject to major variations, both in hours and in days. Many visitors who have budgeted only 2 or 3 days for Venice often express disappointment when, for some unknown reason, a major attraction closes abruptly, sometimes for the entire day. When you arrive, check with the tourist office for a list of the latest open hours.

Ca' d'Oro ✦✦✦ The only problem with the use of this building as an art museum is that the Ca' d'Oro is so opulent that its architecture and decor compete with the works. It was built in the early 1400s, and its name translates as "House of Gold," although the gilding that once covered its facade eroded away long ago, leaving softly textured pink and white stone carved into lacy Gothic patterns. Historians compare its majesty to that of the Ducal Palace. The building was meticulously restored in the early 20th century by philanthropist Baron Franchetti, who attached it to a smaller nearby palazzo (Ca' Duodo), today part of the Ca' d'Oro complex. The interconnected buildings contain the baron's valuable private collection of paintings, sculpture, and furniture, all donated to the Italian government during World War I.

You enter into a stunning courtyard, 46m (50 yd.) from the vaporetto stop. The courtyard has a multicolored patterned marble floor and is filled with statuary. Proceed upstairs to the lavishly appointed palazzo. One of the gallery's major paintings is Titian's voluptuous *Venus.* She coyly covers one breast, but what about the other?

In a special niche reserved for the masterpiece of the Franchetti collection is Andrea Mantegna's icy-cold *St. Sebastian,* the central figure of which is riddled with what must be a record number of arrows. You'll also find works by Carpaccio.

For a delightful break, step out onto the palazzo's loggia, overlooking the Grand Canal, for a view up and down the aquatic waterway and across to the Pescheria, a timeless vignette of an unchanged city.

Cannaregio 3931–3932. ✆ **041-5238790.** Admission 3€ ($2.70). Mon 8am–2pm; Tues–Sun 8:15am–7:15pm. Closed Jan 1, May 1, and Dec 25. Vaporetto: Ca' d'Oro.

Ca' Rezzonico ✦✦ This 17th- and 18th-century palace along the Grand Canal is where Robert Browning set up his bachelor headquarters and eventually died in 1889. Pope Clement XIII also stayed here. It's a virtual treasure house, known for its baroque paintings and furniture. First you enter the **Grand Ballroom** with its allegorical ceiling, and then you proceed through lavishly embellished rooms with Venetian chandeliers, brocaded walls, portraits of patricians, tapestries, gilded furnishings, and touches of chinoiserie. At the end of the first walk is the **Throne Room,** with its allegorical ceilings by Giovanni Battista Tiepolo.

On the first floor you can walk out onto a **balcony** for a view of the Grand Canal as the aristocratic tenants of the 18th century saw it. Another group of rooms follows, including the library. In these salons, look for a bizarre collection of paintings: One, for example, depicts half-clothed women beating up a defenseless naked man (one Amazon is about to stick a pitchfork into his neck, while another looks to crown him with a violin). In the adjoining room, another woman is hammering a spike through a man's skull.

Upstairs is a survey of 18th-century Venetian art. As you enter the main room from downstairs, head for the **first salon** on your right (facing the canal), which contains the best works, paintings from the brush of Pietro Longhi. His most famous work, *The Lady and the Hairdresser,* is the first canvas to the right on the entrance wall. Others depict the life of the idle Venetian rich. On the rest of the floor are bedchambers, a chapel, and salons, some with badly damaged frescoes, including a romp of satyrs.

Fondamenta Rezzonico, Dorsoduro 3136. © 041-2410100. Admission 6.50€ ($5.80) adults, 2.50€ ($2.25) children under 14. Oct–Apr Sat–Thurs 10am–4pm; May–Sept daily 10am–5pm. Vaporetto: Ca' Rezzonico.

Peggy Guggenheim Collection (Collezione Peggy Guggenheim) ★★★

This is one of the most comprehensive and brilliant modern-art collections in the Western world, and it reveals both the foresight and the critical judgment of its founder. The collection is housed in an unfinished palazzo, the former Venetian home of Peggy Guggenheim, who died in 1979. In the tradition of her family, Peggy Guggenheim was a lifelong patron of contemporary painters and sculptors. In the 1940s, she founded the avant-garde Art of This Century Gallery in New York, impressing critics not only with the high quality of the artists she sponsored but also with her methods of displaying them.

As her private collection increased, she decided to find a larger showcase and selected Venice. Today you can wander through the home and enjoy art in an informal and relaxed way.

Max Ernst was one of Peggy Guggenheim's early favorites (she even married him), as was Jackson Pollock (she provided a farmhouse where he could develop his technique). Displayed here are works not only by Pollock and Ernst but also by Picasso (see his 1911 cubist *The Poet*), Duchamp, Chagall, Mondrian, Brancusi, Delvaux, and Dalí, plus a garden of modern sculpture with Giacometti works (some of which he struggled to complete while resisting the amorous intentions of Marlene Dietrich). Temporary modern-art shows sometimes are presented during winter. Since Peggy Guggenheim's death, the collection has been administered by the Solomon R. Guggenheim Foundation, which also operates New York's Guggenheim Museum. In the new wing are a museum shop and a cafe, overlooking the sculpture garden.

In the Palazzo Venier dei Leoni, Calle Venier dei Leoni, Dorsoduro 701. © 041-2405411. Admission 8€ ($7.15); free for children under 9. Wed–Mon 10am–6pm. Apr–Oct Sat open until 10pm. Vaporetto: Accademia.

Naval History Museum (Museo Storico Navale) & Arsenale ★

The Naval History Museum is filled with cannons, ships' models, and fragments of old vessels dating to the days when Venice was supreme in the Adriatic. The prize exhibit is a gilded model of the *Bucintoro,* the great ship of the doge that surely would've made Cleopatra's barge look like an oil tanker. In addition, you'll find models of historic and modern fighting ships, local fishing and rowing craft, and a collection of 24 Chinese junks, as well as a number of maritime *ex voto* (religious paintings in the form of triptychs or altarpieces) from churches of Naples.

If you walk along the canal as it branches off from the museum, you'll arrive at the Ships' Pavilion, where historic vessels are displayed (about 247m/270 yd. from the museum and before the wooden bridge). Proceeding along the canal, you'll soon reach the Arsenale, Campo dell'Arsenale, guarded by stone lions, Neptune with a trident, and other assorted ferocities. You'll spot it readily enough because of its two towers flanking the canal. In its day, the Arsenale turned out galley after galley at speeds usually associated with wartime production.

Campo San Biagio, Castello 2148. ℂ **041-5200276.** Admission 1.50€ ($1.35). Mon–Fri 8am–1:30pm; Sat 8:45am–1pm. Closed holidays. Vaporetto: Arsenale.

CHURCHES & GUILD HOUSES

Much of the great art of Venice lies in its **churches** and *scuole* (guild houses or fraternities). Most of the guild members were drawn from the rising bourgeoisie. The guilds were said to fulfill both the material and the spiritual needs of their (male) members, who often engaged in charitable works in honor of the saint for whom their scuola was named. Many of Venice's greatest artists, including Tintoretto, were commissioned to decorate these guild houses. Some created masterpieces that you can still see today. Narrative canvases that depicted the lives of the saints were called *teleri*.

San Rocco ✶✶✶   Of all Venice's scuole, none is as richly embellished as this, filled with epic canvases by Tintoretto. Born Jacopo Robusti in 1518, Tintoretto became known for paintings of mystical spirituality and phantasmagoric light effects. By a clever trick, he won the competition to decorate this darkly illuminated early-16th-century building. He began painting in 1564, and the work stretched on until his powers as an artist waned; he died in 1594. The paintings sweep across the upper and lower halls, mesmerizing you with a kind of passion play. In the grand hallway, they depict New Testament scenes, devoted largely to episodes in the life of Mary (the *Flight into Egypt* is among the best). In the top gallery are works illustrating scenes from the Old and New Testaments, the most renowned being those devoted to the life of Christ. In a separate room is Tintoretto's masterpiece: his mammoth *Crucifixion.* In it, he showed his dramatic scope and sense of grandeur as an artist, creating a deeply felt scene that fills you with the horror of systematic execution, thus transcending its original subject matter. (Movie trivia: Watch Woody Allen try to pick up Julia Roberts in *Everyone Says I Love You* while she studies the Tintorettos in San Rocco—if you can get past the idea of the lovely Ms. Roberts as an art historian.)

Campo San Rocco, San Polo. ℂ **041-5234864.** Admission 5€ ($4.45) adults, 3.50€ ($3.15) children. Mar 28–Nov 2 daily 9am–5:30pm; Nov 3–30 and Mar 1–27 daily 10am–4pm; Dec–Feb Mon–Sat 7:30am–12:30pm, Sun 7:30am–12:30pm and 2–4pm. Closed Dec 25–Jan 1. Ticket office closes 30 min. before last entrance. Vaporetto: San Tomà.

San Giorgio degli Schiavoni ✶✶   At the St. Antonino Bridge (Fondamenta dei Furlani) is the second important guild house to visit. Between 1502 and 1509, Vittore Carpaccio painted a pictorial cycle here of exceptional merit and interest. His works of **St. George and the Dragon** ✶ are our favorite art in all Venice and certainly the most delightful. For example, in one frame St. George charges the dragon on a field littered with half-eaten bodies and skulls. Gruesome? Not at all. Any moment you expect the director to call "Cut!" The pictures relating to St. Jerome are appealing but don't compete with St. George and his ferocious dragon.

Calle dei Furiani, Castello. ℂ **041-5228828.** Admission 2.50€ ($2.25). Nov–Mar Tues–Sat 10am–12:30pm and 3–6pm, Sun 10am–12:30pm; Apr–Oct Tues–Sat 9:30am–12:30pm and 3:30–6:30pm, Sun 9:30am–12:30pm. Last entrance 20 min. before closing. Vaporetto: San Zaccaria.

Santa Maria Gloriosa dei Frari 👁👁   Known simply as the Frari, this Venetian Gothic church is only a short walk from the San Rocco and is filled with great art. The best work is Titian's *Assumption* over the main altar—a masterpiece of soaring beauty depicting the ascension of the Madonna on a cloud puffed up by floating cherubs. In her robe, but especially in the robe of one of the gaping saints below, "Titian red" dazzles as never before.

On the first altar to the right as you enter is Titian's second major work here: *Madonna Enthroned,* painted for the Pesaro family in 1526. Although it lacks the power and drama of the *Assumption,* it nevertheless is brilliant in its use of color and light effects. But Titian surely would turn redder than his Madonna's robes if he could see the latter-day neoclassical tomb built for him on the opposite wall. The kindest word for it: large.

Facing the tomb is a memorial to Canova, the Italian sculptor who led the revival of classicism. To return to more enduring art, head to the sacristy for a 1488 Giovanni Bellini triptych on wood; the Madonna is cool and serene, one of Bellini's finest portraits of the Virgin. Also, see the almost primitive-looking wood carving by Donatello of St. John the Baptist.

Campo dei Frari, San Polo. © 041-2728611. Admission 2€ ($1.80); free Sun. Mon–Sat 9am–5:30pm; Sun 1–5:30pm. Vaporetto: San Tomà.

Madonna dell'Orto 👁   At this church, a good reason to walk to this remote northern district, you can pay your final respects to Tintoretto. The brick structure with a Gothic front is famed not only because of its paintings by that artist but also because the great master is buried in the chapel to the right of the main altar. At the high altar are his *Last Judgment* (on the right) and *Sacrifice of the Golden Calf* (left), with monumental paintings curving at the top like a Gothic arch. Over the doorway to the right of the altar is Tintoretto's superb portrayal of the presentation of Mary as a little girl at the temple. The composition is unusual in that Mary isn't the focal point; rather, a pointing woman bystander dominates the scene.

The first chapel to the right of the main altar contains a masterly work by Cima de Conegliano, showing the presentation of a sacrificial lamb to the saints (the plasticity of St. John's body evokes Michelangelo). In the first chapel on the left, as you enter, notice the large photo of Giovanni Bellini's *Madonna and Child.* The original, which was noteworthy for its depiction of the eyes and mouths of the mother and child, was stolen as part of a 1994 theft; pending the possibility of its hoped-for return, the photograph was installed in its place. Two other pictures in the apse are *The Presentation of the Cross to St. Peter* and *The Beheading of St. Christopher.*

Campo dell'Orto, Cannaregio 3512. © 041-719933. Admission 1.50€ ($1.35). Mon–Sat 10am–5pm; Sun 1–6pm. Vaporetto: Madonna dell'Orto.

San Zaccaria 👁👁   Behind St. Mark's is this Gothic church with a Renaissance facade, filled with works of art, notably Giovanni Bellini's restored *Madonna Enthroned,* painted with saints (second altar to the left). Many have found this to be one of Bellini's finest Madonnas, and it does have beautifully subdued coloring, although it appears rather static. Many worthwhile works lie in the main body of the church, but for a view of even more of them, apply to the sacristan for entrance to the church's museum, housed in an area once reserved exclusively for nuns. Here you'll find works by Tintoretto, Titian, Il Vecchio, Anthony Van Dyck, and Bassano. The paintings aren't labeled, but the sacristan will point out the names of the artists. In the Sisters' Choir are five armchairs in which the

Venetian doges of yore sat. And if you save the best for last, you can see the faded frescoes of Andrea del Castagno in the shrine honoring San Tarasio.

Campo San Zaccaria, Castello. ℂ 041-5221257. Admission 1€ (90¢) to museum; church free. Mon–Sat 10am–noon; daily 4–6pm. Vaporetto: San Zaccaria.

San Giorgio Maggiore ⭑

This church, on the little island of San Giorgio Maggiore, was designed by the great Renaissance architect Palladio—perhaps as a consolation prize because he wasn't chosen to rebuild the burned-out Doge's Palace. The logical rhythm of the Vicenza architect is played here on a grand scale. But inside it's almost too stark because Palladio wasn't much on gilded adornment. The chief art hangs on the main altar: two epic paintings by Tintoretto, the *Fall of Manna* to the left and the far more successful *Last Supper* to the right. It's interesting to compare Tintoretto's *Cena* with that of Veronese at the Accademia. Afterward, you might want to take the elevator (for 2.50€, $2.25) to the top of the belfry for a view of the greenery of the island itself, the lagoon, and the Doge's Palace across the way. It's unforgettable.

Isola San Giorgio Maggiore, across from Piazzetta San Marco. ℂ 041-5227827. Free admission. Apr–Oct daily 9:30am–12:30pm and 2:30–6pm; Nov–Mar daily 10am–12:30pm and 2:30–4:30pm. Closed for Mass on Sun and feast days 10:45am–noon. Vaporetto: Take the Giudecca-bound vaporetto on Riva degli Schiavoni and get off at the first stop, right in the courtyard of the church.

Santa Maria della Salute ⭑⭑

Like the proud landmark it is, La Salute, the pinnacle of the baroque movement in Venice, stands at the mouth of the Grand Canal overlooking Piazzetta San Marco and opening onto Campo della Salute. One of Venice's most historic churches, it was built by Longhena in the 17th century (work began in 1631) as an offering to the Virgin for delivering the city from the plague. Longhena, almost unknown when he got the commission, dedicated half a century to working on this church and died 5 years before the long-lasting job was completed. Surmounted by a great cupola, the octagonal basilica makes for an interesting visit: It houses a small art gallery in its sacristy (tip the custodian), which includes a marriage feast of Cana by Tintoretto, allegorical paintings on the ceiling by Titian, a mounted St. Mark, and poor St. Sebastian with his inevitable arrow.

Campo della Salute, Dorsoduro. ℂ 041-5225558. Free admission (but offering is expected); sacristy 1.50€ ($1.35). Mar–Nov daily 9am–noon and 3–6pm (to 5:30pm Dec–Feb). Vaporetto: Salute.

Santi Giovanni e Paolo ⭑⭑

This great Gothic church (aka Zanipolo) houses the tombs of many doges. It was built during the 13th and 14th centuries and contains works by many of the most noted Venetian painters. As you enter (right aisle), you'll find a retable by Giovanni Bellini (which includes a St. Sebastian filled with arrows). In the Rosary Chapel are Veronese ceilings depicting New Testament scenes, including *The Assumption of the Madonna*. To the right of the church is one of the world's best-known equestrian statues, that of Bartolomeo Colleoni, sculpted in the 15th century by Andrea del Verrochio. The bronze has long been acclaimed as his masterpiece, although it was completed by another artist. The horse is far more beautiful than the armored military hero, who looks as if he had just stumbled on a three-headed crocodile.

To the left of the pantheon is the **Scuola di San Marco,** with a stunning Renaissance facade (it's now run as a civic hospital). The church requests that Sunday visits be of a religious nature rather than for sightseeing.

Campo SS. Giovanni e Paolo, Castello 6363. ℂ 041-5235913. Free admission. Daily 8am–12:30pm and 3–7pm. Vaporetto: Rialto or Fondamenta Nuove.

THE LIDO ★★

The white sands of the Lido have drawn artists and literary types for centuries. And why not? This is a resort area complete with deluxe hotels, a casino, and stratospheric prices.

But don't expect the Lido of days gone by. The Lido is well past its heyday. A chic crowd still checks into the Excelsior Palace and the Hotel des Bains, but the beach strip is overrun with tourists and opens onto polluted waters. (For swimming, guests use their hotel pools, although they still stroll along the Lido sands and enjoy the views.) Even if you aren't planning to stay in this area, you should come over and explore for an afternoon. There's no denying the appeal of a beach so close to one of the world's most romantic cities, even if it is unfit for swimming. The strips of beachfront in front of the big hotels on the Lido are technically considered private, and the public is discouraged from using the facilities. But because you can use the beachfront on either side of their property, no one seems to really care about shooing nonguests away.

If you don't want to tread on the beachfront property of the rarefied hotels (which have huts lining the beach like those of some tropical paradise), you can try the **Lungomare G. d'Annunzio (Public Bathing Beach)** at the end of the Gran Viale (Piazzale Ettore Sorger), a long stroll from the vaporetto stop. You can book cabins (*camerini*) and enjoy the sand. Rates change seasonally.

Located on the Lido is one of the oldest Jewish cemeteries in Europe. Established in 1386, it still has the oldest surviving gravestone, that of Shemuel ben Shimshon who died in 1389. The **Venice Jewish Cemetery** was abandoned for 200 years and almost completely inaccessible for decades. This once-crumbling cemetery has been restored and is now open to visitors for the first time. If you'd like to explore it, contact the Jewish Museum at $\textcircled{C}$ **041-715359** to arrange a visit. Tickets cost 8€ ($7.15), and tours are Friday at 10:30am and Sunday at 2:30pm. In winter the cemetery is sometimes closed depending on weather conditions.

To reach the Lido, take vaporetto nos. 1, 6, 52, or 82 (the ride takes about 15 min.). The boat departs from a landing stage near the Doge's Palace.

THE GHETTO ★★

The Ghetto of Venice, called the **Ghetto Nuovo,** was instituted in 1516 by the Venetian Republic in the Cannaregio district. It's considered to be the first ghetto in the world and also the best kept. The word *geto* comes from the Venetian dialect and means "foundry" (originally there were two iron foundries here where metals were fused). At one time, Venetian Jews were confined to a walled area and obliged to wear red or yellow marks sewn onto their clothing and distinctive-looking hats. The walls that once enclosed and confined the Ghetto were torn down long ago, but much remains of the past.

There are five synagogues in Venice, each built during the 16th century and each representing a radically different aesthetic and cultural difference among the groups of Jews who built them. The oldest is the **German Synagogue (Sinagoghe Grande Tedesca),** restored after the end of World War II with funds from Germany. Others are the **Spanish Synagogue (Sinagoghe Spagnola),** the oldest continuously functioning synagogue in Europe; the **Italian Synagogue (Sinagoghe Italiana);** the **Levantine-Oriental Synagogue (Sinagoghe Levantina,** aka the **Turkish Synagogue);** and the **Canton Synagogue (Sinagoghe del Canton).**

The best way to visit the synagogues is to take one of the guided tours departing from the **Museo Comunità Ebraica,** Campo di Ghetto Nuovo 2902B (© **041-715359**). It contains a small but worthy collection of artifacts pertaining to the Jewish community of Venice and costs 3€ ($2.70) for adults. From June to September, the museum is open Sunday to Friday 10am to 7pm (Oct–May to 5:45pm). However, the museum is by no means the focal point of your experience: More worthwhile are the walking tours that begin and end here, costing 8€ ($7.15), with free entrance to the museum. The 50-minute tours incorporate a brisk commentary and a stroll through the neighborhood, including visits to the interiors of three of the five synagogues (the ones that you visit depend on various factors). From June to September, the tours depart hourly Sunday to Friday 10:30am to 5:30pm (Oct–May to 3:30pm).

ORGANIZED TOURS

Tours through the streets and canals of Venice are distinctly different from tours through other cities of Italy because of the complete absence of traffic. You can always wander at will through the labyrinth of streets, but many visitors opt for a guided tour to at least familiarize themselves with the city's geography.

American Express, Calle San Moisè, San Marco 1471 (© **041-5200844**), which operates from a historic building a few steps from St. Mark's Square, offers an array of guided city tours. It's open for tours and travel arrangements Monday to Friday 9am to 5:30pm and Saturday 9am to 12:30pm. Call ahead to ask about the current schedule and to make reservations. The offerings include a daily 2-hour guided tour of the city for 29€ ($25.90), and a tour of the islands of the Venetian lagoon for 15€ ($13.40).

If you'd like personalized neighborhood tours, contact the **Venice Travel Advisory Service,** 22 Riverside Dr., New York, NY 10023 (© and fax **212/873-1964**). Born in New York, Samantha Durell is a professional photographer who has lived and worked in Venice for more than 10 years. She conducts private walking tours, assists with advance-planning services, and is an expert in making wedding arrangements in Venice. She knows a wealth of details about shopping, sightseeing, art, history, dining, and entertainment. Morning and afternoon tours, for a maximum of four people, last about 5 hours and cost $250 for two people, $50 for each additional adult, and $25 for each child.

6 Shopping

Venetian glass and lace are known throughout the world. However, selecting quality products in either craft requires a shrewd eye because there's much that's tawdry and shoddily crafted. Some of the glassware hawked isn't worth the cost of shipping it home. Yet other pieces represent some of the world's finest artistic and ornamental glass. Murano is the island famous for its handmade glass. However, you can find little glass-animal souvenirs in shops all over Venice.

For lace, head out to Burano, where the latest of a long line of women put in painstaking hours to produce some of the finest lace in the world.

SHOPPING STROLLS

All the main shopping streets, even the side streets, are touristy and overrun. The greatest concentration of shops is around **Piazza San Marco** and the **Rialto Bridge.** Prices are much higher at San Marco, but the quality of merchandise is also higher. There are two major shopping strolls in Venice.

First, from **Piazza San Marco** you can stroll west toward spacious **Campo Morosini.** You just follow one shop-lined street all the way to its end (although the name will change several times). You begin at Salizzada San Moisè, which becomes Via 22 Marzo and then Calle delle Ostreghe before it opens onto Campo Santa Maria Zobenigo. The street then narrows and changes to Calle Zaguri before widening once more into Campo San Maurizio, finally becoming Calle Piovan before reaching Campo Morosini. The only deviation from this tour is a detour down Calle Vallaressa, between San Moisè and the Grand Canal, which is one of the major shopping arteries with some of the biggest designer names in the business.

The other great shopping stroll wanders from Piazza San Marco to the Rialto in a succession of streets collectively known as the **Mercerie.** It's virtually impossible to get lost because each street name is preceded by the word *merceria,* such as Merceria dell'Orologio, which begins near the clock tower in Piazza San Marco. Many commercial places, mainly shops, line the Mercerie before it reaches the Rialto, which then explodes into one vast shopping emporium.

SHOPPING A TO Z

ANTIQUES   Antichita Santomanco, Frezzeria, San Marco 1504 (© 041-5236643), is for the well-heeled serious collector. It deals in antique furniture, jewels, silver, prints, and old Murano glass. Of course, the merchandise is ever-changing, but you're likely to pick up some little heirloom item in the midst of the clutter. Many of the items date from the Venetian heyday of the 1600s.

BOOKS   The most centrally located bookstore is the **Libreria Sansovino,** Bacino Orseolo, San Marco 84 (© 041-5222623), to the north of Piazza San Marco. It carries both hard- and softcover books in English.

BRASS   Founded in 1913, **Valese Fonditore,** Calle Fiubera, San Marco 793 (© 041-5227282), serves as a showcase for one of the most famous of the several foundries with headquarters in Venice. Many of the brass copies of 18th-century chandeliers produced by this company grace fine homes in the United States and become valuable family heirlooms. Some of the most appealing objects are the 50 or 60 replicas of the brass seahorses that grace the sides of many of the gondolas. A pair of medium-size ones, each about 11 inches tall, begins at 175€ ($156.30).

CARNEVALE MASKS   Venetian masks, considered collectors' items, originated during Carnevale, which takes place the week before the beginning of Lent. In the old days there was a good reason to wear masks during the riotous Carnevale—they helped wives and husbands be unfaithful to one another and priests break their vows of chastity. Things got so out of hand that Carnevale was banned in the late 18th century. But it came back, and the masks went on again.

You can find shops selling masks practically on every corner. As with glass and lace, however, quality varies. Many masks are great artistic expressions, while others are shoddy and cheap. The most sought-after mask is the *Portafortuna* (luck bringer), with its long nose and birdlike visage. *Orientale* masks evoke the heyday of the Serene Republic and its trade with the Far East. The *Bauta* was worn by men to assert their macho qualities, and the *Neutra* blends the facial characteristics of both sexes. The list of masks and their origins seems endless.

The best place to buy Carnevale masks is **Mondonovo,** Rio Terrà Canal, Dorsoduro 3063 (© 041-5287344), where talented artisans labor to produce copies of both traditional and more modern masks, each of which is one-of-a-kind and richly nuanced with references to Venetian lore and traditions. Prices range from

25€ ($22.35) for a fairly basic model to 1,500€ ($1,339.50) for something that you might display on a wall as a piece of sculpture.

DOLLS   The studio/shop **Bambole di Frilly,** Fondamenta dell'Osmarin, Castello 4974 (© **041-5212579**), offers dolls with meticulously painted porcelain faces (they call it a "biscuit") and hand-tailored costumes, including dressy pinafores. Prices begin at 15€ ($13.40) and can go as high as 750€ ($669.75), but even the reasonably priced dolls are made with the same painstaking care.

FABRICS   Select outlets in Venice sell some of the greatest fabrics in the world. **Norelene,** Calle della Chiesa, Dorsoduro 727 (© **041-5237605**), sells lustrous hand-printed silks, velvets, and cottons, plus wall hangings and clothing.

Venetia Studium is at two outlets: Calle Larga XXII Marco, San Marzo 2403 (© **041-5229281**), and a newer shop at Mercerie, San Marco 723 (© **041-5229859**). For years, Lino Lando worked to crack the secret of fabled designer Mariano Fortuny's *plissè* (finely pleated silk). Eventually he found the secret. The result can now be yours in his selection of silk accessories, scarves, Delphos gowns, and even silk lamps.

Gaggio Rich, San Marco, San Stefano 3451–3441 (© **041-5228574**), offers unique items, the most stunning of which are velvets and artistic fabrics with filigree, all inspired by the deep colors and designs of Fortuny. The fabrics are very Venetian and very decadent. You can purchase these fabrics by the meter, or they can be fashioned into clothing, shawls, cushions, or whatever.

Yet another Fortuny-inspired outlet is **Vittorio Trois,** Campo San Maurizio, San Marco 2666 (© **041-5222905**). Trois was selected to receive a priceless legacy. The great Mariano Fortuny revealed his exquisite printing techniques to a friend of Trois, the late Contessa Gozzi, and she passed them on to Trois, who made a business of them. Today you can buy the same Fortuny patterns that stunned your grandparents on their visit to Venice decades ago. The radiant designs look like brocade and are sold by the yard.

FASHION   The **Belvest Boutique,** Calle Vallaresso, San Marco 1305, near Harry's Bar (© **041-5287933**), is one of Venice's finest boutiques, specializing in clothing for women and men, handmade and ready-to-wear. Fabric from some of the world's leading cloth makers is used in the designs. Linked with Vogini, the famous purveyor of leatherwork, the boutique is a bastion of top-quality craftsmanship and high-fashion style.

In need of some new threads for the film festival? Then **La Bottega di Nino,** Mercerie dell'Orologio, San Marco 223 (© **041-5225608**), is the place for elegant cutting-edge male attire as stylish as anything you'll find in Milan. It features the work of many European designers, even some from England, but shines brightest in its Italian names, such as Nino Cerruti and Zenia. The prices are also better for Italian wear.

La Fenice, Calle Larga XXII Marzo, San Marco 2255 (© **041-5231273**), is a large outlet for a stylish assortment of designers from throughout Europe. The most visible of several members of a city-wide chain, it sells women's clothing from designers such as Moschino, Thierry Mügler, German Rena Lang, and the well-received Turkish-born designer Osbek.

By accident we stumbled on **Caberlotto,** San Salvador, San Marco 5114 (© **041-5229242**), with a stunning collection of classic apparel for both women and men, all in jewel-like colors. Head here to see the rich collection of Loro Piana shawls, cashmere sweaters, scarves, and other apparel.

GIFTS The **Bac Art Studio,** San Vio, Dorsoduro 862 (© **041-5228171**), sells paper goods, but it's mainly a graphics gallery, noted for its selection of engravings, posters, and lithographs of Venice at Carnevale time. For the most part, items are reasonably priced, and it's clear that a great deal of care has gone into the choice of merchandise.

Head to **Osvaldo Böhm,** Salizzada San Moisè, San Marco 1349–1350 (© **041-5222255**), for that just-right, and light, souvenir of Venice. It has a rich collection of photographic archives specializing in Venetian art, as well as original engravings and maps, lithographs, watercolors, and Venetian masks. You can also see modern serigraphs by local artists and some fine handcrafted bronzes.

GLASS Venice is crammed with glass shops: It's estimated that there are at least 1,000 in San Marco alone. Unless you go to a top-quality dealer, you'll find that most stores sell both shoddy and high-quality glassware, and often only the most trained eye can tell the difference. A lot of "Venetian glass" isn't from Venice at all, but from the Czech Republic. (Of course, the Czech Republic has some of the finest glassmakers in Europe, so that might not be bad, either.) Buying glass boils down to this: If you like an item, buy it. It might not be high quality, but, then, high quality can cost thousands.

If you're looking for an heirloom, stick to the major houses. One of the oldest (founded in 1866) and largest purveyors of traditional Venetian glass is **Pauly & Co.,** Ponte Consorzi, San Marco 4392 (© **041-5209899**), with more than two dozen showrooms. Part of the premises is devoted to something akin to a museum, where past successes (now antiques) are displayed. Antique items are only rarely offered for sale; but they can be copied and shipped anywhere, and chandeliers can be electrified to match your standards. They begin at about 1,000€ ($893) but can spiral to as much as 500,000€ ($446,500) if you're a Saudi emir who's designing an entire throne room around them.

The art glass sold by **Venini,** Piazzetta Leoncini, San Marco 314 (© **041-5224045**), has caught the attention of collectors from all over the world. Many of its pieces, including anything-but-ordinary lamps, bottles, and vases, are works of art representing the best of Venetian craftsmanship. Its best-known glass has a distinctive swirl pattern in several colors, called a venature. This shop is known for the refined quality of its glass, some of which appears almost transparent. Much of it is very fragile, but the shop learned long ago how to ship it anywhere safely. To visit the furnace, call © **041-739955.**

L'Isola, Campo San Moisè, San Marco 1468 (© **041-5231973**), is the shop of Carlo Moretti, one of the world's best-known contemporary artisans working in glass. You'll find all his signature designs in decanters, glasses, vases, bowls, and paperweights.

Galleria Marina Barovier, Salizzada San Samuele, San Marco 3216 (© **041-5226102**), sells some of the most creative modern glass sculptures in Italy. Since it was opened in the early 1980s by its founder, Marina Barovier, in the suburb of Mestre, it has grown until it's now viewed as one of the most glamorous art galleries in the world of glassmaking. Especially sought after are sculptures by master glassmakers Luco Tagliapietra and American artist Dale Chihuly, whose chandeliers represent amusing or dramatic departures from traditional Venetian forms. Anything sold can be shipped.

At **Vetri d'Arte,** Piazza San Marco 140 (© **041-5200205**), you can find moderately priced glass jewelry for souvenirs and gifts, as well as a selection of pricier crystal jewelry and porcelain dolls.

Luco Tagliapietra, one of the masters of Venetian glass blowing, has his works distributed by **Domus Vetri d'Arte,** Fondamenta Vetrai 82, Murano (© 041-739215). This artisan, with his cutting-edge sense of design, began blowing glass at age 12 and by age 21 was recognized as a master—some even called him a genius in glass. Unlike some Venetian glassmakers, inspired by ancient Greece and Rome, Tagliapietra roams the world for inspiration, finding it even in some Native American cultures.

JEWELRY   Since 1846, **Missiaglia,** Piazza San Marco, San Marco 125 (© 041-5224464), has been the supplier to savvy shoppers from around the world seeking the best jewelry. Go here for a special classic piece, such as hand-crafted jewelry with a Venetian twist—everything from a gold gondolier oar pin to a diamond-studded fan brooch with an ebony Carnevale mask. The specialty is colored precious and semiprecious gemstones set in white or yellow gold.

For antique jewelry, there's no shop finer than **Codognato,** Calle Ascensione, San Marco 1295 (© 041-5225042). Some of the great heirloom jewelry of Europe is sent here when estates are settled.

LACE   Most lace vendors center on Piazza San Marco. Although the price of handmade Venetian lace is high, it's still reasonable considering the painstaking work that goes into the real thing. It can cause damage to a woman's eyesight. Authentic hand-tatted lace is cheaper in Venice than it is back home, and it's even cheaper on the island of Burano, where stores don't have to pay high-priced Venice rents. But no one ever called handmade Burano lace a bargain, even on its home turf.

Regardless of where you buy lace, however, make sure it's the real thing. The lace shops are like the glassware outlets, selling the whole gamut from the shoddy to the exquisite. Much of it—even on Burano—is shoddy, and a lot of it isn't handmade in Venice but machine-made in Taiwan. Shop carefully and know what you're buying. If a price seems too good to be true, it probably is.

For serious purchases, **Jesurum,** Mercerie del Capitello, San Marco 4857 (© 041-5206177), is tops. You'll find Venetian handmade or machine-made lace and embroidery on table, bed, and bath linens, as well as hand-printed swimsuits. Prices are high, but quality and originality are guaranteed and special orders are accepted. The exclusive linens created here are expensive, but the inventory is large enough to accommodate many budgets. Staff members insist that everything sold is made in or around Venice in traditional patterns.

LEATHER   **Marforio,** Campo San Salvador, San Marco 5033 (© 041-5225734), was founded in 1875 and is Italy's oldest and largest leather-goods retail outlet, run by the same family for five generations. It's known for the quality of its leather products, and there's an enormous assortment of famous European labels, including Valentino, Armani, Ferrè, and Cardin, among others.

Bottega Veneta, Calle Vallaresso, San Marco 1337 (© 041-5202816), is primarily known for its woven leather bags. They're sold elsewhere, but the prices are said to be less at the company's flagship outlet in Venice. The shop also sells women's shoes, suitcases, wallets, belts, and high-fashion accessories.

Furla, Mercerie del Capitello, San Marco 4954 (© 041-5230611), is a specialist in women's leather bags but sells belts and gloves as well. Many of the bags are stamped with molds, creating alligator- and lizardlike textures. You'll also find costume jewelry, silk scarves, briefcases, and wallets.

Every kind of leather work is offered at **Vogini,** Ascensione, San Marco 1291, 1292, and 1301, near Harry's Bar (© 041-5222573), especially women's handbags, which are exclusive models. There's also a large assortment of hand-bags in petit-point embroideries and in crocodile, plus an assortment of men's and women's shoes. Brand names include Mosquino and Robert Di Camerino, plus products designed and manufactured by Vogini itself.

MARKETS   If you're looking for some bargain-basement buys, head to one of the little shops lining the **Rialto Bridge.** The shops there branch out to encompass fruit and vegetable markets as well. The Rialto isn't the Ponte Vecchio in Florence, but for what it offers it isn't bad, particularly if your euros are running short. You'll find a wide assortment of merchandise, from angora sweaters to leather gloves. The quality is likely to vary widely, so plunge in with your eyes open.

PAPER   Florence is still the major center in Italy for artistic paper, especially marbleized paper. However, craftsmen in Venice still make marble paper by hand, sheet by sheet. The technique offers unlimited decorative possibilities and the widest range of possible colors. Each sheet of handmade marbleized paper is one of a kind.

Il Papiro, Calle del Piovan, San Marco 2764 (© **041-5223055**), carries absolutely gorgeous stationery, plus photo albums, address books, picture frames, diaries, and boxes covered in artfully printed paper. It is also the best outlet for purchasing leather-bound blank and lined journals, a unique gift.

Stylish **Piazzesi,** Campiello della Feltrina, San Marco 2511 (© **041-5221202**), claims to be Italy's oldest purveyor of writing paper (opened 1900). Some of its elegant lines of stationery require as many as 13 artisans to produce. Most of the production is hand-blocked, marbleized, stenciled, or accented with dyes that are blown onto each of the sheets with a breath-operated tube. If you want impressive paper for your social thank-you notes or wedding invitations, Piazzesi will undoubtedly have it in stock. Also look for papier-mâché masks and Commedia dell'Arte–style statues representing age-old professions such as architects, carpenters, doctors, glassmakers, church officials, and notaries. Seeking something more modern? Consider any of the whimsically decorated containers for CDs and computer disks.

WOOD SCULPTURES   A unique outlet in Venice is **Livio de Marchi,** San Samuele, San Marco 3157 (© **041-5285694**). De Marchi and his staff can take almost any item, from cowboy boots to a Vespa to a woman's handbag, and sculpt it in wood in hyper-real detail. Even if you don't buy anything, just stop in to take a look at these stunning items sculpted from wood.

7 Venice After Dark

For such a fabled city, Venice's nightlife is pretty meager. Who wants to hit the nightclubs when strolling the city at night is more interesting than any spectacle staged inside? Ducking into a cafe or bar for a brief interlude, however, is a good way to break up your evening walk. Although Venice offers gambling and a few other diversions, it is pretty much an early-to-bed town. Most restaurants close at midnight.

The best guide to what's happening is **"Un Ospite di Venezia,"** a free pamphlet (part in English, part in Italian) distributed by the tourist office every 15 days. It lists any music and opera or theatrical presentations, along with art exhibits and local special events.

At least 10 of Venice's historic churches host **concerts,** with a constantly changing schedule. These include the Chiesa di Vivaldi, the Chiesa della Pietà, and the Chiesa Santa Maria Formosa. Many concerts are free; others charge an admission that rarely exceeds 12.50€ ($11.15). For information about what's going on, call ℂ **041-5208722.**

THE PERFORMING ARTS

In January 1996, a dramatic fire left the fabled **Teatro de La Fenice** at Campo San Fantin, the city's main venue for performing arts, a blackened shell and a smoldering ruin. Opera lovers around the world, including Luciano Pavarotti, mourned its loss. The Italian government has pledged $12.5 million for its reconstruction, but restoration efforts have proceeded at the proverbial snail's pace. Who can predict when it will be done? (Some speculate an opening in late 2003.) However, the theater's neoclassical facade survived the blaze and is the subject of sightseeing interest today.

Despite the tragic loss of La Fenice, cultural events have continued in a temporary theater built as a short-term substitute. Designed in the form of a big circus-style tent, within walking distance of Piazzale Roma, is the **Teatro Temporaneo de La Fenice** (aka **PalaFenice**), Isola Tronchetto (ℂ **041-786511**). For a list of other cultural performances in Venice, contact either the tourist office or City Hall, the **Municipio Comunale di Venezia,** at ℂ **041-2748200.**

The **Teatro Goldoni,** Calle Goldoni, near Campo San Luca, San Marco 4650B (ℂ **041-2402011**), honors Carlo Goldoni (1707–93), the most prolific and one of the best of the Italian playwrights. The theater presents a changing repertoire of productions, often plays in Italian but musical presentations as well. The box office is open Monday to Saturday 10am to 1pm and 4:30 to 7pm, and tickets cost 12.50€ to 25€ ($11.15–$22.35).

CAFES

All the cafes on Piazza San Marco offer a simply magical setting, several with full orchestras playing in the background. But you'll pay shockingly high prices (plus a hefty music charge) to enjoy a drink or a snack while you soak in this setting. Prepare yourself for it, and splurge on a beer, a cappuccino, or an ice cream anyway. It'll be the most memorable $15 or $20 (that's *per person*) that you'll drop on your trip.

Venice's most famous spot is **Caffè Florian,** Piazza San Marco, San Marco 56–59 (ℂ **041-5205641**), built in 1720 and elaborately decorated with plush red banquettes, elaborate murals under glass, and Art Nouveau lighting. The Florian has hosted everyone from Casanova to Lord Byron and Goethe. Light lunch is served noon to 3pm, and an English tea is served 3 to 6pm, when you can select from a choice of pastries, ice creams, and cakes. It's open Thursday to Tuesday 9:30am to midnight; it's closed the first week in December and the first week in January.

Previously recommended as a restaurant, **Quadri,** Piazza San Marco, San Marco 120–124 (ℂ **041-5222105**), stands on the opposite side of the square from Florian's and is as elegantly decorated in antique style. It should be: It was founded in 1638. Wagner used to drop in for a drink when he was working on *Tristan und Isolde.* The bar was a favorite with the Austrians during their long-ago occupation. From April to October, it's open daily 9am to midnight; off-season hours are Tuesday to Sunday 9am to midnight (it's closed the first week of Dec and the first week of Jan). The restaurant on the second floor is open the same hours as the cafe.

The 18th-century **Gran Caffè Lavena,** Piazza San Marco, San Marco 133–134 (© **041-5224070**), is a popular but intimate cafe under the piazza's arcades. During his stay in Venice, Richard Wagner was a frequent customer; he composed some of his greatest operas here. This cafe has one of the most beautifully ornate glass chandeliers in town. The best tables are near the plate-glass window in front, although there's plenty of room at the stand-up bar as well. It's open daily 9:30am to 12:30am (closed for a few days in Jan and in Nov and on Tues in winter).

Il Café (also known as Bar Rosso), Campo Santa Margherita, Dorsoduro 2963 (© **041-5287998**), is a bit battered but is a popular spot for those under 30. It's a great place to sit and enjoy a drink while watching the ever-fascinating street scenes of Dorsoduro. The antique samovar, old piano, and fading paint evoke a better day, but the place is still going strong. Sandwiches are served; beer and whisky are the drinks of choice. It's open Monday to Saturday 7am to 1am.

Although **Caffè Chioggia,** Piazza San Marco, San Marco 11 (© **041-5285011**), isn't the only cafe whose entrance opens onto the piazza; it's the only one with a view of the Venetian lagoon (off to one side). Starting around 10am and continuing, with reasonable breaks, until 1:30am, music here might begin with the kind of piano music you'd expect in a bar and end with a jazz trio. Don't expect a full-fledged restaurant: The only food served is light platters and sandwiches. Drinks include whiskey with soda, beer, and endless cups of coffee.

The hippest cafe in Venice today is funky little **Cip's,** on Isola della Giudecca within the Cipriani hotel (© **041-5207744**). Pronounced *chips* (as in potato), this cafe with its summer terrace frames one of the grandest views of Piazza San Marco. If you arrive between May and August, ask for a Bellini, made from prosecco and white-peach purée, or perhaps a *sgroppino,* a slushy mix of lemon gelato and vodka whisked over ice. You can also order the best bitter chocolate gelato in Venice here. Cip's also serves terrific international and Venetian dishes (p. 414). To reach the place, take the vaporetto to Zittelle.

BARS & PUBS

Want more in the way of nightlife? All right, but be warned: The Venetian bar owners might sock it to you when they present the bill.

In addition to the specific recommendations below, you might **barhop around San Francesco Vigna,** where there are a plethora of local watering holes.

The single most famous of all the watering holes of Ernest Hemingway is **Harry's Bar,** Calle Vallaresso, San Marco 1323 (© **041-5285777**). Harry's is known for inventing its own drinks and exporting them around the world, and it's said that carpaccio, the delicate raw-beef dish, was invented here. Fans say that Harry's makes the best Bellini in the world, although many old-time visitors still prefer a vodka martini. (Even Hemingway ordered a Bellini here once, although later he called it a drink for sissies, suggesting that it might be ideal for Fitzgerald.) Harry's Bar is now found around the world, but this is the original (the others are unauthorized knockoffs). Celebrities frequent the place during the various film and art festivals. From April to October, Harry's is open daily 10:30am to 1am (to 11pm in winter).

Bar ai Speci, in the Hotel Panada, Calle dei Specchieri, San Marco 646 (© **041-5209088**), is a charming corner bar only a short walk from St. Mark's. Its richly grained paneling is offset by dozens of antique mirrors whose glittering surfaces reflect the rows of champagne and scotch bottles and the clustered groups of Biedermeier chairs. It's open Monday to Saturday 5pm to midnight.

Bar Ducale, Calle delle Ostreghe, San Marco 2354 (© **041-5210002**), occupies a tiny corner of a building near a bridge over a narrow canal. Customers stand at the zinc bar facing the carved 19th-century Gothic-reproduction shelves. Mimosas are the specialty, but tasty sandwiches are also offered. It's ideal for an early-evening cocktail as you stroll about. Bar Ducale is open daily 7:30am to 9pm.

For the best Americano (sweet vermouth, bitters, and soda), head for **Bonifacio,** Calle degli Albanesi, Castello 4237 (© **041-5227507**), a bar off the beaten track. The Americano was said to have been invented in Venice. The version here costs far less than those at the bars closer to the San Marco area.

A stone's throw from the Rialto Bridge, **Devil's Forest,** Calle Stagneri, San Marco 5185 (© **041-5200623**), is an authentic English pub where you'll find a comfortable balance between the English- and Italian-speaking worlds. A comforting roster of beers and ales is on tap (Guinness, Harp, Kilkenny, and a line of German beers). It's open daily 10am to midnight.

A rival of Devil's Forest, **Hollandaise Volante (The Flying Dutchman),** Campo San Lio, Castello 5658 (© **041-5289349**), is another English-style pub with lots of wood paneling. A young, heavy-drinking crowd patronizes this place, mainly for beer, although fast food is also served.

Inishark Irish Pub, Calle Mondo Novo, Castello 5787 (© **041-5235300**), is the most elegant Irish pub in Venice, drawing a diverse international crowd, mainly young. Between Campo S. Maria Formosa and Salizzada S. Lio, it is decorated with flea-market junk and is often a lot of fun. It's open Tuesday to Sunday 5:30pm to 2am, and it's closed for 20 days in August.

Bar Salus, Campo Santa Margherita, Dorsoduro 3112 (© **041-5285279**), is our favorite gathering spot for a hot night in Venice's Greenwich Village, the Dorsoduro sector. Young people, both locals and visitors, predominate. This cafe has more outdoor seating than all its competitors. When the winds blow in from the Adriatic, you can retreat inside to comfortable booths in a spacious bar.

Cafe Blue, Calle Lunga S. Panalon, Dorsoduro 3778 (© **041-710227**), is ground zero for Venice's expatriate community, including exchange students from around the world. Animated, often crowded, and brightly lit, it is the nerve center for the English-speaking community. Come here to find out what's happening in the city. Open Monday to Friday 8am to 2am, and Saturday 5pm to 2am.

Five minutes from the Rialto Bridge, **Fiddler's Elbow,** Corte dei Pali, Cannaregio 3847 (© **041-5239930**), is called "the Irish pub" by the Venetians and is run by the same people who operate the equally popular Fiddler's Elbow in Florence and Rome. It has the only satellite TV in Venice with all channels: Sky, American, sports, music, whatever. In summer, there's live outdoor music. It's open daily 5pm to 12:30am.

Do Leoni is in the Londra Palace hotel, Riva degli Schiavoni, Castello 4171 (© **041-5200533**). The interior is a rich blend of scarlet-and-gold carpeting with a lion motif, English pub–style furniture, and Louis XVI–style chairs. While sipping your cocktail, you'll enjoy a view of a 19th-century bronze statue, the lagoon, and the foot traffic along the Grand Canal. A piano player entertains Wednesday to Monday. Do Leoni is open daily 12:30 to 2:30pm and 7:30 to 10:30pm (the bar is open 10:30am–12:30am).

Venice's oldest pastry shop, **Guanotto,** Ponte del Lovo, San Marco 4819 (© **041-5208439**), is a gelateria/pasticceria/bar. It's said to have virtually invented the spritzer, a combination of soda water, bitters, and white wine. Its drinks and cocktails are renowned, although enjoying a cappuccino here can take the chill off a rainy day. Guanotto is open Monday to Saturday 8am to 8:30pm, and Sunday noon to 8pm.

WINE BARS

The historic **Cantina do Spade,** Calle do Spade, San Polo 860 (© 041-5210574), beneath an arcade near the main fish-and-fruit market, dates from 1475 and was once frequented by Casanova. The place is completely rustic and bare-bones, but regulars come to order *cicchetti,* the equivalent of Spanish tapas. There's no menu, but the kitchen will occasionally turn out typical Venetian fare. Many diners prefer to order one of the 250 sandwiches. Venetians delight in the 220 types of wine; glasses begin at 1€ (90¢). Cantina do Spade is open daily 9am to 3pm and 6 to 11pm.

Mascareta, Calle Lunga Santa Maria Formosa, Castello 5183 (© 041-5230744), opened in 1995 as a showcase for the rich assortment of Italian wines. Especially prevalent are reds and whites from the Veneto, Sicily, Pulia, and Tuscany, beginning at 1.50€ ($1.35) per glass. There's room for only about 20 people at the cramped tables in this antique building. If you're hungry, you can order simple, cheap platters of cold food. It's open Monday to Saturday 6:30pm to 1am (it's closed mid-Dec to mid-Jan).

At **Vino Vino,** Calle del Caffettier, San Marco 2007A (© 041-5237027), you can choose from more than 250 Italian and imported wines. This place is loved by everyone from snobs to young people to almost-broke tourists. It offers wines by the bottle or the glass, including Italian grappas. Popular and supercheap Venetian dishes are served, including pastas, beans, baccalà (codfish), and polenta. The two rooms are always jammed like a vaporetto in rush hour, and there's takeout service if you can't find a place. It's open Wednesday to Monday 10:30am to midnight.

DINING & DANCING

Near the Accademia, **Il Piccolo Mondo,** Calle Contarini Corfu, Dorsoduro 1056A (© 041-5200371), is open during the day but comes alive with dance music at night. The crowd is often young. It's open daily 10pm to 4am, but the action actually doesn't begin until after midnight. Cover, including the first drink, is 7.50€ ($6.70) Thursday and Friday, and 10€ ($8.95) Saturday.

Martini Scala Club, Campo San Fantin, San Marco 1980 (© 041-5224121), is an elegant restaurant with a piano bar (and a kitchen that stays open late). The piano bar gets going after 10pm and stays open until 3am (it's closed Tues and Wed at lunch).

Early every evening except Wednesday, **Paradiso Perduto,** Fondamenta della Misericordia, Cannaregio 2540 (© 041-720581), functions as a likable tavern, serving well-prepared and reasonably priced platters of seafood Thursday to Monday 7 to 11pm, and Sunday noon to 3pm. After 11pm, a mix of soft recorded music and live piano music creates a backdrop for animated conversation between the neighborhood crowd and visitors. The chitchat continues until at least 2am.

Casanova Music Cafe, Lista di Spagna, Cannaregio 158A (© 041-5347479), is a claustrophobic dance club. It's not the world's greatest, but it is very popular and a good pickup bar for straights. The music is mostly recorded,

Fueled by Cicchetti

Madrid has its tasca hopping, London has its pub-crawling, and Venice has its cantina or *cicchetti* crawl. Venetians thrive on small glasses of wine and bar snacks consumed in these little wine bars.

Drop in to **Enoteca Mascareta,** 5183 Castello, Calle Lunga Santa Maria Formosa (© **041-5230744**), for its wines but also for its superb meats and cheese offered with crusty, freshly baked bread. At **Vivaldi,** 1457 San Polo, Calle de la Madoneta (© **041-5238185**), sample some of the best fried fish and baby octopus in Venice, and save room for the cheese-stuffed sardines (fresh) and their deep-fried fritters fashioned from squid. In a setting of copper kettles and wooden kegs, **Cantina do Mori,** 429 San Polo, Calle del Do Mori (© **041-5225401**), serves some of the best little sandwiches in Venice. The cantina also prepares delectable tapas, some made from oxtail and others made from cured bacon called speck.

The Lilliputian **Vina da Pinto,** 367 San Polo, Campo de le Becarie (© **041-5224599**), is known for preparing the best *baccala mantecato* in the city. This is a creamy paste of salt cod beaten with olive oil to form a paste, which is then spread across crostini.

Finally, the best for last: **Vecio Fritolin,** 2262 Santa Croce, Calle della Regina (© **041-5222881**), one of the last remaining *fritolin* (fry shops) that used to pepper Venice. A small blonde from northern Italy has brought new life to this fritolin, and her *fritto misto,* or mixed fried seafood, was the best that we encountered on a recent trip to Venice.

ranging from alternative to Latin salsa. Come around 11pm, when the dancing begins in earnest. There's a cover of 10€ ($8.95) after 10pm.

GAY CLUBS

There are no gay bars in Venice; you'll have to go to Padua, 35 minutes away by train (see chapter 10). One local count, a distinguished member of the Venetian homosexual community, expressed this point of view to us: "All bars in Venice are gay if you look in the right corner."

CASINOS

Venice is home to only one casino: the **Vendramin-Calergi Palace,** located in the center of town. This cozy venue attracts gamblers from all over the world.

Regardless of where you might happen to drop your euro, know in advance that a jacket (but not a tie) is requested for men, and basketball sneakers and shorts are forbidden. The casino contains slot machines, but more interesting are the roulette wheels, where minimum bets are 5€ ($4.45) and maximum wagers are 180€ ($160.75).

All year round, the action is at this 15th-century home, located on Strada Nuova, Cannaregio 2040 (© **041-5297111**). Incidentally, in 1883 Wagner died in this house, which opens onto the Grand Canal. Admission is 2.50€ ($2.25), and it's open daily 11am to 2:30am. You can try your luck at blackjack, roulette, baccarat, and more.

8 The Lagoon Islands of Murano, Burano & Torcello

If you take a boat from the Grand Canal near San Marco to Murano, Burano, and Torcello, it can take hours. But in about 20 minutes or so, you can head north from Piazza San Marco, coming to the Campo di Santa Maria Formosa and continuing north until you reach the vaporetto stop at Fondamente Nuove. Here you can catch the vaporetto to Murano or the other islands and cut down traveling time considerably. You can spend more time seeing the sights instead of taking a long boat trip with seemingly endless stops.

MURANO 🏵🏵

For centuries, glass blowers on the island of Murano have turned out those fantastic chandeliers that Victorian ladies used to prize so highly. They also produce heavily ornamented glasses so ruby red or so indigo blue that you can't tell whether you're drinking blackberry juice or pure-grain alcohol. Happily, the glass blowers are still plying their trade, although increasing competition (notably from Sweden) has compelled a greater degree of sophistication in design.

Murano remains the chief expedition from Venice, but it's not the most beautiful nearby island. (Burano and Torcello are far more attractive.)

You can combine a tour of Murano with a trip along the lagoon. To reach Murano, take **vaporetto no. 42 or 43** at Riva degli Schiavoni, a short walk from Piazzetta San Marco. The boat docks at the landing platform at Murano where the first furnace awaits conveniently. It's best to go Monday to Friday 10am to noon if you want to see some glass blowing action.

TOURING THE GLASS FACTORIES & OTHER SIGHTS

As you stroll through Murano, you'll find that the factory owners are only too glad to let you come in and see their age-old crafts. While browsing the showrooms, you'll need stiff resistance to keep the salespeople at bay. Bargaining is expected. Don't—repeat *don't*—pay the marked price on any item. That's merely the figure at which to open negotiations.

However, the prices of made-on-the-spot souvenirs aren't negotiable. For example, you might want to buy a horse streaked with blue. The artisan takes a piece of incandescent glass, huffs, puffs, rolls it, shapes it, snips it, and behold—he has shaped a horse. The showrooms of Murano also contain a fine assortment of Venetian crystal beads, available in every hue. You might find some of the best work to be the experiments of apprentices.

While on the island, you can visit the Renaissance palazzo housing the **Museo Vetrario di Murano,** Fondamenta Giustinian 8 (② 041-739586), which contains a spectacular collection of Venetian glass. From April to October, it's open Monday, Tuesday, and Thursday to Sunday from 10am to 5pm (to 4pm Nov–Mar). Admission is 4€ ($3.55).

⌒Finds A Special Glass Museum

For a really special museum, call for an appointment to visit the **Barovier & Toso Museum,** Palazzo Contarini, Fondamenta Vetrai 28, Murano (② 041-739049). Here Angelo Barovier displays rare glass from his private collection acquired over half a century. The museum is open (if you call first) during foundry hours Monday to Friday 9:30am to noon and 2:30 to 5pm.

If you're looking for something different, head to **San Pietro Martire,** Fondamente Vetrai (℃ 041-739704), which dates from the 1300s but was rebuilt in 1511 and is richly decorated with paintings by Tintoretto and Veronese. Its proud possession is a *Madonna and Child Enthroned,* by Giovanni Bellini, plus two superb altarpieces by the same master. The church lies right before the junction with Murano's Grand Canal, about 229m (250 yd.) from the vaporetto landing stage. It's open daily 9am to noon and 3 to 6pm; it's closed for Mass on Sunday morning.

Even more notable is **Santa Maria e Donato,** Campo San Donato (℃ **041-739056**), open daily 9am to noon and 4 to 6pm, with time variations for Sunday Mass. Dating from the 7th century but reconstructed in the 1100s, this building is a stellar example of Venetian Byzantine style, despite its 19th-century restoration. The interior is known for its mosaic floor (a parade of peacocks and eagles, as well as other creatures) and a 15th-century ship's keel ceiling. Over the apse is an outstanding mosaic of the Virgin against a gold background from the early 1200s.

WHERE TO DINE

Ai Vetrai VENETIAN   Ai Vetrai entertains and nourishes its guests in a large room not far from the Canale dei Vetrai. If you're looking for fish prepared in the local style, with arguably the widest selection on Murano, this is it. Most varieties of crustaceans and gilled creatures are available on the spot. However, if you phone ahead and order food for a large party, as the Venetians sometimes do, the owners will prepare what they call "a noble fish." You might begin with spaghetti in green clam sauce and follow with *griglia misto di pesce,* a dish that combines all the seafood of the Adriatic or other types of grilled or baked fish accented with vegetables.

Fondamenta Manin 29. ℃ 041-739293. Reservations recommended. Main courses 8.50€–15€ ($7.60–$13.40). AE, DC, MC, V. Fri–Wed 11:30am–5pm. Closed Jan. Vaporetto: 42 or 61.

BURANO ⭐⭐

Burano became world famous as a center of lacemaking, a craft that reached its pinnacle in the 18th century. The visitor who can spare a morning to visit this island will be rewarded with a charming fishing village far removed in spirit from the grandeur of Venice but only half an hour away by ferry. **Boats** leave from Fondamente Nuove, overlooking the Venetian graveyard (which is well worth the trip all on its own). To reach Fondamente Nuove, take **vaporetto no. 12 or 52** from Riva degli Schiavoni.

EXPLORING THE ISLAND

Once at Burano, you'll discover that the houses of the islanders come in varied colors: sienna, robin's egg or cobalt blue, barn red, butterscotch, and grass green.

Check out the **Scuola di Merletti di Burano,** "Museo del Merletto," Piazza Galuppi 187 (℃ **041-730034**), in the center of the village at Piazza Baldassare Galuppi. From November to March, the museum is open Wednesday to Monday 10am to 4pm (to 5pm Apr–Oct). Admission is 4€ ($3.55). The Burano School of Lace was founded in 1872 as part of a movement aimed at restoring the age-old craft that had earlier declined, giving way to such lace-making centers as Chantilly and Bruges. On the second floor you can see the lacemakers, mostly young women, at their painstaking work, and you can purchase hand-embroidered or handmade lace items.

After visiting the lace school, walk across the square to the **Duomo** and its leaning **campanile** (inside, look for the *Crucifixion,* by Tiepolo). See it while you can, because the bell tower is leaning so precariously that it looks as if it might topple at any moment.

WHERE TO DINE

Ostaria ai Pescatori SEAFOOD   This is your finest choice on Burano. This restaurant opened 200 years ago in a building that was antique even then. Today, Paolo Torcellan and his wife are the gracious owners, serving a cuisine prepared with gusto by his stalwart mother, Iolanda, in her 70s. The place has gained a reputation as the preserver of a type of simple restaurant unique to Burano. Patrons often take the vaporetto from other sections of Venice (the restaurant lies close to the boat landing) to eat at the plain wooden tables set up indoors or on the small square in front. Specialties feature all the staples of the Venetian seaside diet, such as fish soup, *risotto di pesce,* pasta seafarer style, tagliolini in squid ink, and a wide range of crustaceans, plus grilled, fried, and baked fish. Dishes prepared with local game are also available, but you must request them well in advance. Your meal might include a bottle of fruity wine from the region.

Piazza Baldassare Galuppi 371. (✆ 041-730650. Reservations recommended. Main courses 12€–20€ ($10.70–$17.85). AE, DC, MC, V. Thurs–Tues noon–3pm and 6–9:30pm. Closed Jan. Vaporetto: Line 12 or 52.

TORCELLO 🍂🍂

Of all the islands of the lagoon, Torcello, the so-called Mother of Venice, offers the most charm. If Burano is behind the times, Torcello is positively antediluvian. You can stroll across a grassy meadow, traverse an ancient stone bridge, and step back into that time when the Venetians first fled from invading barbarians to create a city of Neptune in the lagoon.

To reach Torcello, take **vaporetto no. 12** from Fondamenta Nuova on Murano. The trip takes about 45 minutes.

Warning: If you go to Torcello on your own, don't listen to the gondoliers who hover at the ferry quay. They'll tell you that the cathedral and the locanda are miles away. Actually, they're both reached after a leisurely 12- to 15-minute stroll along the canal.

EXPLORING THE ISLAND

Torcello has two major attractions: a church with Byzantine mosaics good enough to make Empress Theodora at Ravenna turn as purple with envy as her robe, and a *locanda* (inn) that converts day-trippers into inebriated angels of praise (see "Where to Dine," below). First the spiritual nourishment, then the alcoholic sustenance.

Cattedrale di Torcello, also called **Santa Maria Assunta Isola di Torcello** 🍂 (✆ **041-730084**), was founded in A.D. 639 and subsequently rebuilt. It stands in a lonely grassy meadow beside an 11th-century campanile. The attractions here are its **Byzantine mosaics** 🍂🍂. Clutching her child, the weeping Madonna in the apse is a magnificent sight, and on the opposite wall is a powerful *Last Judgment.* Byzantine artisans, it seems, were at their best in portraying hell and damnation. In their *Inferno,* they've re-created a virtual human stew with the fires stirred by wicked demons. Reptiles slide in and out of the skulls of cannibalized sinners. The church is open daily: April to October 10am to 12:30pm and 2:30 to 6pm (to 5pm Nov–Mar). Admission is 2.50€ ($2.25).

WHERE TO DINE

Locanda Cipriani ⭑⭑ VENETIAN   This place is operated by the same folks behind the Hotel Cipriani and Harry's Bar (actually, by the very cosmopolitan Bonifacio Brass, nephew of Harry Cipriani). This artfully simple locanda is deliberately rustic, light-years removed from the family's grander venues. Menu items are uncompromisingly classic, with deep roots in family tradition. A good example is *filleto di San Pietro alla Carlina* (filet of John Dory in the style of Carla, a late and much-revered matriarch, who made the dish for decades using tomatoes and capers). Also look for carpaccio Cipriani, *risotto alla Torcellano* (with fresh vegetables and herbs from the family's garden), fish soup, *tagliolini verdi gratinati,* and a traditional roster of veal, liver, fish, and beef dishes.

For years the Locanda's five bedrooms were closed but have been newly restored and open to the public. It attracts those seeking an exclusive, remote retreat in an authentic Venetian inn unlike any other in the city. The price is 140€ ($125) per person with half-board. Bedrooms are air-conditioned with a phone, hair dryer, minibar, and safe.

Piazza San Fosca 29, Isola di Torcello. ⓒ **041-730150.** www.locandacipriani.com. Reservations recommended. Main courses 18€–22.50€ ($16.05–$20.10). AE, DC, MC, V. Wed–Mon noon–3pm; Fri–Sat 7–10pm. Closed Jan 15–Feb 15. Vaporetto: Line 12 and 14.

10

The Veneto & the Dolomites

Venice doesn't have a monopoly on art or architectural treasures. Of the cities of interest that you can easily reach from Venice, in the area known as the Veneto, three cities tower above the rest: **Verona,** home of the eternal lovers Romeo and Juliet; **Padua,** the city of Mantegna, with frescoes by Giotto; and **Vicenza,** the city of Palladio, with streets of Renaissance palazzi and hills studded with villas.

In order of interest, we'd rank the three in that order. Outside of Venice, Verona is the most beautiful city in the region for wandering. Padua's many art treasures, including Giotto frescoes, gives it a nod over Vicenza, which lures those who are mainly interested in touring Palladio's villas. If time remains, you can also explore the **Riviera del Brenta,** with its Venetian palazzi, and such historic old cities as **Treviso** and **Bassano del Grappa.**

If you have even more time, you can venture farther afield to the limestone **Dolomites (Dolomiti),** one of Europe's greatest natural attractions.

Some of these peaks in the northeastern Italian Alps soar to 3,200m (10,500 ft.). The Dolomiti are a year-round destination, with two high seasons: midsummer, when the hiking is great, and winter, when the skiers slide in. At times, the Dolomiti form fantastic shapes, combining to create a primordial landscape, with mountain chains resembling the teeth of a giant dragon. Clefts descend precipitously along jagged rocky walls, and at other points a vast, flat tableland, spared nature's fury, emerges.

Readers with an extra day or so to spare might first want to postpone their Dolomite adventure for a detour to **Trieste,** the unofficial capital of **Friuli–Venezia Giulia.** It was Venice's main rival in the Adriatic from the 9th century to the 15th century. Even though Trieste doesn't boast Venice's charm, it is still one of Italy's most interesting ports, with Hapsburg monuments at its core and the world's largest accessible cave on its outskirts.

1 The Riviera del Brenta ★★

The **Brenta Canal,** running from Fusina to Padua, functioned as a mainland extension of Venice during the Renaissance, when wealthy merchants began using the area as a retreat from the city's summer heat. Dubbed the Riviera del Brenta, the 17km (11-mile) stretch along the banks of the canal from Malcontenta to Stra is renowned for its gracious villas, 44 of which are still visible. Meticulous readers of Shakespeare will remember that in *The Merchant of Venice,* Portia's home is a villa at Belmont along the Brenta.

The region's primary architect was **Andrea di Pietro,** known as **Palladio** (1508–80), who designed 19 of the villas. Inspired by ancient Roman architecture, Palladio's singular design—square, perfectly proportioned, functionally elegant—became the standard by which villas were judged. His designs are familiar to Americans as the basis for most state capitals and for Jefferson's Monticello.

ESSENTIALS

GETTING THERE   Consider an all-day guided excursion by **boat** along the Brenta Canal as far as Padua, including many of the most important Renaissance monuments en route. **American Express** (✆ 041-5200844) will sell you tickets for the Burchiello Excursion Boat. From March to October, trips depart from the piers at Venice's Piazza San Marco every Tuesday, Thursday, and Saturday at 9am for a ride that includes a running bilingual commentary from an onboard host. The price is 62.50€ ($55.80) per person, plus 22.50€ ($20.10) for an optional lunch in historic Oriago. You get glimpses of the elegant villas that seem to cling to the shorelines, guided visits through the evocative villas at Malcontenta and Oriago, and a somewhat rushed tour through the most spectacular sights of Padua after the boat docks. At 6:10pm, you board a bus for transit back to Venice.

You can tour the Brenta Riviera by means of **buses** leaving from Venice headed for Padua. The buses, operated by the local **ACTV** line (✆ 041-5287886), depart from the Venetian company's ticket office in Piazzale Roma Monday to Saturday every 15 to 30 minutes starting at 6:10am. A one-way ticket to Villa Foscari is 1.50€ ($1.35) and a one-way fare to the Villa Pisani is 2.25€ ($2).

By car, note that all villas open to the public are on the north bank of the canal directly along Route S11 headed west out of Venice toward Padua. At the APT in Venice, you can pick up the visitor's guide *Riviera del Brenta Venezia,* offering background information on the villas and a map of their locations between Malcontenta and Stra.

VISITOR INFORMATION   Contact the **APT tourist office** of Villa Widmann, Via Nazionale 420, Venezia (✆ 041-424973). From April to September, it's open Tuesday to Saturday 8:30am to 1:30pm and 2 to 4pm; October to March, hours are Friday through Sunday 9:30am to 3:30pm.

TOURING THE VILLAS

The villa closest to Venice that's open for tours is the **Villa Foscari (Villa La Malcontenta)** ✦, Via dei Turisti 9, Malcontenta (✆ 041-5203966), on Route S11 about 4km (2½ miles) west of where the canal empties into the Venetian Lagoon. It was constructed by Palladio for the Foscari family in 1560. A Foscari wife was exiled here for some alleged misdeed she did to her husband, and the unhappiness surrounding the incident gave the name Malcontenta (unhappy one) to the villa and its village. It's open Tuesday and Saturday 9am to noon, with a 7€ ($6.25) admission; you can call Monday to Friday and make reservations to see it on other days.

In Stra, 32km (20 miles) west of Venice on Route S11, stands the **Villa Pisani (Villa Nazionale;** ✆ 049-502074). Built in 1720 as a palatial retreat for Doge Alvise Pisani, it became the Italian home of Napoleon and later served as the initial meeting site of Mussolini and Hitler. Given this historical context, it's no surprise that the villa is the largest and grandest. A reflecting pool out front gives added dimension, and a small army of statues stands guard over the premises. The highlights of a visit are the magnificent Giambattista Tiepolo frescoes, painted on the ballroom ceiling to depict the *Glory of the Pisani Family,* in which family members are surrounded by hovering angels and saints. The villa is open Tuesday to Sunday 9am to 4pm (until 6pm Apr–Sept). Admission is 5€ ($4.45) for both the park and the museum but only 2.50€ ($2.25) to explore just the park.

The Veneto & the Dolomites

Mittewald

Drau

Gail

Weissensee

Millstatter See

AUSTRIA

Forni
Avoltri

Sappada

Vigo

Paluzza

Forni
di Sopra

Ampezzo

SLOVENIA

▲ M. Pramaggiore

Bohinjsko Jazero

A23

S. Francesco

Kobarid

S. Martino
di C.

Digliano

Udine

Tagliamento

S. Giorgio

Pordenone

S13

Pozzuolo

A23

A28

A28

Palmanova

Brugnera

Villalta

A4

SLOVENIA

Annone

Monfalcone

A4

Portogruaro

Livenza

Grignano

Ponte
di Piave

Trieste

*Golfo di
Trieste*

SLOVENIA

CROATIA

The Veneto &
the Dolomites

Venice

Florence

ITALY

✪ Rome

Golfo di Venezia

There are other villas you can visit along the Riviera, each with a stately private home whose owners appreciate and fiercely protect the unique nature of their property. These structures don't follow the gracefully symmetrical rhythms of Palladio: Each appears to be a larger version of the palazzi lining Venice's Grand Canal. Although most villas welcome the occasional appropriately respectful visitor, call in advance before you drop in.

These include the **Villa Sagredo,** Via Sagredo (✆ **049-503174;** after hours, 041-412967), half a mile northwest of the hamlet of Vigonovo. In a suitably gnarled garden, it was built on ancient Roman foundations, and the form it has today dates from around 1700, the result of frequent rebuilding. You must reserve in advance, and the owners prefer scheduled visits Tuesday to Friday 5 to 10pm or Saturday and Sunday 2 to around 8pm. A restaurant and a bar serve simple food and drink. Admission is free.

WHERE TO STAY

Dolo, 15 minutes by car from Venice or Padua, is at the midpoint of the Brenta Canal. It contains several villas from the 17th and 18th centuries, most of which are still inhabited. **Mira** is 10 minutes from Venice and 20 minutes from Padua at the most scenic bend of the Brenta; it's no wonder that several villas lie in the area. The following villas welcome overnight guests.

Villa Ducale ✦✦   This villa, built in 1884 by Count Giulio Rocca, is one of the finest hotels in the area. Restored to its original grandeur, it's graced with Murano glass chandeliers, elaborate frescoes, luxurious fabrics, and antique furnishings. The beautifully outfitted guest rooms overlook the statue-filled grounds and are extremely comfortable.

Riviera Martiri della Libertà 75, 30031 Dolo. ✆ **041-5608020.** Fax 041-5608004. www.villaducale.it. 11 units. 120€–350€ ($107.15–$312.55) double; 170€–500€ ($151.80–$446.50) suite. Rates include breakfast. AE, DC, MC, V. Free parking. **Amenities:** Restaurant; lounge; room service; babysitting; laundry/dry cleaning. *In room:* A/C, TV, minibar, hair dryer, safe.

Villa Margherita ✦✦   This 17th-century villa is on a particularly scenic bend of the Brenta. It features marble columns and fireplaces, marble and terra-cotta floors, frescoes and stucco, a sunny breakfast room, and guest rooms that blend individualized traditional elegance with modern comfort. The rooms come in various shapes and sizes, each with first-rate linen and well-kept bathrooms. An immense park opens up behind the villa.

Via Nazionale 416–417, 30030 Mira, Venezia. ✆ **041-4265800.** Fax 041-4265838. www.villa-margherita.com. 19 units. 199€–254€ ($177.70–$226.80) double. Rates include buffet breakfast. AE, DC, MC, V. **Amenities:** Bar; lounge; bike rental; room service; babysitting; laundry/dry cleaning. *In room:* A/C, TV, minibar, hair dryer, safe.

WHERE TO DINE

Trattoria Nalin VENETIAN/SEAFOOD   Most of the Riviera del Brenta's restaurants focus on seafood, and this one is no exception. In a century-old building, the restaurant has flourished as a family-run enterprise since the 1960s. It's adjacent to the canal near the town center, and you'll probably gravitate to the terrace, where potted shrubs and flowers bloom in summer. The specialties vary with whatever happens to be in season but are likely to include *tagliatelle con salsa di calamaretti* (with squid sauce), *spaghetti al nero* (with octopus ink), crabs from the Venetian lagoon, and variations on polenta and risotto.

Via Nuovissimo 29, Mira. ✆ **041-420083.** Reservations recommended. Main courses 11€–17€ ($9.80–$15.20). AE, DC, MC, V. Tues–Sun noon–2:30pm; Tues–Sat 7:30–10pm. Closed Aug and Dec 26–Jan 12.

Wine Tasting

Important vineyards in the Veneto include **Azienda Vinicola Fratelli Fabiano,** Via Verona 6, 37060 Sona, near Verona (✆ **045-6081111**); and **Fratelli Bolla,** Piazza Cittadella 3, 37122 Verona (✆ **045-8670911**). Smaller, but well respected because of recent improvements to its vintages, is **Nino Franco** (known for its sparkling prosecco), in the hamlet of Valdobbiadene, Via Garibaldi 177, 31049 Treviso (✆ **0423-972051**). For information on these and the dozens of other producers in the Veneto, contact the **Azienda di Promozione Turistica,** Via Delgi Alpini no. 9, Piazza Bra Verona, 37121 Verona (✆ **045-8068680**). If you plan to tour the countryside and do a little wine tasting and vineyard touring, it's best to make an appointment ahead of time and get detailed directions. See also "The Wine Roads from Treviso," on p. 472.

2 Padua ★

40km (25 miles) W of Venice, 81km (50 miles) E of Verona, 233km (144 miles) E of Milan

Padua (Padova) no longer looks as it did when Richard Burton's Petruchio tamed Elizabeth Taylor's Katerina in the Zeffirelli adaptation of *The Taming of the Shrew.* However, it remains a major art center of the Veneto.

Many visitors stay in more affordable Padua and commute to high-priced Venice. Of course, Padua doesn't have the beauty of Venice and suffers from high-rises and urban blight, but its inner core has a wealth of attractions. Its university, Italy's second oldest, adds life and vibrancy, even though such visitors and professors as Dante and Galileo haven't been seen here in a while.

ESSENTIALS

GETTING THERE The **train** is best if you're coming from Venice, Milan, or Bologna. Trains depart for and arrive from Venice once every 30 minutes (trip time: 30 min.), costing 2.25€ ($2) one way. Trains to and from Milan run every hour (trip time: 2½ hr.) for 10€ ($8.95) one way. For information and schedules, call ✆ **848-888088** toll-free in Italy. Padua's main rail terminus is at Piazza Stazione, north of the historic core and outside the 16th-century walls. A bus will connect you to the center.

Buses from Venice arrive every 30 minutes (trip time: 45 min.), costing 2.80€ ($2.50) one way. There are also connections from Vicenza every 30 minutes (trip time: 30 min.) at 2.80€ ($2.50) one way. Padua's bus station is at Via Trieste 42 (✆ **049-8206844**), near Piazza Boschetti, 5 minutes from the rail station.

By car, take A4 west from Venice.

VISITOR INFORMATION The **tourist office** is at Riviera Mugnai 8 (✆ **049-8767911**). It's open Monday to Saturday 9:15am to 5:45pm, and Sunday 9am to noon.

SEEING THE SIGHTS

A university that grew to fame throughout Europe was founded here as early as 1222. The **University of Padua** has remained one of the great centers for learning in Italy. The physics department counts Galileo among its past professors, and Petrarch lectured here. Today its buildings are scattered around the city. The historic main building is called **Il Bo,** after an inn on the site that used an ox as its sign. The chief entrance is on Via Otto Febbraio. Of particular interest is an anatomy theater, which dates from 1594 and was the first of its kind in Europe. For 2.50€ ($2.25), you can join a guided tour of the university. On Tuesday, Thursday, and Saturday, tours depart at 9, 10, and 11am; on Monday, Wednesday, and Friday, they depart at 3, 4, and 5pm. For information, contact the Associazione Guide di Padova at (✆ **049-8209773.**

If you're on a tight schedule, concentrate on the Cappella degli Scrovegni (Giotto frescoes) and the Basilica di Sant'Antonio.

A combination ticket valid for admission to all of Padua's museums costs 7.50€ ($6.70). It is available at the tourist office or any of the city's museums.

Chapel of the Scrovegni (Cappella degli Scrovegni) This modest chapel is the best reason for visiting Padua because it contains remarkable **Giotto frescoes** ✹✹✹. Sometime around 1305 and 1306, Giotto did a cycle of more than 35 frescoes here, which, along with those at Assisi (see chapter 7, "Tuscany & Umbria"), form the basis of his claim to fame. Like an illustrated storybook, the frescoes unfold biblical scenes. The third bottom panel (the lower level on the right) is most often reproduced; it depicts Judas kissing a most skeptical Christ. On the entrance wall is Giotto's *Last Judgment,* in which hell wins out for sheer fascination. The master's representation of the *Vices and Virtues* is bizarre; it reveals the depth of his imagination in personifying nebulous evil and elusive good. One of the most dramatic panels depicts the raising of Lazarus from the dead—a masterfully balanced scene, rhythmically ingenious for its day. The swathed and cadaverous Lazarus, however, looks indecisive on whether he'll rejoin the living. The *Virgin* ✹ on the altar is by the Tuscan sculptor Giovanni Pisano.

Piazza Eremitani 8, off Corso Garibaldi. (✆ **049-8204550.** Admission 7.50€ ($6.70) (including entry to Civil Museums and Palace of Law). Daily 9am–6pm. Bus: 3, 8, 12, or 18.

Civic Museum (Museo Civico di Padova) ✹ This picture gallery is filled with minor works by major Venetian artists, some dating from the 14th century. Look for a wooden Crucifix by Giotto and two miniatures by Giorgione. Other works are Giovanni Bellini's *Portrait of a Young Man* and Jacopo Bellini's miniature *Descent into Limbo,* with its childlike devils. The 15th-century Arras tapestry is also on display. Other works are Veronese's *Martyrdom of St. Primo and St. Feliciano,* plus Tintoretto's *Supper in Simone's House* and *Crucifixion,* probably the finest single painting in the gallery.

Piazza Eremitani 8. (✆ **049-8204550.** Admission included with entry to Cappella degli Scrovegni and to Palace of Law; separate visit 5€ ($4.45). Daily 9am–7pm. Bus: 3, 8, 12, or 18.

Chiesa degli Eremitani ✹ One of Padua's tragedies occurred when this church was bombed on March 11, 1944. Before that, it housed one of the greatest treasures in Italy, the **Ovetari Chapel (Cappella Ovetari),** with the first significant cycle of **frescoes** ✹ **by Andrea Mantegna** (1431–1506). The church was rebuilt, but, alas, you can't resurrect 15th-century frescoes. To the right of the main altar are the fragments left after the bombing. The most interesting fresco saved is a panel depicting the dragging of St. Christopher's body through the streets. Note also the *Assumption of the Virgin.* Like Leonardo, the artist had a keen eye for architectural detail. In the chancel chapel are some magnificent **frescoes** ✹✹ **attributed to Guarineto,** a Venetian student of Giotto.

Piazza Eremitani 9. (✆ **049-8756410.** Free admission (donations accepted). Mon–Sat 8am–12:30pm and 4–6pm; Sun and religious holidays 9:30am–noon and 4–6pm. Bus: 3, 8, 12, or 18.

Padua

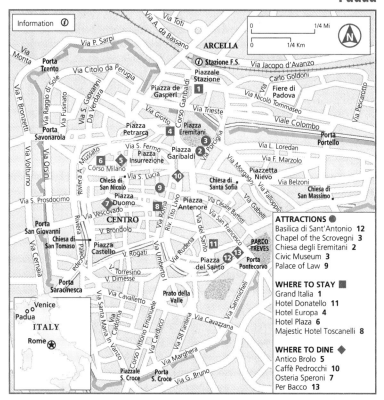

Basilica di Sant'Antonio 🐱🐱   This basilica was built in the 13th century and dedicated to St. Anthony of Padua, who's interred within. It's a synthesis of styles, with mainly Romanesque and Gothic features. Campaniles and minarets combine to give it an Eastern appearance. The imposing **interior** 🐱🐱 is richly frescoed and decorated, filled with pilgrims devoutly touching the saint's **marble tomb in the Saints Chapel** 🐱🐱, a Renaissance masterpiece. One of the more unusual relics is in the treasury: the 7-centuries-old, still-uncorrupted tongue of St. Anthony.

The great art treasures are the **Donatello bronzes** 🐱🐱 at the main altar, with a realistic Crucifix towering over the rest. Seek out as well the **Donatello relief** depicting the removal of Christ from the cross (at the back of the high altar), a unified composition expressing in simple lines and with an unromantic approach the tragedy of Christ and the sadness of the mourners.

Among his other innovations, Donatello restored the lost art of the **equestrian statue** 🐱🐱 with the well-known example in front of the basilica. Although the man it honors (Gattamelata) is of little interest to art lovers, the 1453 statue is of prime importance. The large horse is realistic because Donatello was a master of detail. He cleverly directs the eye to the commanding face of the Venetian military hero, nicknamed "Spotted Cat." Gattamelata was a dead ringer for the late Laurence Olivier.

Piazza del Santo 11. ⓒ **049-8242811.** Free admission. Daily 6:30am–7pm. Bus: 8, 12, 18, 22, M, or T.

Palace of Law (Palazzo della Ragione) ⭐ This palazzo, dating from the early 13th century, is among the most remarkable buildings of northern Italy. It sits in the marketplace, ringed with loggias and with a roof shaped like the hull of a sailing vessel. Climb the steps and enter the grandiose **Salone,** an 82m (270-ft.) assembly hall containing a gigantic 15th-century wooden horse. The walls are richly frescoed with symbolic paintings that replaced the frescoes by Giotto and his assistants that were destroyed by fire in 1420.

Via VIII Febbraio, between Piazza delle Erbe and Piazza dell Frutta. ℂ **049-8205006.** Admission included with entry to Cappella degli Scrovegni and to the Civil Museum; separate visit 5€ ($4.45). Tues–Sun 9am–7pm. Bus: 8 or A.

SHOPPING

Padua is an elegant town with a rich university life, a solid industrial base, and an economy too diversified to rely exclusively on tourism. Therefore, you'll find a wide roster of upscale consumer goods and luxury items, and less emphasis on souvenirs and handcrafts. For insights into the good life *alla Padovese,* trek through the neighborhood around the landmark **Piazza Insurrezione,** especially the **Galleria Borghese,** a conglomeration of shops off Via San Fermo.

Droves of shoppers head to the **Prato delle Valle** on the third Sunday of every month, when more than 200 antiques and collectibles vendors set up shop for the day. The square, one of the largest in all Europe, also hosts a smaller **weekly market** on Saturday. Shoes from nearby Brenta factories are the prevalent product, but the range of goods offered remains eclectic.

The outdoor markets (Mon–Sat) in the twin **Piazza delle Erbe** (for fresh produce) and **Piazza della Frutta** (dry goods), flanking the enormous Palazzo della Ragione, are some of Italy's best.

Specialty shops include **Roberto Callegari,** 8 via Davila (ℂ **049-8755803**), Padua's leading jewelry store, and **L'Antiquario Gemmologo,** 6 Via Davila (ℂ **049-664195**), run by Callegari's brother. He sells antique silver and also has an outstanding collection of jewelry next door. Just for fun, drop in at **Amadio,** Galleria Pedrocchi (ℂ **049-8752150**), which has been specializing in men's sportswear and (an unusual marriage) household furnishings for more than a hundred years. If you found the designer shops of Venice too pricey, you'll encounter the same merchandise by walking along **Via San Fermo,** where you'll find Prada, Armani, Gucci, Hermès, Max Mara, and the like.

WHERE TO STAY

Grand'Italia ⭐⭐ This is the town's finest hotel, surpassing the position long held by the Hotel Plaza. Rated four stars by the government, it lies in a restored building in the heart of the city near the train station. It was built in 1909 as a palazzo in the then-innovative Art Nouveau style, an architecture still in evidence in its terraces, verandas, and balconies. Before the opening of this hotel, the innkeeping at Padua was rather dismal. The Cinel family took over the building and succeeded in bringing back its former luster. The elegant reception hall sets the grace note for the entire hotel. Two living rooms on the second floor, decorated with stucco and gilt, reproduce the Deco style of two rooms of the Louvre in Paris. Bedrooms aren't neglected either. Each is roomy and decorated in a fashionable modern style, with many conveniences, including a hydromassage in the suites. Bathrooms are immaculately kept.

Corso del Popolo 81, 35131 Padova. ℂ **049-8761111.** Fax 049-8750850. www.hotelgranditalia.it/ to_reach.htm. 61 units. 170€ ($151.80) double; 230€ ($205.40) suite. Rates include buffet breakfast. AE, DC, MC, V. **Amenities:** Bar; room service; babysitting; laundry/dry cleaning. *In room:* A/C, TV, minibar, hair dryer.

Hotel Donatello   The Donatello is a renovated hotel with an ideal location near the basilica. Its facade is pierced by an arched arcade, and the chandeliers of its lobby combine with the checkerboard marble floor to create a hospitable ambience. The guest rooms are reasonably comfortable, if unremarkable, and most come with private balconies.

Piazza del Santo 102–104, 35123 Padova. ℂ **049-8750634.** Fax 049-8750829. www.hoteldonatello.net. 45 units (some with tub, some with shower). 130€–145€ ($116.10–$129.50) double; 180€–225€ ($160.75–$200.95) suite. Breakfast 11€ ($9.80). AE, DC, MC, V. Parking 15€ ($13.40). Closed Dec 15–Jan 15. Bus: 3, 8, or 12. **Amenities:** Restaurant; lounge; room service; laundry. *In room:* A/C, TV, minibar, hair dryer, safe.

Hotel Europa   The Europa was built in the 1960s and looks its age, but it's still a good buy. The compact and serviceable guest rooms have simple built-in furnishings and open onto small balconies. The public rooms are enhanced by cubist murals, free-form ceramic plaques, and furniture placed in conversational groupings.

Largo Europa 9, 35137 Padova. ℂ **049-661200.** Fax 049-661508. 64 units (showers only). 133€ ($118.75) double. Rates include breakfast. AE, DC, MC, V. Parking 17€ ($15.20). **Amenities:** Restaurant; bar; room service; laundry. *In room:* A/C, TV, minibar, hair dryer.

Hotel Plaza   Popular with business travelers, the Plaza is one of Padua's leading inns. The guest rooms are comfortable, attractive, and well-maintained. They're the most spacious and up-to-date in town, offering modern bathrooms. The hotel staff is efficient and helpful.

Corso Milano 40, 35139 Padova. ℂ **049-656822.** Fax 049-661117. www.plazapadova.it. 142 units (showers only). 185€ ($165.20) double; 300€ ($267.90) suite. Rates include buffet breakfast. AE, DC, MC, V. Parking 12€ ($10.70). Bus: 5, 7, or 10. **Amenities:** Fine restaurant; bar; room service; laundry. *In room:* A/C, TV, minibar, hair dryer, safe.

Majestic Hotel Toscanelli ✦   This pink hotel has wrought-iron balconies and stone-edged French windows on its facade, plus a Renaissance well and dozens of potted shrubs out front. It's centrally located; you can walk to all the major attractions from here. The inviting breakfast room is surrounded by a garden of green plants. The midsize-to-spacious guest rooms have elegant cherrywood pieces crafted by Tuscan artisans, along with mahogany and white-marble touches. Furnishings are tasteful, with good lighting, adequate desk space, and carpets at your feet. The staff is attentive and helpful.

Via dell'Arco 2, 35122 Padova. ℂ **049-663244.** Fax 049-8760025. www.toscanelli.com. 32 units (25 with shower only). 161€–197€ ($143.75–$175.90) double; from 197€ ($175.90) suite. Rates include buffet breakfast. AE, DC, DISC, MC, V. Parking 16€ ($14.30). Bus: 8. **Amenities:** Bar; room service; babysitting; laundry. *In room:* A/C, TV, minibar, hair dryer, safe.

WHERE TO DINE

Caffè Pedrocchi ✦, Piazzetta Pedrocchi 15 (ℂ **049-8781231**), off Piazza Cavour, is a neoclassical landmark, hailed as Europe's most elegant coffeehouse when it opened in 1831. Its green, white, and red rooms reflect the national colors. On sunny days, you might want to sit on one of the two stone porches; in winter, you'll have plenty to distract you inside. The sprawling bathtub-shaped travertine bar has a brass top and brass lion's feet, and the velvet banquettes have maroon upholstery, red-veined marble tables, and Egyptian Revival chairs. There's also a more conservatively decorated English-style pub, whose entrance is under a covered arcade a few steps away. It's open Tuesday to Sunday 8am to midnight.

Antico Brolo 🏆🏆 ITALIAN   Across from the ornate *Teatro de Padova* (Civic Theater), this is the city's best restaurant. Even though the 16th-century dining room evokes the Renaissance, many patrons prefer a table in the garden, where candlelit tables are set on a terrace. The cuisine follows the tenets of most of Italy, with special emphasis on seasonal ingredients and the traditions of the Veneto and Emilia-Romagna. Especially delicious are the made-on-the-premises *graganelli* (similar to the tubular shape of penne) with garlic sauce, onion soup baked in a crust, chateaubriand with balsamic vinegar, and grilled fish. The perfect dessert is *zuppa inglese,* a cream-enriched equivalent to zabaglione.

Corso Milano 22. © 049-664555. Reservations recommended. Main courses 13€–25€ ($11.60–$22.35). AE, DC, MC, V. Tues–Sun 12:30–2:30pm and 7:30–midnight. Closed Aug 10–20. Bus: 5, 7, or 10.

Osteria Speroni 🅥🅐🅛🅤🅔 SEAFOOD   This affordable fish restaurant occupies a 16th-century building a 3-minute walk from the cathedral. You'll dine in one of the three antique-looking rooms, each with exposed stone. Don't expect a lot of meat on the menu. The best way to begin is with antipasti from the buffet table, where you'll find fried calamari, marinated octopus, garlic-marinated shrimp, and a wide assortment of fried or marinated vegetables. A special pasta is *spaghetti alla busara,* with shrimp, tomatoes, and lots of garlic. Also look for sea bass roasted in a salt crust.

Via Speroni 36. © **049-8753370.** Reservations recommended. Main courses 12.50€–17.50€ ($11.15–$15.65). AE, DC, MC, V. Mon–Sat 12:30–2:30pm and 8–10:30pm. Closed Aug 1–25. Bus: 8, 12, 18, 22, M, or T.

Per Bacco 🏆 ITALIAN   Innovative dishes made from market-fresh ingredients and a wine list with nearly 1,000 labels keep diners coming back for more at this inviting restaurant. For your antipasto selection, begin with a selection of various types of Tuscan salami, a plate worthy of gourmets. We recently enjoyed *tagliatelle alla Norcina* (a pasta with black truffles and Tuscan sausage) and *composizione Per Bacco* (a platter of three meats cooked together).

Piazzale Ponte Corvo 10. © **049-8754664.** Reservations recommended. Main courses 14€–17.50€ ($12.50–$15.65). AE, DC, MC, V. Tues–Sun noon–2:30pm and 7:30–11pm. Closed 3rd week of Aug.

PADUA AFTER DARK

You can hang out with students in town at any of the crowded cafes along **Via Cavour,** or walk over to the wine and beer dives around **Piazza della Frutta** to find out where most of the college crowd is being cool. But other than a quiet stroll through the town's historic core, there's little happening in the city.

We like to spend an evening in Padua at one of the city's wine bars or enotecas. The oldest wine bar is **Enoteca da Severino,** 44 Via del Santo (© **049-6504674**). **Coteglioni,** 1 Via Pietro d'Abano (© **049-8750083**), is more of a restaurant, but it offers live music on weekends.

At this *birreria* (beer tavern), **Victoria,** Via Savonarola 149 (© **049-8721530**), live jazz concerts are presented on Thursday. Otherwise, it's a good nighttime hangout if you like to drink beer and eat pizza and mingle with a fairly young crowd. Many people come here mainly to drink, although you can order plates of food costing 6€ to 7.50€ ($5.35–$6.70). The beer tavern stays open Tuesday to Sunday from 7pm to 2am.

For dancing in Padua, try **Disco-Bar Limbo,** Via San Fermo 44 (© **049-656882**), where electronic games alternate with recorded and (occasionally) live music. About 3km (2 miles) west of Padua are **Disco Extra Extra,** Via Ciamician 5 (© **049-620044**), and its neighbor, **Disco P1,** Viale Giusti 15 (© **049-8601633**).

The leading gay bar is **Flexo,** Via Nicola Tommaseo 96 (© **049-8074707**), open Wednesday to Sunday 9:30pm to at least 2am. The first Saturday of every month is leather night.

3 Palladio's Vicenza ✶✶

203km (126 miles) E of Milan, 68km (42 miles) W of Venice, 52km (32 miles) NE of Verona

In the 16th century, Vicenza was transformed into a virtual laboratory for the architectural experiments of Andrea di Pietro, known as **Palladio** (1508–80). One of the greatest architects of the High Renaissance, he was inspired by the classical art and architecture of ancient Greece and Rome. Palladio peppered the city with palazzi and basilicas, and the surrounding hills with villas for patrician families.

The architect was particularly important to England and America. In the 18th century, Robert Adam was inspired by him, as is reflected by many country homes in England. Then, through the influence of Adam and others even earlier, the spirit of Palladio was brought to America (examples are Jefferson's Monticello and plantation homes in the antebellum South). Palladio even lent his name to this architectural style, Palladianism, which is identified by regularity of form, imposing size, and an adherence to lines established in the ancient world. Visitors arrive in Vicenza today principally to see the works left by Palladio; for this reason, the city was designated a UNESCO World Heritage Site in 1994.

Federico Faggin, inventor of the silicon chip, was born here, and many local computer component industries now prosper on Vicenza's outskirts; its citizens earn one of the highest average incomes in the country.

ESSENTIALS

GETTING THERE   Most visitors arrive from Venice via **train** (trip time: 1 hr.), costing 3.50€ ($3.15) one way. Trains also arrive frequently from Padua (trip time: 25 min.), charging 2.25€ ($2) one way. There are also frequent connections from Milan (trip time: 2½ hr.), at 8.85€ ($8.50) one way. For information and schedules, call © **848-888088** toll-free in Italy. Vicenza's rail station is at Piazza Stazione (Campo Marzio), at the southern edge of Viale Roma.

By car, take A4 west from Venice toward Verona, bypassing Padua.

VISITOR INFORMATION   The **tourist office** is at Piazza Matteotti 12 (© **0444-320854**), open Monday to Saturday 9am to 1pm and 2:30 to 6pm, and Sunday 9am to 1pm.

EXPLORING THE WORLD OF PALLADIO

Basilica Palladiana ✶✶   This basilica was partially designed by Palladio. The loggias rise on two levels; the lower tier has Doric pillars and the upper has Ionic pillars. In its heyday, this building was much frequented by the Vicentino aristocrats, who lavishly spent their gold on villas in the neighboring hills. They met here in a kind of social fraternity, perhaps to talk about the excessive sums being spent on Palladio-designed or -inspired projects. The original basilica was done in the Gothic style and served as the Palazzo della Ragione (Hall of Justice). The roof collapsed following a 1945 bombing but has been subsequently rebuilt. Although there aren't any treasures inside, two or three times a year art exhibits are held here.

Beside the basilica is the 13th-century **Torre Bissara** ✶, soaring almost 82m (270 ft.). Across from the basilica is the **Loggia del Capitanio (Captain of the Guard)** ✶, designed by Palladio in his waning years.

Piazza dei Signori © **0444-323681**. Admission 5€ ($4.45). Tues–Sat 10am–1pm and 3–7pm.

Olympic Theater (Teatro Olimpico) 🎭🎭 Palladio's masterpiece and last work—ideal for performances of classical plays—is one of the world's greatest theaters still in use. It was completed in 1585, 5 years after Palladio's death, by Vincenzo Scamozzi, and the curtain went up on the Vicenza premiere of Sophocles's *Oedipus Rex.* The arena seating area, in the shape of a half moon, is encircled by Corinthian columns and balustrades. The simple proscenium abuts the arena. What's ordinarily the curtain in a conventional theater is here a permanent facade, U-shaped, with a large central arch and a pair of smaller ones flanking it. The permanent stage set represents the ancient streets of Thebes, combining architectural detail with trompe l'oeil. Above the arches (to the left and right) are rows of additional classic statuary on pedestals and in niches. Over the area is a dome, with trompe l'oeil clouds and sky, giving the illusion of an outdoor Roman amphitheater.

Piazza Matteotti. ℂ **0444-222800.** Admission 6€ ($5.35), including entry to the Civic Museum and the Archaeological Museum. Sept–July 3 Tues–Sun 9am–5pm; July 4–Aug Tues–Sun 10am–7pm.

Civic Museum (Museo Civico) 🎭 This museum is housed in one of the most outstanding buildings by Palladio. Begun in the mid–16th century; it wasn't finished until the late 17th century, during the baroque period. Visitors come chiefly to view its excellent collection of Venetian paintings on the second floor. Works by lesser-known artists (Paolo Veneziano, Bartolomeo Montagna, and Jacopo Bassano) hang alongside paintings by giants such as Tintoretto (*Miracle of St. Augustine*), Veronese (*The Cherub of the Balustrade*), and Tiepolo (*Time and Truth*).

In the Palazzo Chiericati, Piazza Matteotti 37–39. ℂ **0444-321348.** Admission 6.50€ ($5.80), including entry to the Olympic Theater and the Archaeological Museum. Sept–July 4 Tues–Sun 9am–5pm; July 5–Aug Tues–Sun 10am–7pm.

Santa Corona This much-altered Gothic church was founded in the mid–13th century. Visit it to see **Giovanni Bellini's *Baptism of Christ*** 🎭🎭 (fifth altar on the left). In the left transept, a short distance away, is another of Vicenza's well-known artworks, this one by Veronese, depicting the **three Wise Men paying tribute to the Christ child** 🎭🎭. The high altar with its intricate marble work is also worth a look. A visit to Santa Corona is more rewarding than a trek to the Duomo, which is only of passing interest.

Via Santa Corona. ℂ **0444-321924.** Free admission. Tues–Sun 8:30am–noon and 2:30–6pm; Mon 4–6pm.

Villa Rotonda 🎭 This is Palladio's most famous villa, featuring his trademark design inspired by the Roman temples. It's listed as a UNESCO World Heritage site. The interior lacks the grand decor of many lesser-known villas, but the exterior is the focus anyway, having inspired Christopher Wren's English country estates, Jefferson's Monticello, and the work of a slew of lesser-known architects designing U.S. state capitols and Southern antebellum homes. The building was begun by Palladio in 1567, although he died (1580) before it was finished; Scamozzi completed the project in 1592. If you aren't here during the limited open hours, you can still view it clearly from the road.

Via della Rotonda 25. ℂ **0444-321793.** Admission 5€ ($4.45) to interior; 2.50€ ($2.25) to grounds. Interior open Wed 10am–noon and 3–6pm; grounds open Tues–Sun 10am–noon and 3–6pm. Closed Nov 5–Mar 14.

Villa Valmarana "Ai Nani" 🎭🎭 The most magnificent thing about this 17th-century villa, built by Palladio disciple Mattoni, is the series of frescoes by Giambattista Tiepolo that, taken together, create an elaborate mythological world. In the garden, you'll find miniature statues, which are the *nani* (dwarves)

La Città del Palladio

His name was Andrea di Pietro, but his friends called him Palladio. In time, he became the most prominent architect of the Italian High Renaissance, living and working in his beloved Vicenza. Despite the destruction of 14 of his buildings during World War II air raids (luckily, they were photographed and documented before their demise), this city remains a living museum of his architectural achievements. Vicenza eventually became known as La Città del Palladio.

Palladio was actually born in Padua in 1508, where he was apprenticed to a stone carver, but he fled in 1523 to Vicenza, where he lived until his death in 1580. In his youth, he journeyed to Rome to study the architecture of the Roman Vitruvius, who had a profound influence on him. Returning to Vicenza, Palladio perfected the "Palladian style," with its use of pilasters and a composite structure on a gigantic scale. The "attic" in his design was often surmounted by statues. One critic of European architecture wrote, "The noble design, the perfect proportions, the rhythm, and the logically vertical order invites devotion." Palladio's treatise on architecture, published in four volumes, is required reading for aspiring architects.

By no means was Palladio a genius, in the way the Florentine Brunelleschi was. No daring innovator, Palladio was more like an academician who went by the rules. Although all his buildings are harmonious, there are no surprises in them. One of his most acclaimed buildings is the **Villa Rotonda** in Vicenza, a cube with a center circular hall crowned by a dome. On each external side is a pillared rectangular portico. The classic features, though dry and masquerading as a temple, captured the public's imagination. This same type of villa soon appeared all over England and America.

The main street of Vicenza, **Corso Andrea Palladio,** honors the man who spent much of his life building villas for the wealthy. The street is a textbook illustration of the great architect's work (or that of his pupils), and a walk along the Corso is one of the most memorable in Italy.

referred to in its name. Winter tours, available by appointment, require a group of 10 or more.

Via Dei Nani 8. © **0444-543976.** Admission 5€ ($4.45). Tues–Sat 10am–noon and 2:30–5:30pm (3–6pm May–Sept). Closed Dec–Feb.

WHERE TO STAY

Hotel Campo Marzio   This contemporary hotel is ideally situated in a peaceful part of the historic center, adjacent to a park. The guest rooms have undergone a complete renovation, and the sunny lobby has a conservatively comfortable decor that extends into the rooms. The tiled bathrooms are small but well equipped.

Viale Roma 21, 36100 Vicenza. © **0444-545700.** Fax 0444-320495. www.hotelcampomarzio.com. 35 units. 148€–227€ ($132.15–$202.70) double. Rates include buffet breakfast. AE, DC, MC, V. Free parking. **Amenities:** Restaurant; lounge; room service; babysitting; laundry. *In room:* A/C, TV, minibar, hair dryer, safe.

Hotel Continental   The Continental is among the best choices for an overnight stop. It has been renovated in a modern style and offers comfortable rooms ranging from small to medium in size. Each comes with a small tiled bathroom.

Viale G. G. Trissino 89, 36100 Vicenza. *(C)* **0444-505476.** Fax 0444-513319. www.continental-hotel.it. 55 units (showers only). 90€–150€ ($80.35–$133.95) double. Rates include breakfast. AE, DC, MC, V. **Amenities:** Restaurant; lounge; room service; laundry/dry cleaning. *In room:* A/C, TV, hair dryer.

Hotel Cristina   The Cristina is a cozy place near the city center, with an inside courtyard where you can park. The recently refurbished decor consists of lots of marble, parquet flooring, and exposed paneling, coupled with comfortable furniture in the public rooms. The high-ceilinged guest rooms are also well furnished, although some are small. The tiled bathrooms are compact.

Corso San Felice e Fortunato 32, 36100 Vicenza. *(C)* **0444-323751.** Fax 0444-543656. www.hotelcristina.com. 34 units (showers only). 130€ ($116.10) double. Rates include buffet breakfast. AE, DC, MC, V. Parking 8.50€ ($7.60). **Amenities:** Lounge; room service; laundry/dry cleaning. *In room:* A/C, TV, hair dryer.

Jolly Hotel Europa ☆   Located just outside town, the Jolly is the area's finest hotel. It's a somewhat sterile but well-run place flying the flags of many nations. It's geared to the business traveler because it's in the Exhibition Center, with easy access to the autostrada, but it can also serve vacationers. The guest rooms are done in a jazzy Italian style and are medium-size. Some bathrooms contain Jacuzzis.

Strada Padana Verso Verona 11, 36100 Vicenza. *(C)* **800/221-2626** in the U.S., or 0444-564111. Fax 0444-564382. www.jollyhotels.it. 127 units (some with shower only). 112.50€–183€ ($100.45–$163.40) double; 233€ ($208.05) suite. Rates include buffet breakfast. AE, DC, MC, V. Free parking. Bus: 1 or 14. **Amenities:** Restaurant; bar; room service; babysitting; laundry. *In room:* A/C, TV, minibar, hair dryer, safe.

WHERE TO DINE

Antica Trattoria Tre Visi ☆ VICENTINO/INTERNATIONAL   Only the Cinzia e Valerio (see below) serves better food. This restaurant opened as a simple tavern in the early 1600s. After many variations, it settled on its current name ("The Three Faces") more than a century ago, in honor of the rulers of Austria, Hungary, and Bavaria, all of whom wielded political influence in the Veneto. The decor is rustic, with a fireplace, ceramic wall decorations, baskets of fresh fruit, tavern chairs, and an open kitchen. Along with the good selection of regional wines, you can enjoy dishes such as *baccalà alla vicentina* (salt codfish), *zuppa di fagioli* (bean soup), and spaghetti with duck sauce. Another specialty is *capretto alla gambalaro* (kid marinated for 4 days in wine, vinegar, and spices, and then roasted). The best-known dessert is the traditional *pincha alla vicentina*, made with yellow flour, raisins, and figs.

Corso Palladio 25. *(C)* **0444-324868.** Reservations required. Main courses 11€–12.50€ ($9.80–$11.15). AE, DC, MC, V. Tues–Sun 12:30–2:30pm; Tues–Sat 7:30–10:30pm. Closed July.

Cinzia e Valerio ☆☆ SEAFOOD   This is Vicenza's best and most elegant restaurant, where you'll be greeted by a polite staff and masses of seasonal flowers. The house fish specialties are time-tested recipes from the Adriatic coast. Your meal might begin with mollusks and shellfish arranged into an elegant platter. Other dishes are risotto flavored with squid, a collection of crab and lobster that might surprise you by its size and weight, and an endless procession of fish cooked any way you prefer.

Piazzetta Porta Padova 65–67. *(C)* **0444-505213.** Reservations recommended. Main courses 11€–20€ ($9.80–$17.85). AE, DC, MC, V. Tues–Sun noon–2:30pm; Tues–Sat 7:30–9:30pm. Closed Aug 4–25 and Dec 26–Jan 1.

Ristorante Grandcaffè Garibaldi VICENTINO/ITALIAN/MEDITER-
RANEAN   The most impressive cafe/restaurant in the town center features a
design worthy of the city of Palladio, with a wide terrace and an ornate ceiling,
marble tables, and a long glass case of sandwiches from which you can make a
selection before you sit down (the waitress will bring your sandwiches to your
table). In the cafe, you can order cheap *panini* (sandwiches) and cappuccino.
Prices are slightly lower if you stand at the bar. There's also an upstairs restaurant with trays of antipasti and fresh fruit set up on a central table. The menu's
array of familiar Italian specialties is among the best in town.

Piazza dei Signori 2. (☎ 0444-542455. Main courses 8€–15€ ($7.15–$13.40). AE, MC, V. Restaurant open
Thurs–Tues 12:30–3pm and 7:30–11:30pm. Cafe open Thurs–Tues 8am–midnight.

VICENZA AFTER DARK

In Vicenza you can enjoy music presented in settings of architectural splendor.
The outdoor **Teatro Olimpico,** Piazza Matteotti (☎ **0444-222800**) hosts cultural events from April to late September. For information about the actual programs being presented, call the theater. Look for a changing program of classical
Greek tragedy (*Oedipus Rex* is an enduring favorite), Shakespearean plays (sometimes translated into Italian), chamber music concerts, and dance recitals. You
can pick up schedules and buy tickets either at the gate or from the series'
administrative headquarters near Vicenza's basilica at **Viarte,** Contra San Marco
33 (☎ **0444-540072**). Tickets are 10€ to 22.50€ ($8.95–$20.10), although in
rare instances some nosebleed seats go for 7.50€ ($6.70).

More esoteric, and with a shorter season, is a series of concerts scheduled in
June, the **Concerti in Villa.** Every year, it includes chamber music performed in
or near often privately owned villas in the city's outskirts. Look for orchestras set
up on loggias or under formal pediments, and audiences sitting on chairs in gardens or inside. Note that these depend on the whims of both local musicians and
villa owners. Contact the tourist office (see "Essentials," earlier in this section)
for details.

4 Verona ★★★

114km (71 miles) W of Venice, 502km (311 miles) NW of Rome, 81km (50 miles) W of Padua

Verona was the setting for the most famous love story in the English language,
Shakespeare's *Romeo and Juliet.* A long-forgotten editor of an old volume of the
Bard's plays once wrote, "Verona, so rich in the associations of real history, has
even a greater charm for those who would live in the poetry of the past." It's not
known if a Romeo or a Juliet ever existed, but the remains of Verona's actual past
are much in evidence today. Its Roman antiquities are unequaled north of
Rome.

In its medieval golden age under the despotic Scaligeri princes, Verona reached
the pinnacle of its influence and prestige, developing into a town that, even today,
is among the great cities of Italy. The best-known member of the ruling Della
Scala family, Cangrande I, was a patron of Dante. His sway over Verona has often
been compared to that of Lorenzo the Magnificent over Florence.

Verona stands in contrast to Venice, even though both are tourist towns.
Despite the day-trippers, most of the people walking the streets of Verona are
actually residents, not visitors. For a city that hit its peak in the 1st century A.D.,
Verona is doing admirably well. However, stick to the inner core and not the
newer sections, which are blighted by industry and tacky urban development.

ESSENTIALS

GETTING THERE A total of 37 **trains** a day make the 2-hour run between Venice and Verona, at 5.25€ ($4.70) one way. From Milan and points west, there are even more connections, some 40 trains a day, taking 2 hours to reach Verona at 6.25€ ($5.60) one way. Six daily trains arrive from Rome; it's a 7-hour trip costing 21.65€ ($19.35) on a regular train, or a 4½-hour trip costing 36.05€ ($32.20) on a *rapido*. Rail arrivals are at Verona's **Stazione Porta Nuova,** Piazza XXV Aprile, south of the centrally located Arena and Piazza Brà; call ✆ **8488-88088** toll-free in Italy for information.

At least six **bus** lines service the area, arriving at Piazza XXV (✆ **045-8004129**).

By car, take A4 west from Venice to the cutoff marked Verona Sud. From points north or south, take A22 and get off at the exit marked Verona Nord.

VISITOR INFORMATION The **main tourist office** is at Piazza Erbe (✆ **045-8000065**). Hours are Monday through Saturday 9am to 3pm. There's **another information office** at the rail station, Piazzale XXV Aprile (✆ **045-8000861**). In summer, it's open daily 9am to 6pm; off-season hours are Monday to Saturday 8am to 2pm.

SPECIAL EVENTS Opera festivals on a scale more human and accessible than those in cities such as Milan are presented in Verona annually between July and August. The setting is the ancient **Arena di Verona** ⚜, a site that's grand enough to accommodate as many elephants as might be needed for a performance of *Aïda*. Schedules change every year, so for more information and tickets, call ✆ **045-8005151.** Prices of tickets vary with view lines and whatever is being staged, but usually they are 18€ to 154€ ($16.05–$137.50).

For tickets and information on the opera or ballet in Verona, **Global Edwards & Edwards** has a U.S. office (1270 Ave. of the Americas, Ste. 2414, New York, NY 10020) from which you can buy tickets before you go, or call ✆ **800/223-6108** or 914/328-2150 (fax 914/328-2752). A personal visit isn't necessary, and the office can mail vouchers or fax a confirmation to allow you to pick up the tickets half an hour before curtain call.

Teatro Romano is known for its Shakespeare Festival from June through August. In recent years, it has included a week of English-language performances by the Royal Shakespeare Company. Festival performances begin in late May and June with jazz concerts. In July and August, there are also a number of ballets (such as Prokofiev's *Romeo and Juliet*) and modern dance performances. Check for a current schedule at ✆ **045-8077111** or with the tourist office.

EXPLORING THE CITY

Verona lies along the Adige River. The city is most often visited on a quick half-day excursion but deserves more time—it's meant for wandering and contemplation. But if you're rushed, head first to the old city.

Opening onto **Piazza dei Signori** ⚜⚜, the handsomest in Verona, is the **Palazzo del Governo,** where Cangrande extended the shelter of his hearth and home to the fleeing Florentine Dante Alighieri. A marble statue of the "divine poet" stands in the center of the square, with an expression as cold as a Dolomite icicle, but unintimidated pigeons perch on his pious head. Facing Dante's back is the late-15th-century **Loggia del Consiglio,** frescoed and surmounted by five statues. Five arches lead into Piazza dei Signori.

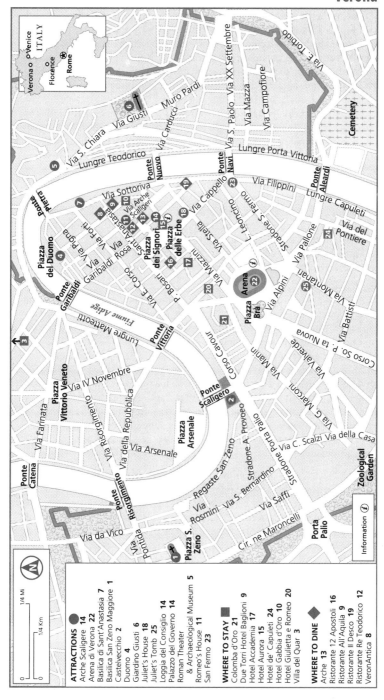

Verona

ITALY

Venice

Verona o

Florence o

Rome ✹

Cemetery

Zoological Garden

ATTRACTIONS ●
Arche Scaligere **14**
Arena di Verona **22**
Basilica di Sant'Anastasia **7**
Basilica San Zeno Maggiore **1**
Castelvecchio **2**
Duomo **4**
Giardino Giusti **6**
Juliet's House **18**
Juliet's Tomb **25**
Loggia del Consiglio **14**
Palazzo del Governo **14**
Roman Theater
& Archaeological Museum **5**
Romeo's House **11**
San Fermo **23**

WHERE TO STAY ■
Colomba d'Oro **21**
Due Torri Hotel Baglioni **9**
Hotel Accademia **17**
Hotel Aurora **15**
Hotel de' Capuleti **24**
Hotel Gabbia d'Oro **10**
Hotel Giulietta e Romeo **20**
Villa del Quar **3**

WHERE TO DINE ◆
Arche **13**
Ristorante 12 Apostoli **16**
Ristorante All'Aquila **9**
Ristorante Il Desco **19**
Ristorante Re Teodorico **12**
VeronAntica **8**

The **Arche Scaligere** are outdoor tombs surrounded by wrought-iron gates that form a kind of open-air pantheon of the Scaligeri princes. One tomb, that of Cangrande della Scala, rests directly over the door of the 12th-century **Santa Maria Antica.** The mausoleum contains many Romanesque features and is crowned by a copy of an equestrian statue (the original is now at the Castelvecchio). The tomb nearest the door is that of Mastino II; the one behind it, and the most lavish of all, is that of Cansignorio.

Piazza delle Erbe (Square of the Herbs) ☆☆ is a lively square, flanked by palaces, that was formerly the Roman city's forum. Today, it's the fruit-and-vegetable market, milling with Veronese shoppers and vendors. In the center is a fountain dating from the 14th century and a Roman statue dubbed *The Virgin of Verona.* The pillar at one end of the square, crowned by a chimera, symbolizes the many years Verona was dominated by Venice. Important buildings include the early-14th-century **House of Merchants (Casa di Mercanti);** the **Torre Gardello,** built by one of the Della Scala princes; the restored former **city hall** and the **Torre Lamberti,** soaring about 79m (260 ft.); the baroque **Palazzo Maffei;** and the **Casa Mazzanti.**

From the vegetable market, you can walk down **Via Mazzini,** the most fashionable street in Verona, to **Piazza Brà,** with its neoclassical town hall and Renaissance palazzo, the **Gran Guardia.**

Arena di Verona ☆☆ The elliptical amphitheater on Piazza Brà, resembling Rome's Colosseum, dates from the 1st century A.D. Four arches of the "outer circle" and a complete "inner ring" still stand, which is rather remarkable because an earthquake hit this area in the 12th century. From Mid-July to mid-August, it's the setting for an opera house, where more than 20,000 people are treated to Verdi and Mascagni. The acoustics are perfect, even after all these centuries, and performances still can be conducted without microphones. Attending an outdoor evening performance (see "Verona After Dark," later in this section) can be one of the highlights of your visit. In one season alone, you might be able to hear *Macbeth, Madama Butterfly, Aïda, Carmen, Rigoletto,* and Verdi's *Requiem.*

Piazza Brà. ✆ 045-8003204. Admission 3€ ($2.70); free the 1st Sun of each month. Tues–Sun 9am–6:30pm (on performance days 9am–3pm).

Castelvecchio ☆☆ Built on the order of Cangrande II in the 14th century, the Old Castle stands beside the Adige River (head out Via Roma) near the Ponte Scaligero, a bridge bombed by the Nazis and subsequently reconstructed. This former seat of the Della Scala family has been turned into an art museum, with important paintings from the Veronese school and other masters of northern Italy. Fourteenth- and 15th-century sculpture are on the ground floor, and on the upper floor you'll see masterpieces of painting from the 15th to 18th centuries.

In the **Sala Monga** is Jacopo Bellini's *St. Jerome,* in the desert with his lion and crucifix. Two sisterlike portraits of Saint Catherina and Veneranda by Vittore Carpaccio grace the **Sala Rizzardi Allegri.** The Bellini family is also represented by a lyrical *Madonna con Bambino,* painted by Giovanni, a master of that subject.

Between the buildings is the most provocative equestrian statue we've ever seen, that of Cangrande I, grinning like a buffoon, with a dragon sticking out of his back. In the **Sala Murari della Corte Brà** is one of the most beguiling portraits in the castle—Giovanni Francesco Caroto's smiling red-haired boy. In the **Sala di Canossa** are Tintoretto's *Madonna Nursing the Child* and *Nativity,* and Veronese's *Deposition from the Cross* and *Pala Bevilacqua Lazise.*

In the **Sala Bolognese Trevenzuoli** is a rare self-portrait of Bernardo Strozzi, and in the **Sala Avena,** among paintings by the most famous Venetian masters, such as Gianbattista and Giandomenico Tiepolo and Guardi, hangs an almost satirical portrait of an 18th-century patrician family by Longhi.

Corso Castelvecchio 2. ✆ **045-594734.** Admission 3€ ($2.70); free 1st Sun of each month. Tues–Sun 9am–7pm. Last admission at 6:30pm.

Basilica San Zeno Maggiore ✪✪ This near-perfect Romanesque church and campanile built between the 9th and 12th centuries is graced with a stunning entrance: two pillars supported by puce-colored marble lions and surmounted by a rose window called the Ruota della Fortuna (Wheel of Fortune). On either side of the portal are bas-reliefs depicting scenes from the Old and New Testaments, as well as a mythological story portraying Theodoric as a huntsman lured to hell (the king of the Goths defeated Odoacer in Verona). The panels on the bronze doors, nearly 50 in all, are a remarkable achievement of medieval art, sculpted perhaps in the 12th century. They reflect a naive handling of their subject (see John the Baptist's head resting on a platter). The artists express themselves with such candor they achieve the power of a child's storybook. The interior, somber and severe, contains a major Renaissance work at the main altar: a triptych by Andrea Mantegna, showing an enthroned Madonna and Child with saints. Although not remarkable in its characterization, it reveals the artist's genius for perspective.

Piazza San Zeno. ✆ **045-8006120.** Admission 2€ ($1.80). Mon–Sat 9:30am–6pm; Sun 1–6pm.

Basilica di Sant'Anastasia ✪ Verona's largest church was built from 1290 to 1481. Its facade isn't complete, yet it's the finest representation of Gothic design in the city. Many artists in the 15th and 16th centuries decorated the interior, but few of the works are worthy of being singled out. The exception is the **Pellegrini Chapel (Cappella Pellegrini),** with terra-cotta reliefs by the Tuscan artist Michele, and the **Giusti Chapel (Cappella Giusti),** with a fresco by Pisanello representing St. George preparing to face his inevitable dragon. The patterned floor is especially impressive. As you enter, look for two *gobbi* (hunchbacks) supporting holy water fonts. The church also has a beautiful **campanile** from the 1300s that's richly decorated with sculpture and frescoes.

Piazza Sant'Anastasia. ✆ **045-8004325.** Admission 2€ ($1.80). Apr–Oct Mon–Sat 9:30am–6:30pm; Sun 1–6pm. Nov–Mar daily 10am–4pm.

Duomo ✪ Verona's cathedral is less interesting than San Zeno Maggiore but still merits a visit. It was begun in the 12th century but not completed until the 17th. A blend of Romanesque and Gothic, its facade contains (lower level) 12th-century sculptured reliefs by Nicolaus depicting scenes of Roland and Oliver, two of the legendary dozen knights attending Charlemagne. In the left aisle (first chapel) is Titian's *Assumption,* the stellar work of the Duomo. The other major work is the **rood screen** in front of the presbytery, with Ionic pillars, designed by Samicheli.

Piazza del Duomo. ✆ **045-595627.** Admission 1.50€ ($1.35). Mar–Oct Mon–Fri 9am–6pm, Sat to 4pm; off-season Mon–Sat 11am–1pm and 1:30–4pm.

San Fermo ✪ This 11th-century Romanesque church forms the foundation of the 14th-century Gothic building surmounting it. Through time, it has been used by both the Benedictines and the Franciscans. The interior is unusual, with a single nave and a splendid roof constructed of wood and exquisitely paneled. The most important work inside is Pisanello's frescoed *Annunciation,* to the left of the main entrance (at the Brenzoni tomb). Delicate and graceful, the work reveals the artist's keen eye for architectural detail and his bizarre animals.

Stradone San Fermo. © 045-8007287. Admission 1.50€ ($1.35). Mon–Sat 10am–4pm; Sun 1–4pm.

Roman Theater (Teatro Romano) & Archaeological Museum (Museo Archeologico) ✦ The Teatro Romano, built in the 1st century A.D., now stands in ruins at the foot of St. Peter's Hill. For nearly a quarter of a century, a Shakespearean festival has been staged here in July and August; of course, a unique theatergoing experience is to see *Romeo and Juliet* or *Two Gentlemen of Verona* in this setting. The theater is across the Adige River (take the Ponte di Pietra). After seeing the remains of the theater, you can take a rickety elevator to the 10th-century Santi Siro e Libera church towering over it. In the cloister of St. Jerome is the Archaeological Museum, with interesting mosaics and Etruscan bronzes.

Rigaste Redentore 2. © 045-8000360. Admission 2.50€ ($2.25); free 1st Sun of each month. Mon 1:30–7:30pm and Tues–Sun 9am–6:30pm.

Giardino Giusti ✦ One of Italy's oldest and most famous gardens, the Giardino Giusti, was created at the end of the 14th century. These well-manicured Italian gardens, studded with cypress trees, form one of the most relaxing and coolest spots in Verona for strolls. You can climb up to the "monster balcony" for an incomparable view of the city.

The layout of the gardens was designed by Agostino Giusti. All its 16th-century characteristics—the grottoes, statues, fountains, box-enclosed flower garden, and maze—have remained intact. In addition to the flower displays, you can admire statues by Lorenzo Muttoni and Alessandro Vittoria, Roman remains, and the great cypress mentioned by Goethe. The gardens, with their adjacent 16th-century palazzo, form one of Italy's most interesting urban complexes. The maze of myrtle hedges faithfully reproduces the 1786 plan of the architect Trezza. Its complicated pattern and small size make it one of the most unusual in Europe. The gardens lie near the Roman Theater, only a few minutes' walk from the heart of the city.

Via Giardino Giusti 2. © 045-8034029. Admission 5€ ($4.45). Apr–Sept daily 9am–8pm (to 7pm off-season).

Juliet's Tomb (Tomba di Giulietta) The so-called Juliet's tomb is sheltered in a Franciscan monastery, which you enter on Via Luigi da Porto, off Via del Pontiere. "A grave? O, no, a lantern . . . For here lies Juliet, and her beauty makes this vault a feasting presence full of light." Don't you believe it! Still, the cloisters, near the Adige River, are graceful. Adjoining the tomb is a museum of frescoes, dedicated to G. B. Cavalcaselle.

Via del Pontiere 5. © 045-8000361. Admission 2.50€ ($2.25); free 1st Sun of each month. Tues–Sun 8:30am–7:30pm.

Juliet's House (Casa di Giulietta) There's no evidence that any family named Capulet lived here, but that hasn't stopped millions of visitors from flocking to this contrived sight. People see the small home, with its balcony and courtyard, and immediately imagine Romeo saying, "But, soft! What light through yonder window breaks? It is the east, and Juliet is the sun!" The house was acquired by the city in 1905. You'll notice that the right breast on a bronze statue of Juliet is much more brightly polished than the left. That's the result of a tradition (having nothing to do with Shakespeare) that calls for visitors to rub this breast as they pass.

So where did Juliet's heartthrob live? At the so-called **Romeo's House (Casi di Romeo),** Via Arche Scaligeri 2, said to have been the home of the Montecchi family, the model for Shakespeare's Montagues. It's been turned into a very good, atmospheric, and affordable restaurant called the **Osteria dal Duca** (© **045-594474**).

Via Cappello 23. © **045-8034303**. Admission 3€ ($2.70). Mon 2–7:30pm; Tues–Sun 9am–7:30pm.

SHOPPING

The byword for shopping in Verona is *elegance,* and shops feature the fashions being touted in Milan and Rome. Don't look for touristy products or rustic crafts and souvenirs; instead, look for more upscale versions of all-Italian fashion and accessories. A worthwhile shop for men is **Class Uomo,** Via San Rocchetto 13B (© **045-595775**), and, for both genders, there's the classic **Armani,** Via Cappello 25 (© **045-594727**).

You'll find a dense concentration of vendors selling antiques or old bric-a-brac in the streets around **Sant'Anastasia,** or head to **Piazza delle Erbe** for a more or less constant roster of merchants in flea market–style kiosks selling dusty, and often junkier, collectibles of yesteryear, along with aromatic herbs, fruits, and vegetables.

WHERE TO STAY

Hotel rooms tend to be scarce during the County Fair in March and during the opera and theater season in July and August.

VERY EXPENSIVE

Due Torri Hotel Baglioni ✿✿✿   This is the inn of choice for the discriminating. It continues to triumph over its closest rival, Gabbia d'Oro (see below). The Baglioni began as the 1400s home of the Scaligeri dynasty. During the 18th and 19th centuries, it hosted VIPs such as Tsar Alexander I. In the 1950s, legendary hotelier Enrico Wallner transformed the palace into a hotel with a stunning collection of antiques. The upscale Cogeta Palace chain bought the property in 1990 and richly restored the entire hotel. Many antiques remain in the public areas and guest rooms—a range of Directoire, Empire, Louis XVIII, and Biedermeier. Most rooms are generous in size, and the Portuguese marble bathrooms come with deluxe toiletries.

Piazza Sant'Anastasia 4, 37121 Verona. © **045-595044**. Fax 045-8004130. www.baglionihotels.com. 90 units. 222€–395€ ($198.25–$352.70) double; from 570€ ($509) suite. Rates include breakfast. AE, DC, MC, V. Parking 27€ ($24.10). **Amenities:** Restaurant; bar; lounge; room service; massage; babysitting; laundry. *In room:* A/C, TV, minibar, hair dryer, safe.

EXPENSIVE

Hotel Gabbia d'Oro ✿   Gabbia d'Oro is sweet and romantic on first impression, particularly for first-time visitors to Europe. But if you look closely, it borders on cutesy, with lots of faux antiquing (by contrast, Due Torri Hotel Baglioni, above, is the real thing). This hotel in an 18th-century palazzo, which opened in 1990, is the first hotel in years to give the Baglioni some competition. Small and discreet, it contains many of the building's original grandiose frescoes, its beamed ceiling, and (in the cozy bar area) much of the carved paneling. The interior courtyard contains potted plants, flowering shrubs, and tables devoted to drinking and dining in clement weather. The guest rooms boast framed engravings, antique furniture, and (in some cases) narrow balconies with wrought-iron detailing overlooking the street or the courtyard. The bathrooms are in marble or tile. Meals are served only for special occasions or on request.

Corso Porta Borsari 4A, 37121 Verona. © **045-8003060**. Fax 045-590293. www.hotelgabbiadoro.it. 27 units. 232€–351€ ($207.20–$313.45) double; 284€–516€ ($253.60–$460.80) suite. Rates include breakfast (in low season). AE, DC, MC, V. Parking 25€ ($22.30). **Amenities:** Dining room (not generally open); bar; room service; massage; babysitting; laundry/dry cleaning. *In room:* A/C, TV, minibar, hair dryer, safe.

MODERATE

Colomba d'Oro ⭐   This hotel is the equal of the Accademia (see below). Colomba d'Oro was built as a villa in the 1600s and later transformed into a monastery. During the 18th and 19th centuries, it served as an inn for travelers and employees of the postal service, and eventually grew into this large hotel. The building is efficiently organized and has an atmosphere somewhere between traditional and contemporary. The medium-size guest rooms are nicely appointed with matching fabrics and comfortable furniture. Some bathrooms are clad in marble.

Via C. Cattaneo 10, 37121 Verona. ☎ **045-595300.** Fax 045-594974. www.colombahotel.com. 51 units (11 with shower only). 150€–192€ ($133.95–$171.45) double; 180€–230€ ($160.75–$205.40) suite. Rates include buffet breakfast. AE, DC, MC, V. Parking 14€ ($12.50). **Amenities:** Lounge; room service. *In room:* A/C, TV, minibar, hair dryer.

Hotel Accademia ⭐   This is one of Verona's few older hotels (dating from the 19th c.) that was custom built rather than being transformed from a monastery or palazzo. It contains Oriental carpets, a medieval tapestry, and a pair of grandiose marble columns flanking the polished stone stairwell leading to the three floors of rooms. The high-ceilinged guest rooms are conservatively traditional and contain excellent furnishings.

Via Scala 12, 37121 Verona. ☎ **045-596222.** Fax 045-8008440. www.accademiavr.it. 98 units (some with shower only). 125€–230€ ($111.60–$205.35) double; 170€–315€ ($151.80–$281.30) suite. Rates include buffet breakfast. AE, DC, MC, V. Parking 15€ ($13.40). **Amenities:** Restaurant; bar; room service; babysitting; laundry/dry cleaning. *In room:* A/C, TV, minibar, hair dryer, safe.

Hotel de' Capuleti   The Capuleti is an attractively pristine place, conveniently a few steps from Juliet's (supposed) tomb and the chapel where she's said to have married Romeo. The reception area has stone floors and leather couches, along with a tastefully renovated decor that's reflected upstairs in the comfortable but small guest rooms. The tiled bathrooms are tiny.

Via del Pontiere 26, 37122 Verona. ☎ **045-8000154.** Fax 045-8032970. www.bestwestern.it. 42 units (showers only). 150€ ($133.95) double. Rates include breakfast. AE, DC, MC, V. Closed Dec 22–Jan 15. **Amenities:** Lounge; room service; laundry. *In room:* A/C, TV, minibar, hair dryer, safe.

INEXPENSIVE

Hotel Aurora   Creaky with age, this landmark budget hostelry still endures. The foundations of this tall and narrow hotel were already at least 400 years old when the building was constructed in the 1500s. In 1994, its owners completed a radical renovation that improved all the hidden systems (structural beams, electricity, plumbing) but retained hints of the building's antique origins. The Aurora is set behind a sienna-colored facade on a square that's transformed every morning, at around 7:30am, into Verona's busiest emporium of fruits and vegetables. Views from all but a few of the simply furnished guest rooms encompass a full or partial look at the activity in the square. The rooms are small, with cramped bathrooms, but the beds are comfortable.

Piazzetta XIV Novembre 2 (off Piazza Erbe), 37121 Verona. ☎ **045-594717.** Fax 045-8010860. 19 units (showers only). 98€–117€ ($87.50–$104.50) double. Rates include breakfast. AE, MC, V. Parking free on street; 12€ ($10.70) in public lot (a 10-min. walk). **Amenities:** Lounge; babysitting. *In room:* A/C, TV, hair dryer.

Hotel Giulietta e Romeo   This place makes a slightly saccharine use of Shakespeare's great love story as its theme. Most of the rooms in this once-stately palazzo look out over the Roman arena. In honor of the maiden Juliet, the hotel maintains at least one marble balcony that might be appropriate in a modern-day revival of the great play. The guest rooms are tastefully modernized, not overly large, and have burnished hardwoods, comfortable furnishings, and lighting that you can actually read by, plus marble-sheathed bathrooms. The service is cordial, and the location is central, though on a quiet side street.

Vicolo Tre Marchetti 3, 37121 Verona. ℂ 045-8003554. Fax 045-8010862. www.giuliettaeromeo.com. 30 units (22 with shower only). 110€–165€ ($98.20–$147.30) double. Rates include breakfast. AE, DC, MC, V. Parking 17€ ($15.20). **Amenities:** Lounge; room service; babysitting; laundry. *In room:* A/C, TV, minibar, hair dryer, safe.

A HOTEL ON THE OUTSKIRTS

Villa del Quar 🏨🏨   This is a patrician villa complex constructed over 14th-century foundations and lying in Verona-Nord, 7km (4¼ miles) north of the heart of Verona. Its pristine elegance evokes that of a Tuscan villa farther south in Italy.

At this Relais & Châteaux property, buildings are arranged around a large courtyard and garden. Once allowed to fall into ruin, the complex today is beautifully restored and set on a 7-acre property. Historic charm coupled with modern comforts characterize the place. It's an ideal base to sneak away to with your own Romeo or Juliet. From your window, you'll have views of the Valpolicella Valley, famous for its wines that have been praised by everybody from Dante to Hemingway. All the rooms are traditionally furnished in an antique neoclassical style. It's not the most convenient location, especially if you prefer a nap in the middle of a day of sightseeing. And you'll probably want a car if you stay here, although it's only a $10 taxi ride into the center of Verona. Otherwise the place makes an idyllic stopover.

Via Quar 12, 37020 Pedemonte (Verona). ℂ 045-6800681. Fax 045-6800604. 22 units. 233€–270€ ($208.05–$241.10) double; from 321€ ($286.65) suite. AE, MC, V. **Amenities:** Fine restaurant; bar; pool; gym; sauna; room service; babysitting; laundry/dry cleaning. *In room:* A/C, TV, minibar, safe.

WHERE TO DINE
EXPENSIVE

Arche 🍴🍴 ITALIAN   This classic restaurant is acclaimed by some as the finest in Verona. We give that honor to Il Desco (see below), but Arche is a close runner-up. It was founded in 1879 by the great-grandfather of owner Giancarlo Gioco, and the seafood dishes are based on recipes passed down from generation to generation, including some discovered in ancient cookbooks. Giancarlo and his wife, Paola, insist on market-fresh fish, with sole, sea bass with porcini mushrooms, and scampi among the favorites. Baked "sea scorpion" with black olives, and the ravioli stuffed with sea bass and served with clam sauce are the finest specialties. The furnishings in this 1420s building are set off by candlelight and fresh flowers.

Via Arche Scaligere 6. ℂ 045-8007415. Reservations required. Main courses 15€–30€ ($13.40–$26.80); fixed-price menus 42.50€–50€ ($37.95–$44.65). AE, DC, MC, V. Mon 8–10pm; Tues–Sat 12:30–2:30pm and 8–10pm. Closed Jan 15–Feb 15.

Ristorante Il Desco 🍴🍴🍴 ITALIAN   The tops in Verona, Il Desco is a handsome restaurant occupying a renovated palazzo that's one of the city's civic prides. The menu steers closer to the philosophy of *cuisine moderne* than anyplace in town. The freshest ingredients are used in the specialties: shrimp purée; potato pie with mushrooms and black truffles; calamari salad with shallots; tortellini with sea bass; risotto with radicchio and truffles; and tagliolini with fresh mint, lemon, and oranges. The wine cellar is superb, and the sommelier will help if you're unfamiliar with regional vintages.

Via Dietro San Sebastiano 7. ℂ 045-595358. Reservations recommended. Main courses 18€–32.50€ ($16.05–$29); tasting menu 92.50€ ($82.60). AE, DC, MC, V. Tues–Sat 12:30–2pm and 7:30–10:30pm. Closed Jan 1–7, June 15–July 4, and Dec 25–26.

MODERATE

Ristorante All'Aquila ITALIAN/INTERNATIONAL   This appealing restaurant boasts an Art Nouveau decor and an impeccably trained staff headed by Sr. Mattia, who trained at Claridge's in London. The menu is almost completely rewritten every 6 months but is likely to include smoked horsemeat with arugula and shaved *parmigiano,* marinated trout with citrus sauce, and tartare of fish with fresh cucumber. Pastas include ravioli with a medley of soft cheeses, spinach, and watercress sauce, and subtly flavored tagliatelle with cream, herb, and egg-yolk sauce. A main course could include braised arugula and eggplant, and perch filets with sage. And dessert choices might be tiramisu and ricotta mousse. The list of mostly Italian wine is comprehensive.

In the Due Torri Hotel Baglioni, Piazza Sant'Anastasia 4. ℂ **045-595044**. Reservations recommended. Main courses 16€–18.50€ ($14.30–$16.50). AE, DC, MC, V. Daily 12:30–2:30pm and 7:30–10pm.

Ristorante Re Teodorico ⟵ REGIONAL/INTERNATIONAL   Ristorante Re Teodorico is perched high on a hill at the edge of town, with a panoramic view of Verona and the Adige. From its entrance, you descend a cypress-lined road to the ledge-hanging restaurant suggestive of a lavish villa. Tables are set out on a wide flagstone terrace edged with classical columns and an arbor of red, pink, and yellow flowering vines. Specialties are homemade pasta, always delectable; swordfish with tomatoes, capers, and fresh basil; and chateaubriand with béarnaise sauce. The dessert specialty is crêpes suzette.

Piazzale di Castel San Pietro 1. ℂ **045-8349990**. Reservations required. Main courses 22.50€–25€ ($20.10–$22.35). AE, DC, MC, V. Thurs–Tues noon–3pm and 7–10pm. Closed Jan.

Ristorante 12 Apostoli ⟵⟵ ITALIAN   Operated by the two Gioco brothers, this is Verona's oldest restaurant, in business for 250 years. It's a festive place, steeped in tradition, with frescoed walls and two dining rooms separated by brick arches. Giorgio, the artist of the kitchen, changes his menu daily, while Franco directs the dining room. For a main course, consider Giorgio's salmon baked in a pastry shell (the fish is marinated the day before, seasoned with garlic, and stuffed with scallops), or chicken stuffed with shredded vegetables and cooked in four layers of paper. To begin, we recommend the tempting *antipasti alla Scaligera.* For dessert, try the homemade cake.

Vicolo Corticella San Marco 3. ℂ **045-596999**. Reservations recommended. Main courses 15€–25€ ($13.40–$22.35). AE, DC, MC, V. Tues–Sun 12:30–2:30pm; Tues–Sat 7:30–10pm. Closed the 1st week in Jan and June 15–July 5.

INEXPENSIVE

VeronAntica INTERNATIONAL   The VeronAntica is a local restaurant on the ground floor of a town house a short block from the river, across from a cobblestone arcade similar to the ones used in Zeffirelli's *Romeo and Juliet.* This place attracts locals, not just tourists. It's made even more romantic at night by a hanging lantern that dimly illuminates the street. The chef knows how to prepare all the classics as well as some innovative dishes. Try *bretelline* (tagliatelle made with rice flour) with rughetta salad and asparagus, or select salmon in papillote with fresh mussels, seafood, and tomatoes. From June to September, you can dine on an open-air terrace.

Via Sottoriva 10. ℂ **045-8004124**. Reservations recommended. Main courses 8.25€–13€ ($7.35–$11.60). AE, DC, MC, V. Sept–June Wed–Mon noon–2:30pm and 7–10:45pm; July–Aug daily noon–10:45pm.

VERONA AFTER DARK

The grande dame of local cafe society is the **Antico Caffè Dante** in the beautiful Piazza dei Signori (© **045-8003593**). Inside Verona's oldest cafe, the setting is rather formal and meals are pricey; so you might want to instead snag an outdoor table, where you can soak in the million-dollar view of one of Verona's loveliest ancient squares.

Oenophiles will think they've died and gone to heaven when they discover the unmatched 80,000-bottle selection at **Bottega del Vino,** Via Scudo di Francia 3 (off Via Mazzini; © **045-8004535**). This atmospheric bottega first opened in 1890, and the old-timers who spend hours in animated conversation seem to have been here ever since. The atmosphere and conviviality are reason enough to come by for a tipple at the well-known bar, where five dozen wines are available by the glass. Regulars, journalists, and local merchants often fill the few wooden tables at mealtimes, ordering simple and affordable but excellent dishes, such as homemade risottos.

Put on your dancing shoes and head for **Disco Berfis Club,** Via Lussemburgo 1 (© **045-508024**), or **Bar/Disco Tribu,** Via Calderara 17 (© **045-566470**), where the rhythms echo what's being broadcast in New York and Milan.

Gays and lesbians can call **Circolo Pink,** Via Scriminari 7 (© **045-8012854**), to get details on gay cultural activities, parties, or newly opened bars. You can call the hot line only Monday or Thursday 9 to 11pm, and Saturday 4 to 6pm.

5 Treviso ★

31km (19 miles) N of Venice

Treviso is known to culinary fans for the cherries grown in its environs and the creation of tiramisu ("pick me up"), a delicious blend of ladyfingers, mascarpone cheese, eggs, cocoa, liqueur, and espresso. Art aficionados know Treviso for its many works by Tomaso da Modena.

Treviso also attracts those interested in fashion who know it as the birthplace of Benetton. Many come here to browse and window-shop the dozens of stores selling fashion and Italian leather goods. Treviso catches visitors wanting to take the wine route as well (see "The Wine Roads from Treviso," below). But mainly Treviso is for connoisseurs, visitors who love the Veneto region so much that they want to spend an extra day visiting Treviso and taking the wine trail. In recent years, the town has begun to emerge as Italy's newest center for artists, fashion designers, filmmakers, and art lovers.

ESSENTIALS

GETTING THERE   There are four **trains** per hour from Venice, a trip of 30 minutes that costs 1.50€ ($1.35) one way, and hourly trains from Udine, a trip of 1½ hours for 6€ ($5.35) one way. Treviso's station (© **848-888088,** toll-free in Italy) is at Piazza Duca d'Aosta on the southern end of town.

The station at Lungosile Mattei 21 gets **buses** on the La Marca bus line (© **0422-577311**) from Bassano del Grappa nine times daily, a trip of 1 hour costing 3.50€ ($3.15) one way. From Padua, buses arrive every 30 minutes; the trip takes 1 hour, 10 minutes, and costs 3.10€ ($2.75) one way. The ACTV line (© **0422-541821**) runs two buses an hour from Venice, a 30-minute trip for 2.25€ ($2).

The Wine Roads from Treviso

The gently rolling foothills of the Dolomites around Treviso are known for producing fine wines. For a view of the ancient vines, take a drive along the two highways known as the **Strade dei Vini del Piave** in honor of the nearby Piave River. Both begin at the medieval town of **Conegliano,** where the tourist office is at XX Settembre 61 (📞 **0438-21230**), open from Tuesday to Friday 9am to 12:30pm and 3 to 6pm, and Saturday and Sunday from 9am to 12:30pm and 2:30 to 6pm.

You won't find route numbers associated with either of these wine roads, and each is badly signposted en route, beginning in central Conegliano. The less interesting is the **Strada del Vino Rosso (Red Wine Road),** running through 40km (25 miles) of humid flatlands southeast of Conegliano. Significant points en route include the scenic hamlets of Oderzo, Motta, and Ponte di Piave.

Much more scenic and evocative is the **Strada del Vino Bianco (White Wine Road),** or, more specifically, the **Strada del Prosecco,** meandering through the foothills of the Dolomites for about 39km (24 miles) northwest of Conegliano, ending at Valdobbiadene. It passes through particularly prestigious regions famous for their sparkling prosecco, a quality white meant to be drunk young, with the characteristic taste and smell of ripe apples, wisteria, and acacia honey. The most charming of the many hamlets you'll encounter (blink an eye and you'll miss them) are San Pietro di Feletto, Follina, and Pieve di Soligno. Each is awash with family-run cantinas, kiosks, and roadside stands, all selling the fermented fruits of the local harvest and offering platters of prosciutto, local cheese, and crusty bread.

The best hotel for establishing a base here is in Conegliano. The **Canon d'Oro,** Via XX Settembre 131, 31015 Conegliano (📞 **0438-34246**), occupies a 15th-century building near the rail station and charges from 75€ ($67) for a double.

If you're looking for a bite to eat in Conegliano, try our favorite restaurant, **Tre Panoce,** Via Vecchia Trevigiano 50 (📞 **0438-60071**). Occupying a 16th-century stone building, it charges around 26€ ($23.20) for full meals that include a celebration of whatever is in season (wine not included). Your pasta could be flavored with radicchio, fresh mushrooms, wild herbs, or local cheese. Tre Panoce is in the hills above Conegliano, half a mile from the town center. It's open from Tuesday to Saturday noon to 2:30pm and 8 to 10pm (closed Aug). The most formal restaurant in town is **Al Salisà,** Via XX Settembre 2 (📞 **0438-24288**), occupying a stone building with 12th-century foundations. The excellent menu includes roasted veal with wild herbs, sea bass with seasonal vegetables and basil-flavored white-wine sauce, and fettuccine with wild duck. Expect to spend 25€ ($22.30) and up for a full meal. It's open from Thursday to Tuesday noon to 3pm and 7:30 to 10:30pm.

By car, take A11 from Venice through Mestre for 10km (6¼ miles); head northeast on A4 for 5km (3 miles), and then take Route S13 for 16km (10 miles) north to Treviso.

VISITOR INFORMATION   The **tourist office** is on Piazza Monte Pietà (℃ 0422-547632). From April to September, it's open Monday to Saturday 9am to 12:30pm and 2:30 to 6pm, and Saturday 9:30am to 12:30pm. From October to March, hours are Monday to Tuesday 9am to 12:30pm, and Wednesday to Saturday 9am to 12:30pm and 3 to 5:30pm.

SEEING THE SIGHTS

The huge Romanesque-Gothic **San Nicolò** ⚘, Via San Nicolo (℃ 0422-3247), boasts some important treasures, including its ornate vaulted ceiling with 14th-century frescoes by Tomaso da Modena on its columns. Even more impressive is the **Dominican Chapter (Capitolo dei Dominicani)** of the **Episcopal Seminary (Seminario Vescovile)**, next door to the church. Here Modena captured in 40 portraits the diverse personalities of a series of Dominican monks seated at their desks. There's no admission fee, and both buildings are open daily 8am to 6:30pm.

No longer a church, **Santa Caterina,** Piazzetta Mario Botter, houses the frescoes composing Modena's depiction of the Christian legend of the Ursula Cycle, with its 11,000 virgins all accounted for. At press time, a restoration program is nearing completion, so it should be open again by the time you arrive. Call the **Civic Museum (Museo Civico),** B. Cavour 24 (℃ 0422-658442), for hours or an appointment. The museum houses the strange *Il Castragatti* (*The Cat Fixer*), by Sebastiano Florigero; a *Crucifixion* by Bassano; and the fresco *San Antonio Abate,* by Pordenone. Hours are Tuesday to Saturday 9am to 12:30pm and 2:30 to 5pm, and Sunday 9am to noon. Admission is 2.50€ ($2.25).

You can visit the **Duomo,** Piazza del Duomo at Via Canoniche 2 (℃ 0422-545720), Monday to Saturday 8am to noon and 3:30 to 7pm, and Sunday 7:30am to 1pm and 3:30 to 8pm. It contains more frescoes by Pordenone, as well as an *Annunciation* by Titian. The crypt is open after 10:30am.

A stroll through **Piazza dei Signori** ⚘ offers views of several interesting Romanesque buildings, including the municipal **bell tower,** the **Palazzo Trecento** ⚘, and the nearby **Loggia dei Cavalieri** on Via Martiri della Libertà.

SHOPPING

The city is known for its production of wrought iron and copper utensils, and the best places to find these goods are **Prior,** Via Palestro 12 (℃ 0422-545886), and **Morandin,** Via Palestro 50 (℃ 0422-543651).

The cherries grown in the surrounding area ripen in June. At that time, you can buy them at all local markets, especially the **open-air market** on Tuesday and Saturday morning sprawling across Via Pescheria. Otherwise, one of the best selections of this fruit is found at **Pam** supermarket, Via Zorgietto 12 (℃ 0422-583913).

WHERE TO STAY

Ca' del' Galletto   This thoroughly modern hotel offers comfortable soundproof guest rooms with serviceable but attractive furnishings. Deluxe rooms also include Jacuzzis. The bathrooms are small but tidily organized. An enclosed garden allows you outdoor privacy in the city.

Via Santa Bona Vecchia 30, 31100 Treviso. ℃ 0422-432550. Fax 0422-432510. www.sevenonline.it/cadel galletto. 75 units (showers only). 130€–155€ ($116.10–$138.40) double; 182.50€ ($162.95) junior suite. Rates include buffet breakfast. AE, DC, MC, V. Free parking. Bus: 5. **Amenities:** Restaurant; bar; lounge; pool; tennis court; gym; sauna; room service; babysitting; laundry/dry cleaning. *In room:* A/C, TV, minibar, hair dryer, safe.

Hotel Al Fogher ☆ We especially recommend this business favorite of wine merchants, just north of the medieval fortifications of Treviso. The decor contrasts antique statuary with modern art prints and marble with glass bricks. The top floor has a panoramic terrace where guests congregate for views over the countryside.

Viale della Repubblica 10, 31100 Treviso. (☎ 800/528-1234 in the U.S., or 0422-432950. Fax 0422-430391. www.bestwestern.com. 55 units. 140€ ($125) double; 165€ ($147.35) suite. Rates include breakfast. AE, DC, MC, V. **Amenities:** Restaurant; bar; lounge; room service; laundry. *In room:* A/C, TV, minibar, hair dryer, safe.

NEARBY ACCOMMODATIONS

Hotel Villa Abbazia ☆☆ *Finds* This is a great little hotel where wine and food lovers often stay. In the historic center of Follina (58km/36 miles north of Treviso), the hotel is in a building that dates from the 16th century. A visit here is like staying in a private home with its own lush garden. Every spacious bedroom is architecturally different with a unique decor, but all are romantic in concept. Sometimes a room will open onto a private terrace. Although it's old, the building is filled with up-to-date facilities, including well-maintained bathrooms. We prefer a room in the main building, but there are equally good units in the annex, a 19th-century Liberty Villa. This was one of many Veneto villas designed for noble families when the patricians of Venice wanted to escape their own grand city. The villa lies along the route of vineyards producing white wines. The staff rents good multigear bikes to guests, with route maps across the relatively flat terrain—perfect in the late summer and early fall when the grapes are ripening. The hotel is a nice antidote to the frenetic pace of Venice and is an idyllic base for touring.

Piazza IV Novembre 3, 30151 Follina (Treviso). (☎ 0438-971277. Fax 0438-970001. www.hotelabbazia.it. 18 units. 175€–200€ ($156.30–$178.60) double; 250€–400€ ($223.25–$357.20) suite. AE, DC, MC, V. **Amenities:** Restaurant; bar; bike rental; room service; babysitting; laundry. *In room:* A/C, TV, minibar, hair dryer, safe.

Villa Condulmer ☆☆ This is the finest place to stay anywhere near Treviso; it's where Giuseppe Verdi fled in 1853 after the Venetian debut of *La Traviata* was met with catcalls. This house was built in 1743 by the Condulmer family, whose wealth and power can be traced to 14th-century ancestor Pope Eugene IV. It passed from the family's hands in the early 19th century, when frescoes by Moretti Laresi were added. You'll find elaborate stucco, marble floors, crystal chandeliers, Oriental carpets, period furnishings, and large, sumptuous guest rooms in the main house as well as in two annexes with lofts. All units have well-kept bathrooms.

Via Zermanese 1, 31020 Zerman di Mogliano Veneto. (☎ 041-457100. Fax 041-457134. www.villa condulmer.com. 50 units. 195€–230€ ($174.15–$205.40) double; 275€ ($245.60) suite. Rates include breakfast. AE, DC, MC, V. Drive 11km (7 miles) south on S13 to Zerman, just outside Mogliano Veneto. **Amenities:** Restaurant; bar; pool; 27-hole golf course; tennis court; room service; babysitting; laundry/dry cleaning. *In room:* A/C, TV, minibar, hair dryer, safe.

WHERE TO DINE

Beccherie VENETIAN This stone-sided building still evokes the era of its construction (1830). The cuisine and the flavorings of the dishes vary with the seasons and include such midwinter game dishes as *faraona in salsa peverada* (guinea hen in peppery sauce) and the spring/summer favorite *pasticcio di melanzane* (eggplant casserole). In between, look for enduring traditions such as fried crabs from the Venetian lagoon served with herb-flavored polenta, salt cod

Vicenza style, osso buco, fiery hot pastas, roasted chicken, or *pasta e fagioli* (pasta and beans) with radicchio.

Piazza Ancilotto 10. ✆ **0422-540871**. Reservations recommended. Main courses 11€–18.50€ ($9.80–$16.50). AE, DC, MC, V. Tues–Sun 12:30–2pm; Tues–Sat 7:30–10pm. Closed July 15–31.

El Toulà da Alfredo ✦ INTERNATIONAL/VENETIAN   This is the restaurant that launched what's now a chain known throughout Italy for its food and service. It offers regional dishes whose inspiration varies with the seasonality of ingredients and the chef's intelligent takes on local traditions. In one of the two Art Nouveau dining rooms, you can order superb versions of risotto with baby peas, pappardelle with baby asparagus tips and herbs, Venetian-style calves' liver, veal kidneys in mustard sauce, *risotto con funghi* (rice with mushrooms), and blinis with caviar. The lengthy dessert roster includes light, sweet sorbets, often made from local fruit. The service is impeccable.

Via Collalto 26. ✆ **0422-540275**. Reservations required Fri–Sat. Main courses 18€–22.50€ ($16.05–$20.10). AE, DC, MC, V. Tues–Sat noon–2:30pm and 7:30–10:30pm; Sun noon–2:30pm. Closed 3 weeks in Aug.

Toni del Spin 〈Value〉 ITALIAN   In the center of Treviso, this is a typical trattoria serving good food at affordable prices. Some excellent dishes of the northern Italian kitchen appear on the menu. Against a rustic backdrop, you can peruse the menu for such delights as risotto with fresh asparagus. A local favorite—perhaps an acquired taste for foreigners—is the *baccala* (dried codfish) cooked in milk with olive oil and onions and baked to perfection in the oven. It comes with a helping of polenta, as does a perfectly roasted and aromatic duck. *Zuppa d'orzo* reveals that barley soup didn't disappear with the Middle Ages. Summer meals are served under an outdoor arbor, and local wines are featured, of course.

Via Inferiore 7. ✆ **0422-543829**. Reservations recommended. Main courses 6€–14€ ($5.35–$12.50). AE, MC, V. Tues–Sat 12:30–2:30pm and Mon–Sat 7:30–10:30pm.

6 Bassano del Grappa ✦

37km (23 miles) N of Venice

At the foot of Mount Grappa in the Valsugana Valley, this hideaway along the Brenta River draws Italian vacationers because of its proximity to the mountains and its panoramic views. Bassano is best known for its liquor, grappa, a brandy usually made from grape pomace left in a winepress, but it's also known for pottery, porcini mushrooms, white asparagus, and radicchio.

ESSENTIALS
GETTING THERE   There's direct **train** service from Trent eight times a day, a 2-hour journey costing 4.15€ ($3.70) one way. There are also trains requiring a change at Castelfranco from Padua and Venice. From Padua, 12 trains per day make the 1-hour trip for 5.05€ ($4.50); from Venice, 16 trains arrive daily, taking 1 hour and 20 minutes for 2.95€ ($2.65). Contact the train station (✆ **848-888088**) for information and schedules.

There are many more **buses** to Bassano than trains. The **FTV** bus line (✆ **0424-30850**) offers service hourly from Vicenza (trip time: 1 hr.) for 2.80€ ($2.50) one way. **CITA** (✆ **0424-8206834**) arrives from Padua every 30 minutes; the trip takes 1 hour and costs 3.25€ ($2.90).

By car from Asolo, take Route 248 for 11km (7 miles) west. From Padua, take the S47 north to Bassano. From Vicenza, take the S47 north and the S53 east. From Verona, take the S47 north and the A4 east.

VISITOR INFORMATION The **tourist office** is at Largo Corona d'Italia 35, off Via Jacopo del Ponte (℡ **0424-524351**); it hands out the *Bassano News,* a monthly information/accommodation guide with a town map. The office is open Monday to Friday 9am to 12:30pm and 2 to 5pm, and Saturday 9am to 12:30pm.

EXPLORING THE TOWN

The village is lovely and the liquor is strong, but there aren't a lot of specific sights. Bassano's best-known landmark is the **Ponte dei Alpini,** a covered wooden bridge over the Brenta, which has been replaced numerous times because of flooding, but each version is faithful to the original 1209 design.

Housing numerous paintings by Basano, the **Civic Museum (Museo Civico)** ✦, in Piazza Garibaldi at Via Museo 12 (℡ **0424-522235**), also has works by Canova, Tiepolo, and others. It's open Tuesday to Saturday 9am to 6:30pm, and Sunday 3:30 to 6:30pm, with an admission of 4€ ($3.55). That ticket will also admit you to the **Palazzo Sturm,** Via Schiavonetti (℡ **0424-524933**), home of the **Ceramics Museum,** featuring 4 centuries of finely crafted regional pottery. In April, May, and October, hours are Tuesday to Saturday 9am to noon and 3:30 to 4:30pm, Sunday 3:30 to 6:30pm. June to September, the museum is open Tuesday to Saturday 9am to noon and 3:30 to 6:30pm, Sunday 10am to 12:30pm and 3:30 to 6:30pm. From November to March, hours are Friday 9am to 12:30pm, Saturday and Sunday 3:30 to 6:30pm. Admission is 3.50€ ($3.15).

If you don't get sick from overindulging on grappa, you might want to pick some up to take home. The best-known distillery is the 18th-century **Nardini,** Via Ponte Vecchio (℡ **0424-567040**), next to the Ponte degli Alpini, where juniper, pear, peach, and plum versions supplement the grape standard. Other grappa shops are **Poli,** Via Gamba (℡ **0424-524426**), and **Bassanina,** Via Angarano 22 (℡ **0424-502140**). Because you're in the heart of grappa country, you can also find good smaller labels such as Folco Portinari, Maschio, Jacopo de Poli, Rino Dal Tosco, Da Ponte, and Carpene Malvolti.

WHERE TO STAY

Al Castello (Value) Opened in the heart of town by the Cattapan family more than 25 years ago, this is a simple hotel outfitted to provide you with a comfortable stay at a bargain rate. This antique town house has been renovated but retains a classical style. The guest rooms are on the small side, but each is comfortable. The tiled bathrooms are a bit cramped.

Piazza Terraglio 19, 36061 Bassano del Grappa. ℡ and fax **0424-228665.** 11 units (showers only). 70€–75€ ($62.50–$67) double. AE, MC, V. Free parking. **Amenities:** Bar; lounge; room service; laundry. *In room:* A/C, TV, hair dryer.

Bonotto Hotel Belvedere ✦ This has been the town's leading hotel since it opened in the 15th century as a place to rest and change horses before traveling on to Venice. The third-floor rooms attest to the hotel's age, with rustic exposed beams. All the guest rooms incorporate classical, Venetian, and Bassanese styles. The hotel recently added five superior doubles and renovated 14 others. The tiled bathrooms are beautifully kept. The public rooms are luxurious, with Oriental rugs and tapestries, fresh flowers, and curvaceous wooden furniture covered with rich fabrics. The lounge houses a baby grand piano, a fireplace, and a wooden ivy-covered balcony.

Piazzale Generale Giardino 14, 36061 Bassano del Grappa. ℡ **0424-529845.** Fax 0424-529849. www.bonotto.it. 87 units. 82€–155€ ($73.20–$138.40) double; 155€–207€ ($138.40–$184.85) junior suite. Rates include breakfast. AE, DC, MC, V. Parking 10€ ($8.95). **Amenities:** Restaurant; bar; lounge; room service; babysitting; laundry/dry cleaning. *In room:* A/C, TV, minibar, hair dryer, safe.

Bonotto Hotel Palladio ☞   This is the Belvedere's sibling (they're 457m/500 yd. apart), but you'd never guess they were related. This hotel's facade is modern, with cut stone and stepped glass panels. The interior is contemporary as well, and the lobby boasts a curved wood-and-brass counter and modern recessed lighting. The guest rooms are modern and streamlined, small to medium in size. The bathrooms are small but tidy.

Via Gramsci 2, 36061 Bassano del Grappa. ✆ **0424-523777.** Fax 0424-524050. www.bonotto.it. 66 units. 78€–132€ ($69.65–$117.90) double. Rates include breakfast. AE, DC, MC, V. Parking 8€ ($7.15). **Amenities:** Bar; lounge; gym; sauna; room service; massage; laundry/dry cleaning. *In room:* A/C, TV, minibar, hair dryer, safe.

ON THE OUTSKIRTS

Villa Palma ☞   This 18th-century villa, which opened as a hotel in 1991, lies just 5km (3 miles) from Bassano. Renovations preserved features such as its beamed and vaulted brick ceilings. The guest rooms are individualized by mixing antiques, carpets, and tapestries to create a comfortable yet elegant atmosphere. Most rooms are fairly spacious, and all have excellent mattresses and fine linen. Some bathrooms have sauna showers or Jacuzzis.

Via Chemin Palma 30, 36065 Mussolente. ✆ **0424-577407.** Fax 0424-87687. 21 units. 162€ ($144.65) double; 228€ ($203.60) suite. Rates include buffet breakfast. AE, DC, MC, V. Free parking. **Amenities:** Restaurant; lounge; room service; babysitting; laundry. *In room:* A/C, TV, minibar, hair dryer, safe.

WHERE TO DINE

Al Sole ☞ VENETIAN   Gian-Franco Chiurato's successful restaurant occupies this cavernous early-19th-century palazzo, where both dining rooms are decorated with local ceramics. The cuisine is rooted in the Veneto's traditions and celebrates two annual crops: In springtime, look for the region's distinctive white asparagus blended into pastas and risottos, used as a garnish for main courses, and often featured as a refreshing course on its own. In autumn and winter, look for similar variations on mushrooms, especially porcini, which are absolutely addictive, with game birds and venison. The rest of the year, expect polenta with codfish, puff pastry layered with local cheeses and mushrooms, homemade bigoli pasta drenched with duck meat and mushrooms, and baked lamb with herbed polenta.

Via Jacopo Vittorelli 41. ✆ **0424-523206.** Reservations recommended. Main courses 10€–15€ ($8.95–$13.40). AE, DC, MC, V. Tues–Sun noon–3pm and 7:30–10pm. Closed 20 days in July.

⌒Moments A Human Chess Game

Seven kilometers (4½ miles) west of Bassano del Grappa on Route 248, **Marostica** hosts the **Game of Life,** a reminder of how far relations between the sexes have actually progressed. The second week of September in even-numbered years, the town square in front of the Castello da Basso is used as a chessboard, and costumed townspeople become its pieces in order to re-create the medieval practice of playing *scacchi* to claim the hand of the kingdom's most beautiful woman (the loser got a homelier maiden). For more information, contact the **Associazione Pro Marostica,** Piazza Castello 1 (✆ **0424-72127**). While you're here, you might want to indulge in the wonderful cherries that are the town's other claim to fame.

Birreria Ottone *(Kids* AUSTRIAN/ITALIAN/VENETO Occupying a 13th-century building across from City Hall, this is the most appealing beer hall in the region. Thanks to generous portions and copious amounts of beer, the site is preferred by extended families and groups of friends, some of whom actually dine. Look for two dining rooms encircled with chiseled stone, marble accents, and ceramic tiles, and food items that include goulash, Wiener schnitzel, frankfurters, roasted lamb, and Venetian-style calves' liver. In spring, look for savory local asparagus.

Via Matteoti 48–50. (℃ **0424-522206.** Reservations recommended Fri–Sat. Main courses 7€–12.50€ ($6.25–$11.15). AE, DC, MC, V. Wed–Mon 12:15–3:15pm; Wed–Sun 7–11pm.

7 Trieste *(★*

116km (72 miles) NE of Venice, 667km (414 miles) NE of Rome, 407km (252 miles) E of Milan

Remote Trieste, a shimmering city with many neoclassical buildings, is perched on the half-moon Gulf of Trieste, which opens into the Adriatic. Trieste has had a long history, with many changes of ownership. The Hapsburg emperor Charles VI declared it a free port in 1719, but by the 20th century it was an ocean outlet for the Austro-Hungarian Empire. After World War I and a secret deal among the Allies, Trieste was ceded to Italy. In 1943, Trieste again fell to foreign troops—this time the Nazis, who were ousted by Tito's Yugoslav army in 1945. In 1954, after much hassle, the American and British troops withdrew as the Italians marched in, with the stipulation that the much-disputed Trieste would be maintained as a free port. Today that status continues. Politics, as always, dominate the agenda here. There's racial tension, and many Italian Fascists and anti-Slav parties are centered in Trieste.

Trieste has known many glamorous literary associations, particularly in the pre–World War II years. As a stop on the Orient Express, it became a famed destination. Dame Agatha Christie came this way, as did Graham Greene. James Joyce, eloping with Nora Barnacle, arrived in 1904. Out of money, Joyce got a job teaching at the Berlitz School and lived in Trieste for nearly 10 years. He wrote *A Portrait of the Artist as a Young Man* here and might have begun his masterpiece *Ulysses* here as well. Poet Rainer Maria Rilke also lived in the area. Author Richard Burton, known for his *Arabian Nights* translations, lived in Trieste from 1871 until he died about 20 years later.

Trieste, squashed between Slovenia and the Adriatic, has been more vulnerable to conditions following the collapse of Yugoslavia than any other city in Italy. Civil war and turmoil have halted the flow of thousands who used to cross the border to buy merchandise—mainly jeans and household appliances. The port has also suffered from crises in the shipbuilding and steel industries. Trieste remains Italy's insurance capital, and one-fourth of its population of 150,000 residents is retired (it has the highest per-capita pensioner population in Italy).

ESSENTIALS

GETTING THERE Trieste is serviced by an **airport** at **Ronchi dei Legionari** (℃ **0481-773224**), 35km (22 miles) northwest of the city. Daily flights on Alitalia connect it with Linate airport in Milan (trip time: 50 min.), Franz Josef Strauss airport in Munich (trip time: 1 hr., 10 min.), and Leonardo da Vinci airport in Rome (trip time: 1 hr., 10 min.).

Trieste lies on a direct **rail** link from Venice. Trip time from Venice is 2½ hours, and a one-way ticket is 7.30€ ($6.50). The station is on Piazza della Libertà (℃ **848-888088,** toll-free in Italy), northwest of the historic center. It's

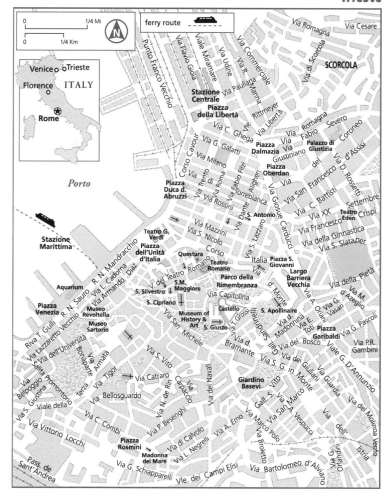

better to fly, drive, or take the train to Trieste. Once here, you'll find a network of **local buses** servicing the region from Corso Cavour (✆ **040-3360300** or 040-425020).

By car, follow A4 northeast from Venice until you reach the end of the line at Trieste.

VISITOR INFORMATION   The **tourist office** is at Via San Nicolò 20 (✆ **040-679611**), open Monday to Friday 9am to 7pm. A **second office** is in Riva III Novembre No. 9 (✆ **040-3478312**), open daily 9am to 7pm.

EXPLORING THE CITY

The heart of Trieste is the neoclassic **Piazza dell'Unità d'Italia** ⨀, Italy's largest square that fronts the sea. Opening onto the square is the town hall with a clock tower, the Palace of the Government, and the main office of the Lloyd Triestino ship line. Flanking it are numerous cafes and restaurants, popular at night with locals who sip an aperitif and then promenade along the seafront esplanade.

After visiting the main square, you might want to view Trieste from an even better vantage point. Head up the hill for another cluster of attractions—you can take an antiquated **tram** leaving from Piazza Oberdan and get off at Obelisco. At the **belvedere,** the city of the Adriatic will spread out before you.

Cathedral of St. Just (Cattedrale di San Giusto)   Dedicated to the patron saint of Trieste, who was martyred in A.D. 303, this basilica was consecrated in 1330, incorporating a pair of churches that had been separate until then. The front is Romanesque style, enhanced by a rose window. Inside, the nave is flanked by two pairs of aisles. To the left of the main altar are the best of the Byzantine mosaics in Trieste (note especially the blue-robed Madonna and child). The main altar and the chapel to the right contain less interesting mosaics. To the left of the basilica entrance is a campanile from the 14th century, which you can scale for a view of Trieste and its bay. At its base are preserved the remains of a Roman temple from the 1st century A.D. You might prefer to take a taxi up to the cathedral and then walk a leisurely 15 minutes back down. From the basilica you can also stroll to the nearby San Giusto Castle (see below).

Piazza Cattedrale, Colle Capitolino. © 040-302874. Free admission. Daily 7:30am–7pm.

St. Just Castle (Castello di San Giusto)   Constructed in the 15th century by the Venetians on the site of a Roman fort, this fortress maintained a sharp eye on the bay, watching for unfriendly visitors arriving by sea. From its bastions, panoramic views of Trieste unfold. Inside is a museum with a collection of arms and armor. The castle's open-air theater hosts a film festival in July and August.

Piazza Cattedrale 3. © 040-309362. Castle 1.50€ ($1.35); museum 1.50€ ($1.35). Castle daily 9am–sunset; museum Tues–Sun 9am–1pm.

Miramare Castle (Castello di Miramare) Overlooking the Bay of Grignano, this castle was built by Archduke Maximilian, the brother of Franz Josef, the Hapsburg emperor of Austria. Maximilian, who married Princess Charlotte of Belgium, was the commander of the Austrian navy in 1854. In an ill-conceived move, he and "Carlotta" sailed to Mexico in 1864, where he became the emperor in an unfortunate, brief reign. He was shot in 1867 in Querétaro, Mexico. His wife lived until 1927 in a château outside Brussels, driven insane by the Mexican episode. On the ground floor, you can visit Maximilian's bedroom (built like a ship's cabin) and Charlotte's, as well as an impressive receiving room and more parlors, including a chinoiserie salon.

Enveloping the castle are magnificently designed grounds (the **Parco di Miramare**), ideal for pleasant strolls. In July and August, a **sound-and-light presentation** in the park depicts Maximilian's tragedy in Mexico. Tickets begin at 5€ ($4.45).

Viale Miramare, Grignano (8km/5 miles northwest of town). © 040-224143. Admission 4€ ($3.55). Daily 9am–6:30pm. Bus: 36.

A ROOM WITH NO VIEW: THE GROTTA GIGANTE

In the heart of the limestone plateau called Carso surrounding Trieste, you can visit the **Grotta Gigante** (© 040-327312), an enormous cavern that's one of the most interesting phenomena of speleology. First explored in 1840 via the top ceiling entrance, this huge room, some 116m (380 ft.) deep, was opened to the public in 1908. It's the biggest single-room cave ever opened to visitors and one of the world's largest underground rooms. You can visit only with a guide on a 40-minute tour. Near the entrance is the Man and Caves Museum, unique in Italy.

Tours of the cave are given April to September 10am to 6pm (every half hour), and October to March 10am to 4pm (every hour). Tours cost 7.50€ ($6.70). If you're driving, take Strada del Friuli beyond the white marble Victory Lighthouse as far as Prosecco. On the freeway, you can take the exit at Prosecco. By public transport, take the tram from Piazza Oberdan and then bus no. 42 to Prosecco.

SHOPPING

Trieste is a great place to shop for antiques. Look for examples of both Biedermeier and Liberty (Italian Art Nouveau) furniture and accessories, and wander at will through the city's densest collection of antiques dealers, the neighborhood around **Piazza dell'Unità d'Italia.** Dealers to look out for are **Davia,** Via dell'Annunziata 6 (© 040-304321), specializing in antique engravings; **Jésu,** Via Felice Venezian 9 (© 040-300719), dealing in small art objects and furniture; and **Dr. Fulvio Rosso,** Via Diaz 13 (© 040-306226), specializing in crystal and porcelain from the turn of the 20th century.

You might also check out the wood carvings from Trieste's most comprehensive collection of half-Austrian, half-Italian accessories, **Paolo Hrovatin,** Borgo Grotte Gigante (© 040-327077).

Fine leather and suede goods fill **Christine Pellettrie,** Piazza della Borso 15 (© 040-366212), where women can find well-crafted shoes, bags, and pants.

Offering both casual and formal attire, **Max Mara,** Corso Italia 20–1 (© 040-636723), features impeccable women's designs, plus shoes and bags. A waterfront shop, **Spangher,** Riva Gulli 8 (© 040-305158), sells trendy sportswear and is an Italianized version of Abercrombie and Fitch.

The 130-year-old **La Bomboniera,** Via XXX Ottobre 3 (© 040-632752), is a candy store as beautifully wrapped as the chocolates it sells, with etched glass, carved walnut shelves, and an elaborate glass chandelier. Besides fine chocolates, it offers traditional sweets and pastries of the region, as well as a few Austro-Hungarian specialties.

WHERE TO STAY

Grand Hotel Duchi d'Aosta   This remains the traditional favorite among upscale travelers to Trieste who want to stay in the center of the city. This glamorous hotel began about 200 years ago as a restaurant for the dock workers who toiled nearby. In 1873, one of the most beautiful facades in Trieste—a white neoclassical shell with delicate carving, arched windows, and a stone crown of heroic sculptures—was erected over the existing building. The design is very much that of an 18th-century palace, enhanced by views over the fountains and lamps of the square and the sea beyond it, while the Victorian public rooms give it a 19th-century ambience. The interior was practically rebuilt in the 1970s, and each guest room boasts antiqued walls and tasteful furniture. The tiled bathrooms are well equipped.

Piazza Unità d'Italia 2, 34121 Trieste. © 040-7600011. Fax 040-366092. 55 units (some with shower only). 259€ ($231.30) double; from 523€ ($467.05) suite. Rates include breakfast. AE, DC, MC, V. Parking 19.50€ ($17.40). **Amenities:** Restaurant; bar; room service; babysitting; laundry/dry cleaning. *In room:* A/C, TV, minibar, hair dryer, safe.

Hotel al Teatro   It's a bit creaky but still an enduring favorite. The theatrical mask carved into the stone arch above the entrance is an appropriate symbol of this hotel, a favorite with many of Trieste's visiting opera stars. It's a few steps from the seaside panorama of Piazza dell'Unità d'Italia and about a 10-minute walk from the station. The slightly old-fashioned guest rooms have parquet floors, lots of space, and comfortable but minimal furniture. The hotel was built in 1830 as a home and served as British army headquarters following World War II.

Capo di Piazza G. Bartoli 1, 34124 Trieste. ☎ 040-366220. Fax 040-366560. 45 units, 35 with bathroom (shower only). 80€ ($71.45) double without bathroom; 105€ ($93.75) double with bathroom. Rates include breakfast. AE, MC, V. **Amenities:** Lounge.

Hotel Greif Maria Theresia 🐟🐟   In the exclusive Barcola district, a 5-minute drive from the city center, this restored villa is the number-one choice for your Trieste layover. It now surpasses the top position long held by the Grand Hotel Duchi d'Aosta (see above). Overlooking the Gulf of Trieste, the building is stylishly furnished and decorated, with exceedingly comfortable bedrooms. All bedrooms come with a medium-size tiled bathroom. Service is efficient, and housekeeping is first-rate. The hotel also has more facilities than any other in the area.

Viale Miramare 109, Barcola, 34136 Trieste. ☎ 040-410115. Fax 040-413053. www.emmeti.it/Welcome/Friuli/Trieste/Alberghi/Greif/index.uk.html. 36 units. 220€ ($196.45) double. AE, DC, MC, V. Free parking. **Amenities:** Restaurant; bar; pool; gym; sauna; room service; laundry/dry cleaning. *In room:* A/C, TV, minibar, hair dryer.

Novo Hotel Impero   This restored member of Fenice hotels occupies a neo-classical building in front of the rail station and still retains much of the original glamour of its facade. Next to the historical center and the business area, it offers tastefully, though sparsely, furnished guest rooms, each with modernized bathrooms.

Via Sant'Anastasio 1, 34132 Trieste. ☎ 040-364242. Fax 040-365023. 50 units (showers only). 124€ ($110.75) double; 180€ ($160.75) suite. Rates include breakfast. AE, DC, MC, V. Parking 10€ ($8.95). **Amenities:** Bar; babysitting; laundry/dry cleaning. *In room:* A/C, TV.

WHERE TO DINE

Al Bragozzo 🐟 SEAFOOD   This is the best-known restaurant at the port, and it's not for landlubbers; only fish and pasta are served. The simply yet creatively prepared meals pay homage to the sea and its heritage by combining the elements of Italian cuisine and the riches of the Mediterranean. Specialties include *spaghetti alla Giorgio* (with tomatoes and herbs), ravioli stuffed with herbs, monkfish braised with artichokes and cooked with white wine, spaghetti with lobster, and many preparations of salmon and shrimp. If you visit in summer, you can dine at the outdoor tables sheltered by a canopy.

Riva Nazario Sauro 22. ☎ 040-303001. Reservations recommended. Main courses 9€–25€ ($8.05–$22.35). AE, DC, MC, V. Tues–Sat noon–3pm and 7–10pm. Closed June 22–July 10 and Dec 25–Jan 10.

Al Granzo 🐟 SEAFOOD   The people of Trieste still flock here today to enjoy seafood, often based on the same recipes that the founding fathers, a trio of brothers, have been serving since 1923. It's one of Trieste's leading seafood restaurants, serving flavor-filled versions of that curious mix of Italian, Austrian, and Yugoslav cuisines known as Triestino. Menu items include *brodetto,* a traditional bouillabaisse spiced with saffron and other herbs; vermicelli with black mussels; and risotto with seafood. Fresh fish are displayed on crushed ice in a wagon, and there's an impressive selection of fresh *contorni* (vegetables, sold individually). A suitable wine would be a local Tocai Friulano, aromatic and somewhat tart. Dessert might be homemade strudel.

Piazza Venezia 7. ☎ 040-306788. Reservations recommended. Main courses 12.50€–17.50€ ($11.15–$15.65); fixed-price menu 30€–40€ ($26.80–$35.70). AE, DC, MC, V. Thurs–Tues 12:30–3pm; Mon–Tues and Thurs–Sat 7:30–10:30pm.

Antica Trattoria Suban ITALIAN/CENTRAL EUROPEAN   This tavern is 4km (2½ miles) north of Trieste in the district of San Giovanni, on a spacious terrace opening onto a hill view. The landscape contains glimpses of the Industrial Age, but the brick and stone walls, the terrace, and the country feeling are still intact. The restaurant is run by descendants of the founding family, and the cuisine is both hearty and delicate, drawing its inspiration from northeastern Italian, Slavic, Hungarian, and Germanic traditions. Dishes include a flavorful risotto with herbs, beef with garlic sauce, a perfectly prepared chicken Kiev, veal croquettes with parmigiano and egg yolks, crepes stuffed with basil and roasted veal, and haunch of veal with roasted potatoes. The chef's handling of grilled meats is adept, and the rich pastries, such as the honey strudel, are worth the calories.

Via Comici 2, at San Giovanni. ℂ 040-54368. Reservations recommended. Main courses 11€–17.50€ ($9.80–$15.65). AE, DC, MC, V. Wed–Sun 12:30–2:30pm; Wed–Mon 7:30–10pm. Closed 15 days in Aug.

Ristorante Harry's Grill ℛ INTERNATIONAL   In Trieste's most upscale hotel, this restaurant manages to be both elegant and relaxed, where you can have an American-style martini followed by a simple plate of pasta or a full meal. The big lace-covered curtains complement the paneling, the polished brass, and the blue Murano chandeliers. In summer, tables are set up in the traffic-free piazza. The outdoor terrace, sheltered by a canopy, has a separate area for bar patrons. The Mediterranean-inspired cuisine is good but not great and includes fresh shrimp with oil and lemon, pasta and risotto dishes, boiled salmon in sauce, calves' liver with onions, *bigoli* (fat spaghetti) with duck meat, and beef filet with red-wine sauce. The adjoining bar (not related to Italy's other famed Harry's Bars) is one of the most popular rendezvous spots in town.

In the Grand Hotel Duchi d'Aosta, Piazza dell'Unità d'Italia 2. ℂ 040-660606. Reservations required. Main courses 15€–20€ ($13.40–$17.85). AE, DC, MC, V. Daily 12:15–3pm and 7:15–10:30pm.

TRIESTE AFTER DARK

Trieste's most impressive theater, the **Teatro Verdi,** Corso Cavour (ℂ **040-6722111**), has been compared to a blend of the Vienna State Opera and Milan's La Scala. Built in 1801 and massively renovated in the mid-1990s, it presents classical concerts and operas throughout the year. Tickets range from 12.50€ to 60€ ($11.15–$53.60).

The town's loveliest cafe, almost adjacent to the above-mentioned theater, is the **Caffè Tommaseo,** Piazza Tommaseo 4–6 (ℂ **040-362666**). The bar adjoining **Ristorante Harry's Grill** is also a popular watering hole.

If you're interested in dancing the night away, the neighborhood around Piazza dell'Unità d'Italia offers the town's most animated disco, **Mandracchio,** Passo di Piazza (ℂ **040-366292**). Its closest rival is **Disco Machiavelli,** Viale Miramare 285 (ℂ **040-44104**), a crowded see-and-be-seen dance hall whose only drawback is its location 6km (3¾ miles) north of Piazza dell'Unità d'Italia.

8 Cortina d'Ampezzo: Gateway to the Dolomites ℛℛ

161km (100 miles) N of Venice, 411km (255 miles) NE of Milan

This chic resort town is your best center for exploring the snowy Dolomiti. Its reputation as a tourist mecca dates from before World War I, but its recent growth has been phenomenal, spurred by the 1956 Olympics held here. Cortina d'Ampezzo draws throngs of nature lovers in summer and both Olympic-caliber and neophyte skiers in winter. (Expect high hotel prices in July and Aug, as well as in the 3 months of winter, Nov–Jan.)

Cortina is in the middle of a valley ringed by enough Dolomite peaks to cause Hannibal's elephants to throw up their trunks and flee in horror. Regardless of which road you choose for a drive, you'll find the scenery rewarding. And Cortina sets an excellent table, inspired by the cuisine of both Venice and Tirol.

ESSENTIALS

GETTING THERE   Frequent **trains** run between Venice and Calalzo di Cadore (trip time: 2½ hr.), 31km (19 miles) south of Cortina. You proceed the rest of the way by bus. For information about schedules, call ✆ **848-888088** in Calalzo. About 14 to 16 **buses** a day connect Calalzo di Cadore with Cortina. Buses arrive at the Cortina bus station on Viale Marconi (✆ **0436-2741**).

By car, take A27 north from Venice and then follow the S51 into Cortina.

VISITOR INFORMATION   The **tourist office** is at Piazzetta San Francesco 8 (✆ **0436-3231**), open daily 9am to 12:30pm and 3 to 6:30pm.

EXPLORING THE PEAKS OF THE DOLOMITES

One of the main attractions in Cortina is to take a **cable car** "halfway to the stars," as the expression goes. On one of them, at least, you'll be just a yodel away from the pearly gates: the **Freccia nel Cielo** ("Arrow of the Sky"). From July 12 to September 28 and December 20 to mid-April beginning at 9am, cars depart from the base behind Cortina's Olympic Stadium every 20 minutes (call ✆ **0436-5052** for departures the rest of the year). Round-trip cost is 15.45€ ($13.80) in winter and 22.50€ ($20.10) in summer. An ascent to the summit of the cable-car run requires two changes en route and an uphill ride through three separate cable-car segments. The first station is Col Druscie, at 1,753m (5,752 ft.); the second is Ra Valles, at 2,447m (8,027 ft.); and the top is Tofana di Mezzo, at 3,214m (10,543 ft.). At Tofana on a clear day, you can see as far as Venice.

Part of the Alps, the snowy peaks of the **Dolomiti** stretch along Italy's northwestern tier, following the line of the Austrian border between the valleys of the Adige and Brenta rivers.

Although the highest peak is the Marmolada (a little shy of 3,350m/11,000 ft. above sea level), the range contains 18 peaks in Italian territory that rise above 3,050m (10,000 ft.). Escaping from the often intense heat of other parts of the country, Italians travel here to breathe the Dolomiti's cool mountain air and to ski and play in resorts such as Cortina.

The mix of limestone and porphyry, combined with the angle of the sun, contributes to the peaks' dramatic coloration. Most pronounced in the morning and at dusk, their colors range from soft pinks to brooding russets. When the sun shines directly overhead, the hues fade to a homogenized dull gray. Fortunately for tourists, trekkers, and skiers, the climate isn't as bone-chilling as it is in the alpine regions of western Italy and in the Alps of the Tirol, farther north.

Throughout the Dolomiti, networks of **hiking trails** are clearly marked with signs, and local tourist offices (as well as most hotel staffs) can help you choose a good hike that suits your time and ability level. Maps of hiking trails are broadly distributed, and any tourist office can refer you to the nearest branch of the Associazione Guide Alpine. If you decide to ramble across the Dolomiti, you'll need stout shoes, warm clothing, and a waterproof jacket (storms erupt quickly at these altitudes). Rustically charming *refugi* (mountain huts) offer the opportunity for an overnight stay or just a rest. (While you're hiking, please refrain from picking the wildflowers because many of them, including the Austrian national flower, the edelweiss, are endangered species. Picking flowers or destroying vegetation is punishable by stiff fines.)

SKIING & OTHER OUTDOOR PURSUITS

DOWNHILL SKIING The **Faloria-Cristallo area** surrounding Cortina is known for its 30km (19 miles) of slopes and 16km (10 miles) of fresh-snow runs. At 1,223m (4,014 ft.) above sea level, Cortina's altitude isn't particularly forbidding (at least, compared with that of other European ski resorts), and though snowfall is usually abundant from late December to early March, a holiday in November or April might leave you stranded without adequate snow. Die-hard Cortina enthusiasts usually compensate for that, at least during the tail end of the season, by remaining only at the surrounding slopes' higher altitudes (there's lots of ski-ability at 2,743m/9,000 ft.) and traversing lower-altitude snowfields by cable car.

As Italy's premier ski resort, Cortina boasts more than 50 cable cars and lifts spread out across the valley of the Boite River. The surrounding mountains contain about two dozen restaurants, about 145km (90 miles) of clearly designated ski trails, and a virtually unlimited number of off-piste trails for cross-country enthusiasts. Cortina boasts plenty of sunshine, a relative lack of crowds, and an array of slopes that will suit intermediate, advanced intermediate, and novice skiers alike. During winter, ski lifts are open daily 9am to between 4 and 5pm, depending on the time of sunset.

Cortina boasts eight distinct ski areas, each with its own challenges and charms. Regrettably, because they sprawl rather disjointedly across the terrain, they're not always easy to interconnect. The most appealing of the ski areas are the **Tofana-Promedes, Forcella Rossa,** and **Faloria-Tondi** complexes. The **Pocol, Mietres,** and **Socepres** areas are specifically for novices; the **Cinque Torre** is valuable for intermediates; and the outlying **Falzarego** is a long, dramatic, and sometimes terrifying downhill jaunt not recommended for anyone except a very competent skier.

Despite the availability of dozens of cable cars originating outside the town center along the valley floor, Cortina's most dramatic cable cars are the **Freccia nel Cielo** ("Arrow to the Sky"), the region's longest and most panoramic (see above), and the **Funivia Faloria** (Faloria chairlift), which begins 183m (200 yd.) east of town, adjacent to the Olympic Ice Stadium. Both of these cable cars are patronized even by visitors who'd never dream of skiing. A single round-trip ticket on either is 22.50€ ($20.10), although if you plan on spending time in Cortina, it's almost always more economical to buy a ski pass (see below).

Ski passes are issued for from 1 to 21 days. They can include access to just the lifts around Cortina (about 50) or to all the ski lifts in the Dolomiti (around 464). By far the better value is the more comprehensive pass. This Dolomiti Super Ski Pass allows you unlimited access to a vast network of chairlifts and gondolas stretching over Cortina and the mountains flanking at least 10 other resorts. The single-day pass is 32.90€ ($29.40), but the daily cost goes down as you increase the days of the pass. For example, a 7-day pass is 170.30€ ($152.10) and a 21-day pass is 395€ ($352.75). The Cortina-only pass sells for about 10% less, but few people opt for it. Children under 8 ski free.

Included in any pass is free transport on any of Cortina's bright yellow ski buses that run the length of the valley in season, connecting the many cable cars. Depending on snowfall, the two ski lifts mentioned above, as well as most of the other lifts in Cortina, are closed from around April 20 to July 15 and September 15 to around December 1. For information, call © **0436-862171.**

CROSS-COUNTRY SKIING The trails start about 3km (2 miles) north of town. Some, but not all, run parallel to the region's roads and highways. For information about their location, instruction, and rental of equipment, contact the **Scuola Italiana Sci Fondo Cortina** in Fiames at ☎ **0436-4903.**

FISHING If you opt to fish in the cold, clear waters of the River Boite, you should first arrange with the tourist office for a permit, which costs 5€ ($4.45) per day. Many visitors, however, prefer to fish in any of the three lakes around Cortina, the best stocked of which is the Lago di Aial. For fishing in any of the lakes, you won't be charged for a permit until you actually catch something—lake access roads leading from Cortina have checkpoints with the Italian equivalent of a park ranger, who charges you a small fee based on the size and weight of your catch. For information on fishing in Cortina and the surrounding region, contact the tourist office at ☎ **0436-3231.**

ICE SKATING In winter, two rinks operate in the **Stadio Olimpico del Ghiaccio,** Via dello Stadio (☎ **0436-2661**). One of the two operates throughout summer, but the other is converted to a concrete surface suitable for in-line skating. Regardless of the season, you'll pay 6.50€ ($5.80), with skates rented for an additional fee.

WHERE TO STAY

If you're looking for the chance to live with a Dolomite family in comfort and informality, ask the tourist office for its list of private homes that take in paying guests (the office won't make the reservations for you, however; you have to do it yourself). Even though nearly 4,700 hotel beds are available, it's best to reserve ahead, especially in August and December 20 to January 7.

Hotel Ancora ✦ This evocative hotel is the domain of the empress of the Dolomiti, Flavia Bertozzi, who gathered its antique sculptures and objets d'art during her trips throughout Italy. The Ancora attracts sporting guests from all over the world, hosts modern art exhibits and classical concerts, and boasts terraces with outdoor tables and umbrellas (the town center for sipping and gossiping). Garlanded wooden balconies encircle the five floors. Most guest rooms open onto these sunny porches, and all are well furnished, comfortable, and especially pleasant; many have sitting areas. Each unit comes with a well-kept bathroom.

Corso Italia 62, 32043 Cortina d'Ampezzo. ☎ **0436-3261.** Fax 0436-3265. www.hotelancoracortina.com. 49 units. 230€–352€ ($205.35–$314.30) double; 420€–550€ ($375.05–$491.15) suite. Winter 186€–290€ ($166.10–$258.95) double; 235€–380€ ($209.85–$339.35) suite. Rates include half-board. AE, DC, MC, V. Closed after Easter to June and Sept 15–Dec 20. Valet parking 20€ ($17.85). **Amenities:** Restaurant; bar; room service; massage; babysitting; laundry. *In room:* TV, minibar, hair dryer, safe.

Hotel Corona _Value_ For anyone interested in modern Italian art, a stop here is an event—the walls are hung with dozens of works. Many of the most important artists of Italy (and a few from France) from 1948 to 1963 are represented by paintings, sculptures, and ceramic bas-reliefs acquired by manager Luciano Rimoldi. The guest rooms are cozy, with varnished pine and local artifacts. The tiled bathrooms are compact. Rimoldi is also a ski instructor (he once coached Princess Grace in her downhill technique) and was head of the Italian ice-hockey team during the 1988 Winter Olympics, where one of his former pupils, Alberto Tomba, began his Olympic domination of alpine events.

Via Val di Sotto 10, 32040 Cortina d'Ampezzo. ☎ **0436-3251.** Fax 0436-867339. www.hotelcorona cortina.it. 46 units (17 with shower only). 160€–380€ ($142.85–$339.30) double. Rates include breakfast. AE, DC, MC, V. Closed Apr 2–July and Sept–Dec 3. **Amenities:** Restaurant; lounge; room service; babysitting; laundry. *In room:* TV, minibar, hair dryer, safe.

Hotel Dolomiti   This hotel offers many amenities, although it's more sterile than our other recommendations. But it's a good bet if you're watching your euros or if you arrive in Cortina off-season, when virtually everything else is closed. Its convenient location on the main road just outside the center of town, coupled with its comfortable, no-nonsense format, has gained it increasing favor with visitors. The guest rooms are predictably furnished and fairly quiet, and the management is helpful. The bathrooms are tidy.

Via Roma 118, 32043 Cortina d'Ampezzo. © 0436-861400. Fax 0436-862140. 42 units (showers only). 65€–110€ ($58.05–$98.25) double. Rates include half-board. AE, DC, MC, V. Parking 15€ ($13.40). **Amenities:** Restaurant; lounge; room service; babysitting. *In room:* TV, minibar, hair dryer.

Hotel Menardi ★ *(Finds)*   This eye-catcher in the upper part of Cortina looks like a great country inn, with wooden balconies and shutters. Its rear windows open onto a flowery meadow and a view of the Dolomite crags. The inn is 100 years old and is run by the Menardi family, who still know how to speak the old Dolomite tongue, Ladino. The guest rooms are decorated in the Tirolean fashion, each with its own distinct personality; bathrooms are on the small side. Considering what you get—the quality of the facilities, the reception, and the food—we'd rate this one of the best values here.

Via Majon 112, 32043 Cortina d'Ampezzo. © **0436-2400.** Fax 0436-862183. www.hotelmenardi.it. 51 units. 110€–180€ ($98.25–$160.75) double. Rates include breakfast. DC, MC, V. Parking 7.50€ ($6.70). Closed Apr 10–June 8 and Sept 20–Dec 19. **Amenities:** Dining room; bar; room service; babysitting; laundry. *In room:* TV, hair dryer, safe.

Miramonti Majestic Grand Hotel ★★   Built in 1893, this hotel, one of the grandest in the Dolomites, is a short distance from the center of town. The rustic interior is filled with warm colors, lots of exposed timbers, and the most elegant crowd in Cortina. The well-furnished guest rooms look like those of a private home, complete with matching accessories, built-in closets, and all the modern extras. The bathrooms boast deluxe toiletries.

Località Peziè 103, 32043 Cortina d'Ampezzo. © **0436-4201.** Fax 0436-867019. 108 units. 145€–510€ ($129.50–$455.45) double; 620€–1,020€ ($553.65–$910.85) suite. Rates include breakfast. AE, DC, MC, V. Closed Apr–June and Sept–Nov. Parking 15€ ($13.40) in garage, free outside. Hotel shuttle to/from town center every 30 min. **Amenities:** Restaurant; bar; pool; spa; concierge; car-rental desk; room service; babysitting; laundry/dry cleaning. *In room:* A/C, TV, minibar; hair dryer, safe.

WHERE TO DINE

Da Beppe Sello *(Value)* ALPINE/INTERNATIONAL/ITALIAN   This down-to-earth and reasonably priced restaurant is located in a Tirolean-style hotel at the edge of the village. Named for the hotel founder's two nicknames, Joseph (Beppe) Menardi (Sello), and run by his multilingual niece, Elisa, it's a bastion of superb regional cuisine. Menu items include venison filet with pears, polenta, and *marmellata di mirtilli* (marmalade made from an alpine berry like a huckleberry or blueberry); pappardelle with rabbit sauce; tagliolini with porcini mushrooms; roast chicken with bay leaves; and filet steak flavored with bacon. You get to keep your plate as a souvenir.

Via Ronco 68. © **0436-3236.** Reservations recommended. Main courses 12.50€–20€ ($11.15–$17.85). AE, DC, MC, V. High season daily 12:30–2pm and 7:30–10pm; low season Wed–Mon 12:30–2pm and 7:30–10pm. Closed Mar 20–May 20 and Sept 20–Nov 20.

El Toulà ★ ITALIAN/VENETIAN   Located 3km (2 miles) east of Cortina toward Pocol, this restaurant offers an even more elegant setting than the Tivoli (see below), but the Tivoli still retains its cutting edge in cuisine. This restaurant is a wood-framed structure with picture windows and a terrace. You get excellently prepared dishes, such as grilled squab with an expertly seasoned sauce and veal braised with white truffle sauce. Try the frittata of sea crabs "Saracen" style, pasta e fagioli Veneto style, pasticcio of eggplant, or Venetian-style calves' liver.

Località Ronco 123. ☎ **0436-3339.** Reservations required. Main courses 16€–22.50€ ($14.30–$20.10). AE, DC, MC, V. Tues–Sun noon–3pm and 8–11pm. Closed Easter to late July and Sept–Christmas.

Ristorante Tivoli 🐾🐾 ALPINE   The low-slung alpine chalet whose rear seems almost buried in the slope of the hillside is Cortina's best restaurant and one of the area's finest. About 1.5km (1 mile) from the resort's center, the Tivoli is beside the road leading to the hamlet of Pocol. The excellence of this restaurant stems from the hardworking efforts of the gracious Calderoni family, who use only the freshest ingredients. Try the stuffed rabbit in onion sauce, wild duck with honey and orange, veal filet with basil and pine nuts, or salmon flavored with saffron. The pastas are made fresh daily. For dessert, you might try an aspic of exotic fruit.

Località Lacedel. ☎ **0436-866400.** Reservations required. Main courses 15€–25€ ($13.40–$22.35). AE, DC, MC, V. High season daily 12:30–2:30pm and 7:30–10pm. Closed Mon off-season. Closed May–June and Oct–Nov.

CORTINA AFTER DARK

In true European alpine resort style, Cortina's bar and disco scene does a roaring business in winter, virtually closes down in spring and autumn, and reopens rather halfheartedly in midsummer. Most clubs lie off or along the pedestrian-only Corso Italia, and by the time you read this, the nightlife landscape will probably feature two or three newcomers. Here are a few of the longtime favorites.

Area, Località Ronco 81–82 (☎ **0436-867393**), keeps up-to-date with the latest nightlife trends of Rome, Milan, and London. You enter a bar on the street level but go down to the basement to dance. A rocking competitor popular mostly with Europeans is the **Bilbo Club,** Galleria Nuovo Centro 7 (☎ **0436-5599**), whose interior is dark, woodsy, and just battered enough that no one minds if you spill your beer. More dancing is available in the cellar of the **Hyppo Dance Hall,** Largo Poste (☎ **0436-2333**).

Less frenetic is **Enoteca Cortina,** Via del Mercato 5 (☎ **0436-862040**), a relaxed wine bar with a carefully polished interior that might remind you of an English pub. Locals happily mingle with skiers in winter and mountain climbers in summer. An equivalent kind of calm is available at the **Piano Bar** in the lobby of the Splendid Hotel Venezia, Corso Italia 209 (☎ **0436-5527**), with soothing music during midwinter and midsummer from dusk until midnight.

THE GREAT DOLOMITE ROAD 🐾🐾🐾

Stretching from Cortina d'Ampezzo in the east to Bolzano in the west, the **Great Dolomite Road (Grande Stada delle Dolomiti)** follows a circuitous route of about 109km (68 miles) and ranks among the grandest scenic drives in all Europe. The first panoramic pass you'll cross is **Falzarego,** about 18km (11 miles) from Cortina and 2,103m (6,900 ft.) above sea level. The next great pass is **Pordoi,** at about 2,240m (7,350 ft.) above sea level, the loftiest point. (You can get out of your car and ride a cable car, the Funiculare Porta Vescovo, between the roadside parking lot and the mountain's summit. At both ends, you'll find alpine-style restaurants, hotels, and cafes. Cable cars depart at 30-min. intervals throughout daylight hours. For fares and more information, contact the tourist office in Cortina.) In spring, edelweiss grows in the surrounding fields; in winter, virtually everything except the surface of the road is blanketed in snow. After crossing the pass, you'll descend to the little resort of **Canazei,** and then much later pass by sea-blue **Carezza Lake.**

9 Trent ⚑

232km (144 miles) NE of Milan, 101km (63 miles) N of Verona

A northern Italian city that basks in its former glory, the medieval Trent (Trento) on the left bank of the Adige is famous as the host of the Council of Trent (1545–63). Beset with difficulties, such as the rising tide of "heretics," the Ecumenical Council convened at Trent, leading to the Counter-Reformation. Trent lies on the main rail line from the Brenner Pass, and many visitors like to stop off here before journeying farther south into Italy.

Although it has an alpine setting, Trent still has a definite Italian flavor. As capitals of provinces go, Trent is rather sleepy and provincial. It hasn't been overly commercialized and is still richly imbued with a lot of architectural charm, with a small array of attractions. Nonetheless, it makes a good refueling stop for those exploring this history-rich part of Italy.

ESSENTIALS

GETTING THERE   Trent lies on the **rail line** for Bologna, Verona, the Brenner Pass, and Munich; trains pass through day and night. The trip from Milan takes 2¾ hours; from Rome, 7 hours. Seven trains per day make the 3½-hour run from Venice. For rail information and schedules, call ✆ **848-88088** toll-free in Italy.

Both the train and the bus stations lie between the Adige River and the public gardens of Trent. The heart of town is to the east of the Adige. From the station, turn on Via Pozzo, which becomes Via Orfane and Via Cavour before reaching the city's heartbeat, Piazza del Duomo.

By car, take A22 north from Verona or south from Bolzano.

VISITOR INFORMATION   The **tourist office** is on Via Manci 2 (✆ **0461-983880**), open daily 9am to 7pm.

EXPLORING THE CITY

Trent is loaded with old-fashioned charm and alpine flair. For a quick glimpse of the old town, head for **Piazza del Duomo** ⚑, dominated by the **Cattedrale di San Vergilio.** Built in the Romanesque style and much restored over the years, it dates from the 12th century. A medieval crypt under the altar holds a certain fascination, and the ruins of a 6th-century Christian basilica were recently discovered beneath the church. You're entitled to visit these remains by paying your admission to the **Diocese Museum (Museum Diocesano)** ⚑, facing the cathedral (✆ **0461-234419**), with its religious artifacts on display relating to the Council of Trent, which met in the Duomo from 1545 to 1563. The museum is open Monday to Saturday 9:30am to 12:30pm and 2:30 to 6pm; it costs 2.50€ ($2.25). The Duomo is open daily 8:30am to noon and 2:30 to 8pm. In the center of the square is a mid-18th-century **Fountain of Neptune (Fontana di Nettuno).**

The ruling prince-bishops of Trent, who held sway until they were toppled by the French in the early 19th century, resided at the medieval **Castello del Buonconsiglio** ⚑ (✆ **0461-233770**), reached from Via Bernardo Clesio 3. The **Historical Museum (Museo Storico),** at the castle (✆ **0461-230482**), contains mementos related to the period of national unification between 1796 and 1948. The museum and castle are open Tuesday to Sunday with this schedule: September 27 to June 24 9am to noon and 2 to 5pm, and June 25 to September 26 10am to 6pm. Admission is 5€ ($4.45).

Trent makes a good base for exploring **Monte Bondone,** a sports resort about 35km (22 miles) from the city center; **Paganella,** slightly more than 19km (12

Wine Tasting

The two most important wine-producing regions of northwestern Italy are the Alto Adige (also known as the Bolzano or Sudtirol region) and Trento. The loftier of the two, the Alto Adige, grows an Italian version of the Gewürztraminers (a fruity white) that are more often found in Germany, Austria, and Alsace. Venerable wine growers include **Alois Lageder** (founded in 1855), Tenuta Loüwengang, Vicolo dei Conti, in the hamlet of Magré (℃ **0471-809500**); and **Schloss Turmhof,** Entiklar, Kurtatsch, 39040 (℃ **0471-880122**). The Trentino area, a short distance to the south, is one of the leading producers of chardonnay and sparkling wines fermented by using methods developed centuries ago.

miles) from Trent (the summit is nearly 2,133m/7,000 ft. high); and the **Brenta Dolomiti.** The last excursion, which requires at least a day for a good look, will reward you with some of the finest mountain scenery in Italy. En route from Trent, you'll pass by **Lake Toblino** and then travel a winding road past jagged boulders. A 10-minute detour from the main road at the turn-off to the Genova valley offers untamed scenery. Take the detour at least to the thunderous **Nardis waterfall.** A good stopover point is the little resort of **Madonna di Campiglio.**

If you don't have time to drive around, you'll get a breezy view over Trent and a heart-thumping aerial ride as well by taking the **cable car** from Ponte di San Lorenzo near the train station up to Sardagna, a village on one of the mountainsides that enclose the city. You might want to pack sandwiches and enjoy an alpine picnic on one of the grassy meadows nearby. The cable car (℃ **0461-232154**) runs daily every 30 minutes from 7am to 10:30pm, and the fare is 2.10€ ($1.90) for an all-day ticket.

SHOPPING

The most memorable food-and-wine shop in town is the **Enoteca del Corso,** Corso 3 Novembre 54 (℃ **0461-916424**), with wines from the region and everywhere else in Italy, as well as the salamis, olives, cheeses, and other salty tidbits that go well with them. Another outlet for the reds and whites produced through the Trentino and the rest of Italy is the **Grado 12,** Largo Carducci 12 (℃ **0461-982496**).

If you're looking for handcrafts, ceramics, woodcarvings, and metal work, head for the largest store of its type in town, **Artigianato E Design,** Via Manci 62 (℃ **0461-234892**).

WHERE TO STAY

Albergo Accademia   This alpine inn behind the Renaissance Santa Maria Maggiore is made up of three buildings that have been joined to create an attractive hotel. One of the structures is believed to be of 11th- or 12th-century origin, based on a brick wall similar to the city walls found during renovation work. According to legend, the older part of the Accademia housed church leaders who attended the Council of Trent in the 16th century. The guest rooms are done in light natural wood, and a suite at the top of the house has a terrace with a view of the town and mountains. The rooms are comfortable and cozy, each with a compact bathroom.

Vicolo Colico 6, Trento. © **0461-233600**. Fax 0461-230174. www.accademiahotel.it. 43 units (showers only). 142€ ($126.80) double; from 196€ ($175.05) suite. Rates include breakfast. AE, DC, MC, V. Parking 11€ ($9.80). Closed Dec 24–Jan 6. **Amenities:** Restaurant; bar; lounge; room service; laundry. *In room:* A/C, TV, minibar, hair dryer.

Hotel Buonconsiglio   Built shortly after World War II and massively renovated in the 1990s, this is an immaculate hotel with pleasant rooms and an English-speaking staff. It's on a busy street near the rail station and has a slight edge over the Accademia (see above). In the lobby is a collection of abstract modern paintings. Each guest room is soundproofed against traffic noise and has a well-kept bathroom.

Via Romagnosi 14–16, 38100 Trento. © **0461-272888**. Fax 0461-272889. www.hotelbuonconsiglio.it. 46 units (with shower only). 110€ ($98.25) double; 160€ ($142.90) suite. Rates include breakfast. AE, DC, MC, V. Parking 7.50€ ($6.70). **Amenities:** Bar; room service; babysitting; laundry. *In room:* A/C, TV, minibar, hair dryer, safe.

WHERE TO DINE

It's almost a requirement to stroll down Trent's Renaissance streets with a gelato from **Torre-Verde-Gelateria Zanella** on Via Suffragio 6 (© **0461-232039**). Many flavors are made from fresh local fruits in season.

Orso Grigio ITALIAN/TRENTINE   This elegant restaurant lies about 27m (30 yd.) from Piazza Fiera, in a building whose origins might go back to the 1500s. When you see the immaculate table linen, well-cared-for plants, and subdued lighting, you'll know something is going right. The menus are seasonally adjusted to take advantage of the finest fresh produce. *Rufioli* (a green tortellini) and *squazzet con polenta* (Trentine-style fried tripe) are two regional specialties. Finish with chocolate mousse. The wines of the province are a special feature here.

Via degli Orti 19. © **0461-984400**. Reservations recommended. Main courses 10€–16€ ($8.95–$14.30). AE, DC, MC, V. Mon–Sat 12:30–2:30pm and 7:30–10pm.

Restaurant Chiesa ✮ *(finds)* TRENTINE   This restaurant offers the largest array of dishes we've ever seen made with apples. Owners Allesandro and Alberto recognized that Eve's favorite fruit, which grows more abundantly around Trent than practically anywhere else, was the base of dozens of traditional recipes. Specialties include risotto with apple, liver paté with apple, perch filet with apple, and a range of other well-prepared specialties (not all of which contain apples).

Via San Marco 64. © **0461-238766**. Reservations recommended. Main courses 11€–16€ ($9.80–$14.30); fixed-price "apple menu" 42.50€ ($37.95). AE, DC, MC, V. Mon–Sat noon–2:30pm and 7:30–10pm.

TRENT AFTER DARK

Trent is an early-to-bed/early-to-rise kind of town. Your most appealing option might be an after-dark stroll around **Piazza del Duomo,** where three bars offer conviviality.

Still in the town center but farther afield, you might be attracted to **Bar Picaro,** Via San Giovanni 36 (© **0461-230145**), where live music attracts the under-30 crowd. More soothing is the hideaway piano bar in **La Cantinotta,** Via San Marco 24 (© **0461-238527**). Every night from 10pm to around 4am, you'll find a singer, usually an Italian who speaks and sings good amounts of English, who will perform stylish songs, including any you might request.

If you want to dance, head for the village of Pergine, 10km (6 miles) east of Trent, to the region's most popular disco, **Paradisi,** Via al Lago 1 (© **0461-532694**). There are at least two bars; one side of the place is devoted to amusing versions of such old-fashioned dances as the waltz and jitterbug; the other features disco.

11

Milan, Lombardy & the Lake District

Among the most progressive of all the Italians, the Lombards have charted an industrial empire unequaled in Italy. Often the dream of the underfed and jobless in the south is to go to Milan for the high wages and the good life, although thousands end up finding neither. Lombardy isn't all about manufacturing, however. Milan is filled to the brim with important attractions, and nearby are old Lombard art cities such as Bergamo and Mantua.

Conquerors from barbarians to Napoleon have marched across the plains of Lombardy, and even Mussolini came to his end here. He and his mistress (both already dead) were strung up in a Milan square as war-weary residents vented their rage.

The **Lake District,** with its flowery promenades, lemon trees, villas, parks, and crystal-blue waters, is an old-fashioned resort area, with some grand old hotels. The lakes themselves—notably Garda, Como, and Maggiore—form one of the most enchanting splashes of scenery in northern Italy. They've attracted poets and writers from Goethe to d'Annunzio. After World War II, the Italian lakes seemed to be largely the domain of matronly English and German types. In our more recent swings through the district, however, we've seen a new, younger crowd, particularly at resorts such as Limone on Lake Garda. Even if your time is limited, you'll want to have at least a look at Lake Garda.

1 Milan ★★★

572km (355 miles) NW of Rome, 140km (87 miles) NE of Turin, 142km (88 miles) N of Genoa

Southern Italians, perhaps resentful of the north's hard-earned prosperity, sometimes declare that the Milanese are like the nearby no-nonsense Swiss. With two million inhabitants, Milan (Milano) is Italy's most dynamic city. Milan is Italy's window on Europe, its most sophisticated and high-tech metropolis, devoid of the dusty history that sometimes paralyzes modern developments in Rome and Florence or the watery rot that seems to pervade Venice.

Part of the work ethic that has catapulted Milan into the 21st century might stem from the Teutonic origins of the Lombards (originally from northwestern Germany), who occupied Milan and intermarried with its population after the collapse of the Roman Empire. In the 14th century, the Viscontis, through their wits, wealth, and marriages with the royalty of England and France, made Milan Italy's strongest city. And Milan initiated a continuing campaign of drainage and irrigation of the Po Valley that helped to make it one of the world's most fertile regions.

Lombardy & the Lake District

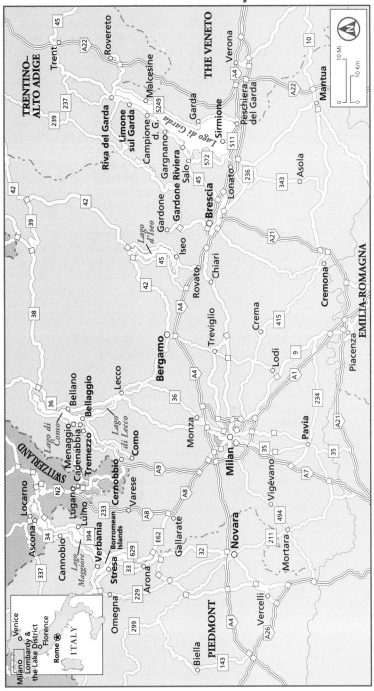

In the 1700s, Milan was dominated by the Hapsburgs, a legacy that left it with scores of neoclassical buildings in its inner core and an abiding appreciation for music and (perhaps) work. In 1848, it was at the heart of the northern Italian revolt against its Austro-Hungarian rulers and, with Piedmont, was at the center of the 19th-century nationalistic passion that swept through Italy and culminated in the country's unification. During this same period, Milan (through the novelist Manzoni) was encouraging the development of a Pan-Italian dialect.

Today, Milan is a commercial powerhouse and, partly because of its 400 banks and major industrial companies, Italy's most influential city. It's the center of publishing, silk production, TV and advertising, and fashion design; it also lies close to Italy's densest collection of automobile-assembly plants, rubber and textile factories, and chemical plants. Milan also boasts La Scala, one of Europe's most prestigious opera houses, and a major commercial university (the alma mater of most of Italy's corporate presidents). In addition, it's the site of several world-renowned annual trade fairs.

With unashamed capitalistic style, Milan has purchased more art than it has produced and has attracted an energetic group of creative intellects. To make it in Milan, in either business or the arts, is to have made it to the top of the pecking order. If you came to Italy to find sunny piazzas and lazy bright afternoons, you won't find them amid the fogs and rains of Milan. You will, however, have placed your finger on the pulse of modern Italy.

ESSENTIALS

GETTING THERE   Milan has three airports: the **Aeroporto di Linate,** 7km (4¼ miles) east of the inner city; the **Aeroporto Malpensa,** 50km (31 miles) northwest; and **Malpensa 2000,** 4km (2½ miles) north of the old Malpensa. Malpensa and Malpensa 2000 are used for most transatlantic flights, whereas Linate is used for flights within Italy and Europe. For general airport and flight information, call ☎ **02-74852200.**

TWA (☎ 800/892-4141; www.twa.com) and **Delta** (☎ 800/241-4141; www.delta.com) both fly nonstop from New York's JFK to Milan. **United** (☎ 800/538-2929; www.ual.com) has service to Milan only from Dulles in Washington, D.C. **Alitalia** (☎ 800/223-5730 in the U.S., or 514/842-8241 in Canada; www.alitalia.it) offers nonstop flights into Milan from New York (JFK), Newark, and Los Angeles. **British Airways** (☎ 800/AIRWAYS; www.british airways.com) has flights from London to Milan.

Malpensa Express trains will whisk arrivals from either Malpensa airport to the Cadorna station in the heart of Milan in about 45 minutes. They run every 30 minutes daily 5:30am to 8pm, and every hour from 9pm to midnight. A one-way ticket costs 9€ ($8.05) for adults and 5€ ($4.45) for children 4 to 12 years old. Alitalia passengers ride the Malpensa Express free.

Buses run between Linate and the Centrale station every 30 minutes daily 6am to 11pm. A bus (no. 73) also runs between Piazza San Babila and Linate airport every 20 minutes daily from 5:35am to 12:30am. **Buses** run from Malpensa and Malpensa 2000 to Stazione Centrale daily every 30 to 45 minutes, costing 4€ ($3.55) one way. For information about buses to and from the airports, call ☎ 02-58583202. This is much cheaper than taking a taxi, which could run you a whopping 65€ ($58.05).

Milan is serviced by the finest **rail connections** in Italy. The main rail station for arrivals is Mussolini's mammoth **Stazione Centrale,** Piazza Duca d'Aosta

(© **848-888088** toll-free in Italy), where you'll find the National Railways information office open daily 7am to 9:30pm. One train per hour arrives from both Genoa and Turin (trip time: 1½–2 hr.), costing 12.25€ ($10.95) one way. Twenty-five trains arrive daily from Venice (trip time: 3 hr.), costing 18.70€ ($16.70), and one train per hour arrives from Florence (trip time: 2½ hr.), costing 27€ to 40.50€ ($24.10–$36.15) one way. Trains from Rome arrive every hour, taking 5 hours for the journey and costing 43.75€ ($39.05) one way. The station is directly northeast of the heart of town; trams, buses, and the Metro link the station to Piazza del Duomo in the very center.

If you're driving to **Milan,** A4 is the principal east-west route for Milan, with A8 coming in from the northwest, A1 from the southeast, and A7 from the southwest. A22 is another major north-south artery, running just east of Lake Garda. But once you arrive, put your car in a garage and keep it there. Don't even try to drive around the crowded, confusing main tourist areas of Milan.

VISITOR INFORMATION   The **Azienda di Promozione Turistica del Milanese,** on Piazza del Duomo at Via Marconi 1 (© **02-72524301**), is open Monday to Friday 8:30am to 8pm, Saturday 9am to 1pm and 2 to 7pm, and Sunday 9am to 1pm and 2 to 6pm in summer (it closes 1 hr. early in winter). There's also a branch at Stazione Centrale (© **02-72524360**), open Monday to Saturday 9am to 6:30pm, and Sunday 9am to 12:30pm and 1:30 to 6pm.

GETTING AROUND   The **subway** system is extensive and efficient, covering most of Milan; in addition, there are buses and trams, making it fairly easy to navigate. Regular tickets cost 1€ (90¢) and are sold at Metro stations and newsstands. Some subway tickets are good for continuing trips on city buses at no extra charge, but they must be used within 75 minutes of purchase. You must stamp your ticket when you board a bus or tram, or risk incurring a fine.

The tourist office and all subway ticket offices sell a **travel pass** for 3€ ($2.70) for 1 day, or 5.50€ ($4.90) for 2 days, good for unlimited use on the city's tram, bus, and subway network.

To phone a **taxi,** dial © **02-4040,** 02-8585, or 02-4000; fares start at 2.50€ ($2.25), with a nighttime surcharge of 3€ ($2.70).

Don't try to drive within the relatively small Cerchia dei Navigli, where all the major attractions are located. It's easy to walk to everything in this area.

FAST FACTS   The **American Express** office is at Via Brera 3 (© **02-72003693** or 02-86460930; Metro: Duomo); it's open Monday to Friday 9am to 5:30pm.

The **U.S. Consulate,** Via Principe Amedeo 2–10 (© **02-29035141;** Metro: Turati), is open Monday to Friday 8:30am to 12:30pm and 1:30 to 5:30pm. The **Canadian Consulate** is at Via Vittorio Pisani 19 (© **02-67581;** Metro: Centrale), open Monday to Friday 9am to noon. The **U.K. Consulate** is at Via San Paolo 7 (© **02-723001;** Metro: Duomo), open Monday to Friday 9:15am to 12:15pm and 2:30 to 4:30pm. The **Australian Consulate** is at Via Borgogna 2 (© **02-777041;** Metro: San Babila), open Monday to Thursday 9am to noon and 2 to 4pm, and Friday 9am to noon.

For the **police,** call © **112;** for an **ambulance,** call © **118;** for any **emergency,** call © **113.** About a 5-minute ride from the Duomo, the **Ospedale Maggiore Policlinico,** Via Francesco Sforza 35 (© **02-55031;** Metro: Crocetta), has English-speaking doctors. You can find an all-night **pharmacy** by phoning © **192.** The pharmacy (© **02-6690735;** Metro: Centrale) at the Stazione Centrale never closes.

SEEING THE SIGHTS

With its spired cathedral, the **Piazza del Duomo** lies at the heart of Milan. The city is encircled by three "rings," one of which is the **Cerchia dei Navigli,** a road that more or less follows the outline of the former medieval walls. The road runs along what was formerly a series of canals—hence the name Navigli. All the major attractions, including Leonardo's *Last Supper,* La Scala, and the Duomo, lie in this ring, which is easily navigated on foot.

The second ring, known both as **Bastioni** and **Viali,** follows the outline of the Spanish Walls from the 16th century. It's now a tram route (no. 29 or 30). A much more recent ring is the **Circonvallazione Esterna,** connecting with the main roads coming into Milan.

In the Cerchia dei Navigli, one of Milan's most important streets, **Via Manzoni,** begins near the Teatro alla Scala and takes you to **Piazza Cavour,** a key point for the traffic arteries. The **Arch of Porta Nuova,** a remnant of the medieval walls, marks the entrance to Via Manzoni. To the northwest of Piazza Cavour is the **Giardini Pubblici,** and to the northwest of these gardens is **Piazza della Repubblica.** From this square, Via Vittorio Pisani leads into **Piazza Duca d'Aosta,** site of the cavernous Stazione Centrale.

At Piazza Cavour, you can head west on Via Fatebenefratelli into the **Brera** district, whose major attraction is the Pinacoteca di Brera. In recent years this district has become a major center in Milan for offbeat shopping and after-dark diversions.

THE TOP ATTRACTIONS

Despite its modern architecture and industry, Milan is still a city of great art. Serious art lovers should budget at least 2 days here. If your schedule is frantic, see the Duomo, the Brera Picture Gallery, and one of the most important galleries of northern Italy, the Ambrosiana Library and Picture Gallery.

Il Duomo & Baptistry ✦✦✦ Milan's impressive lacy Gothic cathedral, 146m (479 ft.) long and 87m (284 ft.) wide at the transepts, ranks with St. Peter's in Rome and the cathedral at Seville, Spain, as among the world's largest. It was begun in 1386 and has seen numerous architects and builders (even Milan's conqueror, Napoleon, added his ideas to the facade). This imposing structure of marble is the grandest and most flamboyant example of the Gothic style in Italy. Ethereal and colossal, its **exterior** ✦✦✦ is a wonder to behold, with its belfries, statues, gables, and pinnacles.

Built in the shape of a Latin cross, the Duomo's interior is divided by soaring pillars into five naves. The overall effect is like a marble-floored Grand Central Terminal (that is, in space), with far greater dramatic intensity. In the **crypt** rests the tomb of San Carlo Borromeo, the cardinal of Milan. To experience the Duomo at its most majestic, you must ascend to the **roof** or **visita ai terrazzo** ✦✦✦, on which you can walk through a forest of pinnacles, turrets, and marble statuary. Alfred, Lord Tennyson, rhapsodized about the panorama of the Alps as seen from this roof. A gilded Madonna towers over the tallest spire.

If you're really interested in antiquity, you might want to explore the **Baptistry (Battistero Paleocristiano),** which you enter through the cathedral. This is a subterranean ruin lying beneath the cathedral's piazza that dates to the 4th century. It's believed that this is the site where Ambrose, the first bishop and the patron saint of the city, baptized Augustine.

Piazza del Duomo. ✆ 02-86463456. Cathedral free; roof via stairs 3.50€ ($3.15), roof via elevator 5€ ($4.45); crypt free; baptistry 1.50€ ($1.35). Cathedral daily 6:45am–6:50pm. Roof daily 9am–5:30pm. Crypt daily 9am–noon and 2:30–6pm. Baptistry Tues–Sun 9:30am–5pm. Metro: Duomo.

**Duomo Museum (Museo del Duomo) & Civic Museum of Contempo-
rary Art (Museo Civico d'Arte Contemporaneau)** ⍟ Housed in the
Palazzo Reale, the Duomo Museum is like a storybook of the cathedral's 6 centuries of history. It has exhibits of statues and decorative sculptures, some from
the 14th century. There are also antique art objects, stained-glass windows (some
from the 15th c.), and ecclesiastical vestments, many as old as the 16th century.

The palazzo also houses the **Civic Museum of Contemporary Art,** which
displays a wide range of pieces created throughout the 20th century. You're often
greeted with some of the best modern art exhibits in Italy, typically the works of
artists who are either world-class or the more daring of the avant-garde. Permanent works include those by Picasso, De Chirico, and Modigliani. There's also a
fine collection of Italian Futurist art.

In the Palazzo Reale, Piazza del Duomo 12 and 14. (C) **02-860358.** Admission 6€ ($5.35) to Duomo
Museum; free to Contemporary Art Museum. Duomo Museum Mon–Sun 9:30am–12:30pm and 3–6pm. Contemporary Art Museum Mon–Sat 9am–5:30pm. Metro: Duomo.

**Ambrosiana Library & Picture Gallery (Biblioteca-Pinacoteca
Ambrosiana)** ⍟⍟ Near the Duomo, the Ambrosiana Library and Picture
Gallery were founded in the early 17th century by Cardinal Federico Borromeo.
On the second floor, the **Picture Gallery** contains a remarkable collection of art,
mostly from the 15th to 17th centuries. Most notable are *Madonna and Angels*
by Botticelli; works by Brueghel (which have impressive detail and are among
the best pieces); paintings by Lombard artists, including Bramantino's *Presepe,*
in earthy primitive colors; a curious miniature *St. Jerome with Crucifix,* by
Andrea Solario; and works by Bernardino Luini. One of the museum's highlights
is room 10, with 10 magnificent **cartoons by Raphael** ⍟⍟⍟, which he prepared for the frescoes of the School of Athens in the Vatican. Another room contains a collection of reproductions from the drawings of Leonardo da Vinci's
Codex Atlanticus. The museum owns a remarkable portrait that Leonardo did of
the musician Gaffurio. The **Library** contains many medieval manuscripts,
which are shown for scholarly examination only.

Piazza Pio XI 2. (C) **02-806921.** Admission 7.50€ ($6.70). Tues–Sun 10am–5:30pm. Metro: Duomo or
Cordusio.

Santa Maria delle Grazie & The Last Supper ⍟⍟ This Gothic church
was erected by the Dominicans in the mid–15th century, and a number of its
more outstanding features, such as the cupola, were designed by the great Bramante. But visitors from all over the world flock here to gaze on a mural in the
convent next door. In what was once a refectory, the incomparable Leonardo da
Vinci adorned one wall with *The Last Supper* (*Il Cenacolo Vinciano*) ⍟⍟⍟.

Commissioned by Ludovico the Moor, the 8.5-by-4.5m (28-by-15-ft.) mural
was finished about 1497; it began to disintegrate almost immediately and was
totally repainted in the 1700s and the 1800s. Its gradual erosion makes for one
of the most intriguing stories in art. In 1943, it narrowly escaped being bombed,
but the bomb demolished the roof; astonishingly, the painting was exposed to
the elements for 3 years before a new roof was built. The current restoration has
been controversial, drawing fire from some art critics (as has the Sistine Chapel
restoration). The chief restorer of *The Last Supper,* Pinin Brambilla Barcilon, said
that the Sistine Chapel was a "simple window wash" compared with the
Leonardo.

It has been suggested that all that's really left of the original *Last Supper* is a
"few isolated streaks of fading color"—that everything else is the application and

Milan

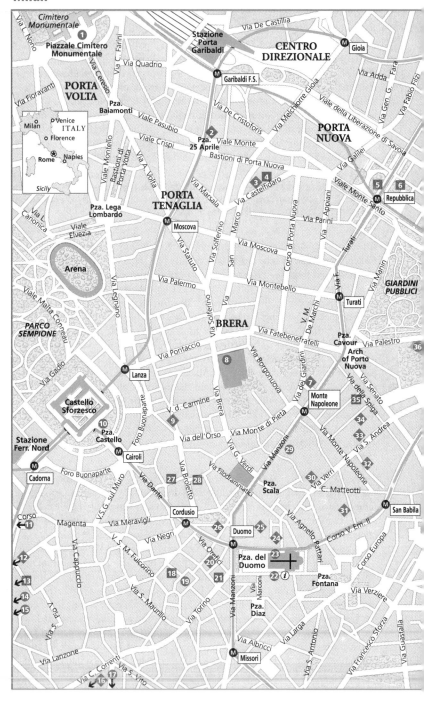

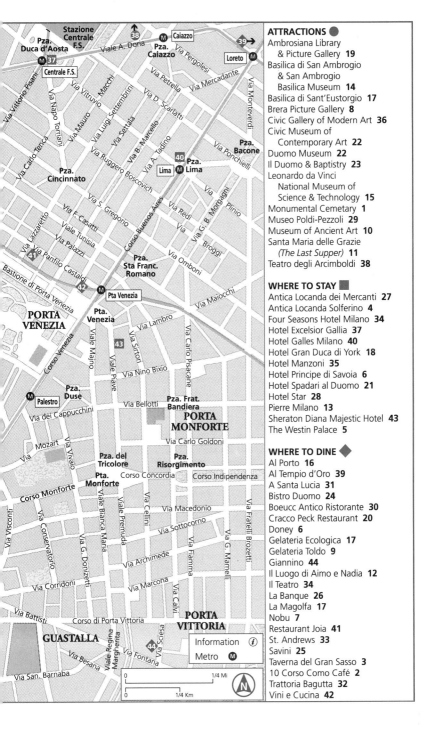

color of artists and restorers who followed. What remains, however, is Leonardo's "outline," and even that is suffering badly. As an Italian newspaper writer put it: "If you want to see *Il Cenacolo,* don't walk—run!" A painting of grandeur, the composition portrays Christ at the moment he announces to his shocked apostles that one of them will betray him. Vasari called the portrait of Judas "a study in perfidy and wickedness."

Only 25 viewers are admitted at a time (be prepared to wait in line), and you're required to pass through antechambers to remove pollutants from your body. After viewing the painting, for 15 minutes only, you must walk through two additional filtration chambers as you exit.

Piazza Santa Maria delle Grazie (off Corso Magenta). © 02-4987588. Free admission to church; 6.50€ ($5.80) to see *The Last Supper.* Church Mon–Sat 7:30am–noon and 3–7pm; Sun 3:30–6:30pm. *The Last Supper* viewings Tues–Sat 9am–6:15pm; Sun 9am–7:15pm. Reservations required for *The Last Supper;* call Mon–Sat 8am–7pm and leave your name. Metro: Cadorna or Conciliazione.

Brera Picture Gallery (Pinacoteca di Brera) ⟨★★★⟩   This is one of Italy's finest galleries, boasting an exceptional collection of works by both Lombard and Venetian masters. Like a Roman emperor, Canova's nude Napoleon, with a toga draped over his shoulder, stands in the courtyard (fittingly, a similar statue ended up in the Duke of Wellington's house in London).

Among the notable pieces, the *Pietà,* by Lorenzo Lotto, is a work of great beauty, as is Gentile Bellini's *St. Mark Preaching in Alexandria* (it was finished by his brother, Giovanni). Seek out Andrea Mantegna's *Virgin and the Cherubs,* from the Venetian school, and Tintoretto's eerie *Finding of the Body of St. Mark.* Three of the most important prizes are **Mantegna's *Dead Christ*** ⟨★★★⟩, **Giovanni Bellini's *La Pietà*** ⟨★★⟩, and **Carpaccio's *St. Stephen Debating*** ⟨★★⟩.

Other paintings include Titian's *St. Jerome,* as well as such Lombard art as Bernardino Luini's *Virgin of the Rose Bush* and Andrea Solario's *Portrait of a Gentleman.* One of the greatest panels is Piero della Francesca's *Virgin and Child Enthroned with Saints and Angels* and the *Kneeling Duke of Urbino in Armor.* Another work to seek out is the *Christ* by Bramante. One wing, devoted to modern art, offers works by such artists as Boccioni, Carrà, and Morandi. One of our favorite paintings in the gallery is **Raphael's *Wedding of the Madonna*** ⟨★★⟩, which has a dancelike quality. The moving *Last Supper at Emmaus* is by Caravaggio.

Via Brera 28. © 02-72263229. Admission 6€ ($5.35). Tues–Sun 8:30am–7:30pm. Metro: Cairoli, Lanza, or Montenapoleone.

MORE ATTRACTIONS

Museo Poldi-Pezzoli ⟨★★⟩   This fabulous museum displays its treasures in a sumptuous, elegant salon setting of antique furnishings, tapestries, frescoes, and Lombard wood carvings (it's much like visiting the Frick Collection in New York or the Isabella Stewart Gardner Museum in Boston). The remarkable collection includes paintings by many of the old masters of northern and central Italy, such as Andrea Mantegna's *Madonna and Child,* Giovanni Bellini's *Cristo Morto,* and Filippo Lippi's *Madonna, Angels, and Saints* (with superb composition). Antonio Pollaiolo's *Portrait of a Lady* is a gorgeous portrait of haunting originality. One room is devoted to Flemish artists, and there's a collection of ceramics and also one of clocks and watches.

Via Manzoni 12. © 02-794889. Admission 6€ ($5.35). Tues–Sun 10am–6pm. Closed Jan 1, Easter, Apr 25, May 1, Aug 15, Nov 1, and Dec 8. Metro: Duomo or Montenapoleone.

Get Thee to a Renaissance Monastery

Certosa (Charter House) of Pavia ⊛, Via Monumento 4 (℃ 0382-925613), marks the pinnacle of the Renaissance statement in Lombardy. The Carthusian monastery is 31km (19 miles) south of Milan and 8km (5 miles) north of Pavia. Founded in 1396 but not completed until years later, it is one of the most harmonious structures in Italy. The facade, studded with medallions and adorned with colored marble and sculptures, was designed in part by Amadeo, who worked on it in the late 15th century. Inside, much of its rich decoration is achieved by frescoes reminiscent of an illustrated storybook.

Through an elegantly decorated portal, you enter the cloister, noted for its exceptional terra-cotta decorations and continuous chain of elaborate "cells," attached villas with their own private gardens and loggia.

Admission is free, but donations are requested. It's open Tuesday to Sunday 9 to 11:30am and 2:30 to 4:30pm. Buses run between Milan and Pavia daily every hour 5am to 10pm, taking 50 minutes and costing 2.60€ ($2.30) one way. Trains leave Milan bound for Pavia once every hour, costing 2€ ($1.80). If you're driving, take Route 35 south from Milan or A7 to Binasco, and continue on Route 35 to Pavia and its Certosa.

Museum of Ancient Art (Museo d'Arte Antica) ⊛ The Castle Sforzesco is an ancient fortress rebuilt by Francesco Sforza, who launched another governing dynasty. It's believed that both Bramante and Leonardo contributed architectural ideas to the fortress. Following extensive World War II bombings, it was painstakingly restored and continues its activity as a Museum of Ancient Art. On the ground floor are sculptures from the 4th century A.D., medieval art mostly from Lombardy, and armor. The most outstanding exhibit, however, is Michelangelo's *Rondanini Pietà*, on which he was working the week he died. In the rooms upstairs, besides a good collection of ceramics, antiques, and bronzes, is the important picture gallery, rich in paintings from the 14th to 18th centuries. Included are works by Lorenzo Veneziano, Mantegna, Lippi, Bellini, Crivelli, Foppa, Bergognone, Cesare da Sesto, Lotto, Tintoretto, Cerano, Procaccini, Morazzone, Guardi, and Tiepolo.

In the Castello Sforzesco, Piazza Castello. ℃ 02-88463703. Free admission. Tues–Sun 9am–5:30pm. Metro: Cairoli.

Leonardo da Vinci National Museum of Science & Technology (Museo Nazionale della Scienza e della Tecnica Leonardo da Vinci) ⊛ *Kids* If you're a fan of Leonardo da Vinci, you'll want to visit this vast museum complex, where you could practically spend a week. For the average visitor, the most interesting section is the Leonardo da Vinci Gallery, which displays copies and models from the Renaissance genius. There's a reconstructed convent pharmacy, a monastic cell, and collections of antique carriages and even sewing machines. You'll also see exhibits relating to astronomy, telecommunications, watchmaking, goldsmithery, motion pictures, and the subjects of classic physics.

Via San Vittore 21. ℃ 02-485551. Admission 6.20€ ($5.55) adults, 4.20€ ($3.75) children and seniors. Tues–Fri 9:30am–5pm; Sat–Sun 9:30am–6:30pm. Metro: San Ambrogio. Bus: 50, 54, 58, or 94.

Civic Gallery of Modern Art (Galleria Civica d'Arte Moderna) This sumptuous palace (the site of many local weddings) houses an important collection of late-19th-century and early-20th-century art, mostly from 1850 to 1918. The palace was built from 1790 to 1793 by noted architect Leopold Pollack and served as the Milanese home of both Napoleon and Eugàne de Beauharnais (son of Josephine from her first marriage). The exhibit space is divided into three collections (the Carlo Grassi, the Vismara, and the Marino Marini), all showing the development of Impressionism and modernism in the Italian, and especially the Lombard, school of painting. Major emphasis is given to the works of Marino Marini, a 20th-century sculptor. Other represented artists include Picasso, Matisse, Rouault, Renoir, Modigliani, Corot, Millet, Manet, Cézanne, Bonnard, and Gauguin.

In the Villa Reale (Villa Comunale), Via Palestro 16. 🕐 **02-76002819.** Free admission. Tues–Sun 9am–5:30pm. Metro: Palestro.

Basilica di Sant'Eustorgio 🕿 The bell tower of this 4th-century basilica dates from the 13th century; it was built in the romantic style by patrician Milanese families. It has the first tower clock in the world, made in 1305. Originally this was the tomb of the Three Wise Men, or the Three Kings (4th c. A.D.). Inside, its greatest treasure is the **Portinari Chapel (Cappella Portinari),** designed by the Florentine Michelozzo in Renaissance style. The chapel is frescoed and contains a bas-relief of angels at the base of the cupola. In the center is an intricately carved tomb containing the remains of St. Peter Martyr, supported by 13th-century marble statuary by Balduccio of Pisa. The basement has a Roman crypt.

Piazza Sant'Eustorgio 1. 🕐 **02-58101583.** Free admission to basilica; chapel and museum 5€ ($4.45). Tues–Sun 9:30am–6pm. Metro: Genova.

Basilica di San Ambrogio 🕿🕿 From the basilica that he constructed on this site in the 4th century A.D.—when he was bishop of Milan and when the city, in turn, was briefly the capital of the Western Roman Empire—St. Ambrose had a profound effect on the development of the early church. Little remains of Ambrose's original church, but the 11th-century structure built in its place and renovated many times since is remarkable. It has a striking atrium, lined with columned porticos and opening to the brick facade, with two ranks of loggias and, on either side, a bell tower. Look carefully at the door on the left, where you'll see a relief of St. Ambrose. This church set a standard for Lombard Romanesque architecture that you'll see imitated many times in your travels throughout the region. In the apse are interesting mosaics from the 12th century. The Lombard tower at the side dates from 1128, and the facade, with its two tiers of arches, is impressive. In the church is the **Museo della Basilica di San Ambrogio,** which contains some frescoes, 15th-century wood paneling, silver and gold objects originally for the altar, paintings, sculpture, and Flemish tapestries.

Piazza San Ambrogio 15. 🕐 **02-86450895.** Free admission to basilica; 1.50€ ($1.35) to museum. Basilica Mon–Sat 7am–noon and 2:30–7pm; Sun 7am–7:45pm. Museum Wed–Sat 10am–noon and 3–5pm; Sun 3–5pm. Closed Aug. Metro: San Ambrogio.

Monumental Cemetery (Cimitero Monumentale) 🕿 This cemetery has catered for more than 100 years to the whims of Milan's elite. The only requirements for burial here are that you're dead and that when you were alive, you were able to buy your way into a plot. Some families have paid up to 28,000€

($25,000) just for the privilege of burying their dead here. The graves are marked not only with brass plates or granite markers but also with Greek temples, elaborate obelisks, or such original works as an abbreviated version of Trajan's Column.

This outdoor museum has become such an attraction that a superintendent has compiled an illustrated guidebook—a sort of "Who Was Who." Among the cemetery's outstanding sights is a sculpted version of *The Last Supper.* Several fine examples of Art Nouveau sculpture dot the hillside, and there's a tasteful example of Liberty-style (Italy's version of Art Nouveau) architecture in a tiny chapel designed to hold the remains of Arturo Toscanini's son, who died in 1906. Among the notables buried here are Toscanini himself and novelist Alessandro Manzoni. In the Memorial Chapel is the tomb of Salvatore Quasimodo, who won the 1959 Nobel prize in literature. Here also rest the ashes of Ermann Einstein, father of the scientist. In the Palanti Chapel is a monument commemorating the 800 Milanese citizens slain in Nazi concentration camps. (A model of this monument is displayed in New York's Museum of Modern Art.) The cemetery is a few blocks east of Stazione Porta Garibaldi, in the urban congestion of Milan, 3km (2 miles) north of Il Duomo.

Piazzale Cimitero Monumentale 1. ℭ **02-6599938.** Free admission. Tues–Sun 8:30am–5:15pm. Metro: Garibaldi. Tram: 3, 4, 11, 12, 14, 29, 30, or 33.

SHOPPING

Milan is one of Europe's top shopping cities, with an incredible concentration of sophisticated, high-style boutiques—and that's only fitting because Milan is the dynamo of the Italian fashion industry. Dolce & Gabbana, Ferré, Krizia, Moschino, Prada, Armani, and Versace have all catapulted to international stardom from design studios based here.

Most shops are closed all day Sunday and Monday (although some open on Mon afternoon). Some stores open at 9am, unless they're very chic, and then they're not likely to open until 10:30am. They remain open, for the most part, until 1pm and then reopen between 3:30 and 7:30pm.

The best time for the savvy shopper to visit Milan is for the **January sales,** when *saldi* (sale) signs appear in the windows. Sales usually begin in mid-January and, in some cases, extend all the way through February. Prices in some emporiums are cut by as much as 50% (but don't count on it). Of course, items offered for sale are most often last season's merchandise, but you can get some good buys. Items bought on sale can't be returned.

THE TOP SHOPPING AREAS

THE GOLDEN TRIANGLE   We recently met a well-heeled shopper from Florida who spent the better part of her vacation in Italy shopping for what she called "the most unbelievable variety of shoes, clothes, and accessories in the world." A walk on the fashion subculture's focal point, **Via Montenapoleone,** heart of the **"Golden Triangle,"** will quickly confirm that impression. It's one of Italy's three great shopping streets. But expect high prices and service that's based on the salesperson's impression of how much money you plan to spend.

CORSO BUENOS AIRES   Bargain hunters leave the Golden Triangle and head for a mile-long stretch of **Corso Buenos Aires,** where you can find style at more affordable prices. Start off at **Piazza Oberdan,** the square closest to the heart of Milan. Clothing abounds on Corso Buenos Aires, especially casual wear and knockoffs of designer goods. But you'll find a vast array of merchandise, from scuba-diving equipment to soft luggage. Saturdays are unbelievably crowded here.

THE BRERA DISTRICT   You'll find more bargains in the **Brera,** the name given to a sprawling shopping district around the Brera Museum. This area is far more attractive than Corso Buenos Aires and has often been compared to New York's Greenwich Village because of its cafes, shops, antiques stores, and art students. Skip the main street, **Via Brera,** and concentrate on the side streets, especially **Via Solferino, Via Madonnina,** and **Via Fiori Chiari.** To get here, start by the La Scala opera house and continue to walk along Via Verdi, which becomes Via Brera. Running off from Via Brera to the left is the pedestrian-only Via Fiori Chiari, good for bric-a-brac and even some fine Art Deco and Art Nouveau pieces. Via Fiori Chiari will lead to another traffic-free street, Via Madonnina, which has some excellent clothing and leather-goods buys. Via Madonnina connects with busy Corso Garibaldi. This will take you to Via Solferino, the third-best shopping street. In addition to traditional clothing and styling, a lot of eye-catching but eccentric modern clothing is sold here.

The best time to visit the Brera area is for the **Mercantone dell'Antiquariato,** which takes place on the third Saturday of each month (it's especially hectic at Christmas time) along Via Brera in the shadow of La Scala. Artists and designers, along with antiques dealers and bric-a-brac peddlers, turn out in droves.

SHOPPING A TO Z

BOOKS   The **American Bookstore,** Via Camperio 16 (© **02-878920;** Metro: Cairoli), will probably have that paperback novel you're looking for or the scholarly volume on Milanese artwork that you should've reviewed before your trip. It stocks only English-language books and periodicals. Milan has one gay bookstore, the **Libreria Babele,** Via San Nicolao 10 (© **02-86915597;** Metro: Cadorna).

DEPARTMENT STORE & MALL   **La Rinascente,** Piazza del Duomo (© **02-88521;** Metro: Duomo), bills itself as Italy's largest fashion department store. In addition to clothing, the basement carries a wide variety of giftware, including handwork from all regions of Italy. There's a ground-floor information desk, and on the seventh floor are a bank, a travel agency, a hairdresser, an Estée Lauder Skincare Center, a coffee bar, and the Brunch and Bistro restaurants.

One of Milan's most famous landmarks, the huge **Galleria Vittorio Emanuele II,** Corso Vittorio Emanuelle II, is reminiscent of a rail station, and the architectural details are impressive, with vaulted glass ceilings merging in a huge central dome, decorative window and door casings, elaborate bas-reliefs, huge arched frescoes, wrought-iron globe lamps, and a decorative tile floor. You can browse in shops that include a Prada boutique and a Rizzoli bookstore or grab a coffee from one of the bistros or restaurants (see the Savini review under "Where to Dine," later in this chapter).

FASHION   In the Brera district, **Accademia,** Via Solferino 11 (© **02-6595961;** Metro: Moscova), is the store for women's outdoor clothing, carrying a variety of classical and casual styles. This is also the place for men who need clothes in hard-to-find dimensions because Accademia offers a "made-to-measure" service; however, it takes more than a month (alterations take 4–5 extra days).

There's always **Il Salvagente,** 16 Via Fratelli Bronzetti (© **02-76110328;** tram: 12; bus: 60 or 73), for the fashion-conscious shopper without an unlimited wallet. On the second floor is the selection of men's clothing; the women's wear, including sweaters, clothes, shoes, and belts, is on the main floor. Here you'll find Versace gowns at cut-rate prices. Of course, it'll be last year's style or something that didn't sell, but who'll ever know?

Ermenegildo Zenga, Via Pietro Verri 3 (☎ 02-76006437; Metro: Montenapoleone), offers a complete range of men's wear, beginning with the Sartorial line of suits, jackets, trousers, and accessories. The "soft line" is dedicated to a younger customer, and the sportswear collection and yachting line allow you to wander the globe with the right apparel. The shop also offers a "made-to-measure" service with a selection of 300 fabrics per season. They can make an outfit in about 4 weeks and then ship it to any destination.

Giorgio Armani, Via San Andrea 9 (☎ 02-76003234; Metro: San Babila), houses the sleek style we've come to expect in a large showroom vaguely reminiscent of an upscale aircraft hangar. Armani's trademark look incorporates unstructured clothing draped loosely over firm bodies—elegant upholstery for elegant people. The big news coming from Armani is the success of a new Giorgio Armani at 31 Via Manzoni (☎ 02-72318645; Metro: Montenapoleone), a three-story megacomplex at the northern end of Milan's Golden Triangle. Armani has told the press, "I want there to be a sense of discovery and surprise every 15 meters throughout the store." It boasts everything from Emporio Armani clothing to an Italian outpost of the famed Nobu sushi restaurants (from New York to London). The store's displays are brilliant.

At **Mila Schön,** Via Montenapoleone 2 (☎ 02-781190; Metro: Montenapoleone), the sophisticated look is casually chic, hip, and expensive. If you're male and relatively muscular, you'll look terrific. Mila's women's line is on the ground floor. Even the somewhat flippant accessories are stratospherically expensive.

Gianfranco Ferré, Via Sant Andrea 15 (☎ 02-794864; Metro: Montenapoleone), is the only outlet in Milan for the famous designer whose fashions are worn by some of the world's most elegant women. The range is wide, from soft knitwear to sensual evening dresses, along with refined leather accessories. Next door to the women's shop is an outlet for the designer's men's clothing. It's closed in August.

Prada, Via della Spiga 1 (☎ 02-76002019; Metro: Montenapoleone), has the best leather goods and other stylish accessories in Milan for women; it's a fashion industry phenomenon. The black nylon backpack is the most popular item. (Prada now has a store in Galleria Vittorio Emanuele as well.)

The Milano base for a famous designer name, **Mario Valentino,** is at via Montenapoleone 10 (☎ 02-798113; Metro: Montenapoleone). High-quality style and high prices are combined in this showcase for leather goods, with fine clothing for both men and women, fashionable shoes, and tasteful accessories.

GIFTS In the tiny **G. Lorenzi,** Via Montenapoleone 9 (☎ 02-76022848; Metro: Montenapoleone) in San Babile, you'll find everything you were looking for in the way of small gifts—and a lot of stuff you've never seen. Many are one-of-a-kind items.

10 Corso Como, 10 Corso Como (☎ 02-653531; Metro: Garibaldi), is the creation of Carla Sozzani, who discovered candlelight and futons back in the 1970s. Today she runs the city's hippest lifestyle shop, selling an eclectic range of merchandise from clothing to household goods in a former coach-repair shop. The outlet also offers a courtyard cafe, a restaurant, and a gallery.

GLASS If you're not going to include Venice in your Italian shopping itinerary, you can patronize **Venini,** Montenapoleone 9, at via Pietro Verri (☎ 02-76000539; Metro: Montenapoleone). This is the Milanese branch of this world-famous Venetian glassmaker. The outlet in Milan stocks one of the most comprehensive collection of Venini's wares outside Venice itself. Look for heirloom vases, precious glasses, and a stunning collection of plates and bowls.

JEWELRY & SILVER At **Mario Buccellati,** Via Montenapoleone 4 (℃ **02-76002153;** Metro: Montenapoleone), you'll find Italy's best-known and most expensive silver and jewels. The designs of the cast-silver bowls, tureens, and christening cups are nothing short of rhapsodic. A real discovery, **Dal Vecchio** (℃ **02-76008740)** is for the devotee of old-fashioned silver and unusual jewelry. This long-established shop features both classic and traditional designs in jewelry. It has many well-crafted pieces in silver and a wide variety of 18-karat gold jewelry.

LACE **Jesurum,** Via Verri 4 (℃ **02-76015045;** Metro: Montenapoleone), is the Milanese outlet of a Venice-based lace company that has been famous since 1870. On a very short street where none of the buildings has an obvious street number, it sells all-lace or lace-edged tablecloths, doilies, and lots of great wedding gifts. It also sells lace blouses and even swimsuits, plus lace by the meter.

LEATHER GOODS & SHOES The prices on the merchandise at **Alfonso Garlando,** Via Madonnina 2 (℃ **02-86463733;** Metro: Cairoli), range up to the very expensive, but the shop's size and its lack of concern for a stylish showroom guarantee a reasonable choice at a reasonable price. It sells shoes for men and women but not children.

The factory outlet **Calzaturificio di Parabiago,** Corso Buenos Aires 52 (℃ **02-29406851;** Metro: Lima), carries classic and casual shoes for men and women. The prices vary from relatively inexpensive to expensive. But most of the merchandise is sold at discount prices along this "street of bargains." Parabiago is one of the major shoe-manufacturing areas of the country. They have another store in Corso Buenos Aires 59 (℃ **02-29408575;** Metro: Porta Venezia).

Gucci, Via Montenapoleone 5 (℃ **02-771271;** Metro: Montenapoleone), is the Milanese headquarters for the most famous leather-goods distributor in Italy. Its shoes, luggage, and wallets for men and women; handbags; and leather accessories usually have the colors of the Italian flag (olive and crimson) stitched in the form of a fairly discreet ribbon across the front.

At **Salvatore Ferragamo,** Via Montenapoleone 3 (℃ **02-76006660;** Metro: Montenapoleone), the label is instantly recognizable and the quality is high. Rigidly controlled by an extended second generation of the original founders, it's still a style-setter. This branch offer shoes, luggage, accessories for women and men, leather jackets, and a small selection of clothing.

LINENS You'll find some great buys (as much as 50% off) in linens at the company headquarters of **Frette,** Via Montenapoleone 21 (℃ **02-76003791;** Metro: Montenapoleone). Frette is one of the finest names in Italian linens, so this is an exceptional deal, especially if you're looking for damask tablecloths in the vibrant colors of Italy—everything from apple green to sunflower yellow.

If you've got the time and are a dedicated shopper, you can head for the **Spaccio Frette** shop at 45 Via Vittorio Veneto in Concorezzo (℃ **039-60461),** in the northeastern outskirts. Remainders from hotel and restaurant orders are sold at even greater discounts than at the main headquarters.

You might also leave Milan altogether and head for **Maton Sargeeant,** 23–25 Via Pace, in Cassinetta di Lugagnano (℃ **02-9422316),** a village 14km (8¾ miles) from Milan. The showroom for this outlet is sheltered above a still-functioning 12th-century mill. The shop sells not only beautiful sheets but also blankets, towels, and other quality linens. To reach it from Milan, take a train at Porta Genova Station heading to Abiategrasso. Do not go unless you've made an appointment in advance. (It's open only Mon–Sat 3–6pm; it's closed July 15–Aug.)

MUSIC   The best music store in Milan is **Messaggerie Musicali,** Gallerie del Corso 2 at Corso Vittorio Emanuele I (© **02-781251;** Metro: Duomo). This outlet offers the largest selection of "things musical" in all of Milan, including CDs, cassettes, and music publications. You can even purchase tickets here for concerts and local musical spectacles.

PAPER & STATIONERY   In the Brera district, **I Giorni di Carta,** Corso Garibaldi 81 (© **02-6552514;** Metro: Moscova), is one of the city's most unusual outlets for stationery, with dozens of colors, textures, and weights. It also sells briefcases, pens and ink, notebooks, lamps, dishes, dolls, and ornamental paperweights.

Papier, 4 Via San Maurilio (© **02-865221;** Metro: Missori), is the premier address for stationery, including "extreme paper" (plasticized and plaited paper given a metallic sheen evoking fabric). Banana-leaf pages from Thailand and Nepal are sold, as are hairy coconut sheets resembling the real thing. History buffs can order the parchment paper.

PERFUME   In the Brera district, **Profumo,** Via Brera 6 (© **02-72023334;** Metro: Duomo), sells some of Italy's most exotic perfumes for women, plus cologne and aftershave lotions for men.

PORCELAIN & CRYSTAL   Since 1735, **Richard Ginori,** Corso Buenos Aires 1 (© **02-29516611;** Metro: Porta Venezia), has manufactured and sold porcelain in many price ranges. A household word in Italy, Ginori sells ovenproof porcelain in both modern and traditional themes, as well as crystal and silverware that the company makes and inventory from other manufacturers, such as Baccarat and Wedgwood.

PRINTS & ENGRAVINGS   **Raimondi di Pettinaroli,** Corso Venezia 6 (© **02-76002412;** Metro: San Babila), is the finest shop in Milan for antique prints and engravings, plus reprints of old engravings made from the original copper plates. Of particular interest are the engravings of Italian cityscapes during the 19th century, many of them treasures that'll be worth framing after you return home.

WHERE TO STAY

In Milan, you'll find some deluxe hotels and an abundance of first- and second-class hotels, most of which are big on comfort but short on romance. In the third- and fourth-class bracket and on the *pensione* (boardinghouse) level are dozens of choices, although the budget hotels in Milan are not nearly as nice as those in Italy's other major cities. If you can afford it, spend more on your hotel in Milan and opt for budget accommodations in Rome, Florence, and Venice, which have clean, comfortable, and often architecturally interesting third- and fourth-class hotels and pensioni.

VERY EXPENSIVE

Four Seasons Hotel Milano ★★★ *Kids*   There is a saying in Milano that guests go to the Principe de Savoia to make their fortunes, but they come to the Four Seasons to spend it. Milan's most exciting five-star hotel opened in 1993 on a side street opening onto Via Montenapoleone's upscale boutiques, near the

Duomo. The building was first a 15th-century monastery, then the residence of the Hapsburg-appointed governor of northern Italy in the 1850s, and later the site of luxury apartments. The medieval facade, many of the frescoes and columns, and the original monastic details were incorporated into a modern edifice accented with bronze, stone floors, glass, pearwood cabinetry, Murano chandeliers, and acres of Fortuny fabrics. The guest rooms are cool, conservative, sleek, and spacious, with a sense of understated luxury. The state-of-the-art bathrooms offer deep soaking tubs, robes, heated marble floors, heated towel racks, steam-resistant mirrors, and fine toiletries. Service is impeccable. Children are pampered with bedtime milk and cookies, video games, and other perks, and the staff can arrange tee times at several area golf courses.

Via Gesù 8, 20121 Milano. ⓒ 02-77088. Fax 02-77085000. www.fourseasons.com. 118 units. 693€ ($618.75) double; from 770€ ($687.50) suite. AE, DC, MC, V. Parking 51€ ($45.55). Metro: Montenapoleone or San Babila. **Amenities:** 2 restaurants (the elegant and acclaimed Il Teatro, reviewed below, and a less formal Mediterranean and vegetarian restaurant); lovely lounge; fitness center and spa; concierge; business center; 24-hr. room service; laundry. *In room:* A/C, TV, dataport, minibar, hair dryer, safe.

Hotel Excelsior Gallia ⭐ This Liberty-style monument was built by the Gallia family in 1933. It's a prominent hotel, once one of Italy's tops—but today it's more of an upscale rail-station hotel. The 1994 renovations combined some of the smaller rooms into larger and more comfortable accommodations. The guest rooms, all lovely, fall into two categories: modern and comfortable in the newer wing and graciously old-fashioned in the original core. All are soundproofed and have marble bathrooms attached. Struggling to regain its former stellar reputation, this is a longtime landmark, but it has been surpassed by some more stylish, high-tech newcomers.

Piazza Duca d'Aosta 9, 20124 Milano. ⓒ **800/225-5843** in the U.S., or 02-67851. Fax 02-66713239. www.excelsiorgallia.it. 237 units. 375€–625€ ($334.90–$558.15) double; from 725€ ($647.45) suite. AE, DC, MC, V. Parking 15€–32.50€ ($13.40–$29). Metro: Stazione Centrale. Tram: 33 or 59. **Amenities:** Elegant restaurant; bar; fitness center; sauna; concierge; room service; massage; babysitting; laundry. *In room:* A/C, TV, dataport, minibar, hair dryer, safe.

Hotel Principe di Savoia ⭐⭐⭐ Only the Four Seasons does it better. The Principe was built in 1927 to fill the need for a luxurious hotel near Stazione Centrale, and it was completely restored in 1991. It offers solid comfort, fine service, and contemporary amenities in an opulent old-world setting of crystal, detailed plasterwork, fine carpets, and polished marble. The guest rooms are spacious, decorated in a 19th-century Lombard style but offering high-tech efficiency. All contain leather chairs and other stylish furniture. The front rooms face the hysterical traffic of Piazza della Repubblica, but the ones in back are more tranquil, opening onto the Alps. The marble bathrooms are extravagant, with robes and deluxe toiletries.

Piazza della Repubblica 17, 20124 Milano. ⓒ **800/325-3535** in the U.S., or 02-62301. Fax 02-653799. www.luxurycollection.com. 399 units. 439€–558€ ($392.05–$498.30) double; from 796€ ($710.85) suite. AE, DC, MC, V. Parking 31€ ($27.70). Metro: Repubblica. **Amenities:** 2 restaurants (the hotel's Doney is reviewed below); bar; indoor pool; health club; sauna; 24-hr. concierge; business services; salon; 24-hr. room service; babysitting; laundry/dry cleaning. *In room:* A/C, TV, dataport, minibar, hair dryer, safe.

Sheraton Diana Majestic Hotel ⭐⭐ This hotel proudly wears its crown once again. Opened in 1908, the Diana Majestic has been brought back to its original splendor with the completion of a $10 million renovation. In restoring the public areas, particular attention was paid to the stucco and decorative details, as well as to the original wooden floors. The 1925 French Art Deco style incorporated during that era is prevalent in the new carpeting and upholstery, leather armchairs, and authentically reproduced furniture. The guest rooms and suites are decorated in classical imperial style, with maximum comfort. All include direct-line phones with personalized voice mail and the terrific beds that are a hallmark of Starwood Hotels. Many overlook the inside garden. The marble bathrooms are simply beautiful.

Viale Piave 42, 20129 Milano. ☎ **800/325-3535** in the U.S. and Canada, or 02-20581. Fax 02-205820-58. www.sheraton.com. 107 units. 360€–490€ ($321.50–$437.55) double; from 900€ ($803.70) suite. Free parking. Metro: Porta Venezia. **Amenities:** Restaurant; bar; fitness center; 24-hr. concierge; business center; 24-hr. room service; laundry. *In room:* A/C, TV, dataport, minibar, hair dryer, safe.

The Westin Palace *⭐*   The Palace stands aloof on a hill near the rail station, with a formal car entrance, a facade boasting tiers of balconies, and an opulent lobby. Geared primarily to business travelers, the Palace is also a fine choice for vacationers and hosts the occasional visiting celeb. The guest rooms are furnished with pastel upholstery and reproductions of Italian antiques, as well as video games, voice mail, and the super-comfortable beds for which Starwood Hotels are known. The elegant bathrooms are in pink- and green-marble.

Piazza della Repubblica 20, 20124 Milano. ☎ **800/325-3535** in the U.S., 167-780525 toll-free in Italy, or 02-63361. Fax 02-654485. www.westin.com. 216 units. 425€–500€ ($379.55–$446.50) double; 750€–2,000€ ($669.75–$1,786) suite. AE, DC, MC, V. Parking 30€–42.50€ ($26.80–$37.95). Metro: Repubblica. **Amenities:** 1 restaurant (Mediterranean); piano bar; fitness center; airport shuttle service; business center; room service; babysitting; laundry. *In room:* A/C, TV, dataport, minibar, hair dryer, safe.

EXPENSIVE

Hotel Galles Milano *⭐*   This is a winning hotel, first built in 1901. In 1990, Italian investors financed an elegant renovation, producing a hotel favored by businesspeople, conventioneers, and visitors looking for reliable, unpretentious lodgings. The guest rooms come in a variety of shapes and sizes, each with comfortable furnishings and bathrooms.

Via Ozanam 1 (Corso Buenos Aires), Milano 20129. ☎ **800/528-1234** in the U.S., or 02-204841. Fax 02-2048422. www.galles.it. 150 units. 206€–361€ ($183.95–$322.35) double; from 310€ ($276.85) suite. Rates include buffet breakfast. AE, DC, MC, V. Parking 21€ ($18.75). Metro: Lima. **Amenities:** Restaurant; bar; Jacuzzi; room service; babysitting; laundry. *In room:* A/C, TV, minibar, hair dryer, safe.

Hotel Spadari al Duomo *⭐* *(Finds*   Near the Duomo, this little charmer is as close as Milan comes to having a boutique hotel. The hip modern decor features a cool blue color scheme, furniture by designer Ugo La Pietra, and the hotel's own collection of contemporary art. The spacious, comfortable bedrooms are chic, each with comfy beds (some have twins), a wide desk, and a bathroom that features a multijet shower and tub.

Via Spadari 11, 20123 Milano. ☎ **02-72002371.** Fax 02-861184. www.spadarihotel.com. 39 units. 208€–268€ ($185.75–$239.30) double; from 288€ ($257.20) suite. Rates include breakfast. AE, DC, MC, V. Parking 21€ ($18.75) per day. Metro: Duomo. Bus: 2, 3, or 27. **Amenities:** Restaurant; bar; room service; babysitting; laundry/dry cleaning. *In room:* A/C, TV, minibar, hair dryer, safe.

Pierre Milano *⭐* *(Finds*   This is a little undiscovered gem. In the central section of the city, close to the Sant'Ambrogio, a church of the Middle Ages, the Pierre is luxury on a small scale. Few hotels in Milan were thought out so well. It's the choice (to borrow from a Marlene Dietrich lyric) "for the laziest gal in town." It's all electronic: a touch of a button and you can turn off your lights, receive messages on your television, and even open or close the draperies in your bedroom. Rooms are beautifully, even luxuriously furnished, with tasteful fabrics and silks and an inviting medley of contemporary and antique furnishings. Each room is individually decorated, and contains a luxurious first-rate tiled bathroom.

Via de Amicis 32, 20123 Milano. © **02-72000581.** Fax 02-8052157. http://milan.realhotels.com/milan hotels/100087-Pierre-Milano-Hotel.htm. 51 units (showers only). 195€–275€ ($174.15–$245.60) double; 400€ ($357.20) suite. AE, DC, MC, V. Parking 26€ ($23.20) per day. Closed: Aug. Metro: Sant'Ambrogio. **Amenities:** Restaurant; coffee shop; laundry/dry cleaning. *In room:* A/C, TV, minibar, hair dryer, safe.

MODERATE TO INEXPENSIVE

Antica Locanda dei Mercanti   This reasonably priced but sophisticated hotel, located in the historic district, is an offbeat choice with charm. It remains a favorite with many movers and shakers in Milan's fashion industry. In 1996, a former model, Paola Ora, gutted the second floor of this late-19th-century building and installed a streamlined hotel, custom-designing each room. The furnishings are upholstered in fine fabrics and the bathrooms are sheathed in marble. Some rooms have canopied beds and all feature fresh flowers, books, and magazines. Don't be startled by the severe-looking monumental entrance or the businesslike appearance of three of the building's four floors, most of which are occupied by crafts studios for the jewelry industry.

Via San Tommaso 6, 20123 Milano. © **02-8054080.** Fax 02-8054090. www.locanda.it. 14 units (showers only). 115€–200€ ($102.70–$178.60) double. AE, MC, V. Parking 17.50€ ($15.65). Tram: 1, 14, or 24. Metro: Cairoli, Cordusio, or Duomo. **Amenities:** Lounge; room service; babysitting; laundry/dry cleaning. *In room:* Hair dryer.

Antica Locanda Solferino 🌟🌟   When this hotel opened in 1976, the neighborhood was a depressed backwater. Today it's an avant-garde community of actors, writers, and poets, and this inn deserves some of the credit. It got off to a great start soon after opening when editors from *GQ* stayed here while working on a fashion feature. Since then, countless celebs and fashion-industry types have either stayed in the old-fashioned rooms or dined in the ground-floor restaurant. Each guest room is unique, furnished with Daumier engravings and Art Nouveau or late-19th-century pieces, as well as well-kept bathrooms. Reserve as far in advance as possible.

Via Castelfidardo 2, 20121 Milano. © **02-6570129.** Fax 02-6571361. www.anticalocandasolferino.it. 11 units. 150€ ($133.95) double. Rates include breakfast. AE, DC, MC, V. Parking 20€ ($17.85) nearby. Metro: Moscova or Repubblica. **Amenities:** Restaurant; lounge; laundry. *In room:* TV, hair dryer.

Hotel Gran Duca di York 🌟🌟   This longtime favorite just keeps getting better. When it was built by the Catholic Church in the 1890s, this Liberty-style palace housed dozens of priests from the Duomo. Among them was the cardinal of Milan, who later became Pope Pius XI. Today anyone can rent one of the pleasantly furnished and well-kept rooms, ranging from small to medium in size, each with a tile bathroom. You'll find a bar in an alcove of the severely elegant lobby, which sports a suit of armor and leather-covered armchairs.

Via Moneta 1A (Piazza Cordusio), 20123 Milano. © **02-874863.** Fax 02-8690344. 33 units. 153€ ($136.65) double; 176€ ($157.15) triple. Rates include breakfast. AE, MC, V. Parking 25€ ($22.35). Closed Aug. Metro: Cordusio or Duomo. **Amenities:** Bar; room service; babysitting; laundry/dry cleaning. *In room:* A/C, TV, hair dryer.

Hotel Manzoni   The Manzoni, built around 1910 and renovated frequently since then, charges reasonable prices considering its location near the most-fashionable shopping streets. Each of its rather small guest rooms contains color-coordinated comfortable furniture and soft carpeting; many have TVs. The tiled bathrooms are also small. A brass-trimmed winding staircase leads from the lobby into a bar and TV lounge.

Via Santo Spirito 20, 20121 Milano. ☎ 02-76005700. Fax 02-784212. 52 units (showers only). 193€ ($172.35) double, 247€ ($220.55) suite. Rates include breakfast. AE, DC, MC, V. Parking 12.50€–30€ ($11.15–$26.80). Metro: Montenapoleone or San Babila. **Amenities:** Restaurant; room service; babysitting; laundry/dry cleaning. *In room:* A/C, TV, hair dryer.

Hotel Star The Ceretti family welcomes guests to its well-run little hotel, a few blocks from La Scala and the Duomo. The lobby has been brightened, and the guest rooms are pleasant, if plain. They range from small to medium, each with a comfortable bed and double-glass windows that cut down on street noise. All rooms contain bathrooms, and 15 units include a personal sauna and a hydromassage tub.

Via dei Bossi 5, 20121 Milano. ☎ 02-801501. Fax 02-861787. www.starhotel.it. 30 units (some with shower only). 150€–165€ ($133.95–$147.35) double. Rates include buffet breakfast. AE, MC, V. Parking 20€–22.50€ ($17.85–$20.10). Closed Aug and Christmas. Metro: Cordusio or Duomo. **Amenities:** Lounge; room service. *In room:* A/C, TV, dataport, minibar, hair dryer, safe.

WHERE TO DINE
VERY EXPENSIVE

A Santa Lucia MEDITERRANEAN/SEAFOOD This festive place is decked out with photographs of pleased celebs, who attest to the skill of its kitchen. You can order such specialties as a savory fish soup, a meal in itself; fried baby squid; or well-prepared sole. Spaghetti *alla vongole* evokes the tang of the sea with its succulent clam sauce. Pizza also reigns supreme: Try either the calzone of Naples or the pizza alla napoletana.

Via San Pietro all'Orto 3. ☎ 02-76023155. Reservations recommended. Main courses 27.50€–30€ ($24.55–$26.80). AE, MC, V. Tues–Sun noon–3pm and 7:30pm–1am. Closed Aug. Metro: San Babila.

Giannino MILANESE/SEAFOOD Giannino enchants its loyal patrons and wins new fans every year. It's one of the top restaurants in all Lombardy and has been since 1899. You have a choice of several attractive rooms, and eyes rivet on the tempting offerings of the *specialità gastronomiche milanesi*. The choice is excellent, including such dishes as breaded veal cutlet and risotto simmered in broth and coated with *parmigiano*. We have special affection for the *tagliolini con scampi al verde* (fresh homemade noodles with prawn tails in herb sauce). Also superb are the cold fish and seafood salad and the beautifully seasoned *orata al cartoccio* (fish baked in a paper bag with shrimp butter and fresh herbs).

Via Amatore Sciesa 8. ☎ 02-55195582. Reservations required. Main courses 19€–25€ ($16.95–$22.35). AE, DC, MC, V. Tues–Sat 12:30–2:30pm; Mon–Sat 7:30–10:30pm. Closed 2 weeks in Aug. Metro: San Babila. Bus: 73.

Il Luogo di Aimo e Nadia *Finds* NORTHERN ITALIAN Some of the most creative cookery in Milan is offered at this somewhat remote outpost of fine cuisine in an avant-garde modern setting. Tastes, fragrances, and colors are innovatively combined on the platter with polish; only top-quality, fresh ingredients are used. The sommelier is often cited as the best in Lombardy, and the wine list is one of the reasons to dine here. The chef's risotto with zucchini flowers, truffles, and porcini mushrooms is another reason to make the trek across town. Veal baked in puff pastry is yet another reason. Another delight, especially in spring, is tagliolini with sweet red peppers, calamari, and fresh vegetables of the season. Desserts are homemade and sumptuous.

Via Montecuccoli 6. ☎ 02-416886. Reservations essential. Jacket and tie preferred. Main courses 20€–45€ ($17.85–$40.20). AE, DC, MC, V. Mon–Fri 12:30–2:15pm and Mon–Sat 8–10:15pm. Closed Aug. Metro: Primaticcio.

Nobu ★★ JAPANESE   This innovative Japanese cuisine, long enjoyed by foodies in such cities as London and New York, has invaded Milan. Yes, that was one of the restaurant's founders, Robert de Niro, we spotted dining here. The kitchen staff here is as brilliant and finely tuned as their New York or London cousins. Sushi chefs create not just sushi but gastronomic pyrotechnics. Those on the see-and-be-seen fashion circuit don't seem to mind the high prices that go with these incredibly fresh fish dishes. Elaborate preparations lead to perfectly balanced flavors. Where can you find a good sea urchin tempura in Milano but at Nobu? The squid pasta is sublime, as is the black cod with miso. If you don't like fish, you might opt for such dishes as chicken in a teriyaki sauce. Cold sake arrives in bamboo pitchers, and you can order light snacks and drinks on the ground floor.

Via Pisoni 1. ⓒ 02-72318645. Reservations required. Fixed-price menu 80€ ($71.45). Tues–Fri noon–2pm; Mon–Sat 7–11pm. Metro: Montenapoleone.

Savini ★★ LOMBARD/INTERNATIONAL   Savini provides a heavenly introduction to Lombard cuisine. Perched in the great glass-enclosed arcade opposite the Duomo, the restaurant draws both out-of-towners and discriminating locals to its terrace and its old-world dining room with crystal chandeliers. Many of the most memorable dishes are unassuming, such as the *cotoletta alla milanese,* tender veal coated with egg batter and bread crumbs and then fried a rich brown. The pièce de résistance, most often ordered before the main course, is *risotto alla milanese*—rice simmered in a veal broth and dressed with whatever the artiste in the kitchen selects. The wine list is excellent.

In the Galleria Vittorio Emanuele II. ⓒ 02-72003433. Reservations required. Main courses 23.50€–28€ ($21–$25). AE, DC, MC, V. Mon–Sat 12:30–2:30pm and 7:30–10:30pm. Closed Dec 26–Jan and Aug 10–25. Metro: Duomo.

EXPENSIVE

Bistro Duomo ★ LOMBARD/ITALIAN   Duomo was created by Gualtiero Marchesi, once hailed by *Time* as one of the world's 10 top chefs. He has moved on to a newer, very expensive restaurant, but he left behind this terraced bistro as a token of love for Milan. It boasts one of the city's best views of the cathedral because it's on the top floor of the Rinascente Center, across from the Duomo. For your antipasti, consider such delights as steamed vegetables with hazelnut oil and toasted almonds, salmon carpaccio with soy sauce, or swordfish salad with fennel and oranges. The potato soup with leeks and black truffles might also get you going. The chefs prepare superb fish dishes, and a meat specialty is a perfectly rendered osso buco.

Via San Raffaele 2. ⓒ 02-877120. Reservations required. Main courses 17.50€–21€ ($15.65–$18.75); fixed-price menus 35€–45€ ($31.25–$40.20). AE, MC, V. Tues–Sat noon–2:30pm; Mon–Sat 7–10:15pm. Closed 2 weeks in Aug (dates vary). Metro: Duomo.

Cracco Peck Restaurant ★★ MILANESE/ITALIAN   Peck's is owned by the famous delicatessen, viewed as the Milanese equivalent of Fauchon's in Paris. It was opened by Francesco Peck, who came to Milan from Prague in the 19th century. His small restaurant went on to become a food empire. Amid shimmering marble and modern Italian paintings, an efficient staff serves an elegant cuisine. The fresh specialties include a classic version of risotto milanese, rack of lamb with fresh rosemary, and *lombo di vitello* (veal) with artichokes, followed by chocolate meringue for dessert. Its cured meats are said to be the richest in Italy.

Via Victor Hugo 4. ⓒ 02-876774. Reservations required. Main courses 27.50€–35€ ($24.55–$31.25). AE, DC, MC, V. Mon–Sat 12:15–2:30pm and 7:15–10:30pm. Closed 10 days in Jan and July 1–21. Metro: Duomo.

Doney ❀ LIGHT FARE/AFTERNOON TEA   Doney, a lavish Liberty-style cafe, emerged from the recent renovations of the Principe di Savoia Hotel looking like a jewel box, with burnished paneling, plush upholstery, and soaring frescoed ceilings. Its menu features elegant but simple salads (including lobster, artichokes, and pears), sandwiches (including smoked salmon on brown bread), vegetarian selections, and steaks. During teatime, you can select from nine kinds of tea and enjoy pastries and finger sandwiches from a trolley. At any hour, the place is a popular meeting point.

In the Principe di Savoia Hotel, Piazza della Repubblica 17. ✆ **02-6230.** Reservations recommended. Main courses 15€–30€ ($13.40–$26.80); afternoon tea 12.50€–22.50€ ($11.15–$20.10). AE, DC, MC, V. Daily 12:30–3pm and 7–11pm (afternoon tea 4–7pm). Metro: Repubblica. Tram: 1, 4, 11, 29, or 30.

Il Teatro ❀ MEDITERRANEAN   This is the culinary showcase of the shopping district's most glamorous hotel, often hosting big names in the fashion business. It's located in a 1400s Milanese palazzo. The patio overlooks a garden, and the dining room is sheathed in burnished paneling and rich leather under a ceiling of tented champagne silk. The menu changes with the seasons but might include a tantalizing *involtini* (a roll layered with foodstuffs) of eggplant with ricotta and mint, crispy crayfish with a purée of tomatoes, and red mullet filet with essence of tomato and black truffles. Everything tastes as fresh as the day it was picked, harvested, or caught. Dessert might be a *mille-feuille croquante*, a pastry layered with walnuts, chocolate mousse, and raspberries.

In the Four Seasons Hotel Milano, Via Gesù 8. ✆ **02-77081435.** Reservations recommended. Main courses 18€–24€ ($16.05–$21.45); fixed-price menus 47.50€–75€ ($42.40–$67). AE, DC, MC, V. Mon–Sat 7:30–11:45pm. Metro: Montenapoleone or San Babila.

Restaurant Joia ❀❀ *Finds* VEGETARIAN/SEAFOOD   One of the most innovative restaurants in Milan is under the helm of Pietro Leemann, a Swiss chef. His vegetarian food is the city's most flavorful, and he prepares a delectable selection of seafood as well. Unusual for a Swiss chef, many of his dishes are nondairy. A specialty and a hit with the patrons here is "six variations on an artichoke." You can also order excellent dried codfish and perfectly roasted sea scallops. We've found the best pasta to be ravioli stuffed with ricotta.

Via Panfilo Castaldi 18. ✆ **02-29522124.** Reservations recommended. Main courses 19.50€–24€ ($17.40–$21.45); fixed-price fish menu 62.50€ ($55.80). AE, DC, MC, V. Mon–Fri 12:30–2:30pm and 8–11:30pm. Closed Aug. Metro: Piazza della Repubblica or Pizza Venezia.

St. Andrews ❀ LOMBARD/INTERNATIONAL   This restaurant boasts one of the finest kitchens in Lombardy. The menu includes an unusual appetizer of steak tartare mixed with caviar and seasonings, John Dory in salt crust, and rack of lamb Provençal style. The dessert specialty is a *tartatelli,* pastry with honey-and-strawberry sauce. At lunch the place seems like a private club and is apt to be filled with businesspeople. The armchairs are covered in black leather, the paneling is dark wood, and the lighting is discreet. The formally attired waiters give superb service.

Via Sant'Andrea 23. ✆ **02-798236.** Reservations required. Main courses 17.50€–40€ ($15.65–$35.70). AE, DC, MC, V. Mon–Sat noon–4pm and 7pm–2am. Closed Aug. Metro: Montenapoleone or San Babila.

Taverna del Gran Sasso ❀ ABRUZZI   The walls of this tavern are crowded ceiling to floor with copper molds, ears of corn, strings of pepper and garlic, and cart wheels. A tall open hearth burns with a charcoal fire, and a Sicilian cart is laden with baskets of bread, dried figs, nuts, and kegs of wine. As you enter, you'll find a mellowed wooden keg of wine with a brass faucet (you're supposed

---

Take a Gelato Break

You can find organic gelato at the **Gelateria Ecologica,** Corso di Porta Ticinese 40 (© **02-58101872;** Metro: Sant'Ambrogio or Missori), in the Ticinese/Navigli neighborhood. It's so popular that there's no need for a sign out front.

In the Brera neighborhood, you'll find the **Gelateria Toldo,** Via Ponte Vetero 11 (© **02-86460863;** Metro: Cordusio or Lanza), where the gelato is wonderfully creamy and many of the sorbetto selections are so fruity and fresh that you can pretend they're healthy.

---

to help yourself, using glass mugs). The cuisine features a number of specialties from the Abruzzi, such as *maccheroni alla chitarra,* a distinctively shaped macaroni with savory meat sauce. Meals are an all-you-can-eat feast.

Piazza Principessa Clotilde 10. © 02-6597578. Reservations not required. All-you-can-eat meal 37.50€ ($33.50); all-you-can-eat fish meal (reserve in advance) 42.50€ ($37.95). AE, DC, MC, V. Mon–Fri noon–2pm and 7–11:30pm; Sat 7:30–10:30pm. Closed Jan 1 and Aug. Metro: Repubblica.

MODERATE

Al Porto ★★ SEAFOOD   Opened in 1907, Al Porto is among the most popular seafood restaurants in Milan, with a lovely glassed-in garden room. Menu items include *orata* (dorado) with pink peppercorns, and *branzini* (sea bass) with white Lugurian wine and olives. You might begin with a warm antipasto and follow with *risotto ai frutti di mare* (seafood risotto) or perhaps the traditional *fritto misto* (a platter of fried assorted seafood). Everything tastes better with a Friuli wine.

Piazzale Generale Cantore. © 02-8321481. Reservations required several days in advance. Main courses 15€–22.50€ ($13.40–$20.10). AE, DC, MC, V. Tues–Sat 12:30–2:30pm; Mon–Sat 7:30–10:30pm. Closed Dec 24–Jan 3 and Aug. Metro: Porta Genova or Sant'Agostino.

Boeucc Antico Ristorante INTERNATIONAL/MILANESE   This restaurant, opened in 1696, is a trio of rooms in an elegant old palace, within walking distance of the Duomo and the major shopping streets. Throughout you'll find soaring stone columns and modern art. In summer, guests gravitate to a terrace for open-air dining. You might enjoy spaghetti in clam sauce, a salad of shrimp with arugula and artichokes, or grilled liver, veal, or beef with aromatic herbs. In season, sautéed zucchini flowers accompany some dishes.

Piazza Belgioioso 2. © 02-76020224. Reservations required. Main courses 15€–22.50€ ($13.40–$20.10). AE. Mon–Fri 12:40–2:30pm; Sun–Fri 7:40–10:30pm. Closed Aug, Easter, and Christmas. Metro: Duomo, Montenapoleone, or San Babila.

La Banque ★ REGIONAL ITALIAN/INTERNATIONAL   In an early 1900s building, Le Banque gets its name from its former role as a bank and is one of Milan's hottest restaurants. The chef often modernizes regional dishes, adding his own touch. The risotto alla milanese, for example, comes in an updated version as a rice timbale with saffron-flavored sauce. Most of the dishes are cooked fast and simply in the best virgin olive oil. Perfectly cooked lobster appears on a bed of barley, and a delicious Lomellina salami is served in mustard sauce. One of the finest pasta dishes is made with clams and fresh zucchini. A superb main course is tender Nebraska beef filet marinated in balsamic vinegar. Diners have free access to the cellar disco.

Via Bassano Porrone 6. © 02-86996565. Reservations required. Main courses 12.50€–19€ ($11.15–$16.95). AE, DC, MC, V. Tues–Sun 6pm–3am. Metro: Cordusio or Duomo.

10 Corso Como Café (Value) ITALIAN/INTERNATIONAL   In the Brera, the hottest cafe is the domain of Carla Sozzani. It's part of her stylish bazaar at 10 Corso Como, which also includes an art gallery, a music room, a boutique, and a bookstore. It pushes the envelope of chic, attracting a big fashion-industry crowd, yet it isn't overpriced. The minimalist decor of cast iron, stained glass, and steel is Milanese modern at its best. Oh, yes, the food. Of course, everyone likes to stay fashionably thin around here, so expect a selection of Mediterranean sushi or sashimi and beautifully flavored Italian fresh vegetables and fish tempura. The pastas have distinctive and original flavors, including one with toasted pine nuts and fresh marjoram. This trendsetter of a place also offers a wide selection of teas from all over the world. On Saturday and Sunday, an American-style brunch is served until 2pm.

Corso Como 10. © **02-29013581.** Reservations recommended. Main courses 12.50€–20€ ($11.15–$17.85). AE, DC, MC, V. Daily 11am–2am. Metro: Garibaldi.

Trattoria Bagutta ✿ INTERNATIONAL   This is Milan's most celebrated trattoria, drawing an artsy crowd. Dating from 1927, the Bagutta is known for the caricatures (framed and frescoed) covering its walls. Of the many bustling dining rooms, the rear one with its picture windows is most enticing. The food draws from the kitchens of Lombardy, Tuscany, and Bologna for inspiration. On offer are assorted antipasti, and main-dish specialties include fried squid and scampi, *lingua e puré* (tongue with mashed potatoes), linguine with shrimp in tomato-cream sauce, and *scaloppine alla Bagutta* (veal baked with fresh tomatoes, mozzarella, and lettuce).

Via Bagutta 14. © **02-76002767.** Reservations required. Main courses 8€–25€ ($7.15–$22.35). AE, DC, MC, V. Mon–Sat 12:30–2:30pm and 7:30–10:30pm. Closed Dec 24, Jan 6, and Aug. Metro: San Babila.

Vini e Cucina TUSCAN/ITALIAN   This monument to modernism, with a sleek decor, draws the fashion crowd, who likes its light menu and well-chosen selections based on the freshest of ingredients. "We serve healthy food without being a health-food restaurant," a waiter told us. Forget about the traditional Milanese trattoria decor when entering here. Seafood, both raw and lightly cooked, is the specialty. Treat yourself to one of the grilled fish dishes or a delectable fish bourguignon. The pasta dishes are also wonderful, without those heavy cream and butter sauces.

Via Tadino 4. © **02-29519840.** Reservations required. Main courses 12€–17€ ($10.70–$15.20). AE, DC, MC, V. Tues–Sun 8–11:30pm. Metro: Porta Venezia.

INEXPENSIVE

Al Tempio d'Oro ITALIAN/INTERNATIONAL   This restaurant near the central rail station offers inexpensive and well-prepared meals. The chef is justifiably proud of his fish soup, Spanish paella, and North African couscous. The crowd scattered among the ceiling columns is relaxed, and they contribute to an atmosphere somewhat like that of a beer hall. No one will mind if you stop by just for a drink.

Via delle Leghe 23. © **02-26145709.** Main courses 6€–15€ ($5.35–$13.40). MC, V. Mon–Sat 6pm–2am. Closed 2 weeks in mid-Aug. Metro: Pasteur.

La Magolfa (Value) PIZZERIA/INTERNATIONAL   La Magolfa, one of the city's dining bargains, offers a great value in pizzas and pastas. The building is a country farmhouse whose origins date from the 1500s, although the restaurant opened only in 1960. It's likely to be crowded with young people, as is every other restaurant in Milan that offers such value. If you don't mind its location away from the center of town, in Zona Ticinese in the southern part of the city, you'll be treated to some hearty food and gargantuan helpings. A general air of conviviality reigns, and there's live music nightly.

Via Magolfa 15. ✆ 02-8321696. Reservations not necessary. Pastas 4€–6€ ($3.55–$5.35); pizza 3.50€–7.50€ ($3.15–$6.70). MC, V. Thurs–Tues noon–3pm and 7pm–2am. Metro: Porta Genova.

ON THE OUTSKIRTS
Antica Osteria del Ponte ✿✿ ITALIAN   One of our favorite restaurants in the area is 29km (18 miles) outside Milan (see the directions below). A country inn since the 18th century, this osteria was taken over 20 years ago by Mr. and Mrs. Ezio Santin, who turned it into one of Lombardy's most acclaimed restaurants. Mr. Santin studied under one of France's greatest chefs, Roger Vergé, and has devised a menu reflecting both lessons learned in France and his own inventive touches. The Santins' son, Maurizio, is the creative pastry chef. On our most recent rounds, we were thrilled by the shrimp marinated with olive oil and lemon sauce and served with caviar and a touch of vanilla. The risotto with fresh young artichoke hearts, anchovies, and parmigiano was among the finest versions of this dish we've ever found. For a regal taste treat, try the baked goose stuffed with foie gras.

From the center of Milan, take the SS Vigevanese until you reach Abiategrasso; then cross the bridge over the Naviglio Canal. At the first traffic light, turn right and follow the directions to Novara/Magenta. Go straight for 3km (2 miles) until you come to an intersection with a signpost marking the way to Cassinetta di Lugagnano. Turn left and follow this sign to the restaurant.

Piazza G. Negri 9, Cassinetta di Lugagnano. ✆ 02-9420034. Reservations required. Main courses 30€–42.50€ ($26.80–$37.95); fixed-price menu 100€ ($89.30). AE, DC, MC, V. Tues–Sat 12:30–2:30pm and 7:30–10:30pm. Closed Aug and Dec 25–Jan 12.

MILAN AFTER DARK
As in Rome, many of the top nightclubs in Milan shut down for the summer, when the cabaret talent and the bartenders pack their bags and head for the hills or the seashore. However, Milan is a big city, and there are always plenty of after-dark diversions. This sprawling metropolis is also one of Europe's cultural centers.

THE PERFORMING ARTS   The most complete list of cultural events appears in the large Milan newspaper, the left-wing *La Repubblica.* Try for a Thursday edition, which usually has the most complete listings.

The world's most famous opera house, **La Scala,** Piazza della Scala (Metro: Duomo), closed December 30, 2001, for a 3-year restoration. It marks the first time since World War II that Italy's leading opera house has been closed for an extended period.

While La Scala remains closed, operas will be presented at the 2,500-seat, newly constructed auditorium, **Teatro degli Arcimboldi,** Zona Bicocca, Viale dell'Innovazione (✆ 02-72003744), on the northern outskirts of Milan. The question remains, do elegantly dressed operagoers want to move from La Scala's glittering social arena to a somewhat rundown part of the city? It lies alongside a new university campus and dreary housing developments. Since the new opera house is difficult to reach by public transportation, the new theater operates shuttle buses departing from the Piazza Duomo between 6:45 and 7pm on the nights of performances. Otherwise, you have to take the Metro to the Precotto stop and from there take a bus (no. 162) to the auditorium.

Tickets are extremely hard to come by and are sold out weeks in advance, costing 20€ to 150€ ($17.85–$133.95). If you're a serious opera fan and don't want to take your chances at the last minute, you can get tickets to Milan's operas before leaving home by contacting a Milanese tour operator called **Agencia Sertur** (© 02-76024314), which usually packages tickets with hotel overnights for out-of-towners. Otherwise, you can check schedules and purchase tickets at www.lascala.milano.it, or phone for tickets by calling © 02-72003339. The opera house is closed in midsummer (late July and all of Aug). The new season begins every year on December 7, although the program for the upcoming season is announced the previous September.

Conservatorio, Via del Conservatorio 12 (© 02-7621101 or 02-76001755; Metro: San Babila), in the San Babila neighborhood, features the finest in classical music. Year-round, a cultured Milanese audience enjoys high-quality programs of, widely varied classical concerts. Tickets cost 15€ to 30€ ($13.40–$26.80).

Piccolo Teatro, Via Rivoli 2, near Via Dante (© 02-72333222; Metro: Cordusio), hosts a wide variety of Italian-language performances. Its director, Giorgio Strehler, is acclaimed as one of the most avant-garde and talented in the world. The theater lies between the Duomo and the Castle of the Sforzas. It's sometimes hard to obtain seats. It's closed August. Tickets cost 17.50€ to 27€ ($15.65–$24.10).

LIVE-MUSIC CLUBS The **Ca'Bianca Club,** Via Lodovico il Moro 117 (© 02-89125777; Metro: Bisceglie), offers live music and dancing on Wednesday night, from folk music to cabaret to Dixieland jazz. This is a private club, but no one at the door will prevent nonmembers from entering. The show, whatever it might be, begins at 10:30pm (closed Sun and closed in Aug). Cover is 15.60€ ($13.95) for the show and the first drink, or 45€ to 110€ ($40.20–$98.25) for dinner.

Capolinea, Via Lodovico il Moro 119 (© 02-89122024; Metro: Bisceglie), is one of the most appealing jazz clubs in town, with a wide variety of performers. Music is performed 10:30pm to 1 or 1:30am. The first drink costs 7.50€ ($6.70) and the others cost 3.50€ to 7€ ($3.15–$6.25). There's also a restaurant that serves affordable meals.

At **Le Scimmie,** Via Ascanio Sforza 49 (© 02-89402874; bus: 59), bands play everything from funk to blues to creative jazz. Doors open nightly around 8pm, and music is presented 10pm to around 3am.

Rolling Stone, Corso XXII Marzo 32 (© 02-733172; tram: 4 or 20), features head-banging rock bands. It's open every night, usually 10:30pm to 4am, but things don't get going until at least midnight. Closed in July and August. Cover on Friday and Saturday is 10€ ($8.95) and other days is 7.50€ ($6.70).

CAFES The decor of the **Berlin Cafe,** Via Gian Giacomo Mora 9 (© 02-8392605; tram: 15, 19, or 24), seems straight out of turn-of-the-20th-century Berlin, with etched glass and marble-topped tables. It's a great spot for coffee or a drink, although we've had gruff service here. A variety of simple snack food is available, primarily during the day, although the cafe is open until midnight.

Boasting a chic crowd of garment-district workers and shoppers, **Cafe Cova,** Via Montenapoleone 8 (© 02-76000578; Metro: Montenapoleone), has been around since 1817, serving pralines, chocolates, brioches, and sandwiches. The more elegant sandwiches contain smoked salmon and truffles. Sip your espresso from fragile gold-rimmed cups at one of the small tables in an elegant inner room or while standing at the prominent bar. It's closed in August and on Sunday year-round. Closing time is in the early evening.

Opened in 1910, the **Pasticceria Taveggia,** Via Visconti di Modrone 2 (© 02-76021257; Metro: San Babila), is one of Milan's most historic cafes. Behind ornate glass doors set into the 19th-century facade, Taveggia makes the best cappuccino and espresso in town, and it offers a variety of brioches, pastries, candies, and tortes. You can enjoy them while standing at the bar or seated in the Victorian tearoom. It's closed in the month of August.

One of the most traditional bakery/cafes in Milan, **Pasticceria Ricci,** 27 Piazza della Repubblica (© 02-66982536; Metro: Piazza della Repubblica), is now a century old. But after 10pm, it surprisingly becomes a well-known rendezvous for single gay men, often attracting the likes of Boy George and other air-kissing celebs.

BARS & PUBS Decorated a bit like a 19th-century bohemian parlor, **Al Teatro,** Corso Garibaldi 16 (© 02-864222; Metro: Garibaldi), is a popular bar across from the Teatro Fossati. It opens Tuesday to Sunday at 5pm and closes (after several changes of ambience) at 2am. Most of the time the crowd seems perfectly happy to drink, gossip, and flirt. In addition to coffee and drinks, it serves toasts and tortes. In fine weather, tables are set out on Corso Garibaldi.

Bar Giamaica, Via Brera 32 (© 02-876723; Metro: Lanza or Borgonvovo), is loud and bustling, with a gruff but humorous style. Everyone on staff has worked here forever. If you want only a drink, you'll have lots of company among the office workers who jostle around the tiny tables, often standing because of the lack of room. It's open as a restaurant Monday to Saturday noon to 2:30pm and 7:30 to 10pm, serving affordable meals. The bar opens at 9am Monday to Saturday and remains open until around 2am; it's closed 1 week in mid-August.

Despite its name, the **Grand Hotel Restaurant,** Via Ascanio Sforza 75 (© 02-89511586; bus: 59), doesn't rent rooms or even pretend to be grand. Instead, it's a large animated restaurant, which frequently offers live music. In summer, the crowds can move quickly from the smoky interior into a sheltered garden. Most visitors come here only for a drink, but if you're hungry you can get a moderately priced meal. The place is open Tuesday to Sunday 8 to 11pm. There's usually no cover.

Our favorite piano bar is **Clue Due,** via Formentini 2 (© 02-86464807; Metro: Lanza). The piano bar is on the second floor, and there's also a disco pub in the basement with no cover. Open daily 9pm to 3am.

World-class beer drinkers in Milan head for the pub, **El Tumbun de San Marc,** via San Marco 20 (© 02-6599507; Metro: Moscova), in the Berra district of the city. One patron said, "It's our version of Cheers." Open Monday to Saturday 12:30 to 2:30pm and 7:30pm to 1am.

One of the most convivial—and also the most crowded pub in Milan—is the Irish-themed **Pogue Mahone's,** via Salmini 1 (© 02-58309726; Metro: Porta Romana). Filled with a young crowd, a mixture of Milanese and visitors, the pub is awash with Irish beer, the drink of choice. Open daily 10am to 2am.

Milan's first brewery is **Birrificio Lambrate,** via Porpora, at the corner of via Adelchi (© 02-70638678; Metro: Lambrate). The beer is made on the premises in three steel kettles. Open Monday to Saturday noon to 2pm and 6pm to 2am.

DANCE CLUBS & NIGHTCLUBS **Killer Plastic,** Viale Umbria 120 (© 02-733996; bus: 92), is a favorite disco. Thursday is gay night, welcoming gay men (and some lesbians) onto the high-tech dance floors, and Saturday is crammed with the cream of the city's *alta moda* (high-fashion) crowd. Other nights, it's fun, high-energy, and exhibitionistic. Doors usually open Thursday to Sunday 10:30pm to around 3am or later, depending on the crowd. The cover is 15€ ($13.40).

Usually packed with a good-looking crowd, **Hollywood,** Corso Como 15 (© **02-6598996;** Metro: Garibaldi or Moscova), is small and has a sound system that's so good that you might get swept up in the fun of it all. It's open Tuesday to Sunday 10:30pm to at least 3am, with a 12.50€ to 15€ ($11.15–$13.40) cover that includes the first drink.

Coquetel, Via Vetere 14 (© **02-8360688;** bus: 59), is loud and wild and celebrates the American-style party-colored cocktail with a whimsy that could only be all Italian. The action around here, coupled with babble from dozens of regulars, ain't exactly sedate. It's open Monday to Saturday 8am to 2am.

The long-enduring disco, **Gimmi's,** via Cellini 2 (© **02-55188069;** Bus: 29, 30, or 63), is a rather classy joint among the more affluent Milanese youth. On-site is a restaurant open Thursday to Tuesday from 8:30 to 10:30pm; the dancing to '60s and '70s music starts after dinner is over. During the week the cover is 10€ ($8.95), including the first drink. On Friday and Saturday the entrance is 16€ ($14.30), also including the first drink. Reservations and a jacket are required for the restaurant.

WINE BARS   Open until late, **La Cantina di Manuela,** via Cadore 30 (© **02-55184931;** bus: 84), is one of the best of the Milanese wine bars, with outdoor tables when the weather is warm. They have a wide selection of reasonably priced Italian wines, plus a number of tasty snacks. Open Monday to Saturday 7:30am to 1am.

One of Milan's best-known caterers, Claudio Sadler, has opened **Sadler Wine & Food,** via Monte Bianco 2A (© **02-4814677;** Metro Amendola Fiera). The bar features some of the best wines and grappas from the northern wine-producing regions of Italy, and also offers a wide choice of the cheese and deli cuts. A convivial crowd in their 20s and 30s patronize the place. Open Monday to Saturday 12:30 to 3:30pm and 7:30 to 11pm.

Another wine bar with a choice of drinks to equal Sadler (see above) is **L'altra Pharmacia,** via Rosimini 3 (© **02-3451300;** Metro: Moscova). On weekends a basement piano bar is a lively place for a rendezvous. Food is also served but it takes second billing to the wines. Open Monday to Saturday noon to 3pm and 7:30pm to 1am.

GAY & LESBIAN CLUBS   **Nuova Idea International,** Via de Castillia 30 (© **02-69007859;** Metro: Garibaldi), is the largest, oldest, and most fun gay disco in Italy, very much tied to Milan's urban bustle. It prides itself on mimicking the large all-gay discos of northern Europe, and it draws young and not-so-young men, many of whom are actors. There are a large video screen and occasional live entertainment. It's open Thursday to Sunday 10pm to 3am. Cover is 10€ ($8.95) on Thursday, Friday, and Sunday, and 16€ ($14.30) on Saturday, including the first drink.

Straights flock to **After Line,** via Sammartini 25 (© **02-6692130;** Metro: Stazione Centrale), but the club enjoys even more popularity among Milan's gay community. Many nights are devoted to themes. Strong drinks and recorded music fill the night air, and the place is very cruisy. Open daily 9pm to 3am.

2 Bergamo ★★
50km (31 miles) NE of Milan, 601km (373 miles) NW of Rome

Bergamo is one of the most characteristic Lombard hill towns. Many of the town's stone fortifications were built on Roman foundations by the medieval Venetians, who looked on Bergamo as one of the gems of their trading network during several centuries of occupation. Set on a hilltop between the Seriana and the Brembana valleys, Bergamo lies in the alpine foothills.

The Upper Town, 274m (900 ft.) above sea level, is buttressed by and terraced on the original Venetian fortifications. About half a mile downhill is the Lower Town (usually identified by residents simply as "Bergamo"), with many 19th-century and early-20th-century buildings lining its wide streets. This modern metropolis and industrial center contains the bus and rail stations, most of the hotels, and the town's commercial and administrative center.

ESSENTIALS
GETTING THERE **Trains** arrive from Milan once every hour, depositing passengers in the center of the Lower Town at Piazza Marconi. The trip takes an hour and costs 5€ ($4.45). For information about rail connections in Bergamo, call ✆ **848-888088** toll-free in Italy.

The **bus station** in Bergamo is across from the train station. For information or schedules, call ✆ **02-801161.** Buses arrive from Milan once every 30 minutes and cost 4.50€ ($4) one way.

If you have a **car** and are coming from Milan, head east on A4.

VISITOR INFORMATION The **tourist office** is on Città Alta, Vicolo Aquila Nera 2 (✆ **035-242226**), open daily 9am to 12:30pm and 2 to 5:30pm.

EXPLORING THE UPPER TOWN (CITTÀ ALTA)
The higher you climb, the more rewarding the view will be. The **Upper Town (Città Alta)** ★★★ is replete with narrow circuitous streets, old squares, splendid monuments, and imposing and austere medieval architecture. To reach the Upper Town, take bus no. 1 or 3, and then walk for 10 minutes up Viale Vittorio Emanuele.

The heart of the Upper Town is **Piazza Vecchia** ★, which has witnessed most of the town's upheavals and a parade of conquerors ranging from Attila to the Nazis. On the square is the Palazzo della Ragione (town hall), an 18th-century fountain, and the Palazzo Nuovo of Scamozzi (town library).

A vaulted arcade connects Piazza Vecchia with **Piazza del Duomo.** Opening onto the latter is the cathedral of Bergamo, which has a baroque overlay.

Basilica di Santa Maria Maggiore & Baptistry ★ Built in the Romanesque style, the church was founded in the 12th century but much later was given a baroque interior and a disturbingly busy ceiling. Displayed are exquisite Flemish and Tuscan tapestries incorporating such themes as the Annunciation and the Crucifixion. The choir, designed by Lotto, dates from the 16th century. In front of the main altar is a series of inlaid panels depicting themes such as Noah's Ark and David and Goliath.

Facing the cathedral is the **baptistry,** dating from Giovanni da Campione's design in the mid–14th century, but it was rebuilt at the end of the 19th century.

Piazza del Duomo. ✆ 035-223327. Free admission. Mon–Sat 8am–noon and 3–6pm; Sun 9am–12:45pm and 3–6pm.

Colleoni Chapel (Cappella Colleoni) ★★   This Renaissance chapel honors the inflated ego of the Venetian military hero Bartolomeo Colleoni, with an inlaid marble facade reminiscent of Florence. It was designed by Giovanni Antonio Amadeo, who's chiefly known for his creation of the Certosa in Pavia (see the box "Get Thee to a Renaissance Monastery," under "The Top Attractions" in section 1). For the condottiere, Amadeo built an elaborate tomb, surmounted by a gilded equestrian statue. (Colleoni, who was once the ruler of the town and under whose watch the town fell to the Republic of Venice, which he then served, was also the subject of one of the world's most famous equestrian statues, now standing on a square in Venice.) The tomb sculpted for his daughter, Medea, is much less elaborate. Giovanni Battista Tiepolo painted most of the frescoes on the ceiling.

Piazza del Duomo. ✆ **035-210061.** Free admission. Mar–Oct Tues–Sun 9am–noon and 2–6:30pm; off-season Tues–Sun 9am–noon and 2:30–4:30pm.

EXPLORING THE LOWER TOWN (CITTÀ BASSA)

Carrara Academy Gallery (Galleria dell'Accademia Carrara) ★★   Filled with a wide-ranging collection of the works of homegrown artists, as well as Venetian and Tuscan masters, the academy draws art lovers from all over the world. The most important works are on the top floor—head here first if your time is limited. The Botticelli portrait of Giuliano de' Medici is well known, and one room contains three versions of Giovanni Bellini's favorite subject, the *Madonna and Child.* It's interesting to compare his work with that of his brother-in-law, Andrea Mantegna, whose *Madonna and Child* is also displayed, as is Vittore Carpaccio's *Nativity of Maria,* seemingly inspired by Flemish painters.

Farther along, you encounter a most original treatment of the old theme of the Madonna and Child, this one by Cosmà Tura of Ferrara. Also displayed are three tables of a predella by Lotto and his *Holy Family with St. Catherine* (wonderful composition) and Raphael's *St. Sebastian.* The entire wall space of another room is taken up with paintings by Moroni (1523–78), a local artist who seemingly did portraits of everybody who could afford it. In the salons to follow, foreign masters, such as Rubens, van der Meer, and Jan Brueghel, are represented along with Guardi's architectural renderings of Venice and Longhi's continuing parade of Venetian high society.

Piazza Dell'Accademia. ✆ **035-399640.** Admission 2.50€ ($2.25). Apr–Sept Tues–Sun 10am–1pm and 3–6:45pm; Oct–Mar Tues–Sun 9:30am–1pm and 2:30–5:45pm.

WHERE TO STAY

Hotel Agnello d'Oro   This is an intimate 17th-century country inn in the heart of the Città Alta. It's an atmospheric setting for good food or a serviceable room. When you enter the cozy reception lounge, ring an old bell to bring the owner away from the kitchen. The guest rooms come in different shapes and sizes, although most are quite small, as are the attached bathrooms; each has a comfortable bed, either a double or a twin.

Via Gombito 22, 24129 Bergamo. ✆ **035-249883.** Fax 035-235612. 20 units (most with shower only). 85€ ($75.90) double. AE, DC, V. Bus: 1, then funicular. **Amenities:** Restaurant; bar; lounge; room service. *In room:* TV, hair dryer.

Hotel Cappello d'Oro   This Best Western affiliate lies in a renovated 150-year-old corner building on a busy street in the center of the Città Bassa. The public rooms and guest rooms are functional, high-ceilinged, and clean. The rooms are adequately but rather plainly furnished and are accompanied by compact tiled bathrooms. If you need a parking space, reserve it along with your room.

Viale Papa Giovanni XXIII 12, 24121 Bergamo. (℡) **035-232503.** Fax 035-242946. www.hotelcappellodoro.it. 92 units. 176€–190€ ($157.15–$169.65) double. Rates include buffet breakfast. AE, DC, MC, V. Parking 15€ ($13.40). **Amenities:** Restaurant; bar; gym; sauna; room service; babysitting; laundry/dry cleaning. *In room:* A/C, TV, minibar, hair dryer.

Hotel Excelsior San Marco ★ This 4-decade-old place at the edge of a city park is about midway between the Città Alta and the Città Bassa, both of which might be visible from the balcony of your room. The lobby features comfy leather chairs and ceiling frescoes depicting the lion of St. Mark. The guest rooms are attractively furnished and comfortable, most medium-size to spacious and all with modernized bathrooms.

Piazza della Repubblica 6, 24122 Bergamo. (℡) **035-366111.** Fax 035-223201. www.hotelsanmarco.com. 158 units (some with shower only). 174€ ($155.40) double; 245€ ($218.80) suite. Rates include breakfast. AE, DC, MC, V. Parking 17.50€ ($15.65) indoors, 10€ ($8.95) outdoors. **Amenities:** Restaurant; bar; pool; fitness center; sauna; room service; babysitting; laundry/dry cleaning. *In room:* A/C, TV, minibar, hair dryer, safe.

WHERE TO DINE

Ristorante da Vittorio ★★★ REGIONAL/INTERNATIONAL This restaurant on the Città Bassa's main boulevard can hold its own with the finest places in Milan. The menu offers more than a dozen risottos, more than 20 pastas, and around 30 meat dishes, as well as just about every kind of fish that swims in Italy's waters. Examples are grilled "fantasy of the sea" with fresh seasonal vegetables, goose breast with a tapenade of black olives, and tartare of salmon with avocado. The service is efficient, directed by members of the Cerea family, who by now are among the best-known citizens of Bergamo.

Viale Papa Giovanni XXIII 23. (℡) **035-218060.** Reservations required. Main courses 25€–37.50€ ($22.35–$33.50); fixed-price dinner 42.50€–90€ ($37.95–$80.35). AE, DC, MC, V. Thurs–Tues noon–3pm and 7:30–10:30pm. Closed 3 weeks in Aug.

BERGAMO AFTER DARK

The opera season lasts from September to November, with a drama being staged from then until April at the **Teatro Donizetti,** Piazza Cavour (℡ **035-4160611).** The tourist office (under "Essentials," above) will provide a pamphlet of upcoming events.

If visiting a *birreria* (beer hall) is what you want, head for **Via Gombito** in the Città Alta. It's lined with places to drink. One of the most popular joints is **Papageno Pub,** Via Colleoni 1B (℡ **035-236624),** which makes the best sandwiches and bruschetta in town. In the Città Bassa, **Capolinea,** Via Giacomo Quarenghi 29 (℡ **035-320981),** has an active bar up front, always packed with a young crowd.

3 Mantua ★★★

40km (25 miles) S of Verona, 153km (95 miles) SE of Milan, 469km (291 miles) NW of Rome, 145km (90 miles) SW of Venice

Mantua (Mantova) had a flowering of art and architecture under the Gonzaga dynasty, who held sway over the city for nearly 4 centuries. Originally an Etruscan settlement and then a Roman colony, it has known many conquerors, including the French and the Austrians in the 18th and 19th centuries. Virgil, the great Latin poet, has remained its most famous son (he was born outside the city in a place called Andes). Verdi set *Rigoletto* here, Romeo (Shakespeare's creation, that is) took refuge here, and writer Aldous Huxley called Mantua "the most romantic city in the world."

Mantua is imposing and at times even austere. It's very much a city of the past, and its historic center is gloriously traffic free.

ESSENTIALS

GETTING THERE   Mantua has excellent **train** connections because it lies on direct lines to Milan, Cremona, Modena, and Verona. Nine trains a day arrive from Milan, taking 2¼ hours and costing 8€ ($7.15) one way. From Cremona, trains arrive every hour (trip time: 1 hr.), costing 3.50€ ($3.15) one way. The train station is on Piazza Don Leoni (© **848-888088**). Take bus no. 3 from outside the station to get to the center of town.

Most visitors arrive by train, but Mantua has good **bus** connections with Brescia; 17 buses a day make a 1¾-hour journey at a cost of 5€ ($4.45) one way. The bus station is on Piazza Mondadori (© **0376-327237**).

If you have a **car** and are in Cremona, continue east along Route 10.

VISITOR INFORMATION   The **tourist office** is at Piazza Andrea Mantegna 6 (© **0376-328253**), open Monday to Saturday 8:30am to 12:30pm and 3 to 6pm, and Sunday 9:30am to 12:30pm.

EXPLORING THE TOWN

The best shopping is at the **open-air market** that operates only on Thursday morning at Piazza delle Erbe and Piazza Sordello. Here you can find a little bit of everything, from cheap clothing (often designer rip-offs) to bric-a-brac. The place is like an outdoor traveling department store.

Museo di Palazzo Ducale ★★★   The ducal apartments of the Gonzagas, with more than 500 rooms and 15 courtyards, are the most remarkable in Italy, certainly when judged from the standpoint of size. Like Rome, the compound wasn't built in a day, or even a century. The earlier buildings, erected to the specifications of the Bonacolsi family, date from the 13th century. The 14th and early 15th centuries saw the rise of the **Castle of St. George (Castello di San Giorgio),** designed by Bartolino da Novara. The Gonzagas also added the **Palatine Basilica of Santa Barbara (Basilica Palatina di Santa Barbara),** by Bertani.

Over the years, the historic monument of Renaissance splendor has lost many of the art treasures collected by Isabella d'Este during the 15th and 16th centuries in her efforts to turn Mantua into *La Città dell'Arte.* Her descendants, the Gonzagas, sold the most precious objects to Charles I of England in 1628, and 2 years later most of the remaining rich collection was looted during the sack of Mantua. Even Napoleon did his bit by carting off some of the objects still there.

What remains of the painting collection is still superb, including works by Tintoretto and Sustermans and a "cut-up" Rubens. The display of classical statuary is impressive, gathered mostly from the various Gonzaga villas at the time of Maria Theresa of Austria. Among the more inspired sights are the **Zodiac Room (Sala dello Zodiaco);** the **Hall of Mirrors (Salone degli Specchi),** with a vaulted ceiling from the beginning of the 17th century; the **River Chamber (Sala del Fume);** the **Apartment of Paradise (Appartamento del Paradiso);** the **Apartment of Troia (Appartamento di Troia),** with frescoes by Giulio Romano; and a scale reproduction of the **Holy Staircase (Scala Santa)** in Rome. The most interesting and best-known room in the castle is the **Bridal Chamber (Camera degli Sposi),** frescoed by Andrea Mantegna. Winged cherubs appear over a balcony at the top of the ceiling. Look for a curious dwarf and a mauve-hatted portrait of Christian I of Denmark. There are many paintings by Domenico Fetti, along with a splendid series of nine tapestries woven in Brussels based on cartoons by Raphael. A cycle of frescoes on the age of chivalry by Pisanello has recently been discovered. A tour guide will point out the many highlights.

Piazza Sordello 40. ☎ 0376-320283. Admission 6.50€ ($5.80). Daily 8:45am–7:15pm. Last admission 1 hr. before closing.

Basilica di Sant'Andrea & Campanil ☆ Built to the specifications of Leon Battista Alberti, this church opens onto Piazza Mantegna, just off Piazza delle Erbe, where you'll find fruit vendors. The actual work was carried out by a pupil of Alberti's, Luca Fancelli. However, before Alberti died in 1472, it's said that, architecturally speaking, he knew that he had "buried the Middle Ages." The church wasn't completed until 1782, when Juvara crowned it with a dome.

As you enter, check out the first chapel to your left, which contains the tomb of the great Mantegna (the paintings are by his son, except for the *Holy Family* by the old master himself). The sacristan will light it for you. In the crypt, you'll encounter a representation of one of the more fanciful legends in the history of church relics: St. Andrew's claim to possess the blood of Christ, "the gift" of St. Longinus, the Roman soldier who's said to have pierced His side. Beside the basilica is a 1414 **campanile** (bell tower).

Piazza Mantegna. ☎ 0376-328504. Free admission. Mon–Sat 8am–noon; daily 3–7pm.

Palazzo Te ☆☆ This Renaissance palace is known for its frescoes by Giulio Romano and his pupils. Fun-loving Federigo II, one of the Gonzagas, had it built as a place where he could slip away to see his mistress, Isabella Boschetto. The name, Te, is said to have been derived from the word *tejeto*, which in the local dialect means "a cut to let the waters flow out." This was once marshland drained by the Gonzagas for their horse farm.

The frescoes in the various rooms, dedicated to everything from horses to Psyche, rely on mythology for subject matter. The **Room of the Giants (Sala dei Giganti),** the best known, has a scene depicting heaven venting its rage on the giants who had moved threateningly against it. Federico's motto was "What the lizards lack is that which tortures me," an obscure reference to the reptile's cold blood as opposed to his hot blood. The **Cupid and Psyche Room (Sala di Amore e Psiche)** forever immortalizes the tempestuous love affair of these swingers; it's decorated with erotic frescoes on the theme of the marriage of Cupid and Psyche, two other "hot bloods."

Viale Te 13. ☎ 0376-323266. Admission 8€ ($7.15). Tues–Sun 9am–6pm; Mon 1–6pm. Last admission 30 min. before closing. Closed Jan 1, May 1, and Dec 25.

WHERE TO STAY

Albergo San Lorenzo ☆ This hotel in the historic center occupies an ancient building that received a 1996 renovation. Restorers paid great attention to the architectural details and the furnishings, most of which are antique. The great service makes you feel right at home. The guest rooms are furnished with dark woods (antique reproductions) and gilded mirrors; the air-conditioning is individually adjustable (a godsend in steamy Mantua), and the bathrooms are tiled. The hotel also offers a panoramic terrace with a view.

Piazza Concordia 14, 46100 Mantova. ☎ 0376-220500. Fax 0376-327194. www.hotelsanlorenzo.it. 32 units. 140€ ($125) double; 155€ ($138.40) junior suite. Rates include buffet breakfast. AE, DC, MC, V. Parking 18€ ($16.05). Amenities: Lounge; laundry. *In room:* A/C, TV, minibar, hair dryer, safe.

Hotel Dante *(Value* This boxy modern hotel is your best bet on a budget. On a narrow street in the busy commercial center, it has a recessed entrance area and a marble-accented interior, parts of which look out over a flagstone-covered courtyard. Some of the simply furnished but clean guest rooms have nice extras. The bathrooms are a bit cramped.

Via Corrado 54, 46100 Mantova. © **0376-326425.** Fax 0376-221141. www.hoteldantemn.it. 40 units. 105€ ($93.75) double. Rates include breakfast. AE, DC, MC, V. Parking 11€ ($9.80) inside, free outside. **Amenities:** Bar; room service; laundry. *In room:* A/C, TV, minibar, hair dryer.

Mantegna Hotel *(Value* This inn is in a commercial section of town, a few blocks from one of the entrances to the old city. The lobby is accented with gray and red marble slabs, along with enlargements of details of paintings by Mantegna. About half of the guest rooms look out over a sunny rear courtyard, though the rooms facing the street are fairly quiet. They're small to medium in size, each with a small bathroom.

Via Fabio Filzi 10B, 46100 Mantova. © **0376-328019.** Fax 0376-368564. www.hotelmantegna.it. 38 units (showers only). 110€ ($98.25) double; 130€ ($116.10) suite. Breakfast 7.50€ ($6.70). AE, DC, DISC, MC, V. Free parking. Closed Dec 24–Jan 6. **Amenities:** Bar; room service; babysitting; laundry/dry cleaning. *In room:* A/C, TV, hair dryer.

Rechigi Hotel ★ Near the center of the old city stands the Rechigi, rivaled only by the San Lorenzo. The lobby is warmly decorated with modern paintings and contains an alcove bar. The owners maintain the property well and have decorated the guest rooms in good taste. Most rooms are medium in size, and all were renovated in 1996. The bathrooms are compact.

Via P. F. Calvi 30, 46100 Mantova. © **0376-320781.** Fax 0376-220291. 57 units (showers only). 118€–139€ ($105.35–$124.15) double; 233€ ($208.05) suite. AE, DC, MC, V. Parking 18€ ($16.05). **Amenities:** Bar; room service; laundry. *In room:* A/C, TV, minibar, hair dryer, safe.

WHERE TO DINE

The local specialty is **donkey stew** (*stracotto di asino*). Legend claims that you'll never be a man until you've sampled it.

Il Cigno Trattoria dei Martini MANTOVANO   This trattoria overlooks a cobblestone square in the old part of Mantua. The exterior is a faded ocher, with wrought-iron cross-hatched window bars within sight of the easy parking on the piazza outside. After passing through a large entrance hall studded with frescoes, you'll come to the bustling dining rooms. The menu offers both freshwater and saltwater fish and dishes such as *agnoli* (a form of pasta) in a light sauce or risotto. *Bollito misto* (a medley of boiled meats) is served with various sauces, including one made of mustard. One excellent pasta, *tortelli di zucca,* is stuffed with pumpkin.

Piazza Carlo d'Arco 1. © **0376-327101.** Reservations recommended. Main courses 12.50€–17.50€ ($11.15–$15.65). AE, DC, MC, V. Wed–Sun 12:30–1:45pm and 7:40–9:45pm. Closed Jan 1–6 and Aug.

L'Aquila Nigra (The Black Eagle) ★★ MANTOVANO/ITALIAN   This restaurant is in a Renaissance mansion on a narrow passageway by the Bonacolsi Palace. The foundations were laid in the 1200s, but the restaurant dates from 1984. In the elegant rooms, you can choose from such dishes as pike from the Mincio River, served with *salsa verde* (green sauce) and polenta, as well as other regional specialties. You also might order *gnocchi alle ortiche* (potato dumplings tinged with puréed nettles), eel marinated in vinegar (one of the most distinctive specialties of Mantua), or *tortelli di zucca* (with a pumpkin base).

Vicolo Bonacolsi 4. ☎ **0376-327180.** Reservations recommended. Main courses 13€–16.50€ ($11.60–$14.75). AE, DC, MC, V. Tues–Sat noon–2pm and 8–10pm (also Sun noon–2pm Apr–May and Sept–Oct). Closed the 2nd week in Aug.

Ristorante Pavesi *Finds* ITALIAN   The Pavesi is located under an ancient arcade on Mantua's most beautiful square. The walls partially date from the 1200s, although the restaurant goes back only before World War II. It's an intimate family-run place with hundreds of antique copper pots hanging from the single-barrel vault of the plaster ceiling; tables spill out into the square in summer. The antipasti table is loaded with delicacies, and specialties include *agnolotti* (a form of tortellini) with meat, cheese, sage, and butter, as well as *risotto alla mantovana* (with pesto). Also try the roast filet of veal (deboned and rolled) and a blend of *fagioli* (white beans) with onions.

Piazza delle Erbe 13. ☎ **0376-323627.** Reservations recommended. Main courses 9.50€–18€ ($8.50–$16.05). AE, DC, MC, V. Daily noon–2:30pm and 7:30–10:30pm. Closed Nov 19–27 and Feb–Mar 7.

MANTUA AFTER DARK

The major cultural venue is the **Teatro Sociale di Mantova,** Piazza Cavallotti (☎ **0376-362739;** www.alessandrobrancaleoni.it), off Corso Vittorio Emanuele. Operas are staged in October, followed by a season of Italian dramas and classical music concerts December to May. Tickets cost 17.50€ to 50€ ($15.65–$44.65). You might also catch a chamber music series in April and May.

If you're just looking for a fun place for a drink, head for **Leoncino Rosso,** Via Giustiziati 33 (☎ **0376-323277**), behind Piazza Erbe. This osteria opened in 1750 and hasn't changed some of its recipes (such as tortellini with nuts or pumpkin) since then. It's closed August and 2 weeks in January. The best selection of beer in town is at **Oblo,** Via Arrivabene 50 (☎ **0376-360676**), which also has a good offering of reasonably priced wines, such as the fizzy red Lambrusco.

4 Lake Garda ✶✶✶

The easternmost of the northern Italian lakes, Lake Garda is also the largest, 52km (32 miles) long and 19km (12 miles) at its widest. Sheltered by mountains, its scenery, especially the part on the western shore that reaches from Limone to Salo, seems almost Mediterranean; you'll see olive, orange, and lemon trees, and even palms. The almost-transparent lake is ringed with four art cities: Trent to the northeast, Brescia to the west, Mantua to the south, and Verona to the east.

The lake's eastern side is more rugged and less developed, but the resort-studded western strip is probably best for first-timers. On the western side, a circuitous road skirts the lake through one molelike tunnel after another. You can park your car at several secluded belvederes and take in the panoramic lakeside views (or stop and take a cruise on the lake; see "Getting Around," below). In spring, the scenery is splashed with color as everything from wild poppies to oleander bursts into bloom.

LAKE GARDA ESSENTIALS

GETTING THERE   Eight buses a day make the 1-hour trip from Trent to Riva del Garde, costing 3.05€ ($2.70) one way. For information and schedules, call the **Autostazione on Viale Trento** in Riva at ☎ **848-888088.** The nearest

train station is at Roverto, a 20-minute ride from Riva. Frequent buses make the 20-minute trip from the train station to Riva, costing 2.50€ ($2.25) one way.

If you have a **car** and are coming from Milan or Brescia, A4 east runs to the southwestern corner of the lake. From Mantua, take A22 north to A4 west. From Verona and points east, take A4 west.

GETTING AROUND   For getting around Lake Garda, you'll need a **car.** Most drivers take the road along the western shore, S572, north to Riva di Garda. For a less-congested drive, try heading back down the lake along its eastern shore on the Gardesana Orientale (S249). S11 runs along the south shore.

The twisting roads following the shores of Lake Garda would be enough to rattle even the most experienced driver. Couple the turns, dimly lit tunnels, and emotional local drivers with convoys of tour buses and trucks that rarely stay in their lane, and you have one of the more frightening drives in Italy. Use your horn around blind curves, and be warned that Sunday is especially risky because everyone on the lake and from the nearby cities seems to take to the roads after a long lunch with lots of heady wine.

Both **ferries** and **hydrofoils** operate on the lake from Easter to September. For schedules and information, contact **Navigazione Lago di Garda** at © **030-914951** (its main office in Desenzano) or 0464-552625 (its Riva del Garda branch). Ferries connect Riva's harbor, Porto San Nicolà, with the major lakeside towns, such as Gardone (trip time: 2½ hr.), costing 5.30€ ($4.75) one way; Sirmione (trip time: 4 hr.), 5.30€ ($4.75) one way; and Desenzano (trip time: 4 hr., 20 min.), 9€ ($8.05) one way.

These ferries provide the best opportunity for admiring the lake's beauty and are quite a bargain. Following the same routes, at about the same times, are a battalion of hydrofoils, which cut the travel time to each of the destinations in half. Transit on any of them requires a supplement of 1.10€ to 3.10€ ($1–$2.75), depending on the distance you intend to travel. If you want to admire the lake from a waterside vantage, a well-recommended mode of attack is to travel in one direction via conventional ferry and return to Riva del Garda by hydrofoil. From early November to late February, there's no transportation offered in or out of Riva del Garda's port, or anywhere else along the lake's northern tier; only very limited transportation options are available from Desenzano, in the south.

RIVA DEL GARDA ☞

Riva del Garda is the lake's oldest and most traditional resort. It consists of both an expanding new district and an old town, the latter centered at **Piazza III Novembre.**

ESSENTIALS

GETTING THERE   Riva del Garda is linked to the Brenner-Modena motorway (Rovereto Sud/Garda Nord exit) and to the railway (Rovereto station); it is near Verona's airport.

VISITOR INFORMATION   The tourist office is located on Giardini di Porta Orientale 8 (© **0464-554444**), which is open as follows: November to March, Monday to Friday 9am to noon and 2:30 to 5:15pm; April to June 15, Monday to Saturday 9am to noon and 3 to 6:15pm; June 16 to September 15, Monday to Saturday 9am to noon and 3 to 6:30pm, Sunday 10am to noon and 4 to 6:30pm; and September 16 to October, Monday to Saturday 9am to noon and 3 to 6:15pm.

SEEING THE SIGHTS

Situated on the northern banks of the lake, between the Benacense plains and towering mountains, Riva offers the advantages of both the Riviera and the Dolomites. Its climate is classically Mediterranean—mild in winter and moderate in summer. Vast areas of rich vegetation combine with the deep blue of the lake. Many people come for the healthy air and climate; others come for business conferences, meetings, and fairs. Riva is popular with tour groups from Germany and England.

Riva is the windsurfing capital of Italy. Windsurfing schools offer lessons and also rent equipment. The best one is **Nautic Club Riva,** Viale Rovereto 132 (© **0464-552453**), closed November to Easter. It has full rentals, including life jackets, wet suits, and boards, for 30€ ($26.80) per day.

If you'd like to explore the area by bike, go to **Super Bike Girelli,** Viale Damiano Chiesa 15–17 (© **0464-556602**), where rentals cost 15€ ($13.40) per day.

Most of the town's shopping consists of unremarkable souvenirs, but a large **open-air market,** the best on Lake Garda, comes to town on the second and fourth Wednesdays of every month. It mainly sprawls along Viale Dante, Via Prati, and Via Pilati. You can buy virtually anything, from alpine handcrafts to busts of Mussolini. While you're shopping, drop in at the **Pasticceria Copat di Fabio Marzari,** Viale Dante 37 (© **0464-551885**), for delectable pastries.

On the harbor, at Piazza III Novembre, you'll see the town's highest building, a 13th-century watchtower, the **Tower of Apponale (Torre d'Apponale).** It isn't open for visits, but the angelic-looking trumpeter adorning its pinnacle has been adopted as the symbol of the town itself. There's also a severe-looking castle, **La Rocca,** Piazza Battisti 3 (© **0464-573869**). Built in 1124 and owned at various times by both the ruling Scaligeri princes of Verona and the Viennese Hapsburgs (who used it as a prison), La Rocca has been turned into a **Civic Museum (Museo Civico La Rocca),** which you might visit on a rainy day to see its exhibits of local artworks and attractions reflecting local traditions. Admission is 2€ ($1.80); it's open from September to June Tuesday to Sunday from 9:30am to 5:30pm (open an hr. later in July and Aug).

WHERE TO STAY

Hotel du Lac et du Parc ★★ This deluxe Spanish-style hotel, the best in town, is set back from the busy road behind a shrub-filled parking lot; it boasts a lovely lakeside beach. The interior of the main building is freshly decorated, with arched windows and lots of comfort. The well-trained staff speaks many languages and seems genuinely concerned with everyone's well-being. The guest rooms are well furnished and come in various shapes and sizes, some boasting balconies with lovely lake views.

Viale Rovereto 44, 38066 Riva del Garda. © **0464-551500.** Fax 0464-555200. www.hoteldulac-riva.it. 170 units (33 bungalows). 130€–280€ ($116.10–$250.05) double; 295€–385€ ($263.45–$343.80) suite; 260€ ($232.20) bungalow for 4. Rates include breakfast. AE, DC, MC, V. Free parking. Closed Oct 20–Mar 20. **Amenities:** 3 restaurants (outdoor barbecues with live music are occasionally offered in summer); bar; 2 outdoor pools (1 for kids, 1 for adults); 1 indoor pool; 2 tennis courts; fitness center; sauna; sailing and windsurfing schools; boat rentals; bike rentals; children's program; concierge; salon; room service; babysitting; laundry/dry cleaning. *In room:* A/C (in some), TV, minibar, hair dryer, safe.

Hotel Sole ★ *Value* This large villa with arched windows and colonnades enjoys the most scenic location on the waterfront and offers luxuries that you'd expect from a more expensive hotel. The character and the quality of the guest rooms vary considerably, but most have lake views and some even have balconies. Some are almost suites, with living-room areas; the smaller ones are less desirable. The staff can help you arrange bike trips and steer you toward the best watersports on the lake.

Piazza III Novembre 35, 38066 Riva del Garda. (C) **0464-552686.** Fax 0464-552811. www.hotelsole.net. 52 units. 115€–135€ ($102.70–$120.55) double; 175€–195€ ($156.30–$174.15) suite. Rates include breakfast. AE, DC, MC, V. Parking 5€ ($4.45). Closed Jan 15–Mar 20 and Nov–Dec 23. **Amenities:** Restaurant; bar; sauna; room service; laundry. *In room:* TV, minibar, hair dryer, safe.

Hotel Venezia 😊 *(Value)*   This is one of the most attractive budget hotels in town. The main section of the Venezia's angular modern building is raised on stilts above a private parking lot set back from the lakefront promenade. The complex is surrounded by trees on a quiet street bordered with flowers and private homes. The guest rooms are pleasantly furnished and well maintained, each with a compact bathroom. Breakfast is served on the open-air sunroof.

Via Franz Kafka 7, 38066 Riva del Garda. (C) 0464-552216. Fax 0464-556031. www.rivadelgarda.com. 21 units (showers only). 83€–105€ ($74.10–$93.75) double. Rates include breakfast. MC, V. Closed Nov–Easter. **Amenities:** Dining room; lounge; attractive outdoor pool. *In room:* TV, hair dryer.

WHERE TO DINE

Il Giardino dell'Abondanza 😊 ITALIAN/SEAFOOD   Set back from the lake on one of the main shopping streets of the resort, San Marco offers superb classic Italian cuisine and excellent service. You might begin with pasta, such as spaghetti with clams or tortellini with prosciutto. The restaurant serves many good fish dishes, including sole and grilled scampi. Among the meat selections, try the tournedos opera or veal cutlet bolognese. During summer, you may dine in the garden.

Viale Roma 20. (C) **0464-554477.** Reservations recommended. Main courses 7.50€–10€ ($6.70–$8.95). AE, MC, V. Tues–Sun noon–2:30pm and 7pm–midnight. Closed Feb.

RIVA AFTER DARK

The best disco is **Discoteca Tiffany,** Giardini di Porta Orientale ((C) **0464-552512**), open only Thursday to Sunday. You can also shake it at **Disco Bar Café Latino,** Via Monte d'Oro 14 ((C) **0464-555785**), open most of the year Wednesday to Sunday 9pm to 2:30am (although the owners will often cut hours to just Fri and Sat in spring and autumn).

LIMONE SUL GARDA 😊

Limone sul Garda lies 10km (6 miles) south of Riva on the western shore of Lake Garda and is one of the liveliest resorts on the lake.

Limone snuggles close to the water at the bottom of a narrow, steep road, so its shopkeepers, faced with no building room, dug right into the rock. There are 4km (2½ miles) of beach for sunbathing, swimming, sailing, and windsurfing. The only way to get around is by walking, but that's part of the fun. You can enjoy tennis, soccer, and other sports, as well as the discos that seem to come and go every year.

If you're bypassing Limone, you might still want to make a detour south of the village to the turnoff to **Tignale,** in the hills. You can climb a modern highway to the town for a sweeping vista of Garda, one of the most scenic spots on the entire lake.

There's a **tourist office** in the City Hall, via IV Novembre 2-C ((C) **0365-918987**); it's open Monday to Friday 8am to noon and 2 to 5:30pm from October to March, and daily 8am to 10pm from April to September.

WHERE TO STAY & DINE

Hotel Capo Reamol 🏊   You won't even get a glimpse of this 1960s hotel from the main highway because it nestles on a series of terraces well below road level. Pull into a roadside area indicated at 2km (1¼ miles) north of Limone; then follow the driveway down a steep, narrow hill.

The guest rooms are well furnished and freshly decorated, ranging from medium size to spacious; some offer balconies overlooking the lake and the gravel beach. The bathrooms are tidily kept.

Via IV Novembre 92, 25010 Limone sul Garda. © **0365-954040**. Fax 0365-954262. www.gardaresort.it/cr.html. 60 units. 125€–185€ ($111.65–$165.20) double; 180€–230€ ($160.75–$205.40) suite. Rates include half-board. AE, DC, MC, V. Closed Nov–Easter. **Amenities:** Restaurant; bar; pool; fitness center; spa; watersports; room service; laundry. *In room:* A/C, TV, minibar, hair dryer, safe.

Hotel Le Palme   Opening directly onto Lake Garda, this Venetian-style villa with period furniture stands in the shade of palm trees 2 centuries old. It offers well-furnished guest rooms, each individually decorated, and compact tiled bathrooms. The second floor has a comfortable reading room with a TV, and the third floor has a wide terrace.

Via Porto 36, 25020 Limone sul Garda. © **0365-954681**. Fax 0365-954120. 28 units (showers only). 75€–125€ ($67–$111.65) double. Rates include buffet breakfast. MC, V. Closed Nov–Easter. **Amenities:** Restaurant; bar; lounge; room service; laundry. *In room:* TV, safe.

GARDONE RIVIERA ★★

On Lake Garda's western shore, 97km (60 miles) east of Milan, **Gardone Riviera** is a bustling resort with a number of good hotels and sporting facilities. Its lakeside promenade attracts a wide range of European tourists for most of the year. When it used to be chic for patrician Italian families to spend their holidays by the lake, many prosperous families built elaborate villas here and in neighboring Fasano, and many of these homes have been converted into inns. The town also has the major sightseeing attraction along the lake, d'Annunzio's Villa Vittoriale.

ESSENTIALS

GETTING THERE   The resort lies 42km (26 miles) south of Riva on the west coast. During the day, buses from Brescia arrive every 30 minutes; the trip takes 1 hour and costs 2.50€ ($2.25) one way. Two buses make the 3-hour trip from Milan, costing 7.50€ ($6.70) one way. For schedule information, call © **030-44061.**

VISITOR INFORMATION   The **tourist office** is at Corso della Repubblica 35 (© **0365-20347**). It's open Monday to Saturday 9am to 12:30pm, and Monday to Wednesday and Friday to Saturday 3 to 6pm.

SEEING THE SIGHTS

There are many scenic hiking trails and walking paths through the area; the staff at your hotel or the tourist office can help you choose a route that fits your available time and ability level. One easy day hike with charming scenery starts from the edge of the lake, near the town center, and goes 3 miles up a gentle hill to the north, taking you to the village of **San Michele.** There you'll find a cluster of ancient houses and a village church, with views over the surrounding landscapes.

Closer to the town center is **Rimbalcello,** on the via Zanardelli (© **0365-21069**), the site of a half-dozen tennis courts that anyone can use for around 10€ ($8.95) an hour. Within the same compound, you'll find access to a free

Wine Tasting

This region produces everything from dry still reds to sparkling whites with a champagnelike zest. **Fratelli Berlucchi,** Via Bruletto 2, Borgonato di Cortefranca, 25040 Brescia (✆ **030-984451**), one of Italy's largest wineries, is especially happy to host visitors. If you'd like to drive around the countryside to taste wine and tour a vineyard, call to make an appointment and get detailed directions.

beach, a disco that rocks and rolls after dark beginning around 9:30pm, and a restaurant.

If you want to get out on the lake, you can rent motorboats or sailboats at **Nautica Benaco,** along the lakefront of the nearby village of Manerba del Garda (✆ **0365-654074**), 14m (9 miles) from Gardone.

Villa Vittoriale ⊛ This villa was the home of Gabriele d'Annunzio (1863–1938), the poet and military adventurer, another Italian who believed in *la dolce vita,* even when he couldn't afford it. Most of the celebrated events in d'Annunzio's life occurred before 1925, including his love affair with Eleonora Duse and his bravura takeover as a self-styled commander of a territory being ceded to Yugoslavia. In the later years of his life, until he died in the winter before World War II, he lived the grand life at his private estate on Garda.

The furnishings and decor passed for avant-garde in their day but now evoke the Radio City Music Hall of the 1930s. D'Annunzio's death mask is of morbid interest, and his bed with a "Big Brother" eye adds a curious touch of Orwell's *1984* (over the poet's bed is a faun casting a nasty sneer). The marble bust of Duse ("the veiled witness" of his work) seems sadly out of place, but the manuscripts and old uniforms perpetuate the legend. In July and August, d'Annunzio plays are presented at the amphitheater on the premises. Villa Vittoriale is a bizarre monument to a hero of yesteryear.

Via Vittoriale 12. ✆ 0365-296511. Admission 5€ ($4.45) to grounds only; 10€ ($8.95) to grounds and villa. Summer daily 8:30am–8pm; winter Tues–Sun 9am–5pm. Head out Via Roma, connecting with Via Colli.

WHERE TO STAY

You can also rent a luxury room at the **Villa Fiordaliso** (see "Where to Dine," below).

Bellevue Hotel *Value* This villa, perched above the main road, offers many terraces surrounded by trees and flowers, and an unforgettable view. You can stay here on a budget, enjoying the advantages of lakeside villa life. The guest rooms come in a variety of shapes and sizes, each with a small bathroom.

Via Zanardelli 81, 25083 Gardone Riviera. ✆ 0365-290088. Fax 0365-290080. www.hotelbellevue gardone.com. 30 units (showers only). 98€ ($87.50) double. Rates include breakfast. V. Free parking. Closed Oct 10–Apr. **Amenities:** Restaurant; lounge; pool; room service. *In room:* TV, hair dryer, safe.

Grand Hotel ⊛⊛ This grand old dame is still the leading lady of Gardone. When it was built in 1881, this was the most fashionable hotel on the lake and one of the biggest resorts in Europe. Famous guests have included Winston Churchill, Gabriele d'Annunzio, and Somerset Maugham. It's only a rumor that Vladimir Nabokov was inspired to write *Lolita* after spotting a young girl here. The main salon's sculpted ceilings, parquet floors, and comfortable chairs make it an ideal spot for reading or watching the lake. For the most part, the guest rooms are spacious and traditionally furnished, always inviting (especially those balconies overlooking the lake). All the bathrooms come with deluxe toiletries.

Via Zanardelli 84, 25083 Gardone Riviera. © **0365-20261.** Fax 0365-22695. www.grangardone.it. 180 units. 135€–150€ ($120.55–$133.95) double; 195€–250€ ($174.15–$223.25) junior suite. Rates include buffet breakfast. Half-board 25€ ($22.35) per person. AE, DC, MC, V. Parking 11€ ($9.80). Closed Nov–Mar. **Amenities:** Restaurant (plus buffet lunches on the garden terrace); bar; pool; room service; massage; babysitting; laundry/dry cleaning. *In room:* A/C, TV, minibar, hair dryer, safe.

Where to Stay Nearby

The nearby town of **Fasano del Garda** is a satellite resort of Gardone Riviera, 2km (1¼ miles) to the north. Many prefer it to Gardone.

Hotel Villa del Sogno ★★★ This 1920s re-creation of a Renaissance villa offers sweeping views of the lake and spacious old-fashioned guest rooms (nine are air-conditioned). The rooms come in various shapes and sizes, and all are elegantly comfortable. The bathrooms are also well equipped, each with deluxe toiletries. This "Villa of the Dream" is far superior to anything in the area and offers a gorgeous, peaceful setting with extensive grounds. The baronial stairway of the interior and many of the ceilings and architectural details were crafted from beautiful woods.

Via Zanardelli 107, 25083 Gardone Riviera. © **0365-290181.** Fax 0365-290230. www.villadelsogno.it. 31 units. 200€–300€ ($178.60–$267.90) double; 380€–430€ ($339.35–$384) suite. Rates include breakfast. AE, DC, MC, V. Free parking. Closed Nov–Mar. **Amenities:** Restaurant; piano bar; pool; tennis court; Jacuzzi; sauna; room service; babysitting; laundry/dry cleaning. *In room:* A/C, TV, minibar, hair dryer, safe.

WHERE TO DINE

Most visitors take their meals at their hotels. However, there are some good independent choices.

Ristorante La Stalla (Kids) INTERNATIONAL This charming restaurant, set in a garden ringed with cypresses on a hill above the lake, is frequented by local families. It occupies a handcrafted stone building with a brick-columned porch and outdoor tables. To get here, follow the signs toward Il Vittoriale (the building was commissioned by d'Annunzio as a horse stable) to a quiet residential street. Depending on what's at the market that day, the specialties might include a selection of freshly prepared antipasti, risotto with cuttlefish, or crepes fondue. Polenta is served with Gorgonzola and walnuts, or you might prefer beef filet in beer sauce. Sunday afternoon can be crowded.

Via dei Colli Strada per Il Vittoriale. © **0365-21038.** Reservations recommended. Main courses 8€–16€ ($7.15–$14.30); fixed-price menu 12.50€ ($11.15). AE, DC, MC, V. Wed–Mon 12:30–2:30pm and 7:30pm–midnight. Closed Jan 8–20.

Villa Fiordaliso ★★★ ITALIAN This deluxe restaurant is in a Liberty-style villa from 1924 with gardens stretching down to the lake. Not only is it the most scenic and beautiful eatery on Lake Garda, but it also serves the finest cuisine. The chef gives his dishes a personal touch; the menu is likely to include a terrine of eel and salmon in herb-and-onion sauce, a timbale of rice and shellfish with curry, and several fish and meats grilled over a fire. Other specialties are ravioli with Bergoss (a salty regional cheese), sardines from a nearby lake baked in an herb crust, and scampi in a sauce of tomatoes and wild onions. This little bastion of fine food has impeccable service to match.

Today this famous villa is owned by Rosa Tosetti, who runs it beautifully and also offers guest rooms in a setting of cypresses, pine trees, and olive trees, near a private beach. Each room is exquisitely furnished. It was here that poet

Gabriele D'Annunzio used to gaze out through the villa's stained-glass windows. It was also here that Mussolini and his lover, Claretta, trysted in the 1940s, and the hotel's one suite is named after her. The six standard rooms cost 175€ to 375€ ($156.25–$334.80), with Claretta's suite costing 475€ ($424.20).

Via Zanardelli 150, 25083 Gardone Riviera. ©️ 0365-20158. www.villafiordaliso.it. Reservations required. Main courses 22.50€–32.50€ ($20.10–$29). AE, DC, MC, V. Wed–Sun 12:30–2pm and 7:30–10pm; Tues 7:30–10:30pm.

SIRMIONE ⭐⭐
Perched at the tip of a narrowing strip on the southern end of Lake Garda, Sirmione juts out 4km (2½ miles) into the lake. Noted for its thermal baths (used to treat deafness), the town is a major resort, just north of the autostrada connecting Milan and Verona. As in many Lake District resorts, things come to life in spring, go full tilt in summer, and then wilt away again in autumn.

ESSENTIALS
GETTING THERE   Sirmione lies 6km (3¾ miles) from the A4 exit and 8km (5 miles) from Desanzano.

Buses run from Brescia and from Verona to Sirmione every hour (trip time from either, depending on traffic: 1 hr.). A one-way ticket from Brescia costs 4€ ($3.55), and from Verona, 3.50€ ($3.15). For information call ©️ **030-223761.**

There's no rail service. The nearest train terminal is at Desenzano, on the Venice-Milan rail line. From here, there's frequent bus service to Sirmione; the bus trip takes 30 minutes and costs 1.30€ ($1.15) one way.

VISITOR INFORMATION   The **tourist office** is at Viale Marconi 2 (©️ **030-916245**). From April to October, it's open daily 9am to 12:30pm and 3 to 6pm; November to March, hours are Monday to Friday 9am to 12:30pm and 3 to 6pm, and Saturday 9am to 12:30pm.

SEEING THE SIGHTS
Known for its beaches (which are invariably crowded in summer), Sirmione is Garda's major lakeside resort. The best beach is **Lido delle Bionde,** which you reach by taking Via Dante near the castle. Here vendors will rent you a chaise longue with an umbrella for 7.50€ ($6.70). If you're feeling more athletic, other vendors will hook you up with a **pedal boat** at 10€ ($8.95) per hour or a **kayak** at 7.50€ ($6.70) per hour.

The resort is filled with souvenir shops, many hawking cheap trinkets aimed at the day-tripper. However, the best buys are found Friday 8am to 1pm when an **outdoor market** blossoms in Piazza Montebaldo. Vendors bring their wares here not only from nearby lake villages but also from towns and villages to the south.

The resort was a favorite of Giosué Carducci, the Italian poet who won the Nobel Prize for literature in 1906. In Roman days it was frequented by another poet, the hedonistic Catullus, who died in 54 B.C. Today the **Grotte di Catullo** ⭐, on Via Catullo 1 (©️ **030-916157**), is the chief sight, an unbeatable combination of Roman ruins and a panoramic lake view. You can wander through the remains of this once-great villa Tuesday to Sunday: March to October 14 8:30am to 7pm, and October 15 to February 8:30am to 5pm. Admission is 4€ ($3.55).

At the entrance to the town stands the moated 13th-century **Castello Scaligera** ⭐, Piazza Castello (©️ **030-916468**), which once belonged to the powerful Scaligeri princes of Verona. You can climb to the top and walk the ramparts. It's open year-round from Tuesday to Sunday 9am to 7pm. Admission is 4€ ($3.55).

WHERE TO STAY

During the peak summer season, you need a hotel reservation to bring a car into this crowded town. However, there's a large parking area at the town entrance. Accommodations are plentiful.

Flaminia Hotel ⭐ *Value*   This is one of the best little hotels in Sirmione, recently renovated with a number of modern facilities and amenities. It's right on the lakefront, with a terrace extending into the water. The guest rooms are made attractive by French doors opening onto private balconies. The rooms come in different shapes and sizes, each with a tiled bathroom. The lounges are furnished in a functional modern style.

Piazza Flaminia 8, 25019 Sirmione. ℂ **030-916078.** Fax 030-916193. www.hotelflaminia.com. 85 units. 103€–134€ ($92–$119.65) double. Rates include breakfast. AE, DC, MC, V. Free parking. **Amenities:** Bar; room service; babysitting; laundry. *In room:* A/C, TV, minibar, hair dryer, safe.

Grand Hotel Terme ⭐   This rambling hotel at the entrance of the old town is on the lake next to the Scaligeri Castle, and it boasts a lovely lakefront garden. Wide marble halls and stairs lead to well-furnished guest rooms ranging from medium in size to spacious, each with a lake view. The tiled bathrooms have deluxe toiletries.

Viale Marconi 1, 25019 Sirmione. ℂ **030-916261.** Fax 030-916568. www.termedisirmione.com. 58 units. 162€–248€ ($144.65–$221.45) double; 388€–502€ ($346.50–$448.30) suite. Rates include breakfast. AE, DC, MC, V. **Amenities:** Restaurant (international/Mediterranean, with outdoor dining); lounge; outdoor pool and indoor thermal pool; fitness center; spa with extensive menu of health and beauty treatments; Jacuzzi; sauna; concierge; car-rental desk; salon; room service; massage; babysitting; laundry/dry cleaning. *In room:* A/C, TV, minibar, hair dryer, safe.

Hotel Olivi ⭐   This hotel benefits from an excellent location on the rise of a hill in a grove of olive trees at the edge of town. The all-glass walls of the public rooms never let you forget that you're in a garden spot. Even the streamlined guest rooms have walls of glass leading onto open balconies. The tiled bathrooms, though a bit small, still have adequate shelf space.

Via San Pietro 5, 25019 Sirmione. ℂ **030-9905365.** Fax 030-916472. www.hotelolivi.it. 67 units. 120€–270€ ($107.15–$241.10) double. Rates include buffet breakfast. Half-board 28€ ($25) extra per person. AE, MC, V. Closed Dec–Jan. **Amenities:** 2 restaurants; bar with outdoor terrace; lounge; pool; room service; babysitting; laundry/dry cleaning. *In room:* A/C, TV, minibar, hair dryer, safe.

Villa Cortine Palace Hotel ⭐⭐   This first-class choice, whose original building dates from 1905, is set apart from the town and surrounded by sumptuous formal gardens. For serenity, atmosphere, professional service, and even good food, there's nothing to equal it in Sirmione. Today all but a handful of its guest rooms are in the new wing, and the reception area is located in the older building. Most rooms are medium to spacious, each with an excellent bathroom containing deluxe toiletries. Most units have balconies and lovely lake views. The formal drawing room boasts lots of gilt and marble—it's positively palatial.

Via Grotte 12, 25019 Sirmione. ℂ **030-9905890.** Fax 030-916390. www.hotelvillacortine.com. 54 units. 290€–650€ ($258.95–$580.45) double with breakfast; 465€ ($415.25) double with half-board. 460€–640€ ($410.80–$571.50) suite with breakfast; 510€–720€ ($455.45–$642.95) suite with half-board. Half-board compulsory June 18–Sept 19. AE, DC, MC, V. Closed end of Oct to Easter. **Amenities:** 2 restaurants (plus barbecue lunches on the private beach); bar; pool; clay tennis court; concierge; room service; babysitting; laundry/dry cleaning. *In room:* A/C, TV, minibar, hair dryer, safe.

WHERE TO DINE

La Rucola ITALIAN   This restaurant lies on a small alley a few steps from the main gate leading into Sirmione. The building looks like a vine-laden, sienna-colored country house (actually, it was a stable 150 years ago). The menu includes fresh salmon, langoustines, mixed grilled fish, and a more limited meat selection. Meats, such as Florentine beefsteak, are most often grilled or flambéed. More innovative items include *gnocchetti di riso* with baby squid and squid ink, and turbot filet with potatoes and zabaglione of spinach. A good pasta dish is spaghetti with clams. Many of the desserts are made for two, including crêpes suzette and banana flambé.

Vicolo Strentelle 5. ✆ **030-916326.** Reservations recommended. Main courses 12.50€–19€ ($11.15–$16.95); fixed-price menu 45€–70€ ($40.20–$62.50). AE, DC, MC, V. Fri–Wed 12:30–2:30pm and 7:30–10:30pm. Closed Jan–Feb 8.

Ristorante Grifone da Luciano 🌟 INTERNATIONAL   One of the most attractive restaurants in town is separated from the castle by a row of shrubbery, a low stone wall, and a moat. From your seat on the flagstone terrace, you'll have a view of the crashing waves and the plants ringing the dining area. The main building is an old stone house surrounded by olive trees, but many diners gravitate toward the low glass-and-metal extension. The staff is charming and fun, and the chef is talented. The food includes many varieties of fish and many standard Italian dishes, such as *gnocchetti dragoncella* (with tomatoes and aromatic herbs), risotto with shellfish, Venetian-style calves' livers with onions, beef filet flambéed with whisky, and *costello di Manzo* (beef cutlets).

Via delle Bisse 5. ✆ **030-916097.** Main courses 10€–17€ ($8.95–$15.20). AE, DC, MC, V. Thurs–Tues noon–2:30pm and 7–10:30pm. Closed Nov–Mar 15.

Vecchia Lugana 🌟🌟🌟 LOMBARD/ITALIAN   The grandest dining along Lake Garda is found here at the base of the peninsula outside town—in fact, Vecchia Lugana ranks as one of the best restaurants in Italy. The guiding light is Pierantonio Ambrosi, who uses only the freshest ingredients prepared with great care. He claims that the important thing is to offer a genuine cuisine in an informal setting. He also cares more about the food's substance and quality than about its artistic arrangement. Every day his staff prepares several kinds of fresh pasta, from tagliatelle to orecchiette, and you can count on it being served with a savory sauce. The chefs are known for their fresh fish, grilled to perfection with a touch of olive oil, lemon sauce, and freshly chopped herbs. The perch filet with fresh artichokes is a delight. For dessert, try one of the pretty fresh-fruit tarts.

Piazzale Vecchia Lugana 1, Lugana di Sirmione. ✆ **030-919012.** Reservations recommended. Main courses 11€–17.50€ ($9.80–$15.65). AE, DC, MC, V. Wed–Sun 12:30–2pm and 7:30–10pm. Closed Jan to mid-Feb.

5 Lake Como 🌟🌟🌟

More than 48km (30 miles) north of Milan, romantic and lovely Lake Como is a shimmering deep blue, spanning 4km (2½ miles) at its widest point. With its flower-filled gardens, villas built for the wealthy of the 17th and 18th centuries, and mild climate, it's among the most scenic spots in Italy. The best way to admire the lake's many faces is to take a boat tour and pull into selected ports of call en route for a meal, an espresso, a stroll, or some shopping or swimming.

LAKE COMO ESSENTIALS

GETTING THERE   Trains arrive daily at Como from Milan every hour. The trip takes 40 minutes, and a one-way fare is 4.60€ ($4.10). The main station, **Stazione San Giovanni,** Piazzale San Gottardo (✆ **848-888088**), lies at the end of Viale Gallio, a 15-minute walk from the center (Piazza Cavour).

The city of Como is 40km (25 miles) north of Milan; you can **drive** there via A9. Once at the Como, a small road (S583) leads to the popular resort of Bellagio.

GETTING AROUND   Bus service connecting the major towns along the lake is offered by **SPT,** Piazza Matteotti (*©* **031-247247**). A one-way fare from Como to the most popular resort of Bellagio is 2.20€ ($1.95). Travel time depends on the traffic.

COMO ⚜

At the southern tip of the lake, 40km (25 miles) north of Milan, Como is known for its silk industry. Most visitors at least pass through here to take a cruise on the lake (see below). But because Como is also an industrial city, this isn't the best place to stay (head instead to one of the more attractive resorts along the lake, such as Bellagio), unless you don't have your own car and are dependent on public transportation (in which case it's the most convenient base).

For centuries, the town's economy has been linked to Milan. Como has been making silk since Marco Polo first returned with silkworms from China (since the end of World War II, Como has left the cultivation of silk to the Chinese and just imports the thread to weave into fabrics). Como's silk makers are major suppliers for the fashion designers of Milan, and big names like Giorgio Armani and Bill Blass come here to discuss the patterns that they want with silk manufacturers.

ESSENTIALS
GETTING THERE   See "Lake Como Essentials," above.

VISITOR INFORMATION   The **tourist office** is at Piazza Cavour 17 (*©* **031-269712**), open Monday to Saturday 9am to 12:30pm and 2:30 to 6pm.

SPECIAL EVENTS   July's **Jazz & Co.** stages five concerts at Piazza San Federale. The tourist office will supply details.

SEEING THE SIGHTS
The heart of Como is **Piazza Cavour,** with its hotels, cafes, and steamers departing for lakeside resorts. Immediately to the west, the **Public Gardens (Giardini Pubblici)** make for a pleasant stroll, especially if you're heading for the **Tempio Voltiano,** Viale Marconi (*©* **031-574705**), which honors native son Alessandro Volta, the physicist and pioneer of electricity. The temple contains memorabilia of his life and experiments. It's open Tuesday to Sunday: April to September 10am to noon and 3 to 6pm, and October to March 10am to noon and 2 to 4pm. Admission costs 2.50€ ($2.25).

From Como, it's easy to take a cruise around the lake; boats departing from the town's piers make calls at every significant settlement along its shores. Stroll down to the **Lungo Lario,** adjacent to Piazza Cavour, and head to the ticket windows of the **Società Navigazione Lago di Como** (*©* **031-304060**). Between Easter and September, half a dozen ferries and almost as many high-speed hydrofoils embark for circumnavigations of the lake. One-way transit from Como to Colico at the northern end of the lake takes 4 hours by ferry and 90 minutes by hydrofoil, and includes stops at each of the towns en route. Transit each way costs 7€ to 10.10€ ($6.25–$9), depending on which boat you take. One-way transit between Como and Bellagio takes 2 hours by ferry and 45 minutes by hydrofoil,

Lake Como

and costs 5.50€ to 8.05€ ($4.90–$7.20) per person. There's no service from Como between October and Easter.

Note: Be warned in advance that much of your view will be obscured by mists thrown up by the hydrofoils, so if you're taking this ride primarily for the view, the slower, cheaper boat is preferable.

To get an overview, take the funicular at Lungolario Trieste (near the main beach at Villa Genio) to the top of **Brunante,** a hill overlooking Como and providing a panoramic view. Departures are every 30 minutes daily, costing 3.55€ ($3.15) round-trip.

The best swimming is at the **Lido Villa Olmo,** Via Cantoni (© **031-570968**), a pool adjoining a sandy stretch of beach for sunbathing. Admission is 6€ ($5.35), and it's open daily 9am to 6pm.

Because this lakeside city has such a thriving silk industry, there's great shopping for scarves, blouses, lingerie, and neckties. Before you buy, you might be interested in knowing more about the history and techniques of the silk indus-try; if that's the case, head for the **Museo Didatico della Sete,** Via Vallegio 3 (© 031-303180). Maintained by a local trade school, it displays antique weav-ing machines and memorabilia going back to the Renaissance concerning the world's most elegant fabric. The relatively expensive admission is 7.75€ ($6.90). It's open Tuesday to Friday 9am to noon and 3 to 6pm.

Not all the silk factories will sell retail to individuals, but the best of those that do are **Binda,** Viale Geno (© 031-303440), and **Martinetti,** Via Torriani 41 (© 031-269053).

Before rushing off on a boat for a tour of the lake, you might want to visit the **Cattedrale di Como** ⭐, Piazza del Duomo (© 031-265244). Construction began in the 14th century in the Lombard Gothic style and continued on through the Renaissance until the 1700s. Frankly, the exterior is more interest-ing than the interior. Dating from 1487, the exterior is lavishly decorated with statues, including those of Pliny the Elder (A.D. 23–79) and the Younger (A.D. 62–113), who one writer once called "the beautiful people of ancient Rome." Inside, look for the 16th-century tapestries depicting scenes from the Bible. The cathedral is open Monday to Saturday 7am to noon and 3 to 7pm.

On the other side of the Duomo lies the colorfully striped **Brolette** (town hall) and, adjoining it, the **Torre del Comune.** Both are from the 13th century.

If time remains, head down the main street, **Via Vittorio Emanuele,** where the five-sided **San Fedele** ⭐, a 12th-century church standing on Piazza San Fedele, rises 2 blocks south of the cathedral. It's known for its unusual pentago-nal apse and a doorway carved with "fatted" figures from the Middle Ages. Far-ther along, you come to the **Garibaldi National Unity Civic Museum (Museo Civico del Risorgimento Garibaldi),** Piazza Medaglie d'Oro Comasche (© 031-271343), the virtual attic of Como, displaying artifacts collected by the city from prehistoric times through World War II. The museum is open Tues-day to Sunday 9:30am to 1pm, and Tuesday to Saturday 9:30am to 12:30pm and 2 to 5pm. Admission is 2.50€ ($2.25).

The art museum of Como is of passing interest: The small **Pinacoteca Palazzo Volpi,** Via Diaz 84 (© 031-269869), has several old and wonderful paintings from the Middle Ages, most of which were taken from the monastery of Santa Margherita del Broletto. Two of the museum's best paintings are anony-mous: that of St. Sebastian riddled with arrows (though appearing quite resigned to the whole thing) and a moving *Youth and Death.* The museum is open Mon-day to Saturday 9:30am to 12:30pm and 2 to 5pm, and Sunday 10am to 1pm. Admission is 3.50€ ($3.15).

After the museum, continue down Via Giovio until you come to the **Porta Vittoria,** a gate from 1192 with five tiers of arches. A short walk away, passing through a dreary commercial area leads you to Como's most interesting church, the 11th-century **Sant'Abbondio** ⭐, a Romanesque gem. From Porta Vittoria, take Viale Cattaneo to Viale Roosevelt, turning left onto Via Sant'Abbondio on which the church stands. Because of its age, it was massively restored in the 19th century. Heavily frescoed, the church has five aisles.

WHERE TO STAY

Hotel Barchetta Excelsior ⭐   This first-class hotel is at the edge of the main square in the commercial section of town. Major additions have been made to the 1957 structure, including an upgrading of the guest rooms, which are com-fortably furnished, most with balconies overlooking the square and the lake. All of the small to medium-size accommodations are soundproof, and most have lake views; some are reserved for nonsmokers. A few of the spotless bathrooms are fitted with Jacuzzis. There's a parking lot behind the hotel, plus a covered garage about 45m (50 yd.) away.

Piazza Cavour 1, 22100 Como. © **031-3221**. Fax 031-302622. www.hotelbarchetta.com. 84 units. 139€–229€ ($124.15–$204.50) double; 242€–273€ ($216.10–$243.80) suite. Rates include buffet breakfast. AE, DC, MC, V. Parking 16.50€ ($14.75). **Amenities:** 2 restaurants; bar; room service; babysitting; laundry/dry cleaning. *In room:* A/C, TV, minibar, hair dryer, safe.

Hotel Metropole & Suisse *Value*   This hotel offers good value. Near the cathedral and the major square that fronts the lake, it's composed of three lower floors dating from around 1700, with upper floors added about 60 years ago. The guest rooms come in various shapes and sizes, rich with character for the most part. All are comfortable and most have lake views. A parking garage and the city marina are nearby.

Piazza Cavour 19, 22100 Como. © **031-269444**. Fax 031-300808. www.hotelmetropolesuisse.com. 71 units (showers only). 160€–184€ ($142.90–$164.30) double. Lower rates off-season. Buffet breakfast 24€ ($21.45). AE, DC, MC, V. Parking 12€ ($10.70). **Amenities:** Recommended restaurant (see below); lounge; sauna; room service; babysitting; laundry/dry cleaning. *In room:* A/C, TV, minibar, hair dryer, safe.

WHERE TO DINE

Ristorante Imbarcadero *🍴* LOMBARD/ITALIAN   Located near the edge of the lake, this restaurant is filled with a pleasing blend of carved Victorian chairs, panoramic windows, and potted palms. The summer terrace set up on the square is ringed with shrubbery and illuminated with evening candlelight. First-class ingredients are deftly handled by the kitchen. The chef makes his own tagliatelle, or you might want to order spaghetti with garlic, oil, and red pepper. The fish dishes are excellent, especially slices of sea bass with braised leek and aromatic vinegar and sage-flavored Como lake whitefish. Try the breaded veal cutlet Milanese style or breast of pheasant flavored with port and shallots. Desserts might include a parfait of almonds, hazelnuts, and apple sorbet flavored with Calvados.

In the Hotel Metropole & Suisse, Piazza Cavour 20. © **031-270166**. Reservations recommended. Main courses 12€–17.50€ ($10.70–$15.65); fixed-price menu 25€ ($22.35). AE, DC, MC, V. Daily 12:30–2:30pm and 7:30–10:30pm. Closed Jan 2–6.

CERNOBBIO 🌟🌟

Cernobbio, 5km (3 miles) northwest of Como and 53km (33 miles) north of Milan, is a small, chic resort frequented by wealthy Europeans, who come largely to check into its famous deluxe hotel, the 16th-century Villa d'Este. However, the town's idyllic setting on the lake is available to everyone, because there are a number of more affordable hotels as well. Call the tourist office for information about other options in the area.

The **tourist office** is at Via Regina 33B (© **031-510198**), open Monday to Saturday 9:30am to 12:30pm and 2:30 to 5:30pm; it's closed January.

WHERE TO STAY & DINE

Grand Hotel Villa d'Este 🌟🌟🌟   This is the grandest hotel on any of Italy's lakes. One of Europe's most legendary hotels, the Villa d'Este was built in 1568 as a lakeside home/pleasure pavilion for Cardinal Tolomeo Gallio. Designed in the neoclassical style by Pellegrino Pellegrini di Valsolda, it passed from owner to illustrious owner for 300 years until it was transformed into a hotel in 1873.

The hotel remains a kingdom unto itself, a splendid palace surrounded by 10 acres of some of the finest gardens in Italy. The interior lives up to the enthralling beauty of the grounds. The silken wall coverings of the Salon Napoleone were embroidered especially for the emperor's visit; the Canova Room includes a statue of Venus by Canova himself; and the Grand Ballroom is suitable for the most festive banquets. The frescoed ceilings, impeccable antiques, and attentive service create one of the world's most envied hotels. Each plush guest room is individually decorated with antiques. Some 34 of the hotel's 166 accommodations are in the Queen's Pavilion, an elegant annex built in 1856. The large marble bathrooms are beautifully appointed.

Via Regina 40, 22012 Cernobbio. ℂ 031-3481. Fax 031-348844. www.villadeste.it. 166 units. 410€–610€ ($366.15–$544.75) double; 660€–798€ ($589.40–$712.60) suite. Rates include breakfast. Spa packages available. AE, DC, MC, V. Closed Nov 15–Mar 1. Free parking. **Amenities:** 3 restaurants; 3 bars; disco; 2 pools; 8 tennis courts; squash court; health club with sauna and steam room; spa with massage and various treatments; watersports; concierge; limo service; salon; room service; babysitting; laundry. *In room:* A/C, TV, minibar, hair dryer, safe.

BELLAGIO ⟨★★★⟩

Sitting on a promontory at the point where Lake Como forks, 77km (48 miles) north of Milan and 29km (18 miles) northeast of Como, Bellagio is one of the prettiest towns in Europe. A sleepy veil hangs over the arcaded streets and little shops. Bellagio has attracted wealthy visitors, even royalty, for centuries (Leopold I of Belgium used to own the 18th-century Villa Giulia). It's not so aristocratic anymore, but it's still going strong as a thriving and lovely resort town, a 45-minute drive north of Como.

The **tourist office** is at Piazza della Chiesa 14 (ℂ **031-950204**). April to October, it's open daily 9am to noon and 3 to 6pm; November to March, hours are Monday and Wednesday to Saturday 8:30am to noon and 3 to 6pm.

SEEING THE SIGHTS

To reach many of the places in Bellagio, you must climb streets that are really stairways. Its lakeside promenade blossoms with flowering shrubbery. From the town, you can take tours of Lake Como, enjoy watersports and tennis, or just lounge at the **Bellagio Lido** (the beach).

You'll probably spend a lot of your time just sunbathing and enjoying that glorious lakeside scenery. Most of the lakefront hotels have their own swimming **beaches.** (The swimmable lakefront section that's maintained by the Grand Hotel Villa Serbelloni is especially well-maintained, but it's only for hotel guests.) Otherwise, you can walk 10 minutes north of the town center to swim in the lake at the free public facilities at **La Punta.** Anyone can rent either of the two **tennis courts,** for around 10€ ($8.95) an hour, at the Grand Hotel Villa Serbelloni, and you can visit that hotel's **fitness center** for a fee of around 15€ ($13.40).

If you're interested in a **boat tour,** in a motorized craft suitable for up to six passengers, **Ezio Giradone** (ℂ 031-950201) will take your group for rides on the lake, priced at around 100€ ($89.30) per hour.

Shoppers gravitate to the clusters of **boutiques** along the Salita Serbelloni and the Salita Mella, in the town center. And although there's not a lot of raucous nightlife in this quiet town, you can always hang out in a couple of bars: **La Divina Commedia,** on Salita Mella ℂ 031-951680, and **Inferno Divino,** on Salita Plinio (ℂ **031-951648** for both bars). Both sometimes have live music.

If you're in the mood for a little sightseeing, check out the **gardens of the Villa Serbelloni** , Piazza della Chiesa (© **031-950204**), the Bellagio Study and Conference Center of the Rockefeller Foundation (not to be confused with the Grand Hotel Villa Serbelloni by the waterside in the village). The landlord here used to be Pliny the Younger. The villa isn't open to the public, but you can visit the park on 1½-hour guided tours starting at 11am and 4pm. Tours are conducted mid-April to mid-October, Tuesday to Sunday, at a cost of 5€ ($4.45); the proceeds go to local charities.

There's also a garden at the **Villa Melzi Museum and Chapel,** Lungolario Marconi, which was built in 1808 for Duca Francesco Melzi d'Eril, vice president of the Italian republic founded by Napoleon. Franz Liszt and Stendhal are among the illustrious guests who've stayed here. The park has many well-known sculptures, and, if you're here in spring, you can enjoy the azaleas. Today it's the property of Conte Gallarti Scotti, who opens it April to October, daily 9am to 6pm. The museum contains a not-very-distinguished collection of Egyptian sculptures. Admission is 5€ ($4.45). For further information, contact the tourist office (see above).

From Como, car ferries sail back and forth across the lake to **Cadenabbia** on the western shore, another lakeside resort with hotels and villas. Directly south of Cadenabbia on the run to Tremezzo, the **Villa Carlotta** (© **0344-40405**) is the most-visited attraction on Lake Como, and with good reason. In a serene setting, the villa is graced with gardens of exotic flowers and blossoming shrubbery, especially rhododendrons and azaleas. Its beauty is tame, formal, and cultivated, indicative of the halcyon life available only to the very rich of the 19th century. Dating from 1847, the estate was named after a Prussian princess, Carlotta, who married the duke of Sachsen-Meiningen. Inside are a number of art treasures, including Canova's *Cupid and Psyche,* and neoclassical statues by Bertel Thorvaldsen, a Danish sculptor who died in 1844. There are also neoclassical paintings, furniture, and a stone-and-bronze table ornament that belonged to Viceroy Eugene Beauharnais. It's open daily: March and October from 9 to 11:30am and 2 to 4:30pm, and April to September from 9am to 6pm. Admission is 6.50€ ($5.80).

WHERE TO STAY & DINE

Grand Hotel Villa Serbelloni   This lavish old hotel is grand indeed. It stands proud at the edge of town against a backdrop of hills, surrounded by beautiful gardens. The public rooms rekindle the spirit of the baroque: a drawing room with a painted ceiling, marble columns, a glittering chandelier, gilt furnishings, and a mirrored neoclassical dining room. The guest rooms are wide-ranging, from elaborate suites with recessed tile bathrooms, baroque furnishings, and lake-view balconies to more simple quarters. The most desirable rooms open onto the lake. You can sunbathe on the waterside terrace or doze under a willow tree.

Via Roma 1, 22021 Bellagio. © **031-950216.** Fax 031-951529. www.villaserbelloni.com. 83 units. 300€–340€ ($267.90–$303.60) double; 560€–680€ ($500.10–$607.25) suite. Rates include buffet breakfast. AE, DC, MC, V. Parking 18€ ($16.05). Closed mid-Nov to Mar. **Amenities:** Formal gourmet restaurant (jacket required for men); lounges; pool; fitness center; Jacuzzi; sauna; children's center; concierge; salon; room service; massage; babysitting; laundry/dry cleaning. *In room:* A/C, TV, minibar, hair dryer, safe.

Hotel du Lac   This little charmer offers the most panoramic views of lake and mountain from its terraced roof garden. The Hotel du Lac was built 150 years ago, when the lake waters came up to the front door. Landfill has since created Piazza Mazzini, and today there's a generous terraced expanse of flagstones in front with cafe tables and an arched arcade. The guest rooms are comfortably furnished. You can bask in the sun or relax in the shade on the rooftop garden, opening onto panoramic views of the lake. The staff can help you arrange golf, watersports, and many local excursions.

Piazza Mazzini 32, 22021 Bellagio. ℂ 031-950320. Fax 031-951624. www.bellagiohoteldulac.com. 47 units (some with shower only). 185€ ($165.20) double. Rates include breakfast. MC, V. Parking 8.50€ ($7.60). Closed Nov–Mar. **Amenities:** Restaurant (with outdoor terrace); bar; access to nearby fitness center and spa; room service; laundry. *In room:* A/C, TV, minibar, hair dryer.

Hotel Florence   The entrance to this green-shuttered villa is under a vaulted arcade near the ferry landing. Wisteria climbs over the iron balustrades of the lake-view terraces, and the entrance hall's vaulted ceilings are supported by massive tim-bers and granite Doric columns. The main section was built around 1720, although most of what you see today was added around 1880. For 150 years, the Florence has been run by the Ketzlar family, and you'll probably be welcomed by the charming Roberta Ketzlar; her brother, Ronald; and their mother, Friedl. The guest rooms are scattered amid spacious sitting and dining areas and often have high ceilings, antiques, and lake views. All have excellent tiled bathrooms.

Piazza Mazzini 45, 22021 Bellagio. ℂ 031-950342. Fax 031-951722. 30 units. 140€–190€ ($125–$169.65) double; 210€–240€ ($187.55–$214.30) suite. Rates include breakfast. AE, DC, DISC, MC, V. Closed Nov–Mar. **Amenities:** Restaurant; bar; room service; laundry. *In room:* TV, hair dryer, safe.

TREMEZZO

Reached by frequent ferries from Bellagio, Tremezzo, 77km (48 miles) north of Milan and 29km (18 miles) north of Como, is another popular west-shore resort that opens onto a panoramic view of Lake Como. Around the town is a district known as Tremezzina, with lush citrus trees, palms, cypresses, and magnolias. Because Tremezzo lies in the middle of the western bank of Como, it's easy to use it as a base for taking scenic drives either to the north of the lake or all the way south to the city of Como. From here, it's also easy to visit Villa Carlotta (see under "Bellagio," above), but accommodations in Tremezzo are much more limited than those in Bellagio.

The **tourist office** is at Via Regina 3 (ℂ **0344-40493**). May to October, it's open Monday to Wednesday and Friday to Saturday 9am to noon and 3:30 to 6:30pm.

WHERE TO STAY

Grand Hotel Tremezzo Palace ★★   Built in 1910 on a terrace several feet above the lakeside road, this hotel is one of the region's best examples of the Ital-ian Liberty style. In 1990 most of it was discreetly modernized, with air-condi-tioning installed on two of the four floors (many guests still reject the air-conditioning in favor of the lakefront breezes). The high-ceilinged rooms are comfortable, traditionally furnished, and priced according to whether they have views of the lake (many of these have balconies) or the rear park and garden.

Via Regina 8, 22019 Tremezzo. ℂ 0344-42491. Fax 0344-40201. www.grandhoteltremezzo.com. 101 units. 193.50€–320€ ($172.80–$285.75) double; 425.50€–484€ ($379.95–$432.20) suite. Rates include break-fast. AE, DC, MC, V. Parking 15€ ($13.40) in a garage; free outside. Closed Nov 15–Feb. **Amenities:** 3 restau-rants; bar; 2 pools; tennis court; billiard room; fitness and beauty center; sauna; heliport; room service; babysitting; laundry. *In room:* A/C, TV, minibar, hair dryer, safe.

Hotel Bazzoni & du Lac ★ *Value*   This hotel is one of the best choices in a resort town filled with grand hotels that offer much less desirable guest rooms. There was an older hotel on this spot during Napoleon's era, but it was bombed by the British 5 days after the official end of World War II. Today the reconstructed hotel is a collection of glass-and-concrete walls, with prominent balconies. Rooms were renovated in 1999, with spruced-up bathrooms. The pleasantly furnished sitting rooms include antique architectural elements from older buildings. A summer restaurant near the entrance is constructed like a small island of glass walls.

Via Regina 26, 22019 Tremezzo. ℂ 0344-40403. Fax 0344-41651. 140 units. 95€–110€ ($84.85–$98.25) double. Rates include breakfast. AE, DC, MC, V. Closed Oct 10–Mar. Ferry from Bellagio or hydrofoil from Como. **Amenities:** 2 restaurants; bar; room service; babysitting; laundry. *In room:* TV, minibar, hair dryer, safe.

Hotel Villa Marie *Value* Enjoying a lakeside location, this intimate little villa will house you well at an affordable price. Guests look out over the lake from the chaise longues in the garden and later retreat to their homey bedrooms, most of which also have lake views. Beds are comfortable, and the bathrooms, though small, are well organized.

Via Regina 30, Tremezzo 20019. ℂ and fax 0344-40427. 13 units (showers only). 93€–110€ ($83.05–$98.25) double; 115€–130€ ($102.70–$116.10) suite. AE, DC, MC, V. Free parking. **Amenities:** Coffee bar; pool. *In room:* TV, minibar, hair dryer, safe.

Where to Stay Nearby

Grand Hotel Victoria *★★* Built in 1806, this is one of the best hotels on the lake. It has been renovated over the years, but lovely old touches remain, such as the ornate plasterwork of the ceiling vaults. The modern furniture and extras in the spacious guest rooms include bathroom tiling designed by Valentino. The beach in front of the hotel is one of the best spots on Lake Como for windsurfing, especially between 3 and 7pm. The staff can help you arrange tee times nearby.

Via Lungolago Castelli 7–11, 22017 Menaggio. ℂ 0344-32003. Fax 0344-32992. www.palacehotel.it. 53 units. 176€–210€ ($157.15–$187.55) double; from 230€ ($205.40) junior suite. Rates include breakfast. Half-board 31€ ($27.70) per person. AE, DC, MC, V. Free parking. **Amenities:** Restaurant (with an outdoor garden that often has live music); bar; pool; tennis court; private boat for guests; room service; babysitting; laundry. *In room:* A/C, TV, minibar, hair dryer, safe.

WHERE TO DINE

Al Veluu *★* LOMBARD/INTERNATIONAL Al Veluu, 1 mile north of the resort in the hills, is an excellent regional restaurant with plenty of relaxed charm and personalized attention from owner Carlo Antonini and his son, Luca. The terrace tables offer a panoramic sweep of the lake, and the rustic dining room with its fireplace and big windows is a welcome refuge in inclement weather. Most of the produce comes freshly picked from the garden; even the butter is homemade, and the best cheeses come from a local farmer. The menu is based on the flavorful cuisine of northern Italy. Examples are *missoltini* (dried fish from the lake, marinated, and grilled with olive oil and vinegar), *penne al Veluu* (with spicy tomato sauce), *risotto al Veluu* (with champagne sauce and fresh green peppers), and an unusual lamb paté.

Via Rogaro 11, Rogaro di Tremezzo. ℂ 0344-40510. Reservations recommended. Main courses 10€–17.50€ ($8.95–$15.65). AE, MC, V. Wed–Mon noon–2pm and 7:30–10pm. Closed Nov–Mar 15.

6 Lake Maggiore *★★*

The waters of Lake Maggiore wash up on the banks of Piedmont and Lombardy in Italy, but its more austere northern basin (Locarno, for example) lies in the mountainous region of Switzerland. It stretches more than 64km (40 miles) and is 10km (6¼ miles) at its widest. A wealth of natural beauty awaits you: mellowed lakeside villas, dozens of lush gardens, sparkling waters, and panoramic views. A veil of mist seems to hover at times, especially in early spring and late autumn.

Maggiore is a most rewarding lake to visit from Milan, especially because of the Borromean Islands in its center (most easily reached from Stresa). If you have time, drive around the entire basin; on a more limited schedule, you might find the resort-studded western shore the most scenic.

LAKE MAGGIORE ESSENTIALS

GETTING THERE   The major resort of the lake, Stresa, is just 1 hour by **train** from Milan on the Milan-Domodossola line. Service is every hour, costing 3.60€ to 7.50€ ($3.20–$6.70) one way, depending on the train. For information and schedules, call ✆ **848-888088.**

If you have a **car** and are in Milan, take an 82km (51-mile) drive northwest along A8 (staying on E62 out of Gallarate until it joins SS33 up the western shore of the lake) to Stresa.

GETTING AROUND   S33 goes up the west side of the lake to Verbania, where it becomes S34 on its way to the Swiss town of Locarno, about 40km (25 miles) away. If you want to drive around the lake, you'll have to clear Swiss Customs before passing through such famed resorts as Ascona and eventually Locarno. From Locarno you can head south again along the eastern, less touristy shore, which becomes SS493 on the Italy side. At Luino, you can cut off on SS233 and then A8 to return to Milan, or continue along the lakeshore (the road becomes SS629) to the southern point again, where you can get E62 back toward Milan.

Cruising Lake Maggiore on modern **boats** and fast **hydrofoils** is great fun. There's a frequent ferry service for cars and passengers between Intra (Verbania) and Laveno. Boats leave from Piazza Marconi along Corso Umberto I in Stresa. For boat schedules, contact the **Navigazione Sul Lago Maggiore,** Viale F. Baracca 1 (✆ **0322-46651**), in the lakeside town of Arona.

STRESA 𝕲𝕲

On the western shore, 655km (406 miles) northwest of Rome and 82km (51 miles) northwest of Milan, Stresa has skyrocketed from a simple village of fisherfolk to a first-class international resort. Its vantage on the lake is almost unparalleled, and its accommodations level is superior to that of other Maggiore resorts in Italy. The scene of sporting activities and an international **Festival of Musical Weeks** (beginning in July), it swings into action in April, stays hopping all summer, and then quiets down at the end of October. For information, call Settimane Musicali (✆ **0323-31095** or 0323-30459).

The **tourist office** is at Via Principe Tommaso 70–72 (✆ **0323-30416**). It's open Monday to Friday from 9am to 6pm from June to September; in other months, hours are 9am to noon and 3 to 6:30pm.

Near the resort of Pallanza, north of Stresa, the **Botanical Gardens (Giardini Botanici) at Villa Taranto** 𝕲𝕲, Via Vittorio Veneto 111, Verbania-Pallanza (✆ **0323-556667**), spread over more than 50 acres of the Castagnola Promontory jutting out into Lake Maggiore. In this dramatic setting between the mountains and the lake, more than 20,000 species of plants from all over the world thrive in a cultivated institution begun in 1931 by a Scotsman, Capt. Neil McEacharn. Plants range from rhododendrons and azaleas to specimens from such faraway places as Louisiana. Seasonal exhibits include fields of Dutch tulips (80,000 of them), Japanese magnolias, giant water lilies, cotton plants, and rare varieties of hydrangeas. The formal gardens are carefully laid out with ornamental fountains, statues, and reflection pools. Among the more ambitious creations is the elaborate irrigation system that pumps water from the lake to all parts of the gardens and the Terrace Gardens, complete with waterfalls and pool. From March 28 to October 31, the gardens are open daily 8:30am to 6:30pm. To arrange an hour-long guided tour (groups only), contact the **Palazzo dei Congressi di Stresa** (© **0323-30389**). You also can take a round-trip **boat ride** from Stresa, docking at the Villa Taranto pier adjoining the entrance to the gardens. You pay an admission of 6.50€ ($5.80).

WHERE TO STAY

Albergo Ariston *Value*   Here's a good bargain. The hotel is listed as third class by the government, but it's quite comfortable. The small guest rooms are well kept and attractively furnished, each containing a well-kept bathroom. Nonguests can stop in for a meal and order lunch or dinner on the terrace, which has a panoramic view of the lake and gardens. Your hosts are the Balconi family.

Corso Italia 60, 28838 Stresa. © and fax **0323-31195.** 11 units (showers only). 80€ ($71.45) double. Rates include breakfast. Half-board 40€ ($35.70) per person. AE, DC, MC, V. Free parking. Closed Dec–Mar. **Amenities:** Restaurant; bar; room service; babysitting; laundry/dry cleaning. *In room:* No phone.

Grand Hotel des Iles Borromées 𝒜𝒜   On the edge of the lake in a flowering garden, this is by far Stresa's leading resort hotel. You can see the Borromean Islands from many rooms, which are furnished in an Italian/French Empire style, including rich ormolu, burnished hardwoods, plush carpets, and pastel colors. The bathrooms look as if every quarry in Italy were scoured for matched marble. The hotel opened in 1863, attracting titled notables and guests such as J. P. Morgan. Hemingway sent the hero of *A Farewell to Arms* here to escape World War I. The elegant public rooms, with two-tone ornate plasterwork and crystal chandeliers, once hosted a top-level meeting among the heads of state of Italy, Great Britain, and France in an attempt to stave off World War II. The hotel also operates a 27-room Residenza in a separate building, where the prices are 20% lower and the rooms are decorated in a modern style. The staff can help you arrange for golf and watersports.

Corso Umberto I 67, 28838 Stresa. © **0323-938938.** Fax 0323-93832405. www.borromees.it. 175 units. 286€–352€ ($255.40–$314.35) double; 364€ ($325.05) junior suite; from 545€ ($486.70) suite. Rates include breakfast. AE, DC, MC, V. Free parking. **Amenities:** Restaurant; piano bar; 2 pools; tennis court; fitness room; spa; sauna; concierge; heliport; room service; babysitting; laundry. *In room:* A/C, TV, minibar, hair dryer, safe.

Hotel Astoria 𝒜   Its flower gardens and roof garden with solarium are reason enough to attract you here. A 5-minute walk from the rail station or the center of Stresa, this hotel fronting the lake was partially rebuilt in 1993, giving an even more modern gloss to a contemporary hotel. Each room has a triangular balcony jutting out for the view. The rooms are streamlined and spacious.

Corso Umberto I 31, 28838 Stresa. © **0323-32566.** Fax 0323-933785. www.stresa.net/hotel/astoria. 99 units. 186€ ($166.10) double; 212€ ($189.30) suite. Rates include breakfast. AE, DC, MC, V. Parking 5.20€ ($4.65). Closed late Oct to Mar. **Amenities:** Restaurant; lounge; pool; gym; Jacuzzi; sauna; room service; babysitting; laundry/dry cleaning. *In room:* A/C, TV, minibar, hair dryer, safe.

Hotel Moderno   A block from the lake and boat-landing stage, the Moderno lies in the center of Stresa. It dates from the turn of the 20th century, but renovations have rendered the building's original lines unrecognizable. The small guest rooms have a personalized decor, good beds, and compact bathrooms.

Via Cavour 33, 28838 Stresa. © **0323-933773.** Fax 0323-933775. www.hms.it. 52 units (with shower only). 115€ ($102.70) double. Rates include breakfast. AE, DC, MC, V. Parking 9€ ($8.05). Closed Nov–Mar. **Amenities:** 3 restaurants; room service; babysitting; laundry. *In room:* TV, hair dryer.

Hotel Villa Aminta ✿   Right across from Isola Bella (see below), this hotel is much valued by lake-loving aficionados. Offering gracious hospitality, it lies only a few minutes' drive from the center. Unlike Grand Hotel des Iles Borromées, which is on the main shore drive, Villa Aminta stands above the drive. Rooms range from midsize to spacious, each tastefully and comfortably decorated. The highest-priced units are those with lake views (as opposed to garden views). The public rooms are splendidly decorated, and the staff at the villa enjoys a deserved reputation for its fine cuisine. The staff can help you arrange for nearby golf, horseback riding, and hiking.

Via Sempione Nord 123, 28838 Stresa. ✆ **0323-933818.** Fax 0323-933955. www.villa-aminta.it. 68 units. 212€ ($189.30) double; from 254€ ($226.80) suite. AE, DC, MC. V. Closed Nov–Feb. **Amenities:** Well-regarded restaurant; coffee shop; pool; tennis court; room service; babysitting; laundry/dry cleaning. *In room:* A/C, TV, minibar, hair dryer, safe.

Regina Palace ✿   We prefer the Grand Hotel des Iles Borromées, but this lakeside palace is still a wonderful choice, especially for traditionalists. The Regina was built in 1908 in a boomerang shape, with a central curve facing the lakefront. Inside, the Art Deco columns of illuminated glass are topped with gilded Corinthian capitals, and a wide marble stairwell is flanked with carved oak lions. The guest roster has included George Bernard Shaw, Ernest Hemingway, Umberto I of Italy, and Princess Margaret. Lately, about half of the guests are American, many with the tour groups that stream through town. The rooms are equipped with all the modern comforts. Many have views of the Borromean Islands.

Corso Umberto I 33, 28049 Stresa. ✆ **0323-936936.** Fax 0323-933776. www.regina-palace.it. 166 units. 350€ ($312.55) double; from 450€ ($401.85) suite. Rates include breakfast. AE, DC, MC, V. Parking 12.50€ ($11.15) in garage; free outside. **Amenities:** 2 restaurants; piano bar; pool; tennis court; 2 squash courts; Jacuzzi; Turkish bath; concierge; room service; laundry. *In room:* A/C, TV, minibar, hair dryer, safe.

WHERE TO DINE

Ristorante Triangolo ✿ NORTHERN ITALIAN   Outside the hotels, this is one of the finest dining choices. At one time or another, almost every middle-class family in Stresa has dined at this popular trattoria. It is pleasant and homey with a helpful though not very articulate staff. Dishes are prepared from time-tested recipes, and nothing served taxes the imagination of the chef. But what you get is very good, especially the oven-grilled salmon served with fresh vegetables and the filet steak with porcini mushrooms. We've found that their Lombard veal dishes are always worthy choices. Every day special dishes are offered—you might want to ask about them—and the menu is frequently changed and always adjusted to take advantage of any season's harvest.

Via Roma 61. ✆ **0323-32736.** Reservations recommended. Main courses 14€–17€ ($12.50–$15.20). AE, DC, MC, V. Wed–Mon noon–2pm and 7–10pm. Closed Dec.

Taverna del Pappagallo *Value* ITALIAN/PIZZA   This formal little garden restaurant and tavern is operated by the Ghiringhelli brothers, who turn out some of the least expensive meals in Stresa. Specialties include gnocchi, many types of scaloppine, *scalamino allo spiedo e fagioli* (grilled sausage with beans), and *saltimbocca alla romana* (a veal-and-prosciutto dish). At night, pizza is king (try the pizza Regina). The service has a personal touch.

Via Principessa Margherita 46. ✆ **0323-30411.** Reservations recommended. Main courses 9€–12.50€ ($8.05–$11.15); pizzas 4€–10€ ($3.55–$8.95). AE, MC, V. Thurs–Mon 11:30am–2:30pm and 6:30–10:30pm.

THE BORROMEAN ISLANDS ★★

In the middle of Lake Maggiore lie the **Borromean Islands,** a chain of tiny islands that were turned into sites of lavish villas and gardens by the Borromeo clan. Boats leave from Stresa about every 30 minutes in summer, and the trip takes 3 hours. The **navigation offices** at Stresa's center port (✆ **0323-30393**) are open daily 7am to 7pm. The best deal is to buy an excursion ticket for 9.50€ ($8.50) entitling you to go back and forth to all three islands during the day.

Dominating the **Isola Bella (Beautiful Island)** ★★★ is the major sight: the 17th-century **Borromeo Palazzo** (✆ **0323-30556**). From the front, the figurines in the garden seem straight off the top of a wedding cake. Napoleon slept here. On conducted tours, you're shown through the airy palace, whose views are remarkable. A special feature is the six grotto rooms, built piece by piece like a mosaic. In addition, there's a collection of quite good tapestries, with gory, cannibalistic animal scenes. Outside, the white peacocks in the garden enchant year after year. From March 27 to October 24, the palace and its grounds are open daily 9am to noon and 1:30 to 5:30pm. Admission is 8.50€ ($7.60).

The largest of the chain, the **Isola Madre (Mother Island)** ★★ is visited chiefly for its **Botanical Garden (Orto Botanico).** You wander through a setting ripe with pomegranates, camellias, wisteria, rhododendrons, bougainvillea, hibiscus, hydrangea, magnolias, and even a cypress tree from the Himalayas. You can also visit the 17th-century **palace** (✆ **0323-31261**), which contains a rich collection of 17th- and 18th-century furnishings. Of particular interest is a collection of 19th-century French and German dolls belonging to Countess Borromeo and the livery of the House of Borromeo. The unique 18th-century marionette theater, complete with scripts, stage scenery, and devices for sound, light, and other special effects, is on display. Peacocks, pheasants, and other birds live and roam freely on the grounds. From March 27 to October 24, the palace is open daily 9am to 12:30pm and 1:30 to 5:30pm. Admission to the palace and grounds is 8€ ($7.15).

The **Isola del Pescatori (Fisher's Island)** ★ doesn't have major sights or lavish villas, but in many ways it's the most colorful. Less a stage setting than its two neighbors, it's inhabited by fisherfolk who live in cottages that haven't been converted to souvenir shops. It's a lovely place for a stroll.

12

Piedmont & Valle d'Aosta

Towering snowcapped alpine peaks; oleander, poplar, and birch trees; sky-blue lakes; river valleys and flowering meadows; the chamois and the wild boar; medieval castles; Roman ruins and folklore; the taste of vermouth on home ground; Fiats and fashion—northwestern Italy is a fascinating area to explore.

The Piedmont (Piemonte) is largely agricultural, though its capital, Turin, is one of Italy's front-ranking industrial cities (with more mechanics per square foot than any other location in Europe). The influence of France is strongly felt, both in the dialect and in the kitchen.

The Valle d'Aosta (really a series of valleys) traditionally has been associated with Piedmont, but in 1948 it was given wide-ranging autonomy. Most of the residents in this least-populated district of Italy speak French. Closing in Valle d'Aosta to the north on the French and Swiss borders are the tallest mountains in Europe, including Mont Blanc (4,809m/ 15,780 ft.), the Matterhorn (4,478m/ 14,690 ft.), and Monte Rosa (4,633m/15,200 ft.). The road tunnels of Great St. Bernard and Mont Blanc (opened in 1965) connect France and Italy.

1 Turin ★★

225km (140 miles) SW of Milan, 174km (108 miles) NW of Genoa, 667km (414 miles) NW of Rome

In Turin (Torino), the capital of Piedmont, the Italian Risorgimento (unification movement) was born. While the United States was fighting its Civil War, Turin became the first capital of a unified Italy, a position that it later lost to Florence. Turin was once the capital of Sardinia. Much of the city's history is associated with the House of Savoy, a dynasty that reigned for 9 centuries, even presiding over the kingdom of Italy when Vittorio Emanuele II was proclaimed king in 1861. The family ruled, at times in name only, until the monarchy was abolished in 1946.

In spite of extensive bombings, Turin found renewed prosperity after World War II, largely because of the Fiat manufacturers based here (it has been called the Detroit of Italy). Many buildings were destroyed, but much of its 17th- and 18th-century look remains. Located on the Po River, Turin is well laid out, with wide streets, historic squares, churches, and parks. For years it has had a reputation as the least-visited and least-known of Italy's major cities, but it has become an increasingly dynamic center for industry and the arts.

Turin's biggest draw, the **Cattedrale di San Giovanni,** home to the **Shroud of Turin,** was damaged by fire in 1997. The Chapel of the Holy Shroud, where the silver reliquary that protects the controversial Christian symbol is usually on display, and the west wing of the neighboring Royal Palace sustained most of the damage. Luckily, the shroud had been moved into the cathedral itself because the dome of its chapel was being renovated.

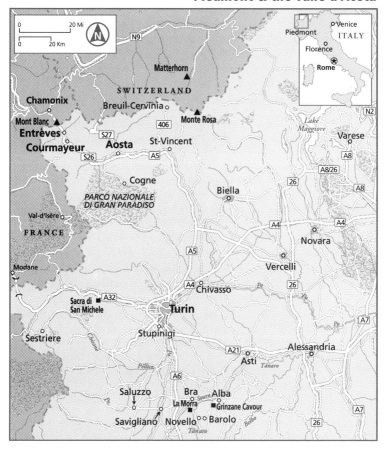

Turin is one of Italy's richest cities, with some million Turinese, many of whom are immigrants who came here to get a piece of the pie. This "Car Capital of Italy" (also now home to high-tech and aerospace industries) is surrounded by some hideous suburbs that are ever-growing, but its Crocietta district is home to some of the most aristocratic residences in Italy, and its inner core is one of grace and harmony. Gianni Agnelli, heir to the Fiat fortune, international playboy extraordinaire, and one of Italy's most influential power brokers, lives in Turin. The city was also once the home of Antonio Gramsci, who staged "occupations" of the Fiat factory and later helped found the Italian Communist Party before dying in a Fascist prison. On a cultural note, Turin is the center of modern Italian writing; it was here that such major authors as Primo Levi, Cesare Pavese, and Italo Calvino were first published. Major exhibitions and shows are being booked all the time.

Note that Turin has been named as the host city for the **Olympic Winter Games** in the year 2006. You can get details on the upcoming event at **www.torino2006.it**. Turin will host the opening and closing ceremonies, the Olympic Village, and the press operations, as well as some of the events. Other events, such as downhill skiing, will be held in small towns just outside Turin.

ESSENTIALS

GETTING THERE   Alitalia flies into the **Caselle International Airport** (Aeroporto Internazionale di Caselle; © **011-5676361**), about 14km (8½ miles) north of Turin. It receives direct scheduled flights from 22 cities (7 domestic and 15 from major European centers); it's used by 13 scheduled carriers operating regular flights. Its Air Passenger Terminal is one of Europe's most technologically advanced structures, capable of handling up to three million passengers a year.

Turin is a major **rail** terminus, with arrivals at **Stazione di Porta Nuova,** Corso Vittorio Emanuele (© **011-531327**), or **Stazione Centrale,** Corso Vittorio Emanuele II (© **011-534435**), in the heart of the city. It takes 1¼ hours to reach Turin by train from Milan, but it takes anywhere from 9 to 11 hours to reach Turin from Rome, depending on the connection. The one-way fare from Milan is 26€ ($23.20); from Rome, 63€ ($56.25).

By car from France via the Mont Blanc Tunnel, you can pick up the autostrada (A5) at Aosta. You can also reach Turin by autostrada from both the French and the Italian Rivieras, and there's an easy link from Milan.

VISITOR INFORMATION   Go to the office of **APT,** Piazza Castello 161 (© **011-535181**), open Monday to Saturday 9:30am to 7pm, and Sunday 9:30am to 3pm. There's another office at the Porta Nuova train station (© **011-531327**), open the same hours.

SPECIAL EVENTS   Turin stages two major cultural fests every year: the **Extra Iorino Festival** in July, with programs devoted to dance, music, and film; and the month-long **Settembre Musica** in September, with dozens of classical music performances in various parts of the city. For details about these festivals, contact the **Assesorato per la Cultura,** Via San Francisco di Paolo 3 (© **011-4424715**).

EXPLORING THE CITY

One of Turin's main arteries is **Corso Vittorio Emanuele II.** The railway station is on this boulevard; follow it east for half a mile and you'll reach the Po River. Turin is also a city of fashion; and you might want to walk along the major shopping street, **Via Roma,** which begins north of the station and leads eventually to two squares that join each other, **Piazza Castello** and **Piazza Reale.**

In the middle of Via Roma is **Piazza San Carlo** ✦✦, the heartbeat of Turin. Begin your explorations here. Although it was heavily bombed during World War II, it's still the loveliest and most unified square in the city. Designed by Carlo di Castellamonte in the 17th century, it covers about 3½ acres. Some of the most prestigious figures in Italy once sat on this square, sipping coffee and plotting the unification of Italy. The two churches are **Santa Cristina** and **San Carlo.**

ATM, the Public Transportation Company of Turin, offers a **"Touristbus"** that takes visitors around the city with a guide. Tours depart from Piazza Castello and last 2 hours. For information, call ATM (© **800-019152** toll-free in Italy), or visit the ATM center at Stazione Porta Nuova (the railway station) Monday to Saturday 7:15am to 7pm, and Sunday 10am to 4:30pm. Tickets cost 6€ ($5.35); tours are Wednesday to Monday at 2:30pm.

Cattedrale di San Giovanni & the Holy Shroud ✦   This Renaissance cathedral, dedicated to John the Baptist, was swept by fire on April 12, 1997, with major damage sustained by Guarini's **Chapel of the Holy Shroud (Cappella della Santissima Sindone)** ✦✦✦, the usual resting place of the relic in

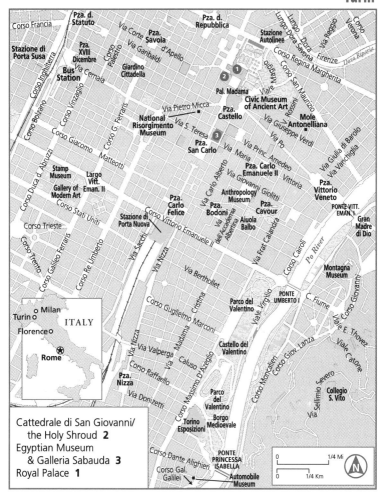

Cattedrale di San Giovanni/
the Holy Shroud **2**
Egyptian Museum
& Galleria Sabauda **3**
Royal Palace **1**

which Jesus Christ was supposedly wrapped after his crucifixion (see "The Mystery of Turin's Holy Shroud," below). Fortunately, the shroud itself was undamaged. The shroud made world headlines in 1998 when it was put on public display for the first time in 20 years. At its unveiling for only the fourth time in this century, on the occasion of the cathedral's 500th anniversary, some three million pilgrims traveled to Turin to see it. Most visitors to the cathedral must content themselves with a series of dramatically backlit photos of the relic near the entrance. The chapel is somberly clad in black marble, but, as if to suggest that better things await in the heavens, it ascends to an airy, light-flooded, six-tiered dome, one of the masterpieces of Italian baroque architecture.

The shroud is rarely on view. It's usually tucked away at the **Holy Shroud Museum (Museo della Santissima Sindone),** Via San Domenico 28 (© **011-4365832**), a small, dusty library/research center near the cathedral that's open only to scholars and church officials.

Piazza San Giovanni. © **011-4360790.** Admission 5€ ($4.45). Daily 9am–noon and 3–7pm. Bus: 63.

Egyptian Museum (Museo Egizio) & Galleria Sabauda 🌟🌟 Two interesting museums are housed in the Guarini-designed 17th-century Science Academy Building. The collection of the **Egyptian Museum** is world-class. Of the statuary, those of Ramses II and Amenhotep II are best known. A room nearby contains a rock temple consecrated by Thutmose III in Nubia. In the crowded wings upstairs, the world of the pharaohs lives on—one of the prized exhibits is the Royal Papyrus, with its valuable chronicle of the Egyptian monarchs from the 1st to the 17th dynasty. The funerary art is exceptionally rare and valuable, especially the chapel built for Maia and his young wife, and an entirely reassembled tomb (of Kha and Merit, 18th dynasty), discovered in good condition at the turn of the 20th century.

Galleria Sabauda presents one of Italy's richest art collections, acquired over a period of centuries by the House of Savoy. The largest exhibit is of Piedmontese masters, but there are many fine examples of Flemish art as well. Of the latter, the best-known painting is Sir Anthony Van Dyck's *Three Children of Charles I.* Other important works are Botticelli's *Venus,* Memling's *Passion of Christ,* Rembrandt's *Sleeping Old Man,* Duccio's *Virgin and Child,* Mantegna's *Holy Conversation,* Jan van Eyck's *The Stigmata of Francis of Assisi,* Veronese's *Dinner in the House of the Pharisee,* Bellotto's *Views of Turin,* intriguing paintings by Brueghel, and a section of the royal collections between 1730 and 1832.

In the Palazzo dell'Accademia delle Scienze, Via Accademia delle Scienze 6. 🕿 **011-5617776** (Egyptian Museum) or 011-547440 (Galleria Sabauda). Egyptian Museum 6€ ($5.35). Galleria Sabauda 4€ ($3.55). Both museums 7.80€ ($6.95). Egyptian Museum and Galleria Tues–Sun 8:30am–7pm. Both closed Jan 1 and Dec 25. Tram: 18.

Royal Palace (Palazzo Reale) The palace that the Savoys called home was begun in 1645. The halls, the columned ballroom by Palagi, the tea salon, and the Queen's Chapel are richly baroque in style. The original architect was Amedeo de Castellamonte, but numerous builders supplied ideas and effort before the palazzo was completed. As in nearly all ducal residences of that period, the most bizarre room is the one bedecked with flowering chinoiserie.

The Throne Room is of interest, as is the tapestry-draped Banqueting Hall. Le Nôtre, the famous Frenchman, mapped out the gardens, which also may be visited along with the Royal Armory (*Armeria Reale*), containing a large collection of arms and armor and many military mementos. Guided tours are offered (in Italian only) every 40 minutes.

The west wing of the palace was damaged when fire spread through the chapel of the neighboring cathedral in 1997. Restoration of this wing could take years.

Piazza Castello. 🕿 **011-4361455.** Admission 6.50€ ($5.80). Tues–Sun 8:30am–6:30pm. Bus: 63.

SHOPPING

The most adventurous shopping is at the **Gran Balôn,** an old-fashioned flea market set up every second Sunday in Piazza della Repubblica (northwest of Piazza Castello).

Some of the best-known drinks in the world are produced in Torino. For the best sampling, head for **Paissa,** Piazza San Carlo 196 (🕿 **011-5628364**), where, among the wine and food items available, you'll find the best deals on Cinzano and Martini & Rossi vermouths.

The Mystery of Turin's Holy Shroud

One of the world's greatest mysteries, the **Santissima Sindone (Holy Shroud)** is the most famous and controversial religious artifact on Earth. The shroud is said to be the one that Joseph of Arimathea wrapped around the body of Christ when he was removed from the cross.

This 3.5m (4-yd.) length of linen reveals, in almost photographic detail, the agonized features of a man who suffered crucifixion. The face of the bearded man is complete with a crown of thorns, and the marks of a thonged whip and bruises are compatible with the torment of carrying a cross. No one has successfully put forth a scientific explanation as to why the imprints of the man on the cloth exist or even how its image became impregnated in the threads. Photography, of course, was centuries away from being invented.

Turin didn't always possess this relic. First mentioned in the Gospel of Matthew, the shroud disappeared in history until it mysteriously "turned up" in Cyprus, centuries after the death of Christ. From Cyprus, it was taken to France, where it was first exhibited in 1354 and immediately denounced as a fraud by a French bishop. In 1578, the shroud was acquired by Duca Emanuele Filiberto, of the House of Savoy, who took it to Turin.

For centuries, the church didn't allow scientists to conduct dating tests of the shroud. The first scientific testing suggested that it was a fraud, probably from the 12th century. In 1988, three teams of scientists (from the United States, Britain, and Italy) each announced that the shroud was a clever forgery, and they estimated the time frame of its fabrication as between 1260 and 1390. Recent findings, however, propose a much earlier dating. Using calculations based on the fact that the shroud was involved in a fire in the 16th century, scientists now say that the shroud is roughly 1,800 years old—a date that could realistically make it the shroud of Christ. In 1997, Avinoam Danin, a plant expert at the University of Jerusalem, analyzed threads from the linen and detected traces of pollen in the flax. This pollen was believed to have dropped into the linen from flowers laid on the shroud. Danin stated that some of those species are found only in the Middle East.

The archbishop of Turin has presented the shroud to the Holy See, and the fact that the Vatican accepted it as a holy relic has increased some world belief in its validity. However, the Vatican has refrained from pronouncing it "the true shroud." The shroud remains encased in a silver casket. Only two keys can unlock the casket, one held by the archbishop of Turin and the other held by the Palatine cardinals, church seniors who are based permanently in the Vatican. The key unlocks only the casket—not the mystery of the shroud.

WHERE TO STAY

Like Milan, Turin is an industrial city first and a tourist center second. Most of its hotels were built after 1945 with an eye toward modern comfort but not necessarily style. Turin also has its own central hotel reservation website, **www.hotelres.it**, with links to many accommodations throughout the city.

EXPENSIVE

Jolly Hotel Principi di Piemonte ★★   A favorite of Fiat executives, this 10-story hotel is in the city center, near the rail station. It dates from 1939, but some of Italy's finest architects and designers were involved in its wholesale revamping. The public rooms are grand, with bas-relief ceilings, gold wall panels, silk draperies, Louis XVI–style chairs, and baroque marble sideboards. The guest rooms, medium-size to spacious, are traditionally furnished and perfectly maintained, containing fine draperies and spreads, upholstered chairs, and generous storage space.

Via Gobetti 15, 10123 Torino. ☎ **800/221-2626** or 800/247-1277 in the U.S., or 011-5577111. Fax 011-5620270. www.jollyhotels.it. 107 units. 208€–235€ ($185.75–$209.85) double; from 302€ ($269.70) suite. Rates include breakfast. AE, DC, MC, V. Parking 17.50€ ($15.65). Bus: 9. **Amenities:** Restaurant; bar; concierge; room service; babysitting; laundry/dry cleaning. *In room:* A/C, TV, minibar, hair dryer.

Relais Villa Sassi ★★   For peace and quiet, head to this 17th-century-style estate 6km (3¾ miles) east of the town center, surrounded by park grounds. The impressive original architectural details are still intact, like the entrance hall's wooden staircase. The drawing room features an overscale mural and life-size baroque figures holding bronze torchiers. The intimate drinking salon has red-velvet walls, a bronze chandelier, and low, cushioned seating. Each guest room has been individually decorated with antiques and reproductions, plus perfectly kept bathrooms. The manager sees that the hotel is run in a personal way.

Via Traforo del Pino 47, 10132 Torino. ☎ **011-8980556.** Fax 011-8980095. www.villasassi.com. 16 units (most with shower only). 217€ ($193.80) double; 260€ ($232.20) junior suite. Rates include breakfast. AE, DC, MC, V. Closed Aug. Tram: 15. Bus: 61. **Amenities:** Restaurant; lounge; room service; laundry. *In room:* A/C, TV, minibar, hair dryer, safe.

MODERATE

Hotel Due Mondi *Value*   Located off Corso Vittorio Emanuele and within walking distance of the railway station and many restaurants, this little hotel is near the top for those seeking old-fashioned yet affordable grace. Everything is smartly outfitted, often in dark patterns and woods. The best rooms are those on the third and fourth floors because they have been recently renewed. The bathrooms are well equipped, with a shower and a little private sauna in each.

Via Saluzzo 3, 10125 Torino. ☎ **011-6505084.** Fax 011-6699383. www.hotelduemondi.it. 42 units. 93€–139€ ($83.05–$124.15) double. Rates include buffet breakfast. AE, DC, MC, V. Closed Aug 10–20. Bus: 52. Tram: 1 or 9. **Amenities:** Lounge; sauna; room service; laundry/dry cleaning. *In room:* A/C, TV, minibar, hair dryer, safe.

Hotel Genio   Built at the end of the 19th century, this four-story hotel stands in the center of town. It was renovated and modernized in 1990, and now contains a comfortable blend of contemporary and early-20th-century furniture. Double-paned windows make the rooms soundproof. They're small but reasonably comfortable, each with a compact bathroom.

Corso Vittorio Emanuele II 47, 10125 Torino. ☎ **011-6505771.** Fax 011-6508264. 120 units. 134€–165€ ($119.65–$147.35) double; 230€ ($205.40) junior suite. Rates include breakfast. AE, DC, MC, V. Parking 15€ ($13.40). Bus: 9 or 18. Tram: 4, 9, 12, or 18. **Amenities:** Bar; room service; babysitting; laundry/dry cleaning. *In room:* A/C, TV, minibar, hair dryer.

Hotel Piemontese   The Piemontese is in a 19th-century building near the railway station, its facade covered with iron balconies and ornate stone trim. The guest rooms range from small to medium, and half of them were renovated in 2001. All are somewhat functionally furnished but equipped with all the standard comforts. Bathrooms are a bit on the small side. Breakfast, taken in a sunny room, is the only meal served, but there are lots of restaurants nearby.

Via Berthollet 21, 10125 Torino. (C) **011-6698101.** Fax 011-6690571. 37 units. 113€–135€ ($100.90–$120.55) double; 150€ ($133.95) suite. Rates include breakfast. AE, DC, MC, V. Parking 7.50€ ($6.70). Tram: 1, 9, or 18. **Amenities:** Lounge; access to nearby sports center with a pool; room service; laundry. *In room:* A/C, TV, minibar, hair dryer, safe.

Victoria Hotel ☆ *Value* One of the city's best bargains, this worthy selection lies between the river and Via Roma. In honor of its namesake, it evokes a bit of the aura of a British manor. You'll think you're back in Devon as you sink in the public living room with its soft armchairs and floral print couches, opening onto a garden. The rooms come in various sizes with individualized decor, each with a midsize bathroom. In the more luxurious bedrooms, you get antiques and canopied beds, but even the standard rooms are well furnished and inviting.

Via Nino Costa 4, 10123 Torino. (C) **011-5611909.** Fax 011-5611806. www.hotelvictoria-torino.com. 98 units. 140€–157€ ($125–$140.20) double. AE, DC, MC, V. Rates include breakfast. Bus: 15. **Amenities:** Coffee shop; room service; babysitting; laundry/dry cleaning. *In room:* A/C, TV, minibar, hair dryer.

INEXPENSIVE

Hotel Dogana Vecchia ☆☆ *Finds* This one is a bit funky but fun. The Dogana Vecchia was built in the 17th century as the headquarters of the postal service. It was later converted to an inn, playing host to the likes of Verdi, Mozart, and Napoleon. The wood-paneled hall continues to evoke the Turin of a century ago. Today, you'll find midsize to spacious bedrooms, each recently renovated and rather charming, despite the faux baroque furnishings. The staff is the most helpful we've encountered in the city.

Via Corte D'Appello 4, 10122 Torino. (C) **011-4366752.** Fax 011-4367194. www.ibow.com/DoganaVecchia/english.html. 50 units (showers only). 110€ ($98.25) double; 135€ ($120.55) triple. Rates include breakfast. AE, DC, MC, V. Bus: 63. Tram: 4. **Amenities:** Bar; room service; laundry/dry cleaning. *In room:* TV, minibar.

WHERE TO DINE
EXPENSIVE

Del Cambio ☆☆ PIEDMONTESE/MEDITERRANEAN At Del Cambio, you dine in a setting of white-and-gilt walls, crystal chandeliers, and gilt mirrors. Opened in 1757, it's the oldest restaurant in Turin. Statesman Camillo Cavour was a loyal patron, and his regular corner is immortalized with a bronze medallion. The chef, who has received many culinary honors, features white truffles in many of his specialties. The assorted fresh antipasti are excellent; the best pasta dish is the regional *agnolotti piemontesi.* Among the main dishes, the agnolotti with truffles and the beef braised in Barolo wine deserve special praise. Some trademark specialties are derived from old recipes of the southwestern Alps: artichokes stewed with bone marrow and truffles, *girello aromatizzato alla piemontese* (flank steak marinated in sugar, salt, and aromatic herbs, then sliced paper-thin and served with *parmigiano* and vegetables), and *tonno di coniglio à la manière antica* (rabbit).

Piazza Carignano 2. (C) **011-543760.** Reservations required. Main courses 16€–20€ ($14.30–$17.85); fixed-price menu 57.50€ ($51.35). AE, DC, MC, V. Mon–Sat 12:30–2:30pm and 8–10:30pm. Bus: 13, 15, or 55.

La Prima Smarrita ☆☆ PIEDMONTESE/MEDITERRANEAN This is the best restaurant in Turin, located a short walk from the city center. The owner, Mr. Grossi, is proud of his vast selection of Italian and international wines, and his fine Piedmontese fare and innovative Mediterranean dishes. Even

Wine Tasting

Reds with rich and complex flavors make up most of the wine output of this rugged high-altitude region near Italy's border with France. One of the most interesting vineyards is headquartered in a 15th-century abbey near the hamlet of Alba, south of Turin: **Antiche Cantine dell'Annunziata,** Abbazia dell'Annunziata, La Morra, 12064 Cuneo (© **0173-50185**). If you'd like to drive through the countryside for a little wine tasting and a vineyard tour, call to make an appointment and get detailed directions.

a simple fish salad with cherry tomatoes and fresh basil is made with flair. Only the best of regional beef goes into the beef filet with mushroom-laced cream sauce. Among the pasta dishes, try *tortelli di borraigine* (fresh pasta stuffed with borage, a type of green, with a savory tomato sauce). You might follow with a main course of sea bass cooked with diced potatoes, green olives, and fresh young artichokes. All the desserts are made fresh daily: Count yourself lucky if the chef has prepared his hazelnut chocolate mousse.

Corso Unione Sovietica 244. © 011-3179657. Reservations required. Main courses 15€–25€ ($13.40–$22.35). AE, DC, MC, V. Daily 12:30–3:30pm and 8pm–1am. Tram: 4. Bus: 63.

MODERATE

El Toulà–Villa Sassi ⚘ PIEDMONTESE/INTERNATIONAL   This 17th-century villa is on the rise of a hill 6km (3¾ miles) east of the town center. The stylish antique-decorated place has seen the addition of a modern dining room with glass walls (most tables have excellent garden views). Some of the food comes from the villa's own farm—not only the vegetables, fruit, and butter, but also the beef. For an appetizer, try the frogs' legs cooked with broth-simmered rice or the *fonduta* (a Piedmont fondue with Fontina cheese and white truffles). If it's featured, try the prized specialty: *camoscio in salmi*—chamois (a goatlike antelope) in a sauce of olive oil, anchovies, and garlic, laced with wine and served with polenta. Other menu items worth noting are agnolotti with a sauce of roasted veal and fresh tomatoes, *nodino di vitello* (roasted veal filet) with rosemary and sage, and braised sturgeon slices with orange-pepper-cinnamon sauce.

In the Villa Sassi, Via Traforo del Pino 47. © 011-8980556. Reservations recommended. Main courses 14€–20€ ($12.50–$17.85); fixed-price menu 45€ ($40.20). AE, DC, MC, V. Mon–Sat noon–2:30pm and 8–10:30pm. Closed Aug, Dec 24, and Jan 6. Tram: 15. Bus: 61.

Vintage 1997 ⚘ PIEDMONTESE SEAFOOD   A fast-rising star, this restaurant looks like an English pub, but the food is unmistakably Italian. The "1997" in the name refers to the year the place opened, but it's already becoming firmly entrenched in the minds of serious foodies. You can partake of the fish-tasting menu or else enjoy the mainly meat-based Piedmontese fare. Meat and fish are wed in an unusual dish—lamb with tuna sauce. Tuna also appears in a delectable starring role in chateaubriand of tuna with fresh spinach. Our favorite pasta is the tortelli stuffed with mozzarella and eggplant and served in a cherry tomato sauce. For dessert, the heavenly choice is chocolate flan with white chocolate ice cream over which a rum sauce is drizzled.

Piazza Solferino 16. © 011-535948. Reservations required. Main courses 9.30€–18.60€ ($8.30–$16.60). Mon–Fri noon–3pm; Mon–Sat 8pm–midnight. Tram: 4 or 10. Bus: 5 or 67.

INEXPENSIVE

Caffé Torino ITALIAN   Opened in 1903, this famous coffeehouse is the best re-creation in Turin of the days of Vittorio Emanuele. It's set on one of the most elegant squares in northern Italy and is decorated with faded frescoes, brass and marble inlays, and a somewhat battered 19th-century formality. Don't be surprised if the staff has all kinds of rules about where and when you can be seated. There's a stand-up bar near the entrance, a rather formal dining room off to the side, and a cafe area with tiny tables and unhurried service.

Piazza San Carlo 204. © 011-545118. Main courses 9€–15€ ($8.05–$13.40). AE, DC, MC, V. Daily 7am–1am. Tram: 13.

Da Mauro (Value) ITALIAN/TUSCAN   Within walking distance of Piazza San Carlo, this place, the best of the town's affordable trattorie, is generally packed. The food is conventional but does have character; the chef borrows freely from most of the gastronomic centers of Italy, although the cuisine is mainly Tuscan. An excellent pasta specialty is the cannelloni. Most main dishes consist of well-prepared fish, veal, and poultry. The desserts are consistently enjoyable.

Via Maria Vittoria 21. © 011-8170604. Reservations not accepted. Main courses 7.50€–17.50€ ($6.70–$15.65). No credit cards. Tues–Sun noon–2:30pm and 7:30–10pm. Closed July. Tram: 13.

Ristorante C'Era una Volta ✿ PIEDMONTESE   This is a good introduction to classic Piedmontese cuisine. Fixed-price meals feature an aperitif, a choice of seven or eight antipasti, and two first and two main courses, with vegetables, dessert, and coffee. The fare includes polenta, crepes, rabbit, and guinea fowl. Piedmont's most typical dish served here is *bagna cauda,* raw vegetables dipped into a sauce made with garlic, anchovies, and olive oil.

Corso Vittorio Emanuele II 41. © 011-655498. Reservations recommended. Main courses 7€–8.50€ ($6.25–$7.60). Fixed-price menu 29€ ($25.90). AE, DC, MC, V. Mon–Sat 8pm–midnight. Closed Aug. Bus: 52, 67, or 68. Tram: 9 or 18.

TURIN AFTER DARK

Turin is the cultural center of northwestern Italy, a major stopover for concert artists performing between Genoa and Milan. The daily newspaper of Piedmont, *La Stampa,* lists complete details of current cultural events.

Classical music concerts are presented at the **Auditorium della RAI,** Via Verde 31 (© **011-8104653**), throughout the year, though mainly in winter. Turin is also home to one of the country's leading opera houses, the **Teatro Regio,** Piazza Castello 215 (© **011-88151**). Concerts and leading ballets are also presented here. The box office (© **011-8815241** or 011-8815242) is open Tuesday to Friday 10:30am to 6pm, and Saturday 10:30am to 4pm (closed in Aug). Opera and other classical productions are presented in summer outside the gardens of the **Palazzo Reale.**

The last remaining government-subsidized (RAI) orchestra performs at Via Nizza 280. The **orchestra hall** (© **011-6640458**) is part of the extensive Lingotto exhibition/conference center that grew out of Fiat's first large-scale automobile assembly plant. Ticket prices vary by performance.

The rest of the city's nightlife is like that of Milan, only smaller. **Alcatraz,** Murazzi del Po (© **011-8128570**), is hypermodern, with an avant-garde design and the latest dance mixes. Its main rivals are **Discoteca Atlantide,** Via Monginevro 10 (© **011-9367783**), and the somewhat corny **Lo Scoppiato,** Via Villarbasse 26 (© **011-338567**), where karaoke contests with local wannabes might either intrigue or repel you. Another karaoke club is **Luca's,** Via Fredour 26 (© **011-7764604**), where sports talk and karaoke contests bring out the exhibitionism of cinematic hopefuls. **Ziegfield Follies,** Via Pomba 7 (© **011-8127395**), offers disco music, restaurant service, and a bar where you might strike up a fun conversation. The more punkish **Exit,** Via Barge 4C (© **011-4348233**), is a pub with live music from north Italian punk bands, techno artists, and rock bands.

Turin has several elegant cafes where you can pass the time sipping coffee, enjoying a cocktail, or simply people-watching. Among the landmarks are **Caffè San Carlo,** Piazza San Carlo 156 (© **011-5617748**), which serves until 1am under a huge chandelier of Murano glass in a glittering setting of gilt, mirrors, and marble. One of our favorites is **Al Bicerin Caffè,** Piazza della Consolata 5 (© **011-4369325**), Turin's oldest cafe dating from 1763. Dumas, Nietzsche, and Puccini have all enjoyed its signature drink—coffee with the famous Giandujotti chocolate, served with whipped cream in the cozy, wood-paneled setting with marble-topped tables and the original 18th-century bar. The name, Bicerin, is Turinese for "something delicious." Right next door is **Il Bacaro Pane e Vino,** Piazza della Consolata 1 (© **011-4369064**), a little wine bar that offers the most delectable sandwiches in an Art Deco setting with subdued lighting. Full meals (some of them Venetian) are also available. For night owls, it stays open until 2am Tuesday to Sunday.

2 Aosta ✦

184km (114 miles) NW of Milan, 126km (78 miles) N of Turin, 745km (462 miles) NW of Rome

Founded by the Emperor Augustus, Aosta has lost much of its quaintness today. It's called the "Rome of the Alps," but that's just tourist propaganda. Aostans number about 40,000 now and live in the shadow of the peaks of Mont Blanc and San Bernardo. The economy is increasingly dependent on tourism.

Lying as it does on a major artery, Aosta makes for an important stop, either for overnighting or as a base for exploring Valle d'Aosta or taking the cable car to the Conca di Pila, the mountain that towers over the town.

ESSENTIALS

GETTING THERE Thirteen **trains** per day run directly from Turin to Aosta (trip time: 2 hr.), costing 6.80€ ($6.05) one way. From Milan, the trip takes 4½ hours and costs 10.10€ ($9) one way; you must change trains at Chivasso. For information and schedules, call (© **0165-262057**) or 1478-88088 toll-free in Italy. The train station is at Piazza Manzetti, only a 5-minute stroll over to the Piazza Chanoux, the very core of Aosta.

By **car** from Turin, take A5 north until it ends, just east of Aosta.

VISITOR INFORMATION The **tourist office** is at Piazza Chanoux 8 (© **0165-236627**), open daily 9am to 1pm and 3 to 8pm.

EXPLORING AOSTA

The town's Roman ruins include the **Arch of Augustus,** built in 24 B.C., the date of the Roman founding of the town. Via Sant'Anselmo, part of the old city from the Middle Ages, leads to the arch. Even more impressive are the ruins of a **Roman theater,** reached by the Porta Pretoria, a major gateway built of huge blocks dating from the 1st century B.C. The ruins are open year-round daily 9am to 7pm; entrance is free. A **Roman forum** is today a small park with a crypt, lying off Piazza San Giovanni near the cathedral.

The town is also enriched by its medieval relics. The Gothic **Collegiata dei Santi Pietro e Orso,** directly off Via Sant'Anselmo (© **0165-262026**), was founded in the 12th century and is characterized by its landmark Romanesque steeple. You can explore the crypt, but the cloisters, with capitals of some three dozen pillars depicting biblical scenes, are more interesting. The church is open daily 9am to 7pm.

A SIDE TRIP TO A GREAT NATIONAL PARK

Aosta is a good base for exploring the **Great Paradise National Park (Parco Nazionale di Gran Paradiso)** ✸✸✸, five lake-filled valleys that in 1865 were a royal hunting ground of Vittorio Emanuele II. Even back then, long before the term *endangered species* was common, he awarded that distinction to the ibex, a nearly extinct species of mountain goat. In 1919, Vittorio Emanuele III gave the property to the Italian state, which established a national park in 1922. The park encompasses some 3,626 sq. km (1,400 sq. miles) of forest, pastureland, and alpine meadows, filled with not only ibex but also the chamois and other animals that roam wild.

The main gateway to the park is **Cogne,** a popular resort. The best time to visit is in June, when the wildflowers are at their most spectacular. You can get a sampling of this rare alpine fauna by visiting the **Paradise Alpine Garden (Giardino Alpino Paradiso),** near the village of Valnontey, a mile south of Cogne. It's open June 10 to September 15, daily 10am to 12:30pm and 2:30 to 5:30pm. Admission costs 2€ ($1.80), free for children under 10. For information about Great Paradise National Park, visit the **park headquarters** at Via Umberto I, Noasca (© **0124-901070**). Cogne lies about 29km (18 miles) south of Aosta and is reached along S35 and S507.

SHOPPING

Valle d'Aosta is known for its wood carvings and wrought-iron work. For a sampling, head for the permanent craft exhibits in the arcades of **Piazza Chanoux,** the center of Aosta. You're not expected to pay the first price quoted, so test your bargaining skill. The market here swells during the last 2 days in January, when dozens of artisans from all around the Italian Alps appear en masse to sell their handcrafts. Count yourself lucky if you pick up some handmade lace from neighboring Cogne. It's highly valued for its workmanship.

Valdostan handcrafts can be found at **IVAT,** Via Xavier de Maistre 1 (© **0165-41462**), where sculpture, bas-relief, and wrought iron are offered. The shop owners can also provide you with a list of local furniture makers. Antique furniture and paintings are the domain of **Bessone,** Via Edouard Aubert 53 (© **0165-40853**).

WHERE TO STAY

Hotel Le Pageot *Value* This hotel is one of the best values in town. It has a modern angular facade of brown brick with big windows and floors crafted from carefully polished slabs of mountain granite. The guest rooms are clean, comfortable, and functional, but not a lot more. The bathrooms are small.

Via Giorgio Carrel 31, 11100 Aosta. © **0165-32433.** Fax 0165-33217. 18 units (showers only). 70€–85€ ($62.50–$75.90) double. MC, V. Parking 5€ ($4.45). **Amenities:** Bar; room service. *In room:* TV, hair dryer.

Hotel Roma *Value* Silvio Lepri and Graziella Nicoli are the owners of this hotel on a peaceful alley in a cubist-style white stucco building. The small guest rooms are modern, simple, and well maintained, with touches of varnished pine and modern bathrooms. The public rooms include a warmly paneled bar area, big windows, and a homey decor filled with bright colors and rustic accessories.

Via Torino 7, 11100 Aosta. ℂ **0165-41000.** Fax 0165-32404. 38 units (showers only). 62€–74€ ($55.35–$66.10) double. AE, DC, MC, V. Parking 5€ ($4.45). **Amenities:** Bar; lounge. *In room:* TV.

Hotel Valle d'Aosta   This modern hotel is one of Aosta's leading choices. Located on a busy road leading from the old town to the entrance of the autostrada, it's a prominent stop for motorists using the Great St. Bernard and Mont Blanc tunnels to and from Italy. The sunny lobby has beige stone floors and deep leather chairs, and an oversize bar. All guest rooms have double windows and views angled toward the mountains. Bathrooms are small.

Corso Ivrea 146, 11100 Aosta. ℂ **0165-41845.** Fax 0165-236660. 104 units (showers only). 87.80€–118€ ($78.40–$105.35) double. Rates include breakfast. AE, DC, MC, V. Free garage parking. **Amenities:** Restaurant; bar; room service; babysitting; laundry. *In room:* TV, minibar, hair dryer.

WHERE TO DINE

Ristorante Le Foyer VALDOSTAN/INTERNATIONAL   This restaurant sits beside a traffic artery on the outskirts of town. The complete Valdostan meals are both flavorful and affordable. In a wood-paneled dining room illuminated by a wall of oversize windows, you can dine on specialties such as salmon, trout, beef tagliata with balsamic vinegar, vegetable flan with fondue, or fresh noodles with smoked salmon and asparagus. There's also a good selection of French and Italian wines.

In the Hotel Valle d'Aosta, Corso Ivrea 146. ℂ **0165-32136.** Reservations recommended. Main courses 6€–17.50€ ($5.35–$15.65). AE, MC, V. Wed–Mon 12:15–1:50pm; Wed–Sun 7:30–9:30pm. Closed Jan 8–25 and July 5–20.

Ristorante Piemonte ⭐ *Finds* VALDOSTAN/INTERNATIONAL   On a relatively traffic-free street, this is a charming, unpretentious trattoria with all the authenticity that its 250-year-old premises deserve. It's known for its savory versions of age-old mountain recipes. You can order at least four set menus, all featuring either truffles or mushrooms, when they're in season. Other tried-and-true favorites are heaping platters of charcuterie, several versions of fondue, risotto with roasted pork, and an array of desserts that might include fresh strawberries from local suppliers. Especially interesting is roast chamois prepared with a Barolo sauce.

Via Porta Pretoria 13. ℂ **0165-40111.** Reservations recommended. Main courses 7.50€–10€ ($6.70–$8.95); fixed-price menus 11€–30€ ($9.80–$26.80). MC, V. Sat–Thurs noon–3pm and 7–10pm. Closed Nov.

Vecchia Aosta VALDOSTAN/INTERNATIONAL   The most unusual restaurant in Aosta lies in the narrow niche between the inner and outer Roman walls of the Porta Pretoria. It's in an old structure that, though modernized, still bears evidence of the superb building techniques of the Romans, whose chiseled stones are sometimes visible between patches of modern wood and plaster. Full meals are served on at least two levels in a labyrinth of nooks and isolated crannies. Highlights include homemade ravioli, beef filet with mushrooms, pepperoni flan, eggs with cheese fondue and truffles, roasted duck with tomatoes and orange sauce, and a cheese-laden version of Valdostan fondue.

Piazza Porta Pretoria 4. ℂ **0165-361186.** Reservations recommended. Main courses 10€–20€ ($8.95–$17.85). AE, DC, MC, V. Thurs–Tues noon–2:30pm and 7:30–10pm. Closed Nov 15–30 and Feb 15–30.

AOSTA AFTER DARK

Sweet Rock Caffè, Via Piccolo St. Bernardo 18 (ℂ **165-553251**), caters to a 25-to-45 crowd, featuring rock and jazz with live music on occasion.

3 Courmayeur & Entrèves: Skiing & Alpine Beauty

COURMAYEUR 🎿🎿

Courmayeur, a 35km (22-mile) drive northwest of Aosta, is Italy's best all-around ski resort, with two "high seasons," attracting skiers in winter and other active types who come to play in the mountain scenery in summer. Its popularity was given a considerable boost with the opening of the Mont Blanc road tunnel (© **0165-89422** or 0165-899196), feeding traffic from France into Italy (estimated trip time: 20 min.). This vital link between France and Italy was closed by a tragic fire in the spring of 1999, and the Mont Blanc tunnel reopening was announced in December of 2001. Setbacks occurred and the opening was delayed. This vital link between France and Italy was closed by a tragic fire in the spring of 1999, but is now hailed by engineers as "the safest in the world" after reopening in spring 2002.

With Europe's highest mountain in the background, Courmayeur sits snugly in a valley. Directly to the north of the resort is the alpine village of Entrèves, sprinkled with a number of chalets (some of which take in paying guests).

ESSENTIALS

GETTING THERE   There's **no direct train service;** you'll have to take the **bus** from Aosta (see section 2 of this chapter). Aosta's bus terminal, Via Carrel (© **0165-841305**), is adjacent to the train station. There's a bus every hour that costs 2.40€ ($2.15) each way or 4.10€ ($3.65) round-trip. Transit time is 1 hour. The last departure from Aosta is at 10:15pm.

By car, take Route S26 west from Aosta (toward Monte Bianco).

VISITOR INFORMATION   The **tourist office** for Courmayeur is on Piazzale Monte Bianco (© **0165-842060**), open daily 9am to 12:30pm and 3 to 6:30pm.

FUN ON & OFF THE SLOPES

The **ski season** begins in mid-December and lasts until sometime in April, depending on snow conditions in the area. The skiing, although good, has little to attract experts, who head instead for Chamonix across Mont Blanc in France; Courmayeur is more for beginners and intermediates. **Lift tickets** in Courmayeur cost 27€ ($24.10) for 1 day, and 85.75€ ($76.55) for 3 days. For **snow reports** in and around Courmayeur, call © **0165-843566.**

Near Courmayeur, you can take one of the most unusual **cable cars** in Europe across Mont Blanc all the way to Chamonix, France. It's a ride across glaciers that's altogether frightening and thrilling. Departures on the **Funivie Monte Bianco** are from La Palud, near Entrèves. The three-stage cable car heads for the intermediate stations, Pavillon and Rifugio Torino, before reaching its peak at Punta Helbronner at 3,430m (11,254 ft.). At the latter, you'll be on the doorstep of the glacier and the celebrated 19km (12-mile) Vallée Blanche ski run to Chamonix, France, usually opened at the beginning of February every year. The round-trip price for the cable-car ride is 27€ ($24.10). Departures are every 20 minutes, and service is daily 8:30am to 12:40pm and 2 to 4pm. At the top are a bar, a snack bar, and a terrace for sunbathing. Bookings are possible at **Esercizio Funivie,** Frazione La Palude 22 (© **0165-89925**).

Many nonskiing visitors come here just for the bracing mountain air and the panoramic views. The shopping is excellent, especially on **Via Roma,** and many of the most prestigious retailers in Milan or Rome maintain branches here.

In **summer** the scenery is gorgeous, with towering Mont Blanc in the distance. Some 32 miles southeast of Courmayeur is the **Parco Nazionale del Gran Paradise,** once the private domain of King Vittorio Emanuele II (1820–78). For more information, see "A Side Trip to a Great National Park," in section 2 of this chapter.

WHERE TO STAY

Courmayeur has a number of attractive hotels, many of which are open seasonally. Always reserve ahead in high season, either summer or winter.

Expensive

Grand Hotel Royal e Golf ★★   This hotel sits in a dramatic location above the heart of the resort town. It is a top choice, exceeded only by the more tranquil and elegant Pavillon (see below). Much of its angular facade is covered with rocks, so it fits in neatly with the mountainous landscape. The guest rooms are of a decent size, with streamlined bathrooms; rooms on the fifth floor have private balconies. The rooms most requested are those with southern exposure, holding a great view of Mont Blanc; those on the north side open onto a valley.

Via Roma 87, 11013 Courmayeur. ✆ **0165-831611.** Fax 0165-842093. www.hotelroyalgolf.com. 86 units. 144.30€–346€ ($128.85–$309) double; 232€–511.25€ ($207.20–$456.55) suite. Rates include breakfast. AE, DC, MC, V. Parking 10€ ($8.95) inside, free outside. **Amenities:** Restaurant; bar; pool; 9-hole golf course called Golf Club Courmayeur & Grandes Jorasses (which lies outside of town at Le Pont-Val Ferret); gym; sauna; concierge; room service; massage; babysitting; laundry/dry cleaning. *In room:* A/C, TV, minibar, hair dryer, safe.

Hotel Pavillon ★★   This is one of the swankiest hotels in town, despite its small size. Designed like a chalet, the hotel is a 4-minute walk south of Courmayeur's inner-city pedestrian zone. The guest rooms feature leather-covered doors and conservative decor; all but two have private balconies. Accommodations range from medium-size to spacious. The hotel is only a short walk from the funicular that goes to Plan Checrouit.

Strada Regionale 62, 11013 Courmayeur. ✆ **0165-846120.** Fax 0165-846122. www.pavillon.it. 50 units. 180€–300€ ($160.75–$267.90) double; 280€–420€ ($250.05–$375.05) suite. Rates include breakfast and dinner. AE, DC, MC, V. Valet parking 6€ ($5.35). Closed May–June 15 and Oct–Dec 2. **Amenities:** 2 restaurants; bar; pool; sauna; room service; massage and spa treatments; babysitting; laundry/dry cleaning. *In room:* TV, minibar, hair dryer, safe.

Moderate

Hotel del Viale   This old-style mountain chalet at the edge of town has an inviting terrace with tables set under trees in fair weather. In chillier months, the rooms inside are cozy and pleasant. The guest rooms, though small, have an alpine charm, each with an efficient tiled bathroom. In winter, guests can gather in the taproom to enjoy après-ski life, drinking at pine tables and warming their feet before the open fire.

Viale Monte Bianco 74, 11013 Courmayeur. ✆ **0165-846712.** Fax 0165-844513. www.hoteldelviale.com. 23 units. 60€–110€ ($53.60–$98.25) double. Rates include breakfast and dinner. AE, DC, MC, V. Parking 6€ ($5.35) inside, free outside. Closed May and Oct–Nov. **Amenities:** Restaurant; lounge; room service; laundry. *In room:* TV, minibar, hair dryer, safe.

Palace Bron ★   About 2km (1¼ miles) from the heart of the resort, this tranquil oasis is one of the plushest hotels in town. You're made to feel like a member of a baronial household. The guest rooms are handsomely furnished and well maintained, ranging from medium to spacious. Winter visitors appreciate its proximity to the many ski lifts. Walking from the chalet to the center of town is a good way to exercise after your formal dinner selected from the kitchen's filling international cuisine. The hotel's piano bar is especially lively in winter.

Località Plan Gorret 41, 11013 Courmayeur. ✆ **0165-846742.** Fax 0165-844015. www.palacebron.it. 27 units (most with shower only). 139€–196€ ($124.15–$175.05) double. AE, DC, MC, V. Closed Easter–July 1 and mid-Sept to Dec 1. **Amenities:** Dining room; bar; valet; room service; babysitting; laundry. *In room:* TV, minibar, hair dryer.

Inexpensive

Hotel Bouton d'Or   This family-owned hotel is named for the buttercups that cover the surrounding hills in summer. French windows lead from the guest rooms onto small balconies. The rooms are a bit cramped, but you'll find reasonable comfort for the price. All units come with well-kept bathrooms. The hotel is about 91m (100 yards, toward the Mont Blanc tunnel) from the most popular restaurant in Courmayeur, Le Vieux Pommier (see below), which is owned by the same family.

Strada Traforo del Monte Bianco 10 (off Piazzale Monte Bianco), 11013 Courmayeur. ✆ **0165-846729.** Fax 0165-842152. www.hotelboutondor.com. 35 units (showers only). 85€–105€ ($75.90–$93.75) double; 92€–113€ ($82.15–$100.90) apt for 3; 170€ ($151.80) apt for 4. Rates include breakfast. AE, DC, MC, V. Free parking. Closed June and Nov. **Amenities:** Bar; sauna; room service. *In room:* TV, hair dryer, safe.

Hotel Courmayeur   This centrally located inn is built so that most of its rooms have unobstructed views of the mountains. It's a small, unpretentious hotel with immaculate rooms and low prices. A number of the guest rooms, furnished in mountain chalet style, also have wooden balconies.

Via Roma 158, 11013 Courmayeur. ✆ **0165-846732.** Fax 0165-845125. www.hotelcourmayeur.com. 26 units (most with shower only). 75€–110€ ($66.95–$98.20) double. Rates include breakfast. AE, DC, MC, V. Free parking. Closed Sept–Nov and May. **Amenities:** Restaurant; bar; room service; babysitting; laundry/dry cleaning. *In room:* TV, hair dryer.

WHERE TO DINE

Cadran Solaire ✦ VALDOSTAN   In the center of town is Courmayeur's most interesting restaurant, named after the sundial (*cadran solaire*) embellishing the upper floor of its chalet facade. It's owned by Leo Garin, whose La Maison de Filippo in Entrèves (see below) is Valle d'Aosta's most popular restaurant. Try to come for a before-dinner drink in the vaulted bar; in the 16th century, the room's massive stones were crafted into long spans by using techniques that the Romans perfected. The rustically elegant dining room has a stone fireplace, a beamed ceiling, and wide plank floors. Specialties change with the season but are likely to include warm goat cheese blended with a salad, noodles with seasonal vegetables, baked cheese-and-spinach casserole, and duck breast with plums. The most sumptuous of all desserts would be the chocolate and pear cake.

Via Roma 122. ✆ **0165-844609.** Reservations required. Main courses 15€–38€ ($13.40–$33.95). AE, MC, V. Wed–Mon 12:30–3pm and 7:30–11pm. Closed May and 2 weeks in Oct.

Leone Rosso VALDOSTAN   This is in a stone- and timber-fronted house in a slightly isolated courtyard, a few paces from the busy pedestrian traffic of Via Roma. It serves well-prepared Valdostan specialties, such as fondues, a thick and steaming regional version of minestrone, *tagliatelle* (flat noodles) with mushrooms and *en papillote* (in parchment), and a selection of creamy desserts. Some meats you grill yourself at your table. Don't confuse this place with the Red Lion pub.

Via Roma 71. ✆ **0165-846726.** Reservations recommended. Main courses 11€–20€ ($9.80–$17.85). AE, MC, V. Daily noon–2pm and 7–10pm. Closed May–June and Oct.

Le Vieux Pommier FRENCH   The hacked-up trunk of the old apple tree that was cut down to build this place was erected inside and serves as the focal point (and namesake) of the restaurant, which is located on the main square. The exposed stone, the copper-covered bar, and the thick pine tables arranged in an octagon create a charming atmosphere. Today Alessandro Casale, the son of the founder, directs the kitchen, assisted by his wife, Lydia. Your meal might consist of three kinds of dried alpine beef, followed by noodles in ham-studded cream sauce or an arrangement of three pastas or four fondues, including a regional variety with Fontina, milk, and egg yolks. Then it's on to chicken supreme en papillote or four or five unusual meat dishes cooked mountain style, right at your table.

Piazzale Monte Bianco 25. (*C*) 0165-842281. Reservations recommended. Main courses 7.50€–15€ ($6.70–$13.40). DC, MC, V. Tues–Sun noon–2pm and 7–9:30pm. Closed Oct and 15 days in May.

COURMAYEUR AFTER DARK

Not to be confused with a less desirable bar of the same name at the end of the same street, the **American Bar,** Via Roma 43 ((*C*) **0165-846707**), is one of the most popular watering holes on the après-ski circuit. It's rowdy and sometimes outrageous, but most often a lot of fun. Most guests end up beside either the open fireplace or the long, crowded bar. The place is open all day every day, until 1:30am in ski season. A few doors down, the **Café della Posta,** Via Roma 51 ((*C*) **0165-842272**), the oldest cafe in Courmayeur, is as sedate as its neighbor is unruly. Many guests prefer to remain in the warmly decorated bar area, never venturing into the large salon with its glowing fireplace. The place changes its stripes throughout the day, opening as a morning cafe at 8:30am.

ENTRÈVES ⊛

Even older than Courmayeur, Entrèves is an ancient community that's small and compact, really a mountain village of wooden houses. Many visitors prefer its alpine charm to the more bustling resort of Courmayeur; they ski the slopes at Courmayeur and enjoy its shopping, dining, and nightlife, but they retreat here to stay in a quieter, less congested setting. Entrèves is reached by a steep and narrow road. Many gourmets visit just to enjoy the regional fare for which the village is known.

Just outside Entrèves on the main highway lies the **Val Veny cable car,** which skiers take in winter to reach the Courmayeur lift system.

Entrèves is 3km (2 miles) north of Courmayeur (signposted off Route 26). Buses from the center of Courmayeur run daily to Entrèves. For more information, contact Courmayeur's tourist office ((*C*) **0165-892060**).

WHERE TO STAY

See also La Brenva (below), which rents 12 guest rooms above its dining room.

La Grange ⊛ *(Value*   This will be one of the first buildings you'll see as you enter this rustic alpine village. A few foundation stones date from the 1300s, when the hotel was a barn. What you'll see today is a stone building whose balconies and gables are outlined against the steep hillside into which it's constructed. The Berthod family transformed a dilapidated property into a rustic and comfortable hotel in 1979. It's enthusiastically managed by Bruna Berthod Perri and her nephew, Stefano Pellin. The unusual decor includes a collection of antique tools and a series of thick timbers, stucco, and exposed stone walls. The guest rooms are imbued with a cozy alpine charm, each with a tiled bathroom. A rich breakfast is the only meal served.

Strada La Brenva 1, 11013 Courmayeur-Entrèves. © **0165-869733.** Fax 0165-869744. www.lagrange-it.com. 23 units (showers only). 77€–129€ ($68.75–$115.20) double; from 155€ ($138.40) suite. Rates include breakfast. AE, DC, MC, V. Free parking. Closed May–June and Oct–Nov. **Amenities:** Bar; lounge; exercise room; sauna; room service. *In room:* TV, minibar, hair dryer.

WHERE TO DINE

La Brenva ★ *Finds* VALDOSTAN/FRENCH. Many skiers make a special trip to Entrèves just for a drink at the old-fashioned bar of this hotel/restaurant. The copper espresso machine topped by a brass eagle and many of the other decorative accessories are at least a century old. The core of the building was constructed in 1884 as a hunting lodge for Vittorio Emanuele. The restaurant consists of exposed stone walls, wide flooring planks, hunting trophies, copper pots, and straw-bottomed chairs. Fires burn in winter, and many diners prefer an aperitif in the unusual salon, within view of the well-chosen paintings. On any given day, the menu could include prosciutto, fonduta for two, carbonada with polenta, scaloppini with fresh mushrooms, Valle d'Aostan beefsteak, and zabaglione for dessert.

Each of the 12 simple and comfortable guest rooms has a bathroom, a TV, a phone, and lots of peace and quiet. Many have covered loggias. With breakfast included, they rent for 78€ to 120€ ($69.65–$107.15) per person. The inn takes a vacation in either May or June.

Via La Palud 12, Frazione Entrèves di Courmayeur, 11013 Courmayeur-Entrèves. © **0165-869780.** Fax 0165-869726. Reservations required. Main courses 9.30€–18.10€ ($8.30–$16.15); fixed-price menus 20€–32.50€ ($17.85–$29). AE, MC, V. Tues–Sun 12:30–2pm and 7:30–10:30pm. Closed May and Oct.

La Maison de Filippo *Value* VALDOSTAN This colorful tavern, the creation of Leo Garin, is for those who enjoy a festive atmosphere and bountiful regional food. The three-story open hallway seems like a rustic barn, with an open, worn wooden staircase leading to the various dining nooks. The outdoor summer beer garden has a full view of Mont Blanc. You pass by casks of nuts, baskets of fresh fruits, bowls of salad, fruit tarts, and loaves of fresh-baked bread. Mr. Garin features local specialties on an all-you-can-eat basis, earning the place the nickname "Chalet of Gluttony." A typical meal might begin with a selection of antipasti, followed by a large platter of about 60 varieties of sausage. Next comes a parade of pasta dishes. For a main course, you can pick everything from fondue to *camoscio* (chamois meat) to trout with almond-butter sauce.

Frazione Entrèves di Courmayeur. © **0165-869797.** Reservations required. Fixed-price menus 30€–35€ ($26.80–$31.25). MC, V. Wed–Mon 12:30–2:30pm and 8–10:30pm. Closed May 16–June and Nov–Dec 20.

13

Genoa & the Italian Riviera

For years the retreat of the wintering wealthy, the Italian Riviera now enjoys a broad base of tourism. It's popular even in winter, although not for swimming (the average Jan temperature hovers around 50°F/10°C). The protection provided by the Ligurian Apennines looming in the background makes for balmy weather. Genoa, dividing the Riviera in two, is the capital of Liguria. It's a big, bustling port that has charm for those willing to take the time to seek out its treasures.

The winding coastline of the Rivieras, particularly the one stretching from the French border to San Remo, is especially familiar to moviegoers as the background for countless flicks about sports-car racing, jewel thieves, and spies. The Mediterranean landscape is dotted with pines, olives, citrus trees, and cypresses. The western Riviera—the **Riviera di Ponente (Setting Sun),** from the border to Genoa—is sometimes known as the Riviera of Flowers (Riviera dei Fiori) because of its profusion of blossoms. Starting at the French border, Ventimiglia is the gateway city to Italy. Along the way you'll encounter the first big resort, Bardighera, followed by San Remo, the major center of tourism. On the eastern Riviera—the **Riviera di Levante (Rising Sun)**—are three dramatically situated small resorts: Rapallo, Santa Margherita, and Portofino (the favorite of the yachting set). **Genoa** itself, with its proud maritime history, is a world apart from the easygoing seaside resorts that surround it: brusque and clamorous, it is one of the most historic, fascinating, and least-visited cities in Italy.

The Ligurians are famous for ceramics, lace, silver and gold filigree, marble, velvet, olive wood, and macramé, and all the towns and villages of the region hold outdoor markets either in the main square or on the waterfront. Haggling is a way of life, so good deals do exist; but English speakers should be warned that prices might not fall as low as they would if you were negotiating in the local dialect.

1 San Remo ✴✴

16km (10 miles) E of the French border, 137km (85 miles) SW of Genoa, 639km (396 miles) NW of Rome

San Remo has been known as a resort ever since Emperor Frederick William wintered in a villa here. In time, Empress Maria Alexandrova, wife of Czar Alexander II, showed up, trailed by a Russian colony that included Tchaikovsky, who composed the Fourth Symphony here during a stay in 1878. Alfred Nobel, the father of dynamite and the founder of the famous prizes in Stockholm, died here in 1896.

The flower-filled resort is today something of a mini-Vegas by the sea, complete with a casino, race track, 18-hole golf course, and the deluxe Royal Hotel. Its climate is the mildest on the western Riviera, and the town offers mile after mile of well-maintained beaches.

The Italian Riviera

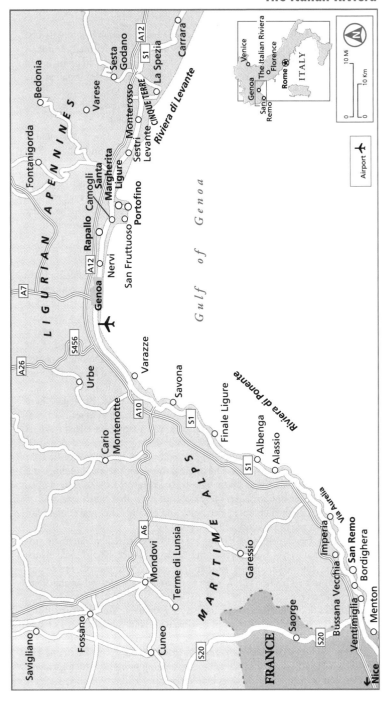

ITALY

Venice
The Italian Riviera
Florence
Genoa
Rome
San Remo

10 Mi
10 Km

Airport

Carrara
A12
S1
Godano
Sesta
Varese
A12
La Spezia
Bedonia
Monterosso
CINQUE TERRE
Levante
Riviera di Levante
Fontanigorda
LIGURIAN APENNINES
Sestri
Santa
Margherita
Ligure
Camogli
Rapallo
Portofino
San Fruttuoso
Nervi
A12
Genoa
Gulf of Genoa
A7
S456
A26
Urbe
Varazze
Savona
A10
S1
Finale Ligure
Riviera di Ponente
Cario
Montenotte
Albenga
Alassio
S1
MARITIME ALPS
A6
Terme di Lunsia
Mondovi
Garessio
Imperia
Via Aurelia
San Remo
Bordighera
Fossano
Savigliano
Cuneo
Saorge
S20
Bussana Vecchia
Ventimiglia
Menton
S20
FRANCE
Nice

ESSENTIALS

GETTING THERE   San Remo lies on the coast between Ventimiglia and Imperia, 10km (6¼ miles) from each, and it's a major stop for many **trains.** A train leaves Genoa heading for the French border once per hour, stopping in San Remo. Rome is 8 hours by train from San Remo. For train information and schedules, call © **848-8880888.**

If you have a **car,** A10, running east-west along the Riviera, is the fastest way to reach San Remo from either the French border or Genoa.

VISITOR INFORMATION   The **tourist office** is on Corso Nuvoloni 1 (© **0184-59059**), open Monday to Saturday 8am to 7pm and Sunday 9am to 1pm.

SAFETY   The harbor, particularly after dark, isn't for the squeamish. If you go wandering, don't go alone and don't carry valuables. Genoa is rougher than Barcelona, more comparable to Marseille. A woman is likely to lose her purse not only in the harbor area but also on any side street running downhill if she doesn't take precautions.

EXPLORING THE RESORT

Even if you're just passing through San Remo, you might want to visit **La Città Vecchia** (also known as **La Pigna**), the old city atop the hill. Far removed in spirit from the burgeoning sterile-looking town down near the water, old San Remo blithely ignores the present, and its tiny houses on narrow, steep lanes capture the past. In the new town, the palm-flanked **Corso dell'Imperatrice** (aka the **Passeggiata dell'Imperatrice**) attracts promenaders; at one end of the passeggiata stands the Russian Orthodox **San Basilio,** boasting onion-shaped domes. For a scenic view, drive to the top of **San Romolo** and **Monte Bignone** (1,300m/4,265 ft.).

Outside of town, you can visit **Bussana Vecchia (Old Bussana),** 8km (5 miles) west of San Remo (it's signposted). Too well inhabited to really be considered a ghost town, Bussana Vecchia is, however, a rather unofficial town. A substantial 1887 earthquake killed thousands of its residents and destroyed many buildings. The survivors, too frightened to stay, started a new Bussana 2km (1¼ miles) closer to the sea. The original town, with several buildings still standing, has gradually been taken over by artist-squatters who've revamped interior spaces (but not exteriors—no reason to draw that much attention to themselves) and hooked up water, electricity, and phones. They live off their art, so haggling can get you a good deal on a painting.

The pebbly **beach** below the Passeggiata dell'Imperatrice is where many visitors spend their days. Beach huts offer showers, snack bars, beach chairs, lounges, and umbrellas. Expect to spend at least 7.50€ ($6.70) for a basic lounge and up to 12.50€ ($11.15) for a more elaborate sun-bed arrangement with an umbrella.

Stylish boutiques line the town's busiest thoroughfare, **Via Matteotti.** Most are devoted to high-style Milan-inspired beachwear and slinky cocktail dresses. Wander up and down the street, making it a point to stop at **Annamoda,** Via Matteotti 141 (© **0184-505550**), and **Moro Gabrielle,** Corso Matteotti 132 (© **0184-531586**), both of which sell sporty-looking as well as formal garments for men and women, with labels such as Versace and YSL.

WHERE TO STAY

EXPENSIVE

Royal Hotel ⊛ Though long past its heyday, this resort is a big name because of its size and facilities. It's complete with terraces and gardens, a forest of palms, bright flowers, and hideaway nooks. Activity revolves around the garden terrace; no one really hangs out in the grand old dowager public lounges. The guest rooms vary considerably: Some are tennis-court size with private balconies, many have sea views, and others face the hills. The furnishings range from traditional to modern. The luxurious fifth-floor rooms have the best views and are more expensive. The bathrooms boast deluxe toiletries.

Corso Imperatrice 80, 18038 San Remo. Ⓒ **0184-5391.** Fax 0184-661445. www.royalhotelsanremo.com. 135 units. 190€–352€ ($169.65–$314.35) double; 320€ ($285.75) suite. Rates include buffet breakfast. AE, DC, MC, V. Parking 10€–18€ ($8.95–$16.05). Closed Oct 10–Dec 20. **Amenities:** 2 restaurants; bar; lounge; pool; minigolf; tennis court; gym; sauna; children's center; concierge; salon; room service; babysitting; laundry/dry cleaning. *In room:* A/C, TV, minibar, hair dryer, safe.

MODERATE

Grand Hotel Londra Like the Royal, this hotel coasts along on past glories, but it's still a worthy choice. Built around 1900 as a two-story hotel, this place was later expanded into the imposing structure you see today. It's in a park with a sea view, within a 10-minute walk of the commercial district. The well-furnished interior is filled with framed engravings, porcelain in illuminated cases, gilt mirrors, and brass detailing. Many of the guest rooms, ranging from medium to spacious, have wrought-iron balconies; all have well-kept bathrooms.

Corso Matuzia 2, 18038 San Remo. Ⓒ **0184-65511.** Fax 0184-668073. www.londrahotelsanremo.com. 130 units. 160€–180€ ($142.90–$160.75) double. Rates include breakfast. AE, DC, MC, V. Free parking. Closed Sept 30–Dec 23. **Amenities:** Restaurant; bar; pool; room service; babysitting; laundry/dry cleaning. *In room:* A/C, TV, minibar, hair dryer.

Hotel Miramare Continental Palace A curved drive leads past palmettos to this traditional building set behind semitropical gardens bordering a busy street. A private underpass gives direct access to the beach. After passing through the well-appointed public rooms, you'll discover a garden with a 300-year-old magnolia, sculptures, and plenty of verdant hideaways. The guest rooms are clean and comfortable, ranging from small to medium; some are in a neighboring annex with garden views. The tiled bathrooms are compact.

Corso Matuzia 9, 18038 San Remo. Ⓒ **0184-667601.** Fax 0184-667655. www.miramaresanremo.it. 59 units (showers only). 94€–186€ ($83.95–$166.10) double; 258€–362€ ($230.40–$323.25) suite. Rates include breakfast. AE, DC, MC, V. Free parking. **Amenities:** Restaurant; lounge; pool; gym; sauna; room service; laundry. *In room:* A/C, TV, minibar, hair dryer.

Suite Hotel Nyala ⊛ Built in 1984 and doubled in size in 1993, this comfortable hotel lies in what was a century ago the English-style park of a villa. Although it's in a residential neighborhood with some impressive antique villas, this is San Remo's most modern hotel. The accommodations are divided among three buildings interconnected with corridors. Most guest rooms have a view over the sea and a sun-filled terrace; about half are junior suites, with a separate sitting area and larger balconies. The rooms are nicely decorated, with tiled bathrooms.

Via Solaro 134, 18038 San Remo. Ⓒ **0184-667668.** Fax 0184-666059. www.nyalahotel.com. 80 units. 135€–270€ ($120.55–$241.10) double; from 200€ ($178.60) suite. Rates include breakfast. AE, DC, MC, V. Free parking. **Amenities:** Dining room; bar; lounge; pool; room service; laundry. *In room:* A/C, TV, minibar, hair dryer, safe.

INEXPENSIVE

Hotel Belsoggiorno   This centrally located hotel is near the Corso dell'Imperatrice, the main seaside walkway, and the beaches. Attractively furnished and inviting, it contains a large reception area, plenty of living rooms for lounging, and TV rooms. The guest rooms are contemporary and functional, if not exactly stylish. Nonetheless, they're quite comfortable, although the bathrooms are small. This hotel also provides a pleasant garden in which to sit and enjoy the sun and plants.

Corso Matuzia 41, 18038 San Remo. ☏ **0184-667631.** Fax 0184-667471. 35 units (showers only). 74€–98€ ($66.10–$87.50) double. Rates include breakfast. Half-board 50€–62€ ($44.65–$55.35) per person. DC, MC, V. Free parking. **Amenities:** Dining room; lounge; room service; babysitting; laundry/dry cleaning. *In room:* A/C, TV, hair dryer, safe.

Hotel Eletto   This hotel, on the main artery of town, stands behind a 19th-century facade with cast-iron balconies and ornate detailing. This pleasant stop has public rooms filled with carved panels, old mirrors, and antique furniture, and guest rooms that are old-fashioned and comfortable. Each comes with a small tiled bathroom. The hotel provides a cabana on the beach.

Corso Matteotti 44, 18038 San Remo. ☏ **0184-531548.** Fax 0184-531506. 24 units. 75€ ($67) double. Half-board 82.50€ ($73.65) per person. Rates include breakfast. AE, MC, V. Free parking. **Amenities:** Dining room; lounge; room service. *In room:* A/C, TV, hair dryer.

Hotel Mariluce *Value*   As you walk along the promenade away from the center, you'll note a flowering garden enclosed on one side by the walls of a Polish church; one wall is emblazoned with a gilded coat of arms. Behind the garden is the building that until 1945 was a refugee center that Poles throughout Europe used for finding friends and relatives. Today it's a reasonably priced hotel, a bargain for San Remo, offering sunny public rooms and simply furnished, small guest rooms with cramped tiled bathrooms. A passage under the street leads from the garden to the beach.

Corso Matuzia 3, 16038 San Remo. ☏ **0184-667805.** Fax 0184-667655. 23 units, 18 with bathroom (showers only). 52€ ($46.45) double without bathroom; 57€ ($50.90) double with bathroom. DC, MC, V. Closed Oct–May. **Amenities:** Lounge. *In room:* No phone.

Hotel Paradiso *Value*   This once-private villa is now one of the most homey accommodations in San Remo, lying in a residential area 100m (328 ft.) from the sea and only a short walk from the heart of the resort. A hearty welcome is extended, and the Paradiso attracts a loyal following. Its garden setting provides for a tranquil oasis in a high-traffic city. The place is not elegant, and its decor is of another day, but it is exceedingly comfortable. Try for a room overlooking the sea, because these also come with private balconies. The bathrooms are tiled and roomy, containing old-fashioned tubs. Guests gather in the evening in the lounge for drinks, or else enjoy cocktails in the garden. A fixed-price menu is changed daily here; it is reasonably priced and always offers some tempting Ligurian recipes.

Via Roccasterone 12, 18038 San Remo. ☏ **0184-571211.** Fax 0184-578176. 40 units. 94€–151€ ($83.95–$134.85) double. Half-board 67€–90€ ($59.85–$80.35) per person. AE, DC, MC, V. Parking 7€ ($6.25). **Amenities:** Restaurant; bar; room service; babysitting; laundry/dry cleaning. *In room:* A/C, TV, mini-bar, hair dryer.

WHERE TO DINE
VERY EXPENSIVE

Paolo e Barbara ★★ LIGURIAN/ITALIAN   Named after the husband-and-wife team that owns it (the Masieris), this restaurant stands near the casino and has caught the imagination of San Remo. It specializes in traditional regional recipes plus a handful of innovative dishes. Meals tend to be drawn-out affairs, so allow adequate time. Depending on the season, the menu might feature a tartare of raw marinated mackerel with garlic mousse and potato, tomato, and basil-flavored garnish; *troffie* (a regional pasta) with fresh pesto; or grilled crayfish with wild rice with fresh herbs, olive oil, and pine nuts. The specialty is an antipasto called *cappon magro*, a mix of steamed fish and vegetables covered with a sauce made of parsley, anchovies, olives, and capers.

Via Roma 47. (*C*) 0184-531653. Reservations recommended. Main courses 18€–22€ ($16.05–$19.65); fixed-price lunch 47€ ($41.95); tasting menu (without wine) 83€ ($74.10). AE, DC, MC, V. Fri–Tues 12:30–2pm and Thurs–Tues 8–10pm.

EXPENSIVE
Da Giannino ✿✿ LIGURIAN/SEAFOOD   This restaurant is still acclaimed as San Remo's finest restaurant, although Paolo e Barbara is closing in fast. In a conservatively elegant setting, you can enjoy such specialties as warm seafood antipasti, a flavorful risotto laced with cheese and a pungently aromatic green sauce, and a selection of main courses that changes with the availability of ingredients. An exotic selection is marinated cuttlefish gratinée. The wine list features many of the better vintages of both France and Italy.

Lungomare Trento e Trieste 23. (*C*) 0184-504014. Reservations required. Main courses 16€–26€ ($14.30–$23.20); fixed-price menus 52€–78€ ($46.45–$69.65). AE, DC, MC, V. Tues–Sat 12:30–2:30pm and 7:30–10pm.

MODERATE
Il Bagatto LIGURIAN/SEAFOOD   Il Bagatto provides good meals in the 16th-century home of an Italian duke, with dark beams and provincial chairs. It's in the shopping district, about 2 blocks from the sea. Our most recent dinner began with a choice of creamy lasagna and savory hors d'oeuvres. Especially pleasing are the scaloppine with artichokes and asparagus and the mixed grill of Mediterranean fish. All orders are accompanied by potatoes and a choice of vegetables, followed by crème caramel. Diners can select from many kinds of Ligurian fish, including sea bass filet in a sauce of fresh peppers and *gallinella*, the quintessential white-flesh Ligurian fish, roasted with potatoes and olives.

Via Matteotti 145. (*C*) 0184-531925. Reservations required. Main courses 10€–13€ ($8.95–$11.60). MC, V. Mon–Sat noon–3pm and 7:30–10pm. Closed July.

La Lanterna SEAFOOD   Many locals recommend La Lanterna, a nautical place near the harbor. Opened around 1917, it's one of the few restaurants that has survived in San Remo from the heady days of its Edwardian grandeur. The crowd can get very fashionable, especially in summer, when outdoor tables are set within view of the harbor. Meals might include an excellent fish soup (*brodetto di pesce con crostini*), a Ligurian fish fry, or a meat dish such as scaloppine in Marsala sauce. Sea bass and red snapper are available, and your selection might be served grilled or perhaps fried with olive oil, herbs, and lemon, or even baked with artichokes, olives, and white-wine sauce.

Via Molo di Ponente al Porto 16. (*C*) 0184-506855. Reservations required Sat–Sun. Main courses 10€–20€ ($8.95–$17.85). AE, MC, V. Tues–Sun 12:30–3pm and 7pm–midnight.

SAN REMO AFTER DARK
Most nightlife revolves around the **San Remo Casino,** Corso Inglesi 18 ((*C*) 0184-5951), in the center of town. For decades, visitors have dined in high style in the restaurant, reserved tables at the roof garden's cabaret, or tested their luck at the gaming tables. Like a white-walled palace, the pristine-looking casino

stands at the top of a steep flight of stone steps above the main artery of town. Its showroom hosts a variety of fashion shows, concerts, and theatrical productions throughout the year. There is no entrance fee for the American gaming rooms; all gaming rooms are open daily from 2:30pm to 3:30am. You'll be required to show a passport, and men must wear jackets and ties. For the slot-machines section, open Sunday to Friday 10am to 3am and Saturday 2:30pm to 3:30am, entrance is free and there's no dress code. The casino restaurant is open nightly 8:30pm to 1:30am, charging 30€ to 50€ ($26.80–$44.65) per person for dinner. Its orchestra plays everything from waltzes to rock. The roof-garden cabaret is open June to September daily, with shows beginning at 10:30pm. If you visit for drinks only (not dinner), the cost is 17.50€ ($15.65) per drink.

You should also check out your hotel's bar or the bar in one of the grand hotels (especially the Royal; see above), whose bars are always open to well-dressed nonguests. You can always strike out for the cafes along **Via Matteotti,** which serve drinks until late at night.

2 Genoa ★★

142km (88 miles) SW of Milan, 501km (311 miles) NW of Rome, 193km (120 miles) NE of Nice

With its dizzying mix of the old and the new, of sophistication and squalor, Genoa is as multilayered as the hills it clings to. It's always been first and foremost a port city: It was an important maritime center for the Roman Empire, the boyhood home of Christopher Columbus, and later one of the largest and wealthiest cities of Renaissance Europe. It's easy to capture glimpses of these former glory days on the narrow lanes and dank alleyways of Genoa's portside old town, where treasure-filled palaces and fine marble churches stand next to laundry-draped tenements. In fact, life within the old medieval walls seems frozen in time. The other Genoa, the modern city that stretches for miles along the coast and climbs the hills, is a city of international business, peaceful parks, and breezy belvederes from which you can enjoy views over this colorful metropolis and the sea that continues to define its identity.

ESSENTIALS

GETTING THERE   Alitalia and other carriers fly into the **Aeroporto Internazionale di Genova Cristoforo Colombo,** 6km (3¾ miles) west of the city center in Sestri Ponente (call ✆ **010-60151** for flight information).

Genoa has good **rail** connections with the rest of Italy; it lies only 1½ hours from Milan, 3 hours from Florence, and 1½ hours from the French border. Genoa has two major rail stations, **Stazione Principe** and **Stazione Brignole.** Chances are, you'll arrive at the Principe, Piazza Acquaverde, nearest to the harbor and the old part of the city. The Brignole, on Piazza Verde, lies in the heart of the modern city. Both trains and municipally operated buses run between the two stations. For train information, call ✆ **848-8880888,** toll-free in Italy.

Genoa is right along the main **autostrada (A10)** that begins at the French border and continues along the Ligurian coastline.

There's a 22-hour **ferry** service to Genoa originating in Palermo (Sicily), costing from 74€ ($66.10) per person. Ferries also leave Porto Torres (Sardinia) for Genoa, costing from 36€ ($32.15). For information, the number to call in Genoa is the **Stazione Marittima** at ✆ **010-2412534.**

VISITOR INFORMATION   The **Azienda di Promozione Turistica** is on Via al Porto Antico (✆ **010-248711**), open daily 9am to 6:30pm. You'll also

Genoa

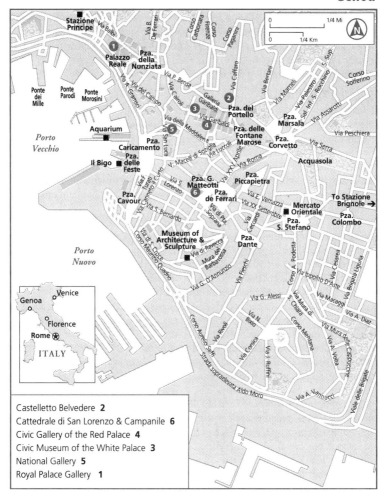

Castelletto Belvedere **2**
Cattedrale di San Lorenzo & Campanile **6**
Civic Gallery of the Red Palace **4**
Civic Museum of the White Palace **3**
National Gallery **5**
Royal Palace Gallery **1**

---

find **information booths** dispensing tourist literature at the rail stations and the airport. The rail-station office at Principe (📞 **010-2462633**) is open Monday to Saturday 9:30am to 6pm; the airport office (📞 **010-6015247**) is open Monday to Saturday 9:30am to 5:30pm.

FAST FACTS   Currency exchange is available at **Basso,** Via Gramsci 217 (📞 **010-2462805**), open Monday to Friday 8am to 6:30pm, and Saturday and Sunday 8:30am to 5:30pm. There are also exchange offices at the Principe rail station, open daily 7am to 10pm.

For assistance in a medical, police, or fire emergency, dial 📞 **113** at any time from any phone in Genoa. For automobile trouble, call **ACI,** Soccorso Stradale, at 📞 **116.**

The city's largest hospital, **Ospedale San Martino,** Largo Rosanna Benzilo 10 (📞 **010-5551**), maintains a roster of emergency services and can link you with an appropriate specialist.

At least one of Genoa's pharmacies remains open 24 hours, based on a revolving schedule that changes from week to week. One of the largest of the city's pharmacies is **Pescetto,** Via Bali 185R (*©* **010-2462697**), across from the Principe rail station.

To call a **taxi,** dial *©* **010-5966.**

SEEING THE SIGHTS

Like a half moon, the port encircles the Gulf of Genoa. Its hills slope down to the water, so walking is an up- and downhill affair. Genoa invites exploring at random more than any other port city along Italy's western coastline. Broad traffic-filled boulevards give way to dark and twisting *vicoli* or alleyways, which offer intrigue and interest at every turn (and danger at night from muggers). The center of the city's maritime life, the harbor in particular is worth a stroll. Sailors from many lands search for adventure and women in the little bars and cabarets occupying the back alleys.

Most of the section of interest lies between the two rail stations, **Stazione Principe,** on the western fringe of the town near the port, and **Stazione Brignole,** to the northeast, opening onto Piazza Verdi. A major artery is **Via XX Settembre,** running between Piazza Ferrari in the west and Piazza della Vittoria in the east. **Via Balbi** is another major artery, beginning east of Stazione Principe, off Piazza Acquaverde. Via Balbi ends at Piazza Nunziata.

From here, a short walk along Via Cairola leads to the most important street in Genoa, **Via Garibaldi,** the street of patricians, on which noble Genovese families erected splendid palazzi in late Renaissance times. The guiding hand behind the general appearance and most of the architecture was Alessi, who grew to fame in the 16th century (he studied under Michelangelo). Aside from the art collections housed in the **Palazzo Bianco** and **Palazzo Rosso** (see below), the street contains a wealth of treasures. The **Palazzo Podesta,** no. 7, hides a beautiful fountain in its courtyard, and the **Palazzo Tursi,** no. 9, now housing the municipal offices, proudly displays artifacts of famous Genoans, such as letters written by Christopher Columbus and the violin of Niccolò Paganini (which is still played on special occasions); visitors are allowed free entry to the building at times when the offices are open (Mon–Friday 8:30am–noon and 1–4pm).

The present harbor is the result of extensive rebuilding, following massive World War II bombardments that crippled its seaside. The best way to view the overall skyline is from a **harbor cruise.** Hour-long cruises on one of the boats in the fleet of the **Cooperativa Battellieri dei Porto di Genova** (*©* **010-265712**) provide a close look at the harbor bustle and at the **Lanterna,** the 110m (360-ft.) tall lighthouse built in 1544. Boats embark daily from Stazione Marittima, located on the harbor, a short distance south of Stazione Principe. The cruises cost 7.50€ ($6.70).

Acquario di Genova *(★★★)* *(Kids)*   The largest aquarium of Europe and one of the biggest attractions in all the land, this site explores the great richness of marine life. Launched for EXPO'92, it honored the fifth centenary of Columbus's arrival in the New World. The 40-tank aquarium was styled like a mammoth ship ready to set sail. Much enlarged since the expo, the aquarium seems to aid you in your discovery of the very mystery of the beginning of life in the ocean. Allow at least 3 hours for this attraction, including the recent addition of a new exhibition center called the Big Blue Ship.

The exhibits are not confined to the Ligurian coastline but range the world, capturing marine life from the great coral reefs of the planet to the tropical rain forests of the Amazon River basin. About every known sea creature you'd want to meet (and dozens you wouldn't) are on parade. The location is a 15-minute walk from Stazione Principe.

Ponte Spinola. ℂ **010-2481204.** Admission 11.25€ ($10.05) adults; 6.75€ ($6.05) ages 2–13; free 2 and under. Mon 10am–6pm; Tues–Fri 9:30am–7:30pm (Thurs to 10pm); Sat–Sun 9:30am–8:30pm. Bus: 12, 18, 19, and 34.

Civic Gallery of the Red Palace (Galleria Civica di Palazzo Rosso) ☆

This 17th-century palace was once the home of the Brignole-Sale, a local aristocratic family that founded a Genovese dynasty. It was restored after having been bombed in World War II and now contains a good collection of paintings, with such exceptional works as *Giuditta* by Veronese, *St. Sebastian* by Guido Reni, and *Cleopatra* by Guercino. The best-known works are Sir Anthony Van Dyck's portrait of Pauline and Anton Giulio Brignole-Sale from the original collection and the magnificent frescoes by Gregorio de Ferrari (*Spring* and *Summer*) and Domenico Piola (*Autumn* and *Winter*). There are also collections of ceramics and sculpture, and a display of gilded baroque statuary. Across from this red palace is the white palace, the Palazzo Bianco (see below).

Via Garibaldi 18. ℂ **010-5572013.** Admission 3€ ($2.70). Tues and Thurs -Fri 9am–1pm; Wed and Sat 9am–7pm; Sun 10am–6pm. Bus: 18, 20, 30, or 35.

Civic Museum of the White Palace (Museo Civico di Palazzo Bianco) ☆

The duchess of Gallier donated this palace, along with her art collection, to the city. Although the palace dates from the 16th century, its appearance is the work of later architects and reflects the most recent advances in museum planning. The most significant paintings, from the Dutch and Flemish schools, include Gerard David's *Polittico della Cervara* and Memling's *Jesus Blessing the Faithful,* as well as works by Sir Anthony Van Dyck and Peter Paul Rubens. A wide-ranging survey of European and local artists is presented, with paintings by Caravaggio, Zurbarán, and Murillo. You'll also find works by Bernardo Strozzi (a whole room) and Alessandro Magnasco (an excellent painting of a scene in a Genovese garden).

Via Garibaldi 11. ℂ **010-5572013.** Admission 3€ ($2.70). Tues and Thurs–Fri 9am–1pm; Wed and Sat 9am–7pm; Sun 10am–6pm. Bus: 18, 20, 30, 34, 35, or 36.

National Gallery (Galleria Nazionale) ☆

This gallery houses a major art collection. Its notable works include Joos van Cleve's *Madonna in Prayer,* Antonello da Messina's *Ecce Homo,* and Giovanni Pisano's *Giustizia.* The gallery is also known for its decorative arts collection (furniture, silver, and ceramics, among other items). The palace itself was designed for the Grimaldi family in the 16th century as a private residence, although the Spinolas took it over eventually.

In the Palazzo Spinola, Piazza della Pellicceria 1. ℂ **010-2477061.** Admission 4€ ($3.55). Tues–Sat 8:30am–7:30pm; Sun 1–8pm. Bus: 18, 20, 30, or 34.

Royal Palace Museum (Museo di Palazzo Reale) ☆

A 5-minute walk from Stazione Principe, the Royal Palace was started in about 1650, and work continued until the early 18th century. It was built for the Balbi family, was sold to the Durazzos, and became one of the royal palaces of the Savoias in 1824. King Charles Albert modified many of the rooms around 1840. As in all Genovese palazzi, some of these subsequent alterations marred the original designs. Its gallery is filled with paintings and sculpture, works by Van Dyck, Tintoretto, G. F. Romanelli, and L. Giordano. Frescoes and antiques from the 17th to the

---

Moments   **Genoa from on High**

From Piazza Portello (at the eastern end of Via Garibaldi), a funicular climbs to the **Castelletto belvedere,** which offers stunning views and refreshing breezes. It costs .30€ (25¢) each way and runs daily 6:40am to midnight.

A similar climb is via the **Granarolo funicular,** leaving from Piazza del Principe, behind the rail station of the same name, and ascending 305m (1,000 ft.) to Porto Granarolo, one of the gates in the city's 17th-century walls; there's a parklike belvedere in front. It costs .75€ (65¢) each way and operates every 15 minutes daily 6am to 11:45pm.

An elevator costing 3.35€ ($3) lifts you to the top of **Il Brigo,** the mast-like tower that is Genoa's new landmark, built to commemorate the 1992 Columbus quincentennial; the observation platform provides an eagle's-eye view of one of Europe's busiest ports. From March to August, it operates Tuesday to Saturday 11am to 1pm and 3 to 6pm, and Sunday from 11am to 1pm and 2:30 to 6:30pm; from September to February, hours are Tuesday to Friday from 11am to 1pm and 2 to 5pm, and Sunday from 11am to 1pm and 2:30 to 5pm.

19th centuries are displayed. Seek out, in particular, the **Hall of Mirrors** and the **Throne Room.**

Via Balbi 10. ℂ 010-2710201. Admission 4€ ($3.55). Mon–Tues 8:15am–1:45pm; Wed–Sun 8:15am–7:15pm. Bus: 18, 19, or 20.

Cattedrale di San Lorenzo & Campanile ✦✦   Genoa is noted for its medieval churches, and this one towers over them all. A British shell fired during World War II almost spelled its doom, but miraculously the explosion never went off. The cathedral is distinguished by its bands of black-and-white marble adorning the **facade** ✦✦ in the Pisan style. In its present form, it dates from the 13th century, although it was erected on the foundation of a much earlier structure. Alessi designed the dome, and the *campanile* (bell tower) dates from the 16th century. The **Chapel of John the Baptist (Cappella di San Giovanni)** ✦, with interesting Renaissance sculpture, is said to contain the remains of the saint for whom it's named. Off the nave and in the vaults, the cathedral **treasury** contains a trove of artifacts acquired during Genoa's heyday as a mercantile empire. Some of the claims are a bit hard to believe, however (a crystal dish reputed to have been used for dinner service at the Last Supper and a blue chalcedony platter on which the head of John the Baptist was placed for its delivery to Salome). Other treasures include an 11th-century arm reliquary of St. Anne and a jewel-studded Byzantine Zaccaria Cross.

Piazza San Lorenzo, Via Tommaso Reggio 17. ℂ **010-2471831.** Admission 5€ ($4.45). Mon–Sat 9–11:30am and 3–6pm. Bus: 42.

SHOPPING

Shopping in Genoa includes a good selection of apparel, antiques, jewelry, and foodstuff. Classic but contemporary **Berti,** Via XII Ottobre 94R (ℂ **010-540026**), carries a line of Burberry items, as well as British-inspired creations by designers such as Valentino and Le Copain. Elegant **Pescetto,** Via Scurreria 8

Rosso (✆ **010-2473433**), offers men's and women's designer outfits and fragrances, plus accessories such as leather bags and wallets.

On a street overrun with goldsmiths, the reputable **Code-villa,** Via Orefici 53R (✆ **010-2472567**), fashions jewelry and small objects out of gold, silver, and a wide variety of precious and semiprecious stones.

In the historic center of town, the **Dallai Libreria Antiquaria,** Piazza de Marini 11R (✆ **010-2472338**), handles first editions and rare books and prints from the 18th and 19th centuries.

Pecchiolo, Via Pisa 13 (✆ **010-3625082**), sells upscale dinnerware and cookware of ceramic, crystal, and silver.

If you'd rather have a one-stop shopping excursion, **La Rinascente,** Via Ettore Vernazza 1 (✆ **010-586995**), and **Coin,** Via XX Settembre (✆ **010-543126**), are the two biggest department stores in town.

The **Mercato Orientale,** the sprawling food market of Genoa, might not be as exotic as it was back in its heyday of the 17th century, but it is still one of Europe's greatest and most colorful markets. A great photo op, you can snap at will at not only the bounty of the Ligurian countryside, including olives, fresh herbs, and citrus fruits, but also every possible known sea creature that's edible (many animals looking like they are not for the faint of heart to consume). The market stands at the edge of the historic core of Genoa and Stazione Brignole on Via XX Settembre, close to Via Consolazione. We like to go early in the morning when it opens Monday to Saturday at 7am, although it is bustling and active until noon.

After you visit the market you can wander the streets just north of here, including **Via Colombo** and **Via San Vincenzo,** which are filled with shops that evoke the late Middle Ages. Each one is devoted to a different delight, from the finest of olive oils, canned pestos, and a series of bakeries and pasticcerias.

WHERE TO STAY

Generally, hotels in Genoa are second-rate, but some good finds await those who search diligently.

Warning: Some of the cheap hotels and pensioni in and around the waterfront are to be avoided. Our recommendations, however, are suitable even for women traveling alone.

EXPENSIVE TO MODERATE

Bristol Palace ★   The late-19th-century Bristol boasts a number of features that'll make your stay in Genoa special, even though it's in the grimy heart of the old town. Its obscure entrance behind colonnades is misleading; the public rooms are decorated nicely with traditional pieces, although both the fabrics and the furnishings are beginning to show their age. The larger of the guest rooms have an old-fashioned elegance, often with chandeliers, Queen Anne desks, and padded headboards. All the rooms contain at least one antique and often several, plus first-rate mattresses. The bathrooms are generally large; some come with whirlpool tubs. The hotel's stairway is one of the most stunning in Genoa.

Via XX Settembre 35, 16121 Genova. ✆ **010-592541.** Fax 010-561756. www.hotelbristolpalace.com. 133 units. 120€–335€ ($107.15–$299.15) double; 620€ ($553.65) suite. Rates include breakfast. AE, DC, MC, V. Parking 17.50€ ($15.65). Bus: 17, 18, 19, 20, 37, or 44. **Amenities:** Restaurant; bar; room service; babysitting; laundry/dry cleaning. *In room:* A/C, TV, minibar, hair dryer.

City Hotel   A good, solid choice, the City occupies a starkly angular stucco-and-travertine building, surrounded by crumbling town houses. The convenient location, near Piazza Corvetto and Via Garibaldi, is one of the best features. Other pluses are a welcoming staff, a comfortable wood-and-granite lobby, guest rooms with parquet floors, and specially designed furniture. The tiled bathrooms are compact.

Via San Sebastiano 6, 16123 Genova. ℂ **010-5545.** Fax 010-586301. www.bestwestern.it/city-ge. 66 units (showers only). 149€–284€ ($133.05–$253.60) double; 199€–495€ ($177.70–$442.05) suite. Rates include breakfast. AE, DC, MC, V. Parking 20€ ($17.85). Bus: 17 or 18. **Amenities:** Restaurant; bar; room service; laundry/dry cleaning. *In room:* A/C, TV, minibar, hair dryer, safe.

Columbus Sea Hotel 🎖 One of the best moderately priced hotels in town, the Columbus Sea looks out at the new cruise-ship terminal. It's warmer and more inviting inside than its cold boxy exterior suggests, with guest rooms that are spacious for the most part, in muted colors with Oriental carpeting. Four rooms are suitable for travelers with disabilities. Each accommodation comes with a compact tiled bathroom. The public rooms are more gracious, with a certain flair.

Via Milano 63, 16126 Genova. ℂ **010-265051.** Fax 010-255226. www.columbussea.com. 80 units (showers only). 152€–218€ ($135.75–$194.65) double; from 262€ ($233.95) junior suite. Rates include buffet breakfast. AE, DC, DISC, MC, V. Free parking. Bus: 1, 3, 7, 8, 18, 19, 20, 30, or 34. **Amenities:** Restaurant; bar; courtesy car; room service; babysitting; laundry/dry cleaning; babysitting. *In room:* A/C, TV, minibar, hair dryer.

Hotel Savoia Majestic 🎖 Situated across from Piazza Principe, the 1887 Savoia still contains some of its original accessories, although its heyday has long since passed. The decor of the high-ceilinged guest rooms ranges from modern to conservatively old-fashioned. Try for a room on the sixth floor for the best harbor views. Some of the bathrooms are unusually large, done in pink marble. Because the rooms vary so widely, your experience will depend entirely on which room you get. You might ask to see a room before you commit. The lobby and reception area are shared with the **Hotel Savoia Continental** (same phone number), where doubles are 149€ ($133.05).

Via Arsenale di Terra 5, 16126 Genova. ℂ **010-261641.** Fax 010-261883. 120 units. 123€–253€ ($109.85–$225.95) double; from 278€ ($248.25) suite. Rates include breakfast. AE, DC, MC, V. Valet parking 15€ ($13.40). Bus: 19, 20, 35, 37, or 41. **Amenities:** Restaurant; lounge; gym; courtesy car; room service; babysitting; laundry/dry cleaning. *In room:* A/C, TV, minibar, hair dryer, safe.

Jolly Hotel Plaza 🎖 A member of the Jolly chain, this hotel is newer than its modified classic facade would suggest. Near Piazza Corvetto, it was built in 1950 to replace an older hotel destroyed during a World War II air raid. In 1992, the hotel was renovated and enlarged, linking two former hotels, the Baglioni Eliseo and the Plaza. The rooms in the old Eliseo are generally more spacious than those in the Plaza (and better decorated). Elegant touches include mother-of-pearl inlay in the doors and marble bathrooms. Special rooms are set aside for nonsmokers or travelers with disabilities.

Via Martin Piaggio 11, 16122 Genova. ℂ **800/221-2626** in the U.S., 800/237-0319 in Canada, or 010-83161. Fax 010-8391850. www.jollyhotels.it. 146 units (showers only). 175€–260€ ($156.30–$232.20) double; 516€ ($460.80) suite. Rates include breakfast. AE, DC, MC, V. Parking 18€ ($16.05) nearby. Bus: 18, 34, or 37. **Amenities:** Restaurant; bar; room service; babysitting; laundry/dry cleaning. *In room:* A/C, TV, minibar, hair dryer.

INEXPENSIVE

Albergo Viale Sauli This hotel is on the second floor of a modern concrete office building, just off a busy shopping street. It's scattered over three floors, each reachable by elevator from the lobby. The high-ceilinged public rooms include a well-managed reception area. Enore Sceresini is the opera-loving owner, and his guests usually include businesspeople, who appreciate cleanliness and comfort. Each guest room has marble floors and a spacious bathroom.

Viale Sauli 5, 16121 Genova. ✆ 010-561397. Fax 010-590092. www.paginegialle.it/vialesauli. 56 units (showers only). 103€ ($92) double. Rates include breakfast. AE, DC, MC, V. Parking 12.50€ ($11.15) nearby. Bus: 33 or 37. **Amenities:** Lounge; room service; laundry. *In room:* A/C, TV, minibar, hair dryer.

Hotel Agnello d'Oro ⟨*Value*⟩ This is one of Genoa's best bargains. When the Doria family owned this structure and everything around it in the 1600s, they carved their family crest on the walls near the top of the alley. The symbol was a golden lamb, and you can still see one at the point where the narrow street joins the busy boulevard leading to Stazione Principe. The hotel, named after the animal on the crest, is a 17th-century building that includes vaulted ceilings and paneling in the lobby. About half of the guest rooms are in a newer wing, but if you want the oldest ones, ask for room nos. 6, 7, or 8.

Vico delle Monachette 6, 16126 Genova. ✆ **010-2462084.** Fax 010-2462327. www.hotelagnellodoro.it. 38 units. 93€ ($83.05) double. Rates include breakfast. AE, DC, MC, V. Parking 10€ ($8.95). Bus: 18, 19, 20, 30, 32, or 41. **Amenities:** Restaurant; bar; room service; babysitting; laundry/dry cleaning. *In room:* A/C, TV.

Hotel Astoria Built in the 1920s but opened as a hotel only in 1978, this place offers lots of polished paneling, wrought-iron accents, beige marble floors, and a baronial carved fireplace. The guest rooms are comfortably furnished and well maintained. In 1998, the entire hotel was renewed, with neatly kept bathrooms. The hotel sits on an uninspiring square that contains a filling station, and its view encompasses a traffic hub and many square blocks of apartment buildings.

Piazza Brignole 4, 16122 Genova. ✆ **010-873316.** Fax 010-8317326. 69 units. 150€ ($133.95) double. Rates include breakfast. AE, DC, MC, V. Parking 12.50€ ($11.15). Bus: 18. **Amenities:** Bar; lounge; room service; laundry. *In room:* A/C, TV, minibar, hair dryer, safe.

Hotel Vittoria Orlandi Because this hotel is built on one of the hillsides for which Genoa is famous, its entrance is under a tunnel opening at a point about a block from Stazione Principe. An elevator will take you up to the reception area. The guest rooms are standardized and fairly basic, and the bathrooms are small but neat. Many rooms have balconies. One appeal of this hotel is its quiet location, sheltered from the boulevards by other buildings.

Via Baldi 33–45, 16126 Genova. ✆ **010-261923.** Fax 010-2462656. www.vittoriaorlandini.com. 41 units. 77.50€–103€ ($69.20–$92) double. AE, DC, MC, V. Bus: 18, 20, 35, 37, or 41. **Amenities:** Lounge; room service; laundry/dry cleaning. *In room:* A/C, TV, minibar.

WHERE TO DINE

Fast food is a Genoese specialty, and any number of storefronts disburse focaccia, the heavenly Ligurian flat bread often stuffed with cheese and topped with herbs, olives, onions, and other vegetables. Two favorites are **La Focacceria di Teobaldo,** Via Balbi 115R (✆ **010-2462294**), and **Il Fornaio di Sattanino,** Via Fiasella 18R (✆ **010-580972**).

Another Genovese favorite is *farinata,* a cross between a ravioli and a crepe, made from chickpea flour and stuffed with spinach and ricotta, lightly fried, and often topped with walnut-cream sauce. Locals say that this delicious concoction gets no better than at the two outlets of **Antica Sciamada,** Via Ravecca 19R and Via San Giorgio 14R.

Da Giacomo ⟨*✦*⟩ LIGURIAN Lots of people think that Da Giacomo is the best restaurant in Genoa; we give an edge to the Gran Gotto, below, but Da Giacomo is very good. The service is excellent, as is the modern dining room, graced with plants. Ligurian cooking is dominated by the sea, and the menu begins with superb seafood antipasti, some of which is raw, carved with the exquisite care that you find in Tokyo. Meat, fish, and poultry dishes are prepared with unusual flair. Pesto accompanies many dishes, especially the pasta. (During the Crusades, it was reported that the Genovese contingent could always be identified by the aroma of pesto surrounding them.) Guests can choose from some of the finest regional wines in Italy, and the desserts are made fresh daily. There's also a piano bar where you can dance.

Corso Italia 1R. © 010-311041. Reservations recommended. Main courses 15€–20€ ($13.40–$17.85); fixed-price menu 37.50€–60€ ($33.50–$53.60). DC, MC, V. Daily 12:30–2:30pm and 7:30–11pm. Bus: 18.

Gran Gotto ☆☆ SEAFOOD   Our pick for Genoa's top restaurant opened in 1937 and has been in the same family since. The emphasis is on seafood, but the meat and pasta dishes aren't neglected. The most typical offering is *trenette al pesto,* paper-thin noodles served with pesto. The delicately simmered risotto is also tempting. The main dishes are reasonably priced and of a high standard, including the mixed fish fry, French baby squid, filet of lamb in a port sauce, and *rognone al cognac* (tender calves' kidneys cooked and delicately flavored in cognac). The *zuppa di pesce* (fish soup) makes a wonderful lunch.

Viale Brigate Bisagno 69R. © 010-583644. Reservations recommended. Main courses 12€–15€ ($10.70–$13.40). AE, DC, MC, V. Mon–Fri 12:30–2:30pm and 7:30–10:30pm; Sat 7:30–10:30pm. Closed Aug 12–31. Bus: 31.

Ristorante Saint Cyr LIGURIAN/PIEDMONTESE   At lunch, this place buzzes with talk of business deals; dinnertime brings a crowd of locals here to enjoy dishes adapted from regional recipes. Menu items change daily, although recent offerings featured rice with truffles and cheese, a timbale of fresh spinach, a charlotte of fish, and a variety of braised meats, each delicately seasoned. Specialties include *scamone* (a certain cut of beef) cooked in Barolo wine and *ravioli al sugo di carne* (with a sauce made from meat juices).

Piazza Marsala 4. © 010-886897. Reservations required. Main courses 15€–17.50€ ($13.40–$15.65). AE, DC, MC, V. Mon–Fri noon–3pm and 8–11pm; Sat 8–11pm. Closed Dec 23–Jan 7 and 2 weeks in Aug. Bus: 33, 34, or 36.

Ristorante Zeffirino LIGURIAN   Located in a cul-de-sac just off one of the busiest boulevards, this place has hosted everyone from Frank Sinatra and Luciano Pavarotti to Pope John Paul II and Liza Minnelli. At least 14 members of the Zeffirino family prepare the best pasta in the city, using recipes collected from all over Italy. These include lesser-known varieties such as quadrucci, pettinati, and cappelletti, as well as the more familiar tagliatelle and lasagna. Next, you can select from a vast array of meat and fish, along with 1,000 kinds of wine. Ligurian specialties, including *risotto alla pescatore* and beef stew with artichokes, are featured. Try a wide array of shellfish, either baked or steamed, served with seasonal vegetables.

Via XX Settembre 20. © 010-591990. Reservations recommended. Main courses 15€–30€ ($13.40–$26.80); fixed-price menu 35€–45€ ($31.25–$40.20). AE, DC, MC, V. Daily noon–midnight. Bus: 17, 18, 19, 20, 37, or 44.

GENOA AFTER DARK

Warning: Keep your wits about you after dark in Genoa, especially in the labyrinthine alleys of the old medieval neighborhoods. The neighborhoods around the bus station and Piazza Matteotti are especially dubious; they're a center for the drug trade and prostitution.

You'll find enough discos to keep you fully occupied every night. The best of them is **Mako,** Corso Italia 28R (© **010-367652**), which has a piano bar, a disco, and a restaurant. Another centrally located contender for the bar/disco trade is **Just One,** Via Brigata Salerno 4R (© **010-3990872**).

A favorite bar with the young and hip is **Le Corbusier,** V.S. Donato 36 (© **010-2468652**), which draws artists and students. Art showings are often staged here, even poetry readings. It's like a literary salon and a welcome change from beach bars with umbrellas.

Looking for a simple pint of beer, some pub grub, and a dose of English humor? Head for the **Britannia Pub,** Vicolo della Cassana, near Piazza de Ferrari (© **010-2474532**), where groups of friends fill a woodsy-looking setting.

The most popular gay spot is **La Cage,** Via Sampierdarena 167R (© **010-6454555**), attracting mainly males 21 to 40. There's a 5€ ($4.45) cover, and it's open Tuesday to Sunday 10pm to 3:30am.

3 Rapallo ⭐

477km (296 miles) NW of Rome, 27km (17 miles) SE of Genoa, 161km (100 miles) S of Milan

Known for years to the chic crowd that lives in the villas on the hillside, Rapallo occupies a remarkable site overlooking the Gulf of Tigullio. In summer the crowded heart of Rapallo takes on a carnival air, as hordes of sunbathers occupy the rocky sands along the beach. In the area is an 18-hole golf course, as well as an indoor pool, a riding club, and a modern harbor.

You can also take a cable car or a bus to the **Montallegro Sanctuary (Santuario di Montallegro).** Inside this 16th-century church are some interesting frescoes and a curious Byzantine icon of the Virgin that allegedly flew here on its own from Dalmatia. The views over the sea and valleys are the main reason to come up here, though, and they're even more breathtaking from the summit of **Monte Rosa,** a short uphill hike away. There are many opportunities for summer **boat trips,** not only to Portofino but also to the Cinque Terre.

Rapallo's long history is often likened to Genoa's. It became part of the Repubblica Superba in 1229, but Rapallo had existed long before that. Its **cathedral** dates from the 6th century, when it was founded by the bishops of Milan. Walls once enclosed the medieval town, but now only the **Saline Gate** remains. Rapallo has also been the scene of many an international meeting, the most notable of which was the 1917 conference of wartime allies.

Today Rapallo is a bit past its heyday, although it was once known as one of Europe's most fashionable resorts, numbering among its residents Ezra Pound and D. H. Lawrence. Other artists, poets, and writers have been drawn to its natural beauty, which has been marred in part by an uncontrolled building boom brought on by tourism. At the innermost corner of the Gulf of Tigullio, Rapallo is still the most famous resort on the Riviera di Levante, a position that it owes to its year-round mild climate.

ESSENTIALS

GETTING THERE   Three **trains** from Genoa stop here each hour from 4:30am to midnight, costing 2.10€ ($1.90) one way. A train also links Rapallo with Santa Margherita every 30 minutes, costing .75€ (65¢) one way. For more information, dial © **848-8880888** toll-free in Italy. From Santa Margherita, a **bus** operated by Tigullio runs every 20 to 25 minutes to Rapallo, costing .70€

(60¢) one way and taking half an hour. The bus information office is at Piazza Vittorio Veneto in Santa Margherita (✆ **0185-288834**).

If you have a **car** and are coming from Genoa, go southeast along A12.

VISITOR INFORMATION   The **tourist office** is at Via Diaz 9 (✆ **0185-230346**), open Monday through Saturday 9:30am to 12:30pm and 2:30 to 5:30pm, and Sunday 9am to 12:30pm.

WHERE TO STAY

Grand Hotel Bristol   This hotel, one of the Riviera's grand old buildings, is still a viable choice, although it has gone downhill recently. Built in 1908, it was reopened in 1984 and the pink-and-white facade was spruced up but basically left unchanged. The interior, however, was gutted. Some guest rooms have private terraces, and all contain electronic window blinds, lots of mirrors, oversize beds, and large bathrooms.

Via Aurelia Orientale 369, 16035 Rapallo. ✆ 0185-273313. Fax 0185-55800. www.tigullio.net/bristol. 91 units. 186.50€–330€ ($166.55–$294.70) double; from 475€ ($424.20) suite. Rates include breakfast. AE, MC, V. Parking 12.50€ ($11.15) in garage; free outside. **Amenities:** 2 restaurants; lounge; pool; salon; room service; massage; babysitting; laundry. *In room:* A/C, TV, minibar, hair dryer.

Hotel Eurotel   With seven floors, this vivid sienna-colored structure is one of the tallest hotels in town, set above the port on a winding road where you'll have to negotiate the oncoming traffic with care. (Many of the units, though, are privately owned condos.) All the guest rooms contain built-in cabinets, arched loggias with views over the gulf of Rapallo, and beds that fold, Murphy-style, into the walls. The tiled bathrooms, though a bit small, are neatly organized.

Via Aurelia di Ponente 22, 16035 Rapallo. ✆ 0185-60981. Fax 0185-50635. www.tigullio.net/eurotel. 65 units. 114€–148€ ($101.80–$132.15) double. Rates include breakfast. AE, DC, MC, V. Parking 13€ ($11.60) in garage; free outside. **Amenities:** Restaurant; bar; pool; room service; massage; babysitting; laundry/dry cleaning. *In room:* A/C, TV, minibar, hair dryer.

Hotel Giulio Cesare *(Value*   This modernized villa, on the coast road about 27m (90 ft.) from the sea, is a bargain. When the genial owner skillfully renovated it, he kept expenses down to keep room rates lower. The guest rooms are furnished with tasteful reproductions and feature views of the Gulf of Tigullio (most have balconies). Ask for the top-floor rooms if you want a quieter room with a better view.

Corso Colombo 52, 16035 Rapallo. ✆ 0185-50685. Fax 0185-60896. www.hotel-giulio-cesare.it. 33 units. 82.65€–113.60€ ($73.80–$101.45) double with breakfast; 70€ ($62.50) per person double with half-board. AE, MC, V. Parking 7.50€ ($6.70). Closed Nov 6–Dec 20. **Amenities:** Dining room; lounge; room service. *In room:* A/C, TV, hair dryer, safe (in most rooms).

Hotel Miramare   On the water near a stone gazebo is this 1929 re-creation of a Renaissance villa, with exterior frescoes that have faded in the salt air. The gardens in front have been replaced by a glass extension that contains a dining area. The accommodations are clean and simple, comfortable, and high-ceilinged; many have iron balconies that stretch toward the harbor.

Lungomare Vittorio Veneto 27, 16035 Rapallo. ✆ 0185-230261. Fax 0185-273570. www.miramarehotel.it. 28 units (7 with shower only). 77€–129€ ($68.75–$115.20) double; 149€ ($133.05) suite. Half-board 82€–98€ ($73.25–$87.50) per person. AE, DC, MC, V. Parking 12.50€ ($11.15). Closed Nov. **Amenities:** Restaurant; lounge; room service; babysitting; laundry/dry cleaning. *In room:* A/C, TV, minibar, hair dryer, safe.

WHERE TO DINE

Ristorante da Monique SEAFOOD   This is one of the most popular seafood restaurants along the harbor, especially in summer, featuring a nautical decor and big windows overlooking the boats in the marina. As you'd expect, fish is the specialty, including seafood salad, fish soup, risotto with shrimp, spaghetti with clams or mussels, grilled fish, and both tagliatelle and scampi "Monique." Some of these dishes might not always hit the mark, but you'll rarely go wrong ordering the grilled fish.

Lungomare Vittorio Veneto 6. (✆) **0185-50541.** Reservations recommended. Main courses 7.50€–15€ ($6.70–$13.40). AE, DC, MC, V. Wed–Mon noon–2:30pm and 7:30–10pm. Closed Jan 7–Feb 10.

Ristorante Elite *Value* SEAFOOD   This popular restaurant is just up a busy avenue from the harbor; the pleasant room, hung with nautical items and paintings of local scenes, is a little less formal than the many seafood restaurants on the waterfront. Mainly fish is served; the offering depends on the catch of the day. Your dinner might consist of mussels marinara, minestrone Genovese style, risotto marinara, *trenette al pesto*, scampi, zuppa di pesce, turbot, or a mixed fish fry. A limited selection of standard meat dishes is available, too. At the peak of the midsummer invasion, the restaurant is likely to be open every day.

Via Milite Ignoto 19. (✆) **0185-50551.** Reservations recommended. Main courses 6€–14€ ($5.35–$12.50); *menù turistico* 17.50€ ($15.65); tasting menu 30€ ($26.80). AE, MC, V. Thurs–Tues noon–2:30pm and 7:30–10pm. Closed Nov.

Ristorante Miramare SEAFOOD/LIGURIAN   This restaurant serves well-prepared unpretentious food in a modern dining room overlooking the sea. Your dinner might include fried calamari, spaghetti with clams, sea bass or turbot baked with potatoes and artichokes, veal in Marsala sauce, or flavorful versions of fish soup.

In the Hotel Miramare, Lungomare Vittorio Veneto 27. (✆) **0185-230261.** Reservations recommended. Main courses 7€–11.50€ ($6.25–$10.25); fixed-price menu 26€ ($23.20). AE, DC, MC, V. Daily 12:30–2:30pm and 7:30–9:30pm.

4 Santa Margherita Ligure ★★

31km (19 miles) E of Genoa, 5km (3 miles) S of Portofino, 477km (296 miles) NW of Rome

Like Rapallo, Santa Margherita Ligure occupies a beautiful position on the Gulf of Tigullio. Its attractive palm-fringed harbor is usually thronged with fun seekers, and the resort offers the widest range of accommodations in all price levels on the eastern Riviera. It has a festive appearance, with a promenade, flower beds, and palms swaying in the wind. As is typical of the Riviera, the town's sandy, pebbly beach is packed with a party crowd in fine weather. Santa Margherita Ligure is linked to Portofino by a narrow road. The climate is mild, even in winter, drawing many retirees from northern Europe.

The town dates from A.D. 262. The official name of Santa Margherita Ligure was given to the town by Vittorio Emanuele II in 1863. Before that, it had many other names, including Porto Napoleone, an 1812 designation from Napoleon.

Santa Margherita's one landmark of note is its namesake **Basilica di Santa Margherita,** just off the seafront on Piazza Caprera (✆ **0185-286555**). The interior is richly embellished, with Italian and Flemish paintings, along with relics of the saint for whom the town was named. Admission is free, and it's open daily 7am to noon and 3 to 7pm.

ESSENTIALS

GETTING THERE   Three **trains** per hour arrive from Genoa daily 4:30am to midnight, costing 1.85€ ($1.65) one way. The train station in Santa Margherita is at Piazza Federico Raoul Nobili. For more information, call

☎ **848-8880888** toll-free in Italy. **Buses** run frequently between Portofino and Santa Margherita Ligure daily, costing 1€ (90¢) one way. You can also catch a bus in Rapallo to Santa Margherita; during the day one leaves every 20 to 25 minutes. For information, call ☎ **0185-5288834.** If you have a **car,** take Route 227 southeast from Genoa.

VISITOR INFORMATION   The **tourist office** is at Via 25 Aprile 2B (☎ **0185-287485**), open Monday to Saturday 9am to 12:30pm and 2:30 to 5:30pm.

WHERE TO STAY
EXPENSIVE
Grand Hotel Miramare 🌟🌟   The top hotel in town, this 1929 palace has kept up with the times better than has the Imperiale (see below). Its 1904 core was the home of Giacomo Costa, who transformed it into a hotel that attracted celebrities such as Laurence Olivier and Vivien Leigh. It was from the terrace here in 1933 that Marconi succeeded in transmitting telegraph and telephone signals a distance of more than 145km (90 miles). Separated from a private stony beach by a busy boulevard, it's a 3-minute walk from the center of town. The guest rooms are classically furnished, with elegant beds and spacious bathrooms. Even some of the standard rooms have large terraces with sea views. The curved outdoor pool adjoins a raised sun terrace dotted with parasols and iron tables.

Via Milite Ignoto 30, 16038 Santa Margherita Ligure. ☎ **800/223-6800** in the U.S., or 0185-287013. Fax 0185-284651. www.grandhotelmiramare.it. 84 units. 145€–191€ ($129.50–$170.55) double; from 360€ ($321.50) suite. Rates include breakfast. AE, DC, MC, V. Parking 15€–17.50€ ($13.40–$15.65). **Amenities:** Restaurant; lounge; lovely pool; skywater (paragliding) school; room service; babysitting; laundry. *In room:* A/C, TV, minibar, hair dryer, safe.

Imperiale Palace Hotel 🌟   The Imperiale looks like a gilded palace. Although still regal, it's fading a bit, and the Miramare (see above) has overtaken it. It's built against a hillside at the edge of the resort, surrounded by semitropical gardens. The public rooms live up to the hotel's name, with vaulted ceilings, satin-covered antiques, ornate mirrors, and inlaid marble floors. The guest rooms vary widely, from royal suites to simple singles away from the sea. Many have elaborate ceilings, balconies, brass beds, chandeliers, and antique furniture, but others are rather sparse. The large tiled or marble bathrooms come with robes and heated towel racks.

Via Pagana 19, 16038 Santa Margherita Ligure. ☎ **0185-288991.** Fax 0185-284223. www.hotel imperiale.com. 93 units. 252€–367€ ($225.05–$327.75) double; 427€–529€ ($381.30–$472.40) suite. Rates include breakfast. AE, DC, MC, V. Free parking. Closed Nov–Mar. **Amenities:** 2 restaurants; 2 bars; pool; recreation center; room service; babysitting; laundry. *In room:* A/C, TV, minibar, hair dryer, safe.

MODERATE
Hotel Continental 🌟   The Continental is the only hotel directly on the water, and the high-ceilinged public rooms give a glimpse of the gardens leading down to a private beach. The guest rooms are filled with comfortable, if somewhat faded, furnishings and often have French windows opening onto wrought-iron balconies. Try for a top-floor room in the main building (the annex contains lackluster lodgings). The view encompasses the curved harbor in the center of town, a few miles away. Since the early 1900s, the Ciana family has managed this property and also the Regina Elena, Metropole, and Laurin.

Via Pagana 8, 16038 Santa Margherita Ligure. ℂ **0185-286512.** Fax 0185-284463. www.hotel-continental.it. 74 units. 134€–176€ ($119.65–$157.15) double. Rates include breakfast. AE, DC, MC, V. Parking 11€–16€ ($9.80–$14.30). **Amenities:** Restaurant; bar; room service; laundry. *In room:* A/C, TV, minibar, hair dryer, safe.

Hotel Regina Elena ⭐   This pastel-painted hotel is along the scenic thoroughfare leading to Portofino. The guest rooms are modern, most opening onto a balcony with a sea view, and bathrooms are tidy. An annex in the garden contains additional units, but they're not as desirable. The hotel was built in 1908 and many turn-of-the-20th-century details remain, including a marble staircase. It's operated by the Ciana family (see listing above), which has been receiving guests for almost 100 years.

Lungomare Milite Ignoto 44, 16038 Santa Margherita Ligure. ℂ **0185-287003.** Fax 0185-284473. www.reginaelena.it. 108 units. 128€–182€ ($114.30–$162.55) double, including breakfast; 164€–234€ ($146.45–$208.95) double with breakfast and dinner. AE, DC, MC, V. Free parking. **Amenities:** Dining room; lounge; pool; Jacuzzi; room service; babysitting; laundry. *In room:* A/C, TV, minibar, hair dryer, safe.

Park Hotel Suisse   Set in a garden above the town center, the Suisse features a panoramic view of the sea and harbor, which lie across the street. It has seven floors, all modern in design, with occasional deep private balconies that are like alfresco living rooms. The medium-size guest rooms that open onto the rear gardens, without a sea view, cost slightly less.

Via Favale 31, 16038 Santa Margherita Ligure. ℂ **0185-289571.** Fax 0185-281469. parkhotelsuisse@libero.it. 85 units (showers only). 118.80€–185.90€ ($106.10–$166.05) double; 176.60€–258.25€ ($157.70–$230.60) suite. Rates include continental breakfast. AE, DC, MC, V. **Amenities:** 2 restaurants; lounge; pool; room service; babysitting; laundry. *In room:* A/C, TV, hair dryer.

INEXPENSIVE

Albergo Conte Verde *(Finds*   This villa offers one of the warmest welcomes in town, with shuttered windows, flower boxes and a small front garden where tables are set out for refreshments. Only 2 blocks from the sea, this third-class hotel has been revamped, and its guest rooms are simple but adequate, ranging from small to medium (the more spacious units also have terraces). All have small tiled bathrooms.

Via Zara 1, 16038 Santa Margherita Ligure. ℂ **0185-287139.** Fax 0185-284211. cverde@zeus.new networks.it. 35 units, 26 with bathroom (showers only). 40€–70€ ($35.70–$62.50) double without bathroom; 50€–100€ ($44.65–$89.30) double with bathroom. Rates include buffet breakfast. AE, DC, MC, V. Parking 12.50€ ($11.15). Closed Jan–Feb. **Amenities:** Bar; gym; babysitting. *In room:* TV, hair dryer, safe.

Hotel Jolanda   Since the 1940s, the Pastine family continues to welcome visitors to its little hotel, a short walk from the sea on a peaceful little street. A patio serves as a kind of open-air living room. The guest rooms are comfortably furnished, ranging from small to medium, each with a well-organized bathroom.

Via Luisito Costa 6, 16038 Santa Margherita Ligure. ℂ **0185-287513.** Fax 0185-284763. www.hoteljolanda.it. 40 units. 85€–122€ ($75.90–$108.95) double with breakfast; 60€–80€ ($53.60–$71.45) per person with half-board. AE, DC, MC, V. Parking 15€ ($13.40). **Amenities:** Restaurant; bar; lounge; room service. *In room:* A/C, TV, minibar, hair dryer, safe.

WHERE TO DINE

Ristorante il Faro ⭐ REGIONAL/ITALIAN   The distinguished culinary background of the Fabbro family is reflected here in one of the town's best restaurants. Roberto Fabbro sets a great table and feeds you well. The atmosphere is comfortable and cozy, and on any night 50 diners can be fed well. High-quality meats and fresh fish dishes are served with flair and style. Try the *gamberi alla*

Santa Margherita, sweet-tasting grilled shrimp in light olive oil, lemon, and mint sauce. The sautéed fish from the Mediterranean is the way to go. Each dish is served with fresh vegetables cooked al dente, for the most part. The pastas are some of the resort's best, especially that Ligurian favorite, trenette with pesto made from only the freshest and most aromatic basil.

Via Maragliano 24A. © **0185-286867**. Reservations recommended. Main courses 7€–15€ ($6.25–$13.40); fixed-price menu 25€ ($22.35). AE, DC, MC, V. Wed–Mon noon–2:30pm and 7:30–10pm. Closed 2 weeks in Nov.

Trattoria Baicin *Value* LIGURIAN   The husband-and-wife owners, Piero and Carmela, make everything fresh daily, from fish soup to gnocchi, and still manage to find time to greet diners at the door. You can get a glimpse of the sea if you sit at one of the tables out front. The owners/cooks are most happy preparing fish, which they buy fresh every morning; the sole, simply grilled, is especially good, and the *fritto misto di pesce* (fish fry) constitutes a memorable feast. Begin your meal with one of the pastas made that morning, especially if *trofie alla genovese* (gnocchi, potatoes, fresh vegetables, and pesto) is available.

Via Algeria 9. © **0185-286763**. Reservations unnecessary. Main courses 10€–15€ ($8.95–$13.40); fixed-price menu 16€ ($14.30). AE, DC, MC, V. Tues–Sun noon–3pm and 7–10:30pm. Closed Nov 1–Dec 15.

Trattoria Cesarina SEAFOOD   This is a very nice trattoria, located beneath the arcade of a short but monumental street running into Piazza Fratelli Bandiere. In an atmosphere of bentwood chairs and discreet lighting, you can enjoy a variety of Ligurian dishes. Specialties include meat, vegetables, and seafood antipasti, along with such classic Italian dishes as taglierini with seafood and *pappardelle* (a flat noodle) in a fragrant sausage sauce, plus seasonal fish such as red snapper or dorado, best when grilled.

Via Mameli 2C. © **0185-286059**. Reservations recommended, especially in midsummer. Main courses 11€–25€ ($9.80–$22.35). AE, DC, MC, V. Wed–Mon 12:30–2:30pm and 7:30–10pm. Closed Jan.

SANTA MARGHERITA LIGURE AFTER DARK
Nightlife here seems geared to sipping wine or cocktails on terraces with sea views, flirting with sunburned strangers, and flip-flopping along the town's sandy beachfront promenades. Folks congregate in the cafes that spill out into the town's two seaside squares, **Piazza Martiri della Liberta** and **Piazza Vittorio Veneto.** But if you want to put on your dancing shoes, head for either of the town's most appealing discos, **Covo di Nord Est,** Via Rossetti 1 (© **0185-286558**), or **Disco Carillon,** Località Paraggi (© **0185-286721**). Both cater to dance and music lovers ages 20 to 40.

Looking for a completely unpretentious place to shoot some pool? Head for the **Old Inn Bar,** Piazza Mazzini 40 (© **0185-286041**), where you can play pool, drink bottled beers, and generally hang out with a crowd of young locals.

5 Portofino ★★★
35km (22 miles) SE of Genoa, 171km (106 miles) S of Milan, 485km (301 miles) NW of Rome

Portofino is about 6km (3¾ miles) south of Santa Margherita Ligure, along one of the most beautiful coastal roads in all Italy. Favored by the yachting set, the resort is in an idyllic location on a harbor, where the water reflects all the pastel-washed little houses running along it. In the 1930s, it enjoyed a reputation with artists; over the next few decades, the town became known as a celebrity hideout. Lots of famous names could be seen arriving by yacht, lounging poolside at the luxury hotels, and vacationing in private villas in the hills, including Rex

Harrison and Elizabeth Taylor. The Splendido Hotel alone has hosted such illustrious guests as the Duke and Duchess of Windsor, Ernest Hemingway, Greta Garbo, Ingrid Bergman, Aristotle Onassis, Clark Gable, and John Wayne. Portofino might not have such star power today, but some rich and powerful people still occupy those private villas, coexisting right alongside all the tourists who pour in by the busloads during the day. And they do pour in—Portofino is almost too beautiful for its own good, and the crowds can be amazing in the high season.

The thing to do in Portofino: Take a walk, preferably before sunset, leading toward the tip of the peninsula. When you come to the entrance of an old castle (where a German baron once lived), step inside the walls to enjoy a lush garden and the views of the town and harbor below; it's open daily 10am to 4pm (to 5pm Oct–Apr), and admission is 1.75€ ($1.55). Continuing on, you'll pass old private villas, towering trees, and much vegetation before you reach the lighthouse (*faro*). Allow an hour at least. When you return to the main piazza, proceed to one of the two little bars, on the left side of the harbor, that rise and fall in popularity.

Before beginning that walk to the lighthouse, however, you can climb the steps from the port leading to the little parish church of **San Giorgio,** built on the site of a sanctuary that Roman soldiers dedicated to the Persian god Mithras. From here you'll get a panoramic view of the port and bay.

In summer, you can also take **boat rides** around the coast to such points as San Fruttuoso. Or set out for a long hike on the paths crossing the Monte Portofino Promontory to the **Abbazia di San Fruttuoso,** about a 2-hour walk from Portofino. The tourist office provides maps.

ESSENTIALS

GETTING THERE   Take the **train** first to Santa Margherita Ligure (see section 4, "Essentials," above); then continue the rest of the way by bus. Tigullio **buses** leave Santa Margherita Ligure once every 30 minutes bound for Portofino, costing 1€ (90¢) one way, and you can buy tickets aboard the bus. Call ✆ **0185-288834** for information and schedules. If you have a **car** and are in Santa Margherita, continue south along the only road, hugging the promontory, until you reach Portofino. In summer, traffic is likely to be heavy.

VISITOR INFORMATION   The **tourist office** is at Via Roma 35 (✆ **0185-269024**). It's open daily: summer 10am to 7pm; off-season 9:30am to 12:30pm and 2 to 7pm.

WHERE TO STAY

Portofino just doesn't have enough hotels, and because of the high demand for rooms, they're all extremely expensive. In July and August, you might be forced to book a room in nearby Santa Margherita Ligure or Rapallo. Make your reservations as far in advance as possible.

Albergo Nazionale   At stage center right on the harbor, this old villa is modest yet well laid out, and it was restored and renovated in the mid-1980s. The suites are tastefully decorated, and the little lounge is a cozy gathering spot, with a brick fireplace, a coved ceiling, antique furnishings, and good reproductions. Most of the guest rooms, furnished in a mix of styles (hand-painted Venetian in some rooms), open onto a view of the harbor. The tiled bathrooms are small but tidy.

Via Roma 8, 16034 Portofino. ✆ 0185-269575. Fax 0185-269138. www.nazionaleportofino.com. 13 units (showers only). 232€ ($207.20) double; 284€–335€ ($253.60–$299.15) suite. Rates include breakfast. MC, V. Parking 17.50€ ($15.65) nearby. Closed Dec 10–Mar 10. **Amenities:** Lounge; room service; laundry. *In room:* A/C, TV, minibar, hair dryer, safe.

Hotel Eden Just 46m (150 ft.) from the harbor in the heart of the village and set in a garden (hence its name), this hotel is a relatively moderately priced choice in an otherwise high-fashion resort town. Although it doesn't have a harbor view, there's a winning vista from the front veranda, where breakfast is served. The guest rooms are small and very simply furnished, although each has a comfortable bed. All have tidily kept bathrooms. *Warning:* Readers have complained that reservations sometimes aren't honored in high season.

Vico Dritto 18, 16034 Portofino. (0185-269091. Fax 0185-269047. www.italyhotels.it. 9 units (showers only). 129.10€–232.40€ ($115.30–$207.55) double. Rates include breakfast. AE, MC, V. Public parking 17€ ($15.20). Closed Dec 1–20. **Amenities:** Bar; room service; babysitting; laundry/dry cleaning. *In room:* A/C, TV, hair dryer, safe.

Hotel Splendido and Splendido Mare 🏨🏨🏨 This spectacular property, reached by a steep and winding road from the port, provides a luxury base for those who moor their yachts in the harbor or have closed down their Palm Beach residences for the summer and can afford its outrageous prices. The four-story structure was built as a monastery during the Middle Ages, but pirates attacked so frequently that the monks abandoned it. Later it became a family summer home. The building opened as a hotel in 1901 and has attracted the likes of Winston Churchill.

There are several levels of public rooms and terraces to maximize the views over the sea, which you'll also enjoy from the guest rooms. Each room is furnished in a personal way, with no two alike. The bathrooms are lovely, clad in marble or tile. Some of the superior rooms are equipped with whirlpool tubs. The hotel has a newer 16-room annex down on the Piazzetta. It might look like a youth hostel on the outside, but the interior has the same glittering qualities as the main house. You can choose the Splendido Mare if you like to immerse yourself in village life, or retreat to the main house for more isolation. The hotel will take you by boat to a private cove with changing cabins and lounge chairs; golf and watersports can be arranged in nearby towns.

Viale Baratta 13, 16034 Portofino. (800/223-6800 in the U.S., or 0185-267801. Fax 0185-267806. www.orient-expresshotels.com. 68 units. 836€–1,305€ ($746.55–$1,165.35) double; from 1,942€ ($1,734.20) suite. Rates include half-board. AE, DC, DISC, MC, V. Parking 20€ ($17.85). Closed Nov 11–Mar 30. **Amenities:** 2 restaurants; 2 bars (1 is a piano bar); heated saltwater pool; tennis court; gym; sauna; private speedboat for excursions and water-skiing; salon; 24-hr. room service; massage; babysitting; laundry/dry cleaning. *In room:* A/C, TV, minibar, hair dryer, safe.

WHERE TO DINE

Da U'Batti SEAFOOD Informal and colorful, this place is on a narrow cobblestone-covered piazza a few steps above the port. A pair of barnacle-encrusted anchors hanging above the arched entrance hint at the seafaring specialties that have become the restaurant's trademark. Owner/sommelier Giancarlo Foppiano serves delectable dishes, which might include a soup of "hen clams," rice with shrimp or crayfish, or fish alla Battista. There is a good selection of grappa, as well as French and Italian wines.

Vico Nuovo 17. (0185-269379. Reservations recommended. Main courses 23.50€–26€ ($21–$23.20); fixed-price menu 62.50€ ($55.80). AE, DC, MC, V. Tues–Sun noon–3pm and 8–11:30pm. Closed Dec–Jan.

Delfino 🏨🏨 SEAFOOD Opened in the 1800s on the village square that fronts the harbor, Delfino is Portofino's most fashionable dining spot (along with Il Pitosforo, below). It has a kind of rustic, informal chic and offers virtually the same type of food as Il Pitosforo, including *troffiette al pesto* (a regional pasta with basil, oil, and pine-nut sauce). The fish dishes are the best bets: zuppa di pesce (a soup made of freshly caught fish with a secret spice blend) and risotto with shrimp, sole, squid, and other sea creatures. The chef also prides himself on his sage-seasoned *vitello all'uccelletto,* roast veal with a gamy taste. Try to get a table near the front so that you can enjoy (or at least be amused by) the parade of visitors and villagers.

Piazza Martiri dell' Olivetta 40. © 0185-269081. Reservations recommended Sat. Main courses 13€–30€ ($11.60–$26.80). AE, DC, MC, V. Apr–Oct daily noon–3pm and 7–11pm; Nov–Mar Tues–Sun noon–2:30pm and 7–10:30pm.

Il Pitosforo ★★ LIGURIAN/ITALIAN   You have to climb some steps to reach this place, which draws raves when the meal is served and often wails when the tab is presented. Although it's not blessed with an especially distinguished decor, its position right on the harbor gives it all the natural charm it needs. Zuppa di pesce is a delectable Ligurian fish soup, or you might prefer the bouil-labaisse. The pastas are especially tasty and include *lasagne al pesto.* Fish dishes feature mussels *alla marinara* and *paella valenciana* for two, and saffron-flavored rice studded with seafood and chicken. Some meat and fish dishes are grilled over hot stones; others are grilled over charcoal.

Molo Umberto I 9. © 0185-269020. Reservations required. Main courses 27€–38€ ($24.10–$33.95). AE, DC, MC, V. Wed–Sun 7:30–11pm. Closed end of Nov to Feb and for lunch Apr–Oct.

Ristorante da Puny SEAFOOD   Da Puny is set up on the stone square that opens onto the harbor. Because of its location, it's practically in the living room of Portofino, within sight of the evening activities of the oh-so-chic and oh-so-tan yachting set. Green-painted tables are set under trees at night on a slate-covered outdoor terrace. The menu includes pappardelle Portofino, antipasto of the house, spaghetti with clams, baked fish with potatoes and olives, fried zucchini flowers, and an array of freshly caught fish.

Piazza Martiri dell'Olivetta 5. © 0185-269037. Reservations required. Main courses 15€–25€ ($13.40–$22.35). No credit cards. Fri–Wed noon–3pm and 7–11pm. Closed Dec 15–Feb 15.

PORTOFINO AFTER DARK

James Jones once called the snug little **La Gritta American Bar,** Calata Marconi 20 (© **0185-269126**), "the nicest waterfront bar this side of Hong Kong." It is indeed very attractive, very friendly, and far enough along the harborside quay to be a little less hectic than other establishments. Stop by for a cocktail, coffee, or other libation (the floating terrace out front is perfect for a drink at sunset). Light fare, such as omelets and salads, is available and affordable. The crowd is often an interesting mix of celebrities, tourists, and U.S. Navy personnel—this is a legendary watering hole from way back. It's open in summer daily 9pm to 3am (in winter, Fri–Wed).

Scafandro American Bar, Calata Marconi 10 (© **0185-269105**), is a chic place that draws the yachting crowd. The three-quarter-round banquettes inside are plush and comfortable, and unusual nautical engravings adorn the walls. From June to September, it's open daily 10am to 3am (open Wed–Mon the rest of the year).

6 The Cinque Terre ★★

Monterosso: 8km (5 miles) E of Genoa, 10km (6¼ miles) W of La Spezia

Among olive and chestnut groves on steep, rocky terrain overlooking the gulf of Genoa, the communities of Corniglia, Manarola, Riomaggiore, and Vernazza offer a glimpse into another time. These rural villages, inaccessible by car, are an agricultural belt where garden and vineyard exist side by side. Together with their "city cousin" Monterosso, they're known as the *Cinque Terre* (five lands). The northernmost town, Monterosso, is the tourist hub of the region, with traffic, crowds, and the only notable glimpse of contemporary urban life here.

The area is best known for its culinary delights, culled from forest, field, and sea. Here the land yields an incredible variety of edible mushrooms; and oregano, borage, rosemary, and sage grow abundantly. The pine nuts essential to pesto are easily collected from the forests, as are chestnuts for making flour and olives for the oil that is the base of all dishes. Garlic and leeks flavor sautéed dishes, and beets turn up unexpectedly in ravioli and other dishes. Fishing boats add their rich hauls of anchovies, mussels, squid, octopus, and shellfish. To wash it all down, vineyards produce Sciacchetra, a DOC wine, rarer than many other Italian varieties because of the low 25% yield characteristic of the Vermentino, Bosco, and Albarola grapes from which it's derived.

Most visitors explore the villages by excursion boat. To avoid these crowds and really get to know the region, you might want to hike along the renowned walking paths that meander scenically for miles across the hills and through the forests.

ESSENTIALS

GETTING THERE   Hourly **trains** run from Genoa to La Spezia, a trip of 1½ hours, where you must backtrack by rail to any of the five towns that you want to visit. Once in the Cinque Terre, local trains, which run frequently between the five stops, offer daily unlimited travel at a cost of 3.25€ ($2.90). Don't expect views, however. The entire ride is within tunnels. For more information, dial © **848-8880888** toll-free in Italy.

If you have a **car** and are coming from Genoa, take A12 and exit at Monterosso, the only town of the five that you can actually approach by car. A gigantic parking lot accommodates visitors, who then travel between the towns by rail, boat, or foot. The **Navigazione Golfo del Porto** plies the waters between Monterosso and Manarola or Riomaggiore five times daily from April to October, whereas **Motobarca Vernazza** runs hourly to Vernazza (© **0187-732987** to reach either company).

VISITOR INFORMATION   The **APT office** for the five villages is in Monterosso, Via Fegina 38 (© **0187-817506**). It's open Monday to Saturday 9am to 1pm and 3 to 5:30pm, and Sunday 9am to 1pm.

EXPLORING THE COAST

Fourteen **walking trails** are laid out for exploring the wilds of the area; they're also a viable way to go from town to town. The APT office (see above) offers a brochure, *Footpaths Along the Cinque Terre and the Eastern Riviera,* which defines and maps out routes ranging as far north as Deiva Marina and as far south as Portovenere; it also suggests several within the boundaries of the Cinque Terre. Walk these trails carefully and get local advice. Some are relatively easy, but others require the endurance of an Olympic athlete.

The easiest route if you want only a short, scenic walk without a major workout is to start at Riomaggiore and stroll to Manarola; it's an easy walk, and the trails are in good shape. If you continue on from Manarola to Corniglia, it's still pretty easy walking, but the trail begins to deteriorate slightly. From Corniglia to Vernazza is a steep walk that takes about 1½ hours, with the trail worsening as you go. The final section from Vernazza to Monterosso is a strenuous 2-hour climb on a narrow trail that's not at all well-maintained. All these routes promise gorgeous scenery along the way. In case you run into trouble, the **local emergency phone number** is © **115**.

The only sandy **beach** in the Cinque Terre is the crowded strand in **Monterosso,** where you can rent a beach chair from a vendor for about 1.25€ ($1.10). **Guvano Beach** is an isolated pebbly strand that stretches just north of Corniglia and is popular with nudists. You can clamber down to it from the Vernazza–Corniglia path, but the drop is steep and treacherous. A weird alternative route takes you through an unused train tunnel, entered from a point near the north end of Corniglia's train station; you must ring the bell at the gated entrance and wait for a custodian to arrive to unburden you of 2.50€ ($2.25), which is good for passage through the dimly lit mile-long gallery that emerges onto the beach at the far end. There's a long rocky beach to the south of **Corniglia,** easily accessible by some quick downhill scrambles from the Corniglia–Manrola path. **Riomaggiore** has a tiny crescent-shaped beach reached by a series of stone steps on the south side of the harbor.

WHERE TO STAY
CORNIGLIA

Albergo & Ristorante da Cedio _Value_   Right outside of the village on the road to Vernazza is one of the most durable inns in the area, an ideal spot for lodging or food during your Cinque Terre sojourn. This stone house, once the private home of a local olive grower and his family, has been turned into a B&B, with four small but comfortably furnished bedrooms in the main building, plus another half dozen scattered throughout the village. We prefer, of course, the accommodations in the main structure, because they open onto views of the water and the town itself. All have well-maintained private bathrooms. Even if you're not a guest, consider the on-site *ristorante,* where in fair weather diners request a table on the flower terrace. Local seafood prepared according to old Ligurian recipes predominate on the menu. Everything is homemade and prepared by the Nunzio family in their kitchen. They grill both meat and fish to perfection on an open hearth. They also make a delectable pasta with the "fruits of the sea," mainly recently caught clams and mussels.

19010 Corniglia. ℂ **0187-812138.** 10 units (showers only). 45€ ($40.20) double. MC, V. Closed Nov–Feb except for some weekend openings. **Amenities:** Restaurant; bar. *In room:* No phone.

IN MONTEROSSO

Hotel Baia   Opened in 1911, this hotel features a private beach and pleasant guest rooms where the whitewashed furniture lends an illusion of size and space. Each comes with a good bed and a small tiled bathroom. What the hotel doesn't offer is air-conditioning or shuttle service, but the train station is only 101m (110 yd.) away.

Via Fegina 88, 19016 Monterosso. ℂ **0187-817512.** Fax 0187-818322. 29 units (showers only). 100€–140€ ($89.30–$125) double. Rates include breakfast. AE, MC, V. Closed Nov–Feb. **Amenities:** Restaurant; bar; room service; babysitting; laundry/dry cleaning. *In room:* TV, minibar.

Hotel Pasquale   This small hotel sits right by the beach, offering both intimacy and privacy because its small number of guest rooms are spread out across four floors. It's modern and has been decorated like a private Genovan home. Bedrooms are small but still comfortable, each furnished with a tiled bathroom. The bar/restaurant is reminiscent of an Italian coffee shop, with gleaming marble floors, glass cases, dark wood wainscoting, and a service counter accented with a brass rail and foot guard.

Via Fegina 4, 19016 Monterosso. ℂ **0187-817477.** Fax 0187-817056. www.pasini.com. 15 units (showers only). 120€ ($107.15) double. Rates include breakfast. AE, MC, V. **Amenities:** Restaurant; cafe; bar; babysitting; laundry. *In room:* A/C, TV, hair dryer.

Hotel Porto Roca ★★   You give up direct beach access to stay here, but it's a small price to pay for accommodations as gracious as these. The hotel is set on a cliff offering panoramic views of the village and harbor, and every corner is filled with antiques, knickknacks, and art. The guest rooms range from medium to spacious, each with a well-kept bathroom. The terrace is alive with lush greenery and an assortment of blossoming white flowers that complement the blue of the bay. The restaurant serves local seafood, and its large dining room offers privacy through the placement of columns and Liberty-style glass screens. In the bar, furniture clusters create cozy pockets for chatting. Its fanciful fireplace adds warmth on cool days.

Via Corone 1, 19016 Monterosso. ℂ **0187-817502.** Fax 0187-817692. www.portoroca.it. 43 units. 161€–255€ ($143.75–$227.70) double. Rates include breakfast. AE, MC, V. Closed Nov–Mar. **Amenities:** Restaurant; lounge; room service; babysitting; laundry/dry cleaning. *In room:* A/C, TV, minibar, safe.

IN MANAROLA

Hotel Marina Piccola   With 10 rooms spread across five floors, this former home is a hotel as vertical as the town that houses it. There's a rustic charm to the small but serviceable guest rooms, which feature wrought-iron beds, old prints, and brass lamps. The tiled bathrooms are small.

Via Lo Scalo 16, 19010 Manarola. ℂ **0187-920103.** Fax 0187-920966. 10 units (showers only). 70€ ($62.50) per person double. Rates include half-board. AE, DC, MC, V. Closed Nov. **Amenities:** Restaurant; bar; laundry. *In room:* Hair dryer.

IN RIOMAGGIORE

Villa Argentina   This hotel's greatest asset is its quiet country setting just outside town. If you don't feel like walking, an efficient shuttle service will transport you into the village. There's no air-conditioning, but each room has a ceiling fan. The guest rooms are small and basic, with cramped bathrooms. Although the Argentina is a no-frills choice, the price is certainly right.

Via de Gaspari 170, 19017 Riomaggiore. ℂ and fax **0187-920213**. villaargentina@libero.it. 15 units (showers only). 78€–103€ ($69.65–$92) double; 132€–156€ ($117.90–$139.30) with half-board. No credit cards. **Amenities:** Restaurant; bar; room service; babysitting; laundry. *In room:* TV, hair dryer, safe, no phone.

IN VERNAZZA

Albergo Barbara *(Finds*   Your window in this pleasant pensione will open onto one of the most enchanting views along the Cinque Terre. Try for room 8, which offers a particularly stunning vista. On the harbor square, the inn is run by Giuseppe and his Swiss wife, Patricia. Try for one of the larger doubles with a view, although there are smaller and cheaper units. The place is simply furnished but clean, with adequate corridor bathrooms. Each bedroom is also equipped with its own sink. Breakfast isn't served but there are cafes nearby.

Piazza Marconi 30, Vernazza, Cinque Terre 19018. ℂ and fax **0187-812398**. 9 units, all with shared bathroom (showers only). 45€ ($40.20) double. Credit cards accepted to hold reservations only; payment is by cash only. Closed Dec–Feb 20. *In room:* No phone.

WHERE TO DINE
IN CORNIGLIA

Da Mananan *(Value* SEAFOOD/LIGURIAN   The locals aren't quite sure when this old house in hilltop Corniglia was built. But of one thing they are certain: the couple who run and cook here serve some of the best and most reasonably priced food along Cinque Terre. The small restaurant is found in the old cellars of this former home. The vegetables are grown along the coastline, and the fresh fish served here has been recently plucked from the sea. Dishes are prepared from old Ligurian recipes handed down from generation to generation. The moment you enter the dining room, you are greeted with the aromatic and basil-infused aroma of pesto, a sauce that will appear later whipped into your homemade pasta. Try the savory platter of steamed mussels, although we gravitate to the grilled catch of the day. The chef claims that many Americans try fresh anchovies here for the first time, having only eaten them canned before.

Via Fieschi 117, Corniglia. ℂ **0187-821166**. Reservations recommended. Main courses 9€–11€ ($8.05–$9.80). No credit cards. Wed–Mon 1–2:30pm and 8–10pm.

IN MONTEROSSO

Il Gigante LIGURIAN   This friendly, simple trattoria, a block off the waterfront in the newer part of town, is one of the best places to introduce yourself to Liguria's flavor-filled cuisine, and there's no better introduction than zuppa di pesce, a fish soup so hearty that it's practically a main course. Another pleasing first course is *minestrone alla genovese,* a bean-and-vegetable soup flavored with pesto. Waiters cite the daily specials, none more delectable than risotto made with freshly plucked shellfish. To go truly Ligurian, opt for the spaghetti with octopus sauce. The mixed grill is another savory offering.

Via IV Novembre 9. ℂ **0187-817401**. Reservations recommended on holidays. Main courses 11€–17€ ($9.80–$15.20). AE, DC, MC, V. Daily noon–3pm and 6:30–10pm (sometimes closed Mon).

IN MANAROLA

Aristide LIGURIAN   This comfortable old trattoria showcases the simplicity of the region's cuisine, combining a few key ingredients in tasty combinations. The weekday fixed-price menu includes wine with the meal, and the weekend version also features antipasto and coffee. House specialties include lasagne al pesto, *penne all'aragosta* (pasta with lobster sauce), and zuppa di pesce, one of the most savory kettles of fish in the "five lands." Traditional recipes have never been forgotten and are always part of the menu.

Via Discovolo 290. ℂ **0187-920000.** Reservations recommended. Main courses 7€–12€ ($6.25–$10.70); fixed-price menu 35€ ($31.25). AE, MC, V. Apr–Sept daily noon–2:30pm and 7–10pm; off-season Tues–Sun noon–2:30pm and 7–10pm.

Marina Piccola LIGURIAN   This simple and completely unpretentious restaurant is next to the inn of the same name (see "Where to Stay," above), right on the water. For a Ligurian palate tantalizer, try *cozze ripieni,* mussels cooked in white wine and served with butter sauce. Squid in its own ink tastes best when combined with homemade spaghetti. Fresh sardines are a local crowd-pleaser, and another homemade pasta, trenette, comes flavored with some of the best-tasting pesto on the coast. Grilled fish is the invariable favorite for a main dish— always fresh and perfectly prepared, though seasoned simply, as is the Ligurian style. Service can be a bit gruff.

Via Lo Scalo 16. ℂ **0187-920103.** Reservations recommended. Main courses 9€–15€ ($8.05–$13.40). AE, DC, MC, V. Wed–Mon noon–3pm and 7–11pm.

IN VERNAZZA

Il Gambero Rosso (*Value* LIGURIAN   Opened 110 years ago, this restaurant overlooks the sea at the harbor. Ask for a table on the terrace to make the most of this setting. The food is typically Ligurian, with house specialties such as ravioli stuffed with fresh fish. The wonderful porcini mushrooms that are harvested in the area figure into some dishes. Many of the recipes were passed by word of mouth from mother to daughter, and a lot of the flavoring is based on the use of herbs and other ingredients that grow in the hills. The pesto is made with the best olive oil and mixed with basil, grated cheese, pine nuts, and fresh marjoram.

Piazza Marconi 7. ℂ **0187-812265.** Reservations recommended Sat–Sun. Main courses 10€–19€ ($8.95–$16.95); fixed-price menu 30€–42.50€ ($26.80–$37.95). AE, DC, MC, V. Tues–Sun 12:30–3pm and 7:30–10:30pm.

14

Campania

Campania is in many ways Italy's most memorable and beautiful region. It forms a fertile crescent around the bays of Naples and Sorrento and stretches inland into a landscape of limestone rocks dotted with patches of fertile soil. The geological oddities of Campania include a smoldering and dangerous volcano (already famous for having destroyed Pompeii and Herculaneum), sulfurous springs that belch steam and smelly gases, and lakes that ancient myths refer to as the gateway to Hades. Its seaside highway is the most beautiful, and probably the most treacherous, in the world, combining danger at every hairpin turn with some of Italy's most reckless drivers. Despite such dark images, Campania is a most captivating region, sought out by native Italians and visitors alike for its combination of earth, sea, and sky. Coupled with this are Europe's densest collection of ancient ruins, each celebrated by classical scholars as among the very best of its kind.

It was off the shores of Campania that Ulysses ordered his crew to tie him to the mast of his ship, ears unstopped, so that he alone would hear the songs of the sirens without throwing himself overboard to sample their pleasures. The ancient Romans dubbed the land "Campania Felix" (pleasant countryside) and constructed hundreds of private villas there. In some ways, the beauty of Campania contributed to the decay of the Roman Empire, as emperors, their senators, and their courtiers spent more time pursuing its pleasures and abandoning the cares of Rome's administrative problems. Even today, seafront land here is so desirable that hoteliers have poured their life savings into buildings that are sometimes bizarrely cantilevered above rock-studded cliffs. Despite an abundance of such hotels, they tend to be profitably overbooked in summer.

Although residents of Campania sometimes stridently defend the cuisine, it's not the most renowned in Italy. The region's produce, however, is superb, its wine is heady, and its pizzas are memorable.

Today Campania typifies the conditions that northern Italians label "the problem of the south." Although the inequities are the most pronounced in **Naples,** the entire region, outside the resorts along the coast, has a lower standard of living and education and higher crime rates, plus less-developed standards of health care, than the more affluent north.

When the English say "see Naples and die," they mean the city and the bay, with majestic Vesuvius in the background. When the Germans use the expression, they mean the **Amalfi Drive.** Indeed, several motorists do die each year on the dangerous coastal road, which is too narrow to accommodate the heavy stream of summer traffic, especially the large tour buses that almost sideswipe one another as they try to pass. When driving along the coast, you sometimes find it difficult to concentrate on the road because of the view. The drive, remarked André Gide, "is so beautiful that nothing more beautiful can be seen on this earth." Those of you who've driven Highway 1 along the California coast will have some idea of what to expect on this gorgeous drive (but toss in terrible traffic and aggressive drivers, and make the scenery even more spectacular).

Sorrento and **Amalfi** are in the vanguard, with the widest range of facilities; **Positano** has more snob appeal and is popular with artists; **Ravello** is still the choice of the discriminating few (such as Gore Vidal) who desire relative seclusion. The gorgeous island of **Capri** (accessible by ferry from Sorrento or Naples) was known to emperors before international travelers discovered it. But the popularity of the resort-studded

Amalfi Coast is a more recent phenomenon. It was discovered by German officers during World War II, and then later by American and English servicemen (Positano was a British rest camp in the last months of the war). When the war was over, many of these servicemen returned, often bringing their families. In time, the fishing villages became major tourism centers, with hotels and restaurants in all price ranges.

In addition to the stunning scenery and the lovely seaside towns, there are some world-class sightseeing attractions—the haunting ruins of **Pompeii** and the Greek temples of the ancient city of **Paestum** are among the highlights of all Italy.

1 Naples ★★

219km (136 miles) SE of Rome, 263km (163 miles) W of Bari

Naples (Napoli) is Italy's most controversial city: You'll either love it or hate it. Is it paradiso or the inferno? It's louder, more intense, more unnerving, but perhaps ultimately more satisfying than almost anywhere else in Italy.

To foreigners unfamiliar with the complexities of the multifarious "Italys" and their regional types, the Neapolitan is still the quintessence of the country and easy to caricature ("O Sole Mio," "Mamma Mia," bel canto). If Sophia Loren (a native who moved elsewhere) evokes the Italian woman for you, you'll find more of her look-alikes here than in any other city. Naples also gave the world Enrico Caruso.

In recent years, Naples has made world headlines for its cultural renaissance and its fight against crime. Despite Mafia-directed crime, political corruption, prostitution, street hoodlums, chaotic traffic, and pervasive unemployment, the longtime mayor of Naples, Antonio Bassolino, has chosen culture as a weapon to clean up the city's image. Since taking office in December 1993, the former Communist party official has made cultural revaluation his top priority—and it seems to be working.

Bassolino received a national government grant of $30 million to make Naples look safer and more presentable, and has been aided by a group of concerned citizens who since 1984 have collected funds for the upkeep of the city's treasures and monuments. The first civic move was to restore and reopen scores of neglected museums and palaces in dilapidated neighborhoods. Muggers, prostitutes, and cars were driven from many historic plazas, especially Piazza del Plebiscito, and from around the San Carlo opera house and Royal Palace areas. All this activity seemed to spark a minor renaissance among the city's musicians, writers, moviemakers, artists, and playwrights. The Neapolitan art scene has been given a shot in the arm.

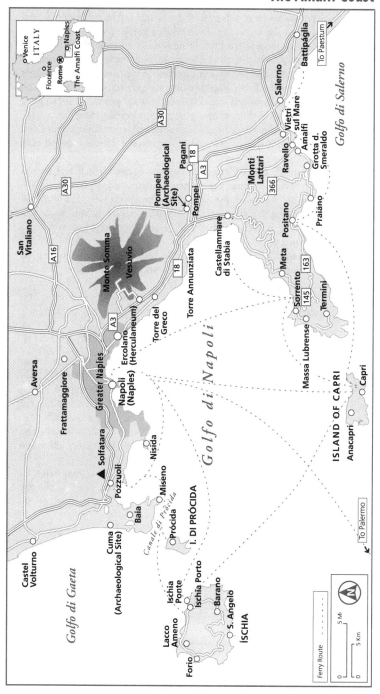

The Amalfi Coast

New rock groups are born in Naples every month, and interest in traditional Neapolitan music is also increasing. Founded by a group of young Neapolitans, the Falso Movimento troupe has brought new life to the city's theatrical scene. Film companies, following in the footsteps of Neapolitan directors such as Francesco Rossi and Gabriele Salvatore, are choosing to shoot in Naples once again. Neapolitan writers are gaining increasing recognition, especially Ermanno Rea for *Mistero Napolitano* and Gabriele Frasca for his poems. And Naples is now becoming popular with a younger generation, especially those from countries to the north. Undeterred by reports of unfavorable conditions, they flood into the city and lend it a new vitality. The hippest scene is at the bars and cafes on Piazza Bellini, near Piazza Dante.

Of course, Naples's deeper ills can't be swept away overnight. There are still major problems here (as in most any congested urban area), especially crime—although a dramatic increase in the number of cops on the street has decreased crime by 25%, leading to a 40% increase in tourism. However, you should still take extreme caution in Naples because theft, especially pickpocketing, remains relatively common.

Naples is on a roll, one shopkeeper told us in perfect English. "Of course, we still have pollution and drugs, and the Camorra [the local Mafia], but we wouldn't really be Naples without that." Art historian Francesca Del Vecchio summed up the change this way: "A few years ago we couldn't sit out in an outdoor cafe because of the traffic and the crime. Now it's like a Mediterranean city again."

ESSENTIALS

GETTING THERE   Domestic flights from Rome and other major Italian cities put you into **Aeroporto Capodichino,** Via Umberto Maddalena (© 081-7896259), 6km (3¾ miles) north of the city. A city **ANM bus** (no. 14) makes the 15-minute run between the airport and Naples's Piazza Garibaldi in front of the main rail terminus. The bus fare is .75€ (65¢); a **taxi** runs about 17.50€ to 20€ ($15.65–$17.85). Domestic flights are available on Alitalia, Alisarda, and Ati. Flying time is 1½ hours from Milan, 1¼ hours from Palermo or Venice, and 50 minutes from Rome.

Frequent **trains** connect Naples with the rest of Italy. One or two trains per hour arrive from Rome, taking 2½ hours and costing from 10€ ($8.95) one way. It's also possible to reach Naples from Milan in about 8 hours, costing from 35€ (31.25) one way.

The city has two main rail terminals: **Stazione Centrale,** at Piazza Garibaldi, and **Stazione Mergellina,** at Piazza Piedigrotta. Most travelers will arrive at Stazione Central, but anybody with an Alitalia ticket can take the **Alitalia Airport Train by FS,** an express train that runs twice a day between Rome's Leonard da Vinci International Airport (Fiumicino) and Naples's Stazione Mergellina. For general rail information, call © 848-888088 toll-free in Italy.

Although driving *in* Naples is a nightmare, **driving** *to* Naples is easy. The Rome-Naples autostrada (A2) passes Caserta 29km (18 miles) north of Naples, and the Naples-Reggio di Calabria autostrada (A3) runs by Salerno, 53km (33 miles) north of Naples.

From Sicily, you can take a **ferry** to Naples that's run by **Tirrenia Lines,** Molo Angionio, Stazione Marritima (© 199-123199 or 081-5800340), in the port area of Palermo. A one-way ticket costs 42.50€ ($37.95) per person for an armchair and 62.50€ ($55.80) per person for a first-class cabin for the 10½-hour trip.

OTTOCALLI

CAPODIMONTE

Albergo dei Poveri

ORTO BOTANICO

ARENACCIA

Airport

VASTO

PIAZZA CAVOUR

Via Materdei

SANTA CHIARA

Piazza Bellini

Piazza S. Domenico

Piazza Dante

MONTESANTO

FUNICULAR

Stazione Cumana

Stazione Centrale

Piazza Garibaldi

CENTRALE

Stazione Circumvesuviana

Piazza del Mercato

Piazza Libri

Università

Via Marinella

Piazza Municipio

Molo Beverello

Stazione Marittima

Galleria Umberto I

Teatro di San Carlo

Royal Palace

Piazza Plebiscito

Piazza d. Martiri

To Chiaia & Mergellina

Bacino del Piliero

Bacino Angiono

Golfo di Napoli

Castel dell'Ovo

| Metro | Ⓜ | Information | ⓘ |
| Church | ✝ | Lighthouse | ✹ |

Aquarium **15**
Cappella San Severo **7**
Carthusian Monastery of San Martino & National Museum of San Martino **10**
Castel Capunana **5**
Castle of the Egg **16**
Catacombs of San Gennaro **2**
Galleria Umberto I **11**
Il Duomo **4**
National Archaeological Museum **3**
National Museum & Gallery of the Capodimonte **1**
New Castle **14**
Royal Palace **13**
San Domenico Maggiore **8**
San Lorenzo Maggiore **6**
Santa Chiara **9**
Teatro di San Carlo **12**

Venice
Florence
ITALY
Rome
Naples

VISITOR INFORMATION   The **Ente Provinciale per il Turismo,** at Piazza dei Martiri 58 (© **081-405311;** bus: 152), is open Monday to Saturday 8:30am to 3:30pm. There are **other offices** at Stazione Centrale (© **081-268779;** Metro: Garibaldi) and at Stazione Mergellina (© **081-7612102**). These offices are open Monday to Saturday 9am to 1pm and 3 to 7pm, and Sunday 9am to 1pm.

GETTING AROUND   The **Metropolitana** line will deliver you from Stazione Centrale in the east all the way to Stazione Mergellina and even beyond to the suburb of Pozzuoli. Get off at Piazza Piedigrotta if you want to take the funicular to Vómero. The Metro uses the same tickets as buses and trams.

It's dangerous to ride **buses** at rush hours—never have we seen such pushing and shoving. Many people prefer to leave the buses to the battle-hardened Neapolitans and take the subway or **tram** nos. 1 or 4, running from Stazione Centrale to Stazione Mergellina. (It'll also let you off at the quayside points where the boats depart for Ischia and Capri.) For a ticket valid for 75 minutes with unlimited transfers during that time, the cost is .75€ (65¢). A ticket for a full day of unlimited travel costs 2.25€ ($2).

If you survive the **taxi** driver's reckless driving, you'll have to do battle only over the bill. Many cab drivers claim that the meter is broken and assess the cost of the ride, always to your disadvantage. Some legitimate surcharges are imposed, such as night drives and extra luggage. However, many drivers deliberately take the scenic route to run up costs. In repeated visits to Naples, we've never yet been quoted an honest fare. We no longer bother with the meter; we estimate what the fare should be, negotiate with the driver, and take off into the night. If you want to take a chance, you can call a radio taxi at © **081-5564444,** 081-5560202, or 081-5707070.

As for **driving** around Naples, we have one word: *don't.*

Funiculars take passengers up and down the steep hills of Naples. The **Funicolare Centrale** (© **800-568866**), for example, connects the lower part of the city to Vómero. Departures, daily 7am to 10pm, are from Piazzetta Duca d'Aosta, just off Via Roma. Be careful not to get stranded by missing the last car back. The same tickets valid for buses and the Metro are good for the funicular.

SPECIAL EVENTS   **Maggio dei Monumenti (May of Monuments)** is sponsored by the Council of Naples, with events occurring every weekend during the month. Each year the theme is slightly different. One of the most interesting parts of this event is a series of guided walks through the historic district, even through the city's underground passages. May is also the month for a variety of exhibits and fairs. Chamber music recitals, concerts, operettas, performances of classic Neapolitan songs, and even soccer matches and horse races add to the celebration. If you're in Naples in May, consult the tourist office for a full program of events, some of which are free.

FAST FACTS   American Express business is handled by **Every Tours,** Piazza Municipio 5 (© **081-5518564;** Metro: Garibaldi), open Monday to Friday 9:30am to 1:30pm and 3:30 to 7pm, and Saturday 9:30am to 1pm.

You'll find the **U.S. Consulate** on Piazza della Repubblica (© **081-5838111;** Metro: Mergellina; tram: 1). Its consular services are open Monday to Friday 8am to 1pm and 2 to 5pm. The **U.K. Consulate** is at Via Dei Mille 40 (© **081-4238911;** Metro: Amedeo), open Monday to Friday 8am to 4pm. Citizens of **Canada, Australia,** and **New Zealand** will need to go to the embassies or consulates in Rome (see "Fast Facts: Rome," in chapter 4).

If you need a drugstore, try **Farmacia Helvethia,** Piazza Garibaldi 11, near Stazione Centrale (✆ **081-5548894;** Metro: Garibaldi).

If you have an emergency, dial ✆ **113** to reach the police, or for an ambulance, call ✆ **118** or **081-7528282.**

For medical care, dial ✆ **113** to find the local **Guarda Medica Permanente,** located in each area of town, or ask for directions at your hotel.

EXPLORING THE CITY

If you arrive by train at Stazione Centrale, in front of **Piazza Garibaldi,** you'll want to escape from that horror by taking one of Naples's major arteries, **Corso Umberto,** in the direction of the Santa Lucia district. Along the water, many boats, such as those heading for Capri and Ischia, leave from **Porto Beverello** (not within walking distance—take a taxi).

Many people confine their visit to the bay-side **Santa Lucia** area and perhaps venture into another section to see an important museum. Most of the major hotels lie along **Via Partenope,** which looks out not only to the Gulf of Naples but also to the Castel dell'Ovo. To the west is the **Mergellina** district, site of many restaurants and dozens of apartment houses. The far western section of the city is known as **Posillipo.**

One of the most important squares is **Piazza del Plebiscito,** north of Santa Lucia. The Palazzo Reale opens onto this square. A satellite is **Piazza Trento e Trieste,** with its Teatro San Carlo and entrance to the famed Galleria Umberto I. To the east is the third most important square, **Piazza Municipio.** From Piazza Trento e Trieste, you encounter the main shopping street, **Via Toledo/Via Roma,** on which you can walk as far as Piazza Dante. From that square, take Via Enrico Pessina to the most important museum, located on **Piazza Museo Nazionale.**

THE TOP MUSEUMS

National Archaeological Museum (Museo Archeologico Nazionale) ✹✹✹   With its Roman and Greek sculpture, this museum contains one of Europe's most valuable archaeological collections—particularly notable are the select Farnese acquisitions and the mosaics and sculpture excavated at Pompeii and Herculaneum. The building dates from the 16th century and was turned into a museum 2 centuries later by Charles and Ferdinand IV of Bourbon.

The nude statues of Armodio and Aristogitone are the most outstanding in one ground-floor room. A famous bas-relief (from a 5th-c. B.C. original) in a nearby salon depicts Orpheus and Eurydice with Mercury. The spear-bearing nude *Doryphorus,* copied from a work by Polyclitus the Elder and excavated at Pompeii, enlivens another room. Also see the gigantic but weary *Farnese Hercules,* a statue of remarkable boldness that was discovered in Rome's Baths of Caracalla and is a copy of an original by Lysippus, the 4th-century B.C. Greek sculptor for Alexander the Great. On a more delicate pedestal is the decapitated

---

(*Tips* **A Museum Note**

Reconfirm any museum's hours before going. Opening hours have been known to change from month to month, depending on how little money is in the city treasury. Even when the opening hours are actually posted, they seem more ornamental than reliable.

but exquisite *Venus* (Aphrodite). The *Psyche of Capua* shows why Aphrodite was jealous. And the *Group of the Farnese Bull* presents a pageant of violence from the days of antiquity; the statue, which is one of the most frequently reproduced, was likewise discovered at the Baths of Caracalla and is a copy of a 2nd- or 3rd-century B.C. Hellenistic statue. The marble group depicts a scene in the legend of Amphion and Zethus, who tied Dirce, wife of Lycus of Thebes, to the horns of a rampaging bull.

The mezzanine galleries are devoted to mosaics excavated from Pompeii and Herculaneum. These include scenes of cockfights, dragon-tailed satyrs, an aquarium, and *Alexander Fighting the Persians,* the finest of all. On the top floor are some of the celebrated bronzes dug out of the Pompeii volcanic mud and the Herculaneum lava. Of particular interest is a Hellenistic portrait of Berenice, a comically drunken satyr, a statue of a sleeping satyr, and Mercury on a rock.

Piazza Museo Nazionale 18–19. ℭ 081-292823. Admission 6€ ($5.35). Mon and Wed–Sun 9am–7pm. Metro: Piazza Cavour.

National Museum & Gallery of the Capodimonte (Museo e Gallerie Nazionale di Capodimonte) ✴✴   This museum and gallery, some of Italy's finest, are housed in the 18th-century Capodimonte Palace, built in the time of Charles III and set in a park. Seven Flemish tapestries, made according to the designs of Bernart van Orley, show grand-scale scenes from the Battle of Pavia (1525), in which the forces of François I of France, more than 25,000 strong, lost to those of Charles V. Van Orley, who lived in a pre-*Guernica* day, obviously considered war not a horror but a romantic ballet.

One of the picture gallery's greatest possessions is Simone Martini's *Coronation,* depicting the brother of Robert of Anjou being crowned king of Naples by the bishop of Toulouse. You'll want to linger over the great Masaccio's *Crucifixion,* a bold expression of grief. The most important room is literally filled with the works of Renaissance masters, notably an *Adoration of the Child,* by Luca Signorelli; a *Madonna and Child,* by Perugino; a panel by Raphael; a *Madonna and Child with Angels,* by Botticelli; and, the most beautiful, Filippino Lippi's *Annunciation and Saints.*

Look for Andrea Mantegna's *St. Eufemia* and portrait of Francesco Gonzaga, his brother-in-law Giovanni Bellini's *Transfiguration,* and Lotto's *Portrait of Bernardo de Rossi* and *Madonna and Child with St. Peter.* In one room is Raphael's *Holy Family and St. John* and a copy of his celebrated portrait of Pope Leo X. Two choice sketches are Raphael's *Moses* and Michelangelo's *Three Soldiers.* Displayed farther on are the Titians, with Danae taking the spotlight from Pope Paul III.

Another room is devoted to Flemish art: Pieter Brueghel's *Blind Men* is outstanding and his *Misanthrope* is devilishly powerful. Other foreign works include Joos van Cleve's *Adoration of the Magi.* You can climb the stairs for a panoramic view of Naples and the bay, a finer landscape than any you'll see inside.

The State Apartments downstairs deserve inspection. Room after room is devoted to gilded mermaids, Venetian sedan chairs, ivory carvings, a porcelain chinoiserie salon, tapestries, the Farnese armory, and a large glass and china collection.

In the Palazzo Capodimonte, Parco di Capodimonte (off Amedeo di Savoia), Via Miano 2. ℭ 081-7499111. Admission 7€ ($6.25). Tues–Sun 8:30am–7:30pm. Bus: 22 or 23.

Carthusian Monastery of San Martino (Certosa di San Martino) & National Museum of San Martino (Museo Nazionale di San Martino) ★★   Magnificently situated on the grounds of the Castel Sant'Elmo, this museum was founded in the 14th century as a Carthusian monastery but fell into decay until the 17th century, when it was reconstructed by architects in the Neapolitan baroque style. The marble-clad **church** ★★ has a ceiling painting of the *Ascension* by Lanfranco in the nave, along with *12 Prophets* by Giuseppe Ribera, who also did the *Institution of the Eucharist* on the left wall of the choir (Lanfranco painted the *Crucifixion* and Guido Reni painted the *Nativity* at the choir's back wall). In the church treasury is Luca Giordano's ceiling fresco of the *Triumph of Judith* (1704) and Ribera's masterful *Descent from the Cross.*

Now a **museum** ★ for the city of Naples, the church displays two stately carriages, historic documents, ships' replicas, china and porcelain, silver, Campagna paintings of the 18th and 19th centuries, military costumes and armor, and a lavishly adorned crib by Cuciniello. The vast collection of *presepi* (Neapolitan Christmas crèches) includes a cast of thousands of peasants and holy figures that have come out of the workshops of Naples's greatest craftsmen over the past 4 centuries. (At press time, a few of the rooms were closed, but they should be opened again by the time you arrive.) A balcony opens onto a panoramic view of Naples and the bay, as well as Vesuvius and Capri. Many people come here just to drink in the view. The colonnaded cloisters have curious skull sculptures on the inner balustrade.

Next to the monastery is the star-shaped **Castel Sant'Elmo** (℃ **081-5784030**), built by the Angevins in a strategic position above the city from 1329 to 1343. It was enlarged in the 16th century and today offers a magnificent 360° panorama of Naples and its bay after a walk through the echoic medieval stone halls now used for conferences and exhibits. Admission is 1.25€ ($1.10).

Largo San Martino 5 (in the Vómero district). ℃ **081-5781769.** Admission 5.50€ ($4.90). Tues–Sun 9am–6:30pm. Funicular: Centrale from Via Toledo.

MORE ATTRACTIONS

New Castle (Castel Nuovo) ★★   The New Castle, housing municipal offices, was built in the late 13th century on orders from Charles I, king of Naples, as a royal residence for the House of Anjou. It was badly ruined and virtually reconstructed in the mid–15th century by the House of Aragón. The castle is distinguished by a trio of imposing round battle towers at its front; between two of the towers, guarding the entrance, is a triumphal arch designed by Francesco Laurana to commemorate the 1442 expulsion of the Angevins by the forces of Alphonso I. It's a masterpiece of the Renaissance. The Palatine Chapel in the center is from the 14th century, and the city commission of Naples meets in the Barons' Hall, designed by Segreta of Catalonia. You'll find some frescoes and sculptures (of minor interest) from the 14th and 15th centuries in the castle.

Piazza del Municipio. ℃ **081-7952003.** Admission 5€ ($4.45). Mon–Sat 9am–7pm. Tram: 1 or 4. Bus: R2.

Impressions

The museum is full, as you know, of lovely Greek bronzes. The only bother is that they all walk about the town at night.

            —Oscar Wilde, letter to Ernest Dowson (October 11, 1897)

Royal Palace (Palazzo Reale) ⭐   This palace was designed by Domenico Fontana in the 17th century, and the eight statues on the facade are of Neapolitan kings. Located in the heart of the city, the square on which the palace stands is one of Naples's most architecturally interesting, with a long colonnade and a church, San Francesco di Paolo, that evokes the style of the Pantheon in Rome. Inside the Palazzo Reale you can visit the royal apartments, adorned in the baroque style with colored marble floors, paintings, tapestries, frescoes, antiques, and porcelain. Charles de Bourbon, son of Philip IV of Spain, became king of Naples in 1734. A great patron of the arts, he installed a library here, one of the finest in the south, with more than 1,250,000 volumes.

Piazza del Plebiscito 1. 𝒞 081-5808216. Admission 4€ ($3.55). Tues–Sat 9am–7pm. Bus: 106 or 150.

Santa Chiara ⭐   On a palazzo-flanked street, this church was built on orders from Robert the Wise, king of Naples, in the early 14th century. It became the church for the House of Anjou. Although World War II bombers heavily blasted it, it has been restored somewhat to its original look, a Gothic style favored by the Provençal architects. The light-filled interior is lined with chapels, each of which contains some leftover bit of sculpture or fresco from the medieval church, but the best three pieces line the wall behind the High Altar. In the center is the towering multilevel tomb of Robert the Wise d'Angio, sculpted by Giovanni and Pacio Bertini in 1343. To its right is Tino di Camaino's tomb of Charles, duke of Calabria; on the left is the 1399 monument to Mary of Durazza. In the choir behind the altar are more salvaged medieval remnants of frescoes and statuary, including bits of a Giotto *Crucifixion*.

Via Benedetto Croce. 𝒞 081-5526280. Free admission. Mon–Sat 7am–12:30pm and 4:30–8pm; Sun 8am–1pm and 4:30–8pm. Metro: Montesanto.

Complesso Museale di Santa Chiara (Museum Complex of St. Clare) You have to exit the church and walk down its left flank to enter this next sight—the most relaxing retreat from the bustle of the city—the 14th-century **Cloisters of the Order of the Clares (Chiostri dell'Ordine di Santa Chiara).** In 1742, Domenico Antonio Vaccaro took the courtyard of these flowering cloisters and lined the four paths to its center with arbors that are supported by columns, each of which is plated with colorfully painted majolica tiles; interspersed among the columns are tiled benches. In the **museum,** rooms off the cloisters are a scattering of Roman and medieval remains.

On the piazza outside is one of Naples's several baroque spires, the **Guglia dell'Immacolata,** a tall pile of statues and reliefs sculpted in 1750.

Via Santa Chiara 49C. 𝒞 081-5526280. Admission 3€ ($2.70). Mon–Sat 9am–1pm and 3:30–5:30pm. Metro: Montesanto.

Aquarium (Acquario)   The Aquarium is in a municipal park, Villa Comunale, between Via Caracciolo and the Riviera di Chiaia. Established by a German naturalist in the 1800s, it's the oldest aquarium in Europe and displays about 200 species of marine plants and fish, all found in the Bay of Naples (they must be a hardy lot).

Inside Villa Comunale, Via Caracciolo 1. 𝒞 081-5833111. Admission 1.50€ ($1.35). Mon–Sat 9am–5pm; Sun 9am–2pm. Bus: R3.

Cappella San Severo   If you want the best example of how baroque can be ludicrously over the top, hauntingly beautiful, and technically brilliant all at once, search out the nondescript entrance to one of Italy's most fanciful chapels.

This 1590 chapel is a festival of marbles, frescoes, and, above all, sculpture—in relief and in the round, masterfully showing off the technical abilities and storytelling of a few relatively unknown Neapolitan baroque masters. At the center is Giuseppe Sammartino's remarkable alabaster *Veiled Christ* (1753), one the most successful and convincing illusions of soft reality crafted from hard stone, depicting the dead Christ lying on pillows under a transparent veil.

Three wall sculptures stand out as well: Francesco Celebrano's 1762 relief of the *Deposition* behind the altar, Antonio Corradini's allegory of *Modesty* (a marble statue of a woman whose nudity is covered only by a decidedly immodest clinging veil), and Francesco Queirolo's virtuoso allegory of *Disillusion*, represented by a man struggling with a rope net carved entirely of marble.

Via F. de Sanctis 19 (near Piazza San Domenico Maggiore). ✆ **081-5518470**. Admission 5€ ($4.45). Wed–Mon 10am–4:30pm. Bus: E1, R1, R3, R4, V10, 24, 42, 105, or 105r.

Castle of the Egg (Castel dell'Ovo)   This 2,000-year-old fortress overlooks the Gulf of Naples. The site was important centuries before the birth of Christ and was fortified by early settlers. In time, a major stronghold to guard the bay was erected and duly celebrated by Virgil. It's said that Virgil built it on an enchanted egg of mystical powers submerged on the floor of the ocean. Legend has it that if the egg breaks, Naples will collapse.

Actually, most of the fortress was constructed by Frederick II and later expanded by the Angevins. Although there's little to see here today, the Castel dell'Ovo is one of the most historic spots in Naples, perhaps the site of the original Greek settlement of Parthenope. In time, it became the villa of Lucullus, the Roman general and philosopher. By the 5th century, the villa had become the home in exile for the last of the western Roman emperors, Romulus Augustulus. The Goths found him too young and stupid to be much of a threat to their ambitions and pensioned him off here. You can still see columns of Lucullus's villa in the dungeons. The view from here is panoramic. The interior of the fortress is not open to the public except for special exhibits.

Porto Santa Lucia (follow Via Console along the seafront from Piazza del Plebiscito to Porto Santa Lucia; Castel dell'Ovo is at the end of the promontory). ✆ **081-2464334**. Free admission. Mon–Sat 9am–5pm; Sun 9am–2pm. Call for schedules. Bus: 152.

Catacombe di San Gennaro (St. Januarius) ☆   A guide will show you through this two-story underground cemetery, dating from the 2nd century and boasting many interesting frescoes and mosaics. You enter the catacombs on Via di Capodimonte (head down an alley going alongside the Madre del Buon Consiglio Church). These wide tunnels lined with early Christian burial niches grew around the tomb of an important pagan family, but they became a pilgrimage site when the bones of San Gennaro himself were transferred here in the 5th century. Along with several well-preserved 6th-century frescoes, there's a depiction of San Gennaro (A.D. 400s) whose halo sports an alpha and an omega and a cross—symbols normally reserved exclusively for Christ's halo. The tour takes you through the upper level of tunnels, passing through several small early basilicas carved from the *tufa* rock. The cemetery remained active until the 11th century, but most of the bones have since been blessed and reinterred in ossuaries on the lower levels (closed to the public). The catacombs survived the centuries intact, but those precious antique frescoes suffered some damage when these tunnels served as an air raid shelter during World War II.

Via di Capodimonte 13. ✆ **081-7411071**. Admission 3€ ($2.70). Tours daily 9:30, 10:15, 11, and 11:45am. Bus: M4.

Wine Tasting

The wines produced in the harsh, hot landscapes of Campania seem stronger, rougher, and, in many cases, more powerful than those grown in gentler climes. Among the most famous are the Lacrymae Christi (Tears of Christ), a white that grows in the volcanic soil near Naples, Herculaneum, and Pompeii; Taurasi, a potent red; and Greco di Tufo, a pungent white laden with the odors of apricots and apples. One of the most frequently visited vineyards is **Mastroberardino**, 75–81 Via Manfredi, Atripalda, 83042 Avellino (✆ **0825-626123**), which is reached by taking the A16 east from Naples. If you'd like to spend a day outside the city, driving through the countryside and doing a little wine tasting, call to make an appointment.

Il Duomo The Cathedral of Naples might not be as impressive as some in other Italian cities, but it merits a visit nonetheless. Consecrated in 1315, it was Gothic in style, but the centuries have witnessed many changes: the facade, for example, is from the 1800s. A curiosity of the Duomo is that it has access to the 4th-century Basilica of St. Restituta, the earliest Christian basilica erected in Naples. But an even greater treasure is the Chapel of San Gennaro (Cappella di San Gennaro), which you enter from the south aisle. The altar is said to contain the blood of St. Gennaro, patron saint of Naples. St. Gennaro might have been a Christian assimilation of Janus, the Roman god. The church contains two vials of the saint's blood, said to liquefy and boil three times annually (the first Sun in May, Sept 19, and Dec 16).

Via del Duomo 147. ✆ **081-449097**. Free admission. Daily 8am–12:30pm and 4:30–7pm. Metro: Piazza Cavour.

San Domenico Maggiore This massive Gothic edifice was built from 1289 to 1324 and then was rebuilt in the Renaissance and early baroque eras. You enter from under the apse end, where you'll see that the body of the church was overhauled in neo-Gothic style in the 1850s. Walk down the left aisle (which is on your right because you're coming in from the wrong end) to the last chapel, where you'll find Luca Giordano's *Crowning of St. Joseph*. Now turn around to attack the church from the proper direction.

The first chapel on the right aisle is a Renaissance masterpiece of design and sculpture by Tuscans Antonio and Romolo da Settignano. The third chapel on the right contains frescoes from 1309 by Roman master Pietro Cavallini (a contemporary of Giotto). The seventh chapel on the right is the **Crucifixion Chapel (Cappella del Crocifisso),** with some Renaissance tombs and a copy of the 12th-century *Crucifixion* painting that spoke to St. Thomas Aquinas. Next door, the theatrical **Sacristy** has a bright ceiling fresco by Francesco Solimena (1706) and small caskets containing the ashes of Aragonese rulers and important courtiers, lining a high shelf. What acts like a right transept was actually a preexisting church grafted onto this one, the **Chiesa Antica di Sant'Angelo a Morfisa,** today an oversize chapel containing lots of finely carved Renaissance tombs.

On Piazza San Domenico is another of Naples's baroque spires, this one a 1737 confection called the **Guglia di San Domenico** by Domenico Antonio Vaccaro.

Piazza San Domenico Maggiore 8A. ✆ **081-459188**. Free admission. Daily 8:30am–noon and 5–7:30pm. Bus: 24, 42, 105, 105r, E1, R1, R3, R4, or V10.

San Lorenzo Maggiore   The greatest of Naples's layered churches was built in 1265 for Charles I over a 6th-century basilica, which lay over many ancient remains. The interior is pure Gothic, with tall pointed arches and an apse off of which radiate nine chapels. This is where, in 1334, Boccaccio first caught sight of Robert of Anjou's daughter Maria, who became "Fiammetta" in his writings. Aside from some gorgeously baroque chapels of inlaid marbles, the highlight of the interior is Tino da Camaino's **canopy tomb of Catherine of Austria** ☆ (1323–25).

San Lorenzo preserves the best and most extensive (still rather paltry) **remains of the ancient Greek and Roman cities** currently open to the public. The church foundations are actually the walls of Neapolis's basilican law courts. In the **cloisters** are excavated bits of the Roman city's treasury and marketplace. In the **crypt** are the rough remains of a Roman-era shop-lined street, a Greek temple, and a medieval building.

Piazza San Gaetano Via Tribunali 316. ℂ **081-290580** or 081-454948 for *scavi* (ruins). Admission to church free; scavi 2.50€ ($2.25). Mon–Sat 10am–5:30pm; Sun 9am–1:30pm Bus: 42, 105, 105r, or E1.

SHOPPING

The shopping in Naples can't compare to that in Milan, Venice, Florence, and Rome. Nevertheless, there are some good buys for those willing to seek them out. The finest shopping area lies around **Piazza dei Martiri** and along such streets as **Via dei Mille, Via Calabritto,** and **Via Chiaia.** There's more commercial shopping between Piazza Trieste e Trento and Piazza Dante along **Via Toledo/Via Roma.**

Coral is much sought after by collectors. Much of the coral is now sent to Naples from Thailand, but it's still shaped into amazing jewelry at one of the workrooms at **Torre del Greco,** on the outskirts of Naples, off the Naples-Pompeii highway. Cameos are also made here. Many of the factories here cater strictly to those endless bus tours and sell shoddy merchandise. The most reliable firm is the century-old **Basilio Liverino,** 61 via Montedoro (ℂ **081-8811225**), which uses the finest Asiatic and Mediterranean coral to make the best cameos in the south of Italy. Its cameos are made from carnelian, a Madagascan shell, and sardonyx, a transparent variety of quartz. Technically, this store will sell only to jewelers, but if you want to make a serious purchase, as opposed to a cheap souvenir, you can call for an appointment; at that time, you can also visit a museum displaying the world's best collection of cameos and corals. The tour buses pull up at **Giovanni Apa,** 1 Via e. De Nicola (ℂ **881-8811155**), but Bruno Gioia will take you beyond the junk and show you a stunning collection of authentic coral pieces and antique cameos.

We never visit Naples without waiting in line to get into a tiny little store, **Marinella,** Riviera di Chiaia 287 (ℂ **081-7644214**), which enjoys worldwide fame. It's worth the wait. Inside you'll find a great collection of accessories for men, along with shirts and sweaters that you'll keep forever. Wherever you look, you encounter a feast of indigo or red ties or else scarves printed in England just for Marinella. Royalty, politicians, and international movie stars are also likely to be waiting in line with you.

Another great menswear store is **Fusaro,** Via Chiaia 32 (ℂ **081-419365**), which is full of everything a smartly dressed man will need for his wardrobe, including suits, ties, shirts, and sweaters. Most suits are tailor-made (some tailoring can even be done the same day!).

Modeled on Milan's galleria, the **Galleria Umberto I,** Via San Carlo (see "Naples After Dark," later in this chapter), was built as part of Naples's urban renewal scheme following an 1884 cholera epidemic. The massive glass- and iron-frame barrel vaults of its four wings and central dome soar some 60m (187 ft.) above the inlaid marble flooring (it had to be largely rebuilt after World War II bomb damage). It makes for a pleasant shopping stroll. You'll find a wide range of stores selling typical area products, from fashion to ceramics.

WHERE TO STAY
EXPENSIVE

Grande Hotel Vesuvio ★★   This is a deluxe and fabled hotel and one of the foremost choices along the Bay of Naples. Built in 1882, the Vesuvio was restored about 50 years later and features a marble-and-stucco facade with curved balconies. The 1930s-style guest rooms have lofty ceilings, cove moldings, parquet floors, and large closets. Traditionalists should request second-floor rooms, decorated in a 1700s style. The marble-clad bathrooms are spacious, with deluxe toiletries. You'll also find a scattering of antiques throughout the echoing halls.

Via Partenope 45, 80121 Napoli. (© **081-7640044.** Fax 081-7644483. www.vesuvio.it. 181 units. 336€ ($300.05) double; from 465€ ($415.25) suite. Rates include buffet breakfast. AE, DC, MC, V. Parking 25€ ($22.35). Bus: 152. **Amenities:** Restaurant; bar; health club; Jacuzzi; sauna; room service; babysitting; laundry/dry cleaning. *In room:* A/C, TV, minibar, hair dryer, safe.

Grand Hotel Parker's ★★   This is the finest hotel in town, surpassing the Vesuvio only because of its more tranquil and scenic location on a hillside avenue. It was created in 1870, when architects cared about the beauty of their work—neoclassic walls, fluted pilasters, and ornate ceilings. The guest rooms are traditionally furnished, some quite formal; each is in a different style, such as Louis XVI, Directoire, Empire, or Charles X. Most guests seek out one of the front rooms where narrow terraces open onto bay views.

Corso Vittorio Emanuele 135, 80121 Napoli. (© **081-7612474.** Fax 081-663527. www.bcedit.it/parkers hotel.htm. 82 units. 240€ ($214.30) double; 350€–750€ ($312.55–$669.75) suite. Rates include breakfast. AE, DC, MC, V. Parking 12.50€ ($11.15). Metro: Piazza Amedeo. **Amenities:** Restaurant; lounge; room service; babysitting; laundry. *In room:* A/C, TV, minibar, hair dryer.

Hotel Excelsior ★   This is the third *luxe* choice for Naples, excelled only by Parker's and the Vesuvio. The Excelsior occupies a dramatic position on the waterfront, with views of Santa Lucia and Vesuvius. After a long decline, the hotel has bounced back under Sheraton (which also owns the posh Vesuvio next door) and boasts elegant details such as Venetian chandeliers, Doric columns, wall-size murals, and bronze torchiers. Most of the spacious guest rooms are furnished in the Empire style, with heavy wood furniture, elegant fabrics, paneled walls, and brass trim. Carrara marble cloaks the walls of the bathrooms.

Via Partenope 48, 80121 Napoli. (© **081-7640111.** Fax 081-7649743. www.excelsior.it. 121 units. 274€–300€ ($244.70–$267.90) double; 465€–1,033€ ($415.20–$922.30) suite. Rates include breakfast. AE, DC, MC, V. Parking 20€ ($17.85). Bus: 140, 152, or C25. **Amenities:** Restaurant; lounge; room service; babysitting; laundry/dry cleaning. *In room:* A/C, TV, minibar, hair dryer, safe.

Hotel Miramare ★   Its roof garden alone is reason enough to stay here, opening as it does onto panoramas of the Gulf of Naples and Vesuvius. In a superb location, seemingly thrust out toward the harbor on a dockside boulevard, the Miramare was originally an aristocratic villa but was transformed into a hotel in 1944 after serving for a short period as the American consulate. Its lobby evokes a little Caribbean hotel with a semitropical look. The guest rooms have been renovated and are pleasantly furnished, with soundproof windows, fax machines, VCRs, and well-kept bathrooms.

Via Nazario Sauro 24, 80132 Napoli. © 081-7647589. Fax 081-7640775. 31 units. 147€–282€ ($131.25–$251.85) double (minimum 2 nights). Rates include buffet breakfast. AE, DC, MC, V. Parking 20€ ($17.85). Bus: 104, 140, or 150. **Amenities:** Bar; lounge; room service; babysitting; laundry. *In room:* A/C, TV/VCR, minibar, hair dryer.

Hotel Santa Lucia ⭐ The Santa Lucia, whose neoclassical facade overlooks a sheltered marina, competes with the nearby Royal (see below) and is better maintained (it ought to be, with rates $65 higher per night). The interior has undergone extensive renovations and is decorated in Neapolitan style, with terrazzo floors. The guest rooms are large, containing quality beds with wrought-iron headboards and ceiling stenciling that lends a classical effect. The tiled bathrooms often contain party-size whirlpools. The rooms in back are quieter but have no views. The balconied front rooms bring you lots of traffic noise but panoramic views of the Bay of Naples in which boats and yachts bob at anchor.

Via Partenope 46, 80121 Napoli. © 081-7640666. Fax 081-7648580. www.santalucia.it. 96 units. 209€–319€ ($186.65–$284.85) double; 359€ ($320.60) suite. Rates include breakfast. AE, DC, MC, V. Parking 20€ ($17.85). Bus: 140, 152, or C25. **Amenities:** Restaurant; bar; room service; babysitting; laundry/dry cleaning. *In room:* A/C, TV, minibar, hair dryer, safe.

MODERATE

Hotel Britannique ⭐ *(Value)* Its bones are a bit creaky with age, but this remains a longtime Neapolitan favorite, especially for traditionalists. It's actually part of the same building as Parker's (see above), but without that hotel's grandness. Nonetheless, the Britannique remains charmingly old-fashioned. The service is old-fashioned, too, in the best sense. The view of the Bay of Naples and even Vesuvius is so compelling that many guests rave about the place. Tropical plants and flowers abound in the garden, but the lobby is a bit seedy. The guest rooms, from small to spacious, have some antiques, but mostly the look is functional. The bathroom plumbing is aging but still humming along.

Corso Vittorio Emanuele 133, 80121 Napoli. © 081-7614145. Fax 081-660457. www.hotelbritannique.it. 155€ ($138.40) double; 176€ ($157.15) junior suite. Rates include breakfast. AE, DC, MC, V. Parking 11€–13€ ($9.80–$11.60). Metro: Piazza Amedeo. Bus: C16 or C28. **Amenities:** Restaurant; bar; lounge; room service; babysitting; laundry/dry cleaning. *In room:* A/C, TV, minibar, hair dryer.

Hotel Majestic ⭐ In a city filled with decaying mansions, the Majestic, built in 1959, qualifies as modern. A favorite with the conference crowd, it's in the antiques district, so at your doorstep will be dozens of boutiques. The guest rooms are cozy, with well-kept bathrooms. The garage is small, so reserve a parking space with your room.

Largo Vasto a Chiaia 68, 80121 Napoli. © 081-416500. Fax 081-410145. www.majestic.it. 112 units. 171€ ($152.70) double; 260€ ($232.20) suite. Rates include breakfast. AE, DC, MC, V. Parking 35€–43€ ($31.25–$38.40). Metro: Piazza Amedeo. **Amenities:** Restaurant; bar; room service; babysitting; laundry/dry cleaning. *In room:* A/C, TV, minibar, hair dryer.

Hotel Paradiso *(Finds)* This hotel might be paradise, but only after you reach it. It's 6km (3¾ miles) from the central station, but one irate driver claimed that it takes about 3½ hours to get here. Once you arrive, however, your nerves will be soothed by the view, one of the most panoramic of any hotel in Italy. The Bay of Naples unfolds before you, and in the distance Vesuvius looms menacingly. The guest rooms range from medium to spacious, each with well-kept bathrooms. From the Paradiso, you can either take taxis to the major attractions or use a funicular that takes you from a hillside site near the hotel to the center of Naples.

Via Catullo 11, 80122 Napoli. © **800/528-1234** in the U.S., or 081-7614161. Fax 081-7613449. www.best western.it. 72 units. 176€ ($157.15) double. Rates include breakfast. AE, DC, MC, V. Parking 12.50€–15€ ($11.15–$13.40) nearby. **Amenities:** Restaurant; lounge; room service; laundry. *In room:* A/C, TV.

Hotel Royal ★ The 10-story Royal is in a desirable location on this busy street beside the bay in Santa Lucia. It's a bustling choice that's often filled with tour groups. You enter a greenery-filled vestibule, where the stairs leading to the modern lobby are flanked by a pair of stone lions. Each of the guest rooms has a balcony and aging modern furniture; some offer a water view. The tiled bathrooms are small but adequate.

Via Partenope 38–44, 80121 Napoli. © **081-7644800.** Fax 081-7645707. www.hotelroyal.it. 251 units. 145€–255€ ($129.50–$227.70) double; 360€ ($321.50) suite. Rates include breakfast. AE, DC, MC, V. Parking 13€–18€ ($11.60–$16.05). Tram: 4. **Amenities:** 2 restaurants; 2 bars; pool; health club; room service; babysitting; laundry/dry cleaning. *In room:* A/C, TV, minibar, hair dryer, safe.

INEXPENSIVE

Albergo San Germano Designed like an Italian version of a Chinese pagoda, this brick-and-concrete hotel is ideal for late-arriving motorists reluctant to negotiate the traffic of Naples. A terraced pool and garden are welcome respites after a day of sightseeing. The guest rooms are clean but simple. All are a bit small—as are the tiled bathrooms—but tidily maintained, with good mattresses.

Via Beccadelli 41, 80125 Napoli. © **081-5705422.** Fax 081-5701546. 105 units (showers only). 129€ ($115.20) double. Rates include breakfast. AE, DC, MC, V. Bus: 152. From the autostrada, follow the signs to Tangenziale Napoli; exit 13km (8 miles) later at Agnano Terme. The hotel is on your right less than a mile from the toll booth. **Amenities:** Restaurant; bar; lounge; pool; room service; babysitting; laundry/dry cleaning. *In room:* A/C, TV, minibar, hair dryer, safe.

Hotel Rex Santa Lucia's most famous budget hotel, the Rex, has played host to cash-conscious visitors from around the world since 1938. Some like it and others don't, but proof of its popularity is that its rooms are often fully booked when other hotels have vacancies. The architecture of the building itself is lavishly ornate, but the guest rooms are simple and some are very cramped. All have small bathrooms.

Via Palepoli 12, 80132 Napoli. © **081-7649389.** Fax 081-7649227. 38 units (showers only). 110€ ($98.25) double. Rates include breakfast. AE, DC, MC, V. Parking 20€ ($17.85). Bus: 152. **Amenities:** Bar; room service; babysitting. *In room:* A/C, TV, hair dryer.

Hotel Serius Built in 1974, this hotel is on a palm-lined street in a calm neighborhood known as Fuorigrotto, a short bus ride north of the center. The paneled, split-level lobby contains an intimate bar and several metal sculptures of horses and birds. The smallish guest rooms are simply furnished, with boldly patterned fabrics and painted furniture. The bathrooms are tiny but for the most part manage to fit in both a tub and a shower.

Viale Augusto 74, 80125 Napoli. © **081-2394844.** Fax 081-2399251. 69 units. 113€ ($100.90) double. Rates include breakfast. AE, MC, V. Free parking. Metro: Piazza Leopardi. **Amenities:** Dining room; bar; room service; laundry. *In room:* A/C, TV, minibar, hair dryer, safe.

WHERE TO DINE

Naples is the home of pizza and spaghetti, and it's great fun to sample the authentic versions. However, if you like subtle cooking and have an aversion to olive oil or garlic, you won't fare as well.

EXPENSIVE

Masaniello ★ *(Finds)* NEAPOLITAN   In a former stable, this hard-to-find restaurant is named for the celebrated leader of a people's uprising in 1647. It prints no menus, so the owner will tell you what's offered. Put yourself in his hands and be prepared for a bounteous feast. The food is cooked to order after elaborate consultations about the taste of each customer. The cuisine is exquisitely prepared and based on only the freshest of ingredients. The traditional dishes based on antique recipes include linguine with *lupini di mare* (Neapolitan clams) and pecorino cheese. The chef is also proud of his special pasta with potatoes; although it sounds like an unlikely combination, it's filled with flavor from the smoked provola cheese and the fresh little tomatoes.

Via Donnalbina 28. ℂ 081-5528863. Reservations recommended. Main courses 10€–35€ ($8.95–$31.25). AE, DC, MC, V. Mon–Sat 12:30–3pm and 8–11:30pm (daily in Dec and May). Bus: C57, R3, or R4.

MODERATE

Don Salvatore ★ SEAFOOD   This restaurant is on the seafront, near the departure point of hydrofoils for Capri. Owner Antonio Aversano takes his wine as seriously as his food. The latter is likely to include linguine with shrimp or squid, an array of fish, and a marvelous assortment of fresh Neapolitan vegetables grown in the countryside. The fish comes right out of the Bay of Naples (which might, but possibly might not, be a plus). Rice comes flavored in a delicate fish broth, and you can get a reasonably priced bottle from the wine cellar, said to be the finest in Campania.

Strada Mergellina 4A. ℂ 081-681817. Reservations recommended. Main courses 8€–14.50€ ($7.15–$12.95). AE, DC, MC, V. Thurs–Tues 1–4pm and 8pm–1am. Metro: Mergellina.

Giuseppone a Mare ★ SEAFOOD   At this restaurant, known for the best and freshest seafood in Campania, you can dine in Neapolitan sunshine on an open-air terrace with a bay view. The only better restaurant is La Cantinella (see below). Diners make their selections from a trolley likely to include everything from crabs to eels. You might precede your fish dinner with some fritters (a batter whipped up with seaweed and fresh squash blossoms). Naturally, the offerings include linguine with clams—the chef also adds squid and mussels. Much of the day's catch is deep-fried a golden brown. The pièce de résistance is an octopus casserole. If the oven's going, you can order a pizza. The restaurant stocks some fine southern Italian wines too, especially from Ischia and Vesuvio.

Via Ferdinando Russo 13. ℂ 081-5756002. Reservations required. Main courses 10€–15€ ($8.95–$13.40). AE, DC, MC, V. Tues–Sat 12:30–3:30pm and 8pm–midnight; Sun 12:30–4pm. Closed Aug 16–31. Bus: 140.

Il Gallo Nero ★ NEAPOLITAN   Gian Paolo Quagliata, with a capable staff, maintains his hillside villa with its period furniture and accessories. In summer, the enthusiastic crowd is served on an elegant terrace. Many of the dishes are based on 100-year-old recipes, although a few are more recent inventions. You might enjoy the Neapolitan linguine with pesto, rigatoni with fresh vegetables, tagliatelle primavera, or macaroni with peas and artichokes. The fish dishes are usually well prepared—grilled, broiled, or sautéed. The meat dishes include slightly more exotic creations, such as prosciutto with orange slices and veal cutlets with artichokes.

Via Torquato Tasso 466. ℂ 081-643012. Reservations recommended. Main courses 10€–17.50€ ($8.95–$15.65); fixed-price menu 42.50€ ($37.95) with meat, 47.50€ ($42.40) with fish. AE, DC, MC, V. Tues–Sat 7pm–midnight; Sun 12:30–3pm. Closed Aug. Metro: Mergellina.

La Cantinella ★★ SEAFOOD   Cantinella serves grilled seafood at its finest. You get the impression of 1920s Chicago as you approach this place, where speakeasy-style doors open after you ring. The restaurant is on a busy street skirting the bay in Santa Lucia. You'll find a well-stocked antipasto table and—get this—a phone on each table. The chefs have a deft way of handling the region's fresh produce and turn out both Neapolitan classics and more imaginative dishes. The menu includes four preparations of risotto (including one with champagne), many kinds of pasta (including penne with vodka and linguine with scampi and seafood), and most of the classic beef and veal dishes of Italy.

Via Cuma 42. ℂ 081-7648684. Reservations required. Main courses 11€–20€ ($9.80–$17.85). AE, DC, MC, V. Oct–Apr daily 12:30–3pm and 7:30pm–midnight. Closed Aug 7–20. Bus: 104, 140, or 150.

La Sacrestia PASTA/SEAFOOD   The trompe l'oeil frescoes on the two-story interior and the name La Sacrestia vaguely suggest the ecclesiastical, but that's not the case. Perched near the top of a seemingly endless labyrinth of streets winding up from the port (take a taxi or go by funicular), this bustling place is sometimes called "the greatest show in town." In summer, a terrace with its flowering arbor provides a view over the harbor lights. Meals emphasize well-prepared dishes with strong doses of Neapolitan drama. You might try what's said to be the most luxurious macaroni dish in Italy ("Prince of Naples"), made with truffles and mild cheeses. Less ornate selections are a full array of pastas and dishes composed of octopus, squid, and shellfish.

Via Orazio 116. ℂ 081-7611051. Reservations required. Main courses 9€–30€ ($8.05–$26.80). AE, DC, MC, V. Daily 12:30–3:30pm and 7:30–11pm. Closed Sun in July. Closed 2 weeks in mid-Aug. Funicular: from Mergellina.

Pizzaria Brandi ★ NEAPOLITAN/PIZZA   Naples is famous for pizza, and this is the place to go to sample the best pies. The most historic pizzeria in Italy, Brandi was opened by Pietro Colicchio in the 19th century. His successor, Raffaele Esposito, was requested one day to prepare a banquet for Margherita di Savoia, the queen of Italy. So successful was the reception of the pizza made with tomato, basil, olive oil, and mozzarella (the colors of the newly united Italy's flag) that the queen accepted the honor of having the dish named after her. Thus was Pizza Margherita born from the kitchens here. Today you can order the pizza that pleased a queen, as well as linguine with scampi, fettuccine "Regina d'Italia," and a full array of seafood dishes. Even Chelsea Clinton gave this place a thumbs up.

Salita Santa Anna di Palazzo. ℂ 081-416928. Reservations required. Main courses 10€–15€ ($8.95–$13.40); pizza from 6€ ($5.35). AE, MC, V. Daily noon–3pm and 6:30pm–midnight. Bus: 106 or 150.

Vini e Cucina ★ *Finds* NEAPOLITAN   The best ragout sauce in all Naples is said to be made at this trattoria, which has only 20 tables. You can get a really satisfying meal, but we must warn you—it's almost impossible to get in. Get there early and resign yourself to a wait. The cooking is the best home-style version of Neapolitan cuisine we've been able to find in this tricky city. The spaghetti, along with that fabulous sauce, is served al dente. The restaurant is in front of the Mergellina station.

Corso Vittorio Emanuele 762. ℂ 081-660302. Reservations recommended. Main courses 4€–7.50€ ($3.55–$6.70). MC, V. Daily 11:30am–3:30pm and 7pm–midnight. Closed Aug 14–28. Metro: Mergellina.

INEXPENSIVE

Dante e Beatrice ★ NEAPOLITAN   Gregarious and unpretentious, and named after the players in one of the great romantic tragedies of the Middle

Ages, Dante e Beatrice opened in 1956 and remains one of the best restaurants in its neighborhood. It specializes in all the staples of the Neapolitan cuisine, serving flavorful portions of lasagna, minestrone, spaghetti with clams, tagliatelle, *pasta e fagioli* (pasta and beans), and grilled fish. Other notable items are maccheroni or spaghetti with seafood, and "frittata" of spaghetti, with a sauce made of mozzarella, prosciutto, and salami, bound together with tomatoes.

Piazza Dante 44–45. ✆ **081-5499438.** Reservations recommended. Main courses 7.50€–15€ ($6.70–$13.40); fixed-price menu 15€–25€ ($13.40–$22.35). AE, DC, MC, V. Thurs–Tues 1:30–4pm and 8–midnight. Closed Aug 15–30. Metro: Dante.

Giovanni Scaturchio PASTRIES   This place has been satisfying and fattening locals since around 1900. Pastries include the entire selection of Neapolitan sweets, cakes, and candies, including brioches soaked in liqueur, *cassate* (pound cake) filled with layered ricotta, Moor's heads, and cheesy ricotta pastries known as *sfogliatelle*. Another specialty is *ministeriale*, a chocolate cake filled with liqueur and chocolate cream.

Piazza San Domenico Maggiore 19. ✆ **081-5516944.** Pastries start at 1.30€ ($1.15) if consumed standing up, or 1.80€ ($1.60) if enjoyed at a table. Daily 7am–8:40pm. Closed 2–3 weeks in Aug.

Ristorante La Fazenda SEAFOOD   It would be hard to find a more typically Neapolitan restaurant than this place. On a clear day, you can see Capri from here. The decor is rustic, loaded with agrarian touches and an assortment of Neapolitan families, lovers, and visitors who have made it one of their preferred places. In summer, the overflow from the dining room spills onto the terrace. Menu specialties include linguine with scampi, fresh grilled fish, sautéed clams, a mixed Italian grill, savory stews, and many chicken dishes, along with lobster with fresh grilled tomatoes. Look for "Mr. Nappo," allegedly "the largest pizza ever."

Via Marechiaro 58A. ✆ **081-5757420.** Reservations required. Main courses 7.50€–15€ ($6.70–$13.40). AE, DC, MC, V. Tues–Sat 1–4pm and 7:30pm–12:30am; Sun 1–5pm; Mon 7:30pm–12:30am. Bus: 140.

Rosolino INTERNATIONAL/ITALIAN/SEAFOOD   This stylish place isn't defined as a nightclub by its owners, but rather as a restaurant with dancing. Set on the waterfront, it's divided into two areas: On Saturday evenings there's a piano bar near the entrance, where you might have a drink before passing into a much larger dining room. Here you can dine within sight of a bandstand reminiscent of the big-band era. In the dining room, there's live Naples-style guitar music on Friday and Saturday nights. The food is traditional—not very imaginative, but well prepared with fresh vegetables. Dishes include rigatoni with zucchini and meat sauce, pusillo (a locally made pasta), an impressive array of fresh shellfish, and such beef dishes as tournedos and veal scaloppine.

Via Nazario Sauro 2–7. ✆ **081-7649873.** Reservations required. Main courses 7.50€–17.50€ ($6.70–$15.65); fixed-price menu 22.50€–35€ ($20.10–$31.25). AE, DC, MC, V. Mon–Sun 12:30–3:30pm; Mon–Sat 7:30pm–midnight. Tram: 1.

Umberto NEAPOLITAN   Off Piazza dei Martiri, Umberto is one of the most atmospheric places to dine; there's even likely to be a dance band playing at dinner. The tasteful dining room has been directed for many a year by the same extended family. The excellent Italian specialties include pizzas, gnocchi with potatoes, grilled meats and fish, savory stews, and a host of pasta dishes.

Via Alabardieri 30. ✆ **081-418555.** Reservations required. Main courses 4.65€–12.90€ ($4.15–$11.50). AE, DC, DISC, MC, V. Tues–Sun 9:30am–4pm and 7pm–midnight. Closed Aug 15–30. Bus: C25 or R3.

Moments Dining in the Past

The city's most unusual dining experience is the weekly banquet at **Simposium,** Via Benedetto Croce 38 (*℃* **081-5518510**), Friday and Saturday at 9pm, or Sunday from noon to 3pm. Reservations are essential. This cultural institution celebrates a different historical era each weekend, with a fascinating lecture followed by a banquet featuring a cuisine based on recipes from that era. Waiters in period costumes serve the banquets. Perhaps the offering will be called *di fine Settecento* (from the end of the 18th c.), accompanied by a live performance of selections from *Don Giovanni.* At the banquet, men sit on one side, women sit on the other, and wine is served in clay pitchers. Don't expect grand cuisine. The food is almost too simplistic—perhaps a plate of gruel, authentic to the time, with overcooked vegetables and a turnover stuffed with something (you're too polite to ask what). But the music and the setting make this one of Naples's hottest reservations. A dinner for two costs about 83.20€ ($74.30), including wine, service charge, tip, and tax.

NAPLES AFTER DARK

A **sunset walk through Santa Lucia** and along the waterfront is one of the lasting pleasures in Naples. You can stroll by the glass-enclosed **Galleria Umberto I,** off Via Roma across from the Teatro San Carlo. The 19th-century gallery is still standing today, although it's a little the worse for wear. It's a kind of social center for Naples, with lots of shopping and dining possibilities.

Naples's oldest cafe, dating from 1860, is the palatial **Gran Caffè Gambrinus,** Via Chiaia 1, near the Galleria Umberto I (*℃* **081-417582**). Along the vaulted ceiling of an inner room, Empire-style caryatids spread their togas in high relief above frescoes of mythological playmates. The cafe is known for its espresso and cappuccino, as well as pastries and cakes whose variety dazzles the eye. You can also order potato-and-rice croquettes and fried pizzas for a light lunch. Cappuccino goes for 2.20€ ($1.95) a table. The cafe is open daily 8am to midnight.

OPERA The **Teatro San Carlo,** Via San Carlo 98, across from the Galleria Umberto (*℃* **081-7972111**), is one of the largest opera houses in Italy, with some of the best acoustics. Built in only 6 months for King Charles's birthday in November 1737, it was restored in a gilded neoclassical style. Grand-scale productions are presented on the main stage. December to October, the box office is open Tuesday to Sunday 10am to 1pm and 4:30 to 6:30pm. Tickets cost 22.50€ to 100€ ($20.10–$89.30).

BARS & CLUBS On its nightclub/cabaret circuit, Naples offers more sucker joints than any other Mediterranean port. If you're starved for action, you'll find plenty of it—and you're likely to end up paying for it dearly.

Chez Moi, Via del Parco Margherita 13 (*℃* **081-407526**), is one of the city's best-managed nightclubs, strictly refusing entrance to anyone who looks like a troublemaker. This is appreciated by the designers, government ministers, and visiting socialites who enjoy the place. The crowd tends to be over 25. The place is open Friday and Saturday 10:30pm to 4 or 5am. Occasionally there's a cabaret act or a live pianist at the bar, but more frequently the music is disco. The cover is 12.50€ to 15€ ($11.15–$13.40).

Madison Street, Via Sgambati 47 (© **338-6175071**), is the largest disco in Naples. The youngish crowd, usually between 18 and 25, mingles and dances and generally has an uninhibited good time. If you tire yourself out on the dance floor, you can watch video movies or videotaped rock concerts on one of several screens. The place is open Tuesday and Thursday to Saturday 10pm to 3am, and Sunday 8pm to 2am. The Friday crowd tends to be older and slightly more sedate. The cover ranges from 7.50€ to 15€ ($6.70–$13.40), depending on the night.

A leading Naples hot spot is **Piazza di Spagna,** Via Petrarca 101 (© **081-5754882**), in Vómero. It features dancing Friday to Sunday from September to July; go after 10pm and expect a 7.50€ to 15€ ($6.70–$13.40) cover.

Most gay nightlife is centered in the Posillipo neighborhood, where you'll find **Tongue,** Via Mazonik 207 (© **081-7690800**). It has a mixed crowd, a large part of whom are gay, dancing to techno music. It is open only on weekends 9pm to 3am and charges a cover of 7.50€ to 15€ ($6.70–$13.40).

2 The Environs of Naples: The Phlaegrean Fields & Herculaneum

THE PHLAEGREAN FIELDS 👁👁

One of the bizarre attractions of southern Italy, the **Phlaegrean Fields (Campi Flegrei)** form a backdrop for a day's exploring west of Naples and along its bay. An explosive land of myth and legend, the fiery fields contain the dormant volcano Solfatara, the cave of the Cumaean Sibyl, Virgil's gateway to the "Infernal Regions," the ruins of thermal baths and amphitheaters built by the Romans, deserted colonies left by the Greeks, and lots more.

The best center for exploring the area is **Pozzuoli,** reached by Metropolitana (subway) from Stazione Centrale in Naples. The fare is .75€ (65¢). Once in Pozzuoli, you can catch one of the SEPSA buses at any bus stop and be in Baia in 20 minutes. You can also go to Cumae on one of these buses or to Solfatara or Lago d'Averno.

SOLFATARA 👁👁   About 12km (7½ miles) west of Naples, near Pozzuoli, is the ancient **Vulcano Solfatara,** Via Solfatara 161 (© **081-5262341**). It hasn't erupted since the final year of the 12th century but has been threatening ever since. It gives off sulfurous gases and releases scalding vapors through cracks in the earth's surface. In fact, Solfatara's activity (or inactivity) has been observed for such a long time that the crater's name was once used by *Webster's* dictionary to define any "dormant volcano" emitting vapors.

You can visit the crater daily 8:30am to 1 hour before sunset at a cost of 4€ ($3.55). From Naples, take bus no. 152 from Piazza Garibaldi or the Metropolitana from Stazione Centrale. Once you get off at the train station, you can board one of the city buses that go up the hill, or you can walk to the crater in about 20 minutes.

POZZUOLI 👁   Just 2km (1¼ miles) from Solfatara, the port of Pozzuoli opens onto a gulf screened from the Bay of Naples by a promontory. The ruins of the **Anfiteatro Flavio** 👁👁, Via Nicola Terracciano 75 (© **081-5266007**), built in the last part of the 1st century, testify to past greatness. One of the finest surviving ancient arenas, it's particularly distinguished by its "wings," which, considering their age, are in good condition. You can see the remains where exotic beasts from Africa were caged before being turned loose in the ring to test

Treading Lightly on Mt. Vesuvius

Stand at the bottom of the great market-place of Pompeii, and look up at the silent streets . . . over the broken houses with their inmost sanctuaries open to the day, away to Mount Vesuvius, bright and snowy in the peaceful distance; and lose all count of time, and heed of other things, in the strange and melancholy sensation of seeing the Destroyed and the Destroyer making this quiet picture in the sun.
—Charles Dickens, *Pictures from Italy*

A volcano that has struck terror in Campania, the towering, pitch-black **Mt. Vesuvius** looms menacingly over the Bay of Naples. August 24, A.D. 79, is the infamous date when Vesuvius burst forth and buried Pompeii, Herculaneum, and Stabiae under its mass of ash and volcanic mud. What many fail to realize is that Vesuvius has erupted periodically ever since (thousands were killed in 1631): The last major spouting of lava occurred in this century (it blew off the ring of its crater in 1906). The last spectacular eruption was on March 31, 1944. The approach to Vesuvius is dramatic, with the terrain growing foreboding as you near the top. Along the way you'll see villas rising on its slopes, and vineyards—the grapes produce an amber-colored wine known as Lacrimae Christi (Tears of Christ); the citizens of ancient Pompeii enjoyed wine from here, as excavations have revealed. Closer to the summit, the soil becomes puce-colored and an occasional wildflower appears.

It might sound like a dubious invitation (Vesuvius, after all, is an active volcano), but it's possible to visit the rim of the crater's mouth. As you look down into its smoldering core, you might recall that Spartacus, a century before the eruption that buried Pompeii, hid in the hollow of the crater, which was then covered with vines.

To reach Vesuvius from Naples, take the Circumvesuviana Railway or (summer only) bus service from Piazza Vittoria, which hooks up with bus connections at Pugliano. You get off the train at the Ercolano station, the 10th stop. Six SITA buses per day go from Herculaneum to the crater of Vesuvius, costing 5€ ($4.45) round-trip. Once at the top, you must be accompanied by a guide, which will cost 2.50€ ($2.25). Assorted willing tour guides are found in the bus parking lot; they are available from early in the morning to about 4:30pm.

their jungle skill against a gladiator. The amphitheater is said to have entertained 40,000 spectators at the height of its glory. You can visit daily 9am to 2:40pm. Admission is 4€ ($3.55). In another part of town, the **Tempio di Serapide** was really the Macellum (market square), and some of its ruined pillars still project upward. It was erected during the reign of the Flavian emperors. You can reach Pozzuoli by subway from Stazione Centrale in Naples.

BAIA In the days of Imperial Rome, the emperors—everybody from Julius Caesar to Hadrian—came here to frolic in the sun while enjoying the comforts of their luxurious villas and Roman baths. It was here that Emperor

Claudius built a grand villa for his first wife, Messalina, who spent her days and nights reveling in debauchery and plotting to have her husband replaced by her lover (for which she was beheaded). And it was here that Claudius was poisoned by his last wife, Agrippina, the controlling mother of Nero. Nero is said to have had Agrippina murdered at nearby Bacoli, with its Pool of Mirabilis—after she had survived his first attempt on her life, a collapsing boat meant to send her to a watery rest. Parts of Baia's illustrious past have been dug out, including both the Temple of Baiae and the Thermal Baths, among the greatest erected in Italy.

You can explore this archaeological district (© **081-8687592;** www.ulixes.it) Tuesday to Sunday 9am to 3pm. Admission is 4€ ($3.55). Ferrovia Cumana trains depart from Stazione Centrale for the 15-minute trip from Naples.

LAGO D'AVERNO 🏛   About 16km (10 miles) west of Naples, a bit north of Baia, is a lake occupying an extinct volcanic crater. Known to the ancients as the **Gateway to Hades,** it was for centuries shrouded in superstition. Its vapors were said to produce illness and even death, and Lake Averno could well have been the source of the expression "Still waters run deep." Facing the lake are the ruins of what has been known as the **Temple of Apollo** from the 1st century A.D. and what was once thought to be the Cave of the Cumaean Sibyl (see below). According to legend, the Sibyl is said to have ferried Aeneas, son of Aphrodite, across the lake, where he traced a mysterious spring to its source, the River Styx. In the 1st century B.C., Agrippa turned it into a harbor for Roman ships by digging out a canal. Take the Napoli–Torre Gaveta bus from Baia to reach the site.

CUMA 🏛   Cuma was one of the first outposts of Greek colonization in what's now Italy. Located 19km (12 miles) west of Naples, it's of interest chiefly because it's said to have contained the **Cave of the Cumaean Sibyl** 🏛. The cave of the oracle, really a gallery, was dug by the Greeks in the 5th century B.C. and was a sacred spot to them. Beloved by Apollo, the Sibyl is said to have written the *Sibylline Oracles,* a group of books of prophecy bought, according to tradition, by Tarquin the Proud. You may visit not only the caves but also the ruins of temples dedicated to Jupiter and Apollo (later converted into Christian churches), daily 9am to 1 hour before sunset; admission is 2€ ($1.80) for adults (children under 18 enter free). On Via Domitiana, to the east of Cuma, you'll pass the **Arco Felice,** an arch about 20m (64 ft.) high, built by Emperor Domitian in the 1st century A.D. Ferrovia Cumana trains run here, departing from Stazione Centrale in Naples.

HERCULANEUM 🏛🏛

The builders of Herculaneum (Ercolano) were still working to repair the damage caused by an A.D. 62 earthquake when Vesuvius erupted on that fateful August day in A.D. 79. Herculaneum, about one-fourth the size of Pompeii, didn't start to come to light again until 1709, when Prince Elbeuf launched the unfortunate fashion of tunneling through it for treasures, more intent on profiting from the sale of objets d'art than on uncovering a Roman town fossilized in time.

Subsequent excavations at the site, the **Ufficio Scavi di Ercolano,** Corso Resina, Ercolano (© **081-7390963**), have been slow and sporadic. In fact, Herculaneum, named after Hercules, is not completely dug out today. One of the obstacles has been that the town was buried under lava, much heavier than that which piled onto Pompeii. Of course, this formed a greater protection for the buildings buried underneath—many of which were more elaborately

Herculaneum

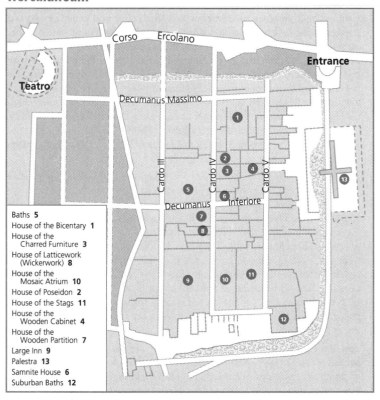

Baths **5**
House of the Bicentary **1**
House of the
  Charred Furniture **3**
House of Latticework
  (Wickerwork) **8**
House of the
  Mosaic Atrium **10**
House of Poseidon **2**
House of the Stags **11**
House of the
  Wooden Cabinet **4**
House of the
  Wooden Partition **7**
Large Inn **9**
Palestra **13**
Samnite House **6**
Suburban Baths **12**

constructed than those at Pompeii because Herculaneum was a seaside resort for patricians. The complication of having the slum of Resina resting over the yet-to-be-excavated district has further impeded progress and urban renewal.

Although all the streets and buildings of Herculaneum hold interest, some ruins merit more attention than others. The **baths (*terme*)** ✫✫✫ are divided between those at the forum and the **Suburban Baths (Terme Suburbane)** ✫ on the outskirts, near the more elegant villas. The municipal baths, which segregated the sexes, are larger, but the ones at the edge of town are more lavishly adorned. The **Palestra** was a kind of sports arena, where games were staged to satisfy the spectacle-hungry denizens. The typical plan for the average town house was to erect it around an uncovered atrium. In some areas, Herculaneum possessed the forerunner of the modern apartment house. Important private homes to seek out are the **House of the Bicentenary (Casa del Bicentenario)** ✫, the **House of the Wooden Cabinet (Casa a Graticcio)** ✫✫, the **House of the Wooden Partition (Casa del Tramezzo di Legno)** ✫, and the **House of Poseidon (Casa di Poseidon)**, as well as the **Amphitheater (Anfiteatro)**, containing the best-known mosaic discovered in the ruins.

The finest example of how the aristocracy lived is the **Casa dei Cervi,** named the **House of the Stags** because of the sculpture found inside. Guides are fond of showing the males on their tours a statue of a drunken Hercules urinating. Some of the best of the houses are locked and can be seen only by permission.

You can visit the ruins daily 8:30am to 3:30pm. Admission is 8€ ($7.15). To reach the archaeological zone, take the regular train service from Naples on the Circumvesuviana Railway, a 20-minute ride that leaves about every half hour from Corso Garibaldi 387, just south of the main train station (you can also catch Circumvesuviana trains underneath the main Stazione Centrale itself; follow the signs). This train will get you to Vesuvius (same stop), Pompeii, and Sorrento. Otherwise, it's a 7km (4⅓-mile) drive on the autostrada to Salerno (turn off at Ercolano).

3 Pompeii ★★★

24km (15 miles) S of Naples, 237km (147 miles) SE of Rome

When Vesuvius erupted in A.D. 79, Pliny the Younger, who later recorded the event, thought the end of the world had come. The ruined Roman city of Pompeii, now dug out from the layers of dried lava that once swept through the settlement, vividly brings to light the life of 19 centuries ago and has sparked the imagination of the world.

Numerous myths have surrounded Pompeii, one of which is that a completely intact city was rediscovered. Actually, the Pompeians (that is, those who escaped) returned to their city when the ashes had cooled and removed some of the most precious treasures from the thriving resort. But they left plenty behind to be uncovered at a later date and carted off to museums throughout Europe and America.

After a long medieval sleep, Pompeii was again brought to life in the late 16th century, quite by accident, by architect Domenico Fontana. However, it was in the mid–18th century that large-scale excavations were launched. Somebody once remarked that Pompeii's second tragedy was its rediscovery, that it really should have been left to slumber for another century or two, when it might have been better excavated and maintained.

ESSENTIALS

GETTING THERE The **Circumvesuviana Railway** (© **081-8575280**) departs Naples every half hour from Piazza Garibaldi. However, be sure you get on the train headed toward *Sorrento* and get off at Pompeii/Scavi (*scavi* means "ruins"). If you get on the Pompeii train, you'll end up in the town of Pompeii and have to transfer there to the other train to get to the ruins. A round-trip ticket costs 1.85€ ($1.65); trip time is 45 minutes each way. Circumvesuviana trains leave Sorrento several times during the day for Pompeii, costing 1.50€ ($1.35) one way. There's an entrance about 46m (50 yd.) from the rail station at the Villa dei Misteri. At the rail station in the town of Pompeii, **bus** connections take you to the entrance to the excavations.

To reach Pompeii by **car** from Naples, take the 22km (14-mile) drive on the autostrada toward Salerno. If you're coming from Sorrento, head east on SS145, where you can connect with A3 (marked Napoli). Then take the signposted turnoff for Pompeii.

VISITOR INFORMATION The **tourist office** is at Via Sacra 1 (© **081-8575347**). It's open Monday to Friday 8am to 3:40pm (until 7pm Apr–Sept), and Saturday 8am to 2pm. The office can fill you in on the **Panatenee Pompeiane,** a festival of the performing arts with a series of classical plays in July and August.

LOGISTICAL TIPS   After you pay for your entrance to the ruins, you'll find a **bookstore,** where you can purchase informative guides to the ruins (available in English and complete with detailed photos) that will help you understand what you're seeing. We highly recommend that you purchase one before you set out.

If you're here on a sunny day, wear sunscreen and bring along a bottle of water. There's almost no place in Pompeii to escape the sun's rays, and it can often be dusty.

EXPLORING THE RUINS

Most people visit the **Ufficio Scavi di Pompeii,** Piazza Esedra (© 081-8610744), the best preserved 2,000-year-old ruins in Europe, on a day trip from Naples (allow at least 4 hr. for even a superficial look at the archaeological site). The ruins are open daily from 8:30am to 3:30pm. Admission is 8.50€ ($7.60).

The most elegant of the patrician villas is the **House of the Vettii (Casa dei Vettii)** 🌟🌟🌟, boasting a courtyard, statuary (such as a two-faced Janus), paintings, and a black-and-red Pompeian dining room known for its frescoes of delicate cupids. The house was occupied by two brothers named Vettii, both of whom were wealthy merchants. As you enter the vestibule, you'll see a painting of Priapus resting his gargantuan phallus on a pair of scales. The guard will reveal other erotic fertility drawings and statuary, although most such material has been removed to the Archaeological Museum in Naples. This house is the best example of a villa and garden that's been restored.

The second most important villa, the **House of the Mysteries (Villa dei Misteri)** 🌟🌟, near the Porto Ercolano, is outside the walls (go along Viale alla Villa dei Misteri). What makes the villa exceptional, aside from its architectural features, are its remarkable frescoes, depicting scenes associated with the sect of Dionysus (Bacchus), one of the cults that flourished in Roman times. Note the Pompeian red in some of the backgrounds. The largest house, called the **House of the Faun (Casa del Fauno)** 🌟🌟 because of a bronze statue of a dancing faun found there, takes up a city block and has four dining rooms and two spacious peristyle gardens. It sheltered the celebrated *Battle of Alexander the Great* mosaic that's now in the Museo Archeologico Nazionale in Naples.

In the center of town is the **Forum (Foro)** 🌟; rather small, it was nonetheless the heart of Pompeian life, known to bakers, merchants, and the aristocrats who lived in the villas. Parts of the Forum were severely damaged in an earthquake 16 years before the eruption of Vesuvius and hadn't been repaired when the final destruction came. Three buildings surrounding the Forum are the **basilica** (the city's largest single structure), the **Temple of Apollo (Tempio di Apollo)** 🌟🌟, and the **Temple of Jupiter (Tempio di Giove)** 🌟🌟. The **Stabian Thermae** 🌟🌟🌟 (baths)—where both men and women lounged between games of knucklebones—are in good condition, among the finest to survive from antiquity. Here you'll see some skeletons. In the **brothel (Lupanare)** are some erotic paintings (tip the guide to see them).

Other buildings of interest include the **Great Theater (Teatro Grande)** 🌟, built in the 5th century B.C. During the Hellenistic period from 200 to 150 B.C., it was largely rebuilt, as it was again by the Romans in the 1st century A.D. This open-air theater could hold 5,000 spectators, many of them bloodthirsty as they screamed for death in the battles between wild animals and gladiators. The **House of the Gilded Cupids (Casa degli Amorini Dorati)** 🌟 was a flamboyant private home; its owner is unknown, although he probably lived during the reign of Nero. Obviously he had theatrical flair, attested to by the gilded and glass cupids known as *amorini.* Even though it's badly ruined, the house contains

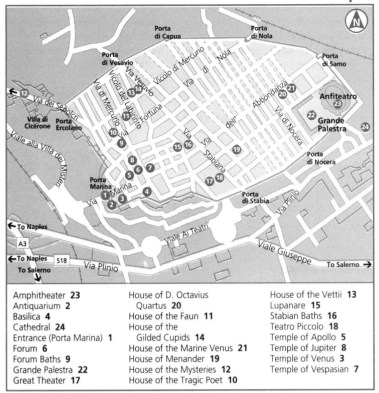

Amphitheater **23**	House of D. Octavius	House of the Vettii **13**
Antiquarium **2**	Quartus **20**	Lupanare **15**
Basilica **4**	House of the Faun **11**	Stabian Baths **16**
Cathedral **24**	House of the	Teatro Piccolo **18**
Entrance (Porta Marina) **1**	Gilded Cupids **14**	Temple of Apollo **5**
Forum **6**	House of the Marine Venus **21**	Temple of Jupiter **8**
Forum Baths **9**	House of Menander **19**	Temple of Venus **3**
Grande Palestra **22**	House of the Mysteries **12**	Temple of Vespasian **7**
Great Theater **17**	House of the Tragic Poet **10**	

a peristyle with one wing raised almost like a stage. The **House of the Tragic Poet (Casa del Poeta Tragico)** gets its name from a mosaic discovered here (later sent to Naples). It depicts a chained watchdog on the doorstep with this warning: Cave Canem ("Beware of the dog").

An ancient **bathhouse** with erotic frescoes has been opened to the public for the first time, although the discovery was made back in the 1980s. The delay in opening was because of lack of funds for restoration. The 2,000-year-old thermal bathhouse was in remarkably good condition and was still adorned with elaborate mosaics, including an indoor waterfall. Controversy centers around eight frescoes in vivid green, reds, and golds. These frescoes depict graphic scenes of various sex acts, including the only known artistic representation of cunnilingus from the Roman era. Some scholars have suggested that they were meant to advertise sexual services available on the upper floor of the baths; other archaeologists maintain they were intended merely to amuse.

WHERE TO STAY

Accommodations in Pompeii appear to be for earnest archaeologists only, with the two below the only really suitable choices (it's easy to drop in for the day from a base elsewhere, so not many people stay overnight). Some hotels in Pompeii aren't considered safe because of robberies. Protect your valuables and your person, and don't wander the streets at night. Most visitors look at the excavations and then seek better accommodations at either Naples or Sorrento.

Hotel Villa dei Misteri   This 1930s hotel is located 229m (250 yd.) from Scavi Station, about 2km (1¼ miles) south of the center of town. It features a little garden and a place to park your car. The family-style welcome might compensate for a certain lack of extras. The place could stand a face-lift, but many readers have expressed their fondness for it. The guest rooms are all bare-bones doubles, with reasonable comfort and well-kept bathrooms.

Via Villa dei Misteri 11, 80045 Pompei-Scavi. ℂ 081-8613593. Fax 081-8622983. www.villadeimisteri.it. 41 units. 50€–57€ ($44.65–$50.90) double, 66€–75€ ($58.95–$67) triple. Breakfast 8€ ($7.15). DC, MC, V. From the Naples rail station Circumvesuviana, take the Sorrento train and get off at the Villa dei Misteri stop. Free parking. **Amenities:** Lounge; pool. *In room:* A/C.

Villa Laura   The Villa Laura is the best hotel in town, although the competition isn't exactly stiff. On a somewhat hidden street, it escapes a lot of the noise that plagues Pompeii hotels. The small guest rooms are comfortably but not spectacularly furnished, with small bathrooms. Try for one with a balcony. The breakfasts are a bit dull.

Via della Salle 13, 80045 Pompeii. ℂ 081-8631024. Fax 081-8504893. www.villaluara.com. 25 units. 75€ ($67) double. Rates include breakfast. AE, DC, MC, V. Parking 5€ ($4.45). **Amenities:** Lounge; babysitting; laundry. *In room:* A/C, TV, minibar, hair dryer, safe.

WHERE TO DINE

Il Principe ✦✦ CAMPANIAN/MEDITERRANEAN   This isn't just Pompeii's leading restaurant; it's one of the best in all of Campania. The decor incorporates the best decorative features of ancient Pompeii, including a scattering of bright frescoes and mosaics. You can dine in its beautiful interior or at a sidewalk table on the town's most important square, with views of the basilica. You might start with carpaccio or a salad of porcini mushrooms, and then follow with one of the pastas, perhaps *spaghetti vongole* (with baby clams). You can also order superb fish dishes, such as sea bass and turbot; *saltimbocca* (sage-flavored veal with ham); or steak Diane. Some of the dishes are based on recipes used in ancient Rome, notably *vermicelli al garum,* an anchovy paste, or *cassata,* a goat-cheese and dried-fruit dessert. If you're fascinated by this culinary innovation, you can call ahead and make arrangements for your party to enjoy a 17-item menu of ancient Roman dishes.

Piazza Bartolo Longo. ℂ 081-8505566. Reservations required. Main courses 15€–25€ ($13.40–$22.35); fixed-price menu 35€ ($31.25). AE, DC, DISC, MC, V. Tues–Sat 12:30–3pm and 8–11:30pm; Sun 12:30–3pm.

Zi Caterina SEAFOOD/NEAPOLITAN   This good choice is in the center of town near the basilica, with two spacious dining rooms. The antipasto table might tempt you with its seafood, but don't rule out the pasta e fagioli with mussels. The chef's special rigatoni, with tomatoes and prosciutto, is tempting, as is the array of fish or one of the live lobsters fresh from the tank.

Via Roma 20. ℂ 081-8507447. Reservations recommended. Main courses 6€–12.50€ ($5.35–$11.15). AE, DC, MC, V. Daily noon–10:30pm.

4 The Emerald Island of Ischia ✦✦

34km (21 miles) W of Naples

Dramatically situated in the Gulf of Gaeta, the island of Ischia is of volcanic origin. Its thermal spas claim cures for most anything that ails you—be it "gout, retarded sexual development, or chronic rheumatism." Called the Emerald Island, Ischia is studded with pine groves and surrounded by sparkling waters

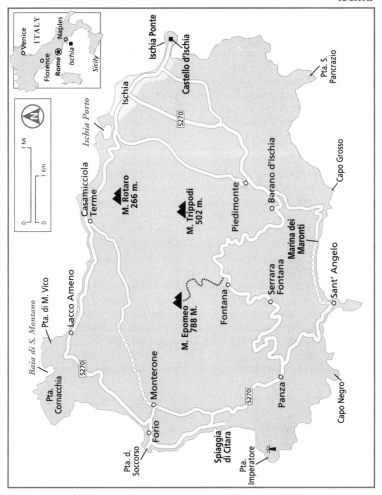

that wash up on many sandy beaches (a popular one is Sant'Angelo). In Greek mythology, it was the home of Typhoeus (Typhon), who created volcanoes and fathered the three-headed canine Cerberus, guardian of the gateway to Hades, and the incongruous Chimera and Sphinx. The island covers just over 47 sq. km (18 sq. miles), and its prominent feature is **Monte Epomeo,** near the center, a volcano that was a powerful force and source of worry for the Greek colonists who settled here in the 8th century B.C.

Today, the 789m (2,590-ft.) peak is dead, having last erupted in the 14th century, but it's still responsible for warming the island's thermal springs. Ischia slumbered for centuries after its early turbulence, although some discerning visitors discovered its charms. Ibsen, for example, lived in a villa near Casamicciola to find the solitude necessary to complete *Peer Gynt.* However, in the 1950s, Ischia was discovered, this time by wealthy Italians who built a slew of first-class hotels in the process of trying to avoid the overrun resorts of Capri.

The island is known for its sandy beaches, health spas (which utilize the hot springs for hydromassage and mud baths), and vineyards producing the red and white Monte Epomeo, the red and white Ischia, and the white Biancolella. The largest community is at **Ischia Porto** on the eastern coast, a circular town seated in the crater of the extinct Monte Epomeo, which functions as the island's main port of call. The most lively town is **Forio** on the western coast, with its many bars along tree-lined streets. The other major communities are **Lacco Ameno** and **Casamicciola Terme,** on the north shore, and **Serrara Fontana** and **Barano d'Ischia,** inland and to the south.

ESSENTIALS

GETTING THERE   The easiest way to get to the island is from Naples, where **hydrofoils** (passengers only) and **ferries** (passengers with their cars) make frequent runs throughout the year (three to seven times a day, depending on the season). The hydrofoil is the most convenient and most expensive option: the 40-minute ride costs 8.80€ to 10€ ($7.85–$8.95) per person each way. The ferry takes twice as long but costs only 5€ ($4.45) for foot passengers. On the ferry, a medium-size vehicle, with as many passengers as will fit inside, costs from 35€ ($31.25) each way. Hydrofoils depart from Naples's Mergellina Pier, near the Hotel Vesuvio; ferries leave from Molo Beverello, near Piazza Municipio. Two companies maintain both hydrofoils and ferries: **Caremar** (© 081-5513882 in Naples, or 081-991953 in Ischia) and **Linee Lauro** (© 081-5522838 in Naples, or 081-8377577 in Ischia). Caremar is somewhat more upscale, with better-maintained ships and a more cooperative staff.

You can also take a **hydrofoil from Sorrento.** These run several times daily, with a fare of 9€ ($8.05) one way. Service is provided by **Linee Marittime Partenopee** (© **081-991888**). No ferry service is available from Sorrento, however.

VISITOR INFORMATION   In Porto d'Ischia, **Azienda Autonoma di Soggiorno e Turismo,** at Corso Vittoria Colonna 108 (© **081-5074211**), is open Monday to Saturday 9am to noon and 2 to 5pm.

ISCHIA PORTO

This harbor actually emerged from the crater of a long-dead volcano. Most of the population and the largest number of hotels are centered in Ischia Porto. The **Castello Aragonese** ✦✦ (© **081-992834**) once guarded the harbor from raids. At the castle lived poet Vittoria Colonna, the confidante of Michelangelo, to whom he wrote celebrated letters.

References to a fortress on this isolated rock date from as early as 474 B.C. Today it's the symbol of Ischia, jutting like a Mediterranean version of France's Mont-St.-Michel from the sea surrounding it. It's connected to the oldest part of town by the Ponte d'Ischia, a narrow bridge barely wide enough for a car. If you're driving, park on the "mainland" side of the bridge and cross on foot. The fortress is privately owned, and you pay 5€ ($4.45) to get inside. It's closed November to February but is open daily otherwise, 9:30am to 7pm.

WHERE TO STAY

Grand Hotel Excelsior ✦✦   Ischia's best hotel was the private retreat of English nobleman James Nihn at the end of the 19th century; early in the 20th century, it was opened as a hotel by the counts of Micangeli. The decor never lets you forget that you're in the lap of luxury, while the lovely pool and private beach never let you forget that you're on the Mediterranean. The public spaces contain multitiered chandeliers, terra-cotta floors, Oriental carpets, and thickly padded furniture. In the guest rooms, curvaceous wrought-iron headboards rise above colorful bedspreads matched to the lampshades, curtains, and sheers. Each room has a private patio beyond French doors and a floral-tiled bathroom.

Via Emanuele Gianturco 19, 80077 Ischia Porto. © 081-991020. Fax 081-984100. www.excelsioriskia.it. 76 units. 216€–352€ ($192.90–$314.35) double; from 538€ ($480.45) suite. Rates include breakfast and dinner. AE, DC, MC, V. Free valet parking. Closed Nov 3–Apr 23. **Amenities:** Restaurant with outdoor terrace; piano bar; 2 pools; minigolf course; fitness room; concierge; room service; babysitting; laundry/dry cleaning. *In room:* A/C, TV, minibar, hair dryer, safe.

Grand Hotel Punta Molino Terme ★★
Standing amid cliffs and olive groves, this modern hotel combines comfort with excellent service and a full spa. The public areas feature a mix of contemporary with 17th- and 18th-century furnishings and stone, marble, or terra-cotta floors. The guest rooms are constantly updated and come in a wide variety of shapes and sizes; however, each is fitted with elegant fabrics and reproductions. Plants and fresh-cut flowers add life and color.

Lungom are Cristoforo Colombo 23, 80070 Ischia Porto. © 081-991544. Fax 081-991562. www.punta molino.it. 84 units. 240€–400€ ($214.30–$357.20) double; from 530€ ($473.30) suite. Rates include breakfast and dinner. AE, DC, MC, V. Free parking. Closed Nov–Apr 14. **Amenities:** Restaurant; lounge; 3 pools (outdoor and indoor); gym; spa (with extensive treatments); sauna; concierge; car-rental desk; room service; babysitting; laundry/dry cleaning. *In room:* A/C, TV, minibar, hair dryer, safe.

Hotel Continental Terme ★
The thermal springs at this sprawling complex are among the largest on the island. There are five thermal water pools (three covered), surrounded by the exotic greenery of 27,340 sq. m (32,700 sq. yd.) of gardens. The public spaces feature polished marble and terra-cotta floors, contemporary Italian seating, and wicker-and-glass tables, accented by cut flowers and plant life. The guest rooms are luxuriously furnished, set in a diverse collection of town house villas scattered throughout the grounds.

Via M. Mazzella 74, 80077 Ischia Porto. © 081-991588. Fax 081-982929. www.ischia.it/contiterme. 244 units. 150€–302€ ($133.95–$269.70) double; from 250€ ($223.25) suite. Rates include breakfast and dinner. AE, DC, MC, V. Free valet parking. Closed Nov–Mar. **Amenities:** Restaurant; 3 bars; pool; 5 thermal pools; gym; spa; salon; room service; babysitting; laundry/dry cleaning. *In room:* A/C, TV, minibar, hair dryer, safe.

Hotel Il Moresco ★
This hotel sits in a sun-dappled park whose pines and palmettos grow close to its arched loggias. From some angles, the Moorish-inspired exterior looks almost like a cubist fantasy. Inside, the straightforward design re-creates a modern oasis in the southern part of Spain, with matador-red tiles coupled with stark-white walls and Iberian furniture. Each well-furnished guest room has a terrace or a balcony and a tidy bathroom.

Via Emanuele Gianturco 16, 80077 Ischia Porto. © 081-981355. Fax 081-992338. www.ilmoresco.it. 70 units. 220€–370€ ($196.45–$330.40) double; from 360€ ($321.50) suite. Rates include breakfast and dinner. AE, DC, MC, V. Closed Oct 27–Mar 23. **Amenities:** Restaurant; bar; 2 pools; fitness center; spa; Jacuzzi; room service; babysitting; laundry/dry cleaning. *In room:* A/C, TV, minibar, hair dryer, safe.

Hotel La Villarosa ★★ (Finds)
This is Ischia's finest pensione, set in a garden of gardenias and banana, eucalyptus, and fig trees. The dining room is in the informal country style, with terra-cotta tiles, lots of French windows, and antique chairs. And what looks like a carriage house in the garden has been converted into an informal tavern with more antiques. The friendly staff maintains the personal atmosphere. The bright and airy guest rooms are well kept, striking a homey tone, with small bathrooms.

Via Giacinto Gigante 5, 80077 Ischia Porto. © 081-991316. Fax 081-992425. 37 units. 140€–180€ ($125–$160.75) double. Rates include breakfast and dinner. AE, DC, MC, V. Closed Nov–Mar. **Amenities:** Dining room; bar; laundry. *In room:* A/C, TV, minibar, hair dryer.

WHERE TO DINE

Ristorante Damiano ✿ NEAPOLITAN This charming restaurant, angled for the best sea views, is located about a mile southwest of the ferry terminal. Damiano Caputo infuses his cuisine with zest and very fresh ingredients. In the rustic setting—long communal tables and fresh flowers—you can select from an array of antipasti, homemade pasta, steamy bowls of minestrone, and some excellent veal and chicken dishes. Our most recently sampled chicken was perfectly grilled in the oven and flavored with olive oil, wine, and fresh tomatoes. The grilled veal was also excellent, served with a tomato and garlic sauce. The chef does wonders with oven-baked rabbit, beautifully flavored and served in a spicy tomato-laced sauce. Desserts include tiramisu and wonderful gelati.

Via delle Vigne. ✆ 081-983032. Reservations recommended. Main courses 10€–20€ ($8.95–$17.85). DC, MC, V. Daily 8pm–midnight; Apr–June and Sept–Oct, also Sun 1–3pm. Closed Nov–Mar.

LACCO AMENO

Jutting up from the water, a rock named **Il Fungo (The Mushroom)** is the landmark natural sight of Lacco Ameno. The spa is the center of the good life (and contains some of the best and most expensive hotels on the island). People come from all over the world either to relax on the beach and be served top-level food or to take the cure. The mineral-rich waters at Lacco Ameno have led to the development of a modern spa with extensive facilities for thermal cures, everything from underwater jet massages to mud baths.

WHERE TO STAY

Hotel La Reginella ✿ Set in a lush garden typical of the island's accommodations, this hotel boasts a Mediterranean decor that combines printed tile floors with light woods and pastel or floral fabrics. Although aging, the guest rooms are still very comfortable, with wood furnishings and well-kept bathrooms.

Piazza Santa Restituta 1, 80076 Lacco Ameno d'Ischia. ✆ **081-994300.** Fax 081-980481. www.albergo lareginella.it. 90 units (showers only). 170€–270€ ($151.80–$241.10) double. Rates include breakfast and dinner. AE, DC, MC, V. Free parking. Closed Nov 3–Mar. **Amenities:** Restaurant; lounge; 2 pools; spa; sauna; car-rental desk; room service; babysitting; laundry/dry cleaning. *In room:* A/C, TV, minibar, hair dryer, safe.

Hotel Regina Isabella e Royal Sporting ✿✿ This resort offers the finest accommodations and service in Lacco Ameno, plus a private beach. The refined setting successfully contrasts contemporary furnishings with rococo and less ornate antique styles. In the medium-to-spacious guest rooms, serene blues and greens are prevalent, and some printed tile floors are offset by earthy brown tiles and woodwork. Most have balconies.

Piazza Santa Restituta, 80076 Lacco Ameno d'Ischia. ✆ **081-994322.** Fax 081-900190. 133 units. 220€–680€ ($196.45–$607.15) double; from 770€ ($687.60) suite. Rates include breakfast and dinner. 3-day minimum stay. AE, DC, MC, V. Free parking. **Amenities:** Restaurant; bar; 2 pools; spa; concierge; room service; massage; babysitting; laundry. *In room:* A/C, TV, minibar, hair dryer, safe.

Hotel Terme di Augusto This hotel, 46m (50 yd.) from the shore, provides excellent service in a setting less ostentatious than that of many competing resorts. It combines prominent arched ceilings, patterned tile floors, and floral drapery and upholstery to create light, airy spaces. The guest rooms are comfortable, with well-maintained bathrooms.

Viale Campo 128, 80076 Lacco Ameno d'Ischia. ✆ **081-994944.** Fax 081-980244. www.termediaugusto.it. 118 units. 146€–198€ ($130.40–$176.80) double. Rates include breakfast and dinner. AE, DC, MC, V. Free parking. Closed Dec 1–27. **Amenities:** Restaurant; bar; 2 pools; tennis courts; gym; Jacuzzi; sauna; salon; room service; massage; babysitting; laundry/dry cleaning. *In room:* A/C, TV, minibar, hair dryer, safe.

Hotel Terme San Montano ★★   This is an oasis of charm and grace, one of our favorite retreats on Ischia. Man Ray was once a faithful guest here, as were opera stars Mario del Monaco and Giuseppe di Stefano. The grounds spread out around the hotel in a luxuriant garden, leading to a private beach. Aged woods, leather, and brass are combined in the furnishings, and marine lamps shed light on almost every room. The headboards resemble a ship's helm, the windows are translated as portholes, and miniature ships and antiquated diving gear are decoratively scattered about. The guest rooms are well cared for and spacious. Rooms with sea views, of course, are the most requested.

Via Monte Vico, 80076 Lacco Ameno d'Ischia. © 081-994033. Fax 081-980242. www.ischiagrandi alberghi.it. 77 units. 155€–200€ ($138.40–$178.60) double; 220€–415€ ($196.45–$370.60) suite. AE, DC, MC, V. Free parking. Closed Nov–Easter. **Amenities:** Restaurant; bar; lounge; 2 pools; tennis courts; squash courts; gym; sauna; water-skiing; boat rental; car-rental desk; room service; massage; babysitting. *In room:* A/C, TV, minibar, hair dryer.

FORIO

A short drive from Lacco Ameno, Forio stands on the west coast of Ischia, opening onto the sea near the Bay of Citara. Long a favorite with artists (filmmaker Lucchino Visconti has a villa here), it's now developing a broader base of tourism. Locals produce some of the finest wines on the island. On the way from Lacco Ameno, stop at the **beach of San Francesco,** with its sanctuary. At sunset, many visitors head for a rocky spur on which sits the church of **Santa Maria del Soccorso.** The lucky ones get to witness the famous "green flash" over the Gulf of Gaeta. It appears on occasion immediately after the sun sets.

WHERE TO STAY

Grande Albergo Mezzatorre ★★   The best hotel in Forio, this complex is built around a 16th-century villa whose stone tower once guarded against invaders; now it houses the least expensive of the doubles. The five postmodern buildings run a few hundred feet downhill to a waterfront bluff. A casual airiness prevails in the public spaces, which contrast soft lighting with terra-cotta floors. The decor in the guest rooms is contemporary, with wooden furniture, bright upholstered seating, and tiled bathrooms.

Via Mezzatorre, 80075 Forio d'Ischia. © 081-986111. Fax 081-986015. www.mezzatorre.it. 59 units. 190€–407€ ($169.65–$363.45) double; 407€–545€ ($363.45–$486.70) suite. Rates include breakfast and dinner. AE, DC, MC, V. Free parking. Closed Nov–Apr. **Amenities:** Restaurant; bar; pool; tennis courts; health club; Jacuzzi; sauna; room service; babysitting; laundry/dry cleaning. *In room:* A/C, TV, minibar, hair dryer, safe.

WHERE TO DINE

La Romantica NEAPOLITAN/ISCHIAN   Near the dry-docked fishing vessels of Forio's old port, this is the most appealing nonhotel restaurant. It occupies a Neapolitan-style building whose facade has been enlarged with a jutting wooden extension that has welcomed everyone from Josephine Baker to heart surgeon Christian Barnard. Your meal might include linguine with clams or scampi or a house specialty, "penne 92," garnished with artichoke hearts and shrimp. Swordfish, grilled and served with lemon sauce or with herb-flavored green sauce, is delicious, as are the baked spigola and several risotto and veal dishes. Weather permitting, you might prefer a seat on the outdoor terrace.

Via Marina 46. © 081-997345. Reservations recommended. Main courses 8€–15€ ($7.15–$13.40). AE, DC, MC, V. Daily noon–3pm and 7pm–midnight. Closed Wed Nov–Mar.

SANT'ANGELO ★

The most charming settlement on Ischia, Sant'Angelo juts out on the southernmost tip. The village of fishers is joined to the "mainland" of Ischia by a 91m

(300-ft.) long lava-and-sand isthmus. Driving into the town is virtually impossible. In summer you might have to park a long way off and walk. Its **beach** is among the best on the island.

WHERE TO STAY

Park Hotel Miramare ⭐ This hotel is right on the sea, although it has no beach to speak of. There is, however, a concrete terrace with chairs and umbrellas, and a stairway that clears the rocky shore, leading into the water. Curved wrought-iron balconies, white wicker, and canopied iron bed frames are recurring decorative elements. Since 1923, the same family has welcomed guests to its old-fashioned accommodations (bathrooms have been recently renewed, however). The dining room features the seafood that the island is known for, and a snack bar offers an informal option. The hotel's health spa is a short walk away, down a flower-lined path. Among its offerings are massage, 12 thermal pools, mud treatments, a sauna, and designated nudist areas.

80070 Sant'Angelo d'Ischia. ℂ **081-999219.** Fax 081-999325. www.hotelmiramare.it. 50 units (showers only). 168€–240€ ($150–$214.30) double; 430€ ($384) suite. Rates include breakfast. AE, DC, MC, V. Closed Nov 11–Apr 6. **Amenities:** 2 restaurants; bar; spa with thermal pools, sauna, and various treatments; salon; room service; massage; babysitting; laundry. *In room:* A/C, TV, minibar, hair dryer, safe.

5 Sorrento ⭐⭐

50km (31 miles) S of Naples, 256km (159 miles) SE of Rome, 50km (31 miles) W of Salerno

Borrowing from Greek mythology, the Romans placed the legendary abode of the sirens (those wicked mermaids who lured seamen to their deaths with their sweet songs) at Sorrento (Surrentum). Ulysses resisted their call by stuffing the ears of his crew with wax and having himself bound to the mast of his ship. Perched on high cliffs overlooking the bays of Naples and Salerno, Sorrento has been sending out its siren call for centuries—luring everybody from Homer to Lord and Lady Astor to busloads of international tourists, who invade every summer.

The streets in summer tend to be as noisy as a carnival. And the traffic is horrendous (no traffic signals in such a bustling city!). The hotels on the "racing strip," **Corso Italia,** need to pass out earplug kits when they tuck you in for the night, although perhaps you'll have a hotel on a cliff side in Sorrento with a view of the sea (and paths and private elevators to take you down).

ESSENTIALS

GETTING THERE Sorrento is served by frequent express **trains** from Naples (trip time: 1 hr.). The high-speed train, called Ferrovia Circumvesuviana, leaves from one floor underground at Stazione Centrale (see "Essentials" in section 1 of this chapter).

By car from Naples, head south on Route 18, cutting west at the junction with Route S145.

VISITOR INFORMATION The **tourist office** is at Via de Maio 35 (ℂ **081-8074033**), which winds down to the port where ships headed for Capri and Naples anchor. It's open Monday to Saturday 9am to 2pm and 4 to 7pm.

EXPLORING THE CITY

For such a famous resort, Sorrento's **beaches** are limited—most of them are just piers extending into the water. Chaise longues and umbrellas line these decks along the rock-strewn coastline. The best beach is **Punta del Capo,** reached by going along Corso Italia to Via del Capo.

If you'd like to go **hiking,** you can explore the green hills above Sorrento. Many of the trails are marked, and the tourist office will advise.

From Sorrento, the more confident drivers among you can undertake the gorgeous but nerve-racking **Amalfi Drive.** If you want to leave the driving to someone else, you can take a blue SITA bus that runs between Sorrento and Salerno or Amalfi. In Sorrento, bus stations with timetables are outside the rail station and in the central piazza.

Although few visitors come to Sorrento to look at churches and monuments, there are some worth exploring. The **Chiesa di San Francesco,** Via San Francesco (© **081-8781269**), dates from the 14th century. This **cloister** ☆ is a pocket of beauty in overcrowded Sorrento, with delicate arches and a garden dotted with flowering vines. The cloister is open daily 9am to 6pm, and admission is free.

If time remains, visit the **Museo Correale di Terranova** ☆, Via Correale (© **081-8781846**), north of Piazza Tasso. A former palace, it has displays of ancient statues, antiques, and Italian art. Here's a chance to introduce yourself to *intarsia,* a technique of making objects with paper-thin pieces of patterned wood. Neapolitan bric-a-brac and other curiosities finish off the exhibits. After a visit to the museum, you can stroll through the gardens. From April to September, it's open Monday and Wednesday to Saturday 9am to 1pm and 5 to 7pm, and Sunday 9am to 12:30pm; off-season hours are Monday and Wednesday to Saturday 9am to 1pm, and Sunday from 9 to 11:30am. Admission is 5€ ($4.45) to the museum and gardens.

Sorrento has better **shopping** than anywhere else along the Amalfi Drive. The city's cobbled alleyways and flower-ringed piazzas encourage strolls, and the best ones for window-shopping are **Piazza Tasso** and **Via San Cesareo,** densely packed with shoppers on weekend afternoons.

Gargiulo & Jannuzzi, Piazza Tasso 1 (© **081-8781041**), is the region's best-known maker of marquetry furniture. Opened in 1863, the shop demonstrates the centuries-old technique in the basement, where an employee will combine multihued pieces of wood veneer to create patterns of arabesques and flowers. The sprawling showrooms feature an array of card tables, clocks, and partners' desks, each inlaid with patterns of elm wood, rosewood, bird's-eye maple, or mahogany. Upstairs is a collection of embroidered table linens, and the outlet has its own ceramic factory. The pottery can be shipped anywhere.

Embroidery and lace are two of the best bargains in Sorrento, and **Luigia Gargiulo,** Corso Italia 48 (© **081-8781081**), comes recommended for embroidered sheets and tablecloths; the shop also offers children's clothing. In **Cuomo's Lucky Store,** Piazza Antica Mura 2–7 (© **081-8785649**), you'll find a little bit of everything made in the area, including displays of porcelain from the 1700s.

One of the most appealing assortments of cameos, meticulously hand-carved from seashells, is available at the reasonably priced **Ciro Bimonte,** Via Giuliani 62 (© **081-8071880**). And if you're feeling underdressed or underaccessorized, consider checking out **Max & Co.,** Corso Italia 62 (© **081-8074408**), which sells clothing of all degrees of formality for men, women, and children.

WHERE TO STAY
EXPENSIVE
Grand Hotel Ambasciatori ☆   The heavily buttressed foundation that prevents this cliffside hotel from plunging into the sea looks like something from a medieval monastery, and it was landscaped to include several rambling gardens

Sorrento

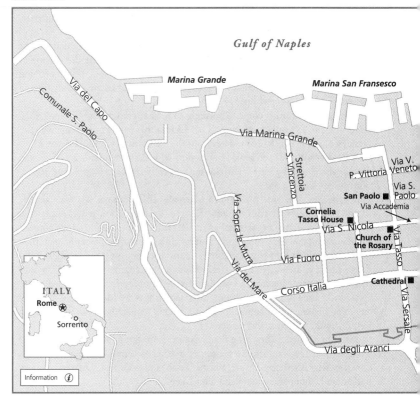

along the precipice. A set of steps and a private elevator lead to the wooden deck of a bathing wharf. Inside, a substantial collection of Oriental carpets and armchairs provides plush comfort. The guest rooms come in a variety of shapes and sizes, each containing a compact tiled bathroom.

Via Califano 18, 80067 Sorrento. © 081-8782025. Fax 081-8071021. www.circumvista.com/ambasciatori. html. 109 units. 210€ ($187.55) double; 315€ ($281.30) suite. Rates include breakfast. AE, DC, MC, V. Free parking. **Amenities:** Restaurant; bar; pool; room service; babysitting; laundry/dry cleaning. *In room:* A/C, TV, minibar, hair dryer, safe.

Grand Hotel Excelsior Vittoria ★★★ This luxury bastion, built between 1834 and 1882 on the edge of a cliff overlooking the Bay of Naples and surrounded by semitropical gardens with lemon and orange trees, combines 19th-century glamour with a modern flair. The terrace theme predominates, especially on the water side, where you can enjoy the cold drinks served at sunset while gazing at Vesuvius. (In summer, the hotel offers a candle-lit dinner on an outdoor terrace with dancing to romantic live music.)

Three elevators will take you down to the harbor to sunbathe and swim. Inside, the atmosphere is old-worldish, especially in the mellow dining room. In 1921, Enrico Caruso stayed in the suite now named for him. The huge guest rooms boast their own drama, some with balconies opening onto the cliffside drop; they have a wide mix of furnishings that include many antique pieces.

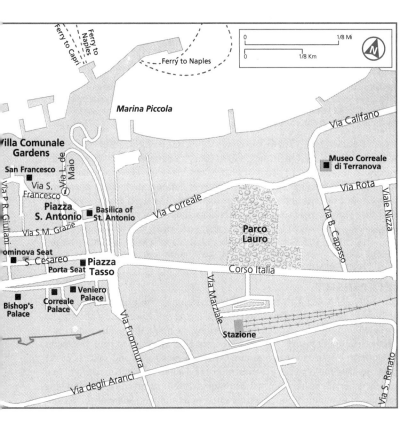

Piazza Tasso 34, 80067 Sorrento. 𝒞 **081-8071044.** Fax 081-8771206. www.exvitt.it. 107 units. 251.60€–296€ ($224.70–$264.35) double; from 446.25€ ($398.50) suite. Rates include breakfast. AE, DC, MC, V. Free parking. **Amenities:** 2 restaurants (elegant indoor venue plus an open-air restaurant in summer); 2 bars; large pool; room service; babysitting; laundry/dry cleaning. *In room:* A/C, TV, minibar, hair dryer, safe.

Hotel Imperial Tramontano ☆☆ This pocket of posh in a semitropical garden is an excellent choice. It was the birthplace of poet Torquato Tasso, yet he'd hardly recognize the palatial villa today. The spacious guest rooms are well furnished, and some have balconies opening onto panoramic sea views. High ceilings and gilt-framed mirrors provide a traditional look. The drawing room is replete with English and Italian antiques. In the garden, you can inhale the sweet-smelling trees and walk down paths of oleander, hydrangea, acacia, coconut palms, and geraniums. An elevator takes guests down to the beach below the main hotel.

Via Vittorio Veneto 1, 80067 Sorrento. 𝒞 **081-8782588.** Fax 081-8072344. www.tramontano.com. 116 units. 250€ ($223.25) double; from 360€ ($321.50) suite. Rates include breakfast. AE, MC, V. Parking 12.50€ ($11.15). Closed Jan–Feb. **Amenities:** Restaurant; bar; lounge; pool; room service; babysitting; laundry/dry cleaning. *In room:* A/C, TV, minibar, hair dryer.

MODERATE

Hotel Bristol ☆ The Bristol was built pueblo style on a hillside at the edge of town, and all but 15 rooms open onto a view of Vesuvius and the Bay of

Naples. (Those 15 open onto a brick wall.) The hotel lures with its contemporary decor and spaciousness and with well-appointed public and private rooms. The guest rooms are warm and inviting, with built-in niceties. Most have balconies overlooking the sea. In summer you can dine on the terrace.

Via Capo 22, 80067 Sorrento. ℭ **081-8784522.** Fax 081-8071910. www.acampora.it. 135 units. 110€–230€ ($98.25–$205.40) double; 160€–290€ ($142.90–$258.95) suite. Rates include buffet breakfast. AE, MC, V. Free parking. **Amenities:** 2 restaurants; bar; pool; mini-golf course; sauna; room service; laundry. *In room:* A/C, TV, minibar, hair dryer, safe.

Hotel Regina *Value*   Evenly spaced rows of balconies jut out over the Regina's well-tended garden. On its uppermost floor, a terrace boasts views of the Mediterranean extending as far as Naples and Vesuvius. The functional rooms have tile floors, private terraces, and well-kept bathrooms. A dozen open onto views from balconies and are the most requested. The hotel employs a helpful staff that provides road maps and offers hints about sightseeing.

Via Marina Grande 10, 80067 Sorrento. ℭ **081-8782722.** Fax 081-8782721. 36 units (showers only). 145€–180€ ($129.50–$160.75) double. Rates include breakfast and dinner. AE, DC, DISC, MC, V. Parking 6€ ($5.35). Closed Nov 15–Jan. **Amenities:** Dining room; lounge; room service; babysitting; laundry. *In room:* A/C (in 10 units), TV, hair dryer.

INEXPENSIVE

La Tonnarella ✸   This is the most desirable of the host of inexpensive inns along Via Capo. There's a marvelous old-fashioned ambience here, with antiques gathered from all over southern Italy adorning the public areas. The panoramas, best seen at sunset from the terraces, are among the finest in Sorrento. Bedrooms range from midsize to spacious, furnished with new pieces and touches of the past, perhaps some pieces left over from the 1800s. Neapolitan tiles are used widely, especially in the compact bathrooms. Although much of the plumbing remains old-fashioned, you're often treated to jet showers. Some of the accommodations open onto their own private terraces. An elevator will take you down to the rock-strewn beach. The hotel also has an excellent restaurant serving a Neapolitan cuisine specializing in fresh fish.

Via Capo 31, 80067 Sorrento. ℭ **081-8781153.** Fax 081-8782169. www.latonnarella.com. 21 units (showers only). 110€–145€ ($98.25–$129.50) double; 150€–165€ ($133.95–$147.35) suite. Half-board 120€ ($107.15) per person extra. Rates include breakfast. AE, MC, V. Free parking. Bus: A. **Amenities:** Restaurant; bar; room service; babysitting; laundry/dry cleaning. *In room:* A/C, TV, hair dryer, safe.

Villa di Sorrento   This is a pleasant villa in the center of town. Architecturally romantic, the Sorrento attracts travelers with its petite wrought-iron balconies, tall shutters, and vines climbing the facade. Some of the comfortably furnished guest rooms contain terraces. The tiled bathrooms are tiny.

Via Fuorimura 4, 80067 Sorrento. ℭ **081-8781068.** Fax 081-8072679. 21 units (showers only). 120€ ($107.15) double. Rates include breakfast. AE, DC, MC, V. Parking 11€ ($9.80) nearby. **Amenities:** Lounge; laundry. *In room:* A/C, TV, hair dryer, safe.

WHERE TO DINE
EXPENSIVE

Don Alfonso ✸✸ SOUTHERN ITALIAN   One of southern Italy's most highly recommended restaurants, this Relais & Châteaux member occupies a turn-of-the-century faux-Pompeian building adjacent to Santa Maria delle Grazie, the centerpiece of the hamlet of Sant'Agata, perched more than 366m (1,200 ft.) above sea level. The chef/co-owner, Alfonso Laccarino, makes it a point to hire as many international assistants as possible, many of whom spend a year here. Alfonso's wife, Livia, directs the dining room and maintains the award-winning wine cellars.

The menu items include lots of organic vegetables and greens from the family's sprawling gardens nearby, adding tremendously to the appeal of a Mediterranean diet of fish and shellfish. The free-range chicken with garlic and homegrown herbs is particularly wonderful, as is the mixed fish fry. Two ongoing favorites are the Neapolitan casseruolla of lobster, squid, clams, mussels, and assorted saltwater fish (for two); and the calamari stuffed with tiny zucchini, sweet pepper, broccoli, and cauliflower and topped with a zabaglione of aged red-wine vinegar.

Don Alfonso also offers three suites, two with kitchens and all with air-conditioning, TVs, and phones. They rent for 125€ ($111.65), including breakfast.

Piazza Sant'Agata 11, Sant'Agata, 10km (6¼ miles) south of Sorrento. © 081-8780026. Reservations recommended. Main courses 30€–35€ ($26.80–$31.25); fixed-price menu 70€–90€ ($62.50–$80.35). AE, DC, MC, V. Wed–Sun 12:30–2:30pm and 8–10:30pm. Closed Mon June–Sept, and Jan 10–Feb 25. By car, follow the signs to Sant'Agata; by bus, take the blue-and-white SITA bus marked SANT'AGATA from the piazza in front of Sorrento's rail station.

MODERATE

L'Antica Trattoria ⭐ CAMPANESE/INTERNATIONAL Inside the weather-beaten walls of what was built 300 years ago as a stable, this 200-year-old restaurant, one of the best in Sorrento, is charming. Although all its food is well prepared, the real highlight is its antipasti. You'll find several varieties of fish cooked in a salt crust, which transforms the dish into a sweetly scented, firm but flaky delicacy, and a daunting array of pastas from lasagna to ravioli (the best is stuffed with seafood). The house special pasta, *spaghetti alla ferrolese,* is made with fish roe, shrimp, red cabbage, and cream. A particularly delicious specialty is seafood *pezzogna,* with pulverized cherry tomatoes, olive oil, garlic, parsley, crushed red pepper, and shellfish. The assortment of ice creams is especially tempting.

Via P. R. Giuliani 33. © 081-8071082. Reservations recommended. Main courses 17.50€–22.50€ ($15.65–$20.10). AE, MC, V. Daily noon–3:30pm and 7–11:30pm. Closed Jan 10–Feb 10.

INEXPENSIVE

La Favorita–O'Parrucchiano NEAPOLITAN/SORRENTINE This is a good choice on the busiest street in town. The building is like an old tavern, with an arched ceiling in the main dining room. On the terrace you can dine in a garden of trees, rubber plants, and statuary. Among the a la carte dishes, classic Italian fare is offered, including ravioli *Caprese* (filled with fresh cheese and covered with tomato sauce), cannelloni, a mixed fish fry from the Bay of Naples, and veal cutlet Milanese. The chef will also prepare a pizza for you.

Corso Italia 71. © 081-8781321. Main courses 7€–12.50€ ($6.25–$11.15). MC, V. Daily noon–3:30pm and 7–11:30pm. Closed Wed Nov 15–Mar 15.

SORRENTO AFTER DARK

At the **Taverna dell' 800,** Via dell'Accademia 29 (© 081-8785970), owner Tony Herculano dispenses flavorful home-style macaroni (pink-tinged, it combines tomatoes with ham, cream, and bacon) and good cheer. From 9pm to midnight, the music of a guitar and a piano duet enlivens a cozy bar with flickering candles. There's no cover charge, and the food is cheap. The joint is open Thursday to Sunday 10am to 2:30am and does lots of business throughout the day as a cafe and pub.

For a dose of Neapolitan-style folklore, head for the **Circolo de Forestière,** Via Luigi de Maio 35 (☎ 081-8773012), a bar/cafe whose views extend out over a flowering terrace and the wide blue bay. Music from the live pianist is interrupted only for episodes of folkloric dancing and cheerful music from a troupe of players.

The town's central square, **Piazza Tasso,** is the site of two worthwhile night-clubs. The one that presents folkloric music is **Fauno** (☎ 081-8781021), where you can slug down a beer or two during the sporadic performances of tarantella. Brief but colorful, they interrupt a program otherwise devoted to recorded dance (usually disco) music. There's usually a cover of 20€ ($17.85). At **The Club** (☎ 081-8773236), dance music blares out to a youngish crowd from through-out Europe and North America. The cover is 7.50€ ($6.70) and includes the first drink. It's open daily 10pm to 3am (depending on the crowd).

6 Capri ★★★

5km (3 miles) off the tip of the Sorrentine peninsula

The island of Capri (pronounced *Cap*-ry, not Ca-*pree*) is one of the loveliest resorts in Italy, a dramatic island soaring upward from the sea, with sweeping views, whitewashed homes and villas, fragrant lemon trees, narrow winding lanes, and flower-filled courtyards. It's completely overrun in summer (actually from Easter to the end of Oct), as throngs of international tourists and vaca-tioning Italians arrive every day to soak up its romantic atmosphere and gor-geous scenery.

Touring the island is relatively simple. You dock at unremarkable **Marina Grande,** the port area. You can then take the funicular up the steep hill to the town of **Capri** above, where you'll find the major hotels, restaurants, cafes, and shops. From Capri, a short bus ride will deliver you to **Anacapri,** also perched at the top of the island near Monte Solaro. The only other settlement you might want to visit is **Marina Piccola,** on the south side of the island, with the major beach. There are also beaches at **Punta Carnea** and **Bagni di Tiberio.**

ESSENTIALS

GETTING THERE   You can get here from either Naples or Sorrento. From Naples's Molo Beverello dock (take a taxi from the train station), the **hydrofoil** takes just 45 minutes. The hydrofoil (*aliscafo*) leaves several times daily (some stop at Sorrento), and a one-way trip costs 9€ ($8.05). Regularly scheduled **ferry** (*traghetto*) service is cheaper but takes longer (about 1½ hr.). Fares are 4.40€ to 5€ ($3.95–$4.45) each way. For ferry and hydrofoil schedules, call (☎ 081-5513882) in Naples. There's no need to check all the dock offices for the best price.

From Sorrento, go to the dock right off Piazza Tasso, where you can board one of the **ferries** run by **Linee Marittime Veloci** (☎ 081-8781430) or **Care-mar** (☎ 081-5513882). Departures are several times per day from 7am to 7pm (the last ferry back leaves Capri at 7:45pm), costing 4.40€ to 10€ ($3.95–$8.95) one way. It's much faster to take one of the **hydrofoils** operated by **Alilauro** (☎ 081-8073024), which depart every hour daily 7am to 5:30pm, take only 30 minutes, and cost 7.50€ ($6.70) one way.

If you make reservations the day before with **Alicost** (☎ 089-875092), you can take a hydrofoil or a ferry to Capri from Positano. Hydrofoils cost 12€ ($10.70) one way, and a ferry ticket goes for 9.50€ ($8.50) one way.

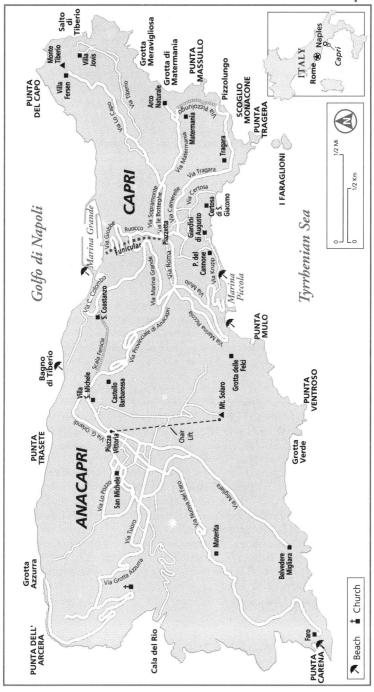

ITALY
Rome
Naples
Capri

1/2 Mi
1/2 Km

Salto di Tiberio
Monte Tiberio
Villa Jovis
Villa Fersen
PUNTA DEL CAPO
Grotta Meravigliosa
Grotta di Matermania
PUNTA MASSULLO
Pizzolungo
Arco Naturale
Via Pizzolungo
Matermania
Via Matermania
SCOGLIO MONACONE
PUNTA TRAGERA
Via Lo Capo
Via Tiberio
Tragara
Via Camerelle
Via Tragara
Via Certosa
I FARAGLIONI
CAPRI
Via Sopramonte
Via le Botteghe
Certosa di S. Giacomo
Marina Grande
Via Giobbe
Ruocco
Piazzetta
Funicular
Giardini di Augusto
Via Roma
P. del Cannone
Via Krupp
Golfo di Napoli
Via C. Colombo
S. Coastanzo
Via Marina Grande
Via Mulo
Via Marina Piccola
Marina Piccola
PUNTA MULO
Tyrrhenian Sea
Scala Fenicia
Via Provinciale di Anacapri
Bagno di Tiberio
Villa S. Michele
Castello Barbarossa
Grotta delle Felci
Mt. Solaro
PUNTA VENTROSO
PUNTA TRASETE
Via G. Orlandi
Piazza Vittoria
Chair Lift
Grotta Verde
ANACAPRI
Via Lo Pozzo
San Michele
Via Nuova del Faro
Via Migliara
Via Tuoro
Materita
Via Grotta Azzurra
Belvedere Migliara
Grotta Azzurra
PUNTA DELL' ARCERA
Cala del Rio
Faro
PUNTA CARENA

Beach   Church

VISITOR INFORMATION Get in touch with the **Tourist Board,** Piazza Umberto I 19 (© 081-8370424), at Capri. From April to September, it's open Monday to Saturday 8:30am to 8:30pm, and Sunday 8:30am to 2:30pm; October to March, hours are Monday to Saturday 9am to 1pm and 3:30 to 6:45pm.

GETTING AROUND There's no need for a car on tiny Capri. The island is serviced by funiculars, taxis, and buses. Capri's hotels are a long way from the docks, so we strongly recommend that you bring as little luggage as possible. If you need a porter, you'll find union headquarters in a building connected to the jetty at Marina Grande. Here you can cajole, coddle, coerce, or connive your way through the hiring process, where the only rule seems to be that there are no rules. But your porter will know where to find any hotel among the winding passageways and steep inclines of the island's arteries. Just bring a sense of humor. (Note that if you have reservations at one of the island's more upscale accommodations, your hotel might have its own porter on duty at the docks to help you with your luggage and get you settled.)

MARINA GRANDE ✸
The least attractive of the island's communities, Marina Grande is the port, bustling daily with the comings and goings of hundreds of visitors. It has a little sand-cum-pebble beach, on which you're likely to see American sailors (on shore leave from Naples) playing ball.

If you're just spending the day on Capri, you might want to see the island's biggest attraction, the **Grotta Azzurra (Blue Grotto)** ✸✸, open daily 9am to 1 hour before sunset. In summer, boats leave frequently from the harbor at Marina Grande to transport passengers to the entrance of the grotto for 15€ ($13.40) round-trip. Once at the grotto, you'll pay 12€ ($10.70) for the small rowboat that takes you inside.

The Blue Grotto is one of the best-known natural sights of the region, although the way passengers are hustled in and out of it makes it a tourist trap. It's truly beautiful, however. Known to the ancients, it was later lost to the world until an artist stumbled on it in 1826. Inside the cavern, light refraction (the sun's rays entering from an opening under the water) achieves the dramatic Mediterranean cerulean color. The effect is stunning, as thousands testify yearly.

If you want, you can take a trip around the entire island, passing not only the Blue Grotto but also the **Baths of Tiberius,** the **Palazzo al Mare** built in the days of the empire, the **Green Grotto** (less known), and the much-photographed rocks called the **Faraglioni.** Motorboats circle the island in about 1½ hours at 17.50€ ($15.65) per person.

Connecting Marina Grande with the town of Capri is a frequently running **funicular** charging 4€ ($3.55) one way. However, the funicular, really a cog railway, doesn't operate off-season (you'll take a bus from Marina Grande to Capri for the same price).

SWIMMING & SUNNING
Although it's a summer resort, Capri doesn't have great sandy beaches because of its mountainous landscape. There are some spots for swimming, most of which have clubs called *stabilimenti balneari,* which you must pay to visit. Most people relax at their hotel swimming pools and take in the gorgeous views from there.

The coastline surrounding Capri is punctuated with jagged rocks that allow for very few sandy beaches. You can head for the **Bagni Nettuno,** Via Grotta

Azzurra 46 (© **081-8371362**), a short distance from the Blue Grotto in Anacapri. Surrounded by scenic cliffsides, with an undeniable drama, it charges 10€ ($8.95). The price includes use of a cabana, towels, and deck chairs. Mid-March to mid-November, it's open daily 9am to sunset. From a point nearby, you can actually swim into the narrow, rocky entrance guarding the Blue Grotto, but this is advisable only after 5pm, when the boat services into the grotto have ended for the day, and only during relatively calm seas.

Another possibility for swimming is the **Bagni di Tiberio,** a sandy beach a short walk from the ruins of an ancient Roman villa. To reach it, you have to board a motorboat departing from Marina Grande for the 15-minute ride to the site. Passage costs 4€ ($3.55) per person, unless you want to walk 30 minutes north from Marina Grande, through rocky landscapes with flowering plants and vineyards.

Closer to the island's south side is the **Marina Piccola,** a usually overcrowded stretch of sand extending between jagged lava rocks. You can rent a small motorboat here from the **Bagni le Sirene** (© **081-8370221**) for around 60€ ($53.60) for the first hour, and 10€ ($8.95) for every hour after that. Prices can vary depending on the boat's size and the luxuries on board.

THE TOWN OF CAPRI ★★★

The main town of Capri is the center of most of the hotels, restaurants, and elegant shops—and the milling throngs. The heart of the resort, **Piazza Umberto I,** is like a grand living room, lined with cafes.

One of the most popular walks from the main square is down Via Vittorio Emanuele, past the deluxe Quisisana hotel, to the **Giardini di Augusto,** the choice spot on Capri for views and relaxation. From this park's perch, you can see the legendary **I Faraglioni,** the rocks once inhabited by the "blue lizard." At the top of the park is a belvedere overlooking emerald waters and Marina Piccola. Nearby you can visit the **Certosa,** a Carthusian monastery erected in the 14th century to honor St. James. It's open Tuesday to Sunday 9am to 2pm and charges no admission.

Back at Piazza Umberto I, head up Via Longano and then Via Tiberio, all the way to Monte Tiberio. Here you'll find the **Villa Jovis** ★★, the splendid ruin of the estate from which Tiberius ruled the empire from A.D. 27 to 37. Actually, the Jovis was one of a dozen villas that the depraved emperor erected on the island. Apparently Tiberius had trouble sleeping, so he wandered from bed to bed, exploring his "nooks of lechery," a young girl one hour, a young boy the next. From the ruins there's a view of both the Bay of Salerno and the Bay of Naples, as well as of the island. You can visit the ruins of the imperial palace daily 9am to 1 hour before sunset for 2.25€ ($2). For information, call the tourist board at © **081-8370424.**

SHOPPING

A little shop on Capri's luxury shopping street, **Carthusia-Profumi di Capri,** Via Camerelle 10 (© **081-8370368**), specializes in perfume made on the island from local herbs and flowers. Since 1948, this shop has attracted such clients as Elizabeth Taylor (before she started touting her own perfume). The scents are unique, and many women consider Carthusia perfumes collector's items.

Carthusia also has a **Perfume Laboratory,** Via Matteotti 2 (© **081-8370368**), which you can visit daily 9:30am to 6pm. There's another **Carthusia shop** in Anacapri, at Via Capodimonte 26 (© **081-8373668**), next to the

Villa Axel Munthe. The shops are closed November to March, but the laboratory remains open year-round.

Capri is famed for its **limoncello,** a liqueur whose recipe was conceived several generations ago by members of the Canali family. It consists of lemon zest (not the juice or pith) mixed with alcohol, sugar, water, and herbs to produce a tart kind of "hyper-lemonade" with a mildly alcoholic lift. It's consumed alone as either an aperitif or a digestive, or it's mixed with vodka or sparkling wines for a lemony cocktail. In 1989, the Canalis formalized their family recipe, established modern distilleries on Capri and in nearby Sorrento, and hired professionals to promote the product as far away as the United States and Japan. Limoncello is sold at **Limoncello di Capri,** 79 Via Roma (© **081-8375561**) in Capri, or at Via Capodimonte 27 (© **081-8372927**) in Anacapri, often in lovely bottles that make nice, affordable gifts.

Shoppers here also look for deals on sandals, cashmere, and jewelry, the town's big bargains. The cobblers at **Canfora,** Via Camerelle 3 (© **081-8370487**), make all the sandals found in their shop. If you don't find what you need, you can order custom-made footwear. The store also sells shoes but doesn't make those. The great sandal maker of Capri is Antonio Viva, holding forth for nearly half a century at **L'Arte del Sandalo Caprese,** via Giuseppe Orlandi 75 in Anacapri (© **081-8373583**). In days of yore, Jackie O and Sophia Loren used to come here to purchase sandals. There are ready-made selections, but this cobbler will also design to order.

You can find a good selection of men's cashmere pullovers at **Russo Uomo,** Piazza Umberto 1 (© **081-8388208**). But for cashmere pullovers for the whole family, go to **Russo Donna,** Via Vittorio Emanuele 55 (© **081-8388207**).

The eight talented jewelers at **La Perla Goielli,** Piazza Umberto 10–21 (© **081-8370641**), work exclusively with gold and gems and can design and create anything you want. Established in 1936 by a local matriarch, Mamma Olympia, this is the most elegant and prestigious jeweler on Capri, with rosters of famous star-quality fans from around Europe and the new world. It's also the local branch of Buccellati, the prestigious silversmith based in Rome. Ask for Angela, or any of her charming children, Giorgio, Giuseppe, or Claudio. Another little charmer we recently stumbled upon quite by accident is **Grazia Vozza Goielli,** via Li Campi 22 (© **081-8374010**), which sells freshwater pearls and a stunning collection of necklaces in peridot, jade, amber, and aquamarine.

WHERE TO STAY

This is a ritzy resort, with correspondingly high prices. If you're really watching your wallet, you might have to visit for the day and return to the mainland for the night. Don't even think of coming in summer without a reservation.

Very Expensive

Grand Hotel Quisisana Capri ✦✦✦ The island's grande dame, this is the favorite of a regular international crowd and a bastion of luxury. The sprawling buildings are painted a distinctive yellow and accented with vines and landscaping. Its guest rooms range from cozy singles to spacious suites—all opening onto wide arcades with a stunning view over the coast. They vary greatly in decor, with traditional and conservatively modern furnishings. All have a lovely, airy style, and all come with comfortable beds and tile or marble bathrooms.

Via Camerelle 2, 80073 Capri. © 081-8370788. Fax 081-8376080. www.quisi.com. 150 units. 245€–490€ ($218.80–$437.55) double; from 455€ ($406.30) suite. Rates include breakfast. AE, DC, MC, V. Closed Nov 1 to mid-Mar. **Amenities:** 2 restaurants; 3 bars; 2 pools (1 indoor, 1 outdoor); tennis courts; limited health club;

spa; sauna; salon; room service; massage; babysitting; laundry/dry cleaning. *In room:* A/C, TV, minibar, hair dryer, safe.

La Scalinatella (Little Steps) ⚜⚜ This delightful hotel is constructed like a private villa above terraces offering a panoramic view. It's an exclusive pair of 200-year-old houses, with a vaguely Moorish design, run by the Morgano family (which also owns the Quisisana, listed above). The ambience is one of unadulterated luxury; all units include a phone beside the bathtub, beds set into alcoves, elaborate wrought-iron accents ringing both the inner stairwell and the ornate balconies, and a sweeping view over the gardens and pool. Half of the accommodations boast two bathrooms each, one with a whirlpool tub.

Via Tragara 8, 80073 Capri. ✆ **081-8370633.** Fax 081-8378291. 30 units. 360€–420€ ($321.50–$375.05) double; 440€–500€ ($392.90–$446.50) junior suite. Rates include breakfast. AE, MC, V. Closed Nov–Easter. **Amenities:** Restaurant; bar; pool; sauna; Jacuzzi; room service; babysitting; laundry/dry cleaning. *In room:* A/C, TV, minibar, hair dryer, safe.

Expensive

Casa Morgano ⚜⚜ *Value* The newest Morgano family property loses out by a hair to La Scalinatella, its next-door neighbor, but with prices $100 a night cheaper, you might not notice the difference. Casa Morgano houses you in grand comfort in 20 of its rooms, which are spacious and deluxe; eight others are quite small. The best units are nos. 201 to 205 and 301 to 305. Most units contain good-size sitting areas along with terraces opening onto sea views. The bathrooms come with a hydromassage bathtub and shower.

Via Tragara 6, 80073 Capri. ✆ **081-8370158.** Fax 081-8370681. www.caprionline.com/morgano. 28 units. 210€–320€ ($187.55–$285.75) double; 330€–385€ ($294.70–$343.80) junior suite. Rates include breakfast. AE, DC, MC, V. **Amenities:** Bar; room service; babysitting; laundry/dry cleaning. *In room:* A/C, TV, minibar, hair dryer, safe.

Hotel Luna ⚜ This first-class hotel stands on a cliff overlooking the sea and the rocks of Faraglioni. The guest rooms are a mix of contemporary Italian pieces and Victorian decor, most with recessed terraces overlooking the garden of flowers and semitropical plants. All are accompanied by tiled bathrooms.

Viale Matteotti 3, 80073 Capri. ✆ **081-8370433.** Fax 081-8377459. www.caprionline.com/luna. 54 units. 200€–305€ ($178.60–$272.35) double. Rates include breakfast. AE, DC, MC, V. Closed Oct 21–Easter. **Amenities:** Restaurant; lounge; pool; health club; Jacuzzi; room service; babysitting; laundry/dry cleaning. *In room:* A/C, TV, minibar, hair dryer, safe.

Hotel Punta Tragara ⚜⚜ This former private villa, designed by Le Corbusier, stands above rocky cliffs at the southwest tip of the most desirable panorama on Capri. With big windows, substantial furniture, and all the modern comforts, each guest room opens onto a terrace or balcony that's brightened with flowers and vines, plus a sweeping view. Bathrooms are spacious. The hotel is isolated from many other island activities, which is either a drawback or a plus, depending on your point of view.

Via Tragara 57, 80073 Capri. ✆ **081-8370844.** Fax 081-8377790. www.hoteltragara.com. 45 units. 200€–240€ ($178.60–$214.30) double; 310€–380€ ($276.85–$339.35) suite. Rates include buffet breakfast. AE, DC, MC, V. Closed Nov–Easter. **Amenities:** Restaurant; lounge; nightclub; pool; Jacuzzi; salon; room service; laundry. *In room:* A/C, TV, minibar, hair dryer, safe.

Villa Brunella ⚜ *Finds* A 10-minute walk from many of Capri's largest hotels, the Brunella was built in the late 1940s as a private villa. In 1963, it was transformed into a pleasant hotel by its present owner, Vincenzo Ruggiero, who named it after his hardworking wife. The hotel has been completely renovated and can hold its own with the other hotels in town. All the doubles have balconies or flowery terraces with sea views. The rooms come in various shapes and sizes, each with a small tiled bathroom.

Via Tragara 24, 80073 Capri. ☎ **081-8370122.** Fax 081-8370430. www.caprionline.com/villabrunella. 20 units. 240€ ($214.30) double; 310€ ($276.85) suite. Rates include breakfast. AE, DC, MC, V. Closed Nov 6–Mar 20. **Amenities:** Restaurant; bar; pool; room service; babysitting; laundry/dry cleaning. *In room:* A/C, TV, minibar, hair dryer, safe.

Moderate

Hotel La Vega   This hotel began in the 1930s as the private home of the family that continues to run it today. It has a clear sea view and is nestled amid trees against a sunny hillside. The oversize guest rooms have decoratively tiled floors; each has a private balcony overlooking the water. Some beds have wrought-iron headboards. Below is a garden of flowering bushes, and on the lower edge is a free-form pool with a grassy border for sunbathing. Breakfast is served on your balcony or on a terrace surrounded by trees and large potted flowers.

Via Occhio Marino 10, 80073 Capri. ☎ **081-8370481.** Fax 081-8370342. 24 units (some with shower only). 190€–210€ ($169.65–$187.55) double. Rates include breakfast. AE, DC, MC, V. Closed Nov–Easter. **Amenities:** Bar; lounge; pool; laundry. *In room:* A/C, TV, minibar, hair dryer, safe.

Hotel Regina Cristina   The white facade of the Regina Cristina rises four stories above one of the most imaginatively landscaped gardens on Capri. It was built in 1959 and has a sunny design of open spaces, sunken lounges, and cool tiles. Each guest room has its own balcony and is very restful. Their sizes range from small to medium, but each has a good mattress and a compact tiled bathroom. In general, the prices are high for what you get, but on Capri in July and August you're sometimes lucky to find a room at any price.

Via Serena 20, 80073 Capri. ☎ **081-8370744.** Fax 081-8370550. www.caprinews.it/reginacristina. 55 units. 165€–210€ ($147.35–$187.55) double; 310€ ($276.85) suite. Rates include breakfast. AE, DC, MC, V. **Amenities:** Restaurant; bar; Jacuzzi; room service; laundry. *In room:* A/C, TV, minibar, hair dryer, safe.

Villa Sarah ✦ *Value*   The modern Sarah, though far removed from the day-trippers from Naples, is still very central. A steep walk from the main square, it seems part of another world, with its private garden and good views. All it lacks is a pool. One of the bargains of the island, it's often fully booked, so reserve ahead in summer. The sea is visible only from the upper floors. Most of the guest rooms are quite small, but some of them make up for this with pleasant terraces. Bathrooms are a bit small as well. Breakfast is sometimes served on the terrace.

Via Tiberio 3A, 80073 Capri. ☎ **081-8377817.** Fax 081-8377215. www.villasarah.it. 20 units. 145€–176€ ($129.50–$157.15) double. Rates include buffet breakfast. AE, MC, V. Closed late Oct to Mar 19. **Amenities:** Bar; room service; babysitting; laundry/dry cleaning. *In room:* A/C, TV, minibar, hair dryer, safe.

Inexpensive

Villa Krupp *Value*   This is a longtime favorite known for its affordable prices. During the early 20th century, Russian revolutionaries Gorky and Lenin called this villa home. Surrounded by shady trees, it offers panoramic views of the sea and the Gardens of Augustus from its terraces. At this family-run place, the front parlor is all glass with views of the seaside and semitropical plants set near Hong Kong chairs, intermixed with painted Venetian-style pieces. Rooms are comfortable and vary in size, with spacious bathrooms.

Via Matteotti 12, 80073 Capri. ☎ **081-8377473.** Fax 081-8376489. 15 units (showers only). 105€–145€ ($93.75–$129.50) double. Rates include breakfast. MC, V. Closed Nov–Mar 15. **Amenities:** Lounge. *In room:* A/C, hair dryer.

WHERE TO DINE
Very Expensive
Da Paolino ✰✰ CAPRESE/ITALIAN   Don't be surprised to spot a visiting celeb at this chic restaurant. The food is about the most authentic Caprese cuisine served on the island. Try everything from a Caprese salad to sautéed ravioli stuffed with fresh cacciotta cheese. The rigatoni pasta with sautéed pumpkin flowers is worthy of *Gourmet* magazine. Equally delectable is the penne with eggplant and fresh mozzarella. Just as enchanting as the food is the dining area placed in a lemon grove. The lemon motif pervades the restaurant, ranging from the waiters' vests to the plates placed before you.

Via Palazzo a Mare 11, Marina Grande. ✆ 081-8376102. Reservations required. Main courses 30€–40€ ($26.80–$35.70). AE, DC, MC, V. June–Oct daily 8–11pm. Closed Wed Nov–April.

Moderate
Ai Faraglioni SEAFOOD/CONTINENTAL   The food is secondary to the scene at this popular restaurant, where tables are set on the main street in nice weather. Stylish and appealing and occupying a stone-sided building at least 150 years old, it has a kitchen that turns out well-prepared European specialties, usually based on seafood from the surrounding waters. Examples are linguine with lobster, seafood crepes, rice Creole, fisherman's risotto, grilled or baked fish, and a wide assortment of meat dishes, such as pappardelle with rabbit. For dessert, try one of the regional pastries mixed with fresh fruit.

Via Camerelle 75. ✆ 081-8370320. Reservations required. Main courses 10€ ($8.95). AE, DC, MC, V. Daily noon–3pm and 7:30–11:30pm. Closed Nov to mid-Mar.

CasaNova ✰ NEAPOLITAN/CAPRESE/SEAFOOD   Run by the D'Alessio family and only a short walk from Piazza Umberto I, this is one of the finest dining rooms on Capri. Its cellar offers a big choice of Italian wines, with most of the favorites of Campania, and its cooks turn out a savory blend of Neapolitan and Italian specialties. You might begin with cheese-filled ravioli and then go on to veal Sorrento or red snapper "crazy waters" (with baby tomatoes). The seafood is always fresh and well prepared. A tempting buffet of antipasti is at hand. In a small wine cellar, you can enjoy a good selection of Italian and foreign wines with a variety of cheeses. Most meals are inexpensive, but some exotic dishes and specialties that appear infrequently can cause your check to soar. Lunch offers some lighter choices such as simple pizzas and salads.

Via Le Botteghe 46. ✆ 081-8377642. Reservations required at dinner in summer. Main courses 12.50€–21€ ($11.15–$18.75). AE, DC, MC, V. Mar–Nov daily noon–3pm and 7–11pm. Closed Dec to mid-Mar.

Da Gemma CAPRESE/SEAFOOD   Da Gemma is reached by passing through a vaulted tunnel beginning at Piazza Umberto I and winding through dark underground passages. The cuisine includes authentic versions of Caprese favorites, with an emphasis on fish, as well as more modern dishes such as pizzas. You might begin with a creamy version of mussel soup, followed by one of many kinds of grilled fish, as well as filets of veal or chicken prepared with lemon and garlic or with Marsala wine. A specialty is a *fritta alla Gemma,* a medley of fried foods that includes fried zucchini blossoms, potato croquettes, fried mozzarella, and a miniature pizza. During warm weather, the site expands from its cramped 14th-century core onto a covered open-air terrace with sweeping views of the Gulf of Naples. (To reach the terrace, you'll have to wander through the same labyrinth of covered passages and then cross the street.)

Via Madre Serafina 6. ✆ 081-8370461. Reservations recommended. Main courses 9€–17.50€ ($8.05–$15.65). AE, DC, MC, V. Daily noon–3pm and 7pm–midnight. Closed Nov–March.

La Cantinella di Capri NEAPOLITAN/FRENCH   One of the most scenically located restaurants, this place occupies a villa (ca. 1750) in a verdant park a short but soothing distance from the town center and a short walk from the Gardens of Augustus. It was acquired in 1996 by the owners of a popular restaurant in Naples. Menu items include lots of pungent sauces and fresh seafood that's sometimes combined into pastas such as linguine *Sant Lucia* (with octopus, squid, whitefish, and tomato sauce). Worth the trip here is the superb fish, including the local pezzogna baked in a salt crust to preserve its aromatic flavors. Try the veal scaloppine prepared with lemon and white wine or parmigiana style. The *pasta fagiole* (beans and pasta) is hearty, and such desserts as tiramisu are invariably velvety smooth.

In the Giardini Augusto, Viale Matteotti 8. *©* 081-8370616. Reservations recommended. Main courses 12€–17.50€ ($10.70–$15.65). AE, DC, MC, V. Tues–Sun 12:30–3pm and 7:30pm–12:30am. Closed Nov–Mar.

La Capannina *©* CAMPANA/ITALIAN   This restaurant has drawn a host of glamorous people, but they come for its lack of pretentiousness. Part of its charm derives from the American-born wife, Aurelia de Angelis, of the fifth-generation owner, who's always on hand to translate or help with menu selections. The three dining rooms are decorated tavern style, although the main draw in summer is the inner courtyard, with ferns and hanging vines. At a table covered with a colored cloth, you can select from baby shrimp au gratin, *pollo* (chicken) *alla Capannina,* or *scaloppine Capannina.* Sicilian macaroni isn't always on the menu; if it is, order it. The most savory skillet of goodies is the *zuppa di pesce,* a soup made with fish from the bay. Some of the dishes were obviously inspired by the nouvelle cuisine school. Wine is from vineyards owned by the restaurant.

Via Le Botteghe 12B–14. *©* 081-8370732. Reservations required for dinner. Main courses 11€–22.50€ ($9.80–$20.10). AE, DC, MC, V. Daily noon–3pm and 7:30pm–midnight. Closed Nov 15–Mar 19.

La Pigna *(Value)* NEAPOLITAN   La Pigna serves the finest meals for the money on the island. Since the place opened in 1875, dining here has been like attending a garden party. It isn't as chic as it once was, but the food is as good as ever. The owner loves flowers almost as much as good food, and the greenhouse ambience includes purple petunias, red geraniums, bougainvillea, and lemon trees. Much of the produce comes from the restaurant's gardens in Anacapri. Try in particular the penne tossed in eggplant sauce, the chicken supreme with mushrooms, or the herb-stuffed rabbit. The dessert specialty is an almond-and-chocolate torte. Another specialty is the homemade liqueurs, one of which is distilled from local lemons. The waiters are courteous and efficient, and the atmosphere is nostalgic, as guitarists stroll by singing sentimental Neapolitan ballads.

Via Lo Palazzo 30. *©* 081-8370280. Reservations recommended. Main courses 12€–18€ ($10.70–$16.05). AE, DC, MC, V. Daily noon–3pm.

Inexpensive

La Cisterna SEAFOOD   This excellent small restaurant is run by brothers Francesco and Salvatore Trama, who extend a warm welcome. Ask what the evening specials are. They might be mama's green lasagna or whatever fish was freshest that afternoon, marinated in wine, garlic, and ginger, and broiled. You could also try the lightly breaded and deep-fried baby squid and octopus, a mouth-watering saltimbocca, spaghetti with clams, and a filling zuppa di pesce. Pizza begins at 3€ ($2.70). La Cisterna is only a short walk from Piazza Umberto I via a labyrinth of covered "tunnels."

Via Madre Serafina 5. *©* 081-8375620. Reservations required. Main courses 7.50€–12€ ($6.70–$10.70). AE, DC, MC, V. Daily noon–3:30pm and 7pm–midnight.

Ristorante al Grottino SEAFOOD/NEAPOLITAN Founded in 1937, this was the retreat of the rich and famous during its 1950s heyday. Ted Kennedy, Ginger Rogers, the Gabor sisters, and Princess Soraya of Iran once dined here, and the place is now popular among ordinary folk. To reach it, you walk down a narrow alley branching off from Piazza Umberto I. Bowing to the influence of the nearby Neapolitan cuisine, the chef offers four different dishes of fried mozzarella, all of which are highly recommended. Try a big plate of the mixed fish fry from the seas of the Campania. The *zuppa di cozze* (mussel soup) is a savory opener, as is the *ravioli alla caprese*. The linguine with scampi is truly wonderful.

Via Longano 27. ✆ **081-8370584.** Reservations required for dinner. Main courses 10€–15€ ($8.95–$13.40). AE, MC, V. Daily noon–3pm and 7pm–midnight. Closed Nov–Mar.

CAPRI AFTER DARK

You'll find some fun nightclubs on the island, all of which you can enter without a cover. They cater to all ages and all nationalities, but only between late April and September. Foremost among them is **Number Two,** Via Camerelle 1 (✆ **081-8377078**).

The presence of these high-tech dance clubs doesn't keep the crowds out of the dozens of cafes, bars, and taverns scattered throughout the narrow streets of Capri's historic center. Among the most appealing is **Taverna Guarracino,** Via Castello 7 (✆ **081-8370514**), an ultramodern yet convivial place to enjoy a beer or a glass of wine.

One of the major pastimes in Capri is cafe-sitting at an outdoor table on Piazza Umberto I. Even some permanent residents (this is a good sign) patronize **Bar Tiberio,** Piazza Umberto I (✆ **081-8370268**), open Thursday to Tuesday 7am to 2am (sometimes to 4am). Larger and a little more comfortable than some of its competitors, this cafe has tables both inside and outside that overlook the busy life of the square.

ANACAPRI ✫✫✫

Even farther up in the clouds than Capri is the town of Anacapri, which is more remote, secluded, and idyllic than the main resort. At one time, Anacapri and Capri were connected only by the *Scala Fenicia,* the Phoenician Stairs (which have been reconstructed a zillion times). Today, however, you can reach Anacapri on a daring bus ride more thrilling than any roller coaster. The fare is 1.80€ ($1.60) round-trip. One visitor remarked that all bus drivers to Anacapri "were either good or dead."

When you disembark at **Piazza della Victoria,** you'll find a village of charming dimensions.

To continue your ascent to the top, hop aboard a chairlift (La Segiovia) to **Monte Solaro** ✫✫, the loftiest citadel on the island at 594m (1,950 ft.). The ride takes about 12 minutes and operates winter, spring, and fall 9:30am to sunset; a round-trip costs 5€ ($4.45). At the top, the panorama of the Bay of Naples is spread before you.

Back in the village below, you can head out on Viale Axel Munthe from Piazza Monumento for a 5-minute walk to the **Villa San Michele** ✫, Capodimonte 34 (✆ **081-8371401**). This was the home of Axel Munthe, the Swedish author (*The Story of San Michele*), physician, and friend of Gustav V, king of Sweden, who visited him several times on the island. The villa is as Munthe (who died in 1949) furnished it, in a harmonious and tasteful way. From the rubble and ruins of an imperial villa built underneath this one by Tiberius, Munthe purchased several marbles, which are displayed inside. You can walk through the gardens for another in a series of endless panoramas of the island. Tiberius used to sleep out here alfresco on hot nights. You can visit the villa daily: May to September 9am to 6pm, April and October 9:30am to 5pm, March 9:30am to 4:30pm, and November to February 10:30am to 3:30pm. Admission is 5€ ($4.45).

WHERE TO STAY
Expensive
Capri Palace ☆☆☆   On the slopes of Monte Solaro, the contemporary, first-class Capri Palace sparkles. Its bold designer obviously loved wide-open spaces and vivid colors. The landscaped gardens with palm trees and plenty of bougainvillea have a large pool, which most guests use as their outdoor living room. Although it lacks the intimate charms of La Scalinatella in Capri (listed earlier in the chapter), it's still a wonderful choice because of its setting. Each of the guest rooms is attractively and comfortably furnished, and from some on a clear day you can see smoking Vesuvius. Many beds (mostly twins) are canopied, and all of them feature quality linens. The bathrooms are tiled or marbled, each with deluxe toiletries. Each of the four special suites has a private pool and private garden.

Via Capodimonte 2, 80071 Anacapri. ⓒ **081-8373800.** Fax 081-8373191. www.capri-palace.com. 80 units. 250€–775€ ($223.20–$691.95) double; 724€–1,130€ ($646.45–$1,008.95) suite. Rates include breakfast. AE, DC, MC, V. Closed Nov 15–Easter. **Amenities:** 2 restaurants; bar; lounge; pool; spa; room service; babysitting; laundry. *In room:* A/C, TV, minibar, hair dryer, safe.

Moderate
Hotel Bella Vista ⓥalue   Only a 2-minute walk from the main piazza, this is a modern vacation retreat with a panoramic view and a distinct sense of a family-run regional inn. Lodged into a mountainside, the hotel is decorated with primary colors and has large living and dining rooms and terraces with sea views. The breakfast and lunch terrace has garden furniture and a rattan-roofed sun shelter. The guest rooms are pleasingly contemporary (a few have a bed mezzanine, a sitting area on the lower level, and a private entrance). The tiled bathrooms are compact.

Via Orlandi 10, 80071 Anacapri. ⓒ **081-8371821.** Fax 081-8370957. syrene@capri.it. 14 units. 200€–275€ ($178.60–$245.60) per person double. Rates include breakfast. AE, MC, V. Closed Nov 1–Easter. **Amenities:** Restaurant; lounge; 3 tennis courts; room service; laundry. *In room:* TV, hair dryer.

Hotel San Michele di Anacapri   This well-appointed hotel offers spacious cliffside gardens and unmarred views as well as enough shady or sunny nooks to please everybody. Guests linger peacefully in its private gardens, where the trees are softened by splashes of color from hydrangea and geraniums. The view includes the Bay of Naples and Vesuvius. Guest rooms contain good beds and tiled bathrooms.

Via Orlandi 1–3, 80071 Anacapri. ⓒ **081-8371427.** Fax 081-8371420. www.sanmichele-capri.com. 60 units. 135€–170€ ($120.55–$151.80) double. Rates include breakfast. AE, MC, DC, V. Closed Nov 6–Mar 31. **Amenities:** Dining room; bar; pool; babysitting; laundry/dry cleaning. *In room:* A/C, TV, hair dryer.

Inexpensive
Hotel Loreley   The Loreley is cozy, with a genial, homey atmosphere. It features an open-air veranda with a bamboo canopy, rattan chairs, and a good view. The guest rooms overlook lemon-bearing trees that have (depending on the season) either scented blossoms or fruit. The rooms are quite large, with unified colors and enough furniture to make a sitting area. Each has a balcony and a well-maintained bathroom. You approach the hotel through a white iron gate,

past a stone wall. It lies off the road toward the sea and is surrounded by fig trees and geraniums.

Via Orlandi 16, 80071 Anacapri. © 081-8371440. Fax 081-8371399. 16 units (showers only). 70€–90€ ($62.50–$80.35) double. Rates include breakfast. AE, MC, V. Closed Nov 8–Mar 19. **Amenities:** Bar; room service; babysitting. *In room:* TV, safe.

WHERE TO DINE

La Rondinella SOUTHERN ITALIAN   Despite the competition from the more formal restaurants in some of Anacapri's hotels, this is the most appealing place, thanks to the likable staff, its garden view, and a location adjacent to the Santa Sophia church. The menu items are tried-and-true versions of classics, yet the chefs manage to produce everything in copious amounts and with lots of robust flavors. Look for succulent homemade ravioli stuffed with cheese and tomatoes; a mixed grill of fresh seafood, braised radicchio, and artichokes; and filet of veal or chicken slathered with mozzarella, tomatoes, and fresh herbs. For dessert, you might try the sugary version of Sicilian tiramisu.

Via Orlandi 295. © 081-8371223. Reservations recommended. Main courses 12€–18€ ($10.70–$16.05). AE, DC, MC, V. Daily noon–3pm and 7pm–midnight. Closed Thurs in winter.

MARINA PICCOLA 🐾

It's a pleasant 20-minute walk from Capri down the hill to the little south-shore fishing village and beach of **Marina Piccola** (treat yourself to a cab or a bus back up the steep hill to Capri). The village opens onto emerald-and-cerulean waters, with the Faraglioni rocks of the sirens jutting out at the far end of the bay. Treat yourself to lunch at **La Canzone del Mare,** Via Marina Piccola 93 (© **081-8370104**), daily noon to 4pm (closed Nov–Easter). Seafood and Neapolitan cuisines are served.

7 Positano 🐾🐾

56km (35 miles) SE of Naples, 16km (10 miles) E of Sorrento, 266km (165 miles) SE of Rome

A Moorish-style hillside village on the southern strip of the Amalfi Drive, Positano opens onto the Tyrrhenian Sea with its legendary (now privately owned) Sirenuse Islands, Homer's siren islands in the *Odyssey,* which form the mini-archipelago of Li Galli (The Cocks). Once, Positano was part of the powerful Republic of the Amalfis, a rival of Venice as a sea power in the 10th century. It's said that the town was "discovered" after World War II when Gen. Mark Clark stationed troops in nearby Salerno. Like many European resorts, it began as a sleepy fishing village that was visited by painters and writers (Paul Klee, Tennessee Williams) and then taken over by visitors in search of bohemia, until a full-scale tourism industry was born.

Today smart boutiques dot the village, and bikinis add vibrant colors to the gray beach, where you're likely to get pebbles in your sand castle. Prices have been rising sharply over the past few years. The .25€- (20¢-) a-night rooms that were popular with sunset-painting artists have gone the way of your baby teeth. The village, you'll soon discover, is impossibly steep. Wear comfortable walking shoes—no heels!

If you make reservations the day before with **Alicost** (© **089-875092**), you can take a hydrofoil or a ferry to Capri from Positano. Hydrofoils cost 12€ ($10.70) one way, and a ferry ticket goes for 9.50€ ($8.50) one way.

ESSENTIALS

GETTING THERE   SITA **buses** leave from Sorrento frequently throughout the day, more often in summer than winter, for the rather thrilling ride to Positano; a one-way fare is 11.50€ ($10.25). For information, call SITA at *©* **089-871016.**

If you have a **car,** Positano lies along Route 145, which becomes Route 163 at the approach to the resort.

VISITOR INFORMATION   The **tourist office** is at Via del Saracino 4 (*©* **089-875067**), open Monday to Friday 8:30am to 2pm, and Saturday June to September 8:30am to noon.

SHOPPING

In a town famous for beach and casual wear, **La Brezza,** Via del Brigantino 1 (*©* **089-875811**), on the shore, has the perfect location for selling its swimsuits, beach towels, and summer clothes. Clothing that's a bit more formal and better suited to a glamorous dinner is at **Nadir,** Via Pasitea 42/46 (*©* **089-875975**). Another sleek fashion option is **Carro Fashion,** Via Pasitea 90 (*©* **089-875780**). The shop at the Hotel Le Sirenuse (below), **Emporio Le Sirenuse,** 109 Via Cristoforo Colombo (*©* **089-811468**), is presided over by Carla Sersale, who has the town's toniest merchandise, everything from ballerina slippers from Porselli (who designs them for Milan's La Scala) to sexy one-piece bathing suits.

If you're in the market for brightly colored, intricately patterned regional pottery, visit **Umberto Carro,** Via Pasitea 98 (*©* **089-811596**), where the focus is on dishes, cookware, and ceramic tiles. For the best collection of ceramics from the Amalfi town of Vietri sul Mare, head for **Ceramica Assunta,** Via Cristoforo Colombo 97 (*©* **089-875008**), known for its colorful ceramics with fine artisanal decorations.

In the overcrowded **Cafiero,** 171 Via Cristoforo Colombo (*©* **089-875838**), you find odd-shaped colored glass bottles and vases. There's nothing like it along the coast.

La Myricae, Piazza Mulini 71 (*©* **089-875882**), has the coast's best selection of antique jewelry, some from the 17th century. There are some excellent buys here in Art Deco jewelry.

WHERE TO STAY
VERY EXPENSIVE

Hotel di San Pietro ★★★   This Relais & Châteaux property, with its gorgeous views, is the most luxurious retreat in the south of Italy. A mile from Positano toward Amalfi, the San Pietro is signaled only by a miniature 17th-century chapel projecting out on a high cliff. The hotel opened in 1970 and has been renovated virtually every winter since. An elevator takes you down to the cliff ledges to a private beach. The suitelike guest rooms are superglamorous with state-of-the-art bathrooms, many with picture windows beside the bathtubs (there's even a huge sunken Roman bath in one suite). Antiques and art objects add to the effect. Room no. 8½ is named for longtime guest Federico Fellini. More recent guests have included Julia Roberts and Sting (not together, of course). Bougainvillea from the terraces reaches into the ceilings of many living rooms.

Via Laurito 2, 84017 Positano. *©* 089-875455. Fax 089-811449. www.ilsanpietro.it. 60 units. 370€–425€ ($330.40–$379.55) double; 510€–800€ ($455.45–$714.40) suite. Rates include breakfast. AE, DC, MC, V. Free parking. Closed Nov 3–Easter. **Amenities:** Restaurant; bar; pool; tennis court; room service; babysitting; laundry. *In room:* A/C, TV, minibar, hair dryer, safe.

Hotel Le Sirenuse ✿✿✿   This is one of southern Italy's greatest resort hotels. It's been long celebrated as a fabled retreat of the rich and famous. Despite stiff competition from San Pietro (see above), Le Sirenuse remains a gem, with simply stunning views. It's better than ever, after the addition of a new high-tech health club and spa in 2000. This old villa a few minutes' walk up from the bay is owned by the Marchesi Sersale family; it was their home until 1951. The family selects all the furnishings, which include fine carved chests, 19th-century paintings and old prints, a spinet piano, upholstered pieces in bold colors, and a Victorian cabinet. The guest rooms, many with Jacuzzis in the luxurious bathrooms, are varied, and all have terraces overlooking the village. Your room might have an iron bed, high and ornate and painted red, as well as a carved chest and refectory tables.

Via Cristoforo Colombo 30, 84017 Positano. ✆ **089-875066.** Fax 089-811798. www.sirenuse.it. 62 units. 253€–374€ ($225.95–$334) double; from 495€ ($442.05) suite. Rates include breakfast. AE, DC, MC, V. Parking 7.50€ ($15.65). **Amenities:** Restaurant (with outdoor terrace dining in summer); lounge; pool; new health club and spa; Jacuzzi; sauna; private excursion boat; room service; massage; babysitting; laundry/dry cleaning. *In room:* A/C, TV, minibar, hair dryer, safe.

EXPENSIVE

Albergo L'Ancora ✿   This hillside villa-turned-hotel has the atmosphere of a private club. The hotel has made massive improvements, including installing an elevator, and is fresh and sunny. Each guest room is like a bird's nest on a cliff, with a private terrace. Well-chosen antiques, such as fine inlaid desks, are mixed with contemporary pieces. All have well-kept bathrooms.

Via Colombo 36, 84017 Positano. ✆ **089-875318.** Fax 089-811784. 18 units. 210€–445€ ($187.55–$397.40) double. Rates include breakfast. AE, DC, MC, V. Free parking. Closed Nov–Apr 1. **Amenities:** Dining room; lounge; room service; laundry. *In room:* A/C, TV, minibar, hair dryer.

Albergo Ristorante Covo dei Saraceni   You'll find this rambling yellow-ochre building, a former fisherman's home, a few steps above the port and immediately above the beach. The side closest to the water culminates in a rounded tower of rough-hewn stone, which makes for an appealing view. The guest rooms range from medium-size to spacious, most with views over the water.

Via Regina Giovanna 5, 84017 Positano. ✆ **089-875400.** Fax 089-875878. www.starnet.it/covo. 58 units (showers only). 192€–238€ ($171.45–$212.55) double; 295€–480€ ($263.45–$428.65) junior suite. Rates include buffet breakfast. AE, DC, MC, V. Parking 15€ ($13.40). Closed mid-Nov to early Mar. **Amenities:** Restaurant; 2 bars; pool; room service; health club; babysitting; laundry. *In room:* A/C, TV, minibar, hair dryer, safe.

Hotel Poseidon ✿   This hotel was built in 1950 by the Aonzo family as their summer residence. In 1955, they enlarged it and transformed it into a hotel; its terraced gardens and panoramic views lure new visitors every year. It's charming, discreet, and elegant, with antique furniture and objects. The Aonzo family still owns and operates the hotel, lending personal service, luxury, and style to each spacious guest room, but without the high rates of San Pietro and Le Sirenuse.

Via Pasitea 148, 84017 Positano. ✆ **089-811111.** Fax 089-875833. www.starnet.it/poseidon. 52 units. 190€–250€ ($169.65–$223.25) double; 310€–410€ ($276.85–$366.15) suite. Rates include breakfast. AE, DC, MC, V. Parking 20€ ($17.85). Closed Jan 9–Apr 18. **Amenities:** Restaurant; bar; pool; health club; salon; room service; babysitting; laundry/dry cleaning. *In room:* A/C, TV, minibar, hair dryer, safe.

Hotel Villa Franca ✿ *(Finds)*   At the top of Positano, about a 10-minute walk from the center, this hotel is a little gem. It offers brightly decorated guest rooms and beautifully tiled bathrooms. The top floor contains somewhat small rooms, but they open onto little balconies with the best views. The finest rooms are the three deluxe corner units; they're more spacious and also have great views of the coast. Ten rooms are in the less inspired annex. The rooftop is the only spot in town with a 360° view of Positano.

Viale Pasitea 318, 84017 Positano. ℂ **089-875655.** Fax 089-875735. www.villafrancahotel.it. 38 units. 196€–310€ ($175.05–$276.85) double. Rates include breakfast. AE, DC, MC, V. Parking 16€ ($14.30). Bus: 318. **Amenities:** Romantic restaurant; bar; lounge; pool; new gym and wellness center; shuttle service to beach; room service; babysitting; laundry. *In room:* A/C, TV, minibar, hair dryer, safe.

Palazzo Murat ✦ This is a delightful little nest, offering quiet and serenity. It was once the retreat of Napoleon's brother-in-law, the king of Naples, who was notorious for confiscating statuary and church art from the former occupants—in this case, an order of Benedictine monks. The jasmine and bougainvillea are so profuse in its garden that they spill over their enclosing wall onto the arbors of the narrow street. The best (and most expensive) rooms are nos. 1 to 5 in the original 18th-century wing, which boasts high ceilings and antiques; the newer annex has smaller and less atmospheric rooms. Only the third-floor rooms have views of the sea. In summer, the hotel often offers classical music concerts on the patio.

Via dei Mulini 23, 84017 Positano. ℂ **089-875177.** Fax 089-811419. www.palazzomurat.it. 28 units. 200€–315€ ($178.60–$281.30) double. Rates include buffet breakfast. AE, DC, MC, V. Parking 20€ ($17.85) nearby. Closed Jan to 1 week before Easter. **Amenities:** Restaurant; lounge; excursion boat; room service; laundry. *In room:* A/C, TV, minibar, hair dryer, safe.

MODERATE

Albergo Miramare ✦ *Finds* On a cliff in the town center, the Miramare is for those who like the personal touch that only a small inn can provide. Guests stay in one of two tastefully furnished buildings amid citrus trees and flamboyant bougainvillea. Your bed (with a firm mattress) will most likely rest under a vaulted ceiling, and the white walls will be thick. The bathrooms have a sense of whimsy, with pink porcelain clamshells as washbasins (the water rushes from a sea-green ceramic fish with coral-pink gills). Nine rooms have a glass wall in the bathroom, so you can enjoy a panoramic sea view while soaking in the tub. The conversation piece is room 210's glass bathtub (once an aquarium) on a flowery terrace. The beach is a 3-minute walk away down a series of stairs.

Via Trara Genoino 27, 84017 Positano. ℂ **089-875002.** Fax 089-875219. 16 units. 180€–190€ ($160.75–$169.65) double. Rates include breakfast. AE, MC, V. Parking 12.50€ ($11.15). Closed Nov–Mar 15. **Amenities:** Lounge; room service; babysitting. *In room:* A/C, TV, minibar, hair dryer, safe.

Buca di Bacco ✦ This is one of the best moderately priced hotels in town, last renovated in 2000. A large terrace opens onto the beach, and you can enjoy cocktails while still in your swimsuit. The oldest and most expensive part, the Buca Residence, was an old seaside mansion at the dawn of the 19th century. The guest rooms are well furnished, most with small balconies facing the sea (the finest accommodations are six superior rooms with full seafront terraces).

Via Rampa Teglia 8, 84017 Positano. ℂ **089-875699.** Fax 089-875731. www.bucadibacco.it. 47 units. 165€–210€ ($147.35–$187.55) double; 275€–330€ ($245.60–$294.70) junior suite. Rates include buffet breakfast. AE, DC, MC, V. Parking 20€ ($17.85). Closed Nov 7–Mar 14. **Amenities:** Restaurant; bar; room service; babysitting; laundry. *In room:* A/C, TV, minibar, hair dryer, safe.

INEXPENSIVE

Casa Albertina Casa Albertina is currently undergoing a renovation that should leave it in great shape for summer 2002. This villa guesthouse, up a steep and winding road, offers a view of the coast from its perch. Guest rooms are gems, color-coordinated in mauve or blue and furnished with well-selected pieces, such as gilt mirrors and fruitwood end tables. Each has wide French doors leading out to a private balcony, and a few have Jacuzzis. You can breakfast on the terra-cotta tiled terrace.

Via Tavolozza 3, 84017 Positano. © 089-875143. Fax 089-811540. www.casaalbertina.it. 20 units. 144€–170€ ($128.60–$151.80) double with breakfast; 207€–227€ ($184.85–$202.70) double with breakfast and dinner. Breakfast and dinner compulsory Apr–Oct. AE, DC, DISC, MC, V. Parking 15€–17.50€ ($13.40–$15.65) nearby. **Amenities:** Restaurant; bar; room service; babysitting; laundry. *In room:* A/C, TV, minibar, hair dryer, safe.

WHERE TO DINE
EXPENSIVE
Buca di Bacco ✸ CAMPANIA/ITALIAN   Right on the beach you'll find one of Positano's top restaurants, opened just days after the end of World War II. Guests often stop for a drink in the bar before heading up to the dining room on a big covered terrace facing the sea. On display are fresh fish, special salads, and fruit, such as luscious black figs and freshly peeled oranges soaked in caramel. An exciting opener is a fresh seafood salad; you might prefer the *zuppa di cozze* (mussels) in a tangy sauce. Other items not to miss are linguine with lobster and *grillata del Golfo*, a unique mixed fish fry. The pasta dishes are homemade and the meats are well prepared with fresh ingredients. Finish with a *limoncello*, the lemon liqueur celebrated along the Amalfi Drive.

Via Rampa Teglia 8. © **089-875699.** Reservations required. Main courses 21€–32€ ($18.75–$28.60). AE, DC, MC, V. Daily 12:30–3:30pm and 8–11pm. Closed Oct 31–Mar.

La Cambusa ✸ CAMPANIA/SEAFOOD   Head here for local fish grilled to perfection. The local fishermen save only the finest catch for owner Luigi Russo (you can see them bringing in their catch early in the morning). The food items are prepared with care, and all the cooking is designed to bring out the natural flavor in the fish. Try the linguine with *cozze* (mussels) or an excellent *patelle* (limpets), a kind of Mediterranean shellfish. Little Neapolitan tomatoes are used for the sauces; they not only add extra flavor to the sauce but also enrich most of the fish dishes. For a special treat, ask for the zucchini soufflé flavored with basil and *parmigiano*.

Piazza Amerigo Vespucci 4. © **089-875432.** Reservations recommended. Main courses 10€–35€ ($8.95–$31.25). AE, DC, MC, V. Daily 12:30–3pm and 7pm–midnight.

Ristorante Le Sirenuse ✸✸ SOUTHERN ITALIAN   This stylish restaurant occupies the third floor of the stellar hotel of the same name (see above). Waiters will tell you that its terrace is "just 80 steps above the level of the sea." Bougainvillea, geraniums, hibiscus, and lemon trees are artfully massed in the terrace corners, and during nice weather the inside dining room closes completely in favor of the alfresco experience. The menu items revolve around what's available at the seafood markets and include linguine le Sirenuse, with lobster, scampi, and crayfish; linguine with artichoke hearts and scampi that's been cooked *en papillote* (in parchment); fresh salads and antipasti; and a grilled medley of fish and shellfish prepared for two or more. Expect lots of Mediterranean herbs, mozzarella, and homemade pastries.

In the Hotel Le Sirenuse, Via Cristoforo Colombo 30. © **089-875066.** Reservations required. Main courses 17€–38€ ($15.20–$33.95); fixed-price menu 60€ ($53.60). AE, DC, MC, V. Daily 1–2:30pm and 8–10pm. Closed Jan 6–Mar 15.

MODERATE

Chez Black SEAFOOD   Chez Black occupies a desirable position near the beach, and in summer it's in the heart of the action. The interior seems like an expensive yacht with varnished ribbing, a glowing sheath of softwood and brass, and semaphore symbols. A stone-edged aquarium holds fresh lobsters, and the racks and racks of local wines give you a vast choice. Seafood is the specialty, as well as a wide selection of pizzas. The best-known dish is the spaghetti with crayfish, but you might be tempted by linguine with fresh pesto, grilled sole, swordfish, or shrimp, plus an array of veal, liver, chicken, and beef dishes. One of the most prized and sought-after dishes is the spicy *zuppa di pesce* (fish soup)—a meal in itself, brimming with succulent finned creatures.

Via del Brigantino 19–21. © 089-875036. Reservations required in summer. Main courses 10€–20€ ($8.95–$17.85). AE, DC, MC, V. Daily 12:30–3pm and 7:30–11pm. Closed Jan–Feb 7.

INEXPENSIVE

Da Adolfo ★★ *(finds* SOUTHERN ITALIAN   Don't even think of coming here via car or taxi because you'd have to descend around 450 rugged stone steps from the highway above. The husband/wife team of Sergio (Italian) and Amanda (Australian) provide a 25-passenger motorboat to take you from Positano's main jetty across the water to the restaurant. (You'll recognize the boat by the large red fish on its side.) During the season when Da Adolfo is open, the boat departs daily every 30 minutes 10am to 1pm, and 4pm to whenever the last customer has left the beach, usually sometime between 6:30 and 8pm or even later on Saturdays in July and August (these late-summer Sat evenings are the only time dinner is served). The shuttle service is free, as is the use of the sands, changing rooms, and freshwater showers maintained by the restaurant. The only things you'll pay for are whatever you eat and drink in the restaurant and the optional rental of a beach chair 3.50€ ($3.15) and an umbrella 2.50€ ($2.25).

Da Adolfo seems like a beachfront restaurant in Greece, complete with pungent summery food, an utter lack of pretension, and sun and fun. Menu items focus on the fish, herbs, mozzarella, and zest of the Mediterranean. Especially appealing are the heaping bowls of mussel soup, slices of fresh mozzarella wrapped in lemon leaves, and *scialetti*, pasta with stewed clams and mussels.

Via Laurito, Località Laurito. © 089-875022. Reservations recommended. Main courses 9€–15€ ($8.05–$13.40). No credit cards. Late May–Sept daily 10am–6pm; July–Aug also Sat 8pm–midnight.

POSITANO AFTER DARK

Music on the Rocks, Spiaggia Grande Via Marina (© 089-875874), is designed on two levels, one of which contains a quieter piano bar. It's owned by the same man who owns the chic Chez Black (see above).

Similar in its choice of music, crowd, and setting is **L'Africana,** Vettica Maggiore (© 089-874042), in the nearby resort of Praiano, about 4 miles from Positano. Local fishermen come in during the most frenzied peak of the dancing and dredge a sinkhole at the edge of the dance floor with nets, pulling up a bountiful catch of seafood for the local restaurants. The contrast of new-age music with old-world folklore is as riveting as it is bizarre. Many chic guests from Positano arrive here by boat. Both clubs open nightly at around 10pm June to August, but only Friday and Saturday in May and September, and they're closed the rest of the year.

8 Amalfi ★★

61km (38 miles) SE of Naples, 18km (11 miles) E of Positano, 34km (21 miles) W of Salerno, 272km (169 miles) SE of Rome

From the 9th to 11th centuries, the seafaring Republic of Amalfi rivaled the great maritime powers of Genoa and Venice. Its maritime code, the Tavole Amalfitane, was followed in the Mediterranean for centuries. But raids by Saracens and a flood in the 14th century devastated the city. Amalfi's power and influence weakened, until it rose again in modern times as the major resort on the Amalfi Drive.

From its position at the slope of the steep Lattari hills, it overlooks the Bay of Salerno. The approach to Amalfi is dramatic, whether you come from Positano or from Salerno. Today Amalfi depends on tourist traffic, and the hotels and pensioni are located right in the milling throng of vacationers. The finest and most highly rated accommodations are on the outskirts.

ESSENTIALS

GETTING THERE   SITA **buses** run every 2 hours during the day from Sorrento, costing 2.05€ ($1.85) one way. There are also SITA bus connections from Positano, costing 1.15€ ($1.05) one way. You can get information about schedules in Amalfi by calling the bus terminal at the waterfront on Piazza Flavio Gioia (© **089-871009**).

By **car** from Positano, continue east along the narrow hairpin turns of the Amalfi Drive (S163).

VISITOR INFORMATION   The **tourist office** is at Corso delle Repubbliche Marinare 19–21 (© **089-871107**), open Monday to Friday 8:30am to 1:30pm and 3 to 5pm, and Saturday 8:30am to noon. It closes early in the winter months.

EXPLORING THE TOWN

Amalfi lays some claim to being a beach resort, and narrow public **beaches** flank the harbor. In addition, between rocky sections of the coast, many of the first-class and deluxe hotels have carved out small stretches of sand reserved for their guests. However, better and more expansive beaches are adjacent to the nearby villages of **Minori** and **Maiori,** a short drive along the coast. Those beaches are lined with a handful of cafes, souvenir kiosks, and restaurants that thrive mostly during the summer. You can reach the villages by buses leaving from Amalfi's Piazza Flavio Gioia at 30-minute intervals during the day. Expect to pay 1.50€ ($1.35) each way.

The **Duomo** ★, Piazza del Duomo (© **089-871059**), evokes Amalfi's rich past. It is named in honor of St. Andrew (Sant'Andrea), whose remains are said to be buried inside the crypt (see below). Reached by climbing steep steps, the cathedral is characterized by its black-and-white facade and mosaics. The one nave and two aisles are all richly baroque. The cathedral dates from the 11th century, although the present structure has been rebuilt. Its bronze doors were made in Constantinople, and its *campanile* (bell tower) is from the 13th century, erected partially in the Romanesque style. The Duomo is open daily 7:30am to 7pm and charges no admission.

You can also visit the **Cloister of Paradise (Chiostro del Paradiso)** ★★, to the left of the Duomo, originally a necropolis for members of the Amalfitan

The Eerie Emerald Grotto

Five kilometers (3 miles) west of Amalfi is the millennia-old **Emerald Grotto (Grotta di Smeraldo)** 🐾🐾. This cavern, known for its light effects, is a chamber of stalactites and stalagmites, some even underwater. You can visit daily 9am to 4pm, provided that the seas are calm enough not to bash boats to pieces as they try to land. The SITA bus (traveling toward Amalfi) departs from Piazza Flavio Gioia at 1-hour intervals throughout the day. En route to Sorrento, it stops at the Emerald Grotto. From the coastal road, you descend via an elevator and then take a boat ride traversing this eerie world for 5€ ($4.45). For more information about SITA buses, call ✆ **089-871009**. However, the best way to go is by boat all the way from Amalfi's docks; it costs 5€ ($4.45) round-trip.

"establishment." This graveyard dates from the 1200s and contains broken columns and statues, as well as sarcophagi. The aura is definitely Moorish, with a whitewashed quadrangle of interlaced arches. One of the treasures is fragments of Cosmatesque work, brightly colored geometric mosaics that once formed parts of columns and altars, a specialty of this region. The arches create an evocative setting for concerts, both piano and vocal, held on Friday nights July to September, with tickets at 1.50€ ($1.35). The cloister is open daily 9am to 7pm and charges 1.50€ ($1.35) admission. You reach the **crypt** from the cloister. Here lie the remains of St. Andrew—that is, everything except his face. The pope donated his face to St. Andrew's in Patras, Greece, but the back half of his head remained here.

A minor attraction, good for that rainy day, is the **Civic Museum (Museo Civico),** Town Hall Piazza Municipio (✆ **089-8736200**), which displays original manuscripts of the Tavoliere Amalfitane. This was the maritime code that governed the entire Mediterranean until 1570. Some exhibits relate to Flavio Gioia, Amalfi's most famous merchant adventurer. Amalfitani claim that he invented the compass in the 12th century. "The sun, the moon, the stars and—Amalfi," locals used to say. What's left from the "attic" of their once-great power is preserved here. The museum is free and open Monday to Saturday 9am to 1pm.

For your most **scenic walk** in Amalfi, start at Piazza del Duomo and head up Via Genova. The classic stroll will take you to the **Valley of the Mills (Valle dei Mulini),** so called because of the paper mills along its rocky reaches (the seafaring republic is said to have acquainted Italy with the use of paper). You'll pass by fragrant gardens and scented citrus groves. If the subject interests you, you can learn more details about the industry at the **Museum of Paper (Museo della Carta),** Via Valle dei Mulini (✆ **089-872615**), filled with antique presses and yellowing manuscripts from yesterday. It's open Tuesday to Thursday and Saturday and Sunday 9am to 1pm. Admission is 1€ (90¢).

SHOPPING

The coast has long been known for its **ceramics,** and the area at **Piazza del Duomo** is filled with hawkers peddling "regional" ware (which often means Asian). But the real thing is still made at nearby **Vietri sul Mare,** 13km (8 miles) west of Amalfi. The pottery made in Vietri is distinguished by its florid colors and sunny motifs. Vietri's best outlet is **Ceramica Solimene,** Via Madonna degli Angeli 7 (✆ **089-210243**), which has been producing quality terra-cotta ceramics for centuries. It's fabled for its production of lead-free surface tiles, dinner and cookware, umbrella holders, and stylish lamps. You might also check out **La Taverna Paradiso,** Via Diego Taiani 1 (© **089-212509**).

In Amalfi itself, look for **limoncello,** a sweet lemon liqueur that tastes best chilled. It's manufactured in town by the **Valle dei Mulin** factories. You can drop by their headquarters on Salita Chiarito 9 to buy a bottle or two (call © **089-873288** or 089-873211 for information). The Aceto Group's product is marketed under the **Limoncello Cata** label and sold at many outlets around town. A bottle of limoncello costs about 8€ ($7.15). At **Antichi Sapori d'Amalfi,** Piazza Duomo 39 (© **089-872062**), you get not only limoncello but also a full array of local products, such as jams, honeys, lemon perfumes, and grappa.

Looking for fancy paper and stationery? You can visit the showroom at **Antonio Cavaliere,** Via Fiume (© **089-871954**). It sells traditional cream-colored, high-fiber paper that seems appropriate for invitations to a royal wedding, as well as versions that amalgamate dried flowers, faintly visible through the surface, into the manufacturing process. The artisan here makes paper completely by hand, using antique methods.

One of Amalfi's best retail outlets is **Criscuolo,** Largo Scario 2 (© **089-871089**). Established by the ancestors of the present owners in 1935 as a site selling only cigarettes and newspapers, it has expanded to specialize in jewelry, including a charming collection of cameos, locally crafted ceramics, and general souvenirs.

At **La Grotta di Mansaniello,** Piazzetta degli Arsenale della Antica Repubblica (© **089-871929**), owner Francesco Mangieri (call him Mao), makes exquisite sculptures from ancient pieces of marble or a stalactite or stalagmite from one of the nearby sea grottoes.

WHERE TO STAY
VERY EXPENSIVE
Hotel Santa Caterina ✸✸✸   This mellow, traditional old choice still reigns supreme as the grande dame of Amalfi. Perched atop a cliff, Santa Caterina has an elevator that'll take you down to a private beach (or you can stroll down the paths past citrus groves and gardens). There you'll find a saltwater swimming pool, a sun deck, a gym, a cafe/bar, and an open-air restaurant. Built in 1880, the structure was destroyed by a rockslide on Christmas Eve 1902, prompting a rebuilding on a "safer" site in 1904. You're housed in the main structure or in one of the small "villas" in the citrus groves. The guest rooms are furnished in good taste, with an eye toward comfort. Most have private balconies facing the sea (the higher the floor, the better the view along the coast). The furniture respects the tradition of the house, and in every room is an antique piece. The bathrooms are spacious and luxurious.

S.S. Amalfitana 9, 84011 Amalfi. © **089-871012.** Fax 089-871351. www.hotelsantacaterina.it. 70 units. 245€–310€ ($218.80–$276.85) double; 545€–830€ ($486.70–$741.20) suite. Rates include breakfast. Dinner 50€ ($44.65) per person. AE, DC, MC, V. Parking 15€ ($13.40) in garage, free outside. **Amenities:** 2 restaurants (with outdoor dining); bar; lounge; saltwater pool by the sea; gym; room service; babysitting; laundry/dry cleaning *In room:* A/C, TV, minibar, hair dryer, safe.

EXPENSIVE
Hotel Belvedere ✸   Lodged below the coastal road outside Amalfi on the drive to Positano, the aptly named Belvedere has one of the best locations in the area. The house originated as a private villa in the 1860s and was transformed

by its present owners into a hotel in 1962. The guest rooms have terraces overlooking the water. They range in shape and size, each with a tiled bathroom. Signor Lucibello, who owns the hotel, sees to it that guests are happy. There's a shuttle bus into Amalfi. An interior elevator will take you down to the pool and the path to the sea.

Via Smeraldo, Conca dei Marini, 84010 Amalfi. ℂ **089-831282.** Fax 089-831439. www.belvederehotel.it. 36 units. 140€–180€ ($125–$160.75) double; 180€–220€ ($160.75–$196.45) suite. AE, DC, MC, V. Free parking. Closed Oct 20–Apr 20. **Amenities:** Restaurant; bar; pool; room service; laundry/dry cleaning. *In room:* A/C, TV, minibar, hair dryer, safe.

Hotel Luna Convento ★★ The second-best hotel in Amalfi (only the Santa Caterina, above, is better) boasts a 13th-century cloister said to have been founded by St. Francis of Assisi. Most of the building, however, was rebuilt in 1975. The long corridors, where monks of old (and, later, Wagner and Ibsen) used to tread, are lined with sitting areas used by the very unmonastic guests seeking a tan. The guest rooms have sea views, terraces, and modern furnishings, although many are uninspired in decor. The drop-dead-gorgeous pool, scooped out of the rocks overlooking the sea, is itself worth a stay here, as is the private beach.

Via Pantaleone Comite 33, 84011 Amalfi. ℂ **089-871002.** Fax 089-871333. www.lunahotel.it. 40 units. 166€–217€ ($148.25–$193.80) double with breakfast; 284€–518€ ($253.60–$462.55) suite. AE, DC, MC, V. Valet parking 16€ ($14.30) in garage, free outside. **Amenities:** Well-recommended restaurant with fabulous views; bar; nightclub; pool; room service; massage; babysitting; laundry/dry cleaning. *In room:* A/C, TV, minibar, hair dryer.

MODERATE

Excelsior Grand Hotel Three kilometers (2 miles) north of Amalfi at Pogerola, the Excelsior is a modern first-class hotel on a high mountain perch. Its structure is unconventional: an octagonal glass tower rising above the central lobby, with exposed mezzanine lounges and an open stairs. All its guest rooms are angled toward the view, so you get the first glimmer of dawn and the last rays of sunset. They're individually designed, with lots of space and good reproductions, as well as some antiques. Transportation to and from the private beach is provided by boat and bus for 8€ ($7.15).

Via Papa Leona, 84011 Amalfi. ℂ **089-830015.** Fax 089-830255. www.venere.it/amalfi/excelsior. 109 units. 115€–170€ ($102.70–$151.80) double. Rates include breakfast. AE, DC, MC, V. Free parking. **Amenities:** Dining room; bar; lounge; pool; room service; babysitting; laundry. *In room:* A/C, TV, minibar, hair dryer.

Hotel Marina Riviera Just 46m (50 yd.) from the beach, this hotel offers guest rooms with terraces overlooking the sea. Directly on the coastal road, it rises against the foot of the hills, with side verandas and balconies. Two adjoining public lounges are traditionally furnished, and a small bar provides drinks whenever you want them. The newly refurbished guest rooms are comfortable, with private balconies.

Via Comite 19, 84011 Amalfi. ℂ **089-872394.** Fax 089-871024. 20 units. 230€–300€ ($205.40–$267.90) double. Rates include breakfast. AE, MC, V. Free parking. Closed Nov–Mar. **Amenities:** Bar; lounge; room service; babysitting; laundry/dry cleaning. *In room:* A/C, TV, minibar, hair dryer, safe.

Hotel Miramalfi On the western edge of Amalfi, the Miramalfi lies below the coastal road on its own beach. The guest rooms are wrapped around the curving contour of the coast and have unobstructed sea views. The stone swimming pier (used for sunbathing, diving, and boarding motorboats for water-skiing) is down a winding cliffside path, past terraces of grapevines. Breakfast is served on one of the main terraces overlooking the sea, or your own balcony. Each room is well equipped, with built-in headboards and cool tile floors.

Via Quasimodo 3, 84011 Amalfi. ℂ **089-871588.** Fax 089-871287. www.miramalfi.it. 49 units. 124€–181€ ($110.75–$161.65) double; 176€–284€ ($157.15–$253.60) suite. Rates include breakfast. Dinner 85€–110€ ($75.90–$98.25) extra per person. AE, DC, MC, V. Parking 11€ ($9.80). Closed Nov. **Amenities:** Dining room; lounge; room service; laundry. *In room:* A/C, TV, minibar, hair dryer, safe.

INEXPENSIVE

Hotel Lidomare *(Value)* One of the best bargains in Amalfi, this pleasant small hotel is a few steps from the sea in a 13th-century building. The high-ceilinged guest rooms are airy and contain a scattering of modern furniture mixed with Victorian-era antiques. The Camera family extends a warm welcome. Breakfast is the only meal served, but you can order it until 11:30am.

Largo Duchi Piccolomini 9, 84011 Amalfi. ℂ **089-871332.** Fax 089-871394. www.lidomare.it. 15 units (8 with shower only). 90€–100€ ($80.35–$89.30) double. Rates include breakfast. AE, MC, V. Parking 12.50€ ($11.15). **Amenities:** Lounge. *In room:* A/C, TV, minibar, hair dryer, safe.

WHERE TO DINE

Gelateria Porto Salvo, Piazza Duomo 22 (ℂ **089-871655**), has the best-tasting gelato along the coast. The wild strawberry (*fragola selvatica*) and candied almond (*mandorle candite*) flavors are to die for. It's closed January to March.

MODERATE

Da Gemma ⭐ SEAFOOD/MEDITERRANEAN Located near the cathedral, Da Gemma is one of Amalfi's best restaurants, with a strong emphasis on fresh seafood. It has been overseen by members of the Grimaldi family for many generations, a fact that caused a lot of fuss when Princess Caroline of Monaco (whose family name is also Grimaldi, but with a link that's very distant) came to dine. The kitchen sends out platefuls of savory spaghetti, grilled or sautéed fish, casseroles, and an enduring favorite—zuppa di pesce, a full meal in its own right and prepared only for two. For dessert, order the *crostata* (pie with jam), the best you're ever likely to have; it's made with pine nuts and homemade marmalades of lemon, orange, and tangerine. In summer, the size of the intimate dining room more than doubles because of its expansion onto a terrace.

Via Frà Gerardo Sassi 9. ℂ **089-871345.** Reservations required. Main courses 12€–28€ ($10.70–$25). AE, DC, MC, V. Thurs–Tues 12:45–2pm and 7:45–10:30pm. Closed Jan 15–Feb 15.

La Caravella–Amalfi ⭐⭐ CAMPANIA The stone building containing this restaurant was a boatyard and marine warehouse during the 1400s. Today, it's one of the most prominent restaurants in town, with a menu featuring authentic Italian specialties. Examples are spaghetti Caravella with seafood sauce and fresh fish with lemon. An even better option is *scialatielli* (wide noodles) with a ragout of shellfish. Grilled fish is also baked in a salt crust to keep the full flavor inside. *Scaloppine alla Caravella* (veal) is served with a tangy clam sauce, and a healthy portion of zuppa di pesce is also ladled out. You can have a platter of the mixed fish fry, with crisp bits of shrimp and squid, followed by a lemon soufflé.

Via Matteo Camera 12. ℂ **089-871029.** Reservations required. Main courses 11€–25€ ($9.80–$22.35). AE, DC, MC, V. Daily noon–2pm and 7:30–10:30pm. Closed Nov, and Tues Sept–July.

Ristorante Luna Convento ITALIAN If you're unable to reserve a table at dinner, try for lunch at this stylish place; there's likely to be less of a crowd, and the sunny view over the town and the sea will be clearer. The restaurant is half indoor/half outdoor and staffed by consummate professionals. The menu items are usually based on seafood and include fresh seafood salad, seafood pastas, baked slices of sea bass or monkfish with herbs and garlic, and *risotto alla pescatore* (fisherman's rice); other choices are chicken, veal, beef, and pork. The antipasti are particularly tantalizing.

If you can't get a reservation even for lunch, perhaps try the restaurant's sibling, the **Ristorante Torre Saracena,** a very short walk away; any staff member will contact it for you. The prices, menu, and hours are more or less the same.

In the Hotel Luna Convento, Via Pantaleone Comite 33. (✆) 089-871002. Reservations recommended. Main courses 14€–18€ ($12.50–$16.05). AE, DC, MC, V. Daily noon–2pm and 7:30–9pm.

9 Ravello ★★★

275km (171 miles) SE of Rome, 66km (41 miles) SE of Naples, 29km (18 miles) W of Salerno

Ravello is one of the loveliest resorts along the Amalfi Drive. It has attracted artists, writers, and celebrities for years (Richard Wagner, Greta Garbo, André Gide, and even D. H. Lawrence, who wrote *Lady Chatterley's Lover* here). Ravello's reigning celebrity at the moment is Gore Vidal, who purchased a villa here as a writing retreat. William Styron set his novel *Set This House on Fire* here. Boccaccio dedicated part of the *Decameron* to Ravello, and John Huston used it as a location for his film *Beat the Devil,* with Bogie.

The sleepy village seems to hang 335m (1,100 ft.) up, between the Tyrrhenian Sea and some celestial orbit. You approach from Amalfi, 6km (3¾ miles) southwest, by a wickedly curving road cutting through the villa- and vine-draped hills that hem in the Valley of the Dragon.

ESSENTIALS

GETTING THERE **Buses** from Amalfi leave for Ravello from the terminal at the waterfront at Piazza Flavio Gioia (✆ **089-871016** for schedules and information) almost every hour 7am to 10pm, costing 1€ (90¢) one way.

If you have a **car** and are in Amalfi, take a circuitous mountain road north of the town (the road is signposted to Ravello).

VISITOR INFORMATION The **tourist office** is at Piazza del Duomo 10 (✆ **089-857096**), open May to September Monday to Saturday 8am to 8pm (to 7pm Oct–Apr).

SPECIAL EVENTS The hilltop town is known for its summer **classical music festivals.** Internationally famed artists sometimes appear. The venues range from the Duomo to the gardens of Villa Rufolo. Tickets, which you can buy at the tourist office, start at 20€ ($17.85).

SEEING THE SIGHTS

Although most of your time will be spent sunbathing, relaxing, strolling, and taking in the view, Ravello has a few outstanding sightseeing attractions too.

Villa Cimbrone ★★   One of Ravello's most aristocratic-looking palaces is the Villa Cimbrone. A 10-minute walk uphill from the main square, it's accessible only via a signposted footpath punctuated with steps and stairs. Built in the 15th century, it was occupied by a wealthy and eccentric Englishman, Lord Grimthorpe, who renovated it to its present status. During his tenure, he entertained such luminaries as Henrik Ibsen, D. H. Lawrence, Virginia Woolf, Greta Garbo, and Tennessee Williams. Lord Grimthorpe died in London in 1917, but his heirs followed his orders and buried his remains near his replica of the Temple of Bacchus.

When you reach the villa's entrance, ring the bell to summon the attendant. You'll be shown vaulted cloisters, evocative architecture, ruined chapels, and panoramic views over the Bay of Salerno. The view from some of the platforms in the garden is simply stunning. Gore Vidal, a nearby resident, referred to the view as "the most beautiful in the world."

You can also stay at the villa because it's now a hotel (see below).

Via Santa Chiara 26. ⟨C⟩ **089-857459.** Admission 4€ ($3.55). Daily 9am–5:30pm.

Villa Rufolo ⋆⋆   The Villa Rufolo was named for the patrician family who founded it in the 11th century. Once the residence of kings and popes, such as Hadrian IV, it's now remembered chiefly for its connection with Richard Wagner. He composed an act of *Parsifal* here in a setting he dubbed the "Garden of Klingsor." He also lived and composed at Palazzo Sasso (see below). Boccaccio was so moved by the spot that he included it as background in one of his tales. The Moorish-influenced architecture evokes Granada's Alhambra, and the large tower was built in what's known as the "Norman–Sicilian" style. You can walk through the flower gardens leading to lookout points over the memorable coastline.

Piazza Duomo. ⟨C⟩ **089-857657.** Admission 3€ ($2.70). Daily 9am–6pm (until 8pm Apr–Sept).

Duomo   It's unusual for such a small place to have a cathedral, but Ravello boasts one because it was once a major bishopric. The building itself dates from the 11th century, but its bronze doors are the work of Barisano da Trani and were crafted in 1179. Its **campanile** (bell tower) was erected in the 13th century. One of its major treasures is the pulpit of the Rufolo family, decorated with intricate mosaics and supported by spiral columns resting on the backs of half a dozen white marble lions. This is the work of Nicoló di Bartolomeo da Foggia in 1272. Another less intricate pulpit from 1130 features two large mosaics of Jonah being eaten and regurgitated by a dragonlike green whale. To the left of the altar is the **Chapel of San Pantaleone (Cappella di San Pantaleone),** the patron saint of Ravello to whom the cathedral is dedicated. His "unleakable" blood is preserved in a cracked vessel. The saint was beheaded at Nicomedia on July 27, A.D. 290. When Ravello holds a festival on that day every year, the saint's blood is said to liquefy. A minor museum of religious artifacts is also on-site.

Piazza Duomo. Duomo free; museum 2.50€ ($2.25). Duomo daily 8am–7pm. Museum Easter–Oct daily 9am–1pm and 3–7pm.

SHOPPING

When Senator Hillary Rodham Clinton came to visit and to call on Gore Vidal, she also visited **Cammeo,** Piazza Duomo 9 (⟨C⟩ **089-857461**), where owner Giorgio Filocamo designed a coral brooch for her. He can make one for you too, or sell you any number of pieces of jewelry in cameos and corals. In the back of the shop, he has collected his most treasured pieces, all worthy of a museum.

Brothers Marco and Piero Cantarella are waiting for you at **Ceramu,** Via Roma 66 (⟨C⟩ **089-858181**), where they'll sell you intricate mosaics in majolica. They also make garden tables with wrought iron or mosaic-bordered mirrors with wood.

WHERE TO STAY

The **Ristorante Garden** (see "Where to Dine," below) also rents rooms.

VERY EXPENSIVE

Hotel Palumbo/Palumbo Residence ⋆⋆ This former 12th-century palace is now a charming boutique hotel. It has been favored by the famous since composer Richard Wagner persuaded the Swiss owners, the Vuilleumiers, to take in paying guests. If you stay, you'll understand why Humphrey Bogart, Ingrid Bergman, Tennessee Williams, and a young John and Jacqueline Kennedy found it ideal. D. H. Lawrence even wrote part of *Lady Chatterley's Lover* while staying here.

The hotel offers gracious living in its drawing rooms full of English and Italian antiques. Most of the snug but elegant guest rooms have their own terraces with glorious views. The original Hotel Palumbo contains by far the more glamorous accommodations; seven functional rooms are in the annex in the garden, but a few have sea views. The bathrooms are often a delight, with gigantic tubs and dual basins.

Via San Giovanni del Toro 16, 84010 Ravello. ℂ **089-857244.** Fax 089-858133. www.hotel-palumbo.it. 21 units. Hotel 400€–600€ ($357.20–$535.80) double; 590€–890€ ($526.85–$794.75) suite. Residence 190€–390€ ($169.65–$348.25) double. Rates include breakfast and dinner. AE, DC, MC, V. Parking 15€ ($13.40). **Amenities:** Open-air restaurant; lounge; access to pool nearby, room service; babysitting; laundry. *In room:* A/C, TV, minibar, hair dryer, safe.

Hotel Rufolo ⋆ *Finds* This little gem of an inn is evocative of a Ravello of an earlier era. Recently enlarged and modernized, the hotel lies in the center between cloisters of pine trees of the Villa Rufolo, from which the hotel takes its name, and the road leading to the Villa Cimbrone. Mr. Schiavo and his family take good care of their guests. The view from the sun decks is superb—chairs are placed on a wide terrace. The attractive pool sits amid an elegantly landscaped garden, overlooking the sea. Some guest rooms are spacious and others are cramped; the suites have Jacuzzis.

Via San Francesco 1, 84010 Ravello. ℂ **089-857133.** Fax 089-857935. www.hotel-rufolo.it. 32 units. 220€–255€ ($196.45–$227.70) double; 410€ ($366.15) suite. Rates include breakfast. AE, DC, MC, V. Parking 10€ ($8.95). **Amenities:** Restaurant; bar; lovely pool; room service; babysitting; laundry/dry cleaning. *In room:* A/C, TV, minibar, hair dryer.

Palazzo Sasso ⋆⋆⋆ At this opulent, idyllic retreat, you're coddled in luxury and comfort. Local resident Gore Vidal calls it a "posh B&B," but it's larger than the other top-notch choice in town, the Palumbo (above). Built in the 1100s for an aristocratic family, this palace began functioning as a hotel in 1880. Richard Wagner composed parts of *Parsifal* here, and Ingrid Bergman found a snug retreat here with producer Roberto Rossellini back in the days when their affair was causing a scandal. The hotel fell into ruin in 1978, but in 1997 it reopened thanks to a flood of money from Virgin Airlines top-dog Richard Branson; it welcomed Plácido Domingo as its first guest. The Sasso is perched 305m (1,000 ft.) above the coast and evokes a Moorish pavilion. The guest rooms are luxurious, even if not overly large, and the views of the Mediterranean compensate for the lack of space. Ask for room nos. 1, 201, 204, or 301, or the grand suite, 304, because they have the most all-encompassing views. The marble bathrooms with brass fixtures come with scales, large tubs, robes, and dual basins.

Via San Giovanni del Toro 28, 84010 Ravello. ℂ **089-818181.** Fax 089-858900. www.palazzosasso.com. 44 units. 220€–255€ ($196.45–$227.70) double; from 410€ ($366.15) suite. Rates include continental breakfast. AE, DC, MC, V. Free parking. **Amenities:** Acclaimed restaurant (open in high season only); bar; 2 pools; room service; massage; babysitting; laundry/dry cleaning. *In room:* A/C, TV, minibar, hair dryer, safe.

Villa Cimbrone ★★ Here you'll find no restaurant and none of the extras offered by more modern hotels. In fact, you can't even drive up to its entrance because there's no road. But despite the inconvenience, few connoisseurs of art and literature would pass up the chance to stay in one of the most historically evocative villas in Ravello (see "Seeing the Sights," above). Amid gardens dotted with statuary, ancient ruins, and late-19th-century re-creations of Greek and Roman temples, it contains only a handful of rooms—high-ceilinged and gracefully furnished with antiques and fine fabrics, and first-rate bathrooms. Most rooms enjoy views over the countryside. The best choices are nos. 10 and 11. The Garbo Suite is the most requested (she had a tryst here in 1938 with her then-lover Leopold Stokowski before dumping him). More recently, Senator Hillary Rodham Clinton slept here. If you arrive by car, park it in the municipal parking lot, a short walk downhill from Ravello's main square, and then call the hotel for a porter who will haul your luggage up the winding paths to the villa.

Via Santa Chiara 26, 84010 Ravello. © 089-857459. Fax 089-857777. www.villacimbrone.it. 13 units. 200€–250€ ($178.60–$223.25) double; 325€ ($290.25) suite. Rates include breakfast. AE, DC, MC, V. Closed Dec–Mar. From the main square of Ravello, walk uphill along a well-marked footpath for an arduous 10 min. **Amenities:** Lounge; room service. *In room:* Minibar, hair dryer, safe.

MODERATE

Hotel Giordano e Villa Maria The older but more obviously modernized of these two hotels is the Giordano, built in the late 1700s as a private manor house of the family that runs it today. In the 1970s, the owners bought the neighboring 19th-century Villa Maria, and the two operate as quasi-independent hotels with shared facilities. Accommodations in the Villa Maria are generally better than those in the Giordano and usually contain high ceilings and antiques and offer sea views. However, a few of the rooms at Villa Maria, rented to late arrivals when the other units are booked, are rather cramped with less-than-adequate mattresses. The Giordano's rooms have garden views and reproductions of traditional furniture. The beach is a 15-minute walk along ancient paths (you can also take a public bus from Ravello's central square every hour).

Via Trinità 14, Via Santa Chiara 2, 84010 Ravello. © 089-857255. Fax 089-857071. www.villamaria.it. 48 units. Hotel Giordano 129€–155€ ($115.20–$138.40) double; 190€–362€ ($169.65–$323.25) suite. Villa Maria 160€–201€ ($142.90–$179.50) double; 310€–407€ ($276.85–$363.45) suite. AE, DC, MC, V. Free parking. **Amenities:** 2 restaurants; bar; pool; room service; laundry. *In room:* A/C, TV, minibar, hair dryer, safe.

INEXPENSIVE

Albergo Toro *Value* Just off the village square with its cathedral, this real bargain is a charming small villa that has been converted into a hotel. You enter the Toro through a garden. It has semimonastic architecture, boasting deeply set arches, long colonnades, and a tranquil character. The guest rooms are a bit plain but still offer reasonable comfort, each containing a small bathroom. The owner is especially proud of the Mediterranean meals he serves.

Viale Wagner 3, 84010 Ravello. © and fax 089-857211. 9 units (showers only). 112.50€ ($100.45) double with breakfast. Dinner 75€ ($67) extra. DC, MC, V. Closed Nov 6–Mar. **Amenities:** Lounge. *In room:* Hair dryer.

Hotel Parsifal This little hotel incorporates part of a convent founded in 1288 by Augustinian monks. The cloister, with stone arches and a tile walk, has a multitude of potted flowers and vines, and the garden spots are the favorites. There are chairs arranged for watching the setting sun. The living rooms have bright and comfortable furnishings, set against pure white walls. The guest rooms, though small, are tasteful. A few have terraces.

Via G. D'Anna 5, 84010 Ravello. ℂ 089-857144. Fax 089-857972. www.hotelparsifal.com. 19 units (some with shower only, some with tub only). 85€–125€ ($75.90–$111.65) double with breakfast and dinner. AE, DC, MC, V. Free parking. **Amenities:** Dining room; lounge; pool. *In room:* TV.

WHERE TO DINE
Most guests take meals at their hotels. But the following are worth a special trip.

Cumpa' Cosimo CAMPANIA   Here's where you're likely to find everyone from the electrician down the street to a movie star looking for the best home cooking in town. Pictures of Jackie O still decorate the walls, a reminder of a long-ago visit. Gore Vidal, who often dines here, recommends it to his visiting guests. The restaurant was opened in 1929 by a patriarch known affectionately as Cumpa' (godfather) Cosimo and his wife, Cumma' (godmother) Chiara. Today their daughter, Netta Bottone, runs the place, turning out well-flavored regional food in generous portions. Menu items include homemade versions of seven pastas, served with your choice of seven sauces. Any of these might be followed by a mixed grill of fish, giant prawns, roasted lamb seasoned with herbs, zuppa di pesce, *frittura di pesce* (fish fry), veal scaloppine, or beefsteak with garlic and wine sauce. Fresh local artichokes, asparagus, and mushrooms are among the vegetables available seasonally.

Via Roma 44–46. ℂ 089-857156. Reservations recommended. Main courses 11€–24€ ($9.80–$21.45). AE, DC, MC, V. Daily noon–3pm and 6:30–10pm.

Ristorante Garden CAMPANIA   This pleasant restaurant's greatest claim to fame was in 1962, when Jacqueline Kennedy dined here with the owner of Fiat. Today some of that old glamour is still visible on the verdant terrace, which was designed to cantilever over the cliff below. The Mansi family offers well-prepared meals that might include one of four kinds of spaghetti, cheese crepes, an array of soups, a well-presented antipasto table, brochettes of grilled shrimp, a mixed fish fry, and sole prepared in several ways.

The restaurant also rents 10 well-scrubbed **guest rooms,** each with its own phone, bathroom, and terrace with a view, for 62.40€ to 78€ ($55.70–$69.65) for a double, including breakfast.

Via Boccaccio 4, 84010 Ravello. ℂ 089-857226. Main courses 7.50€–14€ ($6.70–$12.50). AE, DC, MC, V. Apr–Sept daily noon–3pm and 7:30–10pm; Nov–Mar Wed–Mon noon–3pm and 7:30–10pm.

10 Paestum & Its Glorious Greek Temples ★★★
40km (25 miles) S of Salerno, 100km (62 miles) SE of Naples, 304km (188 miles) SE of Rome

The ancient city of Paestum (Poseidonia) dates from 600 B.C., founded by colonists from the Greek city of Sybaris. It was abandoned for centuries and fell to ruins. But the remnants of its past, excavated in the mid–18th century, are the finest heritage left from the Greek colonies that settled in Italy. The roses of Paestum, praised by the ancients, bloom two times yearly, splashing the landscape of the city with scarlet, a good foil for the salmon-colored temples that still stand in the archaeological garden.

Paestum is an easy day trip from almost anywhere in Campania, even from Naples. You need only an hour or two to explore the temples, and another hour for the museum. Break up the two sights with lunch at Nettuno (see "Where to Dine," below).

ESSENTIALS

GETTING THERE   You must go to Salerno to get to Paestum via public transportation. You can catch a southbound **train,** which departs Salerno with a stop at Paestum about every 2 hours. For schedules, call © **848-888088** toll-free in Italy. A one-way fare is 2.10€ ($1.90), and the journey takes an hour. The **bus** from Salerno leaves from Piazza Concordia (near the rail station) about every 30 minutes. Call © **089-487111** for information. A one-way fare is 2.40€ ($2.15).

By car, from Salerno take S18 south.

VISITOR INFORMATION   The **tourist office** is at Via Magna Grecia 151–156 (© **0828-811016**), in the archaeological zone, open Monday to Saturday 8am to 2pm.

EXPLORING THE TEMPLES

The **basilica** 🏛🏛🏛 is a Doric temple from the 6th century B.C., Italy's oldest temple from the ruins of the Hellenic world. The basilica is characterized by 9 Doric pillars in front and 18 on the sides (they're about 1.5m/5 ft. in diameter). The walls and ceiling long ago gave way to decay. Animals were sacrificed to the gods on the altar.

The **Temple of Neptune (Tempio di Nettuno)** 🏛🏛🏛 is the most impressive of the Greek ruins at Paestum. It and the Temple of Hephaestus ("Theseum") in Athens remain the best-preserved Greek temples in the world, both from around 450 to 420 B.C. Six columns in front are crowned by an entablature, and there are 14 columns on each side. The **Temple of Ceres (Tempio di Cerere)** 🏛🏛, from the 6th century B.C., has 34 columns still standing and a large altar for sacrifices to the gods.

The temple zone is open daily 9am to sunset.

You can visit the **National Archaeological Museum of Paestum (Museo Archeologico Nazionale di Paestum),** Via Magna Grecia 169 (© **0828-811023**), across from the Ceres Temple. It displays the metopes removed from the treasury of the Temple of Hera (Juno) and some of southern Italy's finest tomb paintings from the 4th century B.C. The Diver's Tomb is an extraordinary example of painting from the first half of the 5th century B.C. The museum is open daily 9am to 7pm (it's closed the first and third Mon of every month). Admission is 4€ ($3.55), but there is also a cumulative ticket, which includes the museum and the archaeological area, for 6€ ($5.35).

New discoveries have revealed hundreds of Greek tombs, which have yielded many Greek paintings. Archaeologists have called the finds astonishing. In addition, other excavated tombs were found to contain clay figures in a strongly impressionistic vein.

WHERE TO STAY

Strand Hotel Schuhmann 🏛   If you'd like to stay at a beachside resort while you devote more time to Italy's archaeological past, try the Strand. Set in a pine grove removed from traffic noises, it has a large terrace with a view of the sea and a subtropical garden that overlooks the Gulf of Salerno and the Amalfi Coast to Capri. Its guest rooms are well furnished and maintained, each with a balcony or terrace. The bathrooms are neatly kept. Guests get use of the beach facilities and deck chairs.

Via Marittima, 84063 Paestum. © **0828-851151.** Fax 0828-851183. www.hotelschuhmann.com. 53 units (tubs only). 114€–182€ ($101.80–$162.55) double. AE, DC, MC, V. Free parking. **Amenities:** Restaurant; lounge; room service; laundry. *In room:* A/C, TV, minibar, hair dryer, safe.

WHERE TO DINE

Nettuno Ristorante CAMPANESE/SEAFOOD   Nettuno's only drawback is that throughout most of the year it's open only for lunch. At the edge of Paestum's ruins, it's built from the same beige-colored limestone blocks that were used by the ancient Romans. Its core consists of an ancient tower built in the 2nd century B.C. Seated in the dining room or garden ringed with vines, oleander, and pines, you can order *crespolina*, a savory crepe stuffed with mozzarella and Mediterranean herbs; succulent pastas; a wide selection of fish; and veal, chicken, and beef dishes.

Via Principe di Piemonte, Zona Archeologica. ℂ **0828-811028.** Reservations recommended. Main courses 5€–22.50€ ($4.45–$20.10). AE, DC, MC, V. July–Aug daily noon–3:30pm and 8–11:30pm; Sept–June daily noon–3:30pm.

15

Apulia

The district of Apulia encompasses the southeasternmost section of Italy, the heel of the boot. For many travelers, it's the gateway to Greece from the port of Brindisi. Apulia is little known but fascinating, embracing some of Italy's most poverty-stricken areas and some of its most interesting sections (such as the Trulli District).

The land is rich in archaeological discoveries, and some of its cities were shining sapphires in the crown of *Magna Graecia* (Greater Greece). The Ionian and Adriatic Seas wash up on its shores, which have seen the arrival of diverse civilizations and of the armies seeking to conquer this access route to Rome. The Goths, Germanic hordes, Byzantines, Spanish, and French sought to possess it. Saracen pirates and Turks came to see what riches they might find.

Apulia offers the beauty of marine grottoes and caverns, as well as turquoise seas and sandy beaches. Forests of wind-twisted pines, huge old carob trees, junipers, sage, and rosemary grow near the sea; orchards, vineyards, grain fields, and vegetable gardens grow inland. Flocks of sheep and goats dot the landscape.

In recent years, Apulia has been caught in the eye of the "Albanian Hurricane." Political turmoil and economic upheaval have sent tens of thousands of Albanians to commandeer yachts, ferries, and tugboats and cross the narrow Strait of Otranto into this region. This has adversely affected tourism, leading to massive hotel booking cancellations, presumably because of the fear that the deluge of refugees has made the area undesirable.

Regional officials stress that there's nothing to worry about and promise that Apulia is now more of a bargain than ever. The Albanian presence in most tourist zones is barely noticeable, if at all. Actually, most of the refugees have moved elsewhere or are housed in camps away from the mainstream sites. The regional tourist commissioner, Rossana Di Bello, assured us, "Visitors can visit our land and find peace and tranquility."

1 Foggia: A Base for Exploring the Gargano

97km (60 miles) W of Bari, 174km (108 miles) NE of Naples, 362km (224 miles) SE of Rome

Foggia is the capital of Capitanata, Apulia's northernmost province. A history of tragedy, including a serious earthquake in 1731 and extensive bombing during World War II, has left Foggia with little in the way of attractions, although it's a good base for exploring nearby attractions such as Lucera and Troia. You can also use the city as a base for a day's drive around the Gargano Peninsula. Aside from the ancient cathedral, the city is pleasant but thoroughly modern, with parks and wide boulevards and a decent selection of hotels and restaurants. This is a good place to take care of business—rent a car, exchange money, mail postcards, or whatever, because it's relatively safe, easy to get around, and centrally located.

The 12th-century **Cattedrale della Santa Maria Icona Vetere (𝒞 0881-773482)** lies off Piazza del Lago. The province's largest cathedral, it was constructed in an unusual Norman and Apulian baroque style. Today, after extensive repairs and expansions, the Duomo is an eclectic mix of styles. The present *campanile* **(bell tower)** was built to replace the one destroyed in the 1731 quake. The crypt was built in the Romanesque style, and some of its "excavation" was compliments of Allied bombers in 1943. The cathedral is open daily 8am to noon and 5 to 8pm; admission is free.

The other notable attraction is the **Civic Museum (Museo Civico),** Piazza Nigri (𝒞 **0881-726245**), featuring exhibits on Apulia's archaeology and ethnography. It's housed in the remains of the residence of Frederick II and is open daily 9am to 1pm and also Monday, Tuesday, Thursday, and Friday 5 to 7pm. Admission is 2€ ($1.80).

ESSENTIALS

GETTING THERE   Foggia is at the crossroads of the Lecce–Bologna **rail** line and the Bari-Naples run, so it's easy to get here from just about anywhere in Italy. Trains from Naples arrive four times daily; the trip lasts about 3 hours and costs 10€ ($8.95) one way. Trains arrive from Bari every hour during the day, taking 1½ hours and costing 7€ ($6.25) one way. There are also three trains daily from Rome, which take 4 hours and cost 25€ ($22.35). Trains arrive at Foggia's **Stazione Centrale** in the center of Piazza Vittorio Veneto (𝒞 **848-8880888**).

If you have a **car,** follow Route 90 from Naples directly to Foggia. From Bari, take A14.

VISITOR INFORMATION   The **tourist office** is at Via Senatore Emilio Perrone 17 (𝒞 **0881-723650**), open Monday to Friday 8am to 1pm. In the off-season it's open only in the mornings.

WHERE TO STAY

Grand Hotel Cicolella   The Cicolella is the town's best hotel. The Victorian-era building has been modernized, with glass and marble dominating. The guest rooms are large and pleasantly decorated, each with a small tiled bathroom.

Viale XXIV Maggio 60, 71100 Foggia. 𝒞 **0881-566111.** Fax 0881-778984. 106 units. 170€–192€ ($151.80–$171.45) double; from 192€ ($171.45) suite. AE, DC, V. Parking 10€ ($8.95). **Amenities:** Restaurant; bar; room service; babysitting; laundry. *In room:* A/C, TV, minibar, hair dryer, safe.

Hotel President   About a mile north of the center, this hotel from 1970 is the town's third-best option, ranking under Cicolella and White House. Unpretentious and reasonably comfortable, with a staff that speaks no English (although this shouldn't prove too much of a problem), it provides a tranquil environment removed from urban congestion. The guest rooms are angular and functional, with compact tiled bathrooms.

Viale degli Aviatori 130, 71100 Foggia. 𝒞 **0881-618010.** Fax 0881-1617930. 128 units. 86€ ($76.80) double. Rates include breakfast. DC, MC, V. Parking 3€ ($2.70). Bus: 18 or 19. **Amenities:** Restaurant; bar; room service; babysitting. *In room:* A/C, TV, minibar.

White House Hotel   This first-class hotel is in the heart of Foggia, a few steps from the train station, and it's a good choice for convenience. Its housekeeping is the finest in town, and the guest rooms are comfortably furnished, though

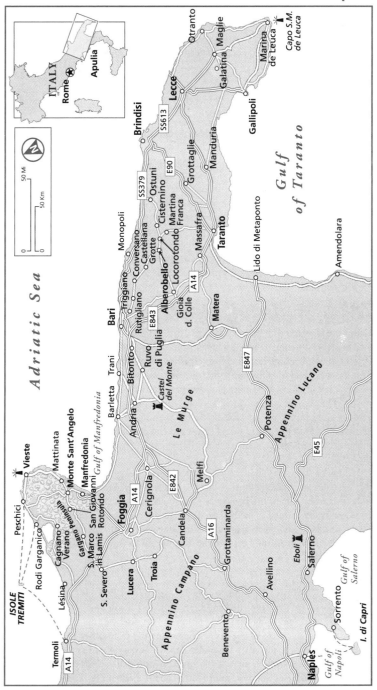

lacking any particular style. They range from small to medium, with compact tiled bathrooms.

Via Sabotino 24, 71100 Foggia. © **0881-721644.** Fax 0881-721646. 40 units. 130€–170€ ($116.10–$151.80) double. AE, DC, MC, V. Parking 10€ ($8.95) nearby. **Amenities:** Bar; lounge; room service; laundry. *In room:* A/C, TV, minibar, hair dryer.

WHERE TO DINE

Two great choices are in the Grand Hotel Cicolella (see above): the **Ristorante Cicolella** and the **Ristorante Infiera.**

Il Ventaglio ★★ ITALIAN   This elegant restaurant is known for its inventive cuisine, among the finest in southern Italy. The chef, who adds a personal touch to everything, says she "never makes the same dish twice." Some of her specialties are *fagottino di pesce* (fish) and *agnolotti ripieni* (pasta stuffed with chopped fish or seasonal vegetables). The *orecchiette* (ear-shaped pasta) comes in clam sauce with the freshest seasonal vegetables. Here's also a chance to sample some of the finest cheeses in the area, such as pecorino, scamorza, and manteca. Service, depending on when you happen to arrive, might be sweet and charming or hysterically overworked.

Via Gaetano Postiglione 6E. © **0881-661500.** Reservations recommended. Main courses 11€–16€ ($9.80–$14.30). AE, DC, MC, V. Tues–Sat 12:30–2:45pm and 8:30–10:45pm; Sun 12:30–2:45pm. Closed Jan 1–9 and Aug 13–31.

2 The Gargano Peninsula ★★★

Called the Gargano, this mountainous wooded promontory is the "spur" of Italy. The best time to come is autumn, when you can enjoy the colors of the Umbra Forest (Foresta Umbra), featuring maples, ashes, cedars, and chestnuts. The world here has a timeless quality. You'll find pristine salt lakes at Lesina and Varano, where you can enjoy swimming and watersports in the mild climate and calm waters. The coast is a series of cliffs, rocks, caves, islets, and beaches. Vegetable gardens grow inland on a landscape dotted with flocks of sheep and goats. In addition to nature's wild and varied landscape, the promontory is rich in historic interest, boasting monuments that are Byzantine, Romanesque, Norman, and medieval.

It'll take a leisurely 7 hours to drive around the Gargano, staying on Route 89. We consider this sometimes-difficult route among the most scenic drives in Italy. In ancient times, the peninsula was an island, until the sediment from a river eventually formed a "bridge" linking it to the mainland. Train service into the peninsula is limited to a private spur along the northwestern coast, so for travelers who want to fully explore the area by bus or car, the gateway will be Manfredonia.

ESSENTIALS

GETTING THERE   We strongly advise readers to rent a car for exploring this difficult-to-access corner of rural southern Italy. But if you absolutely insist on public transport, get ready for some confusion, long delays, and schedules that change frequently. Most of the rail traffic emanating from other parts of Italy originates in Foggia and, to a lesser degree, San Severo. From either of those points, transport by bus or by rail continues to sites that include Manfredonia and Monte Sant'Angelo. For information about these lines, contact either **Ferrovia dello Stato** at © **848-888088;** or, for information about the smaller, local train lines that operate only within the Gargano Peninsula, contact **Ferroveria del Gargano** at © **0881-725188** or 0882-221414.

Alternatively, some sites within the Gargano Peninsula are best accessed by bus lines, or by a combination of bus and train service. For information about buses, and their connections to train lines throughout Gargano, contact **SITA** or **ATAF** (many of their routes and schedules are interconnected and overlap) at 📞 **0881-773117.** The routes include service, usually at intervals of between 60 and 90 minutes every day, between such major settlements as Foggia, Manfredonia, and Vieste, with less frequent connecting service to such hamlets as Mattinata, Monte Sant'Angelo, and Peschici.

If you happen not to have rented a car, you might completely abandon the idea of hassling with the local bus and train routes, and opt instead for participation in one of the generalized tours offered to the peninsula at large. These are offered, among others, by **Gargano Viaggi,** Piazza Roma 7 (📞 **0884-708501**), or **SITA** (📞 **0881-773117**). Both of them, during the peak months of June to mid-September, offer somewhat rushed and anonymous bus tours that depart from Vieste, and follow the coastal road of the Gargano Peninsula, with emphasis on the region's natural beauty, for around 30€ ($26.80) per person. Advance reservations are important.

If you have a **car,** you'll note that three roads dissect the peninsula and connect its major sights. Route 89 runs an 130km (81-mile) circuit around the coast. Route 528 cuts through the heart of the peninsula, starting 8km (5 miles) west of Peschici on the northern coast and running south through the Umbra Forest before ending at Route 272 just west of Monte Sant'Angelo. Route 272 slices east to west through the southern part of the region, from San Marco in Lamis in the west through San Giovanni Rotondo and over to Monte Sant'Angelo, ending on the coast near Punta Rossa.

VISITOR INFORMATION   The **Manfredonia tourist office** is at Piazza del Popolo 11 (📞 **0884-581998**), open Monday to Saturday 9am to 1:30pm. Here you can pick up a map and get advice about touring the Gargano district, including bus and train schedules if you're not driving on your own (important because, in most towns, there are no actual bus stations). The **Vieste tourist office** is at Piazza Kennedy 1 (📞 **0884-708806**), open Monday to Friday 8:30am to 1:30pm. It'll give you information about the many excursion possibilities, especially the excellent beaches along the southern shore.

MANFREDONIA
43km (27 miles) NE of Foggia, 119km (74 miles) NW of Bari, 217km (135 miles) NE of Naples

If you approach Gargano from the south, your first stop, perhaps at lunchtime, will be **Manfredonia,** a small port known for its castle. It was named for Manfred, illegitimate son of Frederick II. In the heyday of the Crusades, this was a bustling port, with knights and pilgrims leaving for the Levant. Much later, the town was noted in World War I documents as the place where the first blow of the conflict was launched—the Austrians bombed the rail station in 1915. Manfredonia is on a rail route from Foggia.

After arriving in town, turn right and go along Viale Aldo Moro to Piazza Marconi. Across the square, Corso Manfredi leads to the **Manfredonia Castello,** built for Manfred and later enlarged by the Angevins. Other bastions were constructed in 1607 by the Spanish, who feared an invasion from Turkey. Regrettably, their fortifications didn't do the job: The Turks arrived in 1620 and destroyed a lot of Manfredonia, leaving only some of its former walls standing. Today the castle is home to the **National Museum of Manfredonia (Museo Nazionale di Manfredonia;** 📞 **0884-587838),** open daily (except the first and fourth Mon of each month) 8:30am to 7:30pm; it charges 2.50€ ($2.25) for admission. The archaeological remnants and finds include a collection of Stone Age objects from area villages, the most striking of which are the Daunian stelae, stone slabs decorated like human torsos and topped with stone heads, the legacy of the Daunian civilization that settled in the region around the 9th century B.C.

Three kilometers (2 miles) outside town is **Santa Maria di Siponto,** a church in a setting of pine woods that once was the site of the ancient city of Siponte, abandoned after being ravaged by an earthquake and a plague. The church, dating from the 11th century, is in the Romanesque style, showing both Tuscan and Arabic influences.

WHERE TO STAY

Hotel Gargano *(Value)*   This is the largest and most appealing hotel in town, a government-rated four-star place that's incredibly bargain priced. The rooms have simple summery furnishings, each facing the sea from a private terrace or veranda. The tiled bathrooms are tiny.

Viale Beccarini 2, 71043 Manfredonia. *(C)* and fax 0884-586021. 46 units (showers only). 90€ ($80.35) double. MC, V. Parking 10€ ($8.95). **Amenities:** Restaurant; bar; pool; room service; laundry. *In room:* A/C, TV, hair dryer.

WHERE TO DINE

Trattoria il Baracchio APULIAN/SEAFOOD   Occupying an early-1900s building close to Piazza Municipio, this is the most appealing restaurant in town, although it serves only lunch. The great selection of antipasti is mostly seafood and vegetarian. Pasta dishes include spaghetti and orecchiette, prepared in simple versions of tomatoes, pesto, and local cheese; with garlic, olive oil, and fresh broccoli; or more elaborately with seafood, especially octopus. Look for aromatic grilled baby lamb and the chef's special, *zuppetta ai rutti di mare,* the area's most savory shellfish soup.

Corso Roma 38. *(C)* 0884-583874. Reservations recommended. Main courses 6.75€–12.50€ ($6.05–$11.15). AE, DC, MC, V. Fri–Wed 12:30–3pm.

MONTE SANT'ANGELO ⊛

60km (37 miles) NE of Foggia, 135km (84 miles) NW of Bari, 233km (144 miles) NE of Naples

The interior's principal town, Monte Sant'Angelo, 16km (10 miles) north of Manfredonia in the great Umbra Forest, is a good place to start your drive. From here you can venture into a landscape of limes, laurels, and towering yews, populated with foxes and gazelles. Narrow passages, streets that are virtually stairways, and little houses washed a gleaming white characterize the town.

The site of Monte Sant'Angelo, standing on a spur, commands panoramic views of the surrounding terrain. Before you leave town, you might want to visit the **Sanctuary of San Michele (Santuario di San Michele),** Via Reale Basilica (*(C)* **0884-561150**), built in the Romanesque-Gothic style. The campanile is octagonal, dating from the last years of the 13th century. The sanctuary commemorates the legend of St. Michael, who's said to have left his red cloak after he appeared to some shepherds in a grotto in 490. You can also visit the grotto—to enter from the church, go through some bronze doors, made in Constantinople in the 11th century. Crusaders stopped here to worship before going to the Holy Land. The sanctuary is open daily 7:30am to 12:30pm and 2:30 to 6:30pm; it charges no admission.

Opposite the campanile is the **Tomb of Rotharis (Tomba di Rotari),** which is said to hold the bones of the king of the Lombards, Rotharis, although it's a baptistry dating from as early as the 12th century.

Continuing past the sanctuary, you'll find the semi-restored ruins of the **Norman Swabian Aragonese Castle (Castello Normanno Aragonese Svevo),** Piazzale Ferri, with a second entrance on the Corso Manfredi (© **0884-587838**); it's open daily 8:30am to 7:30pm and charges 2.50€ ($2.25) for admission. Its Torre dei Giganti was constructed in 837, although most of the castle dates from later in the Middle Ages. From its ramparts is one of the most sweeping views in the Gargano.

You can also visit the **Tancredi Museum (Museo Tancredi),** Piazza San Francesco d'Assisi (© **0884-562098**), exhibiting artifacts used by local farmers and vintners in their trades. From May to September, it's open Monday to Friday 8:30am to 2pm, and on Tuesdays and Thursdays also from 4 to 7pm; off-season hours are Monday to Friday 10:30am to 12:30pm. Admission is 1.50€ ($1.35).

As you wander about, look for local shops selling **wrought-iron goods,** which are among the finest in Italy. Ironwork has a long tradition here, with sons following in their fathers' footsteps. The locals also make wooden furniture and utensils. Most shops are located in an area called **Juno,** in the exact center of town.

WHERE TO STAY

Hotel Rotary   You'll find this 1981 hotel half a mile west of town, amid a sloping terrain with ancient olive groves and almond trees. Because of the hotel's location in relatively high altitudes, ocean breezes usually keep the temperatures comfortable. The newly renovated rooms range from small to medium, with neatly kept bathrooms.

Via per Pulsano km 1, 71037 Monte Sant'Angelo. © and fax **0884-562146.** 70 units (showers only). 62€–73€ ($55.35–$65.20) double. Rates include breakfast. AE, MC, V. Free parking. **Amenities:** Lounge. *In room:* TV, hair dryer.

WHERE TO DINE

Ristorante Medioevo *(Finds* CONTADINA   The Medioevo's dining room takes its name from the weather-beaten but historic neighborhood surrounding it. The cuisine is firmly entrenched in recipes rehearsed by countless generations of *contadine* (peasant women), such as *zuppa di pane cotto* (a savory soup made of chicory and fava beans), homemade pasta (especially orecchiette), and a wide roster of meat or fish and roasted lamb from rocky meadows nearby. The kitchen is particularly proud of its *orecchiette Medioevo* (ear-shaped pasta with a sauce made from roasted lamb, braised arugula, and fresh tomatoes).

Via Castello 21. © **0884-565356.** Reservations recommended. Main courses 15€–27.50€ ($13.40–$24.55). AE, MC, V. Daily 12:30–2:30pm and 7:30–11pm. Closed Nov 15–30 and Mon Oct–June.

THE TREMITI ISLANDS ✦

11km (6¾ miles) NW of Gargano

While you're in the area, consider visiting the jewel-like cluster of the **Isole Tremiti (Tremiti Islands),** northwest of the Gargano Peninsula in the Adriatic. These small limestone islands boast lovely reefs, gin-clear waters, and towering peaks.

Between June and September, when the vast majority of people go to and from the Tremiti Islands, boats and hydrofoils travel from Vieste and Manfredonia. Advance reservations for these ferryboats, especially during the July and August mid-summer crush, are strongly recommended, especially if you bring a car. The rest of the year, the only seaborne access to the islands is via the town of Termilo, in Molise, to the north of Gargano. For information on the (relatively rare) midwinter crossings, call © **0875-705343.** For summer crossings, contact

Gargano Viaggi, at Piazza Roma 7, in Vieste (© **0884-708501**), the local agent for the **Adriatica** line, which operates the boats. Hydrofoil service from Vieste to the Tremiti Islands costs 25€ to 28€ ($22.35–$25) per person, round-trip. A roughly equivalent passage to the Tremiti Islands from Manfredonia goes for 35€ to 40€ ($31.25–$35.70) per person, round-trip, depending on the season. Don't expect frequent connections from either city: Even in the peak travel months of July and August, hydrofoils depart only twice a day, around 8:30am and at 10:15am, and in June and September, they leave only once a day, usually around 9:30am. Transit takes about 2 hours, each way, from Vieste, and about 3 hours, each way, from Manfredonia.

By boat or hydrofoil, you'll arrive at the docks of **San Nicola,** the smaller of the two inhabited islands, where you can explore the **castle** from the 15th century (it's not much of a sight, but the view from there is spectacular). You might also want to visit **Santa Maria a Mare,** which grew out of a 9th-century abbey, one of many monasteries that once stood in the Tremiti. The church has been largely rebuilt over the years, retaining only an intricate mosaic floor and early Byzantine cross from its early history. Pirates plundered all its treasures in 1321.

Transit between the various islands of the Tremiti chain is accomplished via shuttle boats, which operate only between June and September. Transit between San Nicola and the other inhabited island of the chain (San Domino, which is larger than San Nicola, but with a smaller population) costs 1.25€ ($1.10) each way. Departures are frequent, about every hour, and transit time is about 10 minutes each way. San Domino is the largest island of the group, with a rock-strewn shoreline. It's best known for its grottoes—the **Blue Marine Grotto (Grotta del Blu Marino), Salt Grotto (Grotta di Sale),** and **Violet Grotto (Grotta delle Viole),** all stunningly beautiful. The only beaches of the Tremiti are found here, and the **Cala delle Arene,** near the dock, is generally crowded. But you can also make your way to the west and south sides of the island, where the only other approachable beaches (most are at the foot of treacherous cliffs) offer stretches of solitude. As a historical footnote, Charlemagne's quarrelsome Italian father-in-law was exiled on the island, and this is where Augustus banished his daughter, Julia, because of her "excesses" (such as sleeping with nearly every man in Rome).

WHERE TO STAY & DINE

Hotel Gabbiano Built in 1973 and renovated in 2000, this is the most appealing hotel on the island. It lies about half a mile from the port, on San Domino's most beautiful stretch of coast, in a palm garden. The functional guest rooms and tiled bathrooms are a bit cramped, but are well maintained.

Isola San Domino, 71040 San Nicola di Tremiti. © and fax 0882-463410. 40 units (showers only). 80€–115€ ($71.45–$102.70) double with breakfast; 100€–195€ ($89.30–$174.15) double with half-board. AE, DC, MC, V. **Amenities:** Restaurant; bar; room service; babysitting; laundry. *In room:* A/C, TV, minibar, hair dryer; safe.

Hotel San Domino Less desirable than the Gabbiano (see above), this is a government-rated three-star hotel built about a mile from the port. It's within a 5-minute walk from the nearest beach and contains serviceable but simple white guest rooms and cramped tiled bathrooms.

Isola San Domino, 71040 San di Tremiti. © 0882-463404. Fax 0882-463221. 25 units (showers only). 100€–160€ ($89.30–$142.90) double. Rates include half-board. MC, V. **Amenities:** Restaurant; bar; lounge; room service; laundry/dry cleaning. *In room:* A/C, TV, hair dryer.

VIESTE ☆

92km (57 miles) NE of Foggia, 179km (111 miles) NW of Bari, 274km (170 miles) NE of Naples

At Vieste, on the far eastern shore of the Gargano, a legendary monolith stands firmly rooted in the sea. The rock is linked to the woeful tale of Vesta, a beautiful girl supposedly held prisoner on the stone by jealous sirens.

In recent years, the town has blossomed as a summer resort because it offers some of the best **beaches** in the south. If you're just passing through, take time out to walk through the charming medieval quarter, with its whitewashed houses built on terraces overlooking the sea. Vieste is a good center from which to explore the other excellent sandy beaches along the southern shoreline.

WHERE TO STAY

Hotel del Seggio (Value)   This is the best affordable hotel. It occupies a civic monument that, between its construction in the 1600s and around 1910, was the city hall. In 1983, it was renovated to become a hotel. The guest rooms come in a wide range of shapes and sizes, each with a tidily kept tiled bathroom. One edge of the hotel abuts the seafront (and the hotel's private beach); the other is off one of the town's main squares.

Piazza del Seggio/Via Veste 7, 71019 Vieste. © **0884-708123.** Fax 0884-708727. www.vieste.com/seggio. 30 units. 58€–84€ ($51.80–$75) double. Rates include breakfast. July 31–Aug 21 half-board 53€ ($47.35) per person. AE, DC, MC, V. Free parking. **Amenities:** Restaurant; bar; pool; exercise room; room service. *In room:* A/C, TV, minibar, hair dryer, safe.

Pizzomunno Vieste Palace Hotel ☆☆   This deluxe hotel is much better than any other contender in Gargano (with correspondingly high prices) and is proud of its 80% Italian clientele. Its Mediterranean architecture, with five stories growing smaller as they rise, allows lots of private terraces on the fourth and fifth floors. The guest rooms, totally remodeled, are airy and relatively spacious, with big windows and top-grade furnishings. The staff is charming.

Within 27m (30 yd.) is the companion **Hotel La Pineta,** which shares the same management.

Spiaggia di Pizzomunno, 71019 Vieste. © **0884-708741.** Fax 0884-707325. www.pizzomunno.it. 200 units. 260€–720€ ($232.20–$642.95) double; 440€–960€ ($392.90–$857.30) suite. Rates include buffet breakfast. AE, DC, MC, V. Free valet parking. Closed late Oct to mid-Mar. **Amenities:** 2 well-regarded restaurants; 3 bars; nightclub; 2 pools; 3 tennis courts; basketball court; health club and spa; sauna; watersports; concierge; salon; room service; babysitting; laundry/dry cleaning. *In room:* A/C, TV, minibar, hair dryer, safe.

WHERE TO DINE

You can also dine at the wonderful **Ristorante Trabucco** in the Pizzomunno Vieste Palace Hotel (see above).

Al Dragone APULIAN   Near the cathedral is this charming and romantic spot, lit with flickering candles and decorated with raffia-wrapped Chianti bottles. The cuisine is based on the folkloric traditions of old Apulia. Look for seafood pastas, antipasti buffets, lamb roasted with herbs and potatoes, and flavors lush with garlic, rosemary, and pesto. The owners pride themselves on their comprehensive collection of red and white Apulian wines. An excellent example is Patrilione.

Via Duomo 8. © **0884-701212.** Reservations recommended. Main courses 9€–16€ ($8.05–$14.30). AE, DC, MC, V. Wed–Mon noon–3pm and 7–11pm. Closed Nov to mid-Mar.

Box 19 ☆ APULIAN   Box 19 doesn't go the cute folkloric route for tourists; it's a relatively sophisticated dining experience. Despite that, the cuisine is Apulian, with an emphasis on fresh fish, tomato-based pastas, and antipasti offerings that might wow you with their pungent fresh fish (especially anchovies and sardines) and marinated vegetables. (The name? This place opened in the early 1980s in a former car-repair shop—its post-office box was no. 19.)

Via Santa Maria di Merino 13. (© **0884-705229**. Reservations recommended. Main courses 5€–13.50€ ($4.45–$12.05). MC, V. Tues–Sun noon–3pm and 7pm–midnight.

3 Alberobello & the Trulli District ★★

72km (45 miles) NW of Brindisi, 60km (37 miles) SE of Bari, 45km (28 miles) N of Taranto

The center of a triangle made up by Bari, Brindisi, and Taranto, the Valley of Itria has long been known for olive cultivation and the beehive-shaped houses dotting its landscape. These curious structures, called *trulli*, were built at least as early as the 13th century. Their whitewashed limestone walls and conical fieldstone roofs utilize the materials available in the area in such a way that mortar isn't needed to keep the pieces together. Theories abound as to why they aren't built with mortar, the most popular being that the trulli, considered substandard peasant dwellings, had to be easily dismantled in case of a royal visit. See the box "The Mystery of the Trulli," below, for more speculation.

The center of the Trulli District, and home to the greatest concentration of trulli, is Alberobello. Here the streets are lined with some 1,000 of the buildings. You might feel as if you've entered into a child's storybook as you walk through the maze of cobbled streets curving through Italy's most fantastic village. The crowds of visitors will quickly relieve you of any such thoughts, however.

Many of the trulli have been converted into souvenir shops where you can buy everything from postcards to miniature models of the dwellings. Be careful, though: If you enter, you're expected to buy something—and the shop owners will let you know it.

ESSENTIALS

GETTING THERE   FSE **trains** leave Bari every hour (every 2 hr. on Sun) heading to Alberobello. The trip takes about 1¾ hours and costs 6€ ($5.35). To find the trulli, follow Via Mazzini, which turns into Via Garibaldi, until you reach Piazza del Popolo. Turn left on Largo Martellotta, which will take you to the edge of the popular tourist area. If you have a **car,** head south of Bari on S100 and then east (signposted) on S172.

VISITOR INFORMATION   The **tourist office** in Alberobello is off the central square, Piazza del Popolo, at Piazza Ferdinando IV (© **080-4325171**), open daily 8am to noon and 4 to 7pm.

SEEING THE SIGHTS

The best-known of the trulli is the **trullo sovrano (sovereign trullo)** at Piazza Sacramento in Alberobello. The 15m (50-ft.) structure, the only true two-story trullo, was built during the 19th century as headquarters for a religious confraternity and carbonari sect. To find it, head down Corso Vittorio Emanuele until you get to a church, and then take a right. The trullo sovrano is open daily 10am to 1pm and 3 to 7pm, charging no admission.

On the outskirts of Alberobello, you can also visit the small town of **Castellana,** home to a series of caverns that have been carved out over the centuries by water streaming through the rocky soil. A wide stairway leads you down through a tunnel into a cavern called the **Grave.** From here, a series of paths winds through other underground rooms filled with the strange shapes of stalagmites and stalactites. The culmination of the journey into the earth ends with the majestic **Grotta Bianca,** where alabaster concretions are the result of centuries of Mother Nature's work. You can visit the Grotte di Castellana only on guided tours, usually one per hour until early afternoon, at 8€ to 13€ ($7.15–$11.60); call ☎ **080-4998211** for a schedule. Be sure to bring a sweater; the average underground temperature is 59°F (15°C), even on hot summer days.

Most visitors like to buy the hand-painted clay figurines that abound in every souvenir shop. You can also find a good assortment of fabrics and rugs at reasonable prices. One of the most evocative souvenirs would be a miniature re-creation of the region's legendary trulli. Crafted in the same type of stone that was used by the ancient builders, they're small-scale duplicates of the originals, ranging in size from a simple rendering to a replica of an entire village.

WHERE TO STAY

Most people visit the area on a daylong excursion; if you want to stay overnight, know that Alberobello's hotels are limited. You might be able to find individual renovated trulli that are rented to two to eight people for a relatively cheap rate. Call the tourist office for information. Otherwise, the accommodations here are usually more expensive than those in other nearby towns.

Hotel Dei Trulli ⊛   Almost a village unto itself, Dei Trulli offers the experience of living in one of the unique beehive-shaped trulli. Each mini-apartment might have one, two, or three cones, circular buildings wedged together in Siamese fashion. Most have a bedroom with a well-kept bathroom, a small sitting room with a fireplace, and a patio. The complex has the most attractively landscaped grounds.

Via Cadore 32, 70011 Alberobello. ☎ 080-4323555. Fax 080-4323560. htrulli@inmedia.it. 19 units (showers only). 95€ ($84.85) per person. Rates include half-board. AE, MC, V. Free parking. **Amenities:** Restaurant; lounge; pool; room service; babysitting; laundry/dry cleaning. *In room:* A/C, TV, minibar, hair dryer, safe.

Hotel Il Melograno ⊛⊛⊛   This is the most elegant hotel in Apulia and the only Relais & Châteaux south of Naples. Occupying what was the centerpiece for a large farm and estate during the 16th century and enlarged with a discreet modern wing in the mid-1900s, it sits less than a mile from the hamlet of Monopoli, surrounded by a grove of ancient olive trees. Camillo Gurra's polite staff spends long hours maintaining the important antiques and paintings in this charming country inn. The guest rooms range from medium to spacious, each with a well-kept bathroom. The hotel will shuttle guests to a private beach facility nearby with a bar and buffet restaurant right on the Adriatic.

Contrada Torricella, 70043 Monopoli. ☎ 080-6909030. Fax 080-747908. www.melograno.com. 37 units. 260€–370€ ($232.20–$330.40) per person double; 400€–540€ ($357.20–$482.20) per person suite. Rates include breakfast. AE, DC, MC, V. From Alberobello, follow the signs to Monopoli and drive 18km (11 miles) east. **Amenities:** Fine dining room; 2 bars; lounge; 2 pools (1 outdoor, 1 heated indoor); tennis courts; room service; babysitting; laundry/dry cleaning. *In room:* A/C, TV, minibar, hair dryer, safe.

WHERE TO DINE

You can also dine at the superb restaurant in the **Hotel Il Melograno** (see above).

Il Poeta Contadino ⊛⊛ ITALIAN/APULIAN   In the center of Alberobello, beneath the arched and vaulted stone ceilings of what was a barn in the 1700s, this is the region's most elegant restaurant. It's managed by Leonardo Marco and his Canadian-born wife, Carol, who serve sophisticated dishes based mostly on seafood. Their menu changes with the season but is likely to include *involtini* of eggplant, monkfish, and prawns with mussel sauce, as well as *pesce alla Leonardo* (sea bass steamed in water, wine, and oil and served with a chilled sauce of cherry

The Mystery of the Trulli

The architectural mystery of southern Italy, the igloo-shaped trulli are the country's most idiosyncratic homes, built of local limestone without mortar. A hole in the top allows smoke to escape. Southwest of Bari, in an area roughly hemmed in by Gioia del Colle to the west, Ostuni to the south, and the Adriatic coast to the east, these strange whitewashed buildings are roofed with tall spiraling cones of a stone prevalent in the region. Trulli are found nowhere else in the entire country.

The structures look somewhat primitive, giving them an air of being ancient, although most of the existing buildings are less than 2 centuries old. Many are new constructions because the people of the area are attached to their unique architectural form and use it to house businesses as well as homes. The trulli are of a uniformly small size. If more space is needed, local custom dictates the construction of several connected trulli rather than a single larger one. In fact, only one trullo in the entire area dared expand into a two-story structure (see above).

Some locals call trulli signalmen's houses, and others refer to them as monuments and point out obscure symbols that adorn the most tradi-tional ones. These symbols were copied from the emblems that embel-lish the few remaining ancient structures. One of the most puzzling things is that, despite the great attachment to the buildings, no one in the region can tell you how the form came into favor in the first place, what the emblems symbolize, or even why they're called by any of the names associated with them.

Only a few scholars have tackled these questions, in the end making half-hearted suggestions that perhaps the trulli are of Saracenic or

tomatoes, chives, olive oil, black olives, and vinegar). The wine list is one of the region's most comprehensive and has won a *Wine Spectator* award.

Via Indipendenza 21. ℂ 080-4321917. Reservations recommended. Main courses 10€–19€ ($8.95–$16.95). AE, DC, MC, V. Daily noon–3pm and 7–11pm. Closed Mon Oct–June.

Trullo d'Oro ✿ ITALIAN/APULIAN   Housed in several linked trulli, this rustic restaurant is one of the town's best. The cuisine consists mainly of well-prepared local and regional dishes. Specialties are purée of fava beans and chicory leaves, roast lamb with *lampasciuni* (a wild onion), and the chef's spe-cial pasta, orecchiette with bitter greens or tomatoes, olive oil, garlic, and arugula. Southern desserts, such as ricotta cooked with marmalade, are also served.

Via Cavallotti 27. ℂ 080-4321820. Reservations required Sat–Sun. Main courses 16€–42€ ($14.30–$37.50). AE, DC, DISC, MC, V. Tues–Sun noon–3pm and 8–11pm. Closed Jan 3–Feb 3.

4 Lecce ✿✿

40km (25 miles) SE of Brindisi, 87km (54 miles) E of Taranto, 905km (561 miles) SE of Rome

Often called "the Florence of the South," Lecce lies in the heart of the Salento Peninsula, the "heel" of the Italian boot. The town was founded before the time

Greek origin. One line of logic points out that limestone, a calcareous rock found in abundant stratification throughout the region, is easily separated into thin layers that can readily be shaped into crude bricks that don't require mortar when relayered. The dome design allows heat to rise, slightly cooling the living space, a significant factor in the region's brutal summer. Given that the area has long been impoverished, perhaps the design is nothing but good old ingenuity, a means of cheaply constructing homes and businesses with the materials at hand—but that still doesn't explain the hieroglyphics.

One suggestion is that the origin of the trulli had to do with outwitting Ferdinand I of Aragón. This king had prohibited the Apulians from building permanent dwellings because he wanted to be able to move the labor force around as he chose. The clever Apulians thus constructed houses that could be dismantled when they spotted the king's agents. Another theory suggests that during Spanish rule, a tax was levied on individual homes, except for unfurnished homes, for which the trulli qualified when their roofs were removed.

Other theories link them with similar structures in Mycenae and suggest that their origins could be as old as 3000 B.C. Apulia was indeed part of Magna Graecia and thus could have come under that influence. Similarities have been noted between the trulli of Apulia and the "sugarloaf" houses of Syria. It has been suggested that this idea, traveling west, influenced builders in southern Italy who initially used the trulli as tombs. It has also been noted that soldiers returning from the Crusades might have brought these architectural curiosities to Alberobello. Got any theories of your own?

of the ancient Greeks, but it's best known for the architecture, *barocco leccese* (Lecce baroque), of many of its buildings. Dating from Lecce's heyday in the 16th, 17th, and 18th centuries, these structures are made mostly of fine-grained yellow limestone. Masons delighted in working with the golden material; their efforts turned the city into what one architectural critic called a "gigantic bowl of overripe fruit." Alas, recent restorations have taken away much of the color as workers have whitewashed the buildings.

For centuries, Lecce has been neglected by tourists. Perhaps it's for this reason that many of the baroque-style buildings have remained intact—progress hasn't overrun the city with modern development. Lecce's charm lies in these displays of the lighter baroque (although many buildings are now in dire need of repair).

ESSENTIALS

GETTING THERE   Lecce is connected to Brindisi by hourly **train** service on the state-run FS line. For service from points east and south, you'll have to take the FSE line, which isn't known for its speed. Several trains coming from Otranto and Gallipoli enter Lecce each day. The train station is about 2km (1¼ miles) from Piazza Sant'Oronzo, in the center of the old quarter. Call *C* **848-888088** toll-free in Italy for schedules and information.

If you have a **car,** take Route 613 from Brindisi.

VISITOR INFORMATION   The **tourist office** is at Via Monte San Michele (© **0832-214117**), open Monday to Saturday 9am to 1pm.

SPECIAL EVENTS   July and August bring the **Estate Musicale Leccese,** with nightly music and dance. In June and July, plays (and sometimes operas) are staged in the city's public gardens. In September, the churches of Lecce are venues for a **festival of baroque music.** The tourist office will provide complete details.

EXPLORING THE TOWN

Piazza Sant'Oronzo is a good place to begin a stroll through Lecce. The 2nd-century A.D. Roman column erected here, **Colonna Romana,** once stood near its mate in Brindisi, and together they marked the end of the Appian Way. Lightning toppled this column in 1528, and the Brindisians left it lying on the ground until 1661, at which time the citizens of Lecce bought it and set up the pillar in their hometown. St. Oronzo, for whom the square is named, now stands atop it guarding the area. At the southern side of the piazza are the remains of a **Roman amphitheater.** Dating from the 1st century B.C., it accommodated 20,000 fans, who came to watch bloody fights between gladiators and wild beasts.

North of the piazza, Via Umberto I leads to the **Basilica di Santa Croce** ★★ (© **0832-261957**). This ornate display of Leccese baroque architecture took almost 1½ centuries to complete. Architect Gabriele Riccardo began work in the mid–15th century; the final touches weren't added until 1680. The facade bears some similarity to the Spanish plateresque style and is peopled by guardian angels, grotesque demons, and a variety of flora and fauna. St. Benedict and St. Peter are also depicted. The top part of the facade (the flamboyant part) is the work of Antonio Zimbalo, who was called Zingarello (gypsy). The interior is laid out in a Latin cross plan in a simple Renaissance style. The basilica is open daily 7am to 12:30pm and 4 to 7pm. Admission is free.

Down Via Vittorio Emanuele, the **Duomo** ★, Piazza del Duomo (© **0832-308557**), stands in a closed square. The building, which has two facades, was reconstructed between 1659 and 1670 by Zingarello. To the left of the Duomo, the **campanile** towers 64m (210 ft.) above the piazza. The cathedral is open daily 7:30am to 12:30pm and 4 to 7pm, and admission is free. On the opposite side of the cathedral is the **Bishop's Palace (Palazzo Vescovile),** where Lecce's archbishop still lives today. Also in the courtyard is a **seminary,** built between 1694 and 1709 by Giuseppe Cino, who was a student of Zimbalo. Its decorations have been compared to those of a wedding cake. A baroque well, extraordinarily detailed with garlands and clusters of flowers and fruit, stands in the seminary's courtyard.

The collection of bronze statuettes, Roman coins, and other artifacts at the **Provincial Museum (Museo Provinciale)** ★, Viale Gallipoli (© **0832-307415**), will keep your interest for a while. It's worth the time to stop by to have a look at the ornately decorated 13th-century gospel cover. Inlaid with enamel of blue, white, and gold, it's a rare treasure. There's also a small picture gallery. It's open Monday to Friday 9am to 1:30pm and 2:30 to 7pm, and Saturday 9am to 1:30pm. Admission is free.

For an example of the town's traditional wrought-iron goods (trivets, ornamental grills, and the like), shoppers should visit **Salvatore Mancarella,** Via 95 Fanteria 66B (© **0832-634218**). For a different selection of local crafts, including *cartapesta* (papier-mâché), ceramics, and terra cotta, go to **Mostra**

dell'Artigianato, Via Francesco Rubichi 21 (𝄞 **0832-246758**). And if you're interested in any of the wines and foodstuffs of the region, head for a food emporium that's been here as long as anyone can remember, **Enoteca,** Via Cesare Battisti 23 (𝄞 **0832-302832**). Usually, they'll let you taste a glass of whatever wine you're interested in before you buy a bottle.

WHERE TO STAY

Lecce's hotels don't offer the baroque architecture for which the town is famous. Most are modern structures built to accommodate large numbers of visitors who care more about seeing the town and the surrounding area than spending time in their rooms.

Albergo Delle Palme *(Value*   This is the best affordable hotel in town, and it's located within easy walking distance of the major sights. The public rooms, with their overstuffed leather furniture and paneled walls, are warm and inviting. The guest rooms are comfortably decorated with painted iron beds and small sitting areas, and bathrooms are spacious.

Via di Leuca 90, 73100 Lecce. 𝄞 and fax **0832-347171.** www.paginegialle.it/dellepalme-03. 96 units (some with shower only). 88€ ($78.60) double. Rates include breakfast. AE, DC, DISC, MC, V. Free parking. **Amenities:** Restaurant; lounge; room service; laundry. *In room:* A/C, TV, minibar, hair dryer.

Hotel Cristal   This metal-and-glass high-rise is a good choice for comfort at a reasonable price. The marble lobby/lounge area is severe but not sterile and offers a pleasant place to sit and enjoy a drink. The guest rooms vary in size and are decorated monochromatically in purples, pinks, or blues. Each unit comes with a compact, tiled bathroom.

Via Marinosci 16, 73100 Lecce. 𝄞 **0832-372314.** Fax 0832-315109. www.hotelcristal.it. 64 units (showers only). 110€ ($98.25) double. Rates include breakfast. AE, DC, MC, V. Parking 9€ ($8.05). **Amenities:** Bar; room service; babysitting; laundry. *In room:* A/C, TV, fridge, minibar, hair dryer, safe.

Hotel President   Although this hotel is near the historic center of town, it's thoroughly modern. The guest rooms are decorated in the unfortunate browns and oranges popular in the 1970s but are large and comfortable. The look is standardized, almost motel-like, but luckily there's good service. Fresh pastries and breads are the highlights of the breakfast buffet.

Via Salandra 6, 73100 Lecce. 𝄞 **0832-456111.** Fax 0832-456632. 154 units (showers only). 100€–130€ ($89.30–$116.10) double; from 180€ ($160.75) suite. Rates include buffet breakfast. AE, DC, MC, V. Parking 8€ ($7.15). **Amenities:** Restaurant; lounge; car-rental desk; room service; babysitting; laundry/dry cleaning. *In room:* A/C, TV, minibar, hair dryer, safe.

WHERE TO DINE

Be sure to sample some of the specialties of the Salento region, such as a tasty combination of mozzarella and tomato wrapped in a light pastry shell.

I Tre Moschettieri ITALIAN/PIZZA/APULIAN   Although this restaurant has two rooms, most visitors choose to have their meals on the alfresco patio. The tables throughout the restaurant are widely spaced and allow for easy conversation. Offerings from the *cucina rustica* here include a variety of fresh seafood dishes and a vast selection of made-to-order pizzas. Local politicians often frequent this place, where formal service at moderate prices is the rule.

Via Paisiello, 73100 Lecce. 𝄞 **0832-308484.** Reservations recommended. Main courses 8€–14€ ($7.15–$12.50). DC, MC, V. Mon–Sat noon–3pm and 7pm–midnight.

Ristorante Villa G.C. della Monica ⋆ SOUTHERN ITALIAN/INTERNATIONAL   The charming Valente family runs this restaurant in one of Lecce's most stately villas, built of chiseled stone between 1550 and 1600. There are four dining rooms (one available only for private parties) and a flower-strewn terrace overlooking a historic neighborhood near Piazza Mazzini. The menu items are steeped in local culinary traditions and emphasize a regional tubular pasta called *strozzapreti* (a bit smaller than penne), usually served with clams, mussels, crabmeat, and squid. Other specialties are well-seasoned filet steak with black truffles, and fresh fish that seems to taste better when baked in a salt crust to seal in the moisture.

Via SS. Giacomo e Filippo 40. (C) 0832-458432. Reservations recommended. Main courses 7€–12.50€ ($6.25–$11.15). AE, DC, MC, V. Wed–Mon 12:30–3pm and 8–11pm. Closed Jan.

LECCE AFTER DARK

Because of the large student population at the University of Lecce, there's usually something to keep night owls entertained. After nightfall, folks head to the main piazza to join friends for a drink. **Piazzetta del Duca d'Atena** is an especially popular hangout. For a more active night, you might want to head to **Corto Maltese,** Via Giusti 23 (no phone). From Wednesday to Monday 9pm to 2am, crowds gather to dance the night away.

A SIDE TRIP TO GALLIPOLI ⋆

Thirty-seven kilometers (23 miles) southwest of Lecce, on the Gulf of Taranto side of the Salento Peninsula, lies **Gallipoli.** This isn't the Gallipoli infamous in history books as the site of one of the bloodiest battles ever fought; that sad World War I landmark is part of Turkey. The Italian town has a much quieter and less tragic past. Originally named Kallipolis (beautiful city) by the Greeks, the present town still has a distinct Greek look. The medieval quarter, once a small island, is especially inviting to explore, with its twisting lanes and plain, whitewashed houses.

It's best to rent a car for this trip; train service to Gallipoli from Lecce is extremely slow, and public transportation in the area limited. It's a quick 25-minute drive down to the town from Lecce, perfect for a day trip to the beach.

SEEING THE SIGHTS

Many people who come to Gallipoli head straight for the **beaches. Baia Verde,** just south of the town, is especially popular. However, if you take the time to drive down from Lecce, you might as well see what the town has to offer.

One of the most interesting places to visit is the **Civic Museum (Museo Civico),** Via De Pace 108 ((C) **0833-264224**). There's a little of everything here; it's almost as if the townspeople cleaned out their closets and made what they found into a museum. The collection covers several centuries and many aspects of life, from unexploded sea mines to clothing from the 18th century. The museum, just recently renovated, is open in summer daily 9am to 9pm; off-season hours are Monday to Saturday 9am to 1pm and 4 to 6pm.

The Greek **nymphaion,** a fountain elaborately decorated with mythological scenes, can be found in the new town near the bridge. It's the only fountain of this type left in Italy, although there are a few still left in Greece.

The town also has a **cathedral** from the 1400s and a **castle** jutting out into the Ionian sea. The circular fortress has protected the city for centuries; locals fought off Charles of Anjou's men for 7 months here, and troops from England attacked the castle in 1809.

If you drive to Gallipoli, you can continue on to discover the tip of the Salento Peninsula, often called **Finibus Terrae (Land's End).** The Temple of

Minerva that was once used by ancient sailors to trace their course has been replaced with the church of Santa Maria di Leuca, although stones and dolmens that stand in the area are reminders of the long-ago civilization.

Also nearby is **Casarano,** the birthplace of Boniface IX, who was pope from 1339 to 1404. The small church of Casaranello is here; early Christian mosaics adorn the walls.

WHERE TO STAY

Grand Hotel Costa Brada ⚐ This is a contemporary resort with a lot of amenities, including a private beach, more than it is an overnight stopover. It lies about 6km (3¾ miles) from the center of Gallipoli, reached along a scenic road. The gleaming white beach hotel is in a classic Mediterranean design. The public rooms are pristine and simply, though tastefully, furnished. The good-size bedrooms are immaculately kept, with each unit boasting a sea-view balcony and an immaculate tile bathroom. The best units—and these are grabbed up first—are accommodations 110 through 114 because they are larger and offer the best oceanviews. The chefs here are expert at preparing both international and Apulian cuisine, so many guests prefer to book in here on half-board terms.

Strada Litoranea, 73014 Gallipoli. © **0833-202551.** Fax 0833-202555. 87 units. 142€–154€ ($126.80–$137.50) double. Rates include breakfast. AE, DC, MC, V. **Amenities:** 3 restaurants; 2 bars; nightclub; 2 pools; 2 tennis courts; gym; sauna; water-skiing; bike rentals; salon; room service; laundry/dry cleaning. *In room:* A/C, TV, minibar, hair dryer, safe.

WHERE TO DINE

Ristorante Marechiaro REGIONAL The Marechiaro occupies a 1900s villa on a small island connected to the mainland by a bridge. In one of the three dining rooms or on the flowering terrace, you'll enjoy the cuisine of Antonio Giungato. Fish dishes are a staple, including spicy *zuppa di pesce* (fish soup), *risotto alla pescatora* (rice flavored with seafood), and linguine with seafood and a creamy white sauce.

Lungomare Marconi. © **0833-266143.** Reservations recommended. Main courses 11€–17€ ($9.80–$15.20). AE, DC, MC, V. Daily noon–4pm and 7pm–midnight. Closed Tues in winter.

5 Taranto ⚐

71km (44 miles) W of Brindisi, 100km (62 miles) SE of Bari, 533km (330 miles) SE of Rome

Taranto, known to the ancient Greeks as Taras, is said to have been named for a son of Poseidon who rode into the harbor on a dolphin's back. A less fantastic theory, trumpeted by historians, is that a group of Spartans was sent here in 708 B.C. to found a colony. Taranto was once a major center of Magna Graecia and continued as an important port on the Ionian coast throughout the 4th century B.C. A long period of rule under Archytas, a Pythagorean mathematician/philosopher, was the high point in the city's history. According to some, Plato himself came to Taranto during this time to muddle through the mysteries of life with the wise and virtuous ruler.

Ten years of war with the Romans in the 3rd century B.C. ended in defeat for Taranto. Although the city lost much of the power and prestige it had been known for, it did survive the Dark Ages and became an important port once more during the time of the Crusades.

Taranto lent its name to the tarantula, but don't be alarmed; the only spiders here are rather small, harmless brown ones. The dance known today as the *tarantella* also takes its name from this city. (Members of various dancing cults believed that individuals who had been bitten by spiders should dance wildly to rid their bodies of the poison; the inflicted person would sometimes dance for days.) In modern times, the tarantella is characterized by hopping and foot tapping, and it is one of the most popular folk dances of southern Italy.

Taranto is a modern industrial city that many visitors pass by. The once-prosperous old city has begun to crumble, and the economy of the town has hit a slump, in part because the naval forces stationed in Taranto have been scaled back. However, the new city, with its wide promenades and expensive shops, still draws crowds. Come here if only to taste some of Italy's best seafood. Taranto's location on a peninsula between two seas, the Mare Piccolo and Mare Grande, ensures that plenty of oysters, mussels, and other shellfish will wind up on your plate.

ESSENTIALS

GETTING THERE Regular service from both Bari and Brindisi is provided by the FS and FSE **train** lines. Trains leave Bari about once an hour for Taranto; the trip takes 1½ to 2 hours and costs 9.20€ ($8.20). For 3.40€ ($3.05), you can take the hour-long ride from Brindisi; trains leave every 2 hours. The station is on the western outskirts of town; from there, you take a bus or taxi into the center. For information and schedules, call © **099-4714974.**

Three **bus** companies, FSE, SITA, and CTP, provide service to Taranto. From Bari, take the FSE bus, departing every 2 hours. The trip takes from 1 to 2 hours and costs 4.50€ ($4). Call © **099-4532392** for information and schedules.

If you have a **car,** take A14 here from Bari; E90 comes in from Brindisi, and Route 7ter makes the trek west from Lecce.

VISITOR INFORMATION The **tourist office** is at Corso Umberto I 113, near Piazza Garibaldi (© **099-4532392**). It's open Monday to Friday 9am to 1pm and 4:30 to 6:30pm, and Saturday 9am to noon.

EXPLORING THE CITY

For the best view of the city, walk along the waterfront promenade, the **Lungomare Vittorio Emanuele** ✦✦. The heart of the old town, the **Città Vecchia,** lies on an island, separating the Mare Piccolo from the Mare Grande. The modern city, the **Città Moderna,** lies to the north of the Lungomare Vittorio Emanuele.

Evidence of Taranto's former glory as an important city in Magna Graecia can be found at the **Archaeological Museum of Taranto (Museo Archeologico di Taranto)** ✦✦, Corso Umberto 41 (© **099-4532112**), where an assortment of artifacts documenting Pugliese civilization from the Stone Age to modern times is displayed. Most of the items are the results of archaeological digs in the area, especially the excavated necropolis. The museum boasts the world's largest collection of terra-cotta figures, along with a glittering array of Magna Grecian art, such as vases, goldware, marble and bronze sculpture, and mosaics. The designs of many of these works would be considered sophisticated even by today's standards. Admission is 4€ ($3.55). The museum is open Monday to Saturday 9am to 2pm.

If the ornate vases at the National Museum enchanted you, you might want to visit **Grottaglie,** a nearby small town that's the ceramics capital of southeast Italy. Modern styles are crafted here, but most shoppers prefer to purchase traditional pieces, such as the giant vases that originally held laundry or the glazed wine bottles that mimic those of the ancient Greeks. You can buy pieces for a standard 50% discount over what you'd pay anywhere else for Grottaglie pottery, which is sold all over Italy. The whole village looks like one great china shop.

Finds **Tracking Down the Sheik of Araby**

For years, movie buffs have visited the town of **Castellaneta,** birthplace of Rudolph Valentino, the silent-screen actor known for starring roles in *The Sheik* (1921), *Blood and Sand* (1922), and *Four Horsemen of the Apocalypse* (1921). Valentino was born in 1895 at V. Roma 114; for decades, the town's young men modeled themselves, heavily oiled hair and all, after the star. The town still sells mementos and souvenir photos of the matinee idol. In the town piazza stands a statue of Valentino in full costume as the Sheik of Araby.

Castellaneta is also known for its "cave churches" and views of the Gulf of Taranto and the Basilicata mountains. Set high in a ravine, the village isn't easily accessible except by car. From Taranto, take S7 to the turnoff for Castellaneta.

Plates and vases are stacked on the pavements and even on the rooftops. Just walk along, looking to see what interests you; then bargain, bargain, bargain.

WHERE TO STAY

Hotel choices here are limited. In fact, inexpensive accommodations might be impossible to find. Many third- or fourth-class hotels, especially around the waterfront, are unsafe. Proceed with caution. Make reservations in advance—the good hotels, though expensive, fill up fast.

Grand Hotel Delfino ✿ Built in the 1960s and radically renovated in 1994, the Delfino stands on the waterfront, much like a beach club. It's the best place to stay in Taranto. The well-furnished guest rooms are modern and beachy, with tile floors, wooden furniture, and small balconies.

Viale Virgilio 66, 74100 Taranto. ☎ **099-7323232.** Fax 099-7304654. www.grandhoteldelfino.it. 204 units. 100€–140€ ($89.30–$125) double; from 175€ ($156.30) suite. Rates include breakfast. AE, DC, MC, V. Free parking. **Amenities:** Restaurant; bar; lounge; pool; room service; babysitting; laundry/dry cleaning. *In room:* A/C, TV, minibar, hair dryer, safe.

Hotel Palace The Palace is the Delfino's nearest rival, at the eastern end of Lungomare Vittorio Emanuele III, opening onto the Mare Grande. The modern building offers good guest rooms, all with balconies. They range from small to medium, each with a well-kept tiled bathroom.

Viale Virgilio 10, 74100 Taranto. ☎ and fax **099-4594771.** 73 units (showers only). 130€ ($116.10) double. Rates include breakfast. AE, DC, MC, V. Parking 7.50€ ($6.70). **Amenities:** Restaurant; bar; cafe; room service; laundry/dry cleaning. *In room:* A/C, TV, minibar, hair dryer.

WHERE TO DINE

Taranto is blessed with a bountiful supply of seafood; it's fresh from the water, delicious, and inexpensive. However, avoid anything raw—the locals might like some fish dishes this way, but you don't want to risk spending your vacation in the hospital.

Al Gambero ✿ ITALIAN/SEAFOOD This old-time charmer has been thriving since 1952 in a modern-looking building near the rail station. It's devoted to the seafood for which Taranto is famous, with an emphasis on shellfish. Look for such signature dishes as pappardelle with herbs and a lobster-flavored cream sauce, and risotto with shellfish. You have a choice of enjoying your meal alfresco or in one of the rooms overlooking the harbor and the old city fish market. To start your meal, try the *antipasti frutti di mare,* an assortment of seafood hors d'oeuvres. Main courses include *spaghetti al Gambero;* grilled or braised versions of veal, beef, or pork; and *orecchiette alla Pugliese,* the best-known pasta dish of Apulia.

Via del Ponte 4. (*C*) **099-4711190.** Reservations recommended. Main courses 6€–12€ ($5.35–$10.70). AE, DC, MC, V. Tues–Sun noon–3pm and 7–10pm.

L'Assassino ITALIAN/INTERNATIONAL   Described by its owners as "normal but nice," this restaurant is exactly that—nothing too fancy, but a pleasant place for a good, affordable meal. The dining area offers a panoramic view of the water and a wide range of Italian dishes. Of course, L'Assassino has a variety of fresh fish dishes, including *risotto al frutti di mare* (rice with the "fruits of the sea"). Other specialties are orecchiette and spaghetti marinara. The proprietors, who've run the place for more than 30 years, are friendly and provide good service.

Lungomare Vittorio Emanuele III, 29. (*C*) **099-4593447.** Reservations recommended. Main courses 5€–10.50€ ($4.45–$9.40). AE, DC, MC, V. Sat–Thurs noon–4pm and 7pm–midnight.

16

Sicily

Sicily is a land unto itself, proudly different from the rest of Italy in its customs and traditions. On the map, the toe of the Italian boot appears poised to kick Sicily away from the mainland, as if it didn't belong to the rest of the country. The largest of the Mediterranean islands, it's separated from Italy by the 4km (2½-mile) Strait of Messina, a dangerously unstable earthquake zone, making the eventual construction of a bridge doubtful.

Although the island's economy is moving closer to those of Europe and the rest of Italy, its culture is still very much its own. Its vague Arab flavor reminds us that Sicily broke away from the mainland of Africa, not Italy, millions of years ago. Its Greek heritage still lives. Although there are far too many cars in Palermo, and parts of the island are heavily polluted by industrialization, Sicily is still a different country. Life is slower, tradition is respected, and the myths and legends of the past aren't yet forgotten.

Sicily has been inhabited since the Ice Age, and its history is full of natural and political disasters. It has been conquered and occupied over and over: by the Greeks in the 6th to 5th centuries B.C., then the Romans, the Vandals, the Arabs (who created a splendid civilization), the Normans, the Swabians, the fanatically religious House of Aragón, and the Bourbons. When Garibaldi landed at Marsala in 1860, he brought an illusion of freedom, soon dissipated by the patronage system of the Mafia. Besides the invaders, the centuries have brought a series of plagues, volcanic eruptions,

earthquakes, and economic hardships to threaten the interwoven culture of Sicily.

This land has a deep archaeological heritage and is full of sensual sights and experiences: vineyards and fragrant citrus groves, horses with plumes and bells pulling gaily painted carts, masses of blooming almond and cherry trees in February, Greek temples, ancient theaters, complex city architecture, and aromatic Marsala wine. In summer the sirocco whirling out of the Libyan deserts dries the fertile fields, crisping the harvest into a sun-blasted palette of browns. Beaches are plentiful around the island, but most are rocky, crowded, or dirty. The best are at Mondello, outside Palermo, and around Taormina in the east.

If you really want to see most of Sicily's highlights, plan on spending at least 5 to 7 days and moving a few times. Remember that everything is very spread out (Sicily is the largest island in the Mediterranean, 178m/ 110 miles north to south and 282m/ 175 miles wide). Taormina is the most popular resort and is a great place to relax and play in the sun for a couple of days; from here you can visit Mt. Etna. However, the town is rather isolated in the east, so it's not a good base for seeing the island's other major highlights. The quickest and most efficient way to see the majority of Sicily is to fly into Palermo, rent a car, and travel east to Taormina; then return your car and fly back to the mainland from Catania. (Conversely, you can fly into Catania, perhaps from Rome, and end your itinerary in Palermo, returning the car there before flying back to Rome.) You could easily spend a week or more getting to know this fascinating island, one of the most intriguing destinations in Italy.

GETTING TO SICILY

BY PLANE   Flying time from Rome to Palermo is 1 hour.

Alitalia (© 800/223-5730 in the U.S.; toll-free in Italy 1478-65641 for domestic flights or 1478-65642 for international flights; www.alitalia.it/english/index.html) operates at least six flights a day to Palermo from Rome and about half a dozen from Milan (nonstop or with stops in Naples or Rome). From Turin, Venice, Pisa, Genoa, and Bologna, Palermo gets at least one nonstop flight a day and several with a stop at Rome or Naples. Charter flights occasionally land in Trapani, but all other major flights to Sicily land at Catania, with at least one flight a day from Milan, Pisa, Rome, and Turin.

Meridiana (© 800/275-5566 in the U.S., 06-478041 in Rome, or 091-323141 in Palermo) shares some of its flights and reservation functions with Alitalia. Most of the carrier's Sicilian flights operate between Rome and Palermo and can be booked separately or as part of a transatlantic itinerary through Alitalia. Regardless of how you opt to fly, it's cheaper to have your flight to Palermo written into your ticket when you book your flight from North America.

BY TRAIN   Trains from all over Europe arrive at the port at Villa San Giovanni, near Reggio di Calabria, and roll onto enormous barges for the 1-hour crossing to Sicily. Passengers remain in their seats during the short voyage across the Strait of Messina, eventually rolling back onto the tracks at Messina, Sicily.

From Rome, the trip to Palermo takes 11 to 13 hours, depending on the speed of the train. A one-way ticket from Rome to Palermo costs 80€ ($71.45) second class and 116€ ($103.60) first class, with a per-person supplement of 12.50€ ($11.15) for rides on the fastest of the trains. The rail route from Naples takes 9 to 11 hours. From Naples, one-way transit on the slowest of the trains costs 36€ ($32.15) second class and 55€ ($49.10) first class, with a per-person supplement of 11.50€ ($10.25) for access to the faster trains. Aboard any of the trains pulling into Palermo, you can rent a couchette for 16€ to 26€ ($14.30–$23.20) per person, depending on how luxurious it is and the number of persons (between two and six) you share the cabin with.

For fares and information, call © **848-888088** toll-free in Italy.

BY CAR & FERRY   The Autostrada del Sole stretches from Milan to Reggio Calabria, sticking out on the "big toe," the gateway to Sicily. Ferries run from Villa San Giovanni, near Reggio di Calabria, to Messina, and cost around 4.50€ ($4) each way. Vessels of the state railway ferry leave daily at frequent intervals 3:20am to 10:05pm, and it takes 40 minutes to cross. The cost of bringing a car

---

(Tips Safety in Sicily

Sicily is now attracting greater numbers of foreigners, mainly from Europe, especially from England and Germany. Many Americans continue to skip it, though, often because of their fear of the Mafia. However, the Mafia doesn't concern itself with tourists. It does exist (Sicily even made a cameo guest appearance on *The Sopranos*), but its hold seems to have lessened over the years. If you take the usual safety precautions (keep alert and don't flash jewelry), you'll be fine.

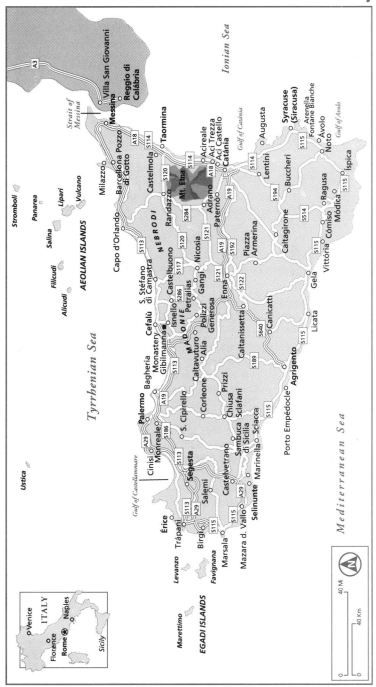

starts at 35€ ($31.25) and depends on the size of the vehicle. For information on both the ferry and train services, call ✆ **848-888088,** from within Italy only.

Driving time from Naples to Sicily is cut considerably by taking one of the vessels operated by **Tirrenia Lines,** Molo Angioino, Stazione Marittima, in Naples (✆ **081-7201111;** www.tirrenia.com). Departures are daily at 8pm for the 10-hour trip from Naples to Palermo. With slight variations for the season, expect to pay around 37€ to 55€ ($33.05–$49.10) for a one-way pedestrian fare, and around 133.50€ ($119.20) for one-way passage with a car and up to two passengers, plus any supplements if you want to rent a cabin. Arrival time in Palermo is 7am the next day.

BY HYDROFOIL (WITHOUT A CAR) If you're interested in shaving time off the ferry crossing, an *aliscafo* (hydrofoil) leaves from Reggio di Calabria. You'll pay 2.75€ ($2.45) each way. You can't take your vehicle on a hydrofoil, so it's less crowded than a ferry. Call ✆ **0903-64044** for schedules and connections.

Near Reggio di Calabria, incidentally, is a much smaller community, Scilla, famous in Homeric legend. You'll spot it during your transit of the Strait of Messina. Mariners of old, including Ulysses, crossed the Strait of Messina from here and faced the menace of the two monsters, Charybdis and Scylla, who—according to myth and legend—delighted in drowning mariners who came too close to their lairs.

1 Taormina ★★★

53km (33 miles) N of Catania, 53km (33 miles) S of Messina, 250km (155 miles) E of Palermo

Taormina was just too good to remain unspoiled. Dating from the 4th century B.C., it hugs the edge of a cliff overlooking the Ionian Sea. Looming in the background is Mt. Etna, an active volcano. Noted for its mild climate, Italy's most beautiful town seems to have no other reason to exist than for the thousands upon thousands of visitors who flock here for shopping, dining, barhopping, and enjoying the nearby beaches.

International tourists pack the main street, Corso Umberto I, from April to October. After that, Taormina quiets down considerably. In spite of the hordes that descend in summer, Taormina is still charming, with much of its medieval character intact. It's filled with intimate piazzas and palazzi dating from the 15th to 19th centuries. You'll find a restaurant for every day of the week, and countless stores sell everything from fine antiques to cheap souvenirs and trinkets.

You can always escape the throngs during the day by seeking out adventures, perhaps climbing Mt. Etna, walking to the Castel Mola, or making a day trip to Syracuse (all described later in this chapter). In summer, of course, you can hang out at the beaches below the town (although Taormina itself isn't right on a beach). At night you can enjoy jazz and disco or just spend some time in a local tavern or restaurant.

A lot of people contributed to putting Taormina on the map. First inhabited by a tribe known as the Siculi, it has known many conquerors, such as the Greeks, Carthaginians, Romans, Saracens, French, and Spanish. Its first tourist is said to have been Goethe, who arrived in 1787 and recorded his impressions in his *Journey to Italy.* Other Germans followed, including a red-haired Prussian, Otto Geleng. Arriving at the age of 20 in Taormina, he recorded its beauties in his painted landscapes, which were exhibited in Paris. They caused much excitement—people had to find out for themselves whether Taormina was really that beautiful.

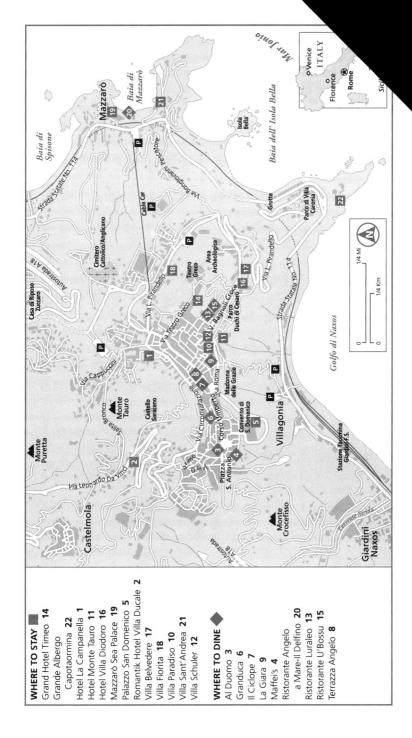

WHERE TO STAY ■
Grand Hotel Timeo **14**
Grande Albergo
  Capotaormina **22**
Hotel La Campanella **1**
Hotel Monte Tauro **11**
Hotel Villa Diodoro **16**
Mazzarò Sea Palace **19**
Palazzo San Domenico **5**
Romantik Hotel Villa Ducale **2**
Villa Belvedere **17**
Villa Fiorita **18**
Villa Paradiso **10**
Villa Sant'Andrea **21**
Villa Schuler **12**

WHERE TO DINE ◆
Al Duomo **3**
Granduca **6**
Il Ciclope **7**
La Giara **9**
Maffei's **4**
Ristorante Angelo
  a Mare-Il Delfino **20**
Ristorante Luraleo **13**
Ristorante U'Bossu **15**
Terrazza Angelo **8**

elm von Gloeden, arrived in 1878 to photograph not
de boys crowned with laurel wreaths. His pictures sent
ocking to Taormina. Von Gloeden's photos, some of
:ial tourist literature to this day, form one of the most
rmina. Souvenir shops still sell his pictures, which,
lalous in their day, seem tame—even innocent—by

steps came a host of celebs hoping to see what all the
ruman Capote, Tennessee Williams, Marlene Dietrich,
Joan Crawford, Rita Hayworth, and Greta Garbo. Always in disguise, sometimes as Harriet Brown, Garbo used Taormina as a vacation retreat from 1950 until her last mysterious arrival in 1979. Many stars, including Garbo, stayed at a villa on the road to Castel Mola owned by Gayelord Hauser, the celebrated dietitian to Hollywood stars of the golden age. In time, another wave of stars arrived, including Elizabeth Taylor and Richard Burton, Cary Grant, and the woman who turned him down, Sophia Loren.

ESSENTIALS

GETTING THERE You can make **rail** connections on the Messina line. It's possible to board a train in Rome for the 8-hour trip to Messina, where you can make connections on to Taormina. Call ✆ **848-888088** for schedules. There are 29 trains a day from both Messina and Catania; trips from both towns take 1 to 1½ hours and cost 8€ ($7.15) one way. The train station at Taormina is a mile from the heart of the resort, below the town. Buses run up a hill every 15 to 45 minutes (schedules vary throughout the year), daily 9am to 9pm; a one-way ticket costs 1.25€ ($1.10). You can also take a cab.

In addition, you can take the train as far as Messina and then hop a Taormina-bound **bus.** There are 14 a day, taking 1½ hours and costing 2.50€ ($2.25) one way. More details are available by calling **Interbus** at ✆ **0942-625301.**

By **car** from Messina, head south along A18. From Catania, continue north along A18.

VISITOR INFORMATION The **tourist office** is in the Palazzo Corvaja, Piazza Santa Caterina (✆ **0942-23243**), open Monday to Saturday 8am to 2pm and 4 to 7pm.

SPECIAL EVENTS The Greek and Roman theaters (see below) offers regular **theatrical performances** July to September. In addition, churches and other venues are the settings for a **summer festival of classical music,** staged from May to September. Each July there's an **international film festival** in the amphitheater.

EXPLORING THE AREA

Many visitors to Taormina come for the beach, although the sands aren't exactly at the resort. To reach the best and most popular beach, the **Lido Mazzarò** ★★, you have to go south of town via a cable car that leaves from Via Pirandello every 15 minutes. A one-way ticket costs 1.50€ ($1.35). This beach is one of the best equipped in Sicily, with bars, restaurants, and hotels. You can rent beach chairs, umbrellas, and watersports equipment at various kiosks from the beginning of April to October. To the right of Lido Mazzarò, past the Capo Sant'Andrea headland, is the region's prettiest cove, where twin crescents of beach sweep from a sand spit out to the miniscule **Isola Bella** islet. You can walk here in a minute from the cable car, but it's more fun to paddle a boat from

Mazzarò around Capo Sant'Andrea, which hides a few grottoes with excellent light effects on the seaward side.

North of Mazzarò are the long, wide beaches of **Spisone** and **Letojanni,** more developed but less crowded than **Giardini,** the large built-up resort beach south of Isola Bella. There's also a local bus that leaves Taormina for Mazzarò, Spisone, and Letojanni, and another that heads down the coast to Giardini; you can catch it outside the town gate on Via Pirandello.

The **Greek Amphitheater (Teatro Greco)** ✷✷✷, Via Teatro Greco (© **0942-23220**), is Taormina's most visited monument, offering a view of rare beauty of Mt. Etna and the seacoast. In the Hellenistic period, the Greeks hewed the theater out of the rocky slope of Mt. Tauro, and the Romans remodeled and modified it greatly. What remains today dates from the 2nd century A.D. The conquering Arabs, who seemed intent on devastating the town, slashed away at it in the 10th century. On the premises is an antiquarium containing artifacts from the classical and early Christian periods. The theater is open daily 9am to 2 hours before sunset. Admission is 4€ ($3.55).

Behind the tourist office, on the other side of Piazza Vittorio Emanuele, is the **Roman Odeon,** a small theater partly covered by the church of Santa Caterina next door. The Romans constructed this theater around A.D. 21, when Taormina was under their rule. Much smaller than the Greek theater and with similar architecture, it was discovered in 1892 by a blacksmith digging in the area. A peristyle (colonnade) was also discovered here, perhaps all that was left of a Greek temple dedicated to Aphrodite. **Santa Caterina** was consecrated to St. Catherine of Alexandria (exact consecration date unknown). It might have been built in the mid–17th century, and the sacristy could have been constructed even earlier. The facade of the sacristy contains two small windows decorated with seashells, the same motif used on the architrave of its doors. The church's open hours are erratic.

Farther along the main drag, **Corso Umberto I,** you arrive at Piazza del Duomo and the **Duomo (cathedral)** of Taormina. Built around 1400 on the ruins of a church from the Middle Ages, this is a fortress cathedral with a Latin-cross plan and a trio of aisles. The nave is held up by half a dozen monolithic columns—three on each side—in pink marble. A fish-scale decoration graces their capitals in honor of the island's maritime tradition. The ceiling of the nave is an attraction, with its wooden beams held up by carved corbels decorated with Arabian scenes. The main portal was reconstructed in 1636, with a large Renaissance-inspired rosette sculpted on it. The cathedral is often open in the early morning or early evening but is likely to be closed during the day. The monsignor apparently opens it when he feels in the mood.

Another thing to do in Taormina is walk through the **Public Garden (Giardino Pubblico),** Via Bagnoli Croce. The flower-filled garden overlooking the sea is a choice spot for views as well as a place to relax. At a bar in the park you can order drinks.

From Taormina, you might want to set out for the nearby village of **Castel Mola** ✷, 3km (2 miles) northwest. This is one of the most beautiful places in eastern Sicily, and you'll have a great view of Mt. Etna if the day is clear. You might also visit **Castello** on the summit of Mt. Tauro, about 3km (2 miles) northwest of Taormina along the Castel Mola road. If you like walking, you might prefer to hike up to it following a footpath. The summit is at 390m (1,280 ft.). Once here, you'll see the ruins of a former acropolis, but most people come for the panoramas.

Meet Mighty Mt. Etna

Warning: Always get the latest report from the tourist office before setting out for a trip to Mt. Etna. Adventurers have been killed by a surprise "belch" (volcanic explosion), and the volcano was erupting again in the summer of 2001.

Looming menacingly over the coast of eastern Sicily, **Mt. Etna** ★★★ is the highest and largest active volcano in Europe—and we do mean active! The peak changes in size over the years but is currently in the neighborhood of 3,292m (10,800 ft.). Etna has been active in modern times (in 1928, the little village of Mascali was buried under its lava), and eruptions in 1971, 1992, and 2001 rekindled Sicilians' fears.

Etna has figured in history and in Greek mythology. Empedocles, the 5th-century-B.C. Greek philosopher, is said to have jumped into its crater as a sign that he was being delivered directly to Mt. Olympus to take his seat among the gods. It was under Etna that Zeus crushed the multi-headed, viper-riddled dragon Typhoeus, thereby securing domination over Olympus. Hephaestus, the god of fire and blacksmiths, made his headquarters in Etna, aided by the single-eyed Cyclops.

The Greeks warned that whenever Typhoeus tried to break out of his prison, lava erupted and earthquakes cracked the land. That must mean that the monster nearly escaped on March 11, 1669, the date of one of the most violent eruptions ever recorded—it destroyed Catania, about 27km (17 miles) away.

For a good view of the ferocious lava-spewing mountain, take one of the trains that circumnavigate the base of the volcano. Board at the **Stazione Giarre,** Via Caronda 490 (© **095-932181**), in Catania, off Viale Leonardo da Vinci. A 4-hour tour from Catania costs 5€ ($4.45). But if

FARTHER AFIELD TO THE ALCANTARA GORGES

To see some beautiful rapids and waterfalls, head outside of town to the **Gole dell'Alcantara** ★ (© **0942-985010**), a series of gorges. Uncharacteristically for Sicily, the waters are extremely cold but quite refreshing in August. It's usually possible to walk up the river May to September (when the water level is low), although you must check locally for current conditions. From the parking lot, you take an elevator partway into the scenic abyss and then continue on foot. You're likely to get wet, so take your bathing suit. If you don't have appropriate shoes, you can rent rubber boots at the entrance. Allow at least an hour for this trip. From October to April, only the entrance is accessible, but the view is always panoramic. It costs 2€ ($1.80) to enter the gorge daily 9am to 5pm. If you're driving, head up SS185 some 17km (11 miles) from Taormina. To get there by bus, take an **Interbus** (© **0942-625301**) for the 20-minute trip departing from Taormina at 9:30am and 12:45pm. There's only one bus back, which leaves at 2:25pm. The round-trip fare is 4.50€ ($4). You can also go by taxi from Taormina, but you'll have to negotiate the fare with your driver. If you'd like a **taxi,** call Franco Nunzio at © **0942-51094.**

you'd prefer a more structured outing, consider a package tour from Taormina. Contact **CST**, Corso Umberto I 101 (✆ **0942-23301**), which organizes tours to Etna Monday to Friday in summer. They cost around 30€ ($26.80).

You can also drive here. Etna lies 31km (19 miles) north of Catania and 60km (37 miles) south of Messina. One of the easiest approaches is via E45 south from Messina or Taormina to Acireale. From here, you can approach by following the signs west going via the little towns of Aci Sant'Antonio and Viagrande, continuing west until you reach the Nicolosi. Allow about 45 minutes from Acireale to Nicolosi. At Nicolosi, you can book one of the official guides from **Funivia del Etna** (✆ **095-911158** or 085-914141). From Nicolosi, the road winds its way up to Rifugio Sapienza, the starting point for all expeditions to the crater. At Rifugio Sapienza, you can get on a cable car that takes you toward the summit. The service runs daily 9am to 4pm and costs 9€ ($8.05).

From Rifugio Sapienza, it's also possible to hike up to the **Torre del Filosofo (Philosopher's Tower)**, at 2,920m (9,580 ft.). The trip there and back takes about 5 hours. At the tower you'll have a panoramic sweep of Etna, with its peaks and craters hissing with steam. This is a difficult hike and not for the faint of heart. The climb is along ashy, pebbly terrain, and once you reach the tower, you have another risky 2-hour hike to the craters. Because the craters can erupt unexpectedly (as they did in the early 1990s, killing 11), all guided tours to the craters have been suspended—if you insist on going all the way, you'll have to do it alone. On the return from the Philosopher's Tower to Rifugio Sapienza, you'll pass Valle de Bove, the original crater of Etna.

SHOPPING

Shopping is easy in Taormina—just find **Corso Umberto I** and go. The trendy shops here sell everything upscale, from lacy linens and fashionable clothing to antique furniture and jewelry. If you're a little more adventurous, you'll want to veer off the Corso and search out the little shops on the side streets.

One of the best outlets for ceramics, in terms of both quality and design, is **Giovanni di Blasi,** 103 Corso Umberto (✆ **0942-24671**), which specializes in the highly valued "white pottery" from Caltagirone.

Mixing the new and the old, **Carlo Panarello,** Corso Umberto I 122 (✆ **0942-23910**), offers Sicilian ceramics (from pots to tables) and also deals in eclectic antique furnishings, paintings, and engravings. A small shop filled with treasures, the **Casa d'Arte Forin,** Corso Umberto I 148 (✆ **0942-23060**), sells Italian antiques, ranging from furniture to prints, silver, and bronze, with an emphasis on Sicilian and Venetian pieces.

Gioielleria Giuseppe Stroscio, Corso Umberto I 169 (✆ **0942-24865**), features antique gold jewelry from 1500 to the early 1900s. The jewelers at **Estro,** Corso Umberto I 205 (✆ **0942-24991**), sell contemporary rings, necklaces, and bracelets. Hand-embroidered lace is the draw at **Galeano** (aka **Concetta**), Corso

Umberto I 233 (© **0942-625144**), where bedspreads and tablecloths are meticulously crafted from fine cotton and linen.

WHERE TO STAY

The hotels in Taormina are the best in Sicily—in fact, they're the finest in Italy south of Amalfi. All price levels and accommodations are available, from sumptuous suites to army cots.

If you're coming primarily to hit the beach, at least in July and August, then consider staying at Mazzarò, 5km (3 miles) from the center (see below), and trekking up the hill for the shopping, nightlife, and dining. At other times, you might want to stay in Taormina itself because it has far more charm and attractions than anything down by the sea.

The curse of Taormina hotels in summer is the noise, not only of traffic but also of visitors who turn the town into an all-night party. If you're a light sleeper and you've chosen a hotel along Corso Umberto, ask for a room in the rear. You might not get a view, but at least you might get a good night's sleep.

If you're driving to the top of Taormina to a hotel, call ahead to see what arrangements can be made for your car. Also ask for clear directions because the narrow one-way streets are bewildering once you get here.

VERY EXPENSIVE

Grand Hotel Timeo ⊛⊛⊛   Hidden in a tranquil private park full of cypresses and magnolias just below the ancient Greek amphitheater, the Timeo opened in 1873 and has hosted everyone from King Umberto II to Liz Taylor and Richard Burton. Old-world elegance and Victorian antiques combine with contemporary conveniences. All the guest rooms are spacious and well furnished, with large marble bathrooms. Guests are greeted with a fruit basket or a bottle of dessert wine on arrival. All the rooms have balconies with a view of the snow-capped volcanic peak of Mount Etna or the sea. Rooms 301 to 316 enjoy the widest panorama. The hotel has a private beach with lounge chairs, umbrellas, and other amenities; the staff will also help you arrange for tee times at nearby golf courses. Because it's so close to the monument, local archaeological authorities are still doing battle with the hotel in court, refusing its right to dig for a swimming pool so close to the Greek ruins.

Via Teatro Greco 59, 98039 Taormina. © **0942-23801.** Fax 0942-628501. www.cormorano.net/framon/ timeo. 87 units. 366€ ($326.85) double; from 465€ ($415.25) suite. Rates include breakfast. AE, DC, MC, V. Parking is free. **Amenities:** Sophisticated restaurant; piano bar; concierge; car-rental desk; shuttle service to the beach; room service; babysitting; laundry. *In room:* A/C, TV, minibar, hair dryer, safe.

Palazzo San Domenico ⊛⊛   Having hosted illustrious guests such as François Mitterrand and Sir Winston Churchill, this is one of Europe's great old hotels, converted from a 14th-century Dominican monastery. It's looking a bit tired these days, though, even after a discreet 1997 renovation. Its position is high up from the coast, on different levels surrounded by magnificent terraced gardens of almond, orange, and lemon trees. The medieval courtyard is planted with semitropical trees and flowers. The encircling enclosed loggia—the old cloister—is decorated with potted palms. Off the loggia are great refectory halls turned into sumptuous lounges. Although antiques are everywhere, the atmosphere is gracious rather than museumlike. The guest rooms, opening off the cloister, are eclectically furnished with elaborate carved beds, provincial pieces, Turkish rugs, and Venetian chairs and dressers in keeping with the building's role as an antique monastery (some look a bit dowdy, however). The most desirable rooms are those overlooking the water.

Piazza San Domenico 5, 98039 Taormina. ☎ **0942-613111.** Fax 0942-625506. www.sandomenico.thi.it. 108 units. 274€–423€ ($244.70–$377.75) double; from 700€ ($625.10) suite. Rates include breakfast. AE, DC, MC, V. Free parking outside; 3 spaces inside (summer only) 15€ ($13.40). **Amenities:** Excellent restaurant; piano bar; heated pool; concierge; conference center; room service; babysitting; laundry. *In room:* A/C, TV, minibar, hair dryer, safe (in most rooms).

EXPENSIVE TO MODERATE

Hotel Monte Tauro   This hotel is built into the side of a hill rising high above the sea. Renovated in the early 1990s, each room has a circular balcony with a sea view, often festooned with flowers. Most rooms are medium in size, each furnished to a high standard, with tiled bathrooms. The social center is the pool, whose cantilevered platform is ringed with dozens of plants.

Via Madonna delle Grazie 3, 98039 Taormina. ☎ **0942-24402.** Fax 0942-24403. www.tao.it/hotelmontetauro. 87 units. 210€ ($187.55) double; from 250€ ($223.25) junior suite. Rates include breakfast. AE, DC, MC, V. Closed Jan 15–Mar. **Amenities:** Restaurant; 2 bars; pool; room service; babysitting; laundry/dry cleaning. *In room:* A/C, TV, minibar, hair dryer, safe.

Hotel Villa Diodoro ✦   This is one of Taormina's better hotels, with tasteful design through and through. There are sunny spots where you can swim, sunbathe, and enjoy the view of mountains, trees, and flowers. The guest rooms are elegant and comfortable, with wrought-iron headboards, terra-cotta floors, balconies, and compact tiled bathrooms. A shuttle bus makes a half-dozen runs per day (June–Oct) to the beach at nearby Lido Caparena.

Via Bagnoli Croce 75, 98039 Taormina. ☎ **0942-23312.** Fax 0942-23391. 99 units (showers only). 165.25€–258.20€ ($147.60–$230.60) double. Rates include breakfast. AE, DC, MC, V. Free parking. **Amenities:** Dining room; lounge; pool; room service; laundry. *In room:* A/C, TV, minibar, hair dryer, safe.

Romantik Hotel Villa Ducale ✦✦   This restored old villa boasts magnificent views of the Mediterranean, the town, and Mt. Etna. Villa Ducale sits on a hillside, a 10-minute uphill walk from the center, in a quiet setting. It's a charming and romantic choice. Each guest room has a veranda with a sea view, an antique Sicilian decor with terra-cotta floors and wrought-iron beds, and a compact tiled bathroom. The service is warm and helpful.

Via Leonardo da Vinci 60, 98039 Taormina. ☎ **0942-28153.** Fax 0942-28710. www.hotelvilladucale.it. 15 units. 155€–238€ ($138.40–$212.55) double; 310€–413€ ($276.85–$368.80) suite. Rates include buffet breakfast. AE, MC, V. Parking 7€ ($6.25). **Amenities:** Lounge; shuttle service to the beach; room service; laundry. *In room:* A/C, TV, minibar, hair dryer, safe.

Villa Belvedere   With a friendly reception, professional maintenance, and an old-fashioned style, this hotel near the Giardino Pubblico offers the same view enjoyed by guests at the more expensive hotels nearby. Guests congregate on the cliffside terrace in the rear to enjoy that view of Sicilian skies and the Ionian Sea, plus the cypress-studded hillside and menacing Mt. Etna. The guest rooms all feature functional furniture with a touch of class. Most rooms have slivers of balconies from which to enjoy views over the neighboring public gardens to the sea, and top-floor rooms have small terraces from which you can glimpse Mt. Etna (and double-paned windows to block noise from the street above). The hotel is located near the cable car and the steps down to the beach.

Via Bagnoli Croci 79, 98039 Taormina. ☎ **0942-23791.** Fax 0942-625830. www.villabelvedere.it. 47 units. 93€–154€ ($83.05–$137.50) double. Rates include breakfast. MC, V. Parking 5.50€ ($4.90). Closed late Nov to mid-Dec and mid-Jan to early Mar. **Amenities:** 2 bars; pool; room service; laundry. *In room:* A/C, TV, hair dryer, safe.

Villa Paradiso   The creation of Signore Salvatore Martorana, this charming hotel is at one end of the town's main street, near the Greek amphitheater. The living room is furnished in a personal manner, with antiques and reproductions. Each individually decorated guest room has a balcony; the tiled bathrooms are a bit cramped. Late May to late October, the hotel offers free access to the private Paradise Beach Club 6km (3¾ miles) east in Letojanni, which has an array of activities and beach facilities.

Via Roma 2, 98039 Taormina. ℂ **0942-23922**. Fax 0942-625800. 35 units. 105.35€–170.45€ ($94.10–$152.20) double; from 131€ ($116.95) junior suite. AE, DC, MC, V. Parking 12€ ($10.70). **Amenities:** Bar; lounge; room service. *In room:* A/C, TV, hair dryer, safe.

INEXPENSIVE

Hotel La Campanella This hotel is rich in plants, paintings, and hospitality. It sits at the top of a seemingly endless flight of stairs, which begin at a sharp curve of the main road leading into town. You climb past terra-cotta pots and the dangling tendrils of a terraced garden, eventually arriving at the house. The owners maintain clean and simple guest rooms, each containing potted plants and homey touches. The tiled bathrooms are tidy.

Via Circonvallazione 3, 98039 Taormina. ℂ **0942-23381**. Fax 0942-625248. 12 units (showers only). 60€ ($53.60) double. Rates include breakfast. No credit cards. **Amenities:** Lounge. *In room:* Hair dryer.

Villa Fiorita ★ (Value) This small inn stretches toward the Greek theater from its position beside the road leading to the top of this cliff-hugging town. Its imaginative decor includes a handful of ceramic stoves, which the owner delights in collecting. A well-maintained flower garden lies alongside an empty but ancient Greek tomb whose stone walls have been classified a national treasure. The guest rooms are arranged in a steplike labyrinth of corridors and stairwells, some of which bend to correspond to the rocky slope on which the hotel was built. Each unit contains a piece of antique furniture, and most have flowery private terraces, plus tiled bathrooms.

Via Pirandello 39, 98039 Taormina. ℂ **0942-24122**. Fax 0942-625967. 25 units (showers only). 105.85€ ($94.55) double; 131.70€ ($117.60) suite. Rates include breakfast. AE, MC, V. Parking 10.35€ ($9.25). **Amenities:** Lounge; pool; room service. *In room:* A/C, TV, hair dryer, safe.

Villa Schuler ★ (Value) Filled with the fragrance of bougainvillea and jasmine, this hotel offers style and comfort at a great price. Family-owned and -run, it sits high above the Ionian Sea, with views of snowcapped Mt. Etna and the Bay of Naxos. The hotel is only a 2-minute stroll from Corso Umberto I and about a 15-minute walk from the cable car to the beach below. The guest rooms are comfortably furnished, and many have a small balcony or terrace with a view of the sea. Breakfast can be served in your room or taken on a terrace with a panoramic sea view. We'd be happy to return here again and again. The service is impeccable.

The most luxurious way to stay here is to book the garden villa suite with its own private access. It's beautifully furnished and spacious with two bathrooms (one with a Jacuzzi). The villa comes with a kitchenette, patio, private garden, and veranda, and costs from 165€ ($147.35) per day for two, including breakfast.

Piazzetta Bastione, Via Roma, 98039 Taormina. ℂ **0942-23481**. Fax 0942-23522. www.villaschuler.com. 26 units. 110€ ($98.25) double; 144€ ($128.60) junior suite. Rates include breakfast. AE, DC, DISC, MC, V. Parking 10€ ($8.95) in garage; free outside. **Amenities:** Bar; lounge; room service; laundry. *In room:* A/C, TV, hair dryer, safe.

WHERE TO STAY NEARBY

If you visit Taormina in summer, you might prefer to stay at **Mazzarò,** about 5km (3 miles) away. This is the major beach and has some fine hotels. A bus for

Mazzarò leaves from the center of Taormina every 30 minutes daily 8am to 9pm (the return-trip schedule is the same). The one-way fare is 1€ (90¢).

Grande Albergo Capotaormina The Grande Albergo is a world unto itself, atop a rugged cape projecting into the Ionian Sea. It was designed by one of Italy's most famous architects, Minoletti. There are five floors with wide sun terraces, plus a saltwater pool at the edge of the cape. Elevators take you through 46m (150 ft.) of solid rock to the beach below. The guest rooms are handsome and well proportioned, with roomy tiled bathrooms and wide glass doors opening onto private terraces.

Via Nazionale 105, 98039 Mazzarò. (𝐂) **0942-572111.** Fax 0942-625467. www.capotaorminahotel.com. 200 units. From 210€ ($187.55) double; from 297.50€ ($265.65) suite. Rates include buffet breakfast. AE, DC, MC. V. Parking 7.50€ ($6.70) in garage; free outside. Closed Oct 30–Mar. **Amenities:** Restaurant; 2 bars; cafe; pool; gym; room service; laundry/dry cleaning. *In room:* A/C, TV, minibar, hair dryer, safe.

Mazzarò Sea Palace The Sea Palace, the leading hotel in Mazzarò, opens onto the most beautiful bay in Sicily and has a private beach. Completed in 1962, it has been renovated frequently since, most recently in the mid-1990s. Big windows let in cascades of light and offer views of the coast. The guest rooms are well furnished, filled with wicker and veneer pieces, along with original art and wood or tile floors; most have panoramic views.

Via Nazionale 147, 98030 Mazzarò. (𝐂) **0942-24004.** Fax 0942-626237. www.mazzaroseapalace.it. 72 units. 274€–388€ ($244.70–$346.50) double; 428€–540€ ($382.20–$482.20) suite. Rates include half-board. AE, DC, MC, V. Parking 15.60€ ($13.95) nearby. **Amenities:** Restaurant; bar; pool; fitness center; room service; babysitting; laundry/dry cleaning. *In room:* A/C, TV, minibar, hair dryer, safe.

Villa Sant'Andrea This hotel lies at the base of the mountain, directly on the sea, and has a private beach. Staying here is like going to a house party at a pretty home. The atmosphere and tasteful refurbishment draw return visits by artists, painters, and other discerning guests. The guest rooms are well maintained and comfortable, although their size and decor vary. Many have balconies or terraces with sea views. The tiled bathrooms are small but adequate. A cable car, just outside the front gates, runs into the heart of Taormina.

Via Nazionale 137, 98030 Taormina Mare. (𝐂) **0942-23125.** Fax 0942-24838. www.framon-hotels.com. 67 units. 174€–308€ ($155.40–$275.05) double. Rates include breakfast. AE, DC, MC, V. Parking 13€ ($11.60). **Amenities:** 2 restaurants; bar; boat rental; room service; babysitting; laundry/dry cleaning. *In room:* A/C, TV, minibar, hair dryer, safe.

WHERE TO DINE
EXPENSIVE

La Giara SICILIAN/ITALIAN The kitchen here is extremely accomplished, turning out flavorful dishes that make the most of fresh ingredients grown in the southern sunshine of Italy. The Art Deco ambience is also inviting—marble floors and columns shaped from stone quarried in the fields outside Syracuse. The pastas are worthy of meals unto themselves, and we're especially fond of the ricotta-stuffed cannelloni served with zucchini cream au gratin, the tagliolini with savory lemon-and-shrimp sauce, and the ravioli stuffed with pesto-flavored eggplant and covered with tomato sauce. The fresh fish of the day is grilled to perfection, and meats are cooked equally well.

Vico la Floresta 1. (𝐂) **0942-23360.** Reservations required. Main courses 15€–23.50€ ($13.40–$21). AE, DC, MC, V. Apr–July and Sept–Oct Tues–Sun 8:15–11pm (Nov–Mar open only Fri–Sat, Aug open daily).

Maffei's *Finds* SICILIAN/SEAFOOD Maffei's is very small, with only 10 tables, but it serves the best fish in Taormina. Every day the chef selects the freshest fish at the market, and you can tell him how you'd like it prepared. We often select the house specialty, swordfish *alla messinese,* braised with tomato sauce, black olives, and capers. The *fritto misto* (a mixed fish fry with calamari, shrimp, swordfish, and sea bream) is superbly light because it's prepared with a good-quality virgin olive oil. Among the desserts are velvety lemon mousse and crepes flambé stuffed with vanilla cream.

Via San Domenico de Guzman 1. © 0942-24055. Reservations required. Main courses 22.50€–45€ ($20.10–$40.20). AE, DC, MC, V. Daily noon–3pm and 7–11pm. Closed early Jan to mid-Feb.

MODERATE

Al Duomo 𝒦 SICILIAN/MESSINESE   Known for its outside terrace dining, this restaurant uses the freshest local produce and regional ingredients. It's an attractive place, with brickwork tiles and inlaid marble tables. The romantic terrace provides a view of the square and the cathedral. Try the stewed lamb with potatoes, pecorino cheese, and red Sicilian wine. Homemade pastas are served with an array of succulent sauces. The fried calamari is sautéed in extra-virgin olive oil and not overcooked. Another marvelous dish is rissolé of fresh anchovies. For dessert, taste a typical almond cake or a Sicilian cassata.

Vico Ebrei 11. © 0942-625656. Reservations required. Main courses 7.50€–15€ ($6.70–$13.40). AE, DC, MC, V. Nov–Mar Mon–Sat noon–2:30pm and 7–11pm; Apr–Oct Thurs–Mon noon–2:30pm and 7–11pm.

Granduca 𝒦 *(Finds* ITALIAN/SICILIAN   This is the most atmospheric choice in town, and it also serves an excellent, carefully executed cuisine. You enter into an antiques store with potted plants and various art objects. Even more alluring is the terrace with its panoramic views. In fair weather, request a table in the beautiful gardens. The competent cookery always focuses on the quality of its ingredients. Our favorite pasta here is spaghetti alla Norma (with tomato sauce, eggplant, and ricotta cheese). If you want something truly Sicilian, ask for pasta with sardines. Pasta also comes with a savory kettle of freshly caught mussels and clams. The best meat dish is *involtini alla Siciliana,* or grilled meat rolls, and at night you can choose a pizza baked in a wood-fired oven.

Corso Umberto 172. © 0942-24983. Reservations recommended. Main courses 9.30€–10€ ($8.30–$8.95); fixed-price menu 7.75€–10.30€ ($6.90–$9.20). AE, DC, MC, V. Daily 12:30–3pm and 7:30pm–midnight. Closed Tues in winter.

Il Ciclope *(Value* SICILIAN/ITALIAN   This is one of the best of Taormina's low-priced trattorie. Set back from the main street, it opens onto the pint-size Piazzetta Salvatore Leone. In summer, try for an outside table. The meals are fairly simple, but the ingredients are fresh and the dishes are well prepared. Try the fish soup or Sicilian squid. If those don't interest you, go for entrecôte Ciclope or grilled shrimp. Most diners begin with a selection from the *antipasti di mare,* a savory assortment of seafood hors d'oeuvres.

Corso Umberto I 203. © 0942-23263. Main courses 17.50€–30€ ($15.65–$26.80). AE, DC, MC, V. Thurs–Tues noon–3pm and 6:30–10pm. Closed Jan 10–Feb 15 and Wed Oct–May.

Ristorante Luraleo *(Value* SICILIAN/INTERNATIONAL   Luraleo offers excellent value for an attractive price. Many diners prefer the flowery terrace, where pastel tablecloths are shaded by a vine-covered arbor. If you prefer to dine indoors, there's a rustic dining room with tile accents, flowers, evening candle-light, racks of wine bottles, and a rich antipasto table. The grilled fish is a good choice, as are pastas (such as homemade macaroni with tomato, eggplant, and basil), regional dishes, and herb-flavored steak. Risotto with salmon and pista-chio nuts is a specialty.

Via Bagnoli Croce 31. (C) **0942-24279.** Reservations recommended. Main courses 15€–25€ ($13.40–$22.35). DC, MC, V. Daily 10am–3pm and 6pm–midnight. Closed Wed in winter.

Ristorante U'Bossu SICILIAN/MEDITERRANEAN   Vines twine around the facade of this small restaurant in a quiet part of town. Amid fresh flowers, wagon-wheel chandeliers, prominently displayed wine bottles, and burnished wooden panels, you can enjoy a meal pungent with the aromas of an herb garden. Start with the complimentary *bruschetta* (grilled bread with oil and garlic or tomato). Specialties include *pasta con la sarde* (with fish) and *involtini di pesce spada* (swordfish stew), and there's a groaning antipasti table. The restaurant is decorated with a folkloric scene from *Cavalleria Rusticana,* and the chef has paid homage to the famed opera by naming his best pasta dish, *maccheroni alla Turiddu,* after the principal character (it contains tuna, olives, capers, onions, wild herbs, tomatoes, and fennel). For dessert, nothing can top the zabaglione with fresh strawberries.

Via Bagnoli Croce 50. (C) **0942-23311.** Reservations recommended. Main courses 7€–13€ ($6.25–$11.60); fixed-price menu 20€ ($17.85). V. Tues–Sun noon–3pm and 6pm–midnight. Closed Jan 10–May 10.

Terrazza Angelo SICILIAN/PIZZA   For years, this old-fashioned rustic place was famous as Giova Rosy, one of the best restaurants in town. Under new management and a new name, it's now receiving mixed reviews. We find it an acceptable but unimaginative choice. It serves a variety of local specialties, such as linguine and risotto dishes. Seafood offerings include *spiedini* (a kabob) with shrimp and lobster dosed with a generous shot of cognac, tagliolini with seafood, and swordfish cooked *in cartoccio* (in a paper bag).

Corso Umberto I 38. (C) **0942-24411.** Reservations recommended. Main courses 10€–12.50€ ($8.95–$11.15). AE, DC, V. Daily noon–3pm and 7pm–midnight. Closed Nov and on Thurs in winter.

WHERE TO DINE NEARBY

Ristorante Angelo a Mare–Il Delfino MEDITERRANEAN/ITALIAN   This late-19th-century structure is in Mazzarò, about 5km (3 miles) from Taormina and a 2-minute walk from the cable-car station. From the flower-filled terrace, there's a view over the bay. The decor and the menu items are inspired by the sea and carefully supervised by the chef/owner. Mussels *delphio* (cooked with garlic, parsley, olive oil, and lemons) and house-style steak (with fresh tomatoes, onions, garlic, capers, and parsley) are specialties. Other good choices are *involtini* (a roll layered with foodstuffs) of fish, cannelloni, *risotto marinara* (fisherman's rice), and anchovies roasted with basil.

Via Nazionale. (C) **0942-23004.** Reservations recommended. Main courses 12€–25€ ($10.70–$22.35). AE, DC, MC, V. Daily noon–3pm and 6pm–midnight. Closed Nov–Mar.

TAORMINA AFTER DARK

Begin your evening at the **Caffè Wunderbar,** Piazza IX Aprile 7, Corso Umberto I ((C) **0942-625302**), a popular spot that was once a favorite watering hole of Tennessee Williams. Beneath a vine-covered arbor, the outdoor section is perched as close to the edge of the cliff as safety allows. We prefer one of the Victorian armchairs beneath chandeliers in the elegant interior. There's a well-stocked bar, as well as a piano bar. It's open daily 8:30am to 2:30am, and closed Tuesday from November to February.

The entire town is geared to having fun, and you'll find a good many bars and clubs. **Bella Blu,** Guardiola Vecchia ((C) **0942-24239**), caters to a high-energy European crowd. At the **Club Septimo,** Via San Pancrazio 50 ((C) **0942-625522**), a sweeping view of the town and the sea is framed with reproductions of ancient Roman columns, and the interior has all the strobe and ultraviolet lights you might want. More elegant than either of these is **La Jarra,** Via La Floresta 1, off Corso Umberto I (② **0942-23360**), the only one of the three that's open year-round.

Other hot spots worth frequenting are **Café Marrakech,** Piazza Garibaldi 2 (② **0942-625692**), which leans heavily on its Moroccan theme, even with Sahara-like tents. In back of the Café Marrakech is a much-frequented mixed club, **Shateulle,** Piazza Garibaldi (② **0942-616175**), which in summer stays open at least until dawn (likely to close at 2 or 3am off-season).

A younger, wilder crowd tends to head for the places down by the water. Here the hottest action is at **Tout Va,** Via Pirandello 70 (② **0942-23824**), an open-air club that offers panoramic views and action late into the night.

EN ROUTE TO SYRACUSE: A STOP AT CATANIA 🌟

Catania is a suitable base if you're planning a jaunt up Mt. Etna. It lies 52km (32 miles) south of Taormina and 60km (37 miles) north of Syracuse. Largely industrial (with sulfur factories), the important port opens onto the Ionian Sea. In 1693, an earthquake virtually leveled the city, and Etna has rained lava on it on many occasions; so its history is fraught with natural disasters.

Somehow Catania has learned to live with Etna, but the volcano's presence is felt everywhere. For example, in certain parts of the city you'll find hardened remains of lava flows, all a sickly purple color. Grottoes in weird shapes, almost fantasylike, line the shores, and boulderlike islands rise from the water.

Catania's present look, earning for it the title of the "baroque city," stems from just after the 1693 earthquake, when the Camastra duke, with several architects and artists, decided to rebuild the city in the baroque style. This reconstruction took the whole 18th century. The most famous artists involved were Alonzo Di Benedetto, Antonino and Francesco Battaglia, Giovanni Vaccarini, and Stefano Ittar. Fragments of solidified black lava were used (first by the Romans and then until the end of the 19th c.) in the construction of walls. This lava, and the way it was positioned into the masonry, gave added strength to the walls.

Splitting the city is **Via Etnea** 🌟, flanked with 18th-century palazzi. The locals are fond of strolling through the **Bellini Garden (Giardini Bellini),** named to honor Vicenzo Bellini, the young (dead at 32) composer of operas such as *Norma* and *La Sonnambula,* who was born in Catania in 1801. If you're interested, you can see the home where he lived until he was 16, now the **Bellini Museum (Museo Belliniano),** Piazza San Francesco 3 (② **095-7150535**). Consisting of five rooms, the museum is organized to trace the composer's musical evolution from cradle to grave. At the entrance, note the painting *Apoteosi di'Bellini* (*Bellini's Apotheosis*), by Michele Rapisardi. Among the relics on display are Bellini's funeral mask, a small bust, and a Girolamo Bozza portrait (*Il Ritratto*). Of particular interest are the several musical manuscripts autographed by Bellini. Admission is free.

Built in the late 11th century, Catania's **Duomo** 🌟, Piazza del Duomo (no phone), honors St. Agatha, the city's patroness. It was rebuilt after the 1693 earthquake, and its most outstanding feature is the curving baroque facade, a Vaccarini masterpiece. The chapel to the right as you enter contains the sarcophagus of Costanza, wife of Frederick III of Aragón, who died in 1363. The southern chapel honors St. Agatha. An elaborate Spanish doorway leads into the reliquary and treasury. Note also the carved choir stalls, illustrating scenes from the life of St. Agatha. Admission is free, and the cathedral is open daily 7:30am to noon and 4:15 to 7pm.

Most rushed visitors today pass through only on their way to or from Catania's airport, which in Sicily is second in importance only to Palermo's. Flights on Alitalia, including those from Rome, arrive at **Aeroporto Fontanarossa** (✆ **095-7306266**), 5km (3 miles) south of the city center. From here, you can take the Alibus (or a taxi) into the Catania train station, where you'll find nine trains per day leaving for Taormina, costing 2.45€ ($2.20) one way. However, there is a bus just outside the airport gate that will take you directly to Taormina in about an hour, costing about 4€ ($3.55). It's much more convenient than getting to the train station.

WHERE TO STAY

Villa Paradiso dell'Etna ✦ If you need to stay near the Fontanarossa airport, you might want to spend the night here, 11km (6¾ miles) from Catania. This elegant hotel lies on the slopes of Etna, surrounded by gardens. It was opened in 1927 and is now restored to its former glory. The villa offers the finest rooms in this area, all with Sicilian antiques and views of the volcano, plus roomy bathrooms.

Via per Viagrande 37, 95030 San Giovanni La Punta. ✆ 095-7512409. Fax 095-7413861. www.paradiso etna.it. 34 units. 210€ ($187.55) double; 325€ ($290.25) suite. Rates include breakfast. AE, DC, MC, V. From Catania, take A18 and exit at Catania Nord; then follow the signs for San Giovanni la Punta. **Amenities:** Restaurant; lounge; pool; room service; laundry. *In room:* A/C, TV, minibar, hair dryer, safe.

WHERE TO DINE

Trattoria La Paglia SICILIAN Our favorite restaurant in town is located in the lively fish market. Just ask for Maria and follow her advice. For an opening, request her *la triaca pasta,* pasta in a fresh bean sauce. For a main course, try any of the fish. If you dare not like Maria's offerings of the day, she'll let you step out in the market and buy a fish you do like, and then she'll cook it to your specifications.

Via Pardo 23. ✆ 095-346838. Reservations unnecessary. Meals 7.50€–13€ ($6.70–$11.60). MC, V. Mon–Sat 12:30–2:30pm and 8–11pm.

2 Syracuse & Ortygia Island ✦✦✦

56km (35 miles) SE of Catania

Of all the Greek cities of antiquity that flourished on the coast of Sicily, Syracuse (Siracusa) was the most important, a formidable competitor of Athens. In its heyday, it dared take on Carthage and even Rome. At one time, its wealth and size were unmatched by any other city in Europe.

Colonists from Corinth founded Syracuse on the Ionian Sea in about 735 B.C. Much of its history was linked to despots, beginning in 485 with Gelon, the tyrant of Gela, who subdued the Carthaginians at Himera. Syracuse came under attack from Athens in 415, but the main Athenian fleet was destroyed and the soldiers on the mainland were captured. They were herded into the Latomia di Cappuccini at Piazza Cappuccini, a stone quarry. The "jail," from which there was no escape, was particularly horrid—the defeated soldiers weren't given food and were packed together like cattle and allowed to die slowly.

Dionysius I was one of the greatest despots, reigning over the city during its height, in the 4th century B.C., when it extended its influence as a sea power. But in A.D. 212, the city fell to the Romans under Marcellus, who sacked its riches and art. In that attack, Syracuse lost its most famous son, the Greek physicist/mathematician Archimedes, who was slain in his study by a Roman soldier.

Although the ruins of Syracuse will be one of the highlights of your trip to Sicily, the city itself has been in a millennia-long decline. Today it's a blend of often unattractive modern development (with supermarkets and high-rises sprouting along speedways) and the ruins of its former glory, a splendor that led Livy to proclaim it "the most beautiful and noble of Greek cities."

A lot of what you'll want to see is on the island of Ortygia, which is filled with not only ancient ruins but also small craft shops and dozens of boutiques. From the mainland, Corso Umberto leads to the Ponte Nuova, which leads to the island. Parking is a serious problem on Ortygia, so if you're driving, park in one of the garages near the bridge and then walk over and explore the island on foot. Allow at least 2 hours to explore, plus another hour to shop along the narrow streets. You'll also want to sit for half an hour or so on Piazza del Duomo, off Via Cavour. This is one of the most elegant squares in Sicily.

The ancient sights are a good half hour's walk back inland from Ortygia, going past a fairly forgettable shopping strip, so you might want to take a cab (they're easily found at all the sights). If you don't see a cab, you can call ℂ **0931-69722,** and one will be sent for you. You'll find buses on Ortygia at Piazza Pancali/Largo XXV Luglio. The harbor front is lined with a collection of 18th- and 19th-century town houses.

Syracuse is a cauldron in summer. You can do as the locals do and head for the sea. The finest **beach** is about 19km (12 miles) away at **Fontane Bianche;** bus nos. 21 and 22 leave from the Syracuse post office, Piazza delle Poste 15. If you're driving, Fontane Bianche lies to the south of the city (it's signposted); take SS115 to reach it. The same buses will take you to **Lido Arenella,** only 8km (5 miles) away but not as good.

ESSENTIALS

GETTING THERE   From other major cities in Sicily, Syracuse is best reached by **train.** It's 1½ hours from Catania, 2 hours from Taormina, and 5 hours from Palermo. Usually you must transfer in Catania. For information, call ℂ **848-888088.** Trains arrive in Syracuse at the station on Via Francesco Crispi, centrally located midway between the archaeological park and Ortygia.

From Catania, 12 SAIS **buses** daily make the 1¼-hour trip to Syracuse. The one-way fare is 4€ ($3.55). Phone **SAIS** (ℂ **0931-66710** in Syracuse or 095-536168 in Catania) for information and schedules.

By **car** from Taormina, continue south along A18 and then E45, past Catania. Although trip time depends on traffic, allow at least 1½ hours.

VISITOR INFORMATION   The **tourist office** is at San Sebastiano 45 (ℂ **0931-67710** or 0931-65201), and there's a branch office at the entrance to the archaeological park. Both are open Monday to Saturday 8:30am to 1:30pm and 3 to 6pm.

SPECIAL EVENTS   Some of the most memorable cultural events in Sicily are presented in May and June of even-numbered years, when actors from the Instituto Nazionale del Dramma Antico present **classical plays** by Aeschylus,

---

⌜**Tips** **Read Before You Go**

Before your trip, you might want to read Mary Renault's novel *The Mask of Apollo,* set in Syracuse in the 5th century B.C. As one critic put it, "It brings the stones to life."

Euripides, and their contemporaries. The setting is the ancient Greek theater (Teatro Greco) in the archaeological park, beneath the open sky. Tickets cost 18€ to 31€ ($16.05–$27.70). For information, schedules, and tickets, write or call **INDA,** Corso G. Matteotti 29, 96100 Siracusa (② **0931-67415** or 1478-82211 from Italy only).

SEEING THE ANCIENT SIGHTS

Archaeological Zone (Zona Archeologica) ★★★   Syracuse's archaeological park contains the town's most important attractions, all on the mainland at the western edge of town, to the immediate north of Stazione Centrale where the trains pull in from other parts of Sicily, including Messina and Taormina. The entrance to the park is down Via Augusto.

On the Temenite Hill, the **Greek Theater (Teatro Greco)** ★★★ was one of the great theaters of the classical period. Hewn from rock during the reign of Hieron I in the 5th century B.C., the ancient seats have been largely eaten away by time. However, you can still stand on the remnants of the stone stage where plays by Euripides were mounted. The theater was much restored in the time of Hieron II in the 3rd century B.C. In the spring of even-numbered years (and in Segesta, in the summer of odd-numbered years), the Italian Institute of Ancient Drama presents classical plays by Euripides, Aeschylus, and Sophocles. (In other words, the show hasn't changed much in 2,000 years!)

Outside the entrance to the Greek Theater is the most famous of the ancient quarries, the **Paradise Quarry (Latomia del Paradiso)** ★★, one of four or five from which stones were hauled to erect the great monuments of Syracuse in its glory days. Upon seeing the cave in the wall, Caravaggio is reputed to have dubbed it the "Ear of Dionysius" because of its unusual shape. But what an ear—it's nearly 61m (200 ft.) long. You can enter the inner chamber of the grotto, where the tearing of paper sounds like a gunshot. Although it's dismissed by some scholars as fanciful, the story goes that the despot Dionysius used to force prisoners into the "ear" at night, where he was able to hear every word they said. Nearby is the **Grotta dei Cordari,** where ropemakers plied their craft.

The **Roman Amphitheater (Anfiteatro Romano)** ★ was created at the time of Augustus. It ranks among the top five amphitheaters left by the Romans in Italy. Like the Greek theater, part of it was carved from rock. Unlike the Greek theater and its classical plays, the Roman amphitheater tended toward gutsier fare. Gladiators (prisoners of war and "exotic" blacks from Africa) faced each other with tridents and daggers, or naked slaves were whipped into the center of a battle to the death between wild beasts. Either way, the victim lost: If his opponent, man or beast, didn't do him in, the crowd would often scream for the ringmaster to slit his throat. The amphitheater is near the entrance to the park, but you can also view it in its entirety from a belvedere on the road.

Via Del Teatro (off intersection of Corso Gelone and Viale Teocrito). ② **0931-66206.** Admission 4€ ($3.55). Apr–Oct daily 9am–6pm; Nov–Mar daily 9am–3pm.

Paolo Orsi Regional Archaeological Museum (Museo Archeologico Regionale Paolo Orsi) ★★   One of the most important archaeological museums in southern Italy surveys the Greek, Roman, and early Christian epochs in sculpture and in fragments of archaeological remains. The museum also has a rich coin collection. The best known of the several excellent statues here is the headless *Venus Anadyomene* (rising from the sea), from the Hellenistic period in the 2nd century B.C. One of the earliest works is of an earth mother suckling two babes, from the 6th century B.C. The pre-Greek vases have great style and elegance.

In the gardens of the Villa Landolina in Akradina, Viale Teocrito 66. © 0931-464022. Admission 8€ ($7.15). Tues–Sat 9am–1pm; Mon and Wed 3:30–6:30pm.

Catacombs of St. John (Catacombe di San Giovanni) ⭐⭐ These honey-combed tunnels of empty coffins evoke the catacombs along the Appian Way in Rome. You enter the world below from the Chiesa di San Giovanni, established in the 3rd century A.D. (the present building is much more recent). Included in the early Christian burial grounds is the crypt of St. Marcianus, which lies under what was reportedly the first cathedral erected in Sicily. The catacombs lie on the mainland, immediately to the east of the archaeological zone.

Warning: Make sure that you exit in plenty of time before closing. Two readers who entered the catacombs after 5pm were accidentally locked in and managed to escape only after a harrowing ordeal of wandering around in the dark.

Piazza San Giovanni, at end of Viale San Giovanni. © 0931-66571. Admission 3€ ($2.70). Open Tues–Sun 9:30am–12:30pm and 2:30–5pm. Closed Feb.

EXPLORING ORTYGIA ISLAND

Ortygia, inhabited for many thousands of years, is also called the Città Vecchia (old city). It contains the town's Duomo, many rows of houses spanning 500 years of building styles, most of the city's medieval and baroque monuments, and some of the most charming vistas in Sicily. In Greek mythology, it's said to have been ruled by Calypso, daughter of Atlas, the sea nymph who detained Ulysses (Odysseus) for 7 years. The island, reached by crossing the Ponte Nuova, is about a mile long and half again as wide.

Heading out the Foro Italico, you'll come to the **Fonte Arethusa** ⭐, also famous in mythology. The river god Alpheius, son of Oceanus, is said to have fallen in love with the sea nymph Arethusa. The nymph turned into this spring or fountain, but Alpheius became a river and "mingled" with his love. According to legend, the spring ran red when bulls were sacrificed at Olympus.

At Piazza del Duomo is the **Duomo** ⭐, which was built over the ruins of the Temple of Minerva and employs the same Doric columns; 26 of the originals are still in place. The temple was erected after Gelon the Tyrant defeated the Carthaginians at Himera in the 5th century B.C. The Christians converted it into a basilica in the 7th century A.D. In 1693, an earthquake caused the facade to collapse, and in the 18th century the cathedral was rebuilt in the baroque style by Palermo architect Andrea Palma. It's open daily 8am to noon and 4 to 7pm. Admission is free.

The irregular **Piazza del Duomo** ⭐ is especially majestic when the facade of the cathedral is dramatically caught by the setting sun or when flood-lit at night. Acclaimed as one of the most beautiful squares in Italy, it's filled with other fine baroque buildings. They include the striking **Palazzo Beneventano del Bosco,** with its lovely courtyard. Opposite it is the **Palazzo del Senato,** with an inner courtyard displaying a senator's carriage from the 1700s. At the far end of the square stands **Santa Lucia,** although it hardly competes with the Duomo.

The other important landmark square is **Piazza Archimede,** with its baroque fountain festooned with dancing jets of water and sea nymphs. This square lies directly northeast of Piazza del Duomo, forming the monumental heart of Ortygia. It, not the cathedral square, is the main square of the old city. On this piazza, original Gothic windows grace the 15th-century **Palazzo Lanzo.** As you wander around Ortygia, you'll find that Piazza Archimede is a great place from which to orient yourself. Wander the narrow streets wherever your feet will take you. When you get lost, you can always ask for directions back to Piazza Archimede.

The **Palazzo Bellomo,** Via Capodieci 14, off Foro Vittorio Emanuele II, dates from the 13th century, with many alterations. Today it's the home of the **Galleria Regionale** ✻ (© **0931-69617**). The palace is fascinating, with its many arches, doors, and stairs, and it also has a fine collection of paintings. The most notable is *Annunciation,* by Antonello da Messina (1474). There's also a noteworthy collection of antiques and porcelain. It's open Monday to Saturday 9am to 1:30pm and Sunday 9 to 11am. Admission is 2.50€ ($2.25).

WHERE TO STAY

The best place to stay here is on Ortygia, at either the Grand Hotel or the Grand Hotel Villa Politi (see below). The island has far more character and charm than "mainland" Syracuse. On the downside, both these hotels might be full, especially during summer. In that case, we've included some backup choices.

EXPENSIVE

Grand Hotel ✻✻   Located on Ortygia, this is among the grandest places to stay in the entire area, in a neck-to-neck race with Villa Politi (see below) for supremacy. It's a first-class hotel in a tranquil location; a private beach is a short shuttle-bus ride away from the main premises. In the early part of the 20th century, it was the most fashionable place in southeastern Sicily, known for its balls and as a gathering point for wealthy Sicilian families and their visitors. Today the guest rooms are spacious and luxuriously furnished, opening onto panoramic sea views and boasting state-of-the-art bathrooms. Some rooms are equipped for travelers with disabilities.

Viale Mazzini 12, 96100 Siracusa. © 0931-464600. Fax 0931-464611. 58 units. 206€ ($183.95) double; 258€ ($230.40) suite. Rates include buffet breakfast. AE, DC, MC, V. Free parking. **Amenities:** Restaurant; bar; room service; laundry. *In room:* A/C, TV, minibar, hair dryer, safe.

Grand Hotel Villa Politi ✻✻   Once known as the grand dame of local hotels, this beautifully restored villa from 1862 is back. Time was when some of the remaining royal heads of pre–World War I Europe checked in for a stay of weeks. Even Winston Churchill came here for some well-deserved R&R, and could be seen with his paints and easel in the garden. The hotel lies in the historic gardens of Latomie dei Cappuccini, opening onto an archaeological dig. The charm and elegance that made the hotel a legend have been renewed. The bedrooms range from midsize to spacious, and each is beautifully furnished, containing tiled bathrooms. The cuisine here is also refined.

Via Politi Laudien 2, 96100 Siracusa. © 0931-412121. Fax 0931-36061. www.villapoliti.com. 100 units (half with shower only). 180€ ($160.75) double; 346€ ($309) suite. Rates include breakfast. AE, DC, MC, V. Free parking. **Amenities:** 2 restaurants; pool; room service; babysitting; laundry/dry cleaning. *In room:* A/C, TV, minibar, hair dryer, safe.

MODERATE

Domus Mariae   Located on Ortygia, this is a less plush but correspondingly less expensive option than the Grand (see above). It's delightful in its own way, a government-rated three-star hotel with a tasteful decor. Directly on the seafront, it opens onto a view of Mt. Etna. Each of its guest rooms is fairly spacious, with a small tiled bathroom.

Via Vittorio Veneto 76, 96100 Siracusa. © 0931-24854. Fax 0931-24858. www.sistemia.it/domusmariae. 12 units (showers only). 118.80€–129.10€ ($106.05–$115.30) double. Rates include buffet breakfast. AE, DC, MC, V. Free parking outside. **Amenities:** Restaurant; bar; lounge; room service. *In room:* A/C, TV, minibar, hair dryer, safe (in most rooms).

Holiday Inn Siracusa   A short drive inland from the Città Vecchia, this branch of the international hotel chain is designed for easy access; it's convenient if you have a car. Each monochromatic guest room is functionally furnished but well kept, with a small tiled bathroom.

Viale Teracati 30–32, 96100 Siracusa. ✆ **0931-463232.** Fax 0931-67115. 87 units (showers only). 125€–165€ ($111.65–$147.35) double. Rates include buffet breakfast. AE, DC, MC, V. Free parking. **Amenities:** Restaurant; lounge; room service; laundry. *In room:* A/C, TV, minibar, hair dryer, safe.

Jolly Hotel   A major stop for tour groups, the six-story Jolly is part of the chain that's Italy's answer to Holiday Inn. You get no surprises, just tropical-style modern rooms that are a bit worn. Each is your basic motel room, with good beds and small bathrooms. At least the view of Mt. Etna and the sea is panoramic. The location is on a dull but busy shopping street, about a 20-minute walk from Ortygia.

Corso Gelone 45, 96100 Siracusa. ✆ **800/221-2626** in the U.S., 800/237-0319 in Canada, or 0931-4611111. Fax 0931-461126. www.jollyhotels.it. 100 units (showers only). 120€–145€ ($107.15–$129.50) double. Rates include breakfast. AE, DC, MC, V. Parking is free. **Amenities:** Restaurant; bar; lounge; room service; laundry. *In room:* A/C, TV, minibar, hair dryer, safe.

INEXPENSIVE

Hotel Bellavista   Family-owned and -run, this hotel lies in the commercial center, close to the archaeological zone. There's an annex in the garden for overflow. The spacious main lounge has leather chairs and semitropical plants. The guest rooms are informal and comfortable; most are furnished with traditional pieces and have sea-view balconies.

Via Diodoro Siculo 4, 96100 Siracusa. ✆ **0931-411355.** Fax 0931-37927. www.sistemia.it/bellavista. 47 units (showers only). 93€ ($83.05) double. Rates include breakfast. AE, MC, V. Free parking. **Amenities:** Restaurant; lounge; gym; sauna; room service. *In room:* A/C, TV.

Hotel Gutkowski ✿ *Finds*   This hotel stands right on the sea in the historic center. It's a little discovery that offers roomy, well-furnished bedrooms, each with a compact, tiled bathroom. Bedrooms are decorated in a tasteful combination of contemporary furnishings and antiques. At the three-story hotel, four of the rooms open onto sea views, and these are grabbed up first.

Lungomare Vittorini 26, 96100 Siracusa. ✆ **0931-465861.** Fax. 0931-480505. www.guthotel.it. 15 units (showers only). 88€ ($78.60) double. Rates include breakfast. AE, MC, V. **Amenities:** Lounge; room service; laundry/dry cleaning. *In room:* A/C, TV, minibar.

Hotel Panorama   Near the entrance to the city, on a rise of Temenite Hill, this bandbox-modern hotel sits on a busy street about 5 minutes from the archaeological park. It's not a motel, but it does provide free parking. The small guest rooms are pleasant and up-to-date, with comfortable but utilitarian furniture and small tiled bathrooms.

Via Necropoli Grotticelle 33, 96100 Siracusa. ✆ **0931-412188.** Fax 0931-412527. 51 units (showers only). 62€ ($55.35) double. Rates include continental breakfast. AE, MC, V. Free parking. **Amenities:** Lounge. *In room:* A/C, TV.

WHERE TO DINE
MODERATE

Gambero Rosso   SICILIAN/MEDITERRANEAN/SEAFOOD   Near the bridge to the Città Vecchia, this large restaurant is in an old tavern, where you can sample Sicilian fare. Two reliable choices are *zuppa di pesce* (fish soup) and *zuppa di cozze* (a plate brimming with fresh mussels in a tasty marinade). The Sicilian cannelloni are good, too. The meat dishes feature a number of choices from the kitchens of Lazio, Tuscany, and Emilia-Romagna. The dining room extends from the restaurant onto a terrace dotted with potted flowers and shrubs that faces the port.

Via Eritrea 2. ℂ **0931-68546**. Reservations recommended. Main courses 10€–17.50€ ($8.95–$15.65). AE, MC, V. Fri–Wed noon–3:30pm and 7:30–11pm.

Giola SEAFOOD/PIZZA   This restaurant occupies the street level of a 250-year-old palace in the heart of the Città Vecchia, a short walk from the cathedral. Despite its understated decor and inexperienced staff, it serves a memorable cuisine. Many specialties emerge from the fragrant kitchen, including a wide array of homemade pastas, a cheese-laden *crespelline* (crepe) of the house, pasta with sardines, *spiedini* with shrimp (a shrimp kabob), and a selection of pungent beef, fish, and veal dishes. There's also a pizzeria on-site.

Via dei Tolomei 5. ℂ **0931-66386**. Reservations recommended. Main courses 6€–11€ ($5.35–$9.80). AE, DC, MC, V. Tues–Sun 12:30–3pm and 7:30pm–midnight.

Ristorante Jonico—a Rutta e Ciauli ✦ SICILIAN   This is one of the best restaurants for the typical cuisine and local wines of Sicily. It's right on the sea, with a panoramic view, about 90m (100 yd.) from Piazzale dei Cappuccini. The decor is pure Liberty (Art Nouveau) style.

The antipasti array is dazzling, and the homemade pasta dishes are superb—try *pasta rusticana* with eggplant, cheese, ham, and herbs (ask one of the English-speaking waiters to explain the many variations) or spaghetti with fresh tuna and herbs. One of the most interesting fish dishes we recently sampled was *spada a pizzaiola* (swordfish in a savory garlic-flavored sauce). Meat specialties include *bistecca siciliana* (tender beef with pulverized tomatoes, eggplant, onions, white wine, and local cheese); sliced veal with eggplant, tomatoes, onions, and slices of local cheese; and delicious fish stew. The dessert specialty is *cassatine siciliane* (mocha-chocolate ice cream capped with sprinkles of coffee-flavored chocolate, all floating in a lake of English custard). There's also a roof garden with a pizzeria serving typical Sicilian pizza.

Riviera Dionisio il Grande 194. ℂ **0931-65540**. Reservations recommended. Main courses 11€–21€ ($9.80–$18.75); pizza 2.50€–6€ ($2.25–$5.35). AE, MC, V. Wed–Mon noon–3pm and 8–10:30pm.

Trattoria Archimede ✦ SEAFOOD   Settle into one of the three large, slightly formal dining rooms here, and prepare to enjoy some of the best-tasting cuisine in Syracuse. This trattoria is an excellent choice for those who want to dine on historic Ortygia. The menu changes constantly, depending on the market, but you'll always find the freshest of Mediterranean fish, grilled or baked to perfection. The owner, Mr. Zammitti, will also prepare fresh pasta dishes (the best is with shellfish) and good-tasting soups. Sometimes ricci or sea urchin is used to flavor the pasta. For dessert, the specialty is a *cassata,* sweetened ricotta flavored with candied pumpkin and enveloped in alternating squares of sponge cake and green-colored almond paste. Candied cherries are often added. The staff is welcoming and attentive.

Via Gemellaro 8. ℂ **0931-69701**. Reservations unnecessary. Main courses 8.50€–15€ ($7.60–$13.40). AE, DC, MC, V. Daily 12:30–3pm and 7:30–11pm. Closed 3 weeks in July.

SYRACUSE AFTER DARK

The region's best disco is **Fontana Bianca,** Viale Dei Lidi (ℂ **0931-790611**), 18km (11 miles) southwest of the town center and open June to September. It contains a walled garden, a pool that at night seems mostly ornamental, and a crowd that's older than you'll find at the student hangouts closer to the town center. Another option is the **Discotecca Malibu,** Via Elorina (© **0931-721888**), about 6km (3¾ miles) southwest of town on SS115, where a younger crowd dances all night at a seaside pavilion that evokes its California namesake.

On a small street near Via Maestanza in Syracuse, **La Nottola,** Via Gargallo 61 (© **0931-60009**), is a stylish jazz club/piano bar/disco that attracts a well-dressed crowd. In midsummer, head for the **Sporting Club Terrauzza** (© **0931-714647**), centerpiece of the village of Terrauzza, about 10km (6¼ miles) southwest of Syracuse, where whoever happens to be vacationing on the local beaches shows up to mingle with local 20-somethings.

A SIDE TRIP TO BAROQUE NOTO ☆☆

From Syracuse, head southwest on A18 for 31km (19 miles) to reach Noto, which is set amid olive groves and almond trees on a plateau overlooking the Asinaro Valley. Noto dates from the 9th century and knew a Greek, a Roman, a Byzantine, an Arab, a Norman, an Aragonese, and even a Spanish culture before 1692, when an earthquake destroyed it. Many Sicilian artists and artisans have worked to rebuild the town into a baroque gem with uniform buildings of soft limestone. It was constructed somewhat like a stage set, with curvaceous and curvilinear accents and pot-bellied wrought-iron balconies on the facades.

To get your bearings, stop first at the **tourist office** at Piazza XVI Maggio, Villetta Ercole, in front of San Domenico church (© **0931-573779**), to pick up a map and some tips about exploring the town on foot. From April to September, office hours are daily 9am to 1pm and 3:30 to 6:30pm; October to March, hours are Monday to Friday 8am to 2pm and 3:30 to 6:30pm.

Mercifully, traffic has been diverted away from Noto's heart, to protect its fragile buildings, on which restoration began in 1987—and not a moment too soon. Your best approach is through the monumental **Royal Gate (Porta Reale),** crowned by three symbols—a dog, a swan, and a tower, representing the town's former allegiance to the Bourbon monarchy. From here, take **Corso Vittorio Emanuele,** going through the **old patricians' quarter.** The rich-looking, honey-colored buildings along this street are some of the most captivating on the island. This street will take you to the three most important piazzas.

You arrive first at **Piazza Immacolata,** dominated by the baroque facade of **San Francesco all'Immacolata,** which still contains notable artworks rescued from a Franciscan church in the old town. Notable works include a painted wooden *Madonna and Child* (1564), believed to be the work of Antonio Monachello. The church is open daily 8:30am to noon and 4 to 7:30pm; admission is free. Immediately to the left stands the **St. Salvador Monastery (Monastero del Santissimo Salvatore),** characterized by an elegant tower, its windows adorned with wrought-iron balconies. When it reopens, it will contain a minor collection of religious art and artifacts.

The next square is **Piazza Municipio,** the most majestic of the trio. It's dominated by the **Palazzo Ducezio,** a graceful town hall with curvilinear elements enclosed by a classical portico, the work of architect Vincenzo Sinatra (no relation to Ol' Blue Eyes). The upper section of this palace was added as late as the 1950s. Its most beautiful room is the Louis XI–style Hall of Representation (*Salone di Rappresentanza*), decorated with gold and stucco. On the vault is a Mazza fresco representing the mythological figure of Ducezio founding Neas (the ancient name of Noto).

On one side of the square, a broad flight of steps leads to the **Duomo,** flanked by two lovely horseshoe-shape hedges. The cathedral was inspired by models of

Borromini's churches in Rome and was completed in 1776. In 1996, the dome collapsed, destroying a large section of the nave, and it's still under repair. The date of completion for the extensive renovations is uncertain. On the far side of the cathedral is the **Palazzo Villadorata,** graced with a classic facade. Its six **extravagant balconies** 🎯🎯 are supported by sculpted buttresses of galloping horses, griffins, and grotesque bald and bearded figures with chubby-cheeked cherubs at their bellies. The palazzo is divided into 90 rooms, the most beautiful being the Yellow Hall (*Salone Giallo*), the Green Hall (*Salone Verde*), and the Red Hall (*Salone Rosso*), with their precious frescoed domes from the 18th century. The charming Feasts Hall (*Salone delle Feste*) is dominated by a fresco representing mythological scenes. In one of its aisles, the palazzo contains a *pinacoteca* (picture gallery) with antique manuscripts, rare books, and portraits of noble families.

The final square is **Piazza XVI Maggio,** dominated by the convex facade of its **Chiesa di San Domenico** 🎯, with two tiers of columns separated by a high cornice. The interior is filled with polychrome marble altars and is open daily 8am to noon and 2 to 5pm. Directly in front of the church is a public garden, the **Villetta d'Ercole,** named for its 18th-century fountain honoring Hercules.

Right off Corso Vittorio Emanuele is one of Noto's most fascinating streets, **Via Nicolaci** 🎯, lined with magnificent baroque buildings.

Noto in summer also is known for some fine **beaches** nearby; the best are 6km (3¾ miles) away at **Noto Marina.** You can catch a bus at the Giardini Pubblici in Noto. The one-way fare is 1.25€ ($1.10).

While wandering the streets, you'll find nothing finer on a hot day than one of the highly praised cones from **Corrado Costanza,** Via Silvio Spaventa 7–9 (© **0931-835243**), open Thursday to Tuesday 7am to 2pm and 4 to 11:30pm. It enjoys local renown for its gelato, the best in the area. The gelati come in various flavors and are often made with fresh fruit.

If you don't have a car, you can reach Noto by AST or SAIS **buses** leaving from Syracuse. The ride takes only 1 hour. From Monday to Saturday, there are 11 buses per day; Sunday, there are 3. A one-way ticket costs 2.50€ ($2.25). Noto is also reached by **train** from Syracuse (nine per day); the trip takes 30 minutes and costs 1.60€ ($1.45) one way. The train station is 20 minutes uphill from the town. For information on schedules call © **091-343811.**

3 Agrigento & the Valley of the Temples 🎯🎯🎯

129km (80 miles) S of Palermo, 175km (109 miles) SE of Trapani, 217km (135 miles) W of Syracuse

Agrigento's amazing Valley of the Temples is one of the most memorable and evocative sights of the ancient world. Greek colonists from Gela (Caltanissetta) called this area Akragas when they established a beachhead in the 6th century B.C. In time, the settlement grew to become one of the most prosperous cities in Magna Graecia. A great deal of that growth is attributed to the despot Phalaris, who ruled from 571 to 555 B.C. and is said to have roasted his victims inside a brass bull. He eventually met the same fate.

Empedocles (ca. 490–430 B.C.), the Greek philosopher and politician (also considered by some the founder of medicine in Italy), was the most famous son of Akragas. He formulated the theory that matter consists of four elements (earth, fire, water, and air), modified by the agents love and strife. In modern times the town produced playwright Luigi Pirandello (1867–1936), who won the Nobel Prize for literature in 1934.

Like nearby Selinunte, the city was attacked by war-waging Carthaginians, beginning in 406 B.C. In the 3rd century B.C., the city changed hands between the Carthaginians and the Romans until it finally succumbed to Roman domination by 210 B.C. It was then known as Agrigentium.

The modern part of Agrigento occupies a hill, and the narrow Casbah-like streets show the influence of the conquering Saracens. Heavy Allied bombing during World War II necessitated much rebuilding. The result is, for the most part, uninspired and not helped by all the cement factories in the area. But below the town stretch the long reaches of the Valley of the Temples (Valle dei Templi), where you'll see some of the greatest Greek ruins in the world.

Visit Agrigento for its past, not for the modern incarnation. However, once you've been awed by the ruined temples, you can visit the *centro storico,* with its tourist boutiques hawking postcards and T-shirts, and enjoy people-watching at a cafe along Via Atenea. When it gets too hot (as it so often does), flee to a beach at nearby San Leone.

ESSENTIALS

GETTING THERE The **train** trip from Palermo takes 1½ hours and costs 6.30€ ($6.05) each way. There are 10 trains daily. The main rail station, **Stazione Centrale,** Piazza Marconi (© 848-888088), is downhill from Piazzale Aldo Moro and Piazza Vittorio Emanuele. From Syracuse by rail, you must first take one of nine daily trains to Ragusa, a 2½-hour trip costing 6€ ($5.35) each way. Three trains a day make the 3½-hour trip from Ragusa to Agrigento, costing 8€ ($7.15) each way.

Omnia, Via Ragazzi del 99, 10 (© 0922-596490), runs four **buses** per day from Palermo to Agrigento. The trip takes 2½ hours and costs 6.50€ ($5.80) one way. **SAIS** buses, Via Favara Vecchia (© 0922-595933), make the 2½-hour trip from Catania several times a day. The one-way fare is 9.50€ ($8.50).

By **car** from Syracuse, take SS115 through Gela. From Palermo, cut southeast along S121, which becomes S188 and S189 before it finally reaches Agrigento and the Mediterranean. Allow about 2½ hours for this jaunt.

VISITOR INFORMATION The **tourist office** is at Via Cesare Battisti 15 (© 0922-20454) or at Via Empedocle 73 (© 0922-20391). Both are open Monday to Friday 8:30am to 2pm, and Wednesday 8:30am to 2:30pm and 3:30 to 6:45pm.

SPECIAL EVENTS The **Settimana Pirandelliana** is a weeklong festival of plays, operas, and ballets staged in Piazza Kaos at the end of July and August. The tourist office can supply details; tickets cost 7.50€ to 15€ ($6.70–$13.40).

WANDERING AMONG THE RUINS

Many writers are fond of suggesting that the Greek ruins in the **Valle dei Templi** be viewed at dawn or sunset, when their mysterious aura is indeed heightened. Regrettably, you can't get very close at those times. Instead, search them out under the cobalt-blue Sicilian sky. The backdrop is idyllic, especially in spring, when the striking almond trees blossom into pink.

Board a bus or climb into your car to investigate. Riding out the Strada Panoramica, you'll first approach (on your left) the **Temple of Juno (Tempio di Giunone)** ★★, erected sometime in the mid–5th century B.C., at the peak of a construction boom honoring the deities. Many of its Doric columns have been restored. As you climb the blocks, note the remains of a cistern as well as a sacrificial altar in front. The temple affords good views of the entire valley.

The **Temple of Concord (Tempio della Concordia)** 🏛️🏛️🏛️, which you come to next, ranks along with the Temple of Hephaestus (the Theseion) in Athens as the best-preserved Greek temple in the world. With 13 columns on its side, 6 in front, and 6 in back, the temple was built in the peripheral hexastyle. You'll see the clearest example in Sicily of what an inner temple was like. In the late 6th century A.D., the pagan structure was transformed into a Christian church, which might have saved it for posterity, although today it has been stripped down to its classical purity.

The **Temple of Hercules (Tempio di Ercole)** 🏛️🏛️ is the oldest, dating from the 6th century B.C. Badly ruined (only eight pillars are standing), it once ranked in size with the Temple of Zeus. At one time the temple sheltered a celebrated statue of Hercules. The infamous Gaius Verres, the Roman magistrate who became an especially bad governor of Sicily, attempted to steal the image as part of his temple-looting tear on the island. Astonishingly, you can still see signs of black searing from fires set by long-ago Carthaginian invaders.

The **Temple of Jove or Zeus (Tempio di Giove)** 🏛️ was the largest in the valley, similar in some respects to the Temple of Apollo at Selinunte, until it was ruined by an earthquake. It even impressed Goethe. In front of the structure was a large altar. The giant on the ground was one of several *telamones* (atlases) used to support the edifice. Carthaginian slave labor built what was then the largest Greek temple in the world and one of the most remarkable.

The so-called **Temple of Castor and Pollux (Tempio di Dioscuri),** with four Doric columns intact, is composed of fragments from different buildings. At various times it has been designated as a temple honoring Castor and Pollux, the twin sons of Leda and deities of seafarers; Demeter (Ceres), the goddess of marriage and of the fertile earth; or Persephone, the daughter of Zeus who became the symbol of spring. Note that on some maps, this temple is called Tempio di Castore e Polluce.

The temples can usually be visited daily 9am until 1 hour before sunset. City bus nos. 8, 9, 10, and 11 run to the valley from the train station in Agrigento.

MORE ATTRACTIONS

The **Regional Archaeological Museum (Museo Regionale Archeologico)** 🏛️, near San Nicola, on Contrada San Nicola at the outskirts of town on the way to the Valle dei Templi (📞 **0922-401565**), is open daily 9am to 1pm and 2 to 6pm. Admission is 4€ ($3.55). Its single most important exhibit is a head of the god Telamon from the Tempio di Giove. The collection of Greek vases is also impressive. Many of the artifacts on display were dug up when Agrigento was excavated. Take bus nos. 8, 9, 10, or 11.

Pirandello's House (Casa di Pirandello), Contrada Caos, Frazione Caos (📞 **0922-511102**), is the former home of the 1934 Nobel Prize winner, known worldwide for his plays *Six Characters in Search of an Author* and *Enrico IV.* He died 2 years after winning the prize and its attendant world acclaim. Although Agrigentans back then might not have liked his portrayal of Italy, all is forgiven now, and Pirandello is the local boy who made good. In fact, the Teatro Luigi Pirandello at Piazza Municipio bears his name. His "casa natale" is now a museum devoted to memorabilia pertaining to the playwright's life, including his study and the murals he painted. His tomb lies under his favorite pine tree: "One night in June I dropped down like a firefly beneath a huge pine tree in the garden." The tomb lies a few hundred yards from the house and grounds, which are open Monday to Saturday 8:30am to 1pm and 4 to n is 2.50€ ($2.25). The birthplace lies outside of town in the ⟨⟩tch bus no. 11 from Piazza Marconi), just west of the temple

⟨⟩E TO STAY

⟨⟩otel Baglio della Luna ★★ *(Finds)*   Enjoying a tranquil and scenic view of the Valley of the Temples is this charming and graceful inn with a flower-garden setting. Classical columns frame the gate leading to the inn, which stands next to the ruined city. Parts of the structure date back to the 13th century, and in the 16th century the site was fortified, later becoming a private Sicilian manor until it was converted into the present little gem of an inn. Villa Athena is better located, but you'll still be charmed by this place. Antiques, bright Italian chintzes, and rugs scattered over wooden floors decorate both the well-furnished bedrooms and the public areas.

Contrada Maddalusa, Valle dei Templi, 92100 Agrigento. ✆ **0922-511061**. Fax 0922-598802. bagliodellaluna@ tin.it. 24 units. 232.40€ ($207.55) double; 335€–468€ ($299.15–$417.90) suite. AE, DC, MC, V. Bus: 1. **Amenities:** Restaurant; coffee shop; room service; babysitting; laundry/dry cleaning. *In room:* A/C, TV, minibar, hair dryer.

Hotel Tre Torri   Though it's near an unattractive commercial district 7km (4⅓ miles) south of Agrigento, this is among the area's busiest hotels. Behind a mock-medieval facade of white stucco, chiseled stone blocks, false crenellations, and crisscrossed iron balconies, the Tre Torri is a favorite with Italian business travelers. The small guest rooms are comfortable, with modern furnishings and compact tiled bathrooms.

Strada Statale 115, Viale Canatello, Villaggio Mosè, 92100 Agrigento. ✆ **0922-606733**. Fax 0922-607839. www.mediatel.it/public/tre-torri. 118 units (showers only). 104€ ($92.85) double. Rates include breakfast. AE, MC, V. Free parking. **Amenities:** 4 restaurants; 3 bars; nightclub; 2 pools; fitness center; sauna; room service; laundry/dry cleaning. *In room:* A/C, TV, hair dryer.

Hotel Villa Athena   This 18th-century villa rises from the landscape in the Valley of the Temples, less than 3km (2 miles) from town. It's worn and overpriced, and it's in dire need of an overhaul; but its location at the archaeological site is so dramatic that we always like to lodge here anyway, if only to see the ruins lit up at night from a hotel bedroom. It would be smart to reserve at least a month in advance. The guest rooms are clean, with little style and tiled bathrooms with aging but still-functioning plumbing. Ask for a room with a view of the temple: The perfect choice would be no. 205, which frames a panorama of the Temple of Concord.

During the day, guests sit in the paved courtyard, enjoying a drink and the fresh breezes. Even if you're not staying here, try to walk through the garden at night for an amazing view of the lit temple. You can also park here during the day and take a 10-minute walk along a trail to the temples.

Via dei Templi 33, 92100 Agrigento. ✆ **0922-596288**. Fax 0922-402180. 40 units. 207€ ($184.85) double. Rates include breakfast. AE, DC, MC, V. Free parking. **Amenities:** Dining room; 2 bars; pool; room service; laundry/dry cleaning. *In room:* A/C, TV, minibar.

WHERE TO DINE

Le Caprice SEAFOOD/SICILIAN   Loyal customers return here for special celebrations and everyday fun. Le Caprice is the only restaurant of any real note in Agrigento; the rest are simple trattorie. Specialties of the house include an antipasto buffet, a mixed fry of fish from the gulf, and rolled pieces of veal in a flavorful sauce. The chef takes justifiable pride in his stuffed swordfish. One German visitor came here 7 nights in a row and ordered the dish each time.

Strada Panoramica dei Templi 51. $\mathcal{C}$ **0922-26469.** Reservations unnecessary. Main courses 11€–20€ ($9.80–$17.85). AE, DC, MC, V. Sat–Thurs 12:30–3pm and 7:30–11pm. Closed July 1–15.

Trattoria del Vigneto SICILIAN   This is a simple place to go for a simple meal. You might try homemade pasta flavored with sardines, pine nuts, and balsamic vinegar; *pasta alla Norma,* with eggplant, ricotta, tomatoes, and fresh basil; or *bistecca vignolo* (steak garnished with prosciutto, mozzarella, and tomatoes). The welcome is sincere and the food is perfectly acceptable and often quite flavorful.

Via Cavalleri Magazzeni 11. $\mathcal{C}$ **0922-414319.** Main courses 8.50€–17.50€ ($7.60–$15.65). V. Wed–Mon noon–2:30pm and 7pm–midnight. Closed Nov.

4 Selinunte ★★

122km (76 miles) SW of Palermo, 113km (70 miles) W of Agrigento, 89km (55 miles) SE of Trapani

Guy de Maupassant called the splendid jumble of ruins at Selinunte "an immense heap of fallen columns, now aligned and placed side by side on the ground like dead soldiers, now having fallen in a chaotic manner." Regardless of what shape they're in, the only reason to visit Selinunte is for its ruins, not for the unappealing modern towns (Mazara del Vallo and Castelvetrano) that have grown up around it.

One of the superb colonies of ancient Greece, Selinunte traces its history to the 7th century B.C., when immigrants from Megara Hyblaea (Syracuse) set out to build a new colony. They succeeded, erecting a city of power and prestige adorned with many temples. But that was calling attention to a good thing. Much of Selinunte's history involves seemingly endless conflicts with the Elymi people of Segesta (see "Segesta," later in this chapter). Siding with Selinunte's rival, Hannibal virtually leveled the city in 409 B.C. The city never recovered its former glory and ultimately fell into decay.

GETTING THERE

From Palermo, Trapani, or Marsala, you can make **rail** connections to Castelvetrano. Once at Castelvetrano, you must board a bus for Selinunte. Call $\mathcal{C}$ **0924-81826** in Palermo for rail information; the trip takes 2 hours and costs 5.75€ ($5.15) each way.

From Agrigento, take one of the four daily **buses** to Castelvetrano, a 2¼-hour trip that costs 5.50€ ($4.90) one way. Buses (about five per day) depart for Selinunte from in front of the rail terminal at Castelvetrano. The one-way fare is 1€ (90¢) for the 20-minute trip. For information, call $\mathcal{C}$ **0922-401352.**

Selinunte is on the southern coast of Sicily and is best explored by **car** because public transportation is awkward. From Agrigento, take Route 115 northwest into Castelvetrano; then follow the signposted secondary road marked SELINUNTE, which leads south to the sea. Allow at least 2 hours to drive here from either Palermo or Agrigento.

EXPLORING THE ARCHAEOLOGICAL GARDEN

Selinunte's temples lie in scattered ruins, the honey-colored stone littering the ground as if an earthquake had struck (as one did in ancient times). Some columns and fragments of temples are still standing, with great columns pointing to the sky. From 9am to dusk daily, you can walk through the monument zone. Parts of it have been partially excavated and reconstructed, as much as is possible with the bits and fragments remaining. Admission is 2€ ($1.80).

The temples, in varying states of preservation, are designated by letters. They're dedicated to such mythological figures as Apollo and Hera (Juno); most date from the 6th and 5th centuries B.C. Near the entrance, the Doric **Temple E** contains fragments of an inner temple. Standing on its ruins before the sun goes down, you can look across the water that washes up on the shores of Africa, from which the Carthaginian fleet emerged to destroy the city. **Temple G,** in scattered ruins north of Temple E, was one of the largest erected in Sicily and was also built in the Doric style. The ruins of the less impressive **Temple F** lie between Temples E and G. Not much remains of Temple F, and little is known about what it was.

After viewing Temples G, F, and E, all near the parking lot at the entrance, you can get in your car and drive along the Strada dei Templi west to the Acropoli. You can also walk here in about 20 minutes. The site of the western temples was the **Acropoli,** which was enclosed within defensive walls and built from the 6th to 5th centuries B.C.

The most impressive site here is **Temple C.** In 1925, 14 of the 17 columns of Temple C were reerected. This is the earliest surviving temple at ancient Selinus, having been built in the 6th century B.C. and probably dedicated to Hercules or Apollo. The pediment, ornamented with a clay Gorgon's head, lies broken on the ground. Temple C towers over the other ruins and gives you a better impression of what all the temples might have looked like at one time. Also here is **Temple A,** which, like the others, remains in scattered ruins.

The streets of the Acropoli were laid out by Hippodamus of Miletus along classical lines, with a trio of principal arteries bisected at right angles by a grid of less important streets. The Acropoli was the site of the town's most important public and religious buildings, and it was also the residence of the town's aristocrats. If you look down below, you can see the site of the town's harbor, now overgrown. After all the earthquake damage, you can only imagine the full glory of this place in its golden era.

The Carthaginian Hannibal treated Selinunte with ferocity. His battle for the city led to the death of 16,000 Selinuntini and the taking of some 5,000 prisoners. The latter begged him for freedom and for their temples to be spared. After receiving payment, he enslaved or killed them and looted the temples and pulled down their walls.

WHERE TO STAY & DINE NEARBY

The site of the ruins contains no hotels, restaurants, or watering holes of note. Most visitors come to visit the temples on a day trip while they're based elsewhere. But there are a handful of accommodations in the seafront village of Marinella, about a mile east of Selinunte. To reach Marinella, you'll travel along a narrow country road.

Hotel Alceste   This hotel, occasionally closed for periods in winter, is about a 15-minute walk from the ruins. The small, recently renovated guest rooms have new furniture, including cramped tiled bathrooms. Most visitors, however, stop only for a visit in the plant-filled courtyard. In summer, there's musical entertainment, dancing, cabaret, and theater in the garden.

Via Alceste 21, 91022 Marinella di Selinunte. ℂ 0924-46184. Fax 0924-46143. 30 units (showers only). 60€–80€ ($53.60–$71.45) double. Rates include breakfast. AE, DC, MC, V. **Amenities:** Restaurant; lounge; room service; laundry. *In room:* A/C, TV, hair dryer, safe.

5 Palermo ★ ★

233km (145 miles) W of Messina, 721km (447 miles) S of Naples, 934km (579 miles) S of Rome

As you arrive in Palermo, you start spotting blond, blue-eyed *bambini* all over the place. Don't be surprised. If fair-haired children don't fit your concept of what a Sicilian should look like, remember that the Normans landed here in 1060 and launched a campaign to wrest control of the island from the Arabs. Today you can see elements of both cultures, notably in Palermo's architecture—a unique style, Norman–Arabic.

The city is Sicily's largest port, its capital, and a jumble of contradictions. Whole neighborhoods remain bombed out and not yet rebuilt from World War II, yet Palermo boasts some of the greatest sights and museums in Sicily. Unemployment, poverty, traffic, crime, and crowding are rampant, and city services just don't run as they should. But amid the decay, you'll find gloriously stuccoed oratories, glittering 12th-century mosaics, art museums, baroque palaces, and busy fish markets bursting with life and color. Palermo is not the most welcoming of towns, and parts of the city can be downright dangerous; but there's a lot of fascinating culture and history to discover if you're the adventurous sort. Thankfully, restoration efforts are underway. More than $60 million has been spent to restore buildings, clean up facades, and repair streets. The picture is mixed, but it's slowly brightening.

ESSENTIALS

GETTING THERE   If you **fly** from Rome or Naples, you'll land at **Falcone e Borsellino–Punta Raisi** (© **1478-65641** for domestic flights, 1478-65642 for international), 31km (19 miles) west of Palermo. You can catch a local airport **bus** from the airport to Piazza Castelnuovo; the fare is 5€ ($4.45). For the same trip, a **taxi** is likely to charge at least 35€ ($31.25)—and more, if the driver thinks he can get away with it. It's also possible to rent a **car** at the airport (all the major firms are represented) and drive into Palermo. Allow 20 to 30 minutes—longer, if traffic is bad—to get to the center of town from the airport.

For information about traveling by **train**, see "Getting to Sicily," at the beginning of this chapter. After a 3½-hour ride from Messina across the north coast, you arrive at Palermo's station at **Piazza Giulio Cesare** (© **091-6161844**), which lies on the east side of town and is linked to the center by buses and taxis.

Palermo has **bus** connections with other major cities, operated by **SAIS,** Via Balsamo 16 (© **091-6166028**). Some 23 buses a day make the 2½-hour trip from Catania; the one-way cost is 11.50€ ($10.25). One bus a day (except Sun) arrives from Syracuse; the trip lasts 4 hours and costs 11€ ($9.80) one way. The bus terminal is near the rail station.

After you arrive by **car** from mainland Italy at Messina, head west on A20, which becomes Route 113, then A20 again, and finally A19 before its final approach to Palermo.

Impressions

I have heard it said that Sicilians can't use the telephone because they need both hands to talk with.

—Anonymous

VISITOR INFORMATION   There are **tourist offices** at strategic points, including the **Palermo airport** (✆ 091-591698) and the main train stations (✆ 091-6165914). The principal office is the **Azienda Autonoma Turismo,** Piazza Castelnuovo 34 (✆ 091-583847), open Monday to Friday 8:30am to 2pm and 2:30 to 6pm, and Saturday 8:30am to 2pm. When you stop in, ask for a good city map and a copy of *Palermo & Provincia Live,* a bimonthly publication with lots of handy tourist information plus an events calendar.

SAFETY   Be especially alert. Palermo is home to some of the most skilled pickpockets on the continent. Don't flaunt expensive jewelry, cameras, or wads of bills. Women who carry handbags are especially vulnerable to purse snatchers on Vespas. It's best to park your car in a garage rather than on the street; wherever you leave it, don't leave valuables inside. Police squads operate mobile centers throughout the town to help combat street crime.

GETTING AROUND   One municipal **bus** ticket costs .75€ (65¢), or you can buy a full-day ticket for 2.50€ ($2.25). For information and schedules, call **AMAT,** Via Borrelli 16 (✆ 091-321333). Most passengers buy their tickets at tobacco shops (*tabacchi*) before boarding. Otherwise, keep some 100L coins handy (euro coins may be accepted by the time you arrive).

If you can afford it, consider renting a **taxi** for the day to explore whatever you want to see in Palermo. Although most drivers speak only a few words of English, it's the best way to get around. Parking is horrendous in Palermo, and it's difficult to find your way around. Many of the major sights are not within walking distance of each other—just tell the driver where to go and where to wait. Call **Radio Taxi** at ✆ 091-512727 or 091-513311. From 9am to 5pm daily, it costs from 12.50€ ($11.15) per hour. On request, they can provide an English-speaking driver.

SPECIAL EVENTS   July brings a month of performances to the **Teatro di Verdura Villa Castelnuovo,** an open-air seaside theater that hosts classical music, jazz, and ballet performances. For information or tickets, contact the **Teatro Politeama Garibaldi** (see "Palermo After Dark," later in this section).

EXPLORING THE OLD TOWN

The "four corners" of the city, the **Quattro Canti di Città** ✿, is in the heart of the old town, at the junction of Corso Vittorio Emanuele and Via Maqueda. The ruling Spanish of the 17th century influenced the design of this grandiose baroque square, replete with fountains and statues. From here you can walk to **Piazza Bellini** ✿, the most attractive square, although it's likely to be under scaffolding for a long time during a renovation project.

Opening onto this square is **Santa Maria dell'Ammiraglio (La Martorana),** which was erected in 1143 (see below). Also fronting the square is **San Cataldo** (1160), in the Arab-Byzantine style (also see below). Here, too, is the late-16th-century **Santa Caterina,** attached to a vast Dominican monastery constructed in 1310. The church contains interesting 18th-century multicolored marble ornamentation.

Adjoining the square is **Piazza Pretoria,** dominated by a fountain designed in Florence in 1554 for a villa but acquired by Palermo about 20 years later. A short walk will take you to **Piazza di Cattedrale** and the Duomo.

Il Duomo ✿   East meets West in this curious spectacle of a cathedral. It was built in the 12th century on the foundation of an earlier basilica that had been converted into a mosque by the Arabs. The impressive Gothic "porch" on the

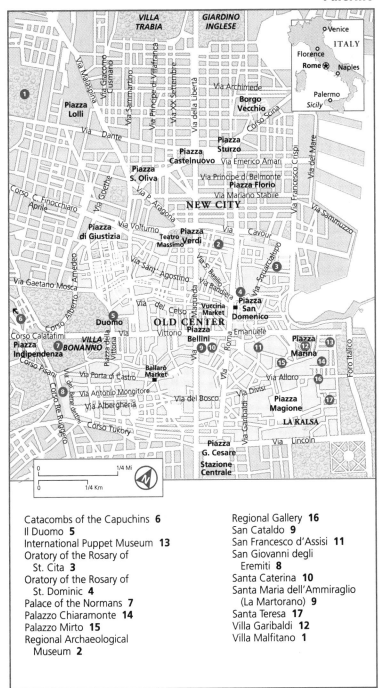

ITALY

Venice
Florence
Rome ⊛
Naples
Palermo
Sicily

Catacombs of the Capuchins **6**
Il Duomo **5**
International Puppet Museum **13**
Oratory of the Rosary of
   St. Cita **3**
Oratory of the Rosary of
   St. Dominic **4**
Palace of the Normans **7**
Palazzo Chiaramonte **14**
Palazzo Mirto **15**
Regional Archaeological
   Museum **2**

Regional Gallery **16**
San Cataldo **9**
San Francesco d'Assisi **11**
San Giovanni degli
   Eremiti **8**
Santa Caterina **10**
Santa Maria dell'Ammiraglio
   (La Martorano) **9**
Santa Teresa **17**
Villa Garibaldi **12**
Villa Malfitano **1**

southern front was built in the 15th century. But the cupola, added in the late 18th century, detracts from the overall appearance, and the interior was revamped at the same time, resulting in a glaring incongruity in styles. The pantheon of royal tombs includes that of the Holy Roman Emperor Frederick II, in red porphyry under a canopy of marble.

Piazza di Cattedrale, Corso Vittorio Emanuele. ✆ **091-334376**. Free admission (donation appreciated). Daily 6:30am–7pm.

Santa Maria dell'Ammiraglio (La Martorana) ✿✿

This church, named for Eloisa Martorana, who in 1194 founded a nearby Benedictine convent, is worth a visit for its glorious Byzantine mosaics. In 1143, the church was founded at the request of George of Antioch, an admiral in the fleet of Roger II. Today this Norman church is concealed behind a baroque facade. You enter through a portico-cum-bell tower that, although constructed free-standing, was connected to the church in the 1500s. The first two bays of the church were added in the 1500s and frescoed in the 1600s. The **mosaics** ✿✿ are stunning, created along strict Byzantine lines. Two panels evoke George of Antioch at the feet of the Madonna and Roger II receiving the crown from Christ. Other subjects depict a trio of Archangels (Gabriel, Raphael, and Michael) and, in the register below, eight prophets.

Piazza Bellini 3. ✆ **091-6161692**. Free admission (donation appreciated). Daily 8am–1pm and 3:30–7pm (closes early Sun).

Palace of the Normans (Palazzo dei Normanni) ✿✿

This palace contains one of the greatest art treasures in Sicily, the **Palatine Chapel (Cappella Palatina)** ✿✿✿. Erected at Roger II's command in the 1130s, it's the finest example of the Arabic–Norman style. The effect of the lushly colored mosaics is awe-inspiring. Dating from 1160, the mosaics in the nave are evocative of those at Monreale's Duomo (see above). If you don't have time to pay a visit to Monreale, you'll have seen the essence of this brilliant type here. Almond-eyed biblical characters from the Byzantine world create a panorama of epic pageantry, illustrating such Gospel scenes as the Nativity. The effect is enhanced by inlaid marble and mosaics, as well as by pillars made of granite shipped from the East. For a look at still more mosaics, this time in a more secular vein depicting scenes of the hunt, head upstairs to the **Hall of Roger II (Sala di Ruggero II)**, the seat of the Sicilian Parliament, where security is likely to be tight.

Piazza del Parlamento. ✆ **091-7054317**. Free palace tours. Chapel Mon–Sat 9am–noon; Mon–Fri 3–5pm; Sun 9–10am and noon–1pm.

Oratory of the Rosary of St. Dominic (Oratorio del Rosario di San Domenico) ✿✿✿

Palermo's most splendid oratory is a gem of stucco decoration by Giacomo Serpotta (1652–1732), a romp of cherubs. Serpotta excelled in the use of marble and polychrome, but it was in stucco that he earned his greatest fame. He worked on this oratory, his masterpiece, from 1714 to 1717. Serpotta depicted the *Joyful Mysteries of the Rosary,* on the left and rear walls, although some of these are the work of Pietro Novelli. Themes throughout the oratory are wide-ranging, depicting a *Flagellation* to an *Allegories of the Virtues.* Serpotta also depicted scenes from the *Apocalypse of St. John.* Particularly graphic is a depiction of a writhing Devil falling from Heaven. At the high altar is a masterpiece by Anthony Van Dyck, *Madonna of the Rosary* (1628). Illustrating the *Coronation of the Virgin,* the ceiling was frescoed by Pietro Novelli.

Via dei Bambinai. ✆ **091-332779**. Free admission. Mon 3–6pm; Tues–Fri 9am–1pm and 3–5:30pm; Sat 9–1am.

Oratory of the Rosary of St. Cita (Oratorio del Rosario di Santa Cita) 🏛🏛

You enter the oratory through the Chiesa di Santa Cita. It was the crowning achievement of Giacomo Serpotta, who worked on it between 1686 and 1718. Cherubs and angels romp with abandon, a delight as they climb onto the window frames or spread garlands of flowers in their pathway; they can also be seen sleeping, eating, and just hugging their knees as if in deep thought. The *Battle of Lepanto* bas-relief is meant to symbolize the horrors of war, and other panels depict such scenes as *The Mystery of the Rosary*. The oratory is a virtual gallery of art—everything from scenes of the flagellation to Jesus in the Garden at Gethsemane. At the high altar is Carlo Maratta's *Virgin of the Rosary* (1690). Allegorical figures protect eight windows along the sidewalls.

Via Valverde 3. (C) 091-332779. Free admission (donation appreciated). Mon–Fri 8:30am–1pm; Sat 9am–1pm.

Regional Archaeological Museum (Museo Archeologico Regionale) 🏛

Occupying a former residence for Philippine friars, this is a noteworthy archaeological collection. Many works displayed were excavated at Selinunte, once one of the major towns in Magna Graecia. See, in particular, the *Sala di Selinunte*, displaying the celebrated metopes that adorned the classical temples, as well as slabs of bas-relief. The gallery also owns important sculpture from the Temple of Himera. The collection of bronzes is exceptional, including the athlete and the stag discovered in the ruins of Pompeii (a Roman copy of a Greek original) and a bronze ram from Syracuse, from the 3rd century B.C. Among the Greek sculpture is *The Pouring Satyr*, excavated at Pompeii (a Roman copy of a Greek original by Praxiteles).

Via Bara Olivella 24. (C) 091-6116807. Admission 4€ ($3.55). Daily 9am–1:30pm; Tues, Wed, and Fri 3–6:30pm.

Regional Gallery (Galleria Regionale della Sicilia) 🏛🏛

The Gothic-Renaissance Palazzo Abatellis houses the Regional Gallery, which shows the evolution of art in Sicily from the 13th to 18th centuries. On the ground floor is the most famous work, the 15th-century fresco *Triumph of Death* 🏛🏛🏛, in all its gory magnificence. A horseback-riding skeleton, representing Death, tramples his victims. Worthy of mention are three majolica plates, valuable specimens of *Loza dorada* manufactured in the workshops of Manises, and the *Giara* produced in the workshops of Malaga at the end of the 13th century.

Francesco Laurana's slanty-eyed *Eleonora d'Aragona* 🏛🏛 is worth seeking out, as are seven grotesque drolleries painted on wood. On the second floor, *L'Annunziata,* by Antonello da Messina, a portrait of the Madonna executed with depth and originality, is one of the most celebrated paintings in Italy. The 13th room contains a very good series of Flemish paintings from the 15th and 16th centuries; the best is the *Trittico Malvagna,* by Jean Gossaert (known as Mabuse).

Via Alloro 4, Palazzo Abatellis. (C) 091-6164317. Admission 4€ ($3.55). Mon–Sat 9am–1pm; Tues and Thurs 3–7:30pm; Sun 9am–1pm.

International Puppet Museum (Museo Internazionale delle Marionette) 🏛🏛

Pupi, as Sicilian puppets are called, have long been considered among the finest versions of the art of the marionette. The puppets are based on characters from traditional French puppetry and street entertainment performances called *chansons de geste.* In the first room is the museum's collection of Sicilian puppets, many presented on stage and operated with strings. The most outstanding artisan here is Gaspara Canino, who achieved fame with his theater

Men of Dishonor

In Sicily, they don't call it the Mafia (from the Arabic *mu'afah*, or "protection"). They call it *Cosa Nostra*, literally "our thing," but, more accurately, "this thing we have." Its origins are debated, but the world's most famed criminal organization seemed to grow out of the convergence of local agricultural overseers working for absentee Bourbon landowners—hired thugs, from the peasant workers' point of view.

Members of the Sicilian Mafia (or "Men of Honor," as they like to be called) traditionally operated as a network of regional bosses who controlled individual towns by setting up puppet regimes of thoroughly corrupt officials. It was a sort of devil's bargain with the national Christian Democrat party, which controlled Italy's government from World War II until 1993 and, despite its law-and-order rhetoric, tacitly left Cosa Nostra alone as long as the bosses got out the party vote.

The Cosa Nostra trafficked in illegal goods, of course, but until the 1960s and 1970s, its income was derived mainly from low-level protection rackets, funneling state money into its own pockets, and ensuring that public contracts were granted to fellow *mafiosi* (all reasons why Sicily has experienced grotesque unchecked industrialization and modern growth at the expense of its heritage and the good of its communities). But the younger generation of Mafia underbosses got into the highly lucrative heroin and cocaine trades in the 1970s, transforming the Sicilian Mafia into a major world player on the international drug trafficking circuit—and raking in the dough. This ignited a clandestine Mafia war that, throughout the late 1970s and 1980s, generated lurid headlines of bloody Mafia hits. The new generation was wiping out the old and turning the balance of power in their favor.

This situation gave rise to the first Mafia turncoats, disgruntled ex-bosses and rank-and-file stoolies who opened up and told their stories, first to police prefect Gen. Alberto Dalla Chiesa (assassinated 1982) and later to crusading magistrates Giovanni Falcone (slaughtered May 23, 1992) and Paolo Borsellino (murdered July 19, 1992), who staged the "maxitrials" of mafiosi that sent hundreds to jail. The magistrates' 1992 murders, especially, garnered public attention to the dishonorable

puppets in the 1800s. In other rooms of the museum you can see results of the marionette art in other countries, including the English Punch and Judy.

Via Butera 1. ℂ **091-328060.** Admission 2.50€ ($2.25). Mon–Fri 9am–1pm and 4–7pm.

San Cataldo   In the Norman heyday of the island in the 12th century, this church was the headquarters of the Knights of the Holy Sepulchre. Today it evokes a Moorish style of architecture, with its perforated window screens and crenellated walls. The bulbous red domes here are often likened by Italians to a eunuch's hat, depicted in many paintings. The interior is rather severe, divided into a trio of aisles. Many of the columns were taken from buildings even older than this Norman edifice. Three domes crown the nave, and the floor is in polychrome marble.

Piazza Bellini 3. Free admission. Mon–Fri 9am–3:30pm; Sat 9am–12:30pm.

methods that defined the new Mafia and, perhaps for the first time, began to stir true shame.

On a broad and culturally important scale, it is these young mafiosi, without a moral center or check on their powers, who have driven many Sicilians to at least secretly break the unwritten code of *omertà*, which translates as "homage" but means "silence," when faced with harboring or even tolerating a man of honor. The Mafia still exists in Palermo, the small towns south of it, and the provincial capitals of Catania, Trapani, and Agrigento. Throughout the rest of Sicily, though, its power has been slipping. The heroin trade is a far cry from construction schemes and protection money, and the Mafia is swiftly outliving its usefulness and its welcome.

Even in Palermo, the grip of Cosa Nostra is loosening. In the closing days of 2000, the city even hosted a United Nations conference on combating organized crime. Palermo's mayor, Leoluca Orlando, proclaimed that his fragile city is "battling a great evil" and paid homage at the conference to those who died fighting the Mafia. As local officials have worked to fight the mafiosi and their corruption and stifling of Sicilian society, their efforts have been hailed as a Palermo Renaissance.

Today civic groups and schools are conducting programs to help people, especially young Sicilians, to aid in loosening the stronghold of the Cosa Nostra. We never thought we'd see it in Sicily, but the **Museo Anti-Mafia**, Via Orfanotrofio 7, Central di Cultura Polivalente (© 091-8461255), operates in the sleepy village of Corleone, outside Palermo. (The village lies a 1-hr. bus ride from Palermo on SAIS transport, with a one-way ticket costing 3.25€/$2.90). Corleone, of course, is a name familiar to all *Godfather* fans. It was depicted as the home of Salvatore Rina, the "boss of all bosses." Rina lived here for nearly a quarter of a century, as Italy's most wanted man. Much of the museum's exhibits consist of photographs documenting Mafia atrocities. Admission is free, and the museum is open Tuesday to Sunday 9am to 1pm and 3:30 to 7:30pm.

San Giovanni degli Eremiti ✮   In an atmosphere appropriate for the recluse it honors, St. John of the Hermits (now deconsecrated), with its twin-columned cloister, is one of the most idyllic spots in Palermo. A medieval veil hangs heavy in the gardens, with their citrus blossoms and flowers, especially on a hot summer day as you wander around in the cloister. Built on the order of Roger II in 1132, the church exhibits its Arabic influence, surmounted by pinkish cupolas, while showing the Norman style as well.

Via dei Benedettini 3. © 091-6515019. Admission 4€ ($3.55). Mon–Sat 9am–1pm and 3–6:30pm; Sun 9am–1pm.

Villa Malfitano ✮✮   One of Palermo's great villas, built in the Liberty style, lies within a spectacular garden. The villa was built in 1886 by Joseph Whitaker, grandson of the famous English gentleman and wine merchant Ingham, who moved to Sicily in 1806 and made a fortune producing Marsala wine. Whitaker arranged to have trees shipped to Palermo from all over the world, and he planted them around his villa. These included such rare species as Dragon's Blood, an enormous banyan tree that is the only example found in Europe. High society in Palermo flocked here for lavish parties, and royalty from Great Britain visited. The villa today is lavishly furnished, with antiques and artifacts from all over the world. The *Sala d'Estate* (Summer Room) is particularly stunning, with trompe l'oeil frescoes covering both the walls and the ceiling.

Via Dante 167. ℭ 091-6816133. Admission 2.50€ ($2.25). Mon–Sat 9am–1pm.

Catacombs of the Capuchins (Catacombe dei Cappuccini) ★ *Finds*   This bizarre site is on the outskirts of the city. The fresco you might have seen in the Regional Gallery, the *Triumph of Death*, dims in comparison with the real thing. These catacombs contained a preservative that helped to mummify the dead. Sicilians (from nobles to maids) were buried here in the 19th century, and it was the custom on Sunday to visit Uncle Luigi and see how he was holding together. If he fell apart, he was wired together or wrapped in burlap sacking. In 1920, the last person was laid to rest here, a little girl almost lifelike in death. Many 19th-century Sicilians are in fine shape, considering—with eyes, hair, and even clothing fairly intact. Some of the expressions on the faces of the skeletons take the fun out of Halloween—this is not a great place to take the kids.

Piazza Cappuccini 1. ℭ 091-212117. Admission 1.25€ ($1.10). Tours Mon–Fri 9am–noon and 3–5pm. Closed holidays.

EXPLORING LA KALSA ★★

Although it's a bit dangerous at night, crumbling La Kalsa is the most interesting neighborhood in Palermo (it's relatively safe during the day, although you should keep your wits about you). Located in the southwestern sector of the old city, it was built by the Arabs as a walled seaside residence for their chief ministers. It's bounded by the port and Via Garibaldi and Via Paternostro to the east and west, and by Corso Vittorio Emanuele and Via Lincoln to the north and south; one of its main thoroughfares is **Via Butero.** Later, much of the Arabs' fine work was destroyed when the Spanish viceroys took over, adding their own architectural interpretations.

One of the neighborhood's most dramatic churches (though not necessarily the oldest) is the fancifully baroque **Santa Teresa,** Piazza Kalsa (ℭ 091-6171658). This church is open only for services, although you can admire it from the outside. If it should happen to be open at the time of your visit, you can see an interior designed by Giacomo Amato (1643–1732). He is known for introducing Roman High Baroque to Palermo, of which Santa Teresa is the most classic example.

Another of the old town's most intriguing antique churches lies only a 5-minute walk northwest of Santa Teresa: the 13th-century **San Francesco d'Assisi** (ℭ 091-6162819). To reach it, begin at the Quattro Canti di Città and walk eastward along **Corso Vittorio Emanuele,** which locals usually refer to simply as "Il Corso." Cross over bustling Via Roma, and then turn right onto Via Paternostro until you reach the church on Piazza San Francesco d'Assisi. Visit the church, if for no other reason than to see its magnificent Cappella Mastrotonio, carved in 1468. Don't count on the church being open, however.

From Piazza San Francesco d'Assisi, follow Via Merlo to the **Palazzo Mirto,** Via Merlo 2 (ℭ 091-6164751), to see how nobility lived in the days when this was an upmarket neighborhood. The palace, a splendid example of a princely residence of the early 20th century, contains its original 18th- and 19th-century furnishings. It's open Monday to Saturday 9am to 10pm, and Sunday 9am to 12:30pm. Admission is 2.50€ ($2.25).

Via Merlo leads into the landmark **Piazza Marina,** one of the most evocative parts of Palermo. The port of La Cala was here, but it silted up in the 1100s. Reminiscent of the American Deep South, a garden is found at the **Villa Garibaldi** in the center of the square. The square is dominated by the **Palazzo Chiaramonte** on the southeast corner, dating from the early 14th century. Renaissance churches occupy the other three corners of this historic square.

SHOPPING

For a touch of local color, join Palermoans for a visit to the **Vucciria,** their main market for meat and fresh vegetables, located off Via Roma in the rear of San Domenico—this is one of Europe's great Casbah-like markets. You'll find mountains of food, from fish to meat and vegetables. The array of wild fennel, long-stemmed artichokes, and blood oranges, as well as giant octopus and squid, will astound you.

Palermo also has a number of other street markets for the adventurous shopper, including the **Capo market,** which has a long line of vendors hawking clothing in stall after stall that winds along Via Vandiera and Via San Agostino in the heart of the city. The food stalls are found mainly at Via Porta Carini and Via Beatri Paolo lying off Via Volturno. Antique vendors with many unusual buys lie along the **Piazza Peranni,** off Corso Vittorio Emanuele.

Two shops in one, **Battaglia,** Via Ruggero Settimo 74 (℃ **091-580224**), sells women's wear. Within it, Hermès offers upscale men's and women's apparel, including ready-to-wear and high-fashion collections. There's also a limited selection of casual and sports shoes, as well as leather accessories, but this shop is really about clothing.

If it comes in linen, **Frette,** Via Ruggero Settimo 12 (℃ **091-585166**) and Via G. Sciutti 85 (℃ **091-343288**), sells it. The shop offers sheets, tablecloths, towels, bedspreads, pajamas, nightgowns, curtains, and tapestries. Call for an appointment at **Miroslava Tasic,** Via Giovan Battista Filippo Basile 6–8–10 (℃ **091-588126**), if you're interested in buying handmade sheets, curtains, towels, tablecloths, or upholstery fabrics in fine cottons, silks, and linens, adorned with embroidery or lace trim.

You'll find traditional fruit-filled tarts as well as *cassata siciliana* (tarts with ricotta-based filling) at **Fratelli Magri,** Via Isidoro Carini 42 (℃ **091-584788**). The shop also makes other types of sweets and in the summer offers gelato, but come here for the authentic high-calorie pastries.

A celebration of local and national confections, **I Peccatucci di Mamma Andrea,** Via Principe di Scordia 67 (℃ **091-334835**), tempts you with the bounty of Sicily's traditional fattening desserts. Examples are pralines, *torrone* (nougat with almonds and honey), *panetoni* (a fruit cake), segments of fruit dripping with Sicilian honey, marzipan, and an age-old specialty known as *ghirlande di croccantini* (a hazelnut torte). Get ready for sugar shock and lots of local color.

One of the most comprehensive bookstores in Palermo is the **Libreria Flaccovio,** Via Ruggero Settimo 37 (℃ **091-589442**). Most of the inventory is in Italian, with good numbers of art books that celebrate the historic legacies of Sicily; a few volumes (but more than any at other outfit in Palermo) are in English.

Four generations have handcrafted tortoise-shell picture frames at **Meli,** Via Dante 294 (℃ **091-6824213**), where you can also find a selection of stylish prints, etchings, and engravings from the 16th to 19th centuries.

For majolica-style stoneware, try **De Simone,** which has been making the stuff in a family-run setup since at least the 1920s. There's a shop at Via Gaetano Daita 13B (© **091-584876**), and both a shop and a factory (which can be visited) at Via Lanza de Scalea 698 (© **091-6711005**). The shops are open Monday to Saturday, but the factory can be visited only Monday to Friday 8am to 5pm. No reservations are necessary.

Sicilian potters have artfully merged influences from the Arab and Christian worlds in their brightly painted trademark stoneware. **Laboratorio Italiano,** Via Principe di Villafranca 42 (© **091-320282**), sells artfully crafted dinner plates, coffee cups, garden ornaments, jardinieres, and chandeliers, any of which can be insured and shipped to wherever you specify.

WHERE TO STAY

The hotel selection is generally not great in Palermo. Choose carefully.

VERY EXPENSIVE

Villa Igiea Grand Hotel 🌟🌟   The Villa Igiea was built in the early 1900s as one of Sicily's aristocratic estates, and today it's a recommended luxury hotel. Set in gardens on the sea, the place is lovely if you're going to spend time here sunning and relaxing. But if you're looking for a base for seeing the city, note that town is a 15-minute taxi ride away. The structure resembles a medieval Sicilian fortress, with crenellated battlements and watchtowers. A circular temple, buttressed with modern scaffolding, still stands in the garden. Everywhere are clusters of antiques. The guest rooms vary from sumptuous suites with terraces to smaller, less glamorous rooms, many a bit worn and faded. The bathrooms have aging but still functional plumbing. The hotel is reached by passing through an industrial port area north of Palermo.

Salita Belmonte 43, 90142 Palermo. © 091-543744. Fax 091-547654. 114 units. 207€–295€ ($184.85–$263.45) double; 436€–454€ ($389.35–$405.40) suite. Rates include breakfast. AE, DC, MC, V. Free parking. **Amenities:** Dining room; bar; pool; tennis court; room service; babysitting; laundry. *In room:* A/C, TV, minibar, hair dryer, safe.

EXPENSIVE

Hotel Centrale Palace 🌟   One of the city's most appealing hotels, a favorite with business travelers, occupies what was an opulent home in the 1600s. About a century ago, it became a hotel; in the 1990s, it was modernized by the Best Western group. Furnishings are mostly functional and modern, with a few period or Empire antiques and Oriental rugs to liven up the decor. The bathrooms were recently renovated. The quietest rooms are on the *cortile,* or side streets, but double-glazing on the front windows blocks traffic noise fairly efficiently. The top-floor breakfast room has views over the Palermo rooftops to Monte Pellegrino.

Corso Vittorio Emanuele 327 (at Via Maqueda), 99134 Palermo. © 091-336666. Fax 091-334881. www. bestwestern.com. 63 units. 206€ ($183.95) double; 266€ ($237.55) junior suite. Rates include buffet breakfast. AE, DC, MC, V. Parking 12€ ($10.70). **Amenities:** Restaurant; bar; gym; sauna; room service; babysitting; laundry/dry cleaning. *In room:* A/C, TV, minibar, hair dryer.

Hotel Principe di Villafranca 🌟 *Finds*   If you'd like a hotel with a homey quality, there is no finer address than this one. A luxurious atmosphere is created with the use of regional antiques, Sicilian marble floors, vaulted ceilings, and tasteful silks that you might find in a palace. In all, there is a museumlike aura about the place, yet it remains informal and inviting. Bedrooms are beautifully furnished, the suites coming with whirlpool bathrooms. The Sicilian decor here extends to even the wardrobes, which were painted by artists in Palmero. Some of the porcelain pieces were made by hand, and most units also contain an antique or two.

Via G. Turrisi Colonna 4, 90141 Palermo. (℃) **091-6118523.** Fax 091-588705. www.principedivillafranca.it. 34 units (some with shower only). 172€ ($153.60) double; 240€ ($214.30) suite. Rates include breakfast. AE, DC, MC, V. **Amenities:** Restaurant; bar; gym; room service; babysitting; laundry/dry cleaning. *In room:* A/C, TV, minibar, hair dryer, safe.

MODERATE

Grande Albergo Sole *(Value)*   This pleasant hotel is in the busy historic center, just steps east of the Quattro Canti. A 1960s remake of a century-old building, it's drearily modern inside, but the staff is wonderful, the price is right, the location is central, and you can usually find a vacancy here due to the hotel's size. Guest rooms are fairly large, furnished with built-in pieces (a few rooms mix in the occasional antique). Units right on the Corso are noticeably noisier. Don't miss the sun terrace on the roof, which has a 360° view of Palermo's rooftops, domes, the fountain, and Quattro Canti below, and the mountains that ring the city beyond.

Corso Vittorio Emanuele 291, 90133 Palermo. (℃) **091-6041111.** Fax 091-6110182. 150 units (showers only). 124€ ($110.75) double. Rates include breakfast. AE, DC, MC, V. Parking 7.50€ ($6.70). **Amenities:** Restaurant; bar; lounge; room service; laundry/dry cleaning. *In room:* A/C, TV, minibar.

Jolly Hotel del Foro Italico *(※)*   Situated off a busy boulevard facing the gulf, this 1960s chain hotel is one of the best in town. The well-organized but small guest rooms contain lots of built-in pieces and comfortable beds, although the bathrooms are small. Try for the quieter rooms on the upper floors (affording at least a glimpse of the Mediterranean) or at the rear.

Via Foro Italico 22, 90133 Palermo. (℃) **800/221-2626** in the U.S., 800/237-0319 in Canada, or 091-6165090. Fax 091-6161441. 235 units (showers only). 132€–162€ ($117.90–$144.65) double; 182€ ($162.55) suite. Rates include breakfast. Half-board 28€ ($25) per person. AE, DC, MC, V. Parking 10€ ($8.95). **Amenities:** Restaurant; bar; pool; room service; laundry. *In room:* A/C, TV, minibar, hair dryer.

President Hotel   Rising eight concrete-and-glass stories above the harbor front, this hotel is one of the better and more moderately priced choices in town. It underwent a complete renovation in 2000. You pass beneath the soaring arcade before entering the informal stone-trimmed lobby. There's nothing stylish about the small guest rooms, but they're comfortably furnished, each with a well-kept bathroom.

Via Francesco Crispi 228, 90139 Palermo. (℃) **091-580733.** Fax 091-611588. 129 units. 125€ ($111.65) double. Rates include breakfast. AE, DC, MC, V. Parking 5€ ($4.45). **Amenities:** Restaurant; bar; room service; laundry/dry cleaning. *In room:* A/C, TV, minibar, hair dryer.

INEXPENSIVE

Hotel Joli   Opening onto a beautiful old square, Piazza Floria, this modest choice lies near the pricey Grand Hotel La Palme, a few blocks from Piazza Castelnuovo. It is near the historic center of Palermo, but in a relatively tranquil location away from some of the blaring noise of traffic. The place is modest but exceptionally clean. The boxy rooms are not large and are simply furnished, but they're welcoming and bright, with compact tiled bathrooms. The best units come with small terraces overlooking the square.

Via Michele Amari 11, 90139 Palermo. (℃) and fax **091-6111765.** www.hoteljoli.com. 30 units. 77€–104€ ($68.75–$92.85) double; from 104€ ($92.85) suite. Rates include breakfast. AE, DC, MC, V. **Amenities:** Bar; room service; babysitting; laundry/dry cleaning. *In room:* A/C, TV, hair dryer.

Hotel Sausele *(Value)* This family-run inn stands out amid the depressing rail station–area hotels. It boasts high ceilings, globe lamps, strikingly clean floors, modern art, and new wooden modular furnishings. The staff is hospitable, and there's a resident St. Bernard named Eva. Rooms on the street can be noisy, so light sleepers should request one overlooking the peaceful courtyard. Rooms are certainly small and modest, but this is a pleasant choice.

Via Vincenzo Errante 12, 90127 Palermo. ℭ **091-6161308.** Fax 091-6167525. www.hotelsausele.it. 36 units (showers only). 77.50€ ($69.20) double. Rates include breakfast. AE, DC, MC, V. Parking 7.50€ ($6.70). **Amenities:** Bar; 2 lounges; room service. *In room:* A/C, TV, hair dryer.

Principe di Belmonte *(Finds)* This hotel has firm beds, large and spotless rooms, and a friendly owner, all in the best part of town. It's also on one of modern Palermo's quieter streets, 1½ blocks down from a pedestrian mall lined with cafes. The time-worn furnishings are plain but sturdy. The bathrooms are large (although some are of the old hold-your-own-shower-nozzle variety and hot water can run scarce). Almost all rooms have TV and balcony. The mini-apartments are great values, with compact kitchens.

Via Principe di Belmonte 25. ℭ 091-331065. Fax 091-6113424. 17 units, 14 with private bathroom (showers only); 6 apts. 60€ ($53.60) double; 69€ ($61.60) apt. AE, DC, MC, V. Free parking in street. **Amenities:** Lounge. *In room:* TV (most units).

WHERE TO DINE
MODERATE

Friends' Bar ✿ SICILIAN About 10km (6¼ miles) north of Palermo, this is one of the finest restaurants in the region. Named after the four friends (*amici*) who opened it in the 1970s, it features an air-conditioned dining room and a gazebolike indoor/outdoor structure that rises from a lush garden. A meal here is an event for many Sicilians, and a reservation (especially for the garden) might be hard to get. The antipasti, rich with marinated vegetables and grilled fish, are loaded onto a buffet table, and the pastas tend to be strong, aromatic, and laced with flavors such as anchovies, fresh basil, and sardines. Grilled swordfish, calamari, and octopus are always worthwhile, and the house wine is redolent with the flavors and sunshine of southern Italy.

Via Filippo Brunelleschi 138, Michelangelo. ℭ 091-201401. Reservations required. Main courses 8.50€–17.50€ ($7.60–$15.65). AE, DC, MC, V. Tues–Sun 12:30–3pm and 8–11pm. Closed 3 weeks in Aug.

La Scuderia ✿✿ INTERNATIONAL/ITALIAN Dedicated professionals direct this restaurant surrounded by trees at the foot of Monte Pellegrino, 5km (3 miles) north of the city center. In summer it has one of the prettiest flowery terraces in town, sought after by everyone from lovers to extended families to vacationing glamour queens. The imaginative cuisine includes a mixed grill of fresh vegetables with a healthy dose of a Sicilian cheese called *caciocavallo*, stuffed turkey cutlet, beef and veal dishes, *involtini* of eggplant or veal, risotto with seafood, and *maccheroni Nettuno* (studded with swordfish, sliced eggplant, and tomato sauce).

Viale del Fante 9. ℭ 091-520323. Reservations recommended. Main courses 12€–20€ ($10.70–$17.85). AE, DC, MC, V. Mon–Sat 12:30–3pm and 8:30pm–midnight. Closed 2 weeks in Aug.

INEXPENSIVE

If you don't have time for a long, drawn-out Sicilian lunch, head for **Antica Focacceria San Francesco,** Mercado Vucciria (ℭ **091-320264**), which has a great selection of little sandwiches. Their pies are often baked with fresh Sicilian fruits.

Capricci di Sicilia *(Value* SICILIAN   Great care goes into the cuisine here, and the chef shops for only the freshest ingredients. To go really local, order *polpette* (fishballs of fresh sardines). Pasta is often flavored with sardines and broccoli, and the spaghetti is succulent when made with sea urchins. The swordfish roulade is always dependable, as are any number of other dishes prepared to bring out maximum flavor. In warm weather, meals can be served in a small garden.

Via Istituto Pignatelli 6 (off Piazza Sturzo). ✆ 091-327777. Reservations recommended. Main courses 15€–30€ ($13.40–$26.80). AE, DC, MC, V. Sept–July daily 1–3:30pm and 8pm–midnight; Aug daily 8pm–midnight

Osteria Fratelli Lo Bizanco *(Value* SICILIAN   Sicily of yesterday lives in this no-frills joint frequented by street vendors and stevedores, with an occasional vegetable trucker dropping in. The owner presides over the establishment with a certain rough flair, inviting you to sample his pasta specialties. On our last visit he was offering pasta with fresh sardines. Many locals, however, ordered the pasta with potatoes, which some diners might find a bit starchy. For a main course, count on the catch of the day, often fresh swordfish steak, or else calamari. Tender beefsteak is also featured, although we noticed many diners making a meal out of pasta *nero di seppia* (a medley of seafood).

V. E. Amari 104. ✆ 091-585816. Reservations recommended. Main courses 3.25€–4.25€ ($2.90–$3.80). No credit cards. Mon–Sat noon–3pm and 7:30–10pm. Bus: 101, 104, 106, 108, or 124.

Santandrea ✶ *(Finds* SEAFOOD/SICILIAN   All the bounty gathered very early that morning at the Vuciria market is prepared with skill and flavor here. In fair weather you can sit out on this old square to the south of Piazza San Domenci, looking at the crumbling buildings from the 19th century. Instead of handing you a menu, the waiter will recite the day's specials to you with obvious pleasure. Go with the mixed antipasti, which always features fresh seafood. The pasta dishes are excellent, notably thin spaghetti prepared with sea urchins, a local delicacy, or spaghetti with fresh sardines. The fresh tagliatelle in a pesto of sun-dried tomatoes, fresh zucchini leaves, and toasted pine nuts is just wonderful. There's always the fresh catch of the day, which is generally grilled but can also be ordered as *timballo di spigola* (cooked to perfection in the oven).

Piazza Sant'Andrea 4. ✆ 091-334999. Reservations required. Main courses 8€–12.50€ ($7.15–$11.15). AE, DC, MC, V. Wed–Mon 1–3pm and 8pm–midnight. Closed Jan. Bus: 101, 103, 104, or 107.

PALERMO AFTER DARK

We always like to begin our evening by heading to the century-old **Caffè Mazzara,** Via Generale Magliocco 15 (✆ **091-321443**). You can sample wonderful Sicilian ice cream, sip a rich coffee, or try a heady Sicilian wine. Besides an espresso bar and pastry shop on the street level, the premises contain a piano bar and pub, plus a well-recommended restaurant. If you can't find a place to eat in Palermo on a Sunday, when virtually everything is shut, Mazzara is a good bet. It's open daily 7:30am to 11pm.

Palermo's most popular dance clubs lie in the city's commercial center. The city's main dance club is **Candelai,** Via Candelai 65 (✆ **091-327151**), which charges a 4€ ($3.55) cover. Mainstream rock blasts throughout the night in this crowded complex of gyrating 20-year-olds. The club is open only Friday to Sunday from 8pm, with no set closing time. **Grant's Club,** Via Principe di Paternò 80 (✆ **091-346772**), is open only Friday and Saturday 10:30pm to at least 3am, depending on the crowd. A charge of 7.50€ to 12.50€ ($6.70–$11.15) includes one drink.

The top gay nightspot in Palermo is **Discopub,** Piazza San Francesco di Paola (© **091-7814698**), where outdoor tables are set out in summer.

If you're looking for relief from Palermo's oppressive heat, consider a short trek north of the city to Mondello, where you'll find an attractive piano bar in the **Mondello Palace Hotel,** Via Principe di Scalea 12 (© **091-450001**).

Palermo is also a cultural center of some note. The opera and ballet seasons last from January to June. The principal venue is the restored **Teatro Massimo,** Via Maqueda (© **091-6053515**), across from the Museo Archeologico. It is the largest indoor stage in Europe, except for the Paris Opera House. Francis Ford Coppola shot a climactic opera scene here for *The Godfather: Part III.* The box office is open Tuesday to Sunday 10am to 4pm, with tickets generally costing from 11€ to 73€ ($9.80–$65.20) for standard seats.

SIDE TRIPS FROM PALERMO
MONREALE

The town of Monreale is 10km (6¼ miles) from Palermo, up Monte Caputo and on the edge of the Conca d'Oro plain. If you don't have a car, you can reach it by taking **bus** no. 389 from Piazza Indipendenza in Palermo.

The Normans under William II founded a Benedictine monastery at Monreale in the 1170s. Eventually a great cathedral was built near the monastery's ruins. Like the Alhambra in Granada, Spain, the **Chiostro del Duomo di Monreale** ✦✦, Piazza Guglielmo il Buono (© **091-6404413**), has a relatively drab facade, giving little indication of the riches inside. The interior is virtually covered with shimmering mosaics illustrating scenes from the Bible. The artwork provides a distinctly original interpretation of the old, rigid Byzantine form of decoration. The mosaics have an Eastern look despite the Western-style robed Christ reigning over his kingdom. The ceiling is ornate, even gaudy. On the north and west facades are two bronze doors depicting biblical stories in relief. The cloisters are also of interest. Built in 1166, they consist of twin mosaic columns, and every other pair bears an original design (the lava inlay was hauled from Mt. Etna). Admission to the cathedral is free; if you visit the cloisters, there's a charge of 4€ ($3.55). The cathedral is open daily 9am to 1pm and 3:30 to 6pm. From July to September, the cloister is open Monday to Saturday 9am to 1pm; Monday, Wednesday, and Friday 3 to 6pm; and Sunday 9am to 12:30pm. In the off-season, ask at the cathedral because hours vary.

You can also visit the **treasury** and the **terraces;** each charges 1.50€ ($1.35) for admission. They're open daily 9:30am to 12:30pm and 3:30 to 5:30pm. The terraces are actually the rooftop of the church, from which you'll be rewarded with a view of the cloisters.

Before or after your visit to Monreale, drop in at **Bar Italia,** Via Benedetto d'Acquisto 1 (© **091-6402421**), near the Duomo. The plain cookies are wonderfully flavorful and fresh; if you go early in the morning, order one of the freshly baked croissants and a cup of cappuccino, Monreale's best.

For a meal, try **La Botte,** Contrada Lenzitti 20 (© **091-414051**), 19km (12 miles) north of Palermo, beside SS186 and uphill from the center of Monreale. Begin with the savory antipasto offerings (marinated tuna, grilled sardines or anchovies, marinated red peppers). Specialties are *gnocchi alla barra* (stuffed with local cheeses and herbs), *delizia tre naccia* (fettuccine with ricotta, mozzarella, eggplant, tomatoes, and Sicilian herbs), and veal layered with cheese, salami, basil, and herbs. Reservations are recommended. It's open Friday to Sunday noon to 2pm and 8 to 11pm (closed June 20–Aug 30); and American Express, Diners Club, MasterCard, and Visa are accepted.

Sampling the Local Vino

Sicily's hot climate and volcanic soil nurture many vineyards, many of which produce just simple table wines. Of the better vintages, the best-known wine is **Marsala**, a sweet dessert wine produced in both amber and ruby tones. One top producer is **Regaleali**, Contrada Regaleali, 93010 Vallelunga, Pratameno Caltanisetta (✆ **0921-542522**), a historic enterprise near Palermo run by the Tasca d'Almerita family. This winery is also known for its sauvignon-based Nozze d'Oro and such full-bodied reds as Rosso del Conte.

One other name that evokes years of wine-making traditions, thanks to the winery's skill at producing Cerasuolo di Vittoria and Moscato di Pantelleria, is **Corvo Duca di Salaparuta**, a 19th-century winery in the hills above Palermo. For information, contact the **Casa Vinicola Duca di Salaparuta**, Via Nazionale, SS113, Casteldaccia, 90014 Palermo (✆ **091-953988**).

If you'd like to tour the countryside and visit any of these wineries, call ahead to make appointments and get detailed directions.

MONDELLO LIDO

When the summer sun burns hot, and when old men on the square seek a place in the shade and bambini tire of their toys, it's beach weather. For Palermo residents, that means **Mondello,** 12km (7½ miles) east. Before this beachfront town started attracting the wealthy class of Palermo, it was a fishing village (and still is), and you can see rainbow-colored fishing boats bobbing in the harbor. A good sandy beach stretches for about a mile and a half, and it's filled to capacity on a July or August day. Some women traveling alone find Mondello more inviting and less intimidating than Palermo. In summer, an express **bus** (no. 6, "Beallo") leaves for Mondello from the central train station in Palermo.

CEFALÙ ⭐⭐

Another good day-trip destination lies 81km (50 miles) east from Palermo, where the fishing village of **Cefalù** is tucked onto every inch of a spit of land underneath an awesome crag called the Rocca. The village is known for its Romanesque cathedral, an outstanding achievement of Arab–Norman architecture (see below). Its beaches, its medley of architectural styles, and its narrow streets were captured in the Oscar-winning *Cinema Paradiso.* You can tour the town in half a day and spend the rest of the time enjoying life on the beach, especially in summer.

From Palermo, 18 **trains** make the 1-hour trip daily, costing 2.85€ ($2.55) one way. For information and schedules, call ✆ **1478-88088. SPISA,** Via Cavour, 2 (✆ **0921-424301**), runs **buses** between Palermo and Cefalù, costing from 4.50€ ($4) one way for the 1½-hour trip. If you're **driving,** follow Route 113 east from Palermo to Cefalù. Driving time is about 1½ hours. You'll have to park at the top of the Rocca and then join lines of visitors walking up and down the narrow steep streets near the water. You'll pass a lot of forgettable shops. In the past few years, it seems that half the denizens of Cefalù have become trinket peddlers and souvenir hawkers.

You'll find the **tourist office** at Corso Ruggero 77 (✆ **0921-421050**), open Monday to Friday 8am to 2:30pm and 3:30 to 7pm; Saturday 9am to 1pm.

Make a beeline to Cefalù's Duomo first thing in the morning so that you can avoid the coach-bus hordes. Resembling a military fortress, the **Duomo** ⭐⭐,

Piazza del Duomo, off Corso Ruggero (© **0921-922021**), was built by Roger II to fulfill a vow he'd made when faced with a possible shipwreck. Construction began in 1131, and, in time, two square towers rose, curiously placed between the sea and a rocky promontory. The architectural line of the cathedral boasts a severe elegance that has earned it a position in many art-history books. The interior, which took a century to complete, overwhelms you with 16 Byzantine and Roman columns supporting towering capitals. The graceful horseshoe arches are one of the island's best examples of the Saracen influence on Norman architecture. The celebrated mosaic of Christ the Pantocrator, one of only three on Sicily, in the dome of the cathedral apse is alone worth the trip. The nearby mosaic of the Virgin with angels and the Apostles is a well-preserved work from 1148. In the transept is a marble statue of the Madonna. Roger's plan to have a tomb placed in the Duomo was derailed by the authorities at Palermo's cathedral, where he rests today. Admission is free, and the church is open daily 8am to noon and 3:30 to 6:30pm.

Before leaving town, try to visit the **Museo Mandralisca,** Via Mandralisca 13 (© **0921-421547**), opposite the cathedral. It has an outstanding art collection, including the 1470 portrait of an unknown by Antonello da Messina. Some art critics have journeyed all the way from Rome just to stare at this handsome work, and it's often featured on Sicilian tourist brochures. Admission is 4€ ($3.55), and it's open daily 9am to 7pm.

If you're feeling hungry, try the rustic seaside trattoria **Al Gabbiano,** Lungomare G. Giardina 17 (© **0921-421495**). Fresh fish is the item to order, from a list of nearly unpronounceable sea creatures. You might begin with *zuppa di cozze,* a luscious mussel soup. The vegetables and pastas are good, too, especially *pennette alla Norma* (with eggplant). If you speak a little Italian, it helps. It's open Thursday to Tuesday noon to 3pm and 7pm to midnight (it's closed mid-Dec to mid-Jan).

SEGESTA ★★

There's only one reason to come to Segesta: to see a single amazing temple in a lonely field. For some visitors, that's reason enough because it's one of the best-preserved ancient temples in all Italy. It takes about an hour to get here from Palermo, and it makes a good brief stop en route to **Erice** (see below).

Segesta was the ancient city of the Elymi, a people of mysterious origin who are linked by some to the Trojans. As the major city in western Sicily, it was brought into a series of conflicts with the rival power nearby, Selinus (Selinunte). From the 6th to 5th centuries B.C., there were near-constant hostilities. The Athenians came from the east to aid the Segestans in 415 B.C., but the expedition ended in disaster, eventually forcing the city to turn for help to Hannibal of Carthage.

Twice in the 4th century B.C., Segesta was besieged and conquered, once by Dionysius and again by Agathocles (a particularly brutal victor who tortured, mutilated, or made slaves of most of the citizenry). Segesta, in time, turned on its old but dubious ally, Carthage. Like all Greek cities of Sicily, it ultimately fell to the Romans.

The main sight in Segesta is its remarkable **Doric temple** ★★★ from the 5th century B.C. Although never completed, it's in an excellent state of preservation (the entablature still remains). The temple was far enough away from the ancient town to have escaped being leveled during the "scorched earth" days of the Vandals and Arabs. From its position on a lonely hill, the Doric temple commands a majestic setting. Although you can scale the hill on foot, you're likely to encounter boys trying to hustle you for a donkey ride (we advise against it—some of these poor animals have saddle sores and seem to be in pain when ridden). In summer, **classical plays** are staged almost nightly at 8:45pm. (Travel agents will have full details and often sell tickets and packages that include transportation.)

There's a cafe in the parking area leading to the temple; otherwise, there are no hotels or restaurants.

There are approximately four **trains** per day between Palermo and Segesta, and buses leave almost hourly. The station is about a 1km (half-mile) walk to the ancient site. Special bus service is usually offered in conjunction with the evening plays. For information, contact either the tourist office in Palermo or **Noema Viaggi,** Via di Marzo 13 (© **091-6254221**). By **car,** drive west from Palermo along A29, branching onto A29dir past Alcamo. From Selinunte, head to Castelvetrano to connect to A29 headed north, branching onto A29dir.

ERICE ★★

Originally established some 3,000 years ago, Erice is an enchanting medieval city. From its thrilling mountaintop setting, two sheer cliffs drop 755m (2,478 ft.) to open up vistas across the plains of Trapani and down the west coast of Sicily. On a clear day, you can even see Cape Bon in Tunisia, but this Sicilian aerie is often shrouded in a mist that only adds to the mystique (or, especially in winter, the misery, when temperatures can really plummet below Sicilian norms and snow and hail are not uncommon).

Erice is a lovely place to spend an afternoon wandering the medieval streets, with their baroque balconies and flowering vines, and drinking in the vistas. The southwest corner of town contains the Villa Balio gardens, originally laid out in the 19th century. Beyond the gardens, a path winds along the cliff edge up to Erice's highest point, the **Castello di Venere** ★, today little more than crumbling Norman-era walls surrounding the sacred site where a temple to Venus once stood. Piercing the walls are several windows and doorways with spectacular views across the countryside.

Erice is noted for its pastries. Stop off at **Maria Grammatica,** via V. Emanuele 14, near Piazza Umberto (© **0923-869390**), to sample sugary almond treats kissed with lemon or citrus juices.

Many people also like to shop for the town's famous rugs, which feature colorful geometric designs. **Maria La Sala** works the loom in her little shop at via V. Emanuele 80 (no phone); also check out **Ceramica Ericina** at via V. Emanuele 7 (© **0923-869140**).

Eight or nine **trains** run to Erice daily from Palermo. If you're driving, follow the A29dir from Palermo or Segesta to the first Trapani exit, and then continue along the signposted switchback road up the mountain.

6 The Aeolian Islands

Lipari: 30km (19 miles) N of Milazzo; Stromboli: 81km (50 miles) N of Milazzo; Vulcano: 20km (12 miles) N of Milazzo

The Aeolian Islands (*Isole Eolie o Lipari*) have been inhabited for more than 3,000 years, in spite of volcanic activity that even now causes the earth to issue forth sulfuric belches, streams of molten lava, and hissing clouds of steam. Ancient Greek sailors believed that these seven windswept islands were the home of Aeolus, god of the winds. He supposedly lived in a cave on Vulcano, keeping the winds of the world in a bag to be opened only with great caution.

Lipari (36 sq. km/14 sq. miles) is the largest and most developed island, **Stromboli** (13 sq. km/5 sq. miles) is the most distant and volcanically active, and **Vulcano** (21 sq. km/8 sq. miles) is the closest island to the Sicilian mainland, with its brooding, potentially volatile cone and therapeutic mud baths. The other islands (**Salina, Filicudi, Alicudi,** and **Panarea**) offer only bare-bones facilities and are visited mainly by day-trippers.

Despite the volcanoes, the area attracts tourists (mainly Germans and Italians) with crystalline waters that have great snorkeling, scuba, and spearfishing, and photogenic beaches composed of hot black sand and rocky outcroppings jutting into the Tyrrhenian Sea. The volcanoes themselves offer hikers the thrill of peering into a bubbling crater.

AEOLIAN ISLANDS ESSENTIALS

GETTING THERE　**Ferry** and **hydrofoil** services to Lipari, Stromboli, and Vulcano are available in Milazzo, on the northeastern coast of Sicily 32km (20 miles) west of Messina, through the **Società Siremar,** Via Dei Mille (© **090-9283242**). The **Società SNAV,** Via L. Rizzo 17 (© **090-9287821**), offers hydrofoil service.

Siremar operates two ferry routes, which are cheaper and slower than the hydrofoils. The Milazzo–Vulcano–Lipari–Salina line leaves Milazzo four to six times daily 7am to 6:30pm. It takes 1½ hours to reach Vulcano, and a one-way ticket costs 5€ ($4.45). Lipari is 2 hours from Milazzo; tickets cost 5.25€ ($4.70) one way. To reach Stromboli, take the Milazzo–Panarea–Stromboli line, which departs from Milazzo at 7am Friday to Wednesday, and at 2:30pm on Thursday. The Stromboli trip takes 5 hours and costs 8.25€ ($7.35) one way.

There's also hydrofoil service. The Milazzo–Vulcano–Lipari–Salina line reaches Vulcano in 50 minutes; a one-way ticket costs 12€ ($10.70). It takes 1 hour to reach Lipari and costs 9.75€ ($8.70) one way. Siremar makes the trip 6 to 12 times daily 7:05am to 7pm; SNAV makes six runs daily 7:30am to 7pm. To reach Stromboli, use the Milazzo–Panarea–Stromboli line, which takes 2½ hours and costs 15€ ($13.40) one way. Siremar trips leave four times daily 6:15am to 3pm. For more information call © **081-3172999** or 199-123199 within Italy.

If you're **driving** from Messina, take S113 west to Palermo until you come to the turnoff for Milazzo.

VISITOR INFORMATION　The **tourist office** in Lipari is at Via Vittorio Emanuele 202 (© **090-9880095**). July and August, it's open daily 8am to 2pm and Monday to Saturday 4:30 to 10pm; September to June, hours are Monday to Friday 8am to 2pm and 4:30 to 7:30pm, and Saturday 8am to 2pm. There's no information center in Stromboli. The **tourist office** in Vulcano, Via Porto di Levante (© **090-9852028**), keeps the same hours as the Lipari office but is open only June to September.

LIPARI ⭐

Homer called it "a floating island, a wall of bronze and splendid smooth sheer cliffs." The offspring of seven volcanic eruptions, Lipari is the largest of the Aeolians. Lipari is also the name of the island's only real town. It's the administrative headquarters of the Aeolian Islands (except autonomous Salina). The town sits on a plateau of red volcanic rock on the southeastern shore, framed by two beaches, Marina Lunga, which functions as the harbor, and Marina Corta.

Its dominant feature is a 16th-century **Spanish castle**, within the walls of which lies a 17th-century cathedral featuring a 16th-century Madonna and an 18th-century silver statue of San Bartolomeo. There's also an **archaeological park** where stratified clues about continuous civilizations dating to 1700 B.C. have been uncovered.

Excellent artifacts from the Stone and Bronze ages, as well as relics from Greek and Roman acropolises that once stood here, are housed next door in the former bishop's palace, now the **Museo Archeologico Eoliano** ★★, Via del Castello (© **090-9880174**), one of Sicily's major archaeological museums. It houses one of the world's finest Neolithic collections. The oldest discoveries date from 4200 B.C. Lustrous red ceramics, known as the "Diana style," come from the last Neolithic period, 3000 to 2500 B.C. Other exhibits are reconstructed necropolises from the Middle Bronze Age and a 6th-century-A.D. depiction of Greek warships. Some 1,200 pieces of painted terra cotta from the 4th and 3rd centuries B.C., including stone theatrical masks, are on exhibit. The museum also houses the only Late Bronze Age (8th c. B.C.) necropolis found in Sicily. It's open daily 9am to 1:30pm and 3 to 6pm. Admission is 4€ ($3.55).

The most popular **beaches** are at **Canneto,** about a 20-minute walk north of Lipari on the eastern coast, and, just north of it, **Spiaggia Bianca** (named for the white sand, an oddity among the region's predominant black sands). To reach the beach from Canneto, take the waterfront road, climb the stairs of Via Marina Garibaldi, and then veer right down a narrow cobbled path for about 297m (325 yd.).

Acquacalda (hot water) is the island's northernmost city, but nobody likes to go on its beaches (the black sand is rocky and unpleasant for walking or lying on). The town is also known for its obsidian and pumice quarries. West of Acquacalda at Quattropani, you can make a steep climb to the **Duomo de Chiesa Barca,** where the point of interest isn't the cathedral but the panoramic view from the church grounds. On the west coast, 4km (2½ miles) from Lipari, the island's other great view is available by making another steep climb to the **Quattrocchi Belvedere.**

Twenty-nine kilometers (18 miles) of road circle the island, connecting all its villages and attractions. Buses run by Lipari's **Autobus Urso Guglielmo,** Via Cappuccini (© **090-9811262**), make 10 circuits of the island per day. The trip to Quattropani and Acquacalda on the north coast costs 1.60€ ($1.45); closer destinations cost 1.30€ ($1.15).

WHERE TO STAY

Hotel Carasco ★★   This is Lipari's grandest hotel, consisting of two buildings connected by an addition, sitting on a bluff by the sea with a staircase leading down to the rocky coast. The interior contrasts with the bright heat of the outdoors; it has brown terra-cotta floors and dark wood furniture upholstered with fabrics striped in shades of brown. Each well-furnished guest room features a ceiling fan and rustic artifacts, with a quality mattress. Views from the ample private balconies are panoramic.

Porto delle Genti, 98055 Lipari. © **090-9811605**. Fax 090-9811828. www.carasco.it. 89 units. 52€–91€ ($46.45–$81.25) double with breakfast; 62€–101€ ($55.35–$90.20) double with breakfast and dinner. AE, DC, MC, V. Closed Nov–Mar. **Amenities:** Restaurant; bar; pool; room service; babysitting; laundry/dry cleaning. *In room:* A/C, hair dryer.

Villa Meligunis ★   This 18th-century villa offers refined Aeolian hospitality. Less than 45m (50 yd.) from the ferry docks, this appealingly contemporary hotel arose from a cluster of 17th-century fishers' cottages at Marina Corta. The guest rooms are rustic but uncluttered and larger than you might expect, usually with views of the harbor and summery furniture. The hotel's name derives from the ancient name that Greek colonists originally gave to Lipari, Meligunia.

Via Marte 7, 98055 Lipari. *©* 090-9812426. Fax 090-9880149. www.netnet.it/villameligunis. 32 units (showers only). 233€–310€ ($208.05–$276.85) double. Rates include breakfast and dinner. AE, DC, MC, V. Free parking nearby. **Amenities:** Restaurant; 2 bars; room service; babysitting; laundry. *In room:* A/C, TV, minibar, hair dryer, safe.

WHERE TO DINE

E Pulera *✯✯* SICILIAN/AEOLIAN   Owned by the same family that owns the Filippino (see below), this restaurant emphasizes its Aeolian origins. Artifacts and maps of the islands fashioned from ceramic tiles are scattered about. Some tables occupy a terrace with a view of a flowering lawn, where you'll probably want to linger. Specialties include a delightful version of *zuppa di pesce alla pescatora* (fisher's soup), *bocconcini di pesce spada* (swordfish ragout), and risotto with crayfish or squid in its own ink. Other good choices are a rich assortment of seafood antipasti that's usually laden with basil and garlic, *involtini* of eggplant, and herb-laden versions of roasted lamb. Desserts might include Aeolian cassata and ricotta mousse with wild strawberries and almonds.

Via Isabella Viniker. *©* **090-9811158.** Reservations recommended. Main courses 17.50€–25€ ($15.65–$22.35). AE, DC, MC, V. Daily 7:30pm–2am. Closed mid-Oct to May.

Filippino *✯✯* SICILIAN   It's a pleasant surprise to find such a fine restaurant in such a remote location. Filippino has thrived in the heart of town, near Town Hall, since 1910, when it was opened by the ancestors of the family that runs it today. You'll dine in one of two large rooms or on an outdoor terrace ringed with flowering shrubs and potted flowers. Menu items are based on old-fashioned Sicilian recipes and prepared with flair. Try the *ravioloni* (large ravioli) stuffed with stone bass and served with salsa macaroni with mozzarella, prosciutto, and ricotta baked in the oven. Veal scaloppini is especially tempting when cooked in Malvasia wine, and the array of fresh fish is broad. We especially enjoyed the *cupolette di pesce spada* with basil ("little dome" of swordfish) and the eggplant capponata. You can also choose to spend the night in one of their double rooms which cost from 60€ to 100€ ($53.60–$89.30).

Piazza Municipio. *©* **090-9811002.** Reservations recommended. Main courses 10€–30€ ($8.95–$26.80). AE, MC, V. Daily noon–2:30pm and 7:30–10:30pm. Closed Mon Oct–Mar.

La Nassa *✯* *(Finds* SICILIAN/AEOLIAN   At this enchanting family-run restaurant, the delectable cuisine of Donna Teresa matches the friendly enthusiasm of her son Bartolo, who has thousands of interesting stories to tell. The food is the most genuine and fresh you can find on the island, prepared respecting both antique traditions and modern taste. After the *sette perle* (seven pearl) appetizer, a combination of fresh fish, sweet shrimp, and spices, you can try the fish roulades, or any kind of fish you like, cooked in every possible way to satisfy your request. Local favorites include *sarago, cernia,* and *dentice,* as delicate in texture as their names are untranslatable. If you are more in a meat mood (which is difficult after you've seen the restaurant's boats coming back with delicious, just-caught fish), you can opt for Teresa's sausages seasoned with Aeolian herbs. As a dessert, try cookies with Malvasia wine, a sweet red wine typical of this area.

Via G. Franza 36. *©* **090-9811319.** Reservations recommended. Main courses 7€–15€ ($6.25–$13.40). AE, MC, V. July–Oct daily 8:30am–3pm and 6pm–midnight; Apr–June closed Thurs. Closed Nov–Easter.

STROMBOLI 🐑🐑

The most distant island in the archipelago, Stromboli achieved notoriety and became a household word in the United States in 1950 with the release of the Roberto Rossellini cinema vérité film starring Ingrid Bergman. The American public was far more interested in the "illicit" affair between Bergman and Rossellini than in the film. Although the affair was tame by today's standards, it temporarily ended Bergman's American film career, and she was denounced on the Senate floor. Movie fans today are more likely to remember Stromboli from the film version of the Jules Verne novel *Journey to the Center of the Earth,* starring James Mason.

The entire surface of Stromboli is the cone of a sluggish but active volcano. Puffs of smoke can be seen during the day. At night on the **Sciara del Fuoco (Slope of Fire)** 🐑🐑, lava glows red-hot on its way down to meet the sea with a loud hiss and a cloud of steam—a memorable vision that might leave you feeling a little too vulnerable.

In fact, the island can serve as a fantasyland for those who were bitten by Hollywood's 1997 volcano-mania. The main attraction is a steep, difficult climb to the lip of the 915m (3,000-ft.) **Gran Cratere** 🐑🐑🐑. The view of bubbling pools of ooze (which glow with heat at night) is accompanied by rising clouds of steam and a sulfuric stench. The journey is a 3-hour hike best taken in early morning or late afternoon to avoid the worst of the brutal sunshine—and even then it requires plenty of sunscreen and water and a good pair of shoes. The law states that you can climb the slope only with a guide. The island's authorized guide company is **Guide Alpine Autorizzate** (✆ **090-986211**), which charges 15€ to 20€ ($13.40–$17.85) per person. It leads groups on the 3-hour trip up the mountain at 6pm, returning at midnight (the trip down takes 2 hr., leaving you an hr. at the rim).

In spite of the volcano and its sloped terrain, there are two settlements. **Ginostra** is on the southwestern shore, little more than a cluster of summer homes with only 15 year-round residents. **Stromboli** is on the northeastern shore, a conglomeration of the villages of Ficogrande, San Vincenzo, and Piscita, where the only in-town attraction is the black-sand beach.

WHERE TO STAY & DINE

As the sun sets and the volcano lights the sky, everybody heads for the island's most popular bar, **Bar Ingrid,** at Piazza San Vicenzo (✆ **090-986385**).

La Locanda del Barbablu 🐑 *Finds*   This is a quirky choice, a charming little isolated Aeolian inn with only a few rooms, standing against turn-of-the-20th-century breakfronts. Rooms are small but comfortably furnished, often with four-poster beds encrusted with cherubs and mother-of-pearl inlay. There's a wide terrace opening onto dramatic views of the volcano and the sea. It's worthwhile to dine in the restaurant even if you're not a guest. The cuisine is inventive, offering dishes such as filet of tuna baked in cloves and cinnamon and flavored with hot peppers.

Via Vittorio Emanuele 17–19, 98050 Stromboli. ✆ 090-986118. Fax 090-986323. 6 units. 90€–175€ ($80.35–$156.30) double. AE, DC, MC, V.

La Sirenetta–Park Hotel 🐑   This is a well-maintained government-rated four-star hotel, with white tile floors and walls offset by contemporary dark wood furniture and trim. The rooms each possess a quality mattress and a small tiled bathroom. Natural wicker furnishings upholstered with blue floral prints grace the public areas. A large terrace overlooks the sea.

Via Marina 33, 98050 Ficogrande, Stromboli. ℂ 090-986025. Fax 090-986124. www.netnet.it/hotel/lasirenetta. 55 units (showers only). 115€–190€ ($102.70–$169.65) double with breakfast; 160€–240€ ($142.90–$214.30) double with breakfast and dinner. AE, DC, MC, V. Closed Nov–Mar 22. **Amenities:** Restaurant; bar; pool; gym; room service; babysitting; laundry/dry cleaning. *In room:* A/C, TV, minibar, hair dryer, safe.

VULCANO ⭐⭐

The island closest to the mainland, the ancient Thermessa, figured heavily in the mythologies of the region. The still-active **Vulcano della Fossa** was thought to be not only the home of Vulcan but also the gateway to Hades. Thucydides, Siculus, and Aristotle each recorded eruptions. Three dormant craters also exist on the island, but a climb to the rim of the active **Gran Cratere (Big Crater)** ⭐⭐⭐ draws the most attention. It hasn't erupted since 1890, but one look inside the sulfur-belching hole makes you understand how it could've inspired the hellish legends surrounding it. The 418m (1,372-ft.) peak is an easier climb than the one on Stromboli, taking just about an hour—though it's just as hot, and the same precautions prevail. Avoid midday, load up on sunscreen and water, and wear good hiking shoes.

Here the risks of mounting a volcano aren't addressed by legislation, so you can make the climb without a guide. Breathing the sulfuric air at the summit has its risks, though, because the steam is tainted with numerous toxins. To get to the peak from Porto Levante, the main port, follow Via Piano away from the sea for about 200m (220 yd.) until you see the first of the CRATERE signs, and then follow the marked trail.

The **Laghetto di Fanghi,** famous free mud baths that reputedly cure every known ailment, are along Via Provinciale a short way from the port. Be warned that the mud discolors everything from cloth to jewelry, which is one explanation for the prevalent nudity. Expect to encounter muddy pools brimming with naked, package-tour Germans. Within sight, the acquacalda features hot-water jets that act as a natural Jacuzzi. Either can scald you if you step or sit on the vents that release the heat, so take care if you decide to enter.

The island offers one of the few smooth beaches in the entire chain, the **Spiaggia Sabbie Nere (Black Sands Beach),** with dark sand so hot in the midday sun that thongs or wading shoes are suggested if you plan to while away your day along the shore. You can find the beach by following signs posted along Via Ponente.

A knowledge of street names is worthless, really, because there are no signs. Not to worry—the locals who gather at the dock are friendly and experienced at giving directions to tongue-tied foreign visitors, especially because all they ever have to point out are the paths to the crater, the mud baths, and the beach. You'll need to spend little time in the village center itself. This is a drab 1970s eyesore filled with souvenir shops and fast-food snack bars.

WHERE TO STAY

Hotel Eolian   This hotel consists of a series of white-sided stucco bungalows in a garden studded with palms and tropical plants. None has a view of the water (that's reserved for the restaurant and bar), but most guests spend their days beside the sea anyway. The guest rooms are medium-size, each with a tiled bathroom. The black sands of the beach lie at the end of a steep staircase.

Località Porto Ponente, 98050 Vulcano. ℂ 090-9852151. Fax 090-9852153. www.eolianhotel.com. 88 units (showers only). 129€–184€ ($115.20–$164.30) double. Rates include breakfast and dinner. AE, DC, MC, V. Closed Oct–Apr. **Amenities:** Restaurant; bar; lounge; tennis court; room service. *In room:* A/C, TV, minibar, hair dryer, safe.

Les Sables Noirs ✮   This is the most elegant place to stay on the island, offering surprising luxury in this remote outpost. Overlooking a black sandy beach, its bedrooms also front a panoramic sweep of the Bay of Ponente. The resort evokes the aura of the Caribbean with its stucco and bamboo. Bedrooms are midsize to spacious, each with a tiled bathroom. The styling in the well-kept units is Mediterranean, idyllic for a beach holiday. Its restaurant, featuring both Sicilian and international recipes, is one of the reasons to stay here.

Porto di Ponente, 98050 Vulcano. ℂ **090-9850.** Fax 090-98522454. www.initalia.it/hotel-messina-lessablesnoirs/pres.htm. 48 units. 165€–260€ ($147.35–$232.20) double. AE, DC, MC, V. **Amenities:** Restaurant,; 2 bars; room service; babysitting; laundry. *In room:* A/C, TV, minibar, hair dryer, safe.

WHERE TO DINE

Restaurant Vincencino SICILIAN   This is the most appealing of the limited number of restaurants convenient to the ferry port. In a rustic setting, you can order filling portions of local specialties. Good choices include house-style macaroni (with ricotta, eggplant, fresh tomatoes, and herbs); spaghetti *Vincencino* (with crayfish, capers, and tomato sauce); grilled fish, including an *involtini* of swordfish; and seafood salad. From October to March, the menu is limited to a simple array of platters served from the bar.

Vulcano Porto. ℂ **090-9852016.** Reservations recommended. Main courses 7.50€–12.50€ ($6.70–$11.15). AE, DC, MC, V. Daily noon–3:30pm and 7–9:30pm.

Appendix A:
Italy in Depth

1 History 101

THE ETRUSCANS

Of all the early inhabitants of Italy, the most significant were the Etruscans. But who were they? No one knows, and the many inscriptions that they left behind (mostly on graves) are of no help because the Etruscan language has never been deciphered by modern scholars. It's thought that they arrived on the eastern coast of Umbria several centuries before Rome was built, around 800 B.C. Their religious rites and architecture show an obvious contact with Mesopotamia; the Etruscans might have been refugees from Asia Minor who traveled westward about 1200 to 1000 B.C. Within 2 centuries, they had subjugated Tuscany and Campania and the Villanova tribes who lived there.

While the Etruscans were building temples at Tarquinia and Caere (present-day Cerveteri), the few nervous Latin tribes who remained outside their sway were gravitating to Rome, then little more than a village of sheepherders. As Rome's power grew, however, it increasingly profited from the strategically important Tiber crossing, where the ancient Salt Way (Via Salaria) turned northeastward toward the central Apennines.

From their base at Rome, the Latins remained free of the Etruscans until about 600 B.C. But the Etruscan advance was inexorable, and although the Latin tribes concentrated their forces at Rome for a last stand, they were swept away by the sophisticated Mesopotamian conquerors. The new

Dateline

- Bronze Age Celts, Teutonic tribes, and others from the Mediterranean and Asia Minor inhabit the peninsula.
- 1000 B.C. Large colonies of Etruscans settle in Tuscany and Campania, quickly subjugating many of the Latin inhabitants of the peninsula.
- 800 B.C. Rome begins to take shape, evolving from a strategically located shepherds' village into a magnet for Latin tribes fleeing the Etruscans.
- 600 B.C. Etruscans occupy Rome, designating it the capital of their empire. The city grows rapidly, and a major seaport opens at Ostia.
- 510 B.C. The Latin tribes, still centered in Rome, revolt against the Etruscans. Alpine Gauls attack from the north, and Greeks living in Sicily destroy the Etruscan navy.
- 250 B.C. The Romans, allied with the Greeks, Phoenicians, and native Sicilians, defeat the Etruscans. Rome flourishes and begins the accumulation of a vast empire.
- 49 B.C. Italy (through Rome) controls the entire Mediterranean world.
- 44 B.C. Julius Caesar is assassinated. His successor, Augustus, transforms Rome from a city of brick into a city of marble.
- 3rd century A.D. Rome declines under a series of incompetent and corrupt emperors.
- 4th century A.D. Rome is fragmented politically as administrative capitals are established in such cities as Milan and Trier, Germany.
- A.D. 395 The empire splits; Constantine establishes a "New Rome" at Constantinople (Byzantium). The

continues

overlords introduced gold tableware and jewelry, bronze urns and terracotta statuary, and the best of Greek and Asia Minor art and culture. They also made Rome the governmental seat of all Latium. Roma is an Etruscan name, and the kings of Rome had Etruscan names: Numa, Ancus, Tarquinius, and even Romulus.

The Estruscans ruled until the Roman revolt around 510 B.C., and by 250 B.C. the Romans and their Campania allies had vanquished the Etruscans, wiping out their language and religion. However, many of the former rulers' manners and beliefs remained and were assimilated into the culture. Even today, certain Etruscan customs and bloodlines are believed to exist in Italy, especially in Tuscany.

The best places to see the legacy left by these mysterious people are in Cerveteri and Tarquinia, outside Rome. Especially interesting is the Etruscan necropolis, just 4 miles southeast of Tarquinia, where thousands of tombs have been discovered. To learn more about the Etruscans, visit the Museo Nazionale di Villa Giulla in Rome.

THE ROMAN REPUBLIC

After the Roman Republic was established in 510 B.C., the Romans continued to increase their power by conquering neighboring communities in the highlands and forming alliances with other Latins in the lowlands. They gave to their Latin allies, and then to conquered peoples, partial or complete Roman citizenship, with the obligation of military service. Citizen colonies were set up as settlements of Roman farmers, and many of the famous cities of Italy originated as colonies. For the most part, these colonies were fortified and linked to Rome by military roads.

The stern Roman republic was characterized by a belief in the gods,

Goths successfully invade Rome's northern provinces.
- 410–55 Rome is sacked by barbarians.
- 475 Rome falls, leaving only the primate of the Catholic Church in control. The pope slowly adopts many of the powers once reserved for the Roman emperor.
- 800 Charlemagne is crowned Holy Roman Emperor by Pope Leo III. Italy dissolves into a series of small warring kingdoms.
- Late 11th century The popes function like secular princes with private armies.
- 1065 The Holy Land falls to the Muslim Turks; the Crusades are launched.
- 1303–77 The Papal Schism occurs; the pope and his entourage move from Rome to Avignon, France.
- 1377 The papacy returns to Rome.
- 1443 Brunelleschi's dome caps the Duomo in Florence as the Renaissance bursts into full bloom.
- 1469–92 Lorenzo il Magnifico rules in Florence as the Medici patron of Renaissance artists.
- 1499 Leonardo da Vinci completes *The Last Supper* in Milan.
- 1508 Michelangelo begins work on the Vatican's Sistine Chapel.
- 1527 Rome is sacked by Charles V of Spain, who is crowned Holy Roman Emperor the following year.
- 1796–97 Napoléon's series of invasions arouses Italian nationalism.
- 1861 The Kingdom of Italy is established.
- 1915–18 Italy enters World War I on the side of the Allies.
- 1922 Fascists march on Rome; Benito Mussolini becomes premier.
- 1929 A concordat between the Vatican and the Italian government is signed, delineating the rights and responsibilities of each party.
- 1935 Italy invades Abyssinia (Ethiopia).
- 1936 Italy signs "Axis" pact with Germany.
- 1940 Italy invades Greece.
- 1943 U.S. Gen. George Patton lands in Sicily and soon controls the island.

continues

the necessity of learning from the past, the strength of the family, education through reading books and performing public service, and, most importantly, obedience. The all-powerful Senate presided as Rome defeated rival powers one after the other and grew to rule the Mediterranean. The Punic Wars with Carthage in the 3rd century B.C. cleared away a major obstacle, although people said later that Rome's breaking of its treaty with Carthage (which led to that city's total destruction) put a curse on Rome.

No figure was more towering during the republic than Julius Caesar, the charismatic conqueror of Gaul—"the wife of every husband and the husband of every wife." After defeating the last resistance of the Pompeians in 45 B.C., he came to Rome and was made dictator and consul for 10 years. By then he was almost a king. Conspirators led by Marcus Junius Brutus stabbed him to death in the Senate on March 15, 44 B.C. Beware the ides of March.

Marc Antony, a Roman general, assumed control by seizing Caesar's papers and wealth. Intent on expanding the Republic, Antony met with Cleopatra at Tarsus in 41 B.C. She seduced him, and he stayed in Egypt for a year. When Antony eventually returned to Rome, still smitten with Cleopatra, he made peace with Caesar's willed successor, Octavius, and, through the pacts of Brundisium, soon found himself married to Octavius's sister, Octavia. This marriage, however, didn't prevent him from openly marrying Cleopatra in 36 B.C. The furious Octavius gathered western legions and defeated Antony at the Battle of Actium on September 2, 31 B.C. Cleopatra fled to Egypt, followed by Antony, who committed suicide in disgrace a year later. Cleopatra, unable to seduce his successor and thus retain her rule of Egypt, followed suit with the help of an asp.

- 1945 Mussolini is killed by a mob in Milan; World War II ends.
- 1946 The Republic of Italy is established.
- 1957 The Treaty of Rome, establishing the European Community (EC), is signed by six nations.
- 1960s The country's economy grows under the EC, but the impoverished south lags behind.
- 1970s Italy is plagued by left-wing terrorism; former premier Aldo Moro is kidnapped and killed.
- 1980s Political changes in Eastern Europe induce Italy's strong Communist Party to modify its program and even to change its name; the Socialists head their first post-1945 coalition government.
- 1994 A conservative coalition, led by Silvio Berlusconi, wins general elections.
- 1995 Following the resignation of Berlusconi, treasury minister Lamberto Dini is named prime minister to head the transitional government.
- 1996 Dini steps down as prime minister, and President Scalfaro dissolves both houses of parliament. In general elections, the center-left coalition known as the Olive Tree sweeps both the Senate and the Chamber of Deputies.
- 1997–98 Twin earthquakes hit Umbria, killing 11 people and destroying precious frescos in Assisi's basilica. Romano Prodi survives a neo-Communist challenge and continues to press for budget cuts in an effort to "join Europe."
- 1999 The euro technically becomes the official currency of Italy and other EU nations.
- 2000 Italy welcomes Jubilee visitors in the wake of political discontent.
- 2001 Billionaire media magnate Silvio Berlusconi is elected prime minister, winning by a landslide and leading the right wing to sweeping victory.
- 2002 Euro notes are introduced into circulation, and lire begin to be withdrawn from circulation over a transition period.

THE ROMAN EMPIRE

By 49 B.C., Italy ruled the entire Mediterranean world, either directly or indirectly, because all political, commercial, and cultural pathways led straight to Rome. The potential for wealth and glory to be found in Rome lured many people, draining other Italian communities of human resources. Foreign imports, especially agricultural imports, hurt local farmers and landowners. Municipal governments faltered, and civil wars ensued. Public order was restored by the Caesars (planned by Julius but brought to fruition under Augustus). On the eve of the birth of Christ, Rome was a mighty empire whose generals had brought the Western world under the sway of Roman law and civilization.

Born Gaius Octavius in 63 B.C., Augustus, the first Roman emperor, reigned from 27 B.C. to A.D. 14. His reign, called "the golden age of Rome," led to the Pax Romana, 2 centuries of peace. He had been adopted by, and eventually became the heir of, his great-uncle Julius Caesar. In Rome you can still visit the remains of the Forum of Augustus, built before the birth of Christ, and the Domus Augustana, where the imperial family lived on Palatine Hill.

The emperors, whose succession started with Augustus's principate after the death of Julius Caesar, brought Rome to new, almost giddy, heights. Augustus transformed the city from brick to marble, much the way Napoleon III transformed Paris many centuries later. But success led to corruption. The emperors wielded autocratic power, and the centuries witnessed a steady decay in the ideals and traditions on which the empire had been founded. The army became a fifth column of barbarian mercenaries, the tax collector became the scourge of the countryside, and for every good emperor (Augustus, Claudius, Trajan, Vespasian, and Hadrian, to name a few) there were three or four debased heads of state (Caligula, Nero, Domitian, Caracalla, and others).

After Augustus died (by poison, perhaps), his widow, Livia—a crafty social climber who had divorced her first husband to marry Augustus—set up her son, Tiberius, as ruler through a series of intrigues and poisonings. A long series of murders ensued, and Tiberius, who ruled during Pontius Pilate's trial and crucifixion of Christ, was eventually murdered in an uprising of landowners. In fact, murder was so common that a short time later, Domitian (A.D. 81–96) became so obsessed with the possibility of assassination that he had the walls of his palace covered in mica so that he could see behind him at all times. (He was killed anyway.)

Excesses and scandal ruled the day: Caligula (a bit overfond of his sister, Drusilla) appointed his horse a lifetime member of the Senate, lavished money on foolish projects, and proclaimed himself a god. Caligula's successor, his uncle Claudius, was deceived and publicly humiliated by one of his wives, the lascivious Messalina (he had her killed for her trouble); he was then poisoned by his final wife, his niece Agrippina, to secure the succession of Nero, her son by a previous marriage. Nero's thanks was later to murder not only his mother but also his wife, Claudius's daughter, and his rival, Claudius's son. The disgraceful Nero was removed as emperor while visiting Greece; he committed suicide with the cry, "What an artist I destroy."

By the 3rd century A.D., corruption had become so prevalent there were 23 emperors in 73 years. How bad were things? So bad that Caracalla, to secure control of the empire, had his brother Geta slashed to pieces while Geta was lying in his mother's arms. Rule of the empire changed hands so frequently that news of the election of a new emperor commonly reached the provinces together with a report of that emperor's assassination.

The 4th-century reforms of Diocletian held the empire together, but at the expense of its inhabitants, who were reduced to tax units. Diocletian reinforced imperial power while paradoxically weakening Roman dominance and prestige by dividing the empire into east and west halves and establishing administrative capitals at outposts such as Milan and Trier, Germany. He instituted not only heavy taxes but also a socioeconomic system that made professions hereditary. This edict was so strictly enforced that the son of a silversmith could be tried as a criminal if he attempted to become a sculptor instead.

Constantine became emperor in A.D. 306, and in 330 he made Constantinople (or Byzantium) the new capital of the Empire, moving the administrative functions away from Rome altogether, partly because the menace of possible barbarian attack in the West had increased greatly. Constantine took the best Roman artisans, politicians, and public figures with him, creating a city renowned for its splendor, intrigue, jealousies, and passion. Constantine was the first Christian emperor, allegedly converting after he saw the True Cross in the heavens, accompanied by the legend "In This Sign Shall You Conquer." He then defeated the pagan Maxentius and his followers in battle.

THE EMPIRE FALLS

The eastern and western sections of the Roman Empire split in 395, leaving Italy without the support it had once received from east of the Adriatic. When the Goths moved toward Rome in the early 5th century, citizens in the provinces, who had grown to hate and fear the cruel bureaucracy set up by Diocletian and followed by succeeding emperors, welcomed the invaders. And then the pillage began.

Rome was first sacked by Alaric, king of the Visigoths, in August 410. The populace made no attempt to defend the city (other than trying vainly to buy him off, a tactic that had worked 3 years before); most people simply fled into the hills or headed to their country estates if they were rich. The feeble Western emperor Honorius hid out in Ravenna the entire time.

More than 40 troubled years passed. Then Attila the Hun invaded Italy to besiege Rome. Attila was dissuaded from attacking, thanks largely to a peace mission headed by Pope Leo I in 452. Yet relief was short-lived: In 455, Gaiseric the Vandal carried out a 2-week sack that was unparalleled in its pure savagery. The empire of the West lasted for only another 20 years; finally, in 476, the sacks and chaos ended the once-mighty city, and Rome was left to the popes, under the nominal auspices of an exarch from Byzantium (Constantinople).

The last would-be Caesars to walk the streets of Rome were both barbarians: The first was Theodoric, who established an Ostrogoth kingdom at Ravenna from 493 to 526; the second was Totila, who held the last chariot races in the Circus Maximus in 549. Totila was engaged in an ongoing battle with Belisarius, the general of the Eastern emperor Justinian, who sought to regain Rome for the Eastern Empire. The city changed hands several times, recovering some of its ancient pride by bravely resisting Totila's forces, but eventually it was entirely depopulated by the continuing battles.

Christianity, a new religion that created a new society, was probably founded in Rome about a decade after the death of Jesus. Gradually gaining strength despite early persecution, it was finally accepted as the official religion. The best way today to relive the early Christian era is to visit Rome's Appian Way and its Catacombs, along Via Appia Antica, built in 312 B.C. According to Christian tradition, it was here that an escaping Peter encountered the vision of Christ. The Catacombs of St. Callixtus form the first cemetery of the Christian community of Rome.

THE MIDDLE AGES

Thus a ravaged Rome entered the Middle Ages, its once-proud population scattered and unrecognizable in rustic exile. A modest population started life again in the swamps of the Campus Martius, while the seven hills, now without water because the aqueducts were cut, stood abandoned and crumbling.

After the fall of the Western Empire, the pope took on more imperial powers, yet there was no political unity. Decades of rule by barbarians and then by Goths were followed by takeovers in different parts of the country by various strong warriors, such as the Lombards. Italy became divided into several spheres of control. In 731, Pope Gregory II renounced Rome's dependence on Constantinople and thus ended the twilight era of the Greek exarch who had nominally ruled Rome.

Papal Rome turned toward Europe, where the papacy found a powerful ally in Charlemagne, a king of the barbarian Franks. In 800, he was crowned emperor by Pope Leo III. The capital that he established at Aachen (Aix-la-Chapelle in French) lay deep within territory known to the Romans a half millennium before as the heart of the barbarian world. Although Charlemagne pledged allegiance to the church and looked to Rome and its pope as the final arbiter in most religious and cultural affairs, he launched northwestern Europe on a course toward bitter political opposition to the meddling of the papacy in temporal affairs.

The successor to Charlemagne's empire was a political entity known as the Holy Roman Empire (962–1806). The new empire defined the end of the Dark Ages but ushered in a period of long, bloody warfare. The Lombard leaders battled Franks. Magyars from Hungary invaded northeastern Lombardy and, in turn, were defeated by the increasingly powerful Venetians. Normans gained military control of Sicily in the 11th century, divided it from the rest of Italy, and altered forever the island's racial and ethnic makeup and its architecture. As Italy dissolved into a fragmented collection of city-states, the papacy fell under the power of Rome's feudal landowners. Eventually, even the process for choosing popes came into the hands of the increasingly Germanic Holy Roman emperors, although this balance of power would very soon shift.

Rome during the Middle Ages was a quaint rural town. Narrow lanes with overhanging buildings filled many areas, such as the Campus Martius, that had previously been showcases of ancient imperial power. Great basilicas were built and embellished with golden-hued mosaics. The forums, mercantile exchanges, temples, and theaters of the Imperial Era slowly disintegrated and collapsed. The decay of ancient Rome was assisted by periodic earthquakes, centuries of neglect, and, in particular, the growing need for building materials. Rome receded into a dusty provincialism. As the seat of the Roman Catholic church, the state was almost completely controlled by priests, who had an insatiable need for new churches and convents.

By the end of the 11th century, the popes shook off control of the Roman aristocracy, rid themselves of what they considered the excessive influence of the emperors at Aachen, and began an aggressive expansion of church influence and acquisitions. The deliberate organization of the church into a format modeled on the hierarchies of the ancient Roman Empire put it on a collision course with the empire and the other temporal leaders of Europe. The result was an endless series of power struggles.

The southern half of the country took a different road when, in the 11th century, the Normans invaded southern Italy, wresting control from the local strongmen and, in Sicily, from the Muslim Saracens who had occupied the region throughout the Dark Ages. To the south, the Normans introduced feudalism, a repressive social system that discouraged individual economic initiative, and whose legacy accounts for the social and economic differences between north and south that persist to this day.

In the mid–14th century, the Black Death ravaged Europe, killing a third of Italy's population. Despite such setbacks, the northern Italian city-states grew wealthy from Crusade booty, trade with one another and with the Middle East, and banking. These wealthy principalities and pseudorepublics ruled by the merchant elite flexed their muscles in the absence of a strong central authority.

THE RENAISSANCE

The story of Italy from the dawn of the Renaissance in the 15th century to the Age of Enlightenment in the 17th and 18th centuries is as varied and fascinating as that of the rise and fall of the empire. The papacy soon became essentially a feudal state, and the pope was a medieval (later Renaissance) prince engaged in many of the worldly activities that brought criticism on the church in later centuries. The 1065 fall of the Holy Land to the Turks catapulted the papacy into the forefront of world politics, primarily because of the Crusades, many of which the popes directly caused or encouraged (but most of which were judged military and economic disasters). During the 12th and 13th centuries, the bitter rivalries that rocked Europe's secular and spiritual bastions took their toll on the Holy Roman Empire, which grew weaker as city-states, buttressed by mercantile and trade-related prosperity, grew stronger and as France emerged as a potent nation in its own right. Each investiture of a new bishop to any influential post resulted in endless jockeying for power among many factions.

These conflicts reached their most visible impasse in 1303 during the Great Schism, when the papacy was moved to the French city of Avignon. For more than 70 years, until 1377, viciously competing popes (one in Rome, another under the protection of the French kings in Avignon) made simultaneous claims to the legacy of St. Peter, underscoring as never before the degree to which the church was both a victim and a victimizer in the temporal world of European politics.

The seat of the papacy was eventually returned to Rome, where successive popes were every bit as interesting as the Roman emperors they had replaced. The great families (Barberini, Medici, Borgia) enhanced their status and fortunes impressively when one of their sons was elected pope. For a look at life during this tumultuous period, you can visit Rome's Castel Sant'Angelo, which became a papal residence in the 14th century.

Despite the centuries that had passed since the collapse of the Roman Empire, the age of siege wasn't yet over. In 1527, Charles V, king of Spain, carried out the worst sack of Rome ever. To the horror of Pope Clement VII (a Medici), the entire city was brutally pillaged by the man who was to be crowned Holy Roman Emperor the next year.

During the years of the Renaissance, the Reformation, and the Counter-Reformation, Rome underwent major physical changes. The old centers of culture reverted to pastures and fields, and great churches and palaces were built with the stones of ancient Rome. This construction boom, in fact, did far more damage to the temples of the Caesars than any barbarian sack had done. Rare marbles were stripped from the imperial baths and used as altarpieces or sent to lime kilns. So enthusiastic was the papal destruction of Imperial Rome that it's a miracle anything is left.

This era is best remembered because of its art. The great ruling families, especially the Medicis in Florence, the Gonzagas in Mantua, and the Estes in Ferrara, not only reformed law and commerce but also sparked a renaissance in art. Out of this period arose such towering figures as Leonardo da Vinci and Michelangelo. Many visitors come to Italy to view what's left of the art and glory of that era—everything from Michelangelo's Sistine Chapel at the Vatican to his statue of *David* in Florence, from Leonardo's *Last Supper* in Milan to the Duomo in Florence, graced by Brunelleschi's dome.

A UNITED ITALY

The 19th century witnessed the final collapse of the Renaissance city-states, which had existed since the end of the 13th century. These units, eventually coming under the control of a *signore* (lord), were essentially regional states, with mercenary soldiers, civil rights, and assistance for their friendly neighbors. Some had attained formidable power under such *signori* as the Estes in Ferrara, the Medicis in Florence, and the Viscontis and Sforzas in Milan.

During the 17th, 18th, and 19th centuries, turmoil continued through a succession of many European dynasties. Napoléon made a bid for power in Italy beginning in 1796, fueling his war machines with what was considered a relatively easy victory. During the Congress of Vienna (1814–15), which followed Napoléon's defeat, Italy was once again divided among many factions: Austria was given Lombardy and Venetia, and the Papal States were returned to the pope. Some duchies were put back into the hands of their hereditary rulers, and southern Italy and Sicily went to a Bourbon dynasty. One historic move, which eventually contributed to the unification of Italy, was the assignment of the former republic of Genoa to Sardinia (which, at the time, was governed by the House of Savoy).

Political unrest became a fact of Italian life, at least some of it encouraged by the rapid industrialization of the north and the almost total lack of industrialization in the south. Despite those barriers, in 1861, thanks to the brilliant efforts of patriots Camillo Cavour (1810–61) and Giuseppe Garibaldi (1807–82), the Kingdom of Italy was proclaimed and Victor Emmanuel (Vittorio Emanuele) II of the House of Savoy, king of Sardinia, became the head of the new monarchy.

Garibaldi, the most respected of all Italian heroes, must be singled out for his efforts, which included taking Sicily, then returning to the mainland and marching north to meet Victor Emmanuel II at Teano, and finally declaring a unified Italy (with the important exception of Rome itself). It must have seemed especially sweet to a man whose efforts at unity had caused him to flee the country fearing for his life on four occasions. It's a tribute to the tenacity of this red-bearded hero that he never gave up, even in the early 1850s, when he was forced to wait out one of his exiles as a candlemaker on Staten Island in New York.

Although the hope, promoted by Europe's theocrats and some of its devout Catholics, of attaining one empire ruled by the pope and the church had long ago faded, there was still a fight, followed by generations of hard feelings, when the Papal States—a strategically and historically important principality under

Impressions

It is not impossible to govern Italians. It is merely useless.

—Benito Mussolini

the pope's temporal jurisdiction—were confiscated by the new Kingdom of Italy.

The establishment of the kingdom, however, didn't signal a complete unification of Italy because Rome was still under papal control and Venetia was still held by Austria. This was partially resolved in 1866, when Venetia joined the rest of Italy after the Seven Weeks' War between Austria and Prussia; in 1871, Rome became the capital of the newly formed country. The Vatican, however, didn't yield its territory to the new order, despite guarantees of nonintervention proffered by the government, and relations between the pope and the country of Italy remained rocky.

THE RISE OF IL DUCE & WORLD WAR II

On October 28, 1922, Benito Mussolini, who had started his Fascist Party in 1919, knew the time was ripe for change. He gathered 50,000 supporters for a march on Rome. Inflation was soaring and workers had just called a general strike, so rather than recognizing a state under siege, King Victor Emmanuel II recognized Mussolini as the new government leader. In 1929, Il Duce defined the divisions between the Italian government and the Vatican by signing a concordat granting political and fiscal autonomy to Vatican City. The agreement also made Roman Catholicism the official state religion—but that designation was removed in 1978 by a revision of the concordat.

During the Spanish Civil War (1936–39), Mussolini's support of Franco's Fascist party, whose members had staged a coup against the democratically elected government of Spain, helped encourage the formation of the "Axis" alliance between Italy and Nazi Germany. Despite having outdated military equipment, Italy added to the general horror of the era by invading Abyssinia (Ethiopia) in 1935. In 1940, Italy invaded Greece through Albania, and, in 1942, it sent thousands of Italian troops to assist Hitler in his disastrous campaign along the Russian front. In 1943, Allied forces, under the command of U.S. Gen. George Patton and British Gen. Bernard Montgomery, landed in Sicily and quickly secured the island as they prepared to move north toward Rome.

In the face of likely defeat and humiliation, Mussolini was overthrown by his own cabinet (Grand Council). The Allies made a separate deal with Victor Emmanuel III, who had collaborated with the Fascists during the previous 2 decades and now easily shifted allegiances. A politically divided Italy watched as battalions of fanatical German Nazis released Mussolini from his Italian jail cell to establish the short-lived Republic of Salò, headquartered on the edge of Lake Garda. Mussolini had hoped for a groundswell of popular opinion in favor of Italian Fascism, but events quickly proved this to be nothing more than a futile dream.

In April 1945, with almost a half-million Italians rising in a mass demonstration against him and the German war machine, Mussolini was captured by Italian partisans as he fled to Switzerland. Along with his mistress, Claretta Petacci, and several other of his intimates, he was shot and strung upside-down from the roof of a Milan gas station.

THE POSTWAR YEARS

Disaffected with the monarchy and its identification with the fallen Fascist dictatorship, Italy's citizens voted in 1946 for the establishment of a republic. The major political party that emerged following World War II was the Christian Democratic Party, a right-of-center group whose leader, Alcide De Gasperi (1881–1954), served as premier until 1953. The second-largest party was the Communist Party; however, by the mid-1970s, it had abandoned its revolutionary program in favor of a democratic form of "Eurocommunism" (in 1991, the Communists even changed their name to the Democratic Party of the Left).

Even though after the war Italy had been stripped of all its overseas colonies, it quickly succeeded in rebuilding its economy, in part because of U.S. aid under the Marshall Plan (1948–52). By the 1960s, as a member of the European Community (founded in Rome in 1957), Italy had become one of the world's leading industrialized nations, prominent in the manufacture of automobiles and office equipment.

But the country continued to be plagued by economic inequities between the prosperous industrialized north and the economically depressed south. It suffered an unprecedented flight of capital (frequently aided by Swiss banks only too willing to accept discreet deposits from wealthy Italians) and an increase in bankruptcies, inflation (almost 20% during much of the 1970s), and unemployment.

During the late 1970s and early 1980s, Italy was rocked by the rise of terrorism, instigated both by neo-Fascists and by left-wing intellectuals from the Socialist-controlled universities of the north.

THE 1990S & INTO THE NEW MILLENNIUM

By the late 19th century, the Mafia had become a kind of shadow government in the south; even to this day, it still controls a number of politicians, national officials, and even judges, although the influence of the *Cosa Nostra* is declining. In the early 1990s, the Italians reeled as many leading politicians were accused of wholesale corruption. As a result, a newly formed right-wing group, led by media magnate Silvio Berlusconi, swept to victory in 1994's general elections. Berlusconi became prime minister at the head of a coalition government. However, in December 1994, he resigned as prime minister after the federalist Northern League Party defected from his coalition and he lost his parliamentary majority. Treasury Minister Lamberto Dini, a nonpolitical banker with international financial credentials, was named to replace Berlusconi.

Dini signed on merely as a transitional player in the topsy-turvy political game. His austere measures enacted to balance Italy's budget, including cuts in pensions and health care, weren't popular among the mostly blue-collar workers or the highly influential labor unions. Aware of a predicted defeat in a no-confidence vote, Dini stepped down. His resignation in January 1996 left beleaguered Italians shouting *"Basta!"* (Enough!). This latest reshuffling in Italy's political deck prompted President Oscar Scalfaro to dissolve both houses of parliament.

Once again the Italians were faced with forming a new government. The elections of April 1996 proved a shocker, not only for the defeated politicians but also for the victors. The center-left coalition known as the Olive Tree, led by Romano Prodi, swept both the Senate and the Chamber of Deputies. The Olive Tree, whose roots stem from the old Communist Party, achieved victory by shifting toward the center and focusing its campaign on a strong platform protecting social benefits and supporting Italy's bid to become a solid member of the European Union.

Prodi carried through on his commitment when he announced a stringent budget for 1997, in a bid to be among the first countries to enter the monetary union. That year saw further upheavals in the Prodi government as he continued to push ahead with cuts to the country's generous social-security system. By autumn, though, Prodi was forced to submit his resignation when he lost critical support in Parliament from the Communist Refounding Party, which balked at pension and welfare cuts in the 1998 budget. The party eventually backed off with its demands, and Prodi was returned to office, where he pledged to see legislation for a 35-hour workweek passed by 2001.

In September 1997, twin earthquakes (5.7 and 5.6 on the Richter scale), with an epicenter just outside Assisi, struck within hours of each other. Umbria sustained considerable damage, especially in Acciano and Assisi, where 11 people were killed and another 13,000 were forced to take refuge in tents. The following 11 days of aftershocks and tremors hindered the recovery effort by the Italian government and relief organizations, and poured salt in the wounds of those left wondering what to do. One of the victims of these quakes was the Basilica of St. Francis in Assisi, where vaults collapsed and magnificent frescoes were reduced to dust.

On the political front, Massimo D'Alema became the first former Communist to lead a Western European government in October 1998, when he formed Italy's 56th postwar government. He replaced departing prime minister Romano Prodi.

As 1999 neared its end, Italy rushed to complete its myriad renovation and restoration projects so that everything would be perfect for the Jubilee. The big financial news of 1999 was Italy's entrance under the euro umbrella.

Italy spent all of 2000 welcoming Jubilee Year visitors from around the world, but everything wasn't a celebration. There is popular disillusionment with the costs of euro membership and with the weakness of the euro against the U.S. dollar and the British pound.

In the spring of 2000, Giuliano Amato, former prime minister and onetime Socialist, returned to power as the leader of Italy's 58th government since the war. For a year, he presided over an unwieldy coalition of a dozen political parties, ranging from former Communists to former Christian Democrats.

The richest man in Italy, billionaire media tycoon Silvio Berlusconi, swept to victory in May 2001 as prime minister, winning with right-wing support. Calling for a "revolution" in Italy, Berlusconi has promised a million and a half new jobs, pension hikes, epic tax cuts, anti-crime bills, and beefed-up public works projects.

In 2002, Italians officially abandoned their long-beloved lire and began trading in euros along with their neighbors to the north, including France and Germany, a total of 12 countries (but not Britain). As the new currency went into effect, counterfeiters and swindlers had a field day. One elderly woman in Southern Italy, cashing a benefit check, unwittingly paid the equivalent of $600 U.S. dollars for a cup of cappuccino. But in general, especially among businesses, the transition went relatively smoothly.

2 A Taste of Italy

Italians are among the world's greatest cooks. Just ask any one of them. Despite the unification of Italy, regional tradition still dominates the various kitchens, ranging from Rome to Lombardy, from the Valle d'Aosta to Sicily. The term "Italian cuisine" has little meaning unless it's more clearly defined as Neapolitan, Roman, Sardinian, Sicilian, Venetian, Piedmontese, Tuscan, or whatever. Each region has a flavor and a taste of its own, as well as a detailed repertoire of local dishes.

Food has always been one of life's great pleasures for the Italians. This has been true even from the earliest days: To judge from the lifelike banquet scenes found in Etruscan tombs, the Etruscans loved food and took delight in enjoying it. The Romans became famous for their never-ending banquets and for their love of exotic treats, such as flamingo tongues.

Although culinary styles vary, Italy abounds in trattorie specializing in local dishes—some of which are a delight for carnivores, such as the renowned *bistecca alla fiorentina* (cut from flavorful Chianina beef and then charcoal-grilled and served with a fruity olive oil). Other dishes, especially those found at the antipasti buffet, would appeal to every vegetarian's heart: peppers, greens, onions, pastas, beans, tomatoes, and fennel.

Incidentally, except in the south, Italians don't use as much garlic in their food as many foreigners seem to believe. Most Italian dishes, especially those in the north, are butter-based. And spaghetti and meatballs isn't an Italian dish, although certain restaurants throughout the country have taken to serving it "for homesick Americans."

See appendix B, "Molto Italiano," for a glossary of menu terms.

CUISINES AROUND THE COUNTRY

Rome is the best place to introduce yourself to Italian cuisine because it boasts specialty restaurants representing every region. Throughout your Roman holiday, you'll encounter such specialties as *zuppa di pesce* (a soup or stew of various fish, cooked in white wine and flavored with herbs), *cannelloni* (tube-shaped pasta baked with any number of stuffings), *riso col gamberi* (rice with shrimp, peas, and mushrooms, flavored with white wine and garlic), *scampi alla griglia* (grilled prawns, one of the best-tasting, albeit expensive, dishes in the city), *quaglie col risotto e tartufi* (quail with rice and truffles), *lepre alla cacciatore* (hare flavored with tomato sauce and herbs), *zabaglione* (a creamy dessert made with sugar, egg yolks, and Marsala), *gnocchi alla romana* (potato-flour dumplings with a meat sauce, covered with grated cheese), *abbacchio* (baby spring lamb, often roasted over an open fire), *saltimbocca alla romana* (literally "jump-in-your-mouth"—thin slices of veal with sage, ham, and cheese), *fritto alla romana* (a mixed fry likely to include everything from brains to artichokes), *carciofi alla romana* (tender artichokes cooked with herbs such as mint and garlic, flavored with white wine), *fettuccine all'uovo* (egg noodles with butter and cheese), *zuppa di cozze* (a hearty bowl of mussels cooked in broth), *fritto di scampi e calamaretti* (baby squid and prawns, fast-fried), *fragoline* (wild strawberries, in this case from the Alban Hills), and *finocchio* (fennel, a celerylike raw vegetable with the flavor of anisette, often eaten as a dessert or in a salad).

From Rome, it's on to **Tuscany,** where you'll encounter the hearty cuisine of the Tuscan hills. The main ingredient for almost any meal is the superb local olive oil, adored for its low acidity and lovely flavor. In Italy's south, the olives

Impressions

In Italy, the pleasure of eating is central to the pleasure of living. When you sit down to dinner with Italians, when you share their food, you are sharing their lives.

—Fred Plotkin, *Italy for the Gourmet Traveler* (1996)

are gathered only after they've fallen off the trees, but here they're handpicked off the trees so that they won't get bruised (ensuring lower acidity and milder aroma). Typical Tuscan pastas are *pappardelle* and *penne* mingled with a variety of sauces, many of which are tomato-based. Tuscans are extremely fond of strong cheeses such as *Gorgonzola, Fontina,* and *parmigiano.* Meat and fish are prepared simply and might seem undercooked, although locals would argue that it's better to let the inherent flavor of the ingredients survive the cooking process.

The next major city to visit is **Venice,** where the cookery is typical of the **Venezia** district. Long ago it was called "tasty, straightforward, and homely" by one food critic, and we concur. Two of the most typical dishes are *fegato alla veneziana* (liver and onions) and *risi e bisi* (rice and fresh peas). Seafood figures heavily in the Venetian diet, and grilled fish is often served with the bitter red radicchio, a lettuce that comes from Treviso.

In **Lombardy,** of which **Milan** is the center, the cookery is more refined and flavorful. No dish here is more famous than *cotoletta alla milanese* (cutlets of tender veal dipped in egg and bread crumbs and fried in olive oil until they're a golden brown)—the Viennese call it Wiener schnitzel. *Osso buco* is the other great dish of Lombardy; this is cooked with the shin bone of veal in a ragout sauce and served on rice and peas. *Risotto alla milanese* is also a classic—rice that can be dressed in almost any way, depending on the chef's imagination. It's often flavored with saffron and butter, to which chicken giblets have been added, and it's seemingly always served with heaps of *Parmigiano-Reggiano* cheese. *Polenta,* a cornmeal mush that's "more than mush," is the staff of life in some parts of northeastern Italy and is eaten in lieu of pasta.

The cooking in the **Piedmont,** of which **Turin** is the capital, and the **Aosta Valley** is different from that in the rest of Italy. Victuals here are said to appeal to strong-hearted men returning from a hard day's work in the mountains. You get such dishes as *bagna cauda,* a sauce made with olive oil, garlic, butter, and anchovies, in which you dip uncooked fresh vegetables. *Fonduta* is also celebrated: It's made with melted Fontina cheese, butter, milk, egg yolks, and, for an elegant touch, white truffles.

In the **Trentino–Alto Adige** area, whose chief towns are **Bolzano, Merano,** and **Trent,** the cooking is naturally influenced by the traditions of the Austrian and Germanic kitchens. South Tirol, of course, used to belong to Austria, and here you get such tasty pastries as strudel.

Liguria, whose chief town is **Genoa,** turns to the sea for a great deal of its cuisine, as reflected by its version of bouillabaisse, a *burrida* flavored with spices. But its most famous food item is *pesto,* a sauce made with fresh basil, garlic, cheese, and walnuts, which is used to dress pasta, fish, and many other dishes.

Emilia-Romagna, with such towns as **Modena, Parma, Bologna, Ravenna,** and **Ferrara,** is one of the great gastronomic centers. Rich in produce, its school of cooking produces many notable pastas now common around Italy: *tagliatelle, tortellini,* and *cappelletti* (larger than tortellini and made in the form of "little hats"). Tagliatelle, of course, are long strips of macaroni, and tortellini are little squares of dough stuffed with chopped pork, veal, or whatever. Equally popular is *lasagne,* which by now everybody has heard of. In Bologna, it's often made by adding finely shredded spinach to the dough. The best-known sausage of the area is *mortadella,* and equally famous is a *cotoletta alla bolognese* (veal cutlet fried with a slice of ham or bacon). The distinctive and famous cheese *Parmigiano-Reggiano* is a product of Parma and also Reggio Emilia. *Zampone* (stuffed pig's foot) is a specialty of Modena. Parma is also known for its ham, which is fashioned into air-cured *prosciutto di Parma.* Served in wafer-thin slices, it's deliciously sweet and hailed by gourmets as the finest in the world.

Much of the cookery of **Campania** (spaghetti with clam sauce, pizzas, and so forth), with **Naples** as its major city, is already familiar to North Americans because so many Neapolitans moved to the New World and opened restaurants. *Mozzarella,* or buffalo cheese, is the classic cheese of this area. Mixed fish fries, done a golden brown, are a staple of nearly every table.

Sicily has a distinctive cuisine, with good, strong flavors and aromatic sauces. A staple of the diet is *maccheroni con le sarde* (spaghetti with pine seeds, fennel, spices, chopped sardines, and olive oil). Fish is good and fresh in Sicily (try swordfish). Among meat dishes, you'll see *involtini siciliani* (rolled meat with a stuffing of egg, ham, and cheese cooked in bread crumbs) on the menu. A *caponata* is a special way of cooking eggplant in a flavorful tomato sauce. The desserts and homemade pastries are excellent, including *cannoli,* cylindrical pastry cases stuffed with ricotta and candied fruit (or chocolate). Their ice creams, called *gelati,* are among the best in Italy.

AND SOME VINO TO WASH IT ALL DOWN

Italy is the largest wine-producing country in the world; as far back as 800 B.C. the Etruscans were vintners. It's said that more soil is used in Italy for the cultivation of grapes than for the growing of food. Many Italian farmers produce wine just for their own consumption or for their relatives in "the big city." However, it wasn't until 1965 that laws were enacted to guarantee regular consistency in wine making. Wines regulated by the government are labeled "DOC" (*Denominazione di Origine Controllata*). If you see "DOCG" on a label (the "G" means *garantita*), that means even better quality control.

THE VINEYARDS OF ITALY

Following traditions established by the ancient Greeks, Italy produces more wine than any other nation. More than 4 million acres of soil are cultivated as vineyards, and recently there has been an increased emphasis on recognizing vintages from lesser-known growers who might or might not be designated as working within a zone of controlled origin and name. (It's considered an honor, and usually a source of profit, to own vines within a DOC. Vintners who are presently limited to marketing their products as unpretentious table wines—*vino di tavola*—often expend great efforts lobbying for an elevated status as a DOC.)

Italy's wine producers range from among the most automated and technologically sophisticated in Europe to low-tech, labor-intensive family plots that turn out just a few hundred bottles per year. You can sometimes save money by buying directly from a producer (the signs beside the highway of any wine-producing district will advertise VENDITA DIRETTA). Not only will you avoid paying the retailer's markup, but you also might get a glimpse of the vines that produced the vintage that you carry home with you.

Useful vocabulary words for such endeavors are *bottiglieria* (a simple wine shop) and *enoteca* (a more upscale shop where many vintages, from several growers, are displayed and sold like magazines in a bookstore). In some cases, you can buy a glass of the product before you buy the bottle, and platters of cold cuts or cheeses are sometimes available to offset the tang (and alcoholic effects) of the wine.

REGIONAL WINES

Here we've cited only a few popular wines. Rest assured that there are hundreds more, and you'll have a great time sampling them to find your own favorites.

Latium: In this major wine-producing region, many of the local wines come from the Castelli Romani, the hill towns around Rome. Horace and Juvenal sang the praises of Latium wines even in imperial times. These wines, experts agree, are best drunk when young, and they're most often white, mellow, and dry (or "demi-sec"). There are seven types, including **Falerno** (straw yellow in color) and **Cecubo** (often served with roast meat). Try also **Colli Albani** (straw yellow with amber tints, served with both fish and meat). The golden yellow wines of **Frascati** are famous, produced in both a demi-sec and a sweet variety, the latter served with dessert.

Tuscany: Tuscan wines rank with some of the finest reds in France. **Chianti** is the best known, and it comes in several varieties. The most highly regarded is **Chianti Classico,** a lively ruby-red wine mellow in flavor with a bouquet of violets. A good label is Antinori. A lesser known but remarkably fine Tuscan wine is **Brunello di Montalcino,** a brilliant garnet red served with roasts and game. The ruby-red, almost purple, **Vino Nobile di Montepulciano** has a rich, rugged body; it's a noble wine that's aged for 4 years. The area around San Gimignano produces a light, sweet white wine called **Vernaccia.** While you're in Tuscany, order the wonderful dessert wine called **Vin Santo,** which tastes almost like sherry and is usually accompanied by biscotti that you dunk into your glass.

Emilia-Romagna: The sparkling **Lambrusco** of this region is, by now, best known by Americans, but this wine can be of widely varying quality. Most of it is a brilliant ruby red. Be more experimental, and try such wines as the dark ruby red **Sangiovese** (with a delicate bouquet) and the golden yellow **Albana,** somewhat sweet. **Trebbiano,** generally dry, is best served with fish.

The Veneto: From this rich breadbasket in northeastern Italy come such world-famous wines as **Bardolino** (a light ruby red often served with poultry), **Valpolicella** (produced in "ordinary quality" and "superior dry," best served with meats), and **Soave** (beloved by W. Somerset Maugham), which has a pale amber color with a light aroma and a velvety flavor. Also try one of the **Cabernets,** either the ruby-red **Cabernet di Treviso** (ideal with roasts and game) or the even deeper ruby-red **Cabernet Franc,** which has a marked herbal bouquet and is served with roasts.

Trentino–Alto Adige: This area produces wine influenced by Austria. Known for its vineyards, the region has some 20 varieties of wine. The straw-yellow, slightly pale-green **Riesling** is served with fish, as is the pale green-yellow **Terlano. Santa Maddalena,** a cross between garnet and ruby, is served with wild fowl and red meats, and **Traminer,** straw yellow, has a distinctive aroma and is served with fish. A **Pinot Bianco,** straw yellow with greenish glints, has a light bouquet and a noble history, and is also served with fish.

Friuli–Venezia Giulia: This area attracts those who enjoy a "brut" wine with a trace of flint. From classic grapes come **Merlot,** deep ruby in color, and several varieties of **Pinot,** including **Pinot Grigio,** whose color ranges from straw yellow to gray-pink (good with fish). Also served with fish, the **Sauvignon** has a straw-yellow color and a delicate bouquet.

Lombardy: These wines are justly renowned—and, if you don't believe us, would you instead take the advice of Leonardo da Vinci, Pliny, and Virgil? These great men have sung the praise of this wine-rich region bordered by the Alps to the north and the Po River to the south. To go with the tasty, refined cuisine of the Lombard kitchen are such wines as **Frecciarossa** (a pale straw-yellow color with a delicate bouquet—order it with fish), **Sassella** (bright ruby red—order it with game, red meat, and roasts), and the amusingly named **Inferno** (a deep ruby red with a penetrating bouquet—order it with meats).

The Piedmont: The finest wines in Italy, mostly red, are said to be produced on the vine-clad slopes of the Piedmont. Of course, **Asti Spumante,** the color of straw with an abundant champagnelike foam, is the prototype of Italian sparkling wines. While traveling through this area of northwestern Italy, you'll want to sample **Barbaresco** (brilliant ruby red with a delicate flavor—order it with red meats), **Barolo** (also brilliant ruby red, best when it mellows into a velvety old age), **Cortese** (pale straw yellow with green glints—order it with fish), and **Gattinara** (an intense ruby-red beauty in youth that changes with age). Piedmont is also the home of **vermouth,** a white wine to which aromatic herbs and spices, among other ingredients, have been added; it's served as an aperitif.

Liguria: This area doesn't have as many wine-producing regions as other parts of Italy, yet it grows dozens of different grapes. These are made into such wines as **Dolceacqua** (lightish ruby red, served with hearty food) and **Vermentino Ligure** (pale yellow with a good bouquet, often served with fish).

Campania: From the volcanic soil of Vesuvius, the wines of Campania have been extolled for 2,000 years. Homer praised the glory of **Falerno,** straw yellow in color. Neapolitans are fond of ordering a wine known as **Lacrima Christi** ("tears of Christ") to accompany many seafood dishes. It comes in amber, red, and pink. With meat dishes, try the dark mulberry-color **Gragnano,** which has a faint bouquet of faded violets. The reds and whites of Ischia and Capri are also justly renowned.

Apulia: The heel of the Italian boot, Apulia, produces more wine than any other part of Italy. Try **Castel del Monte,** which comes in shades of pink, white, and red. Other wines of the region are the dull red **Aleatico di Puglia,** with a mellow taste so sweet and aromatic that it's almost a liqueur; **Barletta,** a highly alcoholic wine made from grapes grown around Troia; the notably pleasant and fragrant **Mistella,** a really fleshy wine usually offered with desserts; the brilliant amber **Moscato della Murge,** aromatic and sweet; **Moscato di Trani,** which is velvety and tastes of a bouquet of faded roses; and **Primitivo di Gioia,** a full-bodied acid wine that, when dry, appears with roasts and, when sweet, appears with desserts. One of the region's best wines to drink with fish is **Torre Giulia,** which is dark yellow tending toward amber—a "brut" wine with a distinctive bouquet.

Sicily: The wines of Sicily, called a "paradise of the grape," were extolled by the ancient poets, including Martial. Caesar himself lavished praise on **Mamertine** when it was served at a banquet honoring his third consulship. **Marsala,** an amber wine served with desserts, is the most famous wine of Sicily; it's velvety and fruity and sometimes used in cooking, as in veal Marsala. The wines made from grapes grown in the volcanic soil of Etna come in both red and white varieties. Also try the **Corvo Bianco di Casteldaccia** (straw yellow, with a distinctive bouquet) and the **Corvo Rosso di Casteldaccia** (ruby red, almost garnet, full-bodied and fruity).

OTHER DRINKS

Italians drink other libations as well. Their most famous drink is **Campari,** bright red in color and flavored with herbs; it has a quinine bitterness to it. It's customary to serve it with ice cubes and soda.

Limoncello, a bright yellow drink made by infusing pure alcohol with lemon zest, has become Italy's second most popular drink. It has long been a staple in the lemon-producing region along the Amalfi Coast in Capri and Sorrento, and recipes for the sweetly potent concoction have been passed down by families there for generations. About a decade ago, restaurants in Sorrento, Naples, and Rome started making their own versions. Visitors to those restaurants as well as the Sorrento peninsula began singing limoncello's praises and requesting bottles to go. Now it's one of the most up-and-coming liqueurs in the world, thanks to heavy advertising promotions.

Beer, once treated as a libation of little interest, is still far inferior to wines produced domestically, but foreign beers, especially those of Ireland and England, are gaining great popularity with Italian youth, especially in Rome. This popularity is mainly because of atmospheric pubs, which now number more than 300 in Rome alone, where young people linger over a pint and a conversation. Most pubs are in the Roman center, and many are licensed by Guinness and its Guinness Italia operations. In a city with 5,000 watering holes, 300 pubs might seem like a drop, but because the clientele is young, the wine industry is trying to devise a plan to keep that drop from becoming a steady stream of Italians who prefer grain to grapes.

High-proof **grappa** is made from the "leftovers" after the grapes have been pressed. Many Italians drink this before or after dinner (some put it into their coffee). It's an acquired taste—to an untrained foreign palate, it often seems rough and harsh.

Appendix B: Molto Italiano

1 Basic Vocabulary

English	Italian	Pronunciation
Thank you	**Grazie**	*graht*-tzee-yey
You're welcome	**Prego**	*prey*-go
Please	**Per favore**	*pehr* fah-*vohr*-eh
Yes	**Sì**	see
No	**No**	noh
Good morning or Good day	**Buongiorno**	bwohn-*djor*-noh
Good evening	**Buona sera**	bwohn-ah *say*-rah
Good night	**Buona notte**	bwohn-ah *noht*-tay
How are you?	**Come sta?**	koh-may *stah*
Very well	**Molto bene**	*mohl*-toh *behn*-ney
Goodbye	**Arrivederci**	ahr-ree-vah-*dehr*-chee
Excuse me (to get attention)	**Scusi**	*skoo*-zee
Excuse me (to get past someone)	**Permesso**	pehr-*mehs*-soh
Where is . . . ?	**Dovè . . . ?**	doh-*vey*
the station	**la stazione**	lah stat-tzee-*oh*-neh
a hotel	**un albergo**	oon ahl-*behr*-goh
a restaurant	**un ristorante**	oon reest-ohr-*ahnt*-eh
the bathroom	**il bagno**	eel *bahn*-nyoh
To the right	**A destra**	ah *dehy*-stra
To the left	**A sinistra**	ah see-*nees*-tra
Straight ahead	**Avanti (*or* sempre diritto)**	ahv-vahn-tee (*sehm*-pray dee-*reet*-toh)
How much is it?	**Quanto costa?**	*kwan*-toh *coh*-sta
The check, please	**Il conto, per favore**	eel kon-toh *pehr* fah-*vohr*-eh
When?	**Quando?**	*kwan*-doh
Yesterday	**Ieri**	ee-*yehr*-ree
Today	**Oggi**	*oh*-jee
Tomorrow	**Domani**	doh-*mah*-nee
Breakfast	**Prima colazione**	*pree*-mah coh-laht-tzee-*ohn*-ay
Lunch	**Pranzo**	*prahn*-zoh
Dinner	**Cena**	*chay*-nah
What time is it?	**Che ore sono?**	kay *or*-ay *soh*-noh
Monday	**Lunedì**	loo-nay-*dee*
Tuesday	**Martedì**	mart-ay-*dee*
Wednesday	**Mercoledì**	mehr-cohl-ay-*dee*

Thursday	**Giovedì**	joh-vay-*dee*
Friday	**Venerdì**	ven-nehr-*dee*
Saturday	**Sabato**	*sah*-bah-toh
Sunday	**Domenica**	doh-*mehn*-nee-kah

NUMBERS

1	**uno** (*oo*-noh)	30	**trenta** (*trayn*-tah)
2	**due** (*doo*-ay)	40	**quaranta** (kwah-*rahn*-tah)
3	**tre** (tray)	50	**cinquanta** (cheen-*kwan*-tah)
4	**quattro** (*kwah*-troh)	60	**sessanta** (sehs-*sahn*-tah)
5	**cinque** (*cheen*-kway)	70	**settanta** (seht-*tahn*-tah)
6	**sei** (say)	80	**ottanta** (oht-*tahn*-tah)
7	**sette** (*set*-tay)	90	**novanta** (noh-*vahnt*-tah)
8	**otto** (*oh*-toh)	100	**cento** (*chen*-toh)
9	**nove** (*noh*-vay)	1,000	**mille** (*mee*-lay)
10	**dieci** (dee-*ay*-chee)	5,000	**cinque milla** (*cheen*-kway *mee*-lah)
11	**undici** (*oon*-dee-chee)	10,000	**dieci milla** (dee-*ay*-chee *mee*-lah)
20	**venti** (*vehn*-tee)		
21	**ventuno** (vehn-*toon*-oh)		
22	**venti due** (*vehn*-tee *doo*-ay)		

2 A Glossary of Architectural Terms

Ambone   A pulpit, either serpentine or simple in form, erected in an Italian church.

Apse   The half-rounded extension behind the main altar of a church; Christian tradition dictates that it be placed at the eastern end of an Italian church, the side closest to Jerusalem.

Atrium   A courtyard, open to the sky, in an ancient Roman house; the term also applies to the courtyard nearest the entrance of an early Christian church.

Baldacchino (also ciborium)   A columned stone canopy, usually placed above the altar of a church; spelled in English *baldachin* or *baldaquin*.

Baptistry   A separate building or a separate area in a church where the rite of baptism is held.

Basilica   Any rectangular public building, usually divided into three aisles by rows of columns. In ancient Rome, this architectural form was frequently used for places of public assembly and law courts; later, Roman Christians adapted the form for many of their early churches.

Caldarium   The steam room of a Roman bath.

Campanile   A bell tower, often detached, of a church.

Capital   The top of a column, often carved and usually categorized into one of three orders: Doric, Ionic, or Corinthian.

Castrum   A carefully planned Roman military camp, whose rectangular form, straight streets, and systems of fortified gates quickly became standardized throughout the Empire; modern cities that began as Roman camps and still more or less maintain their original forms include Chester (England), Barcelona (Spain), and such Italian cities as Lucca, Aosta, Como, Brescia, Florence, and Ancona.

Cavea   The curved row of seats in a classical theater; the most prevalent shape was that of a semicircle.

Cella   The sanctuary, or most sacred interior section, of a Roman pagan temple.

Chancel   Section of a church containing the altar.

Cornice   The decorative flange defining the uppermost part of a classical or neoclassical facade.

Cortile   Courtyard or cloisters ringed with a gallery of arches or lintels set atop columns.

Crypt   A church's main burial place, usually below the choir.

Cupola   A dome.

Duomo   Cathedral.

Forum   The main square and principal gathering place of any Roman town, usually adorned with the city's most important temples and civic buildings.

Grotesques   Carved and painted faces, deliberately ugly, used by everyone from the Etruscans to the architects of the Renaissance; they're especially amusing when set into fountains.

Hypogeum   Subterranean burial chambers, usually of pre-Christian origins.

Loggia   Roofed balcony or gallery.

Lozenge   An elongated four-sided figure that, along with stripes, was one of the distinctive signs of the architecture of Pisa.

Narthex   The anteroom, or enclosed porch, of a Christian church.

Nave   The largest and longest section of a church, usually devoted to sheltering or seating worshipers and often divided by aisles.

Palazzo   A palace or other important building.

Piano Nobile   The main floor of a palazzo (sometimes the second floor).

Pietra Dura   Richly ornate assemblage of semiprecious stones mounted on a flat decorative surface, perfected during the 1600s in Florence.

Pieve   A parish church.

Portico   A porch, usually crafted from wood or stone.

Pulvin   A four-sided stone that serves as a substitute for the capital of a column, often decoratively carved, sometimes into biblical scenes.

Putti   Plaster cherubs whose chubby forms often decorate the interiors of baroque chapels and churches.

Stucco   Colored plaster composed of sand, powdered marble, water, and lime, either molded into statuary or applied in a thin concretelike layer to the exterior of a building.

Telamone   Structural column carved into a standing male form; female versions are called *caryatids*.

Thermae   Roman baths.

Transenna   Stone (usually marble) screen separating the altar area from the rest of an early Christian church.

Travertine   The stone from which ancient and Renaissance Rome was built, it's known for its hardness, light coloring, and tendency to be pitted or flecked with black.

Tympanum   The half-rounded space above the portal of a church, whose semicircular space usually showcases a sculpture.

3 Italian Menu Terms

Abbacchio   Roast haunch or shoulder of lamb baked and served in a casserole and sometimes flavored with anchovies.

Agnolotti   A crescent-shaped pasta shell stuffed with a mix of chopped meat, spices, vegetables, and cheese; when prepared in rectangular versions, the same combination of ingredients is identified as ravioli.

Amaretti   Crunchy, sweet almond-flavored macaroons.

Anguilla alla veneziana   Eel cooked in a sauce made from tuna and lemon.

Antipasti   Succulent tidbits served at the beginning of a meal (before the pasta), whose ingredients might include slices of cured meats, seafood (especially shellfish), and cooked and seasoned vegetables.

Aragosta   Lobster.

Arrosto   Roasted meat.

Baccalà   Dried and salted codfish.

Bagna cauda   Hot and well-seasoned sauce, heavily flavored with anchovies, designed for dipping raw vegetables; literally translated as "hot bath."

Bistecca alla fiorentina   Florentine-style steaks, coated before grilling with olive oil, pepper, lemon juice, salt, and parsley.

Bocconcini   Veal layered with ham and cheese, and then fried.

Bollito misto   Assorted boiled meats served on a single platter.

Braciola   Pork chop.

Bresaola   Air-dried spiced beef.

Bruschetta   Toasted bread, heavily slathered with olive oil and garlic and often topped with tomatoes.

Bucatini   Coarsely textured hollow spaghetti.

Busecca alla Milanese   Tripe (beef stomach) flavored with herbs and vegetables.

Cacciucco ali livornese   Seafood stew.

Calzone   Pizza dough rolled with the chef's choice of sausage, tomatoes, cheese, and so on and then baked into a kind of savory turnover.

Cannelloni   Tubular dough stuffed with meat, cheese, or vegetables and then baked in a creamy white sauce.

Cappellacci alla ferrarese   Pasta stuffed with pumpkin.

Cappelletti   Small ravioli ("little hats") stuffed with meat or cheese.

Carciofi   Artichokes.

Carpaccio   Thin slices of raw cured beef, sometimes in a piquant sauce.

Cassatta alla siciliana   A richly caloric dessert that combines layers of sponge cake, sweetened ricotta cheese, and candied fruit, bound together with chocolate buttercream icing.

Cervello al burro nero   Brains in black-butter sauce.

Cima alla genovese   Baked fillet of veal rolled into a tube-shaped package containing eggs, mushrooms, and sausage.

Coppa   Cured morsels of pork fillet encased in sausage skins, served in slices.

Costoletta alla milanese   Veal cutlet dredged in bread crumbs, fried, and sometimes flavored with cheese.

Cozze   Mussels.

Fagioli   White beans.

Fave   Fava beans.

Fegato alla veneziana   Thinly sliced calves' liver fried with salt, pepper, and onions.

Foccacia   Ideally, concocted from potato-based dough left to rise slowly for several hours and then garnished with tomato sauce, garlic, basil, salt, and pepper and drizzled with olive oil; similar to a deep-dish pizza most popular in the deep south, especially Bari.

Fontina   Rich cow's-milk cheese.

Frittata   Italian omelet.

Fritto misto   A deep-fried medley of whatever small fish, shellfish, and squid are available in the marketplace that day.

Fusilli   Spiral-shaped pasta.

Gelato (produzione propria)   Ice cream (homemade).

Gnocchi   Dumplings usually made from potatoes (*gnocchi alla patate*) or from semolina (*gnocchi alla romana*), often stuffed with combinations of cheese, spinach, vegetables, or whatever combinations strike the chef's fancy.

Gorgonzola   One of the most famous blue-veined cheeses of Europe—strong, creamy, and aromatic.

Granità   Flavored ice, usually with lemon or coffee.

Insalata di frutti di mare   Seafood salad (usually including shrimp and squid) garnished with pickles, lemon, olives, and spices.

Involtini   Thinly sliced beef, veal, or pork, rolled, stuffed, and fried.

Minestrone   A rich and savory vegetable soup usually sprinkled with grated parmigiano and studded with noodles.

Mortadella   Mild pork sausage, fashioned into large cylinders and served sliced; the original lunchmeat bologna (because its most famous center of production is Bologna).

Mozzarella   A nonfermented cheese, made from the fresh milk of a buffalo (or, if unavailable, from a cow), boiled, and then kneaded into a rounded ball, served fresh.

Mozzarella con pomodori (also "caprese")   Fresh tomatoes with fresh mozzarella, basil, pepper, and olive oil.

Nervetti   A northern Italian antipasto made from chewy pieces of calves' foot or shin.

Osso buco   Beef or veal knuckle slowly braised until the cartilage is tender and then served with a highly flavored sauce.

Pancetta   Herb-flavored pork belly, rolled into a cylinder and sliced—the Italian bacon.

Panettone   Sweet yellow-colored bread baked in the form of a brioche.

Panna   Heavy cream.

Pansotti   Pasta stuffed with greens, herbs, and cheeses, usually served with a walnut sauce.

Pappardelle alle lepre   Pasta with rabbit sauce.

Parmigiano   Parmesan, a hard and salty yellow cheese usually grated over pastas and soups but also eaten alone; also known as *granna*. The best is *Parmigiano-Reggiano.*

Peperoni   Green, yellow, or red sweet peppers (not to be confused with pepperoni).

Pesci al cartoccio   Fish baked in a parchment envelope with onions, parsley, and herbs.

Pesto   A flavorful green sauce made from basil leaves, cheese, garlic, marjoram, and (if available) pine nuts.

Piccata al Marsala   Thin escalope of veal braised in a pungent sauce flavored with Marsala wine.

Piselli al prosciutto   Peas with strips of ham.

Pizza   Specific varieties include *capricciosa* (its ingredients can vary widely, depending on the chef's culinary vision and the ingredients at hand), *margherita* (with tomato sauce, cheese, fresh basil, and memories of the first queen of Italy, Marguerite di Savoia, in whose honor it was first made by a Neapolitan chef), *napoletana* (with ham, capers, tomatoes, oregano, cheese, and the distinctive taste of anchovies), *quattro stagione* (translated as "four seasons" because of the array of fresh vegetables in it; it also contains ham and bacon), and *siciliana* (with black olives, capers, and cheese).

Pizzaiola   A process in which something (usually a beefsteak) is covered in a tomato-and-oregano sauce.

Polenta   Thick porridge or mush made from cornmeal flour.

Polenta de uccelli   Assorted small birds roasted on a spit and served with polenta.

Polenta e coniglio   Rabbit stew served with polenta.

Polla alla cacciatore   Chicken with tomatoes and mushrooms cooked in wine.

Pollo all diavola   Highly spiced grilled chicken.

Ragù   Meat sauce.

Ricotta   A soft bland cheese made from cow's or sheep's milk.

Risotto   Italian rice.

Risotto alla milanese   Rice with saffron and wine.

Salsa verde   "Green sauce," made from capers, anchovies, lemon juice and/or vinegar, and parsley.

Saltimbocca   Veal scallop layered with prosciutto and sage; its name literally translates as "jump in your mouth," a reference to its tart and savory flavor.

Salvia   Sage.

Scaloppina alla Valdostana   Escalope of veal stuffed with cheese and ham.

Scaloppine   Thin slices of veal coated in flour and sautéed in butter.

Semifreddo   A frozen dessert; usually ice cream with sponge cake.

Seppia   Cuttlefish (a kind of squid); its black ink is used for flavoring in certain sauces for pasta and also in risotto dishes.

Sogliola   Sole.

Spaghetti   A long, round, thin pasta, variously served: *alla bolognese* (with ground meat, mushrooms, peppers, and so on), *alla carbonara* (with bacon, black pepper, and eggs), *al pomodoro* (with tomato sauce), *al sugo/ragù* (with meat sauce), and *alle vongole* (with clam sauce).

Spiedini   Pieces of meat grilled on a skewer over an open flame.

Strangolaprete   Small nuggets of pasta, usually served with sauce; the name is literally translated as "priest-choker."

Stufato   Beef braised in white wine with vegetables.

Tagliatelle   Flat egg noodles.

Tonno   Tuna.

Tortelli   Pasta dumplings stuffed with ricotta and greens.

Tortellini   Rings of dough stuffed with minced and seasoned meat, and served either in soups or as a full-fledged pasta covered with sauce.

Trenette   Thin noodles served with pesto sauce and potatoes.

Trippe alla fiorentina   Beef tripe (stomach).

Vermicelli   Very thin spaghetti.

Vitello tonnato   Cold sliced veal covered with tuna-fish sauce.

Zabaglione/zabaione   Egg yolks whipped into the consistency of a custard, flavored with Marsala, and served warm as a dessert.

Zampone   Pig's trotter stuffed with spicy seasoned port, boiled and sliced.

Zuccotto   A liqueur-soaked sponge cake, molded into a dome and layered with chocolate, nuts, and whipped cream.

Zuppa inglese   Sponge cake soaked in custard.

Index

HIT THE ROAD WITH FROMMER'S DRIVING TOURS!

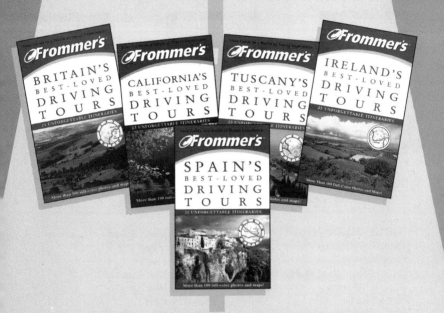

Frommer's Britain's Best-Loved Driving Tours
Frommer's California's Best-Loved Driving Tours
Frommer's Florida's Best-Loved Driving Tours
Frommer's France's Best-Loved Driving Tours
Frommer's Germany's Best-Loved Driving Tours
Frommer's Ireland's Best-Loved Driving Tours
Frommer's Italy's Best-Loved Driving Tours
Frommer's New England's Best-Loved Driving Tours
Frommer's Northern Italy's Best-Loved Driving Tours
Frommer's Scotland's Best-Loved Driving Tours
Frommer's Spain's Best-Loved Driving Tours
Frommer's Tuscany & Umbria's Best-Loved Driving Tours

Frommer's
Portable Guides
Complete Guides for the Short-Term Traveler

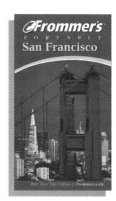

Available at bookstores everywhere.

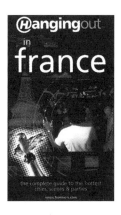

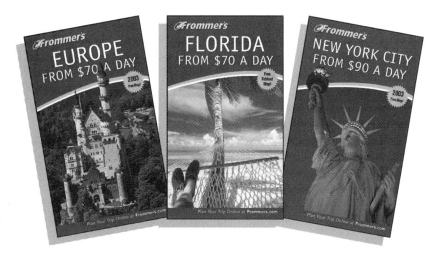

THE UNOFFICIAL GUIDE
FOR PEOPLE
WHO LOVE GOOD VALUE

FROMMER'S® COMPLETE TRAVEL GUIDES

Alaska
Alaska Cruises & Ports of Call
Amsterdam
Argentina & Chile
Arizona
Atlanta
Australia
Austria
Bahamas
Barcelona, Madrid & Seville
Beijing
Belgium, Holland & Luxembourg
Bermuda
Boston
Brazil
British Columbia & the Canadian
   Rockies
Budapest & the Best of Hungary
California
Canada
Cancún, Cozumel & the Yucatán
Cape Cod, Nantucket & Martha's
   Vineyard
Caribbean
Caribbean Cruises & Ports of Call
Caribbean Ports of Call
Carolinas & Georgia
Chicago
China
Colorado
Costa Rica
Denmark
Denver, Boulder & Colorado
   Springs
England
Europe
European Cruises & Ports of Call
Florida

France
Germany
Great Britain
Greece
Greek Islands
Hawaii
Hong Kong
Honolulu, Waikiki & Oahu
Ireland
Israel
Italy
Jamaica
Japan
Las Vegas
London
Los Angeles
Maryland & Delaware
Maui
Mexico
Montana & Wyoming
Montréal & Québec City
Munich & the Bavarian Alps
Nashville & Memphis
Nepal
New England
New Mexico
New Orleans
New York City
New Zealand
Northern Italy
Nova Scotia, New Brunswick &
   Prince Edward Island
Oregon
Paris
Philadelphia & the Amish Country
Portugal
Prague & the Best of the Czech
   Republic

Provence & the Riviera
Puerto Rico
Rome
San Antonio & Austin
San Diego
San Francisco
Santa Fe, Taos & Albuquerque
Scandinavia
Scotland
Seattle & Portland
Shanghai
Singapore & Malaysia
South Africa
South America
South Florida
South Pacific
Southeast Asia
Spain
Sweden
Switzerland
Texas
Thailand
Tokyo
Toronto
Tuscany & Umbria
USA
Utah
Vancouver & Victoria
Vermont, New Hampshire &
   Maine
Vienna & the Danube Valley
Virgin Islands
Virginia
Walt Disney World® & Orlando
Washington, D.C.
Washington State

FROMMER'S® DOLLAR-A-DAY GUIDES

Australia from $50 a Day
California from $70 a Day
Caribbean from $70 a Day
England from $75 a Day
Europe from $70 a Day

Florida from $70 a Day
Hawaii from $80 a Day
Ireland from $60 a Day
Italy from $70 a Day
London from $85 a Day

New York from $90 a Day
Paris from $80 a Day
San Francisco from $70 a Day
Washington, D.C. from $80 a Day

FROMMER'S® PORTABLE GUIDES

Acapulco, Ixtapa & Zihuatanejo
Amsterdam
Aruba
Australia's Great Barrier Reef
Bahamas
Berlin
Big Island of Hawaii
Boston
California Wine Country
Cancún
Charleston & Savannah
Chicago
Disneyland®
Dublin
Florence

Frankfurt
Hong Kong
Houston
Las Vegas
London
Los Angeles
Los Cabos & Baja
Maine Coast
Maui
Miami
New Orleans
New York City
Paris
Phoenix & Scottsdale

Portland
Puerto Rico
Puerto Vallarta, Manzanillo &
   Guadalajara
Rio de Janeiro
San Diego
San Francisco
Seattle
Sydney
Tampa & St. Petersburg
Vancouver
Venice
Virgin Islands
Washington, D.C.

FROMMER'S® NATIONAL PARK GUIDES

Banff & Jasper
Family Vacations in the National
   Parks
Grand Canyon

National Parks of the American
   West
Rocky Mountain

Yellowstone & Grand Teton
Yosemite & Sequoia/ Kings Canyon
Zion & Bryce Canyon

FROMMER'S® MEMORABLE WALKS

Chicago	New York	San Francisco
London	Paris	Washington, D.C.

FROMMER'S® GREAT OUTDOOR GUIDES

Arizona & New Mexico	Northern California	Vermont & New Hampshire
New England	Southern New England	

SUZY GERSHMAN'S BORN TO SHOP GUIDES

Born to Shop: France	Born to Shop: Italy	Born to Shop: New York
Born to Shop: Hong Kong, Shanghai & Beijing	Born to Shop: London	Born to Shop: Paris

FROMMER'S® IRREVERENT GUIDES

Amsterdam	Los Angeles	San Francisco
Boston	Manhattan	Seattle & Portland
Chicago	New Orleans	Vancouver
Las Vegas	Paris	Walt Disney World
London	Rome	Washington, D.C.

FROMMER'S® BEST-LOVED DRIVING TOURS

Britain	Germany	Northern Italy
California	Ireland	Scotland
Florida	Italy	Spain
France	New England	Tuscany & Umbria

HANGING OUT™ GUIDES

Hanging Out in England	Hanging Out in France	Hanging Out in Italy
Hanging Out in Europe	Hanging Out in Ireland	Hanging Out in Spain

THE UNOFFICIAL GUIDES®

Bed & Breakfasts and Country Inns in:	Southwest & South Central Plains	Mid-Atlantic with Kids
California	U.S.A.	Mini Las Vegas
Great Lakes States	Beyond Disney	Mini-Mickey
Mid-Atlantic	Branson, Missouri	New England and New York with Kids
New England	California with Kids	
Northwest	Chicago	New Orleans
Rockies	Cruises	New York City
Southeast	Disneyland®	Paris
Southwest	Florida with Kids	San Francisco
Best RV & Tent Campgrounds in:	Golf Vacations in the Eastern U.S.	Skiing in the West
California & the West	Great Smoky & Blue Ridge Region	Southeast with Kids
Florida & the Southeast	Inside Disney	Walt Disney World®
Great Lakes States	Hawaii	Walt Disney World® for Grown-ups
Mid-Atlantic	Las Vegas	Walt Disney World® with Kids
Northeast	London	Washington, D.C.
Northwest & Central Plains		World's Best Diving Vacations

SPECIAL-INTEREST TITLES

Frommer's Adventure Guide to Australia & New Zealand
Frommer's Adventure Guide to Central America
Frommer's Adventure Guide to India & Pakistan
Frommer's Adventure Guide to South America
Frommer's Adventure Guide to Southeast Asia
Frommer's Adventure Guide to Southern Africa
Frommer's Britain's Best Bed & Breakfasts and Country Inns
Frommer's Caribbean Hideaways
Frommer's Exploring America by RV
Frommer's Fly Safe, Fly Smart
Frommer's France's Best Bed & Breakfasts and Country Inns
Frommer's Gay & Lesbian Europe

Frommer's Italy's Best Bed & Breakfasts and Country Inns
Frommer's New York City with Kids
Frommer's Ottawa with Kids
Frommer's Road Atlas Britain
Frommer's Road Atlas Europe
Frommer's Road Atlas France
Frommer's Toronto with Kids
Frommer's Vancouver with Kids
Frommer's Washington, D.C., with Kids
Israel Past & Present
The New York Times' Guide to Unforgettable Weekends
Places Rated Almanac
Retirement Places Rated

Booked seat 6A, open return.

Rented red 4-wheel drive.

Reserved cabin, no running water.

Discovered space.

:h over 700 airlines, 50,000 hotels, 50 rental car companies and
0 cruise and vacation packages, you can create the perfect get-
ay for you. Choose the car, the room, even the ground you walk on.

Travelocity.com
A Sabre Company
Go Virtually Anywhere.

You Need A Vacation.

700 Airlines, 50,000 Hotels, 50 Rental Car Companies, And A Million Ways To Save Money.

Travelocity.com

A Sabre Company

Go Virtually Anywhere.